D1370736

SELECTED SOLUTIONS MANUAL

Kathleen Thrush Shaginaw
Community College of Philadelphia
Particular Solutions, Inc.

PRINCIPLES OF CHEMISTRY

A MOLECULAR APPROACH

Third Edition

NIVALDO J. TRO

PEARSON

Editor in Chief: Jeanne Zalesky
Senior Acquisitions Editor: Terry Haugen
Marketing Manager: Will Moore
Project Management Team Lead: David Zielonka
Project Manager: Beth Sweeten
Full-Service Project Management/Composition: CodeMantra
Operations Specialist: Maura Zaldivar-Garcia
Cover Art: Quade Paul

PEARSON

www.pearsonhighered.com

1 2 3 4 5 6 7 8 9 10—**V089**—17 16 15 14

ISBN-10: 0-13-388941-6; ISBN-13: 978-0-13-388941-3

Contents

Student Guide to Using This Solutions Manual

The vision behind this solutions manual is to provide guidance that is useful for both the struggling student and the advanced student.

An important feature of this solutions manual is that answers for the review questions are given. This will help in the review of the major concepts in the chapter.

The format of the solutions very closely follows the format in the textbook. Each mathematical problem includes **Given, Find, Conceptual Plan, Solution**, and **Check** sections.

> **Given and Find:** Many students struggle with taking the written problem, parsing the information into categories, and determining the goal of the problem. It is also important to know which pieces of information in the problem are not necessary to solve the problem and if additional information needs to be gathered from sources such as tables in the textbook.

> **Conceptual Plan:** The conceptual plan shows a step-by-step method to solve the problem. In many cases, the given quantities need to be converted to a different unit. Under each of the arrows is the equation, constant, or conversion factor needed to complete this portion of the problem. In the "Problems by Topic" section of the end-of-chapter exercises, the odd-numbered and even-numbered problems are paired. This allows you to use a conceptual plan from an odd-numbered problem in this manual as a starting point to solve the following even-numbered problem. Students should keep in mind that the examples shown are one way to solve the problems. Other mathematically equivalent solutions may be possible.

5.17 **Given:** $m\,(CO_2) = 28.8$ g, $P = 742$ mmHg, and $T = 22\,°C$ **Find:** V

Conceptual Plan: $°C \to K$ and mmHg $\to$ atm and g $\to$ mol then $n, P, T \to V$

$$K = °C + 273.15 \qquad \frac{1\ \text{atm}}{760\ \text{mmHg}} \qquad \frac{1\ \text{mol}}{44.01\ \text{g}} \qquad PV = nRT$$

Solution: $T_1 = 22\,°C + 273.15 = 295$ K, $\quad P = 742\ \text{mmHg} \times \dfrac{1\ \text{atm}}{760\ \text{mmHg}} = 0.976316$ atm,

$n = 28.8\ \text{g} \times \dfrac{1\ \text{mol}}{44.01\ \text{g}} = 0.654397$ mol $\quad PV = nRT$ Rearrange to solve for V.

$$V = \frac{nRT}{P} = \frac{0.654397\ \text{mol} \times 0.08206\ \dfrac{\text{L} \cdot \text{atm}}{\text{mol} \cdot \text{K}} \times 295\ \text{K}}{0.976316\ \text{atm}} = 16.2\ \text{L}$$

Check: The units (L) are correct. The magnitude of the answer (16 L) makes sense because one mole of an ideal gas under standard conditions (273 K and 1 atm) occupies 22.4 L. Although these are not standard conditions, they are close enough for a ballpark check of the answer. Because this gas sample contains 0.65 mole, a volume of 16 L is reasonable.

> **Solution:** The Solution section walks you through solving the problem after the conceptual plan. Equations are rearranged to solve for the appropriate quantity. Intermediate results are shown with additional digits to minimize round-off error. The units are canceled in each appropriate step.

> **Check:** The Check section confirms that the units in the answer are correct. This section also challenges the student to think about whether the magnitude of the answer makes sense. Thinking about what is a reasonable answer can help uncover errors such as calculation errors.

1 Matter, Measurement, and Problem Solving

Review Questions

The Scientific Approach to Knowledge

1.1   (a)   This statement is a theory because it attempts to explain why. It is not possible to observe individual atoms.

       (b)   This statement is an observation.

       (c)   This statement is a law because it summarizes many observations and can explain future behavior.

       (d)   This statement is an observation.

1.3   (a)   Yes, if we divide the mass of the oxygen by the mass of the carbon, the result is always 4/3, a ratio of small whole numbers.

       (b)   Yes, if we divide the mass of the oxygen by the mass of the hydrogen, the result is always 16, a ratio of small whole numbers.

       (c)   These observations suggest that the masses of elements in molecules are ratios of whole numbers (4:3 and 16:1, respectively, for parts (a) and (b)).

       (d)   Atoms combine in small whole number ratios and not as random weight ratios.

The Classification and Properties of Matter

1.5   (a)   Sweat is a homogeneous mixture of water, sodium chloride, and other components.

       (b)   Carbon dioxide is a pure substance that is a compound (two or more elements bonded together).

       (c)   Aluminum is a pure substance that is an element (element 13 in the periodic table).

       (d)   Vegetable soup is a heterogeneous mixture of broth, chunks of vegetables, and extracts from the vegetables.

1.7

Substance	Pure or Mixture	Type
aluminum	pure	element
apple juice	mixture	mixture
hydrogen peroxide	pure	compound
chicken soup	mixture	mixture

1.9   (a)   pure substance that is a compound (one type of molecule that contains two different elements)

       (b)   heterogeneous mixture (two different molecules that are segregated into regions)

       (c)   homogeneous mixture (two different molecules that are randomly mixed)

       (d)   pure substance that is an element (individual atoms of one type)

1.11   (a)   physical property (color can be observed without making or breaking chemical bonds)

       (b)   chemical property (must observe by making or breaking chemical bonds)

       (c)   physical property (the phase can be observed without making or breaking chemical bonds)

       (d)   physical property (density can be observed without making or breaking chemical bonds)

       (e)   physical property (mixing does not involve making or breaking chemical bonds, so this can be observed without making or breaking chemical bonds)

1.13   (a)   chemical property (burning involves breaking and making bonds, so bonds must be broken and made to observe this property)

       (b)   physical property (shininess is a physical property and so can be observed without making or breaking chemical bonds)

       (c)   physical property (odor can be observed without making or breaking chemical bonds)

       (d)   chemical property (burning involves breaking and making bonds, so bonds must be broken and made to observe this property)

1.15   (a)   chemical change (new compounds are formed as methane and oxygen react to form carbon dioxide and water)

       (b)   physical change (vaporization is a phase change and does not involve the making or breaking of chemical bonds)

       (c)   chemical change (new compounds are formed as propane and oxygen react to form carbon dioxide and water)

       (d)   chemical change (new compounds are formed as the metal in the frame is converted to oxides)

1.17   (a)   physical change (vaporization is a phase change and does not involve the making or breaking of chemical bonds)

       (b)   chemical change (new compounds are formed)

       (c)   physical change (vaporization is a phase change and does not involve the making or breaking of chemical bonds)

Units in Measurement

1.19   (a)   To convert from °F to °C, first find the equation that relates these two quantities. $°C = \dfrac{°F - 32}{1.8}$ Now substitute °F into the equation and compute the answer. Note: The number of digits reported in this answer follows significant figure conventions, covered in Section 1.6. $°C = \dfrac{°F - 32}{1.8} = \dfrac{0.}{1.8} = 0.\ °C$

       (b)   To convert from K to °F, first find the equations that relate these two quantities.

             $K = °C + 273.15$ and $°C = \dfrac{°F - 32}{1.8}$

             Because these equations do not directly express K in terms of °F, you must combine the equations and then solve the equation for °F. Substituting for °C:

             $K = \dfrac{°F - 32}{1.8} + 273.15$; rearrange $K - 273.15 = \dfrac{°F - 32}{1.8}$;

             rearrange $1.8(K - 273.15) = (°F - 32)$; finally, $°F = 1.8(K - 273.15) + 32$. Now substitute K into the equation and compute the answer.

             $°F = 1.8(77 - 273.15) + 32 = 1.8(-196.15) + 32 = -353.07 + 32 = -321.07\ °F = -321\ °F$

       (c)   To convert from °F to °C, first find the equation that relates these two quantities. $°C = \dfrac{°F - 32}{1.8}$ Now substitute °F into the equation and compute the answer.

             $°C = \dfrac{-109\ °F - 32\ °F}{1.8} = \dfrac{-141}{1.8} = -78.333\ °C = -78.3\ °C$

       (d)   To convert from °F to K, first find the equations that relate these two quantities.

             $K = °C + 273.15$ and $°C = \dfrac{°F - 32}{1.8}$

             Because these equations do not directly express K in terms of °F, you must combine the equations and then solve the equation for K. Substituting for °C: $K = \dfrac{°F - 32}{1.8} + 273.15$

             Now substitute °F into the equation and compute the answer.

             $K = \dfrac{(98.6 - 32)}{1.8} + 273.15 = \dfrac{66.6}{1.8} + 273.15 = 37.0 + 273.15 = 310.15\ K = 310.2\ K$

1.21   To convert from °F to °C, first find the equation that relates these two quantities: $°C = \dfrac{°F - 32}{1.8}$. Now substitute °F into the equation and compute the answer. Note: The number of digits reported in this answer follows significant figure conventions, covered in Section 1.6. $^\circ C = \dfrac{-80.\ ^\circ F - 32\ ^\circ F}{1.8} = \dfrac{-112}{1.8} = -62.2\ ^\circ C$

Begin by finding the equation that relates the quantity that is given ($^\circ C$) and the quantity you are trying to find (K). $K = {^\circ C} + 273.15$. Because this equation gives the temperature in K directly, simply substitute the correct value for the temperature in $^\circ C$ and compute the answer. $K = -62.\underline{2}22\ ^\circ C + 273.15 = 210.9\ K$

1.23 Use Table 1.2 to determine the appropriate prefix multiplier and substitute the meaning into the expressions.
  (a) $3.8 \times 10^{-8}\ s = 38 \times 10^{-9}\ s$; 10^{-9} implies "nano," so $38 \times 10^{-9}\ s = 38$ nanoseconds $= 38$ ns
  (b) $57 \times 10^{-13}\ g = 5.7 \times 10^{-12}\ g$; 10^{-12} implies "pico," so $5.7 \times 10^{-12}\ g = 5.7$ picograms $= 5.7$ pg
  (c) $5.9 \times 10^{7}\ L = 59 \times 10^{6}\ L$; 10^{6} implies "mega," so $5.9 \times 10^{7}\ L = 59$ megaliters $= 59$ ML
  (d) $9.3 \times 10^{8}\ m = 930 \times 10^{6}\ m$; 10^{6} implies "mega," so $930 \times 10^{6}\ m = 930$ megameters $= 930$ Mm

1.25 (b) **Given:** 515 km   **Find:** dm
       Conceptual Plan: km → m → dm

       $$\frac{1000\ m}{1\ km} \quad \frac{10\ dm}{1\ m}$$

       Solution: $515\ \cancel{km} \times \dfrac{1000\ \cancel{m}}{1\ \cancel{km}} \times \dfrac{10\ dm}{1\ \cancel{m}} = 5.15 \times 10^{6}\ dm$

       Check: The units (dm) are correct. The magnitude of the answer (10^{6}) makes physical sense because a decimeter is a much smaller unit than a kilometer.

       Given: 515 km   **Find:** cm
       Conceptual Plan: km → m → cm

       $$\frac{1000\ m}{1\ km} \quad \frac{100\ cm}{1\ m}$$

       Solution: $515\ \cancel{km} \times \dfrac{1000\ \cancel{m}}{1\ \cancel{km}} \times \dfrac{100\ cm}{1\ \cancel{m}} = 5.15 \times 10^{7}\ cm$

       Check: The units (cm) are correct. The magnitude of the answer (10^{7}) makes physical sense because a centimeter is a much smaller unit than a kilometer or a decimeter.

  (c) **Given:** 122.355 s   **Find:** ms
       Conceptual Plan: s → ms

       $$\frac{1000\ ms}{1\ s}$$

       Solution: $122.355\ \cancel{s} \times \dfrac{1000\ ms}{1\ \cancel{s}} = 1.22355 \times 10^{5}\ ms$

       Check: The units (ms) are correct. The magnitude of the answer (10^{5}) makes physical sense because a millisecond is a much smaller unit than a second.
       Given: 122.355 s   **Find:** ks
       Conceptual Plan: s → ks

       $$\frac{1\ ks}{1000\ s}$$

       Solution: $122.355\ \cancel{s} \times \dfrac{1\ ks}{1000\ \cancel{s}} = 1.22355 \times 10^{-1}\ ks = 0.122355\ ks$

       Check: The units (ks) are correct. The magnitude of the answer (10^{-1}) makes physical sense because a kilosecond is a much larger unit than a second.

  (d) **Given:** 3.345 kJ   **Find:** J
       Conceptual Plan: kJ → J

       $$\frac{1000\ J}{1\ kJ}$$

       Solution: $3.345\ \cancel{kJ} \times \dfrac{1000\ J}{1\ \cancel{kJ}} = 3.345 \times 10^{3}\ J$

       Check: The units (J) are correct. The magnitude of the answer (10^{3}) makes physical sense because a joule is a much smaller unit than a kilojoule.

Given: 3.345×10^3 J (from above)   **Find:** mJ

Conceptual Plan: J → mJ

$$\frac{1000 \text{ mJ}}{1 \text{ J}}$$

Solution: $3.345 \times 10^3 \cancel{\text{ J}} \times \dfrac{1000 \text{ mJ}}{1 \cancel{\text{ J}}} = 3.345 \times 10^6$ mJ

Check: The units (mJ) are correct. The magnitude of the answer (10^6) makes physical sense because a millijoule is a much smaller unit than a joule.

1.27   **Given:** 1 square meter (1 m^2)   **Find:** number of 1 cm squares in 1 square meter

Conceptual Plan: 1 m^2 → cm^2

$$\frac{100 \text{ cm}}{1 \text{ m}}$$

Notice that for squared units, the conversion factors must be squared.

Solution: $1 \cancel{\text{ m}^2} \times \dfrac{(100 \text{ cm})^2}{(1 \cancel{\text{ m}})^2} = 1 \times 10^4$ cm squares $= 10,000.$ squares, so 1×10^4 cm squares

Check: The units of the answer are correct, and the magnitude makes sense. The unit centimeter is smaller than a meter, so the value in square centimeters should be larger than in square meters.

Density

1.29   **Given:** $m = 2.49$ g; $V = 0.349 \text{ cm}^3$ **Find:** d in g/cm^3 and compare to pure copper.

Conceptual Plan: $m, V → d$

$$d = m/V$$

Compare to the published value: d (pure copper) $= 8.96 \text{ g/cm}^3$. (This value is in Table 1.4.)

Solution: $d = \dfrac{2.49 \text{ g}}{0.349 \text{ cm}^3} = 7.13 \dfrac{\text{g}}{\text{cm}^3}$

The density of the penny is much smaller than the density of pure copper (7.13 g/cm^3; 8.96 g/cm^3), so the penny is not pure copper.

Check: The units (g/cm^3) are correct. The magnitude of the answer seems correct. Many coins are layers of metals, so it is not surprising that the penny is not pure copper.

1.31   **Given:** $m = 4.10 \times 10^3$ g; $V = 3.25$ L   **Find:** d in g/cm^3

Conceptual Plan: $m, V → d$ then L → cm^3

$$d = m/V \qquad \frac{1000 \text{ cm}^3}{1 \text{ L}}$$

Solution: $d = \dfrac{4.10 \times 10^3 \text{ g}}{3.25 \cancel{\text{ L}}} \times \dfrac{1 \cancel{\text{ L}}}{1000 \text{ cm}^3} = 1.26 \dfrac{\text{g}}{\text{cm}^3}$

Check: The units (g/cm^3) are correct. The magnitude of the answer seems correct.

1.33   (a)   **Given:** $d = 1.11 \text{ g/cm}^3$; $V = 417$ mL   **Find:** m

Conceptual Plan: $d, V → m$ then cm^3 → mL

$$d = m/V \qquad \frac{1 \text{ mL}}{1 \text{ cm}^3}$$

Solution: $d = m/V$ Rearrange by multiplying both sides of the equation by V. $m = d \times V$

$m = 1.11 \dfrac{\text{g}}{\cancel{\text{cm}^3}} \times \dfrac{1 \cancel{\text{ cm}^3}}{1 \cancel{\text{ mL}}} \times 417 \cancel{\text{ mL}} = 4.63 \times 10^2$ g

Check: The units (g) are correct. The magnitude of the answer seems correct considering that the value of the density is about 1 g/cm^3.

(b)   **Given:** $d = 1.11 \text{ g/cm}^3$; $m = 4.1$ kg   **Find:** V in L

Conceptual Plan: $d, m → V$ then kg → g and cm^3 → L

$$d = m/V \qquad \frac{1000 \text{ g}}{1 \text{ kg}} \qquad \frac{1 \text{ L}}{1000 \text{ cm}^3}$$

Solution: $d = m/V$ Rearrange by multiplying both sides of the equation by V and dividing both sides of the equation by d.

$$V = \frac{m}{d} = \frac{4.1 \text{ kg}}{1.11 \frac{\text{g}}{\text{cm}^3}} \times \frac{1000 \text{ g}}{1 \text{ kg}} = 3.7 \times 10^3 \text{ cm}^3 \times \frac{1 \text{ L}}{1000 \text{ cm}^3} = 3.7 \text{ L}$$

Check: The units (L) are correct. The magnitude of the answer seems correct considering that the value of the density is about 1 g/cm³.

The Reliability of a Measurement and Significant Figures

1.35   To obtain the readings, look to see where the bottom of the meniscus lies. Estimate the distance between two markings on the device.
  (a) 73.3 mL—the meniscus appears to be just above the 73 mL mark.
  (b) 88.2 °C—the mercury is between the 84 °C mark and the 85 °C mark, but it is closer to the lower number.
  (c) 645 mL—the meniscus appears to be just above the 640 mL mark.

1.37   Remember that
  1. interior zeros (zeros between two numbers) are significant.
  2. leading zeros (zeros to the left of the first nonzero number) are not significant. They only serve to locate the decimal point.
  3. trailing zeros (zeros at the end of a number) are categorized as follows:
    • Trailing zeros after a decimal point are always significant.
    • Trailing zeros before an implied decimal point are ambiguous and should be avoided by using scientific notation or by inserting a decimal point at the end of the number.
  (a) 1,0̲5̲0,5̲0̲1 km
  (b) 0̸.0̸0̸2̲0̲ m
  (c) 0̸.0̸0̸0̸0̸0̸0̸0̸0̸0̸0̸0̸0̸0̸0̸0̸2 s
  (d) 0̸.0̸0̸1̲0̲9̲0̲ cm

1.39   Remember all of the rules from Section 1.7.
  (a) Three significant figures. The 3, 1, and 2 are significant (rule 1). The leading zeros only mark the decimal place and are therefore not significant (rule 3).
  (b) Ambiguous. The 3, 1, and 2 are significant (rule 1). The trailing zeros occur before an implied decimal point and are therefore ambiguous (rule 4). Without more information, we would assume three significant figures. It is better to write this as 3.12×10^5 to indicate three significant figures or as 3.12000×10^5 to indicate six (rule 4).
  (c) Three significant figures. The 3, 1, and 2 are significant (rule 1).
  (d) Five significant figures. The 1s, 3, 2, and 7 are significant (rule 1).

1.41   (a) This is not exact because π is an irrational number. The number 3.14 only shows three of the infinite number of significant figures that π has.
  (b) This is an exact conversion because it comes from a definition of the units and so has an unlimited number of significant figures.
  (c) This is a measured number, so it is not an exact number. There are two significant figures.
  (d) This is an exact conversion because it comes from a definition of the units and so has an unlimited number of significant figures.

1.43   (a) 156.9—The 8 is rounded up because the next digit is a 5.
  (b) 156.8—The last two digits are dropped because 4 is less than 5.
  (c) 156.8—The last two digits are dropped because 4 is less than 5.
  (d) 156.9—The 8 is rounded up because the next digit is a 9, which is greater than 5.

Significant Figures in Calculations

1.45   (a) $9.15 \div 4.970 = 1.84$—Three significant figures are allowed to reflect the three significant figures in the least precisely known quantity (9.15).

(b) $1.54 \times 0.03060 \times 0.69 = 0.033$—Two significant figures are allowed to reflect the two significant figures in the least precisely known quantity (0.69). The intermediate answer (0.03251556) is rounded up because the first nonsignificant digit is a 5.

(c) $27.5 \times 1.82 \div 100.04 = 0.500$—Three significant figures are allowed to reflect the three significant figures in the least precisely known quantities (27.5 and 1.82). The intermediate answer (0.50029988) is truncated because the first nonsignificant digit is a 2, which is less than 5.

(d) $(2.290 \times 10^6) \div (6.7 \times 10^4) = 34$—Two significant figures are allowed to reflect the two significant figures in the least precisely known quantity (6.7×10^4). The intermediate answer (34.17910448) is truncated because the first nonsignificant digit is a 1, which is less than 5.

1.47 (a)

$$43.7$$
$$\underline{-2.341}$$
$$41.359 = 41.4$$

Round the intermediate answer to one decimal place to reflect the quantity with the fewest decimal places (43.7). Round the last digit up because the first nonsignificant digit is 5.

(b)

$$17.6$$
$$+2.838$$
$$+2.3$$
$$\underline{+110.77}$$
$$133.508 = 133.5$$

Round the intermediate answer to one decimal place to reflect the quantity with the fewest decimal places (2.3). Truncate nonsignificant digits because the first nonsignificant digit is 0.

(c)

$$19.6$$
$$+58.33$$
$$\underline{-4.974}$$
$$72.956 = 73.0$$

Round the intermediate answer to one decimal place to reflect the quantity with the fewest decimal places (19.6). Round the last digit up because the first nonsignificant digit is 5.

(d)

$$5.99$$
$$\underline{-5.572}$$
$$0.418 = 0.42$$

Round the intermediate answer to two decimal places to reflect the quantity with the fewest decimal places (5.99). Round the last digit up because the first nonsignificant digit is 8.

1.49 Perform operations in parentheses first. Keep track of significant figures in each step by noting the last significant digit in an intermediate result.

(a) $(24.6681 \times 2.38) + 332.58 = 58.\underline{7}10078$

$$\underline{+332.58}$$
$$391.290078 = 391.3$$

The first intermediate answer has one significant digit to the right of the decimal because it is allowed three significant figures [reflecting the quantity with the fewest significant figures (2.38)]. Underline the least significant digit in this answer. Round the next intermediate answer to one decimal place to reflect the quantity with the fewest decimal places (58.7). Round the last digit up because the first nonsignificant digit is 9.

(b) $\dfrac{(85.3 - 21.489)}{0.0059} = \dfrac{63.\underline{8}11}{0.0059} = 1.0\underline{8}1542 \times 10^4 = 1.1 \times 10^4$

The first intermediate answer has one significant digit to the right of the decimal to reflect the quantity with the fewest decimal places (85.3). Underline the last significant digit in this answer. Round the next intermediate answer to two significant figures to reflect the quantity with the fewest significant figures (0.0059). Round the last digit up because the first nonsignificant digit is 8.

(c) $(512 \div 986.7) + 5.44 = 0.5\underline{1}89014$

$$\underline{+5.44}$$
$$5.9589014 = 5.96$$

The first intermediate answer has three significant figures and three significant digits to the right of the decimal, reflecting the quantity with the fewest significant figures (512). Underline the last significant digit in this answer. Round the next intermediate answer to two decimal places to reflect the quantity with the fewest decimal places (5.44). Round the last digit up because the first nonsignificant digit is 8.

(d) $\quad [(28.7 \times 10^5) \div 48.533] + 144.99 = 591\underline{3}5.02$

$$\frac{+144.99}{59280.01} = 59300 = 5.93 \times 10^4$$

The first intermediate answer has three significant figures, reflecting the quantity with the fewest significant figures (28.7×10^5). Underline the most significant digit in this answer. Because the number is so large, when the addition is performed, the last significant digit is the 100s place. Round the next intermediate answer to the 100s place and put in scientific notation to remove any ambiguity. Note that the last digit is rounded up because the first nonsignificant digit is 8.

1.51 **Given:** 11.7 mL liquid; empty flask weight = 124.1 g; flask with liquid weight = 132.8 g $\quad$ **Find:** d in g/mL
Conceptual Plan: Empty flask weight, flask with liquid weight → liquid weight then weight, volume → d

$\qquad\qquad$ (flask with liquid weight) − (flask weight) = liquid weight $\qquad\qquad$ $d = \text{mass/volume} = m/V$

Solution: liquid weight = (flask with liquid weight) − (flask weight) = 132.8 g − 124.1 g = 8.7 g liquid; then

$$\text{density}\,(d) = \frac{\text{mass}}{\text{volume}} = \frac{m}{V} = \frac{8.7\,\text{g}}{11.7\,\text{mL}} = 0.7\underline{4}358974\,\text{g/mL} = 0.74\,\text{g/mL}$$

Check: The units (g/mL) are correct. The magnitude of the answer (0.74) makes physical sense because the volume is greater than the mass.

Unit Conversions

1.53 (a) **Given:** 27.8 L $\quad$ **Find:** cm^3
$\qquad$ **Conceptual Plan: L → cm^3**

$$\frac{1000\,\text{cm}^3}{1\,\text{L}}$$

$\qquad$ **Solution:** $27.8\,\cancel{\text{L}} \times \dfrac{1000\,\text{cm}^3}{1\,\cancel{\text{L}}} = 2.78 \times 10^4\,\text{cm}^3$

$\qquad$ **Check:** The units (cm^3) are correct. The magnitude of the answer (10^4) makes physical sense because cm^3 is much smaller than a liter; so the answer should go up several orders of magnitude. Three significant figures are allowed because of the limitation of 27.8 L (three significant figures).

(b) **Given:** 1898 mg $\quad$ **Find:** kg
$\qquad$ **Conceptual Plan: mg → g → kg**

$$\frac{1\,\text{g}}{1000\,\text{mg}} \quad \frac{1\,\text{kg}}{1000\,\text{g}}$$

$\qquad$ **Solution:** $1898\,\cancel{\text{mg}} \times \dfrac{1\,\cancel{\text{g}}}{1000\,\cancel{\text{mg}}} \times \dfrac{1\,\text{kg}}{1000\,\cancel{\text{g}}} = 1.898 \times 10^{-3}\,\text{kg}$

$\qquad$ **Check:** The units (kg) are correct. The magnitude of the answer (10^{-3}) makes physical sense because a kilogram is a much larger unit than a milligram. Four significant figures are allowed because 1898 mg has four significant figures.

(c) **Given:** 198 km $\quad$ **Find:** cm
$\qquad$ **Conceptual Plan: km → m → cm**

$$\frac{1000\,\text{m}}{1\,\text{km}} \quad \frac{100\,\text{cm}}{1\,\text{m}}$$

$\qquad$ **Solution:** $198\,\cancel{\text{km}} \times \dfrac{1000\,\cancel{\text{m}}}{1\,\cancel{\text{km}}} \times \dfrac{100\,\text{cm}}{1\,\cancel{\text{m}}} = 1.98 \times 10^7\,\text{cm}$

$\qquad$ **Check:** The units (cm) are correct. The magnitude of the answer (10^7) makes physical sense because a kilometer is a much larger unit than a centimeter. Three significant figures are allowed because 198 km has three significant figures.

1.55   (a)   **Given:** 228 cm   **Find:** in

                Conceptual Plan: cm → in

$$\frac{1\ in}{2.54\ cm}$$

                Solution: $228\ \cancel{cm} \times \dfrac{1\ in}{2.54\ \cancel{cm}} = 89.76377953\ in = 89.8\ in$

                Check: The units (in) are correct. The magnitude of the answer (90) makes physical sense because an inch is a larger unit than a centimeter. Three significant figures are allowed because 228 cm has three significant figures.

    (b)   **Given:** 2.55 kg   **Find:** lb

                Conceptual Plan: kg → lb

$$\frac{2.2046\ lb}{1\ kg}$$

                Solution: $2.55\ \cancel{kg} \times \dfrac{2.2046\ lb}{1\ \cancel{kg}} = 5.62173\ lb = 5.62\ lb$

                Check: The units (lb) are correct. The magnitude of the answer (5.6) makes physical sense because a kilogram is a larger unit than a pound. Three significant figures are allowed because 2.55 kg has three significant figures.

    (c)   **Given:** 2.41 L   **Find:** qt

                Conceptual Plan: L → qt

$$\frac{1.057\ qt}{1\ L}$$

                Solution: $2.41\ \cancel{L} \times \dfrac{1.057\ qt}{1\ \cancel{L}} = 2.54737\ qt = 2.55\ qt$

                Check: The units (qt) are correct. The magnitude of the answer (2.6) makes physical sense because a liter is a smaller unit than a quart. Three significant figures are allowed because 2.41 L has three significant figures. Round the last digit up because the first nonsignificant digit is a 7.

    (d)   **Given:** 157 mm   **Find:** in

                Conceptual Plan: mm → m → in

$$\frac{1\ m}{1000\ mm} \qquad \frac{39.37\ in}{1\ m}$$

                Solution: $157\ \cancel{mm} \times \dfrac{1\ \cancel{m}}{1000\ \cancel{mm}} \times \dfrac{39.37\ in}{1\ \cancel{m}} = 6.18109\ in = 6.18\ in$

                Check: The units (in) are correct. The magnitude of the answer (6) makes physical sense because a millimeter is a much smaller unit than an inch. Three significant figures are allowed because 157 mm has three significant figures.

1.57   **Given:** 10.0 km   **Find:** minutes **Other:** running pace = 7.5 miles per hour

       Conceptual Plan: km → mi → hr → min

$$\frac{0.6214\ mi}{1\ km} \qquad \frac{1\ hr}{7.5\ mi} \qquad \frac{60\ min}{1\ hr}$$

       Solution: $10.0\ \cancel{km} \times \dfrac{0.6214\ \cancel{mi}}{1\ \cancel{km}} \times \dfrac{1\ \cancel{hr}}{7.5\ \cancel{mi}} \times \dfrac{60\ min}{1\ \cancel{hr}} = 49.712\ min = 50.\ min = 5.0 \times 10^1\ min$

       Check: The units (min) are correct. The magnitude of the answer (50) makes physical sense because she is running almost 7.5 miles (which would take her 60 min = 1 hr). Two significant figures are allowed because of the limitation of 7.5 mi/hr (two significant figures). Round the last digit up because the first nonsignificant digit is a 7.

1.59   **Given:** 14 km/L   **Find:** miles per gallon

       Conceptual Plan: $\dfrac{\textbf{km}}{\textbf{L}} \rightarrow \dfrac{\textbf{mi}}{\textbf{L}} \rightarrow \dfrac{\textbf{mi}}{\textbf{gal}}$

$$\frac{0.6214\ mi}{1\ km} \qquad \frac{3.785\ L}{1\ gallon}$$

       Solution: $\dfrac{14\ \cancel{km}}{1\ \cancel{L}} \times \dfrac{0.6214\ mi}{1\ \cancel{km}} \times \dfrac{3.785\ \cancel{L}}{1\ gallon} = 32.927986\ \dfrac{miles}{gallon} = 33\ \dfrac{miles}{gallon}$

Check: The units (mi/gal) are correct. The magnitude of the answer (33) makes physical sense because the dominating factor is that a liter is much smaller than a gallon; so the answer should go up. Two significant figures are allowed because of the limitation of 14 km/L (two significant figures). Round the last digit up because the first nonsignificant digit is a 9.

1.61 (a) **Given:** 195 m^2 **Find:** km^2
Conceptual Plan: m^2 → km^2

$$\frac{(1\text{ km})^2}{(1000\text{ m})^2}$$

Notice that for squared units, the conversion factors must be squared.

Solution: $195\text{ m}^2 \times \dfrac{(1\text{ km})^2}{(1000\text{ m})^2} = 1.95 \times 10^{-4}\text{ km}^2$

Check: The units (km^2) are correct. The magnitude of the answer (10^{-4}) makes physical sense because a kilometer is a much larger unit than a meter.

(b) **Given:** 195 m^2 **Find:** dm^2
Conceptual Plan: m^2 → dm^2

$$\frac{(10\text{ dm})^2}{(1\text{ m})^2}$$

Notice that for squared units, the conversion factors must be squared.

Solution: $195\text{ m}^2 \times \dfrac{(10\text{ dm})^2}{(1\text{ m})^2} = 1.95 \times 10^4\text{ dm}^2$

Check: The units (dm^2) are correct. The magnitude of the answer (10^4) makes physical sense because a decimeter is a much smaller unit than a meter.

(c) **Given:** 195 m^2 **Find:** cm^2
Conceptual Plan: m^2 → cm^2

$$\frac{(100\text{ cm})^2}{(1\text{ m})^2}$$

Notice that for squared units, the conversion factors must be squared.

Solution: $195\text{ m}^2 \times \dfrac{(100\text{ cm})^2}{(1\text{ m})^2} = 1.95 \times 10^6\text{ cm}^2$

Check: The units (cm^2) are correct. The magnitude of the answer (10^6) makes physical sense because a centimeter is a much smaller unit than a meter.

1.63 **Given:** 435 acres **Find:** square miles **Other:** 1 acre = 43,560 ft^2; 1 mile = 5280 ft
Conceptual Plan: acres → ft^2 → mi^2

$$\frac{43,560\text{ ft}^2}{1\text{ acre}} \qquad \frac{(1\text{ mi})^2}{(5280\text{ ft})^2}$$

Notice that for squared units, the conversion factors must be squared.

Solution: $435\text{ acres} \times \dfrac{43,560\text{ ft}^2}{1\text{ acres}} \times \dfrac{(1\text{ mi})^2}{(5280\text{ ft})^2} = 0.6796875\text{ mi}^2 = 0.680\text{ mi}^2$

Check: The units (mi^2) are correct. The magnitude of the answer (0.7) makes physical sense because an acre is much smaller than a mi^2; so the answer should go down several orders of magnitude. Three significant figures are allowed because of the limitation of 435 acres (three significant figures). Round the last digit up because the first nonsignificant digit is a 6.

1.65 **Given:** 14 lb **Find:** mL **Other:** 80 mg/0.80 mL; 15 mg/kg body
Conceptual Plan: lb → kg body → mg → mL

$$\frac{1\text{ kg body}}{2.205\text{ lb}} \qquad \frac{15\text{ mg}}{1\text{ kg body}} \qquad \frac{0.80\text{ mL}}{80\text{ mg}}$$

Solution: $14\text{ lb} \times \dfrac{1\text{ kg body}}{2.205\text{ lb}} \times \dfrac{15\text{ mg}}{1\text{ kg body}} \times \dfrac{0.80\text{ mL}}{80\text{ mg}} = 0.9523809524\text{ mL} = 0.95\text{ mL}$

Check: The units (mL) are correct. The magnitude of the answer (1 mL) makes physical sense because it is a reasonable amount of liquid to give to a baby. Two significant figures are allowed because of the statement in the problem. Truncate after the last significant digit because the first nonsignificant digit is a 2.

Cumulative Problems

1.67   **Given:** solar year   **Find:** seconds
        Other: 60 seconds/minute; 60 minutes/hour; 24 hours/solar day; 365.24 solar days/solar year
        Conceptual Plan: yr → day → hr → min → sec

$$\frac{365.24 \text{ day}}{1 \text{ solar yr}} \quad \frac{24 \text{ hr}}{1 \text{ day}} \quad \frac{60 \text{ min}}{1 \text{ hr}} \quad \frac{60 \text{ sec}}{1 \text{ min}}$$

Solution: $1 \text{ solar yr} \times \dfrac{365.24 \text{ day}}{1 \text{ solar yr}} \times \dfrac{24 \text{ hr}}{1 \text{ day}} \times \dfrac{60 \text{ min}}{1 \text{ hr}} \times \dfrac{60 \text{ sec}}{1 \text{ min}} = 3.1556736 \times 10^7 \text{ sec} = 3.1557 \times 10^7 \text{ sec}$

Check: The units (sec) are correct. The magnitude of the answer (10^7) makes physical sense because each conversion factor increases the value of the answer—a second is many orders of magnitude smaller than a year. Five significant figures are allowed because all conversion factors are assumed to be exact except for the 365.24 days/solar year (five significant figures). Round the last digit up because the first nonsignificant digit is a 7.

1.69   (a)   Extensive—The volume of a material depends on how much is present.
        (b)   Intensive—The boiling point of a material is independent of how much material you have; so these values can be published in reference tables.
        (c)   Intensive—The temperature of a material is independent of how much is present.
        (d)   Intensive—The electrical conductivity of a material is independent of how much material you have; so these values can be published in reference tables.
        (e)   Extensive—The energy contained in a material depends on how much is present. If you double the amount of material, you double the amount of energy.

1.71   **Given:** $130 \text{ °X} = 212 \text{ °F}$ and $10 \text{ °X} = 32 \text{ °F}$ **Find:** temperature where $\text{°X} = \text{°F}$.
        Conceptual Plan: Use data to derive an equation relating °X and °F. Then set °F = °X = z and solve for z.
        Solution: Assume a linear relationship between the two temperatures ($y = mx + b$).
        Let $y = \text{°F}$ and let $x = \text{°X}$.
        The slope of the line (m) is the relative change in the two temperature scales:

$$m = \frac{\Delta \text{ °F}}{\Delta \text{ °X}} = \frac{212 \text{ °F} - 32 \text{ °F}}{130 \text{ °X} - 10 \text{ °X}} = \frac{180 \text{ °F}}{120 \text{ °X}} = 1.5$$

Solve for intercept (b) by plugging one set of temperatures into the equation:
$y = 1.5x + b \rightarrow 32 = (1.5)(10) + b \rightarrow 32 = 15 + b \rightarrow b = 17 \rightarrow \text{°F} = (1.5) \text{ °X} + 17$
Set $\text{°F} = \text{°X} = z$ and solve for z.
$z = 1.5z + 17 \rightarrow -17 = 1.5z - z \rightarrow -17 = 0.5z \rightarrow z = -34 \rightarrow -34 \text{ °F} = -34 \text{ °X}$

Check: The units (°F and °X) are correct. Plugging the result back into the equation confirms that the calculations were done correctly. The magnitude of the answer seems correct because it is known that the result is not between 32 °F and 212 °F. The numbers are getting closer together as the temperature drops.

1.73   (a) $1.76 \times 10^{-3}/8.0 \times 10^2 = 2.2 \times 10^{-6}$ Two significant figures are allowed to reflect the quantity with the fewest significant figures (8.0×10^2).
        (b)   Write all figures so that the decimal points can be aligned:
                0.0187
                +0.0002 All quantities are known to four places to the right of the decimal place;
                −0.0030 so the answer should be reported to four places to the right of the
                0.0159 decimal place, or three significant figures.
        (c) $[(136000)(0.000322)/0.082](129.2) = 6.899910244 \times 10^4 = 6.9 \times 10^4$ Round the intermediate answer to two significant figures to reflect the quantity with the fewest significant figures (0.082). Round the last digit up because the first nonsignificant digit is 9.

1.75   (a)   **Given:** cylinder dimensions: length $= 22$ cm; radius $= 3.8$ cm; $d(\text{gold}) = 19.3 \text{ g/cm}^3$; $d(\text{sand}) = 3.00 \text{ g/cm}^3$
                Find: $m(\text{gold})$ and $m(\text{sand})$

Conceptual Plan: $l, r \rightarrow V$ then $d, V \rightarrow m$

$$V = l\pi r^2 \qquad\qquad d = m/V$$

Solution: $V(\text{gold}) = V(\text{sand}) = (22 \text{ cm})(\pi)(3.8 \text{ cm})^2 = 998.0212 \text{ cm}^3$

$d = m/V$ Rearrange by multiplying both sides of equation by V. $\rightarrow m = d \times V$

$$m(\text{gold}) = \left(19.3 \frac{\text{g}}{\text{cm}^3}\right) \times (998.0212 \text{ cm}^3) = 1.926181 \times 10^4 \text{ g} = 1.9 \times 10^4 \text{ g}$$

Check: The units (g) are correct. The magnitude of the answer seems correct considering that the value of the density is ~20 g/cm^3. Two significant figures are allowed to reflect the significant figures in 22 cm and 3.8 cm. Truncate the nonsignificant digits because the first nonsignificant digit is a 2.

$$m(\text{sand}) = \left(3.00 \frac{\text{g}}{\text{cm}^3}\right) \times (998.0212 \text{ cm}^3) = 2.99406 \times 10^3 \text{ g} = 3.0 \times 10^3 \text{ g}$$

Check: The units (g) are correct. The magnitude of the answer seems correct considering that the value of the density is 3 g/cm^3. This number is much lower than the gold mass. Two significant figures are allowed to reflect the significant figures in 22 cm and 3.8 cm. Round the last digit up because the first nonsignificant digit is a 9.

(b)   Comparing the two values 1.9×10^4 g versus 3.0×10^3 g shows a difference in weight of almost a factor of 10. This difference should be enough to trip the alarm and alert the authorities to the presence of the thief.

1.77   **Given:** 3.5 lb of titanium; density (titanium) $= 4.51$ g/cm^3 **Find:** volume in in^3

Conceptual Plan: lb $\rightarrow$ g then $m, d \rightarrow V$ then cm^3 $\rightarrow$ in^3

$$\frac{453.59 \text{ g}}{1 \text{ lb}} \qquad\qquad d = m/V \qquad\qquad \frac{(1 \text{ in})^3}{(2.54 \text{ cm})^3}$$

Solution: $3.5 \text{ lb} \times \dfrac{453.59 \text{ g}}{1 \text{ lb}} = 1.5876 \times 10^3 \text{ g}$

$d = m/V$ Rearrange by multiplying both sides of the equation by V and dividing both sides of the equation by d.

$$V = \frac{m}{d} = \frac{1.5876 \times 10^3 \text{ g}}{4.51 \dfrac{\text{g}}{\text{cm}^3}} = 3.520 \times 10^2 \text{ cm}^3 = 3.5 \times 10^2 \text{ cm}^3 \times \frac{(1 \text{ in})^3}{(2.54 \text{ cm})^3} = 21.480 \text{ in}^3 = 21 \text{ in}^3$$

Check: The units (in^3) are correct. The magnitude of the answer seems correct considering how many grams we have. Two significant figures are allowed to reflect the significant figures in 3.5 lb. Truncate the nonsignificant digits because the first nonsignificant digit is a 4.

1.79   **Given:** cylinder dimensions: length $= 2.16$ in; radius $= 0.22$ in; m $= 41$ g   **Find:** density (g/m^3)

Conceptual Plan: in $\rightarrow$ cm then $l, r \rightarrow V$ then $m, V \rightarrow d$

$$\frac{2.54 \text{ cm}}{1 \text{ in}} \qquad\qquad V = l\pi r^2 \qquad\qquad d = m/V$$

Solution: $2.16 \text{ in} \times \dfrac{2.54 \text{ cm}}{1 \text{ in}} = 5.4864 \text{ cm} = l \qquad\qquad 0.22 \text{ in} \times \dfrac{2.54 \text{ cm}}{1 \text{ in}} = 0.5588 \text{ cm} = r$

$V = l\pi r^2 = (5.4864 \text{ cm})(\pi)(0.5588 \text{ cm})^2 = 5.3820798 \text{ cm}^3$

$$d = \frac{m}{V} = \frac{41 \text{ g}}{5.3820798 \text{ cm}^3} = 7.6178729 \frac{\text{g}}{\text{cm}^3} = 7.6 \frac{\text{g}}{\text{cm}^3}$$

Check: The units (g/cm^3) are correct. The magnitude of the answer seems correct considering that the value of the density of iron (a major component in steel) is 7.86 g/cm^3. Two significant figures are allowed to reflect the significant figures in 0.22 in and 41 g. Truncate the nonsignificant digits because the first nonsignificant digit is a 1.

1.81   **Given:** 185 cubic yards (yd^3) of H$_2$O   **Find:** mass of the H$_2$O (pounds)

Other: $d(\text{H}_2\text{O}) = 1.00$ g/cm^3 at 4 °C

Conceptual Plan: yd^3 $\rightarrow$ m^3 $\rightarrow$ cm^3 $\rightarrow$ g $\rightarrow$ lb

$$\frac{(1 \text{ m})^3}{(1.094 \text{ yd})^3} \quad \frac{(100 \text{ cm})^3}{(1 \text{ m})^3} \quad \frac{1.00 \text{ g}}{1.00 \text{ cm}^3} \quad \frac{1 \text{ lb}}{453.59 \text{ g}}$$

Solution: $185 \text{ yd}^3 \times \dfrac{(1 \text{ m})^3}{(1.094 \text{ yd})^3} \times \dfrac{(100 \text{ cm})^3}{(1 \text{ m})^3} \times \dfrac{1.00 \text{ g}}{1.00 \text{ cm}^3} \times \dfrac{1 \text{ lb}}{453.59 \text{ g}} = 3.114987377 \times 10^5 \text{ lb} = 3.11 \times 10^5 \text{ lb}$

Check: The units (lb) are correct. The magnitude of the answer (10^5) makes physical sense because a pool is not a small object. Three significant figures are allowed because the conversion factor with the least precision is the density ($1.00 \text{ g/cm}^3 - 3$ significant figures) and the initial size has three significant figures. Truncate after the last digit because the first nonsignificant digit is a 4.

1.83   **Given:** 15 liters of gasoline   **Find:** kilometers **Other:** 52 mi/gal in the city

Conceptual Plan: L → gal → mi → km

$$\frac{1 \text{ gallon}}{3.785 \text{ L}} \quad \frac{52 \text{ mi}}{1 \text{ gallon}} \quad \frac{1 \text{ km}}{0.6214 \text{ mi}}$$

Solution: $15 \text{ L} \times \dfrac{1 \text{ gallon}}{3.785 \text{ L}} \times \dfrac{52 \text{ mi}}{1 \text{ gallon}} \times \dfrac{1 \text{ km}}{0.6214 \text{ mi}} = 3.316327941 \times 10^2 \text{ km} = 3.3 \times 10^2 \text{ km}$

Check: The units (km) are correct. The magnitude of the answer (10^2) makes physical sense because the dominating conversion factor is the mileage, which increases the answer. Two significant figures are allowed because the conversion factor with the least precision is 52 mi/gallon (two significant figures) and the initial volume (15 L) has two significant figures. Truncate the last digit because the first nonsignificant digit is a 1. It is best to put the answer in scientific notation so that it is clear how many significant figures are expressed.

1.85   **Given:** radius of nucleus of the hydrogen atom $= 1.0 \times 10^{-13}$ cm; radius of the hydrogen atom $= 52.9$ pm

Find: fractional volume occupied by nucleus

Conceptual Plan: cm → m then pm → m then r → V then V_{atom}, $V_{nucleus}$ → fractional volume occupied

$$\frac{1 \text{ m}}{100 \text{ cm}} \qquad \frac{1 \text{ m}}{10^{12} \text{ pm}} \qquad V = (4/3)\pi r^3 \qquad \frac{V_{nucleus}}{V_{atom}}$$

Solution: $1.0 \times 10^{-13} \text{ cm} \times \dfrac{1 \text{ m}}{100 \text{ cm}} = 1.0 \times 10^{-15} \text{ m}$ and $52.9 \text{ pm} \times \dfrac{1 \text{ m}}{10^{12} \text{ pm}} = 5.29 \times 10^{-11} \text{ m}$

$V = (4/3)\pi r^3$ Substitute into fractional volume equation.

$\dfrac{V_{nucleus}}{V_{atom}} = \dfrac{(4/3)\ \pi r_{nucleus}^3}{(4/3)\ \pi r_{atom}^3}$ Simplify equation.

$\dfrac{V_{nucleus}}{V_{atom}} = \dfrac{r_{nucleus}^3}{r_{atom}^3}$ Substitute numbers and calculate result.

$\dfrac{V_{nucleus}}{V_{atom}} = \dfrac{(1.0 \times 10^{-15} \text{ m})^3}{(5.29 \times 10^{-11} \text{ m})^3} = (1.890359168 \times 10^{-5})^3 = 6.755118686 \times 10^{-15} = 6.8 \times 10^{-15}$

Check: The units (none) are correct. The magnitude of the answer seems correct (10^{-15}) because a proton is so small. Two significant figures are allowed to reflect the significant figures in 1.0×10^{-15} cm. Round the last digits up because the first nonsignificant digit is a 5.

1.87   **Given:** 24.0 kg copper wire; wire is a cylinder of radius $= 1.63$ mm   **Find:** resistance (Ω)

Other: d(copper) $= 8.96 \text{ g/cm}^3$; resistance $= 2.061\ \Omega/\text{km}$

Conceptual Plan: mm → m → cm and kg → g then

$$\frac{10^{-3} \text{ m}}{1 \text{ mm}} \quad \frac{100 \text{ cm}}{1 \text{ m}} \qquad \frac{1000 \text{ g}}{1 \text{ kg}}$$

d, m → V then V, r → l(cm) → m → km → Ω

$$d = m/V \qquad V = l\pi r^2 \qquad \frac{1 \text{ m}}{100 \text{ cm}} \quad \frac{1 \text{ km}}{1000 \text{ m}} \quad \frac{2.061\ \Omega}{1 \text{ km}}$$

Solution: $1.63 \text{ mm} \times \dfrac{10^{-3} \text{ m}}{1 \text{ mm}} \times \dfrac{100 \text{ cm}}{1 \text{ m}} = 0.163 \text{ cm}$ $24.0 \text{ kg} \times \dfrac{1000 \text{ g}}{1 \text{ kg}} = 2.40 \times 10^4 \text{ g}$ then $d = m/V$

Rearrange by multiplying both sides of equation by V to get $m = d \times V$ then divide both sides by d.

$V = \dfrac{m}{d} = \dfrac{2.40 \times 10^4 \text{ g}}{\dfrac{8.96 \text{ g}}{1 \text{ cm}^3}} = 2.6785714 \times 10^3 \text{ cm}^3$ then $V = l\pi r^2$

Rearrange by dividing both sides of the equation by πr^2 to get

$l = \dfrac{V}{\pi r^2} = \dfrac{2.6785714 \times 10^3 \text{ cm}^3}{\pi (0.163 \text{ cm})^2} = 3.2090623 \times 10^4 \text{ cm}$ then

$$3.2090623 \times 10^4 \; \cancel{cm} \times \frac{1 \; \cancel{m}}{100 \; \cancel{cm}} \times \frac{1 \; \cancel{km}}{1000 \; \cancel{m}} \times \frac{2.061 \; \Omega}{1 \; \cancel{km}} = 0.6613877 \; \Omega = \underline{0.661} \; \Omega$$

Check: The units (Ω) are correct. The magnitude of the answer seems correct because we expect a small resistance for a material that is commonly used for electrical wiring. Three significant figures are allowed to reflect the significant figures in 1.63 mm and 24.0 kg. Truncate the nonsignificant digits because the first nonsignificant digit is a 3.

1.89   **Given:** d(liquid nitrogen) $= 0.808$ g/mL; d(gaseous nitrogen) $= 1.15$ g/L; 175 L liquid nitrogen; 10.00 m $\times$ 10.00 m $\times$ 2.50 m room   **Find:** fraction of room air displaced by nitrogen gas

Conceptual Plan: L $\rightarrow$ mL then V_{liquid}, d_{liquid} $\rightarrow$ m_{liquid} then set $m_{liquid} = m_{gas}$ then m_{gas}, d_{gas} $\rightarrow$ V_{gas} then

$$\frac{1000 \; mL}{1 \; L} \qquad\qquad\qquad\qquad d = m/V \qquad\qquad\qquad\qquad\qquad\qquad d = m/V$$

Calculate the V_{room} $\rightarrow$ cm^3 $\rightarrow$ L **then calculate the fraction displaced**

$$V = l \times w \times h \quad \frac{(100 \; cm)^3}{(1 \; m)^3} \quad \frac{1 \; L}{1000 \; cm^3} \qquad\qquad \frac{V_{gas}}{V_{room}}$$

Solution: $175 \; \cancel{L} \times \dfrac{1000 \; mL}{1 \; \cancel{L}} = 1.75 \times 10^5$ mL. Solve for m by multiplying both sides of the equation by V.

$$m = V \times d = 1.75 \times 10^5 \; \cancel{mL} \times \frac{0.808 \; g}{1 \; \cancel{mL}} = 1.\underline{4}14 \times 10^5 \text{ g nitrogen liquid} = 1.\underline{4}14 \times 10^5 \text{ g nitrogen gas}$$

$d = m/V$ Rearrange by multiplying both sides of the equation by V and dividing both sides of the equation by d.

$$V = \frac{m}{d} = \frac{1.\underline{4}14 \times 10^5 \; \cancel{g}}{1.15 \; \dfrac{\cancel{g}}{L}} = 1.2\underline{2}9565 \times 10^5 \text{ L nitrogen gas}$$

$$V_{room} = l \times w \times h = 10.00 \; \cancel{m} \times 10.00 \; \cancel{m} \times 2.50 \; \cancel{m} \times \frac{(100 \; \cancel{cm})^3}{(1 \; \cancel{m})^3} \times \frac{1 \; L}{1000 \; \cancel{cm^3}} = 2.50 \times 10^5 \text{ L}$$

$$\frac{V_{gas}}{V_{room}} = \frac{1.2\underline{2}9565 \times 10^5 \; \cancel{L}}{2.50 \times 10^5 \; \cancel{L}} = 0.491826 = \underline{0.492}$$

Check: The units (none) are correct. The magnitude of the answer seems correct (0.5) because there is a large volume of liquid and the density of the gas is about a factor of 1000 less than the density of the liquid. Three significant figures are allowed to reflect the significant figures in the densities and the volume of the liquid given.

Challenge Problems

1.91   **Given:** mass of black hole (BH) $= 1 \times 10^3$ suns; radius of black hole $=$ one-half the radius of our moon

Find: density (g/cm^3) **Other:** radius of our sun $= 7.0 \times 10^5$ km; average density of our sun $= 1.4 \times 10^3$ kg/m^3; diameter of the moon $= 2.16 \times 10^3$ mi

Conceptual Plan: $d_{BH} = m_{BH}/V_{BH}$

Calculate m_{BH}: $r_{sun} \rightarrow V_{sun}$ km$^3_{sun}$ $\rightarrow$ m$^3_{sun}$ then V_{sun}, $d_{sun} \rightarrow m_{sun}$ then $m_{sun} \rightarrow m_{BH}$ kg $\rightarrow$ g

$$V = (4/3)\pi r^3 \quad \frac{(1000 \; m)^3}{(1 \; km)^3} \qquad\qquad d_{sun} = \frac{m_{sun}}{V_{sun}} \qquad m_{BH} = (1 \times 10^3) \times m_{sun} \quad \frac{1000 \; g}{1 \; kg}$$

Calculate V_{BH}: $dia_{moon} \rightarrow r_{moon} \rightarrow r_{BH}$ mi $\rightarrow$ km $\rightarrow$ m $\rightarrow$ cm then $r \rightarrow V$

$$r_{moon} = 1/2 \; dia_{moon} \text{ for clarity } r_{BH} = 1/2 \; r_{moon} \quad \frac{1 \; km}{0.6214 \; mi} \quad \frac{1000 \; m}{1 \; km} \quad \frac{100 \; cm}{1 \; m} \qquad V = (4/3)\pi r^3$$

Substitute into $d_{BH} = m_{BH}/V_{BH}$

Solution: Calculate m_{BH}: $V_{sun} = (4/3)\pi r^3_{sun} = (4/3)\pi (7.0 \times 10^5 \text{ km})^3 = 1.\underline{4}3675504 \times 10^{18}$ km^3

$$1.\underline{4}3675504 \times 10^{18} \; \cancel{km^3} \times \frac{(1000 \; m)^3}{(1 \; \cancel{km})^3} = 1.\underline{4}3675504 \times 10^{27} \text{ m}^3$$

$d_{sun} = m_{sun}/V_{sun}$. Solve for m by multiplying both sides of the equation by V_{sun}.

$m_{sun} = V_{sun} \times d_{sun}$

$m_{sun} = (1.\underline{4}3675504 \times 10^{27} \text{ m}^3)(1.4 \times 10^3 \text{ kg/m}^3) = 2.\underline{0}11457056 \times 10^{30}$ kg

$m_{BH} = (1 \times 10^3) \times m_{sun} = (1 \times 10^3) \times (2.\underline{0}11457056 \times 10^{30} \text{ kg}) = 2.\underline{0}11457056 \times 10^{33}$ kg

$$2.\underline{0}11457056 \times 10^{33} \; \cancel{kg} \times \frac{1000 \; g}{1 \; \cancel{kg}} = 2.\underline{0}11457056 \times 10^{36} \text{ g}$$

Calculate V_{BH}: $r_{moon} = \frac{1}{2}dia_{moon} = \frac{1}{2}(2.16 \times 10^3 \text{ mi}) = 1.08 \times 10^3 \text{ mi}$

$r_{BH} = \frac{1}{2}r_{moon} = \frac{1}{2}(1.08 \times 10^3 \text{ mi}) = 540. \text{ mi}$

$540. \text{ mi} \times \dfrac{1 \text{ km}}{0.6214 \text{ mi}} \times \dfrac{1000 \text{ m}}{1 \text{ km}} \times \dfrac{100 \text{ cm}}{1 \text{ m}} = 8.6900547 \times 10^7 \text{ cm}$

$V = (4/3)\pi r^3 = (4/3)\pi(8.6900547 \times 10^7 \text{ cm})^3 = 2.74888227 \times 10^{24} \text{ cm}^3$

Substitute into $d_{BH} = \dfrac{m_{BH}}{V_{BH}} = \dfrac{2.011457056 \times 10^{36} \text{ g}}{2.74888227 \times 10^{24} \text{ cm}^3} = 7.31736342 \times 10^{11}\dfrac{\text{g}}{\text{cm}^3} = 7.3 \times 10^{11}\dfrac{\text{g}}{\text{cm}^3}$

Check: The units (g/cm³) are correct. The magnitude of the answer seems correct (10^{12}) because we expect extremely high numbers for black holes. Two significant figures are allowed to reflect the significant figures in the radius of our sun (7.0×10^5 km) and the average density of the sun (1.4×10^3 kg/m³). Truncate the nonsignificant digits because the first nonsignificant digit is a 1.

1.93   **Given:** cubic nanocontainers with an edge length = 25 nanometers
Find: (a) volume of one nanocontainer; (b) grams of oxygen could be contained by each nanocontainer; (c) grams of oxygen inhaled per hour; (d) minimum number of nanocontainers per hour; (e) minimum volume of nanocontainers.
Other: (pressurized oxygen) = 85 g/L; 0.28 g of oxygen per liter; average human inhales about 0.50 L of air per breath and takes about 20 breaths per minute; adult total blood volume = ~5 L.
Conceptual Plan:
(a)   **nm** → **m** → **cm** then l → V then **cm³** → **L**

$\dfrac{1 \text{ m}}{10^9 \text{ nm}}$ $\dfrac{100 \text{ cm}}{1 \text{ m}}$ $V = l^3$ $\dfrac{1 \text{ L}}{1000 \text{ cm}^3}$

(b)   **L** → **g pressurized oxygen**

$\dfrac{85 \text{ g oxygen}}{1 \text{ L nanocontainers}}$

(c)   **hr** → **min** → **breaths** → $\mathbf{L_{air}}$ → $\mathbf{g_{O_2}}$

$\dfrac{60 \text{ min}}{1 \text{ hr}}$ $\dfrac{20 \text{ breath}}{1 \text{ min}}$ $\dfrac{0.50 \text{ L}_{air}}{1 \text{ breath}}$ $\dfrac{0.28 \text{ g}_{CO}}{1 \text{ L}_{air}}$

(d)   **grams oxygen** → **number nanocontainers**

$\dfrac{1 \text{ nanocontainer}}{\text{part (b) grams of oxygen}}$

(e)   **number nanocontainers** → **volume nanocontainers**

$\dfrac{\text{part (a) volume}}{\text{of 1 nanocontainer}}$

Solution:

(a) $25 \text{ nm} \times \dfrac{1 \text{ m}}{10^9 \text{ nm}} \times \dfrac{100 \text{ cm}}{1 \text{ m}} = 2.5 \times 10^{-6} \text{ cm}$

$V = l^3 = (2.5 \times 10^{-6} \text{ cm})^3 = 1.5625 \times 10^{-17} \text{ cm}^3 \times \dfrac{1 \text{ L}}{1000 \text{ cm}^3} = 1.5625 \times 10^{-20} \text{ L} = 1.6 \times 10^{-20} \text{ L}$

(b) $1.5625 \times 10^{-20} \text{ L} \times \dfrac{85 \text{ g oxygen}}{1 \text{ L nanocontainers}} = 1.328125 \times 10^{-18} \dfrac{\text{g pressurized O}_2}{\text{nanocontainer}}$

$= 1.3 \times 10^{-18} \dfrac{\text{g pressurized O}_2}{\text{nanocontainer}}$

(c) $1 \text{ hr} \times \dfrac{60 \text{ min}}{1 \text{ hr}} \times \dfrac{20 \text{ breath}}{1 \text{ min}} \times \dfrac{0.50 \text{ L}_{air}}{1 \text{ breath}} \times \dfrac{0.28 \text{ g O}_2}{1 \text{ L}_{air}} = 1.68 \times 10^2 \text{ g oxygen} = 1.7 \times 10^2 \text{ g oxygen}$

(d) $1.68 \times 10^2 \text{ g oxygen} \times \dfrac{1 \text{ nanocontainer}}{1.3 \times 10^{-18} \text{ g oxygen}} = 1.292307692 \times 10^{20} \text{ nanocontainers}$

$= 1.3 \times 10^{20} \text{ nanocontainers}$

(e) $1.292307692 \times 10^{20}$ nanocontainers $\times \dfrac{1.5625 \times 10^{-20} \, \text{L}}{\text{nanocontainer}} = 2.019230769 \, \text{L} = 2.0 \, \text{L}$

This volume is much too large to be feasible because the volume of blood in the average human is 5 L.

Check:

(a)   The units (L) are correct. The magnitude of the answer (10^{-20}) makes physical sense because these are very, very tiny containers. Two significant figures are allowed, reflecting the significant figures in the starting dimension (25 nm – 2 significant figures). Round the last digit up because the first nonsignificant digit is a 6.

(b)   The units (g) are correct. The magnitude of the answer (10^{-18}) makes physical sense because these are very, very tiny containers and very few molecules can fit inside. Two significant figures are allowed, reflecting the significant figures in the starting dimension (25 nm) and the given concentration (85 g/L) – 2 significant figures in each. Truncate the nonsignificant digits because the first nonsignificant digit is a 2.

(c)   The units (g oxygen) are correct. The magnitude of the answer (10^{2}) makes physical sense because of the conversion factors involved and the fact that air is not very dense. Two significant figures are allowed because it is stated in the problem. Round the last digit up because the first nonsignificant digit is an 8.

(d)   The units (nanocontainers) are correct. The magnitude of the answer (10^{20}) makes physical sense because these are very, very tiny containers and we need a macroscopic quantity of oxygen in these containers. Two significant figures are allowed, reflecting the significant figures in both of the quantities in the calculation – 2 significant figures. Round the last digit up because the first nonsignificant digit is a 9.

(e)   The units (L) are correct. The magnitude of the answer (2) makes physical sense because of the magnitudes of the numbers in this step. Two significant figures are allowed, reflecting the significant figures in both of the quantities in the calculation—2 significant figures. Truncate the nonsignificant digits because the first nonsignificant digit is a 1.

1.95   Assume that all of the spheres are the same size. Let $x =$ the percentage of spheres that are copper (expressed as a fraction); so the volume of copper $= (427 \, \text{cm}^3)x$ and the volume of lead $= (427 \, \text{cm}^3) \, (1 - x)$. Because the density of copper is 8.96 g/cm^3, the mass of copper $= (427 \, \text{cm}^3)x \times \dfrac{8.96 \, \text{g}}{\text{cm}^3} = 3825.92(x)$ g. Because the density of lead is 11.4 g/cm^3, the mass of lead $= (427 \, \text{cm}^3)(1 - x) \times \dfrac{11.46 \, \text{g}}{\text{cm}^3} = 4893.42 \, (1 - x)$ g. Because the total mass is 4.36 kg $= 4360$ g, 4360 g $= 3825.92(x)$ g $+ 4893.42 \, (1 - x)$ g. Solving for x, $1067.50(x)$ g $= 533.42$ g $\rightarrow$ $x = 0.499691$, or 50.% of the spheres are copper.

Check: This answer makes sense because the average density of the spheres $= 4360 \, \text{g}/427 \, \text{cm}^3 = 10.2 \, \text{g/cm}^3$ and the average of the density of copper and the density of lead $= (8.96 + 11.4)/2 \, \text{g/cm}^3 = 10.2 \, \text{g/cm}^3$.

Conceptual Problems

1.97   (c) is the best representation. When solid carbon dioxide (dry ice) sublimes, it changes phase from a solid to a gas. Phase changes are physical changes, so no molecular bonds are broken. This diagram shows molecules with one carbon atom and two oxygen atoms bonded together in every molecule. The other diagrams have no carbon dioxide molecules.

1.99   This problem is similar to Problem 1.28 except that the dimension is changed to 7 cm on each edge.
Given: 7 cm on each edge cube   **Find:** cm^3
Conceptual Plan: Read the information carefully. The cube is 7 cm on each side.
$l, w, h \rightarrow V$
$V = lwh$
in a cube $l = w = h$

Solution: 7 cm $\times$ 7 cm $\times$ 7 cm $= (7 \, \text{cm})^3 = 343 \, \text{cm}^3$, or 343 cubes

1.101   Remember that density $=$ mass/volume.
(a)   The darker-colored box has a heavier mass but a smaller volume, so it is denser than the lighter-colored box.
(b)   The lighter-colored box is heavier than the darker-colored box, and both boxes have the same volume; so the lighter-colored box is denser.
(c)   The larger box is the heavier box, so it cannot be determined with this information which box is denser.

Questions for Group Work

1.103

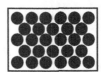
solid element

liquid compound

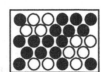
heterogeneous mixture

liquid compound physical change:

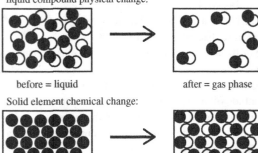

before = liquid   after = gas phase

Solid element chemical change:

before = solid element   after = solid compound

1.105   All of these values can be true because when we round 4.73297 km to three significant figures we get 4.73 km; and if we round this value to one significant figure we get 5 km. The number of digits reported indicates how accurately the distance was measured. The odometer on a car could be used for the first measurement. A trip meter on a car could be used for the second measurement. A long tape measure could be used for the last measurement.

1.107   To convert the height of a student from feet and inches into meters: first convert the feet to inches; then add this to the number of inches, and finally convert the inches to centimeters and to meters. For example, if the height of a student is 5'8.5": $5 \text{ ft} \times \dfrac{12 \text{ in}}{1 \text{ ft}} = 60$ in (exactly); then 60 in + 8.5 in = 68.5 in, and finally

$68.5 \text{ in} \times \dfrac{2.54 \text{ cm}}{1 \text{ in}} \times \dfrac{1 \text{ m}}{100 \text{ cm}} = 1.7399$ m = 1.74 m.

Add all of the heights together to get the sum for your group.

2 Atoms and Elements

Problems by Topic

The Laws of Conservation of Mass, Definite Proportions, and Multiple Proportions

2.1   **Given:** 1.50 g hydrogen; 12.0 g oxygen   **Find:** grams water vapor
Conceptual Plan: total mass reactants = total mass products
Solution: Mass of reactants = 1.50 g hydrogen + 12.0 g oxygen = 13.5 grams
Mass of products = mass of reactants = 13.5 grams water vapor

Check: According to the law of conservation of mass, matter is not created or destroyed in a chemical reaction. So because water vapor is the only product, the masses of hydrogen and oxygen must combine to form the mass of water vapor.

2.3   **Given:** sample 1: 38.9 g carbon, 448 g chlorine; sample 2: 14.8 g carbon, 134 g chlorine
Find: consistent with definite proportions
Conceptual Plan: Determine mass ratio of samples 1 and 2 and compare.

$$\frac{\text{mass of chlorine}}{\text{mass of carbon}}$$

Solution: sample 1: $\dfrac{448 \text{ g chlorine}}{38.9 \text{ g carbon}} = 11.5$ sample 2: $\dfrac{134 \text{ g chlorine}}{14.8 \text{ g carbon}} = 9.05$

Results are not consistent with the law of definite proportions because the ratio of chlorine to carbon is not the same.

Check: According to the law of definite proportions, the mass ratio of one element to another is the same for all samples of the compound.

2.5   **Given:** mass ratio sodium to fluorine = 1.21:1; sample = 28.8 g sodium   **Find:** g fluorine
Conceptual Plan: g sodium → g fluorine

$$\frac{\text{mass of fluorine}}{\text{mass of sodium}}$$

Solution: 28.8 g̶ ̶s̶o̶d̶i̶u̶m̶ $\times \dfrac{1 \text{ g fluorine}}{1.21 \text{ g̶ ̶s̶o̶d̶i̶u̶m̶}} = 23.8$ g fluorine

Check: The units of the answer (g fluorine) are correct. The magnitude of the answer is reasonable because it is less than the grams of sodium.

2.7   **Given:** 1 gram osmium: sample 1 = 0.168 g oxygen; sample 2 = 0.3369 g oxygen
Find: consistent with multiple proportions
Conceptual Plan: Determine mass ratio of oxygen.

$$\frac{\text{mass of oxygen sample 2}}{\text{mass of oxygen sample 1}}$$

Solution: $\dfrac{0.3369 \text{ g oxygen}}{0.168 \text{ g oxygen}} = 2.00$ Ratio is a small whole number. Results are consistent with
multiple proportions.

Check: According to the law of multiple proportions, when two elements form two different compounds, the masses of element B that combine with 1 g of element A can be expressed as a ratio of small whole numbers.

17

2.9   **Given:** sulfur dioxide $=$ 3.49 g oxygen and 3.50 g sulfur; sulfur trioxide $=$ 6.75 g oxygen and 4.50 g sulfur
     Find: mass oxygen per g S for each compound and then determine the mass ratio of oxygen

$$\frac{\text{mass of oxygen in sulfur dioxide}}{\text{mass of sulfur in sulfur dioxide}} \quad \frac{\text{mass of oxygen in sulfur trioxide}}{\text{mass of sulfur in sulfur trioxide}} \quad \frac{\text{mass of oxyen in sulfur trioxide}}{\text{mass of oxyen in sulfur dioxide}}$$

Solution: sulfur dioxide $= \dfrac{3.49 \text{ g oxygen}}{3.50 \text{ g sulfur}} = \dfrac{0.997 \text{ g oxygen}}{1 \text{ g sulfur}}$ sulfur trioxide $= \dfrac{6.75 \text{ g oxygen}}{4.50 \text{ g sulfur}} = \dfrac{1.50 \text{ g oxygen}}{1 \text{ g sulfur}}$

$\dfrac{1.50 \text{ g oxygen in sulfur trioxide}}{0.997 \text{ g oxygen in sulfur dioxide}} = \dfrac{1.50}{1} = \dfrac{3}{2}$. The ratio is converted from 1.50:1 to 3:2 because the law of multiple proportions states that the ratio is in small whole numbers.
Ratio is in small whole numbers and is consistent with multiple proportions.

Check: According to the law of multiple proportions, when two elements form two different compounds, the masses of element B that combine with 1 g of element A can be expressed as a ratio of small whole numbers.

Atomic Theory, Nuclear Theory, and Subatomic Particles

2.11   (a)   Sulfur and oxygen atoms have the same mass. INCONSISTENT with Dalton's atomic theory because only atoms of the same element have the same mass.

         (b)   All cobalt atoms are identical. CONSISTENT with Dalton's atomic theory because all atoms of a given element have the same mass and other properties that distinguish them from atoms of other elements.

         (c)   Potassium and chlorine atoms combine in a 1:1 ratio to form potassium chloride. CONSISTENT with Dalton's atomic theory because atoms combine in simple whole-number ratios to form compounds.

         (d)   Lead atoms can be converted into gold. INCONSISTENT with Dalton's atomic theory because atoms of one element cannot change into atoms of another element.

2.13   (a)   The volume of an atom is mostly empty space. CONSISTENT with Rutherford's nuclear theory because most of the volume of the atom is empty space, throughout which tiny, negatively charged electrons are dispersed.

         (b)   The nucleus of an atom is small compared to the size of the atom. CONSISTENT with Rutherford's nuclear theory because most of the atom's mass and all of its positive charge are contained in a small core called the nucleus.

         (c)   Neutral lithium atoms contain more neutrons than protons. INCONSISTENT with Rutherford's nuclear theory because it did not distinguish where the mass of the nucleus came from other than from the protons.

         (d)   Neutral lithium atoms contain more protons than electrons. INCONSISTENT with Rutherford's nuclear theory because there are as many negatively charged particles outside the nucleus as there are positively charged particles in the nucleus.

2.15   **Given:** drop A $= -6.9 \times 10^{-19}$ C; drop B $= -9.2 \times 10^{-19}$ C; drop C $= -11.5 \times 10^{-19}$ C; drop D $= -4.6 \times 10^{-19}$ C
     Find: the charge on a single electron
     Conceptual Plan: Determine the ratio of charge for each set of drops and determine the charge on an electron.

$$\frac{\text{charge on drop 1}}{\text{charge on drop 2}}$$

Solution: $\dfrac{-6.9 \times 10^{-19} \text{ C drop A}}{-4.6 \times 10^{-19} \text{ C drop D}} = 1.5$ $\dfrac{-9.2 \times 10^{-19} \text{ C drop B}}{-4.6 \times 10^{-19} \text{ C drop D}} = 2$ $\dfrac{-11.5 \times 10^{-19} \text{ C drop C}}{-4.6 \times 10^{-19} \text{ C drop D}} = 2.5$

The ratios obtained are not whole numbers, but they can be converted to whole numbers by multiplying by 2. Therefore, the charge on the electron has to be 1/2 the smallest value experimentally obtained. The charge on the electron $= -2.3 \times 10^{-19}$ C.

Check: The units of the answer (Coulombs) are correct. The magnitude of the answer is reasonable because all of the values experimentally obtained are integer multiples of -2.3×10^{-19}.

2.17   **Given:** charge on body $= -15 \,\mu\text{C}$ **Find:** number of electrons; mass of the electrons
     Conceptual Plan: $\mu\text{C} \rightarrow \text{C} \rightarrow$ **number of electrons** $\rightarrow$ **mass of electrons**

$$\frac{1 \text{ C}}{10^6 \,\mu\text{C}} \quad \frac{1 \text{ electron}}{-1.60 \times 10^{-19} \text{ C}} \qquad \frac{9.11 \times 10^{-28} \text{ g}}{1 \text{ electron}}$$

Solution: $-15 \,\mu\cancel{\text{C}} \times \dfrac{1 \,\cancel{\text{C}}}{10^6 \,\cancel{\mu\text{C}}} \times \dfrac{1 \text{ electron}}{-1.60 \times 10^{-19} \,\cancel{\text{C}}} = 9.\underline{3}75 \times 10^{13} \text{ electrons} = 9.4 \times 10^{13} \text{ electrons}$

$9.\underline{3}75 \times 10^{13} \text{ electrons} \times \dfrac{9.11 \times 10^{-28} \text{ g}}{1 \text{ electron}} = 8.5 \times 10^{-14} \text{ g}$

Check: The units of the answers (number of electrons and grams) are correct. The magnitude of the answers is reasonable because the charge on an electron and the mass of an electron are very small.

2.19   (a)   True: Protons and electrons have equal and opposite charges.
       (b)   True: Protons and electrons have opposite charges, so they will attract each other.
       (c)   True: The mass of the electron is much less than the mass of the neutron.
       (d)   False: The mass of the proton and the mass of the neutron are about the same.

Isotopes and Ions

2.21   For each of the isotopes, determine Z (the number of protons) from the periodic table and determine A (protons + neutrons). Then write the symbol in the form $^A_Z X$.
       (a)   The sodium isotope with 12 neutrons: $Z = 11$; $A = 11 + 12 = 23$ $^{23}_{11}Na$
       (b)   The oxygen isotope with 8 neutrons: $Z = 8$; $A = 8 + 8 = 16$ $^{16}_{8}O$
       (c)   The aluminum isotope with 14 neutrons: $Z = 13$; $A = 13 + 14 = 27$ $^{27}_{13}Al$
       (d)   The iodine isotope with 74 neutrons: $Z = 53$; $A = 53 + 74 = 127$ $^{127}_{53}I$

2.23   (a) $^{14}_{7}N$: $Z = 7$; $A = 14$; protons = $Z = 7$; neutrons = $A - Z = 14 - 7 = 7$
       (b) $^{23}_{11}Na$: $Z = 11$; $A = 23$; protons = $Z = 11$; neutrons = $A - Z = 23 - 11 = 12$
       (c) $^{222}_{86}Rn$: $Z = 86$; $A = 222$; protons = $Z = 86$; neutrons = $A - Z = 222 - 86 = 136$
       (d) $^{208}_{82}Pb$: $Z = 82$; $A = 208$; protons = $Z = 82$; neutrons = $A - Z = 208 - 82 = 126$

2.25   Carbon-14: $A = 14$, $Z = 6$: $^{14}_{6}C$ # protons = $Z = 6$ # neutrons = $A - Z = 14 - 6 = 8$

2.27   In a neutral atom, the number of protons = the number of electrons = Z. For an ion, electrons are lost (cations) or gained (anions).
       (a) Ni^{2+}: $Z = 28 =$ protons; $Z - 2 = 26 =$ electrons
       (b) S^{2-}: $Z = 16 =$ protons; $Z + 2 = 18 =$ electrons
       (c) Br^{-}: $Z = 35 =$ protons; $Z + 1 = 36 =$ electrons
       (d) Cr^{3+}: $Z = 24 =$ protons; $Z - 3 = 21 =$ electrons

2.29   Main-group metal atoms will lose electrons to form a cation with the same number of electrons as the nearest previous noble gas.
       Nonmetal atoms will gain electrons to form an anion with the same number of electrons as the nearest noble gas.
       (a) O^{2-} O is a nonmetal and has 8 electrons. It will gain electrons to form an anion. The nearest noble gas is neon with 10 electrons, so O will gain 2 electrons.
       (b) K^{+} K is a main-group metal and has 19 electrons. It will lose electrons to form a cation. The nearest noble gas is argon with 18 electrons, so K will lose 1 electron.
       (c) Al^{3+} Al is a main-group metal and has 13 electrons. It will lose electrons to form a cation. The nearest noble gas is neon with 10 electrons, so Al will lose 3 electrons.
       (d) Rb^{+} Rb is a main-group metal and has 37 electrons. It will lose electrons to form a cation. The nearest noble gas is krypton with 36 electrons, so Rb will lose 1 electron.

2.31   Main-group metal atoms will lose electrons to form a cation with the same number of electrons as the nearest previous noble gas. Atoms in period 4 and higher lose electrons to form the same ion as the element at the top of the group. Nonmetal atoms will gain electrons to form an anion with the same number of electrons as the nearest noble gas.

Symbol	Ion Formed	Number of Electrons in Ion	Number of Protons in Ion
Ca	Ca^{2+}	18	20
Be	Be^{2+}	2	4
Se	Se^{2-}	36	34
In	In^{3+}	46	49

The Periodic Table and Atomic Mass

2.33   (a)   Na   Sodium is a metal.
          (b)   Mg   Magnesium is a metal.
          (c)   Br   Bromine is a nonmetal.
          (d)   N   Nitrogen is a nonmetal.
          (e)   As   Arsenic is a metalloid.

2.35   (a)   tellurium   Te is in group 6A and is a main-group element.
          (b)   potassium   K is in group 1A and is a main-group element.
          (c)   vanadium   V is in group 5B and is a transition element.
          (d)   manganese   Mn is in group 7B and is a transition element.

2.37   (a)   sodium   Na is in group 1A and is an alkali metal.
          (b)   iodine   I is in group 7A and is a halogen.
          (c)   calcium   Ca is in group 2A and is an alkaline earth metal.
          (d)   barium   Ba is in group 2A and is an alkaline earth metal.
          (e)   krypton   Kr is in group 8A and is a noble gas.

2.39   (a)   N and Ni would not be similar. Nitrogen is a nonmetal; nickel is a metal.
          (b)   Mo and Sn would not be most similar. Although both are metals, molybdenum is a transition metal and tin is a main-group metal.
          (c)   Na and Mg would not be similar. Although both are main-group metals, sodium is in group 1A and magnesium is in group 2A.
          (d)   Cl and F would be most similar. Chlorine and fluorine are both in group 7A. Elements in the same group have similar chemical properties.
          (e)   Si and P would not be most similar. Silicon is a metalloid, and phosphorus is a nonmetal.

2.41   **Given:** Rb-85; mass $=$ 84.9118 amu; 72.15%:Rb-87; mass $=$ 86.9092 amu; 27.85%
        Find: atomic mass Rb
        Conceptual Plan: % abundance → fraction and then find atomic mass

$$\frac{\% \text{ abundance}}{100} \qquad \text{Atomic mass} = \sum_n (\text{fraction of isotope } n) \times (\text{mass of isotope } n)$$

        Solution: Fraction Rb-85 $= \dfrac{72.15}{100} = 0.7215$ Fraction Rb-87 $= \dfrac{27.85}{100} = 0.2785$

$$\text{Atomic mass} = \sum_n (\text{fraction of isotope } n) \times (\text{mass of isotope } n)$$

$$= 0.7215(84.9118 \text{ amu}) + 0.2785(86.9092 \text{ amu}) = 85.47 \text{ amu}$$

        Check: Units of the answer (amu) are correct. The magnitude of the answer is reasonable because it lies between 84.9118 amu and 86.9092 amu and is closer to 84.9118 amu, which has the higher % abundance.

2.43   **Given:** isotope 1, mass $=$ 120.9038 amu, 57.4%; isotope 2, mass $=$ 122.9042 amu.
        Find: atomic mass of the element and identify the element
        Conceptual Plan:
        % abundance isotope 2 → and then % abundance → fraction and then find atomic mass

$$100\% - \% \text{ abundance isotope 1} \qquad \frac{\% \text{ abundance}}{100} \qquad \text{Atomic mass} = \sum_n (\text{fraction of isotope } n) \times (\text{mass of isotope } n)$$

        Solution: $100.0\% - 57.4\%$ isotope 1 $= 42.6\%$ isotope 2

Fraction isotope 1 $= \dfrac{57.4}{100} = 0.574$ Fraction isotope 2 $= \dfrac{42.6}{100} = 0.426$

$$\text{Atomic mass} = \sum_n (\text{fraction of isotope } n) \times (\text{mass of isotope } n)$$

$$= 0.574(120.9038 \text{ amu}) + 0.426(122.9042 \text{ amu}) = 121.8 \text{ amu}$$

From the periodic table, Sb has a mass of 121.757 amu; so it is the closest mass, and the element is antimony.

Check: The units of the answer (amu) are correct. The magnitude of the answer is reasonable because it lies between 120.9038 and 122.9042 and is slightly less than halfway between the two values because the lower value has a slightly greater abundance.

The Mole Concept

2.45   **Given:** 2.7 mol sulfur   **Find:** atoms of sulfur
Conceptual Plan: mol S → atoms S

$$\frac{6.022 \times 10^{23} \text{ atoms}}{\text{mol}}$$

Solution: $2.7 \text{ mol S} \times \dfrac{6.022 \times 10^{23} \text{ atoms S}}{\text{mol S}} = 1.6 \times 10^{24} \text{ atoms S}$

Check: The units of the answer (atoms S) are correct. The magnitude of the answer is reasonable because more than 1 mole of material is present.

2.47   (a)   **Given:** 11.8 g Ar   **Find:** mol Ar
Conceptual Plan: g Ar → mol Ar

$$\frac{1 \text{ mol Ar}}{39.95 \text{ g Ar}}$$

Solution: $11.8 \text{ g Ar} \times \dfrac{1 \text{ mol Ar}}{39.95 \text{ g Ar}} = 0.295 \text{ mol Ar}$

Check: The units of the answer (mol Ar) are correct. The magnitude of the answer is reasonable because less than the mass of 1 mol is present.

(b)   **Given:** 3.55 g Zn   **Find:** mol Zn
Conceptual Plan: g Zn → mol Zn

$$\frac{1 \text{ mol Zn}}{65.38 \text{ g Zn}}$$

Solution: $3.55 \text{ g Zn} \times \dfrac{1 \text{ mol Zn}}{65.38 \text{ g Zn}} = 0.0543 \text{ mol Zn}$

Check: The units of the answer (mol Zn) are correct. The magnitude of the answer is reasonable because less than the mass of 1 mol is present.

(c)   **Given:** 26.1 g Ta   **Find:** mol Ta
Conceptual Plan: g Ta → mol Ta

$$\frac{1 \text{ mol Ta}}{180.95 \text{ g Ta}}$$

Solution: $26.1 \text{ g Ta} \times \dfrac{1 \text{ mol Ta}}{180.95 \text{ g Ta}} = 0.144 \text{ mol Ta}$

Check: The units of the answer (mol Ta) are correct. The magnitude of the answer is reasonable because less than the mass of 1 mol is present.

(d)   **Given:** 0.211 g Li   **Find:** mol Li
Conceptual Plan: g Li → mol Li

$$\frac{1 \text{ mol Li}}{6.941 \text{ g Li}}$$

Solution: $0.211 \text{ g Li} \times \dfrac{1 \text{ mol Li}}{6.941 \text{ g Li}} = 0.0304 \text{ mol Li}$

Check: The units of the answer (mol Li) are correct. The magnitude of the answer is reasonable because less than the mass of 1 mol is present.

2.49   **Given:** 2.54 g silver   **Find:** atoms Ag
Conceptual Plan: g Ag → mol Ag → atoms Ag

$$\frac{1 \text{ mol Ag}}{107.87 \text{ g Ag}} \qquad \frac{6.022 \times 10^{23} \text{ atoms}}{\text{mol}}$$

Solution: $2.54 \ \cancel{g \ Ag} \times \dfrac{1 \ \cancel{mol \ Ag}}{107.87 \ \cancel{g \ Ag}} \times \dfrac{6.022 \times 10^{23} \ atoms \ Ag}{1 \ \cancel{mol \ Ag}} = 1.42 \times 10^{22} \ atoms \ Ag$

Check: The units of the answer (atoms Ag) are correct. The magnitude of the answer is reasonable because less than the mass of 1 mol of Ag is present.

2.51   (a)   **Given:** 5.18 g P   **Find:** atoms P
        Conceptual Plan: g P → mol P → atoms P

$$\dfrac{1 \ mol \ P}{30.97 \ g \ P} \quad \dfrac{6.022 \times 10^{23} \ atoms}{mol}$$

Solution: $5.18 \ \cancel{g \ P} \times \dfrac{1 \ \cancel{mol \ P}}{30.97 \ \cancel{g \ P}} \times \dfrac{6.022 \times 10^{23} \ atoms \ P}{1 \ \cancel{mol \ P}} = 1.01 \times 10^{23} \ atoms \ P$

Check: The units of the answer (atoms P) are correct. The magnitude of the answer is reasonable because less than the mass of 1 mol of P is present.

        (b)   **Given:** 2.26 g Hg   **Find:** atoms Hg
        Conceptual Plan: g Hg → mol Hg → atoms Hg

$$\dfrac{1 \ mol \ Hg}{200.59 \ g \ Hg} \quad \dfrac{6.022 \times 10^{23} \ atoms}{mol}$$

Solution: $2.26 \ \cancel{g \ Hg} \times \dfrac{1 \ \cancel{mol \ Hg}}{200.59 \ \cancel{g \ Hg}} \times \dfrac{6.022 \times 10^{23} \ atoms \ Hg}{1 \ \cancel{mol \ Hg}} = 6.78 \times 10^{21} \ atoms \ Hg$

Check: The units of the answer (atoms Hg) are correct. The magnitude of the answer is reasonable because much less than the mass of 1 mol of Hg is present.

        (c)   **Given:** 1.87 g Bi   **Find:** atoms Bi
        Conceptual Plan: g Bi → mol Bi → atoms Bi

$$\dfrac{1 \ mol \ Bi}{208.98 \ g \ Bi} \quad \dfrac{6.022 \times 10^{23} \ atoms}{mol}$$

Solution: $1.87 \ \cancel{g \ Bi} \times \dfrac{1 \ \cancel{mol \ Bi}}{208.98 \ \cancel{g \ Bi}} \times \dfrac{6.022 \times 10^{23} \ atoms \ Bi}{1 \ \cancel{mol \ Bi}} = 5.39 \times 10^{21} \ atoms \ Bi$

Check: The units of the answer (atoms Bi) are correct. The magnitude of the answer is reasonable because less than the mass of 1 mol of Bi is present.

        (d)   **Given:** 0.082 g Sr   **Find:** atoms Sr
        Conceptual Plan: g Sr → mol Sr → atoms Sr

$$\dfrac{1 \ mol \ Sr}{87.62 \ g \ Sr} \quad \dfrac{6.022 \times 10^{23} \ atoms}{mol}$$

Solution: $0.082 \ \cancel{g \ Sr} \times \dfrac{1 \ \cancel{mol \ Sr}}{87.62 \ \cancel{g \ Sr}} \times \dfrac{6.022 \times 10^{23} \ atoms \ Sr}{1 \ \cancel{mol \ Sr}} = 5.6 \times 10^{20} \ atoms \ Sr$

Check: The units of the answer (atoms Sr) are correct. The magnitude of the answer is reasonable because less than the mass of 1 mol of Sr is present.

2.53   **Given:** 83 mg diamond (carbon)   **Find:** atoms C
        Conceptual Plan: mg C → g C → mol C → atoms C

$$\dfrac{1 \ g \ C}{1000 \ mg \ C} \quad \dfrac{1 \ mol \ C}{12.01 \ g \ C} \quad \dfrac{6.022 \times 10^{23} \ atoms}{mol}$$

Solution: $83 \ \cancel{mg \ C} \times \dfrac{1 \ \cancel{g \ C}}{1000 \ \cancel{mg \ C}} \times \dfrac{1 \ \cancel{mol \ C}}{12.01 \ \cancel{g \ C}} \times \dfrac{6.022 \times 10^{23} \ atoms \ C}{1 \ \cancel{mol \ C}} = 4.2 \times 10^{21} \ atoms \ C$

Check: The units of the answer (atoms C) are correct. The magnitude of the answer is reasonable because less than the mass of 1 mol of C is present.

2.55   **Given:** 1 atom platinum   **Find:** grams Pt
        Conceptual Plan: atoms Pt → mol Pt → g Pt

$$\dfrac{1 \ mol}{6.022 \times 10^{23} \ atoms} \quad \dfrac{195.08 \ g \ Pt}{1 \ mol \ Pt}$$

Solution: $1 \text{ atom Pt} \times \dfrac{1 \text{ mol Pt}}{6.022 \times 10^{23} \text{ atoms Pt}} \times \dfrac{195.08 \text{ g Pt}}{1 \text{ mol Pt}} = 3.239 \times 10^{-22} \text{ g Pt}$

Check: The units of the answer (g Pt) are correct. The magnitude of the answer is reasonable because only 1 atom is in the sample.

Cumulative Problems

2.57   **Given:** 7.83 g HCN sample 1: 0.290 g H; 4.06 g N. 3.37 g HCN sample 2   **Find:** g C in sample 2
    Conceptual Plan: g HCN sample 1 $\rightarrow$ g C in HCN sample 1 $\rightarrow$ ratio g C to g HCN $\rightarrow$ g C in HCN sample 2

$$\text{g HCN} - \text{g H} - \text{g N} \qquad \dfrac{\text{g C}}{\text{g HCN}} \qquad \text{g HCN} \times \dfrac{\text{g C}}{\text{g HCN}}$$

Solution: $7.83 \text{ g HCN} - 0.290 \text{ g H} - 4.06 \text{ g N} = 3.48 \text{ g C}$

$$3.37 \text{ g HCN} \times \dfrac{3.48 \text{ g C}}{7.83 \text{ g HCN}} = 1.50 \text{ g C}$$

Check: The units of the answer (g C) are correct. The magnitude of the answer is reasonable because the sample size is about half the original sample size and the g C are about half the original g C.

2.59   **Given:** in CO, mass ratio O:C = 1.33:1; in compound X, mass ratio O:C = 2:1.   **Find:** formula of X
    Conceptual Plan: Determine the mass ratio of O:O in the two compounds.

    Solution: For 1 gram of C $\dfrac{2 \text{ g O in compound X}}{1.33 \text{ g O in CO}} = 1.5$

So the ratio of O to C in compound X has to be 1.5 : 1, and the formula is C_2O_3.

Check: The answer is reasonable because it fulfills the criteria of multiple proportions and the mass ratio of O:C is 2:1.

2.61   **Given:** $^{4}\text{He}^{2+} = 4.00151 \text{ amu}$ **Find:** charge to mass ratio C/kg
    Conceptual Plan: Determine total charge on $^{4}\text{He}^{2+}$ and then amu $^{4}\text{He}^{2+} \rightarrow$ g $^{4}\text{He}^{2+} \rightarrow$ kg $^{4}\text{He}^{2+}$.

$$\dfrac{+1.60218 \times 10^{-19} \text{ C}}{\text{proton}} \qquad \dfrac{1 \text{ g}}{1.66054 \times 10^{-24} \text{ amu}} \qquad \dfrac{1 \text{ kg}}{1000 \text{ g}}$$

Solution: $\dfrac{2 \text{ protons}}{1 \text{ atom } ^{4}\text{He}^{2+}} \times \dfrac{+1.60218 \times 10^{-19} \text{ C}}{\text{proton}} = \dfrac{3.20436 \times 10^{-19} \text{ C}}{\text{atom } ^{4}\text{He}^{2+}}$

$$\dfrac{4.00151 \text{ amu}}{1 \text{ atom } ^{4}\text{He}^{2+}} \times \dfrac{1.66054 \times 10^{-24} \text{ g}}{1 \text{ amu}} \times \dfrac{1 \text{ kg}}{1000 \text{ g}} = \dfrac{6.64466742 \times 10^{-27} \text{ kg}}{1 \text{ atom } ^{4}\text{He}^{2+}}$$

$$\dfrac{3.20436 \times 10^{-19} \text{ C}}{\text{atom } ^{4}\text{He}^{2+}} \times \dfrac{1 \text{ atom } ^{4}\text{He}^{2+}}{6.64466742 \times 10^{-27} \text{ kg}} = 4.82245 \times 10^{7} \text{ C/kg}$$

Check: The units of the answer (C/kg) are correct. The magnitude of the answer is reasonable when compared to the charge to mass ratio of the electron.

2.63 $^{236}_{90}\text{Th}$ A $-$ Z $=$ number of neutrons. $236 - 90 = 146$ neutrons. So any nucleus with 146 neutrons is an isotone of $^{236}_{90}\text{Th}$.

Some would be $^{238}_{92}\text{U}$, $^{239}_{93}\text{Np}$, $^{241}_{95}\text{Am}$, $^{237}_{91}\text{Pa}$, $^{235}_{89}\text{Ac}$, and $^{244}_{98}\text{Cf}$.

2.65

Symbol	Z	A	Number Protons	Number Electrons	Number Neutrons	Charge
O^{2-}	8	16	8	10	8	2−
Ca^{2+}	20	40	20	18	20	2+
Mg^{2+}	12	25	12	10	13	2+
N^{3-}	7	14	7	10	7	3−

2.67 **Given:** r(nucleus) $= 2.7$ fm; r(atom) $= 70$ pm (assume two significant figures)

Find: vol(nucleus); vol(atom); % vol(nucleus)

Conceptual Plan:

r(nucleus)(fm) $\rightarrow$ r(nucleus)(pm) $\rightarrow$ vol(nucleus) and then r(atom) $\rightarrow$ vol(atom) and then % vol

$$\frac{10^{-15}\text{ m}}{1\text{ fm}} \quad \frac{1\text{ pm}}{10^{-12}\text{ m}} \qquad V = \frac{4}{3}\pi r^3 \qquad\qquad V = \frac{4}{3}\pi r^3 \qquad \frac{\text{vol(nucleus)}}{\text{vol(atom)}} \times 100$$

Solution:

$$2.7\text{ fm} \times \frac{10^{-15}\text{ m}}{\text{fm}} \times \frac{1\text{ pm}}{10^{-12}\text{ m}} = 2.7 \times 10^{-3}\text{ pm} \qquad V_{\text{nucleus}} = \frac{4}{3}\pi\,(2.7 \times 10^{-3}\text{ pm})^3 = 8.2 \times 10^{-8}\text{ pm}^3$$

$$V_{\text{atom}} = \frac{4}{3}\pi(70\text{ pm})^3 = 1.4 \times 10^6\text{ pm}^3 \qquad\qquad \frac{8.2 \times 10^{-8}\text{ pm}^3}{1.4 \times 10^6\text{ pm}^3} \times 100\% = 5.9 \times 10^{-12}\%$$

Check: The units of the answer (% vol) are correct. The magnitude of the answer is reasonable because the nucleus occupies only a very small % of the vol of the atom.

2.69 **Given:** 6.022×10^{23} pennies   **Find:** the amount in dollars; the dollars/person

Conceptual Plan: pennies $\rightarrow$ dollars $\rightarrow$ dollars/person

$$\frac{1\text{ dollar}}{100\text{ pennies}} \quad 6.8\text{ billion people}$$

Solution:

$$6.022 \times 10^{23}\text{ pennies} \times \frac{1\text{ dollar}}{100\text{ pennies}} = 6.022 \times 10^{21}\text{ dollars} \qquad \frac{6.022 \times 10^{21}\text{ dollars}}{6.8 \times 10^9\text{ people}} = 8.9 \times 10^{11}\text{ dollars/person}$$

They are billionaires.

2.71 **Given:** O $= 16.00$ amu when C $= 12.01$ amu   **Find:** mass O when C $= 12.000$ amu

Conceptual Plan: Determine ratio O:C for ^{12}C system; then use the same ratio when C $= 12.00$.

$$\frac{\text{mass O}}{\text{mass C}}$$

Solution: Based on ^{12}C $= 12.00$, O $= 16.00$ and C $= 12.01$; so $\dfrac{\text{mass O}}{\text{mass C}} = \dfrac{16.00\text{ amu}}{12.01\text{ amu}} = \dfrac{1.3322\text{ amu O}}{1\text{ amu C}}$

Based on C $= 12.00$, the ratio has to be the same:

$$12.000\text{ amu C} \times \frac{1.3322\text{ amu O}}{1\text{ amu C}} = 15.986\text{ amu O} = 15.99\text{ amu O}$$

Check: The units of the answer (amu O) are correct. The magnitude of the answer is reasonable because the value for the new mass basis is smaller than the original mass basis; therefore, the mass of O should be less.

2.73 **Given:** Cu sphere: $r = 0.935$ in; $d = 8.96$ g/cm^3 **Find:** number of Cu atoms

Conceptual Plan: r in inch $\rightarrow$ r in cm $\rightarrow$ vol sphere $\rightarrow$ g Cu $\rightarrow$ mol Cu $\rightarrow$ atoms Cu

$$\frac{2.54\text{ cm}}{1\text{ in}} \qquad V = \frac{4}{3}\pi r^3 \qquad \frac{8.96\text{ g}}{\text{cm}^3} \quad \frac{1\text{ mol Cu}}{63.55\text{ g}} \quad \frac{6.022 \times 10^{23}\text{ atoms}}{\text{mol}}$$

Solution: $0.935\text{ in} \times \dfrac{2.54\text{ cm}}{\text{in}} = 2.3749\text{ cm}$

$$\frac{4}{3}\pi(2.3749\text{ cm})^3 \times \frac{8.96\text{ g}}{\text{cm}^3} \times \frac{1\text{ mol Cu}}{63.55\text{ g}} \times \frac{6.022 \times 10^{23}\text{ atoms Cu}}{1\text{ mol Cu}} = 4.76 \times 10^{24}\text{ atoms Cu}$$

Check: The units of the answer (atoms Cu) are correct. The magnitude of the answer is reasonable because about 8 mol Cu are present.

2.75 **Given:** Ti cube: 2.55×10^{24} titanium atoms; $d = 4.50$ g/cm^3 **Find:** e in cm

Conceptual Plan: atoms Ti $\rightarrow$ mol Ti $\rightarrow$ g Ti $\rightarrow$ vol cube $\rightarrow$ e

$$\frac{1\text{ mole}}{6.022 \times 10^{23}\text{ atoms}} \quad \frac{47.87\text{ g Ti}}{1\text{ mol Ti}} \quad \frac{1\text{ cm}^3}{4.50\text{ g}} \qquad V = e^3$$

Solution: 2.55×10^{24} Ti atoms $\times \dfrac{1 \text{ mol Ti}}{6.022 \times 10^{23} \text{ Ti atoms}} \times \dfrac{47.87 \text{ g Ti}}{1 \text{ mole Ti}} \times \dfrac{1 \text{ cm}^3}{4.50 \text{ g Ti}} = 45.0\underline{4}539 \text{ cm}^3$

$V = e^3$ Rearrange to solve for e. $e = \sqrt[3]{V} = \sqrt[3]{45.0\underline{4}539 \text{ cm}^3} = 3.56 \text{ cm}$

Check: The units (cm) are correct. The magnitude of the answer (3.56) makes physical sense because there is over a mole of Ti and the density of Ti is almost 5 g/cm^3.

2.77   **Given:** Li-6 = 6.01512 amu; Li-7 = 7.01601 amu; Li = 6.941 amu
        Find: % abundance Li-6 and Li-7
        Conceptual Plan: Let x = fraction Li-6 then $1 - x$ = fraction Li-7 $\rightarrow$ abundances

$$\text{Atomic mass} = \sum_n (\text{fraction of isotope } n) \times (\text{mass of isotope } n)$$

        Solution: Atomic mass $= \displaystyle\sum_n (\text{fraction of isotope } n) \times (\text{mass of isotope } n)$

$$6.941 = (x)(6.01512 \text{ amu}) + (1 - x)(7.01601 \text{ amu})$$
$$0.07\underline{5}01 = 1.00089x$$
$$x = 0.0\underline{7}494 \qquad 1 - x = 0.92\underline{5}06$$
$$\text{Li-6} = 0.07494 \times 100 = 7.5\% \text{ and Li-7} = 0.92\underline{5}06 \times 100\% = 92.5\%$$

        Check: The units of the answer (%, which gives the relative abundance of each isotope) are correct. The relative abundances are reasonable because Li has an atomic mass closer to the mass of Li-7 than to Li-6.

2.79   **Given:** Alloy of Au and Pd = 67.2 g; 2.49×10^{23} atoms   **Find:** % composition by mass
        Conceptual Plan: atoms Au and Pd $\rightarrow$ mol Au and Pd $\rightarrow$ g Au and Pd $\rightarrow$ g Au

$$\dfrac{1 \text{ mol}}{6.022 \times 10^{23} \text{ atoms}} \qquad \dfrac{196.97 \text{ g Au}}{1 \text{ mol Au}} ; \qquad \dfrac{106.42 \text{ g Pd}}{1 \text{ mol Pd}}$$

        Solution: Let X = atoms Au and Y = atoms Pd; develop expressions that will permit atoms to be related to moles and then to grams.

$$(\text{X atoms Au}) \left(\dfrac{1 \text{ mol Au}}{6.022 \times 10^{23} \text{ atoms Au}} \right) = \dfrac{\text{X}}{6.022 \times 10^{23}} \text{ mol Au}$$

$$(\text{Y atoms Pd}) \left(\dfrac{1 \text{ mol Pd}}{6.022 \times 10^{23} \text{ atoms Pd}} \right) = \dfrac{\text{Y}}{6.022 \times 10^{23}} \text{ mol Pd}$$

$$\text{X + Y} = 2.49 \times 10^{23} \text{ atoms}; \text{ Y} = 2.49 \times 10^{23} - \text{X}$$

$$\left(\dfrac{\text{X}}{6.022 \times 10^{23}} \text{ mol Au} \right) \left(\dfrac{196.97 \text{ g Au}}{\text{mol Au}} \right) = \dfrac{196.97\text{X}}{6.022 \times 10^{23}} \text{ g Au}$$

$$\left(\dfrac{2.49 \times 10^{23} - \text{X}}{6.022 \times 10^{23}} \text{ mol Pd} \right) \left(\dfrac{106.42 \text{ g Pd}}{\text{mol Pd}} \right) = \dfrac{106.42(2.49 \times 10^{23} - \text{X})}{6.022 \times 10^{23}} \text{ g Pd}$$

g Au + g Pd = 67.2 g total

$$\dfrac{196.97\text{X}}{6.022 \times 10^{23}} \text{ g Au} + \dfrac{106.42(2.49 \times 10^{23} - \text{X})}{6.022 \times 10^{23}} \text{ g Pd} = 67.2 \text{ g}$$

$$\text{X} = 1.5\underline{4}26 \times 10^{23} \text{ atoms Au}$$

$$(1.5\underline{4}26 \times 10^{23} \text{ atoms Au}) \left(\dfrac{1 \text{ mol Au}}{6.022 \times 10^{23} \text{ atoms Au}} \right) \left(\dfrac{196.97 \text{ g Au}}{\text{mol Au}} \right) = 50.\underline{4}6 \text{ g Au}$$

$$\left(\dfrac{50.\underline{4}6 \text{ g Au}}{67.2 \text{ g sample}} \right) \times 100 = 75.\underline{0}8\% \text{ Au} = 75.1\% \text{ Au}$$

% Pd = 100.0% − 75.1% Au = 24.9% Pd

        Check: Units of the answer (% composition) are correct.

2.81   **Given:** 0.255 ounce 18K Au   **Find:** atoms Au   **Other:** 18K Au is 75% Au by mass
        Conceptual Plan: ounces 18K Au $\rightarrow$ ounces pure Au $\rightarrow$ g Au $\rightarrow$ mol Au $\rightarrow$ atoms Au

$$\dfrac{75 \text{ oz Au}}{100 \text{ oz 18K Au}} \qquad \dfrac{453.59 \text{ g Au}}{16 \text{ oz Au}} \quad \dfrac{1 \text{ mol Au}}{196.97 \text{ g Au}} \quad \dfrac{6.022 \times 10^{23} \text{ atoms Au}}{1 \text{ mol Au}}$$

Solution: $0.255 \text{ oz } 18\text{K Au} \times \left(\dfrac{75 \text{ oz pure Au}}{100 \text{ oz } 18\text{K Au}}\right) \times \left(\dfrac{453.59 \text{ g}}{16 \text{ oz}}\right) \times \left(\dfrac{1 \text{ mol Au}}{196.97 \text{ g Au}}\right) \times \left(\dfrac{6.022 \times 10^{23} \text{ atoms Au}}{1 \text{ mol Au}}\right)$

$= 1.\underline{6}58 \times 10^{22} \text{ atoms Au} = 1.7 \times 10^{22} \text{ atoms Au}$

Check: The units of the answer (atoms Au) are correct. The magnitude of the answer is reasonable because less than 1 mol of Au is in the sample.

Challenge Problems

2.83   **Given:** sun: $d = 1.4$ g/cm^3, $r = 7 \times 10^8$ m; 100 billion stars/galaxy; 10 billion galaxies/universe

Find: number of atoms in the universe

Conceptual Plan: r **(star) in m** $\rightarrow$ r **(star) in cm** $\rightarrow$ **vol (star)** $\rightarrow$ **g H/star** $\rightarrow$ **mol H star** $\rightarrow$ **atoms H/star**

$$\dfrac{100 \text{ cm}}{1 \text{ m}} \qquad V = \dfrac{4}{3}\pi r^3 \qquad \dfrac{1.4 \text{ g H}}{\text{cm}^3} \qquad \dfrac{1 \text{ mol H}}{1.008 \text{ g}} \qquad \dfrac{6.022 \times 10^{23} \text{atoms}}{1 \text{ mol}}$$

$\rightarrow$ **atoms H/galaxy** $\rightarrow$ **atoms H/universe**

$$\dfrac{100 \times 10^9 \text{ stars}}{\text{galaxy}} \qquad \dfrac{10 \times 10^9 \text{galaxies}}{\text{universe}}$$

Solution: $7 \times 10^8 \text{ m} \times \dfrac{100 \text{ cm}}{\text{m}} = 7 \times 10^{10} \text{ cm}$

$$\dfrac{4}{3}\pi \dfrac{(7 \times 10^{10} \text{ cm})^3}{\text{star}} \times \dfrac{1.4 \text{ g H}}{\text{cm}^3} \times \dfrac{1 \text{ mol H}}{1.008 \text{ g H}} \times \dfrac{6.022 \times 10^{23} \text{ atoms H}}{1 \text{ mol H}} \times \dfrac{100 \times 10^9 \text{ stars}}{1 \text{ galaxy}} \times \dfrac{10 \times 10^9 \text{ galaxies}}{\text{universe}}$$

$$= 1 \times 10^{78} \text{ atoms/universe}$$

Check: The units of the answer (atoms/universe) are correct.

2.85   **Given:** sample $= 1.5886$ g; ^{59}Co $= 58.9332$ amu; ^{60}Co $= 59.9338$ amu; apparent mass $= 58.9901$ amu

Find: mass of ^{60}Co in sample

Conceptual Plan: apparent mass $\rightarrow$ **fraction** ^{60}**Co** $\rightarrow$ **mass** ^{60}**Co**

$$\text{Atomic mass} = \sum_n (\text{fraction of isotope } n) \times (\text{mass of isotope } n)$$

Solution: Let X $=$ fraction of ^{60}Co; so $1.00 - $ X $=$ fraction ^{59}Co

$58.9901 \text{ amu} = (1.00 - \text{X})(58.9332 \text{ amu}) + (\text{X})(59.9338 \text{ amu})$

X $= 0.05\underline{6}86$

1.5886 g sample $\times 0.05\underline{6}86 = 0.090\underline{3}28$ g ^{60}Co $= 0.0903$ g ^{60}Co

Check: The units of the answer (g ^{60}Co) are correct. The magnitude of the answer is reasonable because the apparent mass is very close to the mass ^{59}Co.

2.87   **Given:** $N_2O_3 = \dfrac{\text{mass O}}{\text{mass N}} = \dfrac{12}{7}$; sample X $= \dfrac{\text{mass O}}{\text{mass N}} = \dfrac{16}{7}$ **Find:** Formula of X, next in series

Conceptual Plan: ratio O/N for N_2O_3 $\rightarrow$ **ratio O/N for X** $\rightarrow$ **ratio if O/O**

Solution: $\dfrac{\text{mass O}}{\text{mass N}} = \dfrac{12}{7} = \dfrac{3 \text{ O}}{2 \text{ N}}$ $\dfrac{\text{mass O}}{\text{mass N}} = \dfrac{16}{7} = \dfrac{\text{X O}}{2 \text{ N}}$ $\dfrac{\text{mass O}}{\text{mass O}} = \dfrac{16}{12} = \dfrac{\text{X O}}{3 \text{ O}}$ so, X $= 4$

Therefore, the formula is N_2O_4.

The next member of the series would be N_2O_5.

$\dfrac{\text{mass O}}{\text{mass O}} = \dfrac{5 \text{ O}}{3 \text{ O}} = \dfrac{\text{Y}}{12}$ Y $= 20$ So $\dfrac{\text{mass O}}{\text{mass N}} = \dfrac{20}{7}$

Conceptual Problems

2.89   (a)   This is the law of definite proportions: All samples of a given compound, regardless of their source or how they were prepared, have the same proportions of their constituent elements.

(b)   This is the law of conservation of mass: In a chemical reaction, matter is neither created nor destroyed.

(c)   This is the law of multiple proportions: When two elements form two different compounds, the masses of element B that combine with 1 g of element A can be expressed as a ratio of small whole numbers. In this example the ratio of O from hydrogen peroxide to O from water $= 16{:}8 \rightarrow 2{:}1$, a small whole number ratio.

2.91   Li-6 nucleus   Li-7 nucleus

○○○   ○○○
□□□   □□□□

Since Li-6 has an abundance of 7.5%, in a sample of 1000 atoms, there should, on average, be 75 Li-6 atoms.

2.93   If the amu and mole were not based on the same isotope, the numerical values obtained for an atom of material and a mole of material would not be the same. If, for example, the mole was based on the number of particles in C-12 but the amu was changed to a fraction of the mass of an atom of Ne-20 the number of particles and the number of amu that make up one mole of material would no longer be the same. We would no longer have the relationship where the mass of an atom in amu is numerically equal to the mass of a mole of those atoms in grams.

2.95   The different isotopes of the same element have the same number of protons and electrons, so the attractive forces between the nucleus and the electrons are constant and there is no difference in the radii of the isotopes. Ions, on the other hand, have a different number of electrons than the parent atom from which they are derived. Cations have fewer electrons than the parent atom. The attractive forces are greater because there is a larger positive charge in the nucleus than the negative charge in the electron cloud. So, cations are smaller than the parent atom from which they are derived. Anions have more electrons than the parent. The electron cloud has a greater negative charge than the nucleus, so the anions have larger radii than the parent.

Questions for Group Work

2.97   Each boron atom has 5 protons. The mass of the boron atoms with 5 neutrons is ~10 amu, while the mass of the boron atoms with 6 neutrons is ~11 amu.

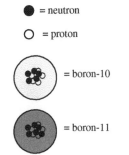

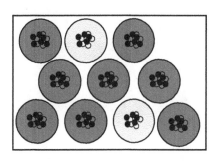

The average mass of boron in the drawing is

$$\text{Atomic mass} = \sum_n (\text{fraction of isotope } n) \times (\text{mass of isotope } n) =$$

$$0.2(10.01294 \text{ amu}) + 0.8(11.00931 \text{ amu}) = 10.810036 \text{ amu}$$

The average mass of boron is

$$\text{Atomic mass} = \sum_n (\text{fraction of isotope } n) \times (\text{mass of isotope } n) =$$

$$0.198(10.01294 \text{ amu}) + 0.802(11.00931 \text{ amu}) = 10.8 \text{ amu}$$

2.99   Electrons: $\dfrac{9.10938 \times 10^{-28} \text{ g}}{1 \text{ electron}} \times \dfrac{6.02214179 \times 10^{23} \text{ electrons}}{1 \text{ mole electrons}} = 5.48580 \times 10^{-4} \text{ g/mol}$

Protons: $\dfrac{1.67262 \times 10^{-24} \text{ g}}{1 \text{ proton}} \times \dfrac{6.02214179 \times 10^{23} \text{ electrons}}{1 \text{ mole electrons}} = 1.00728 \text{ g/mol}$

Neutrons: $\dfrac{1.67493 \times 10^{-24} \text{ g}}{1 \text{ neutron}} \times \dfrac{6.02214179 \times 10^{23} \text{ neutrons}}{1 \text{ mole neutrons}} = 1.00867 \text{ g/mol}$

Carbon-12: $\dfrac{1.992646 \times 10^{-23} \text{ g}}{1 \text{ carbon-12}} \times \dfrac{6.02214179 \times 10^{23} \text{ carbon-12}}{1 \text{ mole carbon-12}} = 12.00000 \text{ g/mol}$

mass of components parts $= \left(6 \text{ mol protons} \times \dfrac{1.00728 \text{ g}}{1 \text{ mol protons}} \right) + \left(6 \text{ mol neutrons} \times \dfrac{1.00867 \text{ g}}{1 \text{ mol neutrons}} \right) +$

$$\left(6 \text{ mol electrons} \times \frac{5.48580 \times 10^{-4} \text{ g}}{1 \text{ mol electrons}} \right) = 6.04368 \text{ g} + 6.05202 \text{ g} + 0.00329148 \text{ g} = 12.09899 \text{ g}$$

The total mass of the protons, neutrons, and electrons weighs 0.09899 g more than the mass of 1 mol of carbon-12 atoms.

Doughnut: $\dfrac{74 \text{ g}}{1 \text{ doughnut}} \times \dfrac{6.02214179 \times 10^{23} \text{ doughnut}}{1 \text{ mole doughnut}} = 4.5 \times 10^{25} \text{ g/mol}$

$74 \text{ g carbon} \times \dfrac{1 \text{ carbon atom}}{1.992646 \times 10^{-23} \text{ g carbon}} = 3.7 \times 10^{24} \text{ carbon atoms}$

3 Molecules, Compounds, and Chemical Equations

Problems by Topic

Chemical Formulas and Molecular View of Elements and Compounds

3.1 The chemical formula gives you the kind of atom and the number of each atom in the compound.
  - (a) $Ca_3(PO_4)_2$ contains: 3 calcium atoms, 2 phosphorus atoms, and 8 oxygen atoms.
  - (b) $SrCl_2$ contains: 1 strontium atom and 2 chlorine atoms.
  - (c) KNO_3 contains: 1 potassium atom, 1 nitrogen atom, and 3 oxygen atoms.
  - (d) $Mg(NO_2)_2$ contains: 1 magnesium atom, 2 nitrogen atoms, and 4 oxygen atoms.

3.3
  - (a) 1 blue = nitrogen, 3 white = hydrogen: NH_3
  - (b) 2 black = carbon, 6 white = hydrogen: C_2H_6
  - (c) 1 yellow = sulfur, 3 red = oxygen: SO_3

3.5
  - (a) Neon is an element, and it is not one of the elements that exists as diatomic molecules; therefore, it is an atomic element.
  - (b) Fluorine is one of the elements that exists as diatomic molecules; therefore, it is a molecular element.
  - (c) Potassium is not one of the elements that exists as diatomic molecules; therefore, it is an atomic element.
  - (d) Nitrogen is one of the elements that exists as diatomic molecules; therefore, it is a molecular element.

3.7
  - (a) CO_2 is a compound composed of a nonmetal and a nonmetal; therefore, it is a molecular compound.
  - (b) $NiCl_2$ is a compound composed of a metal and a nonmetal; therefore, it is an ionic compound.
  - (c) NaI is a compound composed of a metal and a nonmetal; therefore, it is an ionic compound.
  - (d) PCl_3 is a compound composed of a nonmetal and a nonmetal; therefore, it is a molecular compound.

3.9
  - (a) white = hydrogen: a molecule composed of two of the same element; therefore, it is a molecular element.
  - (b) blue = nitrogen, white = hydrogen: a molecule composed of a nonmetal and a nonmetal; therefore, it is a molecular compound.
  - (c) purple = sodium: a substance composed of all the same atoms; therefore, it is an atomic element.

Formulas and Names for Ionic Compounds

3.11 To write the formula for an ionic compound, do the following: (1) Write the symbol for the metal cation and its charge and the symbol for the nonmetal anion and its charge. (2) Adjust the subscript on each cation and anion to balance the overall charge. (3) Check that the sum of the charges of the cations equals the sum of the charges of the anions.
  - (a) magnesium and sulfur: Mg^{2+} S^{2-} MgS cations 2+, anions 2−
  - (b) barium and oxygen: Ba^{2+} O^{2-} BaO cations 2+, anions 2−

     (c)   strontium and bromine: Sr^{2+} Br^- $SrBr_2$ cations 2+, anions 2(1−) = 2−

     (d)   beryllium and chlorine: Be^{2+} Cl^- $BeCl_2$ cations 2+, anions 2(1−) = 2−

3.13   To write the formula for an ionic compound, do the following: (1) Write the symbol for the metal cation and its charge and the symbol for the polyatomic anion and its charge. (2) Adjust the subscript on each cation and anion to balance the overall charge. (3) Check that the sum of the charges of the cations equals the sum of the charges of the anions. Cation = barium: Ba^{2+}

     (a)   hydroxide: OH^- $Ba(OH)_2$ cation 2+, anion 2(1−) = 2−

     (b)   chromate: CrO_4^{2-} $BaCrO_4$ cation 2+, anion 2−

     (c)   phosphate: PO_4^{3-} $Ba_3(PO_4)_2$ cation 3(2+) = 6+, anion 2(3−) = 6−

     (d)   cyanide: CN^- $Ba(CN)_2$ cation 2+, anion 2(1−) = 2−

3.15   To name a binary ionic compound, provide the name of the metal cation followed by the base name of the anion +-*ide*.

     (a) Mg_3N_2:   The cation is magnesium; the anion is from nitrogen, which becomes nitride: magnesium nitride.

     (b) KF: The cation is potassium; the anion is from fluorine, which becomes fluoride: potassium fluoride.

     (c) Na_2O: The cation is sodium; the anion is from oxygen, which becomes oxide: sodium oxide.

     (d) Li_2S: The cation is lithium; the anion is from sulfur, which becomes sulfide: lithium sulfide.

3.17   To name an ionic compound with a metal cation that can have more than one charge, name the metal cation followed by parentheses with the charge in Roman numerals followed by the base name of the anion +-*ide*.

     (a) $SnCl_4$:   The charge on Sn must be 4+ for the compound to be charge neutral: The cation is tin(IV); the anion is from chlorine, which becomes chloride: tin(IV) chloride.

     (b) PbI_2:   The charge on Pb must be 2+ for the compound to be charge neutral: The cation is lead(II); the anion is from iodine, which becomes iodide: lead(II) iodide.

     (c) Fe_2O_3:   The charge on Fe must be 3+ for the compound to be charge neutral: The cation is iron(III); the anion is from oxygen, which becomes oxide: iron(III) oxide.

     (d) CuI_2:   The charge on Cu must be 2+ for the compound to be charge neutral: The cation is copper(II); the anion is from iodine, which becomes iodide: copper(II) iodide.

3.19   To name these compounds, first decide if the metal cation is invariant or can have more than one charge. Then name the metal cation followed by the base name of the anion +-*ide*.

     (a) SnO: Sn can have more than one charge. The charge on Sn must be 2+ for the compound to be charge neutral: the cation is tin(II); the anion is from oxygen, which becomes oxide: tin(II) oxide.

     (b) Cr_2S_3:   Cr can have more than one charge. The charge on Cr must be 3+ for the compound to be charge neutral: the cation is chromium(III); the anion is from sulfur, which becomes sulfide: chromium(III) sulfide.

     (c) RbI: Rb is invariant: the cation is rubidium; the anion is from iodine, which becomes iodide: rubidium iodide.

     (d) $BaBr_2$:   Ba is invariant: the cation is barium; the anion is from bromine, which becomes bromide: barium bromide.

3.21   To name these compounds, first decide if the metal cation is invariant or can have more than one charge. Then name the metal cation followed by the name of the polyatomic anion.

     (a) $CuNO_2$:   Cu can have more than one charge. The charge on Cu must be 1+ for the compound to be charge neutral: The cation is copper(I); the anion is nitrite: copper(I) nitrite.

     (b) $Mg(C_2H_3O_2)_2$:   Mg is invariant: The cation is magnesium; the anion is acetate: magnesium acetate.

     (c) $Ba(NO_3)_2$:   Ba is invariant: The cation is barium; the anion is nitrate: barium nitrate.

     (d) $Pb(C_2H_3O_2)_2$:   Pb can have more than one charge. The charge on Pb must be 2+ for the compound to be charge neutral: The cation is lead(II); the anion is acetate: lead(II) acetate.

     (e) $KClO_3$:   K is invariant: The cation is potassium; the anion is chlorate: potassium chlorate.

     (f) $PbSO_4$:   Pb can have more than one charge. The charge on Pb must be 2+ for the compound to be charge neutral: The cation is lead(II); the anion is sulfate: lead(II) sulfate.

3.23   To write the formula for an ionic compound, do the following: (1) Write the symbol for the metal cation and its charge and the symbol for the nonmetal anion or polyatomic anion and its charge. (2) Adjust the subscript on each cation and anion to balance the overall charge. (3) Check that the sum of the charges of the cations equals the sum of the charges of the anions.

(a)	sodium hydrogen sulfite:	Na^+	HSO_3^-	$NaHSO_3$	cation 1+, anion 1−
(b)	lithium permanganate:	Li^+	MnO_4^-	$LiMnO_4$	cation 1+, anion 1−
(c)	silver nitrate:	Ag^+	NO_3^-	$AgNO_3$	cation 1+, anion 1−
(d)	potassium sulfate:	K^+	SO_4^{2-}	K_2SO_4	cation 2(1+) = 2+, anion 2−
(e)	rubidium hydrogen sulfate:	Rb^+	HSO_4^-	$RbHSO_4$	cation 1+, anion 1−
(f)	potassium hydrogen carbonate:	K^+	HCO_3^-	$KHCO_3$	cation 1+, anion 1−

3.25   Hydrates are named the same way as other ionic compounds with the addition of the term *prefix*hydrate, where the prefix is the number of water molecules associated with each formula unit.

(a)	$CoSO_4 \cdot 7H_2O$	cobalt(II) sulfate heptahydrate
(b)	iridium(III) bromide tetrahydrate	$IrBr_3 \cdot 4H_2O$
(c)	$Mg(BrO_3)_2 \cdot 6H_2O$	magnesium bromate hexahydrate
(d)	potassium carbonate dihydrate	$K_2CO_3 \cdot 2H_2O$

Formulas and Names for Molecular Compounds and Acids

3.27   (a)   CO   The name of the compound is the name of the first element, *carbon*, followed by the base name of the second element, *ox*, prefixed by *mono-* to indicate one and given the suffix *-ide*. Since the prefix ends with "o" and the base name begins with "o," the first "o" is dropped: carbon monoxide.

(b) NI_3 The name of the compound is the name of the first element, *nitrogen*, followed by the base name of the second element, *iod*, prefixed by *tri-* to indicate three and given the suffix *-ide*: nitrogen triiodide.

(c) $SiCl_4$ The name of the compound is the name of the first element, *silicon*, followed by the base name of the second element, *chlor*, prefixed by *tetra-* to indicate four and given the suffix *-ide*: silicon tetrachloride.

(d) N_4Se_4 The name of the compound is the name of the first element, *nitrogen*, prefixed by *tetra-* to indicate four followed by the base name of the second element, *selen*, prefixed by *tetra-* to indicate four and given the suffix *-ide*: tetranitrogen tetraselenide.

(e) I_2O_5 The name of the compound is the name of the first element, *iodine*, prefixed by *di-* to indicate two followed by the base name of the second element, *ox*, prefixed by *penta-* to indicate five and given the suffix *-ide*: diiodine pentaoxide.

3.29   (a)   phosphorus trichloride: PCl_3
         (b)   chlorine monoxide: ClO
         (c)   disulfur tetrafluoride: S_2F_4
         (d)   phosphorus pentafluoride: PF_5
         (e)   diphosphorus pentasulfide: P_2S_5

3.31   (a)   HI: The base name of I is *iod*, so the name is hydroiodic acid.
         (b) HNO_3:   The oxyanion is *nitrate,* which ends in *-ate*; therefore, the name of the acid is nitric acid.
         (c) H_2CO_3:   The oxyanion is *carbonate*, which ends in *-ate*; therefore, the name of the acid is carbonic acid.
         (d) $HC_2H_3O_2$:   The oxyanion is *acetate*, which ends in *-ate*; therefore, the name of the acid is acetic acid.

3.33   (a)   hydrofluoric acid: HF
         (b)   hydrobromic acid: HBr
         (c)   sulfurous acid: H_2SO_3

Formula Mass and the Mole Concept for Compounds

3.35   To find the formula mass, sum the atomic masses of each atom in the chemical formula.

(a) NO_2 formula mass = 1 × (atomic mass N) + 2 × (atomic mass O)
                          = 1 × (14.01 amu) + 2 × (16.00 amu)
                          = 46.01 amu

(b) C_4H_{10} formula mass = 4 × (atomic mass C) + 10 × (atomic mass H)
                          = 4 × (12.01 amu) + 10 × (1.008 amu)
                          = 58.12 amu

(c) $C_6H_{12}O_6$ formula mass $= 6 \times$ (atomic mass C) $+ 12 \times$ (atomic mass H) $+ 6 \times$ (atomic mass O)

$= 6 \times (12.01 \text{ amu}) + 12 \times (1.008 \text{ amu}) + 6 \times (16.00 \text{ amu})$

$= 180.16 \text{ amu}$

(d) $Cr(NO_3)_3$ formula mass $= 1 \times$ (atomic mass Cr) $+ 3 \times$ (atomic mass N) $+ 9 \times$ (atomic mass O)

$= 1 \times (52.00 \text{ amu}) + 3 \times (14.01 \text{ amu}) + 9 \times (16.00 \text{ amu})$

$= 238.03 \text{ amu}$

3.37 (a) **Given:** 72.5 g CCl_4 **Find:** number of moles

Conceptual Plan: g CCl_4 → mole CCl_4

$$\frac{1 \text{ mol}}{153.81 \text{ g } CCl_4}$$

Solution: $72.5 \text{ g } CCl_4 \times \dfrac{1 \text{ mol } CCl_4}{153.81 \text{ g } CCl_4} = 0.47\underline{1}4 \text{ mol } CCl_4 = 0.471 \text{ mol } CCl_4$

Check: The units (mole CCl_4) are correct. The magnitude is appropriate because it is less than 1 mole of CCl_4.

(b) **Given:** 12.4 g $C_{12}H_{22}O_{11}$ **Find:** number of moles

Conceptual Plan: g $C_{12}H_{22}O_{11}$ → mole KNO_3

$$\frac{1 \text{ mol}}{342.296 \text{ g } C_{12}H_{22}O_{11}}$$

Solution:

$$12.4 \text{ g } C_{12}H_{22}O_{11} \times \frac{1 \text{ mol } C_{12}H_{22}O_{11}}{342.296 \text{ g } C_{12}H_{22}O_{11}} = 0.036\underline{2}3 \text{ mol } C_{12}H_{22}O_{11} = 0.0362 \text{ mol } C_{12}H_{22}O_{11}$$

Check: The units (mole $C_{12}H_{22}O_{11}$) are correct. The magnitude is appropriate because there is less than 1 mole of $C_{12}H_{22}O_{11}$.

(c) **Given:** 25.2 kg C_2H_2 **Find:** number of moles

Conceptual Plan: kg CO_2 → g C_2H_2 → mole C_2H_2

$$\frac{1000 \text{ g } C_2H_2}{\text{kg } C_2H_2} \qquad \frac{1 \text{ mol}}{26.036 \text{ g } C_2H_2}$$

Solution: $25.2 \text{ kg } CO_2 \times \dfrac{1000 \text{ g } C_2H_2}{\text{kg } C_2H_2} \times \dfrac{1 \text{ mol } C_2H_2}{26.036 \text{ g } C_2H_2} = 96\underline{7}.9 \text{ mol } C_2H_2 = 968 \text{ mol } C_2H_2$

Check: The units (mole C_2H_2) are correct. The magnitude is appropriate because more than a kilogram of C_2H_2 is present.

(d) **Given:** 12.3 g dinitrogen monoxide   **Find:** number of moles

Conceptual Plan: dinitrogen monoxide → formula and then g N_2O → mole N_2O

$$\frac{1 \text{ mol}}{44.02 \text{ g } N_2O}$$

Solution: Dinitrogen monoxide is N_2O.

$$12.3 \text{ g } N_2O \times \frac{1 \text{ mol } N_2O}{44.02 \text{ g } N_2O} = 0.279\underline{4} \text{ mol } N_2O = 0.279 \text{ mol } N_2O$$

Check: The units (mole N_2O) are correct. The magnitude is appropriate because less than a mole of N_2O is present.

3.39 (a) **Given:** 3.5 g H_2O **Find:** number of molecules

Conceptual Plan: g H_2O → mole H_2O → number H_2O molecules

$$\frac{1 \text{ mol}}{18.02 \text{ g } H_2O} \qquad \frac{6.022 \times 10^{23} \text{ } H_2O \text{ molecules}}{\text{mol } H_2O}$$

Solution: $3.5 \text{ g } H_2O \times \dfrac{1 \text{ mol } H_2O}{18.02 \text{ g } H_2O} \times \dfrac{6.022 \times 10^{23} \text{ } H_2O \text{ molecules}}{\text{mol } H_2O} = 1.\underline{1}70 \times 10^{23} \text{ } H_2O \text{ molecules}$

$= 1.2 \times 10^{23} \text{ } H_2O \text{ molecules}$

Check: The units (H_2O molecules) are correct. The magnitude is appropriate: it is smaller than Avogadro's number, as expected, because there is less than 1 mole of H_2O.

(b)   **Given:** 254 g CBr_4 **Find:** number of molecules
       Conceptual Plan: g CBr_4 → mole CBr_4 → number CBr_4 molecules

$$\frac{1 \text{ mol}}{331.6 \text{ g } CBr_4} \qquad \frac{6.022 \times 10^{23} \text{ } CBr_4 \text{ molecules}}{\text{mol } CBr_4}$$

Solution: $254 \text{ g } CBr_4 \times \dfrac{1 \text{ mol } CBr_4}{331.6 \text{ g } CBr_4} \times \dfrac{6.022 \times 10^{23} \text{ } CBr_4 \text{ molecules}}{\text{mol } CBr_4} = 4.6\underline{1}28 \times 10^{23} \text{ } CBr_4 \text{ molecules}$

$= 4.61 \times 10^{23} \text{ } CBr_4 \text{ molecules}$

Check: The units (CBr_4 molecules) are correct. The magnitude is appropriate: it is smaller than Avogadro's number, as expected, because there is less than 1 mole of CBr_4.

(c)   **Given:** 18.3 g O_2 **Find:** number of molecules
       Conceptual Plan: g O_2 → mole O_2 → number O_2 molecules

$$\frac{1 \text{ mol}}{32.00 \text{ g } O_2} \qquad \frac{6.022 \times 10^{23} \text{ } O_2 \text{ molecules}}{\text{mol } O_2}$$

Solution: $18.3 \text{ g } O_2 \times \dfrac{1 \text{ mol } O_2}{32.00 \text{ g } O_2} \times \dfrac{6.022 \times 10^{23} \text{ } O_2 \text{ molecules}}{\text{mol } O_2} = 3.4\underline{4}38 \times 10^{23} \text{ } O_2 \text{ molecules}$

$= 3.44 \times 10^{23} \text{ } O_2 \text{ molecules}$

Check: The units (O_2 molecules) are correct. The magnitude is appropriate: it is smaller than Avogadro's number, as expected, because there is less than 1 mole of O_2.

(d)   **Given:** 26.9 g C_8H_{10} **Find:** number of molecules
       Conceptual Plan: g C_8H_{10} → mole C_8H_{10} → number C_8H_{10} molecules

$$\frac{1 \text{ mol}}{106.16 \text{ g } C_8H_{10}} \qquad \frac{6.022 \times 10^{23} \text{ } C_8H_{10} \text{ molecules}}{\text{mol } C_8H_{10}}$$

Solution: $26.9 \text{ g } C_8H_{10} \times \dfrac{1 \text{ mol } C_8H_{10}}{106.16 \text{ g } C_8H_{10}} \times \dfrac{6.022 \times 10^{23} \text{ } C_8H_{10} \text{ molecules}}{\text{mol } C_8H_{10}}$

$= 1.5\underline{2}59 \times 10^{23} \text{ } C_8H_{10} \text{ molecules} = 1.53 \times 10^{23} \text{ } C_8H_{10} \text{ molecules}$

Check: The units (C_8H_{10} molecules) are correct. The magnitude is appropriate: it is smaller than Avogadro's number, as expected, because there is less than 1 mole of C_8H_{10}.

3.41   **Given:** 1 H_2O molecule   **Find:** mass in g
       Conceptual Plan: number H_2O molecules → mole H_2O → g H_2O

$$\frac{1 \text{ mol } H_2O}{6.022 \times 10^{23} \text{ } H_2O \text{ molecules}} \qquad \frac{18.02 \text{ g } H_2O}{1 \text{ mol } H_2O}$$

Solution:

$1 \text{ } H_2O \text{ molecule} \times \dfrac{1 \text{ mol } H_2O}{6.022 \times 10^{23} \text{ } H_2O \text{ molecules}} \times \dfrac{18.02 \text{ g } H_2O}{1 \text{ mol } H_2O} = 2.99\underline{2}36 \times 10^{-23} \text{ g } H_2O = 2.992 \times 10^{-23} \text{ g } H_2O$

Check: The units (g H_2O) are correct. The magnitude is appropriate: there is much less than Avogadro's number of molecules, so we have much less than 1 mole of H_2O.

3.43   **Given:** 1.8×10^{17} $C_{12}H_{22}O_{11}$ molecules   **Find:** moles $C_{12}H_{22}O_{11}$; mass of $C_{12}H_{22}O_{11}$ crystal
       Conceptual Plan: molecules $C_{12}H_{22}O_{11}$ → mole $C_{12}H_{22}O_{11}$ → g $C_{12}H_{22}O_{11}$

$$\frac{1 \text{ mol } C_{12}H_{22}O_{11}}{6.022 \times 10^{23} \text{ } C_{12}H_{22}O_{11} \text{ molecules}} \qquad \frac{342.3 \text{ g } C_{12}H_{22}O_{11}}{1 \text{ mol } C_{12}H_{22}O_{11}}$$

Solution:

$1.8 \times 10^{17} \text{ } C_{12}H_{22}O_{11} \text{ molecules} \times \dfrac{1 \text{ mol } C_{12}H_{22}O_{11}}{6.022 \times 10^{23} \text{ molecules } C_{12}H_{22}O_{11}} = 2.9\underline{8}9 \times 10^{-7} \text{ mol } C_{12}H_{22}O_{11}$

$= 3.0 \times 10^{-7} \text{ mol } C_{12}H_{22}O_{11}$

$2.9\underline{8}9 \times 10^{-7} \text{ mol } C_{12}H_{22}O_{11} \times \dfrac{342.3 \text{ g } C_{12}H_{22}O_{11}}{1 \text{ mol } C_{12}H_{22}O_{11}} = 1.0\underline{2}3 \times 10^{-4} \text{ g } C_{12}H_{22}O_{11} = 1.0 \times 10^{-4} \text{ g } C_{12}H_{22}O_{11}$

$= 0.010 \text{ mg } C_{12}H_{22}O_{11}$

Check: The units (mg $C_{12}H_{22}O_{11}$ and g $C_{12}H_{22}O_{11}$) are correct. The magnitude is appropriate: there is much less than Avogadro's number of molecules, so we have much less than 1 mole of $C_{12}H_{22}O_{11}$. And we expect much less than 342 g $C_{12}H_{22}O_{11}$.

Composition of Compounds

3.45   (a)   **Given:** CH_4 **Find:** mass percent C

Conceptual Plan: mass % C $= \dfrac{1 \times \text{molar mass C}}{\text{molar mass } CH_4} \times 100\%$

Solution:

$$1 \times \text{molar mass C} = 1(12.01 \text{ g/mol}) = 12.01 \text{ g C}$$
$$\text{molar mass } CH_4 = 1(12.01 \text{ g/mol}) + 4(1.008 \text{ g/mol}) = 16.04 \text{ g/mol}$$

$$\text{mass \% C} = \dfrac{1 \times \text{molar mass C}}{\text{molar mass } CH_4} \times 100\%$$

$$= \dfrac{12.01 \text{ g/mol}}{16.04 \text{ g/mol}} \times 100\%$$

$$= 74.8\underline{7}53\% = 74.88\%$$

Check: The units (%) are correct. The magnitude is reasonable because it is between 0 and 100% and carbon is the heaviest element.

(b)   **Given:** C_2H_6 **Find:** mass percent C

Conceptual Plan: mass % C $= \dfrac{2 \times \text{molar mass C}}{\text{molar mass } C_2H_6} \times 100\%$

Solution:

$$2 \times \text{molar mass C} = 2(12.01 \text{ g/mol}) = 24.02 \text{ g C}$$
$$\text{molar mass } C_2H_6 = 2(12.01 \text{ g/mol}) + 6(1.008 \text{ g/mol}) = 30.07 \text{ g/mol}$$

$$\text{mass \% C} = \dfrac{2 \times \text{molar mass C}}{\text{molar mass } C_2H_6} \times 100\%$$

$$= \dfrac{24.02 \text{ g/mol}}{30.07 \text{ g/mol}} \times 100\%$$

$$= 79.8\underline{8}03\% = 79.88\%$$

Check: The units (%) are correct. The magnitude is reasonable because it is between 0 and 100% and carbon is the heaviest element.

(c)   **Given:** C_2H_2 **Find:** mass percent C

Conceptual Plan: mass % C $= \dfrac{2 \times \text{molar mass C}}{\text{molar mass } C_2H_2} \times 100\%$

Solution:

$$2 \times \text{molar mass C} = 2(12.01 \text{ g/mol}) = 24.02 \text{ g C}$$
$$\text{molar mass } C_2H_2 = 2(12.01 \text{ g/mol}) + 2(1.008 \text{ g/mol}) = 26.04 \text{ g/mol}$$

$$\text{mass \% C} = \dfrac{2 \times \text{molar mass C}}{\text{molar mass } C_2H_2} \times 100\%$$

$$= \dfrac{24.02 \text{ g/mol}}{26.04 \text{ g/mol}} \times 100\%$$

$$= 92.2\underline{4}27\% = 92.24\%$$

Check: The units (%) are correct. The magnitude is reasonable because it is between 0 and 100% and carbon is the heaviest element.

(d)   **Given:** C_2H_5Cl **Find:** mass percent C

Conceptual Plan: mass % C $= \dfrac{2 \times \text{molar mass C}}{\text{molar mass } C_2H_5Cl} \times 100\%$

Solution:

$$2 \times \text{molar mass C} = 2(12.01 \text{ g/mol}) = 24.02 \text{ g C}$$
$$\text{molar mass } C_2H_5Cl = 2(12.01 \text{ g/mol}) + 5(1.008 \text{ g/mol}) + 1(35.45 \text{ g/mol}) = 64.51 \text{ g/mol}$$

$$\text{mass \% C} = \frac{2 \times \text{molar mass C}}{\text{molar mass C}_2\text{H}_5\text{Cl}} \times 100\%$$

$$= \frac{24.02 \text{ g/mol}}{64.51 \text{ g/mol}} \times 100\%$$

$$= 37.2\underline{3}45\% = 37.23\%$$

Check: The units (%) are correct. The magnitude is reasonable because it is between 0 and 100% and chlorine is heavier than carbon.

3.47   **Given:** NH_3 **Find:** mass percent N

Conceptual Plan: $\text{mass \% N} = \dfrac{1 \times \text{molar mass N}}{\text{molar mass NH}_3} \times 100\%$

Solution:

$$1 \times \text{molar mass N} = 1(14.01 \text{ g/mol}) = 14.01 \text{ g N}$$
$$\text{molar mass NH}_3 = 3(1.008 \text{ g/mol}) + (14.01 \text{ g/mol}) = 17.03 \text{ g/mol}$$

$$\text{mass \% N} = \frac{1 \times \text{molar mass N}}{\text{molar mass NH}_3} \times 100\%$$

$$= \frac{14.01 \text{ g/mol}}{17.03 \text{ g/mol}} \times 100\%$$

$$= 82.2\underline{6}6\% = 82.27\%$$

Check: The units (%) are correct. The magnitude is reasonable because it is between 0 and 100% and nitrogen is the heaviest atom present.

Given: $CO(NH_2)_2$ **Find:** mass percent N

Conceptual Plan: $\text{mass \% N} = \dfrac{2 \times \text{molar mass N}}{\text{molar mass CO(NH}_2)_2} \times 100\%$

Solution:

$$2 \times \text{molar mass N} = 1(14.01 \text{ g/mol}) = 28.02 \text{ g N}$$
$$\text{molar mass CO(NH}_2)_2 = (12.01 \text{ g/mol}) + (16.00 \text{ g/mol}) + 2(14.01 \text{ g/mol}) + 4(1.008 \text{ g/mol}) = 60.06 \text{ g/mol}$$

$$\text{mass \% N} = \frac{2 \times \text{molar mass N}}{\text{molar mass CO(NH}_2)_2} \times 100\%$$

$$= \frac{28.02 \text{ g/mol}}{60.06 \text{ g/mol}} \times 100\%$$

$$= 46.6\underline{5}3\% = 46.65\%$$

Check: The units (%) are correct. The magnitude is reasonable because it is between 0 and 100% and there are two nitrogens and only one carbon and one oxygen per molecule.

Given: NH_4NO_3 **Find:** mass percent N

Conceptual Plan: $\text{mass \% N} = \dfrac{2 \times \text{molar mass N}}{\text{molar mass NH}_4\text{NO}_3} \times 100\%$

Solution:

$$2 \times \text{molar mass N} = 2(14.01 \text{ g/mol}) = 28.02 \text{ g N}$$
$$\text{molar mass NH}_4\text{NO}_3 = 2(14.01 \text{ g/mol}) + 4(1.008 \text{ g/mol}) + 3(16.00 \text{ g/mol}) = 80.05 \text{ g/mol}$$

$$\text{mass \% N} = \frac{2 \times \text{molar mass N}}{\text{molar mass NH}_4\text{NO}_3} \times 100\%$$

$$= \frac{28.02 \text{ g/mol}}{80.05 \text{ g/mol}} \times 100\%$$

$$= 35.00\underline{3}1\% = 35.00\%$$

Check: The units (%) are correct. The magnitude is reasonable because it is between 0 and 100%. The mass of nitrogen is less than the mass of oxygen, and there are two nitrogens and three oxygens per molecule.

Given: $(NH_4)_2SO_4$ **Find:** mass percent N

Conceptual Plan: mass % N $= \dfrac{2 \times \text{molar mass N}}{\text{molar mass } (NH_4)_2SO_4} \times 100\%$

Solution:

$2 \times \text{molar mass N} = 2(14.01 \text{ g/mol}) = 28.02 \text{ g N}$

molar mass $(NH_4)_2SO_4 = 2(14.01 \text{ g/mol}) + 8(1.008 \text{ g/mol}) + (32.07 \text{ g/mol}) + 4(16.00 \text{ g/mol}) = 132.15 \text{ g/mol}$

$$\text{mass \% N} = \frac{2 \times \text{molar mass N}}{\text{molar mass } (NH_4)_2SO_4} \times 100\%$$

$$= \frac{28.02 \text{ g/mol}}{132.15 \text{ g/mol}} \times 100\%$$

$$= 21.20\underline{3}2\% = 21.20\%$$

Check: The units (%) are correct. The magnitude is reasonable because it is between 0 and 100% and the mass of nitrogen is less than the mass of oxygen and sulfur.

The fertilizer with the highest nitrogen content is NH_3 with a N content of 82.27%.

3.49   **Given:** 72.4 g CuF_2; 37.42% F in CuF_2 **Find:** g F in CuF_2
         Conceptual Plan: g CuF_2 $\rightarrow$ g F

$$\frac{37.42 \text{ g F}}{100.0 \text{ g CuF}_2}$$

         Solution: 72.4 g CuF_2 $\times \dfrac{37.42 \text{ g F}}{100.0 \text{ g CuF}_2} = 27.0\underline{9} = 27.1 \text{ g F}$

         Check: The units (g F) are correct. The magnitude is reasonable because it is less than the original mass.

3.51   **Given:** 150 μg I; 76.45% I in KI   **Find:** μg KI
         Conceptual Plan: μg I $\rightarrow$ g I $\rightarrow$ g KI $\rightarrow$ μg KI

$$\frac{1 \text{ g I}}{1 \times 10^6 \, \mu\text{g I}} \quad \frac{100.0 \text{ g KI}}{76.45 \text{ g I}} \quad \frac{1 \times 10^6 \, \mu\text{g KI}}{1 \text{ g KI}}$$

         Solution: 150 μg I $\times \dfrac{1 \text{ g I}}{1 \times 10^6 \, \mu\text{g I}} \times \dfrac{100.0 \text{ g KI}}{76.45 \text{ g I}} \times \dfrac{1 \times 10^6 \, \mu\text{g KI}}{1 \text{ g KI}} = 19\underline{6}.2 \, \mu\text{g KI} = 196 \, \mu\text{g KI}$

         Check: The units (μg KI) are correct. The magnitude is reasonable because it is greater than the original mass.

3.53   (a)   red = oxygen, white = hydrogen: 2H:O H_2O
         (b)   black = carbon, white = hydrogen: C:4H CH_4
         (c)   black = carbon, white = hydrogen, red = oxygen: 2C:6H:O CH_3CH_2OH or C_2H_6O

3.55   (a)   **Given:** 0.0885 mol C_4H_{10} **Find:** mol H atoms
                 Conceptual Plan: mol C_4H_{10} $\rightarrow$ mole H atoms

$$\frac{10 \text{ mol H}}{1 \text{ mol C}_4\text{H}_{10}}$$

                 Solution: 0.0885 mol C_4H_{10} $\times \dfrac{10 \text{ mol H}}{1 \text{ mol C}_4\text{H}_{10}} = 0.885 \text{ mol H atoms}$

                 Check: The units (mol H atoms) are correct. The magnitude is reasonable because it is greater than the original mol C_4H_{10}.

         (b)   **Given:** 1.3 mol CH_4 **Find:** mol H atoms
                 Conceptual Plan: mol CH_4 $\rightarrow$ mole H atoms

$$\frac{4 \text{ mol H}}{1 \text{ mol CH}_4}$$

                 Solution: 1.3 mol CH_4 $\times \dfrac{4 \text{ mol H}}{1 \text{ mol CH}_4} = 5.2 \text{ mol H atoms}$

                 Check: The units (mol H atoms) are correct. The magnitude is reasonable because it is greater than the original mol CH_4.

(c) **Given:** 2.4 mol C_6H_{12} **Find:** mol H atoms
Conceptual Plan: mol C_6H_{12} $\rightarrow$ mole H atoms

$$\frac{12 \text{ mol H}}{1 \text{ mol } C_6H_{12}}$$

Solution: $2.4 \text{ mol } C_6H_{12} \times \dfrac{12 \text{ mol H}}{1 \text{ mol } C_6H_{12}} = 28.8 \text{ mol H atoms} = 29 \text{ mol H atoms}$

Check: The units (mol H atoms) are correct. The magnitude is reasonable because it is greater than the original mol C_6H_{12}.

(d) **Given:** 1.87 mol C_8H_{18} **Find:** mol H atoms
Conceptual Plan: mol C_8H_{18} $\rightarrow$ mole H atoms

$$\frac{18 \text{ mol H}}{1 \text{ mol } C_8H_{18}}$$

Solution: $1.87 \text{ mol } C_8H_{18} \times \dfrac{18 \text{ mol H}}{1 \text{ mol } C_8H_{18}} = 33.66 \text{ mol H atoms} = 33.7 \text{ mol H atoms}$

Check: The units (mol H atoms) are correct. The magnitude is reasonable because it is greater than the original mol C_8H_{18}.

3.57 (a) **Given:** 8.5 g NaCl   **Find:** g Na
Conceptual Plan: g NaCl $\rightarrow$ mole NaCl $\rightarrow$ mol Na $\rightarrow$ g Na

$$\frac{1 \text{ mol NaCl}}{58.44 \text{ g NaCl}} \quad \frac{1 \text{ mol Na}}{1 \text{ mol NaCl}} \quad \frac{22.99 \text{ g Na}}{1 \text{ mol Na}}$$

Solution: $8.5 \text{ g NaCl} \times \dfrac{1 \text{ mol NaCl}}{58.44 \text{ g NaCl}} \times \dfrac{1 \text{ mol Na}}{1 \text{ mol NaCl}} \times \dfrac{22.99 \text{ g Na}}{1 \text{ mol Na}} = 3.344 \text{ g Na} = 3.3 \text{ g Na}$

Check: The units (g Na) are correct. The magnitude is reasonable because it is less than the original g NaCl.

(b) **Given:** 8.5 g Na_3PO_4 **Find:** g Na
Conceptual Plan: g Na_3PO_4 $\rightarrow$ mole Na_3PO_4 $\rightarrow$ mol Na $\rightarrow$ g Na

$$\frac{1 \text{ mol } Na_3PO_4}{163.94 \text{ g } Na_3PO_4} \quad \frac{3 \text{ mol Na}}{1 \text{ mol } Na_3PO_4} \quad \frac{22.99 \text{ g Na}}{1 \text{ mol Na}}$$

Solution: $8.5 \text{ g } Na_3PO_4 \times \dfrac{1 \text{ mol } Na_3PO_4}{163.94 \text{ g } Na_3PO_4} \times \dfrac{3 \text{ mol Na}}{1 \text{ mol } Na_3PO_4} \times \dfrac{22.99 \text{ g Na}}{1 \text{ mol Na}} = 3.576 \text{ g Na} = 3.6 \text{ g Na}$

Check: The units (g Na) are correct. The magnitude is reasonable because it is less than the original g Na_3PO_4.

(c) **Given:** 8.5 g $NaC_7H_5O_2$ **Find:** g Na
Conceptual Plan: g $NaC_7H_5O_2$ $\rightarrow$ mole $NaC_7H_5O_2$ $\rightarrow$ mol Na $\rightarrow$ g Na

$$\frac{1 \text{ mol } NaC_7H_5O_2}{144.10 \text{ g } NaC_7H_5O_2} \quad \frac{1 \text{ mol Na}}{1 \text{ mol } NaC_7H_5O_2} \quad \frac{22.99 \text{ g Na}}{1 \text{ mol Na}}$$

Solution:

$8.5 \text{ g } NaC_7H_5O_2 \times \dfrac{1 \text{ mol } NaC_7H_5O_2}{144.10 \text{ g } NaC_7H_5O_2} \times \dfrac{1 \text{ mol Na}}{1 \text{ mol } NaC_7H_5O_2} \times \dfrac{22.99 \text{ g Na}}{1 \text{ mol Na}} = 1.356 \text{ g Na} = 1.4 \text{ g Na}$

Check: The units (g Na) are correct. The magnitude is reasonable because it is less than the original g $NaC_7H_5O_2$.

(d) **Given:** 8.5 g $Na_2C_6H_6O_7$ **Find:** g Na
Conceptual Plan: g $Na_2C_6H_6O_7$ $\rightarrow$ mole $Na_2C_6H_6O_7$ $\rightarrow$ mol Na $\rightarrow$ g Na

$$\frac{1 \text{ mol } Na_2C_6H_6O_7}{236.1 \text{ g } Na_2C_6H_6O_7} \quad \frac{2 \text{ mol Na}}{1 \text{ mol } Na_2C_6H_6O_7} \quad \frac{22.99 \text{ g Na}}{1 \text{ mol Na}}$$

Solution:

$8.5 \text{ g } Na_2C_6H_6O_7 \times \dfrac{1 \text{ mol } Na_2C_6H_6O_7}{236.1 \text{ g } Na_2C_6H_6O_7} \times \dfrac{2 \text{ mol Na}}{1 \text{ mol } Na_2C_6H_6O_7} \times \dfrac{22.99 \text{ g Na}}{1 \text{ mol Na}} = 1.655 \text{ g Na} = 1.7 \text{ g Na}$

Check: The units (g Na) are correct. The magnitude is reasonable because it is less than the original g $Na_2C_6H_6O_7$.

3.59   **Given:** 5.85 g C_2F_4 **Find:** F atoms

Conceptual Plan: g C_2F_4 → mol C_2F_4 → molecules C_2F_4 → F atoms

$$\frac{1 \text{ mol } C_2F_4}{100.02 \text{ g } C_2F_4} \qquad \frac{6.022 \times 10^{23} \text{ } C_2F_4 \text{ molecules}}{1 \text{ mole } C_2F_4} \qquad \frac{4 \text{ F atoms}}{1 \text{ } C_2F_4 \text{ molecule}}$$

Solution: $5.85 \text{ g } C_2F_4 \times \dfrac{1 \text{ mol g } C_2F_4}{100.02 \text{ g } C_2F_4} \times \dfrac{6.022 \times 10^{23} \text{ } C_2F_4 \text{ molecules}}{1 \text{ mol } C_2F_4} \times \dfrac{4 \text{ F atoms}}{1 \text{ } C_2F_4 \text{ molecules}}$

$$= 1.4\underline{0}89 \times 10^{23} \text{ F atoms} = 1.41 \times 10^{23} \text{ F atoms}$$

Check: The units (F atoms) are correct. The magnitude of the answer (1.41×10^{23}) makes physical sense because there is ~0.06 mole of molecules and there are 4 F atoms in each molecule.

Chemical Formulas from Experimental Data

3.61   (a)   **Given:** 1.651 g Ag; 0.1224 g O   **Find:** empirical formula

Conceptual Plan:

convert mass to mol of each element → write pseudoformula → write empirical formula

$$\frac{1 \text{ mol Ag}}{107.9 \text{ g Ag}} \quad \frac{1 \text{ mol O}}{16.00 \text{ g O}} \qquad \text{divide by smallest number}$$

Solution: $1.651 \text{ g Ag} \times \dfrac{1 \text{ mol Ag}}{107.9 \text{ g Ag}} = 0.01530 \text{ mol Ag}$

$$0.1224 \text{ g O} \times \frac{1 \text{ mol O}}{16.00 \text{ g O}} = 0.007650 \text{ mol O}$$

$Ag_{0.01530} O_{0.007650}$

$$Ag_{\frac{0.01530}{0.007650}} O_{\frac{0.007650}{0.007650}} \rightarrow Ag_2O$$

The correct empirical formula is Ag_2O.

(b)   **Given:** 0.672 g Co; 0.569 g As; 0.486 g O   **Find:** empirical formula

Conceptual Plan:

convert mass to mol of each element → write pseudoformula → write empirical formula

$$\frac{1 \text{ mol Co}}{58.93 \text{ g Co}} \quad \frac{1 \text{ mol As}}{74.92 \text{ g As}} \quad \frac{1 \text{ mol O}}{16.00 \text{ g O}} \qquad \text{divide by smallest number}$$

Solution: $0.672 \text{ g Co} \times \dfrac{1 \text{ mol Co}}{58.93 \text{ g Co}} = 0.0114 \text{ mol Co}$

$$0.569 \text{ g As} \times \frac{1 \text{ mol As}}{74.92 \text{ g As}} = 0.00759 \text{ mol O}$$

$$0.486 \text{ g O} \times \frac{1 \text{ mol O}}{16.00 \text{ g O}} = 0.0304 \text{ mol O}$$

$Co_{0.0114} As_{0.00759} O_{0.0304}$

$$Co_{\frac{0.0114}{0.00759}} As_{\frac{0.00759}{0.00759}} O_{\frac{0.0304}{0.00759}} \rightarrow Co_{1.5}As_1O_4$$

$$Co_{1.5}As_1O_4 \times 2 \rightarrow Co_3As_2O_8$$

The correct empirical formula is $Co_3As_2O_8$.

(c)   **Given:** 1.443 g Se; 5.841 g Br   **Find:** empirical formula

Conceptual Plan:

convert mass to mol of each element → write pseudoformula → write empirical formula

$$\frac{1 \text{ mol Se}}{78.96 \text{ g Se}} \quad \frac{1 \text{ mol Br}}{79.90 \text{ g Br}} \qquad \text{divide by smallest number}$$

Solution: $1.443 \text{ g Se} \times \dfrac{1 \text{ mol Se}}{78.96 \text{ g Se}} = 0.01828 \text{ mol Se}$

$$5.841 \text{ g Br} \times \frac{1 \text{ mol Br}}{79.90 \text{ g Br}} = 0.07310 \text{ mol Br}$$

$Se_{0.01828} Br_{0.07310}$

$$Se_{\frac{0.01828}{0.01828}} Br_{\frac{0.07310}{0.01828}} \rightarrow SeBr_4$$

The correct empirical formula is $SeBr_4$.

3.63   (a)   **Given:** in a 100 g sample: 74.03 g C; 8.70 g H; 17.27 g N   **Find:** empirical formula

Conceptual Plan:

convert mass to mol of each element → **write pseudoformula** → **write empirical formula**

$$\frac{1\ mol\ C}{12.01\ g\ C} \quad \frac{1\ mol\ H}{1.008\ g\ H} \quad \frac{1\ mol\ N}{14.01\ g\ N} \qquad \text{divide by smallest number}$$

Solution: $74.03\ g\ C \times \dfrac{1\ mol\ C}{12.01\ g\ C} = 6.164\ mol\ C$

$8.70\ g\ H \times \dfrac{1\ mol\ H}{1.008\ g\ H} = 8.63\ mol\ H$

$17.27\ g\ N \times \dfrac{1\ mol\ N}{14.01\ g\ N} = 1.233\ mol\ N$

$C_{6.164} H_{8.63} N_{1.233}$

$$C_{\frac{6.164}{1.233}} H_{\frac{8.63}{1.233}} N_{\frac{1.233}{1.233}} \rightarrow C_5H_7N$$

The correct empirical formula is C_5H_7N.

    (b)   **Given:** In a 100 g sample: 49.48 g C; 5.19 g H; 28.85 g N; 16.48 g O   **Find:** empirical formula

Conceptual Plan:

convert mass to mol of each element → **write pseudoformula** → **write empirical formula**

$$\frac{1\ mol\ C}{12.01\ g\ C} \quad \frac{1\ mol\ H}{1.008\ g\ H} \quad \frac{1\ mol\ N}{14.01\ g\ N} \quad \frac{1\ mol\ O}{16.00\ g\ O} \qquad \text{divide by smallest number}$$

Solution: $49.48\ g\ C \times \dfrac{1\ mol\ C}{12.01\ g\ C} = 4.120\ mol\ C$

$5.19\ g\ H \times \dfrac{1\ mol\ H}{1.008\ g\ H} = 5.15\ mol\ H$

$28.85\ g\ N \times \dfrac{1\ mol\ N}{14.01\ g\ N} = 2.059\ mol\ N$

$16.48\ g\ O \times \dfrac{1\ mol\ O}{16.00\ g\ O} = 1.030\ mol\ O$

$C_{4.120} H_{5.15} N_{2.059} O_{1.030}$

$$C_{\frac{4.120}{1.030}} H_{\frac{5.15}{1.030}} N_{\frac{2.059}{1.030}} O_{\frac{1.030}{1.030}} \rightarrow C_4H_5N_2O$$

The correct empirical formula is $C_4H_5N_2O$.

3.65   **Given:** 0.77 mg N; 6.61 mg N_xCl_y **Find:** empirical formula

Conceptual Plan: find mg Cl → **convert mg to g for each element** → **convert mass to mol of each element** →

$$mg\ N_xCl_y - mg\ N \qquad\qquad \frac{1\ g}{1000\ mg} \qquad\qquad \frac{1\ mol\ N}{14.01\ g\ N} \quad \frac{1\ mol\ Cl}{35.45\ g\ Cl}$$

write pseudoformula → **write empirical formula**

    divide by smallest number

Solution: $6.61\ mg\ N_xCl_y - 0.77\ mg\ N = 5.84\ mg\ Cl$

$0.77\ mg\ N \times \dfrac{1\ g\ N}{1000\ mg\ N} \times \dfrac{1\ mol\ N}{14.01\ g\ N} = 5.5 \times 10^{-5}\ mol\ N$

$5.84\ mg\ Cl \times \dfrac{1\ g\ Cl}{1000\ mg\ Cl} \times \dfrac{1\ mol\ Cl}{35.45\ g\ Cl} = 1.6 \times 10^{-4}\ mol\ Cl$

$N_{5.5\times10^{-5}} Cl_{1.6\times10^{-4}}$

$$N_{\frac{5.5\times10^{-5}}{5.5\times10^{-5}}} Cl_{\frac{1.6\times10^{-4}}{5.5\times10^{-5}}} \rightarrow NCl_3$$

The correct empirical formula is NCl_3.

3.67 **(a)** **Given:** empirical formula = C_6H_7N; molar mass = 186.24 g/mol   **Find:** molecular formula

Conceptual Plan: molecular formula = empirical formula $\times$ n $n = \dfrac{\text{molar mass}}{\text{empirical formula mass}}$

Solution: empirical formula mass = 6(12.01 g/mol) + 7(1.008 g/mol) + 1(14.01 g/mol) = 93.13 g/mol

$$n = \frac{\text{molar mass}}{\text{formula molar mass}} = \frac{186.24 \text{ g/mol}}{93.13 \text{ g/mol}} = 1.9998 = 2$$

$$\text{molecular formula} = C_6H_7N \times 2$$
$$= C_{12}H_{14}N_2$$

(b) **Given:** empirical formula = C_2HCl; molar mass = 181.44 g/mol   **Find:** molecular formula

Conceptual Plan: molecular formula = empirical formula $\times$ n $n = \dfrac{\text{molar mass}}{\text{empirical formula mass}}$

Solution: empirical formula mass = 2(12.01 g/mol) + 1(1.008 g/mol) + 1(35.45 g/mol) = 60.48 g/mol

$$n = \frac{\text{molar mass}}{\text{formula molar mass}} = \frac{181.44 \text{ g/mol}}{60.48 \text{ g/mol}} = 3$$

$$\text{molecular formula} = C_2HCl \times 3$$
$$= C_6H_3Cl_3$$

(c) **Given:** empirical formula = $C_5H_{10}NS_2$; molar mass = 296.54 g/mol   **Find:** molecular formula

Conceptual Plan: molecular formula = empirical formula $\times$ n $n = \dfrac{\text{molar mass}}{\text{empirical formula mass}}$

Solution: empirical formula mass = 5(12.01 g/mol) + 10(1.008 g/mol)

$$+ \ 1(14.01 \text{ g/mol}) + 2(32.07) = 148.28 \text{ g/mol}$$

$$n = \frac{\text{molar mass}}{\text{formula molar mass}} = \frac{296.54 \text{ g/mol}}{148.28 \text{ g/mol}} = 2$$

$$\text{molecular formula} = C_5H_{10}NS_2 \times 2$$
$$= C_{10}H_{20}N_2S_4$$

3.69 **Given:** 33.01 g CO_2; 13.51 g H_2O **Find:** empirical formula
Conceptual Plan: mass CO_2, $H_2O \rightarrow$ mol CO_2, $H_2O \rightarrow$ mol C, mol H $\rightarrow$ pseudoformula $\rightarrow$ empirical formula

$$\frac{1 \text{ mol } CO_2}{44.01 \text{ g } CO_2} \quad \frac{1 \text{ mol } H_2O}{18.02 \text{ g } H_2O} \quad \frac{1 \text{ mol C}}{1 \text{ mol } CO_2} \quad \frac{2 \text{ mol H}}{1 \text{ mol } H_2O} \qquad \text{divide by smallest number}$$

Solution: $33.01 \text{ g } CO_2 \times \dfrac{1 \text{ mol } CO_2}{44.01 \text{ g } CO_2} = 0.7501 \text{ mol } CO_2$

$$13.51 \text{ g } H_2O \times \frac{1 \text{ mol } H_2O}{18.02 \text{ g } H_2O} = 0.7497 \text{ mol } H_2O$$

$$0.7501 \text{ mol } CO_2 \times \frac{1 \text{ mol C}}{1 \text{ mol } CO_2} = 0.7501 \text{ mol C}$$

$$0.7497 \text{ mol } H_2O \times \frac{2 \text{ mol H}}{1 \text{ mol } H_2O} = 1.499 \text{ mol H}$$

$$C_{0.7501} H_{1.499}$$

$$C_{\frac{0.7501}{0.7501}} H_{\frac{1.499}{0.7501}} \rightarrow CH_2$$

The correct empirical formula is CH_2.

3.71 **Given:** 4.30 g sample; 8.59 g CO_2; 3.52 g H_2O **Find:** empirical formula
Conceptual Plan: mass CO_2, $H_2O \rightarrow$ mol CO_2, $H_2O \rightarrow$ mol C, mol H $\rightarrow$ mass C, mass H, mass O $\rightarrow$ mol O $\rightarrow$

$$\frac{1 \text{ mol } CO_2}{44.01 \text{ g } CO_2} \quad \frac{1 \text{ mol } H_2O}{18.02 \text{ g } H_2O} \quad \frac{1 \text{ mol C}}{1 \text{ mol } CO_2} \quad \frac{2 \text{ mol H}}{1 \text{ mol } H_2O} \quad \frac{12.01 \text{ g C}}{1 \text{ mol C}} \quad \frac{1.008 \text{ g H}}{1 \text{ mol H}} \quad \text{g sample} - \text{g C} - \text{g H} \quad \frac{1 \text{ mol O}}{16.00 \text{ g O}}$$

pseudoformula $\rightarrow$ empirical formula

divide by smallest number

Solution: $8.59 \text{ g } CO_2 \times \dfrac{1 \text{ mol } CO_2}{44.01 \text{ g } CO_2} = 0.195 \text{ mol } CO_2$

$3.52 \text{ g } H_2O \times \dfrac{1 \text{ mol } H_2O}{18.02 \text{ g } H_2O} = 0.195 \text{ mol } H_2O$

$0.195 \text{ mol } CO_2 \times \dfrac{1 \text{ mol C}}{1 \text{ mol } CO_2} = 0.195 \text{ mol C}$

$0.195 \text{ mol } H_2O \times \dfrac{2 \text{ mol H}}{1 \text{ mol } H_2O} = 0.390 \text{ mol H}$

$0.195 \text{ mol C} \times \dfrac{12.01 \text{ mol C}}{1 \text{ mol C}} = 2.34 \text{ g C}$

$0.390 \text{ mol H} \times \dfrac{1.008 \text{ g H}}{1 \text{ mol H}} = 0.393 \text{ g H}$

$4.30 \text{ g} - 2.34 \text{ g} - 0.393 \text{ g} = 1.57 \text{ g O}$

$1.57 \text{ g O} \times \dfrac{1 \text{ mol O}}{16.00 \text{ g O}} = 0.0981 \text{ mol O}$

$C_{0.195} H_{0.390} O_{0.0981}$

$C_{\frac{0.195}{0.0981}} H_{\frac{0.390}{0.0981}} O_{\frac{0.0981}{0.0981}} \rightarrow C_2H_4O$

The correct empirical formula is C_2H_4O.

Writing and Balancing Chemical Equations

3.73   **Conceptual Plan: write a skeletal reaction $\rightarrow$ balance atoms in more complex compounds $\rightarrow$ balance elements that occur as free elements $\rightarrow$ clear fractions**

      Solution:

Skeletal reaction:	$SO_2(g) + O_2(g) + H_2O(l) \rightarrow H_2SO_4(aq)$
Balance O:	$SO_2(g) + 1/2\, O_2(g) + H_2O(l) \rightarrow H_2SO_4(aq)$
Clear fraction:	$2\, SO_2(g) + O_2(g) + 2\, H_2O(l) \rightarrow 2\, H_2SO_4(aq)$

      Check:

left side	right side
2 S atoms	2 S atoms
8 O atoms	8 O atoms
4 H atoms	4 H atoms

3.75   **Conceptual Plan: write a skeletal reaction $\rightarrow$ balance atoms in more complex compounds $\rightarrow$ balance elements that occur as free elements $\rightarrow$ clear fractions**

      Solution:

Skeletal reaction:	$Na(s) + H_2O(l) \rightarrow H_2(g) + NaOH(aq)$
Balance H:	$Na(s) + H_2O(l) \rightarrow 1/2\, H_2(g) + NaOH(aq)$
Clear fraction:	$2\, Na(s) + 2\, H_2O(l) \rightarrow H_2(g) + 2\, NaOH(aq)$

      Check:

left side	right side
2 Na atoms	2 Na atoms
4 H atoms	4 H atoms
2 O atoms	2 O atoms

3.77   **Conceptual Plan: write a skeletal reaction $\rightarrow$ balance atoms in more complex compounds $\rightarrow$ balance elements that occur as free elements $\rightarrow$ clear fractions**

      Solution:

Skeletal reaction:	$C_{12}H_{22}O_{11}(aq) + H_2O(l) \rightarrow C_2H_5OH(aq) + CO_2(g)$
Balance H:	$C_{12}H_{22}O_{11}(aq) + H_2O(l) \rightarrow 4\, C_2H_5OH(aq) + CO_2(g)$
Balance C:	$C_{12}H_{22}O_{11}(aq) + H_2O(l) \rightarrow 4\, C_2H_5OH(aq) + 4\, CO_2(g)$

      Check:

left side	right side
12 C atoms	12 C atoms
24 H atoms	24 H atoms
12 O atoms	12 O atoms

3.79   (a)   **Conceptual Plan: write a skeletal reaction → balance atoms in more complex compounds → balance elements that occur as free elements → clear fractions**

   Solution: Skeletal reaction: $PbS(s) + HBr(aq) \rightarrow PbBr_2(s) + H_2S(g)$
              Balance Br: $PbS(s) + 2\ HBr(aq) \rightarrow PbBr_2(s) + H_2S(g)$

   Check:

left side	right side
1 Pb atom	1 Pb atom
1 S atom	1 S atom
2 H atoms	2 H atoms
2 Br atoms	2 Br atoms

   (b)   **Conceptual Plan: write a skeletal reaction → balance atoms in more complex compounds → balance elements that occur as free elements → clear fractions**

   Solution: Skeletal reaction: $CO(g) + H_2(g) \rightarrow CH_4(g) + H_2O(l)$
              Balance H: $CO(g) + 3\ H_2(g) \rightarrow CH_4(g) + H_2O(l)$

   Check:

left side	right side
1 C atom	1 C atom
1 O atom	1 O atom
6 H atoms	6 H atoms

   (c)   **Conceptual Plan: write a skeletal reaction → balance atoms in more complex compounds → balance elements that occur as free elements → clear fractions**

   Solution: Skeletal reaction: $HCl(aq) + MnO_2(s) \rightarrow MnCl_2(aq) + H_2O(l) + Cl_2(g)$
              Balance Cl: $4\ HCl(aq) + MnO_2(s) \rightarrow MnCl_2(aq) + H_2O(l) + Cl_2(g)$
              Balance O: $4\ HCl(aq) + MnO_2(s) \rightarrow MnCl_2(aq) + 2\ H_2O(l) + Cl_2(g)$

   Check:

left side	right side
4 H atoms	4 H atoms
4 Cl atoms	4 Cl atoms
1 Mn atom	1 Mn atom
2 O atoms	2 O atoms

   (d)   **Conceptual Plan: write a skeletal reaction → balance atoms in more complex compounds → balance elements that occur as free elements → clear fractions**

   Solution: Skeletal reaction: $C_5H_{12}(l) + O_2(g) \rightarrow CO_2(g) + H_2O(l)$
              Balance C: $C_5H_{12}(l) + O_2(g) \rightarrow 5\ CO_2(g) + H_2O(l)$
              Balance H: $C_5H_{12}(l) + O_2(g) \rightarrow 5\ CO_2(g) + 6\ H_2O(l)$
              Balance O: $C_5H_{12}(l) + 8\ O_2(g) \rightarrow 5\ CO_2(g) + 6\ H_2O(l)$

   Check:

left side	right side
5 C atoms	5 C atoms
12 H atoms	12 H atoms
16 O atoms	16 O atoms

3.81   **Conceptual Plan: write a skeletal reaction → balance atoms in more complex compounds → balance elements that occur as free elements → clear fractions**

   Solution: Skeletal reaction: $Na_2CO_3(aq) + CuCl_2(aq) \rightarrow CuCO_3(s) + NaCl(aq)$
              Balance Na: $Na_2CO_3(aq) + CuCl_2(aq) \rightarrow CuCO_3(s) + 2\ NaCl(aq)$

   Check:

left side	right side
2 Na atoms	2 Na atoms
1 C atom	1 C atom
3 O atoms	3 O atoms
1 Cu atom	1 Cu atom
2 Cl atoms	2 Cl atoms

3.83   (a)   **Conceptual Plan: balance atoms in more complex compounds → balance elements that occur as free elements → clear fractions**

   Solution: Skeletal reaction: $CO_2(g) + CaSiO_3(s) + H_2O(l) \rightarrow SiO_2(s) + Ca(HCO_3)_2(aq)$
              Balance C: $2\ CO_2(g) + CaSiO_3(s) + H_2O(l) \rightarrow SiO_2(s) + Ca(HCO_3)_2(aq)$

	Check:	left side	right side
		2 C atoms	2 C atoms
		8 O atoms	8 O atoms
		1 Ca atom	1 Ca atom
		1 Si atom	1 Si atom
		2 H atoms	2 H atoms

(b) **Conceptual Plan: balance atoms in more complex compounds → balance elements that occur as free elements → clear fractions**

Solution: Skeletal reaction: $Co(NO_3)_3(aq) + (NH_4)_2S(aq) \rightarrow Co_2S_3(s) + NH_4NO_3(aq)$

Balance S: $Co(NO_3)_3(aq) + 3\ (NH_4)_2S(aq) \rightarrow Co_2S_3(s) + NH_4NO_3(aq)$

Balance Co: $2\ Co(NO_3)_3(aq) + 3\ (NH_4)_2S(aq) \rightarrow Co_2S_3(s) + NH_4NO_3(aq)$

Balance N: $2\ Co(NO_3)_3(aq) + 3\ (NH_4)_2S(aq) \rightarrow Co_2S_3(s) + 6\ NH_4NO_3(aq)$

Check:

left side	right side
2 Co atoms	2 Co atoms
12 N atoms	12 N atoms
18 O atoms	18 O atoms
24 H atoms	24 H atoms
3 S atoms	3 S atoms

(c) **Conceptual Plan: balance atoms in more complex compounds → balance elements that occur as free elements → clear fractions**

Solution: Skeletal reaction: $Cu_2O(s) + C(s) \rightarrow Cu(s) + CO(g)$

Balance Cu: $Cu_2O(s) + C(s) \rightarrow 2\ Cu(s) + CO(g)$

Check:

left side	right side
2 Cu atoms	2 Cu atoms
1 O atom	1 O atom
1 C atom	1 C atom

(d) **Conceptual Plan: balance atoms in more complex compounds → balance elements that occur as free elements → clear fractions**

Solution: Skeletal reaction: $H_2(g) + Cl_2(g) \rightarrow HCl(g)$

Balance Cl: $H_2(g) + Cl_2(g) \rightarrow 2\ HCl(g)$

Check:

left side	right side
2 H atoms	2 H atoms
2 Cl atoms	2 Cl atoms

Organic Compounds

3.85 (a) composed of metal cation and polyatomic anion—inorganic compound
(b) composed of carbon and hydrogen—organic compound
(c) composed of carbon, hydrogen, and oxygen—organic compound
(d) composed of metal cation and nonmetal anion—inorganic compound

Cumulative Problems

3.87 **Given:** 165 mL C_2H_5OH; $d = 0.789$ g/cm^3 **Find:** number of molecules

Conceptual Plan: cm^3 → mL:mL C_2H_5OH → g C_2H_5OH → mol C_2H_5OH → molecules C_2H_5OH

$$\frac{1\ cm^3}{1\ mL} \quad \frac{1\ mL\ C_2H_5OH}{0.789\ g\ C_2H_5OH} \quad \frac{1\ mol\ C_2H_5OH}{46.07\ g\ C_2H_5OH} \quad \frac{6.022 \times 10^{23}\ molecules\ C_2H_5OH}{1\ mol\ C_2H_5OH}$$

Solution:

$$165\ mL\ C_2H_5OH \times \frac{0.789\ g\ C_2H_5OH}{cm^3} \times \frac{1\ cm^3}{1\ mL} \times \frac{1\ mol\ C_2H_5OH}{46.07\ g\ C_2H_5OH} \times \frac{6.022 \times 10^{23}\ molecules\ C_2H_5OH}{1\ mol\ C_2H_5OH}$$

$$= 1.7\underline{0}17 \times 10^{24}\ molecules\ C_2H_5OH = 1.70 \times 10^{24}\ molecules\ C_2H_5OH$$

Check: The units (molecules C_2H_5OH) are correct. The magnitude is reasonable because we had more than 2 moles of C_2H_5OH and we have more than two times Avogadro's number of molecules.

3.89   (a)   To write the formula for an ionic compound, do the following: (1) Write the symbol for the metal cation and its charge and the symbol for the nonmetal anion or polyatomic anion and its charge. (2) Adjust the subscript on each cation and anion to balance the overall charge. (3) Check that the sum of the charges of the cations equals the sum of the charges of the anions.

potassium chromate: $K^+CrO_4^{2-}$; K_2CrO_4 cation $2(1+) = 2+$; anion $2-$

Given: K_2CrO_4 **Find:** mass percent of each element

Conceptual Plan: %K, then %Cr, then %O

$$\text{mass \% K} = \frac{2 \times \text{molar mass K}}{\text{molar mass K}_2\text{CrO}_4} \times 100\% \qquad \text{mass \% Cr} = \frac{1 \times \text{molar mass Cr}}{\text{molar mass K}_2\text{CrO}_4} \times 100\% \qquad \text{mass \% O} = \frac{4 \times \text{molar mass O}}{\text{molar mass K}_2\text{CrO}_4} \times 100\%$$

molar mass of K = 39.10 g/mol; molar mass Cr = 52.00 g/mol; molar mass O = 16.00 g/mol

Solution: molar mass K_2CrO_4 = 2(39.10 g/mol) + 1(52.00 g/mol) + 4(16.00 g/mol) = 194.20 g/mol

$$\text{mass \% K} = \frac{2 \times \text{molar mass K}}{\text{molar mass K}_2\text{CrO}_4} \times 100\% \qquad\qquad \text{mass \% Cr} = \frac{1 \times \text{molar mass Cr}}{\text{molar mass K}_2\text{CrO}_4} \times 100\%$$

$$= \frac{2(39.10 \text{ g/mol})}{194.20 \text{ g/mol}} \times 100\% \qquad\qquad = \frac{1(52.00 \text{ g/mol})}{194.20 \text{ g/mol}} \times 100\%$$

$$= \frac{78.20 \text{ g/mol}}{194.20 \text{ g/mol}} \times 100\% \qquad\qquad = \frac{52.00 \text{ g/mol}}{194.20 \text{ g/mol}} \times 100\%$$

$$= 40.27\% \qquad\qquad\qquad\qquad = 26.78\%$$

$$4 \times \text{molar mass O} = 4(16.00 \text{ g/mol}) = 64.00 \text{ g O}$$

$$\text{mass \% O} = \frac{4 \times \text{molar mass O}}{\text{molar mass K}_2\text{CrO}_4} \times 100\%$$

$$= \frac{64.00 \text{ g/mol}}{194.20 \text{ g/mol}} \times 100\%$$

$$= 32.96\%$$

Check: The units (%) are correct. The magnitude is reasonable because each is between 0 and 100% and the total is 100%.

(b)   To write the formula for an ionic compound, do the following: (1) Write the symbol for the metal cation and its charge and the symbol for the nonmetal anion or polyatomic anion and its charge. (2) Adjust the subscript on each cation and anion to balance the overall charge. (3) Check that the sum of the charges of the cations equals the sum of the charges of the anions.

Lead(II) phosphate: Pb^{2+} PO_4^{3-}; $Pb_3(PO_4)_2$ cation $3(2+) = 6+$; anion $2(3-) = 6-$

Given: $Pb_3(PO_4)_2$ **Find:** mass percent of each element

Conceptual Plan: %Pb, then %P, then %O

$$\text{mass \% Pb} = \frac{3 \times \text{molar mass Pb}}{\text{molar mass Pb}_3(\text{PO}_4)_2} \times 100\% \qquad \text{mass \% P} = \frac{2 \times \text{molar mass P}}{\text{molar mass Pb}_3(\text{PO}_4)_2} \times 100\% \qquad \text{mass \% O} = \frac{8 \times \text{molar mass O}}{\text{molar mass Pb}_3(\text{PO}_4)_2} \times 100\%$$

Solution: molar mass $Pb_3(PO_4)_2$ = 3(207.2 g/mol) + 2(30.97 g/mol) + 8(16.00 g/mol) = 811.5 g/mol

$3 \times$ molar mass Pb = 3(207.2 g/mol) = 621.6 g Pb $2 \times$ molar mass P = 2(30.97 g/mol) = 61.94 g P

$$\text{mass \% Pb} = \frac{3 \times \text{molar mass Pb}}{\text{molar mass Pb}_3(\text{PO}_4)_2} \times 100\% \qquad\qquad \text{mass \% P} = \frac{2 \times \text{molar mass P}}{\text{molar mass Pb}_3(\text{PO}_4)_2} \times 100\%$$

$$= \frac{621.6 \text{ g/mol}}{811.5 \text{ g/mol}} \times 100\% \qquad\qquad = \frac{61.94 \text{ g/mol}}{811.5 \text{ g/mol}} \times 100\%$$

$$= 76.60\% \qquad\qquad\qquad\qquad = 7.633\%$$

$$4 \times \text{molar mass O} = 8(16.00 \text{ g/mol}) = 128.0 \text{ g O}$$

$$\text{mass \% O} = \frac{8 \times \text{molar mass O}}{\text{molar mass Pb}_3(\text{PO}_4)_2} \times 100\%$$

$$= \frac{128.0 \text{ g/mol}}{811.5 \text{ g/mol}} \times 100\%$$

$$= 15.77\%$$

Check: The units (%) are correct. The magnitude is reasonable because each is between 0 and 100% and the total is 100%.

(c)   sulfurous acid: H_2SO_3

Given: H_2SO_3 **Find:** mass percent of each element

Conceptual Plan: %H, then %S, then %O

$$\text{mass \% H} = \frac{2 \times \text{molar mass H}}{\text{molar mass } H_2SO_3} \times 100\% \qquad \text{mass \% S} = \frac{1 \times \text{molar mass S}}{\text{molar mass } H_2SO_3} \times 100\% \qquad \text{mass \% O} = \frac{3 \times \text{molar mass O}}{\text{molar mass } H_2SO_3} \times 100\%$$

Solution: molar mass $H_2SO_3 = 2(1.008 \text{ g/mol}) + 1(32.07 \text{ g/mol}) + 3(16.00 \text{ g/mol}) = 82.0\underline{8}6 \text{ g/mol}$

$2 \times$ molar mass $H = 2(1.008 \text{ g/mol}) = 2.016 \text{ g H} \qquad 1 \times$ molar mass $S = 1(32.07 \text{ g/mol}) = 32.07 \text{ g S}$

$$\text{mass \% H} = \frac{2 \times \text{molar mass H}}{\text{molar mass } H_2SO_3} \times 100\% \qquad\qquad \text{mass \% S} = \frac{1 \times \text{molar mass S}}{\text{molar mass } H_2SO_3} \times 100\%$$

$$= \frac{2.016 \text{ g/mol}}{82.0\underline{8}6 \text{ g/mol}} \times 100\% \qquad\qquad\qquad = \frac{32.07 \text{ g/mol}}{82.0\underline{8}6 \text{ g/mol}} \times 100\%$$

$$= 2.456\% \qquad\qquad\qquad\qquad\qquad = 39.07\%$$

$$3 \times \text{molar mass O} = 3(16.00 \text{ g/mol}) = 48.00 \text{ g O}$$

$$\text{mass \% O} = \frac{3 \times \text{molar mass O}}{\text{molar mass } H_2SO_3} \times 100\%$$

$$= \frac{48.00 \text{ g/mol}}{82.0\underline{8}6 \text{ g/mol}} \times 100\%$$

$$= 58.48\%$$

Check: The units (%) are correct. The magnitude is reasonable because each is between 0 and 100% and the total is 100%.

(d)   To write the formula for an ionic compound, do the following: (1) Write the symbol for the metal cation and its charge and the symbol for the nonmetal anion or polyatomic anion and its charge. (2) Adjust the subscript on each cation and anion to balance the overall charge. (3) Check that the sum of the charges of the cations equals the sum of the charges of the anions.

cobalt(II) bromide: $Co^{2+}Br^-$; $CoBr_2$ cation $2+ = 2+$; anion $2(1-) = 2-$

Given: $CoBr_2$ **Find:** mass percent of each element

Conceptual Plan: %Co, then %Br

$$\text{mass \% Co} = \frac{1 \times \text{molar mass Co}}{\text{molar mass } CoBr_2} \times 100\% \qquad \text{mass \% Br} = \frac{2 \times \text{molar mass Br}}{\text{molar mass } CoBr_2} \times 100\%$$

Solution: molar mass $CoBr_2 = (58.93 \text{ g/mol}) + 2(79.90 \text{ g/mol}) = 218.73 \text{ g/mol}$

$1 \times$ molar mass $Co = 1(58.93 \text{ g/mol}) = 58.93 \text{ g Co} \qquad 2 \times$ molar mass $Br = 2(79.90 \text{ g/mol}) = 159.80 \text{ g Br}$

$$\text{mass \% Co} = \frac{1 \times \text{molar mass Co}}{\text{molar mass } CoBr_2} \times 100\% \qquad\qquad \text{mass \% Br} = \frac{2 \times \text{molar mass Br}}{\text{molar mass } CoBr_2} \times 100\%$$

$$= \frac{58.93 \text{ g/mol}}{218.73 \text{ g/mol}} \times 100\% \qquad\qquad\qquad = \frac{159.80 \text{ g/mol}}{218.73 \text{ g/mol}} \times 100\%$$

$$= 26.94\% \qquad\qquad\qquad\qquad\qquad = 73.058\%$$

Check: The units (%) are correct. The magnitude is reasonable because each is between 0 and 100% and the total is 100%.

3.91   **Given:** $32 \text{ g } CF_2Cl_2/\text{mo}$ **Find:** g Cl/yr

Conceptual Plan: g CF_2Cl_2/mo $\rightarrow$ g Cl/mo $\rightarrow$ g Cl/yr

$$\frac{70.90 \text{ g Cl}}{120.91 \text{ g } CF_2Cl_2} \qquad \frac{12 \text{ mo}}{1 \text{ yr}}$$

Solution: $\dfrac{32 \text{ g } CF_2Cl_2}{\text{mo}} \times \dfrac{70.90 \text{ g Cl}}{120.91 \text{ g } CF_2Cl_2} \times \dfrac{12 \text{ mo}}{1 \text{ yr}} = 2.\underline{2}52 \times 10^2 \text{ g Cl/yr} = 2.3 \times 10^2 \text{ g Cl/yr}$

Check: The units (g Cl) are correct. Magnitude is reasonable because it is less than the total CF_2Cl_2/yr.

3.93 **Given:** MCl_3; 65.57% Cl in MCl_3 **Find:** identify M

Conceptual Plan: g Cl → mol Cl → mol M → atomic mass M

$$\frac{1 \text{ mol Cl}}{35.45 \text{ g Cl}} \qquad \frac{1 \text{ mol M}}{3 \text{ mol Cl}} \qquad \frac{g \text{ M}}{\text{mol M}}$$

Solution: in 100 g sample: 65.57 g Cl; 34.43 g M

$$65.57 \text{ g Cl} \times \frac{1 \text{ mol Cl}}{35.45 \text{ g Cl}} \times \frac{1 \text{ mol M}}{3 \text{ mol Cl}} = 0.6165 \text{ mol M} \qquad \frac{34.43 \text{ g M}}{0.6165 \text{ mol M}} = 55.85 \text{ g/mol M}$$

molar mass of 55.85 = Fe

The identity of M = Fe.

3.95 **Given:** in a 100 g sample: 79.37 g C; 8.88 g H; 11.75 g O; molar mass = 272.37 g/mol **Find:** molecular formula

Conceptual Plan:

convert mass to mol of each element → pseudoformula → empirical formula → molecular formula

$$\frac{1 \text{ mol C}}{12.01 \text{ g C}} \quad \frac{1 \text{ mol H}}{1.008 \text{ g H}} \quad \frac{1 \text{ mol O}}{16.00 \text{ g O}} \qquad \text{divide by smallest number} \qquad \text{empirical formula} \times n$$

Solution: $79.37 \text{ g C} \times \dfrac{1 \text{ mol C}}{12.01 \text{ g C}} = 6.609 \text{ mol C}$

$8.88 \text{ g H} \times \dfrac{1 \text{ mol H}}{1.008 \text{ g H}} = 8.81 \text{ mol H}$

$11.75 \text{ g O} \times \dfrac{1 \text{ mol O}}{16.00 \text{ g O}} = 0.7344 \text{ mol O}$

$C_{6.609}H_{8.81}O_{0.7344}$

$C_{\frac{6.609}{0.7344}} H_{\frac{8.81}{0.7344}} O_{\frac{0.7344}{0.7344}} \rightarrow C_9H_{12}O$

The correct empirical formula is $C_9H_{12}O$.

empirical formula mass = 9(12.01 g/mol) + 12(1.008 g/mol) + 1(16.00 g/mol) = 136.19 g/mol

$$n = \frac{\text{molar mass}}{\text{formula molar mass}} = \frac{272.37 \text{ g/mol}}{136.19 \text{ g/mol}} = 2$$

molecular formula = $C_9H_{12}O \times 2 = C_{18}H_{24}O_2$

3.97 **Given:** 13.42 g sample; 39.61 g CO_2; 9.01 g H_2O; molar mass = 268.34 g/mol **Find:** molecular formula

Conceptual Plan:

mass CO_2, H_2O → mol CO_2, H_2O → mol C, mol H → mass C, mass H, mass O → mol O →

$$\frac{1 \text{ mol CO}_2}{44.01 \text{ g CO}_2} \quad \frac{1 \text{ mol H}_2O}{18.02 \text{ g H}_2O} \quad \frac{1 \text{ mol C}}{1 \text{ mol CO}_2} \quad \frac{2 \text{ mol H}}{1 \text{ mol H}_2O} \quad \frac{12.01 \text{ g C}}{1 \text{ mol C}} \quad \frac{1.008 \text{ g H}}{1 \text{ mol H}} \quad \text{g sample} - \text{gC} - \text{gH} \quad \frac{1 \text{ mol O}}{16.00 \text{ g O}}$$

pseudoformula → empirical formula → molecular formula

$$\text{divide by smallest number} \qquad \text{empirical formula} \times n$$

$39.61 \text{ g CO}_2 \times \dfrac{1 \text{ mol CO}_2}{44.01 \text{ g CO}_2} = 0.9000 \text{ mol CO}_2$

$9.01 \text{ g H}_2O \times \dfrac{1 \text{ mol H}_2O}{18.02 \text{ g H}_2O} = 0.500 \text{ mol H}_2O$

$0.9000 \text{ mol CO}_2 \times \dfrac{1 \text{ mol C}}{1 \text{ mol CO}_2} = 0.9000 \text{ mol C}$

$0.500 \text{ mol H}_2O \times \dfrac{2 \text{ mol H}}{1 \text{ mol H}_2O} = 1.00 \text{ mol H}$

$0.9000 \text{ mol C} \times \dfrac{12.01 \text{ g C}}{1 \text{ mol C}} = 10.81 \text{ g C}$

$1.00 \text{ mol H}_2O \times \dfrac{1.008 \text{ g H}}{1 \text{ mol H}} = 1.01 \text{ g H}$

13.42 g − 10.81 g − 1.01 g = 1.60 g O

$1.60 \text{ g O} \times \dfrac{1 \text{ mol O}}{16.00 \text{ g O}} = 0.100 \text{ mol O}$

$$C_{0.9000}\,H_{1.000}O_{0.100}$$

$$\underbrace{C_{0.9000}}_{0.100}\,\underbrace{H_{1.00}}_{0.100}\,\underbrace{O_{0.100}}_{0.100} \rightarrow C_9H_{10}O$$

The correct empirical formula is $C_9H_{10}O$.

$$\text{empirical formula mass} = 9(12.01\ \text{g/mol}) + 10(1.008\ \text{g/mol}) + 1(16.00\ \text{g/mol}) = 134.2\ \text{g/mol}$$

$$n = \frac{\text{molar mass}}{\text{formula molar mass}} = \frac{268.34\ \text{g/mol}}{134.2\ \text{g/mol}} = 2$$

$$\text{molecular formula} = C_9H_{10}O \times 2 = C_{18}H_{20}O_2$$

3.99 $\quad$ **Given:** 4.93 g $MgSO_4 \cdot xH_2O$; 2.41 g $MgSO_4$ $\quad$ **Find:** value of x

Conceptual Plan: g $MgSO_4$ $\rightarrow$ mol $MgSO_4$ then g H_2O $\rightarrow$ mol H_2O then determine mole ratio.

$$\frac{1\ \text{mol } MgSO_4}{120.38\ \text{g } MgSO_4} \qquad \frac{1\ \text{mol } H_2O}{18.02\ \text{g } H_2O} \qquad \frac{\text{mol } HO_2}{\text{mol } MgSO_4}$$

Solution:

$$2.41\ \cancel{\text{g } MgSO_4} \times \frac{1\ \text{mol } MgSO_4}{120.38\ \cancel{\text{g } MgSO_4}} = 0.0200\ \text{mol } MgSO_4$$

Determine g H_2O: 4.93 g $MgSO_4 \cdot xH_2O$ − 2.41 g $MgSO_4$ = 2.52 g H_2O

$$2.52\ \cancel{\text{g } H_2O} \times \frac{1\ \text{mol } H_2O}{18.02\ \cancel{\text{g } H_2O}} = 0.140\ \text{mol } H_2O$$

$$\frac{0.140\ \text{mol } H_2O}{0.0200\ \text{mol } MgSO_4} = 7$$

$$x = 7$$

3.101 $\quad$ **Given:** molar mass = 177 g/mol; g C = 8(g H) $\quad$ **Find:** molecular formula

Conceptual Plan: C_xH_yBrO

Solution: in 1 mol compound, let x = mol C and y = mol H, assume mol Br = 1, assume mol O = 1

$\qquad$ 177 g/mol = x(12.01 g/mol) + y(1.008 g/mol) + 1(79.90 g/mol) + 1(16.00 g/mol)

$\qquad$ x(12.01 g/mol) = 8[y(1.008 g/mol)]

$\qquad$ 177 g/mol = 8y(1.008 g/mol) + y(1.008 g/mol) + 79.90 g/mol + 16.00 g/mol

$\qquad$ 81 = 9y(1.008)

$\qquad$ y = 9 = mol H

$\qquad$ x(12.01) = 8 × 9(1.008)

$\qquad$ x = 6 = mol C

$\qquad$ molecular formula = C_6H_9BrO

Check: molar mass = 6(12.01 g/mol) + 9(1.008 g/mol) + 1(79.90 g/mol) + 1(16.00 g/mol) = 177.0 g/mol

3.103 $\quad$ **Given:** 23.5 mg $C_{17}H_{22}ClNO_4$ $\quad$ **Find:** total number of atoms

Conceptual Plan: mg compound $\rightarrow$ g compound $\rightarrow$ mol compound $\rightarrow$ mol atoms $\rightarrow$ number of atoms

$$\frac{1\ \text{g}}{1000\ \text{mg}} \qquad \frac{1\ \text{mol}}{339.8\ \text{g}} \qquad \frac{45\ \text{mol atoms}}{1\ \text{mol compound}} \qquad \frac{6.022 \times 10^{23}\ \text{atoms}}{1\ \text{mol atoms}}$$

Solution: $23.5\ \cancel{\text{mg}} \times \dfrac{1\ \cancel{\text{g}}}{1000\ \cancel{\text{mg}}} \times \dfrac{1\ \cancel{\text{mol cpd}}}{339.8\ \cancel{\text{g}}} \times \dfrac{45\ \cancel{\text{mol atoms}}}{1\ \cancel{\text{mol cpd}}} \times \dfrac{6.022 \times 10^{23}\ \text{atoms}}{\cancel{\text{mol}}}$

$$= 1.8\underline{7}41 \times 10^{21}\ \text{atoms} = 1.87 \times 10^{21}\ \text{atoms}$$

Check: The units (number of atoms) are correct. The magnitude of the answer is reasonable because the molecule is so complex.

3.105 $\quad$ **Given:** MCl_3; 2.395 g sample; 3.606×10^{-2} mol Cl $\quad$ **Find:** atomic mass M

Conceptual Plan: mol Cl $\rightarrow$ g Cl $\rightarrow$ g X

$$\frac{35.45\ \text{g Cl}}{1\ \text{mol Cl}} \qquad \text{g sample} - \text{g Cl} = \text{g M}$$

mol Cl $\rightarrow$ mol M $\rightarrow$ atomic mass M

$$\frac{1\ \text{mol M}}{3\ \text{mol Cl}} \qquad \frac{\text{g M}}{\text{mol M}}$$

Solution:

$$3.606 \times 10^{-2} \text{ mol Cl} \times \frac{35.45 \text{ g}}{1 \text{ mol Cl}} = 1.278 \text{ g Cl}$$

$$2.395 \text{ g} - 1.278 \text{ g} = 1.117 \text{ g M}$$

$$3.606 \times 10^{-2} \text{ mol Cl} \times \frac{1 \text{ mol M}}{3 \text{ mol Cl}} = 1.202 \times 10^{-2} \text{ mol M}$$

$$\frac{1.117 \text{ g M}}{0.01202 \text{ mol M}} = 92.93 \text{ g/mol M}$$

molar mass of M $= 92.93$ g/mol

3.107   **Given:** X_3P_2; 34.00% P; 100 g sample contains 34.00 g P   **Find:** X

         Conceptual Plan: g P → mol P → mol X

$$\frac{1 \text{ mol P}}{30.97 \text{ g P}} \quad\quad \frac{3 \text{ mol X}}{2 \text{ mol P}}$$

         and then g P → g X → molar mass X

$$100.00 \text{ g sample} - 34.00 \text{ g P} \quad\quad \frac{\text{grams X}}{\text{mol X}}$$

         Solution: $34.00 \text{ g P} \times \dfrac{1 \text{ mol P}}{30.97 \text{ g P}} \times \dfrac{3 \text{ mol X}}{2 \text{ mol P}} = 1.647 \text{ mol X}$

$$100.00 \text{ g sample} - 34.00 \text{ g P} = 66.00 \text{ g X}$$

$$\frac{66.00 \text{ g X}}{1.647 \text{ mol X}} = 40.07 \text{ g/mol} = \text{Ca}$$

         Check: The units (g/mol) are correct. The answer, Ca, is reasonable because Ca_3P_2 is a molecule that exists.

3.109   **Given:** ore is 57.8% $Ca_3(PO_4)_2$ **Find:** mass of ore to get 1.00 kg P

         Conceptual Plan: mass ore → mass $Ca_3(PO_4)_2$ → mass P

         Solution: Assume a 100.0 gram sample of ore.

$$100.0 \text{ g ore} \times \frac{57.8 \text{ g } Ca_3(PO_4)_2}{100.0 \text{ g ore}} \times \frac{61.94 \text{ g P}}{310.18 \text{ g } Ca_3(PO_4)_2} = 11.54 \text{ g P}$$

$$1.00 \text{ kg P} \times \frac{1000 \text{ g P}}{\text{kg P}} \times \frac{100.0 \text{ g ore}}{11.54 \text{ g P}} \times \frac{1 \text{ kg ore}}{1000 \text{ g ore}} = 8.6\underline{6}6 \text{ kg ore} = 8.67 \text{ kg ore}$$

         Check: The units (kg ore) are correct. The magnitude of the answer is reasonable because the amount is greater than 1 kilogram.

Challenge Problems

3.111   **Given:** sample 1: 1.00 g X, 0.472 g Z, X_2Z_3; sample 2: 1.00 g X, 0.630 g Z; sample 3: 1.00 g X, 0.789 g Z

         Find: empirical formula for samples 2 and 3

         Conceptual Plan: moles X remains constant; determine relative moles of Z for three samples.

         Solution: Let X = atomic mass X, Z = atomic mass Z

$$n_X = \frac{1.00 \text{ g X}}{X} \quad\quad n_Z = \frac{0.472 \text{ g Z}}{Z}$$

         for sample 1: $\dfrac{n_X}{n_Z} = \dfrac{2}{3}$

         for sample 2: $\dfrac{0.630 \text{ g}}{0.472 \text{ g}} = 1.33$; mol $= 1.33\, n_Z$

         mol ratio: $\dfrac{n_X}{1.33\, n_Z} = \dfrac{2}{(1.33)3} = \dfrac{2}{4} = \dfrac{1}{2}$

         Empirical formula sample 2: XZ_2

         for sample 3: $\dfrac{0.789 \text{ g}}{0.472 \text{ g}} = 1.67$; mol $= 1.67\, n_Z$

mol ratio: $\dfrac{n_X}{1.67\,n_Z} = \dfrac{2}{(1.67)3} = \dfrac{2}{5}$

Empirical formula sample 3: X_2Z_5

3.113   **Given:** 50.0 g S; 1.00×10^2 g Cl_2; 150. g mixture S_2Cl_2 and SCl_2 **Find:** g S_2Cl_2

Conceptual Plan: total mol S = 2(mol S_2Cl_2) + mol SCl_2; mol $S_2Cl_2 \rightarrow$ g S_2Cl_2

$$\dfrac{135.04\ g}{1\ mol\ S_2Cl_2}$$

then S_2Cl_2 = 135.04 g/mol, SCl_2 = 102.97 g/mol, let x = mol S_2Cl_2, y = mol SCl_2

x(135.04) = g S in S_2Cl_2, y(102.97) = g S in SCl_2

Solution: mol S = 50.0 g̶S̶ $\times \dfrac{1\ mol\ S}{32.1\ g̶S̶}$ = 1.56 mol

$2x$ = mol S in S_2Cl_2, y = mol S in SCl_2

$2x + y = 1.56$

$x(135.04) + y(102.97) = 150.0$

$135.04x + 102.97(1.56 - 2x) = 150.0$

$70.90x = 10.6$

$\qquad x = 0.149\underline{5}$

$\qquad y = 1.26$

$0.149\underline{5}$ m̶o̶l̶ ̶S̶₂̶C̶l̶₂̶ $\times \dfrac{135.04\ g\ S_2Cl_2}{1\ m̶o̶l̶ ̶S̶₂̶C̶l̶₂̶} = 20.\underline{1}88$ g $S_2Cl_2 = 20.2$ g S_2Cl_2

Check: The units (g S_2Cl_2) are correct. The magnitude is reasonable because there would be fewer moles of S_2Cl_2 than SCl_2.

3.115   **Given:** coal = 2.55% S; H_2SO_4; 1.0 metric ton coal

Find: metric ton H_2SO_4 produced

Conceptual Plan: $H_2SO_4 \rightarrow$ %S

$$\dfrac{32.07\ g\ S}{98.09\ g\ H_2SO_4} \times 100\%$$

Solution: $\dfrac{32.07\ g\ S}{98.09\ g\ H_2SO_4} \times 100\% = 32.69\%$ S

Conceptual Plan: metric ton coal $\rightarrow$ kg coal $\rightarrow$ kg S $\rightarrow$ kg H_2SO_4 $\rightarrow$ metric ton H_2SO_4

$$\dfrac{1000\ kg}{metric\ ton}\quad \dfrac{2.55\ kg\ S}{100\ kg\ coal}\quad \dfrac{100\ kg\ H_2SO_4}{32.69\ kg\ S}\quad \dfrac{metric\ ton}{1000\ kg}$$

Solution: 1.0 m̶e̶t̶r̶i̶c̶ ̶t̶o̶n̶ ̶c̶o̶a̶l̶ $\times \dfrac{1000\ kg\ c̶o̶a̶l̶}{1\ m̶e̶t̶r̶i̶c̶ ̶t̶o̶n̶ ̶c̶o̶a̶l̶} \times \dfrac{2.55\ kg̶ ̶S̶}{100\ kg̶-̶c̶o̶a̶l̶} \times \dfrac{100\ kg̶ ̶H̶₂̶S̶O̶₄̶}{32.69\ kg̶ ̶S̶} \times \dfrac{1\ metric\ ton\ H_2SO_4}{1000\ kg̶ ̶H̶₂̶S̶O̶₄̶}$

$= 0.078$ metric ton H_2SO_4

Check: The units (metric ton H_2SO_4) are correct. Magnitude is reasonable because it is more than 2.55% of a metric ton and the mass of H_2SO_4 is greater than the mass of S.

3.117   **Given:** sample 1: 2.52 g sample, 4.23 g CO_2, 1.01 g H_2O; sample 2: 4.14 g, 2.11 g SO_3; sample 3: 5.66 g, 2.27 g HNO_3

Find: empirical formula of the compound

Conceptual Plan: g $CO_2 \rightarrow$ g C $\rightarrow$ %C; g $H_2O \rightarrow$ g H $\rightarrow$ %H; g $SO_2 \rightarrow$ g S $\rightarrow$ %S;

$$\dfrac{12.01\ g\ C}{44.01\ g\ CO_2}\quad \dfrac{g\ C}{g\ sample} \times 100\% \qquad \dfrac{1.01\ g\ H}{18.02\ g\ H_2O}\quad \dfrac{g\ H}{g\ sample} \times 100\% \qquad \dfrac{32.07\ g\ S}{80.07\ g\ SO_2}\quad \dfrac{g\ S}{g\ sample} \times 100\%$$

g $HNO_3 \rightarrow$ g N $\rightarrow$ % N and then $\rightarrow$ % O and then % composition $\rightarrow$ mol of each atom $\rightarrow$

$$\dfrac{14.01\ g\ N}{63.02\ g\ HNO_3}\quad \dfrac{g\ N}{g\ sample} \times 100\% \quad 100\% - \%C - \%H - \%N - \%S = \%O$$

pseudoformula $\rightarrow$ empirical formula

divide by smallest number

Solution: 4.23 g̶-̶C̶O̶₂̶ $\times \dfrac{12.01\ g\ C}{44.01\ g̶-̶C̶O̶₂̶} = 1.15\underline{4}$ g C $\qquad \dfrac{1.15\underline{4}\ g\ C}{2.52\ g\ sample} \times 100\% = 45.\underline{8}1\%$ C

1.01 g̶-̶H̶₂̶O̶ $\times \dfrac{2.02\ g\ H}{18.02\ g̶-̶H̶₂̶O̶} = 0.113\underline{2}$ g H $\qquad \dfrac{0.113\underline{2}\ g\ H}{2.52\ g\ sample} \times 100\% = 4.4\underline{9}\%$ H

$$2.11 \text{ g } \overline{SO_3} \times \frac{32.07 \text{ g S}}{80.07 \text{ g } \overline{SO_3}} = 0.84\underline{5}1 \text{ g S} \qquad \frac{0.8451 \text{ g S}}{4.14 \text{ g sample}} \times 100\% = 20.\underline{4}1\% \text{ S}$$

$$2.27 \text{ g } \overline{HNO_3} \times \frac{14.01 \text{ g N}}{63.02 \text{ g } \overline{HNO_3}} = 0.50\underline{4}6 \text{ g N} \qquad \frac{0.5046 \text{ g N}}{5.66 \text{ g sample}} \times 100\% = 8.9\underline{2}\% \text{ N}$$

$$\% \text{ O} = 100 - 45.\underline{8}1 - 4.4\underline{9} - 20.\underline{4}1 - 8.9\underline{2} = 20.\underline{3}7\% \text{ O}$$

Assume a 100 g sample:

$$45.\underline{8}1 \text{ g } \overline{C} \times \frac{1 \text{ mol C}}{12.01 \text{ g } \overline{C}} = 3.8\underline{1}4 \text{ mol C} \qquad 4.4\underline{9} \text{ g } \overline{H} \times \frac{1 \text{ mol H}}{1.008 \text{ g } \overline{H}} = 4.4\underline{4}5 \text{ mol H}$$

$$20.\underline{4}1 \text{ g } \overline{S} \times \frac{1 \text{ mol S}}{32.07 \text{ g } \overline{S}} = 0.63\underline{6}4 \text{ mol S} \qquad 8.9\underline{2} \text{ g } \overline{N} \times \frac{1 \text{ mol N}}{14.01 \text{ g } \overline{N}} = 0.63\underline{6}7 \text{ mol N}$$

$$20.\underline{3}7 \text{ g } \overline{O} \times \frac{1 \text{ mol O}}{16.00 \text{ g } \overline{O}} = 1.2\underline{7}3 \text{ mol O}$$

$$C_{3.8\underline{1}4} \; H_{4.4\underline{4}5} \; S_{0.63\underline{6}4} \; N_{0.63\underline{6}7} \; O_{1.2\underline{7}3}$$

$$C_{\frac{3.814}{0.6364}} \; H_{\frac{4.445}{0.6364}} \; S_{\frac{0.6364}{0.6364}} \; N_{\frac{0.6367}{0.6364}} \; O_{\frac{1.273}{0.6364}} \rightarrow C_6H_7SNO_2$$

3.119 **Given:** compound is 40% X and 60% Y; atomic mass X = 2 (atomic mass Y) **Find:** empirical formula
Conceptual Plan: mass X and Y → mass ratio X: Y and then g X → mol X and g Y → mol Y and then

$$\frac{\text{g X}}{\text{atomic mass X}} \qquad \frac{\text{g Y}}{\text{atomic mass Y}}$$

mole ratio

Solution: $\dfrac{\text{mass X}}{\text{mass Y}} = \dfrac{40}{60} = \dfrac{2}{3}$ $\quad$ mol X $= \dfrac{2 \text{ g}}{\text{atomic mass X}}$ and mol Y $= \dfrac{3 \text{ g}}{\text{atomic mass Y}}$

But: atomic mass X = 2(atomic mass Y)

mol X $= \dfrac{2 \text{ g}}{2(\text{atomic mass Y})}$ and mol Y $= \dfrac{3 \text{ g}}{\text{atomic mass Y}}$

$\dfrac{\text{mol X}}{\text{mol Y}} = \dfrac{\dfrac{2 \text{ g}}{2(\text{atomic mass Y})}}{\dfrac{3 \text{ g}}{\text{atomic mass Y}}} = \dfrac{1}{3}$ empirical formula: XY_3

Conceptual Problems

3.121 The sphere in the molecular models represents the electron cloud of the atom. On this scale, the nucleus would be too small to see.

3.123 The statement is incorrect because a chemical formula is based on the ratio of atoms combined, not the ratio of grams combined. The statement should read as follows: The chemical formula for ammonia (NH_3) indicates that ammonia contains three hydrogen atoms to each nitrogen atom.

3.125 H_2SO_4: Atomic mass S is approximately twice atomic mass O; both are much greater than atomic mass H. The order of % mass is % O > % S > % H.

Questions for Group Work

3.127 In an ionic bond an electron is transferred from the Na atom to the Cl atom, so a student would move from the Na atom to the Cl atom.
For the covalent bond, a pair of electrons is shared between the O atom and each of the two H atoms.

3.129   Some examples of similarities are:
- The systematic names of both binary ionic compounds and binary molecular compounds contain two words.
- The systematic names of both binary ionic compounds and binary molecular compounds end in –*ide*.
- The systematic names of both binary ionic compounds and binary molecular compounds indicate how many atoms of each element are in the formula.
- The systematic names of both binary ionic compounds and binary molecular compounds name the element listed first first.

Some examples of differences are:
- Only the systematic names of binary molecular compounds contain Greek prefixes.
- There are no polyatomic group names used in generating the systematic name of a binary molecular compound.
- The systematic names of only ionic compounds can have a variety of endings (*-ide*, *-ate*, and *–ite*).
- Binary molecular compounds end in *–ide*.

3.131   **Conceptual Plan: write a skeletal reaction → balance atoms in more complex compounds → balance elements that occur as free elements → clear fractions**

Solution:

Skeletal reaction:	$C_8H_{18}(l) + O_2(g)$	$\rightarrow CO_2(g) + H_2O(g)$
Balance C:	$C_8H_{18}(l) + O_2(g)$	$\rightarrow 8\,CO_2(g) + H_2O(g)$
Balance H:	$C_8H_{18}(l) + O_2(g)$	$\rightarrow 8\,CO_2(g) + 9\,H_2O(g)$
Balance O:	$C_8H_{18}(l) + 25/2\,O_2(g)$	$\rightarrow 8\,CO_2(g) + 9\,H_2O(g)$
Clear fraction:	$2\,C_8H_{18}(l) + 25\,O_2(g)$	$\rightarrow 16\,CO_2(g) + 18\,H_2O(g)$

Check:

left side	right side
16 C atoms	16 C atoms
36 H atoms	36 H atoms
50 O atoms	50 O atoms

4 Chemical Quantities and Aqueous Reactions

Problems by Topic

Reaction Stoichiometry

4.1   **Given:** 4.9 moles C_6H_{14} **Find:** balanced reaction, moles O_2 required
Conceptual Plan: balance the equation then mol C_6H_{14} → mol O_2

$$2\,C_6H_{14}(g) + 19\,O_2(g) \rightarrow 12\,CO_2(g) + 14\,H_2O(g) \qquad \frac{19\ \text{mol}\ O_2}{2\ \text{mol}\ C_6H_{14}}$$

Solution: Skeletal reaction: $C_6H_{14}(aq) + O_2(g) \rightarrow CO_2(g) + H_2O(g)$
             Balance C: $C_6H_{14}(aq) + O_2(g) \rightarrow 6\,CO_2(g) + H_2O(g)$
             Balance H: $C_6H_{14}(aq) + O_2(g) \rightarrow 6\,CO_2(g) + 7\,H_2O(g)$
             Balance O: $C_6H_{14}(aq) + 19/2\,O_2(g) \rightarrow 6\,CO_2(g) + 7\,H_2O(g)$
             Clear fraction: $2\,C_6H_{14}(aq) + 19\,O_2(g) \rightarrow 12\,CO_2(g) + 14\,H_2O(g)$

Check: left side   right side
                                   12 C atoms   12 C atoms
                                   18 H atoms   28 H atoms
                                   38 O atoms   38 O atoms

Solution: $4.9\ \text{mol}\ C_6H_{14} \times \dfrac{19\ \text{mol}\ O_2}{2\ \text{mol}\ C_6H_{14}} = 4\underline{6}.6\ \text{mol}\ O_2 = 47\ \text{mol}\ O_2$

Check: The units of the answer (mol O_2) are correct. The magnitude is reasonable because much more O_2 is needed than C_6H_{14}.

4.3   (a)   **Given:** 1.3 mol N_2O_5 **Find:** mol NO_2
          Conceptual Plan: mol N_2O_5 → mol NO_2

$$\frac{4\ \text{mol}\ NO_2}{2\ \text{mol}\ N_2O_5}$$

          Solution: $1.3\ \text{mol}\ N_2O_5 \times \dfrac{4\ \text{mol}\ NO_2}{2\ \text{mol}\ N_2O_5} = 2.6\ \text{mol}\ NO_2$

          Check: The units of the answer (mol NO_2) are correct. The magnitude is reasonable because it is greater than mol N_2O_5.

       (b)   **Given:** 5.8 mol N_2O_5 **Find:** mol NO_2
          Conceptual Plan: mol N_2O_5 → mol NO_2

$$\frac{4\ \text{mol}\ NO_2}{2\ \text{mol}\ N_2O_5}$$

          Solution: $5.8\ \text{mol}\ N_2O_5 \times \dfrac{4\ \text{mol}\ NO_2}{2\ \text{mol}\ N_2O_5} = 1\underline{1}.6\ \text{mol}\ NO_2 = 12\ \text{mol}\ NO_2$

          Check: The units of the answer (mol NO_2) are correct. The magnitude is reasonable because it is greater than mol N_2O_5.

       (c)   **Given:** 10.5 g N_2O_5 **Find:** mol NO_2
          Conceptual Plan: g N_2O_5 → mol N_2O_5 → mol NO_2

$$\frac{1\ \text{mol}\ N_2O_5}{108.02\ \text{g}\ N_2O_5} \qquad \frac{4\ \text{mol}\ NO_2}{2\ \text{mol}\ N_2O_5}$$

Solution: $10.5 \text{ g N}_2\text{O}_5 \times \dfrac{1 \text{ mol N}_2\text{O}_5}{108.02 \text{ g N}_2\text{O}_5} \times \dfrac{4 \text{ mol NO}_2}{2 \text{ mol N}_2\text{O}_5} = 0.19\underline{4}4 \text{ mol NO}_2 = 0.194 \text{ mol NO}_2$

Check: The units of the answer (mol NO_2) are correct. The magnitude is reasonable because 10 g is about 0.09 mol N_2O_5 and the answer is greater than mol N_2O_5.

(d) **Given:** 1.55 kg N_2O_5 **Find:** mol NO_2
Conceptual Plan: kg N$_2$O$_5$ → g N$_2$O$_5$ → mol N$_2$O$_5$ → mol NO$_2$

$$\dfrac{1000 \text{ g N}_2\text{O}_5}{1 \text{ kg N}_2\text{O}_5} \qquad \dfrac{1 \text{ mol N}_2\text{O}_5}{108.02 \text{ g N}_2\text{O}_5} \qquad \dfrac{4 \text{ mol NO}_2}{2 \text{ mol N}_2\text{O}_5}$$

Solution:

$$1.55 \text{ kg N}_2\text{O}_5 \times \dfrac{1000 \text{ g N}_2\text{O}_5}{1 \text{ kg N}_2\text{O}_5} \times \dfrac{1 \text{ mol N}_2\text{O}_5}{108.02 \text{ g N}_2\text{O}_5} \times \dfrac{4 \text{ mol NO}_2}{2 \text{ mol N}_2\text{O}_5} = 28.\underline{7}0 \text{ mol NO}_2 = 28.7 \text{ mol NO}_2$$

Check: The units of the answer (mol NO_2) are correct. The magnitude is reasonable because 1.55 kg is about 14 mol N_2O_5 and the answer is greater than mol N_2O_5.

4.5 **Given:** 3 mol SiO_2 **Find:** mol C; mol SiC; mol CO
Conceptual Plan: mol SiO$_2$ → mol C → mol SiC → mol CO

$$\dfrac{3 \text{ mol C}}{1 \text{ mol SiO}_2} \qquad \dfrac{1 \text{ mol SiC}}{1 \text{ mol SiO}_2} \qquad \dfrac{2 \text{ mol CO}}{1 \text{ mol SiO}_2}$$

Solution: $3 \text{ mol SiO}_2 \times \dfrac{3 \text{ mol C}}{1 \text{ mol SiO}_2} = 9 \text{ mol C} \qquad 3 \text{ mol SiO}_2 \times \dfrac{1 \text{ mol SiC}}{1 \text{ mol SiO}_2} = 3 \text{ mol SiC}$

$$3 \text{ mol SiO}_2 \times \dfrac{2 \text{ mol CO}}{1 \text{ mol SiO}_2} = 6 \text{ mol CO}$$

Given: 6 mol C **Find:** mol SiO_2; mol SiC; mol CO
Conceptual Plan: mol C → mol SiO$_2$ → mol SiC → mol CO

$$\dfrac{1 \text{ mol SiO}_2}{3 \text{ mol C}} \qquad \dfrac{1 \text{ mol SiC}}{3 \text{ mol C}} \qquad \dfrac{2 \text{ mol CO}}{3 \text{ mol C}}$$

Solution: $6 \text{ mol C} \times \dfrac{1 \text{ mol SiO}_2}{3 \text{ mol C}} = 2 \text{ mol SiO}_2 \qquad 6 \text{ mol C} \times \dfrac{1 \text{ mol SiC}}{3 \text{ mol C}} = 2 \text{ mol SiC}$

$$6 \text{ mol C} \times \dfrac{2 \text{ mol CO}}{3 \text{ mol C}} = 4 \text{ mol CO}$$

Given: 10 mol CO **Find:** mol SiO_2; mol C; mol SiC
Conceptual Plan: mol CO → mol SiO$_2$ → mol C → mol SiC

$$\dfrac{1 \text{ mol SiO}_2}{2 \text{ mol CO}} \qquad \dfrac{3 \text{ mol C}}{2 \text{ mol CO}} \qquad \dfrac{1 \text{ mol SiC}}{2 \text{ mol CO}}$$

Solution: $10 \text{ mol CO} \times \dfrac{1 \text{ mol SiO}_2}{2 \text{ mol CO}} = 5.0 \text{ mol SiO}_2 \qquad 10 \text{ mol C} \times \dfrac{3 \text{ mol C}}{2 \text{ mol CO}} = 15 \text{ mol C}$

$$10 \text{ mol CO} \times \dfrac{1 \text{ mol SiC}}{2 \text{ mol CO}} = 5.0 \text{ mol SiC}$$

Given: 2.8 mol SiO_2 **Find:** mol C; mol SiC; mol CO
Conceptual Plan: mol SiO$_2$ → mol C → mol SiC → mol CO

$$\dfrac{3 \text{ mol C}}{1 \text{ mol SiO}_2} \qquad \dfrac{1 \text{ mol SiC}}{1 \text{ mol SiO}_2} \qquad \dfrac{2 \text{ mol CO}}{1 \text{ mol SiO}_2}$$

Solution: $2.8 \text{ mol SiO}_2 \times \dfrac{3 \text{ mol C}}{1 \text{ mol SiO}_2} = 8.4 \text{ mol C} \qquad 2.8 \text{ mol SiO}_2 \times \dfrac{1 \text{ mol SiC}}{1 \text{ mol SiO}_2} = 2.8 \text{ mol SiC}$

$$2.8 \text{ mol SiO}_2 \times \dfrac{2 \text{ mol CO}}{1 \text{ mol SiO}_2} = 5.6 \text{ mol CO}$$

Given: 1.55 mol C **Find:** mol SiO_2; mol SiC; mol CO
Conceptual Plan: mol C → mol SiO$_2$ → mol SiC → mol CO

$$\dfrac{1 \text{ mol SiO}_2}{3 \text{ mol C}} \qquad \dfrac{1 \text{ mol SiC}}{3 \text{ mol C}} \qquad \dfrac{2 \text{ mol CO}}{3 \text{ mol C}}$$

Solution: $1.55 \text{ mol C} \times \dfrac{1 \text{ mol SiO}_2}{3 \text{ mol C}} = 0.517 \text{ mol SiO}_2$ $1.55 \text{ mol C} \times \dfrac{1 \text{ mol SiC}}{3 \text{ mol C}} = 0.517 \text{ mol SiC}$

$1.55 \text{ mol C} \times \dfrac{2 \text{ mol CO}}{3 \text{ mol C}} = 1.03 \text{ mol CO}$

SiO_2	C	SiC	CO
3	9	3	6
2	**6**	2	4
5.0	15	5.0	**10**
2.8	8.4	2.8	5.6
0.517	**1.55**	0.517	1.03

4.7   **Given:** 4.8 g Fe   **Find:** g HBr; g H_2
Conceptual Plan: g Fe $\rightarrow$ mol Fe $\rightarrow$ mol HBr $\rightarrow$ g HBr

$$\dfrac{1 \text{ mol Fe}}{55.8 \text{ g Fe}} \quad \dfrac{2 \text{ mol HBr}}{1 \text{ mol Fe}} \quad \dfrac{80.9 \text{ g HBr}}{1 \text{ mol HBr}}$$

g Fe $\rightarrow$ mol Fe $\rightarrow$ mol H_2 $\rightarrow$ g H_2

$$\dfrac{1 \text{ mol Fe}}{55.8 \text{ g Fe}} \quad \dfrac{1 \text{ mol H}_2}{1 \text{ mol Fe}} \quad \dfrac{2.02 \text{ g H}_2}{1 \text{ mol H}_2}$$

Solution: $4.8 \text{ g Fe} \times \dfrac{1 \text{ mol Fe}}{55.8 \text{ g Fe}} \times \dfrac{2 \text{ mol HBr}}{1 \text{ mol Fe}} \times \dfrac{80.9 \text{ g HBr}}{1 \text{ mol HBr}} = 1\underline{3}.9 \text{ g HBr} = 14 \text{ g HBr}$

$4.8 \text{ g Fe} \times \dfrac{1 \text{ mol Fe}}{55.8 \text{ g Fe}} \times \dfrac{1 \text{ mol H}_2}{1 \text{ mol Fe}} \times \dfrac{2.02 \text{ g H}_2}{1 \text{ mol H}_2} = 0.17\underline{4} \text{ g H}_2 = 0.17 \text{ g H}_2$

Check: The units of the answers (g HBr, g H_2) are correct. The magnitude of the answers is reasonable because the molar mass of HBr is greater than Fe and the molar mass of H_2 is much less than Fe.

4.9   (a)   **Given:** 2.5 g Ba   **Find:** g $BaCl_2$
Conceptual Plan: g Ba $\rightarrow$ mol Ba $\rightarrow$ mol $BaCl_2$ $\rightarrow$ g $BaCl_2$

$$\dfrac{1 \text{ mol Ba}}{137.33 \text{ g Ba}} \quad \dfrac{1 \text{ mol BaCl}_2}{1 \text{ mol Ba}} \quad \dfrac{208.23 \text{ g BaCl}_2}{1 \text{ mol BaCl}_2}$$

Solution: $2.5 \text{ g Ba} \times \dfrac{1 \text{ mol Ba}}{137.33 \text{ g Ba}} \times \dfrac{1 \text{ mol BaCl}_2}{1 \text{ mol Ba}} \times \dfrac{208.23 \text{ g BaCl}_2}{1 \text{ mol BaCl}_2} = 3.7\underline{9}1 \text{ g BaCl}_2 = 3.8 \text{ g BaCl}_2$

Check: The units of the answer (g $BaCl_2$) are correct. The magnitude of the answer is reasonable because it is larger than grams Ba.

(b)   **Given:** 2.5 g CaO   **Find:** g $CaCO_3$
Conceptual Plan: g CaO $\rightarrow$ mol CaO $\rightarrow$ mol $CaCO_3$ $\rightarrow$ g $CaCO_3$

$$\dfrac{1 \text{ mol CaO}}{56.08 \text{ g CaO}} \quad \dfrac{1 \text{ mol CaCO}_3}{1 \text{ mol CaO}} \quad \dfrac{100.09 \text{ g CaCO}_3}{1 \text{ mol CaCO}_3}$$

Solution:

$2.5 \text{ g CaO} \times \dfrac{1 \text{ mol CaO}}{56.08 \text{ g CaO}} \times \dfrac{1 \text{ mol CaCO}_3}{1 \text{ mol CaO}} \times \dfrac{100.09 \text{ g CaCO}_3}{1 \text{ mol CaCO}_3} = 4.4\underline{6}2 \text{ g CaCO}_3 = 4.5 \text{ g CaCO}_3$

Check: The units of the answer (g $CaCO_3$) are correct. The magnitude of the answer is reasonable because it is larger than grams CaO.

(c)   **Given:** 2.5 g Mg   **Find:** g MgO
Conceptual Plan: g Mg $\rightarrow$ mol Mg $\rightarrow$ mol MgO $\rightarrow$ g MgO

$$\dfrac{1 \text{ mol Mg}}{24.31 \text{ g Mg}} \quad \dfrac{1 \text{ mol MgO}}{1 \text{ mol Mg}} \quad \dfrac{40.31 \text{ g MgO}}{1 \text{ mol MgO}}$$

Solution: $2.5 \text{ g Mg} \times \dfrac{1 \text{ mol Mg}}{24.31 \text{ g Mg}} \times \dfrac{1 \text{ mol MgO}}{1 \text{ mol Mg}} \times \dfrac{40.31 \text{ g MgO}}{1 \text{ mol MgO}} = 4.1\underline{4}5 \text{ g MgO} = 4.1 \text{ g MgO}$

Check: The units of the answer (g MgO) are correct. The magnitude of the answer is reasonable because it is larger than grams Mg.

(d) **Given:** 2.5 g Al **Find:** g Al_2O_3
Conceptual Plan: g Al → mol Al → mol Al_2O_3 → g Al_2O_3

$$\frac{1 \text{ mol Al}}{26.98 \text{ g Al}} \qquad \frac{2 \text{ mol Al}_2O_3}{4 \text{ mol Al}} \qquad \frac{101.96 \text{ g Al}_2O_3}{1 \text{ mol Al}_2O_3}$$

Solution: $2.5 \text{ g Al} \times \dfrac{1 \text{ mol Al}}{26.98 \text{ g Al}} \times \dfrac{2 \text{ mol Al}_2O_3}{4 \text{ mol Al}} \times \dfrac{101.96 \text{ g Al}_2O_3}{1 \text{ mol Al}_2O_3} = 4.7\underline{2}4 \text{ g Al}_2O_3 = 4.7 \text{ g Al}_2O_3$

Check: The units of the answer (g Al_2O_3) are correct. The magnitude of the answer is reasonable because it is larger than grams Al.

4.11 (a) **Given:** 4.85 g NaOH **Find:** g HCl
Conceptual Plan: g NaOH → mol NaOH → mol HCl → g HCl

$$\frac{1 \text{ mol NaOH}}{40.00 \text{ g NaOH}} \qquad \frac{1 \text{ mol HCl}}{1 \text{ mol NaOH}} \qquad \frac{36.46 \text{ g HCl}}{1 \text{ mol HCl}}$$

Solution: $4.85 \text{ g NaOH} \times \dfrac{1 \text{ mol NaOH}}{40.00 \text{ g NaOH}} \times \dfrac{1 \text{ mol HCl}}{1 \text{ mol NaOH}} \times \dfrac{36.46 \text{ g HCl}}{1 \text{ mol HCl}} = 4.4\underline{2}1 \text{ g HCl} = 4.42 \text{ g HCl}$

Check: The units of the answer (g HCl) are correct. The magnitude of the answer is reasonable because it is less than g NaOH.

(b) **Given:** 4.85 g $Ca(OH)_2$ **Find:** g HNO_3
Conceptual Plan: g $Ca(OH)_2$ → mol $Ca(OH)_2$ → mol HNO_3 → g HNO_3

$$\frac{1 \text{ mol Ca(OH)}_2}{74.10 \text{ g Ca(OH)}_2} \qquad \frac{2 \text{ mol HNO}_3}{1 \text{ mol Ca(OH)}_2} \qquad \frac{63.02 \text{ g HNO}_3}{1 \text{ mol HNO}_3}$$

Solution: $4.85 \text{ g Ca(OH)}_2 \times \dfrac{1 \text{ mol Ca(OH)}_2}{74.10 \text{ g Ca(OH)}_2} \times \dfrac{2 \text{ mol HNO}_3}{1 \text{ mol Ca(OH)}_2} \times \dfrac{63.02 \text{ g HNO}_3}{1 \text{ mol HNO}_3} = 8.2\underline{5}0 \text{ g HNO}_3 = 8.25 \text{ g HNO}_3$

Check: The units of the answer (g HNO_3) are correct. The magnitude of the answer is reasonable because it is more than g $Ca(OH)_2$.

(c) **Given:** 4.85 g KOH **Find:** g H_2SO_4
Conceptual Plan: g KOH → mol KOH → mol H_2SO_4 → g H_2SO_4

$$\frac{1 \text{ mol KOH}}{56.11 \text{ g KOH}} \qquad \frac{1 \text{ mol H}_2SO_4}{2 \text{ mol KOH}} \qquad \frac{98.09 \text{ g H}_2SO_4}{1 \text{ mol H}_2SO_4}$$

Solution: $4.85 \text{ g KOH} \times \dfrac{1 \text{ mol KOH}}{56.11 \text{ g KOH}} \times \dfrac{1 \text{ mol H}_2SO_4}{2 \text{ mol KOH}} \times \dfrac{98.09 \text{ g H}_2SO_4}{1 \text{ mol H}_2SO_4} = 4.23\underline{9} \text{ g H}_2SO_4 = 4.24 \text{ g H}_2SO_4$

Check: The units of the answer (g H_2SO_4) are correct. The magnitude of the answer is reasonable because it is less than g KOH.

Limiting Reactant, Theoretical Yield, and Percent Yield

4.13 (a) **Given:** 2 mol Na; 2 mol Br_2 **Find:** limiting reactant
Conceptual Plan: mol Na → mol NaBr

$$\frac{2 \text{ mol NaBr}}{2 \text{ mol Na}} \qquad \text{→ smallest mol amount determines limiting reactant}$$

mol Br_2 → mol NaBr

$$\frac{2 \text{ mol NaBr}}{1 \text{ mol Br}_2}$$

Solution: $2 \text{ mol Na} \times \dfrac{2 \text{ mol NaBr}}{2 \text{ mol Na}} = 2 \text{ mol NaBr}$

$2 \text{ mol Br}_2 \times \dfrac{2 \text{ mol NaBr}}{1 \text{ mol Br}_2} = 4 \text{ mol NaBr}$

Na is the limiting reactant.

Check: The answer is reasonable because Na produced the smallest amount of product.

(b) **Given:** 1.8 mol Na; 1.4 mol Br_2 **Find:** limiting reactant
Conceptual Plan: mol Na → mol NaBr

$$\frac{2 \text{ mol NaBr}}{2 \text{ mol Na}} \qquad \text{→ smallest mol amount determines limiting reactant}$$

$$\text{mol Br}_2 \;\rightarrow\; \text{mol NaBr}$$

$$\frac{2 \text{ mol NaBr}}{1 \text{ mol Br}_2}$$

Solution: $1.8 \;\cancel{\text{mol Na}} \times \dfrac{2 \text{ mol NaBr}}{2 \;\cancel{\text{mol Na}}} = 1.8 \text{ mol NaBr}$

$1.4 \;\cancel{\text{mol Br}_2} \times \dfrac{2 \text{ mol NaBr}}{1 \;\cancel{\text{mol Br}_2}} = 2.8 \text{ mol NaBr}$

Na is the limiting reactant.

Check: The answer is reasonable because Na produced the smallest amount of product.

(c)   **Given:** 2.5 mol Na; 1 mol Br_2 **Find:** limiting reactant

Conceptual Plan: mol Na → mol NaBr

$$\frac{2 \text{ mol NaBr}}{2 \text{ mol Na}} \qquad \rightarrow \textbf{ smallest mol amount determines limiting reactant}$$

mol Br$_2$ → mol NaBr

$$\frac{2 \text{ mol NaBr}}{1 \text{ mol Br}_2}$$

Solution: $2.5 \;\cancel{\text{mol Na}} \times \dfrac{2 \text{ mol NaBr}}{2 \;\cancel{\text{mol Na}}} = 2.5 \text{ mol NaBr}$

$1 \;\cancel{\text{mol Br}_2} \times \dfrac{2 \text{ mol NaBr}}{1 \;\cancel{\text{mol Br}_2}} = 2 \text{ mol NaBr}$

Br$_2$ is the limiting reactant.

Check: The answer is reasonable because Br$_2$ produced the smallest amount of product.

(d)   **Given:** 12.6 mol Na; 6.9 mol Br_2 **Find:** limiting reactant

Conceptual Plan: mol Na → mol NaBr

$$\frac{2 \text{ mol NaBr}}{2 \text{ mol Na}} \qquad \rightarrow \textbf{ smallest mol amount determines limiting reactant}$$

mol Br$_2$ → mol NaBr

$$\frac{2 \text{ mol NaBr}}{1 \text{ mol Br}_2}$$

Solution: $12.6 \;\cancel{\text{mol Na}} \times \dfrac{2 \text{ mol NaBr}}{2 \;\cancel{\text{mol Na}}} = 12.6 \text{ mol NaBr}$

$6.9 \;\cancel{\text{mol Br}_2} \times \dfrac{2 \text{ mol NaBr}}{1 \;\cancel{\text{mol Br}_2}} = 13.8 \text{ mol NaBr} = 14 \text{ mol NaBr}$

Na is the limiting reactant.

Check: The answer is reasonable because Na produced the smallest amount of product.

4.15   The greatest number of Cl_2 molecules will be formed from reaction mixture b and would be 3 molecules Cl_2.

(a)   **Given:** 7 molecules HCl; 1 molecule O_2 **Find:** theoretical yield Cl_2

Conceptual Plan: molecules HCl → molecules Cl$_2$

$$\frac{2 \text{ molecules Cl}_2}{4 \text{ molecules HCl}} \qquad \rightarrow \begin{array}{l}\textbf{smallest mol amount determines} \\ \textbf{limiting reactant}\end{array}$$

molecules O$_2$ → molecules Cl$_2$

$$\frac{2 \text{ molecules Cl}_2}{1 \text{ molecule O}_2}$$

Solution: $7 \;\cancel{\text{molecules HCl}} \times \dfrac{2 \text{ molecules Cl}_2}{4 \;\cancel{\text{molecules HCl}}} = 3 \text{ molecules Cl}_2$

$1 \;\cancel{\text{molecule O}_2} \times \dfrac{2 \text{ molecules Cl}_2}{1 \;\cancel{\text{molecule O}_2}} = 2 \text{ molecules Cl}_2$

theoretical yield $= 2$ molecules Cl_2

(b)   **Given:** 6 molecules HCl; 3 molecules O_2 **Find:** theoretical yield Cl_2

Conceptual Plan: molecules HCl → molecules Cl$_2$

$$\frac{2 \text{ molecules Cl}_2}{4 \text{ molecules HCl}} \qquad \rightarrow \begin{array}{l}\textbf{smallest mol amount determines} \\ \textbf{limiting reactant}\end{array}$$

$$\text{molecules } O_2 \rightarrow \text{molecules } Cl_2$$

$$\frac{2 \text{ molecules } Cl_2}{1 \text{ molecule } O_2}$$

Solution: $6 \text{ molecules HCl} \times \dfrac{2 \text{ molecules } Cl_2}{4 \text{ molecules HCl}} = 3 \text{ molecules } Cl_2$

$3 \text{ molecules } O_2 \times \dfrac{2 \text{ molecules } Cl_2}{1 \text{ molecule } O_2} = 6 \text{ molecules } Cl_2$

theoretical yield $= 3$ molecules Cl_2

(c) **Given:** 4 molecules HCl; 5 molecules O_2 **Find:** theoretical yield Cl_2
Conceptual Plan: molecules HCl $\rightarrow$ molecules Cl_2

$$\frac{2 \text{ molecules } Cl_2}{4 \text{ molecules HCl}} \quad \rightarrow \quad \textbf{smallest mol amount determines}$$
$$\textbf{limiting reactant}$$

molecules $O_2 \rightarrow$ molecules Cl_2

$$\frac{2 \text{ molecules } Cl_2}{1 \text{ molecule } O_2}$$

Solution: $4 \text{ molecules HCl} \times \dfrac{2 \text{ molecules } Cl_2}{4 \text{ molecules HCl}} = 2 \text{ molecules } Cl_2$

$5 \text{ molecules } O_2 \times \dfrac{2 \text{ molecules } Cl_2}{1 \text{ molecule } O_2} = 10 \text{ molecules } Cl_2$

theoretical yield $= 2$ molecules Cl_2

Check: The units of the answer (molecules Cl_2) are correct. The answer is reasonable based on the limiting reactant in each mixture.

4.17 (a) **Given:** 4 mol Ti; 4 mol Cl_2 **Find:** theoretical yield $TiCl_4$
Conceptual Plan: mol Ti $\rightarrow$ mol $TiCl_4$

$$\frac{1 \text{ mol } TiCl_4}{1 \text{ mol Ti}} \quad \rightarrow \quad \textbf{smallest mol amount determines limiting reactant}$$

mol $Cl_2 \rightarrow$ mol $TiCl_4$

$$\frac{1 \text{ mol } TiCl_4}{2 \text{ mol } Cl_2}$$

Solution: $4 \text{ mol Ti} \times \dfrac{1 \text{ mol } TiCl_4}{1 \text{ mol Ti}} = 4 \text{ mol } TiCl_4$

$4 \text{ mol } Cl_2 \times \dfrac{1 \text{ mol } TiCl_4}{2 \text{ mol } Cl_2} = 2 \text{ mol } TiCl_4$

theoretical yield $= 2$ mol $TiCl_4$

Check: The units of the answer (mol $TiCl_4$) are correct. The answer is reasonable because Cl_2 produced the smallest amount of product and is the limiting reactant.

(b) **Given:** 7 mol Ti; 17 mol Cl_2 **Find:** theoretical yield $TiCl_4$
Conceptual Plan: mol Ti $\rightarrow$ mol $TiCl_4$

$$\frac{1 \text{ mol } TiCl_4}{1 \text{ mol Ti}} \quad \rightarrow \quad \textbf{smallest mol amount determines limiting reactant}$$

mol $Cl_2 \rightarrow$ mol $TiCl_4$

$$\frac{1 \text{ mol } TiCl_4}{2 \text{ mol } Cl_2}$$

Solution: $7 \text{ mol Ti} \times \dfrac{1 \text{ mol } TiCl_4}{1 \text{ mol Ti}} = 7 \text{ mol } TiCl_4$

$17 \text{ mol } Cl_2 \times \dfrac{1 \text{ mol } TiCl_4}{2 \text{ mol } Cl_2} = 8.5 \text{ mol } TiCl_4$

theoretical yield $= 7$ mol $TiCl_4$

Check: The units of the answer (mol $TiCl_4$) are correct. The answer is reasonable because Ti produced the smallest amount of product and is the limiting reactant.

(c)   **Given:** 12.4 mol Ti; 18.8 mol Cl_2 **Find:** theoretical yield $TiCl_4$
Conceptual Plan: mol Ti $\rightarrow$ mol $TiCl_4$

$$\frac{1 \text{ mol } TiCl_4}{1 \text{ mol } Ti}$$ $\rightarrow$ **smallest mol amount determines limiting reactant**

mol Cl_2 $\rightarrow$ mol $TiCl_4$

$$\frac{1 \text{ mol } TiCl_4}{2 \text{ mol } Cl_2}$$

Solution: $12.4 \text{ mol Ti} \times \dfrac{1 \text{ mol } TiCl_4}{1 \text{ mol Ti}} = 12.4 \text{ mol } TiCl_4$

$18.8 \text{ mol } Cl_2 \times \dfrac{1 \text{ mol } TiCl_4}{2 \text{ mol } Cl_2} = 9.40 \text{ mol } TiCl_4$

theoretical yield $= 9.40 \text{ mol } TiCl_4$

Check: The units of the answer (mol $TiCl_4$) are correct. The answer is reasonable because Cl_2 produced the smallest amount of product and is the limiting reactant.

4.19   (a)   **Given:** 2.0 g Al; 2.0 g Cl_2 **Find:** theoretical yield in g $AlCl_3$
Conceptual Plan: g Al $\rightarrow$ mol Al $\rightarrow$ mol $AlCl_3$

$$\frac{1 \text{ mol Al}}{26.98 \text{ g Al}} \quad \frac{2 \text{ mol } AlCl_3}{2 \text{ mol Al}}$$ $\rightarrow$ **smallest mol amount determines limiting reactant**

g Cl_2 $\rightarrow$ mol Cl_2 $\rightarrow$ mol $AlCl_3$

$$\frac{1 \text{ mol } Cl_2}{70.90 \text{ g } Cl_2} \quad \frac{2 \text{ mol } AlCl_3}{3 \text{ mol } Cl_2}$$

then mol $AlCl_3$ $\rightarrow$ g $AlCl_3$

$$\frac{133.3 \text{ g } AlCl_3}{1 \text{ mol } AlCl_3}$$

Solution: $2.0 \text{ g Al} \times \dfrac{1 \text{ mol Al}}{26.98 \text{ g Al}} \times \dfrac{2 \text{ mol } AlCl_3}{2 \text{ mol Al}} = 0.0741 \text{ mol } AlCl_3$

$2.0 \text{ g } Cl_2 \times \dfrac{1 \text{ mol } Cl_2}{70.90 \text{ g } Cl_2} \times \dfrac{2 \text{ mol } AlCl_3}{3 \text{ mol } Cl_2} = 0.0188 \text{ mol } AlCl_3$

$0.0188 \text{ mol } AlCl_3 \times \dfrac{133.3 \text{ g } AlCl_3}{1 \text{ mol } AlCl_3} = 2.51 \text{ g } AlCl_3 = 2.5 \text{ g } AlCl_3$

Check: The units of the answer (g $AlCl_3$) are correct. The answer is reasonable because Cl_2 produced the smallest amount of product and is the limiting reactant.

(b)   **Given:** 7.5 g Al; 24.8 g Cl_2 **Find:** theoretical yield in g $AlCl_3$
Conceptual Plan: g Al $\rightarrow$ mol Al $\rightarrow$ mol $AlCl_3$

$$\frac{1 \text{ mol Al}}{26.98 \text{ g Al}} \quad \frac{2 \text{ mol } AlCl_3}{2 \text{ mol Al}}$$ $\rightarrow$ **smallest mol amount determines limiting reactant**

g Cl_2 $\rightarrow$ mol Cl_2 $\rightarrow$ mol $AlCl_3$

$$\frac{1 \text{ mol } Cl_2}{70.90 \text{ g } Cl_2} \quad \frac{2 \text{ mol } AlCl_3}{3 \text{ mol } Cl_2}$$

then mol $AlCl_3$ $\rightarrow$ g $AlCl_3$

$$\frac{133.3 \text{ g } AlCl_3}{1 \text{ mol } AlCl_3}$$

Solution: $7.5 \text{ g Al} \times \dfrac{1 \text{ mol Al}}{26.98 \text{ g Al}} \times \dfrac{2 \text{ mol } AlCl_3}{2 \text{ mol Al}} = 0.2780 \text{ mol } AlCl_3$

$24.8 \text{ g } Cl_2 \times \dfrac{1 \text{ mol } Cl_2}{70.90 \text{ g } Cl_2} \times \dfrac{2 \text{ mol } AlCl_3}{3 \text{ mol } Cl_2} = 0.2332 \text{ mol } AlCl_3$

$0.2332 \text{ mol } AlCl_3 \times \dfrac{133.3 \text{ g } AlCl_3}{1 \text{ mol } AlCl_3} = 31.09 \text{ g } AlCl_3 = 31.1 \text{ g } AlCl_3$

Check: The units of the answer (g $AlCl_3$) are correct. The answer is reasonable because Cl_2 produced the smallest amount of product and is the limiting reactant.

(c) **Given:** 0.235 g Al; 1.15 g Cl_2 **Find:** theoretical yield in g $AlCl_3$

Conceptual Plan: g A → mol Al → mol $AlCl_3$

$$\frac{1\ \text{mol Al}}{26.98\ \text{g Al}} \quad \frac{2\ \text{mol AlCl}_3}{2\ \text{mol Al}}$$

→ **smallest mol amount determines limiting reactant**

g Cl_2 → mol Cl_2 → mol $AlCl_3$

$$\frac{1\ \text{mol Cl}_2}{70.90\ \text{g Cl}_2} \quad \frac{2\ \text{mol AlCl}_3}{3\ \text{mol Cl}_2}$$

then mol $AlCl_3$ → g $AlCl_3$

$$\frac{133.3\ \text{g AlCl}_3}{1\ \text{mol AlCl}_3}$$

Solution: $0.235\ \text{g Al} \times \dfrac{1\ \text{mol Al}}{26.98\ \text{g Al}} \times \dfrac{2\ \text{mol AlCl}_3}{2\ \text{mol Al}} = 0.008710\ \text{mol AlCl}_3$

$1.15\ \text{g Cl}_2 \times \dfrac{1\ \text{mol Cl}_2}{70.90\ \text{g Cl}_2} \times \dfrac{2\ \text{mol AlCl}_3}{3\ \text{mol Cl}_2} = 0.01081\ \text{mol AlCl}_3$

$0.008710\ \text{mol AlCl}_3 \times \dfrac{133.3\ \text{g AlCl}_3}{1\ \text{mol AlCl}_3} = 1.161\ \text{g AlCl}_3 = 1.16\ \text{g AlCl}_3$

Check: The units of the answer (g $AlCl_3$) are correct. The answer is reasonable because Al produced the smallest amount of product and is the limiting reactant.

4.21   **Given:** 28.5 g KCl; 25.7 g Pb^{2+}; 29.4 g $PbCl_2$ **Find:** limiting reactant; theoretical yield $PbCl_2$; % yield

Conceptual Plan: g KCl → mol KCl → mol $PbCl_2$

$$\frac{1\ \text{mol KCl}}{74.55\ \text{g KCl}} \quad \frac{1\ \text{mol PbCl}_2}{2\ \text{mol KCl}}$$

→ **smallest mol amount determines limiting reactant**

g Pb^{2+} → mol Pb^{2+} → mol $PbCl_2$

$$\frac{1\ \text{mol Pb}^{2+}}{207.2\ \text{g Pb}^{2+}} \quad \frac{1\ \text{mol PbCl}_2}{1\ \text{mol Pb}^{2+}}$$

then mol $PbCl_2$ → g $PbCl_2$ then determine % yield

$$\frac{278.1\ \text{g PbCl}_2}{\text{mol PbCl}_2} \qquad \frac{\text{actual yield g PbCl}_2}{\text{theoretical yield g PbCl}_2} \times 100\%$$

Solution: $28.5\ \text{g KCl} \times \dfrac{1\ \text{mol KCl}}{74.55\ \text{g KCl}} \times \dfrac{1\ \text{mol PbCl}_2}{2\ \text{mol KCl}} = 0.1911\ \text{mol PbCl}_2$

$25.7\ \text{g Pb}^{2+} \times \dfrac{1\ \text{mol Pb}^{2+}}{207.2\ \text{g Pb}^{2+}} \times \dfrac{1\ \text{mol PbCl}_2}{1\ \text{mol Pb}^{2+}} = 0.1240\ \text{mol PbCl}_2$ Pb^{2+} is the limiting reactant.

$0.1240\ \text{mol PbCl}_2 \times \dfrac{278.1\ \text{g PbCl}_2}{1\ \text{mol PbCl}_2} = 34.48\ \text{g PbCl}_2$

$\dfrac{29.4\ \text{g PbCl}_2}{34.48\ \text{g PbCl}_2} \times 100\% = 85.2\%$

Check: The theoretical yield has the correct units (g $PbCl_2$) and has a reasonable magnitude compared to the mass of Pb^{2+}, the limiting reactant. The % yield is reasonable, under 100%.

4.23   **Given:** 136.4 kg NH_3; 211.4 kg CO_2; 168.4 kg CH_4N_2O **Find:** limiting reactant; theoretical yield CH_4N_2O; % yield

Conceptual Plan: kg NH_3 → g NH_3 → mol NH_3 → mol CH_4N_2O

$$\frac{1000\ \text{g}}{1\ \text{kg}} \quad \frac{1\ \text{mol NH}_3}{17.03\ \text{g NH}_3} \quad \frac{1\ \text{mol CH}_4\text{N}_2\text{O}}{2\ \text{mol NH}_3}$$

→ **smallest mol amount determines limiting reactant**

kg CO_2 → g CO_2 → mol CO_2 → mol CH_4N_2O

$$\frac{1000\ \text{g}}{1\ \text{kg}} \quad \frac{1\ \text{mol CO}_2}{44.01\ \text{g CO}_2} \quad \frac{1\ \text{mol CH}_4\text{N}_2\text{O}}{1\ \text{mol CO}_2}$$

then mol CH_4N_2O → g CH_4N_2O → kg CH_4N_2O then determine % yield

$$\frac{60.06\ \text{g CH}_4\text{N}_2\text{O}}{1\ \text{mol CH}_4\text{N}_2\text{O}} \quad \frac{1\ \text{kg}}{1000\ \text{g}} \quad \frac{\text{actual yield kg CH}_4\text{N}_2\text{O}}{\text{theoretical yield kg CH}_4\text{N}_2\text{O}} \times 100\%$$

Solution: $136.4\ \text{kg NH}_3 \times \dfrac{1000\ \text{g}}{1\ \text{kg}} \times \dfrac{1\ \text{mol NH}_3}{17.03\ \text{g NH}_3} \times \dfrac{1\ \text{mol CH}_4\text{N}_2\text{O}}{2\ \text{mol NH}_3} = 4004.7\ \text{mol CH}_4\text{N}_2\text{O}$

$211.4\ \text{kg CO}_2 \times \dfrac{1000\ \text{g}}{1\ \text{kg}} \times \dfrac{1\ \text{mol CO}_2}{44.01\ \text{g CO}_2} \times \dfrac{1\ \text{mol CH}_4\text{N}_2\text{O}}{1\ \text{mol CO}_2} = 4803.5\ \text{mol CH}_4\text{N}_2\text{O}$

NH_3 is the limiting reactant.

$$4004.7 \text{ mol } \cancel{CH_4N_2O} \times \frac{60.06 \text{ g } \cancel{CH_4N_2O}}{1 \text{ mol } \cancel{CH_4N_2O}} \times \frac{1 \text{ kg}}{1000 \text{ g}} = 240.\underline{5}2 \text{ kg } CH_4N_2O$$

$$\frac{168.4 \text{ kg } \cancel{CH_4N_2O}}{240.\underline{5}2 \text{ kg } \cancel{CH_4N_2O}} \times 100\% = 70.01\%$$

Check: The theoretical yield has the correct units (kg CH_4N_2O) and has a reasonable magnitude compared to the mass of NH_3, the limiting reactant. The % yield is reasonable, under 100%.

Solution Concentration and Solution Stoichiometry

4.25   (a)   **Given:** 4.3 mol LiCl; 2.8 L solution   **Find:** molarity LiCl
Conceptual Plan: mol LiCl, L solution → molarity

$$\text{molarity (M)} = \frac{\text{amount of solute (in moles)}}{\text{volume of solution (in L)}}$$

Solution: $\dfrac{4.3 \text{ mol LiCl}}{2.8 \text{ L solution}} = 1.\underline{5}4 \text{ M LiCl} = 1.5 \text{ M LiCl}$

Check: The units of the answer (M) are correct. The magnitude of the answer is reasonable. Concentrations are usually between 0 M and 18 M.

(b)   **Given:** 22.6 g $C_6H_{12}O_6$; 1.08 L solution   **Find:** molarity $C_6H_{12}O_6$
Conceptual Plan: g $C_6H_{12}O_6$ → mol $C_6H_{12}O_6$, L solution → molarity

$$\frac{1 \text{ mol } C_6H_{12}O_6}{180.16 \text{ g } C_6H_{12}O_6} \qquad \text{molarity (M)} = \frac{\text{amount of solute (in moles)}}{\text{volume of solution (in L)}}$$

Solution: $22.6 \text{ g } \cancel{C_6H_{12}O_6} \times \dfrac{1 \text{ mol } C_6H_{12}O_6}{180.16 \text{ g } \cancel{C_6H_{12}O_6}} = 0.125\underline{4} \text{ mol } C_6H_{12}O_6$

$$\frac{0.125\underline{4} \text{ mol } C_6H_{12}O_6}{1.08 \text{ L solution}} = 0.116\underline{1} \text{ M } C_6H_{12}O_6 = 0.116 \text{ M } C_6H_{12}O_6$$

Check: The units of the answer (M) are correct. The magnitude of the answer is reasonable. Concentrations are usually between 0 M and 18 M.

(c)   **Given:** 45.5 mg NaCl; 154.4 mL solution   **Find:** molarity NaCl
Conceptual Plan: mg NaCl → g NaCl → mol NaCl, and mL solution → L solution then molarity

$$\frac{1 \text{ g NaCl}}{1000 \text{ mg NaCl}} \quad \frac{1 \text{ mol NaCl}}{58.44 \text{ g NaCl}} \quad \frac{1 \text{ L solution}}{1000 \text{ mL solution}} \qquad \text{molarity (M)} = \frac{\text{amount of solute (in moles)}}{\text{volume of solution (in L)}}$$

Solution: $45.5 \text{ mg } \cancel{NaCl} \times \dfrac{1 \text{ g}}{1000 \text{ mg}} \times \dfrac{1 \text{ mol NaCl}}{58.44 \text{ g } \cancel{NaCl}} = 7.78\underline{6} \times 10^{-4} \text{ mol NaCl}$

$$154.4 \text{ mL solution} \times \frac{1 \text{ L}}{1000 \text{ mL}} = 0.1544 \text{ L}$$

$$\frac{7.78\underline{6} \times 10^{-4} \text{ mol NaCl}}{0.1544 \text{ L}} = 0.00504\underline{3} \text{ M NaCl} = 0.00504 \text{ M NaCl}$$

Check: The units of the answer (M) are correct. The magnitude of the answer is reasonable. Concentrations are usually between 0 M and 18 M.

4.27   (a)   **Given:** 0.150 M KNO_3 **Find:** Molarity NO_3^-
Conceptual Plan: M KNO_3 → M NO_3^-

$$\frac{1 \text{ M } NO_3^-}{1 \text{ M } KNO_3}$$

Solution: $0.150 \text{ M } \cancel{KNO_3} \times \dfrac{1 \text{ M } NO_3^-}{1 \text{ M } \cancel{KNO_3}} = 0.150 \text{ M } NO_3^-$

Check: The units of the answer (M) are correct. The magnitude of the answer (0.150) is reasonable, since there is 1 mole of nitrate ions in each mole of potassium nitrate.

(b)   **Given:** 0.150 M $Ca(NO_3)_2$ **Find:** Molarity NO_3^-
Conceptual Plan: M $Ca(NO_3)_2$ → M NO_3^-

$$\frac{2 \text{ M } NO_3^-}{1 \text{ M } Ca(NO_3)_2}$$

Solution: $0.150 \text{ M Ca(NO}_3)_2 \times \dfrac{2 \text{ M NO}_3^-}{1 \text{ M Ca(NO}_3)_2} = 0.300 \text{ M NO}_3^-$

Check: The units of the answer (M) are correct. The magnitude of the answer (0.300) is reasonable, since there are 2 moles of nitrate ions in each mole of calcium nitrate.

(c)   **Given:** 0.150 M Al(NO$_3$)$_3$ **Find:** Molarity NO$_3^-$
       Conceptual Plan: M Al(NO$_3$)$_3$ → M NO$_3^-$

$$\dfrac{3 \text{ M NO}_3^-}{1 \text{ M Al(NO}_3)_3}$$

Solution: $0.150 \text{ M Al(NO}_3)_3 \times \dfrac{3 \text{ M NO}_3^-}{1 \text{ M Al(NO}_3)_3} = 0.450 \text{ M NO}_3^-$

Check: The units of the answer (M) are correct. The magnitude of the answer (0.450) is reasonable, since there are 3 moles of nitrate ions in each mole of aluminum nitrate.

4.29   (a)   **Given:** 0.556 L; 2.3 M KCl   **Find:** mol KCl
               Conceptual Plan: volume solution × M = mol

               volume solution (L) × M = mol

               Solution: $0.556 \text{ L solution} \times \dfrac{2.3 \text{ mol KCl}}{1 \text{ L solution}} = 1.28 \text{ mol KCl} = 1.3 \text{ mol KCl}$

               Check: The units of the answer (mol KCl) are correct. The magnitude is reasonable because it is less than 1 L of solution.

       (b)   **Given:** 1.8 L; 0.85 M KCl   **Find:** mol KCl
               Conceptual Plan: volume solution × M = mol

               volume solution (L) × M = mol

               Solution: $1.8 \text{ L solution} \times \dfrac{0.85 \text{ mol KCl}}{1 \text{ L solution}} = 1.83 \text{ mol KCl} = 1.5 \text{ mol KCl}$

               Check: The units of the answer (mol KCl) are correct. The magnitude is reasonable because it is less than 2 L of solution.

       (c)   **Given:** 114 mL; 1.85 M KCl   **Find:** mol KCl
               Conceptual Plan: mL solution → L solution, then volume solution × M = mol

               $\dfrac{1 \text{ L}}{1000 \text{ mL}}$ volume solution (L) × M = mol

               Solution: $114 \text{ mL solution} \times \dfrac{1 \text{ L}}{1000 \text{ mL}} \times \dfrac{1.85 \text{ mol KCl}}{1 \text{ L solution}} = 0.2109 \text{ mol KCl} = 0.211 \text{ mol KCl}$

               Check: The units of the answer (mol KCl) are correct. The magnitude is reasonable because it is less than 1 L of solution.

4.31   **Given:** 500.0 mL; 1.3 M NaNO$_3$ **Find:** g NaNO$_3$
        Conceptual Plan: mL solution → L solution, then volume solution × M = mol NaNO$_3$

        $\dfrac{1 \text{ L solution}}{1000 \text{ mL solution}}$ volume solution (L) × M = mol

        then mol NaNO$_3$ → g NaNO$_3$

        $\dfrac{85.00 \text{ g NaNO}_3}{1 \text{ mol NaNO}_3}$

        Solution: $500.0 \text{ mL solution} \times \dfrac{1 \text{ L}}{1000 \text{ mL}} \times \dfrac{1.3 \text{ mol NaNO}_3}{1 \text{ L solution}} \times \dfrac{85.00 \text{ g}}{1 \text{ mol NaNO}_3} = 55.25 \text{ g NaNO}_3 = 55 \text{ g NaNO}_3$

        Check: The units of the answer (g NaNO$_3$) are correct. The magnitude is reasonable for the concentration and volume of solution.

4.33   **Given:** $V_1 = 123$ mL; $M_1 = 1.1$ M glucose; $V_2 = 500.0$ mL   **Find:** M_2
        Conceptual Plan: mL → L then $V_1, M_1, V_2 → M_2$

        $\dfrac{1 \text{ L}}{1000 \text{ mL}}$ $V_1 M_1 = V_2 M_2$

        Solution: $123 \text{ mL} \times \dfrac{1 \text{ L}}{1000 \text{ mL}} = 0.123 \text{ L}$ $500.0 \text{ mL} \times \dfrac{1 \text{ L}}{1000 \text{ mL}} = 0.5000 \text{ L}$

$$M_2 = \frac{V_1 M_1}{V_2} = \frac{(0.123 \text{ L})(1.1 \text{ M})}{(0.5000 \text{ L})} = 0.2\underline{7}1 \text{ M glucose} = 0.27 \text{ M glucose}$$

Check: The units of the answer (M) are correct. The magnitude of the answer is reasonable because it is less than the original concentration.

4.35   **Given:** $V_1 = 50.0$ mL; $M_1 = 12$ M; $M_2 = 0.100$ M   **Find:** V_2
Conceptual Plan: $\text{mL} \rightarrow \text{L}$ then $V_1, M_1, M_2 \rightarrow V_2$

$$\frac{1 \text{ L}}{1000 \text{ mL}} \qquad\qquad V_1 M_1 = V_2 M_2$$

Solution: $50.0 \text{ mL} \times \dfrac{1 \text{ L}}{1000 \text{ mL}} = 0.0500 \text{ L}$

$$V_2 = \frac{V_1 M_1}{M_2} = \frac{(0.0500 \text{ L})(12 \text{ M})}{(0.100 \text{ M})} = 6.0 \text{ L}$$

Check: The units of the answer (L) are correct. The magnitude of the answer is reasonable because the new concentration is much less than the original; the volume must be larger.

4.37   **Given:** 95.4 mL; 0.102 M $CuCl_2$; 0.175 M Na_3PO_4 **Find:** volume Na_3PO_4
Conceptual Plan: $\text{mL CuCl}_2 \rightarrow \text{L CuCl}_2 \rightarrow \text{mol CuCl}_2 \rightarrow \text{mol Na}_3\text{PO}_4 \rightarrow \text{L Na}_3\text{PO}_4 \rightarrow \text{mL Na}_3\text{PO}_4$

$$\frac{1 \text{ L}}{1000 \text{ mL}} \quad \frac{0.102 \text{ mol CuCl}_2}{1 \text{ L}} \quad \frac{2 \text{ mol Na}_3\text{PO}_4}{3 \text{ mol CuCl}_2} \quad \frac{1 \text{ L}}{0.175 \text{ mol Na}_3\text{PO}_4} \quad \frac{1000 \text{ mL}}{1 \text{ L}}$$

Solution: $95.4 \text{ mL CuCl}_2 \times \dfrac{1 \text{ L}}{1000 \text{ mL}} \times \dfrac{0.102 \text{ mol CuCl}_2}{1 \text{ L}} \times \dfrac{2 \text{ mol Na}_3\text{PO}_4}{3 \text{ mol CuCl}_2} \times \dfrac{1 \text{ L}}{0.175 \text{ mol Na}_3\text{PO}_4} \times \dfrac{1000 \text{ mL}}{1 \text{ L}}$

$= 37.0\underline{7} \text{ mL Na}_3\text{PO}_4 = 37.1 \text{ mL Na}_3\text{PO}_4$

Check: The units of the answer (mL Na_3PO_4) are correct. The magnitude of the answer is reasonable because the concentration of Na_3PO_4 is greater.

4.39   **Given:** 25.0 g H_2; 6.0 M H_2SO_4 **Find:** volume H_2SO_4
Conceptual Plan: $\text{g H}_2 \rightarrow \text{mol H}_2 \rightarrow \text{mol H}_2\text{SO}_4 \rightarrow \text{L H}_2\text{SO}_4$

$$\frac{1 \text{ mol H}_2}{2.016 \text{ g H}_2} \quad \frac{3 \text{ mol H}_2\text{SO}_4}{3 \text{ mol H}_2} \quad \frac{1 \text{ L}}{6.0 \text{ mol H}_2\text{SO}_4}$$

Solution: $25.0 \text{ g H}_2 \times \dfrac{1 \text{ mol H}_2}{2.016 \text{ g H}_2} \times \dfrac{3 \text{ mol H}_2\text{SO}_4}{3 \text{ mol H}_2} \times \dfrac{1 \text{ L}}{6.0 \text{ mol H}_2\text{SO}_4} = 2.0\underline{7} \text{ L H}_2\text{SO}_4 = 2.1 \text{ L H}_2\text{SO}_4$

Check: The units of the answer (L H_2SO_4) are correct. The magnitude is reasonable because there are approximately 12 mol H_2 and the mole ratio is 1:1.

4.41   **Given:** 25.0 mL, 1.20 M KCl; 15.0 mL, 0.900 M $Pb(NO_3)_2$; 2.45 g $PbCl_2$
Find: limiting reactant, theoretical yield $PbCl_2$, % yield
Conceptual Plan: **volume KCl solution** $\times$ **M** $\rightarrow$ **mol KCl** $\rightarrow$ **mol** $PbCl_2$

$$\text{volume solution (L)} \times \text{M} = \text{mol} \qquad \frac{1 \text{ mol PbCl}_2}{2 \text{ mol KCl}} \qquad \rightarrow \text{ \textbf{smallest mol amount determines}}$$
$$\text{\textbf{limiting reactant}}$$

volume $Pb(NO_3)_2$ **solution** $\times$ **M** $\rightarrow$ **mol** $Pb(NO_3)_2$ $\rightarrow$ **mol** $PbCl_2$

$$\text{volume solution (L)} \times \text{M} = \text{mol} \qquad \frac{1 \text{ mol PbCl}_2}{1 \text{ mol Pb(NO}_3)_2}$$

then mol $PbCl_2$ $\rightarrow$ **g** $PbCl_2$ **then determine % yield**

$$\frac{278.1 \text{ g PbCl}_2}{\text{mol PbCl}_2} \qquad \frac{\text{actual yield g PbCl}_2}{\text{theoretical yield g PbCl}_2} \times 100\%$$

Solution: $25.0 \text{ mL solution} \times \dfrac{1 \text{ L solution}}{1000 \text{ mL solution}} \times \dfrac{1.20 \text{ mol KCl}}{\text{L solution}} \times \dfrac{1 \text{ mol PbCl}_2}{2 \text{ mol KCl}} = 0.15\underline{0} \text{ mol PbCl}_2$

$15.0 \text{ mL solution} \times \dfrac{1 \text{ L solution}}{1000 \text{ mL solution}} \times \dfrac{0.900 \text{ mol Pb(NO}_3)_2}{\text{L solution}} \times \dfrac{1 \text{ mol PbCl}_2}{1 \text{ mol Pb(NO}_3)_2} = 0.013\underline{5} \text{ mol PbCl}_2$

$0.013\underline{5} \text{ mol PbCl}_2 \times \dfrac{278.1 \text{ g PbCl}_2}{1 \text{ mol PbCl}_2} = 3.7\underline{5}4 \text{ g PbCl}_2$

$\dfrac{2.45 \text{ g PbCl}_2}{3.7\underline{5}4 \text{ g PbCl}_2} \times 100\% = 65.3\%$

Check: The units are correct (g and %). The magnitude of the theoretical yield (3.75) is reasonable since we have much less than a mole of each of the reactants. The magnitude of the percent yield (65.3) is reasonable since the actual yield is a little more than half of the theoretical yield.

Types of Aqueous Solutions and Solubility

4.43   (a)   CsCl is an ionic compound. An aqueous solution is an electrolyte solution, so it conducts electricity.

(b) CH_3OH is a molecular compound that does not dissociate. An aqueous solution is a nonelectrolyte solution, so it does not conduct electricity.

(c) $Ca(NO_2)_2$ is an ionic compound. An aqueous solution is an electrolyte solution, so it conducts electricity.

(d) $C_6H_{12}O_6$ is a molecular compound that does not dissociate. An aqueous solution is a nonelectrolyte solution, so it does not conduct electricity.

4.45   (a) $AgNO_3$ is soluble. Compounds containing NO_3^- are always soluble with no exceptions. The ions in the solution are $Ag^+(aq)$ and $NO_3^-(aq)$.

(b) $Pb(C_2H_3O_2)_2$ is soluble. Compounds containing $C_2H_3O_2^-$ are always soluble with no exceptions. The ions in the solution are $Pb^{2+}(aq)$ and $C_2H_3O_2^-(aq)$.

(c) KNO_3 is soluble. Compounds containing K^+ or NO_3^- are always soluble with no exceptions. The ions in solution are $K^+(aq)$ and $NO_3^-(aq)$.

(d) $(NH_4)_2S$ is soluble. Compounds containing NH_4^+ are always soluble with no exceptions. The ions in solution are $NH_4^+(aq)$ and $S^{2-}(aq)$.

Precipitation Reactions

4.47   (a) $LiI(aq) + BaS(aq) \rightarrow$ Possible products: Li_2S and BaI_2. Li_2S is soluble. Compounds containing S^{2-} are normally insoluble, but Li^+ is an exception. BaI_2 is soluble. Compounds containing I^- are normally soluble, and Ba^{2+} is not an exception. $LiI(aq) + BaS(aq) \rightarrow$ No Reaction

(b) $KCl(aq) + CaS(aq) \rightarrow$ Possible products: K_2S and $CaCl_2$. K_2S is soluble. Compounds containing S^{2-} are normally insoluble, but K^+ is an exception. $CaCl_2$ is soluble. Compounds containing Cl^- are normally soluble, and Ca^{2+} is not an exception. $KCl(aq) + CaS(aq) \rightarrow$ No Reaction

(c) $CrBr_2(aq) + Na_2CO_3(aq) \rightarrow$ Possible products: $CrCO_3$ and $NaBr$. $CrCO_3$ is insoluble. Compounds containing CO_3^{2-} are normally insoluble, and Cr^{2+} is not an exception. $NaBr$ is soluble. Compounds containing Br^- are normally soluble, and Na^+ is not an exception.
$CrBr_2(aq) + Na_2CO_3(aq) \rightarrow CrCO_3(s) + 2\ NaBr(aq)$

(d) $NaOH(aq) + FeCl_3(aq) \rightarrow$ Possible products: $NaCl$ and $Fe(OH)_3$. $NaCl$ is soluble. Compounds containing Na^+ are normally soluble—no exceptions. $Fe(OH)_3$ is insoluble. Compounds containing OH^- are normally insoluble, and Fe^{3+} is not an exception.
$3\ NaOH(aq) + FeCl_3(aq) \rightarrow 3\ NaCl(aq) + Fe(OH)_3(s)$

4.49   (a) $K_2CO_3(aq) + Pb(NO_3)_2(aq) \rightarrow$ Possible products: KNO_3 and $PbCO_3$. KNO_3 is soluble. Compounds containing K^+ are always soluble—no exceptions. $PbCO_3$ is insoluble. Compounds containing CO_3^{2-} are normally insoluble, and Pb^{2+} is not an exception.
$K_2CO_3(aq) + Pb(NO_3)_2(aq) \rightarrow 2\ KNO_3(aq) + PbCO_3(s)$

(b) $Li_2SO_4(aq) + Pb(C_2H_3O_2)_2(aq) \rightarrow$ Possible products: $LiC_2H_3O_2$ and $PbSO_4$. $LiC_2H_3O_2$ is soluble. Compounds containing Li^+ are always soluble—no exceptions. $PbSO_4$ is insoluble. Compounds containing SO_4^{2-} are normally soluble, but Pb^{2+} is an exception.
$Li_2SO_4(aq) + Pb(C_2H_3O_2)_2(aq) \rightarrow 2\ LiC_2H_3O_2(aq) + PbSO_4(s)$

(c) $Cu(NO_3)_2(aq) + MgS(s) \rightarrow$ Possible products: CuS and $Mg(NO_3)_2$. CuS is insoluble. Compounds containing S^{2-} are normally insoluble, and Cu^{2+} is not an exception. $Mg(NO_3)_2$ is soluble. Compounds containing NO_3^- are always soluble—no exceptions.
$Cu(NO_3)_2(aq) + MgS(s) \rightarrow CuS(s) + Mg(NO_3)_2(aq)$

(d) $Sr(NO_3)_2(aq) + KI(aq) \rightarrow$ Possible products: SrI_2 and KNO_3. SrI_2 is soluble. Compounds containing I^- are normally soluble, and Sr^{2+} is not an exception. KNO_3 is soluble. Compounds containing K^+ are always soluble—no exceptions. $Sr(NO_3)_2(aq) + KI(aq) \rightarrow$ No Reaction

Ionic and Net Ionic Equations

4.51   (a) $H^+(aq) + \cancel{Cl^-}(aq) + \cancel{Li^+}(aq) + OH^-(aq) \rightarrow H_2O(l) + \cancel{Li^+}(aq) + \cancel{Cl^-}(aq)$
            $H^+(aq) + OH^-(aq) \rightarrow H_2O(l)$

        (b) $\cancel{Ca^{2+}}(aq) + S^{2-}(aq) + Cu^{2+}(aq) + 2\,\cancel{Cl^-}(aq) \rightarrow CuS(s) + \cancel{Ca^{2+}}(aq) + 2\,\cancel{Cl^-}(aq)$
            $Cu^{2+}(aq) + S^{2-}(aq) \rightarrow CuS(s)$

        (c) $\cancel{Na^+}(aq) + OH^-(aq) + H^+(aq) + \cancel{NO_3^-}(aq) \rightarrow H_2O(l) + \cancel{Na^+}(aq) + \cancel{NO_3^-}(aq)$
            $H^+(aq) + OH^-(aq) + \rightarrow H_2O(l)$

        (d) $6\,\cancel{Na^+}(aq) + 2\,PO_4^{3-}(aq) + 3\,Ni^{2+}(aq) + 6\,\cancel{Cl^-}(aq) \rightarrow Ni_3(PO_4)_2(s) + 6\,\cancel{Na^+}(aq) + 6\,\cancel{Cl^-}(aq)$
            $3\,Ni^{2+}(aq) + 2\,PO_4^{3-}(aq) \rightarrow Ni_3(PO_4)_2(s)$

4.53 $Hg_2^{2+}(aq) + 2\,\cancel{NO_3^-}(aq) + 2\,\cancel{Na^+}(aq) + 2\,Cl^-(aq) \rightarrow Hg_2Cl_2(s) + 2\,\cancel{Na^+}(aq) + 2\,\cancel{NO_3^-}(aq)$
       $Hg_2^{2+}(aq) + 2\,Cl^-(aq) \rightarrow Hg_2Cl_2(s)$

Acid-Base and Gas-Evolution Reactions

4.55   Skeletal reaction: $HBr(aq) + KOH(aq) \rightarrow H_2O(l) + KBr(aq)$
                     acid   base   water   salt
      Net ionic equation: $H^+(aq) + OH^-(aq) \rightarrow H_2O(l)$

4.57   (a)   Skeletal reaction: $H_2SO_4(aq) + Ca(OH)_2(aq) \rightarrow H_2O(l) + CaSO_4(s)$
                           acid   base   water   salt
           Balanced reaction: $H_2SO_4(aq) + Ca(OH)_2(aq) \rightarrow 2\,H_2O(l) + CaSO_4(s)$

        (b)   Skeletal reaction: $HClO_4(aq) + KOH(aq) \rightarrow H_2O(l) + KClO_4(aq)$
                           acid   base   water   salt
           Balanced reaction: $HClO_4(aq) + KOH(aq) \rightarrow H_2O(l) + KClO_4(aq)$

        (c)   Skeletal reaction: $H_2SO_4(aq) + NaOH(aq) \rightarrow H_2O(l) + Na_2SO_4(aq)$
                           acid   base   water   salt
           Balanced reaction: $H_2SO_4(aq) + 2\,NaOH(aq) \rightarrow 2\,H_2O(l) + Na_2SO_4(aq)$

4.59   (a)   Skeletal reaction: $HBr(aq) + NaOH(aq) \rightarrow H_2O(l) + NaBr(aq)$
                           acid   base   water   salt
           Balanced reaction: $HBr(aq) + NaOH(aq) \rightarrow H_2O(l) + NaBr(aq)$
           Complete ionic equation: $H^+(aq) + Br^-(aq) + Na^+(aq) + OH^-(aq) \rightarrow H_2O(l) + Na^+(aq) + Br^-(aq)$
           Net ionic equation: $H^+(aq) + OH^-(aq) \rightarrow H_2O(l)$

        (b)   Skeletal reaction: $HF(aq) + NaOH(aq) \rightarrow H_2O(l) + NaF(aq)$
                           acid   base   water   salt
           Balanced reaction: $HF(aq) + NaOH(aq) \rightarrow H_2O(l) + NaF(aq)$
           Complete ionic equation: $H^+(aq) + F^-(aq) + Na^+(aq) + OH^-(aq) \rightarrow H_2O(l) + Na^+(aq) + F^-(aq)$
           Net ionic equation: $H^+(aq) + OH^-(aq) \rightarrow H_2O(l)$

        (c)   Skeletal reaction: $HC_2H_3O_2(aq) + RbOH(aq) \rightarrow H_2O(l) + RbC_2H_3O_2(aq)$
                           acid   base   water   salt
           Balanced reaction: $HC_2H_3O_2(aq) + RbOH(aq) \rightarrow H_2O(l) + RbC_2H_3O_2(aq)$
           Complete ionic equation: $HC_2H_3O_2(aq) + Rb^+(aq) + OH^-(aq) \rightarrow H_2O(l) + Rb^+(aq) + C_2H_3O_2^-(aq)$
           Net ionic equation: $HC_2H_3O_2(aq) + OH^-(aq) \rightarrow H_2O(l) + C_2H_3O_2^-(aq)$

4.61   (a)   Skeletal reaction: $HBr(aq) + NiS(s) \rightarrow NiBr_2(aq) + H_2S(g)$
                                            gas
           Balanced reaction: $2\,HBr(aq) + NiS(s) \rightarrow NiBr_2(aq) + H_2S(g)$

        (b)   Skeletal reaction: $NH_4I(aq) + NaOH(aq) \rightarrow NH_4OH(aq) + NaI(aq) \rightarrow H_2O(l) + NH_3(g) + NaI(aq)$
                                    decomposes   gas
           Balanced reaction: $NH_4I(aq) + NaOH(aq) \rightarrow H_2O(l) + NH_3(g) + NaI(aq)$

(c) $\quad$ Skeletal reaction: $HBr(aq) + Na_2S(aq) \rightarrow NaBr(aq) + H_2S(g)$

$\qquad\qquad\qquad\qquad\qquad\qquad\qquad\qquad\qquad\quad$ gas

$\qquad$ Balanced reaction: $2\, HBr(aq) + Na_2S(aq) \rightarrow 2\, NaBr(aq) + H_2S(g)$

(d) $\quad$ Skeletal reaction:

$\qquad HClO_4(aq) + Li_2CO_3(aq) \rightarrow H_2CO_3(aq) + LiClO_4(aq) \rightarrow H_2O(l) + CO_2(g) + LiClO_4(aq)$

$\qquad\qquad\qquad\qquad\qquad\qquad$ decomposes $\qquad\qquad\qquad\qquad\qquad$ gas

$\qquad$ Balanced reaction: $2\, HClO_4(aq) + Li_2CO_3(aq) \rightarrow H_2O(l) + CO_2(g) + 2\, LiClO_4(aq)$

Oxidation–Reduction and Combustion

4.63 $\quad$ (a) $\quad$ Ag. The oxidation state of $Ag = 0$. The oxidation state of an atom in a free element is 0.

$\qquad$ (b) $\quad$ Ag^+. The oxidation state of $Ag^+ = +1$. The oxidation state of a monatomic ion is equal to its charge.

$\qquad$ (c) $\quad$ CaF_2. The oxidation state of $Ca = +2$, and the oxidation state of $F = -1$. The oxidation state of a group 2A metal always has an oxidation state of $+2$, and the oxidation of F is -1 because the sum of the oxidation states in a neutral formula unit $= 0$.

$\qquad$ (d) $\quad$ H_2S. The oxidation state of $H = +1$, and the oxidation state of $S = -2$. The oxidation state of H when listed first is $+1$, and the oxidation state of S is -2 because S is in group 6A and the sum of the oxidation states in a neutral molecular unit $= 0$.

$\qquad$ (e) $\quad$ CO_3^{2-}. The oxidation state of $C = +4$, and the oxidation state of $O = -2$. The oxidation state of O is normally -2, and the oxidation state of C is deduced from the formula because the sum of the oxidation states must equal the charge on the ion. (C ox state) $+$ 3(O ox state) $= -2$; (C ox state) $+ 3(-2) = -2$, so C ox state $= +4$.

$\qquad$ (f) $\quad$ CrO_4^{2-}. The oxidation state of $Cr = +6$, and the oxidation state of $O = -2$. The oxidation state of O is normally -2, and the oxidation state of Cr is deduced from the formula because the sum of the oxidation states must equal the charge on the ion. (Cr ox state) $+$ 4(O ox state) $= -2$; (Cr ox state) $+ 4(-2) = -2$, so Cr ox state $= +6$.

4.65 $\quad$ (a) $\quad$ CrO. The oxidation state of $Cr = +2$, and the oxidation state of $O = -2$. The oxidation state of O is normally -2, and the oxidation state of Cr is deduced from the formula because the sum of the oxidation states must $= 0$.

$\qquad\qquad$ (Cr ox state) $+$ (O ox state) $= 0$; (Cr ox state) $+ (-2) = 0$, so $Cr = +2$.

$\qquad$ (b) $\quad$ CrO_3. The oxidation state of $Cr = +6$, and the oxidation state of $O = -2$. The oxidation state of O is normally -2, and the oxidation state of Cr is deduced from the formula because the sum of the oxidation states must $= 0$.

$\qquad\qquad$ (Cr ox state) $+$ 3(O ox state) $= 0$; (Cr ox state) $+ 3\,(-2) = 0$, so $Cr = +6$.

$\qquad$ (c) $\quad$ Cr_2O_3. The oxidation state of $Cr = +3$, and the oxidation state of $O = -2$. The oxidation state of O is normally -2, and the oxidation state of Cr is deduced from the formula because the sum of the oxidation states must $= 0$.

$\qquad\qquad$ 2(Cr ox state) $+$ 3(O ox state) $= 0$; 2(Cr ox state) $+ 3(-2) = 0$, so $Cr = +3$.

4.67 $\quad$ (a) $\qquad\qquad\qquad\qquad$ $4\, Li(s) + O_2(g) \rightarrow 2\, Li_2O(s)$

$\qquad$ Oxidation states; $\qquad$ 0 $\qquad\quad$ 0 $\qquad\quad$ +1 $\;$ −2

$\qquad$ This is a redox reaction because Li increases in oxidation number (oxidation) and O decreases in number (reduction). O_2 is the oxidizing agent, and Li is the reducing agent.

$\qquad$ (b) $\qquad\qquad\qquad\qquad$ $Mg(s) + Fe^{2+}(aq) \rightarrow Mg^{2+}(aq) + Fe(s)$

$\qquad$ Oxidation states; $\qquad$ 0 $\qquad$ +2 $\qquad\quad$ +2 $\qquad\quad$ 0

$\qquad$ This is a redox reaction because Mg increases in oxidation number (oxidation) and Fe decreases in number (reduction). Fe^{2+} is the oxidizing agent, and Mg is the reducing agent.

$\qquad$ (c) $\qquad\qquad\qquad\qquad$ $Pb(NO_3)_2(aq) + Na_2SO_4(aq) \rightarrow PbSO_4(s) + 2\, NaNO_3(aq)$

$\qquad$ Oxidation states; $\qquad$ +2 +5 −2 $\qquad$ +1 +6 −2 $\qquad$ +2 +6 −2 $\qquad$ +1 +5 −2

$\qquad$ This is a not a redox reaction because none of the atoms undergoes a change in oxidation number.

$\qquad$ (d) $\qquad\qquad\qquad\qquad$ $HBr(aq) + KOH(aq) \rightarrow H_2O(l) + KBr(aq)$

$\qquad$ Oxidation states; $\qquad$ +1 −1 $\qquad$ +1 −2 +1 $\qquad$ +1 −2 $\qquad$ +1 −1

$\qquad$ This is a not a redox reaction because none of the atoms undergoes a change in oxidation number.

4.69   (a)   Skeletal reaction: $S(s) + O_2(g) \rightarrow SO_2(g)$

                Balanced reaction: $S(s) + O_2(g) \rightarrow SO_2(g)$

       (b)   Skeletal reaction: $C_3H_6(g) + O_2(g) \rightarrow CO_2(g) + H_2O(g)$

                Balance C: $C_3H_6(g) + O_2(g) \rightarrow 3\,CO_2(g) + H_2O(g)$

                Balance H: $C_3H_6(g) + O_2(g) \rightarrow 3\,CO_2(g) + 3\,H_2O(g)$

                Balance O: $C_3H_6(g) + 9/2\,O_2(g) \rightarrow 3\,CO_2(g) + 3\,H_2O(g)$

                Clear fraction: $2\,C_3H_6(g) + 9\,O_2(g) \rightarrow 6\,CO_2(g) + 6\,H_2O(g)$

       (c)   Skeletal reaction: $Ca(s) + O_2(g) \rightarrow CaO(s)$

                Balance O: $Ca(s) + O_2(g) \rightarrow 2\,CaO(s)$

                Balance Ca: $2\,Ca(s) + O_2(g) \rightarrow 2\,CaO(s)$

       (d)   Skeletal reaction: $C_5H_{12}S(l) + O_2(g) \rightarrow CO_2(g) + H_2O(g) + SO_2(g)$

                Balance C: $C_5H_{12}S(l) + O_2(g) \rightarrow 5\,CO_2(g) + H_2O(g) + SO_2(g)$

                Balance H: $C_5H_{12}S(l) + O_2(g) \rightarrow 5\,CO_2(g) + 6\,H_2O(g) + SO_2(g)$

                Balance S: $C_5H_{12}S(l) + O_2(g) \rightarrow 5\,CO_2(g) + 6\,H_2O(g) + SO_2(g)$

                Balance O: $C_5H_{12}S(l) + 9\,O_2(g) \rightarrow 5\,CO_2(g) + 6\,H_2O(g) + SO_2(g)$

Cumulative Problems

4.71   **Given:** In 100 g solution, 20.0 g $C_2H_6O_2$; density of solution $= 1.03$ g/mL   **Find:** M of solution

           Conceptual Plan: g $C_2H_6O_2$ $\rightarrow$ mol $C_2H_6O_2$ and g solution $\rightarrow$ mL solution $\rightarrow$ L solution

$$\frac{1\text{ mol C}_2\text{H}_6\text{O}_2}{62.07\text{ g C}_2\text{H}_6\text{O}_2} \qquad\qquad \frac{1.00\text{ mL}}{1.03\text{ g}} \qquad\qquad \frac{1\text{ L}}{1000\text{ mL}}$$

           then M $C_2H_6O_2$

$$M = \frac{\text{mol C}_2\text{H}_6\text{O}_2}{\text{L solution}}$$

           Solution:

$$20.0 \text{ g C}_2\text{H}_6\text{O}_2 \times \frac{1\text{ mol C}_2\text{H}_6\text{O}_2}{62.07\text{ g C}_2\text{H}_6\text{O}_2} = 0.32\underline{2}2 \text{ mol C}_2\text{H}_6\text{O}_2$$

$$100.0 \text{ g solution} \times \frac{1.00\text{ mL solution}}{1.03\text{ g solution}} \times \frac{1\text{ L}}{1000\text{ mL}} = 0.097\underline{0}9 \text{ L}$$

$$M = \frac{0.3222 \text{ mol C}_2\text{H}_6\text{O}_2}{0.09709 \text{ L}} = 3.3\underline{1}9 \text{ M C}_2\text{H}_6\text{O}_2 = 3.32 \text{ M C}_2\text{H}_6\text{O}_2$$

           Check: The units of the answer (M $C_2H_6O_2$) are correct. The magnitude of the answer is reasonable because the concentration of solutions is usually between 0 and 18 M.

4.73   **Given:** 2.5 g $NaHCO_3$ **Find:** g HCl

           Conceptual Plan: g $NaHCO_3$ $\rightarrow$ mol $NaHCO_3$ $\rightarrow$ mol HCl $\rightarrow$ g HCl

$$\frac{1\text{ mol NaHCO}_3}{84.01\text{ g NaHCO}_3} \qquad \frac{1\text{ mol HCl}}{1\text{ mol NaHCO}_3} \qquad \frac{36.46\text{ g HCl}}{1\text{ mol HCl}}$$

           Solution: $HCl(aq) + NaHCO_3(aq) \rightarrow H_2O(l) + CO_2(g) + NaCl(aq)$

$$2.5 \text{ g NaHCO}_3 \times \frac{1\text{ mol NaHCO}_3}{84.01\text{ g NaHCO}_3} \times \frac{1\text{ mol HCl}}{1\text{ mol NaHCO}_3} \times \frac{36.46\text{ g HCl}}{1\text{ mol HCl}} = 1.0\underline{8} \text{ g HCl} = 1.1 \text{ g HCl}$$

           Check: The units of the answer (g HCl) are correct. The magnitude of the answer is reasonable because the molar mass of HCl is less than the molar mass of $NaHCO_3$.

4.75   **Given:** 1.0 kg C_8H_{18} **Find:** kg CO_2

           Conceptual Plan: kg C_8H_{18} $\rightarrow$ g C_8H_{18} $\rightarrow$ mol C_8H_{18} $\rightarrow$ mol CO_2 $\rightarrow$ g CO_2 $\rightarrow$ kg CO_2

$$\frac{1000\text{ g}}{1\text{ kg}} \quad \frac{1\text{ mol C}_8\text{H}_{18}}{114.22\text{ g C}_8\text{H}_{18}} \quad \frac{16\text{ mol CO}_2}{2\text{ mol C}_8\text{H}_{18}} \quad \frac{44.01\text{ g CO}_2}{1\text{ mol CO}_2} \quad \frac{1\text{ kg}}{1000\text{ g}}$$

           Solution: $2\,C_8H_{18}(g) + 25\,O_2(g) \rightarrow 16\,CO_2(g) + 18\,H_2O(g)$

$$1.0 \text{ kg C}_8\text{H}_{18} \times \frac{1000\text{ g}}{1\text{ kg}} \times \frac{1\text{ mol C}_8\text{H}_{18}}{114.22\text{ g C}_8\text{H}_{18}} \times \frac{16\text{ mol CO}_2}{2\text{ mol C}_8\text{H}_{18}} \times \frac{44.01\text{ g CO}_2}{1\text{ mol CO}_2} \times \frac{1\text{ kg}}{1000\text{ g}} = 3.0\underline{8} \text{ kg CO}_2 = 3.1 \text{ kg CO}_2$$

Check: The units of the answer (kg CO_2) are correct. The magnitude of the answer is reasonable because the ratio of CO_2 to C_8H_{18} is 8:1.

4.77 **Given:** 3.00 mL $C_4H_6O_3$, $d = 1.08$ g/mL; 1.25 g $C_7H_6O_3$; 1.22 g $C_9H_8O_4$ **Find:** limiting reactant; theoretical yield $C_9H_8O_4$; % yield $C_9H_8O_4$

Conceptual Plan: mL $C_4H_6O_3$ → g $C_4H_6O_3$ → mol $C_4H_6O_3$ → mol $C_9H_8O_4$

$$\frac{1.08 \text{ g } C_4H_6O_3}{1.00 \text{ mL } C_4H_6O_3} \quad \frac{1 \text{ mol } C_4H_6O_3}{102.09 \text{ g } C_4H_6O_3} \quad \frac{1 \text{ mol } C_9H_8O_4}{1 \text{ mol } C_4H_6O_3} \quad \rightarrow \textbf{ smallest mol amount determines limiting reactant}$$

g $C_7H_6O_3$ → mol $C_7H_6O_3$ → mol $C_9H_8O_4$

$$\frac{1 \text{ mol } C_7H_6O_3}{138.12 \text{ g } C_7H_6O_3} \quad \frac{1 \text{ mol } C_9H_8O_4}{1 \text{ mol } C_7H_6O_3}$$

then mol $C_9H_8O_4$ → g $C_9H_8O_4$ **then determine % yield**

$$\frac{180.2 \text{ g } C_9H_8O_4}{1 \text{ mol } C_9H_8O_4} \qquad \frac{\text{actual yield g } C_9H_8O_4}{\text{theoretical yield g } C_9H_8O_4} \times 100\%$$

Solution:

$$3.00 \text{ mL } C_4H_6O_3 \times \frac{1.08 \text{ g } C_4H_6O_3}{\text{mL } C_4H_6O_3} \times \frac{1 \text{ mol } C_4H_6O_3}{102.09 \text{ g } C_4H_6O_3} \times \frac{1 \text{ mol } C_9H_8O_4}{1 \text{ mol } C_4H_6O_3} = 0.03174 \text{ mol } C_9H_8O_4$$

$$1.25 \text{ g } C_7H_6O_3 \times \frac{1 \text{ mol } C_7H_6O_3}{138.12 \text{ g } C_7H_6O_3} \times \frac{1 \text{ mol } C_9H_8O_4}{1 \text{ mol } C_7H_6O_3} = 0.009050 \text{ mol } C_9H_8O_4$$

Salicylic acid is the limiting reactant.

$$0.009050 \text{ mol } C_9H_8O_4 \times \frac{180.2 \text{ g } C_9H_8O_4}{1 \text{ mol } C_9H_8O_4} = 1.631 \text{ g } C_9H_8O_4$$

$$\frac{1.22 \text{ g } C_9H_8O_4}{1.631 \text{ g } C_9H_8O_4} \times 100\% = 74.8\%$$

Check: The theoretical yield has the correct units (g $C_9H_8O_4$) and has a reasonable magnitude compared to the mass of $C_7H_6O_3$, the limiting reactant. The % yield is reasonable, under 100%.

4.79 **Given:** (a) 11 molecules H_2, 2 molecules O_2; (b) 8 molecules H_2, 4 molecules O_2; (c) 4 molecules H_2, 5 molecules O_2; (d) 3 molecules H_2, 6 molecules O_2 **Find:** loudest explosion based on equation

Conceptual Plan: Loudest explosion will occur in the balloon with the mol ratio closest to the balanced equation that contains the most H_2.

Solution: $2H_2(g) + O_2(g) \rightarrow H_2O(l)$

Balloon (a) has enough O_2 to react with 4 molecules H_2; balloon (b) has enough O_2 to react with 8 molecules H_2; balloon (c) has enough O_2 to react with 10 molecules H_2; balloon (d) has enough O_2 for 3 molecules of H_2 to react. Balloon (b) also has the proper stoichiometric ratio of 2 H_2:1O_2 unlike the other three. Therefore balloon (b) will have the loudest explosion because it has the most H_2 that will react.

Check: Answer seems correct because it has the most H_2 with enough O_2 in the balloon to completely react.

4.81 (a) Skeletal reaction: $HCl(aq) + Hg_2(NO_3)_2(aq) \rightarrow Hg_2Cl_2(s) + HNO_3(aq)$
     Balance Cl: $2 HCl(aq) + Hg_2(NO_3)_2(aq) \rightarrow Hg_2Cl_2(s) + 2 HNO_3(aq)$

  (b) Skeletal reaction: $KHSO_3(aq) + HNO_3(aq) \rightarrow H_2O(l) + SO_2(g) + KNO_3(aq)$
     Balanced reaction: $KHSO_3(aq) + HNO_3(aq) \rightarrow H_2O(l) + SO_2(g) + KNO_3(aq)$

  (c) Skeletal reaction: $NH_4Cl(aq) + Pb(NO_3)_2(aq) \rightarrow PbCl_2(s) + NH_4NO_3(aq)$
     Balance Cl: $2 NH_4Cl(aq) + Pb(NO_3)_2(aq) \rightarrow PbCl_2(s) + NH_4NO_3(aq)$
     Balance N: $2 NH_4Cl(aq) + Pb(NO_3)_2(aq) \rightarrow PbCl_2(s) + 2 NH_4NO_3(aq)$

  (d) Skeletal reaction: $NH_4Cl(aq) + Ca(OH)_2(aq) \rightarrow NH_3(g) + H_2O(l) + CaCl_2(aq)$
     Balance Cl: $2 NH_4Cl(aq) + Ca(OH)_2(aq) \rightarrow NH_3(g) + H_2O(l) + CaCl_2(aq)$
     Balance N: $2 NH_4Cl(aq) + Ca(OH)_2(aq) \rightarrow 2 NH_3(g) + H_2O(l) + CaCl_2(aq)$
     Balance H: $2 NH_4Cl(aq) + Ca(OH)_2(aq) \rightarrow 2 NH_3(g) + 2 H_2O(l) + CaCl_2(aq)$

4.83 **Given:** 1.5 L solution; 0.050 M $CaCl_2$; 0.085 M $Mg(NO_3)_2$ **Find:** g Na_3PO_4

Conceptual Plan: V, M $CaCl_2$ → mol $CaCl_2$ and V, M $Mg(NO_3)_2$ → mol $Mg(NO_3)_2$

$$V \times M = \text{mol} \qquad\qquad\qquad V \times M = \text{mol}$$

then (mol CaCl$_2$ + mol Mg(NO$_3$)$_2$) → mol Na$_3$PO$_4$ → g Na$_3$PO$_4$

$$\frac{2 \text{ mol Na}_3\text{PO}_4}{3 \text{ mol (CaCl}_2 + \text{Mg(NO}_3)_2)} \quad \frac{163.94 \text{ g Na}_3\text{PO}_4}{1 \text{ mol Na}_3\text{PO}_4}$$

Solution: 3 CaCl$_2$(aq) + 2 Na$_3$PO$_4$(aq) → Ca$_3$(PO$_4$)$_2$(s) + 6 NaCl(aq)

3 Mg(NO$_3$)$_2$(aq) + 2 Na$_3$PO$_4$(aq) → Mg$_3$(PO$_4$)$_2$(s) + 6 NaCl(aq)

1.5 L × 0.050 M CaCl$_2$ = 0.07$\underline{5}$ mol CaCl$_2$

1.5 L × 0.085 M Mg(NO$_3$)$_2$ = 0.1$\underline{2}$75 mol Mg(NO$_3$)$_2$

$$0.2025 \text{ mol CaCl}_2 \text{ and Mg(NO}_3)_2 \times \frac{2 \text{ mol Na}_3\text{PO}_4}{3 \text{ mol CaCl}_2 \text{ and Mg(NO}_3)_2} \times \frac{163.94 \text{ g Na}_3\text{PO}_4}{1 \text{ mol Na}_3\text{PO}_4} = 22.13 \text{ g Na}_3\text{PO}_4$$

= 22 g Na$_3$PO$_4$

Check: The units of the answer (g Na$_3$PO$_4$) are correct. The magnitude of the answer is reasonable because it is needed to remove both the Ca and Mg ions.

4.85   **Given:** 1.0 L; 0.10 M OH$^-$ **Find:** g Ba

Conceptual Plan: V, M → mol OH$^-$ → mol Ba(OH)$_2$ → mol BaO → mol Ba → g Ba

$$V \times M = \text{mol} \quad \frac{1 \text{ mol Ba(OH)}_2}{2 \text{ mol OH}^-} \quad \frac{1 \text{ mol BaO}}{1 \text{ mol Ba(OH)}_2} \quad \frac{1 \text{ mol Ba}}{1 \text{ mol BaO}} \quad \frac{137.3 \text{ g Ba}}{1 \text{ mol Ba}}$$

Solution: BaO(s) + H$_2$O(l) → Ba(OH)$_2$(aq)

$$1.0 \text{ L} \times \frac{0.10 \text{ mol OH}^-}{\text{L}} \times \frac{1 \text{ mol Ba(OH)}_2}{2 \text{ mol OH}^-} \times \frac{1 \text{ mol BaO}}{1 \text{ mol Ba(OH)}_2} \times \frac{1 \text{ mol Ba}}{1 \text{ mol BaO}} \times \frac{137.3 \text{ g Ba}}{1 \text{ mol Ba}} = 6.8\underline{6}5 \text{ g Ba}$$

= 6.9 g Ba

Check: The units of the answer (g Ba) are correct. The magnitude is reasonable because the molar mass of Ba is large and there are 2 moles hydroxide per mole Ba.

4.87   **Given:** 30.0% NaNO$_3$, $9.00/100 lb; 20.0% (NH$_4$)$_2SO_4$, $8.10/100 lb   **Find:** cost/lb N

Conceptual Plan: mass fertilizer → mass NaNO$_3$ → mass N → cost/lb N

$$\frac{30.0 \text{ lb NaNO}_3}{100 \text{ lb fertilizer}} \quad \frac{16.48 \text{ lb N}}{100 \text{ lb NaNO}_3} \quad \frac{\$9.00}{100 \text{ lb fertilizer}}$$

and mass fertilizer → mass (NH$_4$)$_2$SO$_4$ → mass N → cost/lb N

$$\frac{20.0 \text{ lb (NH}_4)_2\text{SO}_2}{100 \text{ lb fertilizer}} \quad \frac{21.20 \text{ lb N}}{100 \text{ lb (NH}_4)_2\text{SO}_4} \quad \frac{\$8.10}{100 \text{ lb fertilizer}}$$

Solution:

$$100 \text{ lb fertilizer} \times \frac{30.0 \text{ lb NaNO}_3}{100 \text{ lb fertilizer}} \times \frac{16.48 \text{ lb N}}{100 \text{ lb NaNO}_3} = 4.9\underline{4}4 \text{ lb N}$$

$$\frac{\$9.00}{100 \text{ lb fertilizer}} \times \frac{100 \text{ lb fertilizer}}{4.9\underline{4}4 \text{ lb N}} = \$1.82/\text{lb N}$$

$$100 \text{ lb fertilizer} \times \frac{20.0 \text{ lb (NH}_4)_2\text{SO}_4}{100 \text{ lb fertilizer}} \times \frac{21.20 \text{ lb N}}{100 \text{ lb (NH}_4)_2\text{SO}_4} = 4.2\underline{4}0 \text{ lb N}$$

$$\frac{\$8.10}{100 \text{ lb fertilizer}} \times \frac{100 \text{ lb fertilizer}}{4.2\underline{4} \text{ lb N}} = \$1.91/ \text{ lb N}$$

The more economical fertilizer is the NaNO$_3$ because it costs less/lb N.

Check: The units of the cost ($/lb N) are correct. The answer is reasonable because you compare the cost/lb N directly.

4.89   **Given:** 24.5 g Au; 24.5 g BrF$_3$; 24.5 g KF   **Find:** g KAuF$_4$

Conceptual Plan: g Au → mol Au → mol KAuF$_4$

$$\frac{1 \text{ mol Au}}{196.97 \text{ g Au}} \quad \frac{2 \text{ mol KAuF}_4}{2 \text{ mol Au}}$$

g BrF$_3$ → mol BrF$_3$ → mol KAuF$_4$ → smallest mol amount determines limiting reactant

$$\frac{1 \text{ mol BrF}_3}{136.9 \text{ g BrF}_3} \quad \frac{2 \text{ mol KAuF}_4}{2 \text{ mol BrF}_3}$$

g KF → mol KF → mol KAuF$_4$

$$\frac{1 \text{ mol KF}}{58.10 \text{ g KF}} \quad \frac{2 \text{ mol KAuF}_4}{2 \text{ mol KF}}$$

then mol KAuF₄ → g KAuF₄

$$\frac{312.07 \text{ g KAuF}_4}{1 \text{ mol KAuF}_4}$$

$$2 \text{ Au}(s) + 2 \text{ BrF}_3(l) + 2 \text{ KF}(s) \rightarrow \text{Br}_2(l) + 2 \text{ KAuF}_4(s)$$

Oxidation states;   0   +3 −1   +1 −1   0   +1 +3 −1

This is a redox reaction because Au increases in oxidation number (oxidation) and Br decreases in number (reduction). BrF_3 is the oxidizing agent, and Au is the reducing agent.

Solution:

$$24.5 \text{ g Au} \times \frac{1 \text{ mol Au}}{196.97 \text{ g Au}} \times \frac{2 \text{ mol KAuF}_4}{2 \text{ mol Au}} = 0.12\underline{4}4 \text{ mol KAuF}_4$$

$$24.5 \text{ g BrF}_3 \times \frac{1 \text{ mol BrF}_3}{136.90 \text{ g BrF}_3} \times \frac{2 \text{ mol KAuF}_4}{2 \text{ mol BrF}_3} = 0.17\underline{9}0 \text{ mol KAuF}$$

$$24.5 \text{ g KF} \times \frac{1 \text{ mol KF}}{58.10 \text{ g KF}} \times \frac{2 \text{ mol KAuF}_4}{2 \text{ mol KF}} = 0.42\underline{1}7 \text{ mol KAuF}_4$$

$$0.12\underline{4}4 \text{ mol KAuF}_4 \times \frac{312.07 \text{ g KAuF}_4}{1 \text{ mol KAuF}_4} = 38.\underline{8}22 \text{ g KAuF}_4 = 38.8 \text{ g KAuF}_4$$

Check: The units of the answer (g $KAuF_4$) are correct. The magnitude of the answer is reasonable compared to the mass of the limiting reactant Au.

4.91   **Given:** solution may contain Ag^+, Ca^{2+}, and Cu^{2+} **Find:** Determine which ions are present.
Conceptual Plan: Test the solution sequentially with NaCl, Na₂SO₄, and Na₂CO₃ and see if precipitates form.
Solution: Original solution + NaCl yields no reaction: Ag^+ is not present because chlorides are normally soluble, but Ag^+ is an exception.
Original solution with Na_2SO_4 yields a precipitate and solution 2. The precipitate is $CaSO_4$, so Ca^{2+} is present. Sulfates are normally soluble, but Ca^{2+} is an exception.
Solution 2 with Na_2CO_3 yields a precipitate. The precipitate is $CuCO_3$, so Cu^{2+} is present. All carbonates are insoluble.
Net Ionic Equations:

$$Ca^{2+}(aq) + SO_4{}^{2-}(aq) \rightarrow CaSO_4(s)$$
$$Cu^{2+}(aq) + CO_3{}^{2-}(aq) \rightarrow CuCO_3(s)$$

Check: The answer is reasonable because two different precipitates formed and all of the Ca^{2+} was removed before the carbonate was added.

4.93   **Given:** 10.0 kg mixture; 30.35% hexane; 15.85% heptane; 53.80% octane   **Find:** total mass CO_2
Conceptual Plan: kg hexane → kmol hexane → kmol CO₂ → kg CO₂

$$\frac{1 \text{ kmol C}_6\text{H}_{14}}{86.17 \text{ kg C}_6\text{H}_{14}} \qquad \frac{12 \text{ kmol CO}_2}{2 \text{ kmol C}_6\text{H}_{14}} \qquad \frac{44.01 \text{ kg CO}_2}{1 \text{ kmol CO}_2}$$

kg heptane → kmol heptane → kmol CO₂ → kg CO₂

$$\frac{1 \text{ kmol C}_7\text{H}_{16}}{100.20 \text{ kg C}_7\text{H}_{16}} \qquad \frac{7 \text{ kmol CO}_2}{1 \text{ kmol C}_7\text{H}_{16}} \qquad \frac{44.01 \text{ kg CO}_2}{1 \text{ kmol CO}_2}$$

kg octane → kmol octane → kmol CO₂ → kg CO₂

$$\frac{1 \text{ kmol C}_8\text{H}_{18}}{114.22 \text{ kg C}_8\text{H}_{18}} \qquad \frac{16 \text{ kmol CO}_2}{2 \text{ kmol C}_8\text{H}_{18}} \qquad \frac{44.01 \text{ kg CO}_2}{1 \text{ kmol CO}_2}$$

Solution: Balanced Reactions:

$$2 \text{ C}_6\text{H}_{14}(l) + 19 \text{ O}_2(g) \rightarrow 12 \text{ CO}_2(g) + 14 \text{ H}_2\text{O}(l)$$
$$\text{C}_7\text{H}_{16}(l) + 11 \text{ O}_2(g) \rightarrow 7 \text{ CO}_2(g) + 8 \text{ H}_2\text{O}(l)$$
$$2 \text{ C}_8\text{H}_{18}(l) + 25 \text{ O}_2(g) \rightarrow 16 \text{ CO}_2(g) + 18 \text{ H}_2\text{O}(l)$$

$$10.0 \text{ kg mix} \times \frac{30.35 \text{ kg C}_6\text{H}_{14}}{100.0 \text{ kg mix}} \times \frac{1 \text{ kmol C}_6\text{H}_{14}}{86.17 \text{ kg C}_6\text{H}_{14}} \times \frac{12 \text{ kmol CO}_2}{2 \text{ kmol C}_6\text{H}_{14}} \times \frac{44.01 \text{ kg CO}_2}{1 \text{ kmol CO}_2} = 9.3\underline{0}0 \text{ kg CO}_2$$

$$10.0 \text{ kg mix} \times \frac{15.85 \text{ kg C}_7\text{H}_{16}}{100.0 \text{ kg mix}} \times \frac{1 \text{ kmol C}_7\text{H}_{16}}{100.20 \text{ kg C}_7\text{H}_{16}} \times \frac{7 \text{ kmol CO}_2}{1 \text{ kmol C}_7\text{H}_{16}} \times \frac{44.01 \text{ kg CO}_2}{1 \text{ kmol CO}_2} = 4.8\underline{7}3 \text{ kg CO}_2$$

$$10.0 \text{ kg mix} \times \frac{53.80 \text{ kg C}_8\text{H}_{18}}{100.0 \text{ kg mix}} \times \frac{1 \text{ kmol C}_8\text{H}_{18}}{114.22 \text{ kg C}_8\text{H}_{18}} \times \frac{16 \text{ kmol CO}_2}{2 \text{ kmol C}_8\text{H}_{18}} \times \frac{44.01 \text{ kg CO}_2}{1 \text{ kmol CO}_2} = 16.\underline{5}84 \text{ kg CO}_2$$

Total $CO_2 = 9.\underline{3}00$ kg $+ 4.\underline{8}73$ kg $+ 16.\underline{5}84$ kg $= 30.\underline{7}57$ kg $CO_2 = 30.8$ k CO_2

Check: The units of the answer (kg CO_2) are correct. The magnitude of the answer is reasonable because a large amount of CO_2 is produced per mole of hydrocarbon.

Challenge Problems

4.95   **Given:** 15.2 billion L lake water; 1.8×10^{-5} M H_2SO_4; 8.7×10^{-6} M HNO_3 **Find:** kg $CaCO_3$ needed to neutralize
         Conceptual Plan: vol lake $\rightarrow$ mol H_2SO_4 $\rightarrow$ mol H^+ and vol lake $\rightarrow$ mol HNO_3 $\rightarrow$ mol H^+

$$V \times M = \text{mol} \qquad \frac{2 \text{ mol H}^+}{1 \text{ mol H}_2\text{SO}_4} \qquad V \times M = \text{mol} \qquad \frac{1 \text{ mol H}^+}{1 \text{ mol HNO}_3}$$

then total mol H^+ $\rightarrow$ mol CO_3^{2-} $\rightarrow$ mol $CaCO_3$ $\rightarrow$ g $CaCO_3$ $\rightarrow$ kg $CaCO_3$

$$\frac{1 \text{ mol CO}_3^{2-}}{2 \text{ mol H}^+} \qquad \frac{1 \text{ mol CaCO}_3}{1 \text{ mol CO}_3^{2-}} \qquad \frac{100.09 \text{ g CaCO}_3}{1 \text{ mol CaCO}_3} \qquad \frac{1 \text{ kg}}{1000 \text{ g}}$$

Solution: $2H^+(aq) + CO_3^{2-}(aq) \rightarrow H_2O(l) + CO_2(g)$

$$15.2 \times 10^9 \text{ L} \times \frac{1.8 \times 10^{-5} \text{ mol H}_2\text{SO}_4}{\text{L soln}} \times \frac{2 \text{ mol H}^+}{1 \text{ mol H}_2\text{SO}_4} = 547200 \text{ mol H}^+$$

$$15.2 \times 10^9 \text{ L} \times \frac{8.7 \times 10^{-6} \text{ mol HNO}_3}{\text{L soln}} \times \frac{1 \text{ mol H}^+}{1 \text{ mol HNO}_3} = 132240 \text{ mol H}^+$$

Total $H^+ = 547200$ mol H^+ $+ 132240$ mol $H^+ = 67\underline{9}440$ mol H^+

$$67\underline{9}440 \text{ mol H}^+ \times \frac{1 \text{ mol CO}_3^{2-}}{2 \text{ mol H}^+} \times \frac{1 \text{ mol CaCO}_3}{1 \text{ mol CO}_3^{2-}} \times \frac{100.09 \text{ g CaCO}_3}{1 \text{ mol CaCO}_3} \times \frac{1 \text{ kg}}{1000 \text{ g}} = 3.4 \times 10^4 \text{ kg CaCO}_3$$

Check: The units of the answer (kg $CaCO_3$) are correct. The magnitude of the answer is reasonable based on the size of the lake.

4.97   **Given:** 45 μg Pb/dL blood; Vol $= 5.0$ L; 1 mol succimer ($C_4H_6O_4S_2$) $= 1$ mol Pb   **Find:** mass $C_4H_6O_4S_2$ in mg
         Conceptual Plan: volume blood L $\rightarrow$ volume blood dL $\rightarrow$ μg Pb $\rightarrow$ g Pb $\rightarrow$ mol Pb $\rightarrow$

$$\frac{10 \text{ dL}}{1 \text{ L}} \qquad \frac{45 \mu g}{1 \text{ dL}} \qquad \frac{1 \text{ g}}{10^6 \mu g} \qquad \frac{1 \text{ mol Pb}}{207.2 \text{ g Pb}} \qquad \frac{1 \text{ mol succimer}}{1 \text{ mol Pb}}$$

mol succimer $\rightarrow$ g succimer $\rightarrow$ mg succimer

$$\frac{182.23 \text{ g succimer}}{1 \text{ mol succimer}} \qquad \frac{1000 \text{ mg succimer}}{1 \text{ g succimer}}$$

Solution:

$$5.0 \text{ L blood} \times \frac{10 \text{ dL}}{1 \text{ L}} \times \frac{45 \mu g}{1 \text{ dL}} \times \frac{1 \text{ g}}{10^6 \mu g} \times \frac{1 \text{ mol Pb}}{207.2 \text{ g}} \times \frac{1 \text{ mol succimer}}{1 \text{ mol Pb}} \times \frac{182.23 \text{ g succimer}}{1 \text{ mol succimer}} \times \frac{1000 \text{ mg}}{\text{g}}$$

$$= 1.\underline{9}79 \text{ mg succimer} = 2.0 \text{ mg succimer}$$

Check: The units of the answer (mg succimer) are correct. The magnitude is reasonable for the volume of blood and the concentration.

4.99   **Given:** 250 g sample; 67.2 mol % Al   **Find:** theoretical yield in g of Mn
         Conceptual Plan: mol % Al $\rightarrow$ g Al and mol % MnO_2 $\rightarrow$ g MnO_2, then mass % Al

$$\frac{26.98 \text{ g Al}}{1 \text{ mol Al}} \qquad \frac{86.94 \text{ g MnO}_2}{1 \text{ mol MnO}_2} \qquad \frac{\text{g Al}}{\text{total g}} \times 100\%$$

then sample $\rightarrow$ g Al $\rightarrow$ mol Al $\rightarrow$ mol Mn

$$\frac{38.86 \text{ g Al}}{100 \text{ g sample}} \quad \frac{1 \text{ mol Al}}{26.98 \text{ g Al}} \quad \frac{3 \text{ mol Mn}}{4 \text{ mol Al}} \qquad \rightarrow \textbf{smallest mol amount determines limiting reactant}$$

sample $\rightarrow$ g MnO_2 $\rightarrow$ mol MnO_2 $\rightarrow$ mol Mn

$$\frac{61.14 \text{ g MnO}_2}{100 \text{ g sample}} \quad \frac{1 \text{ mol MnO}_2}{86.94 \text{ g MnO}_2} \quad \frac{1 \text{ mol Mn}}{1 \text{ mol MnO}_2}$$

then mol Mn → g Mn

$$\frac{54.94 \text{ g Mn}}{1 \text{ mol Mn}}$$

Solution: $4 \text{ Al}(s) + 3 \text{ MnO}_2(s) \rightarrow 3 \text{ Mn} + 2\text{Al}_2\text{O}_3(s)$

Assume 1 mole: $\quad 0.672 \text{ mol Al} \times \dfrac{26.98 \text{ g Al}}{1 \text{ mol Al}} = 18.13 \text{ g Al}$

$0.328 \text{ mol MnO}_2 \times \dfrac{86.94 \text{ g MnO}_2}{1 \text{ mol MnO}_2} = 28.52 \text{ g MnO}_2$

$\dfrac{18.13 \text{ g Al}}{(18.13 \text{ g Al} + 28.52 \text{ g MnO}_2)} \times 100\% = 38.86\% \text{ Al}$

So 61.14% MnO$_2$

$250 \text{ g sample} \times \dfrac{38.86 \text{ g Al}}{100 \text{ g sample}} \times \dfrac{1 \text{ mol Al}}{26.98 \text{ g Al}} \times \dfrac{3 \text{ mol Mn}}{4 \text{ mol Al}} = 2.701 \text{ mol Mn}$

$250 \text{ g sample} \times \dfrac{61.14 \text{ g MnO}_2}{100 \text{ g sample}} \times \dfrac{1 \text{ mol MnO}_2}{86.94 \text{ g MnO}_2} \times \dfrac{1 \text{ mol Mn}}{1 \text{ mol MnO}_2} = 1.758 \text{ mol Mn}$

$1.758 \text{ mol Mn} \times \dfrac{54.94 \text{ g Mn}}{1 \text{ mol Mn}} = 96.6 \text{ g Mn}$

Check: The units of the answer (g Mn) are correct. The magnitude of the answer is reasonable based on the amount of the limiting reactant, MnO$_2$.

Conceptual Problems

4.101 The correct answer is d. The molar masses of K and O$_2$ are comparable. Because the stoichiometry has a ratio of 4 mol K to 1 mol O$_2$, K will be the limiting reactant when mass of K is less than 4 times the mass of O$_2$.

4.103 **Given:** 1 M solution contains 8 particles **Find:** amount of solute or solvent needed to obtain new concentration
Conceptual Plan: Determine amount of solute particles in each new solution; then determine whether solute (if the number is greater) or solvent (if the number is less) needs to be added to obtain the new concentration.

Solution: Solution (a) contains 12 particles solute. Concentration is greater than the original, so solute needs

to be added. $12 \text{ particles} \times \dfrac{1 \text{ mol}}{8 \text{ particles}} = 1.5 \text{ mol} \quad (1.5 \text{ mol} - 1.0 \text{ mol}) = 0.5 \text{ mol solute added}$

$0.5 \text{ mol solute} \times \dfrac{8 \text{ particles}}{1 \text{ mol solute}} = 4 \text{ solute particles added}$

Solution (a) is obtained by adding 4 particles solute to 1 L of original solution.
Solution (b) contains 4 particles. Concentration is less than the original, so solvent needs to be added.

$4 \text{ particles} \times \dfrac{1 \text{ mol}}{8 \text{ particles}} = 0.5 \text{ mol solute, so 1 L solution contains } 0.5 \text{ mol} = 0.5 \text{ M}$

$(1 \text{ M})(1 \text{ L}) = (0.5 \text{ M})(x) \qquad x = 2 \text{ L}$
Solution (b) is obtained by diluting 1 L of the original solution to 2 L.
Solution (c) contains 6 particles. Concentration is less than the original, so solvent needs to be added.

$6 \text{ particles} \times \dfrac{1 \text{ mol}}{8 \text{ particles}} = 0.75 \text{ mol solute, so 1 L solution contains } 0.75 \text{ mol} = 0.75 \text{ M}$

$(1 \text{ M})(1 \text{ L}) = (0.75 \text{ M})(x) \qquad x = 1.3 \text{ L}$
Solution (c) is obtained by diluting 1 L of the original solution to 1.3 L.

4.105 **Given:** A$_2$X soluble; BY$_2$ soluble; AY insoluble; BX soluble; 2 molecules A$_2$X mixed with 2 molecules BY$_2$
Find: a molecular representation of the mixture; an equation for the reaction

Solution:

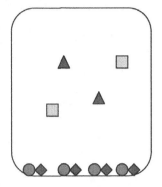

$$A_2X(aq) + BY_2(aq) \rightarrow 2AY(s) + BX(aq)$$

Questions for Group Work

4.107　(1)　Calculate the mass of NaOH needed:

$$100.0 \text{ mL solution} \times \frac{1 \text{ L solution}}{1000 \text{ mL solution}} \times \frac{12 \text{ mol NaOH}}{1 \text{ L solution}} \times \frac{40.00 \text{ g NaOH}}{1 \text{ mol NaOH}} = 48 \text{ g NaOH}$$

Weigh 48 g of solid NaOH and add to the 100.0 mL volumetric flask. Add about 50 mL of distilled water to the flask. Swirl the flask to dissolve the NaOH. Caution should be used, since the flask will become warm. Allow the flask to cool to room temperature. Add distilled water to the mark on the flask. Stopper the flask. Invert the flask several times to create a uniform solution. Allow the flask to cool and add additional distilled water if needed (stopper and agitate the flask after each addition of solvent).

(2)　Calculate the volume of 12 M NaOH solution needed: $M_1V_1 = M_2V_2$ so

$$V_1 = \frac{M_2V_2}{M_1} = \frac{(0.10 \text{ M})(1.00 \text{ L})}{(12 \text{ M})} = 0.0083 \text{ L} = 8.3 \text{ mL}$$

Add 8.3 mL of the 12 M NaOH solution to the 25 mL graduated cylinder. Transfer this solution to the 1.000 L volumetric flask. Add about 15 mL of distilled water to the graduated cylinder. Swirl and then transfer this solution to the 1.000 L volumetric flask. Repeat twice. (Note that the graduated cylinder is a "To Contain" device, so all of the solution in the graduated cylinder needs to be transferred to the 1.000 L volumetric flask). Add distilled water to the mark on the flask. Stopper the flask. Invert the flask several times to create a uniform solution. Allow the flask to cool and add additional distilled water if needed (stopper and agitate the flask after each addition of solvent).

4.109　A precipitation reaction is one in which a solid or precipitate forms upon mixing two solutions. An example is: $2 \text{ KI}(aq) + \text{Pb(NO}_3)_2(aq) \rightarrow \text{PbI}_2(s) + 2 \text{ KNO}_3(aq)$.

In an acid–base reaction, an acid and base are mixed. The $\text{H}^+(aq)$ from the acid combines with the OH^- from the base to form $\text{H}_2\text{O}(l)$. An example is: $\text{HCl}(aq) + \text{NaOH}(aq) \rightarrow \text{H}_2\text{O}(l) + \text{NaCl}(aq)$.

A gas evolution reaction is an aqueous reaction that forms a gas upon mixing two solutions. The reactant types that give rise to gas evolution reactions are: sulfides, carbonates, bicarbonate, sulfites, bisulfites, and ammonium compounds. An example is: $\text{H}_2\text{SO}_4(aq) + \text{Li}_2\text{S}(aq) \rightarrow \text{H}_2\text{S}(g) + \text{Li}_2\text{SO}_4(aq)$.

Oxidation–reduction reactions or redox reactions are reactions in which electrons are transferred from one reactant to the other. An example is: $2 \text{ Na}(s) + \text{Cl}_2(g) \rightarrow 2 \text{ NaCl}(s)$.

Combustion reactions are characterized by the reaction of a substance with O_2 to form one or more oxygen-containing compounds, often including water. Combustion reactions emit heat.

An example is: $\text{CH}_4(g) + 2 \text{ O}_2(g) \rightarrow \text{CO}_2(g) + 2 \text{ H}_2\text{O}(g)$.

5 Gases

Converting Between Pressure Units

5.1   (a)   **Given:** 24.9 in Hg   **Find:** atm
               Conceptual Plan: in Hg → atm

$$\frac{1\ \text{atm}}{29.92\ \text{in Hg}}$$

               Solution: $24.9\ \text{in Hg} \times \dfrac{1\ \text{atm}}{29.92\ \text{in Hg}} = 0.832\ \text{atm}$

               Check: The units (atm) are correct. The magnitude of the answer (< 1) makes physical sense because we started with less than 29.92 in Hg.

      (b)   **Given:** 24.9 in Hg   **Find:** mmHg
               Conceptual Plan: Use answer from part (a) then convert atm → mmHg

$$\frac{760\ \text{mmHg}}{1\ \text{atm}}$$

               Solution: $0.832\ \text{atm} \times \dfrac{760\ \text{mmHg}}{1\ \text{atm}} = 632\ \text{mmHg}$

               Check: The units (mmHg) are correct. The magnitude of the answer (< 760 mmHg) makes physical sense because we started with less than 1 atm.

      (c)   **Given:** 24.9 in Hg   **Find:** psi
               Conceptual Plan: Use answer from part (a) then convert atm → psi

$$\frac{14.7\ \text{psi}}{1\ \text{atm}}$$

               Solution: $0.832\ \text{atm} \times \dfrac{14.7\ \text{psi}}{1\ \text{atm}} = 12.2\ \text{psi}$

               Check: The units (psi) are correct. The magnitude of the answer (< 14.7 psi) makes physical sense because we started with less than 1 atm.

      (d)   **Given:** 24.9 in Hg   **Find:** Pa
               Conceptual Plan: Use answer from part (a) then convert atm → Pa

$$\frac{101{,}325\ \text{Pa}}{1\ \text{atm}}$$

               Solution: $0.832\ \text{atm} \times \dfrac{101{,}325\ \text{Pa}}{1\ \text{atm}} = 8.43 \times 10^4\ \text{Pa}$

               Check: The units (Pa) are correct. The magnitude of the answer ($< 101{,}325$ Pa) makes physical sense because we started with less than 1 atm.

5.3   (a)   **Given:** 31.85 in Hg   **Find:** mmHg
               Conceptual Plan: in Hg → mmHg

$$\frac{25.4\ \text{mmHg}}{1\ \text{in Hg}}$$

               Solution: $31.85\ \text{in Hg} \times \dfrac{25.4\ \text{mmHg}}{1\ \text{in Hg}} = 809.0\ \text{mmHg}$

Check: The units (mmHg) are correct. The magnitude of the answer (809) makes physical sense because inches are larger than millimeters.

(b) **Given:** 31.85 in Hg   **Find:** atm
  Conceptual Plan: Use answer from part (a) then convert mmHg → atm

$$\frac{1 \text{ atm}}{760 \text{ mmHg}}$$

  Solution: $809.0 \text{ mmHg} \times \dfrac{1 \text{ atm}}{760 \text{ mmHg}} = 1.064 \text{ atm}$

  Check: The units (atm) are correct. The magnitude of the answer (>1) makes physical sense because we started with more than 760 mmHg.

(c) **Given:** 31.85 in Hg   **Find:** torr
  Conceptual Plan: Use answer from part (a) then convert mmHg → torr

$$\frac{1 \text{ torr}}{1 \text{ mmHg}}$$

  Solution: $809.0 \text{ mmHg} \times \dfrac{1 \text{ torr}}{1 \text{ mmHg}} = 809.0 \text{ torr}$

  Check: The units (torr) are correct. The magnitude of the answer (809) makes physical sense because both units are of the same size.

(d) **Given:** 31.85 in Hg   **Find:** kPa
  Conceptual Plan: Use answer from part (b) then convert atm → Pa → kPa

$$\frac{101{,}325 \text{ Pa}}{1 \text{ atm}} \quad \frac{1 \text{ kPa}}{1000 \text{ Pa}}$$

  Solution: $1.064 \text{ atm} \times \dfrac{101{,}325 \text{ Pa}}{1 \text{ atm}} \times \dfrac{1 \text{ kPa}}{1000 \text{ Pa}} = 107.9 \text{ kPa}$

  Check: The units (kPa) are correct. The magnitude of the answer (108) makes physical sense because we started with more than 1 atm and there are ~101 kPa in an atm.

Simple Gas Laws

5.5 **Given:** $V_1 = 2.8 \text{ L}$, $P_1 = 755 \text{ mmHg}$, and $V_2 = 3.7 \text{ L}$ **Find:** P_2
  Conceptual Plan: $V_1, P_1, V_2 \rightarrow P_2$
$$P_1 V_1 = P_2 V_2$$
  Solution: $P_1 V_1 = P_2 V_2$ Rearrange to solve for P_2.

$P_2 = P_1 \dfrac{V_1}{V_2} = 755 \text{ mmHg} \times \dfrac{2.8 \text{ L}}{3.7 \text{ L}} = 571.35135 \text{ mmHg} = 5.7 \times 10^2 \text{ mmHg}$

  Check: The units (mmHg) are correct. The magnitude of the answer (570 mmHg) makes physical sense because Boyle's law indicates that as the volume increases, the pressure decreases.

5.7 **Given:** $V_1 = 37.2 \text{ mL}$, $T_1 = 22 \,°\text{C}$, and $T_2 = 81 \,°\text{C}$ **Find:** V_2
  Conceptual Plan: °C → K then $V_1, T_1, T_2 \rightarrow V_2$
$$K = °C + 273.15 \qquad \frac{V_1}{T_1} = \frac{V_2}{T_2}$$
  Solution: $T_1 = 22 \,°\text{C} + 273.15 = 295 \text{ K}$ and $T_2 = 81 \,°\text{C} + 273.15 = 354 \text{ K}$

$\dfrac{V_1}{T_1} = \dfrac{V_2}{T_2}$ Rearrange to solve for V_2. $V_2 = V_1 \dfrac{T_2}{T_1} = 37.2 \text{ mL} \times \dfrac{354 \text{ K}}{295 \text{ K}} = 44.6 \text{ mL}$

  Check: The units (mL) are correct. The magnitude of the answer (45 mL) makes physical sense because Charles's law indicates that as the temperature increases, the volume increases.

5.9 **Given:** $V_1 = 2.76 \text{ L}$, $n_1 = 0.128 \text{ mol}$, and $\Delta n = 0.073 \text{ mol}$ **Find:** V_2
  Conceptual Plan: $n_1 \rightarrow n_2$ then $V_1, n_1, n_2 \rightarrow V_2$
$$n_1 + \Delta n = n_2 \qquad \frac{V_1}{n_1} = \frac{V_2}{n_2}$$

Solution: $n_2 = 0.128 \text{ mol} + 0.073 \text{ mol} = 0.201 \text{ mol}$

$\dfrac{V_1}{n_1} = \dfrac{V_2}{n_2}$ Rearrange to solve for V_2. $V_2 = V_1 \dfrac{n_2}{n_1} = 2.76 \text{ L} \times \dfrac{0.201 \text{ mol}}{0.128 \text{ mol}} = 4.3340625 = 4.33 \text{ L}$

Check: The units (L) are correct. The magnitude of the answer (4 L) makes physical sense because Avogadro's law indicates that as the number of moles increases, the volume increases.

Ideal Gas Law

5.11   **Given:** $n = 0.128 \text{ mol}$, $P = 0.97 \text{ atm}$, and $T = 325 \text{ K}$ **Find:** V
          Conceptual Plan: $n, P, T \rightarrow V$

$$PV = nRT$$

Solution: $PV = nRT$ Rearrange to solve for V. $V = \dfrac{nRT}{P} = \dfrac{0.128 \text{ mol} \times 0.08206 \dfrac{\text{L} \cdot \text{atm}}{\text{mol} \cdot \text{K}} \times 325 \text{ K}}{0.97 \text{ atm}} = 3.5 \text{ L}$

Check: The units (L) are correct. The magnitude of the answer (3.5 L) makes sense because, as you will see in the next section, one mole of an ideal gas under standard conditions (273 K and 1 atm) occupies 22.4 L. Although these are not standard conditions, they are close enough for a ballpark check of the answer. Because this gas sample contains 0.128 moles, a volume of 3.5 L is reasonable.

5.13   **Given:** $V = 28.5 \text{ L}$, $P = 1.8 \text{ atm}$, and $T = 298 \text{ K}$ **Find:** n
          Conceptual Plan: $V, P, T \rightarrow n$

$$PV = nRT$$

Solution: $PV = nRT$ Rearrange to solve for n. $n = \dfrac{PV}{RT} = \dfrac{1.8 \text{ atm} \times 28.5 \text{ L}}{0.08206 \dfrac{\text{L} \cdot \text{atm}}{\text{mol} \cdot \text{K}} \times 298 \text{ K}} = 2.1 \text{ mol}$

Check: The units (mol) are correct. The magnitude of the answer (2 mol) makes sense because, as you will see in the next section, one mole of an ideal gas under standard conditions (273 K and 1 atm) occupies 22.4 L. Although these are not standard conditions, they are close enough for a ballpark check of the answer. Because this gas sample has a volume of 28.5 L and a pressure of 1.8 atm, ~2 mol is reasonable.

5.15   **Given:** $P_1 = 36.0 \text{ psi}$ (gauge P), $V_1 = 11.8 \text{ L}$, $T_1 = 12.0\,^\circ\text{C}$, $V_2 = 12.2 \text{ L}$, and $T_2 = 65.0\,^\circ\text{C}$ **Find:** P_2 and compare
          to $P_{\text{max}} = 38.0 \text{ psi}$ (gauge P)
          Conceptual Plan: $^\circ\text{C} \rightarrow \text{K}$ and gauge $P \rightarrow \text{psi} \rightarrow \text{atm}$ then $P_1, V_1, T_1, V_2, T_2 \rightarrow P_2$

$$K = \,^\circ\text{C} + 273.15 \qquad \text{psi} = \text{gauge P} + 14.7 \quad \dfrac{1 \text{ atm}}{14.7 \text{ psi}} \qquad \dfrac{P_1 V_1}{T_1} = \dfrac{P_2 V_2}{T_2}$$

Solution: $T_1 = 12.0\,^\circ\text{C} + 273.15 = 285.2 \text{ K}$ and $T_2 = 65.0\,^\circ\text{C} + 273.15 = 338.2 \text{ K}$

$P_1 = 36.0 \text{ psi (gauge P)} + 14.7 = 50.7 \text{ psi} \times \dfrac{1 \text{ atm}}{14.7 \text{ psi}} = 3.44898 \text{ atm}$

$P_{\text{max}} = 38.0 \text{ psi (gauge P)} + 14.7 = 52.7 \text{ psi} \times \dfrac{1 \text{ atm}}{14.7 \text{ psi}} = 3.59 \text{ atm}$

$\dfrac{P_1 V_1}{T_1} = \dfrac{P_2 V_2}{T_2}$ Rearrange to solve for P_2. $P_2 = P_1 \dfrac{V_1}{V_2} \dfrac{T_2}{T_1} = 3.44898 \text{ atm} \times \dfrac{11.8 \text{ L}}{12.2 \text{ L}} \times \dfrac{338.2 \text{ K}}{285.2 \text{ K}} = 3.96 \text{ atm}$

This exceeds the maximum tire rating of 3.59 atm or 38.0 psi (gauge P).

Check: The units (atm) are correct. The magnitude of the answer (3.96 atm) makes physical sense because the relative increase in T is greater than the relative increase in V; so P should increase.

5.17   **Given:** m (CO_2) $= 28.8 \text{ g}$, $P = 742 \text{ mmHg}$, and $T = 22\,^\circ\text{C}$ **Find:** V
          Conceptual Plan: $^\circ\text{C} \rightarrow \text{K}$ and $\text{mmHg} \rightarrow \text{atm}$ and $\text{g} \rightarrow \text{mol}$ then $n, P, T \rightarrow V$

$$K = \,^\circ\text{C} + 273.15 \qquad \dfrac{1 \text{ atm}}{760 \text{ mmHg}} \qquad \dfrac{1 \text{ mol}}{44.01 \text{ g}} \qquad PV = nRT$$

Solution: $T_1 = 22\,^\circ\text{C} + 273.15 = 295 \text{ K}$, $P = 742 \text{ mmHg} \times \dfrac{1 \text{ atm}}{760 \text{ mmHg}} = 0.976316 \text{ atm}$,

$$n = 28.8 \ \cancel{g} \times \frac{1 \ mol}{44.01 \ \cancel{g}} = 0.654397 \ mol \quad PV = nRT \ \text{Rearrange to solve for } V.$$

$$V = \frac{nRT}{P} = \frac{0.654397 \ \cancel{mol} \times 0.08206 \ \frac{L \cdot \cancel{atm}}{\cancel{mol} \cdot \cancel{K}} \times 295 \ \cancel{K}}{0.976316 \ \cancel{atm}} = 16.2 \ L$$

Check: The units (L) are correct. The magnitude of the answer (16 L) makes sense because one mole of an ideal gas under standard conditions (273 K and 1 atm) occupies 22.4 L. Although these are not standard conditions, they are close enough for a ballpark check of the answer. Because this gas sample contains 0.65 mole, a volume of 16 L is reasonable.

5.19   **Given:** sample a = 5 gas particles, sample b = 10 gas particles, and sample c = 8 gas particles, with all temperatures and volumes the same   **Find:** sample with largest P
Conceptual Plan: $n, V, T \rightarrow P$
$$PV = nRT$$

Solution: $PV = nRT$ Because V and T are constant, $P \propto n$. The sample with the largest number of gas particles will have the highest P. $P_b > P_c > P_a$.

5.21   **Given:** $P_1 = 755 \ mmHg$, $T_1 = 25 \ °C$, and $T_2 = 1155 \ °C$ **Find:** P_2
Conceptual Plan: $°C \rightarrow K$ and $mmHg \rightarrow atm$ then $P_1, T_1, T_2 \rightarrow P_2$
$$K = °C + 273.15 \qquad \frac{1 \ atm}{760 \ mmHg} \qquad \frac{P_1}{T_1} = \frac{P_2}{T_2}$$

Solution: $T_1 = 25 \ °C + 273.15 = 298 \ K$ and $T_2 = 1155 \ °C + 273.15 = 1428 \ K$

$$P = 755 \ \cancel{mmHg} \times \frac{1 \ atm}{760 \ \cancel{mmHg}} = 0.993421 \ atm \quad \frac{P_1}{T_1} = \frac{P_2}{T_2} \ \text{Rearrange to solve for } P_2.$$

$$P_2 = P_1 \frac{T_2}{T_1} = 0.993421 \ atm \times \frac{1428 \ \cancel{K}}{298 \ \cancel{K}} = 4.76 \ atm$$

Check: The units (atm) are correct. The magnitude of the answer (5 atm) makes physical sense because there is a significant increase in T, which will increase P significantly.

Molar Volume, Density, and Molar Mass of a Gas

5.23   **Given:** STP and m (Ne) = 15.0 g   **Find:** V
Conceptual Plan: $g \rightarrow mol \rightarrow V$
$$\frac{1 \ mol}{20.18 \ g} \qquad \frac{22.414 \ L}{1 \ mol}$$

Solution: $15.0 \ \cancel{g} \times \dfrac{1 \ \cancel{mol}}{20.18 \ \cancel{g}} \times \dfrac{22.414 \ L}{1 \ \cancel{mol}} = 16.7 \ L$

Check: The units (L) are correct. The magnitude of the answer (17 L) makes sense because one mole of an ideal gas under standard conditions (273 K and 1 atm) occupies 22.4 L and we have about 0.75 mol.

5.25   **Given:** H_2, $P = 1655 \ psi$, and $T = 20.0 \ °C$ **Find:** d
Conceptual Plan: $°C \rightarrow K$ and $psi \rightarrow atm$ then $P, T, \mathcal{M} \rightarrow d$
$$K = °C + 273.15 \qquad \frac{1 \ atm}{14.70 \ psi} \qquad d = \frac{P\mathcal{M}}{RT}$$

Solution: $T = 20.0 \ °C + 273.15 = 293.2 \ K \qquad P = 1655 \ \cancel{psi} \times \dfrac{1 \ atm}{14.70 \ \cancel{psi}} = 112.585 \ atm$

$$d = \frac{P\mathcal{M}}{RT} = \frac{112.585 \ \cancel{atm} \times 2.016 \ \frac{g}{\cancel{mol}}}{0.08206 \ \frac{L \cdot \cancel{atm}}{\cancel{K} \cdot \cancel{mol}} \times 293.2 \ \cancel{K}} = 9.434 \ \frac{g}{L}$$

Check: The units (g/L) are correct. The magnitude of the answer (9 g/L) makes physical sense because this is a high pressure; so the gas density will be on the high side.

5.27   **Given:** $V = 248$ mL, $m = 0.433$ g, $P = 745$ mmHg, and $T = 28\,°C$ **Find:** $\mathcal{M}$
Conceptual Plan: $°C \rightarrow K$ and mmHg $\rightarrow$ atm and mL $\rightarrow$ L then $V, m \rightarrow d$ then $d, P, T \rightarrow \mathcal{M}$

$$K = °C + 273.15 \qquad \frac{1\ atm}{760\ mmHg} \qquad \frac{1\ L}{1000\ mL} \qquad d = \frac{m}{V} \qquad d = \frac{p\mathcal{M}}{RT}$$

Solution: $T = 28\,°C + 273.15 = 301$ K $P = 745\ mmHg \times \dfrac{1\ atm}{760\ mmHg} = 0.980263$ atm

$V = 248\ mL \times \dfrac{1\ L}{1000\ mL} = 0.248$ L $d = \dfrac{m}{V} = \dfrac{0.433\ g}{0.248\ L} = 1.74597$ g/L $d = \dfrac{P\mathcal{M}}{RT}$ Rearrange to solve for $\mathcal{M}$.

$$\mathcal{M} = \frac{dRT}{P} = \frac{1.74597\ \dfrac{g}{L} \times 0.08206\ \dfrac{L \cdot atm}{K \cdot mol} \times 301\ K}{0.980263\ atm} = 44.0\ g/mol$$

Check: The units (g/mol) are correct. The magnitude of the answer (44 g/mol) makes physical sense because this is a reasonable number for a molecular weight of a gas.

5.29   **Given:** $m = 38.8$ mg, $V = 224$ mL, $T = 55\,°C$, and $P = 886$ torr   **Find:** $\mathcal{M}$
Conceptual Plan: mg $\rightarrow$ g and mL $\rightarrow$ L and $°C \rightarrow K$ and torr $\rightarrow$ atm then $V, m \rightarrow d$ then $d, P, T \rightarrow \mathcal{M}$

$$\frac{1\ g}{1000\ mg} \qquad \frac{1\ L}{1000\ mL} \qquad K = °C + 273.15 \quad \frac{1\ atm}{760\ torr} \qquad d = \frac{m}{V} \qquad d = \frac{PM}{RT}$$

Solution:

$$m = 38.8\ mg \times \frac{1\ g}{1000\ mg} = 0.0388\ g \quad V = 224\ mL \times \frac{1\ L}{1000\ mL} = 0.224\ L \quad T = 55\,°C + 273.15 = 328\ K$$

$$P = 886\ torr \times \frac{1\ atm}{760\ torr} = 1.165789\ atm \quad d = \frac{m}{V} = \frac{0.0388\ g}{0.224\ L} = 0.173214\ g/L \quad d = \frac{PM}{RT}$$

Rearrange to solve for $\mathcal{M}$. $\mathcal{M} = \dfrac{dRT}{P} = \dfrac{0.173214\ \dfrac{g}{L} \times 0.08206\ \dfrac{L \cdot atm}{K \cdot mol} \times 328\ K}{1.165789\ atm} = 4.00\ g/mol$

Check: The units (g/mol) are correct. The magnitude of the answer (4 g/mol) makes physical sense because this is a reasonable number for a molecular weight of a gas, especially because the density is on the low side.

Partial Pressure

5.31   **Given:** $P_{N_2} = 315$ torr, $P_{O_2} = 134$ torr, $P_{He} = 219$ torr, $V = 2.15$ L, and $T = 25.0\,°C$ **Find:** $P_{Total}, m_{N_2}, m_{O_2}, m_{He}$
Conceptual Plan: $°C \rightarrow K$ and torr $\rightarrow$ atm and $P, V, T \rightarrow n$ then mol $\rightarrow$ g

$$K = °C + 273.15 \qquad \frac{1\ atm}{760\ torr} \qquad PV = nRT \qquad \mathcal{M}$$

and $P_{N_2}, P_{O_2}, P_{He} \rightarrow P_{Total}$

$$P_{Total} = P_{N_2} + P_{O_2} + P_{He}$$

Solution: $T_1 = 25.0\,°C + 273.15 = 298.2$ K, $PV = nRT$ Rearrange to solve for n.

$$n = \frac{PV}{RT} \quad P_{N_2} = 315\ torr \times \frac{1\ atm}{760\ torr} = 0.4144737\ atm \quad n_{N_2} = \frac{0.4144737\ atm \times 2.15\ L}{0.08206\ \dfrac{L \cdot atm}{mol \cdot K} \times 298.2\ K} = 0.03641634\ mol$$

$$0.03641634\ mol \times \frac{28.02\ mol}{1\ mol} = 1.02\ g\ N_2$$

$$P_{O_2} = 134\ torr \times \frac{1\ atm}{760\ torr} = 0.1763158\ atm \quad n_{O_2} = \frac{0.1763158\ atm \times 2.15\ L}{0.08206\ \dfrac{L \cdot atm}{mol \cdot K} \times 298.2\ K} = 0.01549139\ mol$$

$$0.01549139\ mol \times \frac{32.00\ mol}{1\ mol} = 0.496\ g\ O_2$$

$$P_{He} = 219\ torr \times \frac{1\ atm}{760\ torr} = 0.2881579\ atm \quad n_{He} = \frac{0.2881579\ atm \times 2.15\ L}{0.08206\ \dfrac{L \cdot atm}{mol \cdot K} \times 298.2\ K} = 0.02531803\ mol$$

$$0.02531803 \text{ mol} \times \frac{4.003 \text{ mol}}{1 \text{ mol}} = 0.101 \text{ g He and}$$

$P_{\text{Total}} = P_{N_2} + P_{O_2} + P_{He} = 0.414 \text{ atm} + 0.176 \text{ atm} + 0.288 \text{ atm} = 0.878 \text{ atm or}$

$P_{\text{Total}} = P_{N_2} + P_{O_2} + P_{He} = 315 \text{ torr} + 134 \text{ torr} + 219 \text{ torr} = 668 \text{ torr}$

Check: The units (g, g, g, and atm or torr) are correct. The magnitude of the answer (no more than about a gram) makes sense because gases are not very dense and these pressures are < 1 atm. Because all of the pressures are small, the total is < 1 atm or 760 torr.

5.33   **Given:** m (CO_2) = 1.20 g, V = 755 mL, P_{N_2} = 725 mmHg, and T = 25.0 °C   **Find:** P_{Total}
          Conceptual Plan: mL $\rightarrow$ L and °C $\rightarrow$ K and g $\rightarrow$ mol and $n, P, T \rightarrow V$ then atm $\rightarrow$ mmHg

$$\frac{1 \text{ L}}{1000 \text{ mL}} \qquad K = {}^\circ C + 273.15 \qquad \frac{1 \text{ mol}}{44.01 \text{ g}} \qquad\qquad PV = nRT \qquad\qquad \frac{760 \text{ mmHg}}{1 \text{ atm}}$$

finally $P_{CO_2}, P_{N_2} \rightarrow P_{\text{Total}}$

$$P_{\text{Total}} = P_{CO_2} + P_{N_2}$$

Solution: $V = 755 \text{ mL} \times \dfrac{1 \text{ L}}{1000 \text{ mL}} = 0.755 \text{ L} \quad T = 25.0 \,^\circ C + 273.15 = 298.2 \text{ K}$

$n_{CO_2} = 1.20 \text{ g} \times \dfrac{1 \text{ mol}}{44.01 \text{ g}} = 0.0272665 \text{ mol}, \quad PV = nRT \text{ Rearrange to solve for } P.$

$$P = \frac{nRT}{V} = \frac{0.0272665 \text{ mol} \times 0.08206 \dfrac{L \cdot \text{atm}}{\text{mol} \cdot K} \times 298.2 \text{ K}}{0.755 \text{ L}} = 0.883734 \text{ atm}$$

$$P_{CO_2} = 0.883734 \text{ atm} \times \frac{760 \text{ mmHg}}{1 \text{ atm}} = 672 \text{ mmHg}$$

$$P_{\text{Total}} = P_{CO_2} + P_{N_2} = 672 \text{ mmHg} + 725 \text{ mmHg} = 1397 \text{ mmHg or } 1397 \text{ torr} \times \frac{1 \text{ atm}}{760 \text{ torr}} = 1.84 \text{ atm}$$

Check: The units (mmHg) are correct. The magnitude of the answer (1400 mmHg) makes sense because it must be greater than 725 mmHg.

5.35   **Given:** m (N_2) = 1.25 g, m (O_2) = 0.85 g, V = 1.55 L, and T = 18 °C   **Find:** $\chi_{N_2}, \chi_{O_2}, P_{N_2}, P_{O_2}$
          Conceptual Plan: g $\rightarrow$ mol then $n_{N_2}, n_{O_2} \rightarrow \chi_{N_2}$ and $n_{N_2}, n_{O_2} \rightarrow \chi_{O_2}$ and °C $\rightarrow$ K

$$\mathcal{M} \qquad\qquad \chi_{N_2} = \frac{n_{N_2}}{n_{N_2} + n_{O_2}} \qquad \chi_{O_2} = \frac{n_{O_2}}{n_{N_2} + n_{O_2}} \qquad K = {}^\circ C + 273.15$$

then $n, V, T \rightarrow P$

$$PV = nRT$$

Solution: $n_{N_2} = 1.25 \text{ g} \times \dfrac{1 \text{ mol}}{28.02 \text{ g}} = 0.0446110 \text{ mol}, \quad n_{O_2} = 0.85 \text{ g} \times \dfrac{1 \text{ mol}}{32.00 \text{ g}} = 0.026563 \text{ mol},$

$T = 18 \,^\circ C + 273.15 = 291 \text{ K}, \; \chi_{N_2} = \dfrac{n_{N_2}}{n_{N_2} + n_{O_2}} = \dfrac{0.0446110 \text{ mol}}{0.0446110 \text{ mol} + 0.026563 \text{ mol}} = 0.626788 = 0.627,$

$\chi_{O_2} = \dfrac{n_{O_2}}{n_{N_2} + n_{O_2}} = \dfrac{0.026563 \text{ mol}}{0.0446110 \text{ mol} + 0.026563 \text{ mol}} = 0.373212 \text{ We can also calculate this as}$

$\chi_{O_2} = 1 - \chi_{N_2} = 1 - 0.626788 = 0.373212 = 0.373 \quad PV = nRT \text{ Rearrange to solve for } P. \; P = \dfrac{nRT}{V}$

$$P_{N_2} = \frac{0.044611 \text{ mol} \times 0.08206 \dfrac{L \cdot \text{atm}}{\text{mol} \cdot K} \times 291 \text{ K}}{1.55 \text{ L}} = 0.687 \text{ atm}$$

$$P_{O_2} = \frac{0.026563 \text{ mol} \times 0.08206 \dfrac{L \cdot \text{atm}}{\text{mol} \cdot K} \times 291 \text{ K}}{1.55 \text{ L}} = 0.409 \text{ atm}$$

Check: The units (none and atm) are correct. The magnitude of the answers makes sense because the mole fractions should total 1 and because the weight of N_2 is greater than O_2, its mole fraction is larger. The number of moles is $\ll 1$, so we expect the pressures to be < 1 atm, given the V (1.55 L).

5.37   **Given:** $T = 30.0\ °C$, $P_{Total} = 732\ mmHg$, and $V = 722\ mL$ **Find:** P_{H_2} and m_{H_2}

        Conceptual Plan: $T \rightarrow P_{H_2O}$ then $P_{Total}, P_{H_2O} \rightarrow P_{H_2}$ then $mmHg \rightarrow atm$ and $mL \rightarrow L$

            Table 5.3 $P_{Total} = P_{H_2O} + P_{H_2}$ $\dfrac{1\ atm}{760\ mmHg}$ $\dfrac{1\ L}{1000\ mL}$

        and $°C \rightarrow K$ **and** $P, V, T \rightarrow n$ **then** $mol \rightarrow g$

           $K = °C + 273.15$ $PV = nRT$ $\dfrac{2.016\ g}{1\ mol}$

        Solution: Table 5.3 states that at 30 °C, $P_{H_2O} = 31.86\ mmHg$ $P_{Total} = P_{H_2O} + P_{H_2}$

        Rearrange to solve for P_{H_2}. $P_{H_2} = P_{Total} - P_{H_2O} = 732\ mmHg - 31.86\ mmHg = 700.\ mmHg$

        $P_{H_2} = 700.\ mmHg \times \dfrac{1\ atm}{760\ mmHg} = 0.921052\ atm$ $V = 722\ mL \times \dfrac{1\ L}{1000\ mL} = 0.722\ L$

        $T = 30.0\ °C + 273.15 = 303.2\ K,$ $PV = nRT$ Rearrange to solve for n. $n = \dfrac{PV}{RT}$

        $n_{H_2} = \dfrac{0.921052\ atm \times 0.722\ L}{0.08206\ \dfrac{L \cdot atm}{mol \cdot K} \times 303.2\ K} = 0.0267276\ mol$ then $0.0267276\ mol \times \dfrac{2.016\ g}{1\ mol} = 0.0539\ g\ H_2$

        Check: The units (g) are correct. The magnitude of the answer ($\ll 1$ g) makes sense because gases are not very dense, hydrogen is light, the volume is small, and the pressure is ~1 atm.

5.39   **Given:** $T = 25\ °C$, $P_{Total} = 748\ mmHg$, and $V = 0.951\ L$ **Find:** m_{H_2}

        Conceptual Plan: $T \rightarrow P_{H_2O}$ then $P_{Total}, P_{H_2O} \rightarrow P_{H_2}$ then $mmHg \rightarrow atm$ and $mL \rightarrow L$

            Table 5.3 $P_{Total} = P_{H_2O} + P_{H_2}$ $\dfrac{1\ atm}{760\ mmHg}$ $\dfrac{1\ L}{1000\ mL}$

        and $°C \rightarrow K$ $P, V, T \rightarrow n$ **then** $mol \rightarrow g$

           $K = °C + 273.15$ $PV = nRT$ $\dfrac{2.016\ g}{1\ mol}$

        Solution: Table 5.3 states that at 25 °C, $P_{H_2O} = 23.78\ mmHg$ $P_{Total} = P_{H_2O} + P_{H_2}$

        Rearrange to solve for P_{H_2}. $P_{H_2} = P_{Total} - P_{H_2O} = 748\ mmHg - 23.78\ mmHg = 724\ mmHg$

        $P_{H_2} = 724\ mmHg \times \dfrac{1\ atm}{760\ mmHg} = 0.952632\ atm$ $T = 25\ °C + 273.15 = 298\ K,$ $PV = nRT$

        Rearrange to solve for n. $n_{H_2} = \dfrac{PV}{RT} = \dfrac{0.952632\ atm \times 0.951\ L}{0.08206\ \dfrac{L \cdot atm}{mol \cdot K} \times 298\ K} = 0.0370474\ mol$

        $0.0370474\ mol \times \dfrac{2.016\ g}{1\ mol} = 0.0747\ g\ H_2$

        Check: The units (g) are correct. The magnitude of the answer ($\ll 1$ g) makes sense because gases are not very dense, hydrogen is light, the volume is small, and the pressure is ~1 atm.

Reaction Stoichiometry Involving Gases

5.41   **Given:** $m\ (C) = 15.7\ g$, $P = 1.0\ atm$, and $T = 355\ K$ **Find:** V

        Conceptual Plan: $g\ C \rightarrow mol\ C \rightarrow mol\ H_2$ then $n\ (mol\ H_2), P, T \rightarrow V$

                  $\dfrac{1\ mol}{12.01\ g\ C}$ $\dfrac{1\ mol\ H_2}{1\ mol\ C}$ $PV = nRT$

        Solution: $15.7\ g\ C \times \dfrac{1\ mol\ C}{12.01\ g\ C} \times \dfrac{1\ mol\ H_2}{1\ mol\ C} = 1.30724\ mol\ H_2$, $PV = nRT$ Rearrange to solve for V.

        $V = \dfrac{nRT}{P} = \dfrac{1.30724\ mol \times 0.08206\ \dfrac{L \cdot atm}{mol \cdot K} \times 355\ K}{1.0\ atm} = 38\ L$

        Check: The units (L) are correct. The magnitude of the answer (38 L) makes sense because we have more than one mole of gas, so we expect more than 22 L.

5.43   **Given:** $P = 748$ mmHg, $T = 86\,°C$, and $m\,(CH_3OH) = 25.8$ g   **Find:** V_{H_2} and V_{CO}

        Conceptual Plan: g CH$_3$OH $\rightarrow$ mol CH$_3$OH $\rightarrow$ mol H$_2$ and mmHg $\rightarrow$ atm and °C $\rightarrow$ K

$$\frac{1\ \text{mol CH}_3\text{OH}}{32.04\ \text{g CH}_3\text{OH}} \qquad \frac{2\ \text{mol H}_2}{1\ \text{mol CH}_3\text{OH}} \qquad \frac{1\ \text{atm}}{760\ \text{mmHg}} \qquad K = °C + 273.15$$

        then n (mol H$_2$), P, T $\rightarrow$ V and mol H$_2$ $\rightarrow$ mol CO then n (mol CO), P, T $\rightarrow$ V

$$PV = nRT \qquad\qquad \frac{1\ \text{mol CO}}{2\ \text{mol H}_2} \qquad\qquad PV = nRT$$

        Solution: $25.8\ \text{g CH}_3\text{OH} \times \dfrac{1\ \text{mol CH}_3\text{OH}}{32.04\ \text{g CH}_3\text{OH}} \times \dfrac{2\ \text{mol H}_2}{1\ \text{mol CH}_3\text{OH}} = 1.61049\ \text{mol H}_2,$

$$P_{H_2} = 748\ \text{mmHg} \times \frac{1\ \text{atm}}{760\ \text{mmHg}} = 0.984211\ \text{atm}, \quad T = 86\,°C + 273.15 = 359\ K, \quad PV = nRT$$

        Rearrange to solve for V. $V = \dfrac{nRT}{P}$ $V_{H_2} = \dfrac{1.61049\ \text{mol} \times 0.08206\ \frac{L\cdot atm}{mol\cdot K} \times 359\ K}{0.984211\ \text{atm}} = 48.2\ \text{L H}_2$

$$1.61049\ \text{mol H}_2 \times \frac{1\ \text{mol CO}}{2\ \text{mol H}_2} = 0.80525\ \text{mol CO}, \quad V_{CO} = \frac{0.80525\ \text{mol} \times 0.08206\ \frac{L\cdot atm}{mol\cdot K} \times 359\ K}{0.984211\ \text{atm}} = 24.1\ \text{L CO}$$

        Check: The units (L) are correct. The magnitude of the answers (48 L and 24 L) makes sense because we have more than one mole of hydrogen gas and half that of CO, so we expect significantly more than 22 L for hydrogen and half that for CO.

5.45   **Given:** $V = 11.8$ L, and STP   **Find:** $m\,(NaN_3)$

        Conceptual Plan: V_{N_2} $\rightarrow$ mol N$_2$ $\rightarrow$ mol NaN$_3$ $\rightarrow$ g NaN$_3$

$$\frac{1\ \text{mol N}_2}{22.4\ \text{L N}_2} \qquad \frac{2\ \text{mol NaN}_3}{3\ \text{mol N}_2} \qquad \frac{65.02\ \text{g NaN}_3}{1\ \text{mol NaN}_3}$$

        Solution: $11.8\ \text{L N}_2 \times \dfrac{1\ \text{mol N}_2}{22.4\ \text{L N}_2} \times \dfrac{2\ \text{mol NaN}_3}{3\ \text{mol N}_2} \times \dfrac{65.02\ \text{g NaN}_3}{1\ \text{mol NaN}_3} = 22.8\ \text{g NaN}_3$

        Check: The units (g) are correct. The magnitude of the answer (23 g) makes sense because we have about half a mole of nitrogen gas, which translates to even fewer moles of NaN$_3$, so we expect significantly less than 65 g.

5.47   **Given:** $V_{CH_4} = 25.5$ L, $P_{CH_4} = 732$ torr, and $T = 25\,°C$; mixed with $V_{H_2O} = 22.8$ L, $P_{H_2O} = 702$ torr, and $T = 125\,°C$; forms $V_{H_2} = 26.2$ L at STP   **Find:** % yield

        Conceptual Plan: CH$_4$: torr $\rightarrow$ atm and °C $\rightarrow$ K and $P, V, T \rightarrow n_{CH_4} \rightarrow n_{H_2}$

$$\frac{1\ \text{atm}}{760\ \text{torr}} \qquad K = °C + 273.15 \qquad PV = nRT \qquad \frac{3\ \text{mol H}_2}{1\ \text{mol CH}_4}$$

        H$_2$O: torr $\rightarrow$ atm and °C $\rightarrow$ K and $P, V, T \rightarrow n_{H_2O} \rightarrow n_{H_2}$

$$\frac{1\ \text{atm}}{760\ \text{torr}} \qquad K = °C + 273.15 \qquad PV = nRT \qquad \frac{3\ \text{mol H}_2}{1\ \text{mol CH}_4}$$

        Select smaller n_{H_2} as theoretical yield,

        then L_{H_2} $\rightarrow$ mol H$_2$ (actual yield) finally actual yield, theoretical yield $\rightarrow$ % yield

$$\frac{1\ \text{mol H}_2}{22.4\ \text{L H}_2} \qquad\qquad\qquad \% \text{ yield} = \frac{\text{actual yield}}{\text{theoretical yield}} \times 100\%$$

        Solution: CH$_4$: $P_{CH_4} = 732\ \text{torr} \times \dfrac{1\ \text{atm}}{760\ \text{torr}} = 0.963158\ \text{atm}, T = 25\,°C + 273.15 = 298\ K, PV = nRT$

        Rearrange to solve for n. $n = \dfrac{PV}{RT}$ $n_{CH_4} = \dfrac{0.963158\ \text{atm} \times 25.5\ L}{0.08206\ \frac{L\cdot atm}{mol\cdot K} \times 298\ K} = 1.00436\ \text{mol CH}_4$

$$1.00436\ \text{mol CH}_4 \times \frac{3\ \text{mol H}_2}{1\ \text{mol CH}_4} = 3.01308\ \text{mol H}_2$$

        H$_2$O: $P_{H_2O} = 702\ \text{torr} \times \dfrac{1\ \text{atm}}{760\ \text{torr}} = 0.923684\ \text{atm}, T = 125\,°C + 273.15 = 398\ K, n = \dfrac{PV}{RT}$

$$n_{H_2O} = \frac{0.923684\ \text{atm} \times 22.8\ L}{0.08206\ \frac{L\cdot atm}{mol\cdot K} \times 398\ K} = 0.644828\ \text{mol H}_2O \quad 0.644828\ \text{mol H}_2O \times \frac{3\ \text{mol H}_2}{1\ \text{mol H}_2O} = 1.93448\ \text{mol H}_2$$

Water is the limiting reagent because the moles of hydrogen generated is lower.

theoretical yield $= 1.9\underline{3}448$ mol H_2

$$26.2 \text{ L } H_2 \times \frac{1 \text{ mol } H_2}{22.414 \text{ L } H_2} = 1.1\underline{6}891 \text{ mol } H_2 = \text{ actual yield}$$

$$\% \text{ yield} = \frac{\text{actual yield}}{\text{theoretical yield}} \times 100\% = \frac{1.1\underline{6}891 \text{ mol } H_2}{1.9\underline{3}448 \text{ mol } H_2} \times 100\% = 60.4\%$$

Check: The units (%) are correct. The magnitude of the answer (60%) makes sense because it is between 0 and 100%.

5.49   **Given:** $V = 2.00$ L, $P_{Cl_2} = 337$ mmHg, $P_{F_2} = 729$ mmHg, $T = 298$ K   **Find:** limiting reactant and m_{ClF_3}
         Conceptual Plan: Determine limiting reactant by comparing the pressures of each reactant then

$$\frac{3 \text{ mmHg } F_2}{1 \text{ mmHg } Cl_2}$$

mmHg limiting reactant → mmHg ClF_3 and mmHg → atm then

$$\frac{2 \text{ mmHg } ClF_3}{1 \text{ mmHg } Cl_2} \text{ or } \frac{2 \text{ mmHg } ClF_3}{3 \text{ mmHg } F_2} \qquad \frac{1 \text{ atm}}{760 \text{ mmHg}}$$

$$\boldsymbol{P, V, T \rightarrow n \rightarrow m}$$

$$PV = nRT \quad \frac{92.45 \text{ g } ClF_3}{1 \text{ mol } ClF_3}$$

Solution: To determine the limiting reactant, calculate the pressure of fluorine needed to react all of the chlorine and compare to the pressure of fluorine available.

$$337 \text{ mmHg } Cl_2 \times \frac{3 \text{ mmHg } F_2}{1 \text{ mmHg } Cl_2} = 101\underline{1} \text{ mmHg } F_2 \text{ needed.}$$

Because only 729 mmHg F_2 is available, F_2 is the limiting reactant; then

$$P_{ClF_3} = 729 \text{ mmHg } F_2 \times \frac{2 \text{ mmHg } ClF_3}{3 \text{ mmHg } F_2} \times \frac{1 \text{ atm } ClF_3}{760 \text{ mmHg } ClF_3} = 0.639\underline{4}737 \text{ atm } ClF_3. \quad PV = nRT \text{ Rearrange to}$$

solve for n. $n = \dfrac{PV}{RT}$ $\quad n_{ClF_3} = \dfrac{0.639\underline{4}737 \text{ atm } ClF_3 \times 2.00 \text{ L}}{0.08206 \dfrac{\text{L} \cdot \text{atm}}{\text{mol} \cdot \text{K}} \times 298 \text{ K}} = 0.05230\underline{0}387 \text{ mol } ClF_3$

Finally, $0.05230\underline{0}387 \text{ mol } ClF_3 \times \dfrac{92.45 \text{ g } ClF_3}{1 \text{ mol } ClF_3} = 4.8\underline{3}51708 \text{ g } ClF_3 = 4.84 \text{ g } ClF_3$

Check: The units (g) are correct. The magnitude of the answer (5 g) makes sense because we have much less than a mole of fluorine, so we expect a mass much less than the molar mass of ClF_3.

Kinetic Molecular Theory

5.51   (a)   Yes, because the average kinetic energy of a particle is proportional to the temperature in kelvins and the two gases are at the same temperature, they have the same average kinetic energy.
         (b)   No, because the helium atoms are lighter, they must move faster to have the same kinetic energy as argon atoms.
         (c)   No, because the Ar atoms are moving slower to compensate for their larger mass, they will exert the same pressure on the walls of the container.
         (d)   Because He is lighter, it will have the faster rate of effusion.

5.53   **Given:** F_2, Cl_2, Br_2, and $T = 298$ K   **Find:** u_{rms} and KE_{avg} for each gas and relative rates of effusion
         Conceptual Plan: $\mathcal{M}, T \rightarrow u_{rms} \rightarrow KE_{avg}$

$$u_{rms} = \sqrt{\frac{3RT}{M}} \quad KE_{avg} = \frac{1}{2} N_A m u_{rms}^2 = \frac{3}{2} RT$$

Solution:

$$F_2: \mathcal{M} = \frac{38.00 \text{ g}}{1 \text{ mol}} \times \frac{1 \text{ kg}}{1000 \text{ g}} = 0.03800 \text{ kg/mol}, \quad u_{rms} = \sqrt{\frac{3RT}{\mathcal{M}}} = \sqrt{\frac{3 \times 8.314 \dfrac{\text{J}}{\text{K} \cdot \text{mol}} \times 298 \text{ K}}{0.03800 \dfrac{\text{kg}}{\text{mol}}}} = 442 \text{ m/s}$$

Cl_2: $\mathcal{M} = \dfrac{70.90\ \cancel{g}}{1\ mol} \times \dfrac{1\ kg}{1000\ \cancel{g}} = 0.07090\ kg/mol$, $u_{rms} = \sqrt{\dfrac{3RT}{\mathcal{M}}} = \sqrt{\dfrac{3 \times 8.314\dfrac{J}{\cancel{K}\cdot\cancel{mol}} \times 298\ \cancel{K}}{0.07090\ \dfrac{kg}{\cancel{mol}}}} = 324\ m/s$

Br_2: $\mathcal{M} = \dfrac{159.80\ \cancel{g}}{1\ mol} \times \dfrac{1\ kg}{1000\ \cancel{g}} = 0.15980\ kg/mol$, $u_{rms} = \sqrt{\dfrac{3RT}{\mathcal{M}}} = \sqrt{\dfrac{3 \times 8.314\dfrac{J}{\cancel{K}\cdot\cancel{mol}} \times 298\ \cancel{K}}{0.15980\ \dfrac{kg}{\cancel{mol}}}} = 216\ m/s$

All molecules have the same kinetic energy:

$$KE_{avg} = \dfrac{3}{2}RT = \dfrac{3}{2} \times 8.314\ \dfrac{J}{K\cdot mol} \times 298\ K = 3.72 \times 10^3\ J/mol$$

Because the rate of effusion is proportional to $\sqrt{\dfrac{1}{\mathcal{M}}}$, F_2 will have the fastest rate and Br_2 will have the slowest rate.

Check: The units (m/s) are correct. The magnitude of the answer $(200 - 450\ m/s)$ makes sense because it is consistent with what was seen in the text, and the heavier the molecule, the slower the molecule.

5.55   **Given:** $^{238}UF_6$ and $^{235}UF_6$ U-235 $= 235.054$ amu, U-238 $= 238.051$ amu
        Find: ratio of effusion rates $^{238}UF_6/\ ^{235}UF_6$
        Conceptual Plan: $\mathcal{M}(^{238}UF_6), \mathcal{M}(^{235}UF_6) \rightarrow$ **Rate $(^{238}UF_6)$/Rate $(^{235}UF_6)$**

$$\dfrac{Rate(^{238}UF_6)}{Rate(^{235}UF_6)} = \sqrt{\dfrac{\mathcal{M}(^{235}UF_6)}{\mathcal{M}(^{238}UF_6)}}$$

Solution: $^{238}UF_6$: $\mathcal{M} = \dfrac{352.05\ \cancel{g}}{1\ mol} \times \dfrac{1\ kg}{1000\ \cancel{g}} = 0.35205\ kg/mol$,

$^{235}UF_6$: $\mathcal{M} = \dfrac{349.05\ \cancel{g}}{1\ mol} \times \dfrac{1\ kg}{1000\ \cancel{g}} = 0.34905\ kg/mol$,

$$\dfrac{Rate(^{238}UF_6)}{Rate(^{235}UF_6)} = \sqrt{\dfrac{\mathcal{M}(^{235}UF_6)}{\mathcal{M}(^{238}UF_6)}} = \sqrt{\dfrac{0.34905\ \cancel{kg/mol}}{0.35205\ \cancel{kg/mol}}} = 0.99573$$

Check: The units (none) are correct. The magnitude of the answer (<1) makes sense because the heavier molecule has the lower effusion rate because it moves more slowly.

5.57   **Given:** Ne and unknown gas; Ne effusion in 76 s and unknown in 155 s   **Find:** identify unknown gas
        Conceptual Plan: $\mathcal{M}$(Ne), **Rate** (Ne), **Rate**(Unk) $\rightarrow \mathcal{M}$(Unk)

$$\dfrac{Rate(Ne)}{Rate(Unk)} = \sqrt{\dfrac{\mathcal{M}(Unk)}{\mathcal{M}(Ne)}}$$

Solution: Ne: $\mathcal{M} = \dfrac{20.18\ \cancel{g}}{1\ mol} \times \dfrac{1\ kg}{1000\ \cancel{g}} = 0.02018\ kg/mol$, $\dfrac{Rate(Ne)}{Rate(Unk)} = \sqrt{\dfrac{\mathcal{M}(Unk)}{\mathcal{M}(Ne)}}$ Rearrange to solve for

$\mathcal{M}$(Unk). $\mathcal{M}(Unk) = \mathcal{M}(Ne)\left(\dfrac{Rate(Ne)}{Rate(Unk)}\right)^2$ Because Rate $\propto$ 1/(effusion time),

$$\mathcal{M}(Unk) = \mathcal{M}(Ne)\left(\dfrac{Time(Unk)}{Time(Ne)}\right)^2 = 0.02018\ \dfrac{kg}{mol} \times \left(\dfrac{155\ \cancel{s}}{76\ \cancel{s}}\right)^2 = 0.084\ \dfrac{\cancel{kg}}{mol} \times \dfrac{1000\ g}{1\ \cancel{kg}} = 84\ g/mol\ or\ Kr.$$

Check: The units (g/mol) are correct. The magnitude of the answer $(>Ne)$ makes sense because Ne effused faster and so must be lighter.

5.59   Gas A has the higher molar mass because it has the slower average velocity. Gas B will have the higher effusion rate because it has the higher velocity.

Real Gases

5.61   The postulate that the volume of the gas particles is small compared to the space between them breaks down at high pressure. At high pressures, the number of molecules per unit volume increases; so the volume of the gas particles becomes more significant. Because the spacing between the particles is reduced, the molecules themselves occupy a significant portion of the volume.

5.63   **Given:** Ne, $n = 1.000$ mol, $P = 500.0$ atm, and $T = 355.0$ K   **Find:** V(ideal) and V(van der Waals)

Conceptual Plan: $n, P, T \rightarrow V$ and $n, P, T \rightarrow V$

$$PV = nRT \qquad \left(P + \frac{an^2}{V^2}\right)(V - nb) = nRT$$

Solution: $PV = nRT$ Rearrange to solve for V.

$$V = \frac{nRT}{P} = \frac{1.000 \ \text{mol} \times 0.08206 \ \dfrac{\text{L} \cdot \text{atm}}{\text{mol} \cdot \text{K}} \times 355.0 \ \text{K}}{500.0 \ \text{atm}} = 0.05826 \ \text{L}$$

$\left(P + \dfrac{an^2}{V^2}\right)(V - nb) = nRT$ Rearrange to solve to $V = \dfrac{nRT}{\left(P + \dfrac{an^2}{V^2}\right)} + nb$

Using $a = 0.211 \ \text{L}^2 \ \text{atm/mol}^2$ and $b = 0.0171$ L/mol from Table 5.4 and the V from the ideal gas law calculation above, solve for V by successive approximations.

$$V = \frac{1.000 \ \text{mol} \times 0.08206 \ \dfrac{\text{L} \cdot \text{atm}}{\text{mol} \cdot \text{K}} \times 355.0 \ \text{K}}{500.0 \ \text{atm} + \dfrac{0.211 \dfrac{\text{L}^2 \cdot \text{atm}}{\text{mol}^2} \times (1.000 \ \text{mol})^2}{(0.05826 \ \text{L})^2}} + \left(1.000 \ \text{mol} \times 0.0171 \dfrac{\text{L}}{\text{mol}}\right) = 0.068920 \ \text{L}$$

Plug in this new value.

$$V = \frac{1.000 \ \text{mol} \times 0.08206 \ \dfrac{\text{L} \cdot \text{atm}}{\text{mol} \cdot \text{K}} \times 355.0 \ \text{K}}{500.0 \ \text{atm} + \dfrac{0.211 \dfrac{\text{L}^2 \cdot \text{atm}}{\text{mol}^2} \times (1.000 \ \text{mol})^2}{(0.068920 \ \text{L})^2}} + \left(1.000 \ \text{mol} \times 0.0171 \dfrac{\text{L}}{\text{mol}}\right) = 0.070609 \ \text{L}$$

Plug in this new value.

$$V = \frac{1.000 \ \text{mol} \times 0.08206 \ \dfrac{\text{L} \cdot \text{atm}}{\text{mol} \cdot \text{K}} \times 355.0 \ \text{K}}{500.0 \ \text{atm} + \dfrac{0.211 \dfrac{\text{L}^2 \cdot \text{atm}}{\text{mol}^2} \times (1.000 \ \text{mol})^2}{(0.070609 \ \text{L})^2}} + \left(1.000 \ \text{mol} \times 0.0171 \dfrac{\text{L}}{\text{mol}}\right) = 0.070816 \ \text{L}$$

Plug in this new value.

$$V = \frac{1.000 \ \text{mol} \times 0.08206 \ \dfrac{\text{L} \cdot \text{atm}}{\text{mol} \cdot \text{K}} \times 355.0 \ \text{K}}{500.0 \ \text{atm} + \dfrac{0.211 \dfrac{\text{L}^2 \cdot \text{atm}}{\text{mol}^2} \times (1.000 \ \text{mol})^2}{(0.070816 \ \text{L})^2}} + \left(1.000 \ \text{mol} \times 0.0171 \dfrac{\text{L}}{\text{mol}}\right) = 0.070840 \ \text{L} = 0.0708 \ \text{L}$$

The two values are different because we are at very high pressures. The pressure is corrected from 500.0 atm to 542.1 atm, and the final volume correction is 0.0171 L.

Check: The units (L) are correct. The magnitude of the answer (~ 0.07 L) makes sense because we are at such a high pressure and have one mole of gas.

Cumulative Problems

5.65   **Given:** m (penny) $= 2.482$ g, $T = 25 \ °C$, $V = 0.899$ L, and $P_{\text{Total}} = 791$ mmHg   **Find:** % Zn in penny

Conceptual Plan: $T \rightarrow P_{\text{H}_2\text{O}}$ then $P_{\text{Total}}, P_{\text{H}_2\text{O}} \rightarrow P_{\text{H}_2}$ then mmHg $\rightarrow$ atm and $°C \rightarrow$ K

Table 5.3 $\qquad\qquad P_{\text{Total}} = P_{\text{H}_2\text{O}} + P_{\text{H}_2} \qquad\qquad \dfrac{1 \ \text{atm}}{760 \ \text{mmHg}} \qquad$ K $= °C + 273.15$

and $P, V, T \rightarrow n_{H_2} \rightarrow n_{Zn} \rightarrow g_{Zn} \rightarrow \% \text{ Zn}$

$$P V = nRT \quad \frac{1 \text{ mol Zn}}{1 \text{ mol H}_2} \quad \frac{65.38 \text{ g Zn}}{1 \text{ mol Zn}} \quad \%Zn = \frac{g_{Zn}}{g_{penny}} \times 100\%$$

Solution: Table 5.3 states that $P_{H_2O} = 23.78$ mmHg at 25 °C. $P_{Total} = P_{H_2O} + P_{H_2}$ Rearrange to solve for P_{H_2}.

$P_{H_2} = P_{Total} - P_{H_2O} = 791 \text{ mmHg} - 23.78 \text{ mmHg} = 767 \text{ mmHg } P_{H_2} = 767 \text{ mmHg} \times \frac{1 \text{ atm}}{760 \text{ mmHg}} = 1.0092 \text{ atm}$

then $T = 25 °C + 273.15 = 298 \text{ K},$

$PV = nRT$

Rearrange to solve for n. $n_{H_2} = \dfrac{PV}{RT} = \dfrac{1.0092 \text{ atm} \times 0.899 \text{ L}}{0.08206 \dfrac{\text{L} \cdot \text{atm}}{\text{mol} \cdot \text{K}} \times 298 \text{ K}} = 0.0371013 \text{ mol}$

$0.0371013 \text{ mol H}_2 \times \dfrac{1 \text{ mol Zn}}{1 \text{ mol H}_2} \times \dfrac{65.38 \text{ g Zn}}{1 \text{ mol Zn}} = 2.42568 \text{ g Zn}$

$\%Zn = \dfrac{g_{Zn}}{g_{penny}} \times 100\% = \dfrac{2.42568 \text{ g}}{2.482 \text{ g}} \times 100\% = 97.7\% \text{ Zn}$

Check: The units (% Zn) are correct. The magnitude of the answer (98%) makes sense because it should be between 0 and 100%. We expect about 1/22 a mole of gas because our conditions are close to STP and we have ~1 L of gas.

5.67   **Given:** $V = 255$ mL, m (flask) $= 143.187$ g, m (flask + gas) $= 143.289$ g, $P = 267$ torr, and $T = 25 °C$ **Find:** $\mathcal{M}$
Conceptual Plan: °C $\rightarrow$ K and torr $\rightarrow$ atm and mL $\rightarrow$ L and m (flask), m (flask + gas) $\rightarrow$ m (gas)

$$\text{K} = °C + 273.15 \quad \frac{1 \text{ atm}}{760 \text{ torr}} \quad \frac{1 \text{ L}}{1000 \text{ mL}} \qquad m \text{ (gas)} = m \text{ (flask + gas)} - m \text{ (flask)}$$

then $V, m \rightarrow d$ then $d, P, T, \rightarrow \mathcal{M}$

$$d = \frac{m}{V} \qquad d = \frac{P\mathcal{M}}{RT}$$

Solution: $T = 25 °C + 273.15 = 298 \text{ K}, \quad P = 267 \text{ torr} \times \dfrac{1 \text{ atm}}{760 \text{ torr}} = 0.351316 \text{ atm},$

$V = 255 \text{ mL} \times \dfrac{1 \text{ L}}{1000 \text{ mL}} = 0.255 \text{ L},$

$m \text{ (gas)} = m \text{ (flask + gas)} - m \text{ (flask)} = 143.289 \text{ g} - 143.187 \text{ g} = 0.102 \text{ g}$

$d = \dfrac{m}{V} = \dfrac{0.102 \text{ g}}{0.255 \text{ L}} = 0.400 \text{ g/L}, d = \dfrac{P\mathcal{M}}{RT}$ Rearrange to solve for $\mathcal{M}$.

$\mathcal{M} = \dfrac{dRT}{P} = \dfrac{0.400 \dfrac{\text{g}}{\text{L}} \times 0.08206 \dfrac{\text{L} \cdot \text{atm}}{\text{K} \cdot \text{mol}} \times 298 \text{ K}}{0.351316 \text{ atm}} = 27.8 \text{ g/mol}$

Check: The units (g/mol) are correct. The magnitude of the answer (28 g/mol) makes physical sense because this is a reasonable number for a molecular weight of a gas.

5.69   **Given:** $V = 158$ mL, m (gas) $= 0.275$ g, $P = 556$ mmHg, $T = 25 °C$, gas $= 82.66\%$ C and 17.34% H
Find: molecular formula
Conceptual Plan: °C $\rightarrow$ K and mmHg $\rightarrow$ atm and mL $\rightarrow$ L then $V, m \rightarrow d$

$$\text{K} = °C + 273.15 \quad \frac{1 \text{ atm}}{760 \text{ mmHg}} \quad \frac{1 \text{ L}}{1000 \text{ mL}} \qquad d = \frac{m}{V}$$

then $d, P, T, \rightarrow \mathcal{M}$ then $\% \text{ C}, \% \text{ H}, \mathcal{M} \rightarrow$ **formula**

$$d = \frac{P\mathcal{M}}{RT} \qquad \#C = \frac{\mathcal{M} \, 0.8266 \text{ g C}}{12.01 \dfrac{\text{g C}}{\text{mol C}}} \quad \#H = \frac{\mathcal{M} \, 0.1734 \text{ g H}}{1.008 \dfrac{\text{g H}}{\text{mol H}}}$$

Solution: $T = 25 °C + 273.15 = 298 \text{ K}, \quad P = 556 \text{ mmHg} \times \dfrac{1 \text{ atm}}{760 \text{ mmHg}} = 0.731579 \text{ atm},$

$V = 158 \text{ mL} \times \dfrac{1 \text{ L}}{1000 \text{ mL}} = 0.158 \text{ L}, d = \dfrac{m}{V} = \dfrac{0.275 \text{ g}}{0.158 \text{ L}} = 1.74051 \text{ g/L}, d = \dfrac{P\mathcal{M}}{RT}$ Rearrange to solve for $\mathcal{M}$.

$\mathcal{M} = \dfrac{dRT}{P} = \dfrac{1.74051 \dfrac{\text{g}}{\text{L}} \times 0.08206 \dfrac{\text{L} \cdot \text{atm}}{\text{K} \cdot \text{mol}} \times 298 \text{ K}}{0.731579 \text{ atm}} = 58.2 \text{ g/mol},$

$$\#C = \frac{\mathcal{M} \times 0.8266 \text{ g C}}{12.01 \frac{\text{g C}}{\text{mol C}}} = \frac{58.2 \frac{\text{g HC}}{\text{mol HC}} \times \frac{0.8266 \text{ g C}}{1 \text{ g HC}}}{12.01 \frac{\text{g C}}{\text{mol C}}} = 4.00 \frac{\text{mol C}}{\text{mol HC}}$$

$$\#H = \frac{\mathcal{M} \times 0.1734 \text{ g H}}{1.0008 \frac{\text{g H}}{\text{mol H}}} = \frac{58.2 \frac{\text{g HC}}{\text{mol HC}} \times \frac{0.1734 \text{ g H}}{1 \text{ g HC}}}{1.008 \frac{\text{g H}}{\text{mol H}}} = 10.0 \frac{\text{mol H}}{\text{mol HC}} \quad \text{Formula is } C_4H_{10} \text{ or butane.}$$

Check: The answer came up with integer number of C and H atoms in the formula and a molecular weight (58 g/mol) that is reasonable for a gas.

5.71   **Given:** m (NiO) = 24.78 g, T = 40.0 °C, and P_{Total} = 745 mmHg   **Find:** V_{O_2}
Conceptual Plan: $T \rightarrow P_{H_2O}$ then $P_{Total}, P_{H_2O} \rightarrow P_{O_2}$ then mmHg $\rightarrow$ atm and °C $\rightarrow$ K

$$\text{Table 5.3} \qquad P_{Total} = P_{H_2O} + P_{O_2} \qquad \frac{1 \text{ atm}}{760 \text{ mmHg}} \qquad K = °C + 273.15$$

and $g_{NiO} \rightarrow n_{NiO} \rightarrow n_{O_2}$ then $P, V, T \rightarrow n_{O_2}$

$$\frac{1 \text{ mol NiO}}{74.69 \text{ g NiO}} \quad \frac{1 \text{ mol } O_2}{2 \text{ mol NiO}} \qquad PV = nRT$$

Solution: Table 5.3 states that P_{H_2O} = 55.40 mmHg at 40 °C $P_{Total} = P_{H_2O} + P_{O_2}$ Rearrange to solve for P_{O_2}.
$P_{O_2} = P_{Total} - P_{H_2O}$ = 745 mmHg − 55.40 mmHg = 689.6 mmHg

$$P_{O_2} = 689.6 \text{ mmHg} \times \frac{1 \text{ atm}}{760 \text{ mmHg}} = 0.907368 \text{ atm} \quad T = 40.0 °C + 273.15 = 313.2 \text{ K},$$

$$24.78 \text{ g NiO} \times \frac{1 \text{ mol NiO}}{74.69 \text{ mol NiO}} \times \frac{1 \text{ mol } O_2}{2 \text{ mol NiO}} = 0.1658857 \text{ mol } O_2 \quad PV = nRT$$

Rearrange to solve for V. $V_{O_2} = \dfrac{nRT}{P} = \dfrac{0.1658857 \text{ mol} \times 0.08206 \frac{\text{L} \cdot \text{atm}}{\text{mol} \cdot \text{K}} \times 313.2 \text{ K}}{0.907368 \text{ atm}} = 4.70 \text{ L}$

Check: The units (L) are correct. The magnitude of the answer (5 L) makes sense because we have much less than 0.5 mole of NiO, so we get less than a mole of oxygen. Thus, we expect a volume much less than 22 L.

5.73   **Given:** HCl, K_2S to H_2S, V_{H_2S} = 42.9 mL, P_{H_2S} = 752 mmHg, and T = 25.8 °C   **Find:** $m(K_2S)$
Conceptual Plan: read description of reaction and convert words to equation then °C $\rightarrow$ K

$$K = °C + 273.15$$

and mmHg $\rightarrow$ atm **and** mL $\rightarrow$ L then $P, V, T \rightarrow n_{H_2S} \rightarrow n_{K_2S} \rightarrow m_{K_2S}$

$$\frac{1 \text{ atm}}{760 \text{ mmHg}} \qquad \frac{1 \text{ L}}{1000 \text{ mL}} \qquad PV = nRT \quad \frac{1 \text{ mol } K_2S}{1 \text{ mol } H_2S} \quad \frac{1 \text{ mol } K_2S}{110.27 \text{ g } K_2S}$$

Solution: $2 \text{ HCl}(aq) + K_2S(s) \rightarrow H_2S(g) + 2 \text{ KCl}(aq)$

$$T = 25.8 °C + 273.15 = 299.0 \text{ K}, P_{H_2S} = 752 \text{ mmHg} \times \frac{1 \text{ atm}}{760 \text{ mmHg}} = 0.989474 \text{ atm},$$

$$V_{H_2S} = 42.9 \text{ mL} \times \frac{1 \text{ L}}{1000 \text{ mL}} = 0.0429 \text{ L} \quad PV = nRT \text{ Rearrange to solve for } n_{H_2S}.$$

$$n_{H_2S} = \frac{PV}{RT} = \frac{0.989474 \text{ atm} \times 0.0429 \text{ L}}{0.08206 \frac{\text{L} \cdot \text{atm}}{\text{mol} \cdot \text{K}} \times 299.0 \text{ K}} = 0.00173005 \text{ mol}$$

$$0.00173005 \text{ mol } H_2S \times \frac{1 \text{ mol } K_2S}{1 \text{ mol } H_2S} \times \frac{110.27 \text{ g } K_2S}{1 \text{ mol } K_2S} = 0.191 \text{ g } K_2S$$

Check: The units (g) are correct. The magnitude of the answer (0.2 g) makes sense because we have such a small volume of gas generated.

5.75   **Given:** $T = 22\,°C$, $P = 1.02$ atm, and $m = 11.83$ g   **Find:** V_{Total}
        Conceptual Plan: $°C \rightarrow K$ and $g_{(NH_4)_2CO_3} \rightarrow n_{(NH_4)_2CO_3} \rightarrow n_{Gas}$ then $p, n, T \rightarrow V$

$$K = °C + 273.15 \qquad \frac{1\ \text{mol (NH}_4)_2\text{CO}_3}{96.09\ \text{g(NH}_4)_2\text{CO}_3} \quad \frac{(2 + 1 + 1 = 4)\ \text{mol gas}}{1\ \text{mol (NH}_4)_2\text{CO}_3} \qquad PV = nRT$$

Solution: $T = 22\,°C + 273.15 = 295$ K

$$11.83\ \text{g (NH}_4)_2\text{CO}_3 \times \frac{1\ \text{mol (NH}_4)_2\text{CO}_3}{96.09\ \text{g (NH}_4)_2\text{CO}_3} \times \frac{4\ \text{mol gas}}{1\ \text{mol (NH}_4)_2\text{CO}_3} = 0.492455\ \text{mol gas}$$

$PV = nRT$ Rearrange to solve for V_{Gas}.

$$V_{Gas} = \frac{nRT}{P} = \frac{0.492455\ \text{mol gas} \times 0.08206\ \dfrac{\text{L} \cdot \text{atm}}{\text{mol} \cdot \text{K}} \times 295\ \text{K}}{1.02\ \text{atm}} = 11.7\ \text{L}$$

Check: The units (L) are correct. The magnitude of the answer (12 L) makes sense because we have about half a mole of gas generated.

5.77   **Given:** He and air; $V = 855$ mL, $P = 125$ psi, $T = 25\,°C$, $\mathcal{M}(\text{air}) = 28.8$ g/mol   **Find:** $\Delta = m(\text{air}) - m(\text{He})$
        Conceptual Plan: $\text{mL} \rightarrow \text{L}$ and $\text{psi} \rightarrow \text{atm}$ and $°C \rightarrow K$ then $P, T, \mathcal{M} \rightarrow d$

$$\frac{1\ \text{L}}{1000\ \text{mL}} \qquad \frac{1\ \text{atm}}{14.7\ \text{psi}} \qquad K = °C + 273.15 \qquad d = \frac{P\mathcal{M}}{RT}$$

then $d, V \rightarrow m$ **then** $m(\text{air}), m(\text{He}) \rightarrow \Delta$

$$d = \frac{m}{V} \qquad\qquad \Delta = m(\text{air}) - m(\text{He})$$

Solution: $V = 855\ \text{mL} \times \dfrac{1\ \text{L}}{1000\ \text{mL}} = 0.855\ \text{L}$, $P = 125\ \text{psi} \times \dfrac{1\ \text{atm}}{14.7\ \text{psi}} = 8.50340\ \text{atm}$,

$$T = 25\,°C + 273.15 = 298\ \text{K}, d_{\text{air}} = \frac{P\mathcal{M}}{RT} = \frac{8.50340\ \text{atm} \times 28.8\ \dfrac{\text{g air}}{\text{mol air}}}{0.08206\ \dfrac{\text{L} \cdot \text{atm}}{\text{K} \cdot \text{mol}} \times 298\ \text{K}} = 10.0147\ \frac{\text{g air}}{\text{L}}, d = \frac{m}{V}$$

Rearrange to solve for m. $m = dV$

$$m_{\text{air}} = 10.0147\ \frac{\text{g air}}{\text{L}} \times 0.855\ \text{L} = 8.56257\ \text{g air},$$

$$d_{\text{He}} = \frac{PM}{RT} = \frac{8.50340\ \text{atm} \times 4.03\ \dfrac{\text{g He}}{\text{mol He}}}{0.08206\ \dfrac{\text{L} \cdot \text{atm}}{\text{K} \cdot \text{mol}} \times 298\ \text{K}} = 1.40136\ \frac{\text{g He}}{\text{L}},$$

$$m_{\text{He}} = 1.40136\ \frac{\text{g He}}{\text{L}} \times 0.855\ \text{L} = 1.19816\ \text{g He},$$

$$\Delta = m(\text{air}) - m(\text{He}) = 8.56257\ \text{g air} - 1.19816\ \text{g He} = 7.36\ \text{g}$$

Check: The units (g) are correct. We expect the difference to be less than the difference in the molecular weights because we have less than a mole of gas.

5.79   **Given:** flow $= 335$ L/s, $P_{NO} = 22.4$ torr, $T_{NO} = 955$ K, $P_{NH_3} = 755$ torr, $T_{NO} = 298$ K, and NH_3 purity $= 65.2\%$
        Find: flow$_{NH_3}$
        Conceptual Plan: $\text{torr} \rightarrow \text{atm}$ then $P_{NO}, V_{NO}/s, T_{NO} \rightarrow n_{NO}/s \rightarrow n_{NH_3}/s$ (pure)

$$\frac{1\ \text{atm}}{760\ \text{torr}} \qquad\qquad PV = nRT \qquad \frac{4\ \text{mol NH}_3}{4\ \text{mol NO}}$$

then n_{NH_3}/s **(pure)** $\rightarrow n_{NH_3}/s$ **(impure) then** n_{NH_3}/s **(impure),** $P_{NH_3}, T_{NH_3} \rightarrow V_{NH_3}/s$

$$\frac{100\ \text{mol NH}_3\ \text{impure}}{65.2\ \text{mol NH}_3\ \text{pure}} \qquad\qquad\qquad\qquad PV = nRT$$

Solution: $P_{NO} = 22.4\ \text{torr} \times \dfrac{1\ \text{atm}}{760\ \text{torr}} = 0.0294737\ \text{atm}$, $P_{NH_3} = 755\ \text{torr} \times \dfrac{1\ \text{atm}}{760\ \text{torr}} = 0.993421\ \text{atm}$

$PV = nRT$ Rearrange to solve for n_{NO}. Note that we can substitute V/s for V and get n/s as a result.

$$\frac{n_{NO}}{s} = \frac{PV}{RT} = \frac{0.0294737 \text{ atm} \times 335 \text{ L/s}}{0.08206 \frac{\text{L} \cdot \text{atm}}{\text{mol} \cdot \text{K}} \times 955 \text{ K}} = 0.125992 \frac{\text{mol NO}}{s}$$

$$0.125992 \frac{\text{mol NO}}{s} \times \frac{4 \text{ mol NH}_3}{4 \text{ mol NO}} \times \frac{100 \text{ mol NH}_3 \text{ impure}}{65.2 \text{ mol NH}_3 \text{ pure}} = 0.193240 \frac{\text{mol NH}_3 \text{ impure}}{s} \qquad PV = nRT$$

Rearrange to solve for V_{NH_3}. Note that we can substitute n/s for n and get V/s as a result.

$$\frac{V_{NH_3}}{s} = \frac{nRT}{P} = \frac{0.193240 \frac{\text{mol NH}_3 \text{ impure}}{s} \times 0.08206 \times \frac{\text{L} \cdot \text{atm}}{\text{mol} \cdot \text{K}} \times 298 K}{0.993421 \text{ atm}} = 4.76 \frac{\text{L}}{s} \text{ impure NH}_3$$

Check: The units (L) are correct. The magnitude of the answer (5 L/s) makes sense because we expect it to be less than that for the NO. The NO is at a very low concentration and a high temperature. When this converts to a much higher pressure and lower temperature, it will go down significantly even though the ammonia is impure. From a practical standpoint, a low flow rate will make it economical.

5.81   **Given:** $l = 30.0$ cm, $w = 20.0$ cm, $h = 15.0$ cm, 14.7 psi   **Find:** Force (lb)
Conceptual Plan: $l, w, h \rightarrow$ **Surface Area, SA(cm^2)** $\rightarrow$ **Surface Area(in^2)** $\rightarrow$ **Force**

$$SA = 2(lh) + 2(wh) + 2(lw) \qquad \frac{(1 \text{ in})^2}{(2.54 \text{ cm})^2} \qquad \frac{14.7 \text{ lb}}{1 \text{ in}^2}$$

Solution: $SA = 2(lh) + 2(wh) + 2(lw) = 2(30.0 \text{ cm} \times 15.0 \text{ cm}) + 2(20.0 \text{ cm} \times 15.0 \text{ cm}) + 2(30.0 \text{ cm} \times 20.0 \text{ cm}) = 2700 \text{ cm}^2$

$$2700 \text{ cm}^2 \times \frac{(1 \text{ in})^2}{(2.54 \text{ cm})^2} = 418.50 \text{ in}^2, \quad 418.50 \text{ in}^2 \times \frac{14.7 \text{ lb}}{1 \text{ in}^2} = 6150 \text{ lb}. \text{ The can would be crushed.}$$

Check: The units (lb) are correct. The magnitude of the answer (6150 lb) is not unreasonable because there is a large surface area.

5.83   **Given:** $V_1 = 160.0$ L, $P_1 = 1855$ psi, 3.5 L/balloon, $P_2 = 1.0$ atm $= 14.7$ psi, and $T = 298$ K   **Find:** # balloons
Conceptual Plan: $V_1, P_1, P_2 \rightarrow V_2$ **then** L $\rightarrow$ # **balloons**

$$P_1 V_1 = P_2 V_2 \qquad \frac{1 \text{ balloon}}{3.5 \text{ L}}$$

Solution: $P_1 V_1 = P_2 V_2$ Rearrange to solve for V_2. $V_2 = \frac{P_1}{P_2} V_1 = \frac{1855 \text{ psi}}{14.7 \text{ psi}} \times 160.0 \text{ L} = 20190.5 \text{ L},$

$$20190.5 \text{ L} \times \frac{1 \text{ balloon}}{3.5 \text{ L}} = 5800 \text{ balloons}$$

Check: The units (balloons) are correct. The magnitude of the answer (5800) is reasonable because a store does not want to buy a new helium tank very often.

5.85   **Given:** $r_1 = 2.5$ cm, $P_1 = 4.00$ atm, $T = 298$ K, and $P_2 = 1.00$ atm   **Find:** r_2
Conceptual Plan: $r_1 \rightarrow V_1$ **and** $V_1, P_1, P_2 \rightarrow V_2$ **then** $V_2 \rightarrow r_2$

$$V = \frac{4}{3}\pi r^3 \qquad P_1 V_1 = P_2 V_2 \qquad V = \frac{4}{3}\pi r^3$$

Solution: $V = \frac{4}{3}\pi r^3 = \frac{4}{3} \times \pi \times (2.5 \text{ cm})^3 = 65.450 \text{ cm}^3$ $P_1 V_1 = P_2 V_2$ Rearrange to solve for V_2.

$$V_2 = \frac{P_1}{P_2} V_1 = \frac{4.00 \text{ atm}}{1.00 \text{ atm}} \times 65.450 \text{ cm}^3 = 261.80 \text{ cm}^3, \quad V = \frac{4}{3}\pi r^3$$

Rearrange to solve for r. $r = \sqrt[3]{\frac{3V}{4\pi}} = \sqrt[3]{\frac{3 \times 261.80 \text{ cm}^3}{4 \times \pi}} = 4.0 \text{ cm}$

Check: The units (cm) are correct. The magnitude of the answer (4 cm) is reasonable because the bubble will expand as the pressure is decreased.

5.87   **Given:** 2.0 mol CO: 1.0 mol O_2, $V = 2.45$ L, $P_1 = 745$ torr, $P_2 = 552$ torr, and $T = 552$ °C   **Find:** %reacted
Conceptual Plan: From $PV = nRT$, **we know that** $P \propto n$; **looking at the chemical reaction, we see that** $2 + 1 = 3$ **moles of gas gets converted to 2 moles of gas. If all of the gas reacts,** $P_2 = 2/3\ P_1$. **Calculate** $-\Delta P$ **for 100% reacted and for actual case. Then calculate % reacted.**

$$-\Delta P_{100\% \text{ reacted}} = P_1 - \frac{2}{3}P_1 \qquad -\Delta P_{\text{actual}} = P_1 - P_2 \qquad \%\text{reacted} = \frac{\Delta P_{\text{actual}}}{\Delta P_{100\% \text{ reacted}}} \times 100\%$$

Solution: $-\Delta P_{100\% \text{ reacted}} = P_1 - \frac{2}{3}P_1 = 745 \text{ torr} - \frac{2}{3} 745 \text{ torr} = 248.333 \text{ torr}$,

$-\Delta P_{\text{actual}} = P_1 - P_2 = 745 \text{ torr} - 552 \text{ torr} = 193 \text{ torr}$,

$\%\text{reacted} = \dfrac{\Delta P_{\text{actual}}}{\Delta P_{100\% \text{ reacted}}} \times 100\% = \dfrac{193 \text{ torr}}{248.333 \text{ torr} \times 100\%} = 77.7\%$

Check: The units (%) are correct. The magnitude of the answer (78%) makes sense because the pressure would have dropped to 2/3(745 torr) = 497 torr if all of the reactants had reacted. **Note: There are many ways to solve this problem, including calculating the moles of reactants and products using $PV = nRT$.**

5.89   **Given:**

$P(\text{Total})_1 = 2.2 \text{ atm} = P(\text{CO}) + P(O_2)$, $P(\text{Total})_2 = 1.9 \text{ atm} = P(\text{CO}) + P(O_2) + P(CO_2)$, $V = 1.0 \text{ L}$, and $T = 1.0 \times 10^3 \text{ K}$
Find: mass CO_2 made
Conceptual Plan: $P(\text{Total})_1 = 2.2 \text{ atm} = P(\text{CO})_1 + P(O_2)_1$, $P(\text{Total})_2 = 1.9 \text{ atm} = P(\text{CO})_2 + P(O_2)_2 + P(CO_2)_2$. **Let** $x = $ **amount of** $P(O_2)$ **reacted. From stoichiometry:** $P(\text{CO})_2 = P(\text{CO})_1 - 2x$, $P(O_2)_2 = P(O_2)_1 - x$, $P(CO_2)_2 = 2x$. **Thus,** $P(\text{Total})_2 = 1.9 \text{ atm} = P(\text{CO})_1 - 2x + P(O_2)_1 - x + 2x = P(\text{Total})_1 - x$. **Using the initial conditions:** $1.9 \text{ atm} = 2.2 \text{ atm} - x$. **So** $x = 0.3 \text{ atm}$, **and because** $2x = P(CO_2)_2 = 0.6 \text{ atm}$, **then** $P, V, T \rightarrow n \rightarrow \textbf{g}$.

$$PV = nRT \quad \frac{44.01 \text{ g}}{1 \text{ mol}}$$

Solution: $PV = nRT$ Rearrange to solve for n.

$n = \dfrac{PV}{RT} = \dfrac{0.6 \text{ atm} \times 1.0 \text{ L}}{0.08206 \dfrac{\text{L} \cdot \text{atm}}{\text{mol} \cdot \text{K}} \times 1000 \text{ K}} = 0.0073117 \text{ mol}$

$0.0073117 \text{ mol} \times \dfrac{44.01 \text{ g}}{1 \text{ mol}} = 0.321788 \text{ g } CO_2 = 0.3 \text{ g } CO_2$

Check: The units (g) are correct. The magnitude of the answer (0.3 g) makes sense because we have such a small volume at a very high temperature and such a small pressure. This leads us to expect a very small number of moles.

5.91   **Given:** $h_1 = 22.6 \text{ m}$, $T_1 = 22 \,°\text{C}$, and $h_2 = 23.8 \text{ m}$ **Find:** T_2
Conceptual Plan: $°\text{C} \rightarrow \text{K}$ **because** $V_{\text{cylinder}} \propto h$ **we do not need to know** r **to use** $V_1, T_1, T_2 \rightarrow V_2$

$$\text{K} = °\text{C} + 273.15 \qquad\qquad V = \pi r^2 h \qquad\qquad \frac{V_1}{T_1} = \frac{V_2}{T_2}$$

Solution: $T_1 = 22 \,°\text{C} + 273.15 = 295 \text{ K}$, $\dfrac{V_1}{T_1} = \dfrac{V_2}{T_2}$ Rearrange to solve for T_2.

$T_2 = T_1 \times \dfrac{V_2}{V_1} = T_1 \times \dfrac{\pi r^2 h_2}{\pi r^2 h_1} = 295 \text{ K} \times \dfrac{23.8 \text{ m}}{22.6 \text{ m}} = 311 \text{ K}$

Check: The units (K) are correct. We expect the temperature to increase because the volume increased.

5.93   **Given:** He, $V = 0.35 \text{ L}$, $P_{\text{max}} = 88 \text{ atm}$, and $T = 299 \text{ K}$ **Find:** m_{He}
Conceptual Plan: $P, V, T \rightarrow n$ **then** $\text{mol} \rightarrow \textbf{g}$

$$P V = nRT \qquad\qquad \mathcal{M}$$

Solution: $PV = nRT$ Rearrange to solve for n.

$n_{\text{He}} = \dfrac{PV}{RT} = \dfrac{88 \text{ atm} \times 0.35 \text{ L}}{0.08206 \dfrac{\text{L} \cdot \text{atm}}{\text{mol} \cdot \text{K}} \times 299 \text{ K}} = 1.2553 \text{ mol}$, $1.2553 \text{ mol} \times \dfrac{4.003 \text{ g}}{1 \text{ mol}} = 5.0 \text{ g He}$

Check: The units (g) are correct. The magnitude of the answer (5 g) makes sense because the high pressure and the low volume cancel out (remember 22 L/mol at STP). So we expect ~1 mol and so ~4 g.

5.95   **Given:** 15.0 mL HBr in 1.0 min and 20.3 mL unknown hydrocarbon gas in 1.0 min
Find: formula of unknown gas
Conceptual Plan: Because these gases are under the same conditions, $V \propto n$, V, time $\rightarrow$ Rate then

$$\text{Rate} = \frac{V}{\text{time}}$$

$\mathcal{M}$(HBr), Rate (HBr), Rate (Unk) $\rightarrow$ $\mathcal{M}$(Unk)

$$\frac{\text{Rate (HBr)}}{\text{Rate (U)}} = \sqrt{\frac{\mathcal{M}(\text{U})}{\mathcal{M}(\text{HBr})}}$$

Solution: Rate (HBr) $= \dfrac{V}{\text{time}} = \dfrac{15.0 \text{ mL}}{1.0 \text{ min}} = 15.0 \dfrac{\text{mL}}{\text{min}}$, Rate(Unk) $= \dfrac{V}{\text{time}} = \dfrac{20.3 \text{ mL}}{1.0 \text{ min}} = 20.3 \dfrac{\text{mL}}{\text{min}}$,

$\dfrac{\text{Rate(HBr)}}{\text{Rate(Unk)}} = \sqrt{\dfrac{\mathcal{M}(\text{Unk})}{\mathcal{M}(\text{HBr})}}$ Rearrange to solve for $\mathcal{M}$(Unk).

$$\mathcal{M}(\text{Unk}) = \text{M(HBr)}\left(\frac{\text{Rate (HBr)}}{\text{Rate (Unk)}}\right)^2 = 80.91 \frac{\text{g}}{\text{mol}} \times \left(\frac{15.0 \frac{\text{mL}}{\text{min}}}{20.3 \frac{\text{mL}}{\text{min}}}\right)^2 = 44.2 \frac{\text{g}}{\text{mol}} \text{ The formula is } C_3H_8, \text{ or propane.}$$

Check: The units (g/mol) are correct. The magnitude of the answer (<HBr) makes sense because the unknown diffused faster and so must be lighter.

5.97　**Given:** 75.2% by mass nitrogen + 24.8% by mass krypton and $P_{\text{Total}} = 745$ mmHg　**Find:** P_{Kr}
Solution: Assume that 100 g total, so we have 75.2 g N_2 and 24.8 g Kr. Converting these masses to moles,

$$75.2 \text{ g } N_2 \times \frac{1 \text{ mol } N_2}{28.02 \text{ g } N_2} = 2.683797 \text{ mol } N_2 \text{ and } 24.8 \text{ g Kr} \times \frac{1 \text{ mol Kr}}{83.80 \text{ g Kr}} = 0.2959427 \text{ mol Kr}$$

$$P_{\text{Kr}} = \chi_{\text{Kr}}P_{\text{Total}} = \frac{0.2959427 \text{ mol Kr}}{2.683797 \text{ mol } N_2 + 0.2959427 \text{ mol Kr}} \times 745 \text{ mmHg Kr} = 74.0 \text{ mmHg Kr}$$

Check: The units (mmHg) are correct. The magnitude of the answer (74 mmHg) makes sense because the mixture is mostly nitrogen by mass and this dominance is magnified because the molar mass of krypton is larger than the molar mass of nitrogen.

Challenge Problems

5.99　**Given:** CH_4: $V = 155$ mL at STP; O_2: $V = 885$ mL at STP; NO: $V = 55.5$ mL at STP; mixed in a flask: $V = 2.0$ L, $T = 275$ K, and 90.0% of limiting reagent used.　**Find:** Ps of all components and P_{Total}
Conceptual Plan: CH_4: mL $\rightarrow$ L $\rightarrow$ mol_{CH_4} $\rightarrow$ mol_{CO_2} and

$$\frac{1 \text{ L}}{1000 \text{ mL}} \quad \frac{1 \text{ mol}}{22.414 \text{ L}} \quad \frac{1 \text{ mol } CO_2}{1 \text{ mol } CH_4}$$

O_2: mL $\rightarrow$ L $\rightarrow$ mol_{O_2} $\rightarrow$ mol_{CO_2} and NO: mL $\rightarrow$ L $\rightarrow$ mol_{NO} $\rightarrow$ mol_{CO_2}

$$\frac{1 \text{ L}}{1000 \text{ mL}} \quad \frac{1 \text{ mol}}{22.414 \text{ L}} \quad \frac{1 \text{ mol } CO_2}{5 \text{ mol } O_2} \quad \frac{1 \text{ L}}{1000 \text{ mL}} \quad \frac{1 \text{ mol}}{22.414 \text{ L}} \quad \frac{1 \text{ mol } CO_2}{5 \text{ mol NO}}$$

the smallest yield determines the limiting reagent then initial mol_{NO} $\rightarrow$ reacted mol_{NO} $\rightarrow$ final mol_{NO}

NO is the limiting reagent　　90.0%　　0.100 $\times$ initial mol_{NO}

reacted mol_{NO} $\rightarrow$ reacted mol_{CH_4} then initial mol_{CH_4}, reacted mol_{CH_4} $\rightarrow$ final mol_{CH_4} then

$$\frac{1 \text{ mol } CH_4}{5 \text{ mol NO}} \qquad\qquad \text{initial } \text{mol}_{CH_4} - \text{ reacted } \text{mol}_{CH_4} = \text{final } \text{mol}_{CH_4}$$

final mol_{CH_4}, V, T $\rightarrow$ final P_{CH_4} and reacted mol_{NO} $\rightarrow$ reacted mol_{O_2} then

$$PV = nRT \qquad\qquad \frac{5 \text{ mol } O_2}{5 \text{ mol NO}}$$

initial mol_{O_2}, reacted mol_{O_2} $\rightarrow$ final mol_{O_2} then final mol_{O_2} V, T $\rightarrow$ final P_{O_2} and

$$\text{initial } \text{mol}_{O_2} - \text{ reacted } \text{mol}_{O_2} = \text{final } \text{mol}_{O_2} \qquad\qquad PV = nRT$$

final mol_{NO}, V, T $\rightarrow$ final P_{NO} and theoretical mol_{CO_2} from NO $\rightarrow$ final mol_{CO_2}

$$PV = nRT \qquad\qquad 90.0\%$$

final mol_{CO_2}, V, T $\rightarrow$ P_{CO_2} then final mol_{CO_2} $\rightarrow$ mol_{H_2O}, V, T $\rightarrow$ P_{H_2O} and

$$PV = nRT \qquad\qquad \frac{1 \text{ mol } H_2O}{1 \text{ mol } CO_2} \qquad\qquad PV = nRT$$

final mol_{CO_2} $\rightarrow$ mol_{NO_2} then mol_{NO_2}, V, T $\rightarrow$ P_{NO_2} and final mol_{CO_2} $\rightarrow$ mol_{OH} then

$$\frac{1 \text{ mol } NO_2}{1 \text{ mol } CO_2} \qquad\qquad PV = nRT \qquad\qquad \frac{2 \text{ mol OH}}{1 \text{ mol } CO_2}$$

mol_{OH}, V, T $\rightarrow$ P_{OH} finaly $P_{CH_4}, P_{O_2}, P_{NO}, P_{CO_2}, P_{H_2O}, P_{NO_2}, P_{OH} \rightarrow P_{\text{Total}}$

$$PV = nRT \qquad\qquad P_{\text{Total}} = \sum P$$

Solution: CH_4: $155 \text{ mL} \times \dfrac{1 \text{ L}}{1000 \text{ mL}} \times \dfrac{1 \text{ mol } CH_4}{22.414 \text{ L}} \times \dfrac{1 \text{ mol } CO_2}{1 \text{ mol } CH_4} = 0.00691532 \text{ mol } CO_2$,

O_2: $885 \text{ mL} \times \dfrac{1 \text{ L}}{1000 \text{ mL}} \times \dfrac{1 \text{ mol } O_2}{22.414 \text{ L}} = 0.0394843 \text{ mol } O_2 \times \dfrac{1 \text{ mol } CO_2}{5 \text{ mol } O_2} = 0.00789686 \text{ mol } CO_2$

NO: $55.5 \text{ mL} \times \dfrac{1 \text{ L}}{1000 \text{ mL}} \times \dfrac{1 \text{ mol } NO}{22.414 \text{ L}} \times \dfrac{1 \text{ mol } CO_2}{5 \text{ mol } NO} = 0.000495226 \text{ mol } CO_2$.

$0.000495226 \text{ mol } CO_2$ is the smallest yield, so NO is the limiting reagent.

$55.5 \text{ mL} \times \dfrac{1 \text{ L}}{1000 \text{ mL}} \times \dfrac{1 \text{ mol } NO}{22.414 \text{ L}} = 0.00247613 \text{ mol } NO$

reacted mol NO $= 0.900 \times$ mol NO $= 0.900 \times 0.00247613$ mol NO $= 0.00222852$ mol NO,

unreacted mol NO $= 0.100 \times$ mol NO $= 0.100 \times 0.00247613$ mol NO $= 0.000247613$ mol NO,

$0.00222852 \text{ mol } NO \times \dfrac{1 \text{ mol } CH_4}{5 \text{ mol } NO} = 0.000445704 \text{ mol } CH_4$ reacted,

$0.00691532 \text{ mol } CH_4 - 0.000445704 \text{ mol } CH_4$ reacted $= 0.00646962 \text{ mol } CH_4$ then $PV = nRT$

Rearrange to solve for P. $P = \dfrac{nRT}{V} = \dfrac{0.00646962 \text{ mol} \times 0.08206 \dfrac{\text{L} \cdot \text{atm}}{\text{mol} \cdot \text{K}} \times 275 \text{ K}}{2.0 \text{ L}} = 0.0730 \text{ atm } CH_4$ remaining

$0.00222852 \text{ mol } NO \times \dfrac{5 \text{ mol } O_2}{5 \text{ mol } NO} = 0.00222852 \text{ mol } O_2$ reacted

$0.0394843 \text{ mol } O_2 - 0.00222852 \text{ mol } O_2$ reacted $= 0.0372558 \text{ mol } O_2$

$P = \dfrac{nRT}{V} = \dfrac{0.0372558 \text{ mol} \times 0.08206 \dfrac{\text{L} \cdot \text{atm}}{\text{mol} \cdot \text{K}} \times 275 \text{ K}}{2.0 \text{ L}} = 0.420 \text{ atm } O_2$ remaining

$P = \dfrac{nRT}{V} = \dfrac{0.000247613 \text{ mol} \times 0.08206 \dfrac{\text{L} \cdot \text{atm}}{\text{mol} \cdot \text{K}} \times 275 \text{ K}}{2.0 \text{ L}} = 0.00279 \text{ atm } NO$ remaining

$0.00222852 \text{ mol } NO \times \dfrac{1 \text{ mol } CO_2}{5 \text{ mol } NO} = 0.000445704 \text{ mol } CO_2$

$P = \dfrac{nRT}{V} = \dfrac{0.000445704 \text{ mol} \times 0.08206 \dfrac{\text{L} \cdot \text{atm}}{\text{mol} \cdot \text{K}} \times 275 \text{ K}}{2.0 \text{ L}} = 0.00503 \text{ atm } CO_2$ produced

$0.00222852 \text{ mol } NO \times \dfrac{1 \text{ mol } H_2O}{5 \text{ mol } NO} = 0.000445704 \text{ mol } H_2O$

$P = \dfrac{nRT}{V} = \dfrac{0.000445704 \text{ mol} \times 0.08206 \dfrac{\text{L} \cdot \text{atm}}{\text{mol} \cdot \text{K}} \times 275 \text{ K}}{2.0 \text{ L}} = 0.00503 \text{ atm } H_2O$ produced

$0.00222852 \text{ mol } NO \times \dfrac{5 \text{ mol } NO_2}{5 \text{ mol } NO} = 0.00222852 \text{ mol } NO_2$

$P = \dfrac{nRT}{V} = \dfrac{0.00222852 \text{ mol} \times 0.08206 \dfrac{\text{L} \cdot \text{atm}}{\text{mol} \cdot \text{K}} \times 275 \text{ K}}{2.0 \text{ L}} = 0.0251 \text{ atm } NO_2$ produced

$0.00222852 \text{ mol } NO \times \dfrac{2 \text{ mol } OH}{5 \text{ mol } NO} = 0.000891408 \text{ mol } OH$

$P = \dfrac{nRT}{V} = \dfrac{0.000891408 \text{ mol} \times 0.08206 \dfrac{\text{L} \cdot \text{atm}}{\text{mol} \cdot \text{K}} \times 275 \text{ K}}{2.0 \text{ L}} = 0.0101 \text{ atm } OH$ produced

$$P_{Total} = \sum P$$
$$= 0.0730 \text{ atm} + 0.420 \text{ atm} + 0.00279 \text{ atm} + 0.00503 \text{ atm} + 0.00503 \text{ atm} + 0.0251 \text{ atm} + 0.0101 \text{ atm}$$
$$= 0.541 \text{ atm}$$

Check: The units (atm) are correct. The magnitude of the answers is reasonable. The limiting reagent has the lowest pressure. The product pressures are in line with the ratios of the stoichiometric coefficients.

5.101   **Given:** $P_{CH_4} + P_{C_2H_4} = 0.53$ atm and $P_{CO_2} + P_{H_2O} = 2.2$ atm   **Find:** χ_{CH_4}

Conceptual Plan: Write balanced reactions to determine change in moles of gas for CH₄ and C₂H₆.

$$2 \text{ CH}_4(g) + 4 \text{ O}_2(g) \rightarrow 4 \text{ H}_2\text{O}(g) + 2 \text{ CO}_2(g) \text{ and } 2 \text{ C}_2\text{H}_6(g) + 7 \text{ O}_2(g) \rightarrow 6 \text{ H}_2\text{O}(g) + 4 \text{ CO}_2(g) \text{ thus } \quad \frac{6 \text{ mol gases}}{2 \text{ mol CH}_4} \quad \frac{10 \text{ mol gases}}{2 \text{ mol C}_2\text{H}_6}$$

Write expression for final pressure, substituting in data given → χ_{CH_4}.

$$\chi_{CH_4} = \frac{n_{CH_4}}{n_{CH_4} + n_{C_2H_6}} \text{ and } \chi_{C_2H_6} = 1 - \chi_{CH_4}$$

$$P_{CH_4} = \chi_{CH_4} P_{Total} \qquad P_{C_2H_6} = \chi_{C_2H_6} P_{Total} \qquad P_{Final} = \left(\chi_{CH_4} P_{Total} \times \frac{6 \text{ mol gases}}{2 \text{ mol CH}_4} \right) + \left((1 - \chi_{CH_4}) P_{Total} \times \frac{10 \text{ mol gases}}{2 \text{ mol C}_2\text{H}_6} \right)$$

Solution:

$$P_{Final} = \left(\chi_{CH_4} \times 0.53 \text{ atm} \times \frac{6 \text{ mol gases}}{2 \text{ mol CH}_4} \right) + \left((1 - \chi_{CH_4}) \times 0.53 \text{ atm} \times \frac{10 \text{ mol gases}}{2 \text{ mol C}_2\text{H}_6} \right) = 2.2 \text{ atm}$$

Substitute as above for $\chi_{C_2H_6}$, then to solve for $\chi_{CH_4} = 0.42$.

Check: The units (none) are correct. The magnitude of the answer (0.42) makes sense because if it were all methane, the final pressure would have been 1.59 atm and if it were all ethane, the final pressure would have been 2.65 atm. Because we are closer to the latter pressure, we expect the mole fraction of methane to be less than 0.5.

5.103   **Given:** $V = 10$ L, 0.10 mol H_2 initially, $T = 3000$ K, and $P_{final} = 3.0$ atm   **Find:** P_H

Conceptual Plan: Write balanced reaction to determine change in moles of gas.

$$\text{H}_2(g) \rightarrow 2 \text{ H}(g) \text{ thus } \frac{2 \text{ mol H}}{1 \text{ mol H}_2 \text{ reacted}}. \text{ Since } P_{H_2} \, \alpha \, n_{H_2}, \text{ the pressure will increase 1 atm for every 1 atm of } H_2 \text{ that reacts.}$$

$$\textbf{\textit{n, T, V} → } P_{initial} \qquad P_{initial}, P_{final} → \Delta P \qquad \textbf{write expression for } P_H$$

$$PV = nRT \qquad\qquad \Delta P = P_{final} - P_{initial} \qquad P_H = \Delta P \frac{2 \text{ mol H}}{1 \text{ mol H}_2 \text{ reacted}}$$

Solution: $PV = nRT$ Rearrange to solve for P.

$$P = \frac{nRT}{V} = \frac{0.10 \text{ mol} \times 0.08206 \frac{L \cdot atm}{mol \cdot K} \times 3000 \text{ K}}{10 \text{ } L} = 2.4618 \text{ atm } H_2$$

$$\Delta P = P_{final} - P_{initial} = 3.0 \text{ atm} - 2.4618 \text{ atm} = 0.5382 \text{ atm and}$$

$$P_H = \Delta P \frac{2 \text{ mol H}}{1 \text{ atm reacted}} = 0.5382 \text{ atm} \times \frac{2 \text{ mol H}}{1 \text{ atm reacted}} = 1.0764 \text{ atm} = 1.1 \text{ atm H}$$

Check: The units (atm) are correct. The magnitude of the answer (1 atm) makes sense because if all of the hydrogen dissociated, the final pressure would have been 5 atm. Because we are closer to the initial pressure than this maximum pressure, less than half of the hydrogen has dissociated.

5.105   **Given:** CO gas; initial: $V = 0.48$ L, $P = 1.0$ atm, and $T = 275$ K; **final:** $V = 1.3$ L   **Find:** final gas density

Conceptual Plan: $P, V, T → n → m$ then $m, V → d$

$$P V = nRT \qquad \frac{28.01 \text{ g}}{1 \text{ mol}} \qquad\qquad d = m/V$$

Solution: $PV = nRT$ Rearrange to solve for n. $n = \dfrac{PV}{RT} = \dfrac{1.0 \text{ atm} \times 0.48 \text{ } L}{0.08206 \frac{L \cdot atm}{mol \cdot K} \times 275 \text{ K}} = 0.02127047 \text{ mol}$

$$0.02127047 \text{ mol} \times \frac{28.01 \text{ g}}{1 \text{ mol}} = 0.5957859 \text{ g then } d = \frac{m}{V} = \frac{0.5957859 \text{ g}}{1.3 \text{ L}} = 0.4582968 \text{ g/L} = 0.46 \text{ g/L}$$

Check: The units (g/L) are correct. The magnitude of the answer (0.5 g/L) makes sense because this is typical for a gas density.

Conceptual Problems

5.107   Because the passengers have more mass than the balloon, they have more momentum than the balloon. The passengers will continue to travel in their original direction longer. The car is slowing, so the relative position of the passengers is to move forward and the balloon to move backwards. The opposite happens upon acceleration.

5.109   Because each gas will occupy 22.4 L/mole at STP and we have 2 moles of gas, we will have a volume of 44.828 L.

5.111 Br_2 would deviate the most from ideal behavior because it is the largest of the three.

5.113   Because He has the lowest molar mass, it will have the most number of moles and the greatest volume.

Questions for Group Work

5.115   Boyle's law states that the volume of the gas varies inversely to the pressure on the gas, while temperature and number of moles are kept constant ($V \propto 1/P$ or $P_1V_1 = P_2V_2$). Charles's law states that the volume of a gas is directly proportional to the temperature of the gas, while pressure and number of moles are kept constant ($V \propto T$ or $V_1/T_1 = V_2/T_2$). All temperatures must be in degree Kelvin when used in math calculations. Avogadro's law states that the volume of a gas is directly proportional to the number of moles of the gas, while pressure and temperature are kept constant ($V \propto n$ or $V_1/n_1 = V_2/n_2$).

Boyle's law	**Charles's law**	**Avogadro's law**

5.117   (a) $2\,H_2O_2(aq) \rightarrow 2\,H_2O(l) + O_2(g)$

       (b)   Table 5.3 states that $P_{H_2O} = 23.78$ mmHg

       (c) $P_{Total} = P_{H_2O} + P_{O_2}$ Rearrange to solve for P_{O_2}.

            $P_{O_2} = P_{Total} - P_{H_2O} = 763.8$ mmHg $- 23.78$ mmHg $= 740.02$ mmHg

       (d) $P_{O_2} = 740.02 \text{ mmHg} \times \dfrac{1\text{ atm}}{760\text{ mmHg}} = 0.973710526$ atm; $V = 49.5 \text{ mL} \times \dfrac{1\text{ L}}{1000\text{ mL}} = 0.0495$ L;

            $T = 25.0\,°C + 273.15 = 298.15$ K.

            $n_{O_2} = \dfrac{PV}{RT} = \dfrac{0.973710526 \text{ atm} \times 0.0495\text{ L}}{0.08206\,\dfrac{\text{L} \cdot \text{atm}}{\text{mol} \cdot \text{K}} \times 298.15\text{ K}} = 0.00\,197001139$ mol O_2

       (e) $0.00197001139 \text{ mol } O_2 \times \dfrac{2 \text{ mol } H_2O_2}{1 \text{ mol } O_2} \times \dfrac{34.02 \text{ g } H_2O_2}{1 \text{ mol } H_2O_2} = 0.13402381$ g $H_2O_2 = 0.1340$ g H_2O_2

       (f) $5.00 \text{ mL} \times \dfrac{1\text{ L}}{1000\text{ mL}} = 0.0500$ L; $0.00197001139 \text{ mol } O_2 \times \dfrac{2 \text{ mol } H_2O_2}{1 \text{ mol } O_2} = 0.00394002278$ mol H_2O_2

            $[H_2O_2] = \dfrac{0.00394002278 \text{ mol } H_2O_2}{0.00500\text{ L}} = 0.788$ M H_2O_2

       (g)   Perhaps the most difficult part was keeping track of which volumes were liquids and which were gases.

5.119   For an ideal gas, $P = \dfrac{nRT}{V} = \dfrac{1.000 \text{ mol} \times 0.08206\,\dfrac{\text{L} \cdot \text{atm}}{\text{mol} \cdot \text{K}} \times 298\text{ K}}{0.500\text{ L}} = 48.90776$ atm

For van der Waals gas, $\left(P + \dfrac{an^2}{V^2} \right)(V - nb) = nRT$ Rearrange to solve for P.

$P = \dfrac{nRT}{(V - nb)} - \dfrac{an^2}{V^2}$ For He, $a = 0.0342$ L^2 atm/mol^2 and $b = 0.02370$ L/mol from Table 5.4:

$$P = \dfrac{1.000 \text{ mol} \times 0.08206 \dfrac{L \cdot atm}{mol \cdot K} \times 298 \text{ K}}{0.500 \text{ L} - \left(1.000 \text{ mol} \times 0.02370 \dfrac{L}{mol} \right)} - \dfrac{0.0342 \dfrac{L^2 \cdot atm}{mol^2} \times (1.000 \text{ mol})^2}{(0.500 \text{ L})^2} = 51.205 \text{ atm} = 51.2 \text{ atm}$$

The pressure is higher than the ideal gas because there are weak intermolecular forces and the atoms are small.
For Ne, $a = 0.211$ L^2 atm/mol^2 and $b = 0.0171$ L/mol from Table 5.4:

$$P = \dfrac{1.000 \text{ mol} \times 0.08206 \dfrac{L \cdot atm}{mol \cdot K} \times 298 \text{ K}}{0.500 \text{ L} - \left(1.000 \text{ mol} \times 0.0171 \dfrac{L}{mol} \right)} - \dfrac{0.211 \dfrac{L^2 \cdot atm}{mol^2} \times (1.000 \text{ mol})^2}{(0.500 \text{ L})^2} = 49.796 \text{ atm} = 49.8 \text{ atm}$$

The pressure is higher than the ideal gas because there are weak intermolecular forces and the atoms are small.
For H$_2$, $a = 0.244$ L^2 atm/mol^2 and $b = 0.0266$ L/mol from Table 5.4:

$$P = \dfrac{1.000 \text{ mol} \times 0.08206 \dfrac{L \cdot atm}{mol \cdot K} \times 298 \text{ K}}{0.500 \text{ L} - \left(1.000 \text{ mol} \times 0.0266 \dfrac{L}{mol} \right)} - \dfrac{0.244 \dfrac{L^2 \cdot atm}{mol^2} \times (1.000 \text{ mol})^2}{(0.500 \text{ L})^2} = 50.680 \text{ atm} = 50.7 \text{ atm}$$

The pressure is higher than the ideal gas because there are weak intermolecular forces and the atoms are small.
For CH$_4$, $a = 2.25$ L^2 atm/mol^2 and $b = 0.0428$ L/mol from Table 5.4:

$$P = \dfrac{1.000 \text{ mol} \times 0.08206 \dfrac{L \cdot atm}{mol \cdot K} \times 298 \text{ K}}{0.500 \text{ L} - \left(1.000 \text{ mol} \times 0.0428 \dfrac{L}{mol} \right)} - \dfrac{2.25 \dfrac{L^2 \cdot atm}{mol^2} \times (1.000 \text{ mol})^2}{(0.500 \text{ L})^2} = 44.486 \text{ atm} = 44.5 \text{ atm}$$

The pressure is lower than the ideal gas because there are stronger intermolecular forces and the atoms are larger.
For CO$_2$, $a = 3.59$ L^2 atm/mol^2 and $b = 0.0427$ L/mol from Table 5.4:

$$P = \dfrac{1.000 \text{ mol} \times 0.08206 \dfrac{L \cdot atm}{mol \cdot K} \times 298 \text{ K}}{0.500 \text{ L} - \left(1.000 \text{ mol} \times 0.0427 \dfrac{L}{mol} \right)} - \dfrac{3.59 \dfrac{L^2 \cdot atm}{mol^2} \times (1.000 \text{ mol})^2}{(0.500 \text{ L})^2} = 39.114 \text{ atm} = 39.1 \text{ atm}$$

The pressure is lower than the ideal gas because there are stronger intermolecular forces and the atoms are larger.

6 Thermochemistry

Energy Units

6.1   (a)   **Given:** 3.55×10^4 J   **Find:** cal

Conceptual Plan: $J \rightarrow cal$

$$\frac{1 \text{ cal}}{4.184 \text{ J}}$$

Solution: $3.55 \times 10^4 \text{ J} \times \dfrac{1 \text{ cal}}{4.184 \text{ J}} = 8.48 \times 10^3 \text{ cal}$

Check: The units (cal) are correct. The magnitude of the answer (8000) makes physical sense because a calorie is larger than a joule, so the answer decreases.

   (b)   **Given:** 1025 Cal   **Find:** J

Conceptual Plan: $Cal \rightarrow J$

$$\frac{4184 \text{ J}}{1 \text{ Cal}}$$

Solution: $1025 \text{ Cal} \times \dfrac{4184 \text{ J}}{1 \text{ Cal}} = 4.289 \times 10^6 \text{ J}$

Check: The units (J) are correct. The magnitude of the answer (10^6) makes physical sense because a Calorie is much larger than a joule, so the answer increases.

   (c)   **Given:** 355 kJ   **Find:** cal

Conceptual Plan: $kJ \rightarrow J \rightarrow cal$

$$\frac{1000 \text{ J}}{1 \text{ kJ}} \quad \frac{1 \text{ cal}}{4.184 \text{ J}}$$

Solution: $355 \text{ kJ} \times \dfrac{1000 \text{ J}}{1 \text{ kJ}} \times \dfrac{1 \text{ cal}}{4.184 \text{ J}} = 8.48 \times 10^4 \text{ cal}$

Check: The units (cal) are correct. The magnitude of the answer (10^4) makes physical sense because a calorie is much smaller than a kJ, so the answer increases.

   (d)   **Given:** 125 kWh   **Find:** J

Conceptual Plan: $kWh \rightarrow J$

$$\frac{3.60 \times 10^6 \text{ J}}{1 \text{ kWh}}$$

Solution: $125 \text{ kWh} \times \dfrac{3.60 \times 10^6 \text{ J}}{1 \text{ kWh}} = 4.50 \times 10^8 \text{ J}$

Check: The units (J) are correct. The magnitude of the answer (10^8) makes physical sense because a kWh is much larger than a joule, so the answer increases.

6.3   (a)   **Given:** 2285 Cal   **Find:** J

Conceptual Plan: $Cal \rightarrow J$

$$\frac{4184 \text{ J}}{1 \text{ Cal}}$$

Solution: $2285 \text{ Cal} \times \dfrac{4184 \text{ J}}{1 \text{ Cal}} = 9.560 \times 10^6 \text{ J}$

Check: The units (J) are correct. The magnitude of the answer (10^7) makes physical sense because a Calorie is much larger than a joule, so the answer increases.

(b)   **Given:** 2285 Cal   **Find:** kJ

Conceptual Plan: Cal → J → kWh

$$\frac{4184 \text{ J}}{1 \text{ Cal}} \quad \frac{1 \text{ kJ}}{1000 \text{ J}}$$

Solution: $2285 \cancel{\text{Cal}} \times \dfrac{4184 \cancel{\text{J}}}{1 \cancel{\text{Cal}}} \times \dfrac{1 \text{ kJ}}{1000 \cancel{\text{J}}} = 9.560 \times 10^3 \text{ kJ}$

Check: The units (kJ) are correct. The magnitude of the answer (10^4) makes physical sense because a Calorie is larger than a kJ, so the answer increases.

(c)   **Given:** 2285 Cal   **Find:** kWh

Conceptual Plan: Cal → J → kWh

$$\frac{4184 \text{ J}}{1 \text{ Cal}} \quad \frac{1 \text{ kWh}}{3.60 \times 10^6 \text{ J}}$$

Solution: $2285 \cancel{\text{Cal}} \times \dfrac{4184 \cancel{\text{J}}}{1 \cancel{\text{Cal}}} \times \dfrac{1 \text{ kWh}}{3.60 \times 10^6 \cancel{\text{J}}} = 2.656 \text{ kWh}$

Check: The units (kWh) are correct. The magnitude of the answer (3) makes physical sense because a Calorie is much smaller than a kWh, so the answer decreases.

Internal Energy, Heat, and Work

6.5   (d) $\Delta E_{sys} = -\Delta E_{surr}$ If energy change of the system is negative, energy is being transferred from the system to the surroundings, decreasing the energy of the system and increasing the energy of the surroundings. The amount of energy lost by the system must go somewhere, so the amount gained by the surroundings is equal and opposite to that lost by the system.

6.7   (a)   The energy exchange is primarily heat because the skin (part of the surroundings) is cooled. There is a small expansion (work) because water is being converted from a liquid to a gas. The sign of ΔE_{sys} is positive because the surroundings cool.

(b)   The energy exchange is primarily work. The sign of ΔE_{sys} is negative because the system is expanding (doing work on the surroundings).

(c)   The energy exchange is primarily heat. The sign of ΔE_{sys} is positive because the system is being heated by the flame.

6.9   **Given:** 625 kJ heat released; 105 kJ work done on surroundings   **Find:** ΔE_{sys}

Conceptual Plan: interpret language to determine the sign of the two terms then $q, w \rightarrow \Delta E_{sys}$

$$\Delta E = q + w$$

Solution: Because heat is released from the system to the surroundings, $q = -625$ kJ; because the system is doing work on the surroundings, $w = -105$ kJ. $\Delta E = q + w = -625 \text{ kJ} - 105 \text{ kJ} = -730 \text{ kJ} = -7.30 \times 10^2 \text{ kJ}$

Check: The units (kJ) are correct. The magnitude of the answer (-730) makes physical sense because both terms are negative.

6.11   **Given:** 655 J heat absorbed; 344 J work done on surroundings   **Find:** ΔE_{sys}

Conceptual Plan: interpret language to determine the sign of the two terms then $q, w \rightarrow \Delta E_{sys}$

$$\Delta E = q + w$$

Solution: Because heat is absorbed by the system, $q = +655$ J; because the system is doing work on the surroundings, $w = -344$ J. $\Delta E = q + w = 655 \text{ J} - 344 \text{ J} = 311 \text{ J}$.

Check: The units (J) are correct. The magnitude of the answer ($+300$) makes physical sense because the heat term dominates over the work term.

Heat, Heat Capacity, and Work

6.13   Cooler A had more ice after 3 hours because most of the ice in cooler B was melted to cool the soft drinks that started at room temperature. In cooler A, the drinks were already cold; so the ice only needed to maintain this cool temperature.

6.15 **Given:** 1.75 L water; $T_i = 25.0\,°C$; $T_f = 100.0\,°C$; $d = 1.0\,g/mL$ **Find:** q

Conceptual Plan: $L \rightarrow mL \rightarrow g$ and pull C_s from Table 6.4 and $T_i, T_f \rightarrow \Delta T$ then $m, C_s, \Delta T \rightarrow q$

$$\frac{1000\ mL}{1\ L} \qquad \frac{1.0\ g}{1.0\ mL} \qquad 4.18\ \frac{J}{g\cdot°C} \qquad \Delta T = T_f - T_i \qquad q = mC_s\Delta T$$

Solution: $1.75\ \cancel{L} \times \dfrac{1000\ \cancel{mL}}{1\ \cancel{L}} \times \dfrac{1.0\ g}{1.0\ \cancel{mL}} = 17\underline{5}0\ g$ and $\Delta T = T_f - T_i = 100.0\,°C - 25.0\,°C = 75.0\,°C$

then $q = mC_s\Delta T = 17\underline{5}0\ \cancel{g} \times 4.18\ \dfrac{J}{\cancel{g}\cdot\cancel{°C}} \times 75.0\,\cancel{°C} = 5.5 \times 10^5\ J$

Check: The units (J) are correct. The magnitude of the answer (10^6) makes physical sense because there are a large mass, a significant temperature change, and a high specific heat capacity material.

6.17 (a) **Given:** 25 g gold; $T_i = 27.0\,°C$; $q = 2.35\ kJ$ **Find:** T_f

Conceptual Plan: $kJ \rightarrow J$ and pull C_s from Table 6.4 then $m, C_s, q \rightarrow \Delta T$ then $T_i, \Delta T \rightarrow T_f$

$$\frac{1000\ J}{1\ kJ} \qquad 0.128\ \frac{J}{g\cdot°C} \qquad q = mC_s\Delta T \qquad \Delta T = T_f - T_i$$

Solution: $2.35\ \cancel{kJ} \times \dfrac{1000\ J}{1\ \cancel{kJ}} = 23\underline{5}0\ J$ then $q = mC_s\Delta T$. Rearrange to solve for ΔT.

$\Delta T = \dfrac{q}{mC_s} = \dfrac{23\underline{5}0\ J}{25\ \cancel{g} \times 0.128\ \dfrac{J}{\cancel{g}\cdot°C}} = 7\underline{3}4.375\,°C$ finally $\Delta T = T_f - T_i$. Rearrange to solve for T_f.

$T_f = \Delta T + T_i = 7\underline{3}4.375°C + 27.0\,°C = 760\,°C$

Check: The units (°C) are correct. The magnitude of the answer (760) makes physical sense because such a large amount of heat is absorbed and there are a small mass and specific heat capacity. The temperature change should be very large.

(b) **Given:** 25 g silver; $T_i = 27.0\,°C$; $q = 2.35\ kJ$ **Find:** T_f

Conceptual Plan: $kJ \rightarrow J$ and pull C_s from Table 6.4 then $m, C_s, q \rightarrow \Delta T$ then $T_i, \Delta T \rightarrow T_f$

$$\frac{1000\ J}{1\ kJ} \qquad 0.235\ \frac{J}{g\cdot°C} \qquad q = mC_s\Delta T \qquad \Delta T = T_f - T_i$$

Solution: $2.35\ \cancel{kJ} \times \dfrac{1000\ J}{1\ \cancel{kJ}} = 23\underline{5}0\ J$ then $q = mC_s\Delta T$. Rearrange to solve for ΔT.

$\Delta T = \dfrac{q}{mC_s} = \dfrac{23\underline{5}0\ J}{25\ \cancel{g} \times 0.235\ \dfrac{J}{\cancel{g}\cdot°C}} = 4\underline{0}0\,°C$ finally $\Delta T = T_f - T_i$. Rearrange to solve for T_f.

$T_f = \Delta T + T_i = 4\underline{0}0\,°C + 27.0\,°C = 430\,°C$

Check: The units (°C) are correct. The magnitude of the answer (430) makes physical sense because such a large amount of heat is absorbed and there are a small mass and specific heat capacity. The temperature change should be very large. The temperature change should be less than that of the gold because the specific heat capacity is greater.

(c) **Given:** 25 g aluminum; $T_i = 27.0\,°C$; $q = 2.35\ kJ$ **Find:** T_f

Conceptual Plan: $kJ \rightarrow J$ and pull C_s from Table 6.4 then $m, C_s, q \rightarrow \Delta T$ then $T_i, \Delta T \rightarrow T_f$

$$\frac{1000\ J}{1\ kJ} \qquad 0.903\ \frac{J}{g\cdot°C} \qquad q = mC_s\Delta T \qquad \Delta T = T_f - T_i$$

Solution: $2.35\ \cancel{kJ} \times \dfrac{1000\ J}{1\ \cancel{kJ}} = 23\underline{5}0\ J$ then $q = mC_s\Delta T$. Rearrange to solve for ΔT.

$\Delta T = \dfrac{q}{mC_s} = \dfrac{23\underline{5}0\ J}{25\ \cancel{g} \times 0.903\ \dfrac{J}{\cancel{g}\cdot°C}} = 1\underline{0}4.10\,°C$ finally $\Delta T = T_f - T_i$. Rearrange to solve for T_f.

$T_f = \Delta T + T_i = 1\underline{0}4.10\,°C + 27.0\,°C = 130\,°C$

Check: The units (°C) are correct. The magnitude of the answer (130) makes physical sense because such a large amount of heat is absorbed and there is such a small mass. The temperature change should be less than that of the silver because the specific heat capacity is greater.

(d)   **Given:** 25 g water; $T_i = 27.0\,°C$; $q = 2.35$ kJ   **Find:** T_f

Conceptual Plan: kJ $\rightarrow$ J and pull C_s from Table 6.4 then $m, C_s, q \rightarrow \Delta T$ then $T_i, \Delta T \rightarrow T_f$

$$\frac{1000\text{ J}}{1\text{ kJ}} \qquad 4.18\frac{\text{J}}{\text{g}\cdot°\text{C}} \qquad\qquad q = mC_s\Delta T \qquad \Delta T = T_f - T_i$$

Solution: $2.35\text{ kJ} \times \dfrac{1000\text{ J}}{1\text{ kJ}} = 23\underline{5}0$ J then $q = mC_s\Delta T$. Rearrange to solve for ΔT.

$$\Delta T = \frac{q}{mC_s} = \frac{23\underline{5}0\text{ J}}{25\text{ g} \times 4.18\dfrac{\text{J}}{\text{g}\cdot°\text{C}}} = 22.488\,°\text{C finally } \Delta T = T_f - T_i. \text{ Rearrange to solve for } T_f.$$

$$T_f = \Delta T + T_i = 22.488\,°\text{C} + 27.0\,°\text{C} = 49\,°\text{C}$$

Check: The units (°C) are correct. The magnitude of the answer (49) makes physical sense because such a large amount of heat is absorbed and there is such a small mass. The temperature change should be less than that of the aluminum because the specific heat capacity is greater.

6.19   **Given:** $V_i = 0.0$ L; $V_f = 2.5$ L; $P = 1.1$ atm   **Find:** w (J)

Conceptual Plan: $V_i, V_f \rightarrow \Delta V$ then $P, \Delta V \rightarrow w$ (L atm) $\rightarrow w$ (J)

$$\Delta V = V_f - V_i \qquad w = -P\Delta V \qquad \frac{101.3\text{ J}}{1\text{ L}\cdot\text{atm}}$$

Solution: $\Delta V = V_f - V_i = 2.5\text{ L} - 0.0\text{ L} = 2.5$ L then

$$w = -P\Delta V = -1.1\text{ atm} \times 2.5\text{ L} \times \frac{101.3\text{ J}}{1\text{ L}\cdot\text{atm}} = -2.8 \times 10^2 \text{ J}$$

Check: The units (J) are correct. The magnitude of the answer (-280) makes physical sense because this is an expansion (negative work) and we have $\sim$ atmospheric pressure and a small volume of expansion.

6.21   **Given:** $q = 565$ J absorbed; $V_i = 0.10$ L; $V_f = 0.85$ L; $P = 1.0$ atm   **Find:** ΔE_{sys}

Conceptual Plan: $V_i, V_f \rightarrow \Delta V$ and interpret language to determine the sign of the heat

$$\Delta V = V_f - V_i \qquad\qquad q = +565\text{ J}$$

then $P, \Delta V \rightarrow w$ (L atm) $\rightarrow w$ (J) finally $q, w \rightarrow \Delta E_{sys}$

$$w = -P\Delta V \qquad \frac{101.3\text{ J}}{1\text{ L}\cdot\text{atm}} \qquad \Delta E = q + w$$

Solution: $\Delta V = V_f - V_i = 0.85\text{ L} - 0.10\text{ L} = 0.75$ L then

$$w = -P\Delta V = -1.0\text{ atm} \times 0.75\text{ L} \times \frac{101.3\text{ J}}{1\text{ L}\cdot\text{atm}} = -7\underline{5}.975\text{ J} \quad \Delta E = q + w = +565\text{ J} - 7\underline{5}.975\text{ J} = 489\text{ J}$$

Check: The units (J) are correct. The magnitude of the answer (500) makes physical sense because the heat absorbed dominated the small expansion work (negative work).

Enthalpy and Thermochemical Stoichiometry

6.23   **Given:** 1 mol fuel, 3452 kJ heat produced; 11 kJ work done on surroundings   **Find:** ΔE_{sys}, ΔH

Conceptual Plan: interpret language to determine the sign of the two terms then $q \rightarrow \Delta H$ and $q, w \rightarrow \Delta E_{sys}$

$$\Delta H = q_p \qquad\qquad \Delta E = q + w$$

Solution: Because heat is produced by the system to the surroundings, $q = -3452$ kJ; because the system is doing work on the surroundings, $w = -11$ kJ. $\Delta H = q_p = -3452$ kJ and

$$\Delta E = q + w = -3452\text{ kJ} - 11\text{ kJ} = -3463\text{ kJ}.$$

Check: The units (kJ) are correct. The magnitude of the answer (-3500) makes physical sense because both terms are negative. We expect significant amounts of energy from fuels.

6.25   (a)   Combustion is an exothermic process; ΔH is negative.

(b)   Evaporation requires an input of energy, so it is endothermic; ΔH is positive.

(c)   Condensation is the reverse of evaporation, so it is exothermic; ΔH is negative.

6.27   **Given:** 177 mL acetone (C_3H_6O), $\Delta H°_{rxn} = -1658$ kJ; $d = 0.788$ g/mL   **Find:** q

Conceptual Plan: mL acetone $\rightarrow$ g acetone $\rightarrow$ mol acetone $\rightarrow q$

$$\frac{0.788\text{ g}}{1\text{ mL}} \qquad \frac{1\text{ mol}}{58.08\text{ g}} \qquad \frac{-1658\text{ kJ}}{1\text{ mol}}$$

Solution: $177 \text{ mL} \times \dfrac{0.788 \text{ g}}{1 \text{ mL}} \times \dfrac{1 \text{ mol}}{58.08 \text{ g}} \times \dfrac{-1658 \text{ kJ}}{1 \text{ mol}} = -3.98 \times 10^3 \text{ kJ or } 3.98 \times 10^3 \text{ kJ released}$

Check: The units (kJ) are correct. The magnitude of the answer ($\sim -10^3$) makes physical sense because the enthalpy change is negative and we have more than a mole of acetone. We expect more than 1658 kJ to be released.

6.29   **Given:** 5.56 kg nitromethane (CH_3NO_2); $\Delta H^\circ_{rxn} = -1418$ kJ/2 mol nitromethane   **Find:** q
          Conceptual Plan: kg nitromethane → g nitromethane → mol nitromethane → q

$$\dfrac{1000 \text{ g}}{1 \text{ kg}} \qquad \dfrac{1 \text{ mol}}{61.04 \text{ g}} \qquad \dfrac{-1418 \text{ kJ}}{2 \text{ mol}}$$

          Solution: $5.56 \text{ kg} \times \dfrac{1000 \text{ g}}{1 \text{ kg}} \times \dfrac{1 \text{ mol}}{61.04 \text{ g}} \times \dfrac{-1418 \text{ kJ}}{2 \text{ mol}} = -6.46 \times 10^4 \text{ kJ or } 6.46 \times 10^4 \text{ kJ released}$

          Check: The units (kJ) are correct. The magnitude of the answer (-10^4) makes physical sense because the enthalpy change is negative and we have more than a mole of nitromethane. We expect more than 709 kJ to be released.

6.31   **Given:** pork roast, $\Delta H^\circ_{rxn} = -2044$ kJ; q needed $= 1.6 \times 10^3$ kJ, 10% efficiency   **Find:** $m(CO_2)$
          Conceptual Plan: q used → q generated → mol CO_2 → g CO_2

$$\dfrac{100 \text{ kJ generated}}{10 \text{ kJ used}} \qquad \dfrac{3 \text{ mol } CO_2}{2044 \text{ kJ}} \qquad \dfrac{44.01 \text{ g}}{1 \text{ mol}}$$

          Solution: $1.6 \times 10^3 \text{ kJ} \times \dfrac{100 \text{ kJ generated}}{10 \text{ kJ used}} \times \dfrac{3 \text{ mol } CO_2}{2044 \text{ kJ}} \times \dfrac{44.01 \text{ g } CO_2}{1 \text{ mol } CO_2} = 1.0 \times 10^3 \text{ g } CO_2$

          Check: The units (g) are correct. The magnitude of the answer (1000) makes physical sense because the process is not very efficient and a lot of energy is needed.

6.33   **Given:** silver block; $T_{Agi} = 58.5\ ^\circ C$; 100.0 g water; $T_{H_2Oi} = 24.8\ ^\circ C$; $T_f = 26.2\ ^\circ C$ **Find:** mass of silver block
          Conceptual Plan: pull C_s values from table then H_2O: $m, C_s, T_i, T_f → q$ Ag: $C_s, T_i, T_f → m$

$$\text{Ag: } 0.235 \ \dfrac{J}{g \cdot ^\circ C} \quad H_2O: 4.18 \ \dfrac{J}{g \cdot ^\circ C} \qquad\qquad q = mC_s(T_f - T_i) \text{ then set } q_{Ag} = -q_{H_2O}$$

          Solution: $q = mC_s(T_f - T_i)$ substitute in values and set $q_{Ag} = -q_{H_2O}$.

$$q_{Ag} = m_{Ag}C_{Ag}(T_f - T_{Agi}) = m_{Ag} \times 0.235 \ \dfrac{J}{g \cdot ^\circ C} \times (26.2\ ^\circ C - 58.5\ ^\circ C) =$$

$$-q_{H_2O} = -m_{H_2O}C_{H_2O}(T_f - T_{H_2Oi}) = -100.0 \text{ g} \times 4.18 \ \dfrac{J}{g \cdot ^\circ C} \times (26.2\ ^\circ C - 24.8\ ^\circ C)$$

          Rearrange to solve for m_{Ag}.

$$m_{Ag} \times \left(-7.5\underline{9}05 \ \dfrac{J}{g}\right) = -585.2 \text{ J} \rightarrow m_{Ag} = \dfrac{-585.2 \text{ J}}{-7.5\underline{9}05 \ \dfrac{J}{g}} = 77.\underline{0}964 \text{ g Ag} = 77.1 \text{ g Ag}$$

          Check: The units (g) are correct. The magnitude of the answer (77 g) makes physical sense because the heat capacity of water is much greater than the heat capacity of silver.

6.35   **Given:** 31.1 g gold; $T_{Aui} = 69.3\ ^\circ C$; 64.2 g water; $T_{H_2Oi} = 27.8\ ^\circ C$ **Find:** T_f
          Conceptual Plan: pull C_s values from table then $m, C_s, T_i → T_f$

$$\text{Au: } 0.128 \ \dfrac{J}{g \cdot ^\circ C} \quad H_2O: 4.18 \ \dfrac{J}{g \cdot ^\circ C} \qquad q = mC_s(T_f - T_i) \text{ then set } q_{Au} = -q_{H_2O}$$

          Solution: $q = mC_s(T_f - T_i)$ substitute in values and set $q_{Au} = -q_{H_2O}$.

$$q_{Au} = m_{Au}C_{Au}(T_f - T_{Aui}) = 31.1 \text{ g} \times 0.128 \ \dfrac{J}{g \cdot ^\circ C} \times (T_f - 69.3\ ^\circ C) =$$

$$-q_{H_2O} = -m_{H_2O}C_{H_2O}(T_f - T_{H_2Oi}) = -64.2 \text{ g} \times 4.18 \ \dfrac{J}{g \cdot ^\circ C} \times (T_f - 27.8 ^\circ C)$$

          Rearrange to solve for T_f.

$$3.9\underline{8}08 \ \dfrac{J}{^\circ C} \times (T_f - 69.3\ ^\circ C) = -268.\underline{3}56 \ \dfrac{J}{^\circ C} \times (T_f - 27.8\ ^\circ C) \rightarrow$$

$$3.9\underline{8}08 \ \dfrac{J}{^\circ C} T_f - 275.\underline{8}694 \text{ J} = -268.\underline{3}56 \ \dfrac{J}{^\circ C} T_f + 74\underline{6}0.2968 \text{ J} \rightarrow$$

$$268.356 \frac{J}{°C} T_f + 3.9808 \frac{J}{°C} T_f = 275.8694 \text{ J} + 7460.2968 \text{ J} \rightarrow 272.3368 \frac{J}{°C} T_f = 7736.1662 \text{ J} \rightarrow$$

$$T_f = \frac{7736.1662 \text{ J}}{272.3368 \frac{J}{°C}} = 28.4 \text{ °C}$$

Check: The units (°C) are correct. The magnitude of the answer (28) makes physical sense because the heat transfer is dominated by the water (larger mass and larger specific heat capacity). The final temperature should be closer to the initial temperature of water than of gold.

6.37   **Given:** 6.15 g substance A; $T_{Ai} = 20.5$ °C; 25.2 g substance B; $T_{Bi} = 52.7$ °C; $C_s = 1.17$ J/g · °C, $T_f = 46.7$ °C
         Find: specific heat capacity of substance A
         Conceptual Plan: A: m, T_i, T_f → q B: m, C_s, T_i, T_f → q and solve for C_A

$$q = mC_s(T_f - T_i) \qquad \text{then set } q_A = -q_B$$

Solution: $q = mC_s(T_f - T_i)$ substitute in values and set $q_A = -q_B$.

$$q_A = m_A C_A(T_f - T_{Ai}) = 6.15 \text{ g} \times C_A \times (46.7 \text{ °C} - 20.5 \text{ °C}) =$$

$$-q_B = -m_B C_B(T_f - T_{Bi}) = -25.2 \text{ g} \times 1.17 \frac{J}{g \cdot °C} \times (46.7 \text{ °C} - 52.7 \text{ °C})$$

Rearrange to solve for C_A.

$$C_A \times (161.13 \text{ g} \cdot °C) = 176.904 \text{ J} \rightarrow C_A = \frac{176.904 \text{ J}}{161.13 \text{ g} \cdot °C} = 1.097896 \frac{J}{g \cdot °C} = 1.10 \frac{J}{g \cdot °C}$$

Check: The units (J/g · °C) are correct. The magnitude of the answer (1 J/g · °C) makes physical sense because the mass of substance B is greater than the mass of substance A by a factor of ~4.1 and the temperature change for substance A is greater than the temperature change of substance B by a factor of ~4.4; so the heat capacity of substance A will be a little smaller.

Calorimetry

6.39 $\Delta H_{rxn} = q_p$ and $\Delta E_{rxn} = q_V = \Delta H - P\Delta V$. Because combustions always involve expansions, expansions do work and therefore have a negative value. Combustions are always exothermic and therefore have a negative value. This means that ΔE_{rxn} is more negative than $\Delta H°_{rxn}$; so A (-25.9 kJ) is the constant volume process, and B (-23.3 kJ) is the constant pressure process.

6.41   **Given:** 0.514 g biphenyl ($C_{12}H_{10}$); bomb calorimeter; $T_i = 25.8$ °C; $T_f = 29.4$ °C; $C_{cal} = 5.86$ kJ/°C   **Find:** ΔE_{rxn}
         Conceptual Plan: T_i, T_f → ΔT then ΔT, C_{cal} → q_{cal} → q_{rxn} then g $C_{12}H_{10}$ → mol $C_{12}H_{10}$

$$\Delta T = T_f - T_i \qquad q_{cal} = C_{cal}\Delta T \quad q_{cal} = -q_{rxn} \qquad \frac{1 \text{ mol}}{154.20 \text{ g}}$$

then q_{rxn}, mol$C_{12}H_{10}$ → ΔE_{rxn}

$$\Delta E_{rxn} = \frac{q_V}{mol \ C_{12}H_{10}}$$

Solution: $\Delta T = T_f - T_i = 29.4 \text{ °C} - 25.8 \text{ °C} = 3.6 \text{ °C}$ then $q_{cal} = C_{cal}\Delta T = 5.86 \frac{kJ}{°C} \times 3.6 \text{ °C} = 21.096 \text{ kJ}$

then $q_{cal} = -q_{rxn} = -21.096$ kJ and $0.514 \text{ g } C_{12}H_{10} \times \frac{1 \text{ mol } C_{12}H_{10}}{154.20 \text{ g } C_{12}H_{10}} = 0.00333333 \text{ mol } C_{12}H_{10}$ then

$$\Delta E_{rxn} = \frac{q_V}{mol \ C_{12}H_{10}} = \frac{-21.096 \text{ kJ}}{0.00333333 \text{ mol } C_{12}H_{10}} = -6.3 \times 10^3 \text{ kJ/mol}$$

Check: The units (kJ/mol) are correct. The magnitude of the answer (-6000) makes physical sense because such a large amount of heat is generated from a very small amount of biphenyl.

6.43   **Given:** 0.103 g zinc; coffee-cup calorimeter; $T_i = 22.5$ °C; $T_f = 23.7$ °C; 50.0 mL solution; d(solution) $= 1.0$ g/mL;
         $C_{soln} = 4.18$ kJ/g · °C   **Find:** ΔH_{rxn}
         Conceptual Plan: T_i, T_f → ΔT and mL soln → g soln then ΔT, C_{soln} → q_{cal} → q_{rxn} then

$$\Delta T = T_f - T_i \qquad \frac{1.0 \text{ g}}{1.0 \text{ mL}} \qquad q_{soln} = m \ C_{soln} \Delta T \quad q_{soln} = -q_{rxn}$$

g Zn $\rightarrow$ **mol Zn then** q_{rxn}**, mol Zn** $\rightarrow$ ΔH_{rxn}

$$\frac{1 \text{ mol}}{65.38 \text{ g}} \qquad\qquad \Delta H_{rxn} = \frac{q_p}{\text{mol Zn}}$$

Solution: $\Delta T = T_f - T_i = 23.7\,°C - 22.5\,°C = 1.2\,°C$ and $50.0 \text{ mL} \times \dfrac{1.0 \text{ g}}{1.0 \text{ mL}} = 50.0 \text{ g then}$

$q_{soln} = m\, C_{soln}\, \Delta T = 50.0 \text{ g} \times 4.18 \dfrac{\text{J}}{\text{g} \cdot °C} \times 1.2\,°C = 2\underline{5}0.8 \text{ J then } q_{soln} = -q_{rxn} = -2\underline{5}0.8 \text{ J and}$

$0.103 \text{ g Zn} \times \dfrac{1 \text{ mol Zn}}{65.38 \text{ g Zn}} = 0.0015\underline{7}541 \text{ mol Zn then}$

$\Delta H_{rxn} = \dfrac{q_p}{\text{mol Zn}} = \dfrac{-2\underline{5}0.8 \text{ J}}{0.0015\underline{7}541 \text{ mol Zn}} = -1.6 \times 10^5 \text{ J/mol} = -1.6 \times 10^2 \text{ kJ/mol}$

Check: The units (kJ/mol) are correct. The magnitude of the answer (-160) makes physical sense because such a large amount of heat is generated from a very small amount of zinc.

Quantitative Relationships Involving ΔH and Hess's Law

6.45   (a)   Because $A + B \rightarrow 2\,C$ has ΔH_1, then $2\,C \rightarrow A + B$ will have a $\Delta H_2 = -\Delta H_1$. When the reaction direction is reversed, it changes from exothermic to endothermic (or vice versa); so the sign of ΔH changes.

        (b)   Because $A + \frac{1}{2}B \rightarrow C$ has ΔH_1, then $2\,A + B \rightarrow 2\,C$ will have a $\Delta H_2 = 2\,\Delta H_1$. When the reaction amount doubles, the amount of heat (or ΔH) doubles.

        (c)   Because $A \rightarrow B + 2\,C$ has ΔH_1, then $\frac{1}{2}A \rightarrow \frac{1}{2}B + C$ will have a $\Delta H_{1'} = \frac{1}{2}\Delta H_1$. When the reaction amount is cut in half, the amount of heat (or ΔH) is cut in half. Then $\frac{1}{2}B + C \rightarrow \frac{1}{2}A$ will have a $\Delta H_2 = -\Delta H_{1'} = -\frac{1}{2}\Delta H_1$ When the reaction direction is reversed, it changes from exothermic to endothermic (or vice versa); so the sign of ΔH changes.

6.47   Because the first reaction has Fe_2O_3 as a product and the reaction of interest has it as a reactant, we need to reverse the first reaction. When the reaction direction is reversed, ΔH changes.

       $Fe_2O_3(s) \rightarrow 2\,Fe(s) + \frac{3}{2}O_2(g)$ $\Delta H = +824.2 \text{ kJ}$

       Because the second reaction has 1 mole of CO as a reactant and the reaction of interest has 3 moles of CO as a reactant, we need to multiply the second reaction and the ΔH by 3.

       $3[CO(g) + \frac{1}{2}O_2(g) \rightarrow CO_2(g)]$ $\Delta H = 3(-282.7 \text{ kJ}) = -848.1 \text{ kJ}$

       Hess's law states that the ΔH of the net reaction is the sum of the ΔH of the steps.

       The rewritten reactions are as follows:

       $Fe_2O_3(s) \rightarrow 2\,Fe(s) + \frac{3}{2}\cancel{O_2(g)}$ $\Delta H = +824.2 \text{ kJ}$

       $\underline{3\,CO(g) + \frac{3}{2}\cancel{O_2(g)} \rightarrow 3\,CO_2(g)}$ $\underline{\Delta H = -848.1 \text{ kJ}}$

       $Fe_2O_3(s) + 3\,CO(g) \rightarrow 2\,Fe(s) + 3\,CO_2(g)$ $\Delta H_{rxn} = -23.9 \text{ kJ}$

6.49   Because the first reaction has C_5H_{12} as a reactant and the reaction of interest has it as a product, we need to reverse the first reaction. When the reaction direction is reversed, the sign of ΔH changes.

       $5\,CO_2(g) + 6\,H_2O(g) \rightarrow C_5H_{12}(l) + 8\,O_2(g)$ $\Delta H = +3271.5 \text{ kJ}$

       Because the second reaction has 1 mole of C as a reactant and the reaction of interest has 5 moles of C as a reactant, we need to multiply the second reaction and the ΔH by 5.

       $5[C(s) + O_2(g) \rightarrow CO_2(g)]$ $\Delta H = 5(-393.5 \text{ kJ}) = -1967.5 \text{ kJ}$

       Because the third reaction has 2 moles of H_2 as a reactant and the reaction of interest has 6 moles of H_2 as a reactant, we need to multiply the third reaction and the ΔH by 3.

       $3[2\,H_2(g) + O_2(g) \rightarrow 2\,H_2O(g)]$ $\Delta H = 3(-483.5 \text{ kJ}) = -1450.5 \text{ kJ}$

       Hess's law states that the ΔH of the net reaction is the sum of the ΔH of the steps.

       The rewritten reactions are as follows:

       $\cancel{5\,CO_2(g)} + \cancel{6\,H_2O(g)} \rightarrow C_5H_{12}(l) + \cancel{8\,O_2(g)}$ $\Delta H = +3271.5 \text{ kJ}$

       $5\,C(s) + \cancel{5\,O_2(g)} \rightarrow \cancel{5\,CO_2(g)}$ $\Delta H = -1967.5 \text{ kJ}$

       $\underline{6\,H_2(g) + \cancel{3\,O_2(g)} \rightarrow \cancel{6\,H_2O(g)}}$ $\underline{\Delta H = -1450.5 \text{ kJ}}$

       $5\,C(s) + 6\,H_2(g) \rightarrow C_5H_{12}(l)$ $\Delta H_{rxn} = -146.5 \text{ kJ}$

Enthalpies of Formation and ΔH

6.51   (a) $\frac{1}{2} N_2(g) + \frac{3}{2} H_2(g) \rightarrow NH_3(g)$ $\Delta H_f^\circ = -45.9 \text{ kJ/mol}$

      (b) $C(s) + O_2(g) \rightarrow CO_2(g)$ $\Delta H_f^\circ = -393.5 \text{ kJ/mol}$

      (c) $2 Fe(s) + \frac{3}{2} O_2(g) \rightarrow Fe_2O_3(s)$ $\Delta H_f^\circ = -824.2 \text{ kJ/mol}$

      (d) $C(s) + 2 H_2(g) \rightarrow CH_4(g)$ $\Delta H_f^\circ = -74.6 \text{ kJ/mol}$

6.53   **Given:** $N_2H_4(l) + N_2O_4(g) \rightarrow 2 N_2O(g) + 2 H_2O(g)$ **Find:** ΔH_{rxn}°
   Conceptual Plan: $\Delta H_{rxn}^\circ = \sum n_P \Delta H_f^\circ(\text{products}) - \sum n_R \Delta H_f^\circ(\text{reactants})$
   Solution:

Reactant/Product	ΔH_f°(kJ/mol, from Appendix IIB)
$N_2H_4(l)$	50.6
$N_2O_4(g)$	9.16
$N_2O(g)$	81.6
$H_2O(g)$	−241.8

Be sure to pull data for the correct formula and phase.

$\Delta H_{rxn}^\circ = \sum n_P \Delta H_f^\circ(\text{products}) - \sum n_R \Delta H_f^\circ(\text{reactants})$
   $= [2(\Delta H_f^\circ(N_2O(g))) + 2(\Delta H_f^\circ(H_2O(g)))] - [1(\Delta H_f^\circ(N_2H_4(l))) + 1(\Delta H_f^\circ(N_2O_4(g)))]$
   $= [2(81.6 \text{ kJ}) + 2(-241.8 \text{ kJ})] - [1(50.6 \text{ kJ}) + 1(9.16 \text{ kJ})]$
   $= [-320.4 \text{ kJ}] - [59.76 \text{ kJ}]$
   $= -380.2 \text{ kJ}$

Check: The units (kJ) are correct. The answer is negative, which means that the reaction is exothermic. The answer is dominated by the negative heat of formation of water.

6.55   (a)   **Given:** $C_2H_4(g) + H_2(g) \rightarrow C_2H_6(g)$ **Find:** ΔH_{rxn}°
      Conceptual Plan: $\Delta H_{rxn}^\circ = \sum n_P \Delta H_f^\circ(\text{products}) - \sum n_R \Delta H_f^\circ(\text{reactants})$
      Solution:

Reactant/Product	ΔH_f°(kJ/mol, from Appendix IIB)
$C_2H_4(g)$	52.4
$H_2(g)$	0.0
$C_2H_6(g)$	−84.68

Be sure to pull data for the correct formula and phase.

$\Delta H_{rxn}^\circ = \sum n_P \Delta H_f^\circ(\text{products}) - \sum n_R \Delta H_f^\circ(\text{reactants})$
   $= [1(\Delta H_f^\circ(C_2H_6(g)))] - [1(\Delta H_f^\circ(C_2H_4(g))) + 1(\Delta H_f^\circ(H_2(g)))]$
   $= [1(-84.68 \text{ kJ})] - [1(52.4 \text{ kJ}) + 1(0.0 \text{ kJ})]$
   $= [-84.68 \text{ kJ}] - [52.4 \text{ kJ}]$
   $= -137.1 \text{ kJ}$

Check: The units (kJ) are correct. The answer is negative, which means that the reaction is exothermic. Both hydrocarbon terms are negative, so the final answer is negative.

      (b)   **Given:** $CO(g) + H_2O(g) \rightarrow H_2(g) + CO_2(g)$ **Find:** ΔH_{rxn}°
      Conceptual Plan: $\Delta H_{rxn}^\circ = \sum n_P \Delta H_f^\circ(\text{products}) - \sum n_R \Delta H_f^\circ(\text{reactants})$
      Solution:

Reactant/Product	ΔH_f°(kJ/mol, from Appendix IIB)
$CO(g)$	−110.5
$H_2O(g)$	−241.8
$H_2(g)$	0.0
$CO_2(g)$	−393.5

Be sure to pull data for the correct formula and phase.

$$\Delta H^\circ_{rxn} = \sum n_P \Delta H^\circ_f (\text{products}) - \sum n_R \Delta H^\circ_f (\text{reactants})$$
$$= [1(\Delta H^\circ_f(H_2(g))) + 1(\Delta H^\circ_f(CO_2(g)))] - [1(\Delta H^\circ_f(CO(g))) + 1(\Delta H^\circ_f(H_2O(g)))]$$
$$= [1(0.0 \text{ kJ}) + 1(-393.5 \text{ kJ})] - [1(-110.5 \text{ kJ}) + 1(-241.8 \text{ kJ})]$$
$$= [-393.5 \text{ kJ}] - [-352.3 \text{ kJ}]$$
$$= -41.2 \text{ kJ}$$

Check: The units (kJ) are correct. The answer is negative, which means that the reaction is exothermic.

(c) **Given:** $3 NO_2(g) + H_2O(l) \rightarrow 2 HNO_3(aq) + NO(g)$ **Find:** ΔH°_{rxn}
Conceptual Plan: $\Delta H^\circ_{rxn} = \sum n_P \Delta H^\circ_f (\text{products}) - \sum n_R \Delta H^\circ_f (\text{reactants})$
Solution:

Reactant/Product	ΔH°_f (kJ/mol, from Appendix IIB)
$NO_2(g)$	33.2
$H_2O(l)$	−285.8
$HNO_3(aq)$	−207
$NO(g)$	91.3

Be sure to pull data for the correct formula and phase.

$$\Delta H^\circ_{rxn} = \sum n_P \Delta H^\circ_f (\text{products}) - \sum n_R \Delta H^\circ_f (\text{reactants})$$
$$= [2(\Delta H^\circ_f(HNO_3(aq))) + 1(\Delta H^\circ_f(NO(g)))] - [3(\Delta H^\circ_f(NO_2(g))) + 1(\Delta H^\circ_f(H_2O(l)))]$$
$$= [2(-207 \text{ kJ}) + 1(91.3 \text{ kJ})] - [3(33.2 \text{ kJ}) + 1(-285.8 \text{ kJ})]$$
$$= [-322.7 \text{ kJ}] - [-186.2 \text{ kJ}]$$
$$= -137 \text{ kJ}$$

Check: The units (kJ) are correct. The answer is negative, which means that the reaction is exothermic.

(d) **Given:** $Cr_2O_3(s) + 3 CO(g) \rightarrow 2 Cr(s) + 3 CO_2(g)$ **Find:** ΔH°_{rxn}
Conceptual Plan: $\Delta H^\circ_{rxn} = \sum n_P \Delta H^\circ_f (\text{products}) - \sum n_R \Delta H^\circ_f (\text{reactants})$
Solution:

Reactant/Product	ΔH°_f (kJ/mol, from Appendix IIB)
$Cr_2O_3(s)$	−1139.7
$CO(g)$	−110.5
$Cr(s)$	0.0
$CO_2(g)$	−393.5

Be sure to pull data for the correct formula and phase.

$$\Delta H^\circ_{rxn} = \sum n_P \Delta H^\circ_f (\text{products}) - \sum n_R \Delta H^\circ_f (\text{reactants})$$
$$= [2(\Delta H^\circ_f(Cr(s))) + 3(\Delta H^\circ_f(CO_2(g)))] - [1(\Delta H^\circ_f(Cr_2O_3(s))) + 3(\Delta H^\circ_f(CO(g)))]$$
$$= [2(0.0 \text{ kJ}) + 3(-393.5 \text{ kJ})] - [1(-1139.7 \text{ kJ}) + 3(-110.5 \text{ kJ})]$$
$$= [-1180.5 \text{ kJ}] - [-1471.2 \text{ kJ}]$$
$$= 290.7 \text{ kJ}$$

Check: The units (kJ) are correct. The answer is positive, which means that the reaction is endothermic.

6.57   **Given:** form glucose ($C_6H_{12}O_6$) and oxygen from sunlight, carbon dioxide, and water   **Find:** ΔH°_{rxn}
Conceptual Plan: write balanced reaction then $\Delta H^\circ_{rxn} = \sum n_P \Delta H^\circ_f (\text{products}) - \sum n_R \Delta H^\circ_f (\text{reactants})$
Solution: $6 CO_2(g) + 6 H_2O(l) \rightarrow C_6H_{12}O_6(s) + 6 O_2(g)$

Reactant/Product	ΔH°_f (kJ/mol, from Appendix IIB)
$CO_2(g)$	−393.5
$H_2O(l)$	−285.8
$C_6H_{12}O(s)$	−1273.3
$O_2(g)$	0.0

Be sure to pull data for the correct formula and phase.

$$\Delta H_{rxn}^{\circ} = \sum n_P \Delta H_f^{\circ}(\text{products}) - \sum n_R \Delta H_f^{\circ}(\text{reactants})$$
$$= [1(\Delta H_f^{\circ}(C_6H_{12}O_6(s))) + 6(\Delta H_f^{\circ}(O_2(g)))] - [6(\Delta H_f^{\circ}(CO_2(g))) + 6(\Delta H_f^{\circ}(H_2O(l)))]$$
$$= [1(-1273.3 \text{ kJ}) + 6(0.0 \text{ kJ})] - [6(-393.5 \text{ kJ}) + 6(-285.8 \text{ kJ})]$$
$$= [-1273.3 \text{ kJ}] - [-4075.8 \text{ kJ}]$$
$$= +2802.5 \text{ kJ}$$

Check: The units (kJ) are correct. The answer is positive, which means that the reaction is endothermic. The reaction requires the input of light energy, so we expect that this will be an endothermic reaction.

6.59 **Given:** $2 \text{ CH}_3\text{NO}_2(l) + 3/2 \text{ O}_2(g) \rightarrow 2 \text{ CO}_2(g) + 3 \text{ H}_2\text{O}(l) + \text{N}_2(g)$ and $\Delta H_{rxn}^{\circ} = -1418.4 \text{ kJ/mol}$
Find: $\Delta H_f^{\circ}(\text{CH}_3\text{NO}_2(l))$
Conceptual Plan: Fill known values into $\Delta H_{rxn}^{\circ} = \sum n_P \Delta H_f^{\circ}(\text{products}) - \sum n_R \Delta H_f^{\circ}(\text{reactants})$ **and rearrange to solve for $\Delta H_f^{\circ}(\text{CH}_3\text{NO}_2(l))$.**
Solution:

Reactant/Product	ΔH_f°(kJ/mol, from Appendix IIB)
$O_2(g)$	0.0
$CO_2(g)$	−393.5
$H_2O(l)$	−285.8
$N_2(g)$	0.0

Be sure to pull data for the correct formula and phase.

$$\Delta H_{rxn}^{\circ} = \sum n_P \Delta H_f^{\circ}(\text{products}) - \sum n_R \Delta H_f^{\circ}(\text{reactants})$$
$$= [2(\Delta H_f^{\circ}(CO_2(g))) + 3(\Delta H_f^{\circ}(H_2O(l))) + 1(\Delta H_f^{\circ}(N_2(g)))] - [2(\Delta H_f^{\circ}(CH_3NO_2(l))) + 3/2(\Delta H_f^{\circ}(O_2(g)))]$$
$$2(-709.2 \text{ kJ}) = [2(-393.5 \text{ kJ}) + 3(-285.8 \text{ kJ}) + 1(0.0 \text{ kJ})] - [2(\Delta H_f^{\circ}(CH_3NO_2(l)) + 3/2(0.0 \text{ kJ})]$$
$$-1418.4 \text{ kJ} = [-1644.4 \text{ kJ}] - [2(\Delta H_f^{\circ}(CH_3NO_2(l)))]$$
$$\Delta H_f^{\circ}(CH_3NO_2(l)) = -113 \text{ kJ/mol}$$

Check: The units (kJ/mol) are correct. The answer is negative (but not as negative as water and carbon dioxide), which is consistent with an exothermic combustion reaction.

Cumulative Problems

6.61 **Given:** billiard ball$_A$ = system: $m_A = 0.17$ kg, $v_{A1} = 4.5$ m/s slows to $v_{A2} = 3.8$ m/s and $v_{A3} = 0$;
ball$_B$: $m_B = 0.17$ kg, $v_{B1} = 0$ and $v_{B2} = 3.8$ m/s, and KE $= \frac{1}{2} mv^2$ **Find:** $w, q, \Delta E_{sys}$
Conceptual Plan: $m, v \rightarrow$ KE then $\text{KE}_{A3}, \text{KE}_{A1} \rightarrow \Delta E_{sys}$ and $\text{KE}_{A2}, \text{KE}_{A1} \rightarrow q$ and $\text{KE}_{B2}, \text{KE}_{B1} \rightarrow w_B$

$$\text{KE} = \frac{1}{2} mv^2 \qquad \Delta E_{sys} = \text{KE}_{A3} - \text{KE}_{A1} \qquad q = \text{KE}_{A2} - \text{KE}_{A1} \qquad w_B = \text{KE}_{B2} - \text{KE}_{B1}$$

$\Delta E_{sys}, q \rightarrow w_A$ **verify that $w_A = -w_B$ so that no heat is transferred to ball$_B$**
$$\Delta E = q + w$$

Solution: $\text{KE} = \dfrac{1}{2} mv^2$ because m is in kg and v is in m/s; KE will be in kg $\cdot$ m^2/s^2, which is the definition of a joule.

$$\text{KE}_{A1} = \frac{1}{2}(0.17 \text{ kg})\left(4.5 \frac{m}{s}\right)^2 = 1.\underline{7}213 \frac{\text{kg} \cdot \text{m}^2}{\text{s}^2} = 1.\underline{7}213 \text{ J}$$

$$\text{KE}_{A2} = \frac{1}{2}(0.17 \text{ kg})\left(3.8 \frac{m}{s}\right)^2 = 1.\underline{2}274 \frac{\text{kg} \cdot \text{m}^2}{\text{s}^2} = 1.\underline{2}274 \text{ J}$$

$$\text{KE}_{A3} = \frac{1}{2}(0.17 \text{ kg})\left(0 \frac{m}{s}\right)^2 = 0 \frac{\text{kg} \cdot \text{m}^2}{\text{s}^2} = 0 \text{ J},$$

$$\text{KE}_{B1} = \frac{1}{2}(0.17 \text{ kg})\left(0 \frac{m}{s}\right)^2 = 0 \frac{\text{kg} \cdot \text{m}^2}{\text{s}^2} = 0 \text{ J}$$

$$\text{KE}_{B2} = \frac{1}{2}(0.17 \text{ kg})\left(3.8 \frac{m}{s}\right)^2 = 1.\underline{2}274 \frac{\text{kg} \cdot \text{m}^2}{\text{s}^2} = 1.\underline{2}274 \text{ J}$$

$$\Delta E_{sys} = \text{KE}_{A3} - \text{KE}_{A1} = 0 \text{ J} - 1.\underline{7}213 \text{ J} = -1.\underline{7}213 \text{ J} = -1.7 \text{ J}$$
$$q = \text{KE}_{A2} - \text{KE}_{A1} = 1.\underline{2}274 \text{ J} - 1.\underline{7}213 \text{ J} = -0.\underline{4}939 \text{ J} = -0.5 \text{ J}$$

$w_B = KE_{B2} - KE_{B1} = 1.\underline{2}274 \text{ J} - 0 \text{ J} = 1.\underline{2}274 \text{ J}$

$w = \Delta E - q = -1.\underline{7}213 \text{ J} - (-0.\underline{4}939 \text{ J}) = -1.\underline{2}274 \text{ J} = -1.2 \text{ J}$

Because $w_A = -w_B$, no heat is transferred to $ball_B$.

Check: The units (J) are correct. Because the ball is initially moving and is stopped at the end, it has lost energy (negative ΔE_{sys}). As the ball slows due to friction, it is releasing heat (negative q). The kinetic energy is transferred to a second ball, so it does work (w negative).

6.63   **Given:** $H_2O(l) \rightarrow H_2O(g)$ $\Delta H_{rxn}^\circ = +44.01$ kJ/mol; $\Delta T_{body} = -0.50\,^\circ C$, $m_{body} = 95$ kg, $C_{body} = 4.0$ J/g $^\circ C$

Find: m_{H_2O}

Conceptual Plan: kg $\rightarrow$ g then $m_{body}, \Delta T, C_{body} \rightarrow q_{body} \rightarrow q_{rxn}(J) \rightarrow q_{rxn}(kJ) \rightarrow$ mol $H_2O \rightarrow$ g H_2O

$$\frac{1000 \text{ g}}{1 \text{ kg}} \qquad\qquad q_{body} = m_{body}C_{body}\Delta T_{body} \quad q_{rxn} = -q_{body} \quad \frac{1 \text{ kJ}}{1000 \text{ J}} \quad \frac{1 \text{ mol}}{44.01 \text{ kJ}} \quad \frac{18.02 \text{ g}}{1 \text{ mol}}$$

Solution: $95 \text{ kg} \times \dfrac{1000 \text{ g}}{1 \text{ kg}} = 95000 \text{ g}$ then

$$q_{body} = m_{body}C_{body}\Delta T_{body} = 95000 \text{ g} \times 4.0\,\frac{J}{g \cdot {}^\circ C} \times (-0.50\,^\circ C) = -1\underline{9}0000 \text{ J}$$ then

$$q_{rxn} = -q_{body} = 1\underline{9}0000 \text{ J} \times \frac{1 \text{ kJ}}{1000 \text{ J}} \times \frac{1 \text{ mol}}{44.01 \text{ kJ}} \times \frac{18.02 \text{ g}}{1 \text{ mol}} = 78 \text{ g } H_2O$$

Check: The units (g) are correct. The magnitude of the answer (78) makes physical sense because a person can sweat this much on a hot day.

6.65   **Given:** $H_2O(s) \rightarrow H_2O(l)$ $\Delta H_f^\circ(H_2O(s)) = -291.8$ kJ/mol; 355 mL beverage $T_{Bevi} = 25.0\,^\circ C$, $T_{Bevf} = 0.0\,^\circ C$, $C_{Bev} = 4.184$ J/g $^\circ C$, $d_{Bev} = 1.0$ g/mL   **Find:** ΔH_{rxn}° (ice melting) and m_{ice}

Conceptual Plan: $\Delta H_{rxn}^\circ = \sum n_P \Delta H_f^\circ(\text{products}) - \sum n_R \Delta H_f^\circ(\text{reactants})$ **mL $\rightarrow$ g and $T_i, T_f \rightarrow \Delta T$ then**

$$\frac{1.0 \text{ g}}{1.0 \text{ mL}} \qquad \Delta T = T_f - T_i$$

$m_{H_2O}, \Delta T_{H_2O}, C_{H_2O} \rightarrow q_{H_2O} \rightarrow q_{rxn}(J) \rightarrow q_{rxn} (kJ) \rightarrow$ **mol ice $\rightarrow$ g ice**

$$q_{Bev} = m_{Bev}C_{Bev}\Delta T_{Bev} \quad q_{rxn} = -q_{Bev} \quad \frac{1 \text{ kJ}}{1000 \text{ J}} \quad \frac{1 \text{ mol}}{\Delta H_{rxn}^\circ} \quad \frac{18.02 \text{ g}}{1 \text{ mol}}$$

Solution:

Reactant/Product	ΔH_f°(kJ/mol, from Appendix IIB)
$H_2O(s)$	−291.8
$H_2O(l)$	−285.8

Be sure to pull data for the correct formula and phase.

$$\begin{aligned}\Delta H_{rxn}^\circ &= \sum n_P \Delta H_f^\circ(\text{products}) - \sum n_R \Delta H_f^\circ(\text{reactants}) \\ &= [1(\Delta H_f^\circ(H_2O(l)))] - [1(\Delta H_f^\circ(H_2O(s)))] \\ &= [1(-285.8 \text{ kJ})] - [1(-291.8 \text{ kJ})] \\ &= +6.0 \text{ kJ}\end{aligned}$$

$355 \text{ mL} \times \dfrac{1.0 \text{ g}}{1.0 \text{ mL}} = 355 \text{ g}$ and $\Delta T = T_f - T_i = 0.0\,^\circ C - 25.0\,^\circ C = -25.0\,^\circ C$ then

$$q_{Bev} = m_{Bev}C_{Bev}\Delta T_{Bev} = 355 \text{ g} \times 4.184\,\frac{J}{g \cdot {}^\circ C} \times (-25.0\,^\circ C) = -371\underline{3}3 \text{ J}$$ then

$$q_{rxn} = -q_{Bev} = -371\underline{3}3 \text{ J} \times \frac{1 \text{ kJ}}{1000 \text{ J}} \times \frac{1 \text{ mol}}{-6.0 \text{ kJ}} \times \frac{18.02 \text{ g}}{1 \text{ mol}} = 110 \text{ g ice}$$

Check: The units (kJ and g) are correct. The answer is positive, which means that the reaction is endothermic. We expect an endothermic reaction because we know that heat must be added to melt ice. The magnitude of the answer (110 g) makes physical sense because it is much smaller than the weight of the beverage and it would fit in a glass with the beverage.

6.67   **Given:** 25.5 g aluminum; $T_{Ali} = 65.4\,^\circ C$; 55.2 g water; $T_{H_2Oi} = 22.2\,^\circ C$ **Find:** T_f

Conceptual Plan: pull C_s values from table then $m, C_s, T_i \rightarrow T_f$

$$\text{Al: } 0.903\,\frac{J}{g \cdot {}^\circ C} \qquad H_2O: 4.18\,\frac{J}{g \cdot {}^\circ C} \qquad q = mC_s(T_f - T_i) \text{ then set } q_{Al} = -q_{H_2O}$$

Solution: $q = mC_s(T_f - T_i)$ substitute in values and set $q_{Al} = -q_{H_2O}$.

$$q_{Al} = m_{Al}C_{Al}(T_f - T_{Ali}) = 25.5 \text{ g} \times 0.903 \frac{J}{g \cdot °C} \times (T_f - 65.4 \text{ °C}) =$$

$$-q_{H_2O} = -m_{H_2O}C_{H_2O}(T_f - T_{H_2Oi}) = -55.2 \text{ g} \times 4.18 \frac{J}{g \cdot °C} \times (T_f - 22.2 \text{ °C})$$

Rearrange to solve for T_f.

$$23.0265 \frac{J}{°C} \times (T_f - 65.4 \text{ °C}) = -230.736 \frac{J}{°C} \times (T_f - 22.2 \text{ °C}) \rightarrow$$

$$23.0265 \frac{J}{°C} T_f - 1505.93 \text{ J} = -230.736 \frac{J}{°C} T_f + 5122.34 \text{ J} \rightarrow$$

$$-5122.34 \text{ J} - 1505.93 \text{ J} = -230.736 \frac{J}{°C} T_f - 23.0265 \frac{J}{°C} T_f \rightarrow 6628.27 \text{ J} = 253.7625 \frac{J}{°C} T_f \rightarrow$$

$$T_f = \frac{6628.27 \text{ J}}{253.7625 \frac{J}{°C}} = 26.1 \text{ °C}$$

Check: The units (°C) are correct. The magnitude of the answer (26) makes physical sense because the heat transfer is dominated by the water (larger mass and larger specific heat capacity). The final temperature should be closer to the initial temperature of water than of aluminum.

6.69   **Given:** palmitic acid ($C_{16}H_{32}O_2$) $\Delta H_f°(C_{16}H_{32}O_2(s)) = -208$ kJ/mol; sucrose ($C_{12}H_{22}O_{11}$)
$\Delta H_f°(C_{12}H_{22}O_{11}(s)) = -2226.1$ kJ/mol   **Find:** $\Delta H_{rxn}°$ in kJ/mol and Cal/g
Conceptual Plan: write balanced reaction then $\Delta H_{rxn}° = \sum n_P \Delta H_f°(\text{products}) - \sum n_R \Delta H_f°(\text{reactants})$ **then**
kJ/mol $\rightarrow$ J/mol $\rightarrow$ Cal/mol $\rightarrow$ Cal/g

$$\frac{1000 \text{ J}}{1 \text{ kJ}} \qquad \frac{1 \text{ Cal}}{4184 \text{ J}} \qquad \text{PA:} \frac{1 \text{ mol}}{256.42 \text{ g}} \quad \text{S:} \frac{1 \text{ mol}}{342.30 \text{ g}}$$

Solution: Combustion is the combination with oxygen to form carbon dioxide and water (l):
$C_{16}H_{32}O_2(s) + 23 \text{ O}_2(g) \rightarrow 16 \text{ CO}_2(g) + 16 \text{ H}_2O(l)$

Reactant/Product	$\Delta H_f°$ (kJ/mol, from Appendix IIB)
$C_{16}H_{32}O_2(s)$	-208
$O_2(g)$	0.0
$CO_2(g)$	-393.5
$H_2O(l)$	-285.8

Be sure to pull data for the correct formula and phase.

$$\begin{aligned}
\Delta H_{rxn}° &= \sum n_P \Delta H_f°(\text{products}) - \sum n_R \Delta H_f°(\text{reactants}) \\
&= [16(\Delta H_f°(CO_2(g))) + 16(\Delta H_f°(H_2O(l)))] - [1(\Delta H_f°(C_{16}H_{32}O_2(s))) + 23(\Delta H_f°(O_2(g)))] \\
&= [16(-393.5 \text{ kJ}) + 16(-285.8 \text{ kJ})] - [1(-208 \text{ kJ}) + 23(0.0 \text{ kJ})] \\
&= [-10868.8 \text{ kJ}] - [-208 \text{ kJ}] \\
&= -10660.8 \text{ kJ/mol} = -10661 \text{ kJ/mol}
\end{aligned}$$

$$-10660.8 \frac{\text{kJ}}{\text{mol}} \times \frac{1000 \text{ J}}{1 \text{ kJ}} \times \frac{1 \text{ Cal}}{4184 \text{ J}} \times \frac{1 \text{ mol}}{256.42 \text{ g}} = -9.9368 \text{ Cal/g}$$

$C_{12}H_{22}O_{11}(s) + 12 \text{ O}_2(g) \rightarrow 12 \text{ CO}_2(g) + 11 \text{ H}_2O(l)$

Reactant/Product	$\Delta H_f°$ (kJ/mol, from Appendix IIB)
$C_{12}H_{22}O_{11}(s)$	-2226.1
$O_2(g)$	0.0
$CO_2(g)$	-393.5
$H_2O(l)$	-285.8

Be sure to pull data for the correct formula and phase.

$$\Delta H^{\circ}_{rxn} = \sum n_P \Delta H^{\circ}_f (\text{products}) - \sum n_R \Delta H^{\circ}_f (\text{reactants})$$

$$= [12(\Delta H^{\circ}_f(CO_2(g))) + 11(\Delta H^{\circ}_f(H_2O(l)))] - [1(\Delta H^{\circ}_f(C_{12}H_{22}O_{11}(s))) + 12(\Delta H^{\circ}_f(O_2(g)))]$$

$$= [12(-393.5 \text{ kJ}) + 11(-285.8 \text{ kJ})] - [1(-2226.1 \text{ kJ}) + 12(0.0 \text{ kJ})]$$

$$= [-7865.8 \text{ kJ}] - [-2226.1 \text{ kJ}]$$

$$= -5639.7 \text{ kJ/mol}$$

$$-5639.7 \frac{\text{kJ}}{\text{mol}} \times \frac{1000 \text{ J}}{1 \text{ kJ}} \times \frac{1 \text{ Cal}}{4184 \text{ J}} \times \frac{1 \text{ mol}}{342.30 \text{ g}} = -3.938 \text{ Cal/g}$$

Palmitic acid gives more Cal/g than sucrose.

Check: The units (kJ/mol and Cal/g) are correct. The magnitudes of the answers are consistent with the food labels we see every day.

6.71   At constant pressure $\Delta H_{rxn} = q_P$ and at constant volume $\Delta E_{rxn} = q_V = \Delta H_{rxn} - P\Delta V$. Recall that $PV = nRT$. Because the conditions are constant P and a constant number of moles of gas, as T changes the only variable that can change is V. This means that $P\Delta V = nR\Delta T$. Substituting into the equation for ΔE_{rxn}, we get $\Delta E_{rxn} = \Delta H_{rxn} - nR\Delta T$ or $\Delta H_{rxn} = \Delta E_{rxn} + nR\Delta T$.

6.73   **Given:** 16 g peanut butter; bomb calorimeter; $T_i = 22.2\ ^{\circ}C$; $T_f = 25.4\ ^{\circ}C$; $C_{cal} = 120.0 \text{ kJ/}^{\circ}C$
Find: calories in peanut butter
Conceptual Plan: $T_i, T_f \rightarrow \Delta T$ then $\Delta T, C_{cal} \rightarrow q_{cal} \rightarrow q_{rxn} \text{ (kJ)} \rightarrow q_{rxn} \text{ (kJ)} \rightarrow q_{rxn}(\text{Cal})$

$$\Delta T = T_f - T_i \qquad q_{cal} = -C_{cal}\Delta T \quad q_{rxn} = -q_{cal} \qquad \frac{1000 \text{ J}}{1 \text{ kJ}} \qquad \frac{1 \text{ Cal}}{4184 \text{ J}}$$

then q_{rxn} **(Cal)** $\rightarrow$ **Cal/g**

$$\div \text{ 16 g peanut butter}$$

Solution: $\Delta T = T_f - T_i = 25.4\ ^{\circ}C - 22.2\ ^{\circ}C = 3.2\ ^{\circ}C$ then $q_{cal} = C_{cal}\Delta T = 120.0 \frac{\text{kJ}}{^{\circ}C} \times 3.2\ ^{\circ}C = 384 \text{ kJ}$

then $q_{rxn} = -q_{cal} = -384 \text{ kJ} \times \frac{1000 \text{ J}}{1 \text{ kJ}} \times \frac{1 \text{ Cal}}{4184 \text{ J}} = -91.778 \text{ Cal}$ then $\frac{-91.778 \text{ Cal}}{16 \text{ g}} = -5.7 \text{ Cal/g}$

Check: The units (Cal/g) are correct. The magnitude of the answer (6) makes physical sense because there is a significant percentage of fat and sugar in peanut butter. The answer is in line with the answers in Problem 6.69.

6.75   **Given:** $V_1 = 20.0 \text{ L}$ at $P_1 = 3.0 \text{ atm}$; $P_2 = 1.5 \text{ atm}$ let expand at constant T **Find:** $w, q, \Delta E_{sys}$
Conceptual Plan: $V_1, P_1, P_2 \rightarrow V_2$ then $V_1, V_2 \rightarrow \Delta V$ then $P, \Delta V \rightarrow w$ **(L atm)** $\rightarrow w$ **(J)**

$$P_1 V_1 = P_2 V_2 \qquad \Delta V = V_2 - V_1 \qquad w = -P\Delta V \qquad \frac{101.3 \text{ J}}{1 \text{ L atm}}$$

for an ideal gas $\Delta E_{sys} \propto T$; so because this is a constant temperature process, $\Delta E_{sys} = 0$ finally $\Delta E_{sys}, w \rightarrow q$

$$\Delta E = q + w$$

Solution: $P_1 V_1 = P_2 V_2$. Rearrange to solve for V_2. $V_2 = V_1 \dfrac{P_1}{P_2} = (20.0 \text{ L}) \times \dfrac{3.0 \text{ atm}}{1.5 \text{ atm}} = 40. \text{ L}$ and

$\Delta V = V_2 - V_1 = 40. \text{ L} - 20.0 \text{ L} = 20. \text{ L}$ then

$w = -P\Delta V = -1.5 \text{ atm} \times 20. \text{ L} \times \dfrac{101.3 \text{ J}}{1 \text{ L} \cdot \text{atm}} = -3039 \text{ J} = -3.0 \times 10^3 \text{ J}$ $\Delta E = q + w$

Rearrange to solve for q. $q = \Delta E_{sys} - w = +0 \text{ J} - (-3039 \text{ J}) = 3.0 \times 10^3 \text{ J}$

Check: The units (J) are correct. Because there is no temperature change, we expect no energy change ($\Delta E_{sys} = 0$). The piston expands as it does work (negative work), so heat is absorbed (positive q).

6.77   **Given:** 25.3% methane (CH_4), 38.2% ethane (C_2H_6), and the rest propane (C_3H_8) by volume; $V = 1.55 \text{ L tank}$, $P = 755 \text{ mmHg}$, and $T = 298 \text{ K}$ **Find:** heat for combustion
Conceptual Plan: percent composition $\rightarrow$ **mmHg** $\rightarrow$ **atm then** $P, V, T \rightarrow n$ **then**

$$\text{Dalton's law of partial pressures} \qquad \frac{1 \text{ atm}}{760 \text{ mmHg}} \qquad\qquad PV = nRT$$

use data in Problem 6.28 for methane and calculate heat of combustion for ethane and propane

$\Delta H^{\circ}_{rxn}(CH_4) = -802.3 \text{ kJ}$; $\Delta H^{\circ}_{rxn}(C_3H_8) = -2217 \text{ kJ}$ write balanced reaction then $\Delta H^{\circ}_{rxn} = \sum n_P \Delta H^{\circ}_f(\text{products}) - \sum n_R \Delta H^{\circ}_f(\text{reactants})$

then $n, \Delta H \rightarrow q$

Solution: $P_{CH_4} = \dfrac{25.3 \text{ mmHg } CH_4}{100 \text{ mmHg gas}} \times 755 \text{ mmHg gas} \times \dfrac{1 \text{ atm } CH_4}{760 \text{ mmHg}} = 0.2513355 \text{ atm } CH_4$

$$P_{C_2H_6} = \frac{38.2 \text{ mmHg } C_2H_6}{100 \text{ mmHg gas}} \times 755 \text{ mmHg gas} \times \frac{1 \text{ atm } C_2H_6}{760 \text{ mmHg}} = 0.37948684 \text{ atm } C_2H_6$$

$$P_{C_3H_8} = \frac{100 - (25.3 + 38.2) \text{ mmHg } C_3H_8}{100 \text{ mmHg gas}} \times 755 \text{ mmHg gas} \times \frac{1 \text{ atm } C_3H_8}{760 \text{ mmHg}} = 0.36259868 \text{ atm } C_3H_8$$

$PV = nRT$ Rearrange to solve for n.

$$n_{CH_4} = \frac{PV}{RT} = \frac{0.25\underline{1}3355 \text{ atm } CH_4 \times 1.55 \text{ L}}{0.08206 \dfrac{\text{L} \cdot \text{atm}}{\text{mol} \cdot \text{K}} \times 298 \text{ K}} = 0.015\underline{9}3081 \text{ mol } CH_4$$

$$n_{C_2H_6} = \frac{PV}{RT} = \frac{0.37\underline{9}48684 \text{ atm } C_2H_6 \times 1.55 \text{ L}}{0.08206 \dfrac{\text{L} \cdot \text{atm}}{\text{mol} \cdot \text{K}} \times 298 \text{ K}} = 0.024\underline{0}5363 \text{ mol } C_2H_6$$

$$n_{C_2H_6} = \frac{PV}{RT} = \frac{0.36\underline{2}59868 \text{ atm } C_3H_8 \times 1.55 \text{ L}}{0.08206 \dfrac{\text{L} \cdot \text{atm}}{\text{mol} \cdot \text{K}} \times 298 \text{ K}} = 0.022983181 \text{ mol } C_3H_8$$

$C_2H_6(g) + 7/2 \, O_2(g) \rightarrow 2 \, CO_2(g) + 3 \, H_2O(g)$

Reactant/Product	ΔH_f° (kJ/mol, from Appendix IIB)
$C_2H_6(g)$	-84.68
$O_2(g)$	0.0
$CO_2(g)$	-393.5
$H_2O(g)$	-241.8

Be sure to pull data for the correct formula and phase.

$$\begin{aligned}
\Delta H_{rxn}^\circ &= \sum n_P \Delta H_f^\circ (\text{products}) - \sum n_R \Delta H_f^\circ (\text{reactants}) \\
&= [2(\Delta H_f^\circ(CO_2(g))) + 3(\Delta H_f^\circ(H_2O(g)))] - [1(\Delta H_f^\circ(C_2H_6(g))) + 7/2(\Delta H_f^\circ(O_2(g)))] \\
&= [2(-393.5 \text{ kJ}) + 3(-241.8 \text{ kJ})] - [1(-84.68 \text{ kJ}) + 7/2(0.0 \text{ kJ})] \\
&= [-1512.4 \text{ kJ}] - [-84.68 \text{ kJ}] \\
&= -1427.7 \text{ kJ}
\end{aligned}$$

$C_3H_8(g) + 5 \, O_2(g) \rightarrow 3 \, CO_2(g) + 4 \, H_2O(g)$

Reactant/Product	ΔH_f° (kJ/mol, from Appendix IIB)
$C_3H_8(g)$	-103.85
$O_2(g)$	0.0
$CO_2(g)$	-393.5
$H_2O(g)$	-241.8

Be sure to pull data for the correct formula and phase.

$$\begin{aligned}
\Delta H_{rxn}^\circ &= \sum n_P \Delta H_f^\circ (\text{products}) - \sum n_R \Delta H_f^\circ (\text{reactants}) \\
&= [3(\Delta H_f^\circ(CO_2(g))) + 4(\Delta H_f^\circ(H_2O(g)))] - [1(\Delta H_f^\circ(C_3H_8(g))) + 5(\Delta H_f^\circ(O_2(g)))] \\
&= [3(-393.5 \text{ kJ}) + 4(-241.8 \text{ kJ})] - [1(-103.85 \text{ kJ}) + 5(0.0 \text{ kJ})] \\
&= [-2147.7 \text{ kJ}] - [-103.85 \text{ kJ}] \\
&= -2043.9 \text{ kJ}
\end{aligned}$$

$$0.015\underline{9}3081 \text{ mol } CH_4 \times \frac{-802.3 \text{ kJ}}{1 \text{ mol } CH_4} = -12.\underline{7}81289 \text{ kJ}$$

$$0.024\underline{0}5363 \text{ mol } C_2H_6 \times \frac{-1427.7 \text{ kJ}}{1 \text{ mol } C_2H_6} = -34.\underline{3}4137 \text{ kJ}$$

$$0.022983181 \text{ mol } C_3H_8 \times \frac{-2043.9 \text{ kJ}}{1 \text{ mol } C_3H_8} = -46.\underline{9}7532 \text{ kJ}$$

The total heat is $-12.\underline{7}81289 \text{ kJ} - 34.\underline{3}4137 \text{ kJ} - 46.\underline{9}7532 \text{ kJ} = -94.\underline{0}9798 \text{ kJ} = -94.1 \text{ kJ}$

Check: The units (kJ) are correct. The magnitude of the answer (-100 kJ) makes sense because heats of combustion are typically large and negative.

Challenge Problems

6.79   **Given:** 655 kWh/yr; coal is 3.2% S; remainder is C; S emitted as $SO_2(g)$ and gets converted to H_2SO_4 when reacting
        with water   **Find:** $m(H_2SO_4)$/yr
        Conceptual Plan: write balanced reaction then $\Delta H_{rxn}^{\circ} = \sum n_P \Delta H_f^{\circ}(\text{products}) - \sum n_R \Delta H_f^{\circ}(\text{reactants})$
        (because the form of sulfur is not given, assume that all heat is from combustion of only carbon) then
        $kWh \rightarrow J \rightarrow kJ \rightarrow mol\ (C) \rightarrow g\ (C) \rightarrow g\ (S) \rightarrow mol\ (S) \rightarrow mol\ (H_2SO_4) \rightarrow g\ (H_2SO_4)$

$$\frac{3.60 \times 10^6\ J}{1\ kWh} \quad \frac{1\ kJ}{1000\ J} \quad \frac{mol\ C}{\Delta H_f^{\circ}(CO_2(g))} \quad \frac{12.01\ g}{1\ mol} \quad \frac{3.2\ g\ S}{(100.0 - 3.2)\ g\ C} \quad \frac{1\ mol}{32.07\ g} \quad \frac{1\ mol\ H_2SO_4}{1\ mol\ S} \quad \frac{98.09\ g}{1\ mol}$$

Solution: $C(s) + O_2(g) \rightarrow CO_2(g)$. This reaction is the heat of formation of $CO_2(g)$, so
$\Delta H_{rxn}^{\circ} = \Delta H_f^{\circ}(CO_2(g)) = -393.5$ kJ/mol then

$$655\ \text{kWh} \times \frac{3.60 \times 10^6\ J}{1\ \text{kWh}} \times \frac{1\ kJ}{1000\ J} \times \frac{mol\ C}{393.5\ kJ} \times \frac{12.01\ g\ C}{1\ mol\ C} \times \frac{3.2\ g\ S}{(100.0 - 3.2)\ g\ C} \times \frac{1\ mol\ S}{32.07\ g\ S}$$

$$\times \frac{1\ mol\ H_2SO_4}{1\ mol\ S} \times \frac{98.09\ g\ H_2SO_4}{1\ mol\ H_2SO_4} = 7.3 \times 10^3\ g\ H_2SO_4$$

Check: The units (g) are correct. The magnitude (7300) is reasonable, considering this is just one home.

6.81   **Given:** methane combustion, 100% efficiency; $\Delta T = 10.0\ ^{\circ}C$; house = 30.0 m × 30.0 m × 3.0 m;
        $C_s(air) = 30$ J/K · mol; 1.00 mol air = 22.4 L   **Find:** $m\ (CH_4)$
        Conceptual Plan: $l, w, h \rightarrow V(m^3) \rightarrow V(cm^3) \rightarrow V(L) \rightarrow mol\ (air)$ **then** $m, C_s, \Delta T \rightarrow q_{air}\ (J)$

$$V = lwh \qquad \frac{(100\ cm)^3}{(1\ m)^3} \qquad \frac{1\ L}{1000\ cm^3} \qquad \frac{1\ mol\ air}{22.4\ L} \qquad\qquad q = mC_s\Delta T$$

then $q_{air}\ (J) \rightarrow q_{rxn}\ (J) \rightarrow q(kJ)$ **then write balanced reaction for methane combustion**

$$q_{rxn} = -q_{air} \qquad \frac{1\ kJ}{1000\ J}$$

then $\Delta H_{rxn}^{\circ} = \sum n_P \Delta H_f^{\circ}(\text{products}) - \sum n_R \Delta H_f^{\circ}(\text{reactants})$, **and then** $q(kJ) \rightarrow mol\ (CH_4) \rightarrow g(CH_4)$

$$\Delta H_{rxn}^{\circ} \qquad\qquad \frac{16.04\ g}{1\ mol}$$

Solution: $V = lwh = 30.0\ m \times 30.0\ m \times 3.0\ m = 2700\ m^3$, then

$$2700\ m^3 \times \frac{(100\ cm)^3}{(1\ m^3)} \times \frac{1\ L}{1000\ cm^3} \times \frac{1\ mol\ air}{22.4\ L} = 1.20536 \times 10^5\ mol\ air, \text{ and then}$$

$$q = mC_s\Delta T = 1.20536 \times 10^5\ mol \times 30\ \frac{J}{mol \cdot ^{\circ}C} \times 10.0\ ^{\circ}C = 3.6161 \times 10^7\ J \times \frac{1\ kJ}{1000\ J} = 3.6161 \times 10^4\ kJ$$

needed
$CH_4(g) + 2\ O_2(g) \rightarrow CO_2(g) + 2\ H_2O(g)$

Reactant/Product	ΔH_f°(kJ/mol, from Appendix IIB)
$CH_4(g)$	−74.6
$O_2(g)$	0.0
$CO_2(g)$	−393.5
$H_2O(g)$	−241.8

Be sure to pull data for the correct formula and phase.

$\Delta H_{rxn}^{\circ} = \sum n_P \Delta H_f^{\circ}(\text{products}) - \sum n_R \Delta H_f^{\circ}(\text{reactants})$
$\qquad = [1(\Delta H_f^{\circ}(CO_2(g))) + 2(\Delta H_f^{\circ}(H_2O(g)))] - [1(\Delta H_f^{\circ}(CH_4(g))) + 2(\Delta H_f^{\circ}(O_2(g)))]$
$\qquad = [(-393.5\ kJ) + 2(-241.8\ kJ)] - [1(-74.6\ kJ) + 2(0.0\ kJ)]$
$\qquad = [-877.1\ kJ] - [-74.6\ kJ]$
$\qquad = -802.5\ kJ$

$$q_{rxn} = -q_{air} = -3.6161 \times 10^4\ kJ \times \frac{1\ mol\ CH_4}{-802.5\ kJ} \times \frac{16.04\ g\ CH_4}{1\ mol\ CH_4} = 722.8\ g\ CH_4 = 7 \times 10^2\ g\ CH_4$$

Check: The units (g) are correct. The magnitude (700) is not surprising because the volume of a house is large.

6.83 **Given:** $m(\text{ice}) = 9.0$ g; coffee: $T_1 = 90.0\,°C$, $m = 120.0$ g, $C_s = C_{H_2O}$, $\Delta H°_{fus} = 6.0$ kJ/mol **Find:** T_f of coffee

Conceptual Plan: $q_{ice} = -q_{coffee}$ so g(ice) → mol (ice) → q_{fus}(kJ) → q_{fus} (J) → q_{coffee} (J) then

$$\frac{1\ \text{mol}}{18.01\ \text{g}} \qquad \frac{6.0\ \text{kJ}}{1\ \text{mol}} \qquad \frac{1000\ \text{J}}{1\ \text{kJ}} \qquad q_{coffee} = -q_{ice}$$

$q, m, C_s \to \Delta T$ then $T_i, \Delta T \to T_2$; now we have slightly cooled coffee in contact with 0.0 °C water

$$q = mC_s\Delta T \qquad \Delta T = T_2 - T_i$$

so $q_{ice} = -q_{coffee}$ with $m, C_s, T_i \to T_f$

$$q = mC_s(T_f - T_i)\ \text{then set}\ q_{ice} = -q_{coffee}$$

Solution: $9.0\ \text{g} \times \dfrac{1\ \text{mol}}{18.01\ \text{g}} \times \dfrac{6.0\ \text{kJ}}{1\ \text{mol}} \times \dfrac{1000\ \text{J}}{1\ \text{kJ}} = 2.9983 \times 10^3\ \text{J}$, $q_{coffee} = -q_{ice} = -2.9983 \times 10^3\ \text{J}$

$q = mC_s\Delta T$ Rearrange to solve for ΔT. $\Delta T = \dfrac{q}{mC_s} = \dfrac{-2.9983 \times 10^3\ \text{J}}{120.0\ \text{g} \times 4.18\ \dfrac{\text{J}}{\text{g} \cdot °C}} = -5.9775\ °C$ then

$\Delta T = T_2 - T_i$. Rearrange to solve for T_2. $T_2 = \Delta T + T_i = -5.9775\ °C + 90.0\ °C = 84.0225\ °C$

$q = mC_s(T_f - T_i)$ substitute in values and set $q_{H_2O} = -q_{coffee}$.

$q_{H_2O} = m_{H_2O}C_{H_2O}(T_f - T_{H_2Oi}) = 9.0\ \text{g} \times 4.18\ \dfrac{\text{J}}{\text{g} \cdot °C} \times (T_f - 0.0\ °C) =$

$-q_{coffee} = -m_{coffee}C_{coffee}(T_f - T_{coffee2}) = -120.0\ \text{g} \times 4.18\ \dfrac{\text{J}}{\text{g} \cdot °C} \times (T_f - 84.0225\ °C)$

Rearrange to solve for T_f.

$9.0\ \text{g}\ T_f = -120.0\ \text{g}\ (T_f - 84.0225\ °C) \rightarrow 9.0\ \text{g}\ T_f = -120.0\ \text{g}\ T_f + 10082.7\ \text{g} \rightarrow$

$-10082.7\ \text{g} = -129.0\ \dfrac{\text{g}}{°C}\ T_f \rightarrow T_f = \dfrac{-10082.7\ \text{g}}{-129.0\ \dfrac{\text{g}}{°C}} = 78.2\ °C$

Check: The units (°C) are correct. The temperature is closer to the original coffee temperature because the mass of coffee is so much larger than the ice mass.

6.85 $KE = \dfrac{1}{2}mv^2$. For an ideal gas. $v = u_{rms} = \sqrt{\dfrac{3RT}{\mathcal{M}}}$; so $KE_{avg} = \dfrac{1}{2}N_A m u_{rms}^2 = \dfrac{3}{2}RT$ then

$\Delta E_{sys} = KE_2 - KE_1 = \dfrac{3}{2}RT_2 - \dfrac{3}{2}RT_1 = \dfrac{3}{2}R\Delta T$. At constant V, $\Delta E_{sys} = C_V\Delta T$; so $C_V = \dfrac{3}{2}R$.

At constant P, $\Delta E_{sys} = q + w = q_P - P\Delta V = \Delta H - P\Delta V$. Because $PV = nRT$, for one mole of an ideal gas at constant P, $P\Delta V = R\Delta T$; so $\Delta E_{sys} = q + w = q_P - P\Delta V = \Delta H - P\Delta V = \Delta H - R\Delta T$. This gives

$\dfrac{3}{2}R\Delta T = \Delta H - R\Delta T$ or $\Delta H = \dfrac{5}{2}R\Delta T = C_P\Delta T$, so $C_P = \dfrac{5}{2}R$.

6.87 $q = \Delta H = 454\ \text{g} \times \dfrac{1\ \text{mol}}{18.02\ \text{g}} \times \dfrac{40.7\ \text{kJ}}{1\ \text{mol}} = 1025.405\ \text{kJ} = 1030\ \text{kJ}$ and $w = -P\Delta V$. Assume that $P = 1$ atm

(exactly) and $\Delta V = V_G - V_L$, where $V_L = 454\ \text{g} \times \dfrac{1\ \text{mL}}{0.9998\ \text{g}} \times \dfrac{1\ \text{L}}{1000\ \text{mL}} = 0.4540908\ \text{L}$ and $PV = nRT$.

Rearrange to solve for V_G.

$V_G = \dfrac{nRT}{P} = \dfrac{454\ \text{g} \times \dfrac{1\ \text{mol}}{18.02\ \text{g}} \times 0.08206\ \dfrac{\text{L} \cdot \text{atm}}{\text{mol} \cdot \text{K}} \times 373\ \text{K}}{1\ \text{atm}} = 771.1545\ \text{L}$

$\Delta V = V_G - V_L = 771.1545\ \text{L} - 0.4540908\ \text{L} = 770.7004\ \text{L}$ and so

$w = -P\Delta V = -1.0\ \text{atm} \times 770.7004\ \text{L} \times \dfrac{101.3\ \text{J}}{1\ \text{L} \cdot \text{atm}} = -78071.9515\ \text{J} = -7.81 \times 10^4\ \text{J} = -78.1\ \text{kJ}$

Finally, $\Delta E = q + w = 1025.405\ \text{kJ} - 78.0719515\ \text{kJ} = 947.333\ \text{kJ} = 950\ \text{kJ}$.

Conceptual Problems

6.89   (a)   False. When ΔE_{sys} is positive, the system gains energy.

(b)   False. The first law of thermodynamics states that the energy of the universe is constant. Therefore, the energy being gained by the system has to come from the surroundings, and the surroundings lose energy.

(c)   False. When ΔE_{sys} is positive, the system gains energy.

(d)   True. According to the first law of thermodynamics, the energy of the universe is constant. Therefore, the energy gained by the system comes from the surroundings, and the surroundings lose energy equal to the energy gained by the system.

6.91   (a)   At constant P, $\Delta E_{sys} = q + w = q_P + w = \Delta H + w$; so $\Delta E_{sys} - w = \Delta H = q$.

6.93   The aluminum cylinder will be cooler after 1 hour because it has a lower heat capacity than does water (less heat needs to be pulled out for every °C temperature change).

6.95   **Given:** 2418 J heat produced; 5 J work done on surroundings at constant P **Find:** ΔE, ΔH, q, and w
Conceptual Plan: interpret language to determine the sign of the two terms then $q, w \rightarrow \Delta E_{sys}$

$$\Delta E = q + w$$

Solution: Because heat is released from the system to the surroundings, $q = -2418$ J; because the system is doing work on the surroundings, $w = -5$ kJ. At constant P,
$\Delta H = q = -2.418$ kJ; $\Delta E = q + w = -2418$ J $- 5$ J $= -2423$ J $= -2$ kJ.

Check: The units (kJ) are correct. The magnitude of the answer (–2) makes physical sense because both terms are negative and the amount of work done is negligibly small.

6.97   (a)   If ΔV is positive, then $w = -P\Delta V < 0$. Because $\Delta E_{sys} = q + w = q_P + w = \Delta H + w$; if w is negative, then $\Delta H > \Delta E_{sys}$.

Questions for Group Work

6.99   (a)   Gasoline burning is a combustion reaction, which is always exothermic (gasoline engines get very hot when running). $\Delta H < 0$

(b)   Steam condensing is an exothermic process, since the steam loses a lot of heat when it condenses (which is why you can get severely burned from steam). $\Delta H < 0$

(c)   Water boiling is an endothermic process, since the water molecules in steam have more kinetic energy than the molecules in the liquid phase. $\Delta H > 0$

Additional examples of exothermic processes are:

- Liquid water freezing on a cold winter day;
- Reacting an acid and a base, such as HCl with NaOH solutions;
- Any combustion reaction, such as propane burning in a gas grill, alcohol burning in a flaming dessert, or burning wood in a fireplace.

Additional examples of endothermic processes are:

- Snow melting on a spring day;
- Photosynthesis, which converts carbon dioxide and water into glucose and oxygen;
- The reaction in an instant cold pack.

6.101   The reactions in the calorimeter are:

- $C(s, \text{graphite}) + O_2(g) \rightarrow CO_2(g)$ ΔH_1
- $2\,H_2(g) + O_2(g) \rightarrow 2\,H_2O(g)$ ΔH_2
- $C_6H_{12}O_6(s) + 6\,O_2(g) \rightarrow 6\,CO_2(g) + 6\,H_2O(g)$ ΔH_3

The desired reaction is $6\,C(s, \text{graphite}) + 3\,O_2(g) + 6\,H_2(g) \rightarrow C_6H_{12}O_6(s)$. We can get this reaction with the following scheme:

$6\,C(s, \text{graphite}) + \cancel{6\,O_2(g)} \rightarrow \cancel{6\,CO_2(g)}$ $6\Delta H_1$
$6\,H_2(g) + 3\,O_2(g) \rightarrow \cancel{6\,H_2O(g)}$ $3\Delta H_2$
$\cancel{6\,CO_2(g)} + \cancel{6\,H_2O(g)} \rightarrow C_6H_{12}O_6(s) + \cancel{6\,O_2(g)}$ $-\Delta H_3$

$6\,C(s, \text{graphite}) + 3\,O_2(g) + 6\,H_2(g) \rightarrow C_6H_{12}O_6(s)$ $\Delta H = 6\Delta H_1 + 3\Delta H_2 - \Delta H_3$

Plug the results from the three individual reactions into the above equation to calculate the heat of formation of glucose.

7 The Quantum-Mechanical Model of the Atom

Problems by Topic

Electromagnetic Radiation

7.1 **Given:** distance to sun $= 1.496 \times 10^8$ km   **Find:** time for light to travel from sun to Earth

Conceptual Plan: distance km → distance m → time

$$\frac{1000 \text{ m}}{1 \text{ km}} \qquad \text{time} = \frac{\text{distance}}{3.00 \times 10^8 \text{ m/s}}$$

Solution: $1.496 \times 10^8 \text{ km} \times \dfrac{1000 \text{ m}}{1 \text{ km}} \times \dfrac{\text{s}}{3.00 \times 10^8 \text{ m}} = 499 \text{ s}$

Check: The units of the answer (s) are correct. The magnitude of the answer is reasonable because it corresponds to about 8 minutes.

7.3   (i)   By increasing wavelength, the order is d) ultraviolet $<$ c) infrared $<$ b) microwave $<$ a) radio waves.

  (ii)   By increasing energy, the order is a) radio waves $<$ b) microwaves $<$ c) infrared $<$ d) ultraviolet.

7.5   (a)   **Given:** $\lambda = 632.8$ nm   **Find:** frequency (ν)

Conceptual Plan: nm → m → ν

$$\frac{1 \text{ m}}{10^9 \text{ nm}} \qquad \nu = \frac{c}{\lambda}$$

Solution:

$$632.8 \text{ nm} \times \frac{\text{m}}{10^9 \text{ nm}} = 6.328 \times 10^{-7} \text{ m}; \quad \nu = \frac{3.00 \times 10^8 \text{ m}}{\text{s}} \times \frac{1}{6.328 \times 10^{-7} \text{ m}} = 4.74 \times 10^{14} \text{ s}^{-1}$$

Check: The units of the answer (s^{-1}) are correct. The magnitude of the answer seems reasonable because wavelength and frequency are inversely proportional.

  (b)   **Given:** $\lambda = 503$ nm   **Find:** frequency (ν)

Conceptual Plan: nm → m → ν

$$\frac{1 \text{ m}}{10^9 \text{ nm}} \qquad \nu = \frac{c}{\lambda}$$

Solution:

$$503 \text{ nm} \times \frac{1 \text{ m}}{10^9 \text{ nm}} = 5.03 \times 10^{-7} \text{ m}; \quad \nu = \frac{3.00 \times 10^8 \text{ m}}{\text{s}} \times \frac{1}{5.03 \times 10^{-7} \text{ m}} = 5.96 \times 10^{14} \text{ s}^{-1}$$

Check: The units of the answer (s^{-1}) are correct. The magnitude of the answer seems reasonable because wavelength and frequency are inversely proportional.

  (c)   **Given:** $\lambda = 0.052$ nm   **Find:** frequency (ν)

Conceptual Plan: nm → m → ν

$$\frac{1 \text{ m}}{10^9 \text{ nm}} \qquad \nu = \frac{c}{\lambda}$$

Solution: $0.052 \text{ nm} \times \dfrac{1 \text{ m}}{10^9 \text{ nm}} = 5.2 \times 10^{-11} \text{ m}$; $\nu = \dfrac{3.00 \times 10^8 \text{ m}}{\text{s}} \times \dfrac{1}{5.2 \times 10^{-11} \text{ m}} = 5.8 \times 10^{18} \text{ s}^{-1}$

Check: The units of the answer (s^{-1}) are correct. The magnitude of the answer seems reasonable because wavelength and frequency are inversely proportional.

7.7   (a)   **Given:** frequency (ν) from Problem 7.5(a) $= 4.74 \times 10^{14} \text{ s}^{-1}$ **Find:** Energy
        Conceptual Plan: $\nu \rightarrow E$
                $E = h\nu$ $h = 6.626 \times 10^{-34} \text{ J} \cdot \text{s}$

        Solution: $6.626 \times 10^{-34} \text{ J} \cdot \text{s} \times \dfrac{4.74 \times 10^{14}}{\text{s}} = 3.14 \times 10^{-19} \text{ J}$

        Check: The units of the answer (J) are correct. The magnitude of the answer is reasonable because we are talking about the energy of one photon.

        (b)   **Given:** frequency (ν) from Problem 7.5(b) $= 5.96 \times 10^{14} \text{ s}^{-1}$ **Find:** Energy
        Conceptual Plan: $\nu \rightarrow E$
                $E = h\nu \quad h = 6.626 \times 10^{-34} \text{ J} \cdot \text{s}$

        Solution: $6.626 \times 10^{-34} \text{ J} \cdot \text{s} \times \dfrac{5.96 \times 10^{14}}{\text{s}} = 3.95 \times 10^{-19} \text{ J}$

        Check: The units of the answer (J) are correct. The magnitude of the answer is reasonable because we are talking about the energy of one photon.

        (c)   **Given:** frequency (ν) from Problem 7.5(c) $= 5.8 \times 10^{18} \text{ s}^{-1}$ **Find:** Energy
        Conceptual Plan: $\nu \rightarrow E$
                $E = h\nu \quad h = 6.626 \times 10^{-34} \text{ J} \cdot \text{s}$

        Solution: $6.626 \times 10^{-34} \text{ J} \cdot \text{s} \times \dfrac{5.8 \times 10^{18}}{\text{s}} = 3.8 \times 10^{-15} \text{ J}$

        Check: The units of the answer (J) are correct. The magnitude of the answer is reasonable because we are talking about the energy of one photon.

7.9   **Given:** $\lambda = 532 \text{ nm}$ and $E_{\text{pulse}} = 4.88 \text{ mJ}$ **Find:** number of photons
        Conceptual Plan: nm $\rightarrow$ m $\rightarrow$ E_{photon} $\rightarrow$ **number of photons**
                $\dfrac{1 \text{ m}}{10^9 \text{ nm}} \quad E = \dfrac{hc}{\lambda}; h = 6.626 \times 10^{-34} \text{ J} \cdot \text{s} \quad \dfrac{E_{\text{pulse}}}{E_{\text{photon}}}$

        Solution:

$532 \text{ nm} \times \dfrac{1 \text{ m}}{10^9 \text{ nm}} = 5.32 \times 10^{-7} \text{ m}$; $E = \dfrac{6.626 \times 10^{-34} \text{ J} \cdot \text{s} \times \dfrac{3.00 \times 10^8 \text{ m}}{\text{s}}}{5.32 \times 10^{-7} \text{ m}} = 3.7\underline{3}65 \times 10^{-19} \text{ J/photon}$

$4.88 \text{ mJ} \times \dfrac{1 \text{ J}}{1000 \text{ mJ}} \times \dfrac{1 \text{ photon}}{3.7\underline{3}65 \times 10^{-19} \text{ J}} = 1.31 \times 10^{16} \text{ photons}$

        Check: The units of the answer (number of photons) are correct. The magnitude of the answer is reasonable for the amount of energy involved.

7.11   (a)   **Given:** $\lambda = 1500 \text{ nm}$ **Find:** E for 1 mol photons
        Conceptual Plan: nm $\rightarrow$ m $\rightarrow$ E_{photon} $\rightarrow$ $E(\text{J})_{\text{mol}}$ $\rightarrow$ $E(\text{kJ})_{\text{mol}}$
                $\dfrac{1 \text{ m}}{10^9 \text{ nm}} \quad E = \dfrac{hc}{\lambda}; h = 6.626 \times 10^{-34} \text{ J} \cdot \text{s} \quad \dfrac{1 \text{ mol}}{6.022 \times 10^{23} \text{ photons}} \quad \dfrac{1 \text{ kJ}}{1000 \text{ J}}$

        Solution:

$1500 \text{ nm} \times \dfrac{1 \text{ m}}{10^9 \text{ nm}} = 1.500 \times 10^{-6} \text{ m}$; $E = \dfrac{6.626 \times 10^{-34} \text{ J} \cdot \text{s} \times \dfrac{3.00 \times 10^8 \text{ m}}{\text{s}}}{1.500 \times 10^{-6} \text{ m}} = 1.3\underline{2}52 \times 10^{-19} \text{ J/pho}$

$\dfrac{1.3\underline{2}52 \times 10^{-19} \text{ J}}{\text{photon}} \times \dfrac{6.022 \times 10^{23} \text{ photons}}{1 \text{ mol}} \times \dfrac{1 \text{ kJ}}{1000 \text{ J}} = 79.8 \text{ kJ/mol}$

Check: The units of the answer (kJ/mol) are correct. The magnitude of the answer is reasonable for a wavelength in the infrared region.

(b) **Given:** $\lambda = 500$ nm   **Find:** E for 1 mol photons
Conceptual Plan: nm $\rightarrow$ m $\rightarrow$ E_{photon} $\rightarrow$ E_{mol} $\rightarrow$ $E(kJ)_{mol}$

$$\frac{1\ m}{10^9\ nm} \quad E = \frac{hc}{\lambda}; h = 6.626 \times 10^{-34}\ J \cdot s \quad \frac{1\ mol}{6.022 \times 10^{23}\ photons} \quad \frac{1\ kJ}{1000\ J}$$

Solution:

$$500\ \cancel{nm} \times \frac{1\ m}{10^9\ \cancel{nm}} = 5.00 \times 10^{-7}\ m; \quad E = \frac{6.626 \times 10^{-34}\ J \cdot \cancel{s} \times \dfrac{3.00 \times 10^8\ \cancel{m}}{\cancel{s}}}{5.00 \times 10^{-7}\ \cancel{m}} = 3.9\underline{7}56 \times 10^{-19}\ J/photon$$

$$\frac{3.9\underline{7}56 \times 10^{-19}\ \cancel{J}}{\cancel{photon}} \times \frac{6.022 \times 10^{23}\ \cancel{photons}}{1\ mol} \times \frac{1\ kJ}{1000\ \cancel{J}} = 239\ kJ/mol$$

Check: The units of the answer (kJ/mol) are correct. The magnitude of the answer is reasonable for a wavelength in the visible region.

(c) **Given:** $\lambda = 150$ nm   **Find:** E for 1 mol photons
Conceptual Plan: nm $\rightarrow$ m $\rightarrow$ E_{photon} $\rightarrow$ E_{mol} $\rightarrow$ $E(kJ)_{mol}$

$$\frac{1\ m}{10^9\ nm} \quad E = \frac{hc}{\lambda}; h = 6.626 \times 10^{-34}\ J \cdot s \quad \frac{1\ mol}{6.022 \times 10^{23}\ photons} \quad \frac{1\ kJ}{1000\ J}$$

Solution:

$$1.50\ \cancel{nm} \times \frac{1\ m}{10^9\ \cancel{nm}} = 1.50 \times 10^{-7}\ m; \quad E = \frac{6.626 \times 10^{-34}\ J \cdot \cancel{s} \times \dfrac{3.00 \times 10^8\ \cancel{m}}{\cancel{s}}}{1.50 \times 10^{-7}\ \cancel{m}} = 1.3\underline{2}52 \times 10^{-18}\ J/photon$$

$$\frac{1.3\underline{2}52 \times 10^{-18}\ \cancel{J}}{\cancel{photon}} \times \frac{6.022 \times 10^{23}\ \cancel{photons}}{1\ mol} \times \frac{1\ kJ}{1000\ \cancel{J}} = 798\ kJ/mol$$

Check: The units of the answer (kJ/mol) are correct. The magnitude of the answer is reasonable for a wavelength in the ultraviolet region. Note: The energy increases from the IR to the Vis to the UV as expected.

The Wave Nature of Matter and the Uncertainty Principle

7.13   The interference pattern would be a series of light and dark lines.

7.15   **Given:** $m = 9.109 \times 10^{-31}$ kg; $v = 1.55 \times 10^5$ m/s   **Find:** λ
Conceptual Plan: $m, v \rightarrow \lambda$

$$\lambda = \frac{h}{mv}$$

Solution: $\dfrac{6.626 \times 10^{-34}\ \dfrac{kg \cdot m^2}{s^2} \cdot \cancel{s}}{(9.109 \times 10^{-31}\ \cancel{kg})\left(\dfrac{1.55 \times 10^5\ \cancel{m}}{\cancel{s}}\right)} = 4.69 \times 10^{-9}\ m = 4.69\ nm$$

Check: The units of the answer (m) are correct. The magnitude is reasonable because we are looking at an electron.

7.17   **Given:** $m = 143$ g; $v = 95$ mph   **Find:** λ
Conceptual Plan: $m, v \rightarrow \lambda$

$$\lambda = \frac{h}{mv}$$

Solution:
$$\frac{6.626 \times 10^{-34} \frac{\text{kg} \cdot \text{m}^2}{\text{s}^2} \cdot \text{s}}{(143 \text{ g})\left(\dfrac{1 \text{ kg}}{1000 \text{ g}}\right)\left(\dfrac{95 \text{ mi}}{1 \text{ hr}}\right)\left(\dfrac{1.609 \text{ km}}{1 \text{ mi}}\right)\left(\dfrac{1000 \text{ m}}{1 \text{ km}}\right)\left(\dfrac{1 \text{ hr}}{3600 \text{ s}}\right)} = 1.1 \times 10^{-34} \text{ m}$$

The value of the wavelength (1.1×10^{-34} m) is so small that it will not have an effect on the trajectory of the baseball.

Check: The units of the answer (m) are correct. The magnitude of the answer is very small, as would be expected for the de Broglie wavelength of a baseball.

Orbitals and Quantum Numbers

7.19   Because the size of the orbital is determined by the n quantum number, with the size increasing with increasing n, an electron in a $2s$ orbital is closer, on average, to the nucleus than is an electron in a $3s$ orbital.

7.21   The value of l is an integer that lies between 0 and $n - 1$.
   (a)   When $n = 1$, l can only be $l = 0$.
   (b)   When $n = 2$, l can be $l = 0$ or $l = 1$.
   (c)   When $n = 3$, l can be $l = 0$, $l = 1$, or $l = 2$.
   (d)   When $n = 4$, l can be $l = 0$, $l = 1$, $l = 2$, or $l = 3$.

7.23   When $n = 3$: $l = 2$, $m_l = -2, -1, 0, 1, 2$
                    $l = 1$, $m_l = -1, 0, 1$
                    $l = 0$ $m_l = 0$
for a total of 9 orbitals.

7.25   The spin quantum number m_s has only two possible values: $m_s = +\frac{1}{2}$ and $m_s = -\frac{1}{2}$.

7.27   Set c cannot occur together as a set of quantum numbers to specify an orbital. l must lie between 0 and $n - 1$; so for $n = 3$, l can only be as high as 2.

7.29   The $2s$ orbital would be the same shape as the $1s$ orbital but would be larger in size, and the $3p$ orbitals would have the same shape as the $2p$ orbitals but would be larger in size. Also, the $2s$ and $3p$ orbitals would have more nodes.

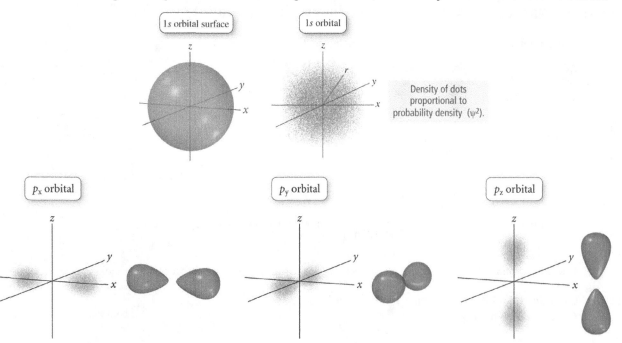

Atomic Spectroscopy

7.31   When the atom emits the photon of energy that was needed to raise the electron to the $n = 2$ level, the photon has the same energy as the energy absorbed to move the electron to the excited state. Therefore, the electron has to be in $n = 1$ (the ground state) following the emission of the photon.

7.33   According to the quantum-mechanical model, the higher the n level, the higher the energy. So the transition from $3p \rightarrow 1s$ would be a greater energy difference than a transition from $2p \rightarrow 1s$. The lower energy transition would have the longer wavelength. Therefore, the $2p \rightarrow 1s$ transition would produce a longer wavelength.

7.35   (a)   **Given:** $n = 2 \rightarrow n = 1$ **Find:** λ
Conceptual Plan: $n = 1, n = 2 \rightarrow \Delta E_{atom} \rightarrow \Delta E_{photon} \rightarrow \lambda$

$$\Delta E_{atom} = E_1 - E_2 \quad \Delta E_{atom} \rightarrow -\Delta E_{photon} \quad E = \frac{hc}{\lambda}$$

Solution:
$\Delta E = E_1 - E_2$

$$= -2.18 \times 10^{-18} \text{ J} \left(\frac{1}{1^2}\right) - \left[-2.18 \times 10^{-18}\left(\frac{1}{2^2}\right)\right] = -2.18 \times 10^{-18} \text{ J} \left[\left(\frac{1}{1^2}\right) - \left(\frac{1}{2^2}\right)\right]$$

$$= -1.6\underline{3}5 \times 10^{-18} \text{ J}$$

$$\Delta E_{photon} = -\Delta E_{atom} = 1.6\underline{3}5 \times 10^{-18} \text{ J}; \lambda = \frac{hc}{E} = \frac{(6.626 \times 10^{-34} \text{ J} \cdot \text{s})(3.00 \times 10^8 \text{ m/s})}{1.6\underline{3}5 \times 10^{-18} \text{ J}} = 1.22 \times 10^{-7} \text{ m}$$

This transition would produce a wavelength in the UV region.

Check: The units of the answer (m) are correct. The magnitude of the answer is reasonable because it is in the region of UV radiation.

(b)   **Given:** $n = 3 \rightarrow n = 1$ **Find:** λ
Conceptual Plan: $n = 1, n = 3 \rightarrow \Delta E_{atom} \rightarrow \Delta E_{photon} \rightarrow \lambda$

$$\Delta E_{atom} = E_1 - E_3 \quad \Delta E_{atom} \rightarrow -\Delta E_{photon} \quad E = \frac{hc}{\lambda}$$

Solution:
$\Delta E = E_1 - E_3$

$$= -2.18 \times 10^{-18} \text{ J} \left(\frac{1}{1^2}\right) - \left[-2.18 \times 10^{-18}\left(\frac{1}{3^2}\right)\right] = -2.18 \times 10^{-18} \text{ J} \left[\left(\frac{1}{1^2}\right) - \left(\frac{1}{3^2}\right)\right]$$

$$= -1.9\underline{3}8 \times 10^{-18} \text{ J}$$

$$\Delta E_{photon} = -\Delta E_{atom} = 1.9\underline{3}8 \times 10^{-18} \text{ J}; \lambda = \frac{hc}{E} = \frac{(6.626 \times 10^{-34} \text{ J} \cdot \text{s})(3.00 \times 10^8 \text{ m/s})}{1.9\underline{3}8 \times 10^{-18} \text{ J}} = 1.03 \times 10^{-7} \text{ m}$$

This transition would produce a wavelength in the UV region.

Check: The units of the answer (m) are correct. The magnitude of the answer is reasonable because it is in the region of UV radiation.

(c)   **Given:** $n = 4 \rightarrow n = 2$ **Find:** λ
Conceptual Plan: $n = 2, n = 4 \rightarrow \Delta E_{atom} \rightarrow \Delta E_{photon} \rightarrow \lambda$

$$\Delta E_{atom} = E_2 - E_4 \quad \Delta E_{atom} \rightarrow -\Delta E_{photon} \quad E = \frac{hc}{\lambda}$$

Solution:
$\Delta E = E_2 - E_4$

$$= -2.18 \times 10^{-18} \text{ J} \left(\frac{1}{2^2}\right) - \left[-2.18 \times 10^{-18}\left(\frac{1}{4^2}\right)\right] = -2.18 \times 10^{-18} \text{ J} \left[\left(\frac{1}{2^2}\right) - \left(\frac{1}{4^2}\right)\right]$$

$$= -4.0\underline{8}8 \times 10^{-19} \text{ J}$$

$$\Delta E_{photon} = -\Delta E_{atom} = 4.0\underline{8}8 \times 10^{-19} \text{ J}; \lambda = \frac{hc}{E} = \frac{(6.626 \times 10^{-34} \text{ J} \cdot \text{s})(3.00 \times 10^8 \text{ m/s})}{4.0\underline{8}8 \times 10^{-19} \text{ J}} = 4.86 \times 10^{-7} \text{ m}$$

This transition would produce a wavelength in the visible region.

Check: The units of the answer (m) are correct. The magnitude of the answer is reasonable because it is in the region of visible light.

(d)   **Given:** $n = 5 \rightarrow n = 2$ **Find:** λ
Conceptual Plan: $n = 2, n = 5 \rightarrow \Delta E_{atom} \rightarrow \Delta E_{photon} \rightarrow \lambda$

$$\Delta E_{atom} = E_2 - E_5 \quad \Delta E_{atom} \rightarrow -\Delta E_{photon} \quad E = \frac{hc}{\lambda}$$

Solution:
$$\Delta E = E_2 - E_5$$

$$= -2.18 \times 10^{-18} \text{ J}\left(\frac{1}{2^2}\right) - \left[-2.18 \times 10^{-18}\left(\frac{1}{5^2}\right)\right] = -2.18 \times 10^{-18} \text{ J}\left[\left(\frac{1}{2^2}\right) - \left(\frac{1}{5^2}\right)\right]$$

$$= -4.5\underline{7}8 \times 10^{-19} \text{ J}$$

$$\Delta E_{photon} = -\Delta E_{atom} = 4.5\underline{7}8 \times 10^{-19} \text{ J}; \lambda = \frac{hc}{E} = \frac{(6.626 \times 10^{-34} \text{ J} \cdot \text{s})(3.00 \times 10^8 \text{ m/s})}{4.5\underline{7}8 \times 10^{-19} \text{ J}} = 4.34 \times 10^{-7} \text{ m}$$

This transition would produce a wavelength in the visible region.

Check: The units of the answer (m) are correct. The magnitude of the answer is reasonable because it is in the region of visible light.

7.37   **Given:** n (initial) $= 7$; $\lambda = 397$ nm   **Find:** n (final)
Conceptual Plan: $\lambda \rightarrow \Delta E_{photon} \rightarrow \Delta E_{atom} \rightarrow n = x, n = 7$

$$E = \frac{hc}{\lambda} \quad \Delta E_{photon} \rightarrow -\Delta E_{atom} \quad \Delta E_{atom} = E_x - E_7$$

Solution: $E = \frac{hc}{\lambda} = \dfrac{(6.626 \times 10^{-34} \text{ J} \cdot \text{s})(3.00 \times 10^8 \text{ m/s})}{(397 \text{ nm})\left(\dfrac{1 \text{ m}}{10^9 \text{ nm}}\right)} = 5.0\underline{0}7 \times 10^{-19} \text{ J}$

$$\Delta E_{atom} = -\Delta E_{photon} = -5.0\underline{0}7 \times 10^{-19} \text{ J}$$

$$\Delta E = E_x - E_7 = -5.0\underline{0}7 \times 10^{-19} = -2.18 \times 10^{-18} \text{ J}\left(\frac{1}{x^2}\right) - \left[-2.18 \times 10^{-18}\left(\frac{1}{7^2}\right)\right]$$

$$= -2.18 \times 10^{-18} \text{ J}\left[\left(\frac{1}{x^2}\right) - \left(\frac{1}{7^2}\right)\right]$$

$$0.2297 = \left(\frac{1}{x^2}\right) - \left(\frac{1}{7^2}\right); \quad 0.25011 = \left(\frac{1}{x^2}\right); \quad x^2 = 3.998; \quad x = 2$$

Check: The answer is reasonable because it is an integer less than the initial value of 7.

Cumulative Problems

7.39   **Given:** 348 kJ/mol   **Find:** λ
Conceptual Plan: kJ/mol $\rightarrow$ kJ/molec $\rightarrow$ J/molec $\rightarrow \lambda$

$$\frac{\text{mol C} - \text{C bonds}}{6.022 \times 10^{23} \text{ C} - \text{C bonds}} \quad \frac{1000 \text{ J}}{1 \text{ kJ}} \quad E = \frac{hc}{\lambda}$$

Solution: $\dfrac{348 \text{ kJ}}{\text{mol C} - \text{C bonds}} \times \dfrac{\text{mol C} - \text{C bonds}}{6.022 \times 10^{23} \text{ C} - \text{C bonds}} \times \dfrac{1000 \text{ J}}{\text{kJ}} = 5.7\underline{7}9 \times 10^{-19} \text{ J}$

$$\lambda = \frac{(6.626 \times 10^{-34} \text{ J} \cdot \text{s})(3.00 \times 10^8 \text{ m/s})}{5.7\underline{7}9 \times 10^{-19} \text{ J}} = 3.44 \times 10^{-7} \text{ m} = 344 \text{ nm}$$

Check: The units of the answer (m or nm) are correct. The magnitude of the answer is reasonable because this wavelength is in the UV region.

7.41 **Given:** $E_{pulse} = 5.0$ watts; $d = 5.5$ mm; hole $= 1.2$ mm; $\lambda = 532$ nm **Find:** photons/s

Conceptual Plan: fraction of beam through hole → fraction of power and then E_{photon} → number photons/s

$$\frac{\text{area hole}}{\text{area beam}} \qquad \text{fraction} \times \text{power} \qquad E = \frac{hc}{\lambda} \qquad \frac{\text{power/s}}{E/\text{photon}}$$

Solution: $A = \pi r^2;\ \dfrac{\pi(0.60\ \text{mm})^2}{\pi(2.75\ \text{mm})^2} = 0.0476 \qquad 0.0476 \times 5.0\ \text{watts} \times \dfrac{\text{J/s}}{\text{watt}} = 0.238\ \text{J/s}$

$$E_{photon} = \frac{(6.626 \times 10^{-34}\ \text{J}\cdot\text{s})(3.00 \times 10^8\ \text{m/s})}{(532\ \text{nm})\left(\dfrac{1\ \text{m}}{10^9\ \text{nm}}\right)} = 3.7\underline{3}6 \times 10^{-19}\ \text{J/photon}$$

$$\frac{0.2\underline{3}8\ \text{J/s}}{3.7\underline{3}6 \times 10^{-19}\ \text{J/photon}} = 6.4 \times 10^{17}\ \text{photons/s}$$

Check: The units of the answer (number of photons/s) are correct. The magnitude of the answer is reasonable.

7.43 **Given:** KE $= 506$ eV **Find:** λ

Conceptual Plan: $\text{KE}_{eV} \rightarrow \text{KE}_J \rightarrow v \rightarrow \lambda$

$$\frac{1.602 \times 10^{-19}\ \text{J}}{1\ \text{eV}} \qquad \text{KE} = 1/2\ mv^2 \qquad \lambda = \frac{h}{mv}$$

Solution:

$$506\ \text{eV}\left(\frac{1.602 \times 10^{-19}\ \text{J}}{1\ \text{eV}}\right)\left(\frac{\text{kg}\cdot\text{m}^2}{\dfrac{\text{s}^2}{\text{J}}}\right) = \frac{1}{2}(9.11 \times 10^{-31}\ \text{kg})\,v^2$$

$$v^2 = \frac{506\ \text{eV}\left(\dfrac{1.602 \times 10^{-19}\ \text{J}}{1\ \text{eV}}\right)\left(\dfrac{\text{kg}\cdot\text{m}^2}{\dfrac{\text{s}^2}{\text{J}}}\right)}{\dfrac{1}{2}(9.11 \times 10^{-31}\ \text{kg})} = 1.7796 \times 10^{14}\ \frac{\text{m}^2}{\text{s}^2}$$

$$v = 1.33 \times 10^7\ \text{m/s} \qquad \lambda = \frac{h}{mv} = \frac{6.626 \times 10^{-34}\dfrac{\text{kg}\cdot\text{m}^2}{\text{s}^2}\cdot\text{s}}{(9.11 \times 10^{-31}\ \text{kg})(1.33 \times 10^7\ \text{m/s})} = 5.47 \times 10^{-11}\ \text{m} = 0.0547\ \text{nm}$$

Check: The units of the answer (m or nm) are correct. The magnitude of the answer is reasonable because a de Broglie wavelength is usually a very small number.

7.45 **Given:** $n = 1 \rightarrow n = \infty$ **Find:** $E;\ \lambda$

Conceptual Plan: $n = \infty, n = 1 \rightarrow \Delta E_{atom} \rightarrow \Delta E_{photon} \rightarrow \lambda$

$$\Delta E_{atom} = E_\infty - E_1 \quad \Delta E_{atom} = \Delta E_{photon} \quad E = \frac{hc}{\lambda}$$

Solution: $\Delta E = E_\infty - E_1 = 0 - \left[-2.18 \times 10^{-18}\left(\dfrac{1}{1^2}\right)\right] = +2.18 \times 10^{-18}\ \text{J}$

$\Delta E_{photon} = \Delta E_{atom} = +2.18 \times 10^{-18}\ \text{J}$

$$\lambda = \frac{hc}{E} = \frac{(6.626 \times 10^{-34}\ \text{J}\cdot\text{s})(3.00 \times 10^8\ \text{m/s})}{2.18 \times 10^{-18}\ \text{J}} = 9.12 \times 10^{-8}\ \text{m} = 91.2\ \text{nm}$$

Check: The units of the answers (J for E and m or nm for part 1) are correct. The magnitude of the answer is reasonable because it would require more energy to completely remove the electron than just moving it to a higher n level. This results in a shorter wavelength.

7.47 (a) **Given:** $n = 1$ **Find:** number of orbitals if $l = 0 \rightarrow n$

Conceptual Plan: value n → values l → values m_l → number of orbitals

$$l = 0 \rightarrow n \qquad\qquad m_l = -1 \rightarrow +1\ \text{total}\ m_l$$

Solution:

$n =$	1	
$l =$	0	1
$m_l =$	0	$-1, 0, +1$

total 4 orbitals

Check: The total orbitals will be equal to the number of l sublevels^2.

(b)   **Given:** $n = 2$ **Find:** number of orbitals if $l = 0 \rightarrow n$
Conceptual Plan: value n $\rightarrow$ values l $\rightarrow$ values m_l $\rightarrow$ number of orbitals

$$l = 0 \rightarrow n \qquad\qquad m_l = -1 \rightarrow +1 \text{ total } m_l$$

Solution:

$$n = 2$$
$$l = 0 \qquad\quad 1 \qquad\qquad 2$$
$$m_l = 0 \qquad -1, 0, +1 \quad -2, -1, 0, 1, 2$$

total 9 orbitals

Check: The total orbitals will be equal to the number of l sublevels^2.

(c)   **Given:** $n = 3$ **Find:** number of orbitals if $l = 0 \rightarrow n$
Conceptual Plan: value n $\rightarrow$ values l $\rightarrow$ values m_l $\rightarrow$ number of orbitals

$$l = 0 \rightarrow n \qquad\qquad m_l = -1 \rightarrow +1 \text{ total } m_l$$

Solution:

$$n = 3$$
$$l = 0 \qquad\quad 1 \qquad\qquad 2 \qquad\qquad\qquad 3$$
$$m_l = 0 \qquad -1, 0, +1 \quad -2, -1, 0, 1, 2 \quad -3, -2, -1, 0, 1, 2, 3$$

total 16 orbitals

Check: The total orbitals will be equal to the number of l sublevels^2.

7.49   **Given:** $\lambda = 1875$ nm; 1282 nm; 1093 nm   **Find:** equivalent transitions
Conceptual Plan: $\lambda \rightarrow E_{photon} \rightarrow E_{atom} \rightarrow n$

$$E = \frac{hc}{\lambda} \quad E_{photon} = -E_{atom} \quad E = -2.18 \times 10^{-18}\,\text{J}\left(\frac{1}{n_f^2} - \frac{1}{n_i^2}\right)$$

Solution: Because the wavelengths of the transitions are longer wavelengths than those obtained in the visual region, the electron must relax to a higher n level. Therefore, we can assume that the electron returns to the $n = 3$ level.

For $\lambda = 1875$ nm: $E = \dfrac{(6.626 \times 10^{-34}\,\text{J} \cdot \text{s})(3.00 \times 10^8\,\text{m/s})}{1875\,\text{nm}\left(\dfrac{1\,\text{m}}{10^9\,\text{nm}}\right)} = 1.060 \times 10^{-19}$ J; 1.060×10^{-19} J $= -1.060 \times 10^{-19}$ J

-1.060×10^{-19} J $= -2.18 \times 10^{-18}\left(\dfrac{1}{3^2} - \dfrac{1}{n^2}\right); n = 4$

For $\lambda = 1282$ nm: $E = \dfrac{(6.626 \times 10^{-34}\,\text{J} \cdot \text{s})(3.00 \times 10^8\,\text{m/s})}{1282\,\text{nm}\left(\dfrac{1\,\text{m}}{10^9\,\text{nm}}\right)} = 1.551 \times 10^{-19}$ J; 1.551×10^{-19} J $= -1.551 \times 10^{-19}$ J

$-1.551 \times 10^{-19} = -2.18 \times 10^{-18}\left(\dfrac{1}{3^2} - \dfrac{1}{n^2}\right); n = 5$

For $\lambda = 1093$ nm: $E = \dfrac{(6.626 \times 10^{-34}\,\text{J} \cdot \text{s})(3.00 \times 10^8\,\text{m/s})}{1093\,\text{nm}\left(\dfrac{1\,\text{m}}{10^9\,\text{nm}}\right)} = 1.819 \times 10^{-19}$ J; 1.819×10^{-19} J $= -1.819 \times 10^{-19}$ J

-1.819×10^{-19} J $= -2.18 \times 10^{-18}\left(\dfrac{1}{3^2} - \dfrac{1}{n^2}\right); n = 6$

Check: The values obtained are all integers, which is correct. The values of n (4, 5, and 6) are reasonable. The values of n increase as the wavelength decreases because the two n levels involved are further apart and more energy is released as the electron relaxes to the $n = 3$ level.

7.51   **Given:** $\Phi = 193$ kJ/mol   **Find:** threshold frequency (ν)
Conceptual Plan: Φ kJ/ mol $\rightarrow$ Φ kJ/ atom $\rightarrow$ Φ J/ atom $\rightarrow$ ν

$$\frac{1\,\text{mol}}{6.022 \times 10^{23}\,\text{atoms}} \qquad \frac{1000\,\text{J}}{1\,\text{kJ}} \qquad \Phi = h\nu$$

Solution: $\nu = \dfrac{\Phi}{h} = \dfrac{\left(\dfrac{193\ \text{kJ}}{1\ \text{mol}}\right)\left(\dfrac{1\ \text{mol}}{6.022 \times 10^{23}\ \text{atoms}}\right)\left(\dfrac{1000\ \text{J}}{1\ \text{kJ}}\right)}{6.626 \times 10^{-34}\ \text{J} \cdot \text{s}} = 4.84 \times 10^{14}\ \text{s}^{-1}$

Check: The units of the answer (s^{-1}) are correct. The magnitude of the answer puts the frequency in the infrared range and is a reasonable answer.

7.53   **Given:** $\nu_{\text{low}} = 30\ \text{s}^{-1}$; $\nu_{\text{hi}} = 1.5 \times 10^4\ \text{s}^{-1}$; speed $= 344\ \text{m/s}$ **Find:** $\lambda_{\text{low}} - \lambda_{\text{hi}}$

     Conceptual Plan: $\nu_{\text{low}} \to \lambda_{\text{low}}$ and $\nu_{\text{hi}} = \lambda_{\text{hi}}$ then $\lambda_{\text{low}} - \lambda_{\text{hi}}$

                   $\lambda\nu = \text{speed}$

     Solution: $\lambda = \dfrac{\text{speed}}{\nu}$ $\lambda_{\text{low}} = \dfrac{344\ \text{m/s}}{30\ \text{s}^{-1}} = 11\ \text{m}$; $\lambda_{\text{hi}} = \dfrac{344\ \text{m/s}}{1.5 \times 10^4\ \text{s}^{-1}} = 0.023\ \text{m}$; $11\ \text{m} - 0.023\ \text{m} = 11\ \text{m}$

     Check: The units of the answer (m) are correct. The magnitude is reasonable because the value is only determined by the low frequency value because of significant figures.

7.55   **Given:** $\lambda = 792\ \text{nm}$; $V = 100.0\ \text{mL}$; $P = 55.7\ \text{mtorr}$; $T = 25\ ^\circ\text{C}$ **Find:** E to dissociate 15.0%

     Conceptual Plan: $\lambda \to E/\text{molecule}$ and then $P, V, T \to n \to$ **molecules**

                     $E = \dfrac{hc}{\lambda}$ $n = \dfrac{PV}{RT}$ $\dfrac{6.022 \times 10^{23}\ \text{molecules}}{1\ \text{mole}}$

     Solution: $E = \dfrac{(6.626 \times 10^{-34}\ \text{J} \cdot \text{s})(3.00 \times 10^8\ \text{m/s})}{792\ \text{nm}\left(\dfrac{1\ \text{m}}{10^9\ \text{nm}}\right)} = 2.51 \times 10^{-19}\ \text{J/molecule}$

$$\dfrac{(55.7\ \text{mtorr})\left(\dfrac{1\ \text{torr}}{1000\ \text{mtorr}}\right)\left(\dfrac{1\ \text{atm}}{760\ \text{torr}}\right)(100.0\ \text{mL})\left(\dfrac{1\ \text{L}}{1000\ \text{mL}}\right)\left(\dfrac{6.022 \times 10^{23}\ \text{molecules}}{1\ \text{mol}}\right)}{\left(\dfrac{0.0821\ \text{L} \cdot \text{atm}}{\text{mol} \cdot \text{K}}\right)(298\ \text{K})} = 1.80 \times 10^{17}\ \text{molecules}$$

     $(1.80 \times 10^{17}\ \text{molecules})(0.150) = 2.70 \times 10^{16}\ \text{molecules dissociated}$

     $(2.51 \times 10^{-19}\ \text{J/molecule})(2.70 \times 10^{16}\ \text{molecules}) = 6.777 \times 10^{-3}\ \text{J} = 6.78 \times 10^{-3}\ \text{J}$

     Check: The units of the answer (J) are correct. The magnitude is reasonable because it is for a part of a mole of molecules.

7.57   **Given:** 20.0 mW; 1.00 hr.; 2.29×10^{20} photons   **Find:** λ

     Conceptual Plan: $\text{mW} \to \text{W} \to \text{J} \to \text{J/photon} \to \lambda$

             $\dfrac{\text{W}}{1000\ \text{mW}}$ $E = \text{W} \times \text{s}$ $\dfrac{E}{\text{number of photons}}$ $\lambda = \dfrac{hc}{E}$

     Solution: $(20.0\ \text{mW})\left(\dfrac{1\ \text{W}}{1000\ \text{mW}}\right)\left(\dfrac{\dfrac{1\ \text{J}}{1\ \text{s}}}{1\ \text{W}}\right)\left(\dfrac{3600\ \text{s}}{2.29 \times 10^{20}\ \text{photons}}\right) = 3.14 \times 10^{-19}\ \text{J/photon}$

$$\dfrac{(6.626 \times 10^{-34}\ \text{J} \cdot \text{s})(3.00 \times 10^8\ \text{m/s})\left(\dfrac{10^9\ \text{nm}}{1\ \text{m}}\right)}{3.14 \times 10^{-19}\ \text{J}} = 632\ \text{nm}$$

     Check: The units of the answer (nm) are correct. The magnitude is reasonable because it is in the red range.

7.59   **Given:** $\lambda = 280\ \text{nm}$, $E_{\text{available}} = 885\ \text{mW}$ for 10. minutes; $\Phi = 0.24$ **Find:** Maximum mol CH_3X dissociated

     Conceptual Plan: $\lambda(\text{nm}) \to \lambda(\text{m}) \to E_{\text{photon}}$ and $\text{mW} \to \text{W}$, min $\to$ s then W, s $\to E_{\text{available}}$

                   $\dfrac{1\ \text{m}}{10^9\ \text{nm}}$ $E = \dfrac{hc}{\lambda}$ $\dfrac{1\ \text{W}}{10^3\ \text{mW}}$ $\dfrac{60\ \text{s}}{1\ \text{min}}$ $1\ \text{W} = 1\ \dfrac{\text{J}}{\text{s}}$

     then $E_{\text{photon}}, E_{\text{used}} \to$ **photons** $\to$ **mol CH_3X dissociated ideal** $\to$ **mol CH_3X dissociated actual**

           $\dfrac{E_{\text{used}}}{E/\text{photon}}$ $\dfrac{1\ \text{mole photons}}{6.022 \times 10^{23}\ \text{photons}}$ $\Phi = \dfrac{\text{number of reaction events}}{\text{number of photons absorbed}}$

Solution:

$$E_{photon} = \frac{(6.626 \times 10^{-34} \text{ J} \cdot \text{s})(3.00 \times 10^8 \text{ m/s})}{(280 \text{ nm})\left(\dfrac{\text{m}}{10^9 \text{ nm}}\right)} = 7.\underline{0}9929 \times 10^{-19} \text{ J/photon}; \quad 885 \text{ mW} \times \frac{1 \text{ W}}{10^3 \text{ mW}} = 0.885 \text{ W}$$

$$10. \text{ min} \times \frac{60 \text{ s}}{1 \text{ min}} = 6.0 \times 10^2 \text{ s then } 0.885 \text{ W} \times \frac{1 \text{ J/s}}{1 \text{ W}} \times 6.0 \times 10^2 \text{ s} = 5\underline{3}1 \text{ J}$$

$$\frac{5\underline{3}1 \text{ J}}{7.\underline{0}9929 \times 10^{-19} \text{ J/photon}} \times \frac{1 \text{ mole photons}}{6.022 \times 10^{23} \text{ photons}} = 1.\underline{2}420 \times 10^{-3} \text{ mol photons}$$

$$\text{mol CH}_3\text{X dissociated ideal} = 1.\underline{2}420 \times 10^{-3} \text{ mol photons} \times \frac{0.24 \text{ mol CH}_3\text{X}}{1.00 \text{ mol photons}} = 3.0 \times 10^{-4} \text{ mol CH}_3\text{X actual}$$

Check: The units of the answer (mol CH$_3$X dissociated) are correct. The magnitude of the answer is reasonable, since the power and quantum yield are low.

Challenge Problems

7.61   (a)   **Given:** $n = 1$; $n = 2$; $n = 3$; $L = 155$ pm   **Find:** E_1, E_2, E_3

        Conceptual Plan: $n \rightarrow E$

$$E_n = \frac{n^2 h^2}{8 \, m \, L^2}$$

        Solution:

$$E_1 = \frac{1^2(6.626 \times 10^{-34} \text{ J} \cdot \text{s})^2}{8(9.11 \times 10^{-31} \text{ kg})(155 \text{ pm})^2\left(\dfrac{1 \text{ m}}{10^{12} \text{ pm}}\right)^2} = \frac{1(6.626 \times 10^{-34})^2 \text{ J}^2\text{s}^2}{8(9.11 \times 10^{-31} \text{ kg})(155 \times 10^{-12})^2 \text{ m}^2}$$

$$= \frac{1(6.626 \times 10^{-34})^2\left(\dfrac{\text{kg} \cdot \text{m}^2}{\text{s}^2}\right)\text{Js}^2}{8(9.11 \times 10^{-31} \text{ kg})(155 \times 10^{-12})^2 \text{ m}^2} = 2.51 \times 10^{-18} \text{ J}$$

$$E_2 = \frac{2^2(6.626 \times 10^{-34} \text{ J} \cdot \text{s})^2}{8(9.11 \times 10^{-31} \text{ kg})(155 \text{ pm})^2\left(\dfrac{1 \text{ m}}{10^{12} \text{ pm}}\right)^2} = \frac{4(6.626 \times 10^{-34})^2 \text{ J}^2\text{s}^2}{8(9.11 \times 10^{-31} \text{ kg})(155 \times 10^{-12})^2 \text{ m}^2}$$

$$= \frac{4(6.626 \times 10^{-34})^2\left(\dfrac{\text{kg} \cdot \text{m}^2}{\text{s}^2}\right)\text{Js}^2}{8(9.11 \times 10^{-31} \text{ kg})(155 \times 10^{-12})^2 \text{ m}^2} = 1.00 \times 10^{-17} \text{ J}$$

$$E_3 = \frac{3^2(6.626 \times 10^{-34} \text{ J} \cdot \text{s})^2}{8(9.11 \times 10^{-31} \text{ kg})(155 \text{ pm})^2\left(\dfrac{1 \text{ m}}{10^{12} \text{ pm}}\right)^2} = \frac{9(6.626 \times 10^{-34})^2 \text{ J}^2\text{s}^2}{8(9.11 \times 10^{-31} \text{ kg})(155 \times 10^{-12})^2 \text{ m}^2}$$

$$= \frac{9(6.626 \times 10^{-34})^2\left(\dfrac{\text{kg} \cdot \text{m}^2}{\text{s}^2}\right)\text{Js}^2}{8(9.11 \times 10^{-31} \text{ kg})(155 \times 10^{-12})^2 \text{ m}^2} = 2.26 \times 10^{-17} \text{ J}$$

        Check: The units of the answers (J) are correct. The answers seem reasonable because the energy is increasing with increasing n level.

    (b)   **Given:** $n = 1 \rightarrow n = 2$ and $n = 2 \rightarrow n = 3$ **Find:** λ

        Conceptual Plan: $n = 1, n = 2 \rightarrow \Delta E_{atom} \rightarrow \Delta E_{photon} \rightarrow \lambda$

$$\Delta E_{atom} = E_2 - E_1 \quad \Delta E_{atom} \rightarrow -\Delta E_{photon} \quad E = \frac{hc}{\lambda}$$

        Solution: Use the energies calculated in part (a).

$$E_2 - E_1 = (1.00 \times 10^{-17} \text{ J} - 2.51 \times 10^{-18} \text{ J}) = 7.49 \times 10^{-18} \text{ J}$$

$$\lambda = \frac{(6.626 \times 10^{-34} \text{ J} \cdot \text{s})(3.00 \times 10^8 \text{ m/s})}{7.49 \times 10^{-18} \text{ J}} = 2.65 \times 10^{-8} \text{ m} = 26.5 \text{ nm}$$

$$E_3 - E_2 = (2.26 \times 10^{-17} \text{ J} - 1.00 \times 10^{-17} \text{ J}) = 1.26 \times 10^{-17} \text{ J}$$

$$\lambda = \frac{(6.626 \times 10^{-34} \text{ J} \cdot \cancel{s})(3.00 \times 10^8 \text{ m/}\cancel{s})}{1.26 \times 10^{-17} \cancel{J}} = 1.58 \times 10^{-8} \text{ m} = 15.8 \text{ nm}$$

These wavelengths are in the UV region.

Check: The units of the answers (m) are correct. The magnitude of the answers is reasonable based on the energies obtained for the levels.

7.63   For the 1s orbital in the Excel® spreadsheet, call the columns as follows: column A as r and column B as $\Psi(1s)$. Make the values for r column A as follows: 0–200. In column B, put the equation for the wave function written as follows: = (POWER(1/3.1415, 1/2))*(1/POWER(53, 3/2))*(EXP(−A2/53)). Go to make chart, choose xy scatter.

e.g., sample values	
r	$\Psi(1s)$
0	7.000146224
1	7.000143491
2	7.000140809
3	7.000138177
4	7.000135594
5	7.00013306
6	7.000130573

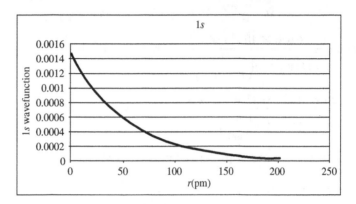

For the 2s orbital in the same Excel® spreadsheet, call the columns as follows: column A as r and column C as $\Psi(2s)$. Use the same values for r in column A: 0–200. In column C, put the equation for the wave function written as follows: = (POWER(1/((32)*(3.1415)), 1/2))*(1/POWER(53,3/2))*(2 − (A2/53))*(EXP(−A2/53)). Go to make chart, choose xy scatter.

e.g., sample values	
r	$\Psi(2s)$
0	7. 0000516979
1	7. 000050253
2	7. 0000488441
3	7. 0000474702
4	7. 0000461307
5	7. 0000448247
6	7. 0000435513

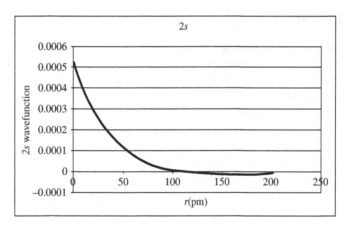

The plot for the 2s orbital extends below the x-axis. The x-intercept represents the radial node of the orbital. The plots differ in that the 1s plot does not contain a node and the slopes of the plots are different.

7.65   **Given:** threshold frequency $= 2.25 \times 10^{14} \text{ s}^{-1}$; $\lambda = 5.00 \times 10^{-7}$ m   **Find:** v of electron
Conceptual Plan: $v \rightarrow \Phi$ and then $\lambda \rightarrow E$ and then $\rightarrow KE \rightarrow v$

$$\Phi = hv \qquad E = \frac{hc}{\lambda} \qquad KE = E - \Phi \quad KE = 1/2 \, mv^2$$

Solution:

$$\Phi = (6.626 \times 10^{-34} \text{ J} \cdot \cancel{s})(2.25 \times 10^{14} \cancel{s^{-1}}) = 1.491 \times 10^{-19} \text{ J};$$

$$E = \frac{(6.626 \times 10^{-34} \text{ J} \cdot \cancel{s})(3.00 \times 10^8 \cancel{m}/\cancel{s})}{5.00 \times 10^{-7} \cancel{m}} = 3.976 \times 10^{-19} \text{ J}$$

$$KE = 3.9\underline{7}6 \times 10^{-19}\,J - 1.4\underline{9}1 \times 10^{-19}\,J = 2.485 \times 10^{-19}\,J; \quad v^2 = \frac{2.485 \times 10^{-19}\,\frac{kg \cdot m^2}{s^2}}{\frac{1}{2}(9.11 \times 10^{-31}\,kg)} = 5.455 \times 10^{11}\,\frac{m^2}{s^2}$$

$$v = 7.39 \times 10^5\,m/s$$

Check: The units of the answer (m/s) are correct. The magnitude of the answer is reasonable for the speed of an electron.

7.67   **Given:** $t = 5.0$ fs; $\lambda_{low} = 722$ nm   **Find:** ΔE and λ_{high}
           Conceptual Plan: $t \rightarrow \Delta E$ and then $\lambda_{low} \rightarrow E_{high} \rightarrow E_{low} \rightarrow \lambda_{high}$

$$\Delta t \times \Delta E \geq \frac{h}{4\pi} \qquad\qquad E = \frac{hc}{\lambda} \quad E - \Delta E \quad \lambda = \frac{hc}{E}$$

Solution: $\dfrac{6.626 \times 10^{-34}\,J \cdot s}{4(3.141)(5.0\,fs)\left(\dfrac{1\,s}{1 \times 10^{15}\,fs}\right)} = 1.0\underline{5}5 \times 10^{-20}\,J$

$$E = \frac{(6.626 \times 10^{-34}\,J \cdot s)(3.00 \times 10^8\,m/s)}{722\,nm\left(\dfrac{1\,m}{10^9\,nm}\right)} = 2.7\underline{5}32 \times 10^{-19}\,J$$

$$2.7\underline{5}32 \times 10^{-19}\,J + 1.0\underline{5}5 \times 10^{-20}\,J = 2.8\underline{5}87 \times 10^{-19}\,J$$

$$\lambda = \frac{(6.626 \times 10^{-34}\,J \cdot s)\left(3.00 \times 10^8\,\dfrac{m}{s}\right)\left(\dfrac{10^9\,nm}{1\,m}\right)}{(2.8\underline{5}87 \times 10^{-19}\,J)} = 695.35\,nm = 695\,nm$$

Check: The units of the answer (nm) are correct. The magnitude of the answer is reasonable because it is a shorter wavelength but it is close to the original wavelength.

Conceptual Problems

7.69   In the Bohr model of the atom, the electron travels in a circular orbit around the nucleus. It is a two-dimensional model. The electron is constrained to move only from one orbit to another orbit. But the electron is treated as a particle that behaves according to the laws of classical physics. The quantum-mechanical model of the atom is three-dimensional. In this model, we treat the electron, an absolutely small particle, differently than we treat particles with classical physics. The electron is in an orbital, which gives us the probability of finding the electron within a volume of space.
           Because the electron in the Bohr model is constrained to a circular orbit, it would theoretically be possible to know both the position and the velocity of the electron simultaneously. This contradicts the Heisenberg uncertainty principle, which states that position and velocity are complementary terms that cannot both be known with precision.

7.71   The transition from a, $n = 4 \rightarrow n = 3$, would result in emitted light with the longest wavelength. Because the n levels get closer together as n increases, the energy difference between the $n = 4$ and 3 levels would be less energy than the energy difference between the $n = 3$ and 2 levels and the $n = 2$ and 1 levels. Because energy and wavelength are inversely proportional, the smaller the energy, the longer the wavelength.

Questions for Group Work

7.73   Light is electromagnetic radiation, a type of energy embodied in oscillating electric and magnetic fields. Light in a vacuum travels at 3.00×10^8 m/s.
           Electromagnetic radiation can be characterized by wavelength, amplitude, and frequency. The wavelength (λ) of the wave is the distance in space between adjacent crests and is measured in units of distance. The amplitude of the wave is the vertical height of a crest. The more closely spaced the waves, that is, the shorter the wavelength, the more energy there is. The amplitude of the electric and magnetic field wave in light determines the intensity or brightness of the light. The higher the amplitude, the more photons are in the wave and so the more energy the wave has.

The frequency, (ν), is the number of cycles (or wave crests) that pass through a stationary point in a given period of time. The units of frequency are cycles per second. The frequency is inversely proportional to the wavelength (λ).

Frequency and wavelength are related by the equation: $\nu = \dfrac{c}{\lambda}$.

For visible light, wavelength determines the color. Red light has a wavelength of 750 nm, the longest wavelength of visible light, and blue has a wavelength of 500 nm. The presence of a variety of wavelengths in white light is responsible for the way we perceive colors in objects. When a substance absorbs some colors while reflecting others, it appears colored. Grass appears green because it reflects primarily the wavelength associated with green light and absorbs the others.

7.75   The magnetic quantum number (m_l) is an integer ranging from $-l$ to $+l$.
(a)   When $l = 0$, $m_l = 0$.
(b)   When $l = 1$, $m_l = -1, 0$, or $+1$.
(c)   When $l = 2$, $m_l = -2, -1, 0, +1$ or $+2$.
(d)   When $l = 20$, $m_l = -20, -19, \ldots, 0, \ldots 19$, or 20, so there are 41 values for m_l.
In the general case, the number of possible values for $m_l = 2l + 1$.

7.77   The $1s$ orbital does not have any nodes. The $2p$ orbitals have a node at the nucleus. Four of the $3d$ orbitals have a cloverleaf shape, with four lobes of electron density around the nucleus and two perpendicular nodal planes. The f orbitals are even more complex. The $4f$ orbitals are shown here. The number of nodes (and nodal planes) depends on the specific orbital.

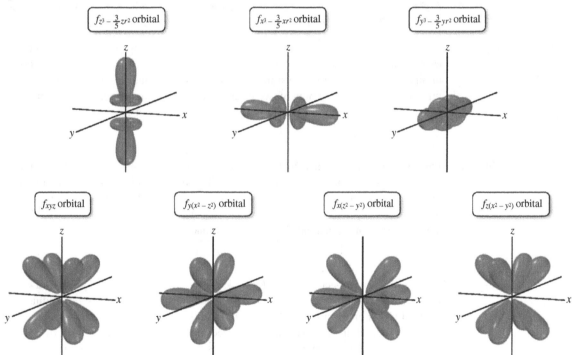

Periodic Properties of the Elements

Problems by Topic

Electron Configurations

8.1   (a)   P   Phosphorus has 15 electrons. Distribute two of these into the $1s$ orbital, two into the $2s$ orbital, six into the $2p$ orbital, two into the $3s$ orbital, and three into the $3p$ orbital. $1s^22s^22p^63s^23p^3$

        (b)   C   Carbon has six electrons. Distribute two of these into the $1s$ orbital, two into the $2s$ orbital, and two into the $2p$ orbital. $1s^22s^22p^2$

        (c)   Na   Sodium has 11 electrons. Distribute two of these into the $1s$ orbital, two into the $2s$ orbital, six into the $2p$ orbital, and one into the $3s$ orbital. $1s^22s^22p^63s^1$

        (d)   Ar   Argon has 18 electrons. Distribute two of these into the $1s$ orbital, two into the $2s$ orbital, six into the $2p$ orbital, two into the $3s$ orbital, and six into the $3p$ orbital. $1s^22s^22p^63s^23p^6$

8.3   (a)   N   Nitrogen has seven electrons and has the electron configuration $1s^22s^22p^3$. Draw a box for each orbital, putting the lowest energy orbital ($1s$) on the far left and proceeding to orbitals of higher energy to the right. Distribute the seven electrons into the boxes representing the orbitals, allowing a maximum of two electrons per orbital and remembering Hund's rule. You can see from the diagram that nitrogen has three unpaired electrons.

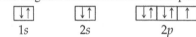

        (b)   F   Fluorine has nine electrons and has the electron configuration $1s^22s^22p^5$. Draw a box for each orbital, putting the lowest energy orbital ($1s$) on the far left and proceeding to orbitals of higher energy to the right. Distribute the nine electrons into the boxes representing the orbitals, allowing a maximum of two electrons per orbital and remembering Hund's rule. You can see from the diagram that fluorine has one unpaired electron.

        (c)   Mg   Magnesium has 12 electrons and has the electron configuration $1s^22s^22p^63s^2$. Draw a box for each orbital, putting the lowest energy orbital ($1s$) on the far left and proceeding to orbitals of higher energy to the right. Distribute the 12 electrons into the boxes representing the orbitals, allowing a maximum of two electrons per orbital and remembering Hund's rule. You can see from the diagram that magnesium has no unpaired electrons.

        (d)   Al   Aluminum has 13 electrons and has the electron configuration $1s^22s^22p^63s^23p^1$. Draw a box for each orbital, putting the lowest energy orbital ($1s$) on the far left and proceeding to orbitals of higher energy to the right. Distribute the 13 electrons into the boxes representing the orbitals, allowing a maximum of two electrons per orbital and remembering Hund's rule. You can see from the diagram that aluminum has one unpaired electron.

8.5 (a) P The atomic number of P is 15. The noble gas that precedes P in the periodic table is neon, so the inner electron configuration is [Ne]. Obtain the outer electron configuration by tracing the elements between Ne and P and assigning electrons to the appropriate orbitals. Begin with [Ne]. Because P is in row 3, add two $3s$ electrons. Next, add three $3p$ electrons as you trace across the p block to P, which is in the third column of the p block.

$$\text{P [Ne] } 3s^2 3p^3$$

(b) Ge The atomic number of Ge is 32. The noble gas that precedes Ge in the periodic table is argon, so the inner electron configuration is [Ar]. Obtain the outer electron configuration by tracing the elements between Ar and Ge and assigning electrons to the appropriate orbitals. Begin with [Ar]. Because Ge is in row 4, add two $4s$ electrons. Next, add ten $3d$ electrons as you trace across the d block. Finally, add two $4p$ electrons as you trace across the p block to Ge, which is in the second column of the p block.

$$\text{Ge [Ar] } 4s^2 3d^{10} 4p^2$$

(c) Zr The atomic number of Zr is 40. The noble gas that precedes Zr in the periodic table is krypton, so the inner electron configuration is [Kr]. Obtain the outer electron configuration by tracing the elements between Kr and Zr and assigning electrons to the appropriate orbitals. Begin with [Kr]. Because Zr is in row 5, add two $5s$ electrons. Next, add two $4d$ electrons as you trace across the d block to Zr, which is in the second column.

$$\text{Zr [Kr] } 5s^2 4d^2$$

(d) I The atomic number of I is 53. The noble gas that precedes I in the periodic table is krypton, so the inner electron configuration is [Kr]. Obtain the outer electron configuration by tracing the elements between Kr and I and assigning electrons to the appropriate orbitals. Begin with [Kr]. Because I is in row 5, add two $5s$ electrons. Next, add ten $4d$ electrons as you trace across the d block. Finally, add five $5p$ electrons as you trace across the p block to I, which is in the fifth column of the p block.

$$\text{I [Kr] } 5s^2 4d^{10} 5p^5$$

8.7 (a) Li is in period 2, and the first column in the s block, so Li has one $2s$ electron.
(b) Cu is in period 4, and the ninth column in the d block $(n-1)$, so Cu should have nine $3d$ electrons. However, it is one of our exceptions, so it has ten $3d$ electrons.
(c) Br is in period 4, and the fifth column of the p block, so Br has five $4p$ electrons.
(d) Zr is in period 5, and the second column of the d block $(n-1)$, so Zr has two $4d$ electrons.

8.9 (a) In period 4, an element with five valence electrons could be V or As.
(b) In period 4, an element with four $4p$ electrons would be in the fourth column of the p block and is Se.
(c) In period 4, an element with three $3d$ electrons would be in the third column of the d block $(n-1)$ and is V.
(d) In period 4, an element with a complete outer shell would be in the sixth column of the p block and is Kr.

Valence Electrons and Simple Chemical Behavior Form the Periodic Table

8.11 (a) Ba is in column 2A, so it has two valence electrons.
(b) Cs is in column 1A, so it has one valence electron.
(c) Ni is in column 8 of the d block, so it has ten valence electrons (eight from the d block and two from the s block).
(d) S is in column 6A, so it has six valence electrons.

8.13 (a) The outer electron configuration ns^2 would belong to a reactive metal in the alkaline earth family.
(b) The outer electron configuration $ns^2 np^6$ would belong to an unreactive nonmetal in the noble gas family.
(c) The outer electron configuration $ns^2 np^5$ would belong to a reactive nonmetal in the halogen family.
(d) The outer electron configuration $ns^2 np^2$ would belong to an element in the carbon family. If $n = 2$, the element is a nonmetal, if $n = 3$ or 4, the element is a metalloid, and if $n = 5$ or 6, the element is a metal.

8.15 Coulomb's law states that the potential energy (E) of two charge particles depends on their charges (q_1 and q_2) and on their separation (r). $E = \dfrac{1}{4\pi\varepsilon_o} \dfrac{q_1 q_2}{r}$. The potential energy is positive for charges of the same sign and negative for charges of opposite signs. The magnitude of the potential energy depends inversely on the separation between the charged particles.

(a)   **Given:** $q_1 = 1-; q_2 = 2+; r = 150$ pm   **Find:** E
Conceptual Plan: Magnitude of Potential Energy depends on the charge and the separation.

$$E = \frac{1}{4\pi\varepsilon_o}\frac{q_1 q_2}{r}$$

Solution: $E = \frac{1}{4\pi\varepsilon_o}\frac{(1-)(2+)}{150} = \frac{-0.0133}{4\pi\varepsilon_o}$

(b)   **Given:** $q_1 = 1-; q_2 = 1+; r = 150$ pm   **Find:** E
Conceptual Plan: Magnitude of Potential Energy depends on the charge and the separation.

$$E = \frac{1}{4\pi\varepsilon_o}\frac{q_1 q_2}{r}$$

Solution: $E = \frac{1}{4\pi\varepsilon_o}\frac{(1-)(1+)}{150} = \frac{-0.00667}{4\pi\varepsilon_o}$

(c)   **Given:** $q_1 = 1-; q_2 = 3+; r = 150$ pm   **Find:** E
Conceptual Plan: Magnitude of Potential Energy depends on the charge and the separation.

$$E = \frac{1}{4\pi\varepsilon_o}\frac{q_1 q_2}{r}$$

Solution: $E = \frac{1}{4\pi\varepsilon_o}\frac{(1-)(3+)}{100} = \frac{-0.0300}{4\pi\varepsilon_o}$

c is most negative and will have the lowest potential energy.

Coulomb's Law and Effective Nuclear Charge

8.17   The valence electrons in nitrogen would experience a greater effective nuclear charge. Be has four protons, and N has seven protons. Both atoms have two core electrons that predominantly contribute to the shielding, while the valence electrons will contribute a slight shielding effect. So Be has an effective nuclear charge of slightly more than 2+, and N has an effective nuclear charge of slightly more than 5+.

8.19   (a)   K(19) [Ar] $4s^1$ $Z_{eff} = Z -$ core electrons $= 19 - 18 = 1+$
(b)   Ca(20) [Ar] $4s^2$ $Z_{eff} = Z -$ core electrons $= 20 - 18 = 2+$
(c)   O(8) [He] $2s^2 2p^4$ $Z_{eff} = Z -$ core electrons $= 8 - 2 = 6+$
(d)   C(6) [He] $2s^2 2p^2$ $Z_{eff} = Z -$ core electrons $= 6 - 2 = 4+$

Atomic Radius

8.21   (a)   Al or In   In atoms are larger than Al atoms because as you trace the path between Al and In on the periodic table, you move down a column. Atomic size increases as you move down a column because the outermost electrons occupy orbitals with a higher principal quantum number that are larger, resulting in a larger atom.

(b)   Si or N   Si atoms are larger than N atoms because as you trace the path between N and Si on the periodic table, you move down a column (atomic size increases) and then to the left across a period (atomic size increases). These effects add together for an overall increase.

(c)   P or Pb   Pb atoms are larger than P atoms because as you trace the path between P and Pb on the periodic table, you move down a column (atomic size increases) and then to the left across a period (atomic size increases). These effects add together for an overall increase.

(d)   C or F   C atoms are larger than F atoms because as you trace the path between C and F on the periodic table, you move to the right within the same period. As you move to the right across a period, the effective nuclear charge experienced by the outermost electrons increases, which results in a smaller size.

8.23   Ca, Rb, S, Si, Ge, F   F is above and to the right of the other elements, so we start with F as the smallest atom. As you trace a path from F to S, you move to the left (size increases) and down (size increases). Next, you move left from S to Si (size increases), then down to Ge (size increases), then to the left to Ca (size increases), and then to the left and down to Rb (size increases). So in order of increasing atomic radii, F<S<Si<Ge<Ca<Rb.

⬤ **Ionic Electron Configurations, Ionic Radii, Magnetic Properties, and Ionization Energy**

8.25   (a) O^{2-} Begin by writing the electron configuration of the neutral atom.

               O $1s^2 2s^2 2p^4$

               Because this ion has a 2− charge, add two electrons to write the electron configuration of the ion.

               O^{2-} $1s^2 2s^2 2p^6$ This is isoelectronic with Ne.

   (b) Br^- Begin by writing the electron configuration of the neutral atom.

               Br $[Ar]\ 4s^2 3d^{10} 4p^5$

               Because this ion has a 1− charge, add one electron to write the electron configuration of the ion.

               Br^- $[Ar]\ 4s^2 3d^{10} 4p^6$ This is isoelectronic with Kr.

   (c) Sr^{2+} Begin by writing the electron configuration of the neutral atom.

               Sr $[Kr]\ 5s^2$

               Because this ion has a 2+ charge, remove two electrons to write the electron configuration of the ion.

               Sr^{2+} $[Kr]$

   (d) Co^{3+} Begin by writing the electron configuration of the neutral atom.

               Co $[Ar]\ 4s^2 3d^7$

               Because this ion has a 3+ charge, remove three electrons to write the electron configuration of the ion. Because it is a transition metal, remove the electrons from the 4s orbital before removing electrons from the 3d orbitals.

               Co^{3+} $[Ar]\ 4s^0 3d^6$

   (e) Cu^{2+} Begin by writing the electron configuration of the neutral atom. Remember, Cu is one of our exceptions.

               Cu $[Ar]\ 4s^1 3d^{10}$

               Because this ion has a 2+ charge, remove two electrons to write the electron configuration of the ion. Because it is a transition metal, remove the electron from the 4s orbital before removing electrons from the 3d orbitals.

               Cu^{2+} $[Ar]\ 4s^0 3d^9$

8.27   (a) V^{5+} Begin by writing the electron configuration of the neutral atom.

               V $[Ar]\ 4s^2 3d^3$

               Because this ion has a 5+ charge, remove five electrons to write the electron configuration of the ion. Because it is a transition metal, remove the electrons from the 4s orbital before removing electrons from the 3d orbitals.

               V^{5+} $[Ar]\ 4s^0 3d^0 = [Ne]\ 3s^2 3p^6$

               [Ne] $\boxed{\downarrow\uparrow}$ $\boxed{\downarrow\uparrow}\boxed{\downarrow\uparrow}\boxed{\downarrow\uparrow}$

                        3s   3p

               V^{5+} is diamagnetic.

   (b) Cr^{3+} Begin by writing the electron configuration of the neutral atom. Remember, Cr is one of our exceptions.

               Cr $[Ar]\ 4s^1 3d^5$

               Because this ion has a 3+ charge, remove three electrons to write the electron configuration of the ion. Because it is a transition metal, remove the electrons from the 4s orbital before removing electrons from the 3d orbitals.

               Cr^{3+} $[Ar]\ 4s^0 3d^3$

               [Ar] $\boxed{}$ $\boxed{\uparrow}\boxed{\uparrow}\boxed{\uparrow}\boxed{}\boxed{}$

                        4s   3d

               Cr^{3+} is paramagnetic.

   (c) Ni^{2+} Begin by writing the electron configuration of the neutral atom.

               Ni $[Ar]\ 4s^2 3d^8$

               Because this ion has a 2+ charge, remove two electrons to write the electron configuration of the ion. Because it is a transition metal, remove the electrons from the 4s orbital before removing electrons from the 3d orbitals.

Ni^{2+} $[Ar] 4s^0 3d^8$

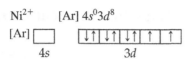
4s   3d

Ni^{2+} is paramagnetic.

(d) Fe^{3+} Begin by writing the electron configuration of the neutral atom.

         Fe $[Ar] 4s^2 3d^6$

         Because this ion has a 3+ charge, remove three electrons to write the electron configuration of the ion. Because it is a transition metal, remove the electrons from the 4s orbital before removing electrons from the 3d orbitals.

         Fe^{3+} $[Ar] 4s^0 3d^5$

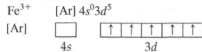
        4s   3d

         Fe^{3+} is paramagnetic.

8.29   (a)   Li or Li^+ A Li atom is larger than Li^+ because cations are smaller than the atoms from which they are formed.

      (b) I^- or Cs^+ An I^- ion is larger than a Cs^+ ion because, although they are isoelectronic, I^- has two fewer protons than Cs^+, resulting in a lesser pull on the electrons and therefore a larger radius.

      (c)   Cr or Cr^{3+} A Cr atom is larger than Cr^{3+} because cations are smaller than the atoms from which they are formed.

      (d)   O or O^{2-} An O^{2-} ion is larger than an O atom because anions are larger than the atoms from which they are formed.

8.31   Because all of the species are isoelectronic, the radius will depend on the number of protons in each species. The fewer the protons, the larger the radius.

      F: $Z = 9$; O: $Z = 8$; Mg: $Z = 12$; Na: $Z = 11$

      So: $O^{2-} > F^- > Na^+ > Mg^{2+}$

8.33   (a)   Br or Bi   Br has a higher ionization energy than Bi because as you trace the path between Br and Bi on the periodic table, you move down a column (ionization energy decreases) and then to the left across a period (ionization energy decreases). These effects sum together for an overall decrease.

      (b)   Na or Rb   Na has a higher ionization energy than Rb because as you trace a path between Na and Rb on the periodic table, you move down a column. Ionization energy decreases as you go down a column because of the increasing size of orbitals with increasing n.

      (c)   As or At   Based on periodic trends alone, it is impossible to tell which has a higher ionization energy because as you trace the path between As and At, you move to the right across a period (ionization energy increases) and then down a column (ionization energy decreases). These effects tend to oppose each other, and it is not obvious which will dominate.

      (d)   P or Sn   P has a higher ionization energy than Sn because as you trace the path between P and Sn on the periodic table, you move down a column (ionization energy decreases) and then to the left across a period (ionization energy decreases). These effects sum together for an overall decrease.

8.35   Because ionization energy increases as you move to the right across a period and increases as you move up a column, the element with the smallest first ionization energy would be the element farthest to the left and lowest on the periodic table. So In has the smallest ionization energy. As you trace a path to the right and up on the periodic table, the next element you reach is Si; continuing up and to the right, you reach N; and continuing to the right, you reach F. So in the order of increasing first ionization energy, the elements are $In < Si < N < F$.

8.37   The jump in ionization energy occurs when you change from removing a valence electron to removing a core electron. To determine where this jump occurs, you need to look at the electron configuration of the atom.

      (a)   Be $1s^2 2s^2$ The first and second ionization energies involve removing 2s electrons, while the third ionization energy removes a core electron; so the jump will occur between the second and third ionization energies.

      (b)   N $1s^2 2s^2 2p^3$ The first five ionization energies involve removing the 2p and 2s electrons, while the sixth ionization energy removes a core electron; so the jump will occur between the fifth and sixth ionization energies.

(c)   O $1s^22s^22p^4$ The first six ionization energies involve removing the $2p$ and $2s$ electrons, while the seventh ionization energy removes a core electron; so the jump will occur between the sixth and seventh ionization energies.

(d)   Li $1s^22s^1$ The first ionization energy involves removing a $2s$ electron, while the second ionization energy removes a core electron; so the jump will occur between the first and second ionization energies.

Electron Affinities and Metallic Character

8.39   (a)   Na or Rb   Na has a more negative electron affinity than Rb. In column 1A, electron affinity becomes less negative as you go down the column.

     (b)   B or S   S has a more negative electron affinity than B. As you trace from B to S in the periodic table, you move to the right, which shows the value of the electron affinity becoming more negative. Also, as you move from period 2 to period 3, the value of the electron affinity becomes more negative. Both of these trends sum together for the value of the electron affinity to become more negative.

     (c)   C or N   C has the more negative electron affinity. As you trace from C to N across the periodic table, you would normally expect N to have the more negative electron affinity. However, N has a half-filled p sublevel, which lends it extra stability; therefore, it is harder to add an electron.

     (d)   Li or F   F has the more negative electron affinity. As you trace from Li to F on the periodic table, you move to the right in the period. As you move to the right across a period, the value of the electron affinity generally becomes more negative.

8.41   (a)   Sr or Sb   Sr is more metallic than Sb because as we trace the path between Sr and Sb on the periodic table, we move to the right within the same period. Metallic character decreases as you move to the right.

     (b)   As or Bi   Bi is more metallic because as we trace a path between As and Bi on the periodic table, we move down a column in the same family (metallic character increases).

     (c)   Cl or O   Based on periodic trends alone, we cannot tell which is more metallic because as we trace the path between O and Cl, we move to the right across a period (metallic character decreases) and then down a column (metallic character increases). These effects tend to oppose each other, and it is not easy to tell which will predominate.

     (d)   S or As   As is more metallic than S because as we trace the path between S and As on the periodic table, we move down a column (metallic character increases) and then to the left across a period (metallic character increases). These effects add together for an overall increase.

8.43   The order of increasing metallic character is S < Se < Sb < In < Ba < Fr. Metallic character decreases as you move left to right across a period and decreases as you move up a column; therefore, the element with the least metallic character will be to the top right of the periodic table. So of these elements, S has the least metallic character. As you move down the column, the next element is Se. As you continue down and to the right, you reach Sb; continuing to the right, you reach In; moving down the column and to the right, you come to Ba; and down the column and to the right is Fr.

Cumulative Problems

8.45   Br: $1s^22s^22p^63s^23p^64s^23d^{10}4p^5$
Kr: $1s^22s^22p^63s^23p^64s^23d^{10}4p^6$
Krypton has a completely filled p sublevel, giving it chemical stability. Bromine needs one electron to achieve a completely filled p sublevel and thus has a highly negative electron affinity. Therefore, it easily takes on an electron and is reduced to the bromide ion, giving it the added stability of the filled p sublevel.

8.47   Write the electron configuration of vanadium.
V: [Ar] $4s^23d^3$
Because this ion has a 3+ charge, remove three electrons to write the electron configuration of the ion. Because it is a transition metal, remove the electrons from the $4s$ orbital before removing electrons from the $3d$ orbitals.
V^{3+}: [Ar] $4s^03d^2$
Both vanadium and the V^{3+} ion have unpaired electrons and are paramagnetic.

8.49   Because K^+ has a 1+ charge, you would need a cation with a similar size and a 1+ charge. Looking at the ions in the same family, Na^+ would be too small and Rb^+ would be too large. If we consider Ar^+ and Ca^+, we would have ions of similar size and charge. Between these two, Ca^+ would be easier to achieve because the first ionization energy of Ca is similar to that of K, while the first ionization energy of Ar is much larger. However, the second ionization energy of Ca is relatively low, making it easy to lose the second electron.

8.51   C has an outer shell electron configuration of ns^2np^2; based on this, you would expect Si and Ge, which are in the same family, to be most like carbon. Ionization energies for both Si and Ge are similar and tend to be slightly lower than that of C, but all are intermediate in the range of first ionization energies. The electron affinities of Si and Ge are close to the electron affinity of C.

8.53   (a)   N: [He] $2s^22p^3$ Mg: [Ne] $3s^2$ O: [He] $2s^22p^4$
             F: [He] $2s^22p^5$ Al: [Ne] $3s^23p^1$
       (b)   Mg > Al > N > O > F
       (c)   Al < Mg < O < N < F (from the table)
       (d)   Mg and Al would have the largest radius because they are in period $n = 3$; Al is smaller than Mg because radius decreases as you move to the right across the period. F is smaller than O and O is smaller than N because as you move to the right across the period, radius decreases.

             The first ionization energy of Al is smaller than the first ionization energy of Mg because Al loses the electron from the $3p$ orbital, which is shielded by the electrons in the $3s$ orbital. Mg loses the electron from the filled $3s$ orbital, which has added stability because it is a filled orbital. The first ionization energy of O is lower than the first ionization energy of N because N has a half-filled $2p$ orbitals, which adds extra stability, thus making it harder to remove the electron. The fourth electron in the O $2p$ orbitals experiences added electron–electron repulsion because it must pair with another electron in the same $2p$ orbital, thus making it easier to remove.

8.55   As you move to the right across a row in the periodic table for the main-group elements, the effective nuclear charge (Z_{eff}) experienced by the electrons in the outermost principal energy level increases, resulting in a stronger attraction between the outermost electrons and the nucleus and therefore a smaller atomic radii.

       Across the row of transition elements, the number of electrons in the outermost principal energy level (highest n value) is nearly constant. As another proton is added to the nucleus with each successive element, another electron is added, but that electron goes into an $n_{highest} - 1$ orbital (a core level). The number of outermost electrons stays constant, and they experience a roughly constant effective nuclear charge, keeping the radius approximately constant after the first couple of elements in the series.

8.57   All of the noble gases have a filled outer quantum level, very high first ionization energies, and positive values for the electron affinity; thus, the noble gases are particularly unreactive. The lighter noble gases will not form any compounds because the ionization energies of both He and Ne are over 2000 kJ/mol. Because ionization energy decreases as you move down a column, you find that the heavier noble gases (Ar, Kr, and Xe) do form some compounds. They have ionization energies that are close to the ionization energy of H and can thus be forced to lose an electron.

8.59   Group 6A: ns^2np^4 Group 7A: ns^2np^5
       The electron affinity of the group 7A elements is more negative than that of the group 6A elements in the same period because group 7A requires only one electron to achieve the noble gas configuration ns^2np^6, while the group 6A elements require two electrons. Adding one electron to the group 6A element will not give them any added stability and leads to extra electron–electron repulsions, so the value of the electron affinity is less negative than that for group 7A.

8.61   35 = Br = [Ar] $4s^23d^{10}4p^5$ 53 = I = [Kr] $5s^24d^{10}5p^5$
       Br and I are both halogens with an outermost electron configuration of ns^2np^5; the next element with the same outermost electron configuration is 85, At.

8.63   **Given:** $r = 100.00$ pm, $q_{proton} = 1.60218 \times 10^{-19}$ C, and $q_{electron} = -1.60218 \times 10^{-19}$ C
       Find: IE in kJ/mol and λ of ionization
       Conceptual Plan: $r, q_{proton}, q_{electron}, \rightarrow E_{atom} \rightarrow E_{mol}$ and then $E_{atom} \rightarrow \lambda$

$$E = \frac{1}{4\pi\varepsilon_0} \frac{q_p q_e}{r} \qquad \frac{1000\,J}{1kJ} \qquad \frac{6.022 \times 10^{23}\,atom}{1mol} \qquad\qquad \lambda = \frac{hc}{E}$$

Solution:

$$E = \frac{1}{(4)(3.141)\left(8.85 \times 10^{-12}\frac{C^2}{J \cdot m}\right)} \times \frac{(1.60218 \times 10^{-19}\,C)(-1.60218 \times 10^{-19}\,C)}{(100.00\,pm)\left(\frac{1\,m}{1 \times 10^{12}\,pm}\right)} = -2.3086 \times 10^{-18}\,\text{J/atom}$$

$$-2.3086 \times 10^{-18}\,\text{J/atom} \times \frac{6.022 \times 10^{23}\,\text{atom}}{1\,\text{mol}} \times \frac{1\,\text{kJ}}{(1000\,J)} = -1.39 \times 10^3\,\text{kJ/mol}$$

$$\text{IE} = 0 - (-1.39 \times 10^3\,\text{kJ/mol}) = 1.39 \times 10^3\,\text{kJ/mol}$$

$$\lambda = \frac{(6.626 \times 10^{-34}\,J \cdot s)(3.00 \times 10^8\,m/s)\left(\frac{1 \times 10^9\,\text{nm}}{1\,m}\right)}{(2.3086 \times 10^{-18}\,J)} = 86.1\,\text{nm}$$

Check: The units of the answer (kJ/mol) are correct. The magnitude of the answer is reasonable because the value is positive and energy must be added to the atom to remove the electron. The units of the wavelength (nm) are correct, and the magnitude is reasonable based on the ionization energy.

8.65 **Given:** Ra, $Z = 88$ **Find:** Z for next two alkaline earth metals

Solution: The next element would lie in period 8, column 2A. The largest currently known element is 116 in period 7, column 6A. To reach period 8, column 2A, you need to add 4 protons and would have $Z = 120$.

The alkaline earth metal following 120 would lie in period 9, column 2A. To reach this column, you need to add 10 d block element protons, 14 f block element protons, 18 g block element protons, 6 p block element protons, and 2 s block element protons. This would give $Z = 170$.

8.67 (a) Because ionization energy increases as you move to the right across a period, the element with the highest first ionization energy would be the element farthest to the right, F.

(b) Because the effective nuclear charge experienced by the outermost electrons increases as you move to the right across a period, which results in a smaller size, the element with the largest atomic radius is the element farthest to the left, B.

(c) Because metallic character decreases as you move left to right across a period, the most metallic element will be the element farthest to the left, B.

(d) In this series of elements we are filling the $2p$ orbitals, the element with three unpaired electrons will have an electron configuration of $1s^2 2s^2 2p^3$, N.

Challenge Problems

8.69 (a) Using Excel®, make a table of radius, atomic number, and density. Using xy scatter, make a chart of radius versus density. With an exponential trendline, estimate the density of argon and xenon. Also make a chart of atomic number versus density. With a linear trendline, estimate the density of argon and xenon.

Element	Atomic Radius (pm)	Atomic Number	Density g/L
He	32	2	0.18
Ne	70	10	0.90
Ar	98	18	
Kr	112	36	3.75
Xe	130	54	
Rn		86	9.73
		118	

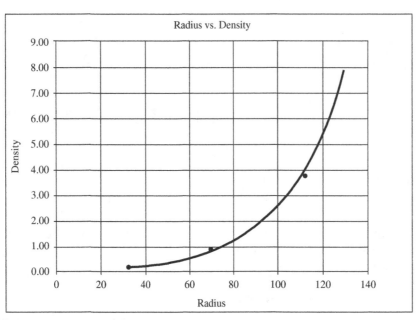

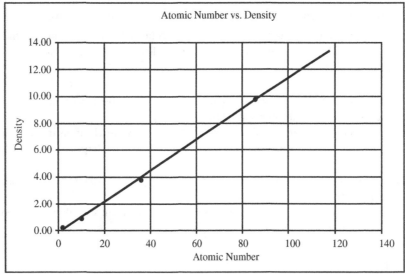

From the radius versus density chart, Ar has a density of ~2 g/L and Xe has a density of ~7.7 g/L. From the atomic number versus density chart, Ar has a density of ~1.8 g/L and Xe has a density of ~6 g/L.

(b)   Using the chart of atomic number versus density, element 118 would be predicted to have a density of ~13 g/L.

(c)   **Given:** Ne: $\mathcal{M} = 20.18$ g/mol; $r = 70$ pm   **Find:** mass of neon; d of neon in g/L

       Conceptual Plan: $\mathcal{M} \rightarrow m_{\text{atom}}$ and then $r \rightarrow \text{vol}_{\text{atom}}$ and then $\rightarrow d$

$$\frac{1 \text{ mol}}{6.022 \times 10^{23} \text{ atoms}} \qquad V = \frac{4}{3}\pi r^3 \qquad d = \frac{m}{V}$$

       Solution: $\dfrac{20.18 \text{ g}}{1 \text{ mol}} \times \dfrac{1 \text{ mol}}{6.022 \times 10^{23} \text{ atoms}} = 3.35 \times 10^{-23}$ g/atom

$$V = \frac{4}{3} \times 3.14 \times (70 \text{ pm})^3 \times \left(\frac{1 \text{ m}}{10^{12} \text{ pm}}\right)^3 \times \frac{1 \text{ L}}{0.0010 \text{ m}^3} = 1.\underline{4}4 \times 10^{-27} \text{ L}$$

$$d = \frac{3.35 \times 10^{-23} \text{ g}}{1.44 \times 10^{-27} \text{ L}} = 2.\underline{3}3 \times 10^4 = 2.3 \times 10^4 \text{ g/L}$$

Check: The units of the answer (g/L) are correct. This density is significantly larger than the actual density of neon gas. This suggests that a liter L of neon is composed primarily of empty space.

(d) **Given:** Ne: $\mathcal{M} = 20.18$ g/mol, $d = 0.90$ g/L; Kr: $\mathcal{M} = 83.80$ g/mol, $d = 3.75$ g/L; Ar: $\mathcal{M} = 39.95$ g/mol
Find: d of argon in g/L
Conceptual Plan: $d \rightarrow$ **mol/L** $\rightarrow$ **atoms/L for Kr and Ne and then atoms/L** $\rightarrow$ **mol/L** $\rightarrow$ **d for Ar**

$$\text{mol} = \frac{\text{mass}}{\text{molar mass}} \qquad \frac{6.022 \times 10^{23} \text{ atoms}}{1 \text{ mol}} \qquad\qquad \frac{1 \text{ mol}}{6.022 \times 10^{23} \text{ atoms}} \quad \frac{39.95 \text{ g}}{1 \text{ mol}}$$

Solution: for Ne: $\dfrac{0.90 \text{ g}}{\text{L}} \times \dfrac{1 \text{ mol}}{20.18 \text{ g}} \times \dfrac{6.022 \times 10^{23} \text{ atoms}}{1 \text{ mol}} = 2.69 \times 10^{22}$ atoms/L

for Kr: $\dfrac{3.75 \text{ g}}{\text{L}} \times \dfrac{1 \text{ mol}}{83.80 \text{ g}} \times \dfrac{6.022 \times 10^{23} \text{ atoms}}{1 \text{ mol}} = 2.69 \times 10^{22}$ atoms/L

for Ar: $\dfrac{2.69 \times 10^{22} \text{ atoms}}{\text{L}} \times \dfrac{1 \text{ mol}}{6.022 \times 10^{23} \text{ atoms}} \times \dfrac{39.95 \text{ g}}{1 \text{ mol}} = 1.78$ g/L

This value is similar to the value calculated in part a. The value of the density calculated from the radius was 2 g/L, and the value of the density calculated from the atomic number was 1.8 g/L.

Check: The units of the answer (g/L) are correct. The value of the answer agrees with the published value.

8.71   The density increases as you move to the right across the first transition series. For the first transition series, the mass increases as you move to the right across the periodic table. However, the radius of the transition series elements stays nearly constant as you move to the right across the periodic table; thus, the volume will remain nearly constant. Because density is mass/volume, the density of the elements increases.

8.73   The longest wavelength would be associated with the lowest energy state next to the ground state of carbon, which has two unpaired electrons. Ground state of carbon:

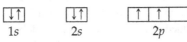

Longest wavelength: One of the p electrons flipped in its orbital, which requires the least amount of energy.

The next wavelength would be associated with the pairing of the two p electrons in the same orbital because this requires energy and raises the energy.

The next wavelength would be associated with the energy needed to promote one of the s electrons to a p orbital.

8.75   The element that would fill the $8s$ and $8p$ orbitals would have atomic number 168. The element is in the noble gas family and would have the properties of noble gases. It would have the electron configuration of [118] $8s^2 5g^{18} 6f^{14} 7d^{10} 8p^6$. The outer shell electron (highest n level) configuration would be $8s^2 8p^6$. The element would be relatively inert, have a first ionization energy less than 1037 kJ/mol (the first ionization energy of Rn), and have a positive electron affinity. It would be difficult to form compounds with most elements but would be able to form compounds with fluorine.

8.77   When you move down the column from Al to Ga, the size of the atom actually decreases because not much shielding is contributed by the $3d$ electrons in the Ga atom, while there is a large increase in the nuclear charge. Therefore, the effective nuclear charge is greater for Ga than for Al, so the ionization energy does not decrease. As you go from In to Tl, the ionization energy actually increases because the $4f$ electrons do not contribute to the shielding of the outermost electrons and there is a large increase in the effective nuclear charge.

8.79   The second electron is added to an ion with a $1-$ charge, so a large repulsive force has to be overcome to add the second electron. Thus, it will require energy to add the second electron, and the second electron affinity will have a positive value.

Conceptual Problems

8.81   If six electrons rather than eight electrons led to a stable configuration, the electron configuration of the stable configuration would be ns^2np^4.

   (a)   A noble gas would have the electron configuration ns^2np^4. This could correspond to the O atom.

   (b)   A reactive nonmetal would have one less electron than the stable configuration. This would have the electron configuration ns^2np^3. This could correspond to the N atom.

   (c)   A reactive metal would have one more electron than the stable configuration. This would have the electron configuration of ns^1. This could correspond to the Li atom.

8.83   (a)   True: An electron in a $3s$ orbital is more shielded than an electron in a $2s$ orbital. This is true because there are more core electrons below a $3s$ orbital.

   (b)   True: An electron in a $3s$ orbital penetrates the region occupied by the core electrons more than electrons in a $3p$ orbital. Examine Figure 8.5 showing the radial distribution functions for the $3s$, $3p$, and $3d$ orbitals. You will see that the $3s$ electrons penetrate more deeply than the $3p$ electrons and more than the $3d$ electrons.

   (c)   False: An electron in an orbital that penetrates closer to the nucleus will experience *less* shielding than an electron in an orbital that does not penetrate as far.

   (d)   True: An electron in an orbital that penetrates close to the nucleus will tend to experience a higher effective nuclear charge than one that does not. Because the orbital penetrates closer to the nucleus, the electron will experience less shielding and therefore a higher effective nuclear charge.

8.85   The $4s$ electrons in calcium have relatively low ionization energies ($IE_1 = 590$ kJ/mol; $IE_2 = 1145$ kJ/mol) because they are valence electrons. The energetic cost for calcium to lose a third electron is extraordinarily high because the next electron to be lost is a core electron. Similarly, the electron affinity of fluorine to gain one electron (-328 kJ/mol) is highly exothermic because the added electron completes fluoride's valence shell. The gain of a second electron by the negatively charged fluoride anion would not be favorable. Therefore, we would expect calcium and fluoride to combine in a 1:2 ratio.

Questions for Group Work

8.87   The orbitals fill in order of increasing energy of the orbitals, which is $1s<2s<2p<3s<3p<4s<3d<4p<5s<4d<5p<6s$. Keep in mind that s subshells can contain two electrons, p subshells can contain six electrons, and d subshells can contain ten electrons.

8.89   (a)   The Br^- and Se^{2-} ions are about the same size because the ions are an isoelectric pair.

   (b)   The Br^- ion is smaller than the Se^{2-} ion because the Br^- ion has a larger nuclear charge and fewer extra electrons than the Se^{2-} ion.

   (c)   The Fr^+ (194 pm) ion is the singly charged cation that is closest in size to the Br^- (195 pm) and Se^{2-} (198 pm) ions because cations are much smaller than their corresponding atoms.

9 Chemical Bonding I: Lewis Theory

Problems by Topic

Valence Electrons and Dot Structures

9.1   N: $1s^22s^22p^3$ $\cdot\ddot{N}:$ The electrons included in the Lewis structure are $2s^22p^3$.

9.3   (a)   Al: $1s^22s^22p^63s^23p^1$

$\cdot\dot{Al}\cdot$

(b) Na^+: $1s^22s^22p^6$

Na^+

(c)   Cl: $1s^22s^22p^63s^23p^5$

$:\ddot{Cl}\cdot$

(d) Cl^-: $1s^22s^22p^63s^23p^6$

$\left[:\ddot{Cl}:\right]^-$

Ionic Lewis Symbols and Lattice Energy

9.5   (a)   NaF: Draw the Lewis symbols for Na and F based on their valence electrons.
Na: $3s^1$ F: $2s^22p^5$

$Na\cdot$ $:\ddot{F}\cdot$

Sodium must lose one electron and be left with the octet from the previous shell, while fluorine needs to gain one electron to get an octet.

Na^+ $\left[:\ddot{F}:\right]^-$

(b)   CaO: Draw the Lewis symbols for Ca and O based on their valence electrons.
Ca: $4s^2$ O: $2s^22p^4$

$\cdot Ca\cdot$ $:\ddot{O}\cdot$

Calcium must lose two electrons and be left with the octet from the previous shell, while oxygen needs to gain two electrons to get an octet.

Ca^{2+} $\left[:\ddot{O}:\right]^{2-}$

(c) $SrBr_2$:   Draw the Lewis symbols for Sr and Br based on their valence electrons.
Sr: $5s^2$ Br: $4s^24p^5$

$\cdot Sr\cdot$ $:\ddot{Br}\cdot$

Strontium must lose two electrons and be left with the octet from the previous shell, while bromine needs to gain one electron to get an octet.

Sr^{2+} $2\left[:\ddot{Br}:\right]^-$

(d) K_2O: Draw the Lewis symbols for K and O based on their valence electrons. K: $4s^1$ O: $2s^22p^4$

$$K\cdot \quad :\ddot{\underset{\cdot\cdot}{O}}\cdot$$

Potassium must lose one electron and be left with the octet from the previous shell, while oxygen needs to gain two electrons to get an octet.

$$2K^+ \quad \left[:\ddot{\underset{\cdot\cdot}{O}}:\right]^{2-}$$

9.7   (a)   Sr and Se: Draw the Lewis symbols for Sr and Se based on their valence electrons.

                 Sr: $5s^2$ Se: $4s^24p^4$

$$\cdot Sr\cdot \quad :\ddot{\underset{\cdot\cdot}{Se}}\cdot$$

Strontium must lose two electrons and be left with the octet from the previous shell, while selenium needs to gain two electrons to get an octet.

$$Sr^{2+} \quad \left[:\ddot{\underset{\cdot\cdot}{Se}}:\right]^{2-}$$

Thus, we need one Sr^{2+} and one Se^{2-}. Write the formula with subscripts (if necessary) to indicate the number of atoms.

               SrSe

(b)   Ba and Cl: Draw the Lewis symbols for Ba and Cl based on their valence electrons.

                 Ba: $6s^2$ Cl: $3s^23p^5$

$$\cdot Ba\cdot \quad :\ddot{\underset{\cdot\cdot}{Cl}}\cdot$$

Barium must lose two electrons and be left with the octet from the previous shell, while chlorine needs to gain one electron to get an octet.

$$Ba^{2+} \quad 2\left[:\ddot{\underset{\cdot\cdot}{Cl}}:\right]^{-}$$

Thus, we need one Ba^{2+} and two Cl^-. Write the formula with subscripts (if necessary) to indicate the number of atoms.

               $BaCl_2$

(c)   Na and S: Draw the Lewis symbols for Na and S based on their valence electrons.

                 Na: $3s^1$ S: $3s^23p^4$

$$Na\cdot \quad :\ddot{\underset{\cdot}{S}}\cdot$$

Sodium must lose one electron and be left with the octet from the previous shell, while sulfur needs to gain two electrons to get an octet.

$$2\,Na^+ \quad \left[:\ddot{\underset{\cdot\cdot}{S}}:\right]^{2-}$$

Thus, we need two Na^+ and one S^{2-}. Write the formula with subscripts (if necessary) to indicate the number of atoms.

               Na_2S

(d)   Al and O: Draw the Lewis symbols for Al and O based on their valence electrons.

                 Al: $3s^23p^1$ O: $2s^22p^4$

$$\cdot \dot{Al}\cdot \quad :\ddot{\underset{\cdot}{O}}\cdot$$

Aluminum must lose three electrons and be left with the octet from the previous shell, while oxygen needs to gain two electrons to get an octet.

$$2\,Al^{3+} \quad 3\left[:\ddot{\underset{\cdot\cdot}{O}}:\right]^{2-}$$

Thus, we need two Al^{3+} and three O^{2-} to lose and gain the same number of electrons. Write the formula with subscripts (if necessary) to indicate the number of atoms.

               Al_2O_3

9.9   As the size of the alkaline metal ions increases down the column, so does the distance between the metal cation and the oxide anion. Therefore, the magnitude of the lattice energy of the oxides decreases, making the formation of the oxides less exothermic and the compounds less stable. Because the ions cannot get as close to each other, they do not release as much energy.

9.11   Cesium is slightly larger than barium, but oxygen is slightly larger than fluorine; so we cannot use size to explain the difference in the lattice energy. However, the charge on the cesium ion is 1+ and the charge on the fluoride ion is 1−, while the charge on the barium ion is 2+ and the charge on the oxide ion is 2−. The coulombic equation states that the magnitude of the potential also depends on the product of the charges. Because the product of the charges for CsF = 1− and the product of the charges for BaO = 4−, the stabilization for BaO relative to CsF should be about four times greater, which is what we see in its much more exothermic lattice energy.

Simple Covalent Lewis Structures, Electronegativity, and Bond Polarity

9.13   (a)   Hydrogen: Write the Lewis symbol of each atom based on the number of valence electrons.

H·   ·H

When the two hydrogen atoms share their electrons, they each get a duet, which is a stable configuration for hydrogen.

H—H

(b)   The halogens: Write the Lewis symbol of each atom based on the number of valence electrons.

:Ẍ·   ·Ẍ:

If the two halogens pair together, each can achieve an octet, which is a stable configuration. So the halogens are predicted to exist as diatomic molecules.

:Ẍ—Ẍ:

(c)   Oxygen: Write the Lewis symbol of each atom based on the number of valence electrons.

:Ö·   ·Ö:

To achieve a stable octet on each oxygen, the oxygen atoms will need to share two electron pairs. So oxygen is predicted to exist as a diatomic molecule with a double bond.

:Ö=Ö:

(d)   Nitrogen: Write the Lewis symbol of each atom based on the number of valence electrons.

·N̈·   ·N̈·

To achieve a stable octet on each nitrogen, the nitrogen atoms will need to share three electron pairs. So nitrogen is predicted to exist as a diatomic molecule with a triple bond.

N̈≡N̈

9.15   (a) PH_3:   Write the Lewis symbol for each atom based on the number of valence electrons.

·P̈·   ·H

Phosphorus will share an electron pair with each hydrogen to achieve a stable octet.

H—P̈—H
    |
    H

(b) SCl_2:   Write the Lewis symbol for each atom based on the number of valence electrons.

:S̈·   :C̈l·

The sulfur will share an electron pair with each chlorine to achieve a stable octet.

:S̈—C̈l:
    |
:C̈l:

(c)   HI: Write the Lewis symbol for each atom based on the number of valence electrons.

H·   ·Ï:

The iodine will share an electron pair with hydrogen to achieve a stable octet.

H—Ï:

(d) CH_4:   Write the Lewis symbol for each atom based on the number of valence electrons.

·Ċ·   H·

The carbon will share an electron pair with each hydrogen to achieve a stable octet.

$$H-\underset{\underset{H}{|}}{\overset{\overset{H}{|}}{C}}-H$$

9.17 (a) Br and Br: pure covalent From Figure 9.7, we find that the electronegativity of Br is 2.8. Because both atoms are the same, the electronegativity difference (ΔEN) = 0, and using Table 9.1, we classify this bond as pure covalent.

(b) C and Cl: polar covalent From Figure 9.7, we find that the electronegativity of C is 2.5 and Cl is 3.0. The electronegativity difference (ΔEN) is ΔEN = 3.0 − 2.5 = 0.5. Using Table 9.1, we classify this bond as polar covalent.

(c) C and S: pure covalent From Figure 9.7, we find that the electronegativity of C is 2.5 and S is 2.5. The electronegativity difference (ΔEN) is ΔEN = 2.5 − 2.5 = 0. Using Table 9.1, we classify this bond as pure covalent.

(d) Sr and O: ionic From Figure 9.7, we find that the electronegativity of Sr is 1.0 and O is 3.5. The electronegativity difference (ΔEN) is ΔEN = 3.5 − 1.0 = 2.5. Using Table 9.1, we classify this bond as ionic.

9.19 CO: Write the Lewis symbol for each atom based on the number of valence electrons.

$\cdot\ddot{C}\cdot$ $:\ddot{O}\cdot$

The carbon will share three electron pairs with oxygen to achieve a stable octet.

The oxygen atom is more electronegative than the carbon atom; so the oxygen will have a partial negative charge, and the carbon will have a partial positive charge.

$:C\!\equiv\!O:$

To estimate the percent ionic character, determine the difference in electronegativity between carbon and oxygen. From Figure 9.7, we find that the electronegativity of C is 2.5 and O is 3.5. The electronegativity difference (ΔEN) is ΔEN = 3.5 − 2.5 = 1.0. From Figure 9.9, we can estimate a percent ionic character of 25%.

Covalent Lewis Structures, Resonance, and Formal Charge

9.21 (a) CI$_4$: Write the correct skeletal structure for the molecule.

$$I-\underset{\underset{I}{|}}{\overset{\overset{I}{|}}{C}}-I$$

Calculate the total number of electrons for the Lewis structure by summing the number of valence electrons of each atom in the molecule.

(number of valence e⁻ for C) + 4(number of valence e⁻ for I) = 4 + 4(7) = 32

Distribute the electrons among the atoms, giving octets to as many atoms as possible. Begin with the bonding electrons; then proceed to lone pairs on terminal atoms and finally to lone pairs on the central atom.

$$:\ddot{I}-\underset{\underset{:\ddot{I}:}{|}}{\overset{\overset{:\ddot{I}:}{|}}{C}}-\ddot{I}:$$

All 32 valence electrons are used.

If any atom lacks an octet, form double or triple bonds as necessary to give them octets. All atoms have octets; the structure is complete.

(b)　N₂O:　Write the correct skeletal structure for the molecule.

N is less electronegative, so it is central.

N—N—O

Calculate the total number of electrons for the Lewis structure by summing the number of valence electrons of each atom in the molecule.

2(number of valence e⁻ for N) + (number of valence e⁻ for O) = 2(5) + 6 = 16

Distribute the electrons among the atoms, giving octets to as many atoms as possible. Begin with the bonding electrons; then proceed to lone pairs on terminal atoms and finally to lone pairs on the central atom.

:N̈—N—Ö:

All 16 valence electrons are used.

If any atom lacks an octet, form double or triple bonds as necessary.

:N≡N—Ö:

All atoms have octets; the structure is complete.

(c)　SiH₄:　Write the correct skeletal structure for the molecule.

H is always terminal, so Si is the central atom.

$$\begin{array}{c} \text{H} \\ | \\ \text{H—Si—H} \\ | \\ \text{H} \end{array}$$

Calculate the total number of electrons for the Lewis structure by summing the number of valence electrons of each atom in the molecule.

(number of valence e⁻ for Si) + 4(number of valence e⁻ for H) = 4 + 4(1) = 8

Distribute the electrons among the atoms, giving octets (or duets for H) to as many atoms as possible. Begin with the bonding electrons; then proceed to lone pairs on terminal atoms and finally to lone pairs on the central atom.

$$\begin{array}{c} \text{H} \\ | \\ \text{H—Si—H} \\ | \\ \text{H} \end{array}$$

All eight valence electrons are used.

If any atom lacks an octet, form double or triple bonds as necessary to give them octets. All atoms have octets; the structure is complete.

(d)　Cl₂CO:　Write the correct skeletal structure for the molecule. C is least electronegative, so it is the central atom.

$$\begin{array}{c} \text{O} \\ \| \\ \text{Cl—C—Cl} \end{array}$$

Calculate the total number of electrons for the Lewis structure by summing the number of valence electrons of each atom in the molecule.

(number of valence e⁻ for C) + 2(number of valence e⁻ for Cl) + (number of valence e⁻ for O)
= 4 + 2(7) + 6 = 24

Distribute the electrons among the atoms, giving octets to as many atoms as possible. Begin with the bonding electrons; then proceed to lone pairs on terminal atoms and finally to lone pairs on the central atom.

$$:\ddot{O}:$$
$$|$$
$$:\ddot{C}l—C—\ddot{C}l:$$

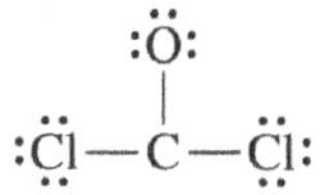

All 24 valence electrons are used.

If any atom lacks an octet, form double or triple bonds as necessary.

$$:O:$$
$$\|$$
$$:\ddot{C}l—C—\ddot{C}l:$$

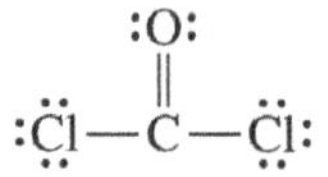

All atoms have octets; the structure is complete.

(e)   H₃COH: Write the correct skeletal structure for the molecule. C is less electronegative, and H is terminal.

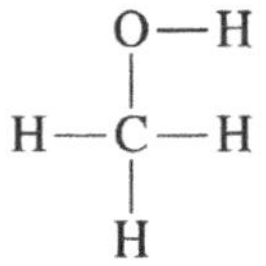

$$O—H$$
$$|$$
$$H—C—H$$
$$|$$
$$H$$

Calculate the total number of electrons for the Lewis structure by summing the number of valence electrons of each atom in the molecule.

(number of valence e⁻ for C) + 4(number of valence e⁻ for H) + (number of valence e⁻ for O)
= 4 + 4(1) + 6 = 14

Distribute the electrons among the atoms, giving octets (or duets for H) to as many atoms as possible. Begin with the bonding electrons; then proceed to lone pairs on terminal atoms and finally to lone pairs on the central atoms.

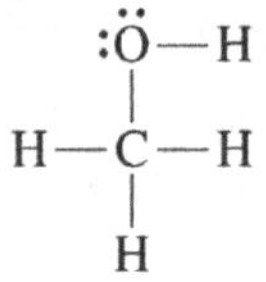

$$:\ddot{O}—H$$
$$|$$
$$H—C—H$$
$$|$$
$$H$$

All 14 valence electrons are used.

If any atom lacks an octet, form double or triple bonds as necessary to give them octets. All atoms have octets (duets for H); the structure is complete.

(f)   OH⁻:   Write the correct skeletal structure for the ion.
O—H

Calculate the total number of electrons for the Lewis structure by summing the number of valence electrons of each atom in the ion and adding 1 for the 1− charge.

(number of valence e⁻ for O) + (number of valence e⁻ for H) + 1 = 6 + 1 + 1 = 8

Distribute the electrons among the atoms, giving octets (or duets for H) to as many atoms as possible. Begin with the bonding electrons; then proceed to lone pairs on terminal atoms and finally to lone pairs on the central atom.

$$:\ddot{O}—H$$

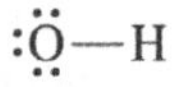

All eight valence electrons are used.

If any atom lacks an octet, form double or triple bonds as necessary to give them octets. Finally, write the Lewis structure in brackets with the charge of the ion in the upper right-hand corner.

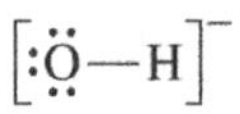

$$\left[:\ddot{O}—H\right]^{-}$$

(g)   BrO⁻:   Write the correct skeletal structure for the ion.
Br—O

Calculate the total number of electrons for the Lewis structure by summing the number of valence electrons of each atom in the ion and adding 1 for the 1− charge.

(number of valence e⁻ for O) + (number of valence e⁻ for Br) + 1 = 6 + 7 + 1 = 14

Distribute the electrons among the atoms, giving octets to as many atoms as possible. Begin with the bonding electrons; then proceed to lone pairs on terminal atoms and finally to lone pairs on the central atom.

$$:\ddot{\text{B}}\text{r}-\ddot{\text{O}}:$$

All 14 valence electrons are used.

If any atom lacks an octet, form double or triple bonds as necessary to give them octets. Finally, write the Lewis structure in brackets with the charge of the ion in the upper right-hand corner.

$$\left[:\ddot{\text{B}}\text{r}-\ddot{\text{O}}:\right]^{-}$$

9.23   (a) SeO_2:   Write the correct skeletal structure for the molecule. Se is less electronegative, so it is central.

O—Se—O

Calculate the total number of electrons for the Lewis structure by summing the number of valence electrons of each atom in the molecule.

(number of valence e⁻ for Se) + 2(number of valence e⁻ for O) = 6 + 2(6) = 18

Distribute the electrons among the atoms, giving octets to as many atoms as possible. Begin with the bonding electrons; then proceed to lone pairs on terminal atoms and finally to lone pairs on the central atom.

$$:\ddot{\text{O}}-\ddot{\text{S}}\text{e}-\ddot{\text{O}}:$$

All 18 valence electrons are used.

If any atom lacks an octet, form double or triple bonds as necessary.

$$:\ddot{\text{O}}-\ddot{\text{S}}\text{e}=\ddot{\text{O}}:$$

All atoms have octets; the structure is complete. However, the double bond can form from either oxygen atom, so there are two resonance forms.

$$:\ddot{\text{O}}-\ddot{\text{S}}\text{e}=\ddot{\text{O}}: \longleftrightarrow :\ddot{\text{O}}=\ddot{\text{S}}\text{e}-\ddot{\text{O}}:$$

Calculate the formal charge on each atom by finding the number of valence electrons and subtracting the number of lone pair electrons and one-half the number of bonding electrons.

	$:\ddot{\text{O}}-\ddot{\text{S}}\text{e}=\ddot{\text{O}}:$			$:\ddot{\text{O}}=\ddot{\text{S}}\text{e}-\ddot{\text{O}}:$	
number of valence electrons	6	6	6	6	6	6
− number of lone pair electrons	6	2	4	4	2	6
− 1/2(number of bonding electrons)	1	3	2	2	3	1
Formal charge	−1	+1	0	0	+1	−1

(b) $CO_3{}^{2-}$:   Write the correct skeletal structure for the ion.

$$\begin{array}{c} \text{O} \\ | \\ \text{O}-\text{C}-\text{O} \end{array}$$

Calculate the total number of electrons for the Lewis structure by summing the number of valence electrons of each atom in the ion and adding 2 for the 2− charge.

3(number of valence e⁻ for O) + (number of valence e⁻ for C) + 2 = 3(6) + 4 + 2 = 24

Distribute the electrons among the atoms, giving octets to as many atoms as possible. Begin with the bonding electrons; then proceed to lone pairs on terminal atoms and finally to lone pairs on the central atom.

$$\begin{array}{c} :\ddot{\text{O}}: \\ | \\ :\ddot{\text{O}}-\text{C}-\ddot{\text{O}}: \end{array}$$

All 24 valence electrons are used.

If any atom lacks an octet, form double or triple bonds as necessary.

$$\ddot{\text{O}}:$$
$$:\ddot{\text{O}}-\text{C}=\ddot{\text{O}}:$$

Finally, write the Lewis structure in brackets with the charge of the ion in the upper right-hand corner.

$$\left[\ :\ddot{\text{O}}-\overset{\displaystyle :\ddot{\text{O}}:}{\text{C}}=\ddot{\text{O}}:\ \right]^{2-}$$

All atoms have octets; the structure is complete. However, the double bond can form from any oxygen atom, so there are three resonance forms.

$$\left[\ :\ddot{\text{O}}-\overset{\displaystyle :\ddot{\text{O}}:}{\text{C}}=\ddot{\text{O}}:\ \right]^{2-} \longleftrightarrow \left[\ :\ddot{\text{O}}=\overset{\displaystyle :\ddot{\text{O}}:}{\text{C}}-\ddot{\text{O}}:\ \right]^{2-} \longleftrightarrow$$

$$\left[\ :\ddot{\text{O}}-\overset{\displaystyle :\text{O}:}{\text{C}}-\ddot{\text{O}}:\ \right]^{2-}$$

Calculate the formal charge on each atom by finding the number of valence electrons and subtracting the number of lone pair electrons and one-half the number of bonding electrons.

$$\left[\ :\ddot{\text{O}}-\overset{\displaystyle :\ddot{\text{O}}:}{\text{C}}=\ddot{\text{O}}:\ \right]^{2-}$$

	O_{left}	O_{top}	O_{right}	C
number of valence electrons	6	6	6	4
− number of lone pair electrons	6	6	4	0
− 1/2(number of bonding electrons)	1	1	2	4
Formal charge	−1	−1	0	0

The sum of the formal charges is −2, which is the overall charge of the ion. The other resonance forms would have the same values for the single- and double-bonded oxygen atoms.

(c) ClO^-:   Write the correct skeletal structure for the ion.

Cl—O

Calculate the total number of electrons for the Lewis structure by summing the number of valence electrons of each atom in the ion and adding 1 for the 1− charge.

(number of valence e$^-$ for O) + (number of valence e$^-$ for Cl) + 1 = 6 + 7 + 1 = 14

Distribute the electrons among the atoms, giving octets to as many atoms as possible. Begin with the bonding electrons; then proceed to lone pairs on terminal atoms and finally to lone pairs on the central atom.

$$:\ddot{\text{Cl}}-\ddot{\text{O}}:$$

All 14 valence electrons are used.

If any atom lacks an octet, form double or triple bonds as necessary to give them octets. Finally, write the Lewis structure in brackets with the charge of the ion in the upper right-hand corner.

$$\left[\ :\ddot{\text{Cl}}-\ddot{\text{O}}:\ \right]^{-}$$

All atoms have octets; the structure is complete.

Calculate the formal charge on each atom by finding the number of valence electrons and subtracting the number of lone pair electrons and one-half the number of bonding electrons.

	Cl	O
number of valence electrons	7	6
− number of lone pair electrons	6	6
− 1/2(number of bonding electrons)	1	1
Formal charge	0	−1

The sum of the formal charges is −1, which is the overall charge of the ion.

(d) NO_2^-:   Write the correct skeletal structure for the ion.

O—N—O

Calculate the total number of electrons for the Lewis structure by summing the number of valence electrons of each atom in the ion and adding 1 for the 1− charge.

2(number of valence e⁻ for O) + (number of valence e⁻ for N) + 1 = 2(6) + 5 + 1 = 18

Distribute the electrons among the atoms, giving octets to as many atoms as possible. Begin with the bonding electrons; then proceed to lone pairs on terminal atoms and finally to lone pairs on the central atom.

:Ö—N̈—Ö:

All 18 valence electrons are used.

If any atom lacks an octet, form double or triple bonds as necessary.

:O̤=N̈—Ö:

Finally, write the Lewis structure in brackets with the charge of the ion in the upper right-hand corner.

$\left[:O̤=N̈—Ö: \right]^-$

All atoms have octets; the structure is complete. However, the double bond can form from either oxygen atom, so there are two resonance forms.

$\left[:O̤=N̈—Ö: \right]^- \longleftrightarrow \left[:Ö—N̈=O̤: \right]^-$

Calculate the formal charge on each atom by finding the number of valence electrons and subtracting the number of lone pair electrons and one-half the number of bonding electrons. Using the left-side structure:

	O	N	O
number of valence electrons	6	5	6
− number of lone pair electrons	4	2	6
− 1/2(number of bonding electrons)	2	3	1
Formal charge	0	0	−1

The sum of the formal charges is −1, which is the overall charge of the ion.

9.25

$$\underset{\text{I}}{\overset{\displaystyle \overset{\text{H}}{\underset{|}{}}}{H—C=S̈}} \qquad \underset{\text{II}}{\overset{\displaystyle \overset{\text{H}}{\underset{|}{}}}{H—S=C̈}}$$

Calculate the formal charge on each atom in structure I by finding the number of valence electrons and subtracting the number of lone pair electrons and one-half the number of bonding electrons.

	H_{left}	H_{top}	C	S
number of valence electrons	1	1	4	6
− number of lone pair electrons	0	0	0	4
− 1/2(number of bonding electrons)	1	1	4	2
Formal charge	0	0	0	0

The sum of the formal charges is 0, which is the overall charge of the molecule. Calculate the formal charge on each atom in structure II by finding the number of valence electrons and subtracting the number of lone pair electrons and one-half the number of bonding electrons.

	H_{left}	H_{top}	S	C
number of valence electrons	1	1	6	4
− number of lone pair electrons	0	0	0	4
− 1/2(number of bonding electrons)	1	1	4	2
Formal charge	0	0	+2	−2

The sum of the formal charges is 0, which is the overall charge of the molecule.

Structure I is the better Lewis structure because it has the least amount of formal charge on each atom.

9.27 $:O \equiv C - \ddot{\underset{..}{O}}:$ does not provide a significant contribution to the resonance hybrid as it has a +1 formal charge on a very electronegative oxygen.

	O_{left}	O_{right}	C
number of valence electrons	6	6	4
− number of lone pair electrons	2	6	0
− 1/2(number of bonding electrons)	3	1	4
Formal charge	+1	−1	0

9.29 CH_3COO^-:   Write the correct skeletal structure for the molecule

Calculate the total number of electrons for the Lewis structure by summing the valence electrons of each atom in the ion and adding 1 for the 1 − charge.

2(number of valence e⁻ for C) + 2(number of valence e⁻ for O) + 3(number of valence e⁻ for H) + 1 = 2(4) + 2(6) + 3(1) + 1 = 24

Distribute the electrons among the atoms, giving octets (or duets for H) to as many atoms as possible. Begin with the bonding electrons, and then proceed to lone pairs on terminal atoms and finally to lone pairs of the central atom.

All 24 valence electrons are used.

If any atom lacks an octet, form double or triple bonds as necessary to give them octets.

Lastly, write the Lewis structure in brackets with the charge of the ion in the upper right-hand corner.

$$
\left[\begin{array}{c} \overset{\displaystyle H}{\underset{\displaystyle H}{\overset{|}{\underset{|}{H-C}}} - C = \overset{\displaystyle :\ddot{O}:}{\ddot{O}} } \end{array} \right]^{-}
$$

All atoms have octets (duets for H); the structure is complete. However, the double bond can form from either oxygen atom, so there are two resonance forms.

$$
\left[\begin{array}{c} H-\overset{\displaystyle H}{\underset{\displaystyle H}{\overset{|}{\underset{|}{C}}}} - C = \overset{\displaystyle :\ddot{O}:}{\ddot{O}} \end{array} \right]^{-} \longleftrightarrow \left[\begin{array}{c} H-\overset{\displaystyle H}{\underset{\displaystyle H}{\overset{|}{\underset{|}{C}}}} - C - \overset{\displaystyle :O:}{\ddot{O}:} \end{array} \right]^{-}
$$

Calculate the formal charge on each atom by finding the number of valence electrons and subtracting the number of lone pair electrons and one-half the number of bonding electrons.

$$
\left[\begin{array}{c} H-\overset{\displaystyle H}{\underset{\displaystyle H}{\overset{|}{\underset{|}{C}}}} - C = \overset{\displaystyle :\ddot{O}:}{\ddot{O}} \end{array} \right]^{-}
$$

	H	$\mathbf{O_{top}}$	$\mathbf{O_{right}}$	**C**
number of valence electrons	1	6	6	4
− number of lone pair electrons	0	6	4	0
− 1/2(number of bonding electrons)	1	1	2	4
Formal charge	0	−1	0	0

The sum of the formal charges is −1, which is the overall charge of the ion. The other resonance form would be the same.

9.31   Calculate the formal charge on each atom by finding the number of valence electrons and subtracting the number of lone pair electrons and one-half the number of bonding electrons.

	N	**O**
number of valence electrons	5	6
− number of lone pair electrons	0	6
− 1/2(number of bonding electrons)	4	1
Formal charge	+1	−1

$$
\begin{array}{c}
\overset{\displaystyle CH_3}{\underset{\displaystyle CH_3}{\overset{|}{\underset{|}{CH_3-N}}}} - \ddot{O}:
\end{array}
$$

Odd-Electron Species, Incomplete Octets, and Expanded Octets

9.33   (a) BCl_3:   Write the correct skeletal structure for the molecule.

B is less electronegative, so it is central.

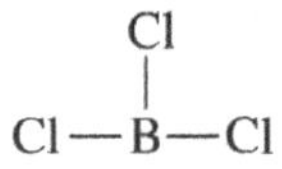

Cl
|
Cl—B—Cl

Calculate the total number of electrons for the Lewis structure by summing the number of valence electrons of each atom in the molecule.

(number of valence e⁻ for B) + 3(number of valence e⁻ for Cl) = 3 + 3(7) = 24

Distribute the electrons among the atoms, giving octets to as many atoms as possible. Begin with the bonding electrons; then proceed to lone pairs on terminal atoms and finally to lone pairs on the central atom.

:C̈l:
|
:C̈l—B—C̈l:

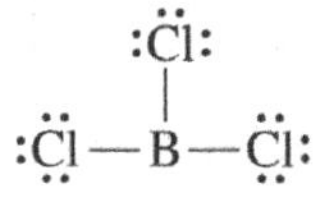

All 24 valence electrons are used.

B has an incomplete octet. If we complete the octet, there is a formal charge of −1 on the B, which is less electronegative than Cl.

(b) NO_2:   Write the correct skeletal structure for the molecule.

N is less electronegative, so it is central.

O—N—O

Calculate the total number of electrons for the Lewis structure by summing the number of valence electrons of each atom in the molecule.

(number of valence e⁻ for N) + 2(number of valence e⁻ for O) = 5 + 2(6) = 17

Distribute the electrons among the atoms, giving octets to as many atoms as possible. Begin with the bonding electrons; then proceed to lone pairs on terminal atoms and finally to lone pairs on the central atom.

Ö=Ṅ—Ö:

⟷   :Ö—Ṅ=Ö

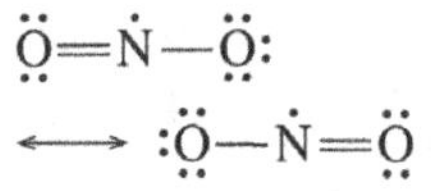

All 17 valence electrons are used.

N has an incomplete octet. It has seven electrons because we have an odd number of valence electrons.

(c) BH_3:   Write the correct skeletal structure for the molecule.

B is less electronegative, so it is central.

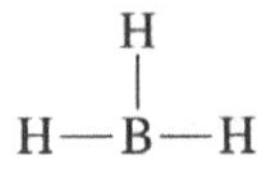

H
|
H—B—H

Calculate the total number of electrons for the Lewis structure by summing the number of valence electrons of each atom in the molecule.

(number of valence e⁻ for B) + 3(number of valence e⁻ for H) = 3 + 3(1) = 6

Distribute the electrons among the atoms, giving octets (or duets for H) to as many atoms as possible. Begin with the bonding electrons; then proceed to lone pairs on terminal atoms and finally to lone pairs on the central atom.

H
|
H—B—H

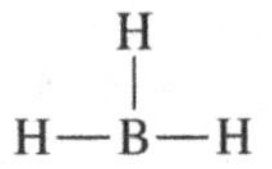

All six valence electrons are used.

B has an incomplete octet. H cannot double-bond, so it is not possible to complete the octet on B with a double bond.

9.35   (a) PO_4^{3-}:   Write the correct skeletal structure for the ion.

$$
\begin{array}{c}
\text{O} \\
| \\
\text{O}-\text{P}-\text{O} \\
| \\
\text{O}
\end{array}
$$

Calculate the total number of electrons for the Lewis structure by summing the number of valence electrons of each atom in the ion and adding 3 for the 3− charge.

$$4(\text{number of valence } e^- \text{ for O}) + (\text{number of valence } e^- \text{ for P}) + 3 = 4(6) + 5 + 3 = 32$$

Distribute the electrons among the atoms, giving octets to as many atoms as possible. Begin with the bonding electrons; then proceed to lone pairs on terminal atoms and finally to lone pairs on the central atom.

$$
\begin{array}{c}
:\ddot{\text{O}}: \\
| \\
:\ddot{\text{O}}-\text{P}-\ddot{\text{O}}: \\
| \\
:\ddot{\text{O}}:
\end{array}
$$

All 32 valence electrons are used.

Finally, write the Lewis structure in brackets with the charge of the ion in the upper right-hand corner.

$$
\left[
\begin{array}{c}
:\ddot{\text{O}}: \\
| \\
:\ddot{\text{O}}-\text{P}-\ddot{\text{O}}: \\
| \\
:\ddot{\text{O}}:
\end{array}
\right]^{3-}
$$

All atoms have octets (duets for H); the structure is complete.

Calculate the formal charge on each atom by finding the number of valence electrons and subtracting the number of lone pair electrons and one-half the number of bonding electrons.

$$
\left[
\begin{array}{c}
:\ddot{\text{O}}: \\
| \\
:\ddot{\text{O}}-\text{P}-\ddot{\text{O}}: \\
| \\
:\ddot{\text{O}}:
\end{array}
\right]^{3-}
$$

	O_{left}	O_{top}	O_{right}	O_{bottom}	P
number of valence electrons	6	6	6	6	5
− number of lone pair electrons	6	6	6	6	0
− 1/2(number of bonding electrons)	1	1	1	1	4
Formal charge	−1	−1	−1	−1	+1

The sum of the formal charges is −3, which is the overall charge of the ion. However, we can write a resonance structure with a double bond to an oxygen because P can expand its octet. This leads to lower formal charges on P and O.

$$
\left[
\begin{array}{c}
:\ddot{\text{O}}: \\
| \\
\ddot{\text{O}}=\text{P}-\ddot{\text{O}}: \\
| \\
:\ddot{\text{O}}:
\end{array}
\right]^{3-}
\longleftrightarrow
\left[
\begin{array}{c}
:\text{O}: \\
\| \\
:\ddot{\text{O}}-\text{P}-\ddot{\text{O}}: \\
| \\
:\ddot{\text{O}}:
\end{array}
\right]^{3-}
\longleftrightarrow
\left[
\begin{array}{c}
:\ddot{\text{O}}: \\
| \\
:\ddot{\text{O}}-\text{P}=\ddot{\text{O}} \\
| \\
:\ddot{\text{O}}:
\end{array}
\right]^{3-}
\longleftrightarrow
\left[
\begin{array}{c}
:\ddot{\text{O}}: \\
| \\
:\ddot{\text{O}}-\text{P}-\ddot{\text{O}}: \\
\| \\
:\text{O}:
\end{array}
\right]^{3-}
$$

Using the leftmost structure, calculate the formal charge on each atom by finding the number of valence electrons and subtracting the number of lone pair electrons and one-half the number of bonding electrons.

	O_{left}	O_{top}	O_{right}	O_{bottom}	P
number of valence electrons	6	6	6	6	5
− number of lone pair electrons	4	6	6	6	0
− 1/2(number of bonding electrons)	2	1	1	1	5
Formal charge	0	−1	−1	−1	0

The sum of the formal charges is −3, which is the overall charge of the ion. These resonance forms would all have the lower formal charges associated with the double-bonded O and P.

(b)   CN⁻:   Write the correct skeletal structure for the ion.

C—N

Calculate the total number of electrons for the Lewis structure by summing the number of valence electrons of each atom in the ion and adding 1 for the 1− charge.

(number of valence e⁻ for C) + (number of valence e⁻ for N) + 1 = 4 + 5 + 1 = 10

Distribute the electrons among the atoms, giving octets to as many atoms as possible. Begin with the bonding electrons; then proceed to lone pairs on terminal atoms and finally to lone pairs on the central atom.

:C—N̈:

All ten valence electrons are used.

If any atom lacks an octet, form double or triple bonds as necessary.

:C≡N:

Finally, write the Lewis structure in brackets with the charge of the ion in the upper right-hand corner.

$$\left[:C≡N:\right]^{-}$$

All atoms have octets; the structure is complete.

Calculate the formal charge on each atom by finding the number of valence electrons and subtracting the number of lone pair electrons and one-half the number of bonding electrons.

$$\left[:C≡N:\right]^{-}$$

	C	N
number of valence electrons	4	5
− number of lone pair electrons	2	2
− 1/2(number of bonding electrons)	3	3
Formal charge	−1	0

The sum of the formal charges is −1, which is the overall charge of the ion.

(c) SO_3^{2-}:   Write the correct skeletal structure for the ion.

```
      O
      |
  O — S — O
```

Calculate the total number of electrons for the Lewis structure by summing the valence electrons of each atom in the ion and adding 2 for the 2− charge.

3(number of valence e⁻ for O) + (number of valence e⁻ for S) + 2 = 3(6) + 6 + 2 = 26

Distribute the electrons among the atoms, giving octets to as many atoms as possible. Begin with the bonding electrons; then proceed to lone pairs on terminal atoms and finally to lone pairs on the central atom.

```
      :Ö:
       |
  :Ö — S — Ö:
```

All 26 valence electrons are used.

Finally, write the Lewis structure in brackets with the charge of the ion in the upper right-hand corner.

$$\left[\begin{array}{c} :\ddot{O}: \\ | \\ :\ddot{O}-S-\ddot{O}: \end{array} \right]^{2-}$$

Calculate the formal charge on each atom by finding the number of valence electrons and subtracting the number of lone pair electrons and one-half the number of bonding electrons.

$$\left[\begin{array}{c} :\ddot{O}: \\ | \\ :\ddot{O}-S-\ddot{O}: \end{array} \right]^{2-}$$

	O_{left}	O_{top}	O_{right}	S
number of valence electrons	6	6	6	6
− number of lone pair electrons	6	6	6	2
− 1/2(number of bonding electrons)	1	1	1	3
Formal charge	−1	−1	−1	+1

The sum of the formal charges is −2, which is the overall charge of the ion. However, we can write a resonance structure with a double bond to an oxygen because S can expand its octet. This leads to a lower formal charge.

$$\left[\begin{array}{c} :\ddot{O}: \\ | \\ \ddot{O}=S-\ddot{O}: \end{array} \right]^{2-} \longleftrightarrow \left[\begin{array}{c} :O: \\ || \\ :\ddot{O}-S-\ddot{O}: \end{array} \right]^{2-} \longleftrightarrow \left[\begin{array}{c} :\ddot{O}: \\ | \\ :\ddot{O}-S=\ddot{O} \end{array} \right]^{2-}$$

Using the leftmost resonance form, calculate the formal charge on each atom by finding the number of valence electrons and subtracting the number of lone pair electrons and one-half the number of bonding electrons.

	O_{left}	O_{top}	O_{right}	S
number of valence electrons	6	6	6	6
− number of lone pair electrons	4	6	6	2
− 1/2(number of bonding electrons)	2	1	1	4
Formal charge	0	−1	−1	0

The sum of the formal charges is −2, which is the overall charge of the ion. These resonance forms would all have the lower formal charge on the double-bonded O and S.

(d) ClO_2^-:   Write the correct skeletal structure for the ion.

O—Cl—O

Calculate the total number of electrons for the Lewis structure by summing the number of valence electrons of each atom in the ion and adding 1 for the 1− charge.

$$2(\text{number of valence e}^- \text{ for O}) + (\text{number of valence e}^- \text{ for Cl}) + 1 = 2(6) + 7 + 1 = 20$$

Distribute the electrons among the atoms, giving octets to as many atoms as possible. Begin with the bonding electrons; then proceed to lone pairs on terminal atoms and finally to lone pairs on the central atom.

$:\ddot{O}-\ddot{C}l-\ddot{O}:$

All 20 valence electrons are used.

Finally, write the Lewis structure in brackets with the charge of the ion in the upper right-hand corner.

$$\left[:\ddot{O}-\ddot{C}l-\ddot{O}: \right]^-$$

All atoms have octets; the structure is complete.

Calculate the formal charge on each atom by finding the number of valence electrons and subtracting the number of lone pair electrons and one-half the number of bonding electrons.

$$\left[:\ddot{O}-\ddot{C}l-\ddot{O}: \right]^{-}$$

	O_{left}	O_{right}	Cl
number of valence electrons	6	6	7
− number of lone pair electrons	6	6	4
− 1/2(number of bonding electrons)	1	1	2
Formal charge	−1	−1	+1

The sum of the formal charges is −1, which is the overall charge of the ion. However, we can write a resonance structure with a double bond to an oxygen because Cl can expand its octet. This leads to a lower formal charge.

$$\left[\ddot{O}=\ddot{C}l-\ddot{O}: \right]^{-} \longleftrightarrow \left[:\ddot{O}-\ddot{C}l=\ddot{O} \right]^{-}$$

Using the leftmost resonance form, calculate the formal charge on each atom by finding the number of valence electrons and subtracting the number of lone pair electrons and one-half the number of bonding electrons.

	O_{left}	O_{right}	Cl
number of valence electrons	6	6	7
− number of lone pair electrons	4	6	4
− 1/2(number of bonding electrons)	2	1	3
Formal charge	0	−1	0

The sum of the formal charges is −1, which is the overall charge of the ion. These resonance forms would all have the lower formal charge on the double-bonded O and Cl.

9.37   (a) PF_5:   Write the correct skeletal structure for the molecule.

$$\begin{array}{c} F \\ | \\ F-P{<}^{F}_{F} \\ | \\ F \end{array}$$

Calculate the total number of electrons for the Lewis structure by summing the number of valence electrons of each atom in the molecule.

(number of valence e⁻ for P) + 5(number of valence e⁻ for F) = 5 + 5(7) = 40

Distribute the electrons among the atoms, giving octets to as many atoms as possible. Begin with the bonding electrons; then proceed to lone pairs on terminal atoms and finally to lone pairs on the central atom. Arrange additional electrons around the central atom, giving it an expanded octet of up to 12 electrons.

$$\begin{array}{c} :\ddot{F}: \\ | \\ :\ddot{F}-P{<}^{\ddot{F}:}_{\ddot{F}:} \\ | \\ :\ddot{F}: \end{array}$$

(b) I_3^-:   Write the correct skeletal structure for the ion.

I—I—I

Calculate the total number of electrons for the Lewis structure by summing the number of valence electrons of each atom in the ion and adding 1 for the 1− charge.

3(number of valence e⁻ for I) + 1 = 3(7) + 1 = 22

Distribute the electrons among the atoms, giving octets to as many atoms as possible. Begin with the bonding electrons; then proceed to lone pairs on terminal atoms and finally to lone pairs on the central atom. Arrange additional electrons around the central atom, giving it an expanded octet of up to 12 electrons.

$$:\ddot{I}—\ddot{I}—\ddot{I}:$$

Finally, write the Lewis structure in brackets with the charge of the ion in the upper right-hand corner.

$$\left[:\ddot{I}—\ddot{I}—\ddot{I}:\right]^-$$

(c)   SF₄: Write the correct skeletal structure for the molecule.

$$\begin{array}{c} F \\ | \\ F—S—F \\ | \\ F \end{array}$$

Calculate the total number of electrons for the Lewis structure by summing the number of valence electrons of each atom in the molecule.

(number of valence e⁻ for S) + 4(number of valence e⁻ for F) = 6 + 4(7) = 34

Distribute the electrons among the atoms, giving octets (or duets for H) to as many atoms as possible. Begin with the bonding electrons; then proceed to lone pairs on terminal atoms and finally to lone pairs on the central atom. Arrange additional electrons around the central atom, giving it an expanded octet of up to 12 electrons.

$$\begin{array}{c} :\ddot{F}: \\ | \\ :\ddot{F}—\ddot{S}—\ddot{F}: \\ | \\ :\ddot{F}: \end{array}$$

(d)   GeF₄: Write the correct skeletal structure for the molecule.

$$\begin{array}{c} F \\ | \\ F—Ge—F \\ | \\ F \end{array}$$

Calculate the total number of electrons for the Lewis structure by summing the number of valence electrons of each atom in the molecule.

(number of valence e⁻ for Ge) + 4(number of valence e⁻ for F) = 4 + 4(7) = 32

Distribute the electrons among the atoms, giving octets to as many atoms as possible. Begin with the bonding electrons; then proceed to lone pairs on terminal atoms and finally to lone pairs on the central atom.

$$\begin{array}{c} :\ddot{F}: \\ | \\ :\ddot{F}—Ge—\ddot{F}: \\ | \\ :\ddot{F}: \end{array}$$

Bond Energies and Bond Lengths

9.39   Bond strength: H₃CCH₃ < H₂CCH₂ < HCCH
Bond length: H₃CCH₃ > H₂CCH₂ > HCCH
Write the Lewis structures for the three compounds. Compare the C—C bonds. Triple bonds are stronger than double bonds, double bonds are stronger than single bonds. Also, single bonds are longer than double bonds, which are longer than triple bonds.

HCCH (10 e⁻)   **H₂CCH₂ (12 e⁻)**   **H₃CCH₃(14 e⁻)**

$$H—C\equiv C—H$$

$$\begin{array}{c} H \\ \diagdown \\ C=C \\ \diagup \diagdown \\ H \end{array} \begin{array}{c} \\ H \\ \diagup \\ \\ H \end{array}$$

$$\begin{array}{c} H \quad H \\ | \quad | \\ H—C—C—H \\ | \quad | \\ H \quad H \end{array}$$

9.41 Rewrite the reaction using the Lewis structures of the molecules involved.

Determine which bonds are broken in the reaction and sum the bond energies of the following:

$\Sigma(\Delta H$'s bonds broken)

$= 4 \, \text{mol}(C\!-\!H) + 1 \, \text{mol}(C\!=\!C) + 1 \, \text{mol}(H\!-\!H)$

$= 4 \, \text{mol}(414 \, \text{kJ/mol}) + 1 \, \text{mol}(611 \, \text{kJ/mol}) + 1 \, \text{mol}(436 \, \text{kJ/mol})$

$= 2703 \, \text{kJ/mol}$

Determine which bonds are formed in the reaction and sum the negatives of the bond energies of the following:

$\Sigma(-\Delta H$'s bonds formed)

$= -6 \, \text{mol}(C\!-\!H) - 1 \, \text{mol}(C\!-\!C)$

$= -6 \, \text{mol}(414 \, \text{kJ/mol}) - 1\text{mol}(347 \, \text{kJ/mol})$

$= -2831 \, \text{kJ/mol}$

Find ΔH_{rxn} by summing the results of the two steps.

$\Delta H_{rxn} = \sum(\Delta H$'s bonds broken$) + \sum(-\Delta H$'s bonds formed$)$

$= 2703 \, \text{kJ/mol} - 2831 \, \text{kJ/mol}$

$= -128 \, \text{kJ/mol}$

Cumulative Problems

9.43 (a) BI$_3$: This is a covalent compound between two nonmetals.
Write the correct skeletal structure for the molecule.

$$\begin{array}{c} I \\ | \\ I\!-\!B\!-\!I \end{array}$$

Calculate the total number of electrons for the Lewis structure by summing the number of valence electrons of each atom in the molecule.

(number of valence e⁻ for B) + 3(number of valence e⁻ for I) = 3 + 3(7) = 24

Distribute the electrons among the atoms, giving octets to as many atoms as possible. Begin with the bonding electrons; then proceed to lone pairs on terminal atoms and finally to lone pairs on the central atom.

$$\begin{array}{c} :\ddot{I}: \\ | \\ :\ddot{I}\!-\!B\!-\!\ddot{I}: \end{array}$$

(b) K$_2$S: This is an ionic compound between a metal and nonmetal.
Draw the Lewis symbols for K and S based on their valence electrons. K: $4s^1$ S: $3s^2 3p^4$

$$\text{K}\cdot \quad \cdot\ddot{\text{S}}:$$

Potassium must lose one electron and be left with the octet from the previous shell, while sulfur needs to gain two electrons to get an octet.

$$2\text{K}^+ \quad \left[:\ddot{\text{S}}:\right]^{2-}$$

(c) HCFO: This is a covalent compound between nonmetals.
Write the correct skeletal structure for the molecule.

$$\begin{array}{c} O \\ | \\ H\!-\!C\!-\!F \end{array}$$

Calculate the total number of electrons for the Lewis structure by summing the number of valence electrons of each atom in the molecule.

(number of valence e⁻ for H) + (number of valence e⁻ for C) + (number of valence e⁻ for F) +

(number of valence e⁻ for O) = 1 + 4 + 7 + 6 = 18

Distribute the electrons among the atoms, giving octets to as many atoms as possible. Begin with the bonding electrons; then proceed to lone pairs on terminal atoms and finally to lone pairs on the central atom.

$$\text{:Ö:} \\ | \\ H - C - \ddot{F}:$$

If any atom lacks an octet, form double or triple bonds as necessary to give them octets.

$$\text{:O:} \\ \| \\ H - C - \ddot{F}:$$

(d) PBr_3: This is a covalent compound between two nonmetals.

Write the correct skeletal structure for the molecule.

$$\text{Br} \\ | \\ Br - P - Br$$

Calculate the total number of electrons for the Lewis structure by summing the number of valence electrons of each atom in the molecule.

(number of valence e^- for P) + 3(number of valence e^- for Br) = 5 + 3(7) = 26

Distribute the electrons among the atoms, giving octets to as many atoms as possible. Begin with the bonding electrons; then proceed to lone pairs on terminal atoms and finally to lone pairs on the central atom.

$$\text{:}\ddot{Br}\text{:} \\ | \\ :\ddot{Br} - P - \ddot{Br}:$$

9.45 (a) $BaCO_3$: Ba^{2+}

$$\left[\begin{array}{c} \text{:}\ddot{O}\text{:} \\ | \\ \ddot{O} = C - \ddot{O}\text{:} \end{array} \right]^{2-}$$

Determine the cation and anion.

$$Ba^{2+} \qquad CO_3^{2-}$$

Write the Lewis symbol for the barium cation based on the valence electrons.

$$Ba \quad 5s^2 \qquad Ba^{2+} \quad 5s^0$$
$$\cdot Ba \cdot \qquad Ba^{2+}$$

Ba must lose two electrons and be left with the octet from the previous shell.

Write the Lewis structure for the covalent anion.

Write the correct skeletal structure for the ion.

$$\text{O} \\ | \\ O - C - O$$

Calculate the total number of electrons for the Lewis structure by summing the number of valence electrons of each atom in the ion and adding two for the 2− charge.

(number of valence e^- for C) + 3(number of valence e^- for O) + 2 = 4 + 3(6) + 2 = 24

Distribute the electrons among the atoms, giving octets to as many atoms as possible. Begin with the bonding electrons; then proceed to lone pairs on terminal atoms and finally to lone pairs on the central atom.

$$\text{:}\ddot{O}\text{:} \\ | \\ :\ddot{O} - C - \ddot{O}:$$

If any atom lacks an octet, form double or triple bonds as necessary.

$$\text{:}\ddot{O}\text{:} \\ | \\ \ddot{O} = C - \ddot{O}:$$

Finally, write the Lewis structure in brackets with the charge of the ion in the upper right-hand corner.

$$\left[\begin{array}{c} \ddot{\text{O}} \\ | \\ \ddot{\text{O}} = \text{C} - \ddot{\text{O}} \end{array} \right]^{2-}$$

The double bond can be between the C and any of the oxygen atoms, so there are resonance structures.

$$\left[\begin{array}{c} \ddot{\text{O}} \\ | \\ \ddot{\text{O}} = \text{C} - \ddot{\text{O}} \end{array} \right]^{2-} \longleftrightarrow \left[\begin{array}{c} \text{O} \\ \| \\ \ddot{\text{O}} - \text{C} - \ddot{\text{O}} \end{array} \right]^{2-} \longleftrightarrow \left[\begin{array}{c} \ddot{\text{O}} \\ | \\ \ddot{\text{O}} - \text{C} = \ddot{\text{O}} \end{array} \right]^{2-}$$

(b) $Ca(OH)_2$: Ca^{2+}

$$2\left[:\ddot{\text{O}} - \text{H} \right]^{-}$$

Determine the cation and anion.

$$Ca^{2+} \qquad OH^-$$

Write the Lewis symbol for the calcium cation based on the valence electrons.

$$Ca \quad 4s^2 \quad Ca^{2+} \quad 4s^0$$

$$\cdot Ca \cdot \qquad Ca^{2+}$$

Ca must lose two electrons and be left with the octet from the previous shell.

Write the Lewis structure for the covalent anion.

Write the correct skeletal structure for the ion.

$$\text{O} - \text{H}$$

Calculate the total number of electrons for the Lewis structure by summing the valence electrons of each atom in the ion and adding one for the 1− charge.

(number of valence e⁻ for H) + (number of valence e⁻ for O) + 1 = 1 + 6 + 1 = 8

Distribute the electrons among the atoms, giving octets (or duets for H) to as many atoms as possible. Begin with the bonding electrons; then proceed to lone pairs on terminal atoms and finally to lone pairs on the central atom.

$$:\ddot{\text{O}} - \text{H}$$

Finally, write the Lewis structure in brackets with the charge of the ion in the upper right-hand corner.

$$\left[:\ddot{\text{O}} - \text{H} \right]^{-}$$

(c) KNO_3: K^+

$$\left[\begin{array}{c} \ddot{\text{O}} \\ | \\ \ddot{\text{O}} = \text{N} - \ddot{\text{O}} \end{array} \right]^{-}$$

Determine the cation and anion.

$$K^+ \qquad NO_3^-$$

Write the Lewis symbol for the potassium cation based on the valence electrons.

$$K \quad 4s^1 \quad K^+ \quad 4s^0$$

$$K \cdot \qquad K^+$$

K must lose one electron and be left with the octet from the previous shell.

Write the Lewis structure for the covalent anion.

Write the correct skeletal structure for the ion.

$$\begin{array}{c} \text{O} \\ | \\ \text{O} - \text{N} - \text{O} \end{array}$$

Calculate the total number of electrons for the Lewis structure by summing the valence electrons of each atom in the ion and adding one for the 1– charge.

(number of valence e⁻ for N) + 3(number of valence e⁻ for O) + 1 = 5 + 3(6) + 1 = 24

Distribute the electrons among the atoms, giving octets to as many atoms as possible. Begin with the bonding electrons; then proceed to lone pairs on terminal atoms and finally to lone pairs on the central atom.

$$
\begin{array}{c}
:\!\ddot{O}\!: \\
| \\
:\!\ddot{O}\!-\!N\!-\!\ddot{O}\!: \\
\ddot{} \ddot{}
\end{array}
$$

If any atom lacks an octet, form double or triple bonds as necessary.

$$
\begin{array}{c}
:\!\ddot{O}\!: \\
| \\
\ddot{O}\!=\!N\!-\!\ddot{O}\!: \\
\ddot{}
\end{array}
$$

Finally, write the Lewis symbol in brackets with the charge of the ion in the upper right-hand corner.

$$
\left[
\begin{array}{c}
:\!\ddot{O}\!: \\
| \\
\ddot{O}\!=\!N\!-\!\ddot{O}\!:
\end{array}
\right]^{-}
$$

The double bond can be between the N and any of the oxygen atoms, so there are resonance structures.

$$
\left[
\begin{array}{c}
:\!\ddot{O}\!: \\
| \\
\ddot{O}\!=\!N\!-\!\ddot{O}\!:
\end{array}
\right]^{-}
\longleftrightarrow
\left[
\begin{array}{c}
:\!O\!: \\
\| \\
:\!\ddot{O}\!-\!N\!-\!\ddot{O}\!:
\end{array}
\right]^{-}
\longleftrightarrow
\left[
\begin{array}{c}
:\!\ddot{O}\!: \\
| \\
:\!\ddot{O}\!-\!N\!=\!\ddot{O}
\end{array}
\right]^{-}
$$

(d)   LiIO: Li⁺

$$
\left[:\!\ddot{I}\!-\!\ddot{O}\!:\right]^{-}
$$

Determine the cation and anion.

Li⁺   IO⁻

Write the Lewis structure for the lithium cation based on the valence electrons.

Li $2s^1$ Li⁺ $2s^0$

Li ·   Li⁺

Li must lose one electron and be left with the octet from the previous shell.

Write the Lewis structure for the covalent anion.

Write the correct skeletal structure for the ion.

I—O

Calculate the total number of electrons for the Lewis structure by summing the number of valence electrons of each atom in the ion and adding one for the 1– charge.

(number of valence e⁻ for I) + (number of valence e⁻ for O) = 7 + 6 + 1 = 14

Distribute the electrons among the atoms, giving octets to as many atoms as possible. Begin with the bonding electrons; then proceed to lone pairs on terminal atoms and finally to lone pairs on the central atom.

$$:\!\ddot{I}\!-\!\ddot{O}\!:$$

Finally, write the Lewis structure in brackets with the charge of the ion in the upper right-hand corner.

$$
\left[:\!\ddot{I}\!-\!\ddot{O}\!:\right]^{-}
$$

9.47   (a)   C₄H₈: Write the correct skeletal structure for the molecule.

$$
\begin{array}{ccc}
H & H \\
| & | \\
H-C-C-H \\
| & | \\
H-C-C-H \\
| & | \\
H & H
\end{array}
$$

Calculate the total number of electrons for the Lewis structure by summing the number of valence electrons of each atom in the molecule.

4(number of valence e⁻ for C) + 8(number of valence e⁻ for H) = 4(4) + 8(1) = 24

Distribute the electrons among the atoms, giving octets (or duets for H) to as many atoms as possible.

$$\begin{array}{cc} H & H \\ | & | \\ H-C-C-H \\ | & | \\ H-C-C-H \\ | & | \\ H & H \end{array}$$

All atoms have octets or duets for H.

(b) C_4H_4:   Write the correct skeletal structure for the molecule.

$$\begin{array}{c} H-C-C-H \\ | \quad | \\ H-C-C-H \end{array}$$

Calculate the total number of electrons for the Lewis structure by summing the number of valence electrons of each atom in the molecule.

4(number of valence e⁻ for C) + 4(number of valence e⁻ for H) = 4(4) + 4(1) = 20

Distribute the electrons among the atoms, giving octets (or duets for H) to as many atoms as possible.

$$\begin{array}{c} H-\ddot{C}-\ddot{C}-H \\ | \quad | \\ H-C-C-H \end{array}$$

Complete octets by forming double bonds on alternating carbons; draw resonance structures.

$$\begin{array}{ccc} H-C-C-H & & H-C{=}C-H \\ \parallel \quad \parallel & \longleftrightarrow & | \quad | \\ H-C-C-H & & H-C{=}C-H \end{array}$$

(c) C_6H_{12}:   Write the correct skeletal structure for the molecule.

$$\begin{array}{c} H \quad H \\ \backslash \; / \\ H \quad C \quad H \\ \backslash \diagup C \diagdown \; C \diagup \\ H \diagup \quad | \quad | \quad \diagdown H \\ H-C \diagdown \quad \diagup C-H \\ H \diagup \quad C \quad \diagdown H \\ \diagup \backslash \\ H \quad H \end{array}$$

Calculate the total number of electrons for the Lewis structure by summing the valence electrons of each atom in the molecule.

6(number of valence e⁻ for C) + 12(number of valence e⁻ for H) = 6(4) + 12(1) = 36

Distribute the electrons among the atoms, giving octets (or duets for H) to as many atoms as possible. Begin with the bonding.

$$\begin{array}{c} H \quad H \\ \backslash \; / \\ H \quad C \quad H \\ \backslash \diagup C \diagdown \; C \diagup \\ H \diagup \quad | \quad | \quad \diagdown H \\ H-C \diagdown \quad \diagup C-H \\ H \diagup \quad C \quad \diagdown H \\ \diagup \backslash \\ H \quad H \end{array}$$

All 36 electrons are used, and all atoms have octets or duets for H.

(d) C_6H_6:   Write the correct skeletal structure for the molecule.

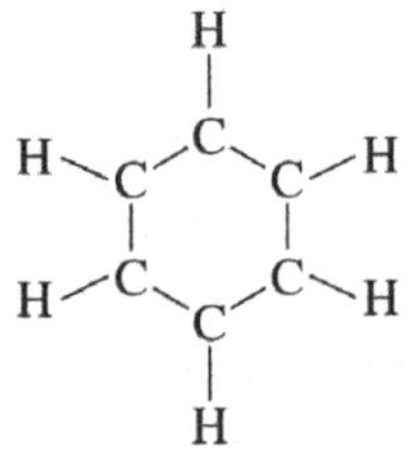

Calculate the total number of electrons for the Lewis structure by summing the number of valence electrons of each atom in the molecule.

6(number of valence e^- for C) + 6(number of valence e^- for H) = 6(4) + 6(1) = 30

Distribute the electrons among the atoms, giving octets (or duets for H) to as many atoms as possible.

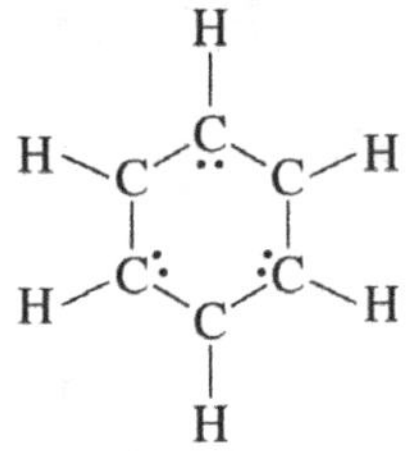

Complete octets by forming double bonds on alternating carbons; draw resonance structures.

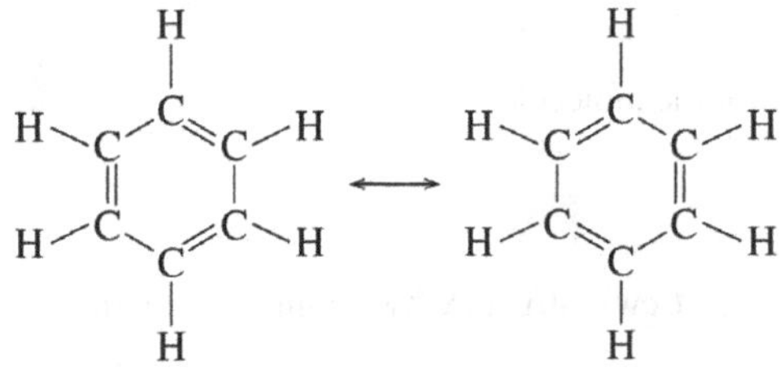

9.49   **Given:** 26.01% C; 4.38% H; 69.52% O; molar mass = 46.02 g/mol
Find: molecular formula and Lewis structure
Conceptual Plan: convert mass to mol of each element → pseudoformula → empirical formula

$$\frac{1\ mol\ C}{12.01\ g\ C} \qquad \frac{1\ mol\ H}{1.008\ g\ H} \qquad \frac{1\ mol\ O}{16.00\ g\ O} \qquad\qquad \text{divide by smallest number}$$

→ molecular formula → Lewis structure

empirical formula × n

Solution: $26.01\ \cancel{g\ C} \times \dfrac{1\ mol\ C}{12.01\ \cancel{g\ C}} = 2.166\ mol\ C$

$4.38\ \cancel{g\ H} \times \dfrac{1\ mol\ H}{1.008\ \cancel{g\ H}} = 4.345\ mol\ H$

$69.52\ \cancel{g\ O} \times \dfrac{1\ mol\ O}{16.00\ \cancel{g\ O}} = 4.345\ mol\ O$

$C_{2.166}H_{4.345}O_{4.345}$

$\dfrac{C_{2.166}H_{4.345}O_{4.345}}{2.166 \quad 2.166 \quad 2.166} \rightarrow CH_2O_2$

The correct empirical formula is CH_2O_2.

empirical formula mass = (12.01 g/mol) + 2(1.008 g/mol) + 2(16.00 g/mol) = 46.03 g/mol

$n = \dfrac{molar\ mass}{formula\ molar\ mass} = \dfrac{46.02\ \cancel{g/mol}}{46.03\ \cancel{g/mol}} = 1$

molecular formula = $CH_2O_2 \times 1$

= CH_2O_2

Write the correct skeletal structure for the molecule.

$$\begin{array}{c} O \\ | \\ H-C-O-H \end{array}$$

Calculate the total number of electrons for the Lewis structure by summing the number of valence electrons of each atom in the molecule.

(number of valence e^- for C) + 2(number of valence e^- for O) + 2(number of valence e^- for H)
= 4 + 2(6) + 2(1) = 18

Distribute the electrons among the atoms, giving octets (or duets for H) to as many atoms as possible. Begin with the bonding electrons; then proceed to lone pairs on terminal atoms and finally to lone pairs on the central atoms.

$$\begin{array}{c} :\ddot{O}: \\ | \\ H-C-\ddot{O}-H \end{array}$$

Complete the octet on C by forming a double bond.

$$\begin{array}{c} :O: \\ \| \\ H-C-\ddot{O}-H \end{array}$$

9.51   To determine the values of the lattice energy, it is necessary to look them up online. The lattice energy of Al_2O_3 is $-15{,}916$ kJ/mol; the value for Fe_2O_3 is $-14{,}774$ kJ/mol. The thermite reaction is exothermic due to the energy released when the Al_2O_3 lattice forms. The lattice energy of Al_2O_3 is more negative than the lattice energy of Fe_2O_3.

9.53 HNO_3 Write the correct skeletal structure for the molecule.

$$\begin{array}{c} O \\ | \\ H-O-N-O \end{array}$$

Calculate the total number of electrons for the Lewis structure by summing the number of valence electrons of each atom in the molecule.

3(number of valence e^- for O) + (number of valence e^- for N) + (number of valence e^- for H) = 3(6) + 5 + 1 = 24

Distribute the electrons among the atoms, giving octets (or duets for H) to as many atoms as possible. Begin with the bonding electrons; then proceed to lone pairs on terminal atoms and finally to lone pairs on the central atom.

$$\begin{array}{c} :\ddot{O}: \\ | \\ H-\ddot{O}-N-\ddot{O}: \end{array}$$

All 24 valence electrons are used.

If any atoms lack an octet, form double or triple bonds as necessary. The double bond can be formed to any of the three oxygen atoms, so there are three resonance forms.

$$\underset{I}{\begin{array}{c} :O: \\ \| \\ H-\ddot{O}-N-\ddot{O}: \end{array}} \longleftrightarrow \underset{II}{\begin{array}{c} :\ddot{O}: \\ | \\ H-\ddot{O}-N=\ddot{O} \end{array}} \longleftrightarrow \underset{III}{\begin{array}{c} :\ddot{O}: \\ | \\ H-\ddot{O}=N-\ddot{O}: \end{array}}$$

All atoms have octets (duets for H); the structure is complete.

To determine which resonance hybrid(s) is most important, calculate the formal charge on each atom in each structure by finding the number of valence electrons and subtracting the number of lone pair electrons and one-half the number of bonding electrons.

	Structure I					**Structure II**				
	O_{left}	O_{top}	O_{right}	N	H	O_{left}	O_{top}	O_{right}	N	H
number of valence electrons	6	6	6	5	1	6	6	6	5	1
− number of lone pair electrons	4	4	6	0	0	4	6	4	0	0
− 1/2(number of bonding electrons)	2	2	1	4	1	2	1	2	4	1
Formal charge	0	0	−1	+1	0	0	−1	0	+1	0

Structure III

	O_{left}	O_{top}	O_{right}	N	H
number of valence electrons	6	6	6	5	1
− number of lone pair electrons	2	6	6	0	0
− 1/2(number of bonding electrons)	3	1	1	4	1
Formal charge	+1	−1	−1	+1	0

The sum of the formal charges is 0 for each structure, which is the overall charge of the molecule. However, in structures I and II, the individual formal charges are lower. These two forms would contribute equally to the structure of HNO_3. Structure III would be less important because the individual formal charges are higher.

9.55 CNO^- Write the skeletal structure:

       C—N—O

Determine the number of valence electrons.

     (valence e^- from C) + (valence e^- from N) + (valence e^- from O) + 1(from the negative charge)

     4 + 5 + 6 + 1 = 16

     :C̈—N—Ö:

Distribute the electrons to complete octets if possible.

$$\left[\ddot{C}=N=\ddot{O} \right]^- \longleftrightarrow \left[:C\equiv N-\ddot{\underset{\cdot\cdot}{O}}: \right]^- \longleftrightarrow \left[:\ddot{C}-N\equiv O: \right]^-$$

         I   II   III

Determine the formal charge on each atom for each structure.

<table>
<tr><td colspan="4">Structure I</td><td colspan="3">Structure II</td></tr>
<tr><td></td><td>C</td><td>N</td><td>O</td><td>C</td><td>N</td><td>O</td></tr>
<tr><td>number of valence electrons</td><td>4</td><td>5</td><td>6</td><td>4</td><td>5</td><td>6</td></tr>
<tr><td>− number of lone pair electrons</td><td>4</td><td>0</td><td>4</td><td>2</td><td>0</td><td>6</td></tr>
<tr><td>− 1/2(number of bonding electrons)</td><td>2</td><td>4</td><td>2</td><td>3</td><td>4</td><td>1</td></tr>
<tr><td>Formal charge</td><td>−2</td><td>+1</td><td>0</td><td>−1</td><td>+1</td><td>−1</td></tr>
</table>

Structure III

	C	N	O
number of valence electrons	4	5	6
− number of lone pair electrons	6	0	2
− 1/2(number of bonding electrons)	1	4	3
Formal charge	−3	+1	+1

Structures I, II, and III all follow the octet rule but have varying degrees of negative formal charge on carbon, which is the least electronegative atom. Also, the amount of formal charge is very high in all three resonance forms. Although structure II is the best of the resonance forms, it has a −1 charge on the least electronegative atom, C, and a +1 charge on the more electronegative atom, N. Therefore, none of these resonance forms contributes strongly to the stability of the fulminate ion and the ion is not very stable.

9.57   (a) C_3H_8:   Write the correct skeletal structure for the molecule.

                 H   H   H
                  | | |
            H—C—C—C—H
                  | | |
                  H   H   H

Calculate the total number of electrons for the Lewis structure by summing the valence electrons of each atom in the molecule.

         3(number of valence e^- for C) + 8(number of valence e^- for H) = 3(4) + 8(1) = 20

Distribute the electrons among the atoms, giving octets (or duets for H) to as many atoms as possible. Begin with the bonding electrons; then proceed to lone pairs on terminal atoms and finally to lone pairs on the central atom.

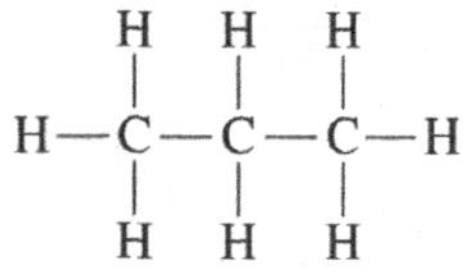

$$
\begin{array}{ccccccc}
 & H & & H & & H & \\
 & | & & | & & | & \\
H & - C & - & C & - & C & - H \\
 & | & & | & & | & \\
 & H & & H & & H &
\end{array}
$$

All 20 valence electrons are used.

(b)   CH$_3$OCH$_3$:   Write the correct skeletal structure for the molecule.

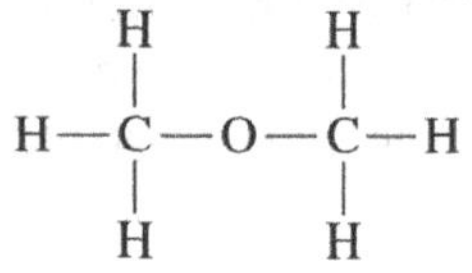

$$
\begin{array}{ccccccc}
 & H & & & & H & \\
 & | & & & & | & \\
H & - C & - & O & - & C & - H \\
 & | & & & & | & \\
 & H & & & & H &
\end{array}
$$

Calculate the total number of electrons for the Lewis structure by summing the valence electrons of each atom in the molecule.

2(number of valence e⁻ for C) + 6(number of valence e⁻ for H) + (number of valence electrons for O) = 2(4) + 6(1) + 6 = 20

Distribute the electrons among the atoms, giving octets (or duets for H) to as many atoms as possible. Begin with the bonding electrons; then proceed to lone pairs on terminal atoms and finally to lone pairs on the central atom.

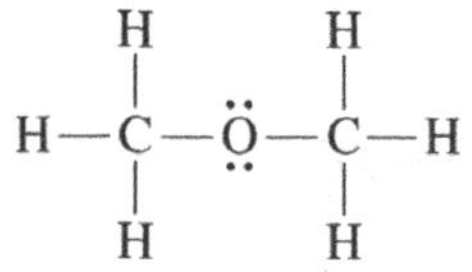

$$
\begin{array}{ccccccc}
 & H & & & & H & \\
 & | & & & & | & \\
H & - C & - & \ddot{\underset{\cdot\cdot}{O}} & - & C & - H \\
 & | & & & & | & \\
 & H & & & & H &
\end{array}
$$

All 20 valence electrons are used.

(c)   CH$_3$COCH$_3$:   Write the correct skeletal structure for the molecule.

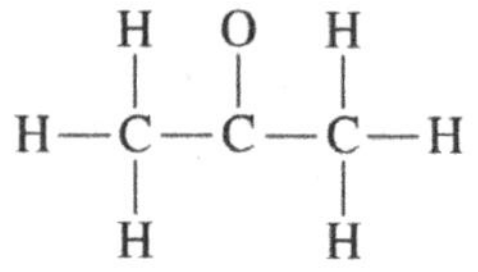

$$
\begin{array}{ccccccc}
 & H & & O & & H & \\
 & | & & | & & | & \\
H & - C & - & C & - & C & - H \\
 & | & & & & | & \\
 & H & & & & H &
\end{array}
$$

Calculate the total number of electrons for the Lewis structure by summing the valence electrons of each atom in the molecule.

3(number of valence e⁻ for C) + 6(number of valence e⁻ for H) + (number of valence electrons for O) = 3(4) + 6(1) + 6 = 24

Distribute the electrons among the atoms, giving octets (or duets for H) to as many atoms as possible. Begin with the bonding electrons; then proceed to lone pairs on terminal atoms and finally to lone pairs on the central atom.

$$
\begin{array}{ccccccc}
 & H & & :\ddot{O}: & & H & \\
 & | & & | & & | & \\
H & - C & - & C & - & C & - H \\
 & | & & & & | & \\
 & H & & & & H &
\end{array}
$$

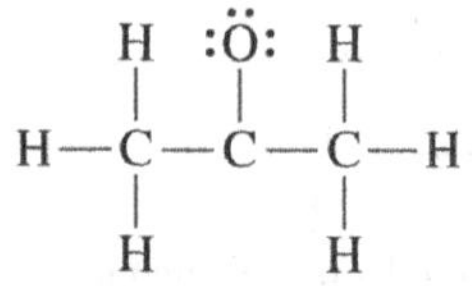

All 24 valence electrons are used.
If any atom lacks an octet, form double or triple bonds to give them octets.

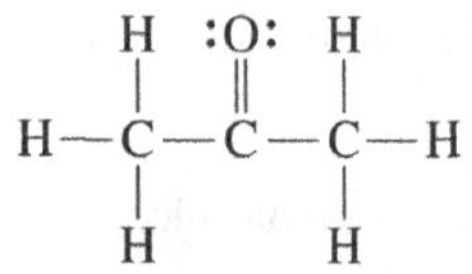

$$
\begin{array}{ccccccc}
 & H & & :\ddot{O}: & & H & \\
 & | & & \| & & | & \\
H & - C & - & C & - & C & - H \\
 & | & & & & | & \\
 & H & & & & H &
\end{array}
$$

All atoms have octets (duets for hydrogen); the structure is complete.

(d)   CH$_3$COOH: Write the correct skeletal structure for the molecule.

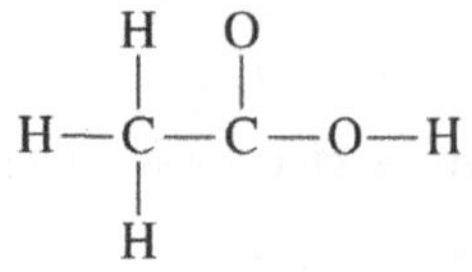

$$
\begin{array}{ccccccc}
 & H & & O & & & \\
 & | & & | & & & \\
H & - C & - & C & - & O & - H \\
 & | & & & & & \\
 & H & & & & &
\end{array}
$$

Calculate the total number of electrons for the Lewis structure by summing the valence electrons of each atom in the molecule.

2(number of valence e⁻ for C) + 4(number of valence e⁻ for H) + 2(number of valence electrons for O) = 2(4) + 4(1) + 2(6) = 24

Distribute the electrons among the atoms, giving octets (or duets for H) to as many atoms as possible. Begin with the bonding electrons; then proceed to lone pairs on terminal atoms and finally to lone pairs on the central atom.

$$\begin{array}{ccc} H & :\ddot{O}: & \\ | & | & \\ H-C-C-\ddot{O}-H \\ | & \\ H & \end{array}$$

All 24 valence electrons are used.

If any atom lacks an octet, form double or triple bonds to give them octets.

$$\begin{array}{ccc} H & :O: & \\ | & \| & \\ H-C-C-\ddot{O}-H \\ | & \\ H & \end{array}$$

All atoms have octets (duets for hydrogen); the structure is complete.

(e)   CH₃CHO: Write the correct skeletal structure for the molecule.

$$\begin{array}{ccc} H & O & \\ | & | & \\ H-C-C-H \\ | & \\ H & \end{array}$$

Calculate the total number of electrons for the Lewis structure by summing the valence electrons of each atom in the molecule.

2(number of valence e⁻ for C) + 4(number of valence e⁻ for H) + (number of valence electrons for O) = 2(4) + 4(1) + (6) = 18

Distribute the electrons among the atoms, giving octets (or duets for H) to as many atoms as possible. Begin with the bonding electrons; then proceed to lone pairs on terminal atoms and finally to lone pairs on the central atom.

$$\begin{array}{ccc} H & :\ddot{O}: & \\ | & | & \\ H-C-C-H \\ | & \\ H & \end{array}$$

All 18 valence electrons are used.

If any atom lacks an octet, form double or triple bonds to give them octets.

$$\begin{array}{ccc} H & :O: & \\ | & \| & \\ H-C-C-H \\ | & \\ H & \end{array}$$

All atoms have octets (duets for hydrogen); the structure is complete.

9.59   HCSNH₂: Write the correct skeletal structure for the molecule.

$$\begin{array}{c} S \\ | \\ H-C-N\diagdown{}^{H}_{H} \end{array}$$

Calculate the total number of electrons for the Lewis structure by summing the number of valence electrons of each atom in the molecule.

(number of valence e⁻ for N) + (number of valence e⁻ for S) + (number of valence e⁻ for C) + 3(number of valence e⁻ for H) = 5 + 6 + 4 + 3(1) = 18

Distribute the electrons among the atoms, giving octets (or duets for H) to as many atoms as possible. Begin with the bonding electrons; then proceed to lone pairs on terminal atoms and finally to lone pairs on the central atoms.

$$
\begin{array}{c}
\ddot{\text{S}} \\
| \\
\text{H}-\text{C}-\ddot{\text{N}}\stackrel{\displaystyle \nearrow \text{H}}{\searrow \text{H}}
\end{array}
$$

Complete the octet on C by forming a double bond.

$$
\begin{array}{c}
\ddot{\text{S}} \\
\text{nonpolar}\parallel \quad \text{polar} \\
\text{H}-\text{C}-\ddot{\text{N}}\stackrel{\displaystyle \nearrow^{\text{polar}} \text{H}}{\searrow_{\text{polar}} \text{H}} \\
\text{nonpolar}\quad\text{polar}
\end{array}
$$

9.61   (a) O_2^-:   Write the correct skeletal structure for the radical.

                    O—O

Calculate the total number of electrons for the Lewis structure by summing the number of valence electrons of each atom in the radical and adding 1 for the 1− charge.

$$2(\text{number of valence e}^- \text{ for O}) + 1 = 2(6) + 1 = 13$$

Distribute the electrons among the atoms, giving octets to as many atoms as possible. Begin with the bonding electrons; then proceed to lone pairs on terminal atoms and finally to lone pairs on the central atom.

$$\left[\cdot\ddot{\text{O}}-\ddot{\text{O}}\!: \right]^-$$

All 13 valence electrons are used.

O has an incomplete octet. It has seven electrons because we have an odd number of valence electrons.

    (b) O^-:   Write the Lewis symbol based on the valence electrons $2s^2 2p^5$.

$$\left[\cdot\ddot{\text{O}}\!: \right]^-$$

    (c)   OH: Write the correct skeletal structure for the molecule.

                    H—O

Calculate the total number of electrons for the Lewis structure by summing the number of valence electrons of each atom in the molecule.

$$(\text{number of valence e}^- \text{ for O}) + (\text{number of valence e}^- \text{ for H}) = 6 + 1 = 7$$

Distribute the electrons among the atoms, giving octets (or duets for H) to as many atoms as possible. Begin with the bonding electrons; then proceed to lone pairs on terminal atoms and finally to lone pairs on the central atom.

$$\text{H}-\ddot{\text{O}}\cdot$$

All seven valence electrons are used.

O has an incomplete octet. It has seven electrons because we have an odd number of valence electrons.

    (d) CH_3OO: Write the correct skeletal structure for the radical.

C is the least electronegative atom, so it is central.

$$
\begin{array}{c}
\text{H} \\
| \\
\text{H}-\text{C}-\text{O}-\text{O} \\
| \\
\text{H}
\end{array}
$$

Calculate the total number of electrons for the Lewis structure by summing the number of valence electrons of each atom in the molecule.

$$3(\text{number of valence e}^- \text{ for H}) + (\text{number of valence e}^- \text{ for C}) + 2(\text{number of valence}$$
$$\text{e}^- \text{ for O}) = 3(1) + 4 + 2(6) = 19$$

Distribute the electrons among the atoms, giving octets (or duets for H) to as many atoms as possible. Begin with the bonding electrons; then proceed to lone pairs on terminal atoms and finally to lone pairs on the central atoms.

$$H-\underset{\underset{H}{|}}{\overset{\overset{H}{|}}{C}}-\ddot{\underset{..}{O}}-\ddot{\underset{..}{O}}\cdot$$

All 19 valence electrons are used.

O has an incomplete octet. It has seven electrons because we have an odd number of valence electrons.

9.63 Rewrite the reaction using the Lewis structures of the molecules involved.

$$H-H(g) + 1/2\ddot{\underset{..}{O}}=\ddot{\underset{..}{O}}(g) \longrightarrow H-\ddot{\underset{..}{O}}-H(g)$$

Determine which bonds are broken in the reaction and sum the bond energies of the following:

$\Sigma(\Delta H$'s bonds broken)
$= 1(H-H) + 1/2(O=O)$
$= 1(436 \text{ kJ/mol}) + 1/2(498)$
$= 685 \text{ kJ/mol}$

Determine which bonds are formed in the reaction and sum the negatives of the bond energies of the following:

$\Sigma(-\Delta H$'s bonds formed)
$= -2 \text{ mol}(O-H)$
$= -2 \text{ mol}(464 \text{ kJ/mol})$
$= -928 \text{ kJ/mol}$

Find ΔH°_{rxn} by summing the results of the two steps.

$\Delta H^{\circ}_{rxn} = \Sigma(\Delta H$'s bonds broken) $+ \Sigma(-\Delta H$'s bonds formed)
$= 685 \text{ kJ/mol} - 928 \text{ kJ/mol}$
$= -243 \text{ kJ/mol}$

$CH_4(g) + 2O_2(g) \rightarrow CO_2(g) + 2H_2O(g)$

Rewrite the reaction using the Lewis structures of the molecules involved.

$$H-\underset{\underset{H}{|}}{\overset{\overset{H}{|}}{C}}-H + 2\ddot{\underset{..}{O}}=\ddot{\underset{..}{O}} \longrightarrow \ddot{\underset{..}{O}}=C=\ddot{\underset{..}{O}} + 2\,H-\ddot{\underset{..}{O}}-H$$

Determine which bonds are broken in the reaction and sum the bond energies of the following:

$\Sigma(\Delta H$'s bonds broken)
$= 4(C-H) + 2(O=O)$
$= 4(414 \text{ kJ/mol}) + 2(498)$
$= 2652 \text{ kJ/mol}$

Determine which bonds are formed in the reaction and sum the negatives of the bond energies of the following:

$\Sigma(-\Delta H$'s bonds formed)
$= -2(C=O) - 4(O-H)$
$= -2(799 \text{ kJ/mol}) - 4(464 \text{ kJ/mol})$
$= -3454 \text{ kJ/mol}$

Find ΔH°_{rxn} by summing the results of the two steps.

$\Delta H^{\circ}_{rxn} = \Sigma(\Delta H$'s bonds broken) $+ \Sigma(-\Delta H$'s bonds formed)
$= 2652 \text{ kJ/mol} - 3454 \text{ kJ/mol}$
$= -802 \text{ kJ/mol}$

Compare the following:

	kJ/mol	**kJ/g**
H_2	-243	-121 (using a molar mass of 2.016)
CH_4	-802	-50.0 (using a molar mass of 16.04)

$$\frac{-243 \text{ kJ}}{\text{mol } H_2} \times \frac{1 \text{ mol } H_2}{2.016 \text{ g } H_2} = \frac{-121 \text{ kJ}}{\text{g } H_2} \qquad \frac{-802 \text{ kJ}}{\text{mol } CH_4} \times \frac{1 \text{ mol } CH_4}{16.04 \text{ g } CH_4} = \frac{-50.0 \text{ kJ}}{\text{g } CH_4}$$

So methane yields more energy per mole, but hydrogen yields more energy per gram.

9.65   (a) Cl_2O_7:   Write the correct skeletal structure for the molecule.

$$\begin{array}{ccccc}
\text{O} & & \text{O} & & \\
| & & | & & \\
\text{O}-\text{Cl}-\text{O}-\text{Cl}-\text{O} \\
| & & | & & \\
\text{O} & & \text{O} & &
\end{array}$$

Calculate the total number of electrons for the Lewis structure by summing the valence electrons of each atom in the molecule.

$$2(\text{number of valence e}^- \text{ for Cl}) + 7(\text{number of valence e}^- \text{ for O}) = 2(7) + 7(6) = 56$$

Distribute the electrons among the atoms, giving octets (or duets for H) to as many atoms as possible. Begin with the bonding electrons; then proceed to lone pairs on terminal atoms and finally to lone pairs on the central atom.

$$\begin{array}{ccccc}
:\ddot{\text{O}}: & & :\ddot{\text{O}}: & & \\
| & & | & & \\
:\ddot{\text{O}}-\text{Cl}-\ddot{\text{O}}-\text{Cl}-\ddot{\text{O}}: \\
| & & | & & \\
:\ddot{\text{O}}: & & :\ddot{\text{O}}: & &
\end{array}$$

Form double bonds to minimize formal charge.

$$\begin{array}{ccccc}
:\text{O}: & & :\text{O}: & & \\
\| & & \| & & \\
\ddot{\text{O}}=\text{Cl}-\ddot{\text{O}}-\text{Cl}=\ddot{\text{O}} \\
\| & & \| & & \\
:\text{O}: & & :\text{O}: & &
\end{array}$$

(b) H_3PO_3:   Write the correct skeletal structure for the molecule.

$$\begin{array}{c}
\text{O} \\
| \\
\text{H}-\text{P}-\text{O}-\text{H} \\
| \\
\text{O} \\
| \\
\text{H}
\end{array}$$

Calculate the total number of electrons for the Lewis structure by summing the valence electrons of each atom in the molecule.

$$(\text{number of valence e}^- \text{ for P}) + 3(\text{number of valence e}^- \text{ for O}) + 3(\text{number of valence e}^- \text{ for H}) = 5 + 3(6) + 3(1) = 26$$

Distribute the electrons among the atoms, giving octets (or duets for H) to as many atoms as possible. Begin with the bonding electrons; then proceed to lone pairs on terminal atoms and finally to lone pairs on central atoms.

$$\begin{array}{c}
:\ddot{\text{O}}: \\
| \\
\text{H}-\text{P}-\ddot{\text{O}}-\text{H} \\
| \\
:\text{O}: \\
| \\
\text{H}
\end{array}$$

Form double bonds to minimize formal charge.

$$\begin{array}{c}
:\text{O}: \\
\| \\
\text{H}-\text{P}-\ddot{\text{O}}-\text{H} \\
| \\
:\text{O}: \\
| \\
\text{H}
\end{array}$$

(c) H_3AsO_4:   Write the correct skeletal structure for the molecule.

$$
\begin{array}{c}
\text{O} \\
| \\
\text{H—O—As—O—H} \\
| \\
\text{O} \\
| \\
\text{H}
\end{array}
$$

Calculate the total number of electrons for the Lewis structure by summing the valence electrons of each atom in the molecule.

(number of valence e⁻ for As) + 4(number of valence e⁻ for O) + 3(number of valence e⁻ for H)
= 5 + 4(6) + 3(1) = 32

Distribute the electrons among the atoms, giving octets (or duets for H) to as many atoms as possible. Begin with the bonding electrons; then proceed to lone pairs on terminal atoms and finally to lone pairs on the central atom.

$$
\begin{array}{c}
:\ddot{\text{O}}: \\
| \\
\text{H—}\ddot{\ddot{\text{O}}}\text{—As—}\ddot{\ddot{\text{O}}}\text{—H} \\
| \\
:\text{O}: \\
| \\
\text{H}
\end{array}
$$

Form double bonds to minimize formal charge.

$$
\begin{array}{c}
:\text{O}: \\
\| \\
\text{H—}\ddot{\ddot{\text{O}}}\text{—As—}\ddot{\ddot{\text{O}}}\text{—H} \\
| \\
:\text{O}: \\
| \\
\text{H}
\end{array}
$$

9.67 $Na^+F^- < Na^+O^{2-} < Mg^{2+}F^- < Mg^{2+}O^{2-} < Al^{3+}O^{2-}$

The lattice energy is proportional to the magnitude of the charge and inversely proportional to the distance between the atoms. Na^+F^- would have the smallest lattice energy because the magnitude of the charges on Na and F are the smallest. $Mg^{2+}F^-$ and Na^+O^{2-} both have the same magnitude formal charge, the O^{2-} is larger than F^- in size, and Na^+ is larger than Mg^{2+}; so Na^+O^{2-} should be less than $Mg^{2+}F^-$. The magnitude of the charge makes $Mg^{2+}O^{2-} < Al^{3+}O^{2-}$.

9.69   **Given:** 7.743% H   **Find:** Lewis structure
Conceptual Plan: %H → %C → mass C, H → mol C, H → pseudoformula → empirical formula

$$100\% - \%H \quad \text{Assume 100 g sample} \quad \frac{1\ \text{mol C}}{12.01\ \text{g}} \quad \frac{1\ \text{mol H}}{1.008\ \text{g}} \quad \text{divide by smallest number}$$

Solution: %C = 100% − 7.743% = 92.257% C
In a 100.00 g sample: 7.743 g H, 92.257 g C

$$7.743\ \text{g H} \times \frac{1\ \text{mol H}}{1.008\ \text{g H}} = 7.682\ \text{mol}$$

$$92.257\ \text{g C} \times \frac{1\ \text{mol C}}{12.01\ \text{g C}} = 7.682\ \text{mol C}$$

$C_{7.682}H_{7.682}$

$$\frac{C_{7.682}H_{7.682}}{7.682 \quad 7.682} \rightarrow CH$$

The smallest molecular formula would be C_2H_2.

Write the correct skeletal structure for the molecule.

$$\text{H—C—C—H}$$

Calculate the total number of electrons for the Lewis structure by summing the valence electrons of each atom in the molecule.

$$2(\text{number of valence e}^- \text{ for C}) + 2(\text{number of valence e}^- \text{ for H}) = 2(4) + 2(1) = 10$$

Distribute the electrons among the atoms, giving octets (or duets for H) to as many atoms as possible. Begin with the bonding electrons; then proceed to lone pairs on terminal atoms and finally to lone pairs on the central atom.

$$\text{H}-\overset{..}{\underset{..}{\text{C}}}-\overset{..}{\underset{..}{\text{C}}}-\text{H}$$

Complete the octet on C by forming a triple bond.

$$\text{H}-\text{C}\equiv\text{C}-\text{H}$$

Challenge Problems

9.71

Step 1:

Bonds broken: $2(\text{S}=\text{O}) + 1(\text{H}-\text{O}) = 2(523 \text{ kJ/mol}) + 1(464 \text{ kJ/mol}) = 1510 \text{ kJ/mol}$
Bonds formed: $-2(\text{S}-\text{O}) - 1(\text{S}=\text{O}) - 1(\text{O}-\text{H}) =$
$-2(265 \text{ kJ/mol}) - 1(523 \text{ kJ/mol}) - 1(464 \text{ kJ/mol}) = -1517 \text{ kJ/mol}$
$$\Delta H_{\text{step}} = -7 \text{ kJ/mol}$$

Step 2:

Bonds broken: $2(\text{S}-\text{O}) + 1(\text{S}=\text{O}) + 1(\text{O}-\text{H}) + 1(\text{O}=\text{O}) =$
$2(265 \text{ kJ/mol}) + 1(523 \text{ kJ/mol}) + 1(464 \text{ kJ/mol}) + 1(498 \text{ kJ/mol}) = 2015 \text{ kJ/mol}$
Bonds formed: $-2(\text{S}-\text{O}) - 1(\text{S}=\text{O}) - 1(\text{O}-\text{H}) - 1(\text{O}-\text{O}) =$
$-2(265 \text{ kJ/mol}) - 1(523 \text{ kJ/mol}) - 1(464 \text{ kJ/mol}) - 1(142 \text{ kJ/mol}) = -1659 \text{ kJ/mol}$
$$\Delta H_{\text{step}} = +356 \text{ kJ/mol}$$

Step 3:

Bonds broken: $2(\text{S}-\text{O}) + 1(\text{S}=\text{O}) + 2(\text{O}-\text{H}) =$
$2 (265 \text{ kJ/mol}) + 1 (523 \text{ kJ/mol}) + 2 (464 \text{ kJ/mol}) = 1981 \text{ kJ/mol}$
Bonds formed: $-2(\text{S}-\text{O}) - 2(\text{S}=\text{O}) - 2(\text{O}-\text{H}) =$
$-2(265 \text{ kJ/mol}) + -2(523 \text{ kJ/mol}) + -2(464 \text{ kJ/mol}) = -2504 \text{ kJ/mol}$
$$\Delta H_{\text{step}} = -523 \text{ kJ/mol}$$

Hess's law states that ΔH for the reaction is the sum of ΔH of the steps:
$\Delta H^{\circ}_{\text{rxn}} = (-7 \text{ kJ/mol}) + (+356 \text{ kJ/mol}) + (-523 \text{ kJ/mol}) = -174 \text{ kJ/mol}$

9.73   **Given:** $\mu = 1.08$ D HCl, 20% ionic and $\mu = 1.82$ D HF, 45% ionic   **Find:** r
Conceptual Plan: $\mu \rightarrow \mu_{\text{calc}} \rightarrow r$

$$\% \text{ ionic character} = \frac{\mu}{\mu_{\text{calc}}} \times 100\%$$

Solution: For HCl $\mu_{\text{calc}} = \dfrac{1.08}{0.20} = 5.4 \text{ D}$ $\dfrac{5.4 \text{ \cancel{D}} \times \dfrac{3.34 \times 10^{-30} \text{ }\cancel{C} \cdot \cancel{m}}{\cancel{D}} \times \dfrac{10^{12} \text{ pm}}{1 \text{ }\cancel{m}}}{1.6 \times 10^{-19} \text{ }\cancel{C}} = 113 \text{ pm}$

For HF $\mu_{calc} = \dfrac{1.82}{0.45} = \underline{4.04}\ D$ $\dfrac{4.04\ \cancel{D} \times \dfrac{3.34 \times 10^{-30}\ \cancel{C} \cdot \cancel{m}}{\cancel{D}} \times \dfrac{10^{12}\ pm}{1\ \cancel{m}}}{1.6 \times 10^{-19}\ \cancel{C}} = 84\ pm$

From Table 9.4, the bond length of HCl = 127 pm, and HF = 92 pm. Both of these values are slightly higher than the calculated values.

9.75   For the four P atoms to be equivalent, they must all be in the same electronic environment. That is, they must all see the same number of bonds and lone pair electrons. The only way to achieve this is with a tetrahedral configuration where the P atoms are at the four points of the tetrahedron.

9.77   **Given:** H_2S_4 linear   **Find:** oxidation number of each S
Write the correct skeletal structure for the molecule.

$$H-S-S-S-S-H$$

Calculate the total number of electrons for the Lewis structure by summing the number of valence electrons of each atom in the molecule.

$$4(\text{number of valence e}^- \text{ for S}) + 2(\text{number of valence e}^- \text{ for H}) = 4(6) + 2(1) = 26$$

Distribute the electrons among the atoms, giving octets (or duets for H) to as many atoms as possible.

$$H-\ddot{\underset{..}{S}}-\ddot{\underset{..}{S}}-\ddot{\underset{..}{S}}-\ddot{\underset{..}{S}}-H$$

Determine the oxidation number on each atom. EN(H) < EN(S), so the electrons in the H — S bond belong to the S atom, while the electrons in the S — S bonds split between the two S atoms.

O. N. = valence electrons − electrons that belong to the atom

$$H-\ddot{\underset{..}{S}}_A-\ddot{\underset{..}{S}}_B-\ddot{\underset{..}{S}}_C-\ddot{\underset{..}{S}}_D-H$$

H = 1 − 0 = +1 for each H
$S_A = 6 - 7 = -1$
$S_B = 6 - 6 = 0$
$S_C = 6 - 6 = 0$
$S_D = 6 - 7 = -1$

9.79   **Given:** $\Delta H_f^\circ(SO_2) = -296.8$ kJ/mol, S(g) = 277.2 kJ/mol, break O=O bond = 498 kJ
Find: S=O bond energy
Conceptual Plan: Use ΔH_f for SO$_2$ and S(g) and the bond energy of O$_2$ to determine heat of atomization of SO$_2$.

Reaction			ΔH (kJ/mol)
$SO_2(g)$	$\rightarrow$	~~S(s, rhombic)~~ + ~~O$_2$(g)~~	+296.8
~~S(s, rhombic)~~	$\rightarrow$	S(g)	+277.2
~~O=O(g)~~	$\rightarrow$	2 O(g)	+498
$SO_2(g)$	$\rightarrow$	S(g) + 2 O(g)	+1072

Write the reaction using the Lewis structure.

$$\ddot{\underset{..}{O}}=\ddot{S}=\ddot{\underset{..}{O}}(g) \longrightarrow S(g) + 2\,O(g)$$

Determine the number and kinds of bonds broken and then ΔH atomization = bonds broken.

ΔH atomization = $2\sum$ (S=O) bonds broken.
1072 kJ/mol = 2 (S=O) bonds broken.
S=O bond energy = 536 kJ/mol.

Check: The S=O bond energy is close to the table value of 523 kJ/mol.

Conceptual Problems

9.81   When we say that a compound is "energy rich," we mean that it gives off a great amount of energy when it reacts. It means that a lot of energy is stored in the compound. This energy is released when the weak bonds in the compound break and much stronger bonds are formed in the product, thereby releasing energy.

9.83   Lewis theory is successful because it allows us to understand and predict many chemical observations. We can use it to determine the formulas of ionic compounds and to account for the low melting points and boiling points of molecular compounds compared to ionic compounds. Lewis theory allows us to predict what molecules or ions will be stable, which will be more reactive, and which will not exist. Lewis theory, however, does not tell us anything about how the bonds in the molecules and ions form. It does not give us a way to account for the paramagnetism of oxygen. And, by itself, Lewis theory does not tell us anything about the shape of the molecule or ion.

Questions for Group Work

9.85   The Lewis dot symbols for the atoms are:

Li·   ·Be·   ·B·   ·C·   ·N: ·O: :F: :Ne:

The formal charge on each atom is the number of valence electrons minus the number of lone pair electrons and one-half the number of bonding electrons. The formal charge is equal to the number of valence electrons because there are no bonds.

9.87   The steps for writing a Lewis structure are:
1.   Write the correct skeletal structure for the molecule or ion.
2.   Calculate the total number of electrons for the Lewis structure by summing the valence electrons of each atom in the molecule or ion. Add an electron for each negative charge on an ion and subtract an electron for each charge on a cation.
3.   Distribute the electrons among the atoms, giving octets (or duets for hydrogen) to as many atoms as possible.
4.   If any atoms lack an octet, form double or triple bonds as necessary to give them octets.
5.   Consider forming resonance structures if it is possible to write two or more Lewis structures for the same molecule or ion. Remember that only electrons move when generating resonance structures. The formal charges of atoms can be used to determine which resonance structures are better than others. The formal charge of an atom in a Lewis structure is the charge it would have if all bonding electrons were shared equally between the bonded atoms. Formal charge = number of valence electrons − (number of lone pair electron +1/2 number of bonding electrons).

10 Chemical Bonding II: Molecular Shapes, Valence Bond Theory, and Molecular Orbital Theory

Problems by Topic

VSEPR Theory and Molecular Geometry

10.1   Four electron groups: A trigonal pyramidal molecular geometry has three bonding groups and one lone pair of electrons, so there are four electron groups on atom A.

10.3   (a)   4 total electron groups, 4 bonding groups, 0 lone pairs
               A tetrahedral molecular geometry has four bonding groups and no lone pairs. So there are four total electron groups, four bonding groups, and no lone pairs.
        (b)   5 total electron groups, 3 bonding groups, 2 lone pairs
               A T-shaped molecular geometry has three bonding groups and two lone pairs. So there are five total electron groups, three bonding groups, and two lone pairs.
        (c)   6 total electron groups, 5 bonding groups, 1 lone pair
               A square pyramidal molecular geometry has five bonding groups and one lone pair. So there are six total electron groups, five bonding groups, and one lone pair.

10.5   (a) PF_3: Electron geometry—tetrahedral; molecular geometry—trigonal pyramidal; bond angle $= 109.5°$
               Because of the lone pair, the bond angle will be less than $109.5°$.
               Draw a Lewis structure for the molecule:
               PF_3 has 26 valence electrons.

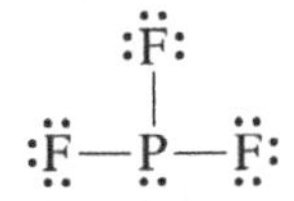

$$:\ddot{F}:$$
$$|$$
$$:\ddot{F}—P—\ddot{F}:$$

               Determine the total number of electron groups around the central atom:
               There are four electron groups on P.
               Determine the number of bonding groups and the number of lone pairs around the central atom:
               There are three bonding groups and one lone pair.
               Use Table 10.1 to determine the electron geometry, molecular geometry, and bond angles:
               Four electron groups give a tetrahedral electron geometry; three bonding groups and one lone pair give a trigonal pyramidal molecular geometry; the idealized bond angles for tetrahedral geometry are $109.5°$. The lone pair will make the bond angle less than idealized.

(b) SBr_2:   Electron geometry—tetrahedral; molecular geometry—bent; bond angle = 109.5°
Because of the lone pairs, the bond angle will be less than 109.5°.
Draw a Lewis structure for the molecule:
SBr_2 has 20 valence electrons.

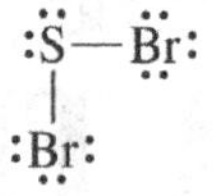

$$:\ddot{S}—\ddot{B}r:$$
$$|$$
$$:\ddot{B}r:$$

Determine the total number of electron groups around the central atom:
There are four electron groups on S.
Determine the number of bonding groups and the number of lone pairs around the central atom:
There are two bonding groups and two lone pairs.
Use Table 10.1 to determine the electron geometry, molecular geometry, and bond angles:
Four electron groups give a tetrahedral electron geometry; two bonding groups and two lone pairs
give a bent molecular geometry; the idealized bond angles for tetrahedral geometry are 109.5°. The
lone pairs will make the bond angle less than idealized.

(c) $CHCl_3$:   Electron geometry—tetrahedral; molecular geometry—tetrahedral; bond angle = 109.5°
Because there are no lone pairs, the bond angle will be 109.5°.
Draw a Lewis structure for the molecule:
$CHCl_3$ has 26 valence electrons.

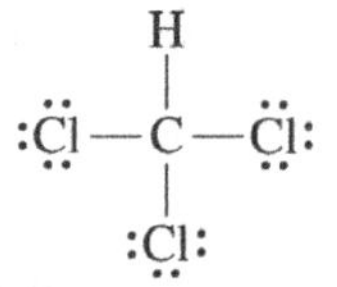

$$H$$
$$|$$
$$:\ddot{C}l—C—\ddot{C}l:$$
$$|$$
$$:\ddot{C}l:$$

Determine the total number of electron groups around the central atom:
There are four electron groups on C.
Determine the number of bonding groups and the number of lone pairs around the central atom:
There are four bonding groups and no lone pairs.
Use Table 10.1 to determine the electron geometry, molecular geometry, and bond angles:
Four electron groups give a tetrahedral electron geometry; four bonding groups and no lone pairs
give a tetrahedral molecular geometry; the idealized bond angles for tetrahedral geometry are 109.5°.
However, because the attached atoms have different electronegativities, the bond angles are less than
idealized.

(d) CS_2:   Electron geometry—linear; molecular geometry—linear; bond angle = 180°
Because there are no lone pairs, the bond angle will be 180°.
Draw a Lewis structure for the molecule:
CS_2 has 16 valence electrons.

$$\ddot{S}=C=\ddot{S}$$

Determine the total number of electron groups around the central atom:
There are two electron groups on C.
Determine the number of bonding groups and the number of lone pairs around the central atom:
There are two bonding groups and no lone pairs.
Use Table 10.1 to determine the electron geometry, molecular geometry, and bond angles:
Two electron groups give a linear geometry; two bonding groups and no lone pairs give a linear mo-
lecular geometry; the idealized bond angle is 180°. The molecule will not deviate from this.

10.7   H$_2$O will have the smaller bond angle because lone pair–lone pair repulsions are greater than lone pair–bonding pair repulsions.

Draw the Lewis structures for both structures:

H$_3$O$^+$ has eight valence electrons.   H$_2$O has eight valence electrons.

$$\left[\begin{array}{c} H \\ | \\ H—\ddot{O}—H \end{array} \right]^+ \qquad\qquad H—\overset{\cdot\cdot}{\underset{\cdot\cdot}{O}}—H$$

There are three bonding groups and   There are two bonding groups and two
one lone pair.   lone pairs.

Both have four electron groups, but the two lone pairs in H$_2$O will cause the bond angle to be smaller because of the lone pair–lone pair repulsions.

10.9   (a)   SF$_4$ Draw a Lewis structure for the molecule:
                         SF$_4$ has 34 valence electrons.

$$:\!\ddot{F}\!: \\ | \\ :\!\ddot{F}\!—\!\ddot{S}\!—\!\ddot{F}\!: \\ | \\ :\!\ddot{F}\!:$$

Determine the total number of electron groups around the central atom:
There are five electron groups on S.
Determine the number of bonding groups and the number of lone pairs around the central atom:
There are four bonding groups and one lone pair.
Use Table 10.1 to determine the electron geometry and molecular geometry:
The electron geometry is trigonal bipyramidal, so the molecular geometry is seesaw.
Sketch the molecule:

$$\begin{array}{c} F \\ | \\ S\!\cdots\!^{^{\backslash\backslash}}\!F \\ | \;\!\blacktriangleright F \\ F \end{array}$$

(b)   ClF$_3$ Draw a Lewis structure for the molecule:
                  ClF$_3$ has 28 valence electrons.

$$:\!\ddot{F}\!: \\ | \\ :\!\ddot{F}\!—\!\ddot{Cl}\!—\!\ddot{F}\!:$$

Determine the total number of electron groups around the central atom:
There are five electron groups on Cl.
Determine the number of bonding groups and the number of lone pairs around the central atom:
There are three bonding groups and two lone pairs.
Use Table 10.1 to determine the electron geometry and molecular geometry:
The electron geometry is trigonal bipyramidal, so the molecular geometry is T-shaped.
Sketch the molecule:

$$\begin{array}{c} F \\ | \\ F—Cl \\ | \\ F \end{array}$$

(c)   IF$_2^-$ Draw a Lewis structure for the ion:
                   IF$_2^-$ has 22 valence electrons.

$$\left[:\!\ddot{F}\!—\!\ddot{I}\!—\!\ddot{F}\!: \right]^-$$

Determine the total number of electron groups around the central atom:
There are five electron groups on I.

Determine the number of bonding groups and the number of lone pairs around the central atom:
There are two bonding groups and three lone pairs.
Use Table 10.1 to determine the electron geometry and molecular geometry:
The electron geometry is trigonal bipyramidal, so the molecular geometry is linear.
Sketch the ion:

$$\left[F - I - F \right]^{-}$$

(d) IBr_4^- Draw a Lewis structure for the ion:
IBr_4^- has 36 valence electrons.

$$\left[\begin{array}{c} :\ddot{Br}: \\ | \\ :\ddot{Br} - \cdot\dot{I} - \ddot{Br}: \\ | \\ :\ddot{Br}: \end{array} \right]^{-}$$

Determine the total number of electron groups around the central atom:
There are six electron groups on I.
Determine the number of bonding groups and the number of lone pairs around the central atom:
There are four bonding groups and two lone pairs.
Use Table 10.1 to determine the electron geometry and molecular geometry:
The electron geometry is octahedral, so the molecular geometry is square planar.
Sketch the ion:

$$\left[\begin{array}{c} Br \diagdown \quad \diagup Br \\ I \\ Br \diagup \quad \diagdown Br \end{array} \right]^{-}$$

10.11   (a) C_2H_2 Draw the Lewis structure:

$$H - C \equiv C - H$$

Atom	Number of Electron Groups	Number of Lone Pairs	Molecular Geometry
Left C	2	0	Linear
Right C	2	0	Linear

Sketch the molecule:

$$H - C \equiv C - H$$

(b) C_2H_4 Draw the Lewis structure:

$$\begin{array}{c} H \diagdown \quad \diagup H \\ C = C \\ H \diagup \quad \diagdown H \end{array}$$

Atom	Number of Electron Groups	Number of Lone Pairs	Molecular Geometry
Left C	3	0	Trigonal planar
Right C	3	0	Trigonal planar

Sketch the molecule:

$$\begin{array}{c} H \diagdown \quad \diagup H \\ C = C \\ H \diagup \quad \diagdown H \end{array}$$

(c) C_2H_6 Draw the Lewis structure:

$$\begin{array}{c} H \quad H \\ | \quad | \\ H - C - C - H \\ | \quad | \\ H \quad H \end{array}$$

Atom	Number of Electron Groups	Number of Lone Pairs	Molecular Geometry
Left C	4	0	Tetrahedral
Right C	4	0	Tetrahedral

Sketch the molecule:

10.13   (a)   Four pairs of electrons give a tetrahedral electron geometry. The lone pair would cause lone pair–bonded pair repulsions and would have a trigonal pyramidal molecular geometry.

(b)   Five pairs of electrons give a trigonal bipyramidal electron geometry. The lone pair occupies an equatorial position to minimize lone pair–bonded pair repulsions, and the molecule would have a seesaw molecular geometry.

(c)   Six pairs of electrons give an octahedral electron geometry. The two lone pairs would occupy opposite positions to minimize lone pair–lone pair repulsions. The molecular geometry would be square planar.

10.15   (a) CH_3OH Draw the Lewis structure and determine the geometry about each interior atom:

Atom	Number of Electron Groups	Number of Lone Pairs	Molecular Geometry
C	4	0	Tetrahedral
O	4	2	Bent

Sketch the molecule:

(b) CH_3OCH_3 Draw the Lewis structure and determine the geometry about each interior atom:

Atom	Number of Electron Groups	Number of Lone Pairs	Molecular Geometry
C	4	0	Tetrahedral
O	4	2	Bent
C	4	0	Tetrahedral

Sketch the molecule:

(c) H_2O_2 Draw the Lewis structure and determine the geometry about each interior atom:

Atom	Number of Electron Groups	Number of Lone Pairs	Molecular Geometry
O	4	2	Bent
O	4	2	Bent

Sketch the molecule:

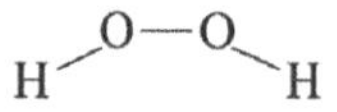

H—O—O—H

Molecular Shape and Polarity

10.17   Draw the Lewis structure for CO_2 and CCl_4; determine the molecular geometry and then the polarity.

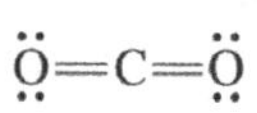

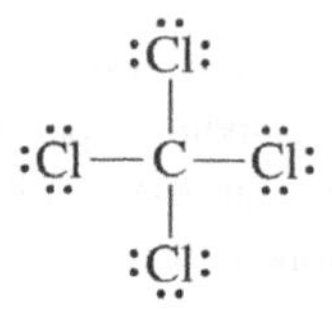

$$:\ddot{C}l—C—\ddot{C}l:$$

$$\ddot{O}=C=\ddot{O}$$

Number of electron groups on C	2	4
Number of lone pairs	0	0
Molecular geometry	linear	tetrahedral

Even though each molecule contains polar bonds, the sum of the bond dipoles gives a net dipole of zero for each molecule.

The linear molecular geometry of CO_2 will have bond vectors that are equal and opposite. ←———→

The tetrahedral molecular geometry of CCl_4 will have bond vectors that are equal and have a net dipole of zero.

10.19   (a) PF_3—polar
Draw the Lewis structure and determine the molecular geometry:
The molecular geometry from Problem 5 is trigonal pyramidal.
Determine whether the molecule contains polar bonds:
The electronegativity of P = 2.1 and F = 4. Therefore, the bonds are polar.

Determine whether the polar bonds add together to form a net dipole:

Because the molecule is trigonal pyramidal, the three dipole moments sum to a nonzero net dipole moment. The molecule is polar. See Table 10.2, in the text to see how dipole moments add to determine polarity.

(b) SBr_2—nonpolar
Draw the Lewis structure and determine the molecular geometry:
The molecular geometry from Problem 5 is bent.
Determine whether the molecule contains polar bonds:
The electronegativity of S = 2.5 and Br = 2.8. Therefore, the bonds are nonpolar.

Even though the molecule is bent, because the bonds are nonpolar, the molecule is nonpolar.

(c) $CHCl_3$—polar
Draw the Lewis structure and determine the molecular geometry:
The molecular geometry from Problem 5 is tetrahedral.
Determine whether the molecule contains polar bonds:
The electronegativity of C = 2.5, H = 2.1, and Cl = 3.0. Therefore, the bonds are polar.

Determine whether the polar bonds add together to form a net dipole:

Because the bonds have different dipole moments due to the different atoms involved, the four dipole moments sum to a nonzero net dipole moment. The molecule is polar. See Table 10.2, in the text to see how dipole moments add to determine polarity.

(d) CS_2—nonpolar
Draw the Lewis structure and determine the molecular geometry:
The molecular geometry from Problem 5 is linear.

Determine whether the molecule contains polar bonds:

The electronegativity of C = 2.5 and S = 2.5. Therefore, the bonds are nonpolar. Also, the molecule is linear, which would result in a zero net dipole even if the bonds were polar.

The molecule is nonpolar. See Table 10.2, in the text to see how dipole moments add to determine polarity.

10.21   (a) SCl_2—polar
Draw the Lewis structure and determine the molecular geometry:

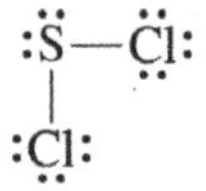

Four electron pairs with two lone pairs give a bent molecular geometry.
Determine whether the molecule contains polar bonds:
The electronegativity of S = 2.5 and Cl = 3.0. Therefore, the bonds are polar.

Determine whether the polar bonds add together to form a net dipole:

Because the molecular geometry is bent, the two dipole moments sum to a nonzero net dipole moment. The molecule is polar. See Table 10.2, in the text to see how dipole moments add to determine polarity.

(b) SCl_4—polar
Draw the Lewis structure and determine the molecular geometry:

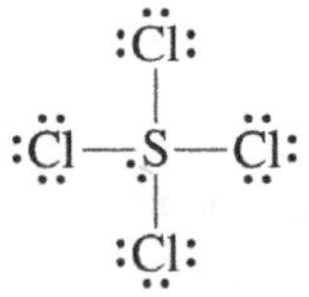

Five electron pairs with one lone pair give a seesaw molecular geometry.
Determine whether the molecule contains polar bonds:
The electronegativity of S = 2.5 and Cl = 3.0. Therefore, the bonds are polar.
Determine whether the polar bonds add together to form a net dipole:
Because the molecular geometry is seesaw, the four equal dipole moments sum to a nonzero net dipole moment. The molecule is polar.
The seesaw molecular geometry will not have offsetting bond vectors.

(c) $BrCl_5$—nonpolar
Draw the Lewis structure and determine the molecular geometry.

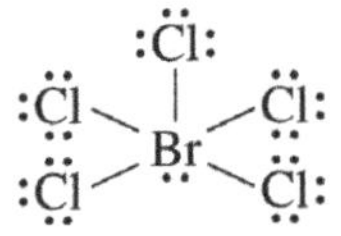

Six electron pairs with one lone pair give square pyramidal molecular geometry.
Determine whether the molecule contains polar bonds:
The electronegativity of Br = 2.8 and Cl = 3.0. The difference is only 0.2; therefore, the bonds are nonpolar. Even though the molecular geometry is square pyramidal, the five bonds are nonpolar; so there is no net dipole. The molecule is nonpolar.

Valence Bond Theory

10.23   (a)   Be $2s^2$ No bonds can form. Beryllium contains no unpaired electrons, so no bonds can form without hybridization.

(b)   P $3s^2 3p^3$ Three bonds can form. Phosphorus contains three unpaired electrons, so three bonds can form without hybridization.

(c)   F $2s^2 2p^5$ One bond can form. Fluorine contains one unpaired electron, so one bond can form without hybridization.

10.25 PH₃ P

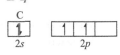

The unhybridized bond angles should be 90°. So without hybridization, there is good agreement between valence bond theory and the actual bond angle of 93.3°.

10.27 C $2s^2 2p^2$

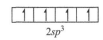

10.29 sp^2 Only sp^2 hybridization of this set of orbitals has a remaining p orbital to form a π bond.
sp^3 hybridization utilizes all three p orbitals.
$sp^3 d^2$ hybridization utilizes all three p orbitals and two d orbitals.

10.31 (a) CCl₄ Write the Lewis structure for the molecule:

$$:\ddot{C}l:$$
$$|$$
$$:\ddot{C}l - C - \ddot{C}l:$$
$$|$$
$$:\ddot{C}l:$$

Use VSEPR to predict the electron geometry:
Four electron groups around the central atom give a tetrahedral electron geometry.
Select the correct hybridization for the central atom based on the electron geometry:
Tetrahedral electron geometry has sp^3 hybridization.
Sketch the molecule and label the bonds:

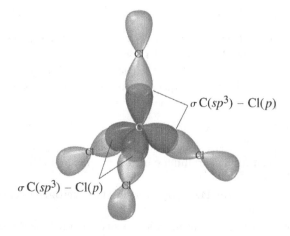

$\sigma\ C(sp^3) - Cl(p)$

$\sigma\ C(sp^3) - Cl(p)$

(b) NH_3 Write the Lewis structure for the molecule:

$$
\begin{array}{c}
H \\
| \\
H-\underset{\displaystyle ..}{N}-H
\end{array}
$$

Use VSEPR to predict the electron geometry:
Four electron groups around the central atom give a tetrahedral electron geometry.
Select the correct hybridization for the central atom based on the electron geometry:
Tetrahedral electron geometry has sp^3 hybridization.
Sketch the molecule and label the bonds:

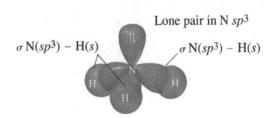

Lone pair in N $sp3$

$\sigma\,N(sp3) - H(s)$ $\sigma\,N(sp3) - H(s)$

(c) OF_2 Write the Lewis structure for the molecule:

$:\ddot{F}-\ddot{O}-\ddot{F}:$

Use VSEPR to predict the electron geometry:
Four electron groups around the central atom give a tetrahedral electron geometry.
Select the correct hybridization for the central atom based on the electron geometry:
Tetrahedral electron geometry has sp^3 hybridization.
Sketch the molecule and label the bonds:

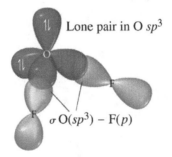

Lone pair in O sp^3

$\sigma\,O(sp3) - F(p)$

(d) CO_2 Write the Lewis structure for the molecule:

$\ddot{O}=C=\ddot{O}$

Use VSEPR to predict the electron geometry:
Two electron groups around the central atom give a linear electron geometry.
Select the correct hybridization for the central atom based on the electron geometry:
Linear electron geometry has sp hybridization.
Sketch the molecule and label the bonds:

$\pi\,C(p_y) - O(p_y)$ $\pi\,C(p_z) - O(p_z)$

$\sigma\,C(sp) - O(p)$

10.33   (a) $COCl_2$ Write the Lewis structure for the molecule:

$$
\begin{array}{c}
:\!O\!: \\
\| \\
:\ddot{C}l-C-\ddot{C}l:
\end{array}
$$

Use VSEPR to predict the electron geometry:
Three electron groups around the central atom give a trigonal planar electron geometry.
Select the correct hybridization for the central atom based on the electron geometry:
Trigonal planar electron geometry has sp^2 hybridization.
Sketch the molecule and label the bonds:

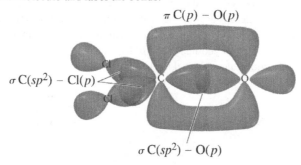

(b) BrF_5 Write the Lewis structure for the molecule:

$$\ddot{:}\overset{\displaystyle :\ddot{F}:}{\underset{\displaystyle :\ddot{F}:}{\overset{\displaystyle |}{\underset{|}{Br}}}}\ddot{:}$$

Use VSEPR to predict the electron geometry:
Six electron pairs around the central atoms gives an octahedral electron geometry.
Select the correct hybridization for the central atom based on the electron geometry:
Octahedral electron geometry has sp^3d^2 hybridization.
Sketch the molecule and label the bonds:

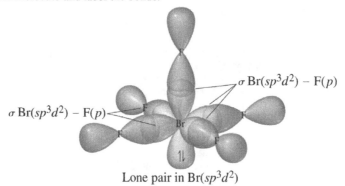

Lone pair in Br(sp^3d^2)

(c) XeF_2 Write the Lewis structure for the molecule:

$:\ddot{F}-\ddot{X}\!e\!-\ddot{F}:$

Use VSEPR to predict the electron geometry:
Five electron groups around the central atom give a trigonal bipyramidal geometry.
Select the correct hybridization for the central atom based on the electron geometry:
Trigonal bipyramidal geometry has sp^3d hybridization.

Sketch the molecule and label the bonds:

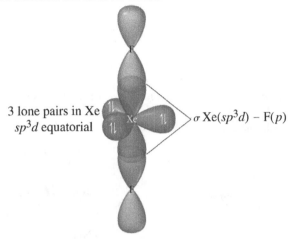

3 lone pairs in Xe
sp^3d equatorial

$\sigma\ Xe(sp^3d) - F(p)$

(d) I_3^- Write the Lewis structure for the molecule:

$$\left[\ddot{\underset{..}{I}} - \underset{..}{\overset{..}{I}} - \ddot{\underset{..}{I}}\ \right]^-$$

Use VSEPR to predict the electron geometry:
Five electron groups around the central atom give a trigonal bipyramidal geometry.
Select the correct hybridization for the central atom based on the electron geometry:
Trigonal bipyramidal geometry has sp^3d hybridization.
Sketch the molecule and label the bonds:

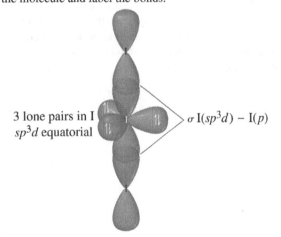

3 lone pairs in I
sp^3d equatorial

$\sigma\ I(sp^3d) - I(p)$

10.35   (a) N_2H_2 Write the Lewis structure for the molecule:

$$H-\ddot{N}=\ddot{N}-H$$

Use VSEPR to predict the electron geometry:
Three electron groups around each interior atom give a trigonal planar electron geometry.
Select the correct hybridization for the central atoms based on the electron geometry:
Trigonal planar electron geometry has sp^2 hybridization.
Sketch the molecule and label the bonds:

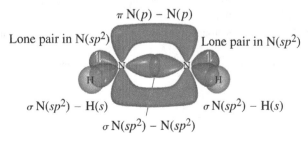

$\pi\ N(p) - N(p)$

Lone pair in $N(sp^2)$ Lone pair in $N(sp^2)$

$\sigma\ N(sp^2) - H(s)$ $\sigma\ N(sp^2) - H(s)$

$\sigma\ N(sp^2) - N(sp^2)$

(b) N_2H_4 Write the Lewis structure for the molecule:

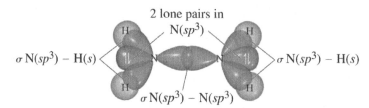

Use VSEPR to predict the electron geometry:
Four electron groups around each interior atom give tetrahedral electron geometry.
Select the correct hybridization for the central atoms based on the electron geometry:
Tetrahedral electron geometry has sp^3 hybridization.
Sketch the molecule and label the bonds:

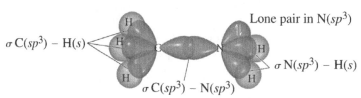

(c) CH_3NH_2 Write the Lewis structure for the molecule:

H
|
H—C—N̈—H
| |
H   H

Use VSEPR to predict the electron geometry:
Four electron groups around the C give a tetrahedral electron geometry around the C atom, and
four electron groups around the N give a tetrahedral geometry around the N atom.
Select the correct hybridization for the central atoms based on the electron geometry:
Tetrahedral electron geometry has sp^3 hybridization of both C and N.
Sketch the molecule and label the bonds:

10.37

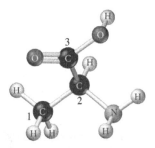

C – 1 and C – 2 each have four electron groups around the atom, which is tetrahedral electron geometry.
Tetrahedral electron geometry is sp^3 hybridization.
C – 3 has three electron groups around the atom, which is trigonal planar electron geometry. Trigonal planar electron
geometry is sp^2 hybridization.
O has four electron groups around the atom, which is tetrahedral electron geometry. Tetrahedral electron geometry is
sp^3 hybridization.
N has four electron groups around the atom, which is tetrahedral electron geometry. Tetrahedral electron geometry is
sp^3 hybridization.

Molecular Orbital Theory

10.39 $1s + 1s$ constructive interference results in a bonding orbital:

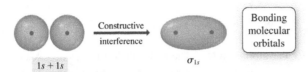

10.41 Be_2^+ has seven electrons. Be_2^- has nine electrons.

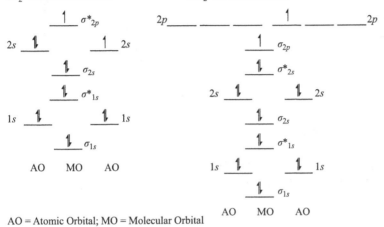

AO = Atomic Orbital; MO = Molecular Orbital

Bond order $= \dfrac{4-3}{2} = \dfrac{1}{2}$ stable   Bond order $= \dfrac{5-4}{2} = \dfrac{1}{2}$ stable

10.43   The bonding and antibonding molecular orbitals from the combination of p_x and p_x atomic orbitals lie along the internuclear axis.

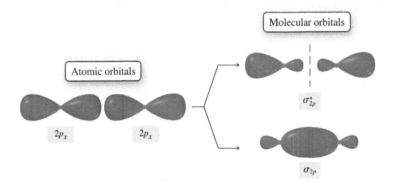

10.45   (a) 4 valence electrons   (b) 6 valence electrons   (c) 8 valence electrons   (d) 9 valence electrons

σ^*_{2p}			
π^*_{2p}			
σ_{2p}			
π_{2p}			
σ^*_{2s}			
σ_{2s}			

Bond order $= \dfrac{2-2}{2} = 0$ Bond order $= \dfrac{4-2}{2} = 1$ Bond order $= \dfrac{6-2}{2} = 2$ Bond order $= \dfrac{7-2}{2} = 2.5$

diamagnetic   paramagnetic   diamagnetic   paramagnetic

10.47   (a)   Write an energy-level diagram for the molecular orbitals in H_2^{2-}. The ion has four valence electrons. Assign the electrons to the molecular orbitals beginning with the lowest energy orbitals and following Hund's rule.

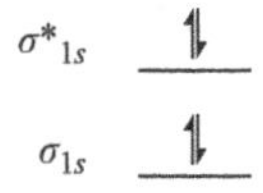

σ^*_{1s} ⥮

σ_{1s} ⥮   Bond order $= \dfrac{2-2}{2} = 0$. With a bond order of 0, the ion will not exist.

   (b)   Write an energy-level diagram for the molecular orbitals in Ne_2. The molecule has 16 valence electrons. Assign the electrons to the molecular orbitals beginning with the lowest energy orbitals and following Hund's rule.

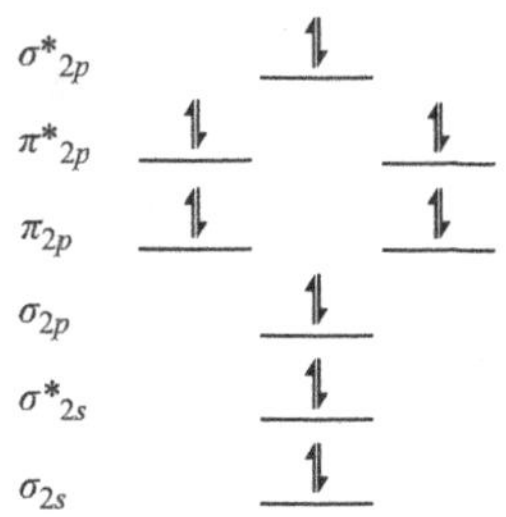

σ^*_{2p} ⥮

π^*_{2p} ⥮   ⥮

π_{2p} ⥮   ⥮

σ_{2p} ⥮

σ^*_{2s} ⥮

σ_{2s} ⥮

Bond order $= \dfrac{8-8}{2} = 0$. With a bond order of 0, the molecule will not exist.

   (c)   Write an energy-level diagram for the molecular orbitals in He_2^{2+}. The ion has two valence electrons. Assign the electrons to the molecular orbitals beginning with the lowest energy orbitals and following Hund's rule.

σ^*_{1s} _____

σ_{1s} ⥮

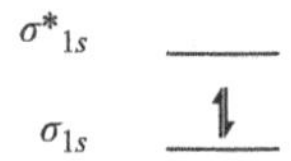

Bond order $= \dfrac{2-0}{2} = 1$. With a bond order of 1, the ion will exist.

   (d)   Write an energy-level diagram for the molecular orbitals in F_2^{2-}. The molecule has 16 valence electrons. Assign the electrons to the molecular orbitals beginning with the lowest energy orbitals and following Hund's rule.

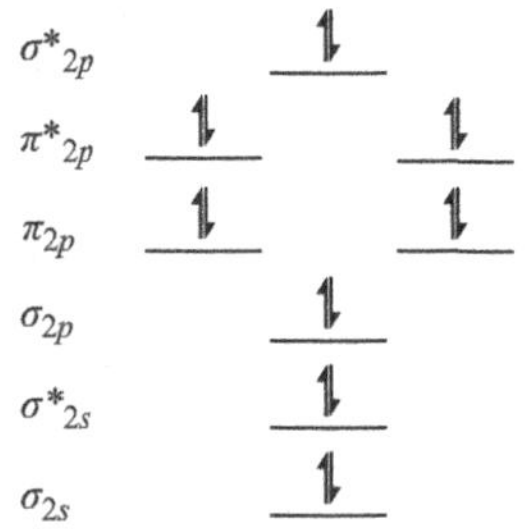

σ^*_{2p} ⥮

π^*_{2p} ⥮   ⥮

π_{2p} ⥮   ⥮

σ_{2p} ⥮

σ^*_{2s} ⥮

σ_{2s} ⥮

Bond order $= \dfrac{8-8}{2} = 0$. With a bond order of 0, the ion will not exist.

10.49 C_2^- has the highest bond order, the highest bond energy, and the shortest bond.
Write an energy-level diagram for the molecular orbitals in each of the C_2 species.
Assign the electrons to the molecular orbitals beginning with the lowest energy orbitals and following Hund's rule for each of the species.

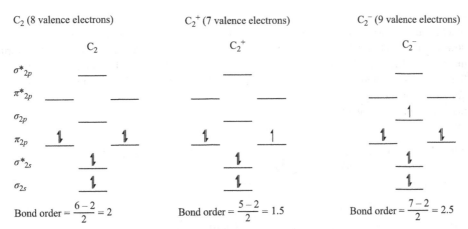

C₂ (8 valence electrons)   C₂⁺ (7 valence electrons)   C₂⁻ (9 valence electrons)

$$\text{Bond order} = \frac{6-2}{2} = 2 \qquad \text{Bond order} = \frac{5-2}{2} = 1.5 \qquad \text{Bond order} = \frac{7-2}{2} = 2.5$$

C_2^- has the highest bond order at 2.5. Bond order is directly related to bond energy, so C_2^- has the largest bond energy; bond order is inversely related to bond length, so C_2^- has the shortest bond length.

Cumulative Problems

10.51   (a) COF_2 Write the Lewis structure for the molecule:

Use VSEPR to predict the electron geometry:
Three electron groups around the central atom give a trigonal planar electron geometry. Three bonding pairs of electrons give a trigonal planar molecular geometry.
Determine whether the molecule contains polar bonds:
The electronegativity of C = 2.5, O = 3.5, and F = 4.0. Therefore, the bonds are polar.
Determine whether the polar bonds add together to form a net dipole:
Even though a trigonal planar molecular geometry normally is nonpolar, because the bonds have different dipole moments, the sum of the dipole moments is not zero. The molecule is polar. See Table 10.2, in the text to see how dipole moments add to determine polarity.
Select the correct hybridization for the central atom based on the electron geometry:
Trigonal planar geometry has sp^2 hybridization.
Sketch the molecule and label the bonds:

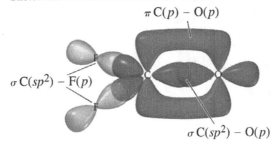

π C(p) – O(p)

σ C(sp²) – F(p)

σ C(sp²) – O(p)

(b) S_2Cl_2 Write the Lewis structure for the molecule:

Use VSEPR to predict the electron geometry:
Four electron groups around the central atom give a tetrahedral electron geometry. Two bonding pairs and two lone pairs of electrons give a bent molecular geometry.
Determine whether the molecule contains polar bonds:
The electronegativity of S = 2.5 and Cl = 3.0. Therefore, the bonds are polar.

Determine whether the polar bonds add together to form a net dipole:

In a bent molecular geometry, the sum of the dipole moments is not zero. As drawn the molecule is polar, however, there is free rotation around the S—S bond, so the molecule can also take on a conformation that is nonpolar. See Table 10.2, in the text to see how dipole moments add to determine polarity.

Select the correct hybridization for the central atom based on the electron geometry:

Tetrahedral geometry has sp^3 hybridization.

Sketch the molecule and label the bonds:

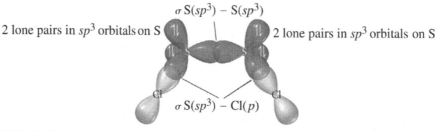

$\sigma\ S(sp^3) - S(sp^3)$

2 lone pairs in sp^3 orbitals on S

2 lone pairs in sp^3 orbitals on S

$\sigma\ S(sp^3) - Cl(p)$

(c) SF_4 Write the Lewis structure for the molecule:

$$:\ddot{F}:$$
$$\quad|$$
$$:\ddot{F}-\underset{\cdot\cdot}{S}-\ddot{F}:$$
$$\quad|$$
$$:\ddot{F}:$$

Use VSEPR to predict the electron geometry:

Five electron groups around the central atom give a trigonal bipyramidal electron geometry.

Four bonding pairs and one lone pair of electrons give a seesaw molecular geometry.

Determine whether the molecule contains polar bonds:

The electronegativity of S = 2.5 and F = 4.0. Therefore, the bonds are polar.

Determine whether the polar bonds add together to form a net dipole:

In a seesaw molecular geometry, the sum of the dipole moments is not zero. The molecule is polar. See Table 10.2, in the text to see how dipole moments add to determine polarity.

Select the correct hybridization for the central atom based on the electron geometry:

Trigonal bipyramidal electron geometry has sp^3d hybridization.

Sketch the molecule and label the bonds:

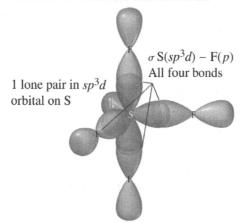

$\sigma\ S(sp^3d) - F(p)$
All four bonds

1 lone pair in sp^3d orbital on S

10.53   (a)   serine

$$\underset{}{H}\quad \underset{}{H}\quad :\underset{}{O}:$$
$$\ \ |\qquad |\qquad \|$$
$$H-\underset{\cdot\cdot}{N}-\underset{1}{\overset{|}{C}}-\underset{2}{\overset{|}{C}}-\underset{\cdot\cdot}{\ddot{O}}_1-H$$
$$\qquad\quad |$$
$$\qquad H-\underset{3}{\overset{|}{C}}-H$$
$$\qquad\qquad\ |$$
$$\qquad\quad :\underset{\cdot\cdot}{O}_2-H$$

C – 1 and C – 3 each have four electron groups around the atom. Four electron groups give a tetrahedral electron geometry; tetrahedral electron geometry has sp^3 hybridization. Four bonding groups and zero lone pairs give a tetrahedral molecular geometry.

C – 2 has three electron groups around the atom. Three electron groups give a trigonal planar geometry; trigonal planar geometry has sp^2 hybridization. Three bonding groups and zero lone pairs give a trigonal planar molecular geometry.

N has four electron groups around the atom. Four electron groups give a tetrahedral electron geometry; tetrahedral electron geometry has sp^3 hybridization. Three bonding groups and one lone pair give a trigonal pyramidal molecular geometry.

O – 1 and O – 2 each have four electron groups around the atom. Four electron groups give a tetrahedral electron geometry; tetrahedral electron geometry has sp^3 hybridization. Two bonding groups and two lone pairs give a bent molecular geometry.

(b)   asparagine

C – 1 and C – 3 each have four electron groups around the atom. Four electron groups give a tetrahedral electron geometry; tetrahedral electron geometry has sp^3 hybridization. Four bonding groups and zero lone pairs give a tetrahedral molecular geometry.

C – 2 and C – 4 each have three electron groups around the atom. Three electron groups give a trigonal planar geometry; trigonal planar geometry has sp^2 hybridization. Three bonding groups and zero lone pairs give a trigonal planar molecular geometry.

N – 1 and N – 2 each have four electron groups around the atom. Four electron groups give a tetrahedral electron geometry; tetrahedral electron geometry has sp^3 hybridization. Three bonding groups and one lone pair give a trigonal pyramidal molecular geometry.

O has four electron groups around the atom. Four electron groups give a tetrahedral electron geometry; tetrahedral electron geometry has sp^3 hybridization. Two bonding groups and two lone pairs give a bent molecular geometry.

(c) cysteine

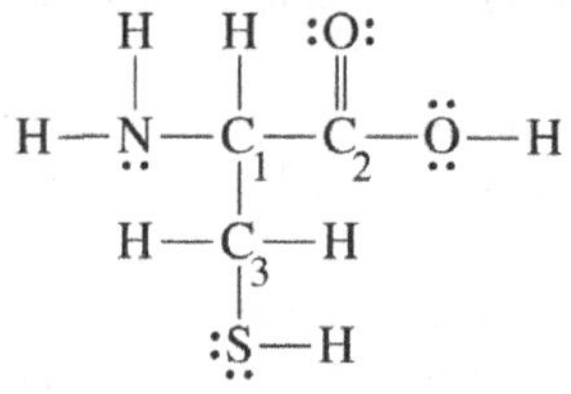

C – 1 and C – 3 each have four electron groups around the atom. Four electron groups give a tetrahedral electron geometry; tetrahedral electron geometry has sp^3 hybridization. Four bonding groups and zero lone pairs give a tetrahedral molecular geometry.

C – 2 has three electron groups around the atom. Three electron groups give a trigonal planar geometry; trigonal planar geometry has sp^2 hybridization. Three bonding groups and zero lone pairs give a trigonal planar molecular geometry.

N has four electron groups around the atom. Four electron groups give a tetrahedral electron geometry; tetrahedral electron geometry has sp^3 hybridization. Three bonding groups and one lone pair give a trigonal pyramidal molecular geometry.

O and S have four electron groups around the atom. Four electron groups give a tetrahedral electron geometry; tetrahedral electron geometry has sp^3 hybridization. Two bonding groups and two lone pairs give bent molecular geometry.

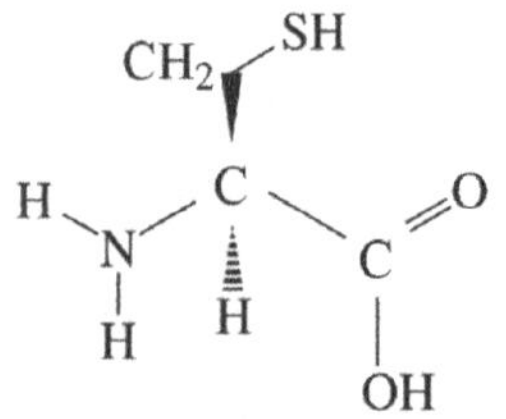

10.55 4π bonds, 25σ bonds; the lone pairs on the Os occupy unhybridized p orbitals, the lone pair on N – 2 occupies an sp^2 orbital; the lone pairs on N – 1, N – 3, and N – 4 occupy sp^3 orbitals.

caffeine

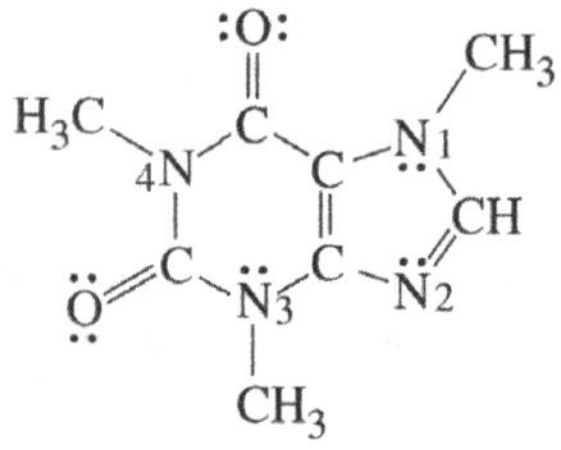

10.57   (a)   Water-soluble: The 4 C—OH bonds, the C = O bond, and the C—O bonds in the ring make the molecule polar. Because of the large electronegativity difference between the C and O, each of the bonds will have a dipole moment. The sum of the dipole moments does *not* give a net zero dipole moment, so the molecule is polar. Because it is polar, it will be water-soluble.

(b)   Fat-soluble: There is only one C—O bond in the molecule. The dipole moment from this bond is not enough to make the molecule polar because of all of the nonpolar components of the molecule. The C—H bonds in the structure lead to a net dipole of zero for most of the sites in the molecule. Because the molecule is nonpolar, it is fat-soluble.

(c)   Water-soluble: The carboxylic acid function (COOH group) along with the N atom in the ring make the molecule polar. Because of the electronegativity difference between the C and O and the C and N atoms, the bonds will have a dipole moment and the net dipole moment of the molecule is *not* zero; so the molecule is polar. Because the molecule is polar, it is water-soluble.

(d)   Fat-soluble: The two O atoms in the structure contribute a very small amount to the net dipole moment of this molecule. The majority of the molecule is nonpolar because there is no net dipole moment around the interior C atoms. Because the molecule is nonpolar, it is fat-soluble.

10.59   BrF (14 valence electrons)

$:\overset{..}{\underset{..}{Br}}—\overset{..}{\underset{..}{F}}:$ no central atom, no hybridization, no electron structure

BrF_2^- (22 valence electrons)

$\left[:\overset{..}{\underset{..}{F}}—\overset{.}{\underset{.}{Br}}—\overset{..}{\underset{..}{F}}:\right]^-$ There are five electron groups on the central atom, so the electron geometry is trigonal bipyramidal. The two bonding groups and three lone pairs give a linear molecular geometry. An electron geometry of trigonal
bipyramidal has sp^3d hybridization.

BrF_3 (28 valence electrons)

$\overset{\textstyle :\overset{..}{F}:}{\underset{\textstyle }{|}}$
$:\overset{..}{\underset{..}{F}}—\overset{.}{\underset{.}{Br}}—\overset{..}{\underset{..}{F}}:$ There are five electron groups on the central atom, so the electron geometry is trigonal bipyramidal. The three bonding groups and two lone pairs give a T-shaped molecular geometry. An electron geometry of
trigonal bipyramidal has sp^3d hybridization.

BrF_4^- (36 valence electrons)

$$\left[\begin{array}{c} :\overset{..}{F}: \\ | \\ :\overset{..}{\underset{..}{F}}—\overset{.}{\underset{.}{Br}}—\overset{..}{\underset{..}{F}}: \\ | \\ :\overset{..}{\underset{..}{F}}: \end{array}\right]^-$$

There are six electron groups on the central atom, so the electron geometry is octahedral. The four
bonding groups and two lone pairs give a square planar molecular geometry. An electron geometry of octahedral has
sp^3d^2 hybridization.

BrF_5 (42 valence electrons)

$$\begin{array}{c} :\overset{..}{F}: \\ :\overset{..}{\underset{..}{F}}\diagdown \, | \diagup \overset{..}{\underset{..}{F}}: \\ \quad Br \\ :\overset{..}{\underset{..}{F}}\diagup \quad \diagdown \overset{..}{\underset{..}{F}}: \end{array}$$

There are six electron groups on the central atom, so the electron geometry is octahedral. The five
bonding groups and one lone pair give a square pyramidal molecular geometry. An electron geometry of octahedral
has sp^3d^2 hybridization.

10.61   Draw the Lewis structure: $C_4H_6Cl_2$ (36 valence electrons)

Even though the C—Cl bonds are polar, the net dipole will be zero because the C—Cl bonds and the C—CH₃
bonds are on opposite sides of the double bond. This will result in bond vectors that cancel each other.

Challenge Problems

10.63   According to valence bond theory, CH_4, NH_3, and H_2O are all sp^3 hybridized. This hybridization results in a tetrahedral
electron group configuration with a 109.5° bond angle. NH_3 and H_2O deviate from this idealized bond angle because
their lone electron pairs exist in their own sp^3 orbitals. The presence of lone pairs lowers the tendency for the central
atom's orbitals to hybridize. As a result, as lone pairs are added, the bond angle moves from the 109.5° hybrid angle
toward the 90° unhybridized angle.

10.65   For each write the Lewis structure:
Determine electron pair geometry around each central atom.
Determine the molecular geometry, determine idealized bond angles, and predict actual bond angles.

NO_2

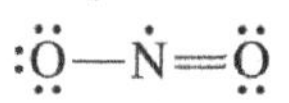

:Ö—Ṅ=Ö

Two bonding groups and a lone electron give a trigonal planar electron geometry; the molecular geometry will be bent. Trigonal planar electron geometry has idealized bond angles of 120°. The bond angle is expected to be slightly less than 120° because of the lone electron occupying the third sp^2 orbital.

NO_2^+

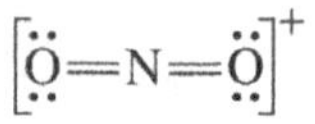

[Ö=N=Ö]⁺

Two bonding groups of electrons and no lone pairs give a linear electron geometry and molecular geometry. Linear electron geometry has a bond angle of 180°.

NO_2^-

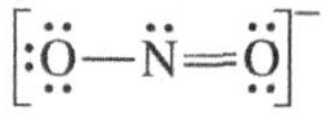

[:Ö—Ṅ=Ö]⁻

Two bonding groups of electrons and one lone pair give a trigonal planar electron geometry; the molecular geometry will be bent.

Trigonal planar electron geometry has idealized bond angles of 120°. The bond angle is expected to be less than 120° because of the lone pair electrons occupying the third sp^2 orbital. Further, the bond angle should be less than the bond angle in NO_2 because the presence of lone pairs lowers the tendency for the central atom's orbitals to hybridize. As a result, as lone pairs are added, the bond angle moves further from the 120° hybrid angle to the 90° unhybridized angle, and the two electrons will increase this tendency.

10.67 CH_3CONH_2 Draw the Lewis structure: (24 valence electrons)

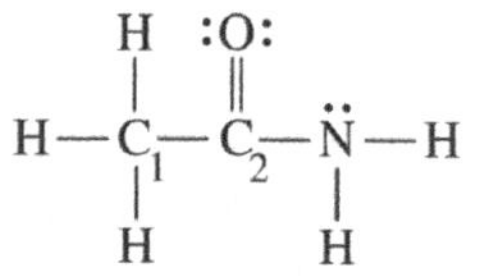

H   :O:
| ||
H—C₁—C₂—Ṅ—H
| |
H   H

Structure I

In structure I: C_1 has four σ bonds and no lone pair. The electron geometry would be tetrahedral.
C_2 has three σ bonds, one π bond, and no lone pair. The electron geometry would be trigonal planar.
N has three σ bonds and one lone pair. The electron geometry would be tetrahedral.
This structure would have a trigonal pyramidal molecular geometry around the nitrogen and would not be planar. A second resonance form can be drawn.

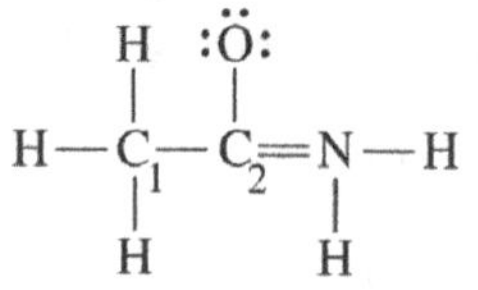

H   :Ö:
| |
H—C₁—C₂=N—H
| |
H   H

Structure II

In structure II: C_1 has four σ bonds and no lone pair. The electron geometry would be tetrahedral.
C_2 has three σ bonds, one π bond, and no lone pair. The electron geometry would be trigonal planar.
N has three σ bonds, one π bond, and no lone pair. The electron geometry would be trigonal planar.
This resonance form would account for a planar configuration around the N.

Conceptual Problems

10.69   Statement a is the best statement.
Statement b neglects the lowering of potential energy that arises from the interaction of the lone pair electrons with the bonding electrons.
Statement c neglects the interaction of the electrons altogether. The molecular geometries are determined by the number and types of electron groups around the central atom.

10.71   In Lewis theory, a covalent bond comes from the sharing of electrons.

A single bond shares two electrons (one pair).
A double bond shares four electrons (two pairs).
A triple bond shares six electrons (three pairs).

In valence bond theory, a covalent bond forms when orbitals overlap. The orbitals can be unhybridized or hybridized orbitals.

A single bond forms when a σ bond is formed from the overlap of an s orbital with an s orbital, an s orbital with a p orbital, or a p orbital and a p orbital overlapping end to end. A σ can also form from the overlap of a hybridized orbital on the central atom with an s orbital or with a p orbital overlapping end to end.
A double bond is a combination of a σ bond and a π bond. The π bond forms from the sideways overlap of a p orbital on each of the atoms involved in the bond. The p orbitals must have the same orientation.
A triple bond is a combination of a σ bond and two π bonds. The π bonds form from the sideways overlap of a p orbital on each of the atoms involved in the bond. The p orbitals must have the same orientation, so each π bond is formed from a different set of p orbitals.

In molecular orbital theory, molecular orbitals form. These are combinations of the atomic orbitals of the atoms involved in the bond. The bonds form when the valence electrons occupy more bonding molecular orbitals than antibonding molecular orbitals. This is calculated by the bond order.

A single bond has a bond order of 1.
A double bond has a bond order of 2.
A triple bond has a bond order of 3.

All three models show the formation of bonds between two atoms. All three models show the formation of the same number of bonds between the atoms involved. Lewis theory tells us only about the number of bonds formed and, combined with VSEPR theory, allows us to predict the shape of the molecule. It does not, however, tell us anything about how the bonds are formed. Valence bond theory addresses the formation of the different types of bonds, sigma and pi. In valence bond theory, the bonds form from the overlap of atomic orbitals on the individual atoms involved in the bonds, and the atoms are localized between the two atoms involved in the bond. Molecular orbital theory approaches the formation of bonds by looking at the entire molecule. The electrons are not restricted to any two individual atoms but are treated as belonging to the whole molecule. The electrons reside in molecular orbitals that are part of the entire molecule rather than being restricted to individual atoms. Each model gives us information about the molecule. The amount and type of information we need determines the model we choose to use.

Questions for Group Work

10.73   Someone might expect methane to have 90° angles because we typically draw Lewis structures with 90° angles. The format to arrange an octet of electrons around an atom is top, bottom, left, and right, implying 90° angles.

10.75 CS_2:   (a)   Draw a Lewis structure for the molecule:
CS_2 has 16 valence electrons

$$\ddot{\text{S}}=\text{C}=\ddot{\text{S}}$$

(b)   Electron geometry – linear; molecular geometry – linear; bond angle = 180°
(c)   Because both C and S have en electronegativity of 2.5, there are no polar bonds.
(d)   Because there are no polar bonds and no lone pairs, the molecule is nonpolar.

NCl_3:   (a)   Draw a Lewis structure for the molecule:
NCl_3 has 26 valence electrons

$$:\ddot{\text{Cl}}-\text{N}-\ddot{\text{Cl}}:$$
$$|$$
$$:\ddot{\text{Cl}}:$$

(b) Electron geometry – tetrahedral; there are three bonding atoms and one lone pair so the molecular geometry – trigonal pyramid; bond angle < 109.5°

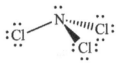

(c) Because both N and Cl have en electronegativity of 3.0, there are no polar bonds.

(d) There are no polar bonds, but there is one lone pair, the molecule is polar.

CF_4:   (a) Draw a Lewis structure for the molecule:

CF_4 has 32 valence electrons

$$:\!\overset{\displaystyle ..}{\underset{\displaystyle ..}{F}}:$$
$$|$$
$$:\!\overset{..}{F}\!-\!C\!-\!\overset{..}{F}:$$
$$|$$
$$:\!\overset{\displaystyle ..}{\underset{\displaystyle ..}{F}}:$$

(b) Electron geometry – tetrahedral; there are four bonding atoms and no lone pair so the molecular geometry –tetrahedral; bond angle = 109.5°

(c) C and F have electronegativities of 2.5 and 4.0, respectively, so there are four polar bonds.

(d) There are four polar bonds, but they cancel each other out, the molecule is nonpolar.

CH_2F_2:   (a) Draw a Lewis structure for the molecule:

CH_2F_2 has 20 valence electrons

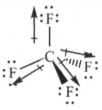

(b) Electron geometry – tetrahedral; there are four bonding atoms and no lone pair so the molecular geometry – tetrahedral; bond angle = 109.5°

(c) C, H, and F have electronegativities of 2.5, 2.1, and 4.0, respectively, so there are four polar bonds.

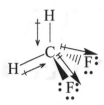

(d)   There are four polar bonds and they do not cancel each other out, the molecule is polar.

10.77   Both N_2^+ and N_2^- have a bond order of 2.5, so the bond lengths and strengths should be similar to each other. For N_2 the bond order = 3, so it has the shortest and strongest bond of these three species. Notice that for N_2 the bonding molecular orbitals are filled with the last valence electron, for N_2^+ the bonding molecular orbital is not filled, and for N_2^- the last electron is in an antibonding molecular orbital (destabilizing).

| N_2 (10 valence electrons) | N_2^+ (9 valence electrons) | N_2^- (11 valence electrons) |

σ^*2p

π^*2p

$\sigma 2p$

$\pi 2p$

σ^*2s

$\sigma 2s$

Bond order = $\dfrac{8-2}{2} = 3$ Bond order = $\dfrac{7-2}{2} = 2.5$ Bond order = $\dfrac{8-3}{2} = 2.5$

11 Liquids, Solids, and Intermolecular Forces

Intermolecular Forces

11.1   (a)   dispersion forces
        (b)   dispersion forces, dipole–dipole forces, and hydrogen bonding
        (c)   dispersion forces and dipole–dipole forces
        (d)   dispersion forces

11.3   (a)   dispersion forces and dipole–dipole forces
        (b)   dispersion forces, dipole–dipole forces, and hydrogen bonding
        (c)   dispersion forces
        (d)   dispersion forces

11.5   (a) CH_4 < (b) CH_3CH_3 < (c) CH_3CH_2Cl < (d) CH_3CH_2OH. The first two molecules only exhibit dispersion forces, so the boiling point increases with increasing molar mass. The third molecule also exhibits dipole–dipole forces, which are stronger than dispersion forces. The last molecule exhibits hydrogen bonding. Because these are by far the strongest intermolecular forces in this group, the last molecule has the highest boiling point.

11.7   (a) CH_3OH has the higher boiling point because it exhibits hydrogen bonding.
        (b) CH_3CH_2OH has the higher boiling point because it exhibits hydrogen bonding.
        (c) CH_3CH_3 has the higher boiling point because it has the larger molar mass.

11.9   (a) Br_2 has the higher vapor pressure because it has the smaller molar mass.
        (b) H_2S has the higher vapor pressure because it does not exhibit hydrogen bonding.
        (c) PH_3 has the higher vapor pressure because it does not exhibit hydrogen bonding.

11.11   (a)   This will not form a homogeneous solution because one is polar and one is nonpolar.
        (b)   This will form a homogeneous solution. There will be ion–dipole interactions between the K^+ and Cl^- ions and the water molecules. There will also be dispersion forces, dipole–dipole forces, and hydrogen bonding between the water molecules.
        (c)   This will form a homogeneous solution. Dispersion forces will be present among all of the molecules.
        (d)   This will form a homogeneous solution. There will be dispersion forces, dipole–dipole forces, and hydrogen bonding among all of the molecules.

Surface Tension, Viscosity, and Capillary Action

11.13   Water will have the higher surface tension because it exhibits hydrogen bonding, a strong intermolecular force. Acetone does not engage in hydrogen bonding.

11.15   Compound A will have the higher viscosity because it can interact with other molecules along the entire molecule. The more branched isomer has a smaller surface area, allowing for fewer interactions. Also, Compound A is very flexible, and the molecules can get tangled with each other.

11.17   In a clean glass tube, the water can generate strong adhesive interactions with the glass (due to the dipoles at the sur-
         face of the glass). Water experiences adhesive forces with glass that are stronger than its cohesive forces, causing it
         to climb the surface of a glass tube. When grease or oil coats the glass, this interferes with the formation of these ad-
         hesive interactions with the glass because oils are nonpolar and cannot interact strongly with the dipoles in the water.
         Without experiencing these strong intermolecular interactions with oil, the water's cohesive forces will be greater and
         water will be drawn away from the surface of the tube.

Vaporization and Vapor Pressure

11.19   The water in the 12-cm diameter beaker will evaporate more quickly because there is more surface area for the mol-
         ecules to evaporate from. The vapor pressure will be the same in the two containers because the vapor pressure is the
         pressure of the gas when it is in dynamic equilibrium with the liquid (evaporation rate = condensation rate). The
         vapor pressure is dependent only on the substance and the temperature. The 12-cm diameter container will reach this
         dynamic equilibrium faster.

11.21   The boiling point and heat of vaporization of oil are much higher than that of water, so it will not vaporize as quickly
         as the water. The evaporation of water cools your skin because evaporation is an endothermic process.

11.23   **Given:** 1065 kJ from candy bar; water $d = 1.00$ g/mL   **Find:** L(H_2O) vaporized at 100.0 °C
         Other: $\Delta H^\circ_{vap} = 40.7$ kJ/mol
         Conceptual Plan: $q \rightarrow$ mol $H_2O \rightarrow$ g $H_2O \rightarrow$ mL $H_2O \rightarrow$ L H_2O

$$\frac{1\ mol}{40.7\ kJ} \qquad \frac{18.02\ g}{1\ mol} \qquad \frac{1.00\ mL}{1.00\ g} \qquad \frac{1\ L}{1000\ mL}$$

   Solution: $1065\ \cancel{kJ} \times \dfrac{1\ \cancel{mol}}{40.7\ \cancel{kJ}} \times \dfrac{18.02\ \cancel{g}}{1\ \cancel{mol}} \times \dfrac{1.00\ \cancel{mL}}{1\ \cancel{g}} \times \dfrac{1\ L}{1000\ \cancel{mL}} = 0.472$ L H_2O

   Check: The units (L) are correct. The magnitude of the answer (<1 L) makes physical sense because we are vapor-
   izing about 26 moles of water.

11.25   **Given:** 0.88 g water condenses on iron block 75.0 g at $T_i = 22$ °C   **Find:** T_f (iron block)
         Other: $\Delta H^\circ_{vap} = 44.0$ kJ/mol; $C_{Fe} = 0.449$ J/g · °C from text
         Conceptual Plan: g $H_2O \rightarrow$ mol $H_2O \rightarrow q_{H_2O}$(kJ) $\rightarrow q_{H_2O}$(J) $\rightarrow q_{Fe}$ then q_{Fe}, m_{Fe}, $T_i \rightarrow T_f$

$$\frac{1\ mol}{18.02\ g} \qquad \frac{-44.0\ kJ}{1\ mol} \qquad \frac{1000\ J}{1\ kJ} \qquad -q_{H_2O} = q_{Fe} \qquad q = mC_s(T_f - T_i)$$

   Solution: $0.88\ \cancel{g} \times \dfrac{1\ \cancel{mol}}{18.02\ \cancel{g}} \times \dfrac{-44.0\ \cancel{kJ}}{1\ \cancel{mol}} \times \dfrac{1000\ J}{1\ \cancel{kJ}} = -2\underline{1}48.72$ J then $-q_{H_2O} = q_{Fe} = 2\underline{1}48.72$ J then

   $q = m\,C_s(T_f - T_i)$. Rearrange to solve for T_f.

$$T_f = \frac{m\,C_s\,T_i + q}{m\,C_s} = \frac{\left(75.0\ \cancel{g} \times 0.449\ \dfrac{\cancel{J}}{\cancel{g}\cdot\cancel{°C}} \times 22\ \cancel{°C}\right) + 2\underline{1}48.72\ \cancel{J}}{75.0\ \cancel{g} \times 0.449\ \dfrac{\cancel{J}}{\cancel{g}\cdot°C}} = 86\ °C$$

   Check: The units (°C) are correct. The temperature rose, which is consistent with heat being added to the block. The
   magnitude of the answer (86 °C) makes physical sense because even though we have $\sim\frac{1}{20}$ of a mole, the energy involved in condensation is very large.

11.27   **Given:**

Temperature (K)	Vapor Pressure (torr)
200	65.3
210	134.3
220	255.7
230	456.0
235	597.0

   Find: $\Delta H^\circ_{vap}(NH_3)$ and normal boiling point

Conceptual Plan: To find the heat of vaporization, use Excel or similar software to make a plot of the natural log of vapor pressure ($\ln P$) as a function of the inverse of the temperature in K ($1/T$). Then fit the points to a line and determine the slope of the line. Because the *slope* $= -\Delta H_{vap}/R$, we find the heat of vaporization as follows:

$$slope = -\Delta H_{vap}/R \rightarrow \Delta H_{vap} = -slope \times R \text{ then } J \rightarrow kJ$$

$$\frac{1\,kJ}{1000\,J}$$

For the normal boiling point, use the equation of the best fit line, substitute 760 torr for the pressure, and calculate the temperature.

Solution: Data was plotted in Excel.

The slope of the best fitting line is -2969.9 K.

$$\Delta H_{vap} = -slope \times R = -(-2969.9\;\cancel{K}) \times \frac{8.314\;J}{\cancel{K}\,mol} = \frac{2.46917 \times 10^4\;\cancel{J}}{mol} \times \frac{1\;kJ}{1000\;\cancel{J}} = 24.7\;\frac{kJ}{mol}$$

$$\ln P = -2969.9\;K\left(\frac{1}{T}\right) + 19.036 \rightarrow$$

$$\ln 760 = -2969.9\;K\left(\frac{1}{T}\right) + 19.036 \rightarrow$$

$$2969.9\;K\left(\frac{1}{T}\right) = 19.036 - 6.63332 \rightarrow$$

$$T = \frac{2969.9\;K}{12.40268} = 239\;K$$

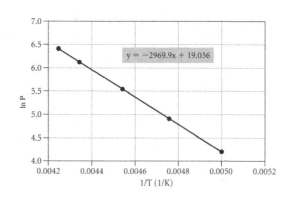

Check: The units (kJ/mol) are correct. The magnitude of the answer (25 kJ/mol) is consistent with other values in the text.

11.29   **Given:** ethanol, $\Delta H^{\circ}_{vap} = 38.56$ kJ/mol; normal boiling point $= 78.4\,^{\circ}C$ **Find:** $P_{Ethanol}$ at $15\,^{\circ}C$
         Conceptual Plan: $^{\circ}C \rightarrow K$ and $kJ \rightarrow J$ then $\Delta H^{\circ}_{vap}, T_1, P_1, T_2 \rightarrow P_2$

$$K = {^{\circ}C} + 273.15 \qquad \frac{1000\,J}{1\,kJ} \qquad \ln\frac{P_2}{P_1} = \frac{-\Delta H_{vap}}{R}\left(\frac{1}{T_2} - \frac{1}{T_1}\right)$$

Solution: $T_1 = 78.4\,^{\circ}C + 273.15 = 351.6$ K; $T_2 = 15\,^{\circ}C + 273.15 = 288$ K;

$$\frac{38.56\;\cancel{kJ}}{mol} \times \frac{1000\;J}{1\;\cancel{kJ}} = 3.856 \times 10^4\;\frac{J}{mol};\quad P_1 = 760\;torr;\quad \ln\frac{P_2}{P_1} = \frac{-\Delta H_{vap}}{R}\left(\frac{1}{T_2} - \frac{1}{T_1}\right).\;\text{Substitute values in}$$

equation. $\ln\dfrac{P_2}{760\;torr} = \dfrac{-3.856 \times 10^4\dfrac{\cancel{J}}{\cancel{mol}}}{8.314\;\dfrac{\cancel{J}}{K\cdot\cancel{mol}}}\left(\dfrac{1}{288\;\cancel{K}} - \dfrac{1}{351.6\;\cancel{K}}\right) = -2.91302 \rightarrow$

$$\frac{P_2}{760\;torr} = e^{-2.91302} = 0.054311 \rightarrow P_2 = 0.054311 \times 760\;torr = 41\;torr$$

Check: The units (torr) are correct. Because 15 °C is significantly below the boiling point, we expect the answer to be much less than 760 torr.

11.31   **Given:** CS_2, $P_{CS_2} = 363$ torr at 25 °C; normal boiling point $= 46.3\,^{\circ}C$ **Find:** ΔH_{vap}
         Conceptual Plan: $^{\circ}C \rightarrow K$ and then $T_1, P_1, T_2, P_2 \rightarrow \Delta H_{vap}$

$$K = {^{\circ}C} + 273.15 \qquad \ln\frac{P_2}{P_1} = \frac{-\Delta H_{vap}}{R}\left(\frac{1}{T_2} - \frac{1}{T_1}\right)$$

Solution: $T_1 = 25\,^{\circ}C + 273.15 = 298.15$ K; $T_2 = 46.3\,^{\circ}C + 273.15 = 319.45$ K; $P_2 = 760$ torr;

$\ln\dfrac{P_2}{P_1} = \dfrac{-\Delta H_{vap}}{R}\left(\dfrac{1}{T_2} - \dfrac{1}{T_1}\right).$ Rearrange to solve for ΔH_{vap}.

$$\Delta H_{vap} = -\frac{R \ln \frac{P_2}{P_1}}{\left(\frac{1}{T_2} - \frac{1}{T_1}\right)} = -\frac{8.314 \frac{J}{K \cdot mol} \ln \frac{760 \text{ torr}}{363 \text{ torr}}}{\left(\frac{1}{319.45 \text{ K}} - \frac{1}{298.15 \text{ K}}\right)} = +27{,}470.27 \frac{J}{mol} = +27 \frac{kJ}{mol}$$

Check: The units (kJ/mol) are correct. The value is reasonable compared to other values seen in this chapter. It also is close to the published value of +27.65 kJ/mol.

Sublimation and Fusion

11.33   **Given:** 47.5 g water freezes   **Find:** energy released **Other:** $\Delta H^\circ_{fus} = 6.02$ kJ/mol from text
Conceptual Plan: g H$_2$O $\rightarrow$ mol H$_2$O $\rightarrow$ q_{H_2O}(kJ) $\rightarrow$ q_{H_2O}(J)

$$\frac{1 \text{ mol}}{18.02 \text{ g}} \qquad \frac{-6.02 \text{ kJ}}{1 \text{ mol}} \qquad \frac{1000 \text{ J}}{1 \text{ kJ}}$$

Solution: $47.5 \text{ g} \times \dfrac{1 \text{ mol}}{18.02 \text{ g}} \times \dfrac{-6.02 \text{ kJ}}{1 \text{ mol}} \times \dfrac{1000 \text{ J}}{1 \text{ kJ}} = -15{,}868.48 \text{ J} = 1.59 \times 10^4$ J or 1.59×10^4 J released

or 15.9 kJ released

Check: The units (J) are correct. The magnitude (15,900 J) makes sense because we are freezing about 2.5 moles of water. Freezing is exothermic, so heat is released.

11.35   **Given:** 8.5 g ice; 255 g water   **Find:** ΔT of water
Other: $\Delta H^\circ_{fus} = 6.02$ kJ/mol; $C_{H_2O} = 4.18$ J/g $\cdot$ °C from text
Conceptual Plan: The first step is to calculate how much heat is removed from the water to melt the ice.
$q_{ice} = -q_{water}$ so **g(ice) $\rightarrow$ mol(ice) $\rightarrow$ q_{fus}(kJ) $\rightarrow$ q_{fus}(J) $\rightarrow$ q_{water}(J) then $q, m, C_s \rightarrow \Delta T_1$**

$$\frac{1 \text{ mol}}{18.02 \text{ g}} \qquad \frac{6.02 \text{ kJ}}{1 \text{ mol}} \qquad \frac{1000 \text{ J}}{1 \text{ kJ}} \qquad q_{water} = -q_{ice} \qquad\qquad q = mC_s \Delta T_1$$

Now we have slightly cooled water (at a temperature of T_1) in contact with 0.0 °C water, and we can calculate a second temperature drop of the water due to mixing of the water that was ice with the water that was initially room temperature; so $q_{ice} = -q_{water}$ **with** $m, C_s \rightarrow \Delta T_2$ **with** ΔT_1 $\Delta T_2 \rightarrow \Delta T_{Total}$.

$$q = m \, C_s \Delta T_2 \text{ then set } q_{ice} = -q_{water} \qquad \Delta T_{Total} = \Delta T_1 + \Delta T_2$$

Solution: $8.5 \text{ g} \times \dfrac{1 \text{ mol}}{18.02 \text{ g}} \times \dfrac{6.02 \text{ kJ}}{1 \text{ mol}} \times \dfrac{1000 \text{ J}}{1 \text{ kJ}} = 2.83962 \times 10^3$ J, $q_{water} = -q_{ice} = -2.83962 \times 10^3$ J

$q = mC_s\Delta T$. Rearrange to solve for ΔT. $\Delta T_1 = \dfrac{q}{mC_s} = \dfrac{-2.83962 \times 10^3 \text{ J}}{255 \text{ g} \times 4.18 \frac{J}{g \cdot °C}} = -2.6641$ °C

$q = mC_s\Delta T$ substitute in values and set $q_{ice} = -q_{H_2O}$

$$q_{ice} = m_{ice} C_{ice}(T_f - T_{icei}) = 8.5 \text{ g} \times 4.18 \frac{\text{J}}{g \cdot °C} \times (T_f - 0.0 °C) =$$

$$-q_{water} = -m_{water}C_{water}\Delta T_{water2} = -255 \text{ g} \times 4.18 \frac{\text{J}}{g \cdot °C} \times \Delta T_{water2} \rightarrow$$

$8.5 \, T_f = -255\Delta T_{water2} = -255(T_f - T_{f1})$. Rearrange to solve for T_f. $8.5 \, T_f + 255 \, T_f = 255 \, T_{f1} \rightarrow$
$263.5 \, T_f = 255 \, T_{f1} \rightarrow T_f = 0.96774 \, T_{f1}$ but $\Delta T_1 = (T_{f1} - T_{i1}) = -2.6641$ °C, which says that
$T_{f1} = T_{i1} - 2.6641$ °C and $\Delta T_{Total} = (T_f - T_{i1})$; so
$\Delta T_{Total} = 0.96774 \, T_{f1} - T_{i1} = 0.96774(T_{i1} - 2.6641 °C) - T_{i1} = -2.5782 °C - 0.03226 \, T_{i1}$.
This implies that the larger the initial temperature of the water, the larger the temperature drop. If the initial temperature was 90 °C, the temperature drop would be 5.6 °C. If the initial temperature was 25 °C, the temperature drop would be 3.5 °C. If the initial temperature was 5 °C, the temperature drop would be 2.8 °C. This makes physical sense because the lower the initial temperature of the water, the less kinetic energy it initially has and the smaller the heat transfer from the water to the melted ice will be.

Check: The units (°C) are correct. The temperature drop from the melting of the ice is only 2.7 °C because the mass of the water is so much larger than that of the ice.

11.37 **Given:** 10.0 g ice $T_i = -10.0\,°C$ to steam at $T_f = 110.0\,°C$ **Find:** heat required (kJ)
Other: $\Delta H^\circ_{fus} = 6.02$ kJ/mol; $\Delta H^\circ_{vap} = 40.7$ kJ/mol; $C_{ice} = 2.09$ J/g·°C; $C_{water} = 4.18$ J/g·°C; $C_{steam} = 2.01$ J/g·°C
Conceptual Plan: Follow the heating curve in Figure 11.24. $q_{Total} = q_1 + q_2 + q_3 + q_4 + q_5$ where $q_1, q_3,$ and q_5 are heating of a single phase then J $\rightarrow$ kJ and q_2 and q_4 are phase transitions.

$$q = m\,C_s(T_f - T_i)$$ $$\frac{1\text{ kJ}}{1000\text{ J}}$$ $$q = m \times \frac{1\text{ mol}}{18.02\text{ g}} \times \frac{\Delta H}{1\text{ mol}}$$

Solution:

$$q_1 = m_{ice}C_{ice}(T_{icef} - T_{icei}) = 10.0\text{ g} \times 2.09\,\frac{\text{J}}{\text{g}\cdot°C} \times (0.0\,°C - (-10.0\,°C)) = 209\text{ J} \times \frac{1\text{ kJ}}{1000\text{ J}} = 0.209\text{ kJ}$$

$$q_2 = m \times \frac{1\text{ mol}}{18.02\text{ g}} \times \frac{\Delta H_{fus}}{1\text{ mol}} = 10.0\text{ g} \times \frac{1\text{ mol}}{18.02\text{ g}} \times \frac{6.02\text{ kJ}}{1\text{ mol}} = 3.3\underline{4}1\text{ kJ}$$

$$q_3 = m_{water}C_{water}(T_{waterf} - T_{wateri}) = 10.0\text{ g} \times 4.18\,\frac{\text{J}}{\text{g}\cdot°C} \times (100.0\,°C - 0.0\,°C) = 4180\text{ J} \times \frac{1\text{ kJ}}{1000\text{ J}} = 4.18\text{ kJ}$$

$$q_4 = m \times \frac{1\text{ mol}}{18.02\text{ g}} \times \frac{\Delta H_{vap}}{1\text{ mol}} = 10.0\text{ g} \times \frac{1\text{ mol}}{18.02\text{ g}} \times \frac{40.7\text{ kJ}}{1\text{ mol}} = 22.5\underline{8}6\text{ kJ}$$

$$q_5 = m_{steam}C_{steam}(T_{steamf} - T_{steami}) = 10.0\text{ g} \times 2.01\,\frac{\text{J}}{\text{g}\cdot°C} \times (110.0\,°C - 100.0\,°C)$$

$$= 201\text{ J} \times \frac{1\text{ kJ}}{1000\text{ J}} = 0.201\text{ kJ}$$

$$q_{Total} = q_1 + q_2 + q_3 + q_4 + q_5 = 0.209\text{ kJ} + 3.3\underline{4}1\text{ kJ} + 4.18\text{ kJ} + 22.5\underline{8}6\text{ kJ} + 0.201\text{ kJ} = 30.5\text{ kJ}$$

Check: The units (kJ) are correct. The total amount of heat is dominated by the vaporization step. Because we have less than 1 mole, we expect less than 41 kJ.

Phase Diagrams

11.39 (a)   solid
(b)   liquid
(c)   gas
(d)   supercritical fluid
(e)   solid/liquid equilibrium
(f)   liquid/gas equilibrium
(g)   solid/liquid/gas equilibrium

11.41 **Given:** nitrogen; normal boiling point = 77.3 K; normal melting point = 63.1 K; critical temperature = 126.2 K; critical pressure = 2.55×10^4 torr; triple point at 63.1 K and 94.0 torr
Find: Sketch phase diagram. Does nitrogen have a stable liquid phase at 1 atm?

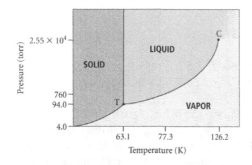

Nitrogen has a stable liquid phase at 1 atm.
Note that the axes are not to scale.

11.43 (a)   0.027 mmHg, the higher of the two triple points
(b)   The rhombic phase is denser because if we start in the monoclinic phase at 100 °C and increase the pressure, we will cross into the rhombic phase.

The Uniqueness of Water

11.45   Water has a low molar mass (18.02 g/mol), yet it is a liquid at room temperature. Water's high boiling point for its molar mass can be understood by examining the structure of the water molecule. The bent geometry of the water molecule and the highly polar nature of the $O-H$ bonds result in a molecule with a significant dipole moment. Water's two $O-H$ bonds (hydrogen directly bonded to oxygen) allow a water molecule to engage in hydrogen bonding with four other water molecules, resulting in a relatively high boiling point.

11.47   Water has an exceptionally high specific heat capacity, which has a moderating effect on the climate of coastal cities. Also, its high ΔH_{vap} causes water evaporation and condensation to have a strong effect on temperature. A tremendous amount of heat can be stored in large bodies of water. Heat will be absorbed or released from large bodies of water preferentially over land around it. In some cities, such as San Francisco, for example, the daily fluctuation in temperature can be less than 10 °C. This same moderating effect occurs over the entire planet, two-thirds of which is covered by water. In other words, without water, the daily temperature fluctuations on our planet might be more like those on Mars, where temperature fluctuations of 63 °C (113 °F) have been measured between early morning and midday.

Types of Solids and Their Structures

11.49   (a)   8 corner atoms $\times$ (1/8 atom/unit cell) = 1 atom/unit cell

   (b)   8 corner atoms $\times$ (1/8 atom/unit cell) + 1 atom in center = (1 + 1) atoms/unit cell = 2 atoms/unit cell

   (c)   8 corner atoms $\times$ (1/8 atom/unit cell) + 6 face-centered atoms $\times$ (1/2 atom/unit cell) = (1 + 3) atoms/unit cell
         = 4 atoms/unit cell

11.51   **Given:** platinum; face-centered cubic structure; $r = 139$ pm   **Find:** edge length of unit cell and density (g/cm^3)

Conceptual Plan: $r \rightarrow l$ and $l \rightarrow V(\text{pm}^3) \rightarrow V(\text{cm}^3)$ and $\mathcal{M}$, FCC structure $\rightarrow m$ then $m, V \rightarrow d$

$$l = 2\sqrt{2}\,r \quad V = l^3 \qquad \frac{(1\ \text{cm})^3}{(10^{10}\ \text{pm})^3} \qquad m = \frac{4\ \text{atoms}}{\text{unit cell}} \times \frac{\mathcal{M}}{N_A} \qquad d = m/V$$

Solution: $l = 2\sqrt{2}\,r = 2\sqrt{2} \times 139\ \text{pm} = 39\underline{3}.151\ \text{pm} = 393\ \text{pm}$ and

$$V = l^3 = (393.151\ \text{pm})^3 \times \frac{(1\ \text{cm})^3}{(10^{10}\ \text{pm})^3} = 6.0\underline{7}684 \times 10^{-23}\ \text{cm}^3\ \text{and}$$

$$m = \frac{4\ \text{atoms}}{\text{unit cell}} \times \frac{\mathcal{M}}{N_A} = \frac{4\ \text{atoms}}{\text{unit cell}} \times \frac{195.08\ \text{g}}{1\ \text{mol}} \times \frac{1\ \text{mol}}{6.022 \times 10^{23}\ \text{atoms}} = 1.29\underline{5}782 \times 10^{-21}\frac{\text{g}}{\text{unit cell}}\ \text{then}$$

$$d = \frac{m}{V} = \frac{1.29\underline{5}782 \times 10^{-21}\ \dfrac{\text{g}}{\text{unit cell}}}{6.0\underline{7}684 \times 10^{-23}\ \dfrac{\text{cm}^3}{\text{unit cell}}} = 21.3\ \frac{\text{g}}{\text{cm}^3}$$

Check: The units (pm and g/cm^3) are correct. The magnitude (393 pm) makes sense because it must be larger than the radius of an atom. The magnitude (21 g/cm^3) is consistent for Pt from Chapter 1.

11.53   **Given:** rhodium; face-centered cubic structure; $d = 12.41$ g/cm^3 **Find:** r(Rh)

Conceptual Plan: $\mathcal{M}$, FCC structure $\rightarrow m$ then $m, V \rightarrow d$ then $V(\text{cm}^3) \rightarrow l(\text{cm}) \rightarrow l(\text{pm})$ then $l \rightarrow r$

$$m = \frac{4\ \text{atoms}}{\text{unit cell}} \times \frac{\mathcal{M}}{N_A} \qquad d = m/V \qquad V = l^3 \qquad \frac{10^{10}\ \text{pm}}{1\ \text{cm}} \qquad l = 2\sqrt{2}\,r$$

Solution: $m = \dfrac{4\ \text{atoms}}{\text{unit cell}} \times \dfrac{\mathcal{M}}{N_A} = \dfrac{4\ \text{atoms}}{\text{unit cell}} \times \dfrac{102.91\ \text{g}}{1\ \text{mol}} \times \dfrac{1\ \text{mol}}{6.022 \times 10^{23}\ \text{atoms}} = 6.83\underline{5}603 \times 10^{-22}\ \dfrac{\text{g}}{\text{unit cell}}$

then $d = \dfrac{m}{V}$. Rearrange to solve for V. $V = \dfrac{m}{d} = \dfrac{6.83\underline{5}603 \times 10^{-22}\ \dfrac{\text{g}}{\text{unit cell}}}{12.41\ \dfrac{\text{g}}{\text{cm}^3}} = 5.50\underline{8}141 \times 10^{-23}\ \dfrac{\text{cm}^3}{\text{unit cell}}$

then $V = l^3$. Rearrange to solve for l.

$$l = \sqrt[3]{V} = \sqrt[3]{5.50\underline{8}141 \times 10^{-23}\ \text{cm}^3} = 3.80\underline{4}828 \times 10^{-8}\ \text{cm} \times \frac{10^{10}\ \text{pm}}{1\ \text{cm}} = 380.\underline{4}828\ \text{pm}\ \text{then}\ l = 2\sqrt{2}r$$

Rearrange to solve for r. $r = \dfrac{1}{2\sqrt{2}} = \dfrac{380.4828 \text{ pm}}{2\sqrt{2}} = 134.5 \text{ pm}$

Check: The units (pm) are correct. The magnitude (135 pm) is consistent with an atomic diameter.

11.55   **Given:** polonium, simple cubic structure $d = 9.3$ g/cm^3; $r = 167$ pm; $\mathcal{M} = 209$ g/mol   **Find:** estimate N_A

   Conceptual Plan: $r \rightarrow l$ and $l \rightarrow V(\text{pm}^3) \rightarrow V(\text{cm}^3)$ then $d, V \rightarrow m$ then $\mathcal{M}, \text{SC structure} \rightarrow m$

$$l = 2r \qquad V = l^3 \qquad \dfrac{(1 \text{ cm})^3}{(10^{10} \text{ pm})^3} \qquad\qquad d = m/V \qquad\qquad m = \dfrac{1 \text{ atom}}{\text{unit cell}} \times \dfrac{\mathcal{M}}{N_A}$$

   Solution: $l = 2r = 2 \times 167$ pm $= 334$ pm and $V = l^3 = (334 \text{ pm})^3 \times \dfrac{(1 \text{ cm})^3}{(10^{10} \text{ pm})^3} = 3.72597 \times 10^{-23}$ cm^3 then

$d = \dfrac{m}{V}$. Rearrange to solve for m. $m = dV = 9.3 \dfrac{\text{g}}{\text{cm}^3} \times \dfrac{3.72597 \times 10^{-23} \text{ cm}^3}{\text{unit cell}} = 3.46515 \times 10^{-22} \dfrac{\text{g}}{\text{unit cell}}$

then $m = \dfrac{1 \text{ atom}}{\text{unit cell}} \times \dfrac{\mathcal{M}}{N_A}$. Rearrange to solve for N_A.

$N_A = \dfrac{1 \text{ atom}}{\text{unit cell}} \times \dfrac{\mathcal{M}}{m} = \dfrac{1 \text{ atom}}{\text{unit cell}} \times \dfrac{209 \text{ g}}{1 \text{ mol}} \times \dfrac{1 \text{ unit cell}}{3.46515 \times 10^{-22} \text{ g}} = 6.0 \times 10^{23} \dfrac{\text{atoms}}{\text{mol}}$

   Check: The units (atoms/mol) are correct. The magnitude (6×10^{23} atoms/mol) is consistent with Avogadro's number.

11.57   (a)   atomic because argon (Ar) is an atom

   (b)   molecular because water (H_2O) is a molecule

   (c)   ionic because potassium oxide (K_2O) is an ionic solid

   (d)   atomic because iron (Fe) is an atom

11.59   LiCl has the highest melting point because it is the only ionic solid in the group. The other three solids are held together by intermolecular forces, while LiCl is held together by stronger coulombic interactions between the cations and anions of the crystal lattice.

11.61   (a) TiO_2 because it is an ionic solid

   (b) $SiCl_4$ because it has a higher molar mass and therefore has stronger dispersion forces

   (c)   Xe because it has a higher molar mass and therefore has stronger dispersion forces

   (d)   CaO because the ions have greater charge and therefore stronger electrostatic interactions

11.63   The Ti atoms occupy the corner positions and the center of the unit cell: 8 corner atoms $\times$ (1/8 atom/unit cell) $+1$ atom in center $= (1 + 1)$ Ti atoms/unit cell $= 2$ Ti atoms/unit cell. The O atoms occupy four positions on the top and bottom faces and two positions inside the unit cell: 4 face-centered atoms $\times$ (1/2 atom/unit cell) $+2$ atoms in the interior $= (2 + 2)$ O atoms/unit cell $= 4$ O atoms/unit cell. Therefore, there are 2 Ti atoms/ unit cell and 4 O atoms/unit cell, so the ratio Ti:O is 2:4, or 1:2. The formula for the compound is TiO_2.

11.65   In CsCl: The Cs atoms occupy the center of the unit cell: 1 atom in center $= 1$ Cs atom/unit cell. The Cl atoms occupy corner positions of the unit cell: 8 corner atoms $\times$ (1/8 atom/unit cell) $= 1$ Cl atom/unit cell. Therefore, there are 1 Cs atom/unit cell and 1 Cl atom/unit cell, so the ratio Cs:Cl is 1:1. The formula for the compound is CsCl, as expected.

   In BaCl$_2$: The Ba atoms occupy the corner positions and the face-centered positions of the unit cell: 8 corner atoms $\times$ (1/8 atom/unit cell) $+$ 6 face-centered atoms $\times$ (1/2 atom/unit cell) $= (1 + 3)$ Ba atoms/unit cell $= 4$ Ba atoms/unit cell. The Cl atoms occupy the eight tetrahedral holes within the unit cell: 8 Cl atoms/unit cell. Therefore, there are 4 Ba atoms/unit cell and 8 Cl atoms/unit cell, so the ratio Ba:Cl is 4:8, or 1:2. The formula for the compound is BaCl$_2$, as expected.

Band Theory

11.67   (a)   Zn should have little or no band gap because it is the only metal in the group.

Cumulative Problems

11.69 The general trend is that melting point increases with increasing molar mass. This is because the electrons of the larger molecules are held more loosely and a stronger dipole moment can be induced more easily. HF is the exception to the rule. It has a relatively high melting point due to strong intermolecular forces due to hydrogen bonding.

11.71 **Given:** $P_{H_2O} = 23.76$ torr at 25 °C; 1.25 g water in 1.5 L container   **Find:** m (H_2O) as liquid

Conceptual Plan: °C → K and torr → atm then P, V, T → mol (g) → g (g) then g (g), g (l)$_i$ → g (l)$_f$

$$K = °C + 273.15 \qquad \frac{1 \text{ atm}}{760 \text{ torr}} \qquad PV = nRT \qquad \frac{18.02 \text{ g}}{1 \text{ mol}} \qquad g\,(l)_f = g\,(l)_i - g\,(g)$$

Solution: $T = 25\,°C + 273.15 = 298$ K, 23.76 torr $\times \dfrac{1 \text{ atm}}{760 \text{ torr}} = 0.0312632$ atm then $PV = nRT$

Rearrange to solve for n. $n = \dfrac{PV}{RT} = \dfrac{0.0312632 \text{ atm} \times 1.5 \text{ L}}{0.08206 \dfrac{\text{L} \cdot \text{atm}}{\text{K} \cdot \text{mol}} \times 298 \text{ K}} = 0.00191768$ mol in the gas phase then

$0.00191768 \text{ mol} \times \dfrac{18.02 \text{ g}}{1 \text{ mol}} = 0.0345566$ g in the gas phase then

g (l)$_f$ = g (l)$_i$ − g (g) = 1.25 g − 0.0345566 g = 1.22 g remaining as liquid. Yes, there is 1.22 g of liquid.

Check: The units (g) are correct. The magnitude (1.2 g) is expected because very little material is expected to be in the gas phase.

11.73 Because we are starting at a temperature that is higher and a pressure that is lower than the triple point, the phase transitions will be gas → liquid → solid, or condensation followed by freezing.

11.75 **Given:** ice: $T_1 = 0\,°C$ exactly, $m = 53.5$ g; water: $T_1 = 75\,°C$, $m = 115$ g   **Find:** T_f

Other: $\Delta H°_{fus} = 6.02$ kJ/mol; $C_{water} = 4.18$ J/g · °C

Conceptual Plan: $q_{ice} = -q_{water}$ so g(ice) → mol(ice) → q_{fus}(kJ) → q_{fus}(J) → q_{water}(J) then

$$\frac{1 \text{ mol}}{18.02 \text{ g}} \qquad \frac{6.02 \text{ kJ}}{1 \text{ mol}} \qquad \frac{1000 \text{ J}}{1 \text{ kJ}} \qquad q_{water} = -q_{ice}$$

q, m, C_s → ΔT then $T_i, \Delta T$ → T_2 now we have slightly cooled water in contact with 0.0 °C water

$$q = mC_s \Delta T \qquad\qquad \Delta T = T_2 - T_i$$

so $q_{ice} = -q_{water}$ with m, C_s, T_i → T_f

$$q = mC_s(T_f - T_i) \text{ then set } q_{ice} = -q_{water}$$

Solution: $53.5 \text{ g} \times \dfrac{1 \text{ mol}}{18.02 \text{ g}} \times \dfrac{6.02 \text{ kJ}}{1 \text{ mol}} \times \dfrac{1000 \text{ J}}{1 \text{ kJ}} = 1.78729 \times 10^4$ J, $q_{water} = -q_{ice} = -1.78729 \times 10^4$ J

$q_{water} = mC_s \Delta T$. Rearrange to solve for ΔT. $\Delta T = \dfrac{q}{mC_s} = \dfrac{-1.78729 \times 10^4 \text{ J}}{115 \text{ g} \times 4.18 \dfrac{\text{J}}{\text{g} \cdot °C}} = -37.1810\,°C$ then

$\Delta T = T_2 - T_i$. Rearrange to solve for T_2. $T_2 = \Delta T + T_i = -37.1810\,°C + 75\,°C = 37.819\,°C$

$q = m\,C_s(T_f - T_i)$ substitute in values and set $q_{ice} = -q_{water}$.

$q_{ice} = m_{ice}C_{ice}(T_f - T_{ice\,i}) = 53.5 \text{ g} \times 4.18 \dfrac{\text{J}}{\text{g} \cdot °C} \times (T_f - 0.0\,°C) =$

$-q_{water} = -m_{water}C_{water}(T_f - T_{water\,2}) = -115 \text{ g} \times 4.18 \dfrac{\text{J}}{\text{g} \cdot °C} \times (T_f - 37.819\,°C)$

Rearrange to solve for T_f.

$53.5\,T_f = -115(T_f - 37.819\,°C) \rightarrow 53.5\,T_f = -115\,T_f + 4349.2\,°C$

$\rightarrow -4346.8\,°C = -168.5\,T_f \rightarrow T_f = \dfrac{-4349.2\,°C}{-168.5} = 25.8\,°C = 26\,°C$

Check: The units (°C) are correct. The temperature is between the two initial temperatures. Because the ice mass is about half the water mass, we are not surprised that the temperature is closer to the original ice temperature.

11.77 **Given:** 1 mole of methanol **Find:** Draw a heating curve beginning at 170 K and ending at 350 K
Other: melting point = 176 K, boiling point = 338 K, ΔH_{fus} = 2.2 kJ/mol, ΔH_{vap} = 35.2 kJ/mol, $C_{s,solid}$ = 105 J/mol·K, $C_{s,liquid}$ = 81.3 J/mol·K, $C_{s,gas}$ = 48 J/mol·K
Conceptual Plan:
Calculate the temperature range of each phase:

$T_{Starting}, T_{Melting} \rightarrow \Delta T_{Solid}$ and $T_{Melting}, T_{Boiling} \rightarrow \Delta T_{Liquid}$ and $T_{Boiling}, T_{Ending} \rightarrow \Delta T_{Gas}$

$\Delta T_{Solid} = T_{Melting} - T_{Starting}$ $\quad\quad\quad \Delta T_{Liquid} = T_{Boiling} - T_{Melting}$ $\quad\quad\quad \Delta T_{Gas} = T_{Ending} - T_{Boiling}$

Because there is 1 mole of methanol, the heat for each phase change is simply the ΔH for that phase change.
Calculate the heat required for each step:

$\Delta T_{Solid}, C_{s,solid} \rightarrow q_{Solid}$ and $\Delta T_{Liquid}, C_{s,liquid} \rightarrow q_{Liquid}$ and $\Delta T_{Gas}, C_{s,gas} \rightarrow q_{Gas}$

$q = C_s \times \Delta T$ $\quad\quad\quad\quad\quad q = C_s \times \Delta T$ $\quad\quad\quad\quad\quad q = C_s \times \Delta T$

Finally, plot each of the segments.
Solution:

$\Delta T_{Solid} = T_{Melting} - T_{Starting} = 176\text{ K} - 170\text{ K} = 6\text{ K};$ $\quad \Delta T_{Liquid} = T_{Boiling} - T_{Melting} = 338\text{ K} - 176\text{ K} = 162\text{ K}$
and $\Delta T_{Gas} = T_{Ending} - T_{Boiling} = 350\text{ K} - 338\text{ K} = 12\text{ K}$

$q_{fus} = \Delta H_{fus} = 2.2\text{ kJ/mol}$ and $q_{vap} = \Delta H_{vap} = 35.2\text{ kJ/mol}$

$q_{Solid} = C_{s,Solid} \times \Delta T_{Solid} = 105 \dfrac{\text{J}}{\text{mol}\cdot\text{K}} \times 6\text{ K} = \underline{6}30\text{ J/mol} = 0.\underline{6}3\text{ kJ/mol}$

$q_{Liquid} = C_{s,Liquid} \times \Delta T_{Liquid} = 81.3 \dfrac{\text{J}}{\text{mol}\cdot\text{K}} \times 162\text{ K} = 13\underline{1}70.6\text{ J/mol} = 13.\underline{1}706\text{ kJ/mol}$ and

$q_{Gas} = C_{s,Gas} \times \Delta T_{Gas} = 48 \dfrac{\text{J}}{\text{mol}\cdot\text{K}} \times 12\text{ K} = 5\underline{7}6\text{ J/mol} = 0.5\underline{7}6\text{ kJ/mol}$

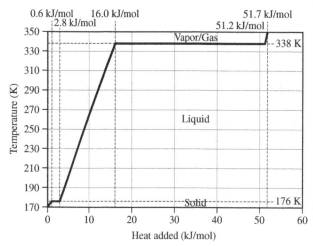

Check: The heating curve has a shape that is similar to that of water.

11.79 **Given:** home: 6.0 m × 10.0 m × 2.2 m; $T = 30\,°C$, P_{H_2O} = 85% of $P^\circ_{H_2O}$ **Find:** $m(H_2O)$ removed
Other: $P^\circ_{H_2O}$ = 31.8 mmHg from text
Conceptual Plan: $l, w, h \rightarrow V(m^3) \rightarrow V(cm^3) \rightarrow V(L)$ and $P^\circ_{H_2O} \rightarrow P_{H_2O}(mmHg) \rightarrow P_{H_2O}(atm)$ and

$V = l\,w\,h$ $\quad \dfrac{(100\text{ cm})^3}{(1\text{ m})^3}$ $\quad \dfrac{1\text{ L}}{1000\text{ cm}^3}$ $\quad\quad P_{H_2O} = 0.85\,P^\circ_{H_2O}$ $\quad \dfrac{1\text{ atm}}{760\text{ mmHg}}$

°C → K then P, V, T → mol(H_2O) → g(H_2O)

K = °C + 273.15 $\quad\quad\quad PV = nRT$ $\quad \dfrac{18.02\text{ g}}{1\text{ mol}}$

Solution: $V = l\,w\,h = 6.0\text{ m} \times 10.0\text{ m} \times 2.2\text{ m} = 1\underline{3}2\text{ m}^3 \times \dfrac{(100\text{ cm})^3}{(1\text{ m})^3} \times \dfrac{1\text{ L}}{1000\text{ cm}^3} = 1.\underline{3}2 \times 10^5\text{ L}$,

$P_{H_2O} = 0.85\,P^\circ_{H_2O} = 0.85 \times 31.8\text{ mmHg} \times \dfrac{1\text{ atm}}{760\text{ mmHg}} = 0.03\underline{5}566\text{ atm}$, $T = 30\,°C + 273.15 = 3\underline{0}3\text{ K}$,

then $PV = nRT$. Rearrange to solve for n.

$$n = \frac{PV}{RT} = \frac{0.035566 \text{ atm} \times 1.32 \times 10^5 \text{ L}}{0.08206 \frac{\text{L} \cdot \text{atm}}{\text{K} \cdot \text{mol}} \times 303 \text{ K}} = 188.81 \text{ mol then } 188.81 \text{ mol} \times \frac{18.02 \text{ g}}{1 \text{ mol}} = 3400 \text{ g to remove}$$

Check: The units (g) are correct. The magnitude of the answer (3400 g) makes sense because the volume of the house is so large. We are removing almost 200 moles of water.

11.81   CsCl has a higher melting point than AgI because of its higher coordination number. In CsCl, one anion bonds to eight cations (and vice versa), while in AgI, one anion bonds only to four cations.

11.83   (a)   Atoms are connected across the face diagonal (c), so $c = 4r$.

   (b)   From the Pythagorean Theorem, $c^2 = a^2 + b^2$; from part (a), $c = 4r$; and for a cubic structure, $a = l, b = l$. So $(4r)^2 = l^2 + l^2 \rightarrow 16r^2 = 2l^2 \rightarrow 8r^2 = l^2 \rightarrow l = \sqrt{8r^2} \rightarrow l = 2\sqrt{2}r$.

11.85   **Given:** diamond, V(unit cell) $= 0.0454 \text{ nm}^3$; $d = 3.52 \text{ g/cm}^3$ **Find:** number of carbon atoms/unit cell

   Conceptual Plan: $V(\text{nm}^3) \rightarrow V(\text{cm}^3)$ then $d, V \rightarrow m \rightarrow \text{mol} \rightarrow \text{atoms}$

$$\frac{(1 \text{ cm})^3}{(10^7 \text{ nm})^3} \qquad d = m/V \quad \frac{1 \text{ mol}}{12.01 \text{ g}} \quad \frac{6.022 \times 10^{23} \text{ atoms}}{1 \text{ mol}}$$

   Solution: $0.0454 \text{ nm}^3 \times \dfrac{(1 \text{ cm})^3}{(10^7 \text{ nm})^3} = 4.54 \times 10^{-23} \text{ cm}^3$ then $d = \dfrac{m}{V}$. Rearrange to solve for m.

$$m = dV = 3.52 \frac{\text{g}}{\text{cm}^3} \times 4.54 \times 10^{-23} \text{ cm}^3 = 1.59808 \times 10^{-22} \text{ g then}$$

$$\frac{1.59808 \times 10^{-22} \text{ g}}{\text{unit cell}} \times \frac{1 \text{ mol}}{12.01 \text{ g}} \times \frac{6.022 \times 10^{23} \text{ atoms}}{1 \text{ mol}} = 8.01 \frac{\text{C atoms}}{\text{unit cell}} = 8 \frac{\text{C atoms}}{\text{unit cell}}$$

   Check: The units (atoms) are correct. The magnitude (8 atoms) makes sense because it is a fairly small number and our answer is within calculation error of an integer.

11.87   (a) $CO_2(s) \rightarrow CO_2(g)$ at 194.7 K

   (b) $CO_2(s) \rightarrow$ triple point at 216.5 K $\rightarrow CO_2(g)$ just above 216.5 K

   (c) $CO_2(s) \rightarrow CO_2(l)$ at somewhat above 216 K $\rightarrow CO_2(g)$ at around 250 K

   (d) $CO_2(s) \rightarrow CO_2(l) \rightarrow$ super critical CO_2. Above the critical point where there is no distinction between liquid and gas. This change occurs at about 300 K.

11.89   **Given:** metal, $d = 7.8748 \text{ g/cm}^3$; $l = 0.28664 \text{ nm}$, body-centered cubic lattice   **Find:** $\mathcal{M}$

   Conceptual Plan: $l \rightarrow V(\text{nm}^3) \rightarrow V(\text{cm}^3)$ then $d, V \rightarrow m$ then m, FCC structure $\rightarrow \mathcal{M}$

$$V = l^3 \quad \frac{(1 \text{ cm})^3}{(10^7 \text{ nm})^3} \qquad d = m/V \qquad m = \frac{2 \text{ atoms}}{\text{unit cell}} \times \frac{\mathcal{M}}{N_A}$$

   Solution: $V = l^3 = (0.28664 \text{ nm})^3 = 0.02355105602 \text{ nm}^3 \times \dfrac{(1 \text{ cm})^3}{(10^7 \text{ nm})^3} = 2.355105602 \times 10^{-23} \text{ cm}^3$ then $d = \dfrac{m}{V}$.

   Rearrange to solve for m. $m = dV = 7.8748 \dfrac{\text{g}}{\text{cm}^3} \times 2.355105602 \times 10^{-23} \text{ cm}^3 = 1.854598559 \times 10^{-22} \text{ g}$

   then $m = \dfrac{2 \text{ atoms}}{\text{unit cell}} \times \dfrac{\mathcal{M}}{N_A}$. Rearrange to solve for $\mathcal{M}$.

$$\mathcal{M} = \frac{\text{unit cell}}{2 \text{ atoms}} \times N_A \times m = \frac{\text{unit cell}}{2 \text{ atoms}} \times \frac{6.022 \times 10^{23} \text{ atoms}}{1 \text{ mol}} \times \frac{1.854598559 \times 10^{-22} \text{ g}}{\text{unit cell}} = 55.842 \frac{\text{g}}{\text{mol}}$$

$$= 55.84 \frac{\text{g}}{\text{mol}} \text{ iron}$$

   Check: The units (g/mol) are correct. The magnitude (55.8 g/mol) makes sense because it is a reasonable atomic mass for a metal and it is close to iron.

Challenge Problems

11.91   **Given:** KCl, rock salt structure   **Find:** density (g/cm^3) **Other:** $r(K^+) = 133$ pm; $r(Cl^-) = 181$ pm from Chapter 8
**Conceptual Plan: Rock salt structure is a face-centered cubic structure with anions at the lattice points and
cations in the holes between lattice sites** → **assume** $r = r(Cl^-)$, **but** $\mathcal{M} = \mathcal{M}(KCl)$
$r(K^+), r(Cl^-) \rightarrow l$ **and** $l \rightarrow V(\text{pm}^3) \rightarrow V(\text{cm}^3)$, **and FCC structure** → m **then** $m, V \rightarrow d$.

$$\text{from Figure 11.43} \quad l = 2r(Cl^-) + 2r(K^+) \quad V = l^3 \quad \frac{(1 \text{ cm})^3}{(10^{10} \text{ pm})^3} \quad m = \frac{4 \text{ formula units}}{\text{unit cell}} \times \frac{\mathcal{M}}{N_A} \quad d = m/V$$

Solution: $l = 2r(Cl^-) + 2r(K^+) = 2(181 \text{ pm}) + 2(133 \text{ pm}) = 628 \text{ pm}$ and

$$V = l^3 = (628 \text{ pm})^3 \times \frac{(1 \text{ cm})^3}{(10^{10} \text{ pm})^3} = 2.4\underline{7}673 \times 10^{-22} \text{ cm}^3 \text{ and}$$

$$m = \frac{4 \text{ formula units}}{\text{unit cell}} \times \frac{\mathcal{M}}{N_A} = \frac{4 \text{ formula units}}{\text{unit cell}} \times \frac{74.55 \text{ g}}{1 \text{ mol}} \times \frac{1 \text{ mol}}{6.022 \times 10^{23} \text{ formula units}}$$

$$= 4.95\underline{1}843 \times 10^{-22} \frac{\text{g}}{\text{unit cell}}$$

$$\text{then } d = \frac{m}{V} = \frac{4.95\underline{1}843 \times 10^{-22} \dfrac{\text{g}}{\text{unit cell}}}{2.4\underline{7}673 \times 10^{-22} \dfrac{\text{cm}^3}{\text{unit cell}}} = 1.9\underline{9}935 \frac{\text{g}}{\text{cm}^3} = 2.00 \frac{\text{g}}{\text{cm}^3}$$

Check: The units (g/cm^3) are correct. The magnitude (2 g/cm^3) is reasonable for a salt density. The published value is
1.98 g/cm^3. This method of estimating the density gives a value that is close to the experimentally measured density.

11.93   Decreasing the pressure will decrease the temperature of liquid nitrogen. Because the nitrogen is boiling, its temperature must be constant at a given pressure. As the pressure decreases, the boiling point decreases, and so does the temperature. Remember that vaporization is an endothermic process, so as the nitrogen vaporizes, it removes heat from
the liquid, dropping its temperature. If the pressure drops below the pressure of the triple point, the phase change will
shift from vaporization to sublimation and the liquid nitrogen will become solid.

11.95   **Given:** cubic closest packing structure = cube with touching spheres of radius = r on alternating corners of a cube
Find: body diagonal of cube and radius of tetrahedral hole

Solution: The cell edge length = l and $l^2 + l^2 = (2r)^2 \rightarrow 2l^2 = 4r^2 \rightarrow l^2 = 2r^2$. Because body
diagonal = BD is the hypotenuse of the right triangle formed by the face diagonal and the cell edge, we have
$(BD)^2 = l^2 + (2r)^2 = 2r^2 + 4r^2 = 6r^2 \rightarrow BD = \sqrt{6}r$. The radius of the tetrahedral hole = r_T is half
the body diagonal minus the radius of the sphere, or

$$r_T = \frac{BD}{2} - r = \frac{\sqrt{6}r}{2} - r = \left(\frac{\sqrt{6}}{2} - 1\right)r = \left(\frac{\sqrt{6} - 2}{2}\right)r = \left(\frac{\sqrt{3}\sqrt{2} - \sqrt{2}\sqrt{2}}{\sqrt{2}\sqrt{2}}\right)r$$

$$= \left(\frac{\sqrt{3} - \sqrt{2}}{\sqrt{2}}\right)r \approx 0.22474r.$$

11.97   **Given:** 1.00 L water, $T_i = 298$ K, $T_f = 373$ K-vapor; $P_{CH_4} = 1.00$ atm   **Find:** $V(CH_4)$
Other: $\Delta H^{\circ}_{comb}(CH_4) = 890.4$ kJ/mol; $C_{water} = 75.2$ J/mol · K; $\Delta H^{\circ}_{vap}(H_2O) = 40.7$ kJ/mol, $d = 1.00$ g/mL
Conceptual Plan: L → mL → g → mol then heat liquid water: $n, C_s, T_i, T_f \rightarrow q_{1water}(J)$

$$\frac{1000 \text{ mL}}{1 \text{ L}} \quad \frac{1.00 \text{ g}}{1.00 \text{ mL}} \quad \frac{1 \text{ mol}}{18.02 \text{ g}} \qquad\qquad q = mC_s(T_f - T_i)$$

vaporize water: $n_{water}, \Delta H^{\circ}_{vap} \rightarrow q_{2water}(J)$ **then calculate total heat** $q_{1water}, q_{2water} \rightarrow q_{water}(J)$ **then**

$$q = n\Delta H \qquad\qquad q_{1water} + q_{2water} = q_{water}$$

$$q_{water}(J) \rightarrow -q_{CH_4 comb}(J) \rightarrow n_{CH_4} \text{ finally } n_{CH_4}, P, T \rightarrow V$$

$$q_{water} = -q_{CH_4 comb} \qquad q = n\Delta H \qquad PV = nRT$$

Solution: $1.00 \text{ L} \times \dfrac{1000 \text{ mL}}{1 \text{ L}} \times \dfrac{1.00 \text{ g}}{1.00 \text{ mL}} \times \dfrac{1 \text{ mol}}{18.02 \text{ g}} = 55.\underline{4}939 \text{ mol } H_2O$

$q_{1water} = n_{water}C_{water}(T_f - T_i) = 55.\underline{4}939 \text{ mol} \times 75.2 \dfrac{J}{\text{mol} \cdot K} \times (373 \text{ K} - 298 \text{ K}) = 3.1\underline{2}98557 \times 10^5 \text{ J}$

$$= 312.\underline{9}8557 \text{ kJ}$$

$$q_{2\text{water}} = n\Delta H = 55.\underline{4}939 \text{ mol} \times 40.7\frac{\text{kJ}}{\text{mol}} = 2.2\underline{5}8602 \times 10^3 \text{ kJ}$$

$$q_{1\text{water}} + q_{2\text{water}} = q_{\text{water}} = 312.\underline{9}8557 \text{ kJ} + 2.2\underline{5}8602 \times 10^3 \text{ kJ} = 2.5\underline{7}158757 \times 10^3 \text{ kJ}$$

$$q_{\text{water}} = -q_{\text{CH}_4\text{comb}} = 2.5\underline{7}158757 \times 10^3 \text{ kJ then } q_{\text{CH}_4\text{comb}} = n\Delta H. \text{ Rearrange to solve for } n.$$

$$n_{\text{CH}_4} = \frac{q_{\text{CH}_4}}{\Delta H_{\text{CH}_4\text{comb}}} = \frac{-2.5\underline{7}158757 \times 10^3 \text{ kJ}}{-890.4 \dfrac{\text{kJ}}{\text{mol}}} = 2.8\underline{8}81262 \text{ mol then } PV = nRT$$

Rearrange to solve for V. $V = \dfrac{nRT}{P} = \dfrac{2.8\underline{8}81262 \text{ mol} \times 0.08206 \dfrac{\text{L} \cdot \text{atm}}{\text{mol} \cdot \text{K}} \times 298 \text{ K}}{1.00 \text{ atm}} = 70.\underline{6}25892 \text{ L} = 70.6 \text{ L}$

Check: The units (L) are correct. The volume (71 L) is reasonable because we are using about 3 moles of methane.

Conceptual Problems

11.99   The melting of an ice cube in a glass of water will not raise or lower the level of the liquid in the glass as long as the ice is always floating in the liquid. This is because the ice will displace a volume of water based on its mass. By the same logic, melting floating icebergs will not raise the ocean levels (assuming that the dissolved solids content, and thus the density, will not change when the icebergs melt). Dissolving ice formations that are supported by land will raise the ocean levels, just as pouring more water into a glass will raise the liquid level in the glass.

11.101   Substance A will have the larger change in vapor pressure with the same temperature change. To understand this, consider the Clausius–Clapeyron equation: $\ln \dfrac{P_2}{P_1} = \dfrac{-\Delta H_{\text{vap}}}{R}\left(\dfrac{1}{T_2} - \dfrac{1}{T_1}\right)$. If we use the same temperatures, we see that $\dfrac{P_2}{P_1} \alpha\, e^{-\Delta H_{\text{vap}}}$. So the smaller the heat of vaporization, the larger the final vapor pressure. We can also consider that the lower the heat of vaporization, the easier to convert the substance from a liquid to a gas. This again leads to Substance A having the larger change in vapor pressure.

11.103 $\Delta H_{\text{sub}} = \Delta H_{\text{fus}} + \Delta H_{\text{vap}}$ as long as the heats of fusion and vaporization are measured at the same temperatures.

11.105   Water has an exceptionally high specific heat capacity, which has a moderating effect on the temperature of the root cellar. A large amount of heat can be stored in a large vat of water. The heat will be absorbed or released from the large bodies of water preferentially over the area around it. As the temperature of the air drops, the water will release heat, keeping the temperature more constant. If the temperature of the cellar falls enough to begin to freeze the water, the heat given off during the freezing will further protect the food in the cellar.

11.107   (a)   In moving from line segment 5 to line segment 4, the water is condensing. Heat is being released, and q is negative.
          (b)   This line represents the heat absorbed when melting ice. The heat is converted to increased kinetic energy of the water molecules as they become more mobile in the liquid phase.
          (c)   For other substances, the following things would change: the melting point, the boiling point, the length of segments, and the slopes of line segments 1, 3, and 5.

Questions for Group Work

11.109   1-hexnaol exhibits hydrogen bonding — it has the highest boiling point. 2-hexanone is polar, but cannot exhibit hydrogen bonding — it has the next highest boiling point. Heptane is nonpolar — it has the lowest boiling point.

11.111   Referring to Figure 11.30, the amount of heat needed to melt one mole of water is 6.02 kJ and the amount of heat needed to boil one mole of water is 40.7 kJ — it takes a lot more heat to boil water than to melt ice, because all of the intermolecular interactions need to be completely broken when boiling but not to melt.
          Referring to Figure 11.30, the amount of heat needed to warm one mole of ice 10 °C is 0.38 kJ (0.941 kJ × (10 °C/25 °C), the amount of heat needed to warm one mole of water 10 °C is 0.75 kJ (7.52 kJ × (10 °C/100 °C) and

the amount of heat needed to warm one mole of steam 10 °C is 0.36 kJ (0.905 kJ × (10 °C/25 °C). It takes more heat to warm water than to warm ice or steam, because there is more motion and disorder in the liquid and gas phases.

11.113   The characteristics of the various cubic crystalline lattices are presented in Figure 11.35.

Cubic Cell Name	Atoms per Unit Cell	Structure	Coordination Number	Edge Length in terms of r	Packing Efficiency (fraction of volume occupied)
Simple Cubic	1		6	$2r$	52%
Body-centered Cubic	2		8	$\dfrac{4r}{\sqrt{3}}$	68%
Face-centered Cubic	4		12	$2\sqrt{2}r$	74%

Note: All of the spheres are identical.

12 Solutions

Solubility

12.1 (a) hexane, toluene, or CCl_4; dispersion forces
  (b) water, methanol, acetone; dispersion, dipole–dipole, hydrogen bonding (except for acetone)
  (c) hexane, toluene, or CCl_4; dispersion forces
  (d) water, acetone, methanol, ethanol; dispersion, ion–dipole

12.3 $HOCH_2CH_2CH_2OH$ would be more soluble in water because it has –OH groups on both ends of the molecule; so it can hydrogen-bond on both ends.

12.5 (a) water; dispersion, dipole–dipole, hydrogen bonding
  (b) hexane; dispersion forces
  (c) water; dispersion, dipole–dipole
  (d) water; dispersion, dipole–dipole, hydrogen bonding

Energetics of Solution Formation

12.7 (a) endothermic
  (b) The lattice energy is greater in magnitude than is the heat of hydration.
  (c)

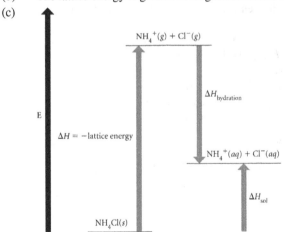

  (d) The solution forms because chemical systems tend toward greater entropy.

12.9 **Given:** $AgNO_3$: lattice energy $= -820.$ kJ/mol, $\Delta H_{soln} = +22.6$ kJ/mol **Find:** $\Delta H_{hydration}$
  Conceptual Plan: lattice energy, $\Delta H_{soln} \rightarrow \Delta H_{hydration}$
  $$\Delta H_{soln} = \Delta H_{solute} + \Delta H_{hydration} \text{ where } \Delta H_{solute} = -\Delta H_{lattice}$$
  Solution:
  $\Delta H_{soln} = \Delta H_{solute} + \Delta H_{hydration}$ where $\Delta H_{solute} = -\Delta H_{lattice}$ so $\Delta H_{hydration} = \Delta H_{soln} + \Delta H_{lattice}$
  $\Delta H_{hydration} = 22.6$ kJ/mol $- 820.$ kJ/mol $= -797$ kJ/mol
  Check: The units (kJ/mol) are correct. The magnitude of the answer (-800 kJ/mol) makes physical sense because the lattice energy is so negative; thus, it dominates the calculation.

12.11 **Given:** LiI: lattice energy $= -7.3 \times 10^2$ kJ/mol, $\Delta H_{\text{hydration}} = -793$ kJ/mol; 15.0 g LiI
Find: ΔH_{soln} and heat evolved
Conceptual Plan: lattice energy, $\Delta H_{\text{hydration}} \rightarrow \Delta H_{\text{soln}}$ and g $\rightarrow$ mol then mol, $\Delta H_{\text{soln}} \rightarrow q$

$$\Delta H_{\text{soln}} = \Delta H_{\text{solute}} + \Delta H_{\text{hydration}} \text{ where } \Delta H_{\text{solute}} = -\Delta H_{\text{lattice}} \qquad \frac{1 \text{ mol}}{133.84 \text{ g}} \qquad q = n\Delta H_{\text{soln}}$$

Solution: $\Delta H_{\text{soln}} = \Delta H_{\text{solute}} + \Delta H_{\text{hydration}}$ where $\Delta H_{\text{solute}} = -\Delta H_{\text{lattice}}$ so $\Delta H_{\text{soln}} = \Delta H_{\text{hydration}} - \Delta H_{\text{lattice}}$
$\Delta H_{\text{soln}} = -793$ kJ/mol $- (-7\underline{3}0$ kJ/mol$) = -6\underline{3}$ kJ/mol $= -6 \times 10^1$ kJ/mol and

$15.0 \text{ g} \times \dfrac{1 \text{ mol}}{133.84 \text{ g}} = 0.112\underline{0}74$ mol then

$q = n\Delta H_{\text{soln}} = 0.112\underline{0}74 \text{ mol} \times -\underline{6}.3 \times 10^1 \dfrac{\text{kJ}}{\text{mol}} = -7$ kJ or 7 kJ released

Check: The units (kJ/mol and kJ) are correct. The magnitude of the answer (-60 kJ/mol) makes physical sense because the lattice energy and the heat of hydration are about the same. The magnitude of the heat (7 kJ) makes physical sense because 15 g is much less than a mole; thus, the amount of heat released is going to be small.

Solution Equilibrium and Factors Affecting Solubility

12.13 The solution is unsaturated because we are dissolving 25 g of NaCl per 100 g of water and the solubility from the figure is ~35 g NaCl per 100 g of water at 25 °C.

12.15 At 40 °C, the solution has 45 g of KNO_3 per 100 g of water, and it can contain up to 63 g of KNO_3 per 100 g of water. At 0 °C, the solubility from the figure is ~14 g KNO_3 per 100 g of water, so ~31 g KNO_3 per 100 g of water will precipitate out of solution.

12.17 Because the solubility of gases decreases as the temperature increases, boiling will cause dissolved oxygen to be removed from the solution.

12.19 Henry's law says that as pressure increases, nitrogen will more easily dissolve in blood. To reverse this process, divers should ascend to lower pressures.

12.21 **Given:** room temperature, 80.0 L aquarium, $P_{\text{Total}} = 1.0$ atm; $\chi_{N_2} = 0.78$ **Find:** m (N_2)
Other: $k_H(N_2) = 6.1 \times 10^{-4}$ M/atm at 25 °C
Conceptual Plan: $P_{\text{Total}}, \chi_{N_2} \rightarrow P_{N_2}$ then $P_{N_2}, k_H(N_2) \rightarrow S_{N_2}$ then L $\rightarrow$ mol $\rightarrow$ g

$$P_{N_2} = \chi_{N_2} P_{\text{Total}} \qquad S_{N_2} = k_H(N_2) P_{N_2} \qquad M = \frac{\text{amount solute (moles)}}{\text{volume solution (L)}} \frac{28.02 \text{ g } N_2}{1 \text{ mol } N_2}$$

Solution: $P_{N_2} = \chi_{N_2} P_{\text{Total}} = 0.78 \times 1.0$ atm $= 0.78$ atm then

$S_{N_2} = k_H(N_2) P_{N_2} = 6.1 \times 10^{-4} \dfrac{\text{M}}{\text{atm}} \times 0.78 \text{ atm} = 4.\underline{7}58 \times 10^{-4}$ M then

$80.0 \text{ L} \times 4.\underline{7}58 \times 10^{-4} \dfrac{\text{mol}}{\text{L}} \times \dfrac{28.02 \text{ g}}{1 \text{ mol}} = 1.1$ g

Check: The units (g) are correct. The magnitude of the answer (1 g) seems reasonable because we have 80 L of water and expect much less than a mole of nitrogen.

Concentrations of Solutions

12.23 **Given:** NaCl and water; 145 g NaCl in 1.00 L solution **Find:** M, m, and mass percent
Other: $d = 1.08$ g/mL
Conceptual Plan: $g_{\text{NaCl}} \rightarrow$ mol and L $\rightarrow$ mL $\rightarrow g_{\text{soln}}$ and $g_{\text{soln}} \ g_{\text{NaCl}} \rightarrow g_{H_2O} \rightarrow kg_{H_2O}$ then

$$\frac{1 \text{ mol NaCl}}{58.44 \text{ g NaCl}} \qquad \frac{1000 \text{ mL}}{1 \text{ L}} \quad \frac{1.08 \text{ g}}{1 \text{ mL}} \qquad g_{H_2O} = g_{\text{soln}} - g_{\text{NaCl}} \qquad \frac{1 \text{ kg}}{1000 \text{ g}}$$

mol, $V \rightarrow$ **M** and mol, $kg_{H_2O} \rightarrow m$ and $g_{\text{soln}} \ g_{\text{NaCl}} \rightarrow$ **mass percent**

$$M = \frac{\text{amount solute (moles)}}{\text{volume solution (L)}} \qquad m = \frac{\text{amount solute (moles)}}{\text{mass solvent (kg)}} \qquad \text{mass percent} = \frac{\text{mass solute}}{\text{mass solution}} \times 100\%$$

Solution: $145 \text{ g NaCl} \times \dfrac{1 \text{ mol NaCl}}{58.44 \text{ g NaCl}} = 2.4\underline{8}1177 \text{ mol NaCl}$ and

$1.00 \text{ L} \times \dfrac{1000 \text{ mL}}{1 \text{ L}} \times \dfrac{1.08 \text{ g}}{1 \text{ mL}} = 10\underline{8}0 \text{ g soln}$ and

$g_{H_2O} = g_{soln} - g_{NaCl} = 10\underline{8}0 \text{ g} - 145 \text{ g} = 9\underline{3}5 \text{ g H}_2\text{O} \times \dfrac{1 \text{ kg}}{1000 \text{ g}} = 0.9\underline{3}5 \text{ kg H}_2\text{O}$ then

$M = \dfrac{\text{amount solute (moles)}}{\text{volume solution (L)}} = \dfrac{2.4\underline{8}1177 \text{ mol NaCl}}{1.00 \text{ L soln}} = 2.48 \text{ M}$ and

$m = \dfrac{\text{amount solute (moles)}}{\text{mass solvent (kg)}} = \dfrac{2.4\underline{8}1177 \text{ mol NaCl}}{0.9\underline{3}5 \text{ kg H}_2\text{O}} = 2.7 \ m$ and

$\text{mass percent} = \dfrac{\text{mass solute}}{\text{mass solution}} \times 100\% = \dfrac{145 \text{ g NaCl}}{10\underline{8}0 \text{ g soln}} \times 100\% = 13.4\% \text{ by mass}$

Check: The units (M, m, and percent by mass) are correct. The magnitude of the answer (2.5 M) seems reasonable because we have 145 g NaCl, which is a couple of moles, and we have 1 L. The magnitude of the answer (2.7 m) seems reasonable because it is a little higher than the molarity, which we expect because we only use the solvent weight in the denominator. The magnitude of the answer (10%) seems reasonable because we have 145 g NaCl and just under 1000 g of solution.

12.25   **Given:** initial solution: 50.0 mL of 5.00 M KI; final solution contains 3.25 g KI in 25.0 mL
Find: final volume to dilute initial solution to
Conceptual Plan: final solution: $g_{KI} \rightarrow$ **mol and** $mL \rightarrow L$ **then** $mol, V \rightarrow M_2$ **then** $M_1, V_1, M_2 \rightarrow V_2$

$\dfrac{1 \text{ mol KI}}{166.00 \text{ g KI}} \qquad \dfrac{1 \text{ L}}{1000 \text{ mL}} \qquad M = \dfrac{\text{amount solute (moles)}}{\text{volume solution (L)}} \qquad M_1 V_1 = M_2 V_2$

Solution: $3.25 \text{ g KI} \times \dfrac{1 \text{ mol KI}}{166.00 \text{ g KI}} = 0.019\underline{5}783 \text{ mol KI}$ and $25.0 \text{ mL} \times \dfrac{1 \text{ L}}{1000 \text{ mL}} = 0.0250 \text{ L}$

then $M = \dfrac{\text{amount solute (moles)}}{\text{volume solution (L)}} = \dfrac{0.019\underline{5}783 \text{ mol KI}}{0.0250 \text{ L soln}} = 0.78\underline{3}132 \text{ M}$ then $M_1 V_1 = M_2 V_2$

Rearrange to solve for V_2. $V_2 = \dfrac{M_1}{M_2} \times V_1 = \dfrac{5.00 \text{ M}}{0.78\underline{3}132 \text{ M}} \times 50.0 \text{ mL} = 319. \text{ mL diluted volume}$

Check: The units (mL) are correct. The magnitude of the answer (320 mL) seems reasonable because we are starting with a concentration of 5 M and ending with a concentration of less than 1 M.

12.27   **Given:** $AgNO_3$ and water; 3.4% Ag by mass, 4.8 L solution   **Find:** m (Ag) **Other:** $d = 1.01 \text{ g/mL}$
Conceptual Plan: $L \rightarrow mL \rightarrow g_{soln} \rightarrow g_{Ag}$

$\dfrac{1000 \text{ mL}}{1 \text{ L}} \qquad \dfrac{1.01 \text{ g}}{1 \text{ mL}} \qquad \dfrac{3.4 \text{ g Ag}}{100 \text{ g soln}}$

Solution: $4.8 \text{ L} \times \dfrac{1000 \text{ mL}}{1 \text{ L}} \times \dfrac{1.01 \text{ g}}{1 \text{ mL}} = 4\underline{8}48 \text{ g soln}$ then

$4\underline{8}48 \text{ g soln} \times \dfrac{3.4 \text{ g Ag}}{100 \text{ g soln}} = 160 \text{ g Ag} = 1.6 \times 10^2 \text{ g Ag}$

Check: The units (g) are correct. The magnitude of the answer (160 g) seems reasonable because we have almost 5000 g of solution.

12.29   **Given:** Ca^{2+} and water; 0.0085% Ca^{2+} by mass, 1.2 g Ca   **Find:** m (water)
Conceptual Plan: $g_{Ca} \rightarrow g_{soln} \rightarrow g_{H_2O}$

$\dfrac{100 \text{ g soln}}{0.0085 \text{ g Ca}} \qquad g_{H_2O} = g_{soln} - g_{Ca}$

Solution: $1.2 \text{ g Ca} \times \dfrac{100 \text{ g soln}}{0.0085 \text{ g Ca}} = 1\underline{4}118 \text{ g soln}$ then

$g_{H_2O} = g_{soln} - g_{Ca} = 1\underline{4}118 \text{ g} - 1.2 \text{ g} = 1.4 \times 10^4 \text{ g water}$

Check: The units (g) are correct. The magnitude of the answer (10^4 g) seems reasonable because we have such a low concentration of Ca.

12.31   **Given:** concentrated HNO_3: 70.3% HNO_3 by mass, $d = 1.41$ g/mL; final solution: 1.15 L of 0.100 M HNO_3
         Find: describe final solution preparation
         Conceptual Plan: $M_2, V_2 \rightarrow \text{mol}_{HNO_3} \rightarrow \text{g}_{HNO_3} \rightarrow \text{g}_{\text{conc acid}} \rightarrow \text{mL}_{\text{conc acid}}$ **then describe method**

$$mol = MV \qquad \frac{63.02 \text{ g } HNO_3}{1 \text{ mol } HNO_3} \qquad \frac{100 \text{ g conc acid}}{70.3 \text{ g } HNO_3} \qquad \frac{1 \text{ mL}}{1.41 \text{ g}}$$

Solution: $mol = MV = 0.100 \dfrac{\text{mol } HNO_3}{1 \text{ L soln}} \times 1.15 \text{ L soln} = 0.115 \text{ mol } HNO_3$ then

$$0.115 \text{ mol } HNO_3 \times \frac{63.02 \text{ g } HNO_3}{1 \text{ mol } HNO_3} \times \frac{100 \text{ g conc acid}}{70.3 \text{ g } HNO_3} \times \frac{1 \text{ mL conc acid}}{1.41 \text{ g conc acid}} = 7.31 \text{ mL conc acid}$$

Prepare the solution by putting about 1.00 L of distilled water in a container. Carefully pour in the 7.31 mL of the concentrated acid, mix the solution, and allow it to cool. Finally, add enough water to generate the total volume of solution (1.15 L). It is important to add acid to water, not the reverse, because such a large amount of heat is released upon mixing.

Check: The units (mL) are correct. The magnitude of the answer (7 mL) seems reasonable because we are starting with such a concentrated solution and diluting it to a low concentration.

12.33   (a)   **Given:** 1.00×10^2 mL of 0.500 M KCl   **Find:** describe final solution preparation
                Conceptual Plan: $\text{mL} \rightarrow \text{L}$ **then** $M, V \rightarrow \text{mol}_{KCl} \rightarrow \text{g}_{KCl}$ **then describe method**

$$\frac{1 \text{ L}}{1000 \text{ mL}} \qquad\qquad mol = MV \qquad \frac{74.55 \text{ g KCl}}{1 \text{ mol KCl}}$$

Solution: $1.00 \times 10^2 \text{ mL} \times \dfrac{1 \text{ L}}{1000 \text{ mL}} = 0.100 \text{ L}$

$$mol = MV = 0.500 \frac{\text{mol KCl}}{1 \text{ L soln}} \times 0.100 \text{ L soln} = 0.0500 \text{ mol KCl}$$

then $0.0500 \text{ mol KCl} \times \dfrac{74.55 \text{ g KCl}}{1 \text{ mol KCl}} = 3.73 \text{ g KCl}$

Prepare the solution by carefully adding 3.73 g KCl to a 100 mL volumetric flask. Add ~75 mL of distilled water and agitate the solution until the salt dissolves completely. Finally, add enough water to generate a total volume of solution (add water to the mark on the flask).

Check: The units (g) are correct. The magnitude of the answer (4 g) seems reasonable because we are making a small volume of solution and the formula weight of KCl is ~75 g/mol.

(b)   **Given:** 1.00×10^2 g of 0.500 m KCl   **Find:** describe final solution preparation
       Conceptual Plan:
       $m \rightarrow \text{mol}_{KCl}/1 \text{ kg solvent} \rightarrow \text{g}_{KCl}/1 \text{ kg solvent}$ **then** $\text{g}_{KCl}/1 \text{ kg solvent, g}_{\text{soln}} \rightarrow \text{g}_{KCl}, \text{g}_{H_2O}$

$$m = \frac{\text{amount solute (moles)}}{\text{mass solvent (kg)}} \qquad \frac{74.55 \text{ g KCl}}{1 \text{ mol KCl}} \qquad\qquad\qquad g_{\text{soln}} = g_{KCl} + g_{H_2O}$$

then describe method

Solution: $m = \dfrac{\text{amount solute (moles)}}{\text{mass solvent (kg)}}$ so $0.500 \ m = \dfrac{0.500 \text{ mol KCl}}{1 \text{ kg } H_2O}$ so

$\dfrac{0.500 \text{ mol KCl}}{1 \text{ kg } H_2O} \times \dfrac{74.55 \text{ g KCl}}{1 \text{ mol KCl}} = \dfrac{37.2\underline{8} \text{ g KCl}}{1000 \text{ g } H_2O}$; $g_{\text{soln}} = g_{KCl} + g_{H_2O}$ so $g_{\text{soln}} - g_{KCl} = g_{H_2O}$

substitute into ratio $\dfrac{37.2\underline{8} \text{ g KCl}}{1037.28 \text{ g solution}} = \dfrac{x \text{ g KCl}}{100 \text{ g solution}}$.

$100 \text{ g solution} \times \dfrac{37.2\underline{8} \text{ g KCl}}{1037.28 \text{ g solution}} = \dfrac{x \text{ g KCl}}{100 \text{ g solution}} \times 100 \text{ g solution}$

$x \text{ g KCl} = \dfrac{372\underline{8} \text{ g KCl}}{1037.28}$; $x \text{ g KCl} = 3.5\underline{9}4015 \text{ g KCl}$

$g_{H_2O} = g_{\text{soln}} - g_{KCl} = 100. \text{ g} - 3.59 \text{ g} = 96.41 \text{ g } H_2O$

Prepare the solution by carefully adding 3.59 g KCl to a container with 96.41 g of distilled water and agitate the solution until the salt dissolves completely.

Check: The units (g) are correct. The magnitude of the answer (3.6 g) seems reasonable because we are making a small volume of solution and the formula weight of KCl is ~75 g/mol.

(c)   **Given:** 1.00×10^2 g of 5.0% KCl by mass   **Find:** describe final solution preparation

        Conceptual Plan: $g_{soln} \rightarrow g_{KCl}$ then $g_{KCl}, g_{soln} \rightarrow g_{H_2O}$

$$\frac{5.0 \text{ g KCl}}{100 \text{ g soln}} \qquad\qquad g_{soln} = g_{KCl} + g_{H_2O}$$

        then describe method

        Solution: 1.00×10^2 g soln $\times \dfrac{5.0 \text{ g KCl}}{100 \text{ g soln}} = 5.0$ g KCl then $g_{soln} = g_{KCl} + g_{H_2O}$

        So $g_{H_2O} = g_{soln} - g_{KCl} = 100.$ g $- 5.0$ g $= 95$ g H_2O

        Prepare the solution by carefully adding 5.0 g KCl to a container with 95 g of distilled water and agitate the solution until the salt dissolves completely.

        Check: The units (g) are correct. The magnitude of the answer (5 g) seems reasonable because we are making a small volume of solution and the solution is 5% by mass KCl.

12.35   (a)   **Given:** 28.4 g of glucose ($C_6H_{12}O_6$) in 355 g water; final volume $= 378$ mL   **Find:** molarity

        Conceptual Plan: mL $\rightarrow$ L and $g_{C_6H_{12}O_6} \rightarrow mol_{C_6H_{12}O_6}$ then $mol_{C_6H_{12}O_6}, V \rightarrow$ **M**

$$\frac{1 \text{ L}}{1000 \text{ mL}} \qquad \frac{1 \text{ mol } C_6H_{12}O_6}{180.16 \text{ g } C_6H_{12}O_6} \qquad M = \frac{\text{amount solute (moles)}}{\text{volume solution (L)}}$$

        Solution: 378 mL $\times \dfrac{1 \text{ L}}{1000 \text{ mL}} = 0.378$ L and

        28.4 g $C_6H_{12}O_6 \times \dfrac{1 \text{ mol } C_6H_{12}O_6}{180.16 \text{ g } C_6H_{12}O_6} = 0.15\underline{7}638$ mol $C_6H_{12}O_6$

        $M = \dfrac{\text{amount solute (moles)}}{\text{volume solution (L)}} = \dfrac{0.15\underline{7}638 \text{ mol } C_6H_{12}O_6}{0.378 \text{ L}} = 0.417$ M

        Check: The units (M) are correct. The magnitude of the answer (0.4 M) seems reasonable because we have 1/8 mole in about 1/3 L.

(b)   **Given:** 28.4 g of glucose ($C_6H_{12}O_6$) in 355 g water; final volume $= 378$ mL   **Find:** molality

        Conceptual Plan: $g_{H_2O} \rightarrow kg_{H_2O}$ and $g_{C_6H_{12}O_6} \rightarrow mol_{C_6H_{12}O_6}$ then $mol_{C_6H_{12}O_6}, kg_{H_2O} \rightarrow m$

$$\frac{1 \text{ kg}}{1000 \text{ g}} \qquad \frac{1 \text{ mol } C_6H_{12}O_6}{180.16 \text{ g } C_6H_{12}O_6} \qquad m = \frac{\text{amount solute (moles)}}{\text{mass solvent (kg)}}$$

        Solution: 355 g $\times \dfrac{1 \text{ kg}}{1000 \text{ g}} = 0.355$ kg and

        28.4 g $C_6H_{12}O_6 \times \dfrac{1 \text{ mol } C_6H_{12}O_6}{180.16 \text{ g } C_6H_{12}O_6} = 0.15\underline{7}638$ mol $C_6H_{12}O_6$

        $m = \dfrac{\text{amount solute (moles)}}{\text{mass solvent (kg)}} = \dfrac{0.15\underline{7}638 \text{ mol } C_6H_{12}O_6}{0.355 \text{ kg}} = 0.444\ m$

        Check: The units (m) are correct. The magnitude of the answer (0.4 m) seems reasonable because we have 1/8 mole in about 1/3 kg.

(c)   **Given:** 28.4 g of glucose ($C_6H_{12}O_6$) in 355 g water; final volume $= 378$ mL   **Find:** percent by mass

        Conceptual Plan: $g_{C_6H_{12}O_6}, g_{H_2O} \rightarrow g_{soln}$ then $g_{C_6H_{12}O_6}, g_{soln} \rightarrow$ **percent by mass**

$$g_{soln} = g_{C_6H_{12}O_6} + g_{H_2O} \qquad \text{mass percent} = \frac{\text{mass solute}}{\text{mass solution}} \times 100\%$$

        Solution: $g_{soln} = g_{C_6H_{12}O_6} + g_{H_2O} = 28.4$ g $+ 355$ g $= 38\underline{3}.4$ g soln then

        mass percent $= \dfrac{\text{mass solute}}{\text{mass solution}} \times 100\% = \dfrac{28.4 \text{ g } C_6H_{12}O_6}{38\underline{3}.4 \text{ g soln}} \times 100\% = 7.41\%$ by mass

        Check: The units (percent by mass) are correct. The magnitude of the answer (7%) seems reasonable because we are dissolving 28 g in 355 g.

(d)   **Given:** 28.4 g of glucose ($C_6H_{12}O_6$) in 355 g water; final volume $= 378$ mL   **Find:** mole fraction

        Conceptual Plan: $g_{C_6H_{12}O_6} \rightarrow mol_{C_6H_{12}O_6}$ and $g_{H_2O} \rightarrow mol_{H_2O}$ then $mol_{C_6H_{12}O_6}, mol_{H_2O} \rightarrow \chi_{C_6H_{12}O_6}$

$$\frac{1 \text{ mol } C_6H_{12}O_6}{180.16 \text{ g } C_6H_{12}O_6} \qquad \frac{1 \text{ mol } H_2O}{18.02 \text{ g } H_2O} \qquad \chi = \frac{\text{amount solute (in moles)}}{\text{total amount of solute and solvent (in moles)}}$$

Solution: $28.4 \ \text{g} \ \cancel{C_6H_{12}O_6} \times \dfrac{1 \ \text{mol} \ C_6H_{12}O_6}{180.16 \ \text{g} \ \cancel{C_6H_{12}O_6}} = 0.15\underline{7}638 \ \text{mol} \ C_6H_{12}O_6$ and

$355 \ \text{g} \ \cancel{H_2O} \times \dfrac{1 \ \text{mol} \ H_2O}{18.02 \ \text{g} \ \cancel{H_2O}} = 19.\underline{7}003 \ \text{mol} \ H_2O$ then

$\chi = \dfrac{\text{amount solute (in moles)}}{\text{total amount of solute and solvent (in moles)}} = \dfrac{0.15\underline{7}638 \ \cancel{\text{mol}}}{0.15\underline{7}638 \ \cancel{\text{mol}} + 19.\underline{7}003 \ \cancel{\text{mol}}} = 0.00794$

Check: The units (none) are correct. The magnitude of the answer (0.008) seems reasonable because we have many more grams of water and water has a much lower molecular weight.

(e)   **Given:** 28.4 g of glucose ($C_6H_{12}O_6$) in 355 g water; final volume = 378 mL   **Find:** mole percent
Conceptual Plan: use answer from part (d) then $\chi_{C_6H_{12}O_6} \rightarrow$ **mole percent**
$$\chi \times 100\%$$

Solution: mole percent $= \chi \times 100\% = 0.00794 \times 100\% = 0.794$ mole percent

Check: The units (%) are correct. The magnitude of the answer (0.8) seems reasonable because we have many more grams of water, water has a much lower molecular weight than glucose, and we are increasing the answer from part (d) by a factor of 100.

12.37   **Given:** 3.0% H_2O_2 by mass, $d = 1.01$ g/mL   **Find:** molarity
Conceptual Plan:
Assume exactly 100 g of solution; $g_{solution} \rightarrow g_{H_2O_2} \rightarrow mol_{H_2O_2}$ **and** $g_{solution} \rightarrow mL_{solution} \rightarrow L_{solution}$
$$\dfrac{3.0 \ \text{g} \ H_2O_2}{100 \ \text{g solution}} \quad \dfrac{1 \ \text{mol} \ H_2O_2}{34.02 \ \text{g} \ H_2O_2} \qquad\qquad \dfrac{1 \ \text{mL}}{1.01 \ \text{g}} \quad \dfrac{1 \ \text{L}}{1000 \ \text{mL}}$$

then $mol_{H_2O_2}, L_{solution} \rightarrow M$
$$M = \dfrac{\text{amount solute (moles)}}{\text{volume solution (L)}}$$

Solution: $100 \ \text{g} \cancel{\text{ solution}} \times \dfrac{3.0 \ \text{g} \ \cancel{H_2O_2}}{100 \ \text{g} \cancel{\text{ solution}}} \times \dfrac{1 \ \text{mol} \ H_2O_2}{34.02 \ \text{g} \ \cancel{H_2O_2}} = 0.08\underline{8}1834 \ \text{mol} \ H_2O_2$ and

$100 \ \text{g} \cancel{\text{ solution}} \times \dfrac{1 \ \text{mL} \cancel{\text{ solution}}}{1.01 \ \text{g} \cancel{\text{ solution}}} \times \dfrac{1 \ \text{L solution}}{1000 \ \text{mL} \cancel{\text{ solution}}} = 0.099\underline{0}099 \ \text{L solution}$ then

$M = \dfrac{\text{amount solute (moles)}}{\text{volume solution (L)}} = \dfrac{0.08\underline{8}1834 \ \text{mol} \ H_2O_2}{0.099\underline{0}099 \ \text{L solution}} = 0.89 \ \text{M} \ H_2O_2.$

Check: The units (M) are correct. The magnitude of the answer (1) seems reasonable because we are starting with a low concentration solution and pure water is ~ 55.5 M.

12.39   **Given:** 36% HCl by mass   **Find:** molality and mole fraction
Conceptual Plan: Assume exactly 100 g of solution; $g_{solution} \rightarrow g_{HCl} \rightarrow mol_{HCl}$ **and** $g_{HCl}, g_{solution} \rightarrow$
$$\dfrac{36 \ \text{g HCl}}{100 \ \text{g solution}} \quad \dfrac{1 \ \text{mol HCl}}{36.46 \ \text{g HCl}} \qquad\qquad g_{soln} = g_{HCl} + g_{H_2O}$$

$g_{solvent} \rightarrow kg_{solvent}$ **then** $mol_{HCl}, kg_{solvent} \rightarrow m$ **and** $g_{solvent} \rightarrow mol_{solvent}$ **then** $mol_{HCl}, mol_{solvent} \rightarrow \chi_{HCl}$
$$\dfrac{1 \ \text{kg}}{1000 \ \text{g}} \qquad m = \dfrac{\text{amount solute (moles)}}{\text{mass solvent (kg)}} \quad \dfrac{1 \ \text{mol} \ H_2O}{18.02 \ \text{g} \ H_2O} \qquad \chi = \dfrac{\text{amount solute (in moles)}}{\text{total amount of solute and solvent (in moles)}}$$

Solution: $100 \ \text{g} \cancel{\text{ solution}} \times \dfrac{36 \ \text{g HCl}}{100 \ \text{g} \cancel{\text{ solution}}} = 36 \ \text{g} \cancel{\text{ HCl}} \times \dfrac{1 \ \text{mol HCl}}{36.46 \ \text{g} \cancel{\text{ HCl}}} = 0.98\underline{7}383 \ \text{mol HCl}$ and

$g_{soln} = g_{HCl} + g_{H_2O}$. Rearrange to solve for $g_{solvent}$. $g_{H_2O} = g_{soln} - g_{HCl} = 100 \ \text{g} - 36 \ \text{g} = 64 \ \text{g} \ H_2O$

$64 \ \text{g} \cancel{H_2O} \times \dfrac{1 \ \text{kg} \ H_2O}{1000 \ \text{g} \cancel{H_2O}} = 0.064 \ \text{kg} \ H_2O$ then

$m = \dfrac{\text{amount solute (moles)}}{\text{mass solvent (kg)}} = \dfrac{0.98\underline{7}383 \ \text{mol HCl}}{0.064 \ \text{kg}} = 15 \ m \ \text{HCl}$ and

$64 \ \text{g} \cancel{H_2O} \times \dfrac{1 \ \text{mol} \ H_2O}{18.02 \ \text{g} \cancel{H_2O}} = 3.\underline{5}5161 \ \text{mol} \ H_2O$ then

$\chi = \dfrac{\text{amount solute (in moles)}}{\text{total amount of solute and solvent (in moles)}} = \dfrac{0.98\underline{7}383 \ \cancel{\text{mol}}}{0.98\underline{7}383 \ \cancel{\text{mol}} + 3.\underline{5}5161 \ \cancel{\text{mol}}} = 0.22$

Check: The units (*m* and unitless) are correct. The magnitude of the answers (15 and 0.2) seems reasonable because we are starting with a high concentration solution and the molar mass of water is much less than that of HCl.

Vapor Pressure of Solutions

12.41   The level has decreased more in the beaker filled with pure water. The dissolved salt in the seawater decreases the vapor pressure and subsequently lowers the rate of vaporization.

12.43   **Given:** 28.5 g of glycerin ($C_3H_8O_3$) in 125 mL water at 30 °C; $P^\circ_{H_2O} = 31.8$ torr   **Find:** P_{H_2O}
   Other: $d(H_2O) = 1.00$ g/mL; glycerin is not ionic solid
   Conceptual Plan: $g_{C_3H_8O_3} \rightarrow mol_{C_3H_8O_3}$ and $mL_{H_2O} \rightarrow g_{H_2O} \rightarrow mol_{H_2O}$ then $mol_{C_3H_8O_3}, mol_{H_2O} \rightarrow \chi_{H_2O}$

$$\frac{1\ mol\ C_3H_8O_3}{92.09\ g\ C_3H_8O_3} \qquad \frac{1.00\ g}{1\ mL} \quad \frac{1\ mol\ H_2O}{18.02\ g\ H_2O} \qquad \chi = \frac{amount\ solute\ (in\ moles)}{total\ amount\ of\ solute\ and\ solvent\ (in\ moles)}$$

   then $\chi_{H_2O}, P^\circ_{H_2O} \rightarrow P_{H_2O}$

$$P_{solution} = \chi_{solvent} P^\circ_{solvent}$$

   Solution: $28.5\ g\ C_3H_8O_3 \times \dfrac{1\ mol\ C_3H_8O_3}{92.09\ g\ C_3H_8O_3} = 0.309\underline{4}799\ mol\ C_3H_8O_3$ and

$$125\ mL \times \frac{1.00\ g}{1\ mL} \times \frac{1\ mol\ H_2O}{18.02\ g\ H_2O} = 6.9\underline{3}6737\ mol\ H_2O \text{ then}$$

$$\chi = \frac{amount\ solute\ (in\ moles)}{total\ amount\ of\ solute\ and\ solvent\ (in\ moles)} = \frac{6.9\underline{3}6737\ mol}{0.309\underline{4}799\ mol + 6.9\underline{3}6737\ mol} = 0.957\underline{2}91 \text{ then}$$

$$P_{solution} = \chi_{solvent} P^\circ_{solvent} = 0.957\underline{2}91 \times 31.8\ torr = 30.4\ torr$$

   Check: The units (torr) are correct. The magnitude of the answer (30 torr) seems reasonable because it is a drop from the pure vapor pressure. Very few moles of glycerin are added, so the pressure will not drop much.

12.45   (a)   **Given:** 50.0 g of heptane (C_7H_{16}) and 50.0 g of octane (C_8H_{18}) at 25 °C; $P^\circ_{C_7H_{16}} = 45.8$ torr; $P^\circ_{C_8H_{18}} = 10.9$ torr
       Find: $P_{C_7H_{16}}, P_{C_8H_{18}}$
       Conceptual Plan: $g_{C_7H_{16}} \rightarrow mol_{C_7H_{16}}$ and $g_{C_8H_{18}} \rightarrow mol_{C_8H_{18}}$ then $mol_{C_7H_{16}}$,

$$\frac{1\ mol\ C_7H_{16}}{100.20\ g\ C_7H_{16}} \quad \frac{1\ mol\ C_8H_{18}}{114.22\ g\ C_8H_{18}} \quad \chi_{C_7H_{16}} = \frac{amount\ C_7H_{16}\ (in\ moles)}{total\ amount\ (in\ moles)}$$

       $mol_{C_8H_{18}} \rightarrow \chi_{C_7H_{16}}, \chi_{C_8H_{18}}$ then $\chi_{C_7H_{16}}, P^\circ_{C_7H_{16}} \rightarrow P_{C_7H_{16}}$ and $\chi_{C_8H_{18}}, P^\circ_{C_8H_{18}} \rightarrow P_{C_8H_{18}}$

$$\chi_{C_8H_{18}} = 1 - \chi_{C_7H_{16}} \qquad P_{C_7H_{16}} = \chi_{C_7H_{16}} P^\circ_{C_7H_{16}} \qquad P_{C_8H_{18}} = \chi_{C_8H_{18}} P^\circ_{C_8H_{18}}$$

       Solution: $50.0\ g\ C_7H_{16} \times \dfrac{1\ mol\ C_7H_{16}}{100.20\ g\ C_7H_{16}} = 0.49\underline{9}002\ mol\ C_7H_{16}$ and

$$50.0\ g\ C_8H_{18} \times \frac{1\ mol\ C_8H_{18}}{114.22\ g\ C_8H_{18}} = 0.43\underline{7}752\ mol\ C_8H_{18} \text{ then}$$

$$\chi_{C_7H_{16}} = \frac{amount\ C_7H_{16}\ (in\ moles)}{total\ amount\ (in\ moles)} = \frac{0.49\underline{9}002\ mol}{0.49\underline{9}002\ mol + 0.43\underline{7}752\ mol} = 0.53\underline{2}693 \text{ and}$$

$$\chi_{C_8H_{18}} = 1 - \chi_{C_7H_{16}} = 1 - 0.53\underline{2}693 = 0.46\underline{7}307 \text{ then}$$
$$P_{C_7H_{16}} = \chi_{C_7H_{16}} P^\circ_{C_7H_{16}} = 0.53\underline{2}693 \times 45.8\ torr = 24.4\ torr \text{ and}$$
$$P_{C_8H_{18}} = \chi_{C_8H_{18}} P^\circ_{C_8H_{18}} = 0.46\underline{7}307 \times 10.9\ torr = 5.09\ torr$$

       Check: The units (torr) are correct. The magnitude of the answers (24 and 5 torr) seems reasonable because we expect a drop in half from the pure vapor pressures because we have roughly a 50:50 mole ratio of the two components.

      (b)   **Find:** P_{Total}
          Conceptual Plan: $P_{C_7H_{16}}, P_{C_8H_{18}} \rightarrow P_{Total}$

$$P_{Total} = P_{C_7H_{16}} + P_{C_8H_{18}}$$

          Solution: $P_{Total} = P_{C_7H_{16}} + P_{C_8H_{18}} = 24.4\ torr + 5.09\ torr = 29.5\ torr$

          Check: The units (torr) are correct. The magnitude of the answer (30 torr) seems reasonable considering the two pressures.

(c) **Find:** mass percent composition of the gas phase

Conceptual Plan: because $n \propto P$ and we are calculating a mass percent, which is a ratio of masses, we can simply convert 1 torr to 1 mole so

$$P_{C_7H_{16}}, P_{C_8H_{18}} \rightarrow n_{C_7H_{16}}, n_{C_8H_{18}} \text{ then } mol_{C_7H_{16}} \rightarrow g_{C_7H_{16}} \text{ and } mol_{C_8H_{18}} \rightarrow g_{C_8H_{18}}$$

$$\frac{100.20 \text{ g } C_7H_{16}}{1 \text{ mol } C_7H_{16}} \qquad \frac{114.22 \text{ g } C_8H_{18}}{1 \text{ mol } C_8H_{18}}$$

then $g_{C_7H_{16}}, g_{C_8H_{18}} \rightarrow$ mass percents

$$\text{mass percent} = \frac{\text{mass solute}}{\text{mass solution}} \times 100\%$$

Solution: so $n_{C_7H_{16}} = 24.4$ mol and $n_{C_8H_{18}} = 5.09$ mol then

$$24.4 \text{ mol } C_7H_{16} \times \frac{100.20 \text{ g } C_7H_{16}}{1 \text{ mol } C_7H_{16}} = 2444.88 \text{ g } C_7H_{16} \text{ and}$$

$$5.09 \text{ mol } C_8H_{18} \times \frac{114.22 \text{ g } C_8H_{18}}{1 \text{ mol } C_8H_{18}} = 581.380 \text{ g } C_8H_{18} \text{ then}$$

$$\text{mass percent} = \frac{\text{mass solute}}{\text{mass solution}} \times 100\% = \frac{2444.88 \text{ g } C_7H_{16}}{2444.88 \text{ g } C_7H_{16} + 581.380 \text{ g } C_8H_{18}} \times 100\%$$

$$= 80.8\% \text{ by mass } C_7H_{16}$$

then $100\% - 80.8\% = 19.2\%$ by mass C_8H_{18}

Check: The units (%) are correct. The magnitude of the answers (81% and 19%) seems reasonable considering the two pressures.

The two mass percents are different because the vapor is richer in the more volatile component (the lighter molecule).

12.47 **Given:** 5.50% NaCl by mass   **Find:** P_{H_2O}

Other: $P^\circ_{H_2O} = 23.78$ torr at 25 °C

Conceptual Plan: Assume exactly 100 g of solution;

$$g_{Solution} \rightarrow g_{NaCl}, \rightarrow mol_{NaCl} \rightarrow mol_{ions} \text{ and } g_{NaCl}, g_{Solution} \rightarrow g_{H_2O} \rightarrow mol_{H_2O}$$

$$\frac{5.50 \text{ g NaCl}}{100 \text{ g solution}} \quad \frac{1 \text{ mol NaCl}}{58.44 \text{ g NaCl}} \quad \frac{2 \text{ mol ions}}{1 \text{ mol NaCl}} \qquad g_{Solution} = g_{NaCl} + g_{H_2O} \quad \frac{1 \text{ mol } H_2O}{18.02 \text{ g } H_2O}$$

then $mol_{ions}, mol_{H_2O} \rightarrow \chi_{H_2O}$ then $\chi_{H_2O}, P^\circ_{H_2O} \rightarrow P_{H_2O}$

$$\chi = \frac{\text{amount solute (in moles)}}{\text{total amount of solute and solvent (in moles)}} \qquad P_{solution} = \chi_{solvent} P^\circ_{solvent}$$

Solution:

$$100 \text{ g solution} \times \frac{5.50 \text{ g NaCl}}{100 \text{ g solution}} = 5.50 \text{ g HCl} \times \frac{1 \text{ mol NaCl}}{58.44 \text{ g NaCl}} \times \frac{2 \text{ mol ions}}{1 \text{ mol NaCl}} = 0.18822724 \text{ mol ions and}$$

$g_{solution} = g_{NaCl} + g_{H_2O}$ Rearrange to solve for g_{H_2O}.

$$g_{H_2O} = g_{solution} - g_{NaCl} = 100.00 \text{ g} - 5.50 \text{ g} = 94.50 \text{ g}_{H_2O}$$

then $94.50 \text{ g } H_2O \times \dfrac{1 \text{ mol } H_2O}{18.02 \text{ g } H_2O} = 5.244173 \text{ mol } H_2O$ then

$$\chi = \frac{\text{amount solute (in moles)}}{\text{total amount of solute and solvent (in moles)}} = \frac{5.244173 \text{ mol}}{0.18822724 \text{ mol} + 5.244173 \text{ mol}} = 0.9653510$$

$$P_{solution} = \chi_{solvent} P^\circ_{solvent} = 0.9653510 \times 23.78 \text{ torr} = 22.96 \text{ torr}$$

Check: The units (torr) are correct. The magnitude of the answer (23 torr) seems reasonable because we have a dilute solution, so the vapor decreases only a small amount.

Freezing Point Depression, Boiling Point Elevation, and Osmosis

12.49 **Given:** 55.8 g of glucose ($C_6H_{12}O_6$) in 455 g water   **Find:** T_f and T_b **Other:** $K_f = 1.86$ °C/m; $K_b = 0.512$ °C/m;

Conceptual Plan: $g_{H_2O} \rightarrow kg_{H_2O}$ and $g_{C_6H_{12}O_6} \rightarrow mol_{C_6H_{12}O_6}$ then $mol_{C_6H_{12}O_6}, kg_{H_2O} \rightarrow m$

$$\frac{1 \text{ kg}}{1000 \text{ g}} \qquad \frac{1 \text{ mol } C_6H_{12}O_6}{180.16 \text{ g } C_6H_{12}O_6} \qquad m = \frac{\text{amount solute (moles)}}{\text{mass solvent (kg)}}$$

$m, K_f \rightarrow \Delta T_f \rightarrow T_f$ and $m, K_b \rightarrow \Delta T_b \rightarrow T_b$

$\Delta T_f = K_f \times m \quad T_f = T_f^\circ - \Delta T_f \qquad \Delta T_b = K_b \times m \quad \Delta T_b = T_b - T_b^\circ$

Solution: $455 \text{ g} \times \dfrac{1 \text{ kg}}{1000 \text{ g}} = 0.455 \text{ kg}$ and $55.8 \text{ g C}_6\text{H}_{12}\text{O}_6 \times \dfrac{1 \text{ mol C}_6\text{H}_{12}\text{O}_6}{180.16 \text{ g C}_6\text{H}_{12}\text{O}_6} = 0.309\underline{7}25 \text{ mol C}_6\text{H}_{12}\text{O}_6$ then

$m = \dfrac{\text{amount solute (moles)}}{\text{mass solvent (kg)}} = \dfrac{0.309\underline{7}25 \text{ mol C}_6\text{H}_{12}\text{O}_6}{0.455 \text{ kg}} = 0.680\underline{7}14 \; m$ then

$\Delta T_f = K_f \times m = 1.86 \dfrac{^\circ\text{C}}{m} \times 0.680\underline{7}14 \; m = 1.27 \text{ }^\circ\text{C}$ then $T_f = T_f^\circ - \Delta T_f = 0.00 \text{ }^\circ\text{C} - 1.27 \text{ }^\circ\text{C} = -1.27 \text{ }^\circ\text{C}$ and

$\Delta T_b = K_b \times m = 0.512 \dfrac{^\circ\text{C}}{m} \times 0.680\underline{7}14 \; m = 0.349 \text{ }^\circ\text{C}$ and $\Delta T_b = T_b - T_b^\circ$ so

$T_b = T_b^\circ + \Delta T_b = 100.000 \text{ }^\circ\text{C} + 0.349 \text{ }^\circ\text{C} = 100.349 \text{ }^\circ\text{C}$

Check: The units ($^\circ$C) are correct. The magnitude of the answers seems reasonable because the molality is ~2/3. The shift in boiling point is less than the shift in freezing point because the constant for boiling is smaller than the constant for freezing.

12.51   **Given:** 10.0 g of naphthalene ($C_{10}H_8$) in 100.0 mL benzene (C_6H_6)   **Find:** T_f and T_b
Other: d(benzene) $= 0.877$ g/cm^3; $K_f = 5.12$ $^\circ$C/m; $K_b = 2.53$ $^\circ$C/m; $T_f^\circ = 5.5$ $^\circ$C; $T_b^\circ = 80.1$ $^\circ$C
Conceptual Plan: $\text{mL}_{C_6H_6} \rightarrow \text{g}_{C_6H_6} \rightarrow \text{kg}_{C_6H_6}$ and $\text{g}_{C_{10}H_8} \rightarrow \text{mol}_{C_{10}H_8}$ then $\text{mol}_{C_{10}H_8}, \text{kg}_{C_6H_6} \rightarrow m$

$$\dfrac{0.877 \text{ g}}{1 \text{ cm}^3} \qquad \dfrac{1 \text{ kg}}{1000 \text{ g}} \qquad \qquad \dfrac{1 \text{ mol C}_{10}\text{H}_8}{128.2 \text{ g C}_{10}\text{H}_8} \qquad \qquad m = \dfrac{\text{amount solute (moles)}}{\text{mass solvent (kg)}}$$

$m, K_f \rightarrow \Delta T_f \rightarrow T_f$ and $m, K_b \rightarrow \Delta T_b \rightarrow T_b$

$\Delta T_f = K_f \times m \quad T_f = T_f^\circ - \Delta T_f \qquad \Delta T_b = K_b \times m \quad \Delta T_b = T_b - T_b^\circ$

Solution: $100.0 \text{ cm}^3 \times \dfrac{0.877 \text{ g}}{1 \text{ cm}^3} \times \dfrac{1 \text{ kg}}{1000 \text{ g}} = 0.0877 \text{ kg}$ and

$10.0 \text{ g C}_{10}\text{H}_8 \times \dfrac{1 \text{ mol C}_{10}\text{H}_8}{128.2 \text{ g C}_{10}\text{H}_8} = 0.0780\underline{0}312 \text{ mol C}_{10}\text{H}_8$ then

$m = \dfrac{\text{amount solute (moles)}}{\text{mass solvent (kg)}} = \dfrac{0.0780\underline{0}312 \text{ mol C}_{10}\text{H}_8}{0.0877 \text{ kg}} = 0.889\underline{4}312 \; m$ then

$\Delta T_f = K_f \times m = 5.12 \dfrac{^\circ\text{C}}{m} \times 0.889\underline{4}312 \; m = 4.55 \text{ }^\circ\text{C}$ then $T_f = T_f^\circ - \Delta T_f = 5.5 \text{ }^\circ\text{C} - 4.55 \text{ }^\circ\text{C} = 0.9\underline{5} \text{ }^\circ\text{C} = 1 \text{ }^\circ\text{C}$

and $\Delta T_b = K_b \times m = 2.53 \dfrac{^\circ\text{C}}{m} \times 0.889\underline{4}312 \; m = 2.25 \text{ }^\circ\text{C}$ and $\Delta T_b = T_b - T_b^\circ$ so

$T_b = T_b^\circ + \Delta T_b = 80.1 \text{ }^\circ\text{C} + 2.25 \text{ }^\circ\text{C} = 82.3\underline{5} \text{ }^\circ\text{C} = 82.4 \text{ }^\circ\text{C}$

Check: The units ($^\circ$C) are correct. The magnitude of the answers seems reasonable because the molality is almost 1. Because the constants are larger for benzene than for water, we expect larger temperature shifts. The shift in boiling point is less than the shift in freezing point because the constant is smaller for freezing.

12.53   **Given:** 17.5 g of unknown nonelectrolyte in 100.0 g water, $T_f = -1.8$ $^\circ$C   **Find:** $\mathcal{M}$
Other: $K_f = 1.86$ $^\circ$C/m
Conceptual Plan: $\text{g}_{H_2O} \rightarrow \text{kg}_{H_2O}$ and $T_f \rightarrow \Delta T_f$ then $\Delta T_f, K_f \rightarrow m$ then $m, \text{kg}_{H_2O} \rightarrow \text{mol}_{Unk}$

$$\dfrac{1 \text{ kg}}{1000 \text{ g}} \qquad\qquad T_f = T_f^\circ - \Delta T_f \qquad\qquad \Delta T_f = K_f \times m \qquad m = \dfrac{\text{amount solute (moles)}}{\text{mass solvent (kg)}}$$

then $\text{g}_{Unk}, \text{mol}_{Unk} \rightarrow \mathcal{M}$

$$\mathcal{M} = \dfrac{\text{g}_{Unk}}{\text{mol}_{Unk}}$$

Solution: $100.0 \text{ g} \times \dfrac{1 \text{ kg}}{1000 \text{ g}} = 0.1000 \text{ kg}$ and $T_f = T_f^\circ - \Delta T_f$ so

$\Delta T_f = T_f^\circ - T_f = 0.00 \text{ }^\circ\text{C} - (-1.8 \text{ }^\circ\text{C}) = +1.8 \text{ }^\circ\text{C}$ $\Delta T_f = K_f \times m$. Rearrange to solve for m.

$m = \dfrac{\Delta T_f}{K_f} = \dfrac{1.8 \text{ }^\circ\text{C}}{1.86 \dfrac{^\circ\text{C}}{m}} = 0.9\underline{6}774 \; m$ then $m = \dfrac{\text{amount solute (moles)}}{\text{mass solvent (kg)}}$ so

$$\text{mol}_{\text{Unk}} = m_{\text{Unk}} \times \text{kg}_{\text{H}_2\text{O}} = 0.9\underline{6}774 \frac{\text{mol Unk}}{\text{kg}} \times 0.1000 \text{ kg} = 0.09\underline{6}774 \text{ mol Unk then}$$

$$\mathcal{M} = \frac{g_{\text{Unk}}}{\text{mol}_{\text{Unk}}} = \frac{17.5 \text{ g}}{0.09\underline{6}774 \text{ mol}} = 180 \frac{\text{g}}{\text{mol}} = 1.8 \times 10^2 \frac{\text{g}}{\text{mol}}$$

Check: The units (g/mol) are correct. The magnitude of the answer (180 g/mol) seems reasonable because the molality is ~0.1 and we have ~18 g. It is a reasonable molecular weight for a solid or liquid.

12.55   **Given:** 24.6 g of glycerin ($C_3H_8O_3$) in 250.0 mL of solution at 298 K   **Find:** Π

Conceptual Plan: $\text{mL}_{\text{soln}} \rightarrow \text{L}_{\text{soln}}$ and $g_{C_3H_8O_3} \rightarrow \text{mol}_{C_3H_8O_3}$ then $\text{mol}_{C_3H_8O_3}, \text{L}_{\text{soln}} \rightarrow \text{M}$ then

$$\frac{1 \text{ L}}{1000 \text{ mL}} \qquad \frac{1 \text{ mol } C_3H_8O_3}{92.09 \text{ g } C_3H_8O_3} \qquad M = \frac{\text{amount solute (moles)}}{\text{volume solution (L)}}$$

M, T $\rightarrow$ Π

$\Pi = MRT$

Solution:

$$250.0 \text{ mL} \times \frac{1 \text{ L}}{1000 \text{ mL}} = 0.2500 \text{ L} \text{ and } 24.6 \text{ g } C_3H_8O_3 \times \frac{1 \text{ mol } C_3H_8O_3}{92.09 \text{ g } C_3H_8O_3} = 0.26\underline{7}130 \text{ mol } C_3H_8O_3 \text{ then}$$

$$M = \frac{\text{amount solute (moles)}}{\text{volume solution (L)}} = \frac{0.26\underline{7}130 \text{ mol } C_3H_8O_3}{0.2500 \text{ L}} = 1.0\underline{6}852 \text{ M then}$$

$$\Pi = MRT = 1.0\underline{6}852 \frac{\text{mol}}{\text{L}} \times 0.08206 \frac{\text{L} \cdot \text{atm}}{\text{K} \cdot \text{mol}} \times 298 \text{ K} = 26.1 \text{ atm}$$

Check: The units (atm) are correct. The magnitude of the answer (26 atm) seems reasonable because the molarity is ~1.

12.57   **Given:** 27.55 mg unknown protein in 25.0 mL solution; $\Pi = 3.22$ torr at 25 °C   **Find:** $\mathcal{M}_{\text{unknown protein}}$

Conceptual Plan: °C $\rightarrow$ K and torr $\rightarrow$ atm then $\Pi, T \rightarrow$ M then $\text{mL}_{\text{soln}} \rightarrow \text{L}_{\text{soln}}$ then

$$K = °C + 273.15 \qquad \frac{1 \text{ atm}}{760 \text{ torr}} \qquad \Pi = MRT \qquad \frac{1 \text{ L}}{1000 \text{ mL}}$$

$\text{L}_{\text{soln}}, \text{M} \rightarrow \text{mol}_{\text{unknown protein}}$ and mg $\rightarrow$ g then $g_{\text{unknown protein}}, \text{mol}_{\text{unknown protein}} \rightarrow \mathcal{M}_{\text{unknown protein}}$

$$M = \frac{\text{amount solute (moles)}}{\text{volume solution (L)}} \qquad \frac{1 \text{ g}}{1000 \text{ mg}} \qquad \mathcal{M} = \frac{g_{\text{unknown protein}}}{\text{mol}_{\text{unknown protein}}}$$

Solution: 25 °C + 273.15 = 298 K and $3.22 \text{ torr} \times \frac{1 \text{ atm}}{760 \text{ torr}} = 0.0042\underline{3}684 \text{ atm } \Pi = MRT \text{ for M}$

$$M = \frac{\Pi}{RT} = \frac{0.0042\underline{3}684 \text{ atm}}{0.08206 \frac{\text{L} \cdot \text{atm}}{\text{K} \cdot \text{mol}} \times 298 \text{ K}} = 1.7\underline{3}258 \times 10^{-4} \frac{\text{mol}}{\text{L}} \text{ then } 25.0 \text{ mL} \times \frac{1 \text{ L}}{1000 \text{ mL}} = 0.0250 \text{ L then}$$

$$M = \frac{\text{amount solute (moles)}}{\text{volume solution (L)}}. \text{ Rearrange to solve for mol}_{\text{unknown protein}}.$$

$$\text{mol}_{\text{unknown protein}} = M \times L = 1.7\underline{3}258 \times 10^{-4} \frac{\text{mol}}{\text{L}} \times 0.0250 \text{ L} = 4.3\underline{3}146 \times 10^{-6} \text{ mol and}$$

$$27.55 \text{ mg} \times \frac{1 \text{ g}}{1000 \text{ mg}} = 0.02755 \text{ g then } \mathcal{M} = \frac{g_{\text{unknown protein}}}{\text{mol}_{\text{unknown protein}}} = \frac{0.02755 \text{ g}}{4.3\underline{3}146 \times 10^{-6} \text{ mol}} = 6.36 \times 10^3 \frac{\text{g}}{\text{mol}}$$

Check: The units (g/mol) are correct. The magnitude of the answer (6400 g/mol) seems reasonable for a large biological molecule. A small amount of material is put into 0.025 L; so the concentration is very small, and the molecular weight is large.

12.59   (a)   **Given:** 0.100 m of K_2S, completely dissociated   **Find:** T_f, T_b

Other: $K_f = 1.86 \text{ °C}/m$; $K_b = 0.512 \text{ °C}/m$

Conceptual Plan: $m, i, K_f \rightarrow \Delta T_f$ then $\Delta T_f \rightarrow T_f$ and $m, i, K_b \rightarrow \Delta T_b$ then $\Delta T_b \rightarrow T_b$

$$\Delta T_f = K_f \times i \times m_{i=3} \qquad T_f = T_f° - \Delta T_f \qquad \Delta T_b = K_b \times i \times m_{i=3} \qquad T_b = T_b° + \Delta T_b$$

Solution: $\Delta T_f = K_f \times i \times m = 1.86 \frac{°C}{m} \times 3 \times 0.100 \text{ } m = 0.558 \text{ °C then}$

$$T_f = T_f° - \Delta T_f = 0.000 \text{ °C} - 0.558 \text{ °C} = -0.558 \text{ °C and}$$

$\Delta T_b = K_b \times i \times m = 0.512 \frac{°C}{m} \times 3 \times 0.100 \, m = 0.154 \, °C$ then

$T_b = T_b° - \Delta T_b = 100.000 \, °C + 0.154 \, °C = 100.154 \, °C$

Check: The units (°C) are correct. The magnitude of the answers (−0.6 °C and 100.2 °C) seems reasonable because the molality of the particles is 0.3. The shift in boiling point is less than the shift in freezing point because the constant for boiling is larger than the constant for freezing.

(b) **Given:** 21.5 g CuCl₂ in 4.50×10^2 g water, completely dissociated   **Find:** T_f, T_b
Other: $K_f = 1.86 \, °C/m$; $K_b = 0.512 \, °C/m$
Conceptual Plan: $g_{H_2O} \rightarrow kg_{H_2O}$ and $g_{CuCl_2} \rightarrow mol_{CuCl_2}$ then $mol_{CuCl_2}, kg_{H_2O} \rightarrow m$

$$\frac{1 \, kg}{1000 \, g} \qquad\qquad \frac{1 \, mol \, CuCl_2}{134.45 \, g \, CuCl_2} \qquad\qquad m = \frac{\text{amount solute (moles)}}{\text{mass solvent (kg)}}$$

$m, i, K_f \rightarrow \Delta T_f \rightarrow T_f$ and $m, i, K_b \rightarrow \Delta T_b \rightarrow T_b$

$\Delta T_f = K_f \times i \times m_{i=3} \quad T_f = T_f° - \Delta T_f \quad \Delta T_b = K_b \times i \times m_{i=3} \quad T_b = T_b° + \Delta T_b$

Solution:

$$4.5 \times 10^2 \, g \times \frac{1 \, kg}{1000 \, g} = 0.450 \, kg \text{ and } 21.5 \, g \, CuCl_2 \times \frac{1 \, mol \, CuCl_2}{134.45 \, g \, CuCl_2} = 0.159911 \, mol \, CuCl_2 \text{ then}$$

$$m = \frac{\text{amount solute (moles)}}{\text{mass solvent (kg)}} = \frac{0.159911 \, mol \, CuCl_2}{0.450 \, kg} = 0.355358 \, m \text{ then}$$

$\Delta T_f = K_f \times i \times m = 1.86 \frac{°C}{m} \times 3 \times 0.355358 \, m = 1.98 \, °C$ then

$T_f = T_f° - \Delta T_f = 0.000 \, °C - 1.98 \, °C = -1.98 \, °C$ and

$\Delta T_b = K_b \times i \times m = 0.512 \frac{°C}{m} \times 3 \times 0.355358 \, m = 0.546 \, °C$ then

$T_b = T_b° - \Delta T_b = 100.000 \, °C + 0.546 \, °C = 100.546 \, °C$

Check: The units (°C) are correct. The magnitude of the answers (−2 °C and 100.5 °C) seems reasonable because the molality of the particles is ~1. The shift in boiling point is less than the shift in freezing point because the constant for boiling is larger than the constant for freezing.

(c) **Given:** 5.5% by mass NaNO₃, completely dissociated   **Find:** T_f, T_b
Other: $K_f = 1.86 \, °C/m$; $K_b = 0.512 \, °C/m$
Conceptual Plan: percent by mass $\rightarrow g_{NaNO_3}, g_{H_2O}$ then $g_{H_2O} \rightarrow kg_{H_2O}$ and $g_{NaNO_3} \rightarrow mol_{NaNO_3}$

$$\text{mass percent} = \frac{\text{mass solute}}{\text{mass solution}} \times 100\% \qquad \frac{1 \, kg}{1000 \, g} \qquad \frac{1 \, mol \, NaNO_3}{85.00 \, g \, NaNO_3}$$

then $mol_{NaNO_3}, kg_{H_2O} \rightarrow m$ **then** $m, i, K_f \rightarrow \Delta T_f \rightarrow T_f$ **and** $m, i, K_b \rightarrow \Delta T_b \rightarrow T_b$

$$m = \frac{\text{amount solute (moles)}}{\text{mass solvent (kg)}} \quad \Delta T_f = K_f \times i \times m_{i=2} \quad T_f = T_f° - \Delta T_f \quad \Delta T_b = K_b \times i \times m_{i=2} \quad T_b = T_b° + \Delta T_b$$

Solution: mass percent $= \frac{\text{mass solute}}{\text{mass solution}} \times 100\%$, so 5.5% by mass NaNO₃ means 5.5 g NaNO₃ and

$100.0 \, g - 5.5 \, g = 94.5 \, g$ water. Then $94.5 \, g \times \frac{1 \, kg}{1000 \, g} = 0.0945 \, kg$ and

$$5.5 \, g \, NaNO_3 \times \frac{1 \, mol \, NaNO_3}{85.00 \, g \, NaNO_3} = 0.064706 \, mol \, NaNO_3 \text{ then}$$

$$m = \frac{\text{amount solute (moles)}}{\text{mass solvent (kg)}} = \frac{0.064706 \, mol \, NaNO_3}{0.0945 \, kg} = 0.68472 \, m \text{ then}$$

$\Delta T_f = K_f \times i \times m = 1.86 \frac{°C}{m} \times 2 \times 0.68472 \, m = 2.5 \, °C$ then

$T_f = T_f° - \Delta T_f = 0.000 \, °C - 2.5 \, °C = -2.5 \, °C$ and

$\Delta T_b = K_b \times i \times m = 0.512 \frac{°C}{m} \times 2 \times 0.68472 \, m = 0.70 \, °C$ then

$T_b = T_b° - \Delta T_b = 100.000 \, °C + 0.70 \, °C = 100.70 \, °C$

Check: The units (°C) are correct. The magnitude of the answers (−2.5 °C and 100.7 °C) seems reasonable because the molality of the particles is ~1. The shift in boiling point is less than the shift in freezing point because the constant for boiling is larger than the constant for freezing.

12.61   **Given:** NaCl complete dissociation; 1.0 L water and $T_f = -10.0\ °C$ **Find:** mass of NaCl

Other: $K_f = 1.86\ °C/m$; $d(\text{water}) = 1.0\ g/mL$

Conceptual Plan:

$$T_f \rightarrow \Delta T_f \text{ then } \Delta T_f, i, K_f \rightarrow m \text{ then } L_{H_2O} \rightarrow mL_{H_2O} \rightarrow g_{H_2O} \rightarrow kg_{H_2O} \text{ then } m, kg_{H_2O} \rightarrow mol_{NaCl}$$

$$T_f = T_f^\circ - \Delta T_f \qquad \Delta T_f = K_f \times i \times m \qquad \frac{1000\ mL}{1\ L} \quad \frac{1.0\ g}{1\ mL} \quad \frac{1\ kg}{1000\ g} \qquad m = \frac{\text{amount solute (moles)}}{\text{mass solvent (kg)}}$$

then $mol_{NaCl} \rightarrow g_{NaCl}$

$$\frac{58.44\ g\ NaCl}{1\ mol\ NaCl}$$

Solution: $T_f = T_f^\circ - \Delta T_f$ so $\Delta T_f = T_f^\circ - T_f = 0.0\ °C - 10.0\ °C = -10.0\ °C$ then $\Delta T_f = K_f \times i \times m$

Rearrange to solve for m. Because the salt completely dissolves, $i = 2$.

$$m = \frac{\Delta T_f}{K_f \times i} = \frac{10.0\ °\!\!\!\!\diagup C}{1.86\ \dfrac{°\!\!\!\!\diagup C}{m} \times 2} = 2.6\underline{8}8172\ m\ NaCl \text{ then } 1.0\ \diagup\!\!\!L \times \frac{1000\ \diagup\!\!\!mL}{1\ \diagup\!\!\!L} \times \frac{1.0\ g}{1\ \diagup\!\!\!mL} \times \frac{1\ kg}{1000\ \diagup\!\!\!g} = 1.0\ kg \text{ then}$$

$$m = \frac{\text{amount solute (moles)}}{\text{mass solvent (kg)}} \text{ so } mol_{NaCl} = m \times kg_{H_2O} = 2.6\underline{8}8172\frac{mol\ NaCl}{\diagup\!\!\!\!kg_{H_2O}} \times 1.0\ \diagup\!\!\!\!kg_{H_2O} = 2.6\underline{8}8172\ mol\ NaCl$$

then $2.6\underline{8}8172\ \diagup\!\!\!\!mol\ \diagup\!\!\!NaCl \times \dfrac{58.44\ g\ NaCl}{1\ \diagup\!\!\!mol\ \diagup\!\!\!NaCl} = 15\underline{7}.097\ g\ NaCl = 160\ g\ NaCl$

Check: The units (g) are correct. The magnitude of the answer (160 g) seems reasonable because the temperature change is moderate and NaCl has a low formula mass.

12.63   **(a)**   **Given:** 0.100 m of $FeCl_3$ **Find:** T_f **Other:** $K_f = 1.86\ °C/m$; $i_{measured} = 3.4$

Conceptual Plan: $m, i, K_f \rightarrow \Delta T_f$ then $\Delta T_f \rightarrow T_f$

$$\Delta T_f = K_f \times i \times m \qquad T_f = T_f^\circ - \Delta T_f$$

Solution: $\Delta T_f = K_f \times i \times m = 1.86\ \dfrac{°C}{\diagup\!\!\!m} \times 3.4 \times 0.100\ \diagup\!\!\!m = 0.632\ °C$ then

$T_f = T_f^\circ - \Delta T_f = 0.000\ °C - 0.632\ °C = -0.632\ °C$

Check: The units (°C) are correct. The magnitude of the answer (−0.6 °C) seems reasonable because the theoretical molality of the particles is 0.4.

(b)   **Given:** 0.085 M of K_2SO_4 at 298 K   **Find:** Π **Other:** $i_{measured} = 2.6$

Conceptual Plan: $M, i, T \rightarrow \Pi$

$$\Pi = i \times MRT$$

Solution: $\Pi = i \times MRT = 2.6 \times 0.085\ \dfrac{\diagup\!\!\!mol}{\diagup\!\!\!L} \times 0.08206\ \dfrac{\diagup\!\!\!L \cdot atm}{K \cdot \diagup\!\!\!mol} \times 298\ K = 5.4\ atm$

Check: The units (atm) are correct. The magnitude of the answer (5 atm) seems reasonable because the molarity of particles is ~0.2 m.

(c)   **Given:** 1.22% by mass $MgCl_2$ **Find:** T_b **Other:** $K_b = 0.512\ °C/m$; $i_{measured} = 2.7$

Conceptual Plan: percent by mass $\rightarrow g_{MgCl_2}, g_{H_2O}$ then $g_{H_2O} \rightarrow kg_{H_2O}$ and $g_{MgCl_2} \rightarrow mol_{MgCl_2}$ then

$$\text{mass percent} = \frac{\text{mass solute}}{\text{mass solution}} \times 100\% \qquad \frac{1\ kg}{1000\ g} \qquad \frac{1\ mol\ MgCl_2}{95.21\ g\ MgCl_2}$$

$mol_{MgCl_2}, kg_{H_2O} \rightarrow m$ then $m, i, K_b \rightarrow \Delta T_b \rightarrow T_b$

$$m = \frac{\text{amount solute (moles)}}{\text{mass solvent (kg)}} \qquad \Delta T_b = K_b \times i \times m \quad T_b = T_b^\circ + \Delta T_b$$

Solution: mass percent $= \dfrac{\text{mass solute}}{\text{mass solution}} \times 100\%$, so 1.22% by mass $MgCl_2$ means 1.22 g $MgCl_2$ and

100.00 g − 1.22 g = 98.78 g water. Then $98.78\ \diagup\!\!\!g \times \dfrac{1\ kg}{1000\ \diagup\!\!\!g} = 0.09878\ kg$ and

$$1.22 \text{ g MgCl}_2 \times \frac{1 \text{ mol MgCl}_2}{95.21 \text{ g MgCl}_2} = 0.012\underline{8}138 \text{ mol MgCl}_2 \text{ then}$$

$$m = \frac{\text{amount solute (moles)}}{\text{mass solvent (kg)}} = \frac{0.012\underline{8}138 \text{ mol MgCl}_2}{0.09878 \text{ kg}} = 0.129\underline{7}21 \text{ } m \text{ then}$$

$$\Delta T_b = K_b \times i \times m = 0.512 \frac{^\circ C}{m} \times 2.7 \times 0.129\underline{7}21 \text{ } \cancel{m} = 0.18 \text{ }^\circ C \text{ then}$$

$$T_b = T_b^\circ - \Delta T_b = 100.000 \text{ }^\circ C + 0.18 \text{ }^\circ C = 100.18 \text{ }^\circ C$$

Check: The units ($^\circ$C) are correct. The magnitude of the answer (100.2 $^\circ$C) seems reasonable because the molality of the particles is $\sim 1/3$.

12.65   **Given:** 1.2 m MX$_2$ in water and $T_b = 101.4 \text{ }^\circ C$ **Find:** i
Other: $K_b = 0.512 \text{ }^\circ C/m$
Conceptual Plan: $T_b \rightarrow \Delta T_b$ then $m, \Delta T_b, K_b \rightarrow i$
$$\Delta T_b = T_b - T_b^\circ \qquad\qquad \Delta T_b = K_b \times i \times m$$
Solution: $\Delta T_b = T_b - T_b^\circ = 101.4 \text{ }^\circ C - 100.0 \text{ }^\circ C = 1.4 \text{ }^\circ C$ then $\Delta T_b = K_b \times i \times m$

Rearrange to solve for i. $i = \dfrac{\Delta T_b}{K_b \times m} = \dfrac{1.4 \text{ } \cancel{^\circ C}}{0.512 \dfrac{\cancel{^\circ C}}{\cancel{m}} \times 1.2 \text{ } \cancel{m}} = 2.2\underline{7}865 = 2.3$

Check: The units (none) are correct. The magnitude of the answer (2.3) seems reasonable because the formula of the salt is MX$_2$, where $i = 3$ if it completely dissociated.

12.67   **Given:** 0.100 M of ionic solution, $\Pi = 8.3$ atm at 25 $^\circ$C   **Find:** i_{measured}
Conceptual Plan: $^\circ$C $\rightarrow$ K then $\Pi, M, T \rightarrow i$
$$K = \text{ }^\circ C + 273.15 \qquad\qquad \Pi = i \times MRT$$
Solution: 25 $^\circ$C + 273.15 = 298 K then $\Pi = i \times MRT$. Rearrange to solve for i.

$$i = \frac{\Pi}{MRT} = \frac{8.3 \text{ } \cancel{\text{atm}}}{0.100 \dfrac{\cancel{\text{mol}}}{\cancel{L}} \times 0.08206 \dfrac{\cancel{L} \cdot \cancel{\text{atm}}}{\text{K} \cdot \cancel{\text{mol}}} \times 298 \text{ } \cancel{K}} = 3.4$$

Check: The units (none) are correct. The magnitude of the answer (3) seems reasonable for an ionic solution with a high osmotic pressure.

Cumulative Problems

12.69   Chloroform is polar and has stronger solute–solvent interactions than does nonpolar carbon tetrachloride.

12.71   **Given:** KClO$_4$: lattice energy = -599 kJ/mol, $\Delta H_{\text{hydration}} = -548$ kJ/mol; 10.0 g KClO$_4$ in 100.00 mL solution
Find: ΔH_{soln} and ΔT **Other:** $C_s = 4.05$ J/g $^\circ$C; $d = 1.05$ g/mL
Conceptual Plan: lattice energy, $\Delta H_{\text{hydration}} \rightarrow \Delta H_{\text{soln}}$ and g $\rightarrow$ mol then mol, $\Delta H_{\text{soln}} \rightarrow q(\text{kJ}) \rightarrow q(\text{J})$
$$\Delta H_{\text{soln}} = \Delta H_{\text{solute}} + \Delta H_{\text{hydration}} \text{ where } \Delta H_{\text{solute}} = -\Delta H_{\text{lattice}} \quad \frac{1 \text{ mol}}{138.55 \text{ g}} \qquad q = n \Delta H_{\text{soln}} \quad \frac{1000 \text{ J}}{1 \text{ kJ}}$$
then mL$_{\text{soln}} \rightarrow$ g$_{\text{soln}}$ then q, g$_{\text{soln}}$, $C_s \rightarrow \Delta T$
$$\frac{1.05 \text{ g}}{1 \text{ mL}} \qquad\qquad q = mC_s \Delta T$$
Solution: $\Delta H_{\text{soln}} = \Delta H_{\text{solute}} + \Delta H_{\text{hydration}}$ where $\Delta H_{\text{solute}} = -\Delta H_{\text{lattice}}$ so $\Delta H_{\text{soln}} = \Delta H_{\text{hydration}} - \Delta H_{\text{lattice}}$

$$\Delta H_{\text{soln}} = -548 \text{ kJ/mol} - (-599 \text{ kJ/mol}) = +51 \text{ kJ/mol} \text{ and } 10.0 \text{ } \cancel{g} \times \frac{1 \text{ mol}}{138.55 \text{ } \cancel{g}} = 0.072\underline{1}761 \text{ mol then}$$

$$q = n \Delta H_{\text{soln}} = 0.072\underline{1}761 \text{ } \cancel{\text{mol}} \times 51 \frac{\text{kJ}}{\cancel{\text{mol}}} = +3.\underline{6}810 \text{ } \cancel{\text{kJ}} \times \frac{1000 \text{ J}}{1 \text{ } \cancel{\text{kJ}}} = +3\underline{6}81.0 \text{ J absorbed then}$$

$$100.0 \text{ } \cancel{\text{mL}} \times \frac{1.05 \text{ g}}{1 \text{ } \cancel{\text{mL}}} = 105 \text{ g. Because heat is absorbed when KClO}_4 \text{ dissolves, the temperature will drop or}$$

$q = -3\underline{6}81.0$ J and $q = mC_s\Delta T$. Rearrange to solve for ΔT.

$$\Delta T = \frac{q}{mC_s} = \frac{-3681.0 \text{ J}}{105 \text{ g} \times 4.05 \frac{\text{J}}{\text{g} \cdot {}^{\circ}\text{C}}} = -8.7 \text{ }^{\circ}\text{C}$$

Check: The units (kJ/mol and °C) are correct. The magnitude of the answer (51 kJ/mol) makes physical sense because the lattice energy is larger than the heat of hydration. The magnitude of the temperature change (-9 °C) makes physical sense because heat is absorbed and the heat of solution is fairly small.

12.73   **Given:** Argon, 0.0537 L; 25 °C, $P_{Ar} = 1.0$ atm to make 1.0 L saturated solution   **Find:** $k_H(Ar)$
           Conceptual Plan: °C → K and P_{Ar}, V, T → mol_{Ar} then $mol_{Ar}, V_{soln}, P_{Ar}$ → $k_H(Ar)$

$$K = {}^{\circ}C + 273.15 \qquad\qquad PV = nRT \qquad\qquad S_{Ar} = k_H(Ar)P_{Ar} \text{ with } S_{Ar} = \frac{mol_{Ar}}{L_{soln}}$$

           Solution: 25 °C + 273.15 = 298 K and $PV = nRT$. Rearrange to solve for n.

$$n = \frac{PV}{RT} = \frac{1.0 \text{ atm} \times 0.0537 \text{ L}}{0.08206 \frac{\text{L} \cdot \text{atm}}{\text{K} \cdot \text{mol}} \times 298 \text{ K}} = 0.00219597 \text{ mol} \text{ then } S_{Ar} = k_H(Ar)P_{Ar} \text{ with } S_{Ar} = \frac{mol_{Ar}}{L_{soln}}$$

           Substitute in values and rearrange to solve for k_H.

$$k_H(Ar) = \frac{mol_{Ar}}{L_{soln} P_{Ar}} = \frac{0.00219597 \text{ mol}}{1.0 \text{ L}_{soln} \times 1.0 \text{ atm}} = 2.2 \times 10^{-3} \frac{\text{M}}{\text{atm}}$$

           Check: The units (M/atm) are correct. The magnitude of the answer (10^{-3}) seems reasonable because it is consistent with other values in the text.

12.75   **Given:** 0.0020 ppm by mass Hg = legal limit; 0.0040 ppm by mass Hg = contaminated water; 50.0 mg Hg ingested
           Find: volume of contaminated water
           Conceptual Plan: mg_{Hg} → g_{Hg} → g_{H_2O} → mL_{H_2O} → L_{H_2O}

$$\frac{1 \text{ g}}{1000 \text{ mg}} \quad \frac{10^6 \text{ g water}}{0.0040 \text{ g Hg}} \quad \frac{1 \text{ mL}}{1.00 \text{ g}} \quad \frac{1 \text{ L}}{1000 \text{ mL}}$$

           Solution: $50.0 \text{ mg Hg} \times \dfrac{1 \text{ g Hg}}{1000 \text{ mg Hg}} \times \dfrac{10^6 \text{ g water}}{0.0040 \text{ g Hg}} \times \dfrac{1 \text{ mL water}}{1.00 \text{ g water}} \times \dfrac{1 \text{ L water}}{1000 \text{ mL water}} = 1.3 \times 10^4 \text{ L water}$

           Check: The units (L) are correct. The magnitude of the answer (10^4 L) seems reasonable because the concentration is so low.

12.77   **Given:** 12.5% NaCl by mass in water at 55 °C; 2.5 L vapor   **Find:** g_{H_2O} in vapor
           Other: $P^{\circ}_{H_2O} = 118$ torr, $i_{NaCl} = 2.0$ (complete dissociation)
           Conceptual Plan: % NaCl by mass → g_{NaCl}, g_{H_2O} then g_{NaCl} → mol_{NaCl} and g_{H_2O} → mol_{H_2O}

$$\frac{12.5 \text{ g NaCl}}{100 \text{ g (NaCl + H}_2\text{O)}} \qquad\qquad \frac{1 \text{ mol NaCl}}{58.44 \text{ g NaCl}} \qquad\qquad \frac{1 \text{ mol H}_2\text{O}}{18.02 \text{ g H}_2\text{O}}$$

           then mol_{NaCl}, mol_{H_2O} → χ_{NaCl} → χ_{H_2O} **then** $\chi_{H_2O}, P^{\circ}_{H_2O}$ → P_{H_2O}

$$\chi = \frac{\text{amount solute (in moles)}}{\text{total amount of solute and solvent (in moles)}} \quad \chi_{H_2O} = 1 - i_{NaCl} \chi_{NaCl} \quad P_{solution} = \chi_{solvent} P^{\circ}_{solvent}$$

           then torr → atm and °C → K P, V, T → mol_{H_2O} → g_{H_2O}

$$\frac{1 \text{ atm}}{760 \text{ torr}} \qquad K = {}^{\circ}C + 273.15 \qquad PV = nRT \qquad \frac{18.02 \text{ g H}_2\text{O}}{1 \text{ mol H}_2\text{O}}$$

           Solution: $\dfrac{12.5 \text{ g NaCl}}{100 \text{ g (NaCl + H}_2\text{O)}}$ means 12.5 g NaCl and (100 g $-$ 12.5 g) = 87.5 g H_2O then

$$12.5 \text{ g NaCl} \times \frac{1 \text{ mol NaCl}}{58.44 \text{ g NaCl}} = 0.213895 \text{ mol NaCl} \text{ and } 87.5 \text{ g H}_2\text{O} \times \frac{1 \text{ mol H}_2\text{O}}{18.02 \text{ g H}_2\text{O}} = 4.85572 \text{ mol H}_2\text{O}$$

           then $\chi = \dfrac{\text{amount solute (in moles)}}{\text{total amount of solute and solvent (in moles)}} = \dfrac{0.213895 \text{ mol}}{0.213895 \text{ mol} + 4.85572 \text{ mol}} = 0.0421916$

           then $\chi_{H_2O} = 1 - i_{NaCl}\chi_{NaCl} = 1 - (2.0 \times 0.0421916) = 0.915617$

           then $P_{solution} = \chi_{solvent} P^{\circ}_{solvent} = 0.915617 \times 118 \text{ torr} = 108.043 \text{ torr H}_2\text{O}$ then

$$108.043 \text{ torr } H_2O \times \frac{1 \text{ atm}}{760 \text{ torr}} = 0.142\underline{1}62 \text{ atm}$$

and $55\,°C + 273.15 = 328 \text{ K}$ then $PV = nRT$. Rearrange to solve for n.

$$n = \frac{PV}{RT} = \frac{0.142\underline{1}62 \text{ atm} \times 2.5 \text{ } L}{0.08206 \dfrac{L \cdot atm}{K \cdot mol} \times 328 \text{ K}} = 0.013\underline{2}04 \text{ mol then}$$

$$0.013\underline{2}04 \text{ mol } H_2O \times \frac{18.02 \text{ g } H_2O}{1 \text{ mol } H_2O} = 0.24 \text{ g } H_2O$$

Check: The units (g) are correct. The magnitude of the answer (0.2 g) seems reasonable because there is very little mass in a vapor.

12.79   **Given:** $T_b = 106.5\,°C$ aqueous solution   **Find:** T_f **Other:** $K_f = 1.86\,°C/m$; $K_b = 0.512\,°C/m$
Conceptual Plan: $T_b \rightarrow \Delta T_b$ then $\Delta T_b, K_b \rightarrow m$ then $m, K_f \rightarrow \Delta T_f \rightarrow T_f$

$$T_b = T_b^\circ + \Delta T_b \qquad\qquad \Delta T_b = K_b \times m \quad \Delta T_f = K_f \times m \qquad T_f = T_f^\circ - \Delta T_f$$

Solution: $T_b = T_b^\circ + \Delta T_b$ so $\Delta T_b = T_b - T_b^\circ = 106.5\,°C - 100.0\,°C = 6.5\,°C$ then $\Delta T_b = K_b \times m$

Rearrange to solve for m. $m = \dfrac{\Delta T_b}{K_b} = \dfrac{6.5\,°C}{0.512 \dfrac{°C}{m}} = 1\underline{2}.695\, m$ then

$$\Delta T_f = K_f \times m = 1.86\,\frac{°C}{m} \times 1\underline{2}.695\, m = 2\underline{3}.6\,°C \text{ then } T_f = T_f^\circ - \Delta T_f = 0.000\,°C - 2\underline{3}.6\,°C = -24\,°C$$

Check: The units (°C) are correct. The magnitude of the answer ($-24\,°C$) seems reasonable because the shift in boiling point is less than the shift in freezing point because the constant for boiling is smaller than the constant for freezing.

12.81   (a)   **Given:** 0.90% NaCl by mass per volume; isotonic aqueous solution at 25 °C; KCl; $i = 1.9$
Find: % KCl by mass per volume
Conceptual Plan: Isotonic solutions will have the same number of particles. Because i is the same,

$$\frac{1 \text{ mol KCl}}{1 \text{ mol NaCl}}$$

the new % mass per volume will be the mass ratio of the two salts.

$$\text{percent by mass per volume} = \frac{\text{mass solute}}{V} \times 100\% \quad \frac{1 \text{ mol NaCl}}{58.44 \text{ g NaCl}} \text{ and } \frac{74.55 \text{ g KCl}}{1 \text{ mol KCl}}$$

Solution: percent by mass per volume $= \dfrac{\text{mass solute}}{V} \times 100\%$

$$= \frac{0.0090 \text{ g NaCl}}{V} \times \frac{1 \text{ mol NaCl}}{58.44 \text{ g NaCl}} \times \frac{1 \text{ mol KCl}}{1 \text{ mol NaCl}} \times \frac{74.55 \text{ g KCl}}{1 \text{ mol KCl}} \times 100\%$$

$$= 1.1\% \text{ KCl by mass per volume}$$

Check: The units (% KCl by mass per volume) are correct. The magnitude of the answer (1.1%) seems reasonable because the molar mass of KCl is larger than the molar mass of NaCl.

(b)   **Given:** 0.90% NaCl by mass per volume; isotonic aqueous solution at 25 °C; NaBr; $i = 1.9$
Find: % NaBr by mass per volume
Conceptual Plan: Isotonic solutions will have the same number of particles. Because i is the same,

$$\frac{1 \text{ mol NaBr}}{1 \text{ mol NaCl}}$$

the new % mass per volume will be the mass ratio of the two salts.

$$\text{percent by mass per volume} = \frac{\text{mass solute}}{V} \times 100\% \quad \frac{1 \text{ mol NaCl}}{58.44 \text{ g NaCl}} \text{ and } \frac{102.89 \text{ g NaBr}}{1 \text{ mol NaBr}}$$

Solution: percent by mass per volume $= \dfrac{\text{mass solute}}{V} \times 100\%$

$$= \frac{0.0090 \text{ g NaCl}}{V} \times \frac{1 \text{ mol NaCl}}{58.44 \text{ g NaCl}} \times \frac{1 \text{ mol NaBr}}{1 \text{ mol NaCl}} \times \frac{102.89 \text{ g NaBr}}{1 \text{ mol NaBr}} \times 100\%$$

$$= 1.6\% \text{ NaBr by mass per volume}$$

Check: The units (% NaBr by mass per volume) are correct. The magnitude of the answer (1.6%) seems reasonable because the molar mass of NaBr is larger than the molar mass of NaCl.

(c)   **Given:** 0.90% NaCl by mass per volume; isotonic aqueous solution at 25 °C; glucose ($C_6H_{12}O_6$); $i = 1.9$
Find: % glucose by mass per volume
Conceptual Plan: Isotonic solutions will have the same number of particles. Because glucose is a nonelectrolyte, the i is not the same; then use the mass ratio of the two compounds.

$$\frac{1.9 \text{ mol } C_6H_{12}O_6}{1 \text{ mol NaCl}} \qquad \text{percent by mass per volume} = \frac{\text{mass solute}}{V} \times 100\% \qquad \frac{1 \text{ mol NaCl}}{58.44 \text{ g NaCl}} \text{ and } \frac{180.16 \text{ g } C_6H_{12}O_6}{1 \text{ mol } C_6H_{12}O_6}$$

Solution: percent by mass per volume $= \dfrac{\text{mass solute}}{V} \times 100\%$

$$= \frac{0.0090 \text{ g NaCl}}{V} \times \frac{1 \text{ mol NaCl}}{58.44 \text{ g NaCl}} \times \frac{1.9 \text{ mol } C_6H_{12}O_6}{1 \text{ mol NaCl}} \times \frac{180.16 \text{ g } C_6H_{12}O_6}{1 \text{ mol } C_6H_{12}O_6} \times 100\%$$

$= 5.3\% \ C_6H_{12}O_6$ by mass per volume

Check: The units (% $C_6H_{12}O_6$ by mass per volume) are correct. The magnitude of the answer (5.3%) seems reasonable because the molar mass of $C_6H_{12}O_6$ is larger than the molar mass of NaCl and we need more moles of $C_6H_{12}O_6$ because it is a nonelectrolyte.

12.83   **Given:** 4.5701 g of $MgCl_2$ and 43.238 g water, $P_{soln} = 0.3624$ atm, $P^\circ_{soln} = 0.3804$ atm at 348.0 K
Find: $i_{measured}$
Conceptual Plan: $g_{MgCl_2} \rightarrow$ mol$_{MgCl_2}$ and $g_{H_2O} \rightarrow$ mol$_{H_2O}$ then $P_{soln}, P^\circ_{soln}, \rightarrow \chi_{MgCl_2}$

$$\frac{1 \text{ mol } MgCl_2}{95.21 \text{ g } MgCl_2} \qquad\qquad \frac{1 \text{ mol } H_2O}{18.02 \text{ g } H_2O} \qquad\qquad P_{Soln} = (1 - \chi_{MgCl_2})P^\circ_{H_2O}$$

then mol$_{MgCl_2}$, mol$_{H_2O}$, $\chi_{MgCl_2} \rightarrow i$

$$\chi_{MgCl_2} = \frac{i(\text{moles } MgCl_2)}{\text{moles } H_2O + i(\text{moles } MgCl_2)}$$

Solution: $4.5701 \text{ g } MgCl_2 \times \dfrac{1 \text{ mol } MgCl_2}{95.21 \text{ g } MgCl_2} = 0.04800021 \text{ mol } MgCl_2$ and

$43.238 \text{ g } H_2O \times \dfrac{1 \text{ mol } H_2O}{18.02 \text{ g } H_2O} = 2.39944506 \text{ mol } H_2O$ then $P_{soln} = (1 - \chi_{MgCl_2})P^\circ_{H_2O}$ so

$\chi_{MgCl_2} = 1 - \dfrac{P_{soln}}{P^\circ_{H_2O}} = 1 - \dfrac{0.3624 \text{ atm}}{0.3804 \text{ atm}} = 0.04731861$. Solve for i.

$i(0.04800021) = 0.04731861(2.39944506 + i(0.04800021)) \rightarrow$

$i(0.04800021 - 0.002271303) = 0.1135384 \rightarrow i = \dfrac{0.1135384}{0.04572891} = 2.483$

Check: The units (none) are correct. The magnitude of the answer (2.5) seems reasonable for $MgCl_2$ because we expect i to be 3 if it completely dissociates. Because Mg is small and doubly charged, we expect a significant drop from 3.

12.85   **Given:** $T_b = 375.3$ K aqueous solution   **Find:** P_{H_2O} **Other:** $P^\circ_{H_2O} = 0.2467$ atm; $K_b = 0.512$ °C/m
Conceptual Plan: $T_b \rightarrow \Delta T_b$ then $\Delta T_b, K_b \rightarrow m$ assume 1 kg water kg$_{H_2O} \rightarrow$ mol$_{H_2O}$ then

$$T_b = T^\circ_b + \Delta T_b \qquad\qquad \Delta T_b = K_b \times m \qquad\qquad \frac{1 \text{ mol } H_2O}{18.02 \text{ g } H_2O}$$

$m \rightarrow$ mol$_{solute}$ then mol$_{H_2O}$, mol$_{solute} \rightarrow \chi_{H_2O}$ then $\chi_{H_2O}, P^\circ_{H_2O} \rightarrow P_{H_2O}$

$$m = \frac{\text{amount solute (moles)}}{\text{mass solvent (kg)}} \qquad \chi_{H_2O} = \frac{\text{moles } H_2O}{\text{moles } H_2O + \text{moles solute}} \qquad P_{H_2O} = \chi_{H_2O}P^\circ_{H_2O}$$

Solution: $T_b = T^\circ_b + \Delta T_b$ so $\Delta T_b = T_b - T^\circ_b = 375.3 \text{ K} - 373.15 \text{ K} = 2.2 \text{ K} = 2.2$ °C then

$\Delta T_b = K_b \times m$. Rearrange to solve for m. $m = \dfrac{\Delta T_b}{K_b} = \dfrac{2.2 \text{ °C}}{0.512 \dfrac{\text{°C}}{m}} = 4.296875 \ m$ then

$1000 \text{ g } H_2O \times \dfrac{1 \text{ mol } H_2O}{18.02 \text{ g } H_2O} = 55.49390 \text{ mol } H_2O$ then

$$m = \frac{\text{amount solute (moles)}}{\text{mass solvent (kg)}} = \frac{x \text{ mol}}{1 \text{ kg}} = 4.\underline{2}96875 \, m \text{ so } x = 4.\underline{2}96875 \text{ mol then}$$

$$\chi_{H_2O} = \frac{\text{moles } H_2O}{\text{moles } H_2O + \text{ moles solute}} = \frac{55.49390 \text{ mol}}{55.49390 \text{ mol} + 4.\underline{2}96875 \text{ mol}} = 0.92\underline{8}1348 \text{ then}$$

$$P_{H_2O} = \chi_{H_2O} P^\circ_{H_2O} = 0.92\underline{8}1348 \times 0.2467 \text{ atm} = 0.229 \text{ atm}$$

Check: The units (atm) are correct. The magnitude of the answer (0.229 atm) seems reasonable because the mole fraction is lowered by ~7%.

12.87 **Given:** equal masses of carbon tetrachloride (CCl_4) and chloroform ($CHCl_3$) at 316 K; $P^\circ_{CCl_4} = 0.354$ atm; $P^\circ_{CHCl_3} = 0.526$ atm   **Find:** χ_{CCl_4}, χ_{CHCl_3} in vapor and P_{CHCl_3} in flask of condensed vapor

Conceptual Plan: assume 100 grams of each $g_{CCl_4} \rightarrow mol_{CCl_4}$ **and** $g_{CHCl_3} \rightarrow mol_{CHCl_3}$ **then**

$$\frac{1 \text{ mol } CCl_4}{153.81 \text{ g } CCl_4} \qquad \frac{1 \text{ mol } CHCl_3}{119.37 \text{ g } CHCl_3}$$

$mol_{CCl_4}, mol_{CHCl_3} \rightarrow \chi_{CCl_4}, \chi_{CHCl_3}$ **then** $\chi_{CCl_4}, P^\circ_{CCl_4} \rightarrow P_{CCl_4}$ **and** $\chi_{CHCl_3}, P^\circ_{CHCl_3} \rightarrow P_{CHCl_3}$ **then**

$$\chi_{CCl_4} = \frac{\text{amount } CCl_4 \text{ (in moles)}}{\text{total amount (in moles)}} \quad \chi_{CHCl_3} = 1 - \chi_{CCl_4} \qquad P_{CCl_4} = \chi_{CCl_4} P^\circ_{CCl_4} \qquad P_{CHCl_3} = \chi_{CHCl_3} P^\circ_{CHCl_3}$$

$P^\circ_{CCl_4}, P_{CHCl_3} \rightarrow P_{Total}$ **then because** $n \, \alpha \, P$ **and we are calculating a mass percent, which is a ratio of masses,**

$$P_{Total} = P_{CCl_4} + P_{CHCl_3}$$

we can simply convert 1 atm to 1 mole so $P_{CCl_4}, P_{CHCl_3} \rightarrow n_{CHCl_4}, n_{CHCl_3}$ **then**

$$\chi_{CCl_4} = \frac{\text{amount } CCl_4 \text{ (in moles)}}{\text{total amount (in moles)}}$$

$mol_{CCl_4}, mol_{CHCl_3} \rightarrow \chi_{CCl_4}, \chi_{CHCl_3}$ **then for the second vapor** $\chi_{CHCl_3}, P^\circ_{CHCl_3} \rightarrow P_{CHCl_3}$

$$\chi_{CHCl_3} = 1 - \chi_{CCl_4} \qquad\qquad\qquad P_{CHCl_3} = \chi_{CHCl_3} P^\circ_{CHCl_3}$$

Solution: $100.00 \text{ g } CCl_4 \times \dfrac{1 \text{ mol } CCl_4}{153.81 \text{ g } CCl_4} = 0.6501\underline{5}279 \text{ mol } CCl_4$ and

$$100.00 \text{ g } CHCl_3 \times \frac{1 \text{ mol } CHCl_3}{119.37 \text{ g } CHCl_3} = 0.8377\underline{3}142 \text{ mol } CHCl_3 \text{ then}$$

$$\chi_{CCl_4} = \frac{\text{amount } CCl_4 \text{ (in moles)}}{\text{total amount (in moles)}} = \frac{0.6501\underline{5}279 \text{ mol}}{0.6501\underline{5}279 \text{ mol} + 0.8377\underline{3}142 \text{ mol}} = 0.4369\underline{6}464 \text{ and}$$

$$\chi_{CHCl_3} = 1 - \chi_{CCl_4} = 1 - 0.4369\underline{6}464 = 0.5630\underline{3}536 \text{ then}$$

$$P_{CCl_4} = \chi_{CCl_4} P^\circ_{CCl_4} = 0.4369\underline{6}464 \times 0.354 \text{ atm} = 0.15\underline{4}685 \text{ atm and}$$

$$P_{CHCl_3} = \chi_{CHCl_3} P^\circ_{CHCl_3} = 0.5630\underline{3}536 \times 0.526 \text{ atm} = 0.29\underline{6}157 \text{ atm then}$$

$$P_{Total} = P_{CCl_4} + P_{CHCl_3} = 0.15\underline{4}685 \text{ atm} + 0.29\underline{6}157 \text{ atm} = 0.45\underline{0}842 \text{ atm then}$$

$$mol_{CCl_4} = 0.15\underline{4}685 \text{ mol and } mol_{CHCl_3} = 0.29\underline{6}157 \text{ mol then}$$

$$\chi_{CCl_4} = \frac{\text{amount } CCl_4 \text{ (in moles)}}{\text{total amount (in moles)}} = \frac{0.15\underline{4}685 \text{ mol}}{0.15\underline{4}685 \text{ mol} + 0.29\underline{6}157 \text{ mol}} = 0.34\underline{3}102 = 0.343 \text{ in the first vapor and}$$

$$\chi_{CHCl_3} = 1 - \chi_{CCl_4} = 1 - 0.34\underline{3}102 = 0.65\underline{6}898 = 0.657 \text{ in the first vapor; then in the second vapor}$$

$$P_{CHCl_3} = \chi_{CHCl_3} P^\circ_{CHCl_3} = 0.65\underline{6}898 \times 0.526 \text{ atm} = 0.34\underline{5}528 \text{ atm} = 0.346 \text{ atm}$$

Check: The units (none and atm) are correct. The magnitude of the answers seems reasonable because we expect the lighter component to be found preferentially in the vapor phase. This effect is magnified in the second vapor.

12.89 **Given:** 49.0% H_2SO_4 by mass, $d = 1.39$ g/cm^3, 25.0 mL diluted to 99.8 cm^3 **Find:** molarity

Conceptual Plan: initial $mL_{solution} \rightarrow g_{solution} \rightarrow g_{H_2SO_4} \rightarrow mol_{H_2SO_4}$ **and final** $mL_{solution} \rightarrow L_{solution}$

$$\frac{1.39 \text{ g}}{1 \text{ mL}} \qquad \frac{49.0 \text{ g } H_2SO_4}{100 \text{ g solution}} \qquad \frac{1 \text{ mol } H_2SO_4}{98.08 \text{ g } H_2SO_4} \qquad\qquad \frac{1 \text{ L}}{1000 \text{ mL}}$$

then $mol_{H_2SO_4}, L_{solution} \rightarrow M$

$$M = \frac{\text{amount solute (moles)}}{\text{volume solution (L)}}$$

Solution:

$$25.0 \text{ mL solution} \times \frac{1.39 \text{ g solution}}{1 \text{ mL solution}} \times \frac{49.0 \text{ g } H_2SO_4}{100 \text{ g solution}} \times \frac{1 \text{ mol } H_2SO_4}{98.08 \text{ g } H_2SO_4} = 0.17\underline{3}6803 \text{ mol } H_2SO_4 \text{ and}$$

$$99.8 \text{ mL solution} \times \frac{1 \text{ L solution}}{1000 \text{ mL solution}} = 0.0998 \text{ L solution then}$$

$$M = \frac{\text{amount solute (moles)}}{\text{volume solution (L)}} = \frac{0.1736803 \text{ mol } H_2SO_4}{0.0998 \text{ L solution}} = 1.74 \text{ M } H_2SO_4$$

Check: The units (M) are correct. The magnitude of the answer (1.74 M) seems reasonable because the solution is ~1/6 surfuric acid.

12.91   **Given:** 10.05 g of unknown compound in 50.0 g water, $T_f = -3.16\,^\circ C$, mass percent composition of the compound is 60.97% C and 11.94% H; the rest is O   **Find:** molecular formula
Other: $K_f = 1.86\,^\circ C/m$; $d = 1.00$ g/mL
Conceptual Plan: $g_{H_2O} \rightarrow kg_{H_2O}$ and $T_f \rightarrow \Delta T_f$ then $\Delta T_f, K_f \rightarrow m$ then $m, kg_{H_2O} \rightarrow mol_{Unk}$

$$\frac{1 \text{ kg}}{1000 \text{ g}} \qquad\qquad T_f = T_f^\circ - \Delta T_f \qquad\qquad \Delta T_f = K_f \times m \qquad\qquad m = \frac{\text{amount solute (moles)}}{\text{mass solvent (kg)}}$$

then $g_{Unk}, mol_{Unk} \rightarrow \mathcal{M} \rightarrow g_C, g_H, g_O \rightarrow mol_C, mol_H, mol_O \rightarrow$ **molecular formula**

$$\mathcal{M} = \frac{g_{Unk}}{mol_{Unk}} \quad \text{mass percents} \qquad \frac{1 \text{ mol C}}{12.01 \text{ g C}} \qquad\qquad \frac{1 \text{ mol H}}{1.008 \text{ g H}} \qquad \frac{1 \text{ mol O}}{16.00 \text{ g O}}$$

Solution: $50.0 \text{ g} \times \dfrac{1 \text{ kg}}{1000 \text{ g}} = 0.0500$ kg and $T_f = T_f^\circ - \Delta T_f$ so

$\Delta T_f = T_f^\circ - T_f = 0.00\,^\circ C - (-3.16\,^\circ C) = +3.16\,^\circ C$ $\Delta T_f = K_f \times m$. Rearrange to solve for m.

$$m = \frac{\Delta T_f}{K_f} = \frac{3.16\,^\circ C}{1.86\,\dfrac{^\circ C}{m}} = 1.69892 \; m \text{ then } m = \frac{\text{amount solute (moles)}}{\text{mass solvent (kg)}} \text{ so}$$

$$mol_{Unk} = m_{Unk} \times kg_{H_2O} = 1.69892 \, \frac{\text{mol Unk}}{\text{kg}} \times 0.0500 \text{ kg} = 0.08494600 \text{ mol Unk then}$$

$$\mathcal{M} = \frac{g_{Unk}}{mol_{Unk}} = \frac{10.05 \text{ g}}{0.08494600 \text{ mol}} = 118.3105 \, \frac{\text{g}}{\text{mol}} \text{ then}$$

$$\frac{118.3105 \text{ g Unk}}{1 \text{ mol Unk}} \times \frac{60.97 \text{ g C}}{100 \text{ g Unk}} \times \frac{1 \text{ mol C}}{12.01 \text{ g C}} = \frac{6.01 \text{ mol C}}{1 \text{ mol Unk}}$$

$$\frac{118.3105 \text{ g Unk}}{1 \text{ mol Unk}} \times \frac{11.94 \text{ g H}}{100 \text{ g Unk}} \times \frac{1 \text{ mol H}}{1.008 \text{ g H}} = \frac{14.0 \text{ mol H}}{1 \text{ mol Unk}} \text{ and}$$

$$\frac{118.3105 \text{ g Unk}}{1 \text{ mol Unk}} \times \frac{(100 - (60.97 + 11.94)) \text{ g O}}{100 \text{ g Unk}} \times \frac{1 \text{ mol O}}{16.00 \text{ g O}} = \frac{2.00 \text{ mol O}}{1 \text{ mol Unk}}$$

So the molecular formula is $C_6H_{12}O_2$.

Check: The units (formula) are correct. The magnitude of the answer (formula with ~118 g/mol) seems reasonable because the molality is ~1.7 and we have ~10 g. It is a reasonable molecular weight for a solid or liquid. The formula does have the correct molar mass.

12.93   **Given:** 100.0 mL solution 13.5% by mass NaCl, $d = 1.12$ g/mL; $T_b = 104.4\,^\circ C$ **Find:** gNaCl or water to add
Other: $K_b = 0.512\,^\circ C/m$; $i_{measured} = 1.8$
Conceptual Plan: $T_b \rightarrow \Delta T_b$ then $\Delta T_b, i, K_b \rightarrow m$ then $mL_{solution} \rightarrow g_{solution} \rightarrow g_{NaCl} \rightarrow mol_{NaCl}$ then

$$\Delta T_b = T_b - T_b^\circ \qquad\qquad \Delta T_b = K_b \times i \times m \qquad \frac{1.12 \text{ g solution}}{1 \text{ mL solution}} \quad \frac{13.5 \text{ g NaCl}}{100 \text{ g solution}} \quad \frac{1 \text{ mol NaCl}}{58.44 \text{ g NaCl}}$$

$m, mol_{NaCl} \rightarrow kg_{H_2O} \rightarrow g_{H_2O}$ and $g_{solution}, g_{NaCl} \rightarrow g_{H_2O}$ then **compare the initial and final g_{H_2O} then**

$$m = \frac{\text{amount solute (moles)}}{\text{mass solvent (kg)}} \quad \frac{1000 \text{ g}}{1 \text{ kg}} \qquad\qquad g_{solution} = g_{NaCl} + g_{H_2O}$$

Calculate the total NaCl in final solution by scaling up the amount from the initial solution. Then calculate the difference between the needed and starting amounts of NaCl.
Solution: $\Delta T_b = T_b - T_b^\circ = 104.4\,^\circ C - 100.0\,^\circ C = 4.4\,^\circ C$ then $\Delta T_b = K_b \times i \times m$

Rearrange to solve for m. $m = \dfrac{\Delta T_b}{K_b \, i} = \dfrac{4.4\,^\circ C}{0.512\,\dfrac{^\circ C}{m} \times 1.8} = 4.774306 \; m$ NaCl then

$$\text{mass of solution} = 10.0 \text{ mL solution} \times \frac{1.12 \text{ g solution}}{1 \text{ mL solution}} = 112 \text{ g solution}$$

$$\text{mass of NaCl} = 112 \text{ g solution} \times \frac{13.5 \text{ g NaCl}}{100 \text{ g solution}} = 15.\underline{1}2 \text{ g NaCl}$$

$$\text{mol NaCl} = 15.12 \text{ g NaCl} \times \frac{1 \text{ mol NaCl}}{58.44 \text{ g NaCl}} = 0.25\underline{8}7269 \text{ mol NaCl}$$

then $m = \dfrac{\text{amount solute (moles)}}{\text{mass solvent (kg)}}$. Rearrange to solve for kg_{H_2O}.

$$\text{kg}_{H_2O} = \frac{\text{mol}_{NaCl}}{m} = \frac{0.25\underline{8}7269 \text{ mol NaCl}}{\dfrac{4.\underline{7}74306 \text{ mol NaCl}}{1 \text{ kg}_{H_2O}}} = 0.05\underline{4}1915 \text{ kg}_{H_2O} \times \frac{1000 \text{ g}_{H_2O}}{1 \text{ kg}_{H_2O}} = 54.\underline{1}915 \text{ g}_{H_2O} \text{ in final solution then}$$

$g_{solution} = g_{NaCl} + g_{H_2O} = 112 \text{ g solution} - 15.\underline{1}2 \text{ g NaCl} = 96.88 \text{ g } H_2O$ in initial solution. Comparing the initial and final solutions, we find that there is a lot more water in the initial solution; so NaCl needs to be added.

In the solution with a boiling point of 104.4 °C, $\dfrac{15.\underline{1}2 \text{ g NaCl}}{54.\underline{1}915 \text{ g } H_2O} = \dfrac{x \text{ g NaCl}}{96.88 \text{ g } H_2O}$. Solve for x g NaCl.

$$x \text{ g NaCl} = \frac{15.\underline{1}2 \text{ g NaCl}}{54.\underline{1}915 \text{ g } H_2O} \times 96.88 \text{ g } H_2O = 27.031 \text{ g NaCl}; \text{ so the amount to be added is}$$

$$27.031 \text{ g NaCl} - 15.\underline{1}2 \text{ g NaCl} = 11.911 \text{ g NaCl} = 12 \text{ g NaCl}$$

Check: The units (g) are correct. The magnitude of the answer (12 g) seems reasonable because there is approximately twice as much water as is desired in the initial solution; so the NaCl amount needs to be approximately doubled.

Challenge Problems

12.95 **Given:** N_2: $k_H(N_2) = 6.1 \times 10^{-4}$ M/atm at 25 °C; 14.6 mg/L at 50 °C and 1.00 atm; $P_{N_2} = 0.78$ atm;
O_2: $k_H(O_2) = 1.3 \times 10^{-3}$ M/atm at 25 °C; 27.8 mg/L at 50 °C and 1.00 atm; $P_{O_2} = 0.21$ atm; and 1.5 L water
Find: $V(N_2)$ and $V(O_2)$
Conceptual Plan: at 25 °C: $P_{Total}, \chi_{N_2} \rightarrow P_{N_2}$ then $P_{N_2}, k_H(N_2) \rightarrow S_{N_2}$ then $L \rightarrow mol$

$$\underset{P_{N_2} = \chi_{N_2} P_{Total}}{} \qquad \underset{S_{N_2} = k_H(N_2) P_{N_2}}{} \qquad \underset{S_{N_2}}{}$$

at 50 °C: $L \rightarrow mL \rightarrow mg \rightarrow g \rightarrow mol$ then $mol_{25\,°C}, mol_{25\,°C} \rightarrow mol_{removed}$ then °C $\rightarrow$ K

$$\frac{1000 \text{ mL}}{1 \text{ L}} \quad \frac{14.6 \text{ mg}}{1 \text{ L}} \quad \frac{1 \text{ g}}{1000 \text{ mg}} \quad \frac{1 \text{ mol}}{28.02 \text{ g}} \qquad mol_{removed} = mol_{25\,°C} - mol_{50\,°C} \qquad K = °C + 273.15$$

then $P, n, T \rightarrow V$

$$PV = nRT$$

at 25 °C: $P_{Total}, \chi_{O_2} \rightarrow P_{O_2}$ then $P_{O_2}, k_H(O_2) \rightarrow S_{O_2}$ then $L \rightarrow mol$

$$\underset{P_{O_2} = \chi_{O_2} P_{Total}}{} \qquad \underset{S_{O_2} = k_H(O_2) P_{O_2}}{} \qquad \underset{S_{O_2}}{}$$

at 50 °C: $L \rightarrow mL \rightarrow mg \rightarrow g \rightarrow mol$ then $mol_{25\,°C}, mol_{25\,°C} \rightarrow mol_{removed}$ then °C $\rightarrow$ K

$$\frac{1000 \text{ mL}}{1 \text{ L}} \quad \frac{27.8 \text{ mg}}{1 \text{ L}} \quad \frac{1 \text{ g}}{1000 \text{ mg}} \quad \frac{1 \text{ mol}}{32.00 \text{ g}} \qquad mol_{removed} = mol_{25\,°C} - mol_{50\,°C} \qquad K = °C + 273.15$$

then $P, n, T \rightarrow V$

$$PV = nRT$$

Solution: at 25 °C: $P_{N_2} = \chi_{N_2} P_{Total} = 0.78 \times 1.0 \text{ atm} = 0.78$ atm then

$$S_{N_2} = k_H(N_2) P_{N_2} = 6.1 \times 10^{-4} \frac{M}{atm} \times 0.78 \text{ atm} = 4.\underline{7}58 \times 10^{-4} \text{ M then}$$

$$1.5 \text{ L} \times 4.\underline{7}58 \times 10^{-4} \frac{mol}{L} = 0.0007\underline{1}370 \text{ mol}$$

at 50 °C: $1.5 \text{ L} \times \dfrac{14.6 \text{ mg}}{1 \text{ L} \cdot \text{atm}} \times 0.78 \text{ atm} \times \dfrac{1 \text{ g}}{1000 \text{ mg}} \times \dfrac{1 \text{ mol}}{28.02 \text{ g}} = 0.0006\underline{0}964 \text{ mol then}$

$mol_{removed} = mol_{25\,°C} - mol_{50\,°C} = 0.0007\underline{1}370 \text{ mol} - 0.0006\underline{0}964 \text{ mol} = 1.\underline{0}39 \times 10^{-4} \text{ mol } N_2$

then 50 °C + 273.15 = 323 K then $PV = nRT$. Rearrange to solve for V.

$$V = \frac{nRT}{P} = \frac{1.039 \times 10^{-4} \text{ mol} \times 0.08206 \frac{\text{L} \cdot \text{atm}}{\text{K} \cdot \text{mol}} \times 323 \text{ K}}{1.00 \text{ atm}} = 0.0027539 \text{ L N}_2$$

at 25 °C: $P_{O_2} = \chi_{O_2} P_{\text{Total}} = 0.21 \times 1.0 \text{ atm} = 0.21 \text{ atm}$ then

$$S_{O_2} = k_H(O_2)P_{O_2} = 1.3 \times 10^{-3} \frac{\text{M}}{\text{atm}} \times 0.21 \text{ atm} = 2.73 \times 10^{-4} \text{ M} \text{ then}$$

$$1.5 \text{ L} \times 2.73 \times 10^{-4} \frac{\text{mol}}{\text{L}} = 0.0004095 \text{ mol}$$

at 50 °C: $1.5 \text{ L} \times \frac{27.8 \text{ mg}}{1 \text{ L} \cdot \text{atm}} \times 0.21 \text{ atm} \times \frac{1 \text{ g}}{1000 \text{ mg}} \times \frac{1 \text{ mol}}{32.00 \text{ g}} = 0.00027366 \text{ mol}$ then

$\text{mol}_{\text{removed}} = \text{mol}_{25\,°\text{C}} - \text{mol}_{50\,°\text{C}} = 0.0004095 \text{ mol} - 0.00027366 \text{ mol} = 1.358 \times 10^{-4} \text{ mol O}_2$

then 50 °C + 273.15 = 323 K then $PV = nRT$. Rearrange to solve for V.

$$V = \frac{nRT}{P} = \frac{1.358 \times 10^{-4} \text{ mol} \times 0.08206 \frac{\text{L} \cdot \text{atm}}{\text{K} \cdot \text{mol}} \times 323 \text{ K}}{1.00 \text{ atm}} = 0.0035994 \text{ L O}_2 \text{ finally}$$

$V_{\text{Total}} = V_{N_2} + V_{O_2} = 0.0027526 \text{ L} + 0.0035994 \text{ L} = 0.0064 \text{ L}$

Check: The units (L) are correct. The magnitude of the answer (0.006 L) seems reasonable because we have so little dissolved gas at room temperature and most is still soluble at 50 °C.

12.97   **Given:** 1.10 g glucose ($C_6H_{12}O_6$) and sucrose ($C_{12}H_{22}O_{11}$) mixture in 25.0 mL solution and $\Pi = 3.78$ atm at 298 K
Find: percent composition of mixture
Conceptual Plan: $\Pi, T \rightarrow M$ then $mL_{\text{soln}} \rightarrow L_{\text{soln}}$ then $L_{\text{soln}}, M \rightarrow \text{mol}_{\text{mixture}}$ then

$$\Pi = MRT \qquad \frac{1 \text{ L}}{1000 \text{ mL}} \qquad M = \frac{\text{amount solute (moles)}}{\text{volume solution (L)}}$$

$\text{mol}_{\text{mixture}}, g_{\text{mixture}} \rightarrow \text{mol}_{C_6H_{12}O_6}, \text{mol}_{C_{12}H_{22}O_{11}}$ then

$g_{\text{mixture}} = \text{mol } C_6H_{12}O_6 \times \frac{180.16 \text{ g } C_6H_{12}O_6}{1 \text{ mol } C_6H_{12}O_6} + \text{mol } C_{12}H_{22}O_{11} \times \frac{342.30 \text{ g } C_{12}H_{22}O_{11}}{1 \text{ mol } C_{12}H_{22}O_{11}}$ with $\text{mol}_{\text{mixture}} = \text{mol}_{C_6H_{12}O_6} + \text{mol}_{C_{12}H_{22}O_{11}}$

$\text{mol}_{C_6H_{12}O_6} \rightarrow g_{C_6H_{12}O_6}$ and $\text{mol}_{C_{12}H_{22}O_{11}} \rightarrow g_{C_{12}H_{22}O_{11}}$ and $g_{C_6H_{12}O_6}, g_{C_{12}H_{22}O_{11}} \rightarrow$ **mass percents**

$$\frac{180.16 \text{ g } C_6H_{12}O_6}{1 \text{ mol } C_6H_{12}O_6} \qquad \frac{342.30 \text{ g } C_{12}H_{22}O_{11}}{1 \text{ mol } C_{12}H_{22}O_{11}} \qquad \text{mass percent} = \frac{\text{mass solute}}{\text{mass solution}} \times 100\%$$

Solution: $\Pi = MRT$. Rearrange to solve for M.

$$M = \frac{\Pi}{RT} = \frac{3.78 \text{ atm}}{0.08206 \frac{\text{L} \cdot \text{atm}}{\text{K} \cdot \text{mol}} \times 298 \text{ K}} = 0.154577 \frac{\text{mol mixture}}{\text{L}} \text{ then } 25.0 \text{ mL} \times \frac{1 \text{ L}}{1000 \text{ mL}} = 0.0250 \text{ L then}$$

$$M = \frac{\text{amount solute (moles)}}{\text{volume solution (L)}} \text{ so}$$

$\text{mol}_{\text{mixture}} = M \times L_{\text{soln}} = 0.154577 \frac{\text{mol mixture}}{\text{L}} \times 0.0250 \text{ L} = 0.00386442 \text{ mol mixture then}$

$g_{\text{mixture}} = \text{mol } C_6H_{12}O_6 \times \frac{180.16 \text{ g } C_6H_{12}O_6}{1 \text{ mol } C_6H_{12}O_6} + \text{mol } C_{12}H_{22}O_{11} \times \frac{342.30 \text{ g } C_{12}H_{22}O_{11}}{1 \text{ mol } C_{12}H_{22}O_{11}}$ with

$\text{mol}_{\text{mixture}} = \text{mol}_{C_6H_{12}O_6} + \text{mol}_{C_{12}H_{22}O_{11}}$ so

$1.10 \text{ g} = \text{mol } C_6H_{12}O_6 \times \frac{180.16 \text{ g } C_6H_{12}O_6}{1 \text{ mol } C_6H_{12}O_6} + (0.00386442 \text{ mol} - \text{mol } C_6H_{12}O_6) \times \frac{342.30 \text{ g } C_{12}H_{22}O_{11}}{1 \text{ mol } C_{12}H_{22}O_{11}} \rightarrow$

$1.10 = 180.16 \times \text{mol } C_6H_{12}O_6 + 1.32279 - 342.30 \times \text{mol } C_6H_{12}O_6 \rightarrow 162.14 \, x \text{ mol } C_6H_{12}O_6 = 0.22279 \rightarrow$

$x \text{ mol } C_6H_{12}O_6 = \frac{0.22279}{162.14} = 0.00137406 \text{ mol } C_6H_{12}O_6 \text{ then}$

$\text{mol}_{C_{12}H_{22}O_{11}} = \text{mol}_{\text{mixture}} - \text{mol}_{C_6H_{12}O_6} = 0.00386442 \text{ mol} - 0.00137406 \text{ mol}$

$= 0.0024904 \text{ mol } C_{12}H_{22}O_{11} \text{ then}$

$0.00137406 \text{ mol } C_6H_{12}O_6 \times \frac{180.16 \text{ g } C_6H_{12}O_6}{1 \text{ mol } C_6H_{12}O_6} = 0.24755 \text{ g } C_6H_{12}O_6 \text{ and}$

$$0.00\underline{2}4904 \ \text{mol} \ \cancel{C_{12}H_{22}O_{11}} \times \frac{342.30 \ \text{g} \ C_{12}H_{22}O_{11}}{1 \ \text{mol} \ \cancel{C_{12}H_{22}O_{11}}} = 0.8\underline{5}245 \ \text{g} \ C_{12}H_{22}O_{11} \ \text{finally}$$

$$\text{mass percent} = \frac{\text{mass solute}}{\text{mass solution}} \times 100\% = \frac{0.2\underline{4}755 \ \text{g} \ \cancel{C_6H_{12}O_6}}{0.2\underline{4}755 \ \text{g} \ \cancel{C_6H_{12}O_6} + 0.8\underline{5}245 \ \text{g} \ \cancel{C_{12}H_{22}O_{11}}} \times 100\%$$

$$= 2\underline{2}.50\% \ C_6H_{12}O_6 \ \text{by mass and} \ 100.00\% - 2\underline{2}.50\% = 7\underline{7}.50\% \ C_{12}H_{22}O_{11} \ \text{by mass}$$

Check: The units (% by mass) are correct. We expect the percent by $C_{12}H_{22}O_{11}$ to be larger than that for $C_6H_{12}O_6$ because the $g_{mixture}/mol_{mixture} = 285$ g/mol, which is closer to $C_{12}H_{22}O_{11}$ than $C_6H_{12}O_6$ and the molar mass of $C_{12}H_{22}O_{11}$ is larger than the molar mass of $C_6H_{12}O_6$. In addition, and most definitively, the masses obtained for sucrose and glucose sum to 1.1 g, the initial amount of solid dissolved.

12.99   **Given:** isopropyl alcohol ($(CH_3)_2CHOH$) and propyl alcohol ($CH_3CH_2CH_2OH$) at 313 K; solution 2/3 by mass isopropyl alcohol $P_{2/3} = 0.110$ atm; solution 1/3 by mass isopropyl alcohol $P_{1/3} = 0.089$ atm
Find: P°_{iso} and P°_{pro} and explain why they are different
Conceptual Plan: Because these are isomers, they have the same molar mass and so the fraction by mass is the same as the mole fraction, so mole fractions, P_{soln}s $\rightarrow P^\circ$s

$$\chi_{iso} = \frac{\text{amount iso (in moles)}}{\text{total amount (in moles)}} \quad \chi_{pro} = 1 - \chi_{iso} \quad P_{iso} = \chi_{iso}P^\circ_{iso} \quad P_{pro} = \chi_{pro}P^\circ_{pro} \ \text{and} \ P_{soln} = P_{iso} + P_{pro}$$

Solution:
Solution 1: $\chi_{iso} = 2/3$ and $\chi_{iso} = 1/3 \ P_{soln} = P_{iso} + P_{pro}$ so $0.110 \ \text{atm} = 2/3P^\circ_{iso} + 1/3P^\circ_{pro}$
Solution 2: $\chi_{iso} = 1/3$ and $\chi_{iso} = 2/3 \ P_{soln} = P_{iso} + P_{pro}$ so $0.089 \ \text{atm} = 1/3P^\circ_{iso} + 2/3P^\circ_{pro}$. We now have two equations and two unknowns and a number of ways to solve this. One way is to rearrange the first equation for P°_{iso} and substitute into the other equation. Thus, $P^\circ_{iso} = 3/2(0.110 \ \text{atm} - 1/3P^\circ_{pro})$ and

$$0.089 \ \text{atm} = \frac{1}{\cancel{3}} \frac{\cancel{3}}{2}(0.110 \ \text{atm} - 1/3 \ P^\circ_{pro}) + \frac{2}{3} P^\circ_{pro} \rightarrow 0.089 \ \text{atm} = 0.0550 \ \text{atm} - \frac{1}{6} P^\circ_{pro} + \frac{2}{3} P^\circ_{pro} \rightarrow$$

$$\frac{1}{2} P^\circ_{pro} = 0.0\underline{3}40 \ \text{atm} \rightarrow P^\circ_{pro} = 0.0\underline{6}80 \ \text{atm} = 0.068 \ \text{atm and then}$$

$$P^\circ_{iso} = 3/2(0.110 \ \text{atm} - 1/3P^\circ_{pro}) = 3/2(0.110 \ \text{atm} - 1/3(0.0\underline{6}80 \ \text{atm})) = 0.131 \ \text{atm}$$

The major intermolecular attractions are between the OH groups. The OH group at the end of the chain in propyl alcohol is more accessible than the one in the middle of the chain in isopropyl alcohol. In addition, the molecular shape of propyl alcohol is a straight chain of carbon atoms, while that of isopropyl alcohol has a branched chain and is more like a ball. The contact area between two ball-like objects is smaller than that of two chain-like objects. The smaller contact area in isopropyl alcohol means that the molecules do not attract each other as strongly as do those of propyl alcohol. As a result of both of these factors, the vapor pressure of isopropyl alcohol is higher.

Check: The units (atm) are correct. The magnitude of the answers seems reasonable because both solution partial pressures are ~ 0.1 atm.

12.101   **Given:** 75.0 g of benzene (C_6H_6) and 75.0 g of toluene (C_7H_8) at 303 K $P^\circ_{Total} = 80.9$ mmHg; 100.0 g of benzene (C_6H_6) and 50.0 g of toluene (C_7H_8) at 303 K $P^\circ_{Total} = 93.9$ mmHg   **Find:** $P^\circ_{C_6H_6}$, $P^\circ_{C_8H_8}$
Conceptual Plan: for each solution,
$g_{C_6H_6} \rightarrow mol_{C_7H_8}$ and $g_{C_7H_8} \rightarrow mol_{C_7H_8}$ then $mol_{C_6H_6}, mol_{C_7H_8} \rightarrow \chi_{C_6H_6}, \chi_{C_7H_8}$ then

$$\frac{1 \ \text{mol} \ C_6H_6}{78.11 \ \text{g} \ C_6H_6} \qquad \frac{1 \ \text{mol} \ C_7H_8}{92.13 \ \text{g} \ C_7H_8} \qquad \chi_{C_6H_6} = \frac{\text{amount} \ C_6H_6 \ (\text{in moles})}{\text{total amount (in moles)}} \qquad \chi_{C_7H_8} = 1 - \chi_{C_6H_6}$$

write expressions relating $\chi_{C_6H_6}, P^\circ_{C_6H_6} \rightarrow P_{C_6H_6}$ **and** $\chi_{C_7H_8}, P^\circ_{C_7H_8} \rightarrow P_{C_8H_{18}}$ **and** $P_{C_6H_6}, P_{C_7H_8} \rightarrow P_{Total}$

$$P_{C_6H_6} = \chi_{C_6H_6}P^\circ_{C_6H_6} \qquad P_{C_7H_8} = \chi_{C_7H_8}P^\circ_{C_7H_8} \qquad P_{Total} = P_{C_6H_6} + P_{C_7H_8}$$

then solve the two simultaneous equations for $P^\circ_{C_6H_6}$ **and** $P^\circ_{C_7H_8}$

Solution: For the first solution: $75.0 \ \text{g} \ \cancel{C_6H_6} \times \frac{1 \ \text{mol} \ C_6H_6}{78.11 \ \text{g} \ \cancel{C_6H_6}} = 0.96\underline{0}18436 \ \text{mol} \ C_6H_6$ and

$$75.0 \ \text{g} \ \cancel{C_7H_8} \times \frac{1 \ \text{mol} \ C_7H_8}{92.13 \ \text{g} \ \cancel{C_7H_8}} = 0.81\underline{4}06708 \ \text{mol} \ C_7H_8 \ \text{then}$$

$$\chi_{C_6H_6} = \frac{\text{amount} \ C_6H_6 \ (\text{in moles})}{\text{total amount (in moles)}} = \frac{0.96\underline{0}18436 \ \cancel{\text{mol}}}{0.96\underline{0}18436 \ \cancel{\text{mol}} + 0.81\underline{4}06708 \ \cancel{\text{mol}}} = 0.54\underline{1}17716 \ \text{and}$$

$$\chi_{C_7H_8} = 1 - \chi_{C_6H_6} = 1 - 0.54\underline{1}17716 = 0.45\underline{8}82284 \ \text{then}$$

$$P_{Total} = P_{C_6H_6} + P_{C_7H_8} = \chi_{C_6H_6}P^\circ_{C_6H_6} + \chi_{C_7H_8}P^\circ_{C_7H_8}$$

$$= 0.54\underline{1}17716P^\circ_{C_6H_6} + 0.45\underline{8}82284P^\circ_{C_7H_8} = 80.9 \text{ mmHg}$$

For the second solution: $100.0 \text{ g } C_6H_6 \times \dfrac{1 \text{ mol } C_6H_6}{78.11 \text{ g } C_6H_6} = 1.28\underline{0}24581 \text{ mol } C_6H_6$ and

$50.0 \text{ g } C_7H_8 \times \dfrac{1 \text{ mol } C_7H_8}{92.13 \text{ g } C_7H_8} = 0.54\underline{2}71139 \text{ mol } C_7H_8$ then

$$\chi_{C_6H_6} = \frac{\text{amount } C_6H_6 \text{ (in moles)}}{\text{total amount (in moles)}} = \frac{1.28\underline{0}24581 \text{ mol}}{1.28\underline{0}24581 \text{ mol} + 0.54\underline{2}71139 \text{ mol}} = 0.702290657 \text{ and}$$

$\chi_{C_7H_8} = 1 - \chi_{C_6H_6} = 1 - 0.702290657 = 0.297\underline{7}09343$ then

$$P_{Total} = P_{C_6H_6} + P_{C_7H_8} = P_{C_7H_{16}} = \chi_{C_6H_6}P^\circ_{C_6H_6} + \chi_{C_7H_8}P^\circ_{C_7H_8}$$

$$= 0.702\underline{2}90657P^\circ_{C_6H_6} + 0.297\underline{7}09343P^\circ_{C_7H_8} = 93.9 \text{ mmHg}$$

Solve the two simultaneous equations for $P^\circ_{C_6H_6}$ and $P^\circ_{C_7H_8}$.

$$P^\circ_{C_6H_6} = \frac{80.9 \text{ mmHg} - 0.45\underline{8}82284P^\circ_{C_7H_8}}{0.54\underline{1}17716} = 149.\underline{4}8894 \text{ mmHg} - 0.84\underline{7}82373\, P^\circ_{C_7H_8} \text{ then}$$

$0.702\underline{2}90657(149.\underline{4}8894 \text{ mmHg} - 0.84\underline{7}82373P^\circ_{C_7H_8}) + 0.297\underline{7}09343P^\circ_{C_7H_8} = 93.9 \text{ mmHg} \rightarrow$

$104.\underline{9}8468 \text{ mmHg} - 0.59\underline{5}41868P^\circ_{C_7H_8} + 0.297\underline{7}09343P^\circ_{C_7H_8} = 93.9 \text{ mmHg} \rightarrow$

$11.\underline{0}8469 \text{ mmHg} = 0.29\underline{7}70935P^\circ_{C_7H_8} \rightarrow$

$$P^\circ_{C_7H_8} = \frac{11.\underline{0}8469 \text{ mmHg}}{0.29\underline{7}70935} = 37.\underline{2}33261 \text{ mmHg} = 37.2 \text{ mmHg} \text{ then}$$

$P^\circ_{C_6H_6} = 149.\underline{4}8894 \text{ mmHg} - 0.84\underline{7}82373P^\circ_{C_7H_8}$

$= 149.\underline{4}8894 \text{ mmHg} - 0.84\underline{7}82373 \times 37.\underline{2}33261 \text{ mmHg} = 117.\underline{9}217 \text{ mmHg} = 118 \text{ mmHg}$

Check: The units (mmHg and mmHg) are correct. The magnitude of the answers (118 mmHg and 37.2 mmHg) seems reasonable because we expect toluene to have a lower vapor pressure than benzene (based on molar mass).

Conceptual Problems

12.103   (a)   The two substances mix because the intermolecular forces among all of the species are roughly equal and there is a pervasive tendency to increase randomness, which happens when the two substances mix.

(b) $\Delta H_{soln} \approx 0$ because the intermolecular forces between themselves are roughly equal to the forces between each other.

(c) ΔH_{solute} and $\Delta H_{solvent}$ are positive, and ΔH_{mix} is negative and equals the sum of ΔH_{solute} and $\Delta H_{solvent}$.

12.105   (d) More solute particles are found in an ionic solution because the solute breaks apart into its ions. The vapor pressure is lowered due to fewer solvent particles in the vapor phase as more solute particles are present.

12.107   The balloon not only loses He, it also takes in N_2 and O_2 from the air surrounding the balloon (due to the tendency for mixing), increasing the density of the gas inside the balloon, thus increasing the density of the balloon.

Questions for Group Work

12.109   The lattice energy, $\Delta H_{lattice}$, is the enthalpy change during the formation of the crystalline solid from the gaseous ions.

The energy required to separate solute particles is called ΔH_{solute} and is always endothermic. For ionic compounds, ΔH_{solute}, the energy required to separate the solute into its constituent particles, is simply the negative of the solute's lattice energy ($\Delta H_{solute} = -\Delta H_{lattice}$), discussed in Section 9.4.

The energy required to separate solvent particles is called $\Delta H_{solvent}$ and is always endothermic.

The energy of mixing solute particles and solvent particles is called ΔH_{mix} and is always exothermic.

The heat of hydration is simply the enthalpy change that occurs when 1 mol of the gaseous solute ions is dissolved in water. In aqueous solutions, $\Delta H_{solvent}$ and ΔH_{mix} can be combined into a single term called the heat of hydration ($\Delta H_{hydration}$) so, $\Delta H_{hydration} = \Delta H_{solvent} + \Delta H_{mix}$. Because the ion–dipole interactions that occur between a dissolved ion and the surrounding water molecules are much stronger than the hydrogen bonds in water, $\Delta H_{\text{hydration}}$ is always largely negative (exothermic) for ionic compounds.

The overall enthalpy change upon solution formation is called the enthalpy of solution (ΔH_{soln}). Using the heat of hydration, we can write the enthalpy of solution as a sum of just two terms, one endothermic and one exothermic: ΔH_{soln} $= \Delta H_{\text{solute}} + \Delta H_{\text{solvent}} + \Delta H_{\text{mix}} = \Delta H_{\text{solute}} + \Delta H_{\text{hydration}} = \text{endothermic}(+) \text{ term} + \text{exothermic}(-) \text{ term}.$

For ionic aqueous solutions, then, the overall enthalpy of solution depends on the relative magnitudes of ΔH_{solute} and $\Delta H_{\text{hydration}}$, with three possible scenarios (in each case we refer to the magnitude or absolute value of ΔH): (1) If $\Delta H_{\text{solute}} < \Delta H_{\text{hydration}}$, the amount of energy required to separate the solute into its constituent ions is less than the energy given off when the ions are hydrated. ΔH_{soln} is therefore negative, the solution process is exothermic, and the solution feels warm to the touch. (2) If $\Delta H_{\text{solute}} > \Delta H_{\text{hydration}}$, the amount of energy required to separate the solute into its constituent ions is greater than the energy given off when the ions are hydrated. ΔH_{soln} is therefore positive and the solution process is endothermic (if a solution forms at all), and the resulting solution feels cool to the touch. (3) If $\Delta H_{\text{solute}} \approx \Delta H_{\text{hydration}}$, the amount of energy required to separate the solute into its constituent ions is about equal to the energy given off when the ions are hydrated. ΔH_{soln} is therefore approximately zero, and the solution process is neither appreciably exothermic nor appreciably endothermic and there is no noticeable change in temperature.

12.111 (a) **Given:** 13.62 g of sucrose ($C_{12}H_{22}O_{11}$) in 241.5 mL water; d (water) $= 0.997$ g/mL **Find:** percent by mass

Conceptual Plan: $d, V \rightarrow g_{H_2O}$ then $g_{C_{12}H_{22}O_{11}}, g_{H_2O} \rightarrow g_{\text{soln}}$ then $g_{C_{12}H_{22}O_{11}}, g_{\text{soln}} \rightarrow$ **percent by mass**

$$d = \frac{m}{V} \qquad g_{\text{soln}} = g_{C_6H_{12}O_6} + g_{H_2O} \qquad \text{mass percent} = \frac{\text{mass solute}}{\text{mass solution}} \times 100\%$$

Solution: $d = \frac{m}{V}$ so $241.5 \text{ mL} \times \dfrac{0.997 \text{ g}}{1 \text{ mL}} = 240.7755 \text{ g}$

$g_{\text{soln}} = g_{C_6H_{12}O_6} + g_{H_2O} = 13.62 \text{ g} + 240.7755 \text{ g} = 254.3955 \text{ g soln then}$

$\text{mass percent} = \dfrac{\text{mass solute}}{\text{mass solution}} \times 100\% = \dfrac{13.62 \text{ g } C_{12}H_{22}O_{11}}{254.3955 \text{ g soln}} \times 100\% = 5.35 \text{ percent by mass}$

Check: The units (percent by mass) are correct. The magnitude of the answer (5%) seems reasonable since we are dissolving 14 g in 241 g.

(b) **Given:** 13.62 g of sucrose ($C_{12}H_{22}O_{11}$) in 241.5 mL water; final volume $= 250.0$ mL **Find:** molarity

Conceptual Plan: $mL \rightarrow L$ and $g_{C_{12}H_{22}O_{11}} \rightarrow mol_{C_{12}H_{22}O_{11}}$ then $mol_{C_{12}H_{22}O_{11}}, V \rightarrow M$

$$\frac{1 \text{ L}}{1000 \text{ mL}} \qquad \frac{1 \text{ mol } C_{12}H_{22}O_{11}}{342.30 \text{ g } C_{12}H_{22}O_{11}} \qquad M = \frac{\text{amount solute (moles)}}{\text{volume solution (L)}}$$

Solution: $250.0 \text{ mL} \times \dfrac{1 \text{ L}}{1000 \text{ mL}} = 0.2500 \text{ L}$ and

$13.62 \text{ g } C_{12}H_{22}O_{11} \times \dfrac{1 \text{ mol } C_{12}H_{22}O_{11}}{342.30 \text{ g } C_{12}H_{22}O_{11}} = 0.03978966 \text{ mol } C_{12}H_{22}O_{11}$

$M = \dfrac{\text{amount solute (moles)}}{\text{volume solution (L)}} = \dfrac{0.03978966 \text{ mol } C_{12}H_{22}O_{11}}{0.2500 \text{ L}} = 0.1592 \text{ M}$

Check: The units (M) are correct. The magnitude of the answer (0.2 M) seems reasonable since we have 1/25 mole in 1/4 L.

(c) **Given:** 13.62 g of sucrose ($C_{12}H_{22}O_{11}$) in 241.5 mL water; d (water) $= 0.997$ g/mL **Find:** molality

Conceptual Plan: $g_{H_2O} \rightarrow kg_{H_2O}$ and $g_{C_6H_{12}O_6} \rightarrow mol_{C_6H_{12}O_6}$ then $mol_{C_6H_{12}O_6}, kg_{H_2O} \rightarrow m$

$$\frac{1 \text{ kg}}{1000 \text{ g}} \qquad \frac{1 \text{ mol } C_{12}H_{22}O_{11}}{342.30 \text{ g } C_{12}H_{22}O_{11}} \qquad m = \frac{\text{amount solute (moles)}}{\text{mass solvent (kg)}}$$

Solution: $g_{H_2O} = 240.7755 \text{ g}$ from part (a); $240.7755 \text{ g} \times \dfrac{1 \text{ kg}}{1000 \text{ g}} = 0.2407755 \text{ kg}$ and

$mol_{C_6H_{12}O_6} = 0.03978966 \text{ mol } C_{12}H_{22}O_{11}$ from part (a);

$m = \dfrac{\text{amount solute (moles)}}{\text{mass solvent (kg)}} = \dfrac{0.03978966 \text{ mol } C_{12}H_{22}O_{11}}{0.2407755 \text{ kg}} = 0.165 \text{ } m$

Check: The units (m) are correct. The magnitude of the answer (0.2 m) seems reasonable since we have 1/25 mole in about 1/4 kg.

13 Chemical Kinetics

Reaction Rates

13.1   (a) $\text{Rate} = -\dfrac{1}{2}\dfrac{\Delta[\text{HBr}]}{\Delta t} = \dfrac{\Delta[\text{H}_2]}{\Delta t} = \dfrac{\Delta[\text{Br}_2]}{\Delta t}$

       (b)   **Given:** first 15.0 s; 0.500 M to 0.455 M   **Find:** average rate

             Conceptual Plan: $t_1, t_2, [\text{HBr}]_1, [\text{HBr}]_2 \rightarrow$ **average rate**

$$\text{Rate} = -\frac{1}{2}\frac{\Delta[\text{HBr}]}{\Delta t}$$

             Solution: $\text{Rate} = -\dfrac{1}{2}\dfrac{[\text{HBr}]_{t_2} - [\text{HBr}]_{t_1}}{t_2 - t_1} = -\dfrac{1}{2}\dfrac{0.455\ \text{M} - 0.500\ \text{M}}{15.0\ \text{s} - 0.0\ \text{s}} = 1.5 \times 10^{-3}\ \text{M}\cdot\text{s}^{-1}$

             Check: The units ($\text{M}\cdot\text{s}^{-1}$) are correct. The magnitude of the answer ($10^{-3}\ \text{M}\cdot\text{s}^{-1}$) makes physical sense because rates are always positive and we are not changing the concentration much in 15 s.

       (c)   **Given:** 0.500 L vessel, first 15.0 s of reaction, and part (b) data   **Find:** mol_{Br_2} formed

             Conceptual Plan: average rate, $t_1, t_2, \rightarrow \Delta[\text{Br}_2]$ **then** $\Delta[\text{Br}_2], \text{L} \rightarrow \text{mol}_{\text{Br}_2}$ **formed**

$$\text{Rate} = \frac{\Delta[\text{Br}_2]}{\Delta t} \qquad\qquad M = \frac{\text{mol}_{\text{Br}_2}}{\text{L}}$$

             Solution: $\text{Rate} = 1.5 \times 10^{-3}\ \text{M}\cdot\text{s}^{-1} = \dfrac{\Delta[\text{Br}_2]}{\Delta t} = \dfrac{\Delta[\text{Br}_2]}{15.0\ \text{s} - 0.0\ \text{s}}$. Rearrange to solve for $\Delta[\text{Br}_2]$.

$$\Delta[\text{Br}_2] = 1.5 \times 10^{-3}\frac{\text{M}}{\cancel{\text{s}}} \times 15.0\ \cancel{\text{s}} = 0.02\underline{2}5\ \text{M then } M = \frac{\text{mol}_{\text{Br}_2}}{\text{L}}. \text{ Rearrange to solve for}$$

             $\text{mol}_{\text{Br}_2}.\ 0.02\underline{2}5\dfrac{\text{mol Br}_2}{\text{L}} \times 0.500\ \text{L} = 0.011\ \text{mol Br}_2$

             Check: The units (mol) are correct. The magnitude of the answer (0.01 mol) makes physical sense because of the stoichiometric coefficient difference and the volume of the vessel, respectively.

13.3   (a) $\text{Rate} = -\dfrac{1}{2}\dfrac{\Delta[\text{A}]}{\Delta t} = -\dfrac{\Delta[\text{B}]}{\Delta t} = \dfrac{1}{3}\dfrac{\Delta[\text{C}]}{\Delta t}$

       (b)   **Given:** $\dfrac{\Delta[\text{A}]}{\Delta t} = -0.100\ \text{M/s}$ **Find:** $\dfrac{\Delta[\text{B}]}{\Delta t}$ and $\dfrac{\Delta[\text{C}]}{\Delta t}$

             Conceptual Plan: $\dfrac{\Delta[\text{A}]}{\Delta t} \rightarrow \dfrac{\Delta[\text{B}]}{\Delta t}$ and $\dfrac{\Delta[\text{C}]}{\Delta t}$

$$\text{Rate} = -\frac{1}{2}\frac{\Delta[\text{A}]}{\Delta t} = -\frac{\Delta[\text{B}]}{\Delta t} = \frac{1}{3}\frac{\Delta[\text{C}]}{\Delta t}$$

             Solution: $\text{Rate} = -\dfrac{1}{2}\dfrac{\Delta[\text{A}]}{\Delta t} = -\dfrac{\Delta[\text{B}]}{\Delta t} = \dfrac{1}{3}\dfrac{\Delta[\text{C}]}{\Delta t}$. Substitute value and solve for the two desired values.

$$-\frac{1}{2}\frac{-0.100\ \text{M}}{\text{s}} = -\frac{\Delta[\text{B}]}{\Delta t} \text{ so } \frac{\Delta[\text{B}]}{\Delta t} = -0.0500\ \text{M}\cdot\text{s}^{-1} \text{ and } -\frac{1}{2}\frac{-0.100\ \text{M}}{\text{s}} = \frac{1}{3}\frac{\Delta[\text{C}]}{\Delta t} \text{ so}$$

$$\frac{\Delta[C]}{\Delta t} = 0.150 \text{ M} \cdot \text{s}^{-1}$$

Check: The units ($M \cdot s^{-1}$) are correct. The magnitude of the answer ($-0.05 \text{ M} \cdot \text{s}^{-1}$) makes physical sense because fewer moles of B are reacting for every mole of A and the change in concentration with time is negative because this is a reactant. The magnitude of the answer ($0.15 \text{ M} \cdot \text{s}^{-1}$) makes physical sense because more moles of C are being formed for every mole of A reacting and the change in concentration with time is positive because this is a product.

13.5   **Given:** $Cl_2(g) + 3 F_2(g) \rightarrow 2 ClF_3(g)$; $\Delta[Cl_2]/\Delta t = -0.012$ M/s   **Find:** $\Delta[F_2]/\Delta t$; $\Delta[ClF_3]/\Delta t$; and Rate
Conceptual Plan: Write the expression for the rate with respect to each species then

$$\text{Rate} = -\frac{\Delta[Cl_2]}{\Delta t} = -\frac{1}{3}\frac{\Delta[F_2]}{\Delta t} = \frac{1}{2}\frac{\Delta[ClF_3]}{\Delta t}$$

rate expression, $\dfrac{\Delta[Cl_2]}{\Delta t} \rightarrow \dfrac{\Delta[F_2]}{\Delta t}; \dfrac{\Delta[ClF_3]}{\Delta t}$; **Rate**

$$\text{Rate} = -\frac{\Delta[Cl_2]}{\Delta t} = -\frac{1}{3}\frac{\Delta[F_2]}{\Delta t} = \frac{1}{2}\frac{\Delta[ClF_3]}{\Delta t}$$

Solution: Rate $= -\dfrac{\Delta[Cl_2]}{\Delta t} = -\dfrac{1}{3}\dfrac{\Delta[F_2]}{\Delta t} = \dfrac{1}{2}\dfrac{\Delta[ClF_3]}{\Delta t}$ so $-\dfrac{\Delta[Cl_2]}{\Delta t} = -\dfrac{1}{3}\dfrac{\Delta[F_2]}{\Delta t}$

Rearrange to solve for $\dfrac{\Delta[F_2]}{\Delta t}$. $\dfrac{\Delta[F_2]}{\Delta t} = 3\dfrac{\Delta[Cl_2]}{\Delta t} = 3(-0.012 \text{ M} \cdot \text{s}^{-1}) = -0.036 \text{ M} \cdot \text{s}^{-1}$ and

$-\dfrac{\Delta[Cl_2]}{\Delta t} = \dfrac{1}{2}\dfrac{\Delta[ClF_3]}{\Delta t}$ Rearrange to solve for $\dfrac{\Delta[ClF_3]}{\Delta t}$.

$$\frac{\Delta[ClF_3]}{\Delta t} = -2\frac{\Delta[Cl_2]}{\Delta t} = -2(-0.012 \text{ M} \cdot \text{s}^{-1}) = 0.024 \text{ M} \cdot \text{s}^{-1}$$

Check: The units ($M \cdot s^{-1}$) are correct. The magnitude of the answers ($-0.036 \text{ M} \cdot \text{s}^{-1}$ and $0.024 \text{ M} \cdot \text{s}^{-1}$) makes physical sense because F_2 is being used at three times the rate of Cl_2, ClF_3 is being formed at two times the rate of Cl_2 disappearance, and Cl_2 has a stoichiometric coefficient of 1.

13.7   (a)   **Given:** $[C_4H_8]$ versus time data   **Find:** average rate between 0 and 10 s and between 40 and 50 s
Conceptual Plan: $t_1, t_2, [C_4H_8]_1, [C_4H_8]_2 \rightarrow$ **average rate**

$$\text{Rate} = -\frac{\Delta[C_4H_8]}{\Delta t}$$

Solution: For 0 to 10 s, Rate $= -\dfrac{[C_4H_8]_{t_2} - [C_4H_8]_{t_1}}{t_2 - t_1} = -\dfrac{0.913 \text{ M} - 1.000 \text{ M}}{10. \text{ s} - 0. \text{ s}} = 8.7 \times 10^{-3} \text{ M} \cdot \text{s}^{-1}$ and

for 40 to 50 s, Rate $= -\dfrac{[C_4H_8]_{t_2} - [C_4H_8]_{t_1}}{t_2 - t_1} = -\dfrac{0.637 \text{ M} - 0.697 \text{ M}}{50. \text{ s} - 40. \text{ s}} = 6.0 \times 10^{-3} \text{ M} \cdot \text{s}^{-1}$

Check: The units ($M \cdot s^{-1}$) are correct. The magnitude of the answers ($10^{-3} \text{ M} \cdot \text{s}^{-1}$) makes physical sense because rates are always positive and we are not changing the concentration much in 10 s. Also, reactions slow as they proceed because the concentration of the reactants is decreasing.

(b)   **Given:** $[C_4H_8]$ versus time data   **Find:** $\dfrac{\Delta[C_2H_4]}{\Delta t}$ between 20 and 30 s

Conceptual Plan: $t_1, t_2, [C_4H_8]_1, [C_4H_8]_2 \rightarrow \dfrac{\Delta[C_2H_4]}{\Delta t}$

$$\text{Rate} = -\frac{\Delta[C_4H_8]}{\Delta t} = \frac{1}{2}\frac{\Delta[C_2H_4]}{\Delta t}$$

Solution: Rate $= -\dfrac{[C_4H_8]_{t_2} - [C_4H_8]_{t_1}}{t_2 - t_1} = -\dfrac{0.763 \text{ M} - 0.835 \text{ M}}{30. \text{ s} - 20. \text{ s}} = 7.2 \times 10^{-3} \text{ M} \cdot \text{s}^{-1} = \dfrac{1}{2}\dfrac{\Delta[C_2H_4]}{\Delta t}$

Rearrange to solve for $\dfrac{\Delta[C_2H_4]}{\Delta t}$. So $\dfrac{\Delta[C_2H_4]}{\Delta t} = 2(7.2 \times 10^{-3} \text{ M} \cdot \text{s}^{-1}) = 1.4 \times 10^{-2} \text{ M} \cdot \text{s}^{-1}$

Check: The units ($M \cdot s^{-1}$) are correct. The magnitude of the answer ($10^{-2} \text{ M} \cdot \text{s}^{-1}$) makes physical sense because the rate of product formation is always positive and we are not changing the concentration much in 10 s. The rate of change of the product is faster than the decline of the reactant because of the stoichiometric coefficients.

13.9   (a)   **Given:** $[Br_2]$ versus time plot
               Find: (i) average rate between 0 and 25 s; (ii) instantaneous rate at 25 s; (iii) instantaneous rate of HBr
               formation at 50 s
               Conceptual Plan: (i) $t_1, t_2, [Br_2]_1, [Br_2]_2 \rightarrow$ **average rate then**

$$Rate = -\frac{\Delta[Br_2]}{\Delta t}$$

(ii) draw tangent at 25 s and determine slope $\rightarrow$ **instantaneous rate then**

$$Rate = -\frac{\Delta[Br_2]}{\Delta t}$$

(iii) draw tangent at 50 s and determine slope $\rightarrow$ **instantaneous rate** $\rightarrow$ $\dfrac{\Delta[HBr]}{\Delta t}$

$$Rate = -\frac{\Delta[Br_2]}{\Delta t} \qquad Rate = \frac{1}{2}\frac{\Delta[HBr]}{\Delta t}$$

Solution:

(i) $Rate = -\dfrac{[Br_2]_{t_2} - [Br_2]_{t_1}}{t_2 - t_1} = -\dfrac{0.75\ M - 1.00\ M}{25\ s - 0.\ s} = 1.0 \times 10^{-2}\ M \cdot s^{-1}$

and (ii) at 25 s:

$Slope = \dfrac{\Delta y}{\Delta x} = \dfrac{0.68\ M - 0.85\ M}{35\ s - 15\ s} = -8.5 \times 10^{-3}\ M \cdot s^{-1}$

because the slope $= \dfrac{\Delta[Br_2]}{\Delta t}$ and $Rate = -\dfrac{\Delta[Br_2]}{\Delta t}$,

then $Rate = -(-8.5 \times 10^{-3}\ M \cdot s^{-1}) = 8.5 \times 10^{-3}\ M \cdot s^{-1}$

(iii) at 50 s:

$Slope = \dfrac{\Delta y}{\Delta x} = \dfrac{0.53\ M - 0.66\ M}{60.\ s - 40.\ s} = -6.5 \times 10^{-3}\ M \cdot s^{-1}$

because the slope $= \dfrac{\Delta[Br_2]}{\Delta t}$ and

$Rate = -\dfrac{\Delta[Br_2]}{\Delta t} = \dfrac{1}{2}\dfrac{\Delta[HBr]}{\Delta t}$, then

$\dfrac{\Delta[HBr]}{\Delta t} = -2\dfrac{\Delta[Br_2]}{\Delta t} = -2(-6.5 \times 10^{-3}\ M \cdot s^{-1}) = 1.3 \times 10^{-2}\ M \cdot s^{-1}$

Check: The units $(M \cdot s^{-1})$ are correct. The magnitude of the first answer is larger than the second answer
because the rate is slowing down and the first answer includes the initial portion of the data. The magnitude of
the answers $(10^{-3}\ M \cdot s^{-1})$ makes physical sense because rates are always positive and we are not changing the
concentration much.

   (b)   **Given:** $[Br_2]$ versus time data and $[HBr]_0 = 0\ M$ **Find:** plot [HBr] with time

Conceptual Plan: Because $Rate = -\dfrac{\Delta[Br_2]}{\Delta t} = \dfrac{1}{2}\dfrac{\Delta[HBr]}{\Delta t}$. **The rate of change of [HBr] will be twice**
that of $[Br_2]$. The plot will start at the origin.
Solution:

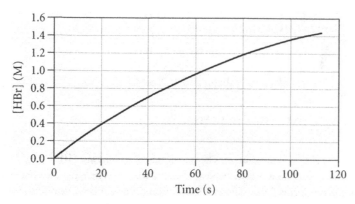

Check: The units (M versus s) are correct. The plot makes sense because the plot has the same general shape of the original plot, except that we are increasing instead of decreasing our concentration axis by a factor of two (to account for the difference in stoichiometric coefficients).

The Rate Law and Reaction Orders

13.11   (a)   **Given:** Rate versus [A] plot   **Find:** reaction order
            Conceptual Plan: Look at shape of plot and match to possibilities.
            Solution: The plot is a linear plot, so Rate $\propto$ [A] or the reaction is first order.

            Check: The order of the reaction is a common reaction order.

        (b)   **Given:** part (a)   **Find:** sketch plot of [A] versus time
            Conceptual Plan: Using the result from part (a), shape plot of [A] versus time should be curved with [A] decreasing. Use 1.0 M as initial concentration.
            Solution:

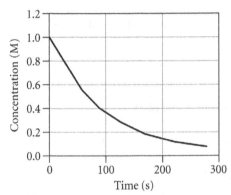

            Check: The plot has a shape that matches the one in the text for first-order plots.

        (c)   **Given:** part (a)   **Find:** write a rate law and estimate k
            Conceptual Plan: Using result from part (a), the slope of the plot is the rate constant.

            Solution: Slope $= \dfrac{\Delta y}{\Delta x} = \dfrac{0.010\,\dfrac{M}{s} - 0.00\,\dfrac{M}{s}}{1.0\,M - 0.0\,M} = 0.010\ s^{-1}$ so Rate $= k\,[A]^1$ or Rate $= k\,[A]$ or

            Rate $= 0.010\ s^{-1}\,[A]$

            Check: The units (s^{-1}) are correct. The magnitude of the answer ($10^{-2}\ s^{-1}$) makes physical sense because of the rate and concentration data. Remember that concentration is in units of M, so plugging the rate constant into the equation has the units of the rate as $M \cdot s^{-1}$, which is correct.

13.13   **Given:** reaction order: (a) first order, (b) second order, and (c) zero order   **Find:** units of k
        Conceptual Plan: Using rate law, rearrange to solve for k.

        $$\text{Rate} = k\,[A]^n,\ \text{where } n = \text{reaction order}$$

        Solution: For all cases, rate has units of $M \cdot s^{-1}$ and [A] has units of M.

        (a)   Rate $= k\,[A]^1 = k\,[A]$ so $k = \dfrac{\text{Rate}}{[A]} = \dfrac{\dfrac{M}{s}}{M} = s^{-1}$

        (b)   Rate $= k\,[A]^2$ so $k = \dfrac{\text{Rate}}{[A]^2} = \dfrac{\dfrac{M}{s}}{M \cdot M} = M^{-1} \cdot s^{-1}$

        (c)   Rate $= k\,[A]^0 = k = M \cdot s^{-1}$

        Check: The units (s^{-1}, $M^{-1} \cdot s^{-1}$, and $M \cdot s^{-1}$) are correct. The units for k change with the reaction order so that the units on the rate remain as $M \cdot s^{-1}$.

13.15   **Given:** A, B, and C react to form products. Reaction is first order in A, second order in B, and zero order in C
Find: (a) rate law; (b) overall order of reaction; (c) factor change in rate if [A] doubled; (d) factor change in rate if [B] doubled; (e) factor change in rate if [C] doubled; and (f) factor change in rate if [A], [B], and [C] doubled
Conceptual Plan:

(a)   **Using general rate law form, substitute values for orders.**

$$\text{Rate} = k\,[A]^m\,[B]^n\,[C]^p,\ \text{where } m, n, \text{and } p = \text{reaction orders}$$

(b)   **Using rate law in part (a), add up all reaction orders.**

$$\textit{overall reaction order} = m + n + p$$

(c)   **Through (f), using rate law from part (a), substitute concentration changes.**

$$\frac{\text{Rate 2}}{\text{Rate 1}} = \frac{k\,[A]_2^1\,[B]_2^2}{k\,[A]_1^1\,[B]_1^2}$$

Solution:

(a) $m = 1, n = 2,$ and $p = 0$ so Rate $= k\,[A]^1\,[B]^2\,[C]^0$ or Rate $= k\,[A][B]^2$

(b)   *overall reaction order* $= m + n + p = 1 + 2 + 0 = 3$, so it is a third-order reaction overall.

(c) $\dfrac{\text{Rate 2}}{\text{Rate 1}} = \dfrac{k\,[A]_2^1\,[B]_2^2}{k\,[A]_1^1\,[B]_1^2}$ and $[A]_2 = 2\,[A]_1,\ [B]_2 = [B]_1,\ [C]_2 = [C]_1$, so $\dfrac{\text{Rate 2}}{\text{Rate 1}} = \dfrac{k\,(2[A]_1)^1\,[B]_1^2}{k\,[A]_1^1\,[B]_1^2} = 2$

so the reaction rate doubles (factor of 2)

(d) $\dfrac{\text{Rate 2}}{\text{Rate 1}} = \dfrac{k\,[A]_2^1\,[B]_2^2}{k\,[A]_1^1\,[B]_1^2}$ and $[A]_2 = [A]_1,\ [B]_2 = 2[B]_1,\ [C]_2 = [C]_1$, so $\dfrac{\text{Rate 2}}{\text{Rate 1}} = \dfrac{k\,[A]_1^1\,(2[B]_1)^2}{k\,[A]_1^1\,[B]_1^2} = 2^2 = 4$

so the reaction rate quadruples (factor of 4)

(e) $\dfrac{\text{Rate 2}}{\text{Rate 1}} = \dfrac{k\,[A]_2^1\,[B]_2^2}{k\,[A]_1^1\,[B]_1^2}$ and $[A]_2 = [A]_1,\ [B]_2 = [B]_1,\ [C]_2 = 2\,[C]_1$, so $\dfrac{\text{Rate 2}}{\text{Rate 1}} = \dfrac{k\,[A]_1^1\,[B]_1^2}{k\,[A]_1^1\,[B]_1^2} = 1$

so the reaction rate is unchanged (factor of 1)

(f) $\dfrac{\text{Rate 2}}{\text{Rate 1}} = \dfrac{k\,[A]_2^1\,[B]_2^2}{k\,[A]_1^1\,[B]_1^2}$ and $[A]_2 = 2[A]_1,\ [B]_2 = 2[B]_1,\ [C]_2 = 2\,[C]_1$, so

$$\frac{\text{Rate 2}}{\text{Rate 1}} = \frac{k\,(2[A]_1)^1\,(2[B]_1)^2}{k\,[A]_1^1\,[B]_1^2} = 2 \times 2^2 = 8,\ \text{so the reaction rate goes up by a factor of 8.}$$

Check: The units (none) are correct. The rate law is consistent with the orders given, and the overall order is larger than any of the individual orders. The factors are consistent with the reaction orders. The larger the order, the larger the factor. When all concentrations are changed, the rate changes the most. If a reactant is not in the rate law, then changing its concentration has no effect on the reaction rate.

13.17   **Given:** table of [A] versus initial rate   **Find:** rate law and k
Conceptual Plan: Using general rate law form, compare rate ratios to determine reaction order.

$$\frac{\text{Rate 2}}{\text{Rate 1}} = \frac{k\,[A]_2^n}{k\,[A]_1^n}$$

Then use one of the concentration/initial rate pairs to determine k.

$$\text{Rate} = k[A]^n$$

Solution: $\dfrac{\text{Rate 2}}{\text{Rate 1}} = \dfrac{k\,[A]_2^n}{k\,[A]_1^n}$ Comparing the first two sets of data $\dfrac{0.210\ \text{M/s}}{0.053\ \text{M/s}} = \dfrac{k\,(0.200\ \text{M})^n}{k\,(0.100\ \text{M})^n}$ and $3.9623 = 2^n$,

so $n = 2$. If we compare the first and the last data sets, $\dfrac{0.473\ \text{M/s}}{0.053\ \text{M/s}} = \dfrac{k\,(0.300\ \text{M})^n}{k\,(0.100\ \text{M})^n}$ and $8.9245 = 3^n$, so $n = 2$.

This second comparison is not necessary, but it increases our confidence in the reaction order. So Rate $= k\,[A]^2$. Selecting the second data set and rearranging the rate equation,

$$k = \frac{\text{Rate}}{[A]^2} = \frac{0.210\,\dfrac{\text{M}}{\text{s}}}{(0.200\ \text{M})^2} = 5.25\ \text{M}^{-1} \cdot \text{s}^{-1},\ \text{so Rate} = 5.25\ \text{M}^{-1} \cdot \text{s}^{-1}[A]^2.$$

Check: The units (none and $\text{M}^{-1} \cdot \text{s}^{-1}$) are correct. The rate law is a common form. The rate is changing more rapidly than the concentration, so second order is consistent. The rate constant is consistent with the units necessary to get rate as M/s, and the magnitude is reasonable because we have a second-order reaction.

13.19   **Given:** table of [A] versus initial rate   **Find:** rate law and k

Conceptual Plan: Using general rate law form, compare rate ratios to determine reaction order.

$$\frac{\text{Rate } 2}{\text{Rate } 1} = \frac{k\,[A]_2^n}{k\,[A]_1^n}$$

Then use one of the concentration/initial rate pairs to determine k.

Solution: $\dfrac{\text{Rate } 2}{\text{Rate } 1} = \dfrac{k\,[A]_2^n}{k\,[A]_1^n}$ Comparing the first two sets of data: $\dfrac{0.16\ \cancel{M/s}}{0.12\ \cancel{M/s}} = \dfrac{\cancel{k}\,(0.0104\ \cancel{M})^n}{\cancel{k}\,(0.0078\ \cancel{M})^n}$ and $1.\underline{3}333 = 1.\underline{3}333^n$

so $n = 1$. If we compare the first and the last data sets: $\dfrac{0.20\ \cancel{M/s}}{0.12\ \cancel{M/s}} = \dfrac{\cancel{k}\,(0.0130\ \cancel{M})^n}{\cancel{k}\,(0.0078\ \cancel{M})^n}$ and $1.\underline{6}667 = 1.\underline{6}667^n$ so $n = 1$.

This second comparison is not necessary, but it increases our confidence in the reaction order. So Rate $= k\,[A]$.

Selecting the second data set and rearranging the rate equation $k = \dfrac{\text{Rate}}{[A]} = \dfrac{0.0104\ \dfrac{M}{s}}{0.16\ M} = 0.065\ s^{-1}$

so Rate $= 0.065\ s^{-1}\,[A]$

Check: The units (none and s^{-1}) are correct. The rate law is a common form. The rate is changing proportionately to the concentration, so first order is consistent. The rate constant is consistent with the units necessary to get rate as M/s and the magnitude is reasonable since we have a first-order reaction.

13.21   **Given:** table of $[NO_2]$ and $[F_2]$ versus initial rate   **Find:** rate law, k, and overall order

Conceptual Plan: Using general rate law form, compare rate ratios to determine reaction order of each reactant. Be sure to choose data that changes only one concentration at a time.

$$\frac{\text{Rate } 2}{\text{Rate } 1} = \frac{k\,[NO_2]_2^m\,[F_2]_2^n}{k\,[NO_2]_1^m\,[F_2]_1^n}$$

Then use one of the concentration/initial rate pairs to determine k.

$$\text{Rate} = k[NO_2]^m\,[F_2]^n$$

Solution: $\dfrac{\text{Rate } 2}{\text{Rate } 1} = \dfrac{k\,[NO_2]_2^m\,[F_2]_2^n}{k\,[NO_2]_1^m\,[F_2]_1^n}$ Comparing the first two sets of data,

$\dfrac{0.051\ \cancel{M/s}}{0.026\ \cancel{M/s}} = \dfrac{\cancel{k}\,(0.200\ M)^m\,(\cancel{0.100\ M})^n}{\cancel{k}\,(0.100\ M)^m\,(\cancel{0.100\ M})^n}$ and $1.\underline{9}615 = 2^m$, so $m = 1$. If we compare the second and third data sets,

$\dfrac{0.103\ \cancel{M/s}}{0.051\ \cancel{M/s}} = \dfrac{\cancel{k}\,(\cancel{0.200\ M})^m\,(0.200\ M)^n}{\cancel{k}\,(\cancel{0.200\ M})^m\,(0.100\ M)^n}$ and $2.\underline{0}196 = 2^n$, so $n = 1$. Other comparisons can be made, but they are not

necessary. They should reinforce these values of the reaction orders. So Rate $= k\,[NO_2][F_2]$. Selecting the

last data set and rearranging the rate equation, $k = \dfrac{\text{Rate}}{[NO_2][F_2]} = \dfrac{0.411\ \dfrac{M}{s}}{(0.400\ M)(0.400\ M)} = 2.57\ M^{-1}\cdot s^{-1}$,

so Rate $= 2.57\ M^{-1}\cdot s^{-1}\,[NO_2][F_2]$ and the reaction is second order overall.

Check: The units (none and $M^{-1}\cdot s^{-1}$) are correct. The rate law is a common form. The rate is changing as rapidly as each concentration is changing, which is consistent with first order in each reactant. The rate constant is consistent with the units necessary to get rate as M/s, and the magnitude is reasonable because we have a second-order reaction.

The Integrated Rate Law and Half-Life

13.23   (a)   The reaction is zero order. Because the slope of the plot is independent of the concentration, there is no dependence on the concentration of the reactant in the rate law.

(b)   The reaction is first order. The expression for the half-life of a first-order reaction is $t_{1/2} = \dfrac{0.693}{k}$, which is independent of the reactant concentration.

(c)   The reaction is second order. The integrated rate expression for a second-order reaction is $\dfrac{1}{[A]_t} = kt + \dfrac{1}{[A]_0}$, which is linear when the inverse of the concentration is plotted versus time.

13.25   **Given:** table of [AB] versus time   **Find:** reaction order, k, and [AB] at 25 s

Conceptual Plan: Look at the data and see if any common reaction orders can be eliminated. If the data does not show an equal concentration drop with time, zero order can be eliminated. Look for changes in the half-life (compare time for concentration to drop to one-half of any value). If the half-life is not constant, the first order can be eliminated. If the half-life is getting longer as the concentration drops, this might suggest second order. Plot the data as indicated by the appropriate rate law. Determine k from the slope of the plot. Finally, calculate the [AB] at 25 s by using the appropriate integrated rate expression.

Solution: By the preceding logic, we can eliminate both the zero-order and the first-order reactions. (Alternatively, you could make all three plots and only one should be linear.) This suggests that we should have a second-order reaction. Plot 1/[AB] versus time.

Because $\dfrac{1}{[AB]_t} = kt + \dfrac{1}{[AB]_0}$, the slope will be the rate constant. The slope can be determined by measuring $\Delta y/\Delta x$ on the plot or by using functions such as "add trendline" in Excel. Thus, the rate constant is 0.0225 M$^{-1} \cdot$ s^{-1}, and the rate law is Rate = 0.0225 M$^{-1} \cdot$ s^{-1}[AB]^2.

Finally, use $\dfrac{1}{[AB]_t} = kt + \dfrac{1}{[AB]_0}$; substitute the values of [AB]$_0$, 25 s, and k; and rearrange to solve for [AB] at 25 s.

$$[AB]_t = \frac{1}{kt + \dfrac{1}{[AB]_0}} = \frac{1}{(0.0225 \text{ M}^{-1} \cdot \text{s}^{-1})(25 \text{ s}) + \left(\dfrac{1}{0.950 \text{ M}}\right)} = 0.619 \text{ M}.$$

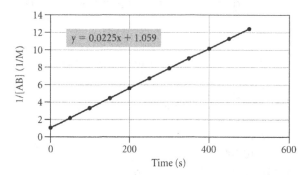

Check: The units (none, M$^{-1} \cdot$ s^{-1}, and M) are correct. The rate law is a common form. The plot was extremely linear, confirming second-order kinetics. The rate constant is consistent with the units necessary to get rate as M/s, and the magnitude is reasonable because we have a second-order reaction. The [AB] at 25 s is between the values at 0 s and 50 s.

13.27   **Given:** table of [C$_4$H$_8$] versus time   **Find:** reaction order, k, and reaction rate when [C$_4$H$_8$] = 0.25 M

Conceptual Plan: Look at the data and see if any common reaction orders can be eliminated. If the data does not show an equal concentration drop with time, zero order can be eliminated. Look for changes in half-life (compare time for concentration to drop to one-half of any value). If the half-life is not constant, the first order

can be eliminated. If the half-life is getting longer as the concentration drops, this might suggest second order. Plot the data as indicated by the appropriate rate law. Determine k from the slope of the plot. Finally, calculate the reaction rate when [C$_4$H$_8$] = 0.25 M by using the rate law.

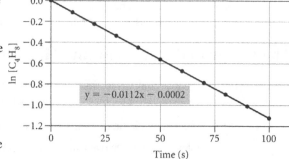

Solution: By the preceding logic, we can see that the reaction is most likely first order. It takes about 60 s for the concentration to be cut in half for any concentration. Plot ln [C$_4$H$_8$] versus time. Because ln[A]$_t = -kt +$ ln[A]$_0$, the negative of the slope will be the rate constant. The slope can be determined by measuring $\Delta y/\Delta x$ on the plot or by using functions such as "add trendline" in Excel. Thus, the rate constant is 0.0112 s^{-1}, and the rate law is Rate = 0.0112 s^{-1}[C$_4$H$_8$]. Finally, use Rate = 0.0112 s^{-1}[C$_4$H$_8$] and substitute the values of [C$_4$H$_8$]: Rate = 0.0112 s^{-1}[0.25 M] = 2.8 $\times$ 10^{-3} M $\cdot$ s^{-1}.

Check: The units (none, s^{-1}, and $M \cdot s^{-1}$) are correct. The rate law is a common form. The plot was extremely linear, confirming first-order kinetics. The rate constant is consistent with the units necessary to get rate as M/s, and the magnitude is reasonable because we have a first-order reaction. The rate when $[C_4H_8] = 0.25$ M is consistent with the average rate using 90 s and 100 s.

13.29 **Given:** plot of ln [A] versus time has slope $= -0.0045$/s; $[A]_0 = 0.250$ M
Find: (a) k, (b) rate law, (c) $t_{1/2}$, and (d) [A] after 225 s
Conceptual Plan:
(a) A plot of ln [A] versus time is linear for a first-order reaction. Using $\ln[A]_t = -kt + \ln[A]_0$, the rate constant is the negative of the slope.
(b) Rate law is first order. Add rate constant from part (a).
(c) For a first-order reaction, $t_{1/2} = \dfrac{0.693}{k}$. Substitute k from part (a).
(d) Use the integrated rate law, $\ln[A]_t = -kt + \ln[A]_0$, and substitute k and the initial concentration.
Solution:
(a) Because the rate constant is the negative of the slope, $k = 4.5 \times 10^{-3}\ s^{-1}$.
(b) Because the reaction is first order, Rate $= 4.5 \times 10^{-3}\ s^{-1}$ [A].
(c) $t_{1/2} = \dfrac{0.693}{k} = \dfrac{0.693}{0.0045/s} = 1.5 \times 10^2\ s$
(d) $\ln[A]_t = -kt + \ln[A]_0$ and substitute k and the initial concentration. So
$\ln[A]_t = -(0.0045/s)(225\ s) + \ln 0.250\ M = -2.39879$ and $[A]_{250\ s} = e^{-2.39879} = 0.0908$ M

Check: The units (s^{-1}, none, s, and M) are correct. The rate law is a common form. The rate constant is consistent with value of the slope. The half-life is consistent with a small value of k. The concentration at 225 s is consistent with being between one and two half-lives.

13.31 **Given:** decomposition of SO_2Cl_2, for order; $k = 1.42 \times 10^{-4}\ s^{-1}$
Find: (a) $t_{1/2}$, (b) t to decrease to 25% of $[SO_2Cl_2]_0$, (c) t to 0.78 M when $[SO_2Cl_2]_0 = 1.00$ M, and
(d) $[SO_2Cl_2]$ after 2.00×10^2 s and 5.00×10^2 s when $[SO_2Cl_2]_0 = 0.150$ M
Conceptual Plan:
(a) $k \rightarrow t_{1/2}$
$t_{1/2} = \dfrac{0.693}{k}$
(b) $[SO_2Cl_2]_0$, 25% of $[SO_2Cl_2]_0$, $k \rightarrow t$
$\ln[A]_t = -kt + \ln[A]_0$
(c) $[SO_2Cl_2]_0$, $[SO_2Cl_2]_t$, $k \rightarrow t$
$\ln[A]_t = -kt + \ln[A]_0$
(d) $[SO_2Cl_2]_0$, t, $k \rightarrow [SO_2Cl_2]_t$
$\ln[A]_t = -kt + \ln[A]_0$

Solution:

(a) $t_{1/2} = \dfrac{0.693}{k} = \dfrac{0.693}{1.42 \times 10^{-4}\ s^{-1}} = 4.88 \times 10^3\ s$

(b) $[SO_2Cl_2]_t = 0.25\ [SO_2Cl_2]_0$. Because $\ln[SO_2Cl_2]_t = -kt + \ln[SO_2Cl_2]_0$, rearrange to solve for t.

$t = -\dfrac{1}{k} \ln \dfrac{[SO_2Cl_2]_t}{[SO_2Cl_2]_0} = -\dfrac{1}{1.42 \times 10^{-4}\ s^{-1}} \ln \dfrac{0.25\ [\cancel{SO_2Cl_2]_0}}{[\cancel{SO_2Cl_2]_0}} = 9.8 \times 10^3\ s$

(c) $[SO_2Cl_2]_t = 0.78$ M; $[SO_2Cl_2]_0 = 1.00$ M. Because $\ln[SO_2Cl_2]_t = -kt + \ln[SO_2Cl_2]_0$, rearrange to

solve for t. $t = -\dfrac{1}{k} \ln \dfrac{[SO_2Cl_2]_t}{[SO_2Cl_2]_0} = -\dfrac{1}{1.42 \times 10^{-4}\ s^{-1}} \ln \dfrac{0.78\ \cancel{M}}{1.00\ \cancel{M}} = 1.7 \times 10^3\ s$

(d) $[SO_2Cl_2]_0 = 0.150$ M and 2.00×10^2 s in
$\ln[SO_2Cl_2]_t = -(1.42 \times 10^{-4}\ s^{-1})(2.00 \times 10^2\ s) + \ln 0.150\ M = -1.92552 \rightarrow$
$[SO_2Cl_2]_t = e^{-1.92552} = 0.146$ M
$[SO_2Cl_2]_0 = 0.150$ M and 5.00×10^2 s in

$$\ln[SO_2Cl_2]_t = -(1.42 \times 10^{-4} \text{ s}^{-1})(5.00 \times 10^2 \text{ s}) + \ln 0.150 \text{ M} = -1.96812 \rightarrow$$
$$[SO_2Cl_2]_t = e^{-1.96812} = 0.140 \text{ M}$$

Check: The units (s, s, s, and M) are correct. The rate law is a common form. The half-life is consistent with a small value of k. The time to 25% is consistent with two half-lives. The time to 0.78 M is consistent with being less than one half-life. The final concentrations are consistent with the time being less than one half-life.

13.33   **Given:** $t_{1/2}$ for radioactive decay of U-238 $= 4.5$ billion years and independent of $[\text{U-238}]_0$
Find: t to decrease by 10%; number U-238 atoms today, when 1.5×10^{18} atoms formed 13.8 billion years ago
Conceptual Plan: $t_{1/2}$ **independent of concentration implies first-order kinetics,** $t_{1/2} \rightarrow k$ **then**

$$t_{1/2} = \frac{0.693}{k}$$

90% of [U-238]$_0$, $k \rightarrow t$ and [U-238]$_0$, t, $k \rightarrow$ [U-238]$_t$

$$\ln[A]_t = -kt + \ln[A]_0 \qquad \ln[A]_t = -kt + \ln[A]_0$$

Solution: $t_{1/2} = \dfrac{0.693}{k}$ Rearrange to solve for k. $k = \dfrac{0.693}{t_{1/2}} = \dfrac{0.693}{4.5 \times 10^9 \text{ yr}} = 1.54 \times 10^{-10} \text{ yr}^{-1}$ then

$[\text{U-238}]_t = 0.90 \, [\text{U-238}]_0$. Because $\ln[\text{U-238}]_t = -kt + \ln[\text{U-238}]_0$, rearrange to solve for t.

$$t = -\frac{1}{k} \ln \frac{[\text{U-238}]_t}{[\text{U-238}]_0} = -\frac{1}{1.54 \times 10^{-10} \text{ yr}^{-1}} \ln \frac{0.90 \, [\text{U-238}]_0}{[\text{U-238}]_0} = 6.8 \times 10^8 \text{ yr}$$

and $[\text{U-238}]_0 = 1.5 \times 10^{18}$ atoms; $t = 13.8 \times 10^9$ yr

$$\ln[\text{U-238}]_t = -kt + \ln[\text{U-238}]_0 = -(1.54 \times 10^{-10} \text{ yr}^{-1})(13.8 \times 10^9 \text{ yr})$$

$$+\ln(1.5 \times 10^{18} \text{ atoms}) = 39.726797 \rightarrow$$

$$[\text{U-238}]_t = e^{39.726797} = 1.8 \times 10^{17} \text{ atoms}$$

Check: The units (yr and atoms) are correct. The time to 10% decay is consistent with less than one half-life. The final concentration is consistent with the time being about three half-lives.

The Effect of Temperature and the Collision Model

13.35

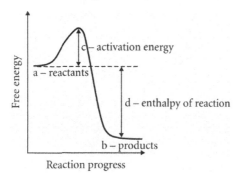

13.37   **Given:** activation energy $= 56.8$ kJ/mol, frequency factor $= 1.5 \times 10^{11}$/s, 25 °C   **Find:** rate constant
Conceptual Plan: **°C $\rightarrow$ K and kJ/mol $\rightarrow$ J/mol then** $E_a, T, A \rightarrow k$

$$K = {}^\circ C + 273.15 \qquad \frac{1000 \text{ J}}{1 \text{ kJ}} \qquad k = Ae^{-E_a/RT}$$

Solution: $T = 25 \,^\circ\text{C} + 273.15 = 298 \text{ K}$ and $\dfrac{56.8 \text{ kJ}}{\text{mol}} \times \dfrac{1000 \text{ J}}{1 \text{ kJ}} = 5.68 \times 10^4 \dfrac{\text{J}}{\text{mol}}$ then

$$k = Ae^{-E_a/RT} = (1.5 \times 10^{11} \text{ s}^{-1})e^{\dfrac{-5.68 \times 10^4 \frac{\text{J}}{\text{mol}}}{\left(8.314 \frac{\text{J}}{\text{K} \cdot \text{mol}}\right) 298 \text{ K}}} = 17 \text{ s}^{-1}$$

Check: The units (s^{-1}) are correct. The rate constant is consistent with a large activation energy and a large frequency factor.

13.39   **Given:** plot of ln k versus $1/T$ (in K) is linear with a slope of -7445 K   **Find:** E_a

Conceptual Plan: Because $\ln k = \dfrac{-E_a}{R}\left(\dfrac{1}{T}\right) + \ln A$ **plot of ln k versus $1/T$ will have a slope $= -E_a/R$.**

Solution: Because the slope $= -7445$ K $= -E_a/R$, then

$$E_a = -(\text{slope})R = -(-7445\ \cancel{K})\left(8.314\frac{\cancel{J}}{\cancel{K}\cdot\text{mol}}\right)\left(\frac{1\ \text{kJ}}{1000\ \cancel{J}}\right) = 61.90\ \frac{\text{kJ}}{\text{mol}}$$

Check: The units (kJ/mol) are correct. The activation energy is typical for many reactions.

13.41   **Given:** table of rate constant versus T **Find:** E_a and A

Conceptual Plan: Because $\ln k = \dfrac{-E_a}{R}\left(\dfrac{1}{T}\right) +$

ln A, a plot of ln k versus $1/T$ will have a slope $= -E_a/R$ and an intercept $= \ln A$.
Solution: The slope can be determined by measuring $\Delta y/\Delta x$ on the plot or by using functions such as "add trendline" in Excel. Because the slope $= -30189$ K $= -E_a/R$, then
$E_a = -(\text{slope})R$

$$= -(-30189\ \cancel{K})\left(8.314\ \frac{\cancel{J}}{\cancel{K}\cdot\text{mol}}\right)\left(\frac{1\ \text{kJ}}{1000\ \cancel{J}}\right)$$

$$= 251\ \frac{\text{kJ}}{\text{mol}}\ \text{and intercept} = 27.399 = \ln A \text{ then}$$

$$A = e^{\text{intercept}} = e^{27.399} = 7.93 \times 10^{11}\ \text{s}^{-1}.$$

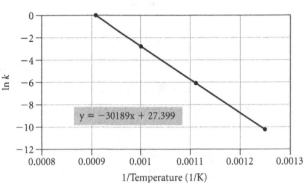

Check: The units (kJ/mol and s^{-1}) are correct. The plot was extremely linear, confirming Arrhenius behavior. The activation energy and frequency factor are typical for many reactions.

13.43   **Given:** table of rate constant versus T **Find:** E_a and A

Conceptual Plan: Because $\ln k = \dfrac{-E_a}{R}\left(\dfrac{1}{T}\right) + \ln A$, a plot of ln k versus $1/T$ will have a slope $= -E_a/R$ and an intercept $= \ln A$.
Solution: The slope can be determined by measuring $\Delta y/\Delta x$ on the plot or by using functions such as "add trendline" in Excel. Because the slope $= -2767.2$ K $= -E_a/R$, then
$E_a = -(\text{slope})R$

$$= -(-2767.2\ \cancel{K})\left(8.314\ \frac{\cancel{J}}{\cancel{K}\cdot\text{mol}}\right)\left(\frac{1\ \text{kJ}}{1000\ \cancel{J}}\right)$$

$$= 23.0\ \frac{\text{kJ}}{\text{mol}}\ \text{and intercept} = 25.112 = \ln A \text{ then}$$

$$A = e^{\text{intercept}} = e^{25.112} = 8.05 \times 10^{10}\ \text{s}^{-1}.$$

Check: The units (kJ/mol and s^{-1}) are correct. The plot was extremely linear, confirming Arrhenius behavior. The activation energy and frequency factor are typical for many reactions.

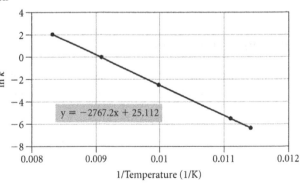

13.45   **Given:** rate constant $= 0.0117/\text{s}$ at 400.0 K and $0.689/\text{s}$ at 450.0 K   **Find:** (a) E_a and (b) rate constant at 425 K
Conceptual Plan:
(a) $k_1, T_1, k_2, T_2, \rightarrow E_a$ then J/mol $\rightarrow$ kJ/mol

$$\ln\left(\frac{k_2}{k_1}\right) = \frac{E_a}{R}\left(\frac{1}{T_1} - \frac{1}{T_2}\right) \qquad \frac{1\ \text{kJ}}{1000\ \text{J}}$$

(b) $E_a, k_1, T_1, T_2 \rightarrow k_2$

$$\ln\left(\frac{k_2}{k_1}\right) = \frac{E_a}{R}\left(\frac{1}{T_1} - \frac{1}{T_2}\right)$$

Solution:

(a) $\ln\left(\dfrac{k_2}{k_1}\right) = \dfrac{E_a}{R}\left(\dfrac{1}{T_1} - \dfrac{1}{T_2}\right)$. Rearrange to solve for E_a.

$$E_a = \dfrac{R\ln\left(\dfrac{k_2}{k_1}\right)}{\left(\dfrac{1}{T_1} - \dfrac{1}{T_2}\right)} = \dfrac{8.314\ \dfrac{J}{K \cdot mol}\ \ln\left(\dfrac{0.689\ s^{-1}}{0.0117\ s^{-1}}\right)}{\left(\dfrac{1}{400.0\ K} - \dfrac{1}{450.0\ K}\right)} = 1.22 \times 10^5\ \dfrac{J}{mol} \times \dfrac{1\ kJ}{1000\ J} = 122\ \dfrac{kJ}{mol}$$

(b) $\ln\left(\dfrac{k_2}{k_1}\right) = \dfrac{E_a}{R}\left(\dfrac{1}{T_1} - \dfrac{1}{T_2}\right)$ with $k_1 = 0.0117/s$, $T_1 = 400.0$ K, $T_2 = 425$ K. Rearrange to solve for k_2.

$$\ln k_2 = \dfrac{E_a}{R}\left(\dfrac{1}{T_1} - \dfrac{1}{T_2}\right) + \ln k_1 = \dfrac{1.22 \times 10^5\ \dfrac{J}{mol}}{8.314\ \dfrac{J}{K \cdot mol}}\left(\dfrac{1}{400.0\ K} - \dfrac{1}{425.0\ K}\right) + \ln 0.0117\ s^{-1} = -2.2902 \rightarrow$$

$$k_2 = e^{-2.2902} = 0.101\ s^{-1}$$

Check: The units (kJ/mol and s^{-1}) are correct. The activation energy is typical for a reaction. The rate constant at 425 K is between the values given at 400 K and 450 K.

13.47   **Given:** rate constant doubles from 10.0 °C to 20.0 °C   **Find:** E_a

Conceptual Plan: $°C \rightarrow K$ then $k_1, T_1, k_2, T_2 \rightarrow E_a$ then J/mol $\rightarrow$ kJ/mol

$$K = °C + 273.15 \qquad \ln\left(\dfrac{k_2}{k_1}\right) = \dfrac{E_a}{R}\left(\dfrac{1}{T_1} - \dfrac{1}{T_2}\right) \qquad \dfrac{1\ kJ}{1000\ J}$$

Solution: $T_1 = 10.0\ °C + 273.15 = 283.2$ K and $T_2 = 20.0\ °C + 273.15 = 293.2$ K and $k_2 = 2\ k_1$ then

$\ln\left(\dfrac{k_2}{k_1}\right) = \dfrac{E_a}{R}\left(\dfrac{1}{T_1} - \dfrac{1}{T_2}\right)$. Rearrange to solve for E_a.

$$E_a = \dfrac{R\ln\left(\dfrac{k_2}{k_1}\right)}{\left(\dfrac{1}{T_1} - \dfrac{1}{T_2}\right)} = \dfrac{8.314\ \dfrac{J}{K \cdot mol}\ \ln\left(\dfrac{2\ k_1}{k_1}\right)}{\left(\dfrac{1}{283.2\ K} - \dfrac{1}{293.2\ K}\right)} = 4.7851 \times 10^4\ \dfrac{J}{mol} \times \dfrac{1\ kJ}{1000\ J} = 47.85\ \dfrac{kJ}{mol}$$

Check: The units (kJ/mol) are correct. The activation energy is typical for a reaction.

13.49   Reaction a would have the faster rate because the orientation factor p would be larger for this reaction because the reactants are symmetrical.

Reaction Mechanisms

13.51   Because the first reaction is the slow step, it is the rate-determining step. Using this first step to determine the rate law, Rate $= k_1\ [AB]^2$. Because this is the observed rate law, this mechanism is consistent with the experimental data.

13.53   (a)   The overall reaction is the sum of the steps in the mechanism:

$$Cl_2(g) \underset{k_2}{\overset{k_1}{\rightleftharpoons}} 2\ \cancel{Cl(g)}$$

$$\cancel{Cl(g)} + CHCl_3(g) \overset{k_3}{\rightarrow} HCl(g) + \cancel{CCl_3(g)}$$

$$\underline{\cancel{Cl(g)} + \cancel{CCl_3(g)} \overset{k_4}{\rightarrow} CCl_4(g)}$$

$$Cl_2(g) + CHCl_3(g) \rightarrow HCl(g) + CCl_4(g)$$

(b)   The intermediates are the species that are generated by one step and consumed by other steps. These are $Cl(g)$ and $CCl_3(g)$.

(c)   Because the second step is the rate-determining step, Rate $= k_3\ [Cl]\ [CHCl_3]$. Because Cl is an intermediate, its concentration cannot appear in the rate law. Using the fast equilibrium in the first step, we see that $k_1[Cl_2] = k_2[Cl]^2$ or $[Cl] = \sqrt{\dfrac{k_1}{k_2}}[Cl_2]$. Substituting this into the first rate expression, we get

Rate $= k_3\sqrt{\dfrac{k_1}{k_2}}[Cl_2]^{1/2}[CHCl_3]$. Simplifying this expression, we see that Rate $= k[Cl_2]^{1/2}[CHCl_3]$.

Catalysis

13.55 Heterogeneous catalysts require a large surface area because catalysis can only happen at the active sites on the surface. A greater surface area means greater opportunity for the substrate to react, which results in a speedier reaction.

13.57 Assume rate ratio $\propto k$ ratio (because concentration terms will cancel each other) and $k = A\,e^{-E_a/RT}$.
$T = 25\,°C + 273.15 = 298\ K$, $E_{a_1} = 1.25 \times 10^5\ J/mol$, and $E_{a_2} = 5.5 \times 10^4\ J/mol$. Ratio of rates will be

$$\frac{k_2}{k_1} = \frac{\cancel{A}\,e^{-E_{a_2}/RT}}{\cancel{A}\,e^{-E_{a_1}/RT}} = \frac{e^{\frac{-5.5 \times 10^4 \frac{\cancel{J}}{\cancel{mol}}}{\left(8.314 \frac{\cancel{J}}{K\,\cdot\,\cancel{mol}}\right)298\,\cancel{K}}}}{e^{\frac{-1.25 \times 10^5 \frac{\cancel{J}}{\cancel{mol}}}{\left(8.314 \frac{\cancel{J}}{K\,\cdot\,\cancel{mol}}\right)298\,\cancel{K}}}} = \frac{e^{-22.199}}{e^{-50.453}} = 10^{12}$$

Cumulative Problems

13.59 **Given:** table of $[CH_3CN]$ versus time $\quad$ **Find:** (a) reaction order, k; (b) $t_{1/2}$; and (c) t for 90% conversion
Conceptual Plan: (a) and (b) Look at the data and see if any common reaction orders can be eliminated. If the data does not show an equal concentration drop with time, zero order can be eliminated. Look for changes in the half-life (compare time for concentration to drop to one-half of any value). If the half-life is not constant, the first order can be eliminated. If the half-life is getting longer as the concentration drops, this might suggest second order. Plot the data as indicated by the appropriate rate law, or if it is first order and there is an obvious half-life in the data, a plot is not necessary. Determine k from the slope of the plot (or using the half-life equation for first order). (c) Finally, calculate the time to 90% conversion using the appropriate integrated rate equation.
Solution: (a) and (b) By the preceding logic, we can see that the reaction is first order. It takes 15.0 h for the concentration to be cut in half for any concentration (1.000 M to 0.501 M, 0.794 M to 0.398 M, and 0.631 M to 0.316 M), so

$t_{1/2} = 15.0\ h$. Then use $t_{1/2} = \dfrac{0.693}{k}$ and rearrange to solve for k.

$k = \dfrac{0.693}{t_{1/2}} = \dfrac{0.693}{15.0\ h} = 0.0462\ h^{-1}$

(c) $[CH_3CN]_t = 0.10\,[CH_3CN]_0$. Because $\ln[CH_3CN]_t = -kt + \ln[CH_3CN]_0$, rearrange to solve for t.

$t = -\dfrac{1}{k}\ln\dfrac{[CH_3CN]_t}{[CH_3CN]_0} = -\dfrac{1}{0.0462\ h^{-1}}\ln\dfrac{0.10\ \cancel{[CH_3CN]_0}}{\cancel{[CH_3CN]_0}} = 49.8\ h$

Check: The units (none, h^{-1}, h, and h) are correct. The rate law is a common form. The data showed a constant half-life very clearly. The rate constant is consistent with the units necessary to get rate as M/s, and the magnitude is reasonable because we have a first-order reaction. The time to 90% conversion is consistent with a time between three and four half-lives.

13.61 **Given:** Rate $= k\,\dfrac{[A][C]^2}{[B]^{1/2}} = 0.0115\ M/s$ at certain initial concentrations of A, B, and C; double A and C

concentration and triple B concentration $\quad$ **Find:** reaction rate

Conceptual Plan: $[A]_1, [B]_1, [C]_1$, Rate 1, $[A]_2, [B]_2, [C]_2 \rightarrow$ **Rate 2**

$$\frac{\text{Rate 2}}{\text{Rate 1}} = \frac{k\dfrac{[A]_2[C]_2^2}{[B]_2^{1/2}}}{k\dfrac{[A]_1[C]_1^2}{[B]_1^{1/2}}}$$

Solution: $\dfrac{\text{Rate 2}}{\text{Rate 1}} = \dfrac{k\dfrac{[A]_2[C]_2^2}{[B]_2^{1/2}}}{k\dfrac{[A]_1[C]_1^2}{[B]_1^{1/2}}}$. Rearrange to solve for Rate 2. Rate 2 $= \dfrac{k\dfrac{[A]_2[C]_2^2}{[B]_2^{1/2}}}{k\dfrac{[A]_1[C]_1^2}{[B]_1^{1/2}}}$,

Rate 1 $[A]_2 = 2[A]_1$, $[B]_2 = 3[B]_1$, $[C]_2 = 2[C]_1$, and Rate 1 = 0.0115 M/s so

$$\text{Rate 2} = \frac{k\dfrac{2\,[\cancel{A_1}](2\,[\cancel{C_1}])^2}{(3\,[\cancel{B_1}])^{1/2}}}{k\dfrac{[\cancel{A_1}]\,[\cancel{C_1}]^2}{[\cancel{B_1}]^{1/2}}}\, 0.0115\,\frac{\text{M}}{\text{s}} = \frac{2^3}{3^{1/2}}\,0.0115\,\frac{\text{M}}{\text{s}} = 0.0531\frac{\text{M}}{\text{s}}$$

Check: The units $(\text{M} \cdot \text{s}^{-1})$ are correct. They should increase because we have a factor of eight (2^3) divided by the square root of three (1.73).

13.63 **Given:** table of P_{Total} versus time **Find:** rate law, k, and P_{Total} at 2.00×10^4 s
Conceptual Plan: Because two moles of gas are generated for each mole of CH_3CHO decomposed,
$P_{CH_3CHO} = P^\circ_{\text{Total}} - (P_{\text{Total}} - P^\circ_{\text{Total}})$. **Look at the data and see if any common reaction orders can be eliminated. If the data does not show an equal P_{Total} rise (or P_{CH_3CHO} drop) with time, zero order can be eliminated. It does appear that the half-life is getting longer, so the first order can be eliminated. Plot the data as indicated by the appropriate rate law. Determine k from the slope of the plot. Finally, calculate the P_{CH_3CHO} at 2.00×10^4 s using the appropriate integrated rate expression and convert this to P_{Total} using the reaction stoichiometry.**
Solution: Calculate $P_{CH_3CHO} = P^\circ_{\text{Total}} - (P_{\text{Total}} - P^\circ_{\text{Total}})$.

Time (s)	P_{Total} (atm)	P_{CH_3CHO}(atm)
0	0.22	0.22
1000	0.24	0.20
3000	0.27	0.17
7000	0.31	0.13

By the preceding logic, we can eliminate both the zero-order and the first-order reactions. (Alternatively, you could make all three plots, and only one should be linear.) This suggests that we should have a second-order reaction. Plot $1/P_{CH_3CHO}$ versus time. Because $\dfrac{1}{P_{CH_3CHO}} = kt + \dfrac{1}{P^\circ_{CH_3CHO}}$, the slope will be the rate constant. The slope can be determined by

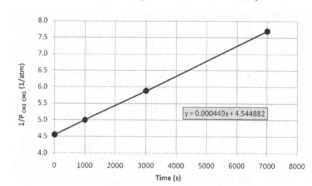

measuring $\Delta y/\Delta x$ on the plot or by using functions such as "add trendline" in Excel. Thus, the rate constant is $4.5 \times 10^{-4}\,\text{atm}^{-1} \cdot \text{s}^{-1}$, and the rate law is Rate $= 4.5 \times 10^{-4}\,\text{atm}^{-1} \cdot \text{s}^{-1}\,P_{CH_3CHO}$.

Finally, use $\dfrac{1}{P_{CH_3CHO}} = kt + \dfrac{1}{P^\circ_{CH_3CHO}}$; substitute the values of $P^\circ_{CH_3CHO}$, 2.00×10^4 s, and k and rearrange to solve for $P^\circ_{CH_3CHO}$ at 2.00×10^4 s.

$$P_{CH_3CHO} = \frac{1}{kt + \dfrac{1}{P^\circ_{CH_3CHO}}} =$$

$$\frac{1}{(4.5 \times 10^{-4}\,\text{atm}^{-1} \cdot \cancel{s}^{-1})(2.00 \times 10^4\,\cancel{s}) + \left(\dfrac{1}{0.22\,\text{atm}}\right)} = 0.07\underline{3}8255\,\text{atm} = 0.074\,\text{atm}$$

Finally, from the first equation in the solution, $P_{\text{Total}} = 2P^\circ_{\text{Total}} - P_{CH_3CHO} = 2(0.22\,\text{atm}) - 0.07\underline{3}8255\,\text{atm} = 0.3\underline{6}6175\,\text{atm} = 0.37\,\text{atm}$.

Check: The units (none, atm$^{-1} \cdot$ s^{-1}, and atm) are correct. The rate law is a common form. The plot was extremely linear, confirming second-order kinetics. The rate constant is consistent with the units necessary to get rate as atm/s, and the magnitude is reasonable because we have a second-order reaction. The P_{Total} at 2.00×10^4 s is consistent with the changes we see in the data table through 7000 s.

13.65   **Given:** N_2O_5 decomposes to NO_2 and O_2, first order in $[N_2O_5]$; $t_{1/2} = 2.81$ h at 25 °C; $V = 1.5$ L, $P^\circ_{N_2O_5} = 745$ torr
Find: P_{O_2} after 215 minutes
Conceptual Plan: Write a balanced reaction. Then $t_{1/2} \rightarrow k$ then °C $\rightarrow$ K and torr $\rightarrow$ atm then

$$N_2O_5 \rightarrow 2\,NO_2 + \tfrac{1}{2}O_2 \qquad t_{1/2} = \frac{0.693}{k} \qquad K = °C + 273.15 \qquad \frac{1\ atm}{760\ torr}$$

$P^\circ_{N_2O_5}, V, T \rightarrow n/V$ **then min $\rightarrow$ h then $[N_2O_5]_0, t, k \rightarrow [N_2O_5]_t$ then $[N_2O_5]_0, [N_2O_5]_t \rightarrow [O_2]_t$**

$$PV = nRT \qquad \frac{1\ h}{60\ min} \qquad \ln [A]_t = -kt + \ln [A]_0 \qquad [O_2]_t = ([N_2O_5]_0 - [N_2O_5]_t) \times \frac{1/2\ mol\ O_2}{1\ mol\ N_2O_5}$$

then $[O_2]_t, V, T \rightarrow P^\circ_{O_2}$ and finally atm $\rightarrow$ torr

$$PV = nRT \qquad \frac{760\ torr}{1\ atm}$$

Solution: $t_{1/2} = \dfrac{0.693}{k}$ and rearrange to solve for k. $k = \dfrac{0.693}{t_{1/2}} = \dfrac{0.693}{2.81\ h} = 0.246619$ h^{-1}. Then

$T = 25\ °C + 273.15 = 298$ K. $745\ \text{torr} \times \dfrac{1\ atm}{760\ torr} = 0.980263$ atm then $PV = nRT$. Rearrange to solve for n/V.

$\dfrac{n}{V} = \dfrac{P}{RT} = \dfrac{0.980263\ atm}{0.08206 \dfrac{L \cdot atm}{K \cdot mol} \times 298\ K} = 0.0400862$ M then $215\ \text{min} \times \dfrac{1\ h}{60\ min} = 3.58333$ h

Because $\ln [N_2O_5]_t = -kt + \ln [N_2O_5]_0 = -(0.246619\ h^{-1})(3.58333\ h) + \ln (0.0400862\ M) = -4.10044 \rightarrow$
$[N_2O_5]_t = e^{-4.10044} = 0.0165654$ M then

$[O_2]_t = ([N_2O_5]_0 - [N_2O_5]_t) \times \dfrac{1/2\ mol\ O_2}{1\ mol\ N_2O_5} = \left(0.0400862\ \dfrac{mol\ N_2O_5}{L} - 0.0165654\ \dfrac{mol\ N_2O_5}{L}\right) \times \dfrac{1/2\ mol\ O_2}{1\ mol\ N_2O_5}$

$= 0.0117604$ M O_2
then finally $PV = nRT$ and rearrange to solve for P.

$P = \dfrac{n}{V}RT = 0.0117604\ \dfrac{mol}{L} \times 0.08206\ \dfrac{L\ atm}{K \cdot mol} \times 298\ K = 0.287587\ atm \times \dfrac{760\ torr}{1\ atm} = 219$ torr

Check: The units (torr) are correct. The pressure is reasonable because it must be less than one-half of the original pressure.

13.67   **Given:** I_2 formation from I atoms, second order in I; $k = 1.5 \times 10^{10}$ M$^{-1} \cdot$ s^{-1}, $[I]_0 = 0.0100$ M
Find: t to decrease by 95%
Conceptual Plan: $[I]_0, [I]_t, k \rightarrow t$

$$\frac{1}{[A]_t} = kt + \frac{1}{[A]_0}$$

Solution: $[I]_t = 0.05\,[I]_0 = 0.05 \times 0.0100$ M $= 0.0005$ M. Because $\dfrac{1}{[I]_t} = kt + \dfrac{1}{[I]_0}$. Rearrange to solve for t.

$t = \dfrac{1}{k}\left(\dfrac{1}{[I]_t} - \dfrac{1}{[I]_0}\right) = \dfrac{1}{(1.5 \times 10^{10}\ M^{-1} \cdot s^{-1})}\left(\dfrac{1}{0.0005\ M} - \dfrac{1}{0.0100\ M}\right) = 1.267 \times 10^{-7}$ s $= 1 \times 10^{-7}$ s

Check: The units (s) are correct. We expect the time to be extremely small because the rate constant is so large.

13.69   **Given:** $AB(aq) \rightarrow A(g) + B(g)$; $k = 0.0118$ M$^{-1} \cdot$ s^{-1}; 250.0 mL of 0.100 M AB; collect gas over water
$T = 25.0$ °C, $P_{Total} = 755.1$ mmHg, and $V = 200.0$ mL; $P^\circ_{H_2O} = 23.8$ mmHg   **Find:** t
Conceptual Plan: $P_{Total}, P_{H_2O} \rightarrow P_A + P_B$ then mmHg $\rightarrow$ atm and mL $\rightarrow$ L

$$P_{Total} = P_{H_2O} + P_A + P_B \qquad \frac{1\ atm}{760\ mmHg} \qquad \frac{1\ L}{1000\ mL}$$

and °C $\rightarrow$ K $P, V, T \rightarrow n_{A+B} \rightarrow \Delta n_{AB}$ then $[AB]_0, V_{AB}, \Delta n_{AB} \rightarrow [AB]$ then $k, [AB] \rightarrow t$

$$K = °C + 273.15 \quad PV = nRT \quad \Delta n_{AB} = \tfrac{1}{2}n_{A+B} \qquad [AB] = [AB]_0 - \dfrac{\Delta n_{AB}}{V_{AB} \times \dfrac{1\ L}{1000\ mL}} \qquad \dfrac{1}{[AB]_t} = kt + \dfrac{1}{[AB]_0}$$

Solution: $P_{Total} = P_{H_2O} + P_A + P_B$. Rearrange to solve for $P_A + P_B$. $P_A + P_B = P_{Total} - P_{H_2O} = 755.1$ mmHg -23.8 mmHg $= 731.3$ mmHg

$$P_A + P_B = 731.3 \text{ mmHg} \times \frac{1 \text{ atm}}{760 \text{ mmHg}} = 0.96223684 \text{ atm} \quad V = 200.0 \text{ mL} \times \frac{1 \text{ L}}{1000 \text{ mL}} = 0.2000 \text{ L},$$

$T = 25.0\,^\circ\text{C} + 273.15 = 298.2$ K, $PV = nRT$. Rearrange to solve for n. $n = \dfrac{PV}{RT}$

$$n_{A+B} = \frac{0.96223684 \text{ atm} \times 0.2000 \text{ L}}{0.08206 \dfrac{\text{L} \cdot \text{atm}}{\text{mol} \cdot \text{K}} \times 298.2 \text{ K}} = 0.0078645309 \text{ mol A} + \text{B. Because one mole each of A and B are}$$

generated for each mole of AB reacting, $\Delta n_{AB} = \frac{1}{2}n_{A+B} = \frac{1}{2}(0.0078645309 \text{ mol A} + \text{B}) = 0.0039322655 \text{ mol AB}$

then $[\text{AB}] = [\text{AB}]_0 - \dfrac{\Delta n_{AB}}{V_{AB} \times \dfrac{1 \text{ L}}{1000 \text{ mL}}} = 0.100 \text{ M} - \dfrac{0.0039322655 \text{ mol AB}}{250.0 \text{ mL} \times \dfrac{1 \text{ L}}{1000 \text{ mL}}} = 0.100 \text{ M} - 0.015729062 \text{ M}$

$= 0.0842709$ M.

Because $\dfrac{1}{[\text{AB}]_t} = kt + \dfrac{1}{[\text{AB}]_0}$, rearrange to solve for t.

$$t = \frac{1}{k}\left(\frac{1}{[\text{AB}]_t} - \frac{1}{[\text{AB}]_0}\right) = \frac{1}{(0.0118 \text{ M}^{-1} \cdot \text{s}^{-1})}\left(\frac{1}{0.0842709 \text{ M}} - \frac{1}{0.100 \text{ M}}\right) = 158.1773 \text{ s} = 160 \text{ s}$$

Check: The units (s) are correct. The magnitude of the answer (160 s) makes sense because the rate constant is $0.0118 \text{ M}^{-1}\text{s}^{-1}$ and a small volume of gas is generated.

13.71   (a)   There are two elementary steps in the reaction mechanism because there are two peaks in the reaction progress diagram.

         (b)

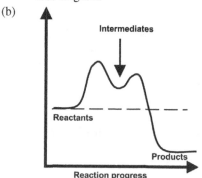

         (c)   The first step is the rate-limiting step because it has the higher activation energy.

         (d)   The overall reaction is exothermic because the products are at a lower energy than the reactants.

13.73   **Given:** n-butane desorption from single crystal aluminum oxide, first order; $k = 0.128$ s^{-1} at 150 K; initially completely covered

       Find: (a) $t_{1/2}$; (b) t for 25% and for 50% to desorb; (c) fraction remaining after 10 s and 20 s

       Conceptual Plan: (a) $k \rightarrow t_{1/2}$ (b) $[C_4H_{10}]_0, [C_4H_{10}]_t, k \rightarrow t$ (c) $[C_4H_{10}]_0, t, k \rightarrow [C_4H_{10}]_t$

$$t_{1/2} = \frac{0.693}{k} \qquad\qquad \ln[A]_t = -kt + \ln[A]_0 \qquad \ln[A]_t = -kt + \ln[A]_0$$

       Solution:

       (a) $t_{1/2} = \dfrac{0.693}{k} = \dfrac{0.693}{0.128 \text{ s}^{-1}} = 5.41 \text{ s}$

       (b) $\ln[C_4H_{10}]_t = -kt + \ln[C_4H_{10}]_0$. Rearrange to solve for t. For 25% desorbed, $[C_4H_{10}]_t = 0.75 [C_4H_{10}]_0$

            and $t = -\dfrac{1}{k} \ln \dfrac{[C_4H_{10}]_t}{[C_4H_{10}]_0} = -\dfrac{1}{0.128 \text{ s}^{-1}} \ln \dfrac{0.75 [C_4H_{10}]_0}{[C_4H_{10}]_0} = 2.2 \text{ s}$. For 50% desorbed,

$$[C_4H_{10}]_t = 0.50\ [C_4H_{10}]_0 \text{ and } t = -\frac{1}{k}\ln\frac{[C_4H_{10}]_t}{[C_4H_{10}]_0} = -\frac{1}{0.128\ s^{-1}}\ln\frac{0.50\ [C_4H_{10}]_0}{[C_4H_{10}]_0} = 5.4\ s.$$

(c)   For 10 s, $\ln[C_4H_{10}]_t = -kt + \ln[C_4H_{10}]_0 = -(0.128\ s^{-1})(10\ s) + \ln(1.00) = -1.28 \rightarrow$
$[C_4H_{10}]_t = e^{-1.28} = 0.28 = $ fraction covered.
For 20 s, $\ln[C_4H_{10}]_t = -kt + \ln[C_4H_{10}]_0 = -(0.128\ s^{-1})(20\ s) + \ln(1.00) = -2.56 \rightarrow$
$[C_4H_{10}]_t = e^{-2.56} = 0.077 = $ fraction covered.

Check: The units (s, s, s, none, and none) are correct. The half-life is reasonable considering the size of the rate constant. The time to 25% desorbed is less than one half-life. The time to 50% desorbed is the half-life. The fraction at 10 s is consistent with about two half-lives. The fraction covered at 20 s is consistent with about four half-lives.

13.75   (a)   **Given:** table of rate constant versus T **Find:** E_a and A
Conceptual Plan: First, convert temperature data into kelvin (°C + 273.15 = K). Because

$$\ln k = \frac{-E_a}{R}\left(\frac{1}{T}\right) + \ln A \text{ a plot of } \ln k \text{ versus } 1/T \text{ will have a slope} = -E_a/R \text{ and an intercept} = \ln A.$$

Solution: The slope can be determined by measuring $\Delta y/\Delta x$ on the plot or by using functions such as "add trendline" in Excel. Because the slope $= -10759\ K = -E_a/R$, then

$E_a = -(\text{slope})R$

$= -(-10759\ K)\left(8.314\ \dfrac{J}{K\cdot mol}\right)\left(\dfrac{1\ kJ}{1000\ J}\right)$

$= 89.5\ \dfrac{kJ}{mol}$

and intercept $= 26.769 = \ln A$ then
$A = e^{\text{intercept}} = e^{26.769} = 4.22 \times 10^{11}\ s^{-1}.$

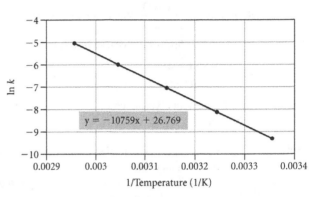

y = -10759x + 26.769

1/Temperature (1/K)

Check: The units (kJ/mol and s^{-1}) are correct. The plot was extremely linear, confirming Arrhenius behavior. The activation and frequency factor are typical for many reactions.

(b)   **Given:** part (a) results   **Find:** k at 15 °C
Conceptual Plan: °C $\rightarrow$ K then $T, E_a, A \rightarrow k$

$$°C + 273.15 = K \qquad \ln k = \frac{-E_a}{R}\left(\frac{1}{T}\right) + \ln A$$

Solution: 15 °C + 273.15 = 288 K then

$$\ln k = \frac{-E_a}{R}\left(\frac{1}{T}\right) + \ln A = \frac{-89.5\ \dfrac{kJ}{mol} \times \dfrac{1000\ J}{1\ kJ}}{8.314\ \dfrac{J}{K\cdot mol}}\left(\frac{1}{288\ K}\right) + \ln(4.22 \times 10^{11}\ s^{-1}) = -10.610 \rightarrow$$

$k = e^{-10.610} = 2.5 \times 10^{-5}\ M^{-1}\cdot s^{-1}$

Check: The units ($M^{-1}\cdot s^{-1}$) are correct. The value of the rate constant is less than the value at 25 °C.

(c)   **Given:** part (a) results, 0.155 M C_2H_5Br and 0.250 M OH^- at 75 °C   **Find:** initial reaction rate
Conceptual Plan: °C $\rightarrow$ K then $T, E_a, A \rightarrow k$ then $k,\ [C_2H_5Br],\ [OH^-] \rightarrow$ initial reaction rate

$$°C + 273.15 = K \qquad \ln k = \frac{-E_a}{R}\left(\frac{1}{T}\right) + \ln A \qquad\qquad \text{Rate} = k[C_2H_5Br][OH^-]$$

Solution: 75 °C + 273.15 = 348 K then

$$\ln k = \frac{-E_a}{R}\left(\frac{1}{T}\right) + \ln A = \frac{-89.5\ \dfrac{kJ}{mol} \times \dfrac{1000\ J}{1\ kJ}}{8.314\ \dfrac{J}{K\cdot mol}}\left(\frac{1}{348\ K}\right) + \ln(4.22 \times 10^{11}\ s^{-1}) = -4.1656 \rightarrow$$

$k = e^{-4.1656} = 1.5521 \times 10^{-2}\ M^{-1}\cdot s^{-1}$

Rate $= k[C_2H_5Br][OH^-] = (1.5521 \times 10^{-2}\ M^{-1} \cdot s^{-1})(0.155\ M)(0.250\ M) = 6.0 \times 10^{-4}\ M \cdot s^{-1}$

Check: The units $(M \cdot s^{-1})$ are correct. The value of the rate is reasonable considering the value of the rate constant (larger than in the table) and the fact that the concentrations are less than 1 M.

13.77   (a)   No, because the activation energy is zero. This means that the rate constant $(k = Ae^{-E_a/RT})$ will be independent of temperature.

       (b)   No bond is broken, and the two radicals (CH_3) attract each other.

       (c)   Formation of diatomic gases from atomic gases

13.79   **Given:** $t_{1/2}$ for radioactive decay of C-14 $= 5730$ years; bone has 19.5% C-14 in living bone

      Find: age of bone

      Conceptual Plan: Radioactive decay implies first-order kinetics, $t_{1/2} \rightarrow k$ **then 19.5% of [C-14]$_0$,** $k \rightarrow t$

$$t_{1/2} = \frac{0.693}{k} \qquad\qquad\qquad \ln[A]_t = -kt + \ln[A]_0$$

      Solution: $t_{1/2} = \dfrac{0.693}{k}$. Rearrange to solve for k. $k = \dfrac{0.693}{t_{1/2}} = \dfrac{0.693}{5730\ \text{yr}} = 1.20942 \times 10^{-4}\ \text{yr}^{-1}$ then

      $[\text{C-14}]_t = 0.195[\text{C-14}]_0$. Because $\ln[\text{C-14}]_t = -kt + \ln[\text{C-14}]_0$, rearrange to solve for t.

$$t = -\frac{1}{k}\ln\frac{[\text{C-14}]_t}{[\text{C-14}]_0} = -\frac{1}{1.20942 \times 10^{-4}\ \text{yr}^{-1}}\ln\frac{0.195[\text{C-14}]_0}{[\text{C-14}]_0} = 1.35 \times 10^4\ \text{yr}$$

      Check: The units (yr) are correct. The time to 19.5% decay is consistent with the time being between two and three half-lives.

13.81   (a)   For each, check that all steps sum to overall reaction and that the predicted rate law is consistent with experimental data (Rate $= k[H_2][I_2]$).

         For the first mechanism, the single step is the overall reaction. The rate law is determined by the stoichiometry, so Rate $= k[H_2][I_2]$, and the mechanism is valid.

         For the second mechanism, the overall reaction is the sum of the steps in the mechanism:

$$I_2(g) \underset{k_2}{\overset{k_1}{\rightleftharpoons}} 2\ \cancel{I(g)}$$

$$H_2(g) + 2\ \cancel{I(g)} \overset{k_3}{\rightarrow} 2\ HI(g) \quad \text{So the sum matches the overall reaction.}$$

$$\overline{H_2(g) + I_2(g) \rightarrow 2\ HI(g)}$$

         Because the second step is the rate-determining step, Rate $= k_3[H_2][I]^2$. Because I is an intermediate, its concentration cannot appear in the rate law. Using the fast equilibrium in the first step, we see that

         $k_1[I_2] = k_2[I]^2$ or $[I]^2 = \dfrac{k_1}{k_2}[I_2]$. Substituting this into the first rate expression, we get Rate $= k_3 \dfrac{k_1}{k_2}[H_2][I_2]$, and the mechanism is valid.

      (b)   To distinguish between mechanisms, you could look for the buildup of I(g), the intermediate in the second mechanism.

13.83   (a)   For a zero-order reaction, the rate is independent of the concentration. If the first half goes in the first 100 minutes, the second half will go in the second 100 minutes. This means that none or 0% will be left at 200 minutes.

      (b)   For a first-order reaction, the half-life is independent of concentration. This means that if half of the reactant decomposes in the first 100 minutes, half of this (or another 25% of the original amount) will decompose in the second 100 minutes. This means that at 200 minutes, 50% + 25% = 75% has decomposed or 25% remains.

      (c)   For a second-order reaction, $t_{1/2} = \dfrac{1}{k[A]_0} = 100$ min, and the integrated rate expression is $\dfrac{1}{[A]_t} = kt + \dfrac{1}{[A]_0}$.

         We can rearrange the first expression to solve for k as $k = \dfrac{1}{100\ \text{min}\ [A]_0}$. Substituting this and 200 minutes

         into the integrated rate expression, we get $\dfrac{1}{[A]_t} = \dfrac{200\ \cancel{\text{min}}}{100\ \cancel{\text{min}}\ [A]_0} + \dfrac{1}{[A]_0} \rightarrow \dfrac{1}{[A]_t} = \dfrac{3}{[A]_0} \rightarrow \dfrac{[A]_t}{[A]_0} = \dfrac{1}{3}$ or

         33% remains.

13.85 Using the energy diagram shown and using Hess's law, we can see that the activation energy for the decomposition is equal to the activation energy for the formation reaction plus the heat of formation of 2 moles of HI, or $E_{a\ \text{formation}} = E_{a\ \text{decomposition}} + 2\Delta H_f^{\circ}(\text{HI})$. So $E_{a\ \text{formation}} = 185\ \text{kJ} + 2\ \text{mol}(-5.65\ \text{kJ/mol}) = 174\ \text{kJ}$.

Check: Because the reaction is endothermic, we expect the activation energy in the reverse direction to be less than that in the forward direction.

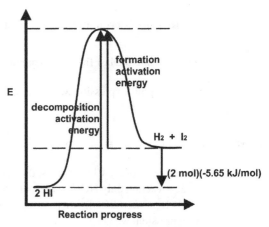

Note: energy axis is not to scale.

Challenge Problems

13.87 (a) Because the rate-determining step involves the collision of two molecules, the expected reaction order would be second order.

(b) The proposed mechanism is

$$CH_3NC + CH_3NC \underset{k_2}{\overset{k_1}{\rightleftharpoons}} CH_3NC^* + CH_3NC \qquad \text{(fast)}$$

$$CH_3NC^* \overset{k_3}{\rightarrow} CH_3CN \qquad \text{(slow)}$$

$$\overline{CH_3NC \rightarrow CH_3CN} \qquad \text{So the sum matches the overall reaction.}$$

CH_3NC^* is the activated molecule. Because the second step is the rate-determining step, Rate $= k_3[CH_3NC^*]$. Because CH_3NC^* is an intermediate, its concentration cannot appear in the rate law. Using the fast equilibrium in the first step, we see that $k_1[CH_3NC]^2 = k_2[CH_3NC^*][CH_3NC]$ or $[CH_3NC^*] = \dfrac{k_1}{k_2}[CH_3NC]$. Substituting this into the first rate expression, we get Rate $= k_3\dfrac{k_1}{k_2}[CH_3NC]$, which simplifies to Rate $= k[CH_3NC]$.

This matches the experimental observation of first order, and the mechanism is valid.

13.89 Rate $= k[A]^2$ and Rate $= -\dfrac{d[A]}{dt}$, so $\dfrac{d[A]}{dt} = -k[A]^2$. Moving the A terms to the left and the t and constants to the right, we have $\dfrac{d[A]}{[A]^2} = -k\,dt$. Integrating, we get $\displaystyle\int_{[A]_0}^{[A]} \dfrac{d[A]}{[A]^2} = -\int_0^t k\,dt$. When we evaluate this integral,

$-[A]^{-1}\Big|_{[A]_0}^{[A]} = -kt\Big|_0^t \rightarrow -[A]_t^{-1} - (-[A]_0^{-1}) = -kt \rightarrow [A]_t^{-1} = kt + [A]_0^{-1}$ or $\dfrac{1}{[A]_t} = kt + \dfrac{1}{[A]_0}$, which is the desired integrated rate law.

13.91 For this mechanism, the overall reaction is the sum of the steps in the mechanism:

$$Cl_2(g) \underset{k_2}{\overset{k_1}{\rightleftharpoons}} 2\ Cl(g)$$

$$Cl(g) + CO(g) \underset{k_4}{\overset{k_3}{\rightleftharpoons}} ClCO(g)$$

$$\underline{ClCO(g) + Cl_2(g) \overset{k_5}{\rightarrow} Cl_2CO(g) + Cl(g)}$$

$$CO(g) + 2\ Cl_2(g) \rightarrow Cl_2CO(g) + 2\ Cl(g)$$

No overall reaction is given. Because the third step is the rate-determining step, Rate $= k_5[ClCO][Cl_2]$. Because ClCO is an intermediate, its concentration cannot appear in the rate law. Using the fast equilibrium in the second step, we see that $k_3[Cl][CO] = k_4[ClCO]$ or $[ClCO] = \dfrac{k_3}{k_4}[Cl][CO]$. Substituting this expression into the first rate expression, we get Rate $= k_5\dfrac{k_3}{k_4}[Cl][CO][Cl_2]$. Because Cl is an intermediate, its concentration cannot appear in the rate law. Using the fast equilibrium in the first step, we see that $k_1[Cl_2] = k_2[Cl]^2$ or $[Cl] = \sqrt{\dfrac{k_1}{k_2}}\,[Cl_2]$. Substituting this

expression into the last first rate expression, we get Rate $= k_5 \dfrac{k_3}{k_4} \sqrt{\dfrac{k_1}{k_2}}\,[Cl_2]\,[CO]\,[Cl_2] = k_5 \dfrac{k_3}{k_4} \sqrt{\dfrac{k_1}{k_2}}\,[CO]\,[Cl_2]^{3/2}$.

Simplifying this expression, we see Rate $= k\,[CO]\,[Cl_2]^{3/2}$.

13.93   For the elementary reaction $2\,NOCl(g) \underset{k_{-1}}{\overset{k_1}{\rightleftharpoons}} 2\,NO(g) + Cl_2(g)$, we see that $k_1[NOCl]^2 = k_{-1}[NO]^2[Cl_2]$.

For each mole of NOCl that reacts, one mole of NO and one-half mole of Cl_2 are generated. Because before any reaction only NOCl is present, $[NO] = 2[Cl_2]$. Substituting this into the first expression, we get $k_1[NOCl]^2 = k_{-1}(2[Cl_2])^2[Cl_2] \rightarrow k_1[NOCl]^2 = 4k_{-1}[Cl_2]^3$. Rearranging and substituting the specific values into this expression, we get

$$[Cl_2] = \sqrt[3]{\dfrac{k_1}{4k_{-1}}}\,[NOCl]^{2/3} = \sqrt[3]{\dfrac{7.8 \times 10^{-2}\,\dfrac{L^2}{mol^2 \cdot s}}{4\left(4.7 \times 10^2\,\dfrac{L^2}{mol \cdot s}\right)}}\left(0.12\,\dfrac{mol}{L}\right)^{2/3} = 0.00842235\,\dfrac{mol}{L}\,Cl_2$$

$$= 0.0084\,M\,Cl_2 \text{ and } [NO] = 2[Cl_2] = 2\left(0.00842235\,\dfrac{mol}{L}\right) = 0.0168445\,\dfrac{mol}{L}\,NO = 0.017\,M\,NO$$

Conceptual Problems

13.95   Reactant concentrations drop more quickly for first-order reactions than for second-order reactions, so reaction A must

be second order. A plot of $1/[A]$ versus time will be linear $\left(\dfrac{1}{[A]_t} = kt + \dfrac{1}{[A]_0}\right)$. Reaction B is first order. A plot of

$\ln[A]$ versus time will be linear $(\ln[A]_t = -kt + \ln[A]_0)$.

Questions for Group Work

13.97   It is very tempting to think that the same descriptor that relates the concentration change to the rate change is the order of the reaction. This statement is incorrect, because the reaction order is first order. For a first-order reaction, Rate $= k[A]^1$, so doubling the concentration of A doubles the reaction rate. For a second-order reaction, Rate $= k[A]^2$, so doubling the concentration of A quadruples the reaction rate $(2^2 = 4)$.

13.99   Using Excel, the slope is the negative of the rate constant $(\ln[A]_t = -kt + \ln[A]_0)$. The rate constants are 0.2711 s^{-1}, 0.3959 s^{-1}, and 0.5728 s^{-1}, for 25.0 °C, 35.0 °C, and 45.0 °C, respectively.

13.101   A catalyst will speed up a reaction by reducing the activation energy. The reaction is still first order, as seen by the linear plots of $\ln[A]$ versus t.

Using Excel, the slope is the negative of the rate constant $(\ln[A]_t = -kt + \ln[A]_0)$. The rate constants are 3.246 s^{-1}, 4.215 s^{-1}, and 5.269 s^{-1}, for 25.0 °C, 35.0 °C, and 45.0 °C, respectively.

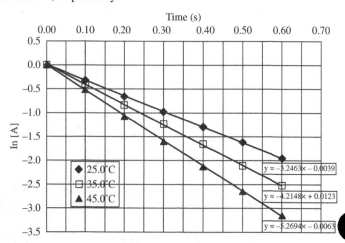

Since $\ln k = \dfrac{-E_a}{R}\left(\dfrac{1}{T}\right) + \ln A$ a plot of $\ln k$ versus $1/T$ will have a slope $= -E_a/R$ and an intercept $= \ln A$.

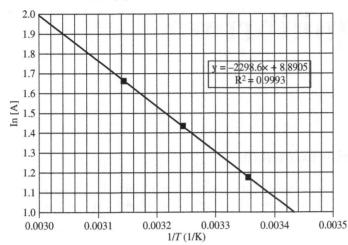

$y = -2298.6x + 8.8905$
$R^2 = 0.9993$

Since the slope $= -2298.6\text{ K} = -E_a/R$ then

$$E_a = -(-2298.6\ K)\left(8.314\ \dfrac{J}{K\cdot\text{mol}}\right)\left(\dfrac{1\text{ kJ}}{1000\ J}\right)$$

$$= 19.1\ \dfrac{\text{kJ}}{\text{mol}}$$

The activation energy has been cut by about a third by adding a catalyst.

14 Chemical Equilibrium

Problems by Topic

Equilibrium and the Equilibrium Constant

14.1 The equilibrium constant is defined as the concentrations of the products raised to their stoichiometric coefficients divided by the concentrations of the reactants raised to their stoichiometric coefficients.

(a) $K = \dfrac{[SbCl_3][Cl_2]}{[SbCl_5]}$

(b) $K = \dfrac{[NO]^2[Br_2]}{[BrNO]^2}$

(c) $K = \dfrac{[CS_2][H_2]^4}{[CH_4][H_2S]^2}$

(d) $K = \dfrac{[CO_2]^2}{[CO]^2[O_2]}$

14.3 With an equilibrium constant of 1.4×10^{-5}, the value of the equilibrium constant is small; therefore, the concentration of reactants will be greater than the concentration of products. This is independent of the initial concentration of the reactants and products.

14.5 (i) has 10 H_2 and 10 I_2
(ii) has 7 H_2 and 7 I_2 and 6 HI
(iii) has 5 H_2 and 5 I_2 and 10 HI
(iv) has 4 H_2 and 4 I_2 and 12 HI
(v) has 3 H_2 and 3 I_2 and 14 HI
(vi) has 3 H_2 and 3 I_2 and 14 HI

(a) Concentrations of (v) and (vi) are the same, so the system reached equilibrium at (v).
(b) If a catalyst was added to the system, the system would reach the conditions at (v) sooner because a catalyst speeds up the reaction but does not change the equilibrium conditions.
(c) The final figure (vi) would have the same amount of reactants and products because a catalyst speeds up the reaction but does not change the equilibrium concentrations.

14.7 (a) If you reverse the reaction, invert the equilibrium constant. So
$$K' = \frac{1}{K_p} = \frac{1}{2.26 \times 10^4} = 4.42 \times 10^{-5}.$$

The reactants will be favored.
(b) If you multiply the coefficients in the equation by a factor, raise the equilibrium constant to the same factor.
So $K' = (K_p)^{1/2} = (2.26 \times 10^4)^{1/2} = 1.50 \times 10^2$. The products will be favored.
(c) Begin with the reverse of the reaction and invert the equilibrium constant.
$$K_{reverse} = \frac{1}{K_p} = \frac{1}{2.26 \times 10^4} = 4.42 \times 10^{-5}$$

Then multiply the reaction by 2 and raise the value of $K_{reverse}$ to the second power.
$K' = (K_{reverse})^2 = (4.42 \times 10^{-5})^2 = 1.95 \times 10^{-9}$. The reactants will be favored.

14.9   To find the equilibrium constant for reaction 3, you need to combine reactions 1 and 2 to get reaction 3. Begin by reversing reaction 2; then multiply reaction 1 by 2 and add the two new reactions. When you add reactions, you multiply the values of K.

$$N_2(g) + O_2(g) \rightleftharpoons 2\,\cancel{NO}(g) \qquad K_1 = \frac{1}{K_p} = \frac{1}{2.1 \times 10^{30}} = 4.\underline{7}6 \times 10^{-31}$$

$$2\,\cancel{NO}(g) + Br_2(g) \rightleftharpoons 2\,NOBr(g) \qquad K_2 = (K_p)^2 = (5.3)^2 = 28.09$$

$$\overline{N_2(g) + O_2(g) + Br_2(g) \rightleftharpoons 2\,NOBr(g) \qquad K_3 = K_1 K_2 = (4.\underline{7}6 \times 10^{-31})(28.09) = 1.3 \times 10^{-29}}$$

K_p, K_c, and Heterogeneous Equilibria

14.11   (a)   **Given:** $K_p = 6.26 \times 10^{-22}$ $T = 298$ K   **Find:** K_c
        Conceptual Plan: $K_p \rightarrow K_c$
                 $K_p = K_c(RT)^{\Delta n}$

        Solution: Δn = mol product gas − mol reactant gas = $2 - 1 = 1$

$$K_c = \frac{K_p}{(RT)^{\Delta n}} = \frac{6.26 \times 10^{-22}}{\left(0.08206 \dfrac{L \cdot atm}{mol \cdot K} \times 298\ K\right)^1} = 2.56 \times 10^{-23}$$

        Check: Substitute into the equation and confirm that you get the original value of K_p.

$$K_p = K_c(RT)^{\Delta n} = (2.56 \times 10^{-23})\left(0.08206 \dfrac{L \cdot atm}{mol \cdot K} \times 298\ K\right)^1 = 6.26 \times 10^{-22}$$

        (b)   **Given:** $K_p = 7.7 \times 10^{24}$ $T = 298$ K   **Find:** K_c
        Conceptual Plan: $K_p \rightarrow K_c$
                 $K_p = K_c(RT)^{\Delta n}$

        Solution: Δn = mol product gas − mol reactant gas = $4 - 2 = 2$

$$K_c = \frac{K_p}{(RT)^{\Delta n}} = \frac{7.7 \times 10^{24}}{\left(0.08206 \dfrac{L \cdot atm}{mol \cdot K} \times 298\ K\right)^2} = 1.3 \times 10^{22}$$

        Check: Substitute into the equation and confirm that you get the original value of K_p.

$$K_p = K_c(RT)^{\Delta n} = (1.3 \times 10^{22})\left(0.08206 \dfrac{L \cdot atm}{mol \cdot K} \times 298\ K\right)^2 = 7.7 \times 10^{24}$$

        (c)   **Given:** $K_p = 81.9$ $T = 298$ K   **Find:** K_c
        Conceptual Plan: $K_p \rightarrow K_c$
                 $K_p = K_c(RT)^{\Delta n}$

        Solution: Δn = mol product gas − mol reactant gas = $2 - 2 = 0$

$$K_c = \frac{K_p}{(RT)^{\Delta n}} = \frac{81.9}{\left(0.08206 \dfrac{L \cdot atm}{mol \cdot K} \times 298\ K\right)^0} = 81.9$$

        Check: Substitute into the equation and confirm that you get the original value of K_p.

$$K_p = K_c(RT)^{\Delta n} = (81.9)\left(0.08206 \dfrac{L \cdot atm}{mol \cdot K} \times 298\ K\right)^0 = 81.9$$

14.13   (a)   Because H_2O is a liquid, it is omitted from the equilibrium expression. $K_{eq} = \dfrac{[HCO_3^-][OH^-]}{[CO_3^{2-}]}$

        (b)   Because $KClO_3$ and KCl are both solids, they are omitted from the equilibrium expression. $K_{eq} = [O_2]^3$

        (c)   Because H_2O is a liquid, it is omitted from the equilibrium expression. $K_{eq} = \dfrac{[H_3O^+][F^-]}{[HF]}$

        (d)   Because H_2O is a liquid, it is omitted from the equilibrium expression. $K_{eq} = \dfrac{[NH_4^+][OH^-]}{[NH_3]}$

Relating the Equilibrium Constant to Equilibrium Concentrations and Equilibrium Partial Pressures

14.15   **Given:** at equilibrium: $[CO] = 0.105$ M, $[H_2] = 0.114$ M, $[CH_3OH] = 0.185$ M   **Find:** K_c
Conceptual Plan: Balanced reaction → equilibrium expression → K_c

Solution: $K_c = \dfrac{[CH_3OH]}{[CO][H_2]^2} = \dfrac{(0.185)}{(0.105)(0.114)^2} = 136$

Check: The answer is reasonable because the concentration of products is greater than the concentration of reactants and the equilibrium constant should be greater than 1.

14.17   At 500 K: **Given:** at equilibrium: $[N_2] = 0.115$ M, $[H_2] = 0.105$ M, and $[NH_3] = 0.439$ M   **Find:** K_c
Conceptual Plan: Balanced reaction → equilibrium expression → K_c

Solution: $K_c = \dfrac{[NH_3]^2}{[N_2][H_2]^3} = \dfrac{(0.439)^2}{(0.115)(0.105)^3} = 1.45 \times 10^3$

Check: The value is reasonable because the concentration of products is greater than the concentration of reactants.

At 575 K: **Given:** at equilibrium: $[N_2] = 0.110$ M, $[NH_3] = 0.128$ M, $K_c = 9.6$ **Find:** $[H_2]$
Conceptual Plan: Balanced reaction → equilibrium expression → $[H_2]$

Solution: $K_c = \dfrac{[NH_3]^2}{[N_2][H_2]^3}$ $9.6 = \dfrac{(0.128)^2}{(0.110)(x)^3}$ $x = 0.249$ M

Check: Plug the value for x back into the equilibrium expression and check the value.

$$9.6 = \dfrac{(0.128)^2}{(0.110)(0.249)^3}$$

At 775 K: **Given:** at equilibrium: $[N_2] = 0.120$ M, $[H_2] = 0.140$ M, $K_c = 0.0584$ **Find:** $[NH_3]$
Conceptual Plan: Balanced reaction → equilibrium expression → $[NH_3]$

Solution: $K_c = \dfrac{[NH_3]^2}{[N_2][H_2]^3}$ $0.0584 = \dfrac{(x)^2}{(0.120)(0.140)^3}$ $x = 0.00439$ M

Check: Plug the value for x back into the equilibrium expression and check the value.

$$0.0584 = \dfrac{(0.00439)^2}{(0.120)(0.140)^3}$$

14.19   **Given:** $P_{NO} = 118$ torr; $P_{Br_2} = 176$ torr, $K_p = 28.4$ **Find:** P_{NOBr}
Conceptual Plan: torr → atm and then balanced reaction → equilibrium expression → P_{NOBr}

$$\frac{1\ atm}{760\ torr}$$

Solution: $P_{NO} = 118\ torr \times \dfrac{1\ atm}{760\ torr} = 0.15\underline{5}3$ atm $P_{Br_2} = 176\ torr \times \dfrac{1\ atm}{760\ torr} = 0.23\underline{1}6$ atm

$K_p = \dfrac{P_{NOBr}^2}{P_{NO}^2 P_{Br_2}}$ $28.4 = \dfrac{x^2}{(0.15\underline{5}3)^2(0.23\underline{1}6)}$ $x = 0.398$ atm $= 303$ torr

Check: Plug the value for x back into the equilibrium expression and check the value.

$$28.4 = \dfrac{(0.398)^2}{(0.15\underline{5}3)^2(0.23\underline{1}6)}$$

14.21   **Given:** $P_{A,\ initial} = 1.32$ atm; $P_{A,\ eq} = 0.25$ atm   **Find:** K_p
Conceptual Plan: 1. **Prepare Initial, Change, and Equil (ICE) table.**
2. **Calculate pressure change for known value.**
3. **Calculate pressure changes for other reactants/products.**
4. **Determine equilibrium pressures.**
5. **Write the equilibrium expression and determine K_p.**

Solution: $A(g) \rightleftharpoons 2B(g)$

	P_A	P_B
Initial	1.32 atm	0.00
Change	$-x$	$+2x$
Equil	0.25 atm	$2x$

$$x = 1.32 - 0.25 = 1.07 \text{ atm}$$
$$2x = 2(1.07 \text{ atm}) = 2.14 \text{ atm} = P_B$$

$$K_p = \frac{P_B^2}{P_A} = \frac{(2.14)^2}{(0.25)} = 1\underline{8}.32 = 18$$

14.23   **Given:** $[Fe^{3+}]_{initial} = 1.0 \times 10^{-3}$ M; $[SCN^-]_{initial} = 8.0 \times 10^{-4}$ M; $[FeSCN^{2+}]_{eq} = 1.7 \times 10^{-4}$ M   **Find:** K_c
Conceptual Plan: 1. **Prepare Initial, Change, and Equil (ICE) table.**
                        2. **Calculate concentration change for known value.**
                        3. **Calculate concentration changes for other reactants/products.**
                        4. **Determine equilibrium concentration.**
                        5. **Write the equilibrium expression and determine K_c.**

Solution: $Fe^{3+}(aq) + SCN^-(aq) \rightleftharpoons FeSCN^{3+}(aq)$

	$[Fe^{3+}]$	$[SCN^-]$	$[FeSCN^{3+}]$
Initial	1.0×10^{-3}	8.0×10^{-4}	0.00
Change	-1.7×10^{-4}	-1.7×10^{-4}	$+1.7 \times 10^{-4}$
Equil	8.3×10^{-4}	6.3×10^{-4}	1.7×10^{-4}

$$K_c = \frac{[FeSCN^{2+}]}{[Fe^{3+}][SCN^-]} = \frac{(1.7 \times 10^{-4})}{(8.3 \times 10^{-4})(6.3 \times 10^{-4})} = 3.3 \times 10^2$$

14.25   **Given:** 3.67 L flask, 0.763 g H_2 initial, 96.9 g I_2 initial, 90.4 g HI equilibrium   **Find:** K_c
Conceptual Plan: g $\rightarrow$ mol $\rightarrow$ M and then

$$n = \frac{g}{molar\ mass} \qquad M = \frac{n}{V}$$

1. **Prepare Initial, Change, and Equil (ICE) table.**
2. **Calculate concentration change for known value.**
3. **Calculate concentration changes for other reactants/products.**
4. **Determine equilibrium concentration.**
5. **Write the equilibrium expression and determine K_c.**

Solution: $0.763 \text{ g } H_2 \times \dfrac{1 \text{ mol } H_2}{2.016 \text{ g } H_2} = 0.37\underline{8}5 \text{ mol } H_2$ $\dfrac{0.37\underline{8}5 \text{ mol } H_2}{3.67 \text{ L}} = 0.103 \text{ M}$. This is an initial concentration.

$96.9 \text{ g } I_2 \times \dfrac{1 \text{ mol } I_2}{253.8 \text{ g } I_2} = 0.38\underline{1}8 \text{ mol } I_2$ $\dfrac{0.38\underline{1}8 \text{ mol } I_2}{3.67 \text{ L}} = 0.104 \text{ M}$. This is an initial concentration.

$90.4 \text{ g HI} \times \dfrac{1 \text{ mol HI}}{127.9 \text{ g HI}} = 0.70\underline{6}8 \text{ mol HI}$ $\dfrac{0.70\underline{6}8 \text{ mol HI}}{3.67 \text{ L}} = 0.193 \text{ M}$. This is an equilibrium
concentration.

$$H_2(g) + I_2(g) \rightleftharpoons 2 HI(g)$$

	$[H_2]$	$[I_2]$	$[HI]$
Initial	0.103	0.104	0.00
Change	-0.0965	-0.0965	$+0.193$
Equil	0.0065	0.0075	0.193

Because HI gained 0.193 M, H_2 and I_2 had to lose 0.193/2 = 0.0965 M from the stoichiometry of the balanced reaction.

$$K_c = \frac{[HI]^2}{[H_2][I_2]} = \frac{(0.193)^2}{(0.0065)(0.0075)} = 764$$

The Reaction Quotient and Reaction Direction

14.27   **Given:** $K_c = 8.5 \times 10^{-3}$; $[NH_3] = 0.166$ M; $[H_2S] = 0.166$ M   **Find:** Will solid form or decompose?
         Conceptual Plan: Calculate Q → **compare** Q → **and** K_c

         Solution: $Q = [NH_3][H_2S] = (0.166)(0.166) = 0.0276$

         $Q = 0.0276$ and $K_c = 8.5 \times 10^{-3}$ so $Q > K_c$ and the reaction will shift to the left; so more solid will form.

14.29   **Given:** 6.55 g Ag_2SO_4, 1.5 L solution, $K_c = 1.1 \times 10^{-5}$ **Find:** Will more solid dissolve?
         Conceptual Plan: g Ag_2SO_4 → **mol** Ag_2SO_4 → **[**Ag_2SO_4**]** → **[**Ag^+**], [**SO_4^{2-}**]** → **calculate** Q **and compare to** K_c

         $$\frac{1 \text{ mol } Ag_2SO_4}{311.81 \text{ g}} \qquad [\ ] = \frac{\text{mol } Ag_2SO_4}{\text{vol solution}} \qquad Q = [Ag^+]^2[SO_4^{2-}]$$

         Solution: $6.55 \text{ g } Ag_2SO_4 \left(\dfrac{1 \text{ mol } Ag_2SO_4}{311.81 \text{ g } Ag_2SO_4} \right) = 0.0210 \text{ mol } Ag_2SO_4$

         $$\frac{0.0210 \text{ mol } Ag_2SO_4}{1.5 \text{ L solution}} = 0.01\underline{4}0 \text{ M } Ag_2SO_4$$

         $[Ag^+] = 2[Ag_2SO_4] = 2(0.01\underline{4}0 \text{ M}) = 0.02\underline{8}0 \text{ M}$ $[SO_4^{2-}] = [Ag_2SO_4] = 0.01\underline{4}0$ M

         $Q = [Ag^+]^2[SO_4^{2-}] = (0.02\underline{8}0)^2(0.01\underline{4}0) = 1.1 \times 10^{-5}$

         $Q = K_c$, so the system is at equilibrium and is a saturated solution. Therefore, if more solid is added, it will not dissolve.

Finding Equilibrium Concentrations from Initial Concentrations and the Equilibrium Constant

14.31   (a)   **Given:** $[A] = 1.0$ M, $[B] = 0.0$ M; $K_c = 2.0$; $a = 1, b = 1$ **Find:** $[A]$, $[B]$ at equilibrium
                Conceptual Plan: Prepare an ICE table, calculate Q**, compare** Q **and** K_c**, predict the direction of the reaction, represent the change with** x**, sum the table, determine the equilibrium values, put the equilibrium values in the equilibrium expression, and solve for** x**. Determine** $[A]$ **and** $[B]$**.**
                Solution: $A(g) \rightleftharpoons B(g)$

	[A]	[B]
Initial	1.0	0.00
Change	$-x$	x
Equil	$1 - x$	x

$Q = \dfrac{[B]}{[A]} = \dfrac{0}{1} = 0$ $Q < K$ Therefore, the reaction will proceed to the right by x.

$K_c = \dfrac{[B]}{[A]} = \dfrac{(x)}{(1-x)} = 2.0$ $x = 0.67$

$[A] = 1 - 0.67 = 0.33$ M $[B] = 0.67$ M

Check: Plug the values into the equilibrium expression: $K_c = \dfrac{0.67}{0.33} = 2.0$.

         (b)   **Given:** $[A] = 1.0$ M, $[B] = 0.0$ M; $K_c = 2.0$; $a = 2, b = 2$ **Find:** $[A]$, $[B]$ at equilibrium
                Conceptual Plan: Prepare an ICE table, calculate Q**, compare** Q **and** K_c**, predict the direction of the reaction, represent the change with** x**, sum the table, determine the equilibrium values, put the equilibrium values in the equilibrium expression, and solve for** x**. Determine** $[A]$ **and** $[B]$**.**
                Solution: $2 A(g) \rightleftharpoons 2 B(g)$

	[A]	[B]
Initial	1.0	0.00
Change	$-2x$	$2x$
Equil	$1 - 2x$	$2x$

$$Q = \frac{[B]^2}{[A]^2} = \frac{0}{1} = 0 \qquad\qquad Q < K \text{ Therefore, the reaction will proceed to the right by } x.$$

$$K_c = \frac{[B]^2}{[A]^2} = \frac{(2x)^2}{(1-2x)^2} = 2.0 \qquad\qquad x = 0.2\underline{9}3$$

$$[A] = 1 - 2(0.293) = 0.4\underline{1}4 = 0.41 \text{ M} \qquad [B] = 2(0.293) = 0.5\underline{8}6 = 0.59 \text{ M}$$

Check: Plug the values into the equilibrium expression: $K_c = \dfrac{(0.59)^2}{(0.41)^2} = 2.1.$

(c) **Given:** $[A] = 1.0$ M, $[B] = 0.0$ M; $K_c = 2.0$; $a = 1, b = 2$ **Find:** $[A]$, $[B]$ at equilibrium
Conceptual Plan: Prepare an ICE table, calculate Q, compare Q and K_c, predict the direction of the reaction, represent the change with x, sum the table, determine the equilibrium values, put the equilibrium values in the equilibrium expression, and solve for x. Determine $[A]$ and $[B]$.
Solution: $A(g) \rightleftharpoons 2\,B(g)$

	[A]	[B]
Initial	1.0	0.00
Change	$-x$	$2x$
Equil	$1 - x$	$2x$

$$Q = \frac{[B]^2}{[A]} = \frac{0}{1} = 0 \qquad\qquad Q < K \text{ Therefore, the reaction will proceed to the right by } x.$$

$$K_c = \frac{[B]^2}{[A]} = \frac{(2x)^2}{(1-x)} = 2.0 \quad 4x^2 + 2x - 2 = 0 \qquad \text{Solve using the quadratic equation, Appendix I.}$$

$$x = -1 \text{ or } x = 0.50; \text{ therefore, } x = 0.50.$$

$$[A] = 1 - 0.50 = 0.50 \text{ M} \qquad\qquad [B] = 2x = 2(0.50) = 1.\underline{0} \text{ M} = 1.0 \text{ M}$$

Check: Plug the values into the equilibrium expression: $K_c = \dfrac{(1.0)^2}{0.50} = 2.0.$

14.33   **Given:** $[N_2O_4] = 0.0;500$ M, $[NO_2] = 0.0$ M; $K_c = 0.513$ **Find:** $[N_2O_4]$, $[NO_2]$ at equilibrium
Conceptual Plan: Prepare an ICE table, calculate Q, compare Q and K_c, predict the direction of the reaction, represent the change with x, sum the table, determine the equilibrium values, put the equilibrium values in the equilibrium expression, and solve for x. Determine $[N_2O_4]$ and $[NO_2]$.
Solution: $N_2O_4(g) \rightleftharpoons 2\,NO_2(g)$

	$[N_2O_4]$	$[NO_2]$
Initial	0.0500	0.00
Change	$-x$	$2x$
Equil	$0.0500 - x$	$2x$

$$Q = \frac{[NO_2]^2}{[N_2O_4]} = \frac{0}{0.0500} = 0 \quad Q < K \text{ Therefore, the reaction will proceed to the right by } x.$$

$$K_c = \frac{[NO_2]^2}{[N_2O_4]} = \frac{(2x)^2}{(0.0500 - x)} = 0.513 \quad 4x^2 + 0.513x - 0.02565 = 0$$

$$\frac{-b \pm \sqrt{b^2 - 4ac}}{2a} = \frac{-0.513 \pm \sqrt{(0.513)^2 - 4(4)(-0.02565)}}{2(4)} = \frac{-0.513 \pm \sqrt{0.6735}}{2(4)}$$

$$x = -0.1667 \text{ or } x = 0.0385 \text{ Therefore, } x = 0.0385.$$
$$[N_2O_4] = 0.0500 - 0.0385 = 0.0115 \text{ M} \qquad [NO_2] = 2x = 2(0.0385) = 0.0770 \text{ M}$$

Check: Plug the values into the equilibrium expression: $K_c = \dfrac{(0.0770)^2}{0.0115} = 0.516.$

14.35   **Given:** [CO] = 0.10 M, [CO$_2$] = 0.0 M; K_c = 4.0 × 10^3 **Find:** [CO$_2$] at equilibrium
        Conceptual Plan: Prepare an ICE table, calculate Q, compare Q and K_c, predict the direction of the reaction, represent the change with x, sum the table, determine the equilibrium values, put the equilibrium values in the equilibrium expression, and solve for x. Determine [CO] and [CO$_2$].
        Solution: NiO(s) + CO(g) ⇌ Ni(s) + CO$_2$(g)

	[CO]	[CO$_2$]
Initial	0.10	0.0
Change	$-x$	x
Equil	0.10 − x	x

$Q = \dfrac{[CO_2]}{[CO]} = \dfrac{0}{(0.10)} = 0$ $Q < K$ Therefore, the reaction will proceed to the right by x.

$K_c = \dfrac{[CO_2]}{[CO]} = \dfrac{x}{(0.10 - x)} = 4.0 \times 10^3$ $4.0 \times 10^3(0.10 - x) = x$

$x = 0.09998$
[CO$_2$] = 0.09998 M = 0.100 M

Check: Because the equilibrium constant is so large, the reaction goes essentially to completion; therefore, it is reasonable that the concentration of the product is 0.0999 M.

14.37   **Given:** [HC$_2$H$_3$O$_2$] = 0.210 M, [H$_3$O$^+$] = 0.0, [C$_2$H$_3$O$_2^-$] = 0.0, K_c = 1.8 × 10^{-5}
        Find: [HC$_2$H$_3$O$_2$], [H$_3$O$^+$], [C$_2$H$_3$O$_2^-$] at equilibrium
        Conceptual Plan: Prepare an ICE table, calculate Q, compare Q and K_c, predict the direction of the reaction, represent the change with x, sum the table, determine the equilibrium values, put the equilibrium values in the equilibrium expression, and solve for x. Determine [HC$_2$H$_3$O$_2$], [H$_3$O$^+$], and [C$_2$H$_3$O$_2^-$].
        Solution: HC$_2$H$_3$O$_2$(aq) + H$_2$O(l) ⇌ H$_3$O$^+$(aq) + C$_2$H$_3$O$_2^-$(aq)

	[HC$_2$H$_3$O$_2$]	[H$_3$O$^+$]	[C$_2$H$_3$O$_2^-$]
Initial	0.210	0.0	0.0
Change	$-x$	x	x
Equil	0.210 − x	x	x

$Q = \dfrac{[H_3O^+][C_2H_3O_2^-]}{[HC_2H_3O_2]} = \dfrac{0}{(0.210)} = 0$ $Q < K$ Therefore, the reaction will proceed to the right by x.

$K_c = \dfrac{[H_3O^+][C_2H_3O_2^-]}{[HC_2H_3O_2]} = \dfrac{(x)(x)}{(0.210 - x)} = 1.8 \times 10^{-5}$

Assume that x is small compared to 0.210.
$x^2 = 0.210(1.8 \times 10^{-5})$

$x = 0.00194$ Check assumption: $\dfrac{0.00194}{0.210} \times 100 = 0.92\%$; assumption is valid.

[H$_3$O$^+$] = [C$_2$H$_3$O$_2^-$] = 0.00194 M
[HC$_2$H$_3$O$_2$] = 0.210 − 0.00194 = 0.2081 = 0.208 M

Check: Plug the values into the equilibrium expression: $K_c = \dfrac{(0.00194)(0.00194)}{(0.208)} = 1.81 \times 10^{-5}$.

The answer is the same to two significant figures with the true value, so the answers are valid.

14.39   **Given:** P_{Br_2} = 755 torr, P_{Cl_2} = 735 torr, P_{BrCl} = 0.0, K_p = 1.11 × 10^{-4} **Find:** P_{BrCl} at equilibrium
        Conceptual Plan: Torr → atm and then prepare an ICE table, calculate Q, compare Q and K_c, predict the direction of the reaction, represent the change with x, sum the table, determine the equilibrium values, put the equilibrium values in the equilibrium expression, and solve for x. Determine P_{BrCl}.
        Solution:

$P_{Br_2} = 755 \text{ torr} \times \dfrac{1 \text{ atm}}{760 \text{ torr}} = 0.9934$ atm $P_{Cl_2} = 735 \text{ torr} \times \dfrac{1 \text{ atm}}{760 \text{ torr}} = 0.9671$ atm

$$Br_2(g) + Cl_2(g) \rightleftharpoons 2\,BrCl\,(g)$$

	P_{Br_2}	P_{Cl_2}	P_{BrCl}
Initial	0.9934	0.9671	0.0
Change	$-x$	$-x$	$2x$
Equil	$0.9934 - x$	$0.9671 - x$	$2x$

$$Q = \frac{P_{BrCl}^2}{P_{Br_2}P_{Cl_2}} = \frac{0}{(0.9934)(0.9671)} = 0 \quad Q < K \quad \text{Therefore, the reaction will proceed to the right by } x.$$

$$K_p = \frac{P_{BrCl}^2}{P_{Br_2}P_{Cl_2}} = \frac{(2x)^2}{(0.9934 - x)(0.9671 - x)} = 1.11 \times 10^{-4}$$

Assume that x is small compared to 0.9934 and 0.9671.

$$\frac{(2x)^2}{(0.9934)(0.9671)} = 1.11 \times 10^{-4} \quad 4x^2 = 1.066 \times 10^{-4}$$

$x = 0.00516\text{ atm} = 3.92\text{ torr}$

$P_{BrCl} = 2x = 2(3.92\text{ torr}) = 7.84\text{ torr}$

Check: Plug the values into the equilibrium expression:

$$K_c = \frac{(2(0.00516))^2}{(0.9934 - 0.00516)(0.9671 - 0.00516)} = 1.120 \times 10^{-4} = 1.12 \times 10^{-4}.$$

This is within 0.01×10^{-4} of the true value; therefore, the answers are valid.

14.41   (a)   **Given:** $[A] = 1.0\text{ M}, [B] = [C] = 0.0, K_c = 1.0$ **Find:** [A], [B], [C] at equilibrium

Conceptual Plan: Prepare an ICE table, calculate Q, compare Q and K_c, predict the direction of the reaction, represent the change with x, sum the table, determine the equilibrium values, put the equilibrium values in the equilibrium expression, and solve for x. Determine [A], [B], and [C].

Solution: $A(g) \rightleftharpoons B(g) + C(g)$

	[A]	[B]	[C]
Initial	1.0	0.0	0.0
Change	$-x$	x	x
Equil	$1.0 - x$	x	x

$$Q = \frac{[B][C]}{[A]} = \frac{0}{(1.0)} = 0 \quad Q < K \quad \text{Therefore, the reaction will proceed to the right by } x.$$

$$K_c = \frac{[B][C]}{[A]} = \frac{(x)(x)}{(1.0 - x)} = 1.0$$

$x^2 = 1.0(1.0 - x)$

$x^2 + x - 1 = 0$

$$\frac{-b \pm \sqrt{b^2 - 4ac}}{2a} = \frac{-1 \pm \sqrt{1^2 - 4(1)(-1)}}{2(1)}$$

$x = 0.618$ or $x = -1.618$ Therefore, $x = 0.618$.

$[B] = [C] = x = 0.618 = 0.62\text{ M}$

$[A] = 1.0 - 0.618 = 0.382 = 0.38\text{ M}$

Check: Plug the values into the equilibrium expression:

$$K_c = \frac{(0.62)(0.62)}{(0.38)} = 1.01 = 1.0, \text{ which is the equilibrium constant; so the values are correct.}$$

(b)   **Given:** $[A] = 1.0\text{ M}, [B] = [C] = 0.0, K_c = 0.010$ **Find:** [A], [B], [C] at equilibrium

Conceptual Plan: Prepare an ICE table, calculate Q, compare Q and K_c, predict the direction of the reaction, represent the change with x, sum the table, determine the equilibrium values, put the equilibrium values in the equilibrium expression, and solve for x. Determine [A], [B], and [C].

Solution:

$$A(g) \rightleftharpoons B(g) + C(g)$$

	[A]	[B]	[C]
Initial	1.0	0.0	0.0
Change	$-x$	x	x
Equil	$1.0 - x$	x	x

$Q = \dfrac{[B][C]}{[A]} = \dfrac{0}{(1.0)} = 0$ $Q < K$ Therefore, the reaction will proceed to the right by x.

$K_c = \dfrac{[B][C]}{[A]} = \dfrac{(x)(x)}{(1.0 - x)} = 0.010$

$x^2 = 0.010(1.0 - x)$

$x^2 + 0.010x - 0.010 = 0$

$\dfrac{-b \pm \sqrt{b^2 - 4ac}}{2a} = \dfrac{-(0.010) \pm \sqrt{(0.010)^2 - 4(1)(-0.010)}}{2(1)}$

$x = 0.09\underline{5}12$ or $x = -0.1051$ Therefore, $x = 0.09\underline{5}12$.

$[B] = [C] = x = 0.09\underline{5}12 = 0.095$ M

$[A] = 1.0 - 0.09\underline{5}12 = 0.\underline{9}0488 = 0.9$ M

Check: Plug the values into the equilibrium expression:

$K_c = \dfrac{(0.095)(0.095)}{(0.\underline{9}0)} = 0.0\underline{1}003 = 0.01$, which is the equilibrium constant; so the values are correct.

(c) **Given:** [A] = 1.0 M, [B] = [C] = 0.0, $K_c = 1.0 \times 10^{-5}$ **Find:** [A], [B], [C] at equilibrium
Conceptual Plan: Prepare an ICE table, calculate Q, compare Q and K_c, predict the direction of the reaction, represent the change with x, sum the table, determine the equilibrium values, put the equilibrium values in the equilibrium expression, and solve for x. Determine [A], [B], and [C].
Solution:

$$A(g) \rightleftharpoons B(g) + C(g)$$

	[A]	[B]	[C]
Initial	1.0	0.0	0.0
Change	$-x$	x	x
Equil	$1.0 - x$	x	x

$Q = \dfrac{[B][C]}{[A]} = \dfrac{0}{(1.0)} = 0$ $Q < K$ Therefore, the reaction will proceed to the right by x.

$K_c = \dfrac{[B][C]}{[A]} = \dfrac{(x)(x)}{(1.0 - x)} = 1.0 \times 10^{-5}$

Assume that x is small compared to 1.0.

$x^2 = 1.0(1.0 \times 10^{-5})$

$x = 0.003\underline{1}6$ Check assumption: $\dfrac{0.003\underline{1}6}{1.0} \times 100 = 0.32\%$; assumption is valid.

$[B] = [C] = x = 0.003\underline{1}6 = 0.0032$ M

$[A] = 1.0 - 0.003\underline{1}6 = 0.9968 = 1.0$ M

Check: Plug the values into the equilibrium expression:

$K_c = \dfrac{(0.0032)(0.0032)}{(1.0)} = 1.\underline{0}24 \times 10^{-5} = 1.0 \times 10^{-5}$,

which is the equilibrium constant; so the values are correct.

Le Châtelier's Principle

14.43 **Given:** $CO(g) + Cl_2(g) \rightleftharpoons COCl_2(g)$ at equilibrium **Find:** What is the effect of each of the following?

(a) $COCl_2$ is added to the reaction mixture: Adding $COCl_2$ increases the concentration of $COCl_2$ and causes the reaction to shift to the left.

(b) Cl_2 is added to the reaction mixture: Adding Cl_2 increases the concentration of Cl_2 and causes the reaction to shift to the right.

(c) $COCl_2$ is removed from the reaction mixture: Removing the $COCl_2$ decreases the concentration of $COCl_2$ and causes the reaction to shift to the right.

14.45 **Given:** $2\ KClO_3(s) \rightleftharpoons 2\ KCl(s) + 3\ O_2(g)$ at equilibrium **Find:** What is the effect of each of the following?

(a) O_2 is removed from the reaction mixture: Removing the O_2 decreases the concentration of O_2 and causes the reaction to shift to the right.

(b) KCl is added to the reaction mixture: Adding KCl does not cause any change in the reaction. KCl is a solid, and the concentration remains constant; so the addition of more solid does not change the equilibrium concentration.

(c) $KClO_3$ is added to the reaction mixture: Adding $KClO_3$ does not cause any change in the reaction. $KClO_3$ is a solid, and the concentration remains constant; so the addition of more solid does not change the equilibrium concentration.

(d) O_2 is added to the reaction mixture: Adding O_2 increases the concentration of O_2 and causes the reaction to shift to the left.

14.47 (a) **Given:** $I_2(g) \rightleftharpoons 2I(g)$ at equilibrium **Find:** the effect of increasing the volume.

The chemical equation has 2 moles of gas on the right and 1 mole of gas on the left. Increasing the volume of the reaction mixture decreases the pressure and causes the reaction to shift to the right (toward the side with more moles of gas particles).

(b) **Given:** $2H_2S(g) \rightleftharpoons 2H_2(g) + S_2(g)$ **Find:** the effect of decreasing the volume.

The chemical equation has 3 moles of gas on the right and 2 moles of gas on the left. Decreasing the volume of the reaction mixture increases the pressure and causes the reaction to shift to the left (toward the side with fewer moles of gas particles).

(c) **Given:** $I_2(g) + Cl_2(g) \rightleftharpoons 2ICl(g)$ **Find:** the effect of decreasing the volume.

The chemical equation has 2 moles of gas on the right and 2 moles of gas on the left. Decreasing the volume of the reaction mixture increases the pressure but causes no shift in the reaction because the moles are equal on both sides.

14.49 **Given:** $C(s) + CO_2(g) \rightleftharpoons 2CO(g)$ is endothermic. **Find:** the effect of increasing the temperature.

Because the reaction is endothermic, we can think of the heat as a reactant: Increasing the temperature is equivalent to adding a reactant, causing the reaction to shift to the right. This will cause an increase in the concentration of products and a decrease in the concentration of reactant; therefore, the value of K will increase.

Find: the effect of decreasing the temperature

Because the reaction is endothermic, we can think of the heat as a reactant: Decreasing the temperature is equivalent to removing a reactant, causing the reaction to shift to the left. This will cause a decrease in the concentration of products and an increase in the concentration of reactants; therefore, the value of K will decrease.

14.51 **Given:** $C(s) + 2\ H_2(g) \rightleftharpoons CH_4(g)$ is exothermic. **Find:** Determine which will favor CH_4.

(a) Adding more C to the reaction mixture does *not* favor CH_4. Adding C does not cause any change in the reaction. C is a solid, and the concentration remains constant; so the addition of more solid does not change the equilibrium concentration.

(b) Adding more H_2 to the reaction mixture favors CH_4. Adding H_2 increases the concentration of H_2, causing the reaction to shift to the right.

(c) Raising the temperature of the reaction mixture does *not* favor CH_4. Because the reaction is exothermic, we can think of heat as a product. Raising the temperature is equivalent to adding a product, causing the reaction to shift to the left.

(d)   Lowering the volume of the reaction mixture favors CH_4. The chemical equation has 1 mole of gas on the right and 2 moles of gas on the left. Decreasing the volume of the reaction mixture increases the pressure and causes the reaction to shift to the right (toward the side with fewer moles of gas particles).

(e)   Adding a catalyst to the reaction mixture does *not* favor CH_4. A catalyst added to the reaction mixture only speeds up the reaction; it does not change the equilibrium concentration.

(f)   Adding neon gas to the reaction mixture does *not* favor CH_4. Adding an inert gas to a reaction mixture at a fixed volume has no effect on the equilibrium.

Cumulative Problems

14.53   (a)   To find the value of K for the new equation, combine the two given equations to yield the new equation. Reverse equation 1 and use $1/K_1$, then add to equation 2. To find K for equation 3, use $(1/K_1)(K_2)$.

$$HbO_2(aq) \rightleftharpoons \cancel{Hb(aq)} + O_2(aq) \qquad K_1 = 1/1.8$$
$$\cancel{Hb(aq)} + CO(aq) \rightleftharpoons HbCO(aq) \qquad K_2 = 306$$
$$\overline{HbO_2(aq) + CO(aq) \rightleftharpoons HbCO(aq) + O_2(aq) \qquad K_3 = K_1K_2 = (1/1.8)(306) = 170}$$

      (b)   **Given:** $O_2 = 20\%$, $CO = 0.10\%$ **Find:** The ratio $\dfrac{[HbCO]}{[HbO_2]}$

          Conceptual Plan: Determine the equilibrium expression and then determine $\dfrac{[HbCO]}{[HbO_2]}$.

          Solution: $K = \dfrac{[HbCO][O_2]}{[HbO_2][CO]}$ $170 = \dfrac{[HbCO](20.0)}{[HbO_2](0.10)}$ $\dfrac{[HbCO]}{[HbO_2]} = 170\left(\dfrac{0.10}{20.0}\right) = \dfrac{0.85}{1.0}$

          Because the ratio is almost 1:1, 0.10% CO will replace about 50% of the O_2 in the blood. The CO blocks the uptake of O_2 by the blood and is therefore highly toxic.

14.55   (a)   **Given:** 4.45 g CO_2, 10.0 L, 1200 K, 2.00 g C, $K_p = 5.78$ **Find:** total pressure

          Conceptual Plan: g CO_2 → mol CO_2 and g C → mol C and then determine limiting reactant

                        $\dfrac{1 \text{ mol } CO_2}{44.01 \text{ g } CO_2}$ $\dfrac{1 \text{ mol C}}{12.01 \text{ g C}}$

          and then mol CO_2 → P_{CO_2}. Prepare an ICE table, represent the change with x, sum the table,

                      $PV = nRT$

          determine the equilibrium values, put the equilibrium values in the equilibrium expression, and solve for x.

          Solution: $CO_2(g) + C(s) \rightleftharpoons 2 CO(g)$

$$4.45 \text{ g } \cancel{CO_2} \times \dfrac{1 \text{ mol}}{44.01 \text{ g } \cancel{CO_2}} = 0.101\underline{1} \text{ mol } CO_2 \qquad 2.00 \text{ g } \cancel{C} \times \dfrac{1 \text{ mol}}{12.01 \text{ g } \cancel{C}} = 0.166\underline{5} \text{ mol C}$$

          Because the stoichiometry is 1:1, the CO_2 is the limiting reactant.

$$P_{CO_2} = \dfrac{(0.101\underline{1} \text{ } \cancel{mol})\left(\dfrac{0.08206 \text{ } \cancel{L} \text{ atm}}{\cancel{mol} \text{ K}}\right)(1200 \text{ K})}{10.0 \text{ } \cancel{L}} = 0.995\underline{6} \text{ atm}$$

$$CO_2(g) + C(s) \rightleftharpoons 2 CO(g)$$

	P_{CO_2}	P_{CO}
Initial	0.996	0.0
Change	$-x$	$2x$
Equil	$0.996 - x$	$2x$

          The reaction will proceed to the right by x.

$$K_p = \dfrac{P_{CO}^2}{P_{CO_2}} = \dfrac{(2x)^2}{(0.996 - x)} = 5.78. \text{ Solve using the quadratic equation, found in Appendix I.}$$

$$x = 0.678 \text{ atm}$$
$$P_{CO_2} = 0.996 \text{ atm} - 0.678 \text{ atm} = 0.318 \text{ atm} \quad P_{CO} = 2(0.678 \text{ atm}) = 1.35\underline{6} \text{ atm}$$
$$P_{total} = 1.67 \text{ atm}$$

Check: Plug the values for the partial pressure into the equilibrium expression. $\dfrac{(1.356)^2}{0.318} = 5.78$, which is the value of the equilibrium constant.

(b) **Given:** 4.45 g CO_2, 10.0 L, 1200 K, 0.50 g C, $K_p = 5.78$ **Find:** total pressure

Conceptual Plan: g CO_2 → mol CO_2 and g C → mol C and then determine limiting reactant

$$\frac{1 \text{ mol } CO_2}{44.01 \text{ g } CO_2} \qquad \frac{1 \text{ mol C}}{12.01 \text{ g C}}$$

and then mol CO_2 → P_{CO_2} and mol C → mol CO → P_{CO}

$$PV = nRT \qquad\qquad PV = nRT$$

Solution: $CO_2(g) + C(s) \rightleftharpoons 2\,CO(g)$

$$4.45 \text{ g } CO_2 \times \frac{1 \text{ mol}}{44.01 \text{ g } CO_2} = 0.101\underline{1} \text{ mol } CO_2 \qquad 0.50 \text{ g } C \times \frac{1 \text{ mol}}{12.01 \text{ g } C} = 0.041\underline{6} \text{ mol C}$$

Because the stoichiometry is 1:1, the C is the limiting reactant; therefore, the moles of CO formed will be determined from the reaction, not the equilibrium.

$$0.041\underline{6} \text{ mol C} \times \frac{2 \text{ mol CO}}{1 \text{ mol C}} = 0.0.83\underline{2} \text{ mol CO}$$

	$CO_2(g)$	+ C(s)	$\rightleftharpoons$ 2 CO(g)
Initial	0.1011	0.041$\underline{6}$	0.0
Change	−0.041$\underline{6}$	−0.041$\underline{6}$	2(0.041$\underline{6}$)
Equil	0.059$\underline{5}$	0	0.083$\underline{2}$

$$P_{CO_2} = \frac{(0.059\underline{5} \text{ mol})\left(\dfrac{0.08206 \text{ L atm}}{\text{mol K}}\right)(1200 \text{ K})}{10.0 \text{ L}} = 0.58\underline{6} \text{ atm}$$

$$P_{CO} = \frac{(0.083\underline{2} \text{ mol})\left(\dfrac{0.08206 \text{ L atm}}{\text{mol K}}\right)(1200 \text{ K})}{10.0 \text{ L}} = 0.81\underline{9} \text{ atm}$$

$$P_{total} = 0.58\underline{6} + 0.81\underline{9} = 1.405 = 1.41 \text{ atm}$$

Check: The pressure is less than the equilibrium pressure, which is reasonable because the C was the limiting reactant.

14.57 **Given:** $V = 10.0$ L, $T = 650$ K, 1.0 g MgO, $P_{CO_2} = 0.026$ atm, $K_p = 0.0260$
Find: mass $MgCO_3$ when volume is 0.100 L

Conceptual Plan: P (10.0 L) → P (0.100 L). **Prepare an ICE table, represent the change with x, sum the table, determine the equilibrium value, put the equilibrium values in the equilibrium expression, and solve for x. Then determine moles CO_2, the limiting reactant, and the mass of $MgCO_3$ formed.**

$$P_1V_1 = P_2V_2 \quad PV = nRT$$

$$P_1V_1 = P_2V_2 \quad (0.0260 \text{ atm})(10.0 \text{ L}) = (x)(0.100 \text{ L}) \quad x = 2.60 \text{ atm}$$

$$MgCO_3(s) \rightleftharpoons MgO_3(s) + CO_2(g)$$

	P_{CO_2}
Initial	2.60
Change	−x
Equil	2.60 − x

$$K_p = P_{CO_2} = 0.026 = 2.60 - x \qquad x = 2.5\underline{7}9 \text{ atm}$$

$$n_{CO_2} = \frac{(2.5\underline{7}9 \text{ atm})10.0 \text{ L}}{\left(\dfrac{0.08206 \text{ L atm}}{\text{mol K}}\right)(650 \text{ K})} = 0.48\underline{3}5 \text{ mol } CO_2 \quad 1.0 \text{ g MgO} \times \frac{1 \text{ mol}}{40.30 \text{ g MgO}} = 0.024\underline{8} \text{ mol MgO}$$

Therefore, MgO is the limiting reactant and produces 0.0248 mol $MgCO_3$.

$$0.0248 \ \cancel{\text{mol } MgCO_3} \times \frac{84.31 \text{ g } MgCO_3}{1 \ \cancel{\text{mol } MgCO_3}} = 2.09 \text{ g } MgCO_3$$

14.59   **Given:** $C_2H_4(g) + Cl_2(g) \rightleftharpoons C_2H_4Cl_2(g)$ is exothermic   **Find:** Which of the following will maximize $C_2H_4Cl_2$?

(a)   Increasing the reaction volume will not maximize $C_2H_4Cl_2$. The chemical equation has 1 mole of gas on the right and 2 moles of gas on the left. Increasing the volume of the reaction mixture decreases the pressure and causes the reaction to shift to the left (toward the side with more moles of gas particles).

(b)   Removing $C_2H_4Cl_2$ as it forms will maximize $C_2H_4Cl_2$. Removing the $C_2H_4Cl_2$ will decrease the concentration of $C_2H_4Cl_2$ and will cause the reaction to shift to the right, producing more $C_2H_4Cl_2$.

(c)   Lowering the reaction temperature will maximize $C_2H_4Cl_2$. The reaction is exothermic, so we can think of heat as a product. Lowering the temperature will cause the reaction to shift to the right, producing more $C_2H_4Cl_2$.

(d)   Adding Cl_2 will maximize $C_2H_4Cl_2$. Adding Cl_2 increases the concentration of Cl_2, so the reaction shifts to the right, which will produce more $C_2H_4Cl_2$.

14.61   **Given:** reaction 1 at equilibrium: $P_{H_2} = 0.958$ atm, $P_{I_2} = 0.877$ atm, $P_{HI} = 0.020$ atm; reaction 2: $P_{H_2} = P_{I_2} = 0.621$ atm, $P_{HI} = 0.101$ atm   **Find:** Is reaction 2 at equilibrium? If not, what is the P_{HI} at equilibrium?
Conceptual Plan: Use equilibrium partial pressures to determine K_p. Use K_p to determine whether reaction 2 is at equilibrium. Prepare an ICE table, calculate Q, compare Q and K_p, predict the direction of the reaction, represent the change with x, sum the table, determine the equilibrium values, put the equilibrium values in the equilibrium expression, and solve for x. Determine P_{HI}.
Solution: $H_2(g) + I_2(g) \rightleftharpoons 2HI(g)$

	P_{H_2}	P_{I_2}	P_{HI}
Reaction 1:	0.958	0.877	0.020

$$K_p = \frac{P_{HI}^2}{P_{H_2}P_{I_2}} = \frac{(0.020)^2}{(0.958)(0.877)} = 4.7\underline{6}10 \times 10^{-4}$$

$$Q = \frac{P_{HI}^2}{P_{H_2}P_{I_2}} = \frac{(0.101)^2}{(0.621)(0.621)} = 0.0264 \ Q > K, \text{ so the reaction shifts to the left.}$$

	$H_2(g)$	$+$ $I_2(g)$	$\rightleftharpoons$ $2 HI(g)$
Reaction 2:	P_{H_2}	P_{I_2}	P_{HI}
Initial	0.621	0.621	0.101
Change	x	x	$-2x$
Equil	$0.621 + x$	$0.621 + x$	$0.101 - 2x$

$$K_p = \frac{P_{HI}^2}{P_{H_2}P_{I_2}} = \frac{(0.101 - 2x)^2}{(0.621 + x)(0.621 + x)} = 4.7\underline{6}10 \times 10^{-4}$$

$$\sqrt{\frac{(0.101 - 2x)^2}{(0.621 + x)(0.621 + x)}} = \sqrt{4.7\underline{6}10 \times 10^{-4}}$$

$$\frac{(0.101 - 2x)}{(0.621 + x)} = 2.1\underline{8}2 \times 10^{-2}$$

$x = 0.04325 = 0.0433$
$P_{H_2} = P_{I_2} = 0.621 + x = 0.621 + 0.0433 = 0.664$ atm
$P_{HI} = 0.101 - 2x = 0.101 - 2(0.0433) = 0.0144$ atm

Check: Plug the values into the equilibrium expression:

$$K_p = \frac{(0.0144)^2}{(0.664)^2} = 4.703 \times 10^{-4} = 4.70 \times 10^{-4}; \text{ this value is close to the original equilibrium constant.}$$

14.63   **Given:** 200.0 L container; 1.27 kg N_2; 0.310 kg H_2; 725 K; $K_p = 5.3 \times 10^{-5}$ **Find:** mass in g of NH_3 and % yield
Conceptual Plan: $K_p \rightarrow K_c$ and then kg $\rightarrow$ g $\rightarrow$ mol $\rightarrow$ M and then prepare an ICE table. Represent

$$K_p = K_c(RT)^{\Delta n} \qquad \frac{1000 \text{ g}}{\text{kg}} \quad \frac{\text{g}}{\text{molar mass}} \quad \frac{\text{mol}}{\text{vol}}$$

Check: Plug the values for the partial pressure into the equilibrium expression. $\dfrac{(1.356)^2}{0.318} = 5.78$, which is the value of the equilibrium constant.

(b) **Given:** 4.45 g CO_2, 10.0 L, 1200 K, 0.50 g C, $K_p = 5.78$ **Find:** total pressure

Conceptual Plan: g $CO_2 \rightarrow$ mol CO_2 and g C $\rightarrow$ mol C and then determine limiting reactant

$$\frac{1 \text{ mol } CO_2}{44.01 \text{ g } CO_2} \qquad\qquad \frac{1 \text{ mol C}}{12.01 \text{ g C}}$$

and then mol $CO_2 \rightarrow P_{CO_2}$ and mol C $\rightarrow$ mol CO $\rightarrow P_{CO}$

$$PV = nRT \qquad\qquad\qquad PV = nRT$$

Solution: $CO_2(g) + C(s) \rightleftharpoons 2\,CO(g)$

$$4.45 \text{ g } CO_2 \times \frac{1 \text{ mol}}{44.01 \text{ g } CO_2} = 0.1011 \text{ mol } CO_2 \qquad 0.50 \text{ g C} \times \frac{1 \text{ mol}}{12.01 \text{ g C}} = 0.0416 \text{ mol C}$$

Because the stoichiometry is 1:1, the C is the limiting reactant; therefore, the moles of CO formed will be determined from the reaction, not the equilibrium.

$$0.0416 \text{ mol C} \times \frac{2 \text{ mol CO}}{1 \text{ mol C}} = 0.0832 \text{ mol CO}$$

	$CO_2(g)$	+	$C(s)$	$\rightleftharpoons$	$2\,CO(g)$
Initial	0.1011		0.0416		0.0
Change	-0.0416		-0.0416		$2(0.0416)$
Equil	0.0595		0		0.0832

$$P_{CO_2} = \frac{(0.0595 \text{ mol})\left(\dfrac{0.08206 \text{ L atm}}{\text{mol K}}\right)(1200 \text{ K})}{10.0 \text{ L}} = 0.586 \text{ atm}$$

$$P_{CO} = \frac{(0.0832 \text{ mol})\left(\dfrac{0.08206 \text{ L atm}}{\text{mol K}}\right)(1200 \text{ K})}{10.0 \text{ L}} = 0.819 \text{ atm}$$

$$P_{total} = 0.586 + 0.819 = 1.405 = 1.41 \text{ atm}$$

Check: The pressure is less than the equilibrium pressure, which is reasonable because the C was the limiting reactant.

14.57 **Given:** $V = 10.0$ L, $T = 650$ K, 1.0 g MgO, $P_{CO_2} = 0.026$ atm, $K_p = 0.0260$
Find: mass $MgCO_3$ when volume is 0.100 L

Conceptual Plan: $P\,(10.0 \text{ L}) \rightarrow P\,(0.100 \text{ L})$. **Prepare an ICE table, represent the change with** x, **sum the table, determine the equilibrium value, put the equilibrium values in the equilibrium expression, and solve for** x. **Then determine moles** CO_2, **the limiting reactant, and the mass of** $MgCO_3$ **formed.**

$$P_1V_1 = P_2V_2 \quad PV = nRT$$

$$P_1V_1 = P_2V_2 \quad (0.0260 \text{ atm})(10.0 \text{ L}) = (x)(0.100 \text{ L}) \quad x = 2.60 \text{ atm}$$

$$MgCO_3(s) \rightleftharpoons MgO_3(s) + CO_2(g)$$

		P_{CO_2}
Initial		2.60
Change		$-x$
Equil		$2.60 - x$

$$K_p = P_{CO_2} = 0.026 = 2.60 - x \qquad x = 2.579 \text{ atm}$$

$$n_{CO_2} = \frac{(2.579 \text{ atm})10.0 \text{ L}}{\left(\dfrac{0.08206 \text{ L atm}}{\text{mol K}}\right)(650 \text{ K})} = 0.4835 \text{ mol } CO_2 \quad 1.0 \text{ g MgO} \times \frac{1 \text{ mol}}{40.30 \text{ g MgO}} = 0.0248 \text{ mol MgO}$$

Therefore, MgO is the limiting reactant and produces 0.0248 mol $MgCO_3$.

$$0.0248 \ \cancel{\text{mol MgCO}_3} \times \frac{84.31 \ \text{g MgCO}_3}{1 \ \cancel{\text{mol MgCO}_3}} = 2.09 \ \text{g MgCO}_3$$

14.59   **Given:** $C_2H_4(g) + Cl_2(g) \rightleftharpoons C_2H_4Cl_2(g)$ is exothermic   **Find:** Which of the following will maximize $C_2H_4Cl_2$?

(a)   Increasing the reaction volume will not maximize $C_2H_4Cl_2$. The chemical equation has 1 mole of gas on the right and 2 moles of gas on the left. Increasing the volume of the reaction mixture decreases the pressure and causes the reaction to shift to the left (toward the side with more moles of gas particles).

(b)   Removing $C_2H_4Cl_2$ as it forms will maximize $C_2H_4Cl_2$. Removing the $C_2H_4Cl_2$ will decrease the concentration of $C_2H_4Cl_2$ and will cause the reaction to shift to the right, producing more $C_2H_4Cl_2$.

(c)   Lowering the reaction temperature will maximize $C_2H_4Cl_2$. The reaction is exothermic, so we can think of heat as a product. Lowering the temperature will cause the reaction to shift to the right, producing more $C_2H_4Cl_2$.

(d)   Adding Cl_2 will maximize $C_2H_4Cl_2$. Adding Cl_2 increases the concentration of Cl_2, so the reaction shifts to the right, which will produce more $C_2H_4Cl_2$.

14.61   **Given:** reaction 1 at equilibrium: $P_{H_2} = 0.958$ atm, $P_{I_2} = 0.877$ atm, $P_{HI} = 0.020$ atm; reaction 2: $P_{H_2} = P_{I_2} = 0.621$ atm, $P_{HI} = 0.101$ atm   **Find:** Is reaction 2 at equilibrium? If not, what is the P_{HI} at equilibrium?
Conceptual Plan: Use equilibrium partial pressures to determine K_p. Use K_p to determine whether reaction 2 is at equilibrium. Prepare an ICE table, calculate Q, compare Q and K_p, predict the direction of the reaction, represent the change with x, sum the table, determine the equilibrium values, put the equilibrium values in the equilibrium expression, and solve for x. Determine P_{HI}.
Solution: $H_2(g) + I_2(g) \rightleftharpoons 2HI(g)$

	P_{H_2}	P_{I_2}	P_{HI}
Reaction 1:	0.958	0.877	0.020

$$K_p = \frac{P_{HI}^2}{P_{H_2}P_{I_2}} = \frac{(0.020)^2}{(0.958)(0.877)} = 4.7\underline{6}10 \times 10^{-4}$$

$$Q = \frac{P_{HI}^2}{P_{H_2}P_{I_2}} = \frac{(0.101)^2}{(0.621)(0.621)} = 0.0264 \ Q > K, \text{ so the reaction shifts to the left.}$$

$$H_2(g) \ + \ I_2(g) \ \rightleftharpoons \ 2 \ HI(g)$$

Reaction 2:	P_{H_2}	P_{I_2}	P_{HI}
Initial	0.621	0.621	0.101
Change	x	x	$-2x$
Equil	$0.621 + x$	$0.621 + x$	$0.101 - 2x$

$$K_p = \frac{P_{HI}^2}{P_{H_2}P_{I_2}} = \frac{(0.101 - 2x)^2}{(0.621 + x)(0.621 + x)} = 4.7\underline{6}10 \times 10^{-4}$$

$$\sqrt{\frac{(0.101 - 2x)^2}{(0.621 + x)(0.621 + x)}} = \sqrt{4.7\underline{6}10 \times 10^{-4}}$$

$$\frac{(0.101 - 2x)}{(0.621 + x)} = 2.1\underline{8}2 \times 10^{-2}$$

$x = 0.04325 = 0.0433$
$P_{H_2} = P_{I_2} = 0.621 + x = 0.621 + 0.0433 = 0.664$ atm
$P_{HI} = 0.101 - 2x = 0.101 - 2(0.0433) = 0.0144$ atm

Check: Plug the values into the equilibrium expression:

$$K_p = \frac{(0.0144)^2}{(0.664)^2} = 4.703 \times 10^{-4} = 4.70 \times 10^{-4}; \text{ this value is close to the original equilibrium constant.}$$

14.63   **Given:** 200.0 L container; 1.27 kg N_2; 0.310 kg H_2; 725 K; $K_p = 5.3 \times 10^{-5}$ **Find:** mass in g of NH_3 and % yield
Conceptual Plan: $K_p \rightarrow K_c$ and then kg $\rightarrow$ g $\rightarrow$ mol $\rightarrow$ M and then prepare an ICE table. Represent

$$K_p = K_c(RT)^{\Delta n} \qquad \frac{1000 \ \text{g}}{\text{kg}} \quad \frac{\text{g}}{\text{molar mass}} \quad \frac{\text{mol}}{\text{vol}}$$

the change with x, sum the table, determine the equilibrium values, put the equilibrium values in the equilibrium expression, and solve for x. Determine [NH_3]. Then M $\rightarrow$ mol $\rightarrow$ g and then determine

$$\text{M} \times \text{vol} \quad \text{mol} \times \text{molar mass}$$

theoretical yield NH₃ $\rightarrow$ % yield.

$$\text{determine limiting reactant } \frac{\text{actual yield}}{\text{theoretical yield}}$$

Solution: $K_p = K_c(RT)^{\Delta n}$ $\quad K_c = \dfrac{K_p}{(RT)^{\Delta n}} = \dfrac{5.3 \times 10^{-5}}{\left(\left(0.08206 \frac{\text{L} \cdot \text{atm}}{\text{mol} \cdot \text{K}}\right)(725\text{K})\right)^{-2}} = 0.1\underline{8}76$

$$n_{N_2} = 1.27 \text{ kg N}_2 \times \frac{1000 \text{ g}}{\text{kg}} \times \frac{1 \text{ mol N}_2}{28.02 \text{ g N}_2} = 45.\underline{3}25 \text{ mol N}_2 \quad [N_2] = \frac{45.\underline{3}25 \text{ mol}}{200.0 \text{ L}} = 0.22\underline{6}63 \text{ M}$$

$$n_{H_2} = 0.310 \text{ kg H}_2 \times \frac{1000 \text{ g}}{\text{kg}} \times \frac{1 \text{ mol H}_2}{2.016 \text{ g H}_2} = 153.\underline{7}7 \text{ mol H}_2 \quad [H_2] = \frac{153.77 \text{ mol}}{200.0 \text{ L}} = 0.76\underline{8}85 \text{ M}$$

$$N_2(g) + 3 H_2(g) \rightleftharpoons 2 NH_3(g)$$

Reaction 1:	[N₂]	[H₂]	[NH₃]
Initial	0.2266	0.7689	0.0
Change	$-x$	$-3x$	$2x$
Equil	$0.2266 - x$	$0.7689 - 3x$	$2x$

Reaction shifts to the right.

$$K_c = \frac{[NH_3]^2}{[N_2][H_2]^3} = \frac{(2x)^2}{(0.2266 - x)(0.7689 - 3x)^3} = 0.1876$$

Assume that x is small compared to 0.2268 and $3x$ is small compared to 0.7689.

$$\frac{(2x)^2}{(0.2266)(0.7689)^3} = 0.1877 \quad x = 0.06951$$

Check assumptions: $\dfrac{0.06951}{0.2268} \times 100\% = 30.6$, which is not valid, and $\dfrac{3(0.06951)}{0.7689} \times 100\% = 27.1\%$

Use method of successive substitution to solve for x. This yields $x = 0.0460$.

[NH_3] $= 2x = 2(0.0460) = 0.0920$ M

Check: Plug the values into the equilibrium expression:

$$K_c = \frac{(0.0920)^2}{(0.2266 - 0.0460)((0.7689 - 3(0.0460))^3} = 0.1866;$$

this value is close to the original equilibrium constant.

Determine grams NH₃: $\dfrac{0.0920 \text{ mol NH}_3}{\text{L}} \times 200.0 \text{ L} \times \dfrac{17.03 \text{ g NH}_3}{\text{mol NH}_3} = 31\underline{3}.4 \text{ g} = 3.1 \times 10^2 \text{ g}$

Determine the theoretical yield: Determine the limiting reactant:

$$1.27 \text{ kg N}_2 \times \frac{1000 \text{ g}}{\text{kg}} \times \frac{1 \text{ mol N}_2}{28.02 \text{ g N}_2} \times \frac{2 \text{ mol NH}_3}{1 \text{ mol N}_2} \times \frac{17.03 \text{ g NH}_3}{\text{mol NH}_3} = 15\underline{4}4 \text{ g NH}_3$$

$$0.310 \text{ kg H}_2 \times \frac{1000 \text{ g}}{\text{kg}} \times \frac{1 \text{ mol H}_2}{2.016 \text{ g H}_2} \times \frac{2 \text{ mol NH}_3}{3 \text{ mol H}_2} \times \frac{17.03 \text{ g NH}_3}{\text{mol NH}_3} = 1746 \text{ g NH}_3$$

N₂ produces the least amount of NH₃; therefore, it is the limiting reactant, and the theoretical yield is 1.54×10^3 g NH₃.

% yield $= \dfrac{3.1 \times 10^2 \text{ g}}{1.54 \times 10^3 \text{ g}} \times 100 = 20.\%$

14.65 **Given:** at equilibrium: $P_{CO} = 0.30$ atm; $P_{Cl_2} = 0.10$ atm; $P_{COCl_2} = 0.60$ atm, add 0.40 atm Cl₂
Find: P_{CO} when system returns to equilibrium
Conceptual Plan: Use equilibrium partial pressures to determine K_p. For the new conditions, prepare an ICE table, represent the change with x, sum the table, determine the equilibrium values, put the equilibrium values in the equilibrium expression, and solve for x. Determine P_{CO}.

Solution: $CO(g) + Cl_2(g) \rightleftharpoons COCl_2(g)$

Condition 1:	P_{CO}	P_{Cl_2}	P_{COCl_2}
	0.30	0.10	0.60

$$K_p = \frac{P_{COCl_2}}{P_{CO}P_{Cl_2}} = \frac{(0.60)}{(0.30)(0.10)} = 20$$

$$CO(g) + Cl_2(g) \rightleftharpoons COCl_2(g)$$

Condition 2:	P_{CO}	P_{Cl_2}	P_{COCl_2}
Initial	0.30	$0.10 + 0.40$	0.60
Change	$-x$	$-x$	$+x$
Equil	$0.30 - x$	$0.50 - x$	$0.60 + x$

Reaction shifts to the right because the concentration of Cl_2 was increased.

$$K_p = \frac{P_{COCl_2}}{P_{CO}P_{Cl_2}} = \frac{(0.60 + x)}{(0.30 - x)(0.50 - x)} = 20$$

$$20x^2 - 17x + 2.4 = 0$$

$$\frac{-b \pm \sqrt{b^2 - 4ac}}{2a} = \frac{-(-17) \pm \sqrt{(-17)^2 - 4(20)(2.4)}}{2(20)}$$

$x = 0.67$ or 0.18 so, $x = 0.18$

$P_{CO} = 0.30 - 0.18 = 0.12$ atm; $P_{Cl_2} = 0.50 - 0.18 = 0.32$; $P_{COCl_2} = 0.60 + 0.18 = 0.78$ atm

Check: Plug the values into the equilibrium expression:

$$K_p = \frac{(0.78)}{(0.12)(0.32)} = 20.3 = 20;$$ this is the same as the original equilibrium constant.

14.67 **Given:** $K_p = 0.76$; P_{total} at equilibrium $= 1.00$ atm   **Find:** $P_{initial}$ CCl_4
Conceptual Plan: Prepare an ICE table, represent the P_{CCl_4} with A and the change with x, sum the table, determine the equilibrium values, use the total pressure, and solve for A in terms of x. Determine partial pressure of each at equilibrium, use the equilibrium expression to determine x, and determine A.
Solution: $CCl_4(g) \rightleftharpoons C(s) + 2 Cl_2(g)$

	P_{CCl_4}	P_C	P_{Cl_2}
Initial	A	constant	0.00
Change	$-x$		$+2x$
Equil	$A - x$		$2x$

$P_{Total} = P_{CCl_4} + P_{Cl_2}$ $1.0 = A - x + 2x$ $A = 1 - x$

$P_{CCl_4} = (A - x) = (1 - x) - x = 1 - 2x$; $P_{Cl_2} = (2x)$

$$K_p = \frac{P_{Cl_2}^2}{P_{CCl_4}} = \frac{(2x)^2}{(1 - 2x)} = 0.76$$

$4x^2 + 1.52x - 0.76 = 0$ $x = 0.285$ or -0.665 so $x = 0.285$

$A = 1 - x = 1.0 - 0.285 = 0.715 = 0.72$ atm

Check: Plug the values into the equilibrium expression:

$$K_p = \frac{P_{Cl_2}^2}{P_{CCl_4}} = \frac{(2x)^2}{(A - x)} = \frac{(2(0.285))^2}{(0.715 - 0.285)} = 0.756 = 0.76;$$ the original equilibrium is constant.

14.69 **Given:** $V = 0.654$ L, $T = 1000$ K, $K_p = 3.9 \times 10^{-2}$ **Find:** mass CaO at equilibrium
Conceptual Plan: $K_p \rightarrow P_{CO_2} \rightarrow n_{(CO_2)} \rightarrow n_{(CaO)} \rightarrow g$

$$PV = nRT \qquad \text{stoichiometry} \qquad g = n(\text{molar mass})$$

Solution: Because $CaCO_3$ and CaO are solids, they are not included in the equilibrium expression.

$$K_p = P_{CO_2} = 3.9 \times 10^{-2} \quad n = \frac{PV}{RT} = \frac{(3.9 \times 10^{-2} \text{ atm})(0.654 \text{ L})}{\left(0.08206 \frac{\text{L} \cdot \text{atm}}{\text{mol} \cdot \text{K}}\right)(1000 \text{ K})} = 3.\underline{1}08 \times 10^{-4} \text{ mol } CO_2$$

$$3.\underline{1}08 \times 10^{-4} \text{ mol } CO_2 \times \frac{1 \text{ mol } CaO}{1 \text{ mol } CO_2} \times \frac{56.1 \text{ g } CaO}{1 \text{ mol } CaO} = 0.0174 \text{ g} = 0.0174 \text{ g } CaO$$

Check: The small value of K would give a small amount of products, so we would not expect to have a large mass of CaO formed.

14.71   **Given:** $K_p = 3.10$, initial $P_{CO} = 215$ torr, $P_{Cl_2} = 245$ torr   **Find:** mole fraction $COCl_2$

Conceptual Plan: *P* in torr → *P* in atm. **Prepare an ICE table, represent the change with *x*, sum the table,**

$$\frac{1 \text{ atm}}{760 \text{ torr}}$$

determine the equilibrium values, use the total pressure, and solve for mole fraction.

$$\frac{P_{COCl_2}}{P_{Total}}$$

Solution: $P_{CO} = (215 \text{ torr})\left(\dfrac{1 \text{ atm}}{760 \text{ torr}}\right) = 0.28\underline{2}9 \text{ atm} \qquad P_{Cl_2} = (245 \text{ torr})\left(\dfrac{1 \text{ atm}}{760 \text{ torr}}\right) = 0.32\underline{2}4 \text{ atm}$

$$CO(g) \quad + \quad Cl_2(g) \rightleftharpoons COCl_2(g)$$

	CO	Cl₂	COCl₂
Initial	0.28$\underline{2}$9	0.32$\underline{2}$4	0
Change	$-x$	$-x$	$+x$
Equil	0.28$\underline{2}$9 $- x$	0.32$\underline{2}$4 $- x$	x

$Q < K$, so the reaction shifts to the right.

$$K_p = \frac{P_{COCl_2}}{P_{CO}P_{Cl_2}} = \frac{x}{(0.28\underline{2}9 - x)(0.32\underline{2}4 - x)} = 3.10 \text{ so, } 3.10x^2 - 2.87643x + 0.2827 = 0$$

Solve using quadratic expression in Appendix I.

$x = 0.81\underline{6}1$ or $0.11\underline{1}7$ so $x = 0.1117$

$P_{CO} = 0.28\underline{2}9 - 0.11\underline{1}7 = 0.17\underline{1}2 \qquad P_{Cl_2} = 0.32\underline{2}4 - 0.11\underline{1}7 = 0.21\underline{0}7 \qquad P_{COCl_2} = 0.11\underline{1}7$

$$\text{mole fraction } COCl_2 = \frac{P_{COCl_2}}{P_{CO} + P_{Cl_2} + P_{COCl_2}} = \frac{0.11\underline{1}7}{0.17\underline{1}2 + 0.21\underline{0}7 + 0.11\underline{1}7} = 0.22\underline{6}3 = 0.226$$

Check: Plug the equilibrium pressures into the equilibrium expression:

$$K_p = \frac{0.11\underline{1}7}{(0.17\underline{1}2)(0.21\underline{0}7)} = 3.0966 = 3.10, \text{ which is the equilibrium constant; so the answer is reasonable.}$$

Challenge Problems

14.73   (a)   **Given:** $P_{NO} = 522$ torr, $P_{O_2} = 421$ torr; at equilibrium, $P_{total} = 748$ torr   **Find:** K_p

Conceptual Plan: Prepare an ICE table, represent the change with *x*, sum the table, determine the equilibrium values, use the total pressure, and solve for *x*. torr → atm → K_p

Solution: $2 NO(g) + O_2(g) \rightleftharpoons 2 NO_2(g)$

	P_{NO}	P_{O_2}	P_{NO_2}
Initial	522 torr	421 torr	0.00
Change	$-2x$	$-x$	$+2x$
Equil	$522 - 2x$	$421 - x$	$2x$

$P_{Total} = P_{NO} + P_{O_2} + P_{NO_2} \quad 748 = 522 - 2x + (421 - x) + 2x$

$x = 195$ torr $P_{NO} = (522 - 2(195)) = 132$ torr;

$P_{O_2} = (421 - 195) = 226$ torr; $P_{NO_2} = 2(195) = 390$ torr

$$P_{NO} = 132 \text{ torr} \times \frac{1 \text{ atm}}{760 \text{ torr}} = 0.17\underline{3}7 \text{ atm}; \quad P_{O_2} = 226 \text{ torr} \times \frac{1 \text{ atm}}{760 \text{ torr}} = 0.29\underline{7}4 \text{ atm};$$

$$P_{NO_2} = 390 \text{ torr} \times \frac{1 \text{ atm}}{760 \text{ torr}} = 0.51\underline{3}2 \text{ atm}$$

$$K_p = \frac{P_{NO_2}^2}{P_{NO}^2 P_{O_2}} = \frac{(0.51\underline{3}2)^2}{(0.17\underline{3}7)^2(0.29\underline{7}4)} = 29.35 = 29.3$$

(b)   **Given:** $= P_{NO} = 255$ torr, $P_{O_2} = 185$ torr, $K_p = 29.3$ **Find:** equilibrium P_{NO_2}
Conceptual Plan:
torr $\rightarrow$ atm and then prepare an ICE table. Represent the change with x, sum the table,

$$\frac{\text{atm}}{760 \text{ torr}}$$

**determine the equilibrium values, put the equilibrium values in the equilibrium expression, and solve
for x. Determine P_{NO_2}.**

Solution: $P_{NO} = 255 \text{ torr} \times \dfrac{1 \text{ atm}}{760 \text{ torr}} = 0.33\underline{5}5 \text{ atm}$ $P_{O_2} = 185 \text{ torr} \times \dfrac{1 \text{ atm}}{760 \text{ torr}} = 0.24\underline{3}4 \text{ atm}$

$$2 \text{ NO}(g) \ + \ O_2(g) \ \rightleftharpoons \ 2 \text{ NO}_2(g)$$

	P_{NO}	P_{O_2}	P_{NO_2}
Initial	0.3355	0.2434	0.00
Change	$-2x$	$-x$	$+2x$
Equil	$0.3355 - 2x$	$0.2434 - x$	$2x$

$$K_p = \frac{P_{NO_2}^2}{P_{NO}^2 P_{O_2}} = \frac{(2x)^2}{(0.3355 - 2x)^2(0.2434 - x)} = 29.3$$

$-117.2x^3 + 63.847x^2 - 12.867x + 0.80282 = 0$. Solve using successive approximations or a cubic equation
calculator found on the Internet.

$x = 0.11\underline{1}3$ $P_{NO_2} = 2x = 2(0.11\underline{1}3) = 0.22\underline{2}6$ atm
$P_{NO} = (0.3355 - 2(0.1113)) = 0.1129$ $P_{O_2} = (0.2434 - 0.1113) = 0.1321$

$$0.22\underline{2}6 \text{ atm} \times \frac{760 \text{ torr}}{1 \text{ atm}} = 169.2 \text{ torr} = 169 \text{ torr}$$

Check: Plug the values into the equilibrium expression:

$$K_p = \frac{(0.22\underline{2}6)^2}{(0.1129)^2(0.1321)} = 29.428 = 29.4; \text{ this is within 0.1 of the original equilibrium constant.}$$

14.75   **Given:** P_{NOCl} at equilibrium $= 115$ torr; $K_p = 0.27$, $T = 700$ K   **Find:** initial pressure NO, Cl_2
Conceptual Plan: torr $\rightarrow$ atm and then prepare an ICE table. Represent the change with x, sum the table,

$$\frac{\text{atm}}{760 \text{ torr}}$$

**determine the equilibrium values, put the equilibrium values in the equilibrium expression, and determine
initial pressure.**

Solution: $115 \text{ torr} \times \dfrac{1 \text{ atm}}{760 \text{ torr}} = 0.15\underline{1}3 \text{ atm}$

$$2 \text{ NO}(g) \ + \ Cl_2(g) \ \rightleftharpoons \ 2 \text{ NOCl}(g)$$

	P_{NO}	P_{Cl_2}	P_{NOCl}
Initial	A	A	0.00
Change	$-2x$	$-x$	$+2x$
Equil	$A - 2x$	$A - x$	0.151
	$A - 0.151$	$A - 0.0756$	

Let $A =$ initial pressure of NO and Cl_2.

$2x = 0.151$ $x = 0.0756$

$$K_p = \frac{P_{NOCl}^2}{P_{NO}^2 \, P_{Cl_2}} = \frac{(0.151)^2}{(A - 0.151)^2(A - 0.0756)} = 0.27$$

$0.27A^3 - 0.1019A^2 + 0.01231A - 0.023266 = 0$. Solve using successive approximations or a cubic equation
calculator found on the Internet.

$A = 0.566$

$P_{NO} = P_{Cl_2} = A = 0.566$ atm $= 430$ torr

Check: Plug the values into the equilibrium expression:

$$K_p = \frac{P_{NOCl}^2}{P_{NO}^2 P_{Cl_2}} = \frac{(0.151)^2}{(0.566 - 0.151)^2(0.566 - 0.0756)} = 0.2699 = 0.27$$

This is the same as the original equilibrium constant.

14.77   **Given:** $P = 0.750$ atm, density $= 0.520$ g/L, $T = 337\ °C$ **Find:** K_c

Conceptual Plan: Prepare an ICE table, represent the P_{NO_2} with A and the change with x, sum the table, determine the equilibrium values, use the total pressure, and solve for A in terms of x. Determine partial pressure of each at equilibrium in terms of x, use the density to determine the apparent molar mass, and use

$$d = \frac{PM}{RT}$$

the mole fraction (in terms of P) and the molar mass of each

$$\chi_A = \frac{P_A}{P_{Total}}$$

gas to determine x.

Solution: $2\ NO_2(g) \rightleftharpoons 2\ NO(g) + O_2(g)$

	P_{NO_2}	P_{NO}	P_{O_2}
Initial	A	0.00	0.00
Change	$-2x$	$+2x$	$+x$
Equil	$A - 2x$	$2x$	x

$P_{Total} = P_{NO_2} + P_{NO} + P_{O_2}$ $0.750 = A - 2x + 2x + x$ $A = 0.750 - x$

$P_{NO_2} = (A - 2x) = (0.750 - x) - 2x = (0.750 - 3x); P_{NO} = 2x; P_{O_2} = x$

$$d = \frac{PM}{RT}\quad M = \frac{dRT}{P} = \frac{\left(0.520\ \dfrac{g}{L}\right)\left(0.08206\ \dfrac{L \cdot atm}{mol \cdot K}\right)(610\ K)}{0.750\ atm} = 34.71\ g/mol$$

$$M = \chi_{NO_2}M_{NO_2} + \chi_{NO}M_{NO} + \chi_{O_2}M_{O_2} = \frac{P_{NO_2}}{P_{total}}M_{NO_2} + \frac{P_{NO}}{P_{total}}M_{NO} + \frac{P_{O_2}}{P_{total}}M_{O_2}$$

$P_{Total}M = P_{NO_2}M_{NO_2} + P_{NO}M_{NO} + P_{O_2}M_{O_2}$

$(0.750)(34.7) = (0.750 - 3x)(46.0) + 2x(30.0) + x(32.0)$

$x = 0.184$

$$K_p = \frac{P_{NO}^2 P_{O_2}}{P_{NO_2}^2} = \frac{(2x)^2(x)}{(0.750 - 3x)^2} = \frac{(2(0.184))^2(0.184)}{(0.750 - 3(0.184))^2} = 0.6356$$

$$K_p = K_c(RT)^{\Delta n}\quad 0.6356 = K_c\left(\left(0.08206\frac{L \cdot atm}{mol \cdot K}\right)(610\ K)\right)^1$$

$K_c = 1.27 \times 10^{-2}$

14.79   **Given:** $P_{total} = 3.0$ atm, mole fraction $O_2 = 0.12$, $T = 600$ K   **Find:** K_p

Conceptual Plan: mole fraction $\rightarrow P_{O_2} \rightarrow P_{SO_2} \rightarrow P_{SO_3} \rightarrow K_p$

$$\text{mol fraction} = \frac{P_{O_2}}{P_{Total}}\qquad \frac{2P_{SO_2}}{P_{O_2}}\qquad P_{SO_3} = P_{Total} - P_{SO_2} - P_{O_2}\qquad K_p = \frac{P_{SO_2}^2 P_{O_2}}{P_{SO_3}^2}$$

Solution: $P_{O_2} = (0.12)(3.0) = 0.36$ atm $P_{SO_2} = 2P_{O_2} = 2(0.36\ atm) = 0.72$ atm

$$P_{SO_3} = 3.0 - 0.36 - 0.72 = 1.92\quad K_p = \frac{P_{SO_2}^2 P_{O_2}}{P_{SO_3}^2} = \frac{(0.72)^2(0.36)}{(1.92)^2} = 0.0506 = 5.1 \times 10^{-2}$$

Conceptual Problems

14.81   Yes, the direction will depend on the volume. If the initial moles of A and B are equal, the initial concentrations of

A and B are equal regardless of the volume. Because $K_c = \dfrac{[B]^2}{[A]} = 1$, if the volume is such that the $[A] = [B] < 1.0$, then $Q < K$ and the reaction goes to the right to reach equilibrium. However, if the volume is such that the $[A] = [B] > 1.0$, then $Q > K$ and the reaction goes to the left to reach equilibrium.

14.83   An examination of the data shows that when $P_A = 1.0$, then $P_B = 1.0$; therefore, $K_p = \dfrac{P_B^b}{P_A^a} = \dfrac{(1.0)^b}{(1.0)^a} = 1.0$.

Therefore, the value of the numerator and denominator must be equal. We see from the data that $P_B = \sqrt{P_A}$, so $P_B^2 = P_A$. Because the stoichiometric coefficients become exponents in the equilibrium expression, $a = 1$ and $b = 2$.

14.85   Looking at the plot, at equilibrium $[A] = 0.59$ M and $[B] = 0.78$ M.

Since $A(g) \rightleftharpoons 2 B(g)$, $K = \dfrac{[B]^2}{[A]} = \dfrac{(0.78)^2}{0.59} = 1.0$. This value is reasonable, since the concentrations of the reactant

and product are similar.

Questions for Group Work

14.87   (a) $K = \dfrac{[NH_3]^2}{[N_2][H_2]^3}$

(b)   Adding H_2 will increase the denominator and not change the numerator.

(c)   Since the denominator is larger, Q will be less than K.

(d)   Since $Q < K$, the denominator needs to be decreased—so the reaction will shift to the right or in the forward direction.

(e)   Yes, the reaction will shift to return Q to K.

14.89   (a) $x^2/(0.2 - x) = 1.3 \times 10^4 \rightarrow x^2 = 1.3 \times 10^4(0.2 - x) \rightarrow x^2 = 2.6 \times 10^3 - 1.3 \times 10^4x$
$\rightarrow x^2 + 1.3 \times 10^4x - 2.6 \times 10^3 = 0$

$x = \dfrac{-b \pm \sqrt{b^2 - 4ac}}{2a} = \dfrac{-1.3 \times 10^4 \pm \sqrt{(1.3 \times 10^4)^2 - (4)(1)(-2.6 \times 10^3)}}{(2)(1)} = -13{,}000.2$ or 0.199997.

The x is small approximation is not valid.

(b) $x^2/(0.2 - x) = 1.3 \rightarrow x^2 = 1.3 (0.2 - x) \rightarrow x^2 = 0.26 - 1.3x \rightarrow x^2 + 1.3x - 0.26 = 0$

$x = \dfrac{-b \pm \sqrt{b^2 - 4ac}}{2a} = \dfrac{-1.3 \pm \sqrt{(1.3)^2 - (4)(1)(-0.26)}}{(2)(1)} = -1.47614$ or 0.176136.

The x is small approximation is not valid.

(c) $x^2/(0.2 - x) = 1.3 \times 10^{-4} \rightarrow x^2 = 1.3 \times 10^{-4}(0.2 - x) \rightarrow x^2 = 2.6 \times 10^{-5} - 1.3 \times 10^{-4}x$
$\rightarrow x^2 + 1.3 \times 10^{-4}x - 2.6 \times 10^{-5} = 0$

$x = \dfrac{-b \pm \sqrt{b^2 - 4ac}}{2a} = \dfrac{-1.3 \times 10^{-4} \pm \sqrt{(1.3 \times 10^{-4})^2 - (4)(1)(-2.6 \times 10^{-5})}}{(2)(1)}$
$= -0.00516443$ or 0.00503443.

The x is small approximation is valid.

(d) $x^2/(0.01 - x) = 1.3 \times 10^{-4} \rightarrow x^2 = 1.3 \times 10^{-4}(0.01 - x) \rightarrow x^2 = 1.3 \times 10^{-6} - 1.3 \times 10^{-4}x$
$\rightarrow x^2 + 1.3 \times 10^{-4}x - 1.3 \times 10^{-6} = 0$

$x = \dfrac{-b \pm \sqrt{b^2 - 4ac}}{2a} = \dfrac{-1.3 \times 10^{-4} \pm \sqrt{(1.3 \times 10^{-4})^2 - (4)(1)(-1.3 \times 10^{-6})}}{(2)(1)}$
$= -0.00120703$ or 0.00107703.

The x is small approximation is not valid.

In order for the x is small approximation to be valid in the expression $x^2/(y - x) = z$, $y/z > {\sim}1000$. So y needs to be much larger than z.

15 Acids and Bases

Problems by Topic

The Nature and Definitions of Acids and Bases

15.1 (a) acid $HNO_3(aq) \rightarrow H^+(aq) + NO_3^-(aq)$
     (b) acid $NH_4^+(aq) \rightarrow H^+(aq) + NH_3(aq)$
     (c) base $KOH(aq) \rightarrow K^+(aq) + OH^-(aq)$
     (d) acid $HC_2H_3O_2(aq) \rightarrow H^+(aq) + C_2H_3O_2^-(aq)$

15.3 (a) Because H_2CO_3 donates a proton to H_2O, it is the acid. After H_2CO_3 donates the proton, it becomes HCO_3^-, the conjugate base. Because H_2O accepts a proton, it is the base. After H_2O accepts the proton, it becomes H_3O^+, the conjugate acid.
     (b) Because H_2O donates a proton to NH_3, it is the acid. After H_2O donates the proton, it becomes OH^-, the conjugate base. Because NH_3 accepts a proton, it is the base. After NH_3 accepts the proton, it becomes NH_4^+, the conjugate acid.
     (c) Because HNO_3 donates a proton to H_2O, it is the acid. After HNO_3 donates the proton, it becomes NO_3^-, the conjugate base. Because H_2O accepts a proton, it is the base. After H_2O accepts the proton, it becomes H_3O^+, the conjugate acid.
     (d) Because H_2O donates a proton to C_5H_5N, it is the acid. After H_2O donates the proton, it becomes OH^-, the conjugate base. Because C_5H_5N accepts a proton, it is the base. After C_5H_5N accepts the proton, it becomes $C_5H_5NH^+$, the conjugate acid.

15.5 (a) Cl^- $HCl(aq) + H_2O(l) \rightarrow H_3O^+(aq) + Cl^-(aq)$
     (b) HSO_3^- $H_2SO_3(aq) + H_2O(l) \rightleftharpoons H_3O^+(aq) + HSO_3^-(aq)$
     (c) CHO_2^- $HCHO_2(aq) + H_2O(l) \rightleftharpoons H_3O^+(aq) + CHO_2^-(aq)$
     (d) F^- $HF(aq) + H_2O(l) \rightleftharpoons H_3O^+(aq) + F^-(aq)$

15.7 $H_2PO_4^-(aq) + H_2O(l) \rightleftharpoons H_3O^+(aq) + HPO_4^{2-}(aq)$
     $H_2PO_4^-(aq) + H_2O(l) \rightleftharpoons H_3PO_4(aq) + OH^-(aq)$

Acid Strength and K_a

15.9 (a) HNO_3 is a strong acid.
     (b) HCl is a strong acid.
     (c) HBr is a strong acid.
     (d) H_2SO_3 is a weak acid. $H_2SO_3(aq) + H_2O(l) \rightleftharpoons H_3O^+(aq) + HSO_3^-(aq)$

$$K_{a_1} = \frac{[H_3O^+][HSO_3^-]}{[H_2SO_3]}$$

15.11 (a) contains no HA, 10 H^+, and 10 A^-
      (b) contains 3 HA, 3 H^+, and 7 A^-
      (c) contains 9 HA, 1 H^+, and 1 A^-
      So solution a > solution b > solution c.

15.13　(a)　F^- is a stronger base than is Cl^-.

　　　　　　F^- is the conjugate base of HF (a weak acid); Cl^- is the conjugate base of HCl (a strong acid); the weaker the acid, the stronger the conjugate base.

　　　(b)　NO_2^- is a stronger base than is NO_3^-.

　　　　　　NO_2^- is the conjugate base of HNO_2 (a weak acid); NO_3^- is the conjugate base of HNO_3 (a strong acid); the weaker the acid, the stronger the conjugate base.

　　　(c)　ClO^- is a stronger base than is F^-.

　　　　　　F^- is the conjugate base of HF ($K_a = 3.5 \times 10^{-4}$); ClO^- is the conjugate base of HClO ($K_a = 2.9 \times 10^{-8}$); HClO is the weaker acid; the weaker the acid, the stronger the conjugate base.

Autoionization of Water and pH

15.15　(a)　**Given:** $K_w = 1.0 \times 10^{-14}$, $[H_3O^+] = 9.7 \times 10^{-9}$ M　　**Find:** $[OH^-]$

　　　　　　Conceptual Plan: $[H_3O^+] \rightarrow [OH^-]$

$$K_w = 1.0 \times 10^{-14} = [H_3O^+][OH^-]$$

　　　　　　Solution:

　　　　　　$K_w = 1.0 \times 10^{-14} = (9.7 \times 10^{-9})[OH^-]$

　　　　　　$[OH^-] = 1.0 \times 10^{-6}$ M

　　　　　　$[OH^-] > [H_3O^+]$ so the solution is basic.

　　　(b)　**Given:** $K_w = 1.0 \times 10^{-14}$, $[H_3O^+] = 2.2 \times 10^{-6}$ M　　**Find:** $[OH^-]$

　　　　　　Conceptual Plan: $[H_3O^+] \rightarrow [OH^-]$

$$K_w = 1.0 \times 10^{-14} = [H_3O^+][OH^-]$$

　　　　　　Solution:

　　　　　　$K_w = 1.0 \times 10^{-14} = (2.2 \times 10^{-6})[OH^-]$

　　　　　　$[OH^-] = 4.5 \times 10^{-9}$ M

　　　　　　$[H_3O^+] > [OH^-]$ so the solution is acidic.

　　　(c)　**Given:** $K_w = 1.0 \times 10^{-14}$, $[H_3O^+] = 1.2 \times 10^{-9}$ M　　**Find:** $[OH^-]$

　　　　　　Conceptual Plan: $[H_3O^+] \rightarrow [OH^-]$

$$K_w = 1.0 \times 10^{-14} = [H_3O^+][OH^-]$$

　　　　　　Solution:

　　　　　　$K_w = 1.0 \times 10^{-14} = (1.2 \times 10^{-9})[OH^-]$

　　　　　　$[OH^-] = 8.3 \times 10^{-6}$ M

　　　　　　$[OH^-] > [H_3O^+]$ so the solution is basic.

15.17　(a)　**Given:** $[H_3O^+] = 1.7 \times 10^{-8}$ M　　**Find:** pH and pOH

　　　　　　Conceptual Plan: $[H_3O^+] \rightarrow$ pH $\rightarrow$ pOH

$$pH = -\log[H_3O^+] \quad pH + pOH = 14$$

　　　　　　Solution: pH $= -\log(1.7 \times 10^{-8}) = 7.77$　　pOH $= 14.00 - 7.77 = 6.23$

　　　　　　pH > 7 so the solution is basic.

　　　(b)　**Given:** $[H_3O^+] = 1.0 \times 10^{-7}$ M　　**Find:** pH and pOH

　　　　　　Conceptual Plan: $[H_3O^+] \rightarrow$ pH $\rightarrow$ pOH

$$pH = -\log[H_3O^+] \quad pH + pOH = 14$$

　　　　　　Solution: pH $= -\log(1.0 \times 10^{-7}) = 7.00$　　pOH $= 14.00 - 7.00 = 7.00$

　　　　　　pH $= 7$ so the solution is neutral.

　　　(c)　**Given:** $[H_3O^+] = 2.2 \times 10^{-6}$ M　　**Find:** pH and pOH

　　　　　　Conceptual Plan: $[H_3O^+] \rightarrow$ pH $\rightarrow$ pOH

$$pH = -\log[H_3O^+] \quad pH + pOH = 14$$

　　　　　　Solution: pH $= -\log(2.2 \times 10^{-6}) = 5.66$　　pOH $= 14.00 - 5.66 = 8.34$

　　　　　　pH < 7 so the solution is acidic.

15.19 $pH = -\log[H_3O^+]$ $K_w = 1.0 \times 10^{-14} = [H_3O^+][OH^-]$

$[H_3O^+]$	$[OH^-]$	pH	Acidic or basic
7.1×10^{-4}	1.4×10^{-11}	**3.15**	acidic
3.7×10^{-9}	2.7×10^{-6}	8.43	basic
8×10^{-12}	1×10^{-3}	**11.1**	basic
6.3×10^{-4}	**1.6×10^{-11}**	3.20	acidic

$[H_3O^+] = 10^{-3.15} = 7.1 \times 10^{-4}$ $[OH^-] = \dfrac{1.0 \times 10^{-14}}{7.1 \times 10^{-4}} = 1.4 \times 10^{-11}$

$[OH^-] = \dfrac{1.0 \times 10^{-14}}{3.7 \times 10^{-9}} = 2.7 \times 10^{-6}$ $pH = -\log(3.7 \times 10^{-9}) = 8.43$

$[H_3O^+] = 10^{-11.1} = 8 \times 10^{-12}$ $[OH^-] = \dfrac{1.0 \times 10^{-14}}{8 \times 10^{-12}} = 1 \times 10^{-3}$

$[H_3O^+] = \dfrac{1.0 \times 10^{-14}}{1.6 \times 10^{-11}} = 6.3 \times 10^{-4}$ $pH = -\log(6.3 \times 10^{-4}) = 3.20$

15.21   **Given:** $K_w = 2.4 \times 10^{-14}$ at 37 °C   **Find:** $[H_3O^+]$, pH
Conceptual Plan: $K_w \rightarrow [H_3O^+] \rightarrow pH$
$K_w = [H_3O^+][OH^-]$ $pH = -\log[H_3O^+]$
Solution: $H_2O(l) + H_2O(l) \rightleftharpoons H_3O^+(aq) + OH^-(aq)$
$K_w = [H_3O^+][OH^-]$
$[H_3O^+] = [OH^-] = \sqrt{K_w} = \sqrt{2.4 \times 10^{-14}} = 1.5 \times 10^{-7}$
$pH = -\log[H_3O^+] = -\log(1.5 \times 10^{-7}) = 6.82$

Check: The value of K_w increased, indicating more products formed; so the $[H_3O^+]$ increases and the pH decreases from the values at 25 °C.

15.23   (a)   **Given:** $[H_3O^+] = 0.044$ M   **Find:** pH
Conceptual Plan: $[H_3O^+] \rightarrow pH$
$pH = -\log[H_3O^+]$
Solution: $pH = -\log(0.044) = 1.3\underline{5}7 = 1.36$

(b)   **Given:** $[H_3O^+] = 0.045$ M   **Find:** pH
Conceptual Plan: $[H_3O^+] \rightarrow pH$
$pH = -\log[H_3O^+]$
Solution: $pH = -\log(0.045) = 1.3\underline{4}7 = 1.35$

(c)   **Given:** $[H_3O^+] = 0.046$ M   **Find:** pH
Conceptual Plan: $[H_3O^+] \rightarrow pH$
$pH = -\log[H_3O^+]$
Solution: $pH = -\log(0.046) = 1.3\underline{3}7 = 1.34$

If the pH of the solution did not carry as many decimal places as the significant digits to the right of the decimal point, you would not be able to distinguish a difference in the pH of solutions b and c. Also, solution a would have a pH that was too high.

Acid Solutions

15.25   (a)   **Given:** 0.15 M HCl (strong acid)   **Find:** $[H_3O^+]$, $[OH^-]$, pH
Conceptual Plan: $[HCl] \rightarrow [H_3O^+] \rightarrow pH$ and then $[H_3O^+] \rightarrow [OH^-]$
$[HCl] \rightarrow [H_3O^+]$ $pH = -\log[H_3O^+]$ $[H_3O^+][OH^-] = 1.0 \times 10^{-14}$

Solution: 0.15 M HCl = 0.15 M H_3O^+ $pH = -\log(0.15) = 0.82$
$[OH^-] = 1.0 \times 10^{-14}/0.15$ M $= 6.7 \times 10^{-14}$

Check: HCl is a strong acid with a relatively high concentration, so we expect the pH to be low and the [OH⁻] to be small.

(b) **Given:** 0.025 M HNO_3 (strong acid)   **Find:** $[H_3O^+]$, $[OH^-]$, pH

Conceptual Plan: $[HNO_3] \rightarrow [H_3O^+] \rightarrow pH$ and then $[H_3O^+] \rightarrow [OH^-]$

$$[HNO_3] \rightarrow [H_3O^+] \quad pH = -\log[H_3O^+] \qquad [H_3O^+][OH^-] = 1.0 \times 10^{-14}$$

Solution: $0.025 \text{ M } HNO_3 = 0.025 \text{ M } H_3O^+ \quad pH = -\log(0.025) = 1.60$

$$[OH^-] = 1.0 \times 10^{-14}/0.025 \text{ M} = 4.0 \times 10^{-13}$$

Check: HNO_3 is a strong acid, so we expect the pH to be low and the [OH⁻] to be small.

(c) **Given:** 0.072 M HBr and 0.015 M HNO_3 (strong acids)   **Find:** $[H_3O^+]$, $[OH^-]$, pH

Conceptual Plan: $[HBr] + [HNO_3] \rightarrow [H_3O^+] \rightarrow pH$ and then $[H_3O^+] \rightarrow [OH^-]$

$$[HBr] + [HNO_3] \rightarrow [H_3O^+] \quad pH = -\log[H_3O^+] \qquad [H_3O^+][OH^-] = 1.0 \times 10^{-14}$$

Solution: $0.072 \text{ M HBr} = 0.072 \text{ M } H_3O^+$ and $0.015 \text{ M } HNO_3 = 0.015 \text{ M } H_3O^+$

$$\text{Total } H_3O^+ = 0.072 \text{ M} + 0.015 \text{ M} = 0.087 \text{ M} \quad pH = -\log(0.087) = 1.06$$

$$[OH^-] = 1.0 \times 10^{-14}/0.087 \text{ M} = 1.1 \times 10^{-13}$$

Check: HBr and HNO_3 are both strong acids that completely dissociate. This gives a relatively high concentration, so we expect the pH to be low and the [OH⁻] to be small.

(d) **Given:** $HNO_3 = 0.855\%$ by mass, $d_{\text{solution}} = 1.01$ g/mL   **Find:** $[H_3O^+]$, $[OH^-]$, pH

Conceptual Plan:

% mass $HNO_3 \rightarrow$ g $HNO_3 \rightarrow$ mol HNO_3 and then g soln $\rightarrow$ mL soln $\rightarrow$ L soln $\rightarrow$ M HNO_3

$$\frac{\%}{100} \qquad \frac{\text{mol } HNO_3}{63.018 \text{ g } HNO_3} \qquad\qquad \frac{1.01 \text{ g soln}}{\text{mL soln}} \quad \frac{1000 \text{ mL soln}}{\text{L soln}} \quad \frac{\text{mol } HNO_3}{\text{L soln}}$$

M $HNO_3 \rightarrow$ M $H_3O^+ \rightarrow$ pH and then $[H_3O^+] \rightarrow [OH^-]$

$$[HNO_3] \rightarrow [H_3O^+] \quad pH = -\log[H_3O^+] \qquad [H_3O^+][OH^-] = 1.0 \times 10^{-14}$$

Solution: $\dfrac{0.855 \text{ g } HNO_3}{100 \text{ g soln}} \times \dfrac{1 \text{ mol } HNO_3}{63.018 \text{ g } HNO_3} \times \dfrac{1.01 \text{ g soln}}{\text{mL soln}} \times \dfrac{1000 \text{ mL soln}}{\text{L soln}} = 0.137 \text{ M } HNO_3$

$$0.137 \text{ M } HNO_3 = 0.137 \text{ M } H_3O^+ \quad pH = -\log(0.137) = 0.863$$

$$[OH^-] = 1.00 \times 10^{-14}/0.137 \text{ M} = 7.30 \times 10^{-14}$$

Check: HNO_3 is a strong acid that completely dissociates. This gives a relatively high concentration, so we expect the pH to be low and the [OH⁻] to be small.

15.27 (a) **Given:** pH = 1.25, 0.250 L   **Find:** g HI

Conceptual Plan: pH $\rightarrow [H_3O^+] \rightarrow$ [HI] $\rightarrow$ mol HI $\rightarrow$ g HI

$$pH = -\log[H_3O^+] \quad [H_3O^+] \rightarrow [HI] \quad \text{mol} = MV \quad \frac{127.9 \text{ g HI}}{1 \text{ mol HI}}$$

Solution: $[H_3O^+] = 10^{-1.25} = 0.056 \text{ M} = [HI] \qquad \dfrac{0.056 \text{ mol HI}}{L} \times 0.250 \text{ L} \times \dfrac{127.9 \text{ g HI}}{1 \text{ mol HI}} = 1.8 \text{ g HI}$

(b) **Given:** pH = 1.75, 0.250 L   **Find:** g HI

Conceptual Plan: pH $\rightarrow [H_3O^+] \rightarrow$ [HI] $\rightarrow$ mol HI $\rightarrow$ g HI

$$pH = -\log[H_3O^+] \quad [H_3O^+] \rightarrow [HI] \quad \text{mol} = MV \quad \frac{127.9 \text{ g HI}}{1 \text{ mol HI}}$$

Solution: $[H_3O^+] = 10^{-1.75} = 0.0178 \text{ M} = [HI] \qquad \dfrac{0.0178 \text{ mol HI}}{L} \times 0.250 \text{ L} \times \dfrac{127.9 \text{ g HI}}{1 \text{ mol HI}} = 0.57 \text{ g HI}$

(c) **Given:** pH = 2.85, 0.250 L   **Find:** g HI

Conceptual Plan: pH $\rightarrow [H_3O^+] \rightarrow$ [HI] $\rightarrow$ mol HI $\rightarrow$ g HI

$$pH = -\log[H_3O^+] \quad [H_3O^+] \rightarrow [HI] \quad \text{mol} = MV \quad \frac{127.9 \text{ g HI}}{1 \text{ mol HI}}$$

Solution: $[H_3O^+] = 10^{-2.85} = 0.0014 \text{ M} = [HI]$ $\quad \dfrac{0.0014 \text{ mol HI}}{L} \times 0.250\,L \times \dfrac{127.9 \text{ g HI}}{1 \text{ mol HI}} = 0.045 \text{ g HI}$

15.29 **Given:** 224 mL HCl, 27.2 °C, 1.02 atm, 1.5 L solution   **Find:** pH

Conceptual Plan: vol HCl → mol HCl → [HCl] → [H$_3$O$^+$] → pH

$$PV = nRT \qquad M = \dfrac{\text{mol HCl}}{\text{vol soln}} \qquad [HCl] = [H_3O^+] \qquad pH = -\log[H_3O^+]$$

Solution: $n = \dfrac{(1.02 \text{ atm})(224 \text{ mL})\left(\dfrac{1\,L}{1000 \text{ mL}}\right)}{\left(\dfrac{0.08206\,L\,\text{atm}}{\text{mol K}}\right)((27.2 + 273.15)\,K)} = 0.00927 \text{ mol}$

$[HCl] = \dfrac{0.00927 \text{ mol}}{1.5 \text{ L}} = 0.006\underline{1}8 \text{ M} = [H_3O^+]$ $pH = -\log(0.006\underline{1}8) = 2.21$

15.31 **Given:** 0.100 M benzoic acid, $K_a = 6.5 \times 10^{-5}$ **Find:** $[H_3O^+]$, pH

Conceptual Plan: Write a balanced reaction. Prepare an ICE (Initial, Change, Equil) table, represent the change with x, sum the table, determine the equilibrium values, put the equilibrium values in the equilibrium expression, and solve for x. Determine [H$_3$O$^+$] and pH.

Solution: $HC_7H_5O_2(aq) + H_2O(l) \rightleftharpoons H_3O^+(aq) + C_7H_5O_2^-(aq)$

	$[HC_7H_5O_2]$	$[H_3O^+]$	$[C_7H_5O_2^-]$
Initial	0.100 M	0.0	0.0
Change	$-x$	x	x
Equil	$0.100 - x$	x	x

$K_a = \dfrac{[H_3O^+][C_7H_5O_2^-]}{[HC_7H_5O_2]} = \dfrac{(x)(x)}{(0.100 - x)} = 6.5 \times 10^{-5}$

Assume that x is small compared to 0.100.

$x^2 = (6.5 \times 10^{-5})(0.100) \qquad x = 2.5 \times 10^{-3} \text{ M} = [H_3O^+]$

Check assumption: $\dfrac{2.5 \times 10^{-3}}{0.100} \times 100\% = 2.5\%$; assumption is valid.

$pH = -\log(2.5 \times 10^{-3}) = 2.60$

15.33 (a) **Given:** 0.500 M HNO$_2$, $K_a = 4.6 \times 10^{-4}$ **Find:** pH

Conceptual Plan: Write a balanced reaction. Prepare an ICE table, represent the change with x, sum the table, determine the equilibrium values, put the equilibrium values in the equilibrium expression, and solve for x. Determine [H$_3$O$^+$] and pH.

Solution: $HNO_2(aq) + H_2O(l) \rightleftharpoons H_3O^+(aq) + NO_2^-(aq)$

	$[HNO_2]$	$[H_3O^+]$	$[NO_2^-]$
Initial	0.500 M	0.0	0.0
Change	$-x$	x	x
Equil	$0.500 - x$	x	x

$K_a = \dfrac{[H_3O^+][NO_2^-]}{[HNO_2]} = \dfrac{(x)(x)}{(0.500 - x)} = 4.6 \times 10^{-4}$

Assume that x is small compared to 0.500.

$x^2 = (4.6 \times 10^{-4})(0.500) \qquad x = 0.015 \text{ M} = [H_3O^+]$

Check assumption: $\dfrac{0.015}{0.500} \times 100\% = 3.0\%$; assumption is valid.

$pH = -\log(0.015) = 1.82$

(b) **Given:** 0.100 M HNO_2, $K_a = 4.6 \times 10^{-4}$ **Find:** pH
Conceptual Plan: Write a balanced reaction. Prepare an ICE table, represent the change with x, sum the table, determine the equilibrium values, put the equilibrium values in the equilibrium expression, and solve for x. Determine $[H_3O^+]$ and pH.

Solution: $HNO_2(aq) + H_2O(l) \rightleftharpoons H_3O^+(aq) + NO_2^-(aq)$

	$[HNO_2]$	$[H_3O^+]$	$[NO_2^-]$
Initial	0.100 M	0.0	0.0
Change	$-x$	x	x
Equil	$0.100 - x$	x	x

$K_a = \dfrac{[H_3O^+][NO_2^-]}{[HNO_2]} = \dfrac{(x)(x)}{(0.100 - x)} = 4.6 \times 10^{-4}$

Assume that x is small compared to 0.100.

$x^2 = (4.6 \times 10^{-4})(0.100)$ $x = 0.0068 \text{ M} = [H_3O^+]$

Check assumption: $\dfrac{0.0068}{0.100} \times 100\% = 6.8\%$; assumption is not valid; solve using the quadratic equation.

$x^2 = (4.6 \times 10^{-4})(0.100 - x)$ $x^2 + 4.6 \times 10^{-4}x - 4.6 \times 10^{-5} = 0$

$x = 0.00656$

$pH = -\log(0.00656) = 2.18$

(c) **Given:** 0.0100 M HNO_2, $K_a = 4.6 \times 10^{-4}$ **Find:** pH
Conceptual Plan: Write a balanced reaction. Prepare an ICE table, represent the change with x, sum the table, determine the equilibrium values, put the equilibrium values in the equilibrium expression, and solve for x. Determine $[H_3O^+]$ and pH.

Solution: $HNO_2(aq) + H_2O(l) \rightleftharpoons H_3O^+(aq) + NO_2^-(aq)$

	$[HNO_2]$	$[H_3O^+]$	$[NO_2^-]$
Initial	0.0100 M	0.0	0.0
Change	$-x$	x	x
Equil	$0.0100 - x$	x	x

$K_a = \dfrac{[H_3O^+][NO_2^-]}{[HNO_2]} = \dfrac{(x)(x)}{(0.0100 - x)} = 4.6 \times 10^{-4}$

Assume that x is small compared to 0.100.

$x^2 = (4.6 \times 10^{-4})(0.0100)$ $x = 0.0021 \text{ M} = [H_3O^+]$

Check assumption: $\dfrac{0.0021}{0.0100} \times 100\% = 21\%$; assumption is not valid; solve with the quadratic equation.

$x^2 = (4.6 \times 10^{-4})(0.0100 - x)$ $x^2 + 4.6 \times 10^{-4}x - 4.6 \times 10^{-6} = 0$

$x = 0.0019$

$pH = -\log(0.0019) = 2.72$

15.35   **Given:** 15.0 mL glacial acetic, $d = 1.05$ g/mL, dilute to 1.50 L, $K_a = 1.8 \times 10^{-5}$ **Find:** pH
Conceptual Plan: mL acetic acid $\rightarrow$ g acetic acid $\rightarrow$ mol acetic acid $\rightarrow$ M and then write a balanced reaction.

$$\frac{1.05 \text{ g}}{\text{mL}} \qquad \frac{\text{mol acetic acid}}{60.05 \text{ g}} \qquad M = \frac{\text{mol}}{L}$$

Prepare an ICE table, represent the change with x, sum the table, determine the equilibrium values, put the equilibrium values in the equilibrium expression, and solve for x. Determine $[H_3O^+]$ and pH.

Solution: $15.0 \text{ mL} \times \dfrac{1.05 \text{ g}}{\text{mL}} \times \dfrac{1 \text{ mol}}{60.05 \text{ g}} \times \dfrac{1}{1.50 \text{ L}} = 0.1749 \text{ M}$

$$HC_2H_3O_2(aq) + H_2O(l) \rightleftharpoons H_3O^+(aq) + C_2H_3O_2^-(aq)$$

	$[HC_2H_3O_2]$	$[H_3O^+]$	$[C_2H_3O_2^-]$
Initial	0.1749 M	0.0	0.0
Change	$-x$	x	x
Equil	$0.1749 - x$	x	x

$$K_a = \frac{[H_3O^+][C_2H_3O_2^-]}{[HC_2H_3O_2]} = \frac{(x)(x)}{(0.1749 - x)} = 1.8 \times 10^{-5}$$

Assume that x is small compared to 0.1749.

$$x^2 = (1.8 \times 10^{-5})(0.1749) \qquad x = 0.00177 \text{ M} = [H_3O^+]$$

Check assumption: $\dfrac{0.00177}{0.1749} \times 100\% = 1.0\%$; assumption is valid.

$$pH = -\log(0.00177) = 2.75$$

15.37   **Given:** 0.185 M HA, pH = 2.95   **Find:** K_a
Conceptual Plan: pH → $[H_3O^+]$ and then write a balanced reaction. Prepare an ICE table, calculate equilibrium concentrations, and plug into the equilibrium expression to solve for K_a.
Solution: $[H_3O^+] = 10^{-2.95} = 0.00112 \text{ M} = [A^-]$

$$HA(aq) + H_2O(l) \rightleftharpoons H_3O^+(aq) + A^-(aq)$$

	$[HA]$	$[H_3O^+]$	$[A^-]$
Initial	0.185 M	0.0	0.0
Change	$-x$	x	x
Equil	$0.185 - 0.00112$	0.00112	0.00112

$$K_a = \frac{[H_3O^+][A^-]}{[HA]} = \frac{(0.00112)(0.00112)}{(0.185 - 0.00112)} = 6.82 \times 10^{-6}$$

15.39   **Given:** 0.125 M HCN, $K_a = 4.9 \times 10^{-10}$ **Find:** % ionization
Conceptual Plan: Write a balanced reaction. Prepare an ICE table, represent the change with x, sum the table, determine the equilibrium values, put the equilibrium values in the equilibrium expression, solve for x, and then x → % ionization.

$$\% \text{ ionization} = \frac{x}{[HCN]_{original}} \times 100\%$$

Solution: $$HCN(aq) + H_2O(l) \rightleftharpoons H_3O^+(aq) + CN^-(aq)$$

	$[HCN]$	$[H_3O^+]$	$[CN^-]$
Initial	0.125 M	0.0	0.0
Change	$-x$	x	x
Equil	$0.125 - x$	x	x

$$K_a = \frac{[H_3O^+][CN^-]}{[HCN]} = \frac{(x)(x)}{(0.125 - x)} = 4.9 \times 10^{-10}$$

Assume that x is small compared to 0.125.

$$x^2 = (4.9 \times 10^{-10})(0.125) \qquad x = 7.83 \times 10^{-6}$$

$$\% \text{ ionization} = \frac{7.83 \times 10^{-6}}{0.125} \times 100\% = 0.0063\% \text{ ionized}$$

15.41   (a)   **Given:** 1.00 M $HC_2H_3O_2$, $K_a = 1.8 \times 10^{-5}$ **Find:** % ionization
Conceptual Plan: Write a balanced reaction. Prepare an ICE table, represent the change with x, sum the table, determine the equilibrium values, put the equilibrium values in the equilibrium expression, solve for x, and then x → % ionization.

$$\% \text{ ionization} = \frac{x}{[HC_2H_3O_2]_{original}} \times 100\%$$

Solution: $HC_2H_3O_2(aq) + H_2O(l) \rightleftharpoons H_3O^+(aq) + C_2H_3O_2^-(aq)$

	$[HC_2H_3O_2]$	$[H_3O^+]$	$[C_2H_3O_2^-]$
Initial	1.00 M	0.0	0.0
Change	$-x$	x	x
Equil	$1.00 - x$	x	x

$$K_a = \frac{[H_3O^+][C_2H_3O_2^-]}{[HC_2H_3O_2]} = \frac{(x)(x)}{(1.00 - x)} = 1.8 \times 10^{-5}$$

Assume that x is small compared to 1.00.

$x^2 = (1.8 \times 10^{-5})(1.00) \qquad x = 0.00424$

$\% \text{ ionization} = \dfrac{0.00424}{1.00} \times 100\% = 0.42\% \text{ ionized}$

(b)   **Given:** 0.500 M $HC_2H_3O_2$, $K_a = 1.8 \times 10^{-5}$ **Find:** % ionization
Conceptual Plan: Write a balanced reaction. Prepare an ICE table, represent the change with x, sum the table, determine the equilibrium values, put the equilibrium values in the equilibrium expression, solve for x, and then $x \rightarrow$ % ionization.

$$\% \text{ ionization} = \frac{x}{[HC_2H_3O_2]_{\text{original}}} \times 100\%$$

Solution: $HC_2H_3O_2(aq) + H_2O(l) \rightleftharpoons H_3O^+(aq) + C_2H_3O_2^-(aq)$

	$[HC_2H_3O_2]$	$[H_3O^+]$	$[C_2H_3O_2^-]$
Initial	0.500 M	0.0	0.0
Change	$-x$	x	x
Equil	$0.500 - x$	x	x

$$K_a = \frac{[H_3O^+][C_2H_3O_2^-]}{[HC_2H_3O_2]} = \frac{(x)(x)}{(0.500 - x)} = 1.8 \times 10^{-5}$$

Assume that x is small compared to 0.500.

$x^2 = (1.8 \times 10^{-5})(0.500) \qquad x = 0.00300$

$\% \text{ ionization} = \dfrac{0.00300}{0.500} \times 100\% = 0.60\% \text{ ionized}$

(c)   **Given:** 0.100 M $HC_2H_3O_2$, $K_a = 1.8 \times 10^{-5}$ **Find:** % ionization
Conceptual Plan: Write a balanced reaction. Prepare an ICE table, represent the change with x, sum the table, determine the equilibrium values, put the equilibrium values in the equilibrium expression, solve for x, and then $x \rightarrow$ % ionization.

$$\% \text{ ionization} = \frac{x}{[HC_2H_3O_2]_{\text{original}}} \times 100\%$$

Solution: $HC_2H_3O_2(aq) + H_2O(l) \rightleftharpoons H_3O^+(aq) + C_2H_3O_2^-(aq)$

	$[HC_2H_3O_2]$	$[H_3O^+]$	$[C_2H_3O_2^-]$
Initial	0.100 M	0.0	0.0
Change	$-x$	x	x
Equil	$0.100 - x$	x	x

$$K_a = \frac{[H_3O^+][C_2H_3O_2^-]}{[HC_2H_3O_2]} = \frac{(x)(x)}{(0.100 - x)} = 1.8 \times 10^{-5}$$

Assume that x is small compared to 0.100.

$x^2 = (1.8 \times 10^{-5})(0.100) \qquad x = 0.00134$

$\% \text{ ionization} = \dfrac{0.00134}{0.100} \times 100\% = 1.3\% \text{ ionized}$

(d)   **Given:** 0.0500 M $HC_2H_3O_2$, $K_a = 1.8 \times 10^{-5}$ **Find:** % ionization
Conceptual Plan: Write a balanced reaction. Prepare an ICE table, represent the change with x, sum the table, determine the equilibrium values, put the equilibrium values in the equilibrium expression, solve for x, and then $x \rightarrow$ % ionization.

$$\text{\% ionization} = \frac{x}{[HC_2H_3O_2]_{\text{original}}} \times 100\%$$

Solution: $HC_2H_3O_2(aq) + H_2O(l) \rightleftharpoons H_3O^+(aq) + C_2H_3O_2^-(aq)$

	$[HC_2H_3O_2]$	$[H_3O^+]$	$[C_2H_3O_2^-]$
Initial	0.0500 M	0.0	0.0
Change	$-x$	x	x
Equil	$0.0500 - x$	x	x

$$K_a = \frac{[H_3O^+][C_2H_3O_2^-]}{[HC_2H_3O_2]} = \frac{(x)(x)}{(0.0500 - x)} = 1.8 \times 10^{-5}$$

Assume that x is small compared to 0.0500.

$$x^2 = (1.8 \times 10^{-5})(0.0500) \qquad x = 9.49 \times 10^{-4}$$

$$\text{\% ionization} = \frac{9.49 \times 10^{-4}}{0.0500} \times 100\% = 1.9\% \text{ ionized}$$

15.43   **Given:** 0.148 M HA, 1.55% dissociation   **Find:** K_a
Conceptual Plan: M $\rightarrow$ [H$_3$O$^+$] $\rightarrow$ K_a and then write a balanced reaction, determine equilibrium concentration, and plug into the equilibrium expression.

Solution: (0.148 M HA)(0.0155) = 0.002294 $[H_3O^+] = [A^-]$

$$HA(aq) + H_2O(l) \rightleftharpoons H_3O^+(aq) + A^-(aq)$$

	[HA]	$[H_3O^+]$	$[A^-]$
Initial	0.148 M	0.0	0.0
Change	$-x$	x	x
Equil	$0.148 - 0.002294$	0.002294	0.002294

$$K_a = \frac{[H_3O^+][A^-]}{[HA]} = \frac{(0.002294)(0.002294)}{(0.148 - 0.002294)} = 3.61 \times 10^{-5}$$

15.45   (a)   **Given:** 0.250 M HF, $K_a = 3.5 \times 10^{-4}$ **Find:** pH, % dissociation
Conceptual Plan: Write a balanced reaction. Prepare an ICE table, represent the change with x, sum the table, determine the equilibrium values, put the equilibrium values in the equilibrium expression, solve for x, and then $x \rightarrow$ % ionization.

$$\text{\% ionization} = \frac{x}{[HF]_{\text{original}}} \times 100\%$$

Solution: $HF(aq) + H_2O(l) \rightleftharpoons H_3O^+(aq) + F^-(aq)$

	[HF]	$[H_3O^+]$	$[F^-]$
Initial	0.250 M	0.0	0.0
Change	$-x$	x	x
Equil	$0.250 - x$	x	x

$$K_a = \frac{[H_3O^+][F^-]}{[HF]} = \frac{(x)(x)}{(0.250 - x)} = 3.5 \times 10^{-4}$$

Assume that x is small compared to 0.250.

$$x^2 = (3.5 \times 10^{-4})(0.250) \qquad x = 0.00935 \text{ M} = [H_3O^+]$$

$$\frac{0.00935}{0.250} \times 100\% = 3.7\%$$

$$pH = -\log(0.00935) = 2.03$$

(b)   **Given:** 0.100 M HF, $K_a = 3.5 \times 10^{-4}$ **Find:** pH, % dissociation
Conceptual Plan: Write a balanced reaction. Prepare an ICE table, represent the change with x, sum the table, determine the equilibrium values, put the equilibrium values in the equilibrium expression, solve for x, and then $x \rightarrow$ % ionization.

$$\% \text{ ionization} = \frac{x}{[\text{HF}]_{\text{original}}} \times 100\%$$

Solution: $HF(aq) + H_2O(l) \rightleftharpoons H_3O^+(aq) + F^-(aq)$

	[HF]	[H₃O⁺]	[F⁻]
Initial	0.1000 M	0.0	0.0
Change	$-x$	x	x
Equil	$0.100 - x$	x	x

$$K_a = \frac{[H_3O^+][F^-]}{[HF]} = \frac{(x)(x)}{(0.100 - x)} = 3.5 \times 10^{-4}$$

Assume that x is small compared to 0.100.

$$x^2 = (3.5 \times 10^{-4})(0.100) \qquad x = 0.00592 \text{ M} = [H_3O^+]$$

$$\frac{0.00592}{0.100} \times 100\% = 5.9\%$$

$x > 5.0\%$ Therefore, assumption is invalid; solve using the quadratic equation.

$$x^2 + 3.5 \times 10^{-4}x - 3.5 \times 10^{-5} = 0$$

$x = 0.00574$ or -0.00609

$\text{pH} = -\log(0.00574) = 2.24$

$$\% \text{ dissociation} = \frac{0.00574}{0.100} \times 100\% = 5.7\%$$

(c)   **Given:** 0.050 M HF, $K_a = 3.5 \times 10^{-4}$ **Find:** pH, % dissociation
Conceptual Plan: Write a balanced reaction. Prepare an ICE table, represent the change with x, sum the table, determine the equilibrium values, put the equilibrium values in the equilibrium expression, solve for x, and then $x \rightarrow$ % ionization.

$$\% \text{ ionization} = \frac{x}{[\text{HF}]_{\text{original}}} \times 100\%$$

Solution: $HF(aq) + H_2O(l) \rightleftharpoons H_3O^+(aq) + F^-(aq)$

	[HF]	[H₃O⁺]	[F⁻]
Initial	0.050 M	0.0	0.0
Change	$-x$	x	x
Equil	$0.050 - x$	x	x

$$K_a = \frac{[H_3O^+][F^-]}{[HF]} = \frac{(x)(x)}{(0.050 - x)} = 3.5 \times 10^{-4}$$

Assume that x is small compared to 0.050.

$$x^2 = (3.5 \times 10^{-4})(0.050) \qquad x = 0.00418 \text{ M} = [H_3O^+]$$

$$\frac{0.00418}{0.050} \times 100\% = 8.4\%$$

Assumption is invalid; solve using the quadratic equation.

$$x^2 + 3.5 \times 10^{-4}x - 1.75 \times 10^{-5} = 0$$

$x = 0.00401$ or -0.00436

$\text{pH} = -\log(0.00401) = 2.40$

$$\% \text{ dissociation} = \frac{0.00401}{0.050} \times 100\% = 8.0\%$$

15.47 $H_3PO_4(aq) + H_2O(l) \rightleftharpoons H_3O^+(aq) + H_2PO_4^-(aq)$ $K_{a_1} = \dfrac{[H_3O^+][H_2PO_4^-]}{[H_3PO_4]}$

$H_2PO_4^-(aq) + H_2O(l) \rightleftharpoons H_3O^+(aq) + HPO_4^{2-}(aq)$ $K_{a_2} = \dfrac{[H_3O^+][HPO_4^{2-}]}{[H_2PO_4^-]}$

$HPO_4^{2-}(aq) + H_2O(l) \rightleftharpoons H_3O^+(aq) + PO_4^{3-}(aq)$ $K_{a_3} = \dfrac{[H_3O^+][PO_4^{3-}]}{[HPO_4^{2-}]}$

15.49   (a)   **Given:** 0.350 M H_3PO_4, $K_{a_1} = 7.5 \times 10^{-3}$, $K_{a_2} = 6.2 \times 10^{-8}$ **Find:** $[H_3O^+]$, pH
Conceptual Plan: K_{a_1} is much larger than K_{a_2}, so use K_{a_1} to calculate $[H_3O^+]$. Write a balanced reaction. Prepare an ICE table, represent the change with x, sum the table, determine the equilibrium values, put the equilibrium values in the equilibrium expression, and solve for x.

Solution: $H_3PO_4(aq) + H_2O(l) \rightleftharpoons H_3O^+(aq) + H_2PO_4^-(aq)$

	$[H_3PO_4]$	$[H_3O^+]$	$[H_2PO_4^-]$
Initial	0.350 M	0.0	0.0
Change	$-x$	x	x
Equil	$0.350 - x$	x	x

$K_a = \dfrac{[H_3O^+][H_2PO_4^-]}{[H_3PO_4]} = \dfrac{(x)(x)}{(0.350 - x)} = 7.5 \times 10^{-3}$

Assume that x is small compared to 0.350.

$x^2 = (7.5 \times 10^{-3})(0.350)$ $x = 0.0512$ M $= [H_3O^+]$

Check assumption: $\dfrac{0.0512}{0.350} \times 100\% = 14.6\%$; assumption is not valid.

$x^2 + 7.5 \times 10^{-3}x - 0.002625 = 0$ $x = 0.04\underline{7}62 = [H_3O^+]$

$pH = -\log(0.04\underline{7}62) = 1.32$

(b)   **Given:** 0.350 M $H_2C_2O_4$, $K_{a_1} = 6.0 \times 10^{-2}$, $K_{a_2} = 6.0 \times 10^{-5}$ **Find:** $[H_3O^+]$, pH
Conceptual Plan: K_{a_1} is much larger than K_{a_2}, so use K_{a_1} to calculate $[H_3O^+]$. Write a balanced reaction. Prepare an ICE table, represent the change with x, sum the table, determine the equilibrium values, put the equilibrium values in the equilibrium expression, and solve for x.

Solution: $H_2C_2O_4(aq) + H_2O(l) \rightleftharpoons H_3O^+(aq) + HC_2O_4^-(aq)$

	$[H_2C_2O_4]$	$[H_3O^+]$	$[HC_2O_4^-]$
Initial	0.350 M	0.0	0.0
Change	$-x$	x	x
Equil	$0.350 - x$	x	x

$K_{a_1} = \dfrac{[H_3O^+][HC_2O_4^-]}{[H_2C_2O_4]} = \dfrac{(x)(x)}{(0.350 - x)} = 6.0 \times 10^{-2}$

$x^2 + 6.0 \times 10^{-2}x - 0.021 = 0$ $x = 0.1\underline{1}80 = 0.12$ M $[H_3O^+]$

$pH = -\log(0.1\underline{1}80) = 0.93$

Base Solutions

15.51   (a)   **Given:** 0.15 M NaOH   **Find:** $[OH^-]$, $[H_3O^+]$, pH, pOH
Conceptual Plan: $[NaOH] \rightarrow [OH^-] \rightarrow [H_3O^+] \rightarrow$ pH $\rightarrow$ pOH
$K_w = [H_3O^+][OH^-]$ pH $= -\log[H_3O^+]$ pH $+$ pOH $= 14$

Solution: $[OH^-] = [NaOH] = 0.15$ M

$$[H_3O^+] = \frac{K_w}{[OH^-]} = \frac{1.0 \times 10^{-14}}{0.15\ M} = 6.7 \times 10^{-14}\ M$$

$$pH = -\log(6.7 \times 10^{-14}) = 13.17$$

$$pOH = 14.00 - 13.17 = 0.83$$

(b) **Given:** 1.5×10^{-3} M $Ca(OH)_2$ **Find:** $[OH^-], [H_3O^+]$, pH, pOH

Conceptual Plan: $[Ca(OH)_2] \rightarrow [OH^-] \rightarrow [H_3O^+] \rightarrow pH \rightarrow pOH$

$$K_w = [H_3O^+][OH^-]\quad pH = -\log[H_3O^+]\quad pH + pOH = 14$$

Solution: $[OH^-] = 2[Ca(OH)_2] = 2(1.5 \times 10^{-3}) = 0.0030\ M$

$$[H_3O^+] = \frac{K_w}{[OH^-]} = \frac{1.0 \times 10^{-14}}{0.0030\ M} = 3.\underline{3}3 \times 10^{-12}\ M$$

$$pH = -\log(3.\underline{3}3 \times 10^{-12}) = 11.48$$

$$pOH = 14.00 - 11.48 = 2.52$$

(c) **Given:** 4.8×10^{-4} M $Sr(OH)_2$ **Find:** $[OH^-], [H_3O^+]$, pH, pOH

Conceptual Plan: $[Sr(OH)_2] \rightarrow [OH^-] \rightarrow [H_3O^+] \rightarrow pH \rightarrow pOH$

$$K_w = [H_3O^+][OH^-]\quad pH = -\log[H_3O^+]\quad pH + pOH = 14$$

Solution: $[OH^+] = [Sr(OH)_2] = 2(4.8 \times 10^{-4}) = 9.6 \times 10^{-4}\ M$

$$[H_3O^-] = \frac{K_w}{[OH^-]} = \frac{1.0 \times 10^{-14}}{9.6 \times 10^{-4}\ M} = 1.\underline{0}4 \times 10^{-11}\ M$$

$$pH = -\log(1.\underline{0}4 \times 10^{-11}) = 10.98$$

$$pOH = 14.00 - 10.98 = 3.02$$

(d) **Given:** 8.7×10^{-5} M KOH **Find:** $[OH^-], [H_3O^+]$, pH, pOH

Conceptual Plan: $[KOH] \rightarrow [OH^-] \rightarrow [H_3O^+] \rightarrow pH \rightarrow pOH$

$$K_w = [H_3O^+][OH^-]\quad pH = -\log[H_3O^+]\quad pH + pOH = 14$$

Solution: $[OH^-] = [KOH] = 8.7 \times 10^{-5}\ M$

$$[H_3O^+] = \frac{K_w}{[OH^-]} = \frac{1.0 \times 10^{-14}}{8.7 \times 10^{-5}\ M} = 1.\underline{1} \times 10^{-10}\ M$$

$$pH = -\log(1.\underline{1} \times 10^{-10}) = 9.96$$

$$pOH = 14.00 - 9.96 = 4.04$$

15.53 **Given:** 3.85% KOH by mass, $d = 1.01$ g/mL **Find:** pH

Conceptual Plan:

% mass $\rightarrow$ g KOH $\rightarrow$ mol KOH and mass soln $\rightarrow$ mL soln $\rightarrow$ L soln $\rightarrow$ M KOH $\rightarrow$ [OH$^-$]

$$\frac{1\ mol\ KOH}{56.11\ g\ KOH}\qquad\qquad \frac{1.01\ g\ soln}{mL\ soln}\quad \frac{1000\ mL\ soln}{1\ L\ soln}\quad \frac{mol\ KOH}{L\ soln}$$

$\rightarrow$ pOH $\rightarrow$ pH

$$pOH = -\log[OH^-]\ pH + pOH = 14$$

Solution: $\dfrac{3.85\ \text{g KOH}}{100.0\ \text{g soln}} \times \dfrac{1\ mol\ KOH}{56.11\ \text{g KOH}} \times \dfrac{1.01\ \text{g soln}}{\text{mL soln}} \times \dfrac{1000\ \text{mL soln}}{1\ L\ soln} = 0.69\underline{3}0\ M\ KOH$

$[OH^-] = [KOH] = 0.69\underline{3}0\ M$; $pOH = -\log(0.69\underline{3}0) = 0.159$; $pH = 14.000 - 0.159 = 13.841$

15.55 **Given:** 3.55 L, pH = 12.4; 0.855 M KOH **Find:** Vol

Conceptual Plan: $pH \rightarrow [H_3O^+] \rightarrow [OH^-]$ and then $V_1M_1 = V_2M_2$

$$[H_3O^+] = 10^{-pH}\quad 1.0 \times 10^{-14} = [H_3O^+][OH^-]\qquad V_1M_1 = V_2M_2$$

Solution: $[H_3O^+] = 10^{-12.4} = 3.98 \times 10^{-13}$ $1.0 \times 10^{-14} = 3.98 \times 10^{-13}[OH^-]$

$[OH^-] = 0.025\underline{1}3$

$V_1M_1 = V_2M_2$ $V_1(0.855\ M) = (3.55\ L)(0.0251\ M)$ $V_1 = 0.104\ L$

15.57 (a) $NH_3(aq) + H_2O(l) \rightleftharpoons NH_4^+(aq) + OH^-(aq)$ $\qquad K_b = \dfrac{[NH_4^+][OH^-]}{[NH_3]}$

(b) $HCO_3^-(aq) + H_2O(l) \rightleftharpoons H_2CO_3(aq) + OH^-(aq)$ $\qquad K_b = \dfrac{[H_2CO_3][OH^-]}{[HCO_3^-]}$

(c) $CH_3NH_2(aq) + H_2O(l) \rightleftharpoons CH_3NH_3^+(aq) + OH^-(aq)$ $\qquad K_b = \dfrac{[CH_3NH_3^+][OH^-]}{[CH_3NH_2]}$

15.59 **Given:** 0.15 M NH_3, $K_b = 1.76 \times 10^{-5}$ **Find:** $[OH^-]$, pH, pOH

Conceptual Plan: Write a balanced reaction. Prepare an ICE table, represent the change with x, sum the table, determine the equilibrium values, put the equilibrium values in the equilibrium expression, and solve for x.

$x = [OH^-] \rightarrow [pOH] \rightarrow pH$

$\qquad pOH = -log[OH^-] \quad pH + pOH = 14$

Solution: $NH_3(aq) + H_2O(l) \rightleftharpoons NH_4^+(aq) + OH^-(aq)$

	$[NH_3]$	$[NH_4^+]$	$[OH^-]$
Initial	0.15 M	0.0	0.0
Change	$-x$	x	x
Equil	$0.15 - x$	x	x

$K_b = \dfrac{[NH_4^+][OH^-]}{[NH_3]} = \dfrac{(x)(x)}{(0.15 - x)} = 1.76 \times 10^{-5}$

Assume that x is small.

$x^2 = (1.76 \times 10^{-5})(0.15) \quad x = [OH^-] = 0.00162 \text{ M}$

$pOH = -log(0.00162) = 2.79$

$pH = 14.00 - 2.79 = 11.21$

15.61 **Given:** $pK_b = 10.4$, 455 mg/L caffeine **Find:** pH

Conceptual Plan: $pK_b \rightarrow K_b$ and then mg/L $\rightarrow$ g/L $\rightarrow$ mol/L and then write a balanced reaction. Prepare an ICE table, represent the change with x, sum the table, determine the equilibrium values, put the equilibrium values in the equilibrium expression, and solve for x.

$x = [OH^-] \rightarrow [pOH] \rightarrow pH$

$\qquad pOH = -log[OH^-] \quad pH + pOH = 14$

Solution: $K_b = 10^{-10.4} = 3.98 \times 10^{-11}$

$\dfrac{455 \text{ mg caffeine}}{L \text{ soln}} \times \dfrac{g \text{ caffeine}}{1000 \text{ mg caffeine}} \times \dfrac{1 \text{ mol caffeine}}{194.20 \text{ g}} = 0.002343 \text{ M caffeine}$

$C_8H_{10}N_4O_2(aq) + H_2O(l) \rightleftharpoons HC_8H_{10}N_4O_2^+(aq) + OH^-(aq)$

	$[C_8H_{10}N_4O_2]$	$[HC_8H_{10}N_4O_2^+]$	$[OH^-]$
Initial	0.002343	0.0	0.0
Change	$-x$	x	x
Equil	$0.002343 - x$	x	x

$K_b = \dfrac{[HC_8H_{10}N_4O_2^+][OH^-]}{[C_8H_{10}N_4O_2]} = \dfrac{(x)(x)}{(0.002343 - x)} = 3.98 \times 10^{-11}$

Assume that x is small.

$x^2 = (3.98 \times 10^{-11})(0.002343) \quad x = [OH^-] = 3.05 \times 10^{-7} \text{ M}$

$\dfrac{3.05 \times 10^{-7} \text{ M}}{0.002343} \times 100\% = 0.013\%$; assumption is valid.

$pOH = -log(3.05 \times 10^{-7}) = 6.5$

$pH = 14.00 - 6.5 = 7.5$

15.63 **Given:** 0.150 M morphine, pH $= 10.5$ **Find:** K_b

Conceptual Plan:

pH → pOH → [OH⁻] and then write a balanced equation, prepare an ICE table, and determine

pH + pOH = 14   pOH = −log[OH⁻]

equilibrium concentrations → K_b.

Solution: pOH $= 14.0 - 10.5 = 3.5$ $[OH^-] = 10^{-3.5} = 3.16 \times 10^{-4} = [\text{Hmorphine}^+]$

$$\text{morphine}(aq) + H_2O(l) \rightleftharpoons \text{Hmorphine}^+(aq) + OH^-(aq)$$

	[morphine]	[Hmorphine⁺]	[OH⁻]
Initial	0.150 M	0.0	0.0
Change	−x	x	x
Equil	0.150 − x	3.16×10^{-4}	3.16×10^{-4}

$$K_b = \frac{[\text{Hmorphine}^+][OH^-]}{[\text{morphine}]} = \frac{(3.16 \times 10^{-4})(3.16 \times 10^{-4})}{(0.150 - 3.16 \times 10^{-4})} = 6.67 \times 10^{-7} = 7 \times 10^{-7}$$

Acid–Base Properties of Ions and Salts

15.65 (a)   pH neutral: Br⁻ is the conjugate base of a strong acid; therefore, it is pH-neutral.

(b)   weak base: ClO⁻ is the conjugate base of a weak acid; therefore, it is a weak base.
$$ClO^-(aq) + H_2O(l) \rightleftharpoons HClO(aq) + OH^-(aq)$$

(c)   weak base: CN⁻ is the conjugate base of a weak acid; therefore, it is a weak base.
$$CN^-(aq) + H_2O(l) \rightleftharpoons HCN(aq) + OH^-(aq)$$

(d)   pH neutral: Cl⁻ is the conjugate base of a strong acid; therefore, it is pH-neutral.

15.67 **Given:** $[F^-] = 0.140$ M, $K_a(HF) = 3.5 \times 10^{-4}$ **Find :** $[OH^-]$, pOH

Conceptual Plan: Determine K_b. Write a balanced reaction. Prepare an ICE table, represent the change

$$K_b = \frac{K_w}{K_a}$$

with x, sum the table, determine the equilibrium values, put the equilibrium values in the equilibrium expression, and solve for x. Determine $[OH^-]$ → pOH → pH.

pOH = −log[OH⁻]   pH + pOH = 14

Solution: $F^-(aq) + H_2O(l) \rightleftharpoons HF(aq) + OH^-(aq)$

	[F⁻]	[HF]	[OH⁻]
Initial	0.140 M	0.0	0.0
Change	−x	x	x
Equil	0.140 − x	x	x

$$K_b = \frac{K_w}{K_a} = \frac{1 \times 10^{-14}}{3.5 \times 10^{-4}} = 2.86 \times 10^{-11} = \frac{(x)(x)}{(0.140 - x)}$$

Assume that x is small.

$x = 2.0 \times 10^{-6} = [OH^-]$ pOH $= -\log(2.0 \times 10^{-6}) = 5.70$

pH $= 14.00 - 5.70 = 8.30$

15.69 (a)   weak acid: NH_4^+ is the conjugate acid of a weak base; therefore, it is a weak acid.
$$NH_4^+(aq) + H_2O(l) \rightleftharpoons H_3O^+(aq) + NH_3(aq)$$

(b)   pH-neutral: Na⁺ is the counterion of a strong base; therefore, it is pH-neutral.

(c)   weak acid: The Co^{3+} cation is a small, highly charged metal cation; therefore, it is a weak acid.
$$Co(H_2O)_6^{3+}(aq) + H_2O(l) \rightleftharpoons Co(H_2O)_5(OH)^{2+}(aq) + H_3O^+(aq)$$

(d)   weak acid: $CH_2NH_3^+$ is the conjugate acid of a weak base; therefore, it is a weak acid.
$$CH_2NH_3^+(aq) + H_2O(l) \rightleftharpoons H_3O^+(aq) + CH_2NH_2(aq)$$

15.71   (a)   acidic: $FeCl_3$ Fe^{3+} is a small, highly charged metal cation; therefore, it is acidic. Cl^- is the conjugate base of a strong acid; therefore, it is pH-neutral.

        (b)   basic: NaF Na^+ is the counterion of a strong base; therefore, it is pH-neutral. F^- is the conjugate base of a weak acid; therefore, it is basic.

        (c)   pH-neutral: $CaBr_2$ Ca^{2+} is the counterion of a strong base; therefore, it is pH-neutral. Br^- is the conjugate base of a strong acid; therefore, it is pH-neutral.

        (d)   acidic: NH_4Br NH_4^+ is the conjugate acid of a weak base; therefore, it is acidic. Br^- is the conjugate base of a strong acid; therefore, it is pH-neutral.

        (e)   acidic: $C_6H_5NH_3NO_2$ $C_6H_5NH_3^+$ is the conjugate acid of a weak base; therefore, it is a weak acid. NO_2^- is the conjugate base of a weak acid; therefore, it is a weak base. To determine pH, compare K values.

$$K_a(C_6H_5NH_3^+) = \frac{1.0 \times 10^{-14}}{3.9 \times 10^{-10}} = 2.6 \times 10^{-5} \quad K_b(NO_2^-) = \frac{1.0 \times 10^{-14}}{4.6 \times 10^{-4}} = 2.2 \times 10^{-11}$$

$K_a > K_b$; therefore, the solution is acidic.

15.73   **Conceptual Plan:** Identify each species and determine whether it is acidic, basic, or neutral.

$NaCl$ pH-neutral: Na^+ is the counterion of a strong base; therefore, it is pH-neutral. Cl^- is the conjugate base of a strong acid; therefore, it is pH-neutral.

NH_4Cl acidic: NH_4^+ is the conjugate acid of a weak base; therefore, it is acidic. Cl^- is the conjugate base of a strong acid; therefore, it is pH-neutral.

$NaHCO_3$ basic: Na^+ is the counterion of a strong base; therefore, it is pH-neutral. HCO_3^- is the conjugate base of a weak acid; therefore, it is basic.

NH_4ClO_2 acidic: NH_4^+ is the conjugate acid of a weak base; therefore, it is a weak acid. ClO_2^- is the conjugate base of a weak acid; therefore, it is a weak base. $K_a(NH_4^+) = 5.6 \times 10^{-10}$ $K_b(ClO_2^-) = 9.1 \times 10^{-13}$

$NaOH$ strong base

Increasing acidity: $NaOH < NaHCO_3 < NaCl < NH_4ClO_2 < NH_4Cl$

15.75   (a)   **Given: 0.10 M NH_4Cl Find: pH**

        Conceptual Plan: Identify each species and determine which will contribute to pH. Write a balanced reaction. Prepare an ICE table, represent the change with x, sum the table, determine the equilibrium values, put the equilibrium values in the equilibrium expression, and solve for x. Determine $[H_3O^+] \rightarrow$ pH.

        Solution: NH_4^+ is the conjugate acid of a weak base; therefore, it is acidic. Cl^- is the conjugate base of a strong acid; therefore, it is pH-neutral.

$$NH_4^+(aq) + H_2O(l) \rightleftharpoons NH_3(aq) + H_3O^+(aq)$$

	$[NH_4^+]$	$[NH_3]$	$[H_3O^+]$
Initial	0.10	0.0	0.0
Change	$-x$	x	x
Equil	$0.10 - x$	x	x

$$K_a = \frac{K_w}{K_b} = \frac{1.0 \times 10^{-14}}{1.76 \times 10^{-5}} = 5.\underline{68} \times 10^{-10} = \frac{(x)(x)}{(0.10 - x)}$$

Assume that x is small.

$x = 7.\underline{54} \times 10^{-6} = [H_3O^+]$ pH $= -\log(7.\underline{54} \times 10^{-6}) = 5.12$

        (b)   **Given: 0.10 M $NaC_2H_3O_2$ Find: pH**

        Conceptual Plan: Identify each species and determine which will contribute to pH. Write a balanced reaction. Prepare an ICE table, represent the change with x, sum the table, determine the equilibrium values, put the equilibrium values in the equilibrium expression, and solve for x. Determine $[OH^-] \rightarrow$ pOH $\rightarrow$ pH.

        pOH $= -\log[OH^-]$ pH + pOH = 14

        Solution: Na^+ is the counterion of a strong base; therefore, it is pH-neutral. $C_2H_3O_2^-$ is the conjugate base of a weak acid; therefore, it is basic.

$$C_2H_3O_2^-(aq) + H_2O(l) \rightleftharpoons HC_2H_3O_2(aq) + OH^-(aq)$$

	$[C_2H_3O_2^-]$	$[HC_2H_3O_2]$	$[OH^-]$
Initial	0.10	0.0	0.0
Change	$-x$	x	x
Equil	$0.10 - x$	x	x

$$K_b = \frac{K_w}{K_a} = \frac{1.0 \times 10^{-14}}{1.8 \times 10^{-5}} = 5.\underline{5}6 \times 10^{-10} = \frac{(x)(x)}{(0.10 - x)}$$

Assume that x is small.

$x = 7.\underline{4}6 \times 10^{-6} = [OH^-]$　　pOH $= -\log(7.\underline{4}6 \times 10^{-6}) = 5.13$

pH $= 14.00 - 5.13 = 8.87$

(c)　**Given:** 0.10 M NaCl　**Find:** pH

Conceptual Plan: Identify each species and determine which will contribute to pH.

Solution: Na^+ is the counterion of a strong base; therefore, it is pH-neutral. Cl^- is the conjugate base of a strong acid; therefore, it is pH-neutral.

pH $= 7.0$

15.77　**Given:** 0.15 M KF　**Find:** concentration of all species

Conceptual Plan: Identify each species and determine which will contribute to pH. Write a balanced reaction. Prepare an ICE table, represent the change with x, sum the table, determine the equilibrium values, put the equilibrium values in the equilibrium expression, and solve for x. Then $[OH^-] \rightarrow [H_3O^+]$.

$$K_w = [H_3O^+][OH^-]$$

Solution: K^+ is the counterion of a strong base; therefore, it is pH-neutral. F^- is the conjugate base of a weak acid; therefore, it is basic.

$$F^-(aq) + H_2O(l) \rightleftharpoons HF(aq) + OH^-(aq)$$

	$[F^-]$	$[HF]$	$[OH^-]$
Initial	0.15 M	0.0	0.0
Change	$-x$	x	x
Equil	$0.15 - x$	x	x

$$K_b = \frac{K_w}{K_a} = \frac{1.0 \times 10^{-14}}{3.5 \times 10^{-4}} = 2.\underline{8}6 \times 10^{-11} = \frac{(x)(x)}{(0.15 - x)}$$

Assume that x is small.

$x = 2.1 \times 10^{-6} = [OH^-] = [HF]$　　　$[H_3O^+] = \dfrac{K_w}{[OH^-]} = \dfrac{1 \times 10^{-14}}{2.1 \times 10^{-6}} = 4.8 \times 10^{-9}$

$[K^+] = 0.15$ M

$[F^-] = (0.15 - 2.1 \times 10^{-6}) = 0.15$ M

$[HF] = 2.1 \times 10^{-6}$

$[OH^-] = 2.1 \times 10^{-6}$

$[H_3O^+] = 4.8 \times 10^{-9}$

Molecular Structure and Acid Strength

15.79　(a)　HCl is the stronger acid. HCl is the weaker bond; therefore, it is more acidic.

　　　　(b)　HF is the stronger acid. F is more electronegative than is O, so the bond is more polar and more acidic.

　　　　(c)　H_2Se is the stronger acid. The H—Se bond is weaker; therefore, it is more acidic.

15.81　(a)　H_2SO_4 is the stronger acid because it has more oxygen atoms.

　　　　(b)　$HClO_2$ is the stronger acid because it has more oxygen atoms.

　　　　(c)　HClO is the stronger acid because Cl is more electronegative than is Br.

　　　　(d)　CCl_3COOH is the stronger acid because Cl is more electronegative than is H.

15.83 S^{2-} is the stronger base. Base strength is determined from the corresponding acid. The weaker the acid, the stronger the base. H_2S is the weaker acid because it has a stronger bond.

Lewis Acids and Bases

15.85 (a) Lewis acid: Fe^{3+} has an empty d orbital and can accept lone pair electrons.
   (b) Lewis acid: BH_3 has an empty p orbital to accept a lone pair of electrons.
   (c) Lewis base: NH_3 has a lone pair of electrons to donate.
   (d) Lewis base: F^- has lone pair electrons to donate.

15.87 (a) Fe^{3+} accepts an electron pair from H_2O; so Fe^{3+} is the Lewis acid, and H_2O is the Lewis base.
   (b) Zn^{2+} accepts an electron pair from NH_3; so Zn^{2+} is the Lewis acid, and NH_3 is the Lewis base.
   (c) The empty p orbital on B accepts an electron pair from $(CH_3)_3N$; so BF_3 is the Lewis acid, and $(CH_3)_3N$ is the Lewis base.

Cumulative Problems

15.89 (a) weak acid. The beaker contains 10 HF molecules, 2 H_3O^+ ions, and 2 F^- ions. Because both the molecule and the ions exist in solution, the acid is a weak acid.
   (b) strong acid. The beaker contains 12 H_3O^+ ions and 12 L^- ions. Because the molecule is completely ionized in solution, the acid is a strong acid.
   (c) weak acid. The beaker contains 10 $HCHO_2$ molecules, 2 H_3O^+ ions, and 2 CHO_2^- ions. Because both the molecule and the ions exist in solution, the acid is a weak acid.
   (d) strong acid. The beaker contains 12 H_3O^+ ions and 12 NO_3^- ions. Because the molecule is completely ionized in solution, the acid is a strong acid.

15.91 $HbH^+(aq) + O_2(aq) \rightleftharpoons HbO_2(aq) + H^+(aq)$
   Using Le Châtelier's principle, if the $[H^+]$ increases, the reaction will shift left, and if the $[H^+]$ decreases, the reaction will shift right. So if the pH of blood is too acidic (low pH; $[H^+]$ increased), the reaction will shift to the left. This will cause less of the HbO_2 in the blood and decrease the oxygen-carrying capacity of the hemoglobin in the blood.

15.93 **Given:** 4.00×10^2 mg $Mg(OH)_2$, 2.00×10^2 mL HCl solution, pH $= 1.3$
   Find: volume neutralized, % neutralized
   Conceptual Plan:
   mg $Mg(OH)_2$ $\rightarrow$ g $Mg(OH)_2$ $\rightarrow$ mol $Mg(OH)_2$ and then pH $\rightarrow$ $[H_3O^+]$ and then mol $Mg(OH)_2$

   $$\frac{1 \text{ g } Mg(OH)_2}{1000 \text{ mg}} \qquad \frac{1 \text{ mol } Mg(OH)_2}{58.326 \text{ g}} \qquad\qquad pH = -\log [H_3O^+]$$

   mol OH^- $\rightarrow$ mol H_3O^+ $\rightarrow$ vol H_3O^+ $\rightarrow$ % neutralized

   $$\frac{2 \text{ OH}^-}{Mg(OH)_2} \quad \frac{H_3O^+}{OH^-} \qquad \frac{\text{mol } H_3O^+}{M(H_3O^+)} \qquad \frac{\text{vol HCl neutralized}}{\text{total vol HCl}} \times 100\%$$

   Solution: $[H_3O^+] = 10^{-1.3} = 0.05012 \text{ M} = 0.05 \text{ M}$

   $$4.00 \times 10^2 \text{ mg } Mg(OH)_2 \times \frac{\text{g } Mg(OH)_2}{1000 \text{ mg } Mg(OH)_2} \times \frac{1 \text{ mol } Mg(OH)_2}{58.326 \text{ g } Mg(OH)_2} \times \frac{2 \text{ mol OH}^-}{1 \text{ mol } Mg(OH)_2}$$

   $$\times \frac{1 \text{ mol } H_3O^+}{1 \text{ mol OH}^-} \times \frac{1 \text{ } L}{0.0501 \text{ mol } H_3O^+} \times \frac{1000 \text{ mL}}{L} = 273.8 \text{ mL} = 3 \times 10^2 \text{ mL neutralized}$$

   The stomach contains 2.00×10^2 mL HCl at pH $= 1.3$, and 4.00×10^2 mg will neutralize 274 mL of pH 1.3 HCl; so all of the stomach acid will be neutralized.

15.95 **Given:** pH of Great Lakes acid rain $= 4.5$, West Coast $= 5.4$
   Find: $[H_3O^+]$ and ratio of Great Lakes/West Coast
   Conceptual Plan: pH $\rightarrow$ $[H_3O^+]$ and then ratio of $[H_3O^+]$ Great Lakes to West Coast
   $$pH = -\log[H_3O^+]$$

Solution: Great Lakes: $[H_3O^+] = 10^{-4.5} = \underline{3}.16 \times 10^{-5}$ M   West Coast: $[H_3O^+] = 10^{-5.4} = \underline{3}.98 \times 10^{-6}$ M

$$\frac{\text{Great Lakes}}{\text{West Coast}} = \frac{3.16 \times 10^{-5} \text{ M}}{3.98 \times 10^{-6} \text{ M}} = \underline{7}.94 = 8 \text{ times more acidic}$$

15.97   **Given:** 6.5×10^2 mg aspirin, 8 oz water, $pK_a = 3.5$ **Find:** pH of solution
       Conceptual Plan:
       mg aspirin → g aspirin → mol aspirin and ounces → quart → L and then [aspirin] and pK_a

$$\frac{1 \text{ g aspirin}}{1000 \text{ mg}} \quad \frac{1 \text{ mol aspirin}}{180.15 \text{ g}} \qquad\qquad \frac{1 \text{ qt}}{32 \text{ oz}} \quad \frac{1 \text{ L}}{1.0567 \text{ qt}} \quad \frac{\text{mol aspirin}}{\text{L soln}} \quad pK_a = -\log K_a$$

       → K_a. Write a balanced reaction. Prepare an ICE table, represent the change with x, sum the table, determine the equilibrium values, put the equilibrium values in the equilibrium expression, and solve for x. Determine $[H_3O^+]$ → pH.

$$pH = -\log[H_3O^+]$$

Solution: $\dfrac{6.5 \times 10^2 \text{ mg aspirin}}{8 \text{ oz}} \times \dfrac{1 \text{ g aspirin}}{1000 \text{ mg aspirin}} \times \dfrac{1 \text{ mol aspirin}}{180.15 \text{ g}} \times \dfrac{32 \text{ oz}}{1 \text{ qt}} \times \dfrac{1.0567 \text{ qt}}{1 \text{ L}} = 0.015\underline{3}$ M

$$K_a = 10^{-3.5} = \underline{3}.16 \times 10^{-4}$$

$$\text{aspirin}(aq) + H_2O(l) \rightleftharpoons H_3O^+(aq) + \text{aspirin}^-(aq)$$

	[aspirin]	[H$_3$O$^+$]	[aspirin$^-$]
Initial	0.015$\underline{3}$ M	0.0	0.0
Change	$-x$	x	x
Equil	0.015$\underline{3}$ $-x$	x	x

$$K_a = \frac{[H_3O^+][\text{aspirin}^-]}{[\text{aspirin}]} = \frac{(x)(x)}{(0.0153 - x)} = \underline{3}.16 \times 10^{-4}$$

$$x^2 + 3.16 \times 10^{-4}x - 4.83 \times 10^{-6} = 0 \quad x = \underline{2}.04 \times 10^{-3} \text{ M} = [H_3O^+]$$

$$pH = -\log(\underline{2}.04 \times 10^{-3}) = 2.69 = 2.7$$

15.99   (a)   **Given:** 0.0100 M HClO$_4$ **Find:** pH
             Conceptual Plan: [HClO$_4$] → [H$_3$O$^+$] → pH

$$[HClO_4] \rightarrow [H_3O^+] \quad pH = -\log[H_3O^+]$$

             Solution: HClO$_4$ is a strong acid so: 0.0100 M HClO$_4$ = 0.0100 M H$_3$O$^+$ pH = $-\log(0.0100)$ = 2.000

       (b)   **Given:** 0.115 M HClO$_2$, $K_a = 1.1 \times 10^{-2}$ **Find:** pH
             Conceptual Plan: Write a balanced reaction. Prepare an ICE table, represent the change with x, sum the table, determine the equilibrium values, put the equilibrium values in the equilibrium expression, and solve for x. Determine $[H_3O^+]$ and pH.
             Solution: $HClO_2(aq) + H_2O(l) \rightleftharpoons H_3O^+(aq) + ClO_2^-(aq)$

	[HClO$_2$]	[H$_3$O$^+$]	[ClO$_2^-$]
Initial	0.115 M	0.0	0.0
Change	$-x$	x	x
Equil	0.115 $-x$	x	x

$$K_a = \frac{[H_3O^+][ClO_2^-]}{[HClO_2]} = \frac{(x)(x)}{(0.115 - x)} = 1.1 \times 10^{-2}$$

Assume that x is small compared to 0.115.

$$x^2 = (1.1 \times 10^{-2})(0.115) \quad x = 0.035\underline{6} \text{ M} = [H_3O^+]$$

Check assumption: $\dfrac{0.035\underline{6}}{0.115} \times 100\% = 31.0\%$; assumption is not valid; solve with the quadratic equation.

$$x^2 + 1.1 \times 10^{-2}\,x - 0.001265 = 0$$
$$x = 0.03\underline{0}49 \text{ or } -0.0415$$
$$\text{pH} = -\log(0.03\underline{0}49) = 1.52$$

(c) **Given:** 0.045 M Sr(OH)$_2$ **Find:** pH
Conceptual Plan: $[\text{Sr(OH)}_2] \rightarrow [\text{OH}^-] \rightarrow [\text{H}_3\text{O}^+] \rightarrow \text{pH}$

$$K_w = [\text{H}_3\text{O}^+][\text{OH}^-] \quad \text{pH} = -\log[\text{H}_3\text{O}^+] \quad \text{pH} + \text{pOH} = 14$$

Solution: Sr(OH)$_2$ is a strong base so: $[\text{OH}^-] = 2[\text{Sr(OH)}_2] = 2(0.045) = 0.090$ M

$$[\text{H}_3\text{O}^+] = \frac{K_w}{[\text{OH}^-]} = \frac{1.0 \times 10^{-14}}{0.090 \text{ M}} = 1.\underline{1}1 \times 10^{-13} \text{ M}$$

$$\text{pH} = -\log(1.\underline{1}1 \times 10^{-13}) = 12.95$$

(d) **Given:** 0.0852 KCN, K_a(HCN) $= 4.9 \times 10^{-10}$ **Find:** pH
Conceptual Plan: Identify each species and determine which will contribute to pH. Write a balanced reaction. Prepare an ICE table, represent the change with x, sum the table, determine the equilibrium values, put the equilibrium values in the equilibrium expression, and solve for x. Determine $[\text{OH}^-] \rightarrow \text{pOH} \rightarrow \text{pH}$.

$$\text{pOH} = -\log[\text{OH}^-] \quad \text{pH} + \text{pOH} = 14$$

Solution: K$^+$ is the counterion of a strong base; therefore, it is pH-neutral. CN$^-$ is the conjugate base of a weak acid; therefore, it is basic.

$$\text{CN}^-(aq) + \text{H}_2\text{O}(l) \rightleftharpoons \text{HCN}(aq) + \text{OH}^-(aq)$$

	[CN$^-$]	[HCN]	[OH$^-$]
Initial	0.0852 M	0.0	0.0
Change	$-x$	x	x
Equil	$0.0852 - x$	x	x

$$K_b = \frac{K_w}{K_a} = \frac{1.0 \times 10^{-14}}{4.9 \times 10^{-10}} = 2.\underline{0}4 \times 10^{-5} = \frac{(x)(x)}{(0.0852 - x)}$$

Assume that x is small.

$$x = 1.\underline{3}2 \times 10^{-3} \text{ M} = [\text{OH}^-] \quad \text{pOH} = -\log(1.\underline{3}2 \times 10^{-3}) = 2.88$$
$$\text{pH} = 14.00 - 2.88 = 11.12$$

(e) **Given:** 0.155 NH$_4$Cl, K_b (NH$_3$) $= 1.76 \times 10^{-5}$ **Find:** pH
Conceptual Plan: Identify each species and determine which will contribute to pH. Write a balanced reaction. Prepare an ICE table, represent the change with x, sum the table, determine the equilibrium values, put the equilibrium values in the equilibrium expression, and solve for x. Determine $[\text{H}_3\text{O}^+] \rightarrow \text{pH}$.
Solution: NH$_4{}^+$ is the conjugate acid of a weak base; therefore, it is acidic. Cl$^-$ is the conjugate base of a strong acid; therefore, it is pH-neutral.

$$\text{NH}_4{}^+(aq) + \text{H}_2\text{O}(l) \rightleftharpoons \text{NH}_3(aq) + \text{H}_3\text{O}^+(aq)$$

	[NH$_4{}^+$]	[NH$_3$]	[H$_3$O$^+$]
Initial	0.155 M	0.0	0.0
Change	$-x$	x	x
Equil	$0.155 - x$	x	x

$$K_a = \frac{K_w}{K_b} = \frac{1 \times 10^{-14}}{1.76 \times 10^{-5}} = 5.6\underline{8}2 \times 10^{-10} = \frac{(x)(x)}{(0.155 - x)}$$

Assume that x is small.

$$x = 9.3\underline{8}5 \times 10^{-6} \text{ M} = [\text{H}_3\text{O}^+] \qquad \text{pH} = -\log(9.3\underline{8}5 \times 10^{-6}) = 5.028$$

15.101　(a)　sodium cyanide = NaCN, nitric acid = HNO_3
　　　　　　$H^+(aq) + CN^-(aq) \rightleftharpoons HCN(aq)$

　　　　(b)　ammonium chloride = NH_4Cl, sodium hydroxide = NaOH
　　　　　　$NH_4^+(aq) + OH^-(aq) \rightleftharpoons NH_3(aq) + H_2O(l)$

　　　　(c)　sodium cyanide = NaCN, ammonium bromide = NH_4Br
　　　　　　$NH_4^+(aq) + CN^-(aq) \rightleftharpoons NH_3(aq) + HCN(aq)$

　　　　(d)　potassium hydrogen sulfate = $KHSO_4$, lithium acetate = $LiC_2H_3O_2$
　　　　　　$HSO_4^-(aq) + C_2H_3O_2^-(aq) \rightleftharpoons SO_4^{2-}(aq) + HC_2H_3O_2(aq)$

　　　　(e)　sodium hypochlorite = NaClO, ammonia $\overset{\pm}{=}$ NH_3
　　　　　　No reaction; both are bases.

15.103　**Given:** 1.00 M urea, pH = 7.050　**Find:** K_a Hurea$^+$
　　　　Conceptual Plan: pH → pOH → [OH$^-$] → K_b(urea) → K_a(Hurea$^+$). Write a balanced reaction.
　　　　　　　　　　　　　$pH + pOH = 14$　　$pOH = -\log[OH^-]$
　　　　Prepare an ICE table, represent the change with x, sum the table, determine the equilibrium values, put the equilibrium values in the equilibrium expression, and determine K_b.
　　　　Solution: $pOH = 14.000 - 7.050 = 6.950$　　$[OH^-] = 10^{-6.950} = 1.122 \times 10^{-7}$ M

$$urea(aq) + H_2O(l) \rightleftharpoons Hurea^+(aq) + OH^-(aq)$$

	[urea]	[Hurea$^+$]	[OH$^-$]
Initial	1.00	0.0	0.0
Change	$-x$	x	x
Equil	$1.00 - 1.1\underline{2}2 \times 10^{-7}$	$1.1\underline{2}2 \times 10^{-7}$	$1.1\underline{2}2 \times 10^{-7}$

$$K_b = \frac{[Hurea^+][OH^-]}{[urea]} = \frac{(1.1\underline{2}2 \times 10^{-7})(1.1\underline{2}2 \times 10^{-7})}{(1.00 - 1.1\underline{2}2 \times 10^{-7})} = 1.2\underline{5}89 \times 10^{-14}$$

$$K_a = \frac{K_w}{K_b} = \frac{1.00 \times 10^{-14}}{1.2\underline{5}89 \times 10^{-14}} = 0.79\underline{4}3 = 0.794$$

15.105　**Given:** $Ca(Lact)_2$, $[Ca^{2+}] = 0.26$ M, pH = 8.40　**Find:** K_a lactic acid
　　　　Conceptual Plan: $[Ca^{2+}] →$ [Lact$^-$]; determine K_b lactate ion. Prepare an ICE table, represent the
　　　　　　　　　　　$\dfrac{2 \text{ mol lactate ion}}{1 \text{ mol } Ca^{2+}}$

　　　　change with x, sum the table, and determine the equilibrium constant. $K_b → K_a$
　　　　　　　　　　　　　　　　　　　　$K_a = \dfrac{K_w}{K_b}$

　　　　Solution: 0.26 M $Ca^{2+} \left(\dfrac{2 \text{ mol Lact}^-}{1 \text{ mol } Ca^{2+}} \right) = 0.52$ M Lact$^-$

$$Lact^-(aq) + H_2O(l) \rightleftharpoons HLact(aq) + OH^-(aq)$$

	[Lact$^-$]	[HLact]	[OH$^-$]
Initial	0.52 M	0	0
Change	$-x$	$+x$	$+x$
Equil	$0.52 - x$	x	x

$$pH = 8.40 \quad [H_3O^+] = 10^{-8.40} = 4.0 \times 10^{-9} \quad [OH^-] = \frac{1.0 \times 10^{-14}}{4.0 \times 10^{-9}} = 2.5 \times 10^{-6} = x$$

$$K_b = \frac{[HLact][OH^-]}{[Lact^-]} = \frac{(2.5 \times 10^{-6})(2.5 \times 10^{-6})}{(0.52 - 2.5 \times 10^{-6})} = 1.2 \times 10^{-11}$$

$$K_a = \frac{K_w}{K_b} = \frac{(1.0 \times 10^{-14})}{(1.2 \times 10^{-11})} = 8.3 \times 10^{-4}$$

Challenge Problems

15.107   The calculation is incorrect because it neglects the contribution from the autoionization of water. HI is a strong acid, so $[H_3O^+]$ from HI $= 1.0 \times 10^{-7}$.

$$H_2O(l) + H_2O(l) \rightleftharpoons H_3O^+(aq) + OH^-(aq)$$

	$[H_2O]$	$[H_3O^+]$	$[OH^-]$
Initial		1×10^{-7}	0.0
Change	$-x$	x	x
Equil		$1 \times 10^{-7} + x$	x

$K_w = [H_3O^+][OH^-] = 1.0 \times 10^{-14}$
$\quad (1 \times 10^{-7} + x)(x) = 1.0 \times 10^{-14} \quad x^2 + 1 \times 10^{-7}x - 1.0 \times 10^{-14} = 0$
$x = 6.18 \times 10^{-8}$
$[H_3O^+] = (1 \times 10^{-7} + x) = (1 \times 10^{-7} + 6.18 \times 10^{-8}) = 1.618 \times 10^{-7}$
$pH = -\log(1.618 \times 10^{-7}) = 6.79$

15.109   **Given:** 0.00115 M HCl, 0.01000 M $HClO_2$, $K_a = 1.1 \times 10^{-2}$ **Find:** pH
Conceptual Plan: Use HCl to determine $[H_3O^+]$. Use $[H_3O^+]$ and $HClO_2$ to determine dissociation of $HClO_2$. Write a balanced reaction, prepare an ICE table, calculate equilibrium concentrations, and plug into the equilibrium expression.

Solution: 0.00115 M HCl $= 0.00115$ M H_3O^+

$$HClO_2(aq) + H_2O(l) \rightleftharpoons H_3O^+(aq) + ClO_2^-(aq)$$

	$[HClO_2]$	$[H_3O^+]$	$[ClO_2^-]$
Initial	0.0100 M	0.00115 M	0.0
Change	$-x$	x	x
Equil	$0.01000 - x$	$0.00115 + x$	x

$K_a = \dfrac{[H_3O^+][ClO_2^-]}{[HClO_2]} = \dfrac{(0.00115 + x)(x)}{(0.0100 - x)} = 1.1 \times 10^{-2}$

$x^2 + 0.01215x - 1.1 \times 10^{-4} = 0 \quad x = 0.006045$
$[H_3O^+] = 0.00115 + 0.006045 = 0.007195$
$pH = -\log(0.007195) = 2.14$

15.111   **Given:** 1.0 M HA, $K_a = 1.0 \times 10^{-8}$, $K = 4.0$ for reaction 2   **Find:** $[H^+]$, $[A^-]$, $[HA_2^-]$
Conceptual Plan: Combine reaction 1 and reaction 2; then determine the equilibrium expression and the value of K. Prepare an ICE table, calculate equilibrium concentrations, and plug into the equilibrium expression.

Solution:

$$HA(aq) \rightleftharpoons H^+(aq) + A^-(aq) \qquad K = 1.0 \times 10^{-8}$$
$$HA(aq) + A^-(aq) \rightleftharpoons HA_2^+(aq) \qquad K = 4.0$$
$$2\,HA(aq) \rightleftharpoons H^+(aq) + HA_2^+(aq) \qquad K = 4.0 \times 10^{-8}$$

	$[HA]$	$[H^+]$	$[HA_2^+]$
Initial	1.0 M	0.0	0.0
Change	$-2x$	x	x
Equil	$1.0 - 2x$	x	x

$K = \dfrac{[H^+][HA_2^-]}{[HA]^2} = 4.0 \times 10^{-8} = \dfrac{(x)(x)}{(1.0 - 2x)^2}$

Take the square root of both sides of the equation. $x = 1.\underline{9}992 \times 10^{-4}$

$$HA(aq) \rightleftharpoons H^+(aq) + A^-(aq) \qquad K = 1.0 \times 10^{-8}$$

	[HA]	[H⁺]	[A⁻]
Initial	1.0 M	1.9992×10^{-4}	0.0
Change	$-y$	y	y
Equil	$1.0 - y$	$1.9992 \times 10^{-4} + y$	y

$$K = \frac{[H^+][A^-]}{[HA]} = 1.0 \times 10^{-8} = \frac{(1.9992 \times 10^{-4} + y)(y)}{(1.0 - y)}$$

Assume y is small compared to 1.0

$y^2 + 1.9992 \times 10^{-4}y - 1 \times 10^{-8} = 0 \qquad y = 4.\underline{1}4 \times 10^{-5}$

$[H^+] = x + y = 1.\underline{9}992 \times 10^{-4} + 4.\underline{2}9 \times 10^{-5} = 2.4 \times 10^{-4}$

$[A^-] = y = 4.14 \times 10^{-5}$

$[HA_2^-] = x = 2.0 \times 10^{-4}$

15.113   **Given:** 0.200 mol NH₄CN, 1.00 L, K_b (NH₃) $= 1.76 \times 10^{-5}$, K_a (HCN) $= 4.9 \times 10^{-10}$ **Find:** pH
Conceptual Plan: K_b NH₃ → K_a NH₄⁺; K_a HCN → K_b CN⁻ **Prepare an ICE table, represent the**

$$K_a K_b = K_w$$

change with x, sum the table, and determine the equilibrium conditions.

Solution: $K_a(\text{NH}_4^+) = \dfrac{1.0 \times 10^{-14}}{1.76 \times 10^{-5}} = 5.68 \times 10^{-10} \qquad K_b(\text{CN}^-) = \dfrac{1.0 \times 10^{-14}}{4.9 \times 10^{-10}} = 2.0 \times 10^{-5}$

0.200 M NH₄CN = 0.200 M NH₄⁺ and 0.200 M CN⁻

Because the value for K for CN⁻ is greater than the K for NH₄⁺, the CN⁻ reaction will be larger and the solution will be basic.

$$CN^-(aq) + H_2O(l) \rightleftharpoons HCN(aq) + OH^-(aq)$$

	[CN⁻]	[HCN]	[OH⁻]
Initial	0.200 M	0	0
Change	$-x$	$+x$	$+x$
Equil	$0.200 - x$	x	x

$K_b = \dfrac{[\text{HCN}][\text{OH}^-]}{[\text{CN}^-]} \qquad 2.0 \times 10^{-5} = \dfrac{(x)(x)}{(0.200 - x)}$ Solve using the quadratic equation.

$x = 0.0020 = [\text{OH}^-]$

$[H_3O^+] = \dfrac{1.0 \times 10^{-14}}{0.0020} = 5.0 \times 10^{-12} \quad \text{pH} = -\log(5.0 \times 10^{-12}) = 11.30$

15.115   **Given:** mixture Na₂CO₃ and NaHCO₃ = 82.2 g, 1.0 L, pH = 9.95, K_a (H₂CO₃) $= K_{a_1} = 4.3 \times 10^{-7}$,
$K_{a_2} = 5.6 \times 10^{-11}$
Find: mass NaHCO₃
Conceptual Plan: Let x = g NaHCO₃, y = g Na₂CO₃ → **mol NaHCO₃, Na₂CO₃** → **[NaHCO₃], [Na₂CO₃]**

$$\frac{1 \text{ mol NaHCO}_3}{84.01 \text{ g}} \qquad \frac{1 \text{ mol Na}_2\text{CO}_3}{105.99 \text{ g}} \qquad M = \frac{\text{mol}}{L}$$

→ **[HCO₃⁻], [CO₃²⁻], K_a (HCO₃⁻)** → **K_b(CO₃²⁻). Prepare an ICE table, represent the change with z,**

$$\frac{1 \text{ mol HCO}_3^-}{1 \text{ mol NaHCO}_3} \quad \frac{1 \text{ mol CO}_3^{2-}}{1 \text{ mol Na}_2\text{CO}_3} \quad K_b = \frac{K_w}{K_a}$$

sum the table, and determine the equilibrium conditions.

Solution: Let x = g NaHCO₃ and y = g Na₂CO₃ $x + y = 82.2$, so $y = 82.2 - x$

$\text{mol NaHCO}_3 = x \text{ g } \cancel{\text{NaHCO}_3}\left(\dfrac{1 \text{ mol}}{84.01 \text{ g } \cancel{\text{NaHCO}_3}}\right) = \dfrac{x}{84.01}$

$$[HCO_3^-] = \left(\frac{\frac{x}{84.01}\ \text{mol NaHCO}_3}{1\ \text{L}}\right)\frac{1\ \text{mol HCO}_3^-}{1\ \text{mol NaHCO}_3} = \frac{x}{84.01}\ \text{M HCO}_3^-$$

$$\text{mol Na}_2\text{CO}_3 = 82.2 - x\ \text{g Na}_2\text{CO}_3\left(\frac{1\ \text{mol}}{105.99\ \text{g Na}_2\text{CO}_3}\right) = \frac{82.2 - x}{105.99}\ \text{Na}_2\text{CO}_3$$

$$[CO_3^{2-}] = \left(\frac{\frac{82.2 - x}{105.99}\ \text{mol Na}_2\text{CO}_3}{1\ \text{L}}\right)\frac{1\ \text{mol CO}_3^{2-}}{1\ \text{mol Na}_2\text{CO}_3} = \frac{82.2 - x}{105.99}\ \text{M CO}_3^{2-}$$

Because the pH of the solution is basic, it is the hydrolysis of CO_3^{2-} that dominates in the solution.

$$K_b(CO_3^{2-}) = \frac{1.0 \times 10^{-14}}{5.6 \times 10^{-11}} = 1.79 \times 10^{-4} \text{ and } [H_3O^+] = 10^{-9.95} = 1.12 \times 10^{-10} \qquad [OH^-] = \frac{1.0 \times 10^{-14}}{1.12 \times 10^{-10}}$$

$$= 8.93 \times 10^{-5}$$

$$CO_3^{2-}(aq) + H_2O(l) \rightleftharpoons HCO_3^-(aq) + OH^-(aq)$$

	$[CO_3^{2-}]$	$[HCO_3^-]$	$[OH^-]$
Initial	$\dfrac{82.2 - x}{105.99}$	$\dfrac{x}{84.01}$	
Change	$-z$	$+z$	
Equil	$\left(\dfrac{82.2 - x}{105.99}\right) - z$	$\left(\dfrac{x}{84.01}\right) + z$	8.93×10^{-5}

$$K_b(CO_3^{2-}) = 1.79 \times 10^{-4} = \frac{[HCO_3^-][OH^-]}{[CO_3^{2-}]} = \frac{\left(\left(\dfrac{x}{84.01}\right) - z\right)(8.93 \times 10^{-5})}{\left(\dfrac{82.2 - x}{105.99}\right) - z} \text{ Assume that } z \text{ is small.}$$

$$\frac{1.79 \times 10^{-4}}{8.93 \times 10^{-5}} = \frac{\left(\dfrac{x}{84.01}\right)}{\left(\dfrac{82.2 - x}{105.99}\right)} \qquad x = 50.38 = 50.4\ \text{g NaHCO}_3$$

Conceptual Problems

15.117   Solution b would be most acidic.
   (a)   0.0100 M HCl (strong acid) and 0.0100 M KOH (strong base) because the concentrations are equal, the acid and base will completely neutralize each other, and the resulting solution will be pH-neutral.
   (b)   0.0100 M HF (weak acid) and 0.0100 M KBr (salt). K_a (HF) $= 3.5 \times 10^{-4}$. The weak acid will produce an acidic solution. K^+ is the counterion of a strong base and is pH-neutral. Br^- is the conjugate base of a strong acid and is pH-neutral.
   (c)   0.0100 M NH_4Cl (salt) and 0.0100 M CH_3NH_3Br. $K_b(NH_3) = 1.8 \times 10^{-5}$, $K_b(CH_3NH_2) = 4.4 \times 10^{-4}$. NH_4^+ is the conjugate acid of a weak base, and $CH_3NH_3^+$ is the conjugate acid of a weak base. Cl^- and Br^- are the conjugate bases of strong acids and will be pH-neutral. The solution will be acidic. However, because the K_a for the conjugate acid in this solution is smaller than the K_a for HF, the solution will be acidic, but not as acidic as HF.
   (d)   0.100 M NaCN (salt) and 0.100 M $CaCl_2$. Na^+ and Ca^{2+} ions are the counterions of strong bases; therefore, they are pH-neutral. Cl^- is the conjugate base of a strong acid and is pH-neutral. CN^- is the conjugate base of a weak acid and will produce a basic solution.

15.119 $CH_3COOH < CH_2ClCOOH < CHCl_2COOH < CCl_3COOH$
   Because Cl is more electronegative than is H, as you add Cl, you increase the number of electronegative atoms, which pulls the electron density away from the O—H group, polarizing the O—H bond, making it more acidic.

Questions for Group Work

15.121   Acids have the following general properties: a sour taste, the ability to dissolve many metals, the ability to turn blue litmus paper red, and the ability to neutralize bases.

Bases have the following general properties: a bitter taste, a slippery feel, the ability to turn red litmus paper blue, and the ability to neutralize acids.

15.123   (a)   A strong acid completely ionizes in solution, and the pH will equal the $-\log$ of the acid concentration. An example is HCl. A weak acid only partially ionizes in solution and the pH will be greater than the $-\log$ of the acid concentration. An example is HF. Table 15.3 lists the strong acids. If the acid is not in this table, it is a weak acid.

(b)   For a strong acid, HA, pH $= -\log[\text{HA}]$.

(c)   For a weak acid, write a balanced reaction for the ionization of the acid. Prepare an ICE table; represent the change with x; sum the table and determine the equilibrium values; put the equilibrium values in the equilibrium expression and solve for x. Finally, determine $[\text{H}_3\text{O}^+]$ and pH ($-\log[\text{H}_3\text{O}^+]$).

(d)   Since $K_a \times K_b = K_w$, $K_b = K_w/K_a$. The larger the K_a the smaller the K_b.

(e)   Since $K_w = [\text{H}_3\text{O}^+] \times [\text{OH}^-]$, $[\text{H}_3\text{O}^+] = K_w/[\text{OH}^-]$. The larger the $[\text{OH}^-]$ the smaller the $[\text{H}_3\text{O}^+]$.

15.125   An Arrhenius acid is a substance that produces H^+ in aqueous solution. An example is HCl.

A Bronsted–Lowry base is a proton (H^+) acceptor. Examples are H_2O and F^-.

A Lewis acid is an electron pair acceptor. An example is BF_3.

16 Aqueous Ionic Equilibrium

The Common Ion Effect and Buffers

16.1   The only solution in which HNO_2 will ionize less is (d) 0.10 M $NaNO_2$. It is the only solution that generates a common ion NO_2^- with nitrous acid.

16.3   (a)   **Given:** 0.15 M $HCHO_2$ and 0.10 M $NaCHO_2$ **Find:** pH **Other:** $K_a(HCHO_2) = 1.8 \times 10^{-4}$
Conceptual Plan: M $NaCHO_2 \rightarrow$ M CHO_2^- then M $HCHO_2$, M $CHO_2^- \rightarrow [H_3O^+] \rightarrow$ pH

$$NaCHO_2(aq) \rightarrow Na^+(aq) + CHO_2^-(aq) \qquad \text{ICE table} \qquad pH = -\log[H_3O^+]$$

Solution: Because one CHO_2^- ion is generated for each $NaCHO_2$, $[CHO_2^-] = 0.10$ M CHO_2^-.

$$HCHO_2(aq) + H_2O(l) \rightleftharpoons H_3O^+(aq) + CHO_2^-(aq)$$

	[HCHO₂]	[H₃O⁺]	[CHO₂⁻]
Initial	0.15	≈0.00	0.10
Change	−x	+x	+x
Equil	0.15 − x	+x	0.10 + x

$$K_a = \frac{[H_3O^+][CHO_2^-]}{[HCHO_2]} = 1.8 \times 10^{-4} = \frac{x(0.10 + x)}{0.15 - x} \text{ Assume that } x \text{ is}$$

small $(x \ll 0.10 < 0.15)$, so $\dfrac{x(0.10 + \cancel{x})}{0.15 - \cancel{x}} = 1.8 \times 10^{-4} = \dfrac{x(0.10)}{0.15}$ and

$x = 2.7 \times 10^{-4}$ M $= [H_3O^+]$. Confirm that the more stringent assumption is valid.

$\dfrac{2.7 \times 10^{-4}}{0.10} \times 100\% = 0.27\%$, so the assumption is valid. Finally,

$pH = -\log[H_3O^+] = -\log(2.7 \times 10^{-4}) = 3.57$.

Check: The units (none) are correct. The magnitude of the answer makes physical sense because pH should be greater than $-\log(0.15) = 0.82$ because this is a weak acid and there is a common ion effect.

(b)   **Given:** 0.12 M NH_3 and 0.18 M NH_4Cl **Find:** pH   **Other:** $K_b(NH_3) = 1.76 \times 10^{-5}$
Conceptual Plan: M $NH_4Cl \rightarrow$ M NH_4^+ then M NH_3, M $NH_4^+ \rightarrow [OH^-] \rightarrow [H_3O^+] \rightarrow$ pH

$$NH_4Cl(aq) \rightarrow NH_4^+(aq) + Cl^-(aq) \qquad \text{ICE table} \quad K_w = [H_3O^+][OH^-] \quad pH = -\log[H_3O^+]$$

Solution: Because one NH_4^+ ion is generated for each NH_4Cl, $[NH_4^+] = 0.18$ M NH_4^+.

$$NH_3(aq) + H_2O(l) \rightleftharpoons NH_4^+(aq) + OH^-(aq)$$

	[NH₃]	[NH₄⁺]	[OH⁻]
Initial	0.12	0.18	≈0.00
Change	−x	+x	+x
Equil	0.12 − x	0.18 + x	+x

$$K_b = \frac{[NH_4^-][OH^-]}{[NH_3]} = 1.76 \times 10^{-5} = \frac{(0.18 + x)x}{0.12 - x}$$

Copyright © 2016 Pearson Education, Inc.

Assume that x is small ($x \ll 0.12 < 0.18$), so $\dfrac{(0.18 + \cancel{x})x}{0.12 - \cancel{x}} = 1.76 \times 10^{-5} = \dfrac{(0.18)x}{0.12}$ and

$x = 1.\underline{1}73333 \times 10^{-5}\,\text{M} = [\text{OH}^-]$. Confirm that the more stringent assumption is valid.

$\dfrac{1.\underline{1}73333 \times 10^{-5}}{0.12} \times 100\% = 9.8 \times 10^{-3}\%$, so the assumption is valid.

$K_w = [\text{H}_3\text{O}^+][\text{OH}^-]$, so $[\text{H}_3\text{O}^+] = \dfrac{K_w}{[\text{OH}^-]} = \dfrac{1.0 \times 10^{-14}}{1.\underline{1}73333 \times 10^{-5}} = 8.\underline{5}2273 \times 10^{-10}\,\text{M}$.

Finally, $\text{pH} = -\log[\text{H}_3\text{O}^+] = -\log(8.\underline{5}2273 \times 10^{-10}) = 9.07$

Check: The units (none) are correct. The magnitude of the answer makes physical sense because the pH should be less than $14 + \log(0.12) = 13.1$ because this is a weak base and there is a common ion effect.

16.5   **Given:** 0.15 M $\text{HC}_7\text{H}_5\text{O}_2$ in pure water and in 0.10 M $\text{NaC}_7\text{H}_5\text{O}_2$
Find: % ionization in both solutions **Other:** $K_a(\text{HC}_7\text{H}_5\text{O}_2) = 6.5 \times 10^{-5}$
Conceptual Plan: pure water: M $\text{HC}_7\text{H}_5\text{O}_2$ $\rightarrow$ [H_3O^+] $\rightarrow$ % ionization then in $\text{NaC}_7\text{H}_5\text{O}_2$ solution:

$$\text{ICE table} \qquad \% \text{ ionization} = \frac{[\text{H}_3\text{O}^+]_{\text{equil}}}{[\text{HC}_7\text{H}_5\text{O}_2]_0} \times 100\%$$

M $\text{NaC}_7\text{H}_5\text{O}_2$ $\rightarrow$ M $\text{C}_7\text{H}_5\text{O}_2{}^-$ then M $\text{HC}_7\text{H}_5\text{O}_2$, M $\text{C}_7\text{H}_5\text{O}_2{}^-$ $\rightarrow$ [H_3O^+] $\rightarrow$ % ionization

$$\text{NaC}_7\text{H}_5\text{O}_2(aq) \rightarrow \text{Na}^+(aq) + \text{C}_7\text{H}_5\text{O}_2{}^-(aq) \qquad\qquad \text{ICE table} \qquad \% \text{ ionization} = \frac{[\text{H}_3\text{O}^+]_{\text{equil}}}{[\text{HC}_7\text{H}_5\text{O}_2]_0} \times 100\%$$

Solution: in pure water:
$$\text{HC}_7\text{H}_5\text{O}_2(aq) + \text{H}_2\text{O}(l) \rightleftharpoons \text{H}_3\text{O}^+(aq) + \text{C}_7\text{H}_5\text{O}_2{}^-(aq)$$

	[$\text{HC}_7\text{H}_5\text{O}_2$]	[H_3O^+]	[$\text{C}_7\text{H}_5\text{O}_2{}^-$]
Initial	0.15	≈ 0.00	0.00
Change	$-x$	$+x$	$+x$
Equil	$0.15 - x$	$+x$	$+x$

$K_a = \dfrac{[\text{H}_3\text{O}^+][\text{C}_7\text{H}_5\text{O}_2{}^-]}{[\text{HC}_7\text{H}_5\text{O}_2]} = 6.5 \times 10^{-5} = \dfrac{x^2}{0.15 - x}$

Assume that x is small ($x \ll 0.10$), so $\dfrac{x^2}{0.15 - \cancel{x}} = 6.5 \times 10^{-5} = \dfrac{x^2}{0.15}$ and $x = 3.\underline{1}225 \times 10^{-3}\,\text{M} = [\text{H}_3\text{O}^+]$. Then

$\% \text{ ionization} = \dfrac{[\text{H}_3\text{O}^+]_{\text{equil}}}{[\text{HC}_7\text{H}_5\text{O}_2]_0} \times 100\% = \dfrac{3.\underline{1}225 \times 10^{-3}}{0.15} \times 100\% = 2.1\%$, which also confirms that the assumption

is valid (because it is less than 5%). In $\text{NaC}_7\text{H}_5\text{O}_2$ solution: Because one $\text{C}_7\text{H}_5\text{O}_2{}^-$ ion is generated for each $\text{NaC}_7\text{H}_5\text{O}_2$, $[\text{C}_7\text{H}_5\text{O}_2{}^-] = 0.10\,\text{M}\,\text{C}_7\text{H}_5\text{O}_2{}^-$.

$$\text{HC}_7\text{H}_5\text{O}_2(aq) + \text{H}_2\text{O}(l) \rightleftharpoons \text{H}_3\text{O}^+(aq) + \text{C}_7\text{H}_5\text{O}_2{}^-(aq)$$

	[$\text{HC}_7\text{H}_5\text{O}_2$]	[H_3O^+]	[$\text{C}_7\text{H}_5\text{O}_2{}^-$]
Initial	0.15	≈ 0.00	0.10
Change	$-x$	$+x$	$+x$
Equil	$0.15 - x$	$+x$	$0.10 + x$

$K_a = \dfrac{[\text{H}_3\text{O}^+][\text{C}_7\text{H}_5\text{O}_2{}^-]}{[\text{HC}_7\text{H}_5\text{O}_2]} = 6.5 \times 10^{-5} = \dfrac{x(0.10 + x)}{0.15 - x}$ Assume that x is small ($x \ll 0.10 < 0.15$), so

$\dfrac{x(0.10 + \cancel{x})}{0.15 - \cancel{x}} = 6.5 \times 10^{-5} = \dfrac{x(0.10)}{0.15}$ and $x = 9.\underline{7}5 \times 10^{-5}\,\text{M} = [\text{H}_3\text{O}^+]$. Then

$\% \text{ ionization} = \dfrac{[\text{H}_3\text{O}^+]_{\text{equil}}}{[\text{HC}_7\text{H}_5\text{O}_2]_0} \times 100\% = \dfrac{9.\underline{7}5 \times 10^{-5}}{0.15} \times 100\% = 0.065\%$, which also confirms that the assumption is valid (because it is less than 5%). The percent ionization in the sodium benzoate solution is less than that in pure water because of the common ion effect. An increase in one of the products (benzoate ion) shifts the equilibrium to the left, so less acid dissociates.

Check: The units (%) are correct. The magnitude of the answer makes physical sense because the acid is weak, so the percent ionization is low. With a common ion present, the percent ionization decreases.

16.7   (a)   **Given:** 0.15 M HF   **Find:** pH **Other:** $K_a(HF) = 3.5 \times 10^{-4}$
Conceptual Plan: M HF $\rightarrow$ **[H$_3$O$^+$]** $\rightarrow$ **pH**
ICE table   pH $= -\log[H_3O^+]$

Solution:

$$HF(aq) + H_2O(l) \rightleftharpoons H_3O^+(aq) + F^-(aq)$$

	[HF]	**[H$_3$O$^+$]**	**[F$^-$]**
Initial	0.15	≈ 0.00	0.00
Change	$-x$	$+x$	$+x$
Equil	$0.15 - x$	$+x$	$+x$

$K_a = \dfrac{[H_3O^+][F^-]}{[HF]} = 3.5 \times 10^{-4} = \dfrac{x^2}{0.15 - x}$ Assume that x is small ($x \ll 0.15$), so

$\dfrac{x^2}{0.15 - x} = 3.5 \times 10^{-4} = \dfrac{x^2}{0.15}$ and $x = 7.2457 \times 10^{-3}$ M $= [H_3O^+]$. Confirm that the

assumption is valid. $\dfrac{7.2457 \times 10^{-3}}{0.15} \times 100\% = 4.8\% < 5\%$, so the assumption is valid.

Finally, pH $= -\log[H_3O^+] = -\log(7.2457 \times 10^{-3}) = 2.14$.

Check: The units (none) are correct. The magnitude of the answer makes physical sense because the pH should be greater than $-\log(0.15) = 0.82$ because this is a weak acid.

   (b)   **Given:** 0.15 M NaF   **Find:** pH **Other:** $K_a(HF) = 3.5 \times 10^{-4}$
Conceptual Plan: M NaF $\rightarrow$ **M F$^-$ and K_a** $\rightarrow$ **K_b, then M F$^-$** $\rightarrow$ **[OH$^-$]** $\rightarrow$ **[H$_3$O$^+$]** $\rightarrow$ **pH**
NaF(aq) $\rightarrow$ Na$^+$(aq) + F$^-$(aq) $K_w = K_a K_b$ ICE table $K_w = [H_3O^+][OH^-]$ pH $= -\log[H_3O^+]$

Solution:
Because one F$^-$ ion is generated for each NaF, [F$^-$] = 0.15 M F$^-$. Because $K_w = K_a K_b$, rearrange to solve for K_b.

$K_b = \dfrac{K_w}{K_a} = \dfrac{1.0 \times 10^{-14}}{3.5 \times 10^{-4}} = 2.8571 \times 10^{-11}$

$$F^-(aq) + H_2O(l) \rightleftharpoons HF(aq) + OH^-(aq)$$

	[F$^-$]	**[HF]**	**[OH$^-$]**
Initial	0.15	0.00	≈ 0.00
Change	$-x$	$+x$	$+x$
Equil	$0.15 - x$	$+x$	$+x$

$K_b = \dfrac{[HF][OH^-]}{[F^-]} = 2.8571 \times 10^{-11} = \dfrac{x^2}{0.15 - x}$

Assume that x is small ($x \ll 0.15$), so $\dfrac{x^2}{0.15 - x} = 2.8571 \times 10^{-11} = \dfrac{x^2}{0.15}$ and $x = 2.0702 \times 10^{-6}$ M $=$

[OH$^-$].

Confirm that the assumption is valid. $\dfrac{2.0702 \times 10^{-6}}{0.15} \times 100\% = 0.0014\% < 5\%$, so the assumption is valid.

$K_w = [H_3O^+][OH^-]$, so $[H_3O^+] = \dfrac{K_w}{[OH^-]} = \dfrac{1.0 \times 10^{-14}}{2.0702 \times 10^{-6}} = 4.8305 \times 10^{-9}$ M.

Finally, $pH = -\log[H_3O^+] = -\log(4.8305 \times 10^{-9}) = 8.32$.

Check: The units (none) are correct. The magnitude of the answer makes physical sense because the pH should be slightly basic because the fluoride ion is a very weak base.

(c)   **Given:** 0.15 M HF and 0.15 M NaF   **Find:** pH **Other:** $K_a(HF) = 3.5 \times 10^{-4}$
     Conceptual Plan: M NaF $\rightarrow$ M F$^-$ then M HF, M F$^-$ $\rightarrow$ [H$_3$O$^+$] $\rightarrow$ pH

$$NaF(aq) \rightarrow Na^+(aq) + F^-(aq) \qquad\qquad ICE\ table \qquad pH = -\log[H_3O^+]$$

Solution: Because one F$^-$ ion is generated for each NaF, [F$^-$] = 0.15 M F$^-$.

$$HF(aq) + H_2O(l) \rightleftharpoons H_3O^+(aq) + F^-(aq)$$

	[HF]	**[H$_3$O$^+$]**	**[F$^-$]**
Initial	0.15	≈ 0.00	0.15
Change	$-x$	$+x$	$+x$
Equil	$0.15 - x$	$+x$	$0.15 + x$

$$K_a = \frac{[H_3O^+][F^-]}{[HF]} = 3.5 \times 10^{-4} = \frac{x(0.15 + x)}{0.15 - x}$$

Assume that x is small ($x \ll 0.15$), so

$$\frac{x(0.15 + \cancel{x})}{0.15 - \cancel{x}} = 3.5 \times 10^{-4} = \frac{x(\cancel{0.15})}{\cancel{0.15}} \text{ and } x = 3.5 \times 10^{-4}\ M = [H_3O^+].$$

Confirm that the assumption is valid. $\dfrac{3.5 \times 10^{-4}}{0.15} \times 100\% = 0.23\% < 5\%$, so the assumption is valid.

Finally, $pH = -\log[H_3O^+] = -\log(3.5 \times 10^{-4}) = 3.46$.

Check: The units (none) are correct. The magnitude of the answer makes physical sense because the pH should be greater than that in part (a) (2.14) because of the common ion effect suppressing the dissociation of the weak acid.

16.9   When an acid (such as HCl) is added, it will react with the conjugate base of the buffer system as follows: $HCl + NaC_2H_3O_2 \rightarrow HC_2H_3O_2 + NaCl$. When a base (such as NaOH) is added, it will react with the weak acid of the buffer system as follows: $NaOH + HC_2H_3O_2 \rightarrow H_2O + NaC_2H_3O_2$. The reaction generates the other buffer system component.

16.11   (a)   **Given:** 0.15 M HCHO$_2$ and 0.10 M NaCHO$_2$ **Find:** pH   **Other:** $K_a(HCHO_2) = 1.8 \times 10^{-4}$
     Conceptual Plan: Identify acid and base components then M NaCHO$_2$ $\rightarrow$ M CHO$_2^-$ then

$$acid = HCHO_2 \qquad base = CHO_2^- \qquad\qquad NaCHO_2(aq) \rightarrow Na^+(aq) + CHO_2^-(aq)$$

     K_a, M HCHO$_2$, M CHO$_2^-$ $\rightarrow$ pH.

$$pH = pK_a + \log\frac{[base]}{[acid]}$$

Solution: Acid = HCHO$_2$, so [acid] = [HCHO$_2$] = 0.15 M. Base = CHO$_2^-$. Because one CHO$_2^-$ ion is generated for each NaCHO$_2$, [CHO$_2^-$] = 0.10 M CHO$_2^-$ = [base]. Then

$$pH = pK_a + \log\frac{[base]}{[acid]} = -\log(1.8 \times 10^{-4}) + \log\frac{0.10\ M}{0.15\ M} = 3.57.$$

Note that to use the Henderson–Hasselbalch equation, the assumption that x is small must be valid. This was confirmed in Problem 16.3.

Check: The units (none) are correct. The magnitude of the answer makes physical sense because the pH should be less than the pK_a of the acid because there is more acid than base. The answer agrees with Problem 16.3.

(b)   **Given:** 0.12 M NH$_3$ and 0.18 M NH$_4$Cl   **Find:** pH   **Other:** $K_b(NH_3) = 1.76 \times 10^{-5}$
     Conceptual Plan: Identify acid and base components then M NH$_4$Cl $\rightarrow$ M NH$_4^+$ and K_b $\rightarrow$ pK_b $\rightarrow$ pK_a

$$acid = NH_4^+ \qquad base = NH_3 \qquad NH_4Cl(aq) \rightarrow NH_4^+(aq) + Cl^-(aq) \qquad pK_b = -\log K_b \qquad 14 = pK_a + pK_b$$

     then pK_a, M NH$_3$, M NH$_4^+$ $\rightarrow$ pH.

$$pH = pK_a + \log\frac{[base]}{[acid]}$$

Solution: Base $= NH_3$, [base] $= [NH_3] = 0.12$ M. Acid $= NH_4^+$. Because one NH_4^+ ion is generated for each NH_4Cl, $[NH_4^+] = 0.18$ M $NH_4^+ = $ [acid].

Because K_b $(NH_3) = 1.76 \times 10^{-5}$, $pK_b = -\log K_b = -\log(1.76 \times 10^{-5}) = 4.75$. Because $14 = pK_a + pK_b$,

$$pK_a = 14 - pK_b = 14 - 4.75 = 9.25. \text{ Then } pH = pK_a + \log \frac{[\text{base}]}{[\text{acid}]} = 9.25 + \log \frac{0.12 \text{ M}}{0.18 \text{ M}} = 9.07.$$

Note that to use the Henderson–Hasselbalch equation, the assumption that x is small must be valid. This was confirmed in Problem 16.3.

Check: The units (none) are correct. The magnitude of the answer makes physical sense because the pH should be less than the pK_a of the acid because there is more acid than base. The answer agrees with Problem 16.3 within the error of the value.

16.13 (a) **Given:** 0.125 M HClO and 0.150 M KClO **Find:** pH **Other:** $K_a(\text{HClO}) = 2.9 \times 10^{-8}$
Conceptual Plan: Identify acid and base components then M KClO → M ClO⁻ then

$$\text{acid} = \text{HClO} \qquad \text{base} = \text{ClO}^- \qquad \text{KClO}(aq) \rightarrow \text{K}^+(aq) + \text{ClO}^-(aq)$$

M HClO, M ClO⁻ → pH.

$$pH = pK_a + \log \frac{[\text{base}]}{[\text{acid}]}$$

Solution: Acid $= $ HClO, so [acid] $= $ [HClO] $= 0.125$ M. Base $= $ ClO⁻. Because one ClO⁻ ion is generated for each KClO, [ClO⁻] $= 0.150$ M ClO⁻ $= $ [base]. Then

$$pH = pK_a + \log \frac{[\text{base}]}{[\text{acid}]} = -\log(2.9 \times 10^{-8}) + \log \frac{0.150 \text{ M}}{0.125 \text{ M}} = 7.62.$$

Check: The units (none) are correct. The magnitude of the answer makes physical sense because the pH should be greater than the pK_a of the acid because there is more base than acid.

(b) **Given:** 0.175 M $C_2H_5NH_2$ and 0.150 M $C_2H_5NH_3Br$ **Find:** pH **Other:** $K_b(C_2H_5NH_2) = 5.6 \times 10^{-4}$
Conceptual Plan: Identify acid and base components then M $C_2H_5NH_3Br$ → M $C_2H_5NH_3^+$ and

$$\text{acid} = C_2H_5NH_3^+ \qquad \text{base} = C_2H_5NH_2 \qquad C_2H_5NH_3Br(aq) \rightarrow C_2H_5NH_3^+(aq) + Br^-(aq)$$

$$K_b \rightarrow pK_b \rightarrow pK_a \text{ than } pK_a, \text{ M } C_2H_5NH_2, \text{ M } C_2H_5NH_3^+ \rightarrow pH.$$

$$pK_b = -\log K_b \qquad 14 = pK_a + pK_b \qquad\qquad pH = pK_a + \log \frac{[\text{base}]}{[\text{acid}]}$$

Solution:
Base $= C_2H_5NH_2$, so [base] $= [C_2H_5NH_2] = 0.175$ M. Acid $= C_2H_5NH_3^+$. Because one $C_2H_5NH_3^+$ ion is generated for each $C_2H_5NH_3Br$, $[C_2H_5NH_3^+] = 0.150$ M $= $ [acid].
Because $K_b(C_2H_5NH_2) = 5.6 \times 10^{-4}$, $pK_b = -\log K_b = -\log(5.6 \times 10^{-4}) = 3.25$.
Because $14 = pK_a + pK_b$, $pK_a = 14 - pK_b = 14 - 3.25 = 10.75$. Then

$$pH = pK_a + \log \frac{[\text{base}]}{[\text{acid}]} = 10.75 + \log \frac{0.175 \text{ M}}{0.150 \text{ M}} = 10.82.$$

Check: The units (none) are correct. The magnitude of the answer makes physical sense because the pH should be greater than the pK_a of the acid because there is more base than acid.

(c) **Given:** 10.0 g $HC_2H_3O_2$ and 10.0 g $NaC_2H_3O_2$ in 150.0 mL solution **Find:** pH
Other: $K_a(HC_2H_3O_2) = 1.8 \times 10^{-5}$
Conceptual Plan: Identify acid and base components then mL → L and g $HC_2H_3O_2$ → mol $HC_2H_3O_2$

$$\text{acid} = HC_2H_3O_2 \qquad \text{base} = C_2H_3O_2^- \qquad\qquad \frac{1 \text{ L}}{1000 \text{ mL}} \qquad \frac{1 \text{ mol } HC_2H_3O_2}{60.05 \text{ g } HC_2H_3O_2}$$

then mol $HC_2H_3O_2$, L → M $HC_2H_3O_2$ and g $NaC_2H_3O_2$ → mol $NaC_2H_3O_2$ then

$$M = \frac{\text{mol}}{L} \qquad\qquad \frac{1 \text{ mol } NaC_2H_3O_2}{82.03 \text{ g } NaC_2H_3O_2}$$

mol $NaC_2H_3O_2$, L → M $NaC_2H_3O_2$ → M $C_2H_3O_2^-$ then M $HC_2H_3O_2$, M $C_2H_3O_2^-$ → pH.

$$M = \frac{\text{mol}}{L} \qquad NaC_2H_3O_2(aq) \rightarrow Na^+(aq) + C_2H_3O_2^-(aq) \qquad pH = pK_a + \log \frac{[\text{base}]}{[\text{acid}]}$$

Solution: $150.0 \text{ mL} \times \dfrac{1 \text{ L}}{1000 \text{ mL}} = 0.1500$ L and

$$10.0 \text{ g } \cancel{\text{HC}_2\text{H}_3\text{O}_2^-} \times \frac{1 \text{ mol HC}_2\text{H}_3\text{O}_2}{60.05 \text{ g } \cancel{\text{HC}_2\text{H}_3\text{O}_2}} = 0.16\underline{6}528 \text{ mol HC}_2\text{H}_3\text{O}_2$$

$$\text{then M} = \frac{\text{mol}}{\text{L}} = \frac{0.16\underline{6}528 \text{ mol HC}_2\text{H}_3\text{O}_2}{0.1500 \text{ L}} = 1.1\underline{1}019 \text{ M HC}_2\text{H}_3\text{O}_2 \text{ and}$$

$$10.0 \text{ g } \cancel{\text{NaC}_2\text{H}_3\text{O}_2^-} \times \frac{1 \text{ mol NaC}_2\text{H}_3\text{O}_2}{82.03 \text{ g } \cancel{\text{NaC}_2\text{H}_3\text{O}_2}} = 0.12\underline{1}907 \text{ mol NaC}_2\text{H}_3\text{O}_2 \text{ then}$$

$$\text{M} = \frac{\text{mol}}{\text{L}} = \frac{0.12\underline{1}907 \text{ mol NaC}_2\text{H}_3\text{O}_2}{0.1500 \text{ L}} = 0.81\underline{2}713 \text{ M NaC}_2\text{H}_3\text{O}_2. \text{ Acid} = \text{HC}_2\text{H}_3\text{O}_2, \text{ so [acid]} =$$

$[\text{HC}_2\text{H}_3\text{O}_2] = 1.1\underline{1}019 \text{ M and base} = \text{C}_2\text{H}_3\text{O}_2^-.$ Because one $\text{C}_2\text{H}_3\text{O}_2^-$ ion is generated for each $\text{NaC}_2\text{H}_3\text{O}_2$, $[\text{C}_2\text{H}_3\text{O}_2^-] = 0.81\underline{2}713 \text{ M C}_2\text{H}_3\text{O}_2^- = [\text{base}].$ Then

$$\text{pH} = \text{p}K_a + \log \frac{[\text{base}]}{[\text{acid}]} = -\log(1.8 \times 10^{-5}) + \log \frac{0.81\underline{2}713 \cancel{\text{M}}}{1.1\underline{1}019 \cancel{\text{M}}} = 4.61.$$

Check: The units (none) are correct. The magnitude of the answer makes physical sense because the pH should be less than the $\text{p}K_a$ of the acid because there is more acid than base.

16.15   (a)   **Given:** 50.0 mL of 0.15 M HCHO_2 and 75.0 mL of 0.13 M NaCHO_2 **Find:** pH
              Other: $K_a(\text{HCHO}_2) = 1.8 \times 10^{-4}$
              Conceptual Plan: Identify acid and base components then mL HCHO_2, mL NaCHO_2 → total mL then

acid = HCHO_2 base = CHO_2^- total mL = mL HCHO_2 + mL NaCHO_2

              mL HCHO_2, M HCHO_2, total mL → buffer M HCHO_2 and

$M_1 V_1 = M_2 V_2$

              mL NaCHO_2, M NaCHO_2, total mL → buffer M NaCHO_2 → buffer M CHO_2^- then

$M_1 V_1 = M_2 V_2$ $\text{NaCHO}_2(aq) \rightarrow \text{Na}^+(aq) + \text{CHO}_2^-(aq)$

              K_a, M HCHO_2, M CHO_2^- → pH.

$\text{pH} = \text{p}K_a + \log \frac{[\text{base}]}{[\text{acid}]}$

              Solution: total mL = mL HCHO_2 + mL NaCHO_2 = 50.0 mL + 75.0 mL = 125.0 mL. Then because $M_1 V_1 = M_2 V_2$, rearrange to solve for M_2.

$$M_2 = \frac{M_1 V_1}{V_2} = \frac{(0.15 \text{ M})(50.0 \text{ mL})}{125.0 \text{ mL}} = 0.060 \text{ M HCHO}_2 \text{ and}$$

$$M_2 = \frac{M_1 V_1}{V_2} = \frac{(0.13 \text{ M})(75.0 \text{ mL})}{125.0 \text{ mL}} = 0.078 \text{ M NaCHO}_2. \text{ Acid} = \text{HCHO}_2, \text{ so [acid]} = [\text{HCHO}_2] =$$

0.060 M. Base = CHO_2^-. Because one CHO_2^- ion is generated for each NaCHO_2, $[\text{CHO}_2^-] =$

$$0.078 \text{ M CHO}_2^- = [\text{base}]. \text{ Then pH} = \text{p}K_a + \log \frac{[\text{base}]}{[\text{acid}]} = -\log(1.8 \times 10^{-4}) + \log \frac{0.078 \cancel{\text{M}}}{0.060 \cancel{\text{M}}} = 3.86.$$

Check: The units (none) are correct. The magnitude of the answer makes physical sense because the pH should be greater than the $\text{p}K_a$ of the acid because there is more base than acid.

      (b)   **Given:** 125.0 mL of 0.10 M NH_3 and 250.0 mL of 0.10 M NH_4Cl **Find:** pH
              Other: $K_b(\text{NH}_3) = 1.76 \times 10^{-5}$
              Conceptual Plan: Identify acid and base components then mL NH_3, mL NH_4Cl → total mL then

acid = NH_4^+ base = NH_3 total mL = mL NH_3 + mL NH_4Cl

              mL NH_3, M NH_3, total mL → buffer M NH_3 and

$M_1 V_1 = M_2 V_2$

              mL NH_4Cl, M NH_4Cl, total mL → buffer M NH_4Cl → buffer M NH_4^+ and K_b → pK_b → pK_a then

$M_1 V_1 = M_2 V_2$ $\text{NH}_4\text{Cl}(aq) \rightarrow \text{NH}_4^+(aq) + \text{Cl}^-(aq)$ $\text{p}K_b = -\log K_b$ $14 = \text{p}K_a + \text{p}K_b$

              pK_a, M NH_3, M NH_4^+ → pH.

$\text{pH} = \text{p}K_a + \log \frac{[\text{base}]}{[\text{acid}]}$

Solution: total mL = mL NH_3 + mL NH_4Cl = 125.0 mL + 250.0 mL = 375.0 mL. Then because $M_1 V_1 = M_2 V_2$, rearrange to solve for M_2.

$$M_2 = \frac{M_1 V_1}{V_2} = \frac{(0.10 \text{ M})(125.0 \text{ mL})}{375.0 \text{ mL}} = 0.03\underline{3333} \text{ M } NH_3 \text{ and}$$

$$M_2 = \frac{M_1 V_1}{V_2} = \frac{(0.10 \text{ M})(250.0 \text{ mL})}{375.0 \text{ mL}} = 0.06\underline{6667} \text{ M } NH_4Cl. \text{ Base} = NH_3, [\text{base}] = [NH_3] =$$

$0.03\underline{3333}$ M acid = NH_4^+. Because one NH_4^+ ion is generated for each NH_4Cl, $[NH_4^+]$ = $0.06\underline{6667}$ M NH_4^+ = [acid]. Because $K_b(NH_3) = 1.76 \times 10^{-5}$,

$pK_b = -\log K_b = -\log(1.76 \times 10^{-5}) = 4.75$. Because $14 = pK_a + pK_b$,

$$pK_a = 14 - pK_b = 14 - 4.75 = 9.25. \text{ Then pH} = pK_a + \log \frac{[\text{base}]}{[\text{acid}]} = 9.25 + \log \frac{0.03\underline{3333} \text{ M}}{0.06\underline{6667} \text{ M}} = 8.95.$$

Check: The units (none) are correct. The magnitude of the answer makes physical sense because the pH should be less than the pK_a of the acid because there is more acid than base.

16.17 **Given:** NaF/HF buffer at pH = 4.00 **Find:** [NaF]/[HF] **Other:** $K_a(HF) = 3.5 \times 10^{-4}$
Conceptual Plan: Identify acid and base components then pH, $K_a \rightarrow$ [NaF]/[HF].

$$\text{acid = HF} \qquad \text{base = } F^- \qquad pH = pK_a + \log \frac{[\text{base}]}{[\text{acid}]}$$

Solution: $pH = pK_a + \log \frac{[\text{base}]}{[\text{acid}]} = -\log(3.5 \times 10^{-4}) + \log \frac{[NaF]}{[HF]} = 4.00.$ Solve for [NaF]/[HF].

$$\log \frac{[NaF]}{[HF]} = 4.00 - 3.46 = 0.54 \rightarrow \frac{[NaF]}{[HF]} = 10^{0.54} = 3.5.$$

Check: The units (none) are correct. The magnitude of the answer makes physical sense because the pH is greater than the pK_a of the acid; so there needs to be more base than acid.

16.19 **Given:** 150.0 mL buffer of 0.15 M benzoic acid at pH = 4.25 **Find:** mass sodium benzoate
Other: $K_a(HC_7H_5O_2) = 6.5 \times 10^{-5}$
Conceptual Plan: Identify acid and base components then pH, K_a, $[HC_7H_5O_2] \rightarrow [NaC_7H_5O_2]$

$$\text{acid = } HC_7H_5O_2 \qquad \text{base = } C_7H_5O_2^- \qquad pH = pK_a + \log \frac{[\text{base}]}{[\text{acid}]}$$

mL $\rightarrow$ L then $[NaC_7H_5O_2]$, L $\rightarrow$ mol $NaC_7H_5O_2 \rightarrow$ g $NaC_7H_5O_2$.

$$\frac{1 \text{ L}}{1000 \text{ mL}} \qquad\qquad M = \frac{\text{mol}}{\text{L}} \qquad\qquad \frac{144.11 \text{ g } NaC_7H_5O_2}{1 \text{ mol } NaC_7H_5O_2}$$

Solution: $pH = pK_a + \log \frac{[\text{base}]}{[\text{acid}]} = -\log(6.5 \times 10^{-5}) + \log \frac{[NaC_7H_5O_2]}{0.15 \text{ M}} = 4.25.$ Solve for $[NaC_7H_5O_2]$.

$$\log \frac{[NaC_7H_5O_2]}{0.15 \text{ M}} = 4.25 - 4.1870866 = 0.06291 \rightarrow \frac{[NaC_7H_5O_2]}{0.15 \text{ M}} = 10^{0.06291} = 1.1\underline{5}59 \rightarrow$$

$[NaC_7H_5O_2] = 0.1\underline{7}338$ M.

Convert to moles using $M = \frac{\text{mol}}{\text{L}}$.

$$\frac{0.1\underline{7}338 \text{ mol } NaC_7H_5O_2}{1 \text{ L}} \times 0.150 \text{ L} = 0.026007 \text{ mol } NaC_7H_5O_2 \times \frac{144.11 \text{ g } NaC_7H_5O_2}{1 \text{ mol } NaC_7H_5O_2} = 3.7 \text{ g } NaC_7H_5O_2.$$

Check: The units (g) are correct. The magnitude of the answer makes physical sense because the volume of solution is small and the concentration is low; so much less than a mole is needed.

16.21 (a) **Given:** 250.0 mL buffer of 0.250 M $HC_2H_3O_2$ and 0.250 M $NaC_2H_3O_2$ **Find:** initial pH
Other: $K_a(HC_2H_3O_2) = 1.8 \times 10^{-5}$
Conceptual Plan: Identify acid and base components then M $NaC_2H_3O_2 \rightarrow$ M $C_2H_3O_2^-$ then

$$\text{acid = } HC_2H_3O_2 \qquad \text{base = } C_2H_3O_2^- \qquad NaC_2H_3O_2(aq) \rightarrow Na^+(aq) + C_2H_3O_2^-(aq)$$

M HC$_2$H$_3$O$_2$, M C$_2$H$_3$O$_2$$^-$ → pH.

$$pH = pK_a + \log \frac{[base]}{[acid]}$$

Solution: Acid = HC$_2$H$_3$O$_2$, so [acid] = [HC$_2$H$_3$O$_2$] = 0.250 M. Base = C$_2$H$_3$O$_2$$^-$. Because one C$_2H_3O_2$$^-$ ion is generated for each NaC$_2$H$_3$O$_2$, [C$_2$H$_3$O$_2$$^-$] = 0.250 M C$_2H_3O_2$$^-$ = [base]. Then

$$pH = pK_a + \log \frac{[base]}{[acid]} = -\log(1.8 \times 10^{-5}) + \log \frac{0.250\ M}{0.250\ M} = 4.74.$$

Check: The units (none) are correct. The magnitude of the answer makes physical sense because the pH is equal to the pK$_a$ of the acid because there are equal amounts of acid and base.

(b)   **Given:** 250.0 mL buffer of 0.250 M HC$_2$H$_3$O$_2$ and 0.250 M NaC$_2$H$_3$O$_2$, add 0.0050 mol HCl   **Find:** pH
Other: K_a(HC$_2$H$_3$O$_2$) = 1.8 × 10^{-5}
Conceptual Plan: Part I: Stoichiometry:
mL → L then [NaC$_2$H$_3$O$_2$], L → mol NaC$_2$H$_3$O$_2$ and [HC$_2$H$_3$O$_2$], L → mol HC$_2$H$_3$O$_2$

$\frac{1\ L}{1000\ mL}$ $M = \frac{mol}{L}$ $M = \frac{mol}{L}$

write balanced equation then

HCl + NaC$_2$H$_3$O$_2$ → HC$_2$H$_3$O$_2$ + NaCl

mol NaC$_2$H$_3$O$_2$, mol HC$_2$H$_3$O$_2$, mol HCl → mol NaC$_2$H$_3$O$_2$, mol HC$_2$H$_3$O$_2$ then

set up stoichiometry table

Part II: Equilibrium:
mol NaC$_2$H$_3$O$_2$, mol HC$_2$H$_3$O$_2$, L, K_a → pH

$$pH = pK_a + \log \frac{[base]}{[acid]}$$

Solution: $250.0\ mL \times \dfrac{1\ L}{1000\ mL} = 0.2500\ L$ then

$\dfrac{0.250\ mol\ HC_2H_3O_2}{1\ L} \times 0.250\ L = 0.0625\ mol\ HC_2H_3O_2$ and

$\dfrac{0.250\ mol\ NaC_2H_3O_2}{1\ L} \times 0.250\ L = 0.0625\ mol\ NaC_2H_3O_2$. Set up a table to track changes:

	HCl(*aq*) +	NaC$_2$H$_3$O$_2$(*aq*) →	HC$_2$H$_3$O$_2$(*aq*) +	NaCl(*aq*)
Before addition	≈0.00 mol	0.0625 mol	0.0625 mol	0.00 mol
Addition	0.0050 mol	—	—	—
After addition	≈0.00 mol	0.0575 mol	0.0675 mol	0.0050 mol

Because the amount of HCl is small, there are still significant amounts of both buffer components; so the Henderson–Hasselbalch equation can be used to calculate the new pH.

$$pH = pK_a + \log \frac{[base]}{[acid]} = -\log(1.8 \times 10^{-5}) + \log \frac{\dfrac{0.0575\ mol}{0.250\ L}}{\dfrac{0.0675\ mol}{0.250\ L}} = 4.68$$

Check: The units (none) are correct. The magnitude of the answer makes physical sense because the pH dropped slightly when acid was added.

(c)   **Given:** 250.0 mL buffer of 0.250 M HC$_2$H$_3$O$_2$ and 0.250 M NaC$_2$H$_3$O$_2$, add 0.0050 mol NaOH
Find: pH   **Other:** K_a(HC$_2$H$_3$O$_2$) = 1.8 × 10^{-5}
Conceptual Plan: Part I: Stoichiometry:
mL → L then [NaC$_2$H$_3$O$_2$], L → mol NaC$_2$H$_3$O$_2$ and [HC$_2$H$_3$O$_2$], L → mol HC$_2$H$_3$O$_2$

$\frac{1\ L}{1000\ mL}$ $M = \frac{mol}{L}$ $M = \frac{mol}{L}$

write balanced equation then

NaOH + HC$_2$H$_3$O$_2$ → H$_2$O + NaC$_2$H$_3$O$_2$

mol NaC$_2$H$_3$O$_2$, mol HC$_2$H$_3$O$_2$, mol NaOH → mol NaC$_2$H$_3$O$_2$, mol HC$_2$H$_3$O$_2$ then

set up stoichiometry table

Part II: Equilibrium:
mol $NaC_2H_3O_2$, mol $HC_2H_3O_2$, L, K_a → pH

$$pH = pK_a + \log \frac{[base]}{[acid]}$$

Solution: $250.0 \text{ mL} \times \dfrac{1 \text{ L}}{1000 \text{ mL}} = 0.2500 \text{ L}$ then

$\dfrac{0.250 \text{ mol } HC_2H_3O_2}{1 \text{ L}} \times 0.2500 \text{ L} = 0.0625 \text{ mol } HC_2H_3O_2$ and

$\dfrac{0.250 \text{ mol } NaC_2H_3O_2}{1 \text{ L}} \times 0.2500 \text{ L} = 0.0625 \text{ mol } NaC_2H_3O_2$. Set up a table to track changes:

$$NaOH(aq) + HC_2H_3O_2(aq) \rightarrow NaC_2H_3O_2(aq) + H_2O(l)$$

Before addition	≈0.00 mol	0.0625 mol	0.0625 mol	—
Addition	0.0050 mol	—	—	—
After addition	≈0.00 mol	0.0575 mol	0.0675 mol	—

Because the amount of NaOH is small, there are still significant amounts of both buffer components; so the Henderson–Hasselbalch equation can be used to calculate the new pH.

$$pH = pK_a + \log \frac{[base]}{[acid]} = -\log(1.8 \times 10^{-5}) + \log \frac{\dfrac{0.0675 \text{ mol}}{0.2500 \text{ L}}}{\dfrac{0.0575 \text{ mol}}{0.2500 \text{ L}}} = 4.81$$

Check: The units (none) are correct. The magnitude of the answer makes physical sense because the pH rose slightly when base was added.

16.23   (a)   **Given:** 500.0 mL pure water   **Find:** initial pH and after adding 0.010 mol HCl
                     Conceptual Plan: Pure water has a pH of 7.00 then mL → L then mol HCl, L → $[H_3O^+]$ → pH

$$\frac{1 \text{ L}}{1000 \text{ mL}} \qquad\qquad M = \frac{mol}{L} \qquad pH = -\log[H_3O^+]$$

                     Solution: Pure water has a pH of 7.00, so initial pH $= 7.00$, $500.0 \text{ mL} \times \dfrac{1 \text{ L}}{1000 \text{ mL}} = 0.5000 \text{ L}$, then

$M = \dfrac{mol}{L} = \dfrac{0.010 \text{ mol } HCl}{0.5000 \text{ L}} = 0.020 \text{ M HCl}$. Because HCl is a strong acid, it dissociates completely; so

$pH = -\log[H_3O^+] = -\log(0.020) = 1.70$.

                     Check: The units (none) are correct. The magnitude of the answers makes physical sense because the pH starts neutral and then drops significantly when acid is added and no buffer is present.

   (b)   **Given:** 500.0 mL buffer of 0.125 M $HC_2H_3O_2$ and 0.115 M $NaC_2H_3O_2$
                     Find: initial pH and after adding 0.010 mol HCl **Other:** $K_a(HC_2H_3O_2) = 1.8 \times 10^{-5}$
                     Conceptual Plan: initial pH:
                     Identify acid and base components then M $NaC_2H_3O_2$ → M $C_2H_3O_2^-$ then

$$acid = HC_2H_3O_2 \qquad base = C_2H_3O_2^- \qquad NaC_2H_3O_2(aq) \rightarrow Na^+(aq) + C_2H_3O_2^-(aq)$$

                     M $HC_2H_3O_2$, M $C_2H_3O_2^-$ → pH

$$pH = pK_a + \log \frac{[base]}{[acid]}$$

                     pH after HCl addition: Part I: Stoichiometry:
                     mL → L then $[NaC_2H_3O_2]$, L → mol $NaC_2H_3O_2$ and $[HC_2H_3O_2]$, L → mol $HC_2H_3O_2$

$$\frac{1 \text{ L}}{1000 \text{ mL}} \qquad\qquad M = \frac{mol}{L} \qquad\qquad M = \frac{mol}{L}$$

                     write balanced equation then

$$HCl + NaC_2H_3O_2 \rightarrow HC_2H_3O_2 + NaCl$$

                     mol $NaC_2H_3O_2$, mol $HC_2H_3O_2$, mol HCl → mol $NaC_2H_3O_2$, mol $HC_2H_3O_2$ then

$$\text{set up stoichiometry table}$$

Part II: Equilibrium:
mol $NaC_2H_3O_2$, mol $HC_2H_3O_2$, L, K_a $\rightarrow$ pH

$$pH = pK_a + \log \frac{[base]}{[acid]}$$

Solution: Initial pH: Acid = $HC_2H_3O_2$, so [acid] = $[HC_2H_3O_2]$ = 0.125 M. Base = $C_2H_3O_2^-$. Because one $C_2H_3O_2^-$ ion is generated for each $NaC_2H_3O_2$, $[C_2H_3O_2^-]$ = 0.115 M $C_2H_3O_2^-$ = [base]. Then

$$pH = pK_a + \log \frac{[base]}{[acid]} = -\log(1.8 \times 10^{-5}) + \log \frac{0.115\ \text{M}}{0.125\ \text{M}} = 4.71.$$

pH after HCl addition:

$$500.0\ \cancel{mL} \times \frac{1\ L}{1000\ \cancel{mL}} = 0.5000\ L \text{ then } \frac{0.125\ \text{mol } HC_2H_3O_2}{1\ \cancel{L}} \times 0.5000\ \cancel{L} = 0.0625\ \text{mol } HC_2H_3O_2 \text{ and}$$

$$\frac{0.115\ \text{mol } NaC_2H_3O_2}{1\ \cancel{L}} \times 0.5000\ \cancel{L} = 0.0575\ \text{mol } NaC_2H_3O_2. \text{ Set up a table to track changes:}$$

$$HCl(aq) + NaC_2H_3O_2(aq) \rightarrow HC_2H_3O_2(aq) + NaCl(aq)$$

Before addition	$\approx$0.00 mol	0.0575 mol	0.0625 mol	0.00 mol
Addition	0.010 mol	—	—	—
After addition	$\approx$0.00 mol	0.0475 mol	0.0725 mol	0.10 mol

Because the amount of HCl is small, there are still significant amounts of both buffer components; so the Henderson–Hasselbalch equation can be used to calculate the new pH.

$$pH = pK_a + \log \frac{[base]}{[acid]} = -\log(1.8 \times 10^{-5}) + \log \frac{\dfrac{0.0475\ \cancel{mol}}{\cancel{0.5000\ L}}}{\dfrac{0.0725\ \cancel{mol}}{\cancel{0.5000\ L}}} = 4.56$$

Check: The units (none) are correct. The magnitude of the answers makes physical sense because the pH started below the pK_a of the acid and it dropped slightly when acid was added.

(c)   **Given:** 500.0 mL buffer of 0.155 M $C_2H_5NH_2$ and 0.145 M $C_2H_5NH_3Cl$
       Find: initial pH and after adding 0.010 mol HCl **Other:** $K_b(C_2H_5NH_2) = 5.6 \times 10^{-4}$
       Conceptual Plan: initial pH:
       Identify acid and base components then M $C_2H_5NH_3Cl$ $\rightarrow$ M $C_2H_5NH_3^+$

         acid = $C_2H_5NH_3^+$ base = $C_2H_5NH_2$ $C_2H_5NH_3Cl(aq) \rightarrow C_2H_5NH_3^+(aq) + Cl^-(aq)$

       and $K_b \rightarrow pK_b \rightarrow pK_a$ then pK_a, M $C_2H_5NH_2$, M $C_2H_5NH_3^+$ $\rightarrow$ pH

    $pK_b = -\log K_b$ $14 = pK_a + pK_b$ $pH = pK_a + \log \frac{[base]}{[acid]}$

       pH after HCl addition: Part I: Stoichiometry:
       mL $\rightarrow$ L then $[C_2H_5NH_2]$, L $\rightarrow$ mol $C_2H_5NH_2$ and

     $\frac{1\ L}{1000\ mL}$ $M = \frac{mol}{L}$

       $[C_2H_5NH_3Cl]$, L $\rightarrow$ mol $C_2H_5NH_3Cl$ write balanced equation then

         $M = \frac{mol}{L}$ $HCl + C_2H_5NH_2 \rightarrow C_2H_5NH_3Cl$

       mol $C_2H_5NH_2$, mol $C_2H_5NH_3Cl$, mol HCl $\rightarrow$ mol $C_2H_5NH_2$, mol $C_2H_5NH_3Cl$ then

               set up stoichiometry table

       Part II: Equilibrium:
       mol $C_2H_5NH_2$, mol $C_2H_5NH_3Cl$, L, K_a $\rightarrow$ pH

           $pH = pK_a + \log \frac{[base]}{[acid]}$

       Solution: Base = $C_2H_5NH_2$, so [base] = $[C_2H_5NH_2]$ = 0.155 M. Acid = $C_2H_5NH_3^+$. Because one $C_2H_5NH_3^+$ ion is generated for each $C_2H_5NH_3Cl$, $[C_2H_5NH_3^+]$ = 0.145 M $C_2H_5NH_3^+$ = [acid]. Because $K_b(C_2H_5NH_2) = 5.6 \times 10^{-4}$, $pK_b = -\log K_b = -\log(5.6 \times 10^{-4}) = 3.25$. Because $14 = pK_a + pK_b$, $pK_a = 14 - pK_b = 14 - 3.25 = 10.75$ then

$$pH = pK_a + \log \frac{[base]}{[acid]} = 10.75 + \log \frac{0.155\ \text{M}}{0.145\ \text{M}} = 10.78.$$

pH after HCl addition: $500.0 \text{ mL} \times \dfrac{1 \text{ L}}{1000 \text{ mL}} = 0.5000 \text{ L}$ then

$\dfrac{0.155 \text{ mol } C_2H_5NH_2}{1 \text{ L}} \times 0.5000 \text{ L} = 0.0775 \text{ mol } C_2H_5NH_2$ and

$\dfrac{0.145 \text{ mol } C_2H_5NH_3Cl}{1 \text{ L}} \times 0.5000 \text{ L} = 0.0725 \text{ mol } C_2H_5NH_3Cl.$ Set up a table to track changes:

$$HCl(aq) \ + \ C_2H_5NH_2(aq) \rightarrow C_2H_5NH_3Cl(aq)$$

	HCl(aq)	C₂H₅NH₂(aq)	C₂H₅NH₃Cl(aq)
Before addition	≈ 0.00 mol	0.0775 mol	0.0725 mol
Addition	0.010 mol	—	—
After addition	≈ 0.00 mol	0.0675 mol	0.0825 mol

Because the amount of HCl is small, there are still significant amounts of both buffer components; so the Henderson–Hasselbalch equation can be used to calculate the new pH.

$$pH = pK_a + \log \frac{[\text{base}]}{[\text{acid}]} = 10.75 + \log \frac{\dfrac{0.0675 \text{ mol}}{0.5000 \text{ L}}}{\dfrac{0.0825 \text{ mol}}{0.5000 \text{ L}}} = 10.66$$

Check: The units (none) are correct. The magnitude of the answers makes physical sense because the initial pH should be greater than the pK_a of the acid because there is more base than acid and the pH drops slightly when acid is added.

16.25   **Given:** 350.00 mL 0.150 M HF and 0.150 M NaF buffer
Find: mass NaOH to raise pH to 4.00 and mass NaOH to raise pH to 4.00 with buffer concentrations raised to 0.350 M
Other: $K_a(HF) = 3.5 \times 10^{-4}$
Conceptual Plan: Identify acid and base components. Because [NaF] = [HF], then initial pH = pK_a

$$\text{acid} = HF \qquad \text{base} = F^- \qquad pH = pK_a$$

final pH, pK_a → [NaF]/[HF] and mL → L then [HF], L → mol HF and [NaF], L → mol NaF

$$pH = pK_a + \log \frac{[\text{base}]}{[\text{acid}]} \qquad \frac{1 \text{ L}}{1000 \text{ mL}} \qquad M = \frac{\text{mol}}{L} \qquad M = \frac{\text{mol}}{L}$$

then write balanced equation then

$$NaOH + HF \rightarrow NaF + H_2O$$

mol HF, mol NaF, [NaF]/[HF] → mol NaOH → g NaOH.

$$\text{set up stoichiometry table} \qquad \frac{40.00 \text{ g NaOH}}{1 \text{ mol NaOH}}$$

Finally, when the buffer concentrations are raised to 0.350 M, simply multiply the g NaOH by the ratio of concentrations (0.350 M/0.150 M).
Solution: initial pH = $pK_a = -\log(3.5 \times 10^{-4}) = 3.46$ then

$$pH = pK_a + \log \frac{[\text{base}]}{[\text{acid}]} = -\log(3.5 \times 10^{-4}) + \log \frac{[NaF]}{[HF]} = 4.00. \text{ Solve for [NaF]/[HF].}$$

$$\log \frac{[NaF]}{[HF]} = 4.00 - 3.46 = 0.54 \rightarrow \frac{[NaF]}{[HF]} = 10^{0.54} = 3.5. \quad 350.0 \text{ mL} \times \frac{1 \text{ L}}{1000 \text{ mL}} = 0.3500 \text{ L}$$ then

$$\frac{0.150 \text{ mol HF}}{1 \text{ L}} \times 0.3500 \text{ L} = 0.0525 \text{ mol HF and} \frac{0.150 \text{ mol NaF}}{1 \text{ L}} \times 0.3500 \text{ L} = 0.0525 \text{ mol NaF}$$

Set up a table to track changes:

	NaOH(aq)	+	HF(aq)	→	NaF(aq)	+	H₂O(aq)
Before addition	≈ 0.00 mol		0.0525 mol		0.0525 mol		—
Addition	x		—		—		—
After addition	≈ 0.00 mol		$(0.0525 - x)$ mol		$(0.0525 + x)$ mol		—

Because $\dfrac{[NaF]}{[HF]} = 3.5 = \dfrac{(0.0525 + x) \text{ mol}}{(0.0525 - x) \text{ mol}}$, solve for x. Note that the ratio of moles is the same as the ratio of concentrations because the volume for both terms is the same. $3.5(0.0525 - x) = (0.0525 + x) \rightarrow$
$0.18375 - 3.5x = 0.0525 + x \rightarrow 0.13125 = 4.5x \rightarrow x = 0.029167$ mol NaOH then

$$0.029167 \text{ mol NaOH} \times \frac{40.00 \text{ g NaOH}}{1 \text{ mol NaOH}} = 1.1667 \text{ g NaOH} = 1.2 \text{ g NaOH.}$$

To scale the amount of NaOH up to a 0.350 M HF and NaF solution, multiply the NaOH mass by the ratio of concentrations. $1.1667 \text{ g NaOH} \times \dfrac{0.350 \text{ M}}{0.150 \text{ M}} = 2.7 \text{ g NaOH}$

Check: The units (g) are correct. The magnitude of the answers makes physical sense because there is much less than a mole of each of the buffer components; so there must be much less than a mole of NaOH. The higher the buffer concentrations, the higher the buffer capacity and the mass of NaOH it can neutralize.

16.27 (a) Yes, this will be a buffer because NH_3 is a weak base and NH_4^+ is its conjugate acid. The ratio of base to acid is 0.10/0.15 = 0.67, so the pH will be within 1 pH unit of the pK_a.

(b) No, this will not be a buffer solution because HCl is a strong acid and NaOH is a strong base.

(c) Yes, this will be a buffer because HF is a weak acid and the NaOH will convert 20.0/50.0 = 40% of the acid to its conjugate base.

(d) No, this will not be a buffer solution because both components are bases.

(e) No, this will not be a buffer solution because both components are bases.

16.29 (a) **Given:** blood buffer 0.024 M HCO_3^- and 0.0012 M H_2CO_3, $pK_a = 6.1$ **Find:** initial pH
Conceptual Plan: Identify acid and base components then M HCO_3^-, M $H_2CO_3 \rightarrow$ pH.

$$\text{acid} = H_2CO_3 \qquad\qquad \text{base} = HCO_3^- \qquad\qquad pH = pK_a + \log \frac{[\text{base}]}{[\text{acid}]}$$

Solution: Acid = H_2CO_3, so [acid] = $[H_2CO_3]$ = 0.0012 M. Base = HCO_3^-, so [base] = $[HCO_3^-]$ =

0.024 M HCO_3^-. Then $pH = pK_a + \log \dfrac{[\text{base}]}{[\text{acid}]} = 6.1 + \log \dfrac{0.024 \text{ M}}{0.0012 \text{ M}} = 7.4.$

Check: The units (none) are correct. The magnitude of the answer makes physical sense because the pH is greater than the pK_a of the acid because there is more base than acid.

(b) **Given:** 5.0 L of blood buffer   **Find:** mass HCl to lower pH to 7.0
Conceptual Plan: final pH, $pK_a \rightarrow [HCO_3^-]/[H_2CO_3]$ then $[HCO_3^-]$, L $\rightarrow$ mol HCO_3^- and

$$pH = pK_a + \log \frac{[\text{base}]}{[\text{acid}]} \qquad\qquad\qquad M = \frac{\text{mol}}{L}$$

$[H_2CO_3]$, L $\rightarrow$ mol H_2CO_3 then write balanced equation then

$$M = \frac{\text{mol}}{L} \qquad\qquad H^+ + HCO_3^- \rightarrow H_2CO_3$$

mol HCO_3^-, mol H_2CO_3, $[HCO_3^-]/[H_2CO_3] \rightarrow$ mol HCl $\rightarrow$ g HCl

$$\text{set up stoichiometry table} \qquad \frac{36.46 \text{ g HCl}}{1 \text{ mol HCl}}$$

Solution: $pH = pK_a + \log \dfrac{[\text{base}]}{[\text{acid}]} = 6.1 + \log \dfrac{[HCO_3^-]}{[H_2CO_3]} = 7.0.$ Solve for $[HCO_3^-]/[H_2CO_3]$.

$$\log \frac{[HCO_3^-]}{[H_2CO_3]} = 7.0 - 6.1 = 0.9 \rightarrow \frac{[HCO_3^-]}{[H_2CO_3]} = 10^{0.9} = 7.9433. \text{ Then}$$

$$\frac{0.024 \text{ mol } HCO_3^-}{1 \text{ L}} \times 5.0 \text{ L} = 0.12 \text{ mol } HCO_3^- \text{ and } \frac{0.0012 \text{ mol } H_2CO_3}{1 \text{ L}} \times 5.0 \text{ L} = 0.0060 \text{ mol } H_2CO_3.$$

Because HCl is a strong acid, [HCl] = $[H^+]$, and set up a table to track changes:

	$H^+(aq)$	+	$HCO_3^-(aq)$	$\rightarrow$	$H_2CO_3(aq)$
Before addition	≈0.00 mol		0.12 mol		0.0060 mol
Addition	x		—		—
After addition	≈0.00 mol		$(0.12 - x)$ mol		$(0.0060 + x)$ mol

Because $\dfrac{[HCO_3^-]}{[H_2CO_3]} = 7.9433 = \dfrac{(0.12 - x) \text{ mol}}{(0.0060 + x) \text{ mol}}$, solve for x. Note that the ratio of moles is the same as the

ratio of concentrations because the volume for both terms is the same.

$7.9433(0.0060 + x) = (0.12 - x) \rightarrow 0.0476598 + 7.9433x = 0.12 - x \rightarrow 8.9433x = 0.07234 \rightarrow$

$x = 0.0080888 \text{ mol HCl}$ then $0.0080888 \text{ mol HCl} \times \dfrac{36.46 \text{ g HCl}}{1 \text{ mol HCl}} = 0.29492 \text{ g HCl} = 0.3 \text{ g HCl}$

Check: The units (g) are correct. The amount of acid needed is small because the concentrations of the buffer components are very low and the buffer starts only 0.4 pH unit above the final pH.

(c) **Given:** 5.0 L of blood buffer   **Find:** mass NaOH to raise pH to 7.8
Conceptual Plan: final pH, pK_a → $[HCO_3^-]/[H_2CO_3]$ then $[HCO_3^-]$, L → mol HCO_3^- and

$$pH = pK_a + \log \dfrac{[\text{base}]}{[\text{acid}]} \qquad\qquad M = \dfrac{\text{mol}}{\text{L}}$$

$[H_2CO_3]$, L → mol H_2CO_3 then write balanced equation then

$$M = \dfrac{\text{mol}}{\text{L}} \qquad OH^- + H_2CO_3 \rightarrow HCO_3^- + H_2O$$

mol HCO_3^-, mol H_2CO_3, $[HCO_3^-]/[H_2CO_3]$ → mol NaOH → g NaOH

$$\text{set up stoichiometry table} \qquad \dfrac{40.00 \text{ g NaOH}}{1 \text{ mol NaOH}}$$

Solution: $pH = pK_a + \log \dfrac{[\text{base}]}{[\text{acid}]} = 6.1 + \log \dfrac{[HCO_3^-]}{[H_2CO_3]} = 7.8$

Solve for $[HCO_3^-]/[H_2CO_3]$. $\log \dfrac{[HCO_3^-]}{[H_2CO_3]} = 7.8 - 6.1 = 1.7 \rightarrow \dfrac{[HCO_3^-]}{[H_2CO_3]} = 10^{1.7} = 50.11872$. Then

$\dfrac{0.024 \text{ mol } HCO_3^-}{1 \text{ L}} \times 5.0 \text{ L} = 0.12 \text{ mol } HCO_3^-$ and $\dfrac{0.0012 \text{ mol } H_2CO_3}{1 \text{ L}} \times 5.0 \text{ L} = 0.0060 \text{ mol } H_2CO_3$.

Because NaOH is a strong base, $[NaOH] = [OH^-]$, and set up a table to track changes:

	$OH^-(aq)$	+	$H_2CO_3(aq)$	→	$HCO_3^-(aq)$	+	$H_2O(l)$
Before addition	≈ 0.00 mol		0.0060 mol		0.12 mol		—
Addition	x		—		—		—
After addition	≈ 0.00 mol		$(0.0060 - x)$ mol		$(0.12 + x)$ mol		—

Because $\dfrac{[HCO_3^-]}{[H_2CO_3]} = 50.11872 = \dfrac{(0.12 + x) \text{ mol}}{(0.0060 - x) \text{ mol}}$, solve for x. Note that the ratio of moles is the same as the ratio of concentrations because the volume for both terms is the same.
$50.11872(0.0060 - x) = (0.12 + x) \rightarrow 0.30071 - 50.11872x = 0.12 + x \rightarrow 51.11872x = 0.18071$
$\rightarrow x = 0.0035351 \text{ mol NaOH}$ then

$0.0035351 \text{ mol NaOH} \times \dfrac{40.00 \text{ g NaOH}}{1 \text{ mol NaOH}} = 0.14140 \text{ g NaOH} = 0.14 \text{ g NaOH}$

Check: The units (g) are correct. The amount of base needed is small because the concentrations of the buffer components are very low.

16.31 **Given:** $HC_2H_3O_2/KC_2H_3O_2$, $HClO_2/KClO_2$, NH_3/NH_4Cl, and $HClO/KClO$ potential buffer systems to create buffer at pH = 7.20   **Find:** best buffer system and ratio of component masses
Other: $K_a(HC_2H_3O_2) = 1.8 \times 10^{-5}$, $K_a(HClO_2) = 1.1 \times 10^{-2}$, $K_b(NH_3) = 1.76 \times 10^{-5}$, $K_a(HClO) = 2.9 \times 10^{-8}$
Conceptual Plan: Calculate pK_a of all potential buffer acids for the base K_b → pK_b → pK_a and

$$pK_a = -\log K_a \qquad\qquad pK_b = -\log K_b \quad 14 = pK_a + pK_b$$

choose the pK_a that is closest to 7.20. Then pH, K_a → [base]/[acid] → mass base/mass acid.

$$pH = pK_a + \log \dfrac{[\text{base}]}{[\text{acid}]} \qquad \dfrac{\mathcal{M}\,(\text{base})}{\mathcal{M}\,(\text{acid})}$$

Solution: for $HC_2H_3O_2/KC_2H_3O_2$:$pK_a = -\log K_a = -\log(1.8 \times 10^{-5}) = 4.74$;
for $HClO_2/KClO_2$:$pK_a = -\log K_a = -\log(1.1 \times 10^{-2}) = 1.96$;
for NH_3/NH_4Cl :$pK_b = -\log K_b = -\log(1.76 \times 10^{-5}) = 4.75$
Because $14 = pK_a + pK_b$, $pK_a = 14 - pK_b = 14 - 4.75 = 9.25$;
and for $HClO/KClO$:$pK_a = -\log K_a = -\log(2.9 \times 10^{-8}) = 7.54$. So the $HClO/KClO$ buffer system has the pK_a

that is closest to 7.20. So $pH = pK_a + \log \dfrac{[\text{base}]}{[\text{acid}]} = 7.54 + \log \dfrac{[KClO]}{[HClO]} = 7.20$. Solve for $[KClO]/[HClO]$.

$$\log \frac{[\text{KClO}]}{[\text{HClO}]} = 7.20 - 7.54 = -0.34 \rightarrow \frac{[\text{KClO}]}{[\text{HClO}]} = 10^{-0.34} = 0.457088. \text{ Then convert to mass ratio using}$$

$$\frac{\mathcal{M}\,(\text{base})}{\mathcal{M}\,(\text{acid})}, 0.457088\, \frac{\dfrac{\text{KClO mol}}{L}}{\dfrac{\text{HClO mol}}{L}} \times \frac{\dfrac{90.55 \text{ g KClO}}{\text{mol KClO}}}{\dfrac{52.46 \text{ g HClO}}{\text{mol HClO}}} = 0.79\frac{\text{g KClO}}{\text{g HClO}}.$$

Check: The units (none and g base/g acid) are correct. The buffer system with the K_a closest to 10^{-7} is the best choice. The magnitude of the answer makes physical sense because the buffer needs more acid than base (and this fact is not overcome by the heavier molar mass of the base).

16.33   **Given:** 500.0 mL of 0.100 M HNO_2/0.150 M KNO_2 buffer and (a) 250 mg NaOH, (b) 350 mg KOH, (c) 1.25 g HBr and (d) 1.35 g HI   **Find:** whether buffer capacity is exceeded

Conceptual Plan: mL $\rightarrow$ L then [HNO_2], L $\rightarrow$ mol HNO_2 and [KNO_2], L $\rightarrow$ mol KNO_2

$$\frac{1\text{ L}}{1000\text{ mL}} \qquad\qquad M = \frac{\text{mol}}{\text{L}} \qquad\qquad M = \frac{\text{mol}}{\text{L}}$$

then calculate moles of acid or base to be added to the buffer mg $\rightarrow$ g $\rightarrow$ mol then

$$\frac{1\text{ g}}{1000\text{ mg}}\quad \mathcal{M}$$

compare the added amount to the buffer amount of the opposite component. Ratio of base/acid must be between 0.1 and 10 to maintain the buffer integrity.

Solution: $500.00 \text{ mL} \times \dfrac{1\text{ L}}{1000\text{ mL}} = 0.5000\text{ L}$ then $\dfrac{0.100 \text{ mol } HNO_2}{1\text{ L}} \times 0.5000\text{ L} = 0.0500 \text{ mol } HNO_2$ and

$$\frac{0.150 \text{ mol } KNO_2}{1\text{ L}} \times 0.5000\text{ L} = 0.0750 \text{ mol } KNO_2$$

(a)   For NaOH: $250 \text{ mg NaOH} \times \dfrac{1\text{ g NaOH}}{1000 \text{ mg NaOH}} \times \dfrac{1 \text{ mol NaOH}}{40.00 \text{ g NaOH}} = 0.00625 \text{ mol NaOH}$. Because the buffer

contains 0.0500 mol acid, the amount of acid is reduced by $0.00625/0.0500 = 12.5\%$ and the ratio of base/acid is still between 0.1 and 10. The buffer capacity is not exceeded.

(b)   For KOH: $350 \text{ mg KOH} \times \dfrac{1\text{ g KOH}}{1000 \text{ mg KOH}} \times \dfrac{1 \text{ mol KOH}}{56.11 \text{ g KOH}} = 0.00624 \text{ mol KOH}$. Because the buffer

contains 0.0500 mol acid, the amount of acid is reduced by $0.00624/0.0500 = 12.5\%$ and the ratio of base/acid is still between 0.1 and 10. The buffer capacity is not exceeded.

(c)   For HBr: $1.25 \text{ g HBr} \times \dfrac{1 \text{ mol HBr}}{80.91 \text{ g HBr}} = 0.0154493 \text{ mol HBr}$. Because the buffer contains 0.0750 mol base,

the amount of acid is reduced by $0.0154/0.0750 = 20.6\%$ and the ratio of base/acid is still between 0.1 and 10. The buffer capacity is not exceeded.

(d)   For HI: $1.35 \text{ g HI} \times \dfrac{1 \text{ mol HI}}{127.91 \text{ g HI}} = 0.0105543 \text{ mol HI}$. Because the buffer contains 0.0750 mol base, the

amount of acid is reduced by $0.0106/0.0750 = 14.1\%$ and the ratio of base/acid is still between 0.1 and 10. The buffer capacity is not exceeded.

Titrations, pH Curves, and Indicators

16.35   (i)   The equivalence point of a titration is where the pH rises sharply as base is added. The pH at the equivalence point is the midpoint of the sharp rise at ~50 mL added base. For (a), the pH = ~8, and for (b), the pH = ~7.

(ii)   Graph (a) represents a weak acid, and graph (b) represents a strong acid. A strong acid titration starts at a lower pH, has a flatter initial region, and has a sharper rise at the equivalence point than does a weak acid. The pH at the equivalence point of a strong acid is neutral, while the pH at the equivalence point of a weak acid is basic.

16.37 **Given:** 20.0 mL 0.200 M KOH and 0.200 M CH_3NH_2 titrated with 0.100 M HI

(a) **Find:** volume of base to reach equivalence point

Conceptual Plan: The answer for both titrations will be the same because the initial concentration and volumes of the bases are the same. Write balanced equation then mL → L then

$$HI + KOH \rightarrow KI + H_2O \text{ and } HI + KOH \rightarrow CH_3NH_3I \qquad \frac{1 \text{ L}}{1000 \text{ mL}}$$

[base], L → mol base then set mol base = mol acid and [HI], mol HI → L HI → mL HI.

$$M = \frac{mol}{L} \qquad \text{balanced equation has 1 : 1 stoichiometry} \qquad M = \frac{mol}{L} \qquad \frac{1000 \text{ mL}}{1 \text{ L}}$$

Solution: $20.0 \text{ mL base} \times \dfrac{1 \text{ L}}{1000 \text{ mL}} = 0.0200 \text{ L base then}$

$\dfrac{0.200 \text{ mol base}}{1 \text{ L}} \times 0.0200 \text{ L} = 0.00400 \text{ mol base. So mol base} = 0.00400 \text{ mol} = \text{mol HI then}$

$0.00400 \text{ mol HI} \times \dfrac{1 \text{ L HI}}{0.100 \text{ mol HI}} = 0.0400 \text{ L HI} \times \dfrac{1000 \text{ mL}}{1 \text{ L}} = 40.0 \text{ mL HI for both titrations.}$

Check: The units (mL) are correct. The volume of acid is twice the volume of bases because the concentration of the base is twice that of the acid in each case. The answer for both titrations is the same because the stoichiometry is the same for both titration reactions.

(b) The pH at the equivalence point will be neutral for KOH (because it is a strong base), and it will be acidic for CH_3NH_2 (because it is a weak base and will produce a conjugate acid when titrated).

(c) The initial pH will be lower for CH_3NH_2 (because it is a weak base and will only partially dissociate) and not raise the pH as high as KOH will (because it is a strong base and so dissociates completely) at the same base concentration.

(d) The titration curves will look like the following:

KOH: CH_3NH_2:

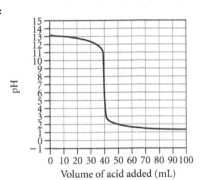 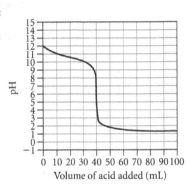

Important features to include are a high initial pH (if strong base pH is over 13 and is lower for a weak base), flat initial region (very flat for strong base, not as flat for weak base where pH halfway to equivalence point is the pK_b of the base), sharp drop at equivalence point, pH at equivalence point (neutral for strong base and lower for weak base), and then a flattening out at low pH.

16.39 (a) The equivalence point of a titration is where the pH rises sharply as base is added. The volume at the equivalence point is ~30 mL. The pH at the equivalence point is the midpoint of the sharp rise at ~30 mL added base, which is a pH = ~9.

(b) At 0 mL, the pH is calculated by doing an equilibrium calculation of a weak acid in water (as done in Chapter 15).

(c) The pH halfway to the equivalence point is equal to the pK_a of the acid, or ~15 mL.

(d) The pH at the equivalence point, or ~30 mL, is calculated by doing an equilibrium problem with the K_b of the acid. At the equivalence point, all of the acid has been converted to its conjugate base.

(e) Beyond the equivalence point (30 mL), there is excess base. All of the acid has been converted to its conjugate base, so the pH is calculated by focusing on this excess base concentration.

16.41 **Given:** 35.0 mL of 0.175 M HBr titrated with 0.200 M KOH

(a) **Find:** initial pH

Conceptual Plan: Because HBr is a strong acid, it will dissociate completely; so initial

$pH = -\log[H_3O^+] = -\log[HBr].$

Solution: $pH = -\log[HBr] = -\log 0.175 = 0.757$

Check: The units (none) are correct. The pH is reasonable because the concentration is greater than 0.1 M, and when the acid dissociates completely, the pH becomes less than 1.

(b)   **Find:** volume of base to reach equivalence point

        Conceptual Plan: Write balanced equation then mL → L then [HBr], L → mol HBr then

$$HBr + KOH \rightarrow KBr + H_2O \qquad \frac{1\ L}{1000\ mL} \qquad M = \frac{mol}{L}$$

        set mol acid (HBr) = mol base (KOH) and [KOH], mol KOH → L KOH → mL KOH.

$$\text{balanced equation has 1:1 stoichiometry} \qquad M = \frac{mol}{L} \qquad \frac{1000\ mL}{1\ L}$$

        Solution: $35.0\ \cancel{mL\ HBr} \times \dfrac{1\ L}{1000\ \cancel{mL}} = 0.0350\ L\ HBr$ then

$$\frac{0.175\ mol\ HBr}{1\ \cancel{L}} \times 0.0350\ \cancel{L} = 0.006125\ mol\ HBr$$

        So mol acid = mol HBr = 0.006125 mol = mol KOH then

$$0.006125\ \cancel{mol\ KOH} \times \frac{1\ L}{0.200\ \cancel{mol\ KOH}} = 0.030625\ \cancel{L\ KOH} \times \frac{1000\ mL}{1\ \cancel{L}} = 30.6\ mL\ KOH$$

        Check: The units (mL) are correct. The volume of base is a little less than the volume of acid because the concentration of the base is a little greater than that of the acid.

(c)   **Find:** pH after adding 10.0 mL of base

        Conceptual Plan: Use calculations from part (b). Then mL → L then [KOH], L → mol KOH then

$$\frac{1\ L}{1000\ mL} \qquad M = \frac{mol}{L}$$

        mol HBr, mol KOH → mol excess HBr and L HBr, L KOH → total L then

$$\text{set up stoichiometry table} \qquad L\ HBr + L\ KOH = \text{total L}$$

        mol excess HBr, L → [HBr] → pH.

$$M = \frac{mol}{L} \qquad pH = -\log[HBr]$$

        Solution: $10.0\ \cancel{mL\ KOH} \times \dfrac{1\ L}{1000\ \cancel{mL}} = 0.0100\ L\ KOH$ then

$$\frac{0.200\ mol\ KOH}{1\ \cancel{L}} \times 0.0100\ \cancel{L} = 0.00200\ mol\ KOH$$

        Because KOH is a strong base, [KOH] = [OH⁻], and set up a table to track changes:

	KOH(aq)	+ HBr(aq)	→ KBr(aq)	+ H₂O(l)
Before addition	≈0.00 mol	0.006125 mol	0.00 mol	—
Addition	0.00200 mol	—	—	—
After addition	≈0.00 mol	0.004125 mol	0.00200 mol	—

        Then 0.0350 L HBr + 0.0100 L KOH = 0.0450 L total volume.

        So mol excess acid = mol HBr = 0.004125 mol in 0.0450 L so

$$[HBr] = \frac{0.004125\ mol\ HBr}{0.0450\ L} = 0.0916667\ M\ \text{and}$$

$$pH = -\log[HBr] = -\log 0.0916667 = 1.038$$

        Check: The units (none) are correct. The pH is a little higher than the initial pH, which is expected because this is a strong acid.

(d)   **Find:** pH at equivalence point

        Solution: Because this is a strong acid–strong base titration, the pH at the equivalence point is neutral, or 7.

(e)   **Find:** pH after adding 5.0 mL of base beyond the equivalence point

        Conceptual Plan: Use calculations from parts (b) and (c). Then the pH is only dependent on the amount of excess base and the total solution volumes.

mL excess → L excess then [KOH], L excess → mol KOH excess

$$\frac{1\,L}{1000\,mL} \qquad\qquad M = \frac{mol}{L}$$

then L HBr, L KOH to equivalence point, L KOH excess → total L then

L HBr + L KOH to equivalence point + L KOH excess = total L

mol excess KOH, total L → [KOH] = [OH⁻] → [H₃O⁺] → pH

$$M = \frac{mol}{L} \qquad\qquad K_w = [H_3O^+][OH^-] \qquad pH = -\log[H_3O^+]$$

Solution: $5.0\,\cancel{mL\,KOH} \times \dfrac{1\,L}{1000\,\cancel{mL}} = 0.0050\,L\,KOH$ excess then

$\dfrac{0.200\,mol\,KOH}{1\,\cancel{L}} \times 0.0050\,\cancel{L} = 0.0010\,mol\,KOH$ excess. Then $0.0350\,L\,HBr + 0.0306\,L\,KOH + 0.0050\,L$

$KOH = 0.0706\,L$ total volume. $[KOH\,excess] = \dfrac{0.0010\,mol\,KOH\,excess}{0.0706\,L} = 0.014\underline{1}64\,M\,KOH$ excess.

Because KOH is a strong base, [KOH] excess = [OH⁻]. $K_w = [H_3O^+][OH^-]$, so

$$[H_3O^+] = \frac{K_w}{[OH^-]} = \frac{1.0 \times 10^{-14}}{0.014\underline{1}64} = 7.0\underline{6} \times 10^{-13}\,M.$$

Finally, $pH = -\log[H_3O^+] = -\log(7.0\underline{6} \times 10^{-13}) = 12.15.$

Check: The units (none) are correct. The pH is rising sharply at the equivalence point, so the pH after 5 mL past the equivalence point should be quite basic.

16.43 **Given:** 25.0 mL of 0.115 M RbOH titrated with 0.100 M HCl

(a) **Find:** initial pH

Conceptual Plan: Because RbOH is a strong base, it will dissociate completely, so
[RbOH] = [OH⁻] → [H₃O⁺] → pH.

$$K_w = [H_3O^+][OH^-] \qquad pH = -\log[H_3O^+]$$

Solution: Because RbOH is a strong base, [RbOH] excess = [OH⁻]. $K_w = [H_3O^+][OH^-]$, so

$$[H_3O^+] = \frac{K_w}{[OH^-]} = \frac{1.0 \times 10^{-14}}{0.115} = 8.6\underline{9}565 \times 10^{-14}\,M \text{ and}$$

$pH = -\log[H_3O^+] = -\log(8.6\underline{9}565 \times 10^{-14}) = 13.06.$

Check: The units (none) are correct. The pH is reasonable because the concentration is greater than 0.1 M, and when the base dissociates completely, the pH becomes greater than 13.

(b) **Find:** volume of acid to reach equivalence point

Conceptual Plan: Write balanced equation then mL → L then [RbOH], L → mol RbOH then

$$HCl + RbOH \rightarrow RbCl + H_2O \qquad \frac{1\,L}{1000\,mL} \qquad\qquad M = \frac{mol}{L}$$

set mol base (RbOH) = mol acid (HCl) and [HCl], mol HCl → L HCl → mL HCl.

balanced equation has 1:1 stoichiometry $\qquad M = \dfrac{mol}{L} \qquad \dfrac{1000\,mL}{1\,L}$

Solution: $25.0\,\cancel{mL\,RbOH} \times \dfrac{1\,L}{1000\,\cancel{mL}} = 0.0250\,L\,RbOH$ then

$\dfrac{0.115\,mol\,RbOH}{1\,\cancel{L}} \times 0.0250\,\cancel{L} = 0.00287\underline{5}\,mol\,RbOH.$ So mol base = mol RbOH = $0.00287\underline{5}\,mol = mol$

HCl then $0.00287\underline{5}\,\cancel{mol\,HCl} \times \dfrac{1\,L}{0.100\,\cancel{mol\,HCl}} = 0.0287\underline{5}\,\cancel{L\,HCl} \times \dfrac{1000\,mL}{1\,\cancel{L}} = 28.8\,mL\,HCl.$

Check: The units (mL) are correct. The volume of acid is greater than the volume of base because the concentration of the base is a little greater than that of the acid.

(c) **Find:** pH after adding 5.0 mL of acid

Conceptual Plan: Use calculations from part (b). Then mL → L then [HCl], L → mol HCl then

$$\frac{1\,L}{1000\,mL} \qquad\qquad M = \frac{mol}{L}$$

mol RbOH, mol HCl → mol excess RbOH and L RbOH, L HCl → total L then
set up stoichiometry table   L RbOH + L HCl = total L

mol excess RbOH, L → [RbOH] = [OH⁻] → [H₃O⁺] → pH.

$$M = \frac{mol}{L} \qquad\qquad K_w = [H_3O^+][OH^-] \quad pH = -\log[H_3O^+]$$

Solution: 5.0 m̶L̶ ̶H̶C̶l̶ $\times \dfrac{1\ L}{1000\ m̶L̶} = 0.0050$ L HCl then $\dfrac{0.100\ mol\ HCl}{1\ L̶} \times 0.0050\ L̶ = 0.00050$ mol HCl

Because HCl is a strong acid, [HCl] = [H₃O⁺]. Set up a table to track changes:

HCl(aq) + RbOH(aq) → RbCl(aq) + H₂O(l)

	HCl(aq)	RbOH(aq)	RbCl(aq)	H₂O(l)
Before addition	0.00 mol	0.002875 mol	0.00 mol	—
Addition	0.00050 mol	—	—	—
After addition	≈0.00 mol	0.002375 mol	0.00050 mol	—

Then 0.0250 L RbOH + 0.0050 L HCl = 0.0300 L total volume. So mol excess base = mol RbOH =

0.002375 mol in 0.0300 L, so $[RbOH] = \dfrac{0.002375\ mol\ RbOH}{0.0300\ L} = 0.0791667$ M. Because RbOH is a strong

base, [RbOH] excess = [OH⁻]. $K_w = [H_3O^+][OH^-]$ so $[H_3O^+] = \dfrac{K_w}{[OH^-]} = \dfrac{1.0 \times 10^{-14}}{0.0791667}$

$= 1.26316 \times 10^{-13}$ M and pH $= -\log[H_3O^+] = -\log(1.26316 \times 10^{-13}) = 12.90$

Check: The units (none) are correct. The pH is a little lower than the initial pH, which is expected because this is a strong base.

(d) **Find:** pH at equivalence point
Solution: Because this is a strong acid–strong base titration, the pH at the equivalence point is neutral, or 7.

(e) **Find:** pH after adding 5.0 mL of acid beyond the equivalence point
Conceptual Plan: Use calculations from parts (b) and (c). Then the pH is only dependent on the amount of excess acid and the total solution volumes. Then
mL excess → L excess then [HCl], L excess → mol HCl excess

$\frac{1\ L}{1000\ mL}$ $M = \frac{mol}{L}$

then L RbOH, L HCl to equivalence point, L HCl excess → total L then
L RbOH + L HCl to equivalence point + L HCl excess = total L

mol excess HCl, total L → [HCl] = [H₃O⁺] → pH

$M = \frac{mol}{L}$ $pH = -\log[H_3O^+]$

Solution: 5.0 m̶L̶ ̶H̶C̶l̶ $\times \dfrac{1\ L}{1000\ m̶L̶} = 0.0050$ L HCl excess then

$\dfrac{0.100\ mol\ HCl}{1\ L̶} \times 0.0050\ L̶ = 0.00050$ mol HCl excess. Then 0.0250 L RbOH + 0.0288 L HCl + 0.0050 L

HCl = 0.0588 L total volume. $[HCl\ excess] = \dfrac{0.00050\ mol\ HCl\ excess}{0.0588\ L} = 0.0085034$ M HCl excess

Because HCl is a strong acid, [HCl] excess = [H₃O⁺].
Finally, pH $= -\log[H_3O^+] = -\log(0.0085034) = 2.07$.

Check: The units (none) are correct. The pH is dropping sharply at the equivalence point, so the pH after 5 mL past the equivalence point should be quite acidic.

16.45   **Given:** 20.0 mL of 0.105 M HC₂H₃O₂ titrated with 0.125 M NaOH **Other:** $K_a(HC_2H_3O_2) = 1.8 \times 10^{-5}$
(a) **Find:** initial pH
Conceptual Plan: Because HC₂H₃O₂ is a weak acid, set up an equilibrium problem using the initial concentration.
So M HC₂H₃O₂ → [H₃O⁺] → pH

ICE table $pH = -\log[H_3O^+]$

Solution:

$$HC_2H_3O_2(aq) + H_2O(l) \rightleftharpoons H_3O^+(aq) + C_2H_3O_2^-(aq)$$

	$[HC_2H_3O_2]$	$[H_3O^+]$	$[C_2H_3O_2^-]$
Initial	0.105	≈ 0.00	0.00
Change	$-x$	$+x$	$+x$
Equil	$0.105 - x$	$+x$	$+x$

$K_a = \dfrac{[H_3O^+][C_2H_3O_2^-]}{[HC_2H_3O_2]} = 1.8 \times 10^{-5} = \dfrac{x^2}{0.105 - x}$. Assume that x is small ($x \ll 0.105$), so

$\dfrac{x^2}{0.105 - \not{x}} = 1.8 \times 10^{-5} = \dfrac{x^2}{0.105}$ and $x = 1.\underline{3}748 \times 10^{-3}$ M $= [H_3O^+]$. Confirm that the assumption is

valid. $\dfrac{1.\underline{3}748 \times 10^{-3}}{0.105} \times 100\% = 1.3\% < 5\%$, so the assumption is valid. Finally,

$pH = -\log[H_3O^+] = -\log(1.\underline{3}748 \times 10^{-3}) = 2.86$.

Check: The units (none) are correct. The magnitude of the answer makes physical sense because the pH should be greater than $-\log(0.105) = 0.98$ because this is a weak acid.

(b)   **Find:** volume of base to reach equivalence point
Conceptual Plan: Write a balanced equation then mL $\rightarrow$ L then $[HC_2H_3O_2]$, L $\rightarrow$ mol $HC_2H_3O_2$ then

$$HC_2H_3O_2 + NaOH \rightarrow NaC_2H_3O_2 + H_2O \qquad \dfrac{1\,L}{1000\,mL} \qquad\qquad M = \dfrac{mol}{L}$$

set mol acid($HC_2H_3O_2$) = mol base(NaOH) and [NaOH], mol NaOH $\rightarrow$ L NaOH $\rightarrow$ mL NaOH.

$$\text{balanced equation has 1:1 stoichiometry} \qquad M = \dfrac{mol}{L} \qquad \dfrac{1000\,mL}{1\,L}$$

Solution: $20.0 \text{ mL } HC_2H_3O_2 \times \dfrac{1\,L}{1000\,mL} = 0.0200 \text{ L } HC_2H_3O_2$

then $\dfrac{0.105 \text{ mol } HC_2H_3O_2}{1\,L} \times 0.0200\,L = 0.00210 \text{ mol } HC_2H_3O_2$

So mol acid = mol $HC_2H_3O_2$ = 0.00210 mol = mol NaOH then

$0.00210 \text{ mol NaOH} \times \dfrac{1\,L}{0.125 \text{ mol NaOH}} = 0.0168 \text{ L NaOH} \times \dfrac{1000\,mL}{1\,L} = 16.8 \text{ mL NaOH}$

Check: The units (mL) are correct. The volume of base is a little less than the volume of acid because the concentration of the base is a little greater than that of the acid.

(c)   **Find:** pH after adding 5.0 mL of base
Conceptual Plan: Use calculations from part (b). Then mL $\rightarrow$ L then [NaOH], L $\rightarrow$ mol NaOH then

$$\dfrac{1\,L}{1000\,mL} \qquad\qquad M = \dfrac{mol}{L}$$

mol $HC_2H_3O_2$, mol NaOH $\rightarrow$ mol excess $HC_2H_3O_2$, mol $C_2H_3O_2^-$ and

$$\text{set up stoichiometry table}$$

L $HC_2H_3O_2$, L NaOH $\rightarrow$ total L then

$$\text{L } HC_2H_3O_2 + \text{L NaOH} = \text{total L}$$

mol excess $HC_2H_3O_2$, L $\rightarrow$ $[HC_2H_3O_2]$ and mol excess $C_2H_3O_2^-$, L $\rightarrow$ $[C_2H_3O_2^-]$ then

$$M = \dfrac{mol}{L} \qquad\qquad M = \dfrac{mol}{L}$$

M $HC_2H_3O_2$, M $C_2H_3O_2^-$ $\rightarrow$ $[H_3O^+]$ $\rightarrow$ pH.

$$\text{ICE table} \qquad pH = -\log[H_3O^+]$$

Solution: $5.0 \text{ mL NaOH} \times \dfrac{1 \text{ L}}{1000 \text{ mL}} = 0.0050 \text{ L NaOH}$ then

$\dfrac{0.125 \text{ mol NaOH}}{1 \text{ L}} \times 0.0050 \text{ L} = 0.000625 \text{ mol NaOH}$. Set up a table to track changes:

$$\text{NaOH}(aq) \ + \ \text{HC}_2\text{H}_3\text{O}_2(aq) \rightarrow \text{NaC}_2\text{H}_3\text{O}_2(aq) \ + \ \text{H}_2\text{O}(l)$$

	NaOH	HC₂H₃O₂	NaC₂H₃O₂	H₂O
Before addition	0.00 mol	0.00210 mol	0.00 mol	—
Addition	0.000625 mol	—	—	—
After addition	≈ 0.00 mol	0.001475 mol	0.000625 mol	—

Then $0.0200 \text{ L HC}_2\text{H}_3\text{O}_2 + 0.0050 \text{ L NaOH} = 0.0250 \text{ L}$ total volume. Then

$[\text{HC}_2\text{H}_3\text{O}_2] = \dfrac{0.001475 \text{ mol HC}_2\text{H}_3\text{O}_2}{0.0250 \text{ L}} = 0.0590 \text{ M}$ and $[\text{NaC}_2\text{H}_3\text{O}_2] = \dfrac{0.000625 \text{ mol C}_2\text{H}_3\text{O}_2^-}{0.0250 \text{ L}} = 0.025 \text{ M}$.

Because one $\text{C}_2\text{H}_3\text{O}_2^-$ ion is generated for each $\text{NaC}_2\text{H}_3\text{O}_2$, $[\text{C}_2\text{H}_3\text{O}_2^-] = 0.025 \text{ M C}_2\text{H}_3\text{O}_2^-$.

$$\text{HC}_2\text{H}_3\text{O}_2(aq) + \text{H}_2\text{O}(l) \rightleftharpoons \text{H}_3\text{O}^+(aq) + \text{C}_2\text{H}_3\text{O}_2^-(aq)$$

	[HC₂H₃O₂]	[H₃O⁺]	[C₂H₃O₂⁻]
Initial	0.0590	≈ 0.00	0.025
Change	$-x$	$+x$	$+x$
Equil	$0.0590 - x$	$+x$	$0.025 + x$

$K_a = \dfrac{[\text{H}_3\text{O}^+][\text{C}_2\text{H}_3\text{O}_2^-]}{[\text{HC}_2\text{H}_3\text{O}_2]} = 1.8 \times 10^{-5} = \dfrac{x(0.025 + x)}{0.0590 - x}$ Assume that x is small ($x \ll 0.025 < 0.0590$), so

$\dfrac{x(0.025 + x)}{0.0590 - x} = 1.8 \times 10^{-5} = \dfrac{x(0.025)}{0.0590}$ and $x = 4.248 \times 10^{-5} \text{ M} = [\text{H}_3\text{O}^+]$. Confirm that the assumption is valid.

$\dfrac{4.248 \times 10^{-5}}{0.025} \times 100\% = 0.17\% < 5\%$, so the assumption is valid.

Finally, $\text{pH} = -\log[\text{H}_3\text{O}^+] = -\log(4.248 \times 10^{-5}) = 4.37$.

Check: The units (none) are correct. The pH is a little higher than the initial pH, which is expected because some of the acid has been neutralized.

(d) **Find:** pH at one-half the equivalence point
Conceptual Plan: Because this is a weak acid–strong base titration, the pH at one-half the equivalence point is the pK_a of the weak acid.
Solution: $\text{pH} = \text{p}K_a = -\log K_a = -\log(1.8 \times 10^{-5}) = 4.74$.

Check: The units (none) are correct. Because this is a weak acid–strong base titration, the pH at one-half the equivalence point is the pK_a of the weak acid; so it should be a little below 5.

(e) **Find:** pH at equivalence point
Conceptual Plan: Use calculations from part (b). Then because all of the weak acid has been converted to its conjugate base, the pH is only dependent on the hydrolysis reaction of the conjugate base. The mol $\text{C}_2\text{H}_3\text{O}_2^-$ = initial mol $\text{HC}_2\text{H}_3\text{O}_2$ and L $\text{HC}_2\text{H}_3\text{O}_2$, L NaOH to equivalence point → total L then

$$\text{L HC}_2\text{H}_3\text{O}_2 + \text{L NaOH} = \text{total L}$$

mol excess $\text{C}_2\text{H}_3\text{O}_2^-$, L → $[\text{C}_2\text{H}_3\text{O}_2^-]$ and K_a → K_b then do an equilibrium calculation:

$$\text{M} = \dfrac{\text{mol}}{\text{L}} \qquad\qquad K_w = K_a K_b$$

$[\text{C}_2\text{H}_3\text{O}_2^-], K_b$ → $[\text{OH}^-]$ → $[\text{H}_3\text{O}^+]$ → pH.

$$\text{set up ICE table} \quad K_w = [\text{H}_3\text{O}^+][\text{OH}^-] \quad \text{pH} = -\log[\text{H}_3\text{O}^+]$$

Solution: mol $\text{C}_2\text{H}_3\text{O}_2^-$ = initial mol $\text{HC}_2\text{H}_3\text{O}_2$ = 0.00210 mol and total volume = L $\text{HC}_2\text{H}_3\text{O}_2$ + L NaOH = 0.020 L + 0.0168 L = 0.0368 L then

$$[C_2H_3O_2^-] = \frac{0.00210 \text{ mol } C_2H_3O_2^-}{0.0368 \text{ L}} = 0.0570652 \text{ M and } K_w = K_aK_b. \text{ Rearrange to solve for } K_b.$$

$$K_b = \frac{K_w}{K_a} = \frac{1.0 \times 10^{-14}}{1.8 \times 10^{-5}} = 5.5556 \times 10^{-10}. \text{ Set up an ICE table:}$$

$$C_2H_3O_2^-(aq) + H_2O(l) \rightleftharpoons HC_2H_3O_2(aq) + OH^-(aq)$$

	$[C_2H_3O_2^-]$	$[HC_2H_3O_2]$	$[OH^-]$
Initial	0.0570652	≈0.00	≈0.00
Change	−x	+x	+x
Equil	0.0570652 − x	+x	+x

$$K_b = \frac{[HC_2H_3O_2][OH^-]}{[C_2H_3O_2^-]} = 5.5556 \times 10^{-10} = \frac{x^2}{0.0570652 - x}. \text{ Assume that } x \text{ is small } (x \ll 0.057), \text{ so}$$

$$\frac{x^2}{0.0570652 - \cancel{x}} = 5.5556 \times 10^{-10} = \frac{x^2}{0.0570652} \text{ and } x = 5.6306 \times 10^{-6} \text{ M} = [OH^-]. \text{ Confirm that the}$$

$$\text{assumption is valid. } \frac{5.6306 \times 10^{-6}}{0.0570652} \times 100\% = 0.0099\% < 5\%, \text{ so the assumption is valid.}$$

$$K_w = [H_3O^+][OH^-], \text{ so } [H_3O^+] = \frac{K_w}{[OH^-]} = \frac{1.0 \times 10^{-14}}{5.6305 \times 10^{-6}} = 1.7760 \times 10^{-9} \text{ M}.$$

Finally, $pH = -\log[H_3O^+] = -\log(1.7760 \times 10^{-9}) = 8.75$.

Check: The units (none) are correct. Because this is a weak acid–strong base titration, the pH at the equivalence point is basic.

(f) **Find:** pH after adding 5.0 mL of base beyond the equivalence point
Conceptual Plan: Use calculations from parts (b) and (c). Then the pH is only dependent on the amount of excess base and the total solution volumes.
mL excess → L excess then [NaOH], L excess → mol NaOH excess

$$\frac{1 \text{ L}}{1000 \text{ mL}} \qquad\qquad M = \frac{mol}{L}$$

then L $HC_2H_3O_2$, L NaOH to equivalence point, L NaOH excess → total L then

$$\text{L } HC_2H_3O_2 + \text{L NaOH to equivalence point} + \text{L NaOH excess} = \text{total L}$$

mol excess NaOH, total L → [NaOH] = [OH⁻] → [H₃O⁺] → pH

$$M = \frac{mol}{L} \qquad K_w = [H_3O^+][OH^-] \quad pH = -\log[H_3O^+]$$

Solution: $5.0 \text{ mL NaOH} \times \frac{1 \text{ L}}{1000 \text{ mL}} = 0.0050 \text{ L NaOH excess then}$

$\frac{0.125 \text{ mol NaOH}}{1 \text{ L}} \times 0.0050 \text{ L} = 0.000625 \text{ mol NaOH excess. Then } 0.0200 \text{ L } HC_2H_3O_2 + 0.0168 \text{ L NaOH}$

$+ 0.0050 \text{ L NaOH} = 0.0418 \text{ L total volume.}$

$$[NaOH \text{ excess}] = \frac{0.000625 \text{ mol NaOH excess}}{0.0418 \text{ L}} = 0.0149522 \text{ M NaOH excess. Because NaOH is a strong}$$

base, [NaOH] excess = [OH⁻]. The strong base overwhelms the weak base, which becomes insignificant in the

$$\text{calculation. } K_w = [H_3O^+][OH^-], \text{ so } [H_3O^+] = \frac{K_w}{[OH^-]} = \frac{1.0 \times 10^{-14}}{0.0149522} = 6.688 \times 10^{-13} \text{ M}.$$

Finally, $pH = -\log[H_3O^+] = -\log(6.688 \times 10^{-13}) = 12.17$.

Check: The units (none) are correct. The pH is rising sharply at the equivalence point, so the pH after 5 mL past the equivalence point should be quite basic.

16.47   **Given:** 25.0 mL of 0.175 M CH_3NH_2 titrated with 0.150 M HBr **Other:** $K_b(CH_3NH_2) = 4.4 \times 10^{-4}$

(a)   **Find:** initial pH

Conceptual Plan: Because CH_3NH_2 is a weak base, set up an equilibrium problem using the initial concentration, so M CH_3NH_2 → $[OH^-]$ → $[H_3O^+]$ → pH.

ICE table $K_w = [H_3O^+][OH^-]$ pH $= -\log[H_3O^+]$

Solution:

$$CH_3NH_2(aq) + H_2O(l) \rightleftharpoons CH_3NH_3^+(aq) + OH^-(aq)$$

	$[CH_3NH_2]$	$[CH_3NH_3^+]$	$[OH^-]$
Initial	0.175	0.00	≈ 0.00
Change	$-x$	$+x$	$+x$
Equil	$0.175 - x$	$+x$	$+x$

$$K_b = \frac{[CH_3NH_3^+][OH^-]}{[CH_3NH_2]} = 4.4 \times 10^{-4} = \frac{x^2}{0.175 - x}$$

Assume that x is small

$(x \ll 0.175)$, so $\dfrac{x^2}{0.175 - \cancel{x}} = 4.4 \times 10^{-4} = \dfrac{x^2}{0.175}$ and $x = 8.\underline{7}750 \times 10^{-3}$ M $= [OH^-]$.

Confirm that the assumption is valid. $\dfrac{8.\underline{7}750 \times 10^{-3}}{0.175} \times 100\% = 5.0\%$, so the assumption is valid.

$K_w = [H_3O^+][OH^-]$, so $[H_3O^+] = \dfrac{K_w}{[OH^-]} = \dfrac{1.0 \times 10^{-14}}{8.\underline{7}750 \times 10^{-3}} = 1.\underline{1}396 \times 10^{-12}$ M.

Finally, pH $= -\log[H_3O^+] = -\log(1.\underline{1}396 \times 10^{-12}) = 11.94$.

Check: The units (none) are correct. The magnitude of the answer makes physical sense because the pH should be less than $14 + \log(0.175) = 13.2$ because this is a weak base.

(b)   **Find:** volume of acid to reach equivalence point

Conceptual Plan: Write a balanced equation, then mL → L then $[CH_3NH_2]$, L → mol CH_3NH_2

$HBr + CH_3NH_2 \rightarrow CH_3NH_3Br + H_2O$ $\dfrac{1\,L}{1000\,mL}$ $M = \dfrac{mol}{L}$

then set mol base $[CH_3NH_2]$ = mol acid (HBr) and [HBr], mol HBr → L HBr → mL HBr.

balanced equation has 1:1 stoichiometry $M = \dfrac{mol}{L}$ $\dfrac{1000\,mL}{1\,L}$

Solution: $25.0 \text{ mL } \cancel{CH_3NH_2} \times \dfrac{1\,L}{1000\,\cancel{mL}} = 0.0250 \text{ L } CH_3NH_2$ then

$\dfrac{0.175 \text{ mol } CH_3NH_2}{1\,\cancel{L}} \times 0.0250\,\cancel{L} = 0.004375 \text{ mol } CH_3NH_2$. So mol base $=$ mol $CH_3NH_2 = 0.004375$ mol

$=$ mol HBr then $0.004\underline{3}75 \text{ mol HBr} \times \dfrac{1\,L}{0.150 \text{ mol HBr}} = 0.0291667 \text{ L HBr} \times \dfrac{1000\,mL}{1\,\cancel{L}} = 29.2 \text{ mL HBr}.$

Check: The units (mL) are correct. The volume of acid is greater than the volume of base because the concentration of the base is a little greater than that of the acid.

(c)   **Find:** pH after adding 5.0 mL of acid

Conceptual Plan: Use calculations from part (b). Then mL → L then [HBr], L → mol HBr

$\dfrac{1\,L}{1000\,mL}$ $M = \dfrac{mol}{L}$

then mol CH_3NH_2, mol HBr → mol excess CH_3NH_2 and L CH_3NH_2, L HBr → total L.

set up stoichiometry table   L CH_3NH_2 + L HBr = total L

Because there are significant concentrations of both the acid and the conjugate base species, this is a

buffer solution; so the Henderson–Hasselbalch equation $\left(\text{pH} = pK_a + \log \dfrac{[base]}{[acid]} \right)$ can be used.

$$[C_2H_3O_2^-] = \frac{0.00210 \text{ mol } C_2H_3O_2^-}{0.0368 \text{ L}} = 0.0570652 \text{ M and } K_w = K_aK_b. \text{ Rearrange to solve for } K_b.$$

$$K_b = \frac{K_w}{K_a} = \frac{1.0 \times 10^{-14}}{1.8 \times 10^{-5}} = 5.\underline{5}556 \times 10^{-10}. \text{ Set up an ICE table:}$$

$$C_2H_3O_2^-(aq) + H_2O(l) \rightleftharpoons HC_2H_3O_2(aq) + OH^-(aq)$$

	$[\mathbf{C_2H_3O_2^-}]$	$[\mathbf{HC_2H_3O_2}]$	$[\mathbf{OH^-}]$
Initial	0.0570652	≈0.00	≈0.00
Change	−x	+x	+x
Equil	0.0570652 − x	+x	+x

$$K_b = \frac{[HC_2H_3O_2][OH^-]}{[C_2H_3O_2^-]} = 5.\underline{5}556 \times 10^{-10} = \frac{x^2}{0.0570652 - x}. \text{ Assume that } x \text{ is small } (x \ll 0.057), \text{ so}$$

$$\frac{x^2}{0.0570652 - \cancel{x}} = 5.\underline{5}556 \times 10^{-10} = \frac{x^2}{0.0570652} \text{ and } x = 5.6306 \times 10^{-6} \text{ M} = [OH^-]. \text{ Confirm that the}$$

assumption is valid. $\dfrac{5.6306 \times 10^{-6}}{0.0570652} \times 100\% = 0.0099\% < 5\%$, so the assumption is valid.

$$K_w = [H_3O^+][OH^-], \text{ so } [H_3O^+] = \frac{K_w}{[OH^-]} = \frac{1.0 \times 10^{-14}}{5.\underline{6}305 \times 10^{-6}} = 1.\underline{7}760 \times 10^{-9} \text{ M}.$$

Finally, pH $= -\log[H_3O^+] = -\log(1.\underline{7}760 \times 10^{-9}) = 8.75$.

Check: The units (none) are correct. Because this is a weak acid–strong base titration, the pH at the equivalence point is basic.

(f) **Find:** pH after adding 5.0 mL of base beyond the equivalence point
Conceptual Plan: Use calculations from parts (b) and (c). Then the pH is only dependent on the amount of excess base and the total solution volumes.
mL excess → L excess then [NaOH], L excess → mol NaOH excess

$$\frac{1 \text{ L}}{1000 \text{ mL}} \qquad\qquad M = \frac{\text{mol}}{\text{L}}$$

then L HC$_2$H$_3$O$_2$, L NaOH to equivalence point, L NaOH excess → total L then

$$\text{L HC}_2\text{H}_3\text{O}_2 + \text{L NaOH to equivalence point} + \text{L NaOH excess} = \text{total L}$$

mol excess NaOH, total L → [NaOH] = [OH$^-$] → [H$_3$O$^+$] → pH

$$M = \frac{\text{mol}}{\text{L}} \qquad\qquad K_w = [H_3O^+][OH^-] \quad pH = -\log[H_3O^+]$$

Solution: $5.0 \cancel{\text{ mL NaOH}} \times \dfrac{1 \text{ L}}{1000 \cancel{\text{ mL}}} = 0.0050 \text{ L NaOH excess then}$

$\dfrac{0.125 \text{ mol NaOH}}{1 \cancel{\text{ L}}} \times 0.0050 \cancel{\text{ L}} = 0.000625 \text{ mol NaOH excess. Then } 0.0200 \text{ L HC}_2\text{H}_3\text{O}_2 + 0.0168 \text{ L NaOH}$

$+ 0.0050 \text{ L NaOH} = 0.0418 \text{ L total volume}.$

$$[\text{NaOH excess}] = \frac{0.000625 \text{ mol NaOH excess}}{0.0418 \text{ L}} = 0.0149522 \text{ M NaOH excess. Because NaOH is a strong}$$

base, [NaOH] excess = [OH$^-$]. The strong base overwhelms the weak base, which becomes insignificant in the

calculation. $K_w = [H_3O^+][OH^-]$, so $[H_3O^+] = \dfrac{K_w}{[OH^-]} = \dfrac{1.0 \times 10^{-14}}{0.0149522} = 6.\underline{6}88 \times 10^{-13} \text{ M}.$

Finally, pH $= -\log[H_3O^+] = -\log(6.\underline{6}88 \times 10^{-13}) = 12.17$.

Check: The units (none) are correct. The pH is rising sharply at the equivalence point, so the pH after 5 mL past the equivalence point should be quite basic.

16.47   **Given:** 25.0 mL of 0.175 M CH_3NH_2 titrated with 0.150 M HBr **Other:** $K_b(CH_3NH_2) = 4.4 \times 10^{-4}$

(a)   **Find:** initial pH

          Conceptual Plan: Because CH_3NH_2 is a weak base, set up an equilibrium problem using the initial con-centration, so M $CH_3NH_2 \rightarrow [OH^-] \rightarrow [H_3O^+] \rightarrow$ pH.

$$\text{ICE table} \quad K_w = [H_3O^+][OH^-] \quad pH = -\log[H_3O^+]$$

          Solution:

$$CH_3NH_2(aq) + H_2O(l) \rightleftharpoons CH_3NH_3{}^+(aq) + OH^-(aq)$$

	$[CH_3NH_2]$	$[CH_3NH_3{}^+]$	$[OH^-]$
Initial	0.175	0.00	≈ 0.00
Change	$-x$	$+x$	$+x$
Equil	$0.175 - x$	$+x$	$+x$

$$K_b = \frac{[CH_3NH_3{}^+][OH^-]}{[CH_3NH_2]} = 4.4 \times 10^{-4} = \frac{x^2}{0.175 - x}$$

Assume that x is small

$(x \ll 0.175)$, so $\dfrac{x^2}{0.175 - \not{x}} = 4.4 \times 10^{-4} = \dfrac{x^2}{0.175}$ and $x = 8.7750 \times 10^{-3}$ M $= [OH^-]$.

Confirm that the assumption is valid. $\dfrac{8.7750 \times 10^{-3}}{0.175} \times 100\% = 5.0\%$, so the assumption is valid.

$K_w = [H_3O^+][OH^-]$, so $[H_3O^+] = \dfrac{K_w}{[OH^-]} = \dfrac{1.0 \times 10^{-14}}{8.7750 \times 10^{-3}} = 1.1396 \times 10^{-12}$ M.

Finally, pH $= -\log[H_3O^+] = -\log(1.1396 \times 10^{-12}) = 11.94$.

Check: The units (none) are correct. The magnitude of the answer makes physical sense because the pH should be less than $14 + \log(0.175) = 13.2$ because this is a weak base.

(b)   **Find:** volume of acid to reach equivalence point

          Conceptual Plan: Write a balanced equation, then mL $\rightarrow$ L then $[CH_3NH_2]$, L $\rightarrow$ mol CH_3NH_2

$$HBr + CH_3NH_2 \rightarrow CH_3NH_3Br + H_2O \qquad \frac{1\ L}{1000\ mL} \qquad\qquad M = \frac{mol}{L}$$

          then set mol base $[CH_3NH_2]$ = mol acid (HBr) and [HBr], mol HBr $\rightarrow$ L HBr $\rightarrow$ mL HBr.

$$\text{balanced equation has 1:1 stoichiometry} \qquad M = \frac{mol}{L} \qquad \frac{1000\ mL}{1\ L}$$

Solution: 25.0 m̶L̶ ̶C̶H̶₃̶N̶H̶₂̶ $\times \dfrac{1\ L}{1000\ \not{mL}} = 0.0250$ L CH_3NH_2 then

$\dfrac{0.175\ mol\ CH_3NH_2}{1\ \not{L}} \times 0.0250\ \not{L} = 0.004375$ mol CH_3NH_2. So mol base = mol CH_3NH_2 = 0.004375 mol

= mol HBr then 0.004375 m̶o̶l̶ ̶H̶B̶r̶ $\times \dfrac{1\ L}{0.150\ \not{mol\ HBr}} = 0.0291667$ L̶ ̶H̶B̶r̶ $\times \dfrac{1000\ mL}{1\ \not{L}} = 29.2$ mL HBr.

Check: The units (mL) are correct. The volume of acid is greater than the volume of base because the concen-tration of the base is a little greater than that of the acid.

(c)   **Find:** pH after adding 5.0 mL of acid

          Conceptual Plan: Use calculations from part (b). Then mL $\rightarrow$ L then [HBr], L $\rightarrow$ mol HBr

$$\frac{1\ L}{1000\ mL} \qquad\qquad M = \frac{mol}{L}$$

          then mol CH_3NH_2, mol HBr $\rightarrow$ mol excess CH_3NH_2 and L CH_3NH_2, L HBr $\rightarrow$ total L.

$$\text{set up stoichiometry table} \qquad\qquad L\ CH_3NH_2 + L\ HBr = \text{total L}$$

Because there are significant concentrations of both the acid and the conjugate base species, this is a buffer solution; so the Henderson–Hasselbalch equation $\left(\text{pH} = pK_a + \log \dfrac{[\text{base}]}{[\text{acid}]} \right)$ can be used.

Convert K_b to K_a using $K_w = K_a K_b$. Also note that the ratio of concentrations is the same as the ratio of moles because the volume is the same for both species.

Solution: $5.0 \text{ mL HBr} \times \dfrac{1 \text{ L}}{1000 \text{ mL}} = 0.0050 \text{ L HBr}$ then $\dfrac{0.150 \text{ mol HBr}}{1 \text{ L}} \times 0.0050 \text{ L} = 0.00075 \text{ mol HBr}$

Set up a table to track changes:

$$\text{HBr}(aq) + \text{CH}_3\text{NH}_2(aq) \rightarrow \text{CH}_3\text{NH}_3\text{Br}(aq)$$

Before addition	0.00 mol	0.004375 mol	0.00 mol	
Addition	0.00075 mol	—	—	then $K_w = K_a K_b$ so
After addition	≈0.00 mol	0.003625 mol	0.000750 mol	

$K_a = \dfrac{K_w}{K_b} = \dfrac{1.0 \times 10^{-14}}{4.4 \times 10^{-4}} = 2.2727 \times 10^{-11}$ M. Then use the Henderson–Hasselbalch equation because the

solution is a buffer. $\text{pH} = \text{p}K_a + \log \dfrac{[\text{base}]}{[\text{acid}]} = -\log(2.2727 \times 10^{-11}) + \log \dfrac{0.003625}{0.000750} = 11.33$

Check: The units (none) are correct. The pH is a little lower than the last pH, which is expected because some of the base has been neutralized.

(d) **Find:** pH at one-half the equivalence point
Conceptual Plan: Because this is a weak base–strong acid titration, the pH at one-half the equivalence point is the pK_a of the conjugate acid of weak base.
Solution: $\text{pH} = \text{p}K_a = -\log K_a = -\log(2.2727 \times 10^{-11}) = 10.64$

Check: The units (none) are correct. Because this is a weak acid–strong base titration, the pH at one-half the equivalence point is the pK_a of the conjugate acid of the weak base; so it should be a little below 11.

(e) **Find:** pH at equivalence point
Conceptual Plan: Use previous calculations. Because all of the weak base has been converted to its conjugate acid, the pH is only dependent on the hydrolysis reaction of the conjugate acid. The mol $\text{CH}_3\text{NH}_3^+ =$ initial mol CH_3NH_2 and
L CH_3NH_2, L HBr to equivalence point $\rightarrow$ total L then mol CH_3NH_3^+, L $\rightarrow$ [CH_3NH_3^+]

$$\text{L CH}_3\text{NH}_2 + \text{L HBr} = \text{total L} \qquad\qquad M = \dfrac{\text{mol}}{\text{L}}$$

then do an equilibrium calculation: [CH_3NH_3^+], $K_a \rightarrow$ [H_3O^+] $\rightarrow$ pH.

$$\text{set up ICE table} \qquad \text{pH} = -\log[\text{H}_3\text{O}^+]$$

Solution: mol base = mol acid = mol $\text{CH}_3\text{NH}_3^+ = 0.004375$ mol. Then total volume = L CH_3NH_3^+

L HBr $= 0.0250 \text{ L} + 0.0292 \text{ L} = 0.0542$ then $[\text{CH}_3\text{NH}_3^+] = \dfrac{0.004375 \text{ mol CH}_3\text{NH}_3^+}{0.0542 \text{ L}} = 0.0807196$ M.

Set up an ICE table:

$$\text{CH}_3\text{NH}_3^+(aq) + \text{H}_2\text{O}\,(l) \rightleftharpoons \text{CH}_3\text{NH}_2(aq) + \text{H}_3\text{O}^+(aq)$$

	[CH_3NH_3^+]	[CH_3NH_2]	[H_3O^+]
Initial	0.0807196	≈0.00	≈0.00
Change	$-x$	$+x$	$+x$
Equil	$0.0807196 - x$	$+x$	$+x$

$K_a = \dfrac{[\text{CH}_3\text{NH}_2]\,[\text{H}_3\text{O}^+]}{[\text{CH}_3\text{NH}_3^+]} = 2.2727 \times 10^{-11} = \dfrac{x^2}{0.0807196 - x}$. Assume that x is small ($x \ll 0.0807$), so

$\dfrac{x^2}{0.0807196 - x} = 2.2727 \times 10^{-11} = \dfrac{x^2}{0.0807196}$ and $x = 1.3544 \times 10^{-6} = [\text{H}_3\text{O}^+]$.

Confirm that the assumption is valid. $\dfrac{1.3544 \times 10^{-6}}{0.0807106} \times 100\% = 0.0017\% < 5\%$, so the assumption is valid.

Finally, pH $= -\log[H_3O^+] = -\log(1.\underline{3}544 \times 10^{-6}) = 5.87$.

Check: The units (none) are correct. Because this is a weak base–strong acid titration, the pH at the equivalence point is acidic.

(f) **Find:** pH after adding 5.0 mL of acid beyond the equivalence point
Conceptual Plan: Use calculations from parts (b) and (c). Then the pH is only dependent on the amount of excess acid and the total solution volumes.
mL excess → L excess then [HBr], L excess → mol HBr excess

$$\frac{1\ L}{1000\ mL} \qquad\qquad M = \frac{mol}{L}$$

then L CH$_3$NH$_2$, L HBr to equivalence point, L HBr excess → total L then

$$L\ CH_3NH_2 + L\ HBr\ \text{to equivalence point} + L\ HBr\ \text{excess} = \text{total L}$$

mol excess HBr, total L → [HBr] = [H$_3$O$^+$] → pH

$$M = \frac{mol}{L} \qquad\qquad pH = -\log[H_3O^+]$$

Solution: $5.0\ \text{mL HBr} \times \dfrac{1\ L}{1000\ \text{mL}} = 0.0050\ \text{L HBr excess then}$

$\dfrac{0.150\ \text{mol HBr}}{1\ L} \times 0.0050\ L = 0.00075\ \text{mol HBr excess}$. Then $0.0250\ \text{L CH}_3\text{NH}_2 + 0.0292\ \text{L HBr} +$

$0.0050\ \text{L HBr} = 0.0592\ \text{L total volume}$.

$[\text{HBr excess}] = \dfrac{0.00075\ \text{mol HBr excess}}{0.0592\ \text{L}} = 0.01\underline{2}669\ \text{M HBr excess}$

Because HBr is a strong acid, [HBr] excess $= [H_3O^+]$. The strong acid overwhelms the weak acid, which becomes insignificant in the calculation. Finally, pH $= -\log[H_3O^+] = -\log(0.01\underline{2}669) = 1.90$.

Check: The units (none) are correct. The pH is dropping sharply at the equivalence point, so the pH after 5 mL past the equivalence point should be quite acidic.

16.49 (i) Acid a is more concentrated because the equivalence point (where sharp pH rise occurs) is at a higher volume of added base.

(ii) Acid b has the larger K_a because the pH at a volume of added base equal to half the equivalence point volume is lower.

16.51 **Given:** 0.229 g unknown monoprotic acid titrated with 0.112 M NaOH and curve
Find: molar mass and pK_a of acid
Conceptual Plan: The equivalence point is where sharp pH rise occurs. The pK_a is the pH at a volume of added base equal to half the equivalence point volume. Then mL NaOH → L NaOH

$$\frac{1\ L}{1000\ mL}$$

then [NaOH], L NaOH → mol NaOH = mol acid then mol NaOH, g acid → molar mass.

$$M = \frac{mol}{L} \qquad\qquad \frac{\text{g acid}}{\text{mol acid}}$$

Solution: The equivalence point is at 25 mL NaOH. The pH at $0.5 \times 25\ \text{mL} = 13\ \text{mL is} \sim 3 = \text{p}K_a$. Then

$25\ \text{mL NaOH} \times \dfrac{1\ L}{1000\ \text{mL}} = 0.025\ \text{L NaOH then}$

$\dfrac{0.112\ \text{mol NaOH}}{1\ L} \times 0.025\ L = 0.0028\ \text{mol NaOH} = 0.0028\ \text{mol acid then}$

$\text{molar mass} = \dfrac{0.229\ \text{g acid}}{0.0028\ \text{mol acid}} = 82\ \text{g/mol}$.

Check: The units (none and g/mol) are correct. The pK_a is consistent with a weak acid. The molar mass is reasonable for an acid (> 1 g/mol).

16.53 **Given:** 20.0 mL of 0.115 M sulfurous acid (H$_2$SO$_3$) titrated with 0.1014 M KOH   **Find:** volume of base added
Conceptual Plan: Because this is a diprotic acid, each proton is titrated sequentially. Write balanced equations.

$$H_2SO_3 + OH^- \rightarrow HSO_3^- + H_2O \text{ and } HSO_3^- + OH^- \rightarrow SO_3^{2-} + H_2O$$

Then mL $\rightarrow$ L then $[H_2SO_3]$, L $\rightarrow$ mol H_2SO_3 then set mol base (H_2SO_3) $=$ mol acid (KOH) and

$$\frac{1\,L}{1000\,mL} \qquad\qquad M = \frac{mol}{L} \qquad\qquad \textit{balanced equation has 1:1 stoichiometry} \text{ (1 st equivalence point)}$$

[KOH], mol KOH $\rightarrow$ L KOH $\rightarrow$ mL KOH the volume to the second equivalence point will be

$$M = \frac{mol}{L} \qquad\qquad \frac{1000\,mL}{1\,L}$$

double the volume to the first equivalence point.

Solution: $20.0 \,\cancel{mL\,H_2SO_3} \times \dfrac{1\,L}{1000\,\cancel{mL}} = 0.0200\,L\,H_2SO_3$ then $\dfrac{0.115\,mol\,H_2SO_3}{1\,\cancel{L}} \times 0.0200\,\cancel{L} = 0.00230$

mol H_2SO_3. So mol base $=$ mol $H_2SO_3 = 0.00230$ mol $=$ mol KOH then

$$0.00230\,\cancel{mol\,KOH} \times \frac{1\,L}{0.1014\,\cancel{mol\,KOH}} = 0.02268245\,\cancel{L\,KOH} \times \frac{1000\,ml}{1\,\cancel{L}} = 22.7\,mL\,KOH$$

to the first equivalence point. The volume to the second equivalence point is simply twice this amount, or 45.4 mL, to the second equivalence point.

Check: The units (mL) are correct. The volume of base is greater than the volume of acid because the concentration of the acid is a little greater than that of the base. The volume to the second equivalence point is twice the volume to the first equivalence point.

16.55   Because the exact conditions of the titration are not given, a rough calculation will suffice. Recall that at the equivalence point the moles of acid and base are equal. If it is assumed that the concentrations of the acid and the base are equal, then the total volume of the solution will have doubled. Assuming an acid and base concentration of 0.1 M, then the conjugate base formed must have a concentration of ~0.05 M. From earlier calculations, it can be seen that

the $K_b = \dfrac{K_w}{K_a} = \dfrac{[OH^-]^2}{0.05}$; thus, $[OH^-] = \sqrt{\dfrac{0.05\,K_w}{K_a}} = \sqrt{\dfrac{5 \times 10^{-16}}{K_a}}$ and the pH $= 14 + \log\sqrt{\dfrac{5 \times 10^{-16}}{K_a}}$.

(a)   For HF, the $K_a = 3.5 \times 10^{-4}$; so the above equation approximates the pH at the equivalence point of ~8.0. Looking at Table 16.1, phenol red or *m*-nitrophenol will change at the appropriate pH range.

(b)   For HCl, the pH at the equivalence point is 7 because HCl is a strong acid. Looking at Table 16.1, alizarin, bromthymol blue, *m*-nitrophenol or phenol red will change at the appropriate pH range.

(c)   For HCN, the $K_a = 4.9 \times 10^{-10}$; so the preceding equation approximates the pH at the equivalence point of ~11.0. Looking at Table 16.1, alizarin yellow R will change at the appropriate pH range.

Solubility Equilibria

16.57   For the dissolution reaction, start with the ionic compound as a solid and put it in equilibrium with the appropriate cation and anion, making sure to include the appropriate stoichiometric coefficients. The K_{sp} expression is the product of the concentrations of the cation and anion concentrations raised to their stoichiometric coefficients.

(a) $BaSO_4(s) \rightleftharpoons Ba^{2+}(aq) + SO_4^{2-}(aq)$ and $K_{sp} = [Ba^{2+}]\,[SO_4^{2-}]$

(b) $PbBr_2(s) \rightleftharpoons Pb^{2+}(aq) + 2\,Br^-(aq)$ and $K_{sp} = [Pb^{2+}]\,[Br^-]^2$

(c) $Ag_2CrO_4(s) \rightleftharpoons 2\,Ag^+(aq) + CrO_4^{2-}(aq)$ and $K_{sp} = [Ag^+]^2\,[CrO_4^{2-}]$

16.59   **Given:** ionic compound formula and Table 16.2 of K_{sp} values   **Find:** molar solubility (*S*)
Conceptual Plan: Since the balanced chemical equation for the dissolution of A_mX_n is $A_mX_n(s) \rightleftharpoons mA^{n+}(aq) + nX^{m-}(aq)$, the expression of the solubility product constant of A_mX_n is $K_{sp} = [A^{n+}]^m[X^{m-}]^n$. The molar solubility of a compound, A_mX_n, can be computed directly from K_{sp} by solving for *S* in the expression $K_{sp} = (mS)^m(nS)^n = m^mn^nS^{m+n}$.

Solution:

(a)   For AgBr, $K_{sp} = 5.35 \times 10^{-13}$, $A = Ag^+$, $m = 1$, $X = Br^-$, and $n = 1$; so $K_{sp} = 5.35 \times 10^{-13} = S^2$.

Rearrange to solve for *S*. $S = \sqrt{5.35 \times 10^{-13}} = 7.31 \times 10^{-7}$ M.

(b)   For $Mg(OH)_2$, $K_{sp} = 2.06 \times 10^{-13}$, $A = Mg^{2+}$, $m = 1$, $X = OH^-$, and $n = 2$; so $K_{sp} = 2.06 \times 10^{-13} = 2^2S^3$.

Rearrange to solve for *S*. $S = \sqrt[3]{\dfrac{2.06 \times 10^{-13}}{4}} = 3.72 \times 10^{-5}$ M.

(c)   For CaF_2, $K_{sp} = 1.46 \times 10^{-10}$, $A = Ca^{2+}$, $m = 1$, $X = F^-$, and $n = 2$; so $K_{sp} = 1.46 \times 10^{-10} = 2^2 S^3$.

Rearrange to solve for S. $S = \sqrt[3]{\dfrac{1.46 \times 10^{-10}}{4}} = 3.32 \times 10^{-4}$ M.

Check: The units (M) are correct. The molar solubilities are much less than 1 and dependent not only on the value of the K_{sp}, but also on the stoichiometry of the ionic compound. The more ions generated, the greater the molar solubility for the same value of the K_{sp}.

16.61   **Given:** ionic compound formula and molar solubility (S)   **Find:** K_{sp}
Conceptual Plan: The expression of the solubility product constant of A_mX_n is $K_{sp} = [A^{n+}]^m[X^{m-}]^n$. The molar solubility of a compound, A_mX_n, can be computed directly from K_{sp} by solving for S in the expression $K_{sp} = (mS)^m(nS)^n = m^m n^n S^{m+n}$.
Solution:
(a)   For MX, $S = 3.27 \times 10^{-11}$ M, $A = M^+$, $m = 1$, $X = X^-$, and $n = 1$; so $K_{sp} = S^2 = (3.27 \times 10^{-11})^2 = 1.07 \times 10^{-21}$.
(b)   For PbF_2, $S = 5.63 \times 10^{-3}$ M, $A = Pb^{2+}$, $m = 1$, $X = F^-$, and $n = 2$; so $K_{sp} = 2^2 S^3 = 2^2(5.63 \times 10^{-3})^3 = 7.14 \times 10^{-7}$.
(c)   For MgF_2, $S = 2.65 \times 10^{-4}$ M, $A = Mg^{2+}$, $m = 1$, $X = F^-$, and $n = 2$; so $K_{sp} = 2^2 S^3 = 2^2(2.65 \times 10^{-4})^3 = 7.44 \times 10^{-11}$.

Check: The units (none) are correct. The K_{sp} values are much less than 1 and dependent not only on the value of the solubility, but also on the stoichiometry of the ionic compound. The more ions generated, the smaller the K_{sp} for the same value of the S.

16.63   **Given:** ionic compound formulas AX and AX_2 and $K_{sp} = 1.5 \times 10^{-5}$ **Find:** higher molar solubility (S)
Conceptual Plan: The expression of the solubility product constant of A_mX_n is $K_{sp} = [A^{n+}]^m[X^{m-}]^n$. The molar solubility of a compound, A_mX_n, can be computed directly from K_{sp} by solving for S in the expression $K_{sp} = (mS)^m(nS)^n = m^m n^n S^{m+n}$.
Solution: For AX, $K_{sp} = 1.5 \times 10^{-5}$, $m = 1$, and $n = 1$; so $K_{sp} = 1.5 \times 10^{-5} = S^2$. Rearrange to solve for S.
$S = \sqrt{1.5 \times 10^{-5}} = 3.9 \times 10^{-3}$ M. For AX_2, $K_{sp} = 1.5 \times 10^{-5}$, $m = 1$, and $n = 2$; so $K_{sp} = 1.5 \times 10^{-5} = 2^2 S^3$.

Rearrange to solve for S. $S = \sqrt[3]{\dfrac{1.5 \times 10^{-5}}{4}} = 1.6 \times 10^{-2}$ M. Because 10^{-2} M $> 10^{-3}$ M, AX_2 has a higher molar solubility.

Check: The units (M) are correct. The more ions generated, the greater the molar solubility for the same value of the K_{sp}.

16.65   **Given:** $Fe(OH)_2$ in 100.0 mL solution   **Find:** grams of $Fe(OH)_2$ **Other:** $K_{sp} = 4.87 \times 10^{-17}$
Conceptual Plan: The expression of the solubility product constant of A_mX_n is $K_{sp} = [A^{n+}]^m[X^{m-}]^n$. The molar solubility of a compound, A_mX_n, can be computed directly from K_{sp} by solving for S in the expression $K_{sp} = (mS)^m(nS)^n = m^m n^n S^{m+n}$. Then solve for S, then mL $\rightarrow$ L then

$$\frac{1\,L}{1000\,mL}$$

$S, L \rightarrow$ mol $Fe(OH)_2 \rightarrow$ g $Fe(OH)_2$.

$$M = \frac{mol}{L} \qquad \frac{89.87 \text{ g } Fe(OH)_2}{1 \text{ mol } Fe(OH)_2}$$

Solution:
For $Fe(OH)_2$, $K_{sp} = 4.87 \times 10^{-17}$, $A = Fe^{2+}$, $m = 1$, $X = OH^-$, and $n = 2$; so $K_{sp} = 4.87 \times 10^{-17} = 2^2 S^3$.

Rearrange to solve for S. $S = \sqrt[3]{\dfrac{4.87 \times 10^{-17}}{4}} = 2.30050 \times 10^{-6}$ M. Then $100.0 \text{ mL} \times \dfrac{1\,L}{1000\,mL} = 0.1000$ L

then $\dfrac{2.30050 \times 10^{-6} \text{ mol } Fe(OH)_2}{1\,L} \times 0.1000\,L = 2.30050 \times 10^{-7}$ mol $Fe(OH)_2$

and mass $Fe(OH)_2 = 2.30050 \times 10^{-7}$ mol $Fe(OH)_2 \times \dfrac{89.87 \text{ g } Fe(OH)_2}{1 \text{mol } Fe(OH)_2} = 2.07 \times 10^{-5}$ g $Fe(OH)_2$

Check: The units (g) are correct. The solubility rules from Chapter 4 (most hydroxides are insoluble) suggest that very little $Fe(OH)_2$ will dissolve; so the magnitude of the answer is not surprising.

16.67 (a) **Given:** BaF_2 **Find:** molar solubility (S) in pure water **Other:** $K_{sp}(BaF_2) = 2.45 \times 10^{-5}$
**Conceptual Plan: The expression of the solubility product constant of A_mX_n is $K_{sp} = [A^{n+}]^m[X^{m-}]^n$.
The molar solubility of a compound, A_mX_n, can be computed directly from K_{sp} by solving for S in the
expression $K_{sp} = (mS)^m(nS)^n = m^mn^nS^{m+n}$.**
Solution: For BaF_2, $K_{sp} = 2.45 \times 10^{-5}$, $A = Ba^{2+}$, $m = 1$, $X = F^-$, and $n = 2$; so $K_{sp} = 2.45 \times 10^{-5} = 2^2S^3$.

Rearrange to solve for S. $S = \sqrt[3]{\dfrac{2.45 \times 10^{-5}}{4}} = 1.83 \times 10^{-2}$ M.

(b) **Given:** BaF_2 **Find:** molar solubility (S) in 0.10 M $Ba(NO_3)_2$ **Other:** $K_{sp}(BaF_2) = 2.45 \times 10^{-5}$
Conceptual Plan: M $Ba(NO_3)_2 \rightarrow$ M Ba^{2+} then M $Ba^{2+}, K_{sp} \rightarrow S$

$$Ba(NO_3)_2(s) \rightarrow Ba^{2+}(aq) + 2\,NO_3^-(aq) \qquad \text{ICE table}$$

Solution: Because one Ba^{2+} ion is generated for each $Ba(NO_3)_2$, $[Ba^{2+}] = 0.10$ M.

$BaF_2(s) \rightleftharpoons Ba^{2-}(aq) + 2\,F^-(aq)$

Initial	0.10	0.00
Change	S	$2S$
Equil	$0.10 + S$	$2S$

$K_{sp}(BaF_2) = [Ba^{2+}][F^-]^2 = 2.45 \times 10^{-5} = (0.10 + S)(2S)^2$

Assume that $S \ll 0.10$, $2.45 \times 10^{-5} = (0.10)(2S)^2$, and $S = 7.83 \times 10^{-3}$ M. Confirm that the assumption

is valid. $\dfrac{7.83 \times 10^{-3}}{0.10} \times 100\% = 7.8\% > 5\%$, so the assumption is not valid. Because expanding the expression will give a third-order polynomial, that is not easily solved directly, solve by successive approximations.
Substitute $S = 7.83 \times 10^{-3}$ M for the S term that is part of a sum (i.e., the one in $(0.10 + S)$). Thus, $2.45 \times 10^{-5} = (0.10 + 7.83 \times 10^{-3})(2S)^2$ and $S = 7.53 \times 10^{-3}$ M. Substitute this new S value again. Thus, $2.45 \times 10^{-5} = (0.10 + 7.53 \times 10^{-3})(2S)^2$ and $S = 7.55 \times 10^{-3}$ M. Substitute this new S value again. Thus, $2.45 \times 10^{-5} = (0.10 + 7.55 \times 10^{-3})(2S)^2$ and $S = 7.55 \times 10^{-3}$ M. So the solution has converged and $S = 7.55 \times 10^{-3}$ M.

(c) **Given:** BaF_2 **Find:** molar solubility (S) in 0.15 M NaF **Other:** $K_{sp}(BaF_2) = 2.45 \times 10^{-5}$
Conceptual Plan: M NaF $\rightarrow$ M F^- then M $F^-, K_{sp} \rightarrow S$

$$NaF(S) \rightarrow Na^+(aq) + F^-(aq) \qquad \text{ICE table}$$

Solution: Because one F^- ion is generated for each NaF, $[F^-] = 0.15$ M.

$BaF_2(s) \rightleftharpoons Ba^{2-}(aq) + 2\,F^-(aq)$

Initial	0.00	0.15
Change	S	$2S$
Equil	S	$0.15 + 2S$

$K_{sp}(BaF_2) = [Ba^{2+}][F^-]^2 = 2.45 \times 10^{-5} = (S)(0.15 + 2S)^2$

Because $2S \ll 0.15$, $2.45 \times 10^{-5} = (S)(0.15)^2$ and $S = 1.09 \times 10^{-3}$ M. Confirm that the assumption is

valid. $\dfrac{2(1.09 \times 10^{-3})}{0.15} \times 100\% = 1.5\% < 5\%$, so the assumption is valid.

Check: The units (M) are correct. The solubility of the BaF_2 decreases in the presence of a common ion. The effect of the anion is greater because the K_{sp} expression has the anion concentration squared.

16.69 **Given:** $Ca(OH)_2$ **Find:** molar solubility (S) in buffers at (a) pH $= 4$, (b) pH $= 7$, and (c) pH $= 9$
Other: $K_{sp}(Ca(OH)_2) = 4.68 \times 10^{-6}$
Conceptual Plan: pH $\rightarrow [H_3O^+] \rightarrow [OH^-]$ then M $OH^-, K_{sp} \rightarrow S$

$$[H_3O^+] = 10^{-pH} \qquad K_w = [H_3O^+][OH^-] \qquad \text{set up ICE table}$$

Solution:

(a)   pH = 4, so $[H_3O^+] = 10^{-pH} = 10^{-4} = 1 \times 10^{-4}$ M then $K_w = [H_3O^+][OH^-]$ so

$$[OH^-] = \frac{K_w}{[H_3O^+]} = \frac{1.0 \times 10^{-14}}{1 \times 10^{-4}} = 1 \times 10^{-10} \text{ M then}$$

$$Ca(OH)_2(s) \rightleftharpoons Ca^{2+}(aq) + 2\,OH^-(aq)$$

Initial	0.00	1×10^{-10}
Change	S	—
Equil	S	1×10^{-10}

$K_{sp}(Ca(OH)_2) = [Ca^{2+}][OH^-]^2 = 4.68 \times 10^{-6} = S(1 \times 10^{-10})^2$ and $S = 5 \times 10^{14}$ M

(b)   pH = 7, so $[H_3O^+] = 10^{-pH} = 10^{-7} = 1 \times 10^{-7}$ M then $K_w = [H_3O^+][OH^-]$ so

$$[OH^-] = \frac{K_w}{[H_3O^+]} = \frac{1.0 \times 10^{-14}}{1 \times 10^{-7}} = 1 \times 10^{-7} \text{ M then}$$

$$Ca(OH)_2(s) \rightleftharpoons Ca^{2+}(aq) + 2\,OH^-(aq)$$

Initial	0.00	1×10^{-7}
Change	S	—
Equil	S	1×10^{-7}

$K_{sp}(Ca(OH)_2) = [Ca^{2+}][OH^-]^2 = 4.68 \times 10^{-6} = S(1 \times 10^{-7})^2$ and $S = 5 \times 10^8$ M

(c)   pH = 9, so $[H_3O^+] = 10^{-pH} = 10^{-9} = 1 \times 10^{-9}$ M then $K_w = [H_3O^+][OH^-]$ so

$$[OH^-] = \frac{K_w}{[H_3O^+]} = \frac{1.0 \times 10^{-14}}{1 \times 10^{-9}} = 1 \times 10^{-5} \text{ M then}$$

$$Ca(OH)_2(s) \rightleftharpoons Ca^{2+}(aq) + 2\,OH^-(aq)$$

Initial	0.00	1×10^{-5}
Change	S	—
Equil	S	1×10^{-5}

$K_{sp}(Ca(OH)_2) = [Ca^{2+}][OH^-]^2 = 4.68 \times 10^{-6} = S(1 \times 10^{-5})^2$ and $S = 5 \times 10^4$ M

Check: The units (M) are correct. The solubility of the $Ca(OH)_2$ decreases as the pH increases (and the hydroxide ion concentration increases). These molar solubilities are not achievable because the saturation point of pure $Ca(OH)_2$ is ~30 M. The bottom line is that as long as the hydroxide concentration can be controlled with a buffer, the $Ca(OH)_2$ will be very soluble.

16.71   (a) $BaCO_3$ will be more soluble in acidic solutions because CO_3^{2-} is basic. In acidic solutions, it can be converted to HCO_3^- and H_2CO_3. These species are not CO_3^{2-}, so they do not appear in the K_{sp} expression.

(b)   CuS will be more soluble in acidic solutions because S^{2-} is basic. In acidic solutions, it can be converted to HS^- and H_2S. These species are not S^{2-}, so they do not appear in the K_{sp} expression.

(c)   AgCl will not be more soluble in acidic solutions because Cl^- will not react with acidic solutions because HCl is a strong acid.

(d) PbI_2 will not be more soluble in acidic solutions because I^- will not react with acidic solutions because HI is a strong acid.

16.73   **Given:** 0.015 M NaF and 0.010 M $Ca(NO_3)_2$ **Find:** Will a precipitate form? If so, identify it.
Other: $K_{sp}(CaF_2) = 1.46 \times 10^{-10}$
Conceptual Plan: Look at all possible combinations and consider the solubility rules from Chapter 4. Salts of alkali metals (Na) are very soluble, so NaF and $NaNO_3$ will be very soluble. Nitrate compounds are very soluble, so $NaNO_3$ will be very soluble. The only possibility for a precipitate is CaF_2. Determine whether a precipitate will form by determining the concentration of the Ca^{2+} and F^- in solution. Then compute the reaction quotient, Q. If $Q > K_{sp}$, a precipitate will form.
Solution: Because the only possible precipitate is CaF_2, calculate the concentrations of Ca^{2+} and F^-. NaF(s) $\rightarrow$ $Na^+(aq) + F^-(aq)$. Because one F^- ion is generated for each NaF, $[F^-] = 0.015$ M.

$Ca(NO_3)_2(s) \rightarrow Ca^{2+}(aq) + 2\ NO_3^-(aq)$. Because one Ca^{2+} ion is generated for each $Ca(NO_3)_2$, $[Ca^{2+}] = 0.010$ M. Then calculate Q (CaF_2), A = Ca^{2+}, $m = 1$, X = F⁻, and $n = 2$. Because $Q = [A^{n+}]^m\ [X^{m-}]^n$, Q (CaF_2) = $[Ca^{2+}]\ [F^-]^2 = (0.010)\ (0.015)^2 = 2.3 \times 10^{-6} > 1.46 \times 10^{-10} = K_{sp}(CaF_2)$; so a precipitate will form.

Check: The units (none) are correct. The solubility of the CaF_2 is low, and the concentrations of ions are extremely large compared to the K_{sp}; so a precipitate will form.

16.75   **Given:** 75.0 mL of NaOH with pOH = 2.58 and 125.0 mL of 0.018 M $MgCl_2$ **Find:** Will a precipitate form? If so, identify it. **Other:** $K_{sp}(Mg(OH)_2) = 2.06 \times 10^{-13}$

Conceptual Plan: Look at all possible combinations and consider the solubility rules from Chapter 4. Salts of alkali metals (Na) are very soluble, so NaOH and NaCl will be very soluble. Chloride compounds are generally very soluble, so $MgCl_2$ and NaCl will be very soluble. The only possibility for a precipitate is $Mg(OH)_2$. Determine whether a precipitate will form by determining the concentration of the Mg^{2+} and OH⁻ in solution. Because pH, not NaOH concentration, is given, pOH → [OH⁻] then

$$[OH^-] = 10^{-pOH}$$

mix solutions and calculate diluted concentrations mL NaOH, mL $MgCl_2$ → mL total then

$$mL\ NaOH + mL\ MgCl_2 = total\ mL$$

mL, initial M → final M then compute the reaction quotient, Q.

$$M_1V_1 = M_2V_2$$

If $Q > K_{sp}$, a precipitate will form.

Solution: Because the only possible precipitate is $Mg(OH)_2$, calculate the concentrations of Mg^{2+} and OH⁻. For NaOH at pOH = 2.58, so $[OH^-] = 10^{-pOH} = 10^{-2.58} = 2.63027 \times 10^{-3}$ M and $MgCl_2(s) \rightarrow Mg^{2+}(aq) + 2\ Cl^-(aq)$. Because one Mg^{2+} ion is generated for each $MgCl_2$, $[Mg^{2+}] = 0.018$ M. Then total mL = mL NaOH + mL $MgCl_2$ = 75.0 mL + 125.0 mL = 200.0 mL. Then $M_1\ V_1 = M_2V_2$;

rearrange to solve for M_2. $M_2 = M_1 \dfrac{V_1}{V_2} = 2.63027 \times 10^{-3}$ M OH⁻ $\times \dfrac{75.0\ mL}{200.0\ mL} = 9.8635 \times 10^{-4}$ M OH⁻ and

$M_2 = M_1 \dfrac{V_1}{V_2} = 0.018$ M $Mg^{2+} \times \dfrac{125.0\ mL}{200.0\ mL} = 1.125 \times 10^{-2}$ M Mg^{2+}. Calculate $Q(Mg(OH)_2)$, A = Mg^{2+},

$m = 1$, X = OH⁻, and $n = 2$. Because $Q = [A^{n+}]^m\ [X^{m-}]^n$, $Q(Mg(OH)_2) = [Mg^{2+}]\ [OH^-]^2 = (1.125 \times 10^{-2})(9.8635 \times 10^{-4})^2 = 1.1 \times 10^{-8} > 2.06 \times 10^{-13} = K_{sp}(Mg(OH)_2)$; so a precipitate will form.

Check: The units (none) are correct. The solubility of the $Mg(OH)_2$ is low, and the NaOH (a base) is high enough that the product of the concentration of ions is large compared to the K_{sp}; so a precipitate will form.

16.77   **Given:** KOH as precipitation agent in (a) 0.015 M $CaCl_2$, (b) 0.0025 M $Fe(NO_3)_2$, and (c) 0.0018 M $MgBr_2$

Find: concentration of KOH necessary to form a precipitate

Other: $K_{sp}(Ca(OH)_2) = 4.68 \times 10^{-6}$, $K_{sp}(Fe(OH)_2) = 4.87 \times 10^{-17}$, $K_{sp}(Mg(OH)_2) = 2.06 \times 10^{-13}$

Conceptual Plan: The solubility rules from Chapter 4 state that most hydroxides are insoluble, so all precipitates will be hydroxides. Determine the concentration of the cation in solution. Because all metals have an oxidation state of +2 and [OH⁻] = [KOH], all of the K_{sp} = [cation] [KOH]²; so [KOH] = $\sqrt{\dfrac{K_{sp}}{[cation]}}$.

Solution:

(a) $CaCl_2(s) \rightarrow Ca^{2+}(aq) + 2\ Cl^-(aq)$. Because one Ca^{2+} ion is generated for each $CaCl_2$, $[Ca^{2+}] = 0.015$ M.

Then $[KOH] = \sqrt{\dfrac{K_{sp}}{[cation]}} = \sqrt{\dfrac{4.68 \times 10^{-6}}{0.015}} = 0.018$ M KOH.

(b) $Fe(NO_3)_2(s) \rightarrow Fe^{2+}(aq) + 2\ NO_3^-(aq)$. Because one Fe^{2+} ion is generated for each $Fe(NO_3)_2$, $[Fe^{2+}] = 0.0025$ M.

Then $[KOH] = \sqrt{\dfrac{K_{sp}}{[cation]}} = \sqrt{\dfrac{4.87 \times 10^{-17}}{0.0025}} = 1.4 \times 10^{-7}$ M KOH.

(c) $MgBr_2(s) \rightarrow Mg^{2+}(aq) + 2\ Br^-(aq)$. Because one Mg^{2+} ion is generated for each $MgBr_2$, $[Mg^{2+}] = 0.0018$ M.

Then $[KOH] = \sqrt{\dfrac{K_{sp}}{[cation]}} = \sqrt{\dfrac{2.06 \times 10^{-13}}{0.0018}} = 1.1 \times 10^{-5}$ M KOH.

Check: The units (none) are correct. Because all cations have an oxidation state of +2, it can be seen that the [KOH] needed to precipitate the hydroxide is lower the smaller the K_{sp}.

Complex Ion Equilbria

16.79   **Given:** solution with 1.1×10^{-3} M $Zn(NO_3)_2$ and 0.150 M NH_3 **Find:** $[Zn^{2+}]$ at equilibrium
          Other: $K_f(Zn(NH_3)_4^{2+}) = 2.8 \times 10^9$
          Conceptual Plan: Write a balanced equation and expression for K_f. Use initial concentrations to set up an ICE table. Because the K_f is so large, assume that reaction essentially goes to completion. Solve for $[Zn^{2+}]$ at equilibrium.
          Solution: $Zn(NO_3)_2(s) \rightarrow Zn^{2+}(aq) + 2\,NO_3^-(aq)$. Because one Zn^{2+} ion is generated for each $Zn(NO_3)_2$, $[Zn^{2+}] = 1.1 \times 10^{-3}$ M. Balanced equation is:

$$Zn^{2+}(aq) \;+\; 4\,NH_3(aq) \;\rightleftharpoons\; Zn(NH_3)_4^{2+}(aq)$$

	$[Zn^{2+}]$	$[NH_3]$	$[Zn(NH_3)_4^{2+}]$
Initial	1.1×10^{-3}	0.150	0.00
Change	$\approx 1.1 \times 10^{-3}$	$\approx -4(1.1 \times 10^{-3})$	$\approx 1.1 \times 10^{-3}$
Equil	x	0.1456	1.1×10^{-3}

Set up an ICE table with initial concentrations. Because K_f is so large and because initially $[NH_3] > 4[Zn^{2+}]$, the reaction essentially goes to completion; then write equilibrium expression and solve for x.

$$K_f = \frac{[Zn(NH_3)_4^{2+}]}{[Zn^{2+}][NH_3]^4} = 2.8 \times 10^9 = \frac{1.1 \times 10^{-3}}{x\,(0.1456)^4}.$$ So $x = 8.7 \times 10^{-10}$ M Zn^{2+}. Because x is insignificant compared to the initial concentration, the assumption is valid.

Check: The units (M) are correct. Because K_f is so large, the reaction essentially goes to completion and $[Zn^{2+}]$ is extremely small.

Cumulative Problems

16.81   **Given:** 150.0 mL solution of 2.05 g sodium benzoate and 2.47 g benzoic acid   **Find:** pH
          Other: $K_a(HC_7H_5O_2) = 6.5 \times 10^{-5}$
          Conceptual Plan: g $NaC_7H_5O_2$ $\rightarrow$ mol $NaC_7H_5O_2$ and g $HC_7H_5O_2$ $\rightarrow$ mol $HC_7H_5O_2$

$$\frac{1\ mol\ NaC_7H_5O_2}{144.10\ g\ NaC_7H_5O_2} \qquad\qquad \frac{1\ mol\ HC_7H_5O_2}{122.12\ g\ HC_7H_5O_2}$$

Because the two components are in the same solution, the ratio of [base]/[acid] = (mol base)/(mol acid). Then K_a, mol $NaC_7H_5O_2$, mol $HC_7H_5O_2$ $\rightarrow$ pH.

$$pH = pK_a + \log\frac{[base]}{[acid]}$$

Solution: $2.05\ \cancel{g\ NaC_7H_5O_2} \times \dfrac{1\ mol\ NaC_7H_5O_2}{144.10\ \cancel{g\ NaC_7H_5O_2}} = 0.0142262$ mol $NaC_7H_5O_2$ and

$2.47\ \cancel{g\ HC_7H_5O_2} \times \dfrac{1\ mol\ HC_7H_5O_2}{122.12\ \cancel{g\ HC_7H_5O_2}} = 0.0202260$ mol $HC_7H_5O_2$ then

$$pH = pK_a + \log\frac{[base]}{[acid]} = pK_a + \log\frac{mol\ base}{mol\ acid} = -\log(6.5 \times 10^{-5}) + \log\frac{0.0142262\ \cancel{mol}}{0.0202260\ \cancel{mol}} = 4.03$$

Check: The units (none) are correct. The magnitude of the answer makes physical sense because the pH is a little lower than the pK_a of the acid because there is more acid than base in the buffer solution.

16.83   **Given:** 150.0 mL of 0.25 M $HCHO_2$ and 75.0 ml of 0.20 M NaOH   **Find:** pH **Other:** $K_a(HCHO_2) = 1.8 \times 10^{-4}$
          Conceptual Plan: In this buffer, the base is generated by converting some of the formic acid to the formate ion. Part I: Stoichiometry:
          mL $\rightarrow$ L then L, initial $HCHO_2$ M $\rightarrow$ mol $HCHO_2$ then mL $\rightarrow$ L then

$$\frac{1\ L}{1000\ mL} \qquad\qquad M = \frac{mol}{L} \qquad\qquad \frac{1\ L}{1000\ mL}$$

L, initial NaOH M → mol NaOH then write a balanced equation then

$$M = \frac{mol}{L} \qquad\qquad NaOH + HCHO_2 \rightarrow H_2O + NaCHO_2$$

mol HCHO$_2$, mol NaOH → mol NaCHO$_2$, mol HCHO$_2$ then

set up stoichiometry table

Part II: Equilibrium:

Because the two components are in the same solution, the ratio of [base]/[acid] = (mol base)/(mol acid). Then K_a, mol NaCHO$_2$, mol HCHO$_2$ → pH.

$$pH = pK_a + log\frac{[base]}{[acid]}$$

Solution: $150.0 \text{ mL} \times \dfrac{1 \text{ L}}{1000 \text{ mL}} = 0.1500 \text{ L}$ then

$0.1500 \text{ L HCHO}_2 \times \dfrac{0.25 \text{ mol HCHO}_2}{1 \text{ L HCHO}_2} = 0.03\underline{7}5 \text{ mol HCHO}_2$

Then $75.0 \text{ mL} \times \dfrac{1 \text{ L}}{1000 \text{ mL}} = 0.0750 \text{ L}$ then $0.0750 \text{ L NaOH} \times \dfrac{0.20 \text{ mol NaOH}}{1 \text{ L NaOH}} = 0.015 \text{ mol NaOH}$ then set up a

table to track changes:

$$NaOH(aq) + HCHO_2(aq) \rightarrow NaCHO_2(aq) + H_2O(l)$$

	NaOH	HCHO$_2$	NaCHO$_2$	H$_2$O
Before addition	0.00 mol	0.0375 mol	0.00 mol	—
Addition	0.015 mol	—	—	—
After addition	≈0.00 mol	0.0225 mol	0.015 mol	—

Because the amount of NaOH is small, there are significant amounts of both buffer components; so the Henderson–Hasselbalch equation can be used to calculate the pH.

$$pH = pK_a + log\frac{[base]}{[acid]} = pK_a + log\frac{mol \; base}{mol \; acid} = -log(1.8 \times 10^{-4}) + log\frac{0.015 \; mol}{0.0225 \; mol} = 3.57$$

Check: The units (none) are correct. The magnitude of the answer makes physical sense because the pH is a little lower than the pK_a of the acid because there is more acid than base in the buffer solution.

16.85 **Given:** 1.0 L of buffer of 0.25 mol NH$_3$ and 0.25 mol NH$_4$Cl; adjust to pH = 8.75
Find: mass NaOH or HCl   **Other:** $K_b(NH_3) = 1.76 \times 10^{-5}$
Conceptual Plan: To decide which reagent needs to be added to adjust pH, calculate the initial pH. Because the mol NH$_3$ = mol NH$_4$Cl, the pH = pK_a so $K_b \rightarrow pK_b \rightarrow pK_a$ then

acid = NH$_4^+$ base = NH$_3$ $\qquad pK_b = -log \, K_b \quad 14 = pK_a + pK_b$

final pH, $pK_a \rightarrow$ [NH$_3$]/[NH$_4^+$] then [NH$_3$], L → mol [NH$_3$] and [NH$_4^+$], L → mol [NH$_4^+$]

$$pH = pK_a + log\frac{[base]}{[acid]} \qquad\qquad M = \frac{mol}{L} \qquad\qquad M = \frac{mol}{L}$$

then write a balanced equation then

$H^+ + NH_3 \rightarrow NH_4^+$

mol NH$_3$, mol NH$_4^+$, [NH$_3$]/[NH$_4^+$] → mol HCl → g HCl.

set up stoichiometry table $\dfrac{36.46 \text{ g HCl}}{1 \text{ mol HCl}}$

Solution: Because $K_b(NH_3) = 1.76 \times 10^{-5}$, $pK_b = -log \, K_b = -log(1.76 \times 10^{-5}) = 4.75$. Because $14 = pK_a + pK_b$, $pK_a = 14 - pK_b = 14 - 4.75 = 9.25$. Because the desired pH is lower (8.75), HCl (a strong acid) needs to be

added. Then $pH = pK_a + log\dfrac{[base]}{[acid]} = 9.25 + log\dfrac{[NH_3]}{[NH_4^+]} = 8.75.$ Solve for $\dfrac{[NH_3]}{[NH_4^+]}$.

$log\dfrac{[NH_3]}{[NH_4^+]} = 8.75 - 9.25 = -0.50 \rightarrow \dfrac{[NH_3]}{[NH_4^+]} = 10^{-0.50} = 0.3\underline{1}623.$ Then

$\dfrac{0.25 \text{ mol NH}_3}{1 \text{ L}} \times 1.0 \text{ L} = 0.25 \text{ mol NH}_3$ and

$\dfrac{0.25 \text{ mol NH}_4\text{Cl}}{1 \ \cancel{L}} \times 1.0 \ \cancel{L} = 0.25 \text{ mol NH}_4\text{Cl} = 0.25 \text{ mol NH}_4{}^+$. Because HCl is a strong acid, [HCl] = [H$^+$], and set up a table to track changes:

	H$^+$(aq)	+	NH$_3$(aq)	→	NH$_4{}^+$(aq)
Before addition	≈0.00 mol		0.25 mol		0.25 mol
Addition	x		—		—
After addition	≈0.00 mol		(0.25 − x) mol		(0.25 + x) mol

Because $\dfrac{[\text{NH}_3]}{[\text{NH}_4{}^+]} = 0.31623 = \dfrac{(0.25 - x) \ \cancel{\text{mol}}}{(0.25 + x) \ \cancel{\text{mol}}}$, solve for x. Note that the ratio of moles is the same as the ratio of concentrations, because the volume for both terms is the same. $0.31623(0.25 + x) = (0.25 - x) \rightarrow 0.0790575 + 0.31623x = 0.25 - x \rightarrow 1.31623x = 0.17094 \rightarrow x = 0.12987$ mol HCl then

$0.12987 \ \cancel{\text{mol HCl}} \times \dfrac{36.46 \text{ g HCl}}{1 \ \cancel{\text{mol HCl}}} = 4.7 \text{ g HCl}$

Check: The units (g) are correct. The magnitude of the answer makes physical sense because there is much less than a mole of each of the buffer components; so there must be much less than a mole of HCl.

16.87   (a)   **Given:** potassium hydrogen phthalate = KHP = KHC$_8$H$_4$O$_4$ titration with NaOH
           Find: balanced equation
           Conceptual Plan: The reaction will be a titration of the acid proton, leaving the phthalate ion intact.
           Solution: NaOH(aq) + KHC$_8$H$_4$O$_4$(aq) → Na$^+$(aq) + K$^+$(aq) + C$_8$H$_4$O$_4{}^{2-}$(aq) + H$_2$O(l)

           Check: An acid–base reaction generates a salt (soluble here) and water. There is only one acidic proton in KHP.

      (b)   **Given:** 0.5527 g KHP titrated with 25.87 mL of NaOH solution   **Find:** [NaOH]
           Conceptual Plan:
           g KHP → mol KHP → mol NaOH and mL → L then mol NaOH and mL → M NaOH

           $\dfrac{1 \text{ mol KHP}}{204.22 \text{ g KHP}}$ 1:1 from balanced equation $\dfrac{1 \text{ L}}{1000 \text{ mL}}$ $M = \dfrac{\text{mol}}{\text{L}}$

           Solution: $0.5527 \ \cancel{\text{g KHP}} \times \dfrac{1 \text{ mol KHP}}{204.22 \ \cancel{\text{g KHP}}} = 0.002706395 \text{ mol KHP}$; mol KHP = mol acid = mol base =

           0.002706395 mol NaOH then $25.87 \ \cancel{\text{mL}} \times \dfrac{1 \text{ L}}{1000 \ \cancel{\text{mL}}} = 0.02587 \text{ L}$ then

           $[\text{NaOH}] = \dfrac{0.002706395 \text{ mol NaOH}}{0.02587 \text{ L}} = 0.1046 \text{ M NaOH}$

           Check: The units (M) are correct. The magnitude of the answer makes physical sense because there is much less than a mole of acid. The magnitude of the moles of acid and base is smaller than the volume of base in liters.

16.89   **Given:** 0.25 mol weak acid with 10.0 mL of 3.00 M KOH diluted to 1.500 L has pH = 3.85   **Find:** pK_a of acid
       Conceptual Plan: mL → L then M KOH, L → mol KOH then write a balanced reaction

           $\dfrac{1 \text{ L}}{1000 \text{ mL}}$ $M = \dfrac{\text{mol}}{\text{L}}$ KOH + HA → NaA + H$_2$O

       added mol KOH, initial mol acid → equil. mol KOH, equil. mol acid then

               set up stoichiometry table

       equil. mol KOH, equil. mol acid, pH → pK_a

              $\text{pH} = \text{p}K_a + \log \dfrac{[\text{base}]}{[\text{acid}]}$

       Solution: $10.00 \ \cancel{\text{mL}} \times \dfrac{1 \text{ L}}{1000 \ \cancel{\text{mL}}} = 0.01000 \text{ L}$ then $0.01000 \ \cancel{\text{L KOH}} \times \dfrac{3.00 \text{ mol KOH}}{1 \ \cancel{\text{L KOH}}} = 0.0300 \text{ mol KOH}$

Because KOH is a strong base, [KOH] = [OH$^-$], and set up a table to track changes:

$$KOH(aq) \; + \; HA(aq) \rightarrow KA(aq) \; + \; H_2O(l)$$

Before addition	≈ 0.00 mol	0.25 mol	0.00 mol	—
Addition	0.0300 mol	—	—	—
After addition	≈ 0.00 mol	0.22 mol	0.0300 mol	—

Because the ratio of base to acid is between 0.1 and 10, it is a buffer solution. Note that the ratio of moles is the same as the ratio of concentrations because the volume for both terms is the same.

$$pH = pK_a + \log \frac{[base]}{[acid]} = pK_a + \log \frac{0.0300 \text{ mol}}{0.22 \text{ mol}} = 3.85. \text{ Solve for } pK_a.$$

$$pK_a = 3.85 - \log \frac{0.0300 \text{ mol}}{0.22 \text{ mol}} = 4.72$$

Check: The units (none) are correct. The magnitude of the answer makes physical sense because there is more acid than base at equilibrium; so the pK_a is higher than the pH of the solution.

16.91   **Given:** 0.867 g diprotic acid titrated with 32.2 mL of 0.182 M Ba(OH)$_2$ solution   **Find:** molar mass of acid
Conceptual Plan: Write a balanced reaction then mL $\rightarrow$ L then M Ba(OH)$_2$, L $\rightarrow$ mol Ba(OH)$_2$ $\rightarrow$ mol acid

$$H_2A + Ba(OH)_2 \rightarrow BaA + 2H_2O \qquad \frac{1 \text{ L}}{1000 \text{ ml}} \qquad M = \frac{mol}{L} \qquad 1:1$$

then mol acid, g acid $\rightarrow$ $\mathcal{M}$.

$$\mathcal{M} = \frac{g \text{ acid}}{mol \text{ acid}}$$

Solution: $32.2 \text{ mL} \times \dfrac{1 \text{ L}}{1000 \text{ mL}} = 0.0322 \text{ L}$ then

$$0.0322 \text{ L Ba(OH)}_2 \times \frac{0.182 \text{ mol Ba(OH)}_2}{1 \text{ L Ba(OH)}_2} = 0.0058604 \text{ mol Ba(OH)}_2 \times \frac{1 \text{ mol H}_2A}{1 \text{ mol Ba(OH)}_2} = 0.0058604 \text{ mol H}_2A$$

then $\mathcal{M} = \dfrac{g \text{ acid}}{mol \text{ acid}} = \dfrac{0.867 \text{ g H}_2A}{0.0058604 \text{ mol H}_2A} = 148 \text{ g/mol}$

Check: The units (g/mol) are correct. The magnitude of the answer makes physical sense because there is much less than a mole of acid and about half a gram of acid, so the molar mass will be high. The number is reasonable for an acid (must be >20 g/mol—lightest acid is HF).

16.93   **Given:** saturated CaCO$_3$ solution; precipitate 1.00×10^2 mg CaCO$_3$ **Find:** volume of solution evaporated
Other: $K_{sp}(CaCO_3) = 4.96 \times 10^{-9}$
Conceptual Plan: mg CaCO$_3$ $\rightarrow$ g CaCO$_3$ $\rightarrow$ mol CaCO$_3$

$$\frac{1 \text{ g CaCO}_3}{1000 \text{ mg CaCO}_3} \qquad \frac{1 \text{ mol CaCO}_3}{100.09 \text{ g CaCO}_3}$$

The expression of the solubility product constant of A$_m$X$_n$ is $K_{sp} = [A^{n+}]^m [X^{m-}]^n$. The molar solubility of a compound, A$_m$X$_n$, can be computed directly from K_{sp} by solving for S in the expression $K_{sp} = (mS)^m (nS)^n = m^n n^n S^{m+n}$. Then mol CaCO$_3$, S $\rightarrow$ L.

$$M = \frac{mol}{L}$$

Solution: $1.00 \times 10^2 \text{ mg CaCO}_3 \times \dfrac{1 \text{ g CaCO}_3}{1000 \text{ mg CaCO}_3} \times \dfrac{1 \text{ mol CaCO}_3}{100.09 \text{ g CaCO}_3} = 9.99101 \times 10^{-4} \text{ mol CaCO}_3$ then

$K_{sp} = 4.96 \times 10^{-9}$, A = Ca^{2+}, $m = 1$, X = CO$_3^{2-}$, and $n = 1$; so $K_{sp} = 4.96 \times 10^{-9} = S^2$.
Rearrange to solve for S. $S = \sqrt{4.96 \times 10^{-9}} = 7.04273 \times 10^{-5}$ M. Finally,

$$9.99101 \times 10^{-4} \text{ mol CaCO}_3 \times \frac{1 \text{ L}}{7.04273 \times 10^{-5} \text{ mol CaCO}_3} = 14.2 \text{ L}.$$

Check: The units (L) are correct. The volume should be large because the solubility is low.

16.95   **Given:** $[Ca^{2+}] = 9.2$ mg/dL and K_{sp} $(Ca_2P_2O_7) = 8.64 \times 10^{-13}$ **Find:** $[P_2O_7^{4-}]$ to form precipitate
Conceptual Plan: mg Ca^{2+}/dL $\rightarrow$ g Ca^{2+}/dL $\rightarrow$ mol Ca^{2+}/dL $\rightarrow$ mol Ca^{2+}/L then

$$\frac{1 \text{ g } Ca^{2+}}{1000 \text{ mg } Ca^{2+}} \qquad \frac{1 \text{ mol } Ca^{2+}}{40.08 \text{ g } Ca^{2+}} \qquad \frac{10 \text{ dL}}{1 \text{ L}}$$

write a balanced equation and expression for K_{sp}. Then $[Ca^{2+}]$, $K_{sp} \rightarrow [P_2O_7^{4-}]$.

Solution: $9.2\dfrac{\text{mg } Ca^{2+}}{dL} \times \dfrac{1 \text{ g } Ca^{2+}}{1000 \text{ mg } Ca^{2+}} \times \dfrac{1 \text{ mol } Ca^{2+}}{40.08 \text{ g } Ca^{2+}} \times \dfrac{10 \text{ dL}}{1 \text{ L}} = 2.\underline{2}9541 \times 10^{-3}$ M Ca^{2+} then write

equation $Ca_2P_2O_7(s) \rightarrow 2\ Ca^{2+}(aq) + P_2O_7^{4-}(aq)$. So $K_{sp} = [Ca^{2+}]^2\ [P_2O_7^{4-}] = 8.64 \times 10^{-13} =$
$(2.\underline{2}9541 \times 10^{-3})^2\ [P_2O_7^{4-}]$. Solve for $[P_2O_7^{4-}]$ then $[P_2O_7^{4-}] = 1.6 \times 10^{-7}$ M.

Check: The units (M) are correct. Because K_{sp} is so small and the calcium concentration is relatively high, the diphosphate concentration required is at a very low level.

16.97   **Given:** CuX in 0.150 M NaCN   **Find:** molar solubility (S)
Other: $K_f(Cu(CN)_4^{2-}) = 1.0 \times 10^{25}$, $K_{sp}(CuX) = [Cu^{2+}][X^{2-}] = 1.27 \times 10^{-36}$
Conceptual Plan: Identify the appropriate solid and complex ion. Write balanced equations for dissolving the solid and forming the complex ion. Add these two reactions to get the desired overall reaction. Using the rules from Chapter 14, multiply the individual reaction Ks to get the overall K for the sum of these reactions. Then M NaCN, $K \rightarrow S$.

ICE table

Solution: Identify the solid as MX and the complex ion as $M(CN)_4^{2-}$. Write the individual reactions and add them together.

$CuX(s) \rightleftharpoons Cu^{+}(aq) + X^{2-}(aq)$ $\qquad\qquad K_{sp} = 1.27 \times 10^{-36}$

$\dfrac{Cu^{2+}(aq) + 4\ CN^-(aq) \rightleftharpoons Cu(CN)_4^{2-}(aq)}{Cu(s) + 4\ CN^-(aq) \rightleftharpoons Cu(CN)_4^{2-}(aq) + X^{2-}(aq)} \qquad K_f = 1.0 \times 10^{25}$

Because the overall reaction is the simple sum of the two reactions, the overall reaction $K = K_f K_{sp} = (1.0 \times 10^{25}) \times (1.27 \times 10^{-36}) = 1.\underline{2}7 \times 10^{-11}$. $NaCN(s) \rightarrow Na^+(aq) + CN^-(aq)$. Because one CN^- ion is generated for each $NaCN$, $[CN^-] = 0.150$ M. Set up an ICE table:

$$Cu(s) + 4\ CN^-(aq) \rightleftharpoons Cu(CN)_4^{2-}(aq) + X^{2-}(aq)$$

	$[CN^-]$	$[Cu(CN)_4^{2-}]$	$[X^{2-}]$
Initial	0.150	0.00	0.00
Change	$-4S$	$+S$	$+S$
Equil	$0.150 - 4S$	$+S$	$+S$

$K = \dfrac{[Cu(CN)_4^{2-}]\ [X^{2-}]}{[CN^-]^4} = 1.\underline{2}7 \times 10^{-11} = \dfrac{S^2}{(0.150 - 4S)^4}$

Assume that S is small ($4S \ll 0.150$); so $\dfrac{S^2}{(0.150 - 4S)^4} = 1.\underline{2}7 \times 10^{-11} = \dfrac{S^2}{(0.150)^4}$ and $S = 8.0183 \times 10^{-8} =$

8.0×10^{-8} M. Confirm that the assumption is valid. $\dfrac{4(8.\underline{0}183 \times 10^{-8})}{0.150} \times 100\% = 0.00021\% \ll 5\%$, so the assumption is valid.

Check: The units (M) are correct. Because K_f is large, the overall K is larger than the original K_{sp} and the solubility of MX increases over that of pure water ($\sqrt{1.27 \times 10^{-36}} = 1.13 \times 10^{-18}$ M).

16.99   **Given:** 100.0 mL of 0.36 M NH_2OH and 50.0 mL of 0.26 M HCl and $K_b(NH_2OH) = 1.10 \times 10^{-8}$ **Find:** pH
Conceptual Plan: Identify acid and base components mL $\rightarrow$ L then $[NH_2OH]$, L $\rightarrow$ mol NH_2OH

$$\text{acid} = NH_3OH^+ \qquad \text{base} = NH_2OH \qquad \frac{1 \text{ L}}{1000 \text{ mL}} \qquad M = \frac{\text{mol}}{\text{L}}$$

then mL $\rightarrow$ L then [HCl], L $\rightarrow$ mol HCl then write balanced equation then

$$\frac{1 \text{ L}}{1000 \text{ mL}} \qquad M = \frac{\text{mol}}{\text{L}} \qquad HCl + NH_2OH \rightarrow NH_3OHCl$$

mol NH_2OH, mol HCl → mol excess NH_2OH, mol NH_3OH^+.

set up stoichiometry table

Because there are significant amounts of both the acid and the conjugate base species, this is a buffer solution; so the Henderson–Hasselbalch equation $\left(pH = pK_a + \log \dfrac{[base]}{[acid]} \right)$ can be used. Convert K_b to K_a using $K_w = K_a K_b$. Also note that the ratio of concentrations is the same as the ratio of moles because the volume is the same for both species.

Solution: $100 \text{ mL } NH_2OH \times \dfrac{1 \text{ L}}{1000 \text{ mL}} = 0.1000 \text{ L } NH_2OH$ then

$\dfrac{0.36 \text{ mol } NH_2OH}{1 \text{ L}} \times 0.1000 \text{ L} = 0.036 \text{ mol } NH_2OH$. $50.0 \text{ mL } HCl \times \dfrac{1 \text{ L}}{1000 \text{ mL}} = 0.0500 \text{ L } HCl$ then

$\dfrac{0.26 \text{ mol } HCl}{1 \text{ L}} \times 0.0500 \text{ L} = 0.013 \text{ mol } HCl$.

Set up a table to track changes:

$$HCl(aq) + NH_2OH(aq) \rightarrow NH_3OHCl(aq)$$

	$HCl(aq)$	$NH_2OH(aq)$	$NH_3OHCl(aq)$
Before addition	0.00 mol	0.036 mol	0.00 mol
Addition	0.013 mol	—	—
After addition	$\approx$0.00 mol	0.023 mol	0.013 mol

Then $K_w = K_a K_b$, so $K_a = \dfrac{K_w}{K_b} = \dfrac{1.0 \times 10^{-14}}{1.10 \times 10^{-8}} = 9.\underline{0}909 \times 10^{-7}$ M.

Then use the Henderson–Hasselbalch equation because the solution is a buffer. Note that the ratio of moles is the same as the ratio of concentrations because the volume for both terms is the same.

$$pH = pK_a + \log \frac{[base]}{[acid]} = -\log(9.\underline{0}909 \times 10^{-7}) + \log \frac{0.023 \text{ mol}}{0.013 \text{ mol}} = 6.2\underline{8}918 = 6.29.$$

Check: The units (none) are correct. The magnitude of the answer makes physical sense because the pH should be more than the pK_a of the acid because there is more base than acid.

16.101   **Given:** $(CH_3)_2NH/(CH_3)_2NH_2Cl$ buffer at pH $= 10.43$ **Find:** relative masses of $(CH_3)_2NH$ and $(CH_3)_2NH_2Cl$
     Other: $K_b((CH_3)_2NH) = 5.4 \times 10^{-4}$
     Conceptual Plan: $K_b \rightarrow pK_b \rightarrow pK_a$ then pH, $pK_a \rightarrow [(CH_3)_2NH] / [(CH_3)_2NH_2^+]$ then

$$pK_b = -\log K_b \qquad 14 = pK_a + pK_b \qquad \text{acid} = (CH_3)_2NH_2^+ \qquad \text{base} = (CH_3)_2NH \qquad pH = pK_a + \log \frac{[base]}{[acid]}$$

$[(CH_3)_2NH] / [(CH_3)_2NH_2^+] \rightarrow g(CH_3)_2NH / g(CH_3)_2NH_2^+$

$$\frac{45.09 \text{ g}(CH_3)_2NH}{1 \text{ mol } (CH_3)_2NH} \qquad \frac{1 \text{ mol } (CH_3)_2NH_2Cl}{81.54 \text{ g } (CH_3)_2NH_2Cl}$$

Solution: Because $K_b((CH_3)_2NH) = 5.4 \times 10^{-4}$, $pK_b = -\log K_b = -\log(5.4 \times 10^{-4}) = 3.27$. Because $14 = pK_a + pK_b$, $pK_a = 14 - pK_b = 14 - 3.27 = 10.73$. Because $[acid] = [(CH_3)_2NH_2^+] = [(CH_3)_2NH_2Cl]$ and $[base] = [(CH_3)_2NH]$, then $pH = pK_a + \log \dfrac{[base]}{[acid]} = 10.73 + \log \dfrac{[(CH_3)_2NH]}{[(CH_3)_2NH_2Cl]} = 10.43$. Solve for

$$\frac{[(CH_3)_2NH]}{[(CH_3)_2NH_2Cl]}. \; \log \frac{[(CH_3)_2NH]}{[(CH_3)_2NH_2Cl]} = 10.43 - 10.73 = -0.30 \rightarrow \frac{[(CH_3)_2NH]}{[(CH_3)_2NH_2Cl]} = 10^{-0.30} = 0.\underline{5}01187.$$

Then $\dfrac{0.\underline{5}01187 \text{ mol}(CH_3)_2NH}{1 \text{ mol}(CH_3)_2NH_2Cl} \times \dfrac{45.09 \text{ g}(CH_3)_2NH}{1 \text{ mol}(CH_3)_2NH} \times \dfrac{1 \text{ mol}(CH_3)_2NH_2Cl}{81.54 \text{ g}(CH_3)_2NH_2Cl} = \dfrac{0.\underline{2}77146 \text{ g}(CH_3)_2NH}{\text{g}(CH_3)_2NH_2Cl}$

$= \dfrac{0.28 \text{ g } (CH_3)_2NH}{\text{g } (CH_3)_2NH_2Cl}$ or $\dfrac{3.6 \text{ g } (CH_3)_2NH_2Cl}{\text{g } (CH_3)_2NH}$.

Check: The units (g/g) are correct. The magnitude of the answer makes physical sense because there are more moles of acid than base in the buffer (pH $<$ pK_a) and the molar mass of the acid is greater than the molar mass of the base. Thus, the ratio of the mass of the base to the mass of the acid is expected to be less than 1.

16.103   **Given:** $HC_7H_5O_2/C_7H_5O_2Na$ buffer at pH $= 4.55$, complete dissociation of $C_7H_5O_2Na$, $d = 1.01$ g/mL; $T_f = -2.0\,°C$
    Find: $[HC_7H_5O_2]$ and $[C_7H_5O_2Na]$ **Other:** $K_a(HC_7H_5O_2) = 6.5 \times 10^{-5}$, $K_f = 1.86\,°C/m$
    Conceptual Plan: $K_a \rightarrow pK_a$ then pH, $pK_a \rightarrow [C_7H_5O_2Na]\,/\,[HC_7H_5O_2]$ and $T_f \rightarrow \Delta T_f$ then

$$pK_a = -\log K_a \qquad \text{acid} = HC_7H_5O_2 \qquad \text{base} = C_7H_5O_2^{-} \qquad pH = pK_a + \log\frac{[\text{base}]}{[\text{acid}]} \qquad T_f = T_f^{\circ} - \Delta T_f$$

$\Delta T_f, i, K_f \rightarrow m$ **then assume 1 kg water (or 1000 g water)**

$$\Delta T_f = K_f \times m \qquad\qquad m = \frac{\text{amount solute (moles)}}{\text{mass solvent (kg)}}$$

**Assume that $HC_7H_5O_2$ does not dissociate and that $C_7H_5O_2Na$ completely dissociates, then mol particles =
mol $HC_7H_5O_2$ + 2(mol $C_7H_5O_2Na$). Use $[C_7H_5O_2Na]\,/\,[HC_7H_5O_2]$ and total mol particles = mol $[HC_7H_5O_2]$
+ 2(mol $C_7H_5O_2Na$) to solve for mol $HC_7H_5O_2$ and mol $C_7H_5O_2Na$. Then
mol $HC_7H_5O_2$ $\rightarrow$ g mol $HC_7H_5O_2$ and mol $C_7H_5O_2Na$ $\rightarrow$ g $C_7H_5O_2Na$ then**

$$\frac{122.12\ \text{g}\ HC_7H_5O_2}{1\ \text{mol}\ HC_7H_5O_2} \qquad\qquad \frac{144.10\ \text{g}\ C_7H_5O_2Na}{1\ \text{mol}\ HC_7H_5O_2Na}$$

g mol $HC_7H_5O_2$, g $C_7H_5O_2Na$, g water $\rightarrow$ g solution $\rightarrow$ mL solution $\rightarrow$ L solution then

$$\text{g mol}\ HC_7H_5O_2 + \text{g}\ C_7H_5O_2Na + \text{g water} = \text{g solution} \qquad d = \frac{1\ \text{mL}}{1.01\ \text{g}} \qquad \frac{1\ \text{L}}{1000\ \text{mL}}$$

mol $HC_7H_5O_2$, L $\rightarrow$ M $HC_7H_5O_2$ and mol $C_7H_5O_2Na$, L $\rightarrow$ M $C_7H_5O_2Na$.

$$M = \frac{\text{mol}}{L} \qquad\qquad\qquad M = \frac{\text{mol}}{L}$$

Solution: Because $K_a(HC_7H_5O_2) = 6.5 \times 10^{-5}$, $pK_a = -\log K_a = -\log(6.5 \times 10^{-5}) = 4.19$. Because [acid] $=$
$[HC_7H_5O_2]$ and [base] $= [C_7H_5O_2^{-}] = [C_7H_5O_2Na]$, then

$$pH = pK_a + \log\frac{[\text{base}]}{[\text{acid}]} = 4.19 + \log\frac{[C_7H_5O_2Na]}{[HC_7H_5O_2]} = 4.55.\ \text{Solve for } \frac{[C_7H_5O_2Na]}{[HC_7H_5O_2]}.$$

$$\log\frac{[C_7H_5O_2Na]}{[HC_7H_5O_2]} = 4.55 - 4.19 = 0.36 \rightarrow \frac{[C_7H_5O_2Na]}{[HC_7H_5O_2]} = 10^{0.36} = 2.29087.\ \text{Then } T_f = T_f^{\circ} - \Delta T_f,\ \text{so}$$

$$\Delta T_f = T_f^{\circ} - T_f = 0.0\,°C - (-2.0\,°C) = 2.0\,°C \text{ then } \Delta T_f = K_f \times m.\ \text{Rearrange to solve for } m.$$

$$m = \frac{\Delta T_f}{K_f} = \frac{2.0\,°C}{1.86\,\dfrac{°C}{m}} = 1.07527\ \frac{\text{mol particles}}{\text{kg solvent}}.\ \text{Assume that 1 kg water, so we have 1.07527 mol particles.}$$

Assume that $HC_7H_5O_2$ does not dissociate and that $C_7H_5O_2Na$ completely dissociates; then 1.07527 mol particles =
mol $HC_7H_5O_2$ + 2(mol $C_7H_5O_2Na$). Use $[C_7H_5O_2Na]/[HC_7H_5O_2] = 2.29087$ and 1.07527 mol particles =
mol $[HC_7H_5O_2]$ + 2(mol $C_7H_5O_2Na$) to solve for mol $HC_7H_5O_2$ and mol $C_7H_5O_2Na$. So mol $C_7H_5O_2Na =$
2.29087(mol $HC_7H_5O_2$) $\rightarrow$ 1.07527 mol particles = mol $HC_7H_5O_2$ + 2(2.29087 mol $HC_7H_5O_2$) $\rightarrow$
1.07527 mol particles = 5.58174 mol $HC_7H_5O_2$ $\rightarrow$ mol $HC_7H_5O_2 = 0.192641$ mol and
mol $C_7H_5O_2Na = 2.29087 \times$ mol $HC_7H_5O_2 = 2.29087 \times 0.192641$ mol $HC_7H_5O_2 = 0.441315$ mol $C_7H_5O_2Na$

$$0.192641\ \text{mol}\ HC_7H_5O_2 \times \frac{122.12\ \text{g}\ HC_7H_5O_2}{1\ \text{mol}\ HC_7H_5O_2} = 23.5253\ \text{g}\ HC_7H_5O_2 \text{ and}$$

$$0.441315\ \text{mol}\ C_7H_5O_2Na \times \frac{144.10\ \text{g}\ C_7H_5O_2Na}{1\ \text{mol}\ C_7H_5O_2Na} = 63.5935\ \text{g}\ C_7H_5O_2Na \text{ then}$$

23.5253 g mol $HC_7H_5O_2$ + 63.5935 g $C_7H_5O_2Na$ + 1000 g water = 1087.119 g solution then

$$1087.119\ \text{g solution} \times \frac{1\ \text{mL}}{1.01\ \text{g}} \times \frac{1\ \text{L}}{1000\ \text{mL}} = 1.076355\ \text{L. Finally,}$$

$$\frac{0.192641\ \text{mol}\ HC_7H_5O_2}{1.076355\ \text{L}} = 0.178975\ \text{M}\ HC_7H_5O_2 = 0.18\ \text{M}\ HC_7H_5O_2 \text{ and}$$

$$\frac{0.441315\ \text{mol}\ C_7H_5O_2Na}{1.076355\ \text{L}} = 0.410009\ \text{M}\ C_7H_5O_2Na = 0.41\ \text{M}\ C_7H_5O_2Na.$$

Check: The units (M and M) are correct. The magnitude of the answer makes physical sense because there are more
moles of base than acid in the buffer (pH $> pK_a$).

Challenge Problems

16.105   **Given:** 10.0 L of 75 ppm $CaCO_3$ and 55 ppm $MgCO_3$ (by mass)
Find: mass Na_2CO_3 to precipitate 90.0% of ions
Other: $K_{sp}(CaCO_3) = 4.96 \times 10^{-9}$ and $K_{sp}(MgCO_3) = 6.82 \times 10^{-6}$
Conceptual Plan: Assume that the density of water is 1.00 g/mL, L water → mL water → g water then

$$\frac{1000\ mL}{1\ L} \qquad \frac{1.00\ g\ water}{1\ mL}$$

g water → g $CaCO_3$ → mol $CaCO_3$ → mol Ca^{2+} and g water → g $MgCO_3$ → mol $MgCO_3$ then

$$\frac{75\ g\ CaCO_3}{10^6\ g\ water} \quad \frac{1\ mol\ CaCO_3}{100.09\ g\ CaCO_3} \quad \frac{1\ mol\ Ca^{2+}}{1\ mol\ CaCO_3} \qquad \frac{55\ g\ MgCO_3}{10^6\ g\ water} \quad \frac{1\ mol\ MgCO_3}{84.32\ g\ MgCO_3}$$

mol $MgCO_3$ → mol Mg^{2+} then comparing the two K_{sp} values, essentially all of the Ca^{2+} will

$$\frac{1\ mol\ Mg^{2+}}{1\ mol\ MgCO_3}$$

precipitate before the Mg^{2+} will begin to precipitate. Because 90.0% of the ions are to be precipitates, 10.0% of the ions will be left in solution (all will be Mg^{2+}).

$$(0.100)(mol\ Ca^{2+} + mol\ Mg^{2+})$$

Calculate the moles of ions remaining in solution. Then mol Mg^{2+}, L → M Mg^{2+}.

$$M = \frac{mol}{L}$$

The solubility product constant (K_{sp}) is the equilibrium expression for a chemical equation representing the dissolution of an ionic compound. The expression of the solubility product constant of A_mX_n is $K_{sp} = [A^{n+}]^m[X^{m-}]^n$. Use this equation to M Mg^{2+}, K_{sp} → M CO_3^{2-} then M CO_3^{2-}, L → mol CO_3^{2-}

$$\text{for ionic compound, } A_mX_n, K_{sp} = [A^{n+}]^m[X^{m-}]^n \qquad M = \frac{mol}{L}$$

then mol CO_3^{2-} → mol Na_2CO_3 → g Na_2CO_3.

$$\frac{1\ mol\ CO_3^{2-}}{1\ mol\ Na_2CO_3} \qquad \frac{105.99\ g\ Na_2CO_3}{1\ mol\ Na_2CO_3}$$

Solution: $10.0\ L \times \dfrac{1000\ mL}{1\ L} \times \dfrac{1.00\ g\ water}{1\ mL} = 1.00 \times 10^4$ g water then

$$1.00 \times 10^4\ g\ water \times \frac{75\ g\ CaCO_3}{10^6\ g\ water} \times \frac{1\ mol\ CaCO_3}{100.09\ g\ CaCO_3} \times \frac{1\ mol\ Ca^{2+}}{1\ mol\ CaCO_3} = 0.0074933\ mol\ Ca^{2+}\ and$$

$$1.00 \times 10^4\ g\ water \times \frac{55\ g\ MgCO_3}{10^6\ g\ water} \times \frac{1\ mol\ MgCO_3}{84.32\ g\ MgCO_3} \times \frac{1\ mol\ Mg^{2+}}{1\ mol\ MgCO_3} = 0.0065228\ mol\ Mg^{2+}\ so\ the\ ions$$

remaining in solution after 90.0% precipitate out = $(0.100)(mol\ Ca^{2+} + mol\ Mg^{2+})$
= $(0.100)(0.0074933\ mol\ Ca^{2+} + 0.0065228\ mol\ Mg^{2+}) = 0.00140161\ mol\ ions$

so $\dfrac{0.00140161\ mol\ Mg^{2+}}{10.0\ L} = 0.000140161$ M Mg^{2+}. Then $K_{sp} = 6.82 \times 10^{-6}, A = Mg^{2+}, m = 1, X = CO_3^{2-}$, and

$n = 1$; so $K_{sp} = 6.82 \times 10^{-6} = [Mg^{2+}][CO_3^{2-}] = (0.00140161)[CO_3^{2-}]$. Rearrange to solve for $[CO_3^{2-}]$.
So $[CO_3^{2-}] = 0.0486583$ M. Then

$$\frac{0.0486583\ mol\ CO_3^{2-}}{1\ L} \times 10.0\ L \times \frac{1\ mol\ Na_2CO_3}{1\ mol\ CO_3^{2-}} \times \frac{105.99\ g\ Na_2CO_3}{1\ mol\ Na_2CO_3} = 51.6\ g\ Na_2CO_3.$$

Check: The units (g) are correct. The mass is reasonable to put in a washing machine load.

16.107   **Given:** 1.00 L of 0.100 M $Mg(NO_3)_2$ **Find:** volume of 0.100 M Na_2CO_3 to precipitate 99% of Mg^{2+} ions
Other: $K_{sp}(MgCO_3) = 6.82 \times 10^{-6}$
Conceptual Plan:
Because 99% of the Mg^{2+} ions are to be precipitated, 1% of the ions will be left in solution.

$$(0.01)(0.100\ M\ Mg^{2+})$$

Let x = required volume (in L). Calculate the amount of CO_3^{2-} added and the amount of Mg^{2+} that does not precipitate and remains in solution. Use these to calculate the $[Mg^{2+}]$ and $[CO_3^{2-}]$. The solubility product

constant (K_{sp}) is the equilibrium expression for a chemical equation representing the dissolution of an ionic compound. The expression of the solubility product constant of $A_m X_n$ is $K_{sp} = [A^{n+}]^m [X^{m-}]^n$. Substitute these expressions in this equation to $[Mg^{2+}]$, $[CO_3^{2-}]$, $K_{sp} \rightarrow x$.

$$\text{for ionic compound, } A_m X_n, K_{sp} = [A^{n+}]^m [X^{m-}]^n$$

Solution: Because 99% of the Mg^{2+} ions are to be precipitated, 1% of the ions will be left in solution, or $(0.01)(0.100 \text{ M } Mg^{2+}) = 0.001 \text{ M } Mg^{2+}$. Let x = required volume (in L). The volume of the solution after precipitation is $(1.00 + x)$. The amount of CO_3^{2-} added = $(0.100 \text{ M})(x \text{ L}) = 0.100x \text{ mol } CO_3^{2-}$. The amount of Mg^{2+} that does not precipitate and remains in solution is $(0.100 \text{ M})(1.00 \text{ L})(0.001) = 1.00 \times 10^{-3} \text{ mol}$, and the amount that precipitates $= 0.099 \text{ mol}$, which is also equal to the amount of CO_3^{2-} used. The amount of CO_3^{2-} remaining in solution is $(0.10x - 0.099)$. Thus, $[Mg^{2+}] = 1.00 \times 10^{-3} \text{mol}/(1.00 + x) \text{ L}$ and $[CO_3^{2-}] = (0.10x - 0.099) \text{ mol}/(1.00 + x) \text{ L}$. Then $K_{sp} = 6.82 \times 10^{-6}$, $A = Mg^{2+}$, $m = 1$, $X = CO_3^{2-}$, and

$n = 1$; so $K_{sp} = 6.82 \times 10^{-6} = [Mg^{2+}][CO_3^{2-}] = \dfrac{(1.00 \times 10^{-3})(0.10x - 0.099)}{(1.00 + x)^2}$. Rearrange to solve for x.

$1.00 + 2.00x + x^2 = \dfrac{1.0 \times 10^{-4}x - 9.9 \times 10^{-5}}{6.82 \times 10^{-6}} \rightarrow 0 = x^2 - 12.6628x + 15.5161$. Using quadratic equation, $x = 1.3\underline{7}5 \text{ L} = 1.4 \text{ L}$.

Check: The units (L) are correct. The necessary concentration is very low, so the volume is fairly large.

16.109   **Given:** 1.0 L solution with 0.10 M $Ba(OH)_2$ and excess $Zn(OH)_2$ **Find:** pH
               Other: $K_{sp}(Zn(OH)_2) = 3 \times 10^{-15}$, $K_f(Zn(OH)_4^{2-}) = 2 \times 10^{15}$
               Conceptual Plan: Because $[Ba(OH)_2] = 0.10$ M, $[OH^-] = 0.20$ M. Write balanced equations for the solubility of $Zn(OH)_2$ and reaction with excess OH^- and expressions for K_{sp} and K_f. Use initial concentrations to set up an ICE table. Solve for $[OH^-]$ at equilibrium. Then $[OH^-] \rightarrow [H_3O^+] \rightarrow$ pH.

$$K_w = [H_3O^+][OH^-] \quad pH = -\log [H_3O^+]$$

Solution: Write two reactions and combine.

$Zn(OH)_2(s) \rightleftharpoons Zn^{2+}(aq) + 2\,OH^-(aq)$ with $K_{sp} = [Zn^{2+}][OH^-]^2 = 3 \times 10^{-15}$

$Zn^{2+}(aq) + 4\,OH^-(aq) \rightleftharpoons Zn(OH)_4^{2-}(aq)$ with $K_f = \dfrac{[Zn(OH)_4^{2-}]}{[Zn^{2+}][OH^-]^4} = 2 \times 10^{15}$

$\overline{Zn(OH)_2(s) + 2\,OH^-(aq) \rightleftharpoons Zn(OH)_4^{2-}(aq)}$

$$\text{with } K = K_{sp}K_f = [Zn^{2+}][OH^-]^2 \frac{[Zn(OH)_4^{2-}]}{[Zn^{2+}][OH^-]^4} = (3 \times 10^{-15})(2 \times 10^{15})$$

$K = \dfrac{[Zn(OH)_4^{2-}]}{[OH^-]^2} = 6$. Set up an ICE table with initial concentration and solve for x.

$$Zn(OH)_2(s) + 2\,OH^-(aq) \rightleftharpoons Zn(OH)_4^{2-}(aq)$$

	$[OH^-]$	$[Zn(OH)_4^{2-}]$
Initial	0.20	0.00
Change	$-2x$	x
Equil	$0.20 - 2x$	x

$$K = \frac{[Zn(OH)_4^{2-}]}{[OH^-]^2} = \frac{x}{(0.20 - 2x)^2} = 6$$

$x = 6(0.20 - 2x)^2 \rightarrow x = 6(4x^2 - 0.80x + 0.040) \rightarrow x = 24x^2 - 4.8x + 0.24 \rightarrow$
$0 = 24x^2 - 5.8x + 0.24$. Using quadratic equation, $x = 0.05\underline{3}0049 \rightarrow$
$[OH^-] = 0.20 - 2x = 0.20 - 2(0.0530049) = 0.093990 \text{ M } OH^-$. Then $K_w = [H_3O^+][OH^-]$, so

$[H_3O^+] = \dfrac{K_w}{[OH^-]} = \dfrac{1.0 \times 10^{-14}}{0.093990} = 1.0\underline{6}394 \times 10^{-13} \text{ M}$. Finally,

$pH = -\log [H_3O^+] = -\log(1.0\underline{6}394 \times 10^{-13}) = 12.97$.

Check: The units (none) are correct. Because the pH of the solution before the addition of the $Zn(OH)_2$ is 13.30, the reaction decreases the $[OH^-]$ and the pH drops.

Conceptual Problems

16.111   If the concentration of the acid is greater than the concentration of the base, then the pH will be less than the pK_a. If the concentration of the acid is equal to the concentration of the base, then the pH will be equal to the pK_a. If the concentration of the acid is less than the concentration of the base, then the pH will be greater than the pK_a.

    (a) $pH < pK_a$

    (b) $pH > pK_a$

    (c) $pH = pK_a$, the OH^- will convert half of the acid to base

    (d) $pH > pK_a$, the OH^- will convert more than half of the acid to base

16.113   Only (a) is the same for all three solutions. The volume to the first equivalence point will be the same because the number of moles of acid is the same. The pH profiles of the three titrations will be different.

16.115   (a)   The solubility will be unchanged because the pH is constant and no common ions are added.

    (b)   The solubility will be less because extra fluoride ions are added, suppressing the solubility of the fluoride ionic compound.

    (c)   The solubility will increase because some of the fluoride ion will be converted to HF; so more of the ionic compound can be dissolved.

Questions for Group Work

16.117   In each case, you must add the conjugate acid to a weak base or the conjugate base to a weak acid. (Additionally, you can make a buffer by adding a little strong acid to a weak base or a little strong base to a weak acid. The product of the neutralization is the conjugate you need.)

    (a)   an acetate salt, such as sodium acetate, potassium acetate, rubidium acetate, ... (The cation may vary.)

    (b)   nitrous acid

    (c)   an ammonium salt, such as ammonium chloride, ammonium bromide, ammonium iodide, ammonium nitrate, ... (The anion may vary.)

    (d)   formic acid

    (e)   a phosphate salt or a dihydrogen phosphate salt, such as Na_3PO_4 or NaH_2PO_4, Li_3PO_4 or LiH_2PO_4, K_3PO_4 or KH_2PO_4, ... (The cations may vary.)

16.119   Students will take roles of H^+, $C_2H_3O_2^-$, Na^+, and Cl^-. As HCl (H^+ and Cl^-) is added, the H^+ will pair with $C_2H_3O_2^-$, neutralizing the acetate ion and becoming acetic acid. Since acetic acid is a weak acid, it will remain primarily undissociated and the amount of H^+ ions in solution will not significantly change.

16.121   The molar solubility, S, is simply the solubility in units of moles per liter (mol/L). The molar solubility of a compound, A_mX_n, can be computed directly from K_{sp} by solving for S in the expression: $K_{sp} = (mS)^m (nS)^n = m^m n^n S^{m+n}$. As an example, for $Ca(OH)_2$, $K_{sp} = 4.68 \times 10^{-6}$, $A = Ca^{2+}$, $m = 1$, $X = OH^-$, and $n = 2$ so $K_{sp} = 4.68 \times 10^{-6} = 2^2 S^3$. Rearrange to solve for S. $S = \sqrt[3]{\dfrac{4.68 \times 10^{-6}}{4}} = 1.05 \times 10^{-2}$ M. The solubility rules in Chapter 4 predict that hydroxides are not very soluble, which agrees with the calculated value of S.

17 Free Energy and Thermodynamics

Entropy, the Second Law of Thermodynamics, and the Direction of Spontaneous Change

17.1 a and c are spontaneous processes.

17.3 System B has the greatest entropy. There is only one energetically equivalent arrangement for System A. However, the particles of System B may exchange positions for a second energetically equivalent arrangement.

17.5 (a) $\Delta S > 0$ because a gas is being generated.

(b) $\Delta S < 0$ because 2 moles of gas are being converted to 1 mole of gas.

(c) $\Delta S < 0$ because a gas is being converted to a solid.

(d) $\Delta S < 0$ because 4 moles of gas are being converted to 2 moles of gas.

17.7 (a) $\Delta S_{sys} > 0$ because 6 moles of gas are being converted to 7 moles of gas. Because $\Delta H < 0$ and $\Delta S_{surr} > 0$, the reaction is spontaneous at all temperatures.

(b) $\Delta S_{sys} < 0$ because 2 moles of different gases are being converted to 2 moles of one gas. Because $\Delta H > 0$ and $\Delta S_{surr} < 0$, the reaction is nonspontaneous at all temperatures.

(c) $\Delta S_{sys} < 0$ because 3 moles of gas are being converted to 2 moles of gas. Because $\Delta H > 0$ and $\Delta S_{surr} < 0$, the reaction is nonspontaneous at all temperatures.

(d) $\Delta S_{sys} > 0$ because 9 moles of gas are being converted to 10 moles of gas. Because $\Delta H < 0$ and $\Delta S_{surr} > 0$, the reaction is spontaneous at all temperatures.

17.9 (a) **Given:** $\Delta H^{\circ}_{rxn} = -287$ kJ, $T = 298$ K **Find:** ΔS_{surr}

Conceptual Plan: kJ $\rightarrow$ J then $\Delta H^{\circ}_{rxn}, T \rightarrow \Delta S_{surr}$

$$\frac{1000 \text{ J}}{1 \text{ kJ}} \qquad \Delta S_{surr} = \frac{-\Delta H_{sys}}{T}$$

Solution: $-287 \text{ kJ} \times \dfrac{1000 \text{ J}}{1 \text{ kJ}} = -287{,}000 \text{ J}$ then

$$\Delta S_{surr} = \frac{-\Delta H_{sys}}{T} = \frac{-(-287{,}000 \text{ J})}{298 \text{ K}} = 963 \text{ J/K}$$

Check: The units (J/K) are correct. The magnitude of the answer (10^3 J/K) makes sense because the kJ and the temperature started with similar values and then a factor of 10^3 was applied.

(b) **Given:** $\Delta H^{\circ}_{rxn} = -287$ kJ, $T = 77$ K **Find:** ΔS_{surr}

Conceptual Plan: kJ $\rightarrow$ J then $\Delta H^{\circ}_{rxn}, T \rightarrow \Delta S_{surr}$

$$\frac{1000 \text{ J}}{1 \text{ kJ}} \qquad \Delta S_{surr} = \frac{-\Delta H_{sys}}{T}$$

Solution:
$-287 \text{ kJ} \times \dfrac{1000 \text{ J}}{1 \text{ kJ}} = -287{,}000 \text{ J}$ then $\Delta S_{surr} = \dfrac{-\Delta H_{sys}}{T} = \dfrac{-(-287{,}000 \text{ J})}{77 \text{ K}} = 3.73 \times 10^3 \text{ J/K}$

Check: The units (J/K) are correct. The magnitude of the answer (4×10^3 J/K) makes sense because the temperature is much lower than in part (a); so the answer should increase.

(c)   **Given:** $\Delta H^{\circ}_{rxn} = +127$ kJ, $T = 298$ K   **Find:** ΔS_{surr}

Conceptual Plan: kJ $\rightarrow$ J then $\Delta H^{\circ}_{rxn}, T \rightarrow \Delta S_{surr}$

$$\frac{1000 \text{ J}}{1 \text{ kJ}} \qquad\qquad \Delta S_{surr} = \frac{-\Delta H_{sys}}{T}$$

Solution: $+127 \text{ kJ} \times \dfrac{1000 \text{ J}}{1 \text{ kJ}} = +127{,}000$ J then $\Delta S_{surr} = \dfrac{-\Delta H_{sys}}{T} = \dfrac{-127{,}000 \text{ J}}{298 \text{ K}} = -426$ J/K

Check: The units (J/K) are correct. The magnitude of the answer (-400 J/K) makes sense because the kJ are less and of the opposite sign than in part (a); so the answer should decrease.

(d)   **Given:** $\Delta H^{\circ}_{rxn} = +127$ kJ, $T = 77$ K   **Find:** ΔS_{surr}

Conceptual Plan: kJ $\rightarrow$ J then $\Delta H^{\circ}_{rxn}, T \rightarrow \Delta S_{surr}$

$$\frac{1000 \text{ J}}{1 \text{ kJ}} \qquad\qquad \Delta S_{surr} = \frac{-\Delta H_{sys}}{T}$$

Solution: $+127 \text{ kJ} \times \dfrac{1000 \text{ J}}{1 \text{ kJ}} = +127{,}000$ J then

$$\Delta S_{surr} = \frac{-\Delta H_{sys}}{T} = \frac{-127{,}000 \text{ J}}{77 \text{ K}} = -1650 \, \frac{\text{J}}{\text{K}} = -1.65 \times 10^3 \text{ J/K}$$

Check: The units (J/K) are correct. The magnitude of the answer (-2×10^3 J/K) makes sense because the temperature is much lower than in part (c); so the answer should increase.

17.11   (a)   **Given:** $\Delta H^{\circ}_{rxn} = -125$ kJ, $\Delta S^{\circ}_{rxn} = +253$ J/K, $T = 298$ K   **Find:** ΔS_{univ} and spontaneity

Conceptual Plan: kJ $\rightarrow$ J then $\Delta H^{\circ}_{rxn}, T \rightarrow \Delta S_{surr}$ then $\Delta S_{rxn}, \Delta S_{surr} \rightarrow \Delta S_{univ}$

$$\frac{1000 \text{ J}}{1 \text{ kJ}} \qquad\qquad \Delta S_{surr} = \frac{-\Delta H_{sys}}{T} \qquad\qquad \Delta S_{univ} = \Delta S_{sys} + \Delta S_{surr}$$

Solution: $-125 \text{ kJ} \times \dfrac{1000 \text{ J}}{1 \text{ kJ}} = -125{,}000$ J then $\Delta S_{surr} = \dfrac{-\Delta H_{sys}}{T} = \dfrac{-(-125{,}000 \text{ J})}{298 \text{ K}} = 419.4631$ J/K then

$\Delta S_{univ} = \Delta S_{sys} + \Delta S_{surr} = +253$ J/K $= +419.4631$ J/K $= +672$ J/K; so the reaction is spontaneous.

Check: The units (J/K) are correct. The magnitude of the answer ($+670$ J/K) makes sense because both terms are positive; so the reaction is spontaneous.

(b)   **Given:** $\Delta H^{\circ}_{rxn} = +125$ kJ, $\Delta S^{\circ}_{rxn} = -253$ J/K, $T = 298$ K   **Find:** ΔS_{univ} and spontaneity

Conceptual Plan: kJ $\rightarrow$ J then $\Delta H^{\circ}_{rxn}, T \rightarrow \Delta S_{surr}$ then $\Delta S_{rxn}, \Delta S_{surr} \rightarrow \Delta S_{univ}$

$$\frac{1000 \text{ J}}{1 \text{ kJ}} \qquad\qquad \Delta S_{surr} = \frac{-\Delta H_{sys}}{T} \qquad\qquad \Delta S_{univ} = \Delta S_{sys} + \Delta S_{surr}$$

Solution: $+125 \text{ kJ} \times \dfrac{1000 \text{ J}}{1 \text{ kJ}} = +125{,}000$ J then $\Delta S_{surr} = \dfrac{-\Delta H_{sys}}{T} = \dfrac{-(+125{,}000 \text{ J})}{298 \text{ K}} = -419.4631$ J/K then

$\Delta S_{univ} = \Delta S_{sys} + \Delta S_{surr} = -253$ J/K $- 419.4631$ J/K $= -672$ J/K; so the reaction is nonspontaneous.

Check: The units (J/K) are correct. The magnitude of the answer (-670 J/K) makes sense because both terms are negative; so the reaction is nonspontaneous.

(c)   **Given:** $\Delta H^{\circ}_{rxn} = -125$ kJ, $\Delta S^{\circ}_{rxn} = -253$ J/K, $T = 298$ K   **Find:** ΔS_{univ} and spontaneity

Conceptual Plan: kJ $\rightarrow$ J then $\Delta H^{\circ}_{rxn}, T \rightarrow \Delta S_{surr}$ then $\Delta S_{rxn}, \Delta S_{surr} \rightarrow \Delta S_{univ}$

$$\frac{1000 \text{ J}}{1 \text{ kJ}} \qquad\qquad \Delta S_{surr} = \frac{-\Delta H_{sys}}{T} \qquad\qquad \Delta S_{univ} = \Delta S_{sys} + \Delta S_{surr}$$

Solution: $-125 \text{ kJ} \times \dfrac{1000 \text{ J}}{1 \text{ kJ}} = -125{,}000$ J then $\Delta S_{surr} = \dfrac{-\Delta H_{sys}}{T} = \dfrac{-(-125{,}000 \text{ J})}{298 \text{ K}} = +419.4631$ J/K

then $\Delta S_{univ} = \Delta S_{sys} + \Delta S_{surr} = -253$ J/K $+ 419.4631$ J/K $= +166$ J/K; so the reaction is spontaneous.

Check: The units (J/K) are correct. The magnitude of the answer (170 J/K) makes sense because the larger term is positive; so the reaction is spontaneous.

(d)   **Given:** $\Delta H^{\circ}_{rxn} = -125$ kJ, $\Delta S^{\circ}_{rxn} = -253$ J/K, $T = 555$ K   **Find:** ΔS_{univ} and spontaneity

       Conceptual Plan: kJ $\rightarrow$ J then $\Delta H^{\circ}_{rxn}, T \rightarrow \Delta S_{surr}$ then $\Delta S_{rxn}, \Delta S_{surr} \rightarrow \Delta S_{univ}$

$$\frac{1000 \text{ J}}{1 \text{ kJ}} \qquad\qquad \Delta S_{surr} = \frac{-\Delta H_{sys}}{T} \qquad\qquad \Delta S_{univ} = \Delta S_{sys} + \Delta S_{surr}$$

       Solution: $-125 \text{ kJ} \times \dfrac{1000 \text{ J}}{1 \text{ kJ}} = -125{,}000$ J then $\Delta S_{surr} = \dfrac{-\Delta H_{sys}}{T} = \dfrac{-(-125{,}000 \text{ J})}{555 \text{ K}} = +22\underline{5}.225$ J/K

       then $\Delta S_{univ} = \Delta S_{sys} + \Delta S_{surr} = -253$ J/K $+ 22\underline{5}.225$ J/K $= -28$ J/K; so the reaction is nonspontaneous.

       Check: The units (J/K) are correct. The magnitude of the answer (-30 J/K) makes sense because the larger term is negative; so the reaction is nonspontaneous.

Standard Entropy Changes and Gibbs Free Energy

17.13   (a)   **Given:** $\Delta H^{\circ}_{rxn} = -125$ kJ, $\Delta S_{rxn} = +253$ J/K, $T = 298$ K   **Find:** ΔG and spontaneity

       Conceptual Plan: J/K $\rightarrow$ kJ/K then $\Delta H^{\circ}_{rxn}, \Delta S_{rxn}, T \rightarrow \Delta G$

$$\frac{1 \text{ kJ}}{1000 \text{ J}} \qquad\qquad \Delta G = \Delta H_{rxn} - T\Delta S_{rxn}$$

       Solution: $+253 \dfrac{\text{J}}{\text{K}} \times \dfrac{1 \text{ kJ}}{1000 \text{ J}} = +0.253$ kJ/K then

       $\Delta G = \Delta H_{rxn} - T\Delta S_{rxn} = -125 \text{ kJ} - (298 \text{ K})\left(0.253 \dfrac{\text{kJ}}{\text{K}}\right) = -2.00 \times 10^2$ kJ $= -2.00 \times 10^5$ J; so the reaction is spontaneous.

       Check: The units (kJ) are correct. The magnitude of the answer (-200 kJ) makes sense because both terms are negative; so the reaction is spontaneous.

   (b)   **Given:** $\Delta H^{\circ}_{rxn} = +125$ kJ, $\Delta S_{rxn} = -253$ J/K, $T = 298$ K   **Find:** ΔG and spontaneity

       Conceptual Plan: J/K $\rightarrow$ kJ/K then $\Delta H^{\circ}_{rxn}, \Delta S_{rxn}, T \rightarrow \Delta G$

$$\frac{1 \text{ kJ}}{1000 \text{ J}} \qquad\qquad \Delta G = \Delta H_{rxn} - T\Delta S_{rxn}$$

       Solution: $-253 \dfrac{\text{J}}{\text{K}} \times \dfrac{1 \text{ kJ}}{1000 \text{ J}} = -0.253$ kJ/K then

       $\Delta G = \Delta H_{rxn} - T\Delta S_{rxn} = +125 \text{ kJ} - (298 \text{ K})\left(-0.253 \dfrac{\text{kJ}}{\text{K}}\right) = +200. \text{ kJ} = +2.00 \times 10^2$ kJ $= +2.00 \times 10^5$ J; so the reaction is nonspontaneous.

       Check: The units (kJ) are correct. The magnitude of the answer ($+200$ kJ) makes sense because both terms are positive; so the reaction is nonspontaneous.

   (c)   **Given:** $\Delta H^{\circ}_{rxn} = -125$ kJ, $\Delta S_{rxn} = -253$ J/K, $T = 298$ K   **Find:** ΔG and spontaneity

       Conceptual Plan: J/K $\rightarrow$ kJ/K then $\Delta H^{\circ}_{rxn}, \Delta S_{rxn}, T \rightarrow \Delta G$

$$\frac{1 \text{ kJ}}{1000 \text{ J}} \qquad\qquad \Delta G = \Delta H_{rxn} - T\Delta S_{rxn}$$

       Solution: $-253 \dfrac{\text{J}}{\text{K}} \times \dfrac{1 \text{ kJ}}{1000 \text{ J}} = -0.253$ kJ/K then

       $\Delta G = \Delta H_{rxn} - T\Delta S_{rxn} = -125 \text{ kJ} - (298 \text{ K})\left(-0.253 \dfrac{\text{kJ}}{\text{K}}\right) = -4\underline{9}.606 \text{ kJ} = -5.0 \times 10^1$ kJ $= -5.0 \times 10^4$ J; so the reaction is spontaneous.

       Check: The units (kJ) are correct. The magnitude of the answer (-50 kJ) makes sense because the larger term is negative; so the reaction is spontaneous.

   (d)   **Given:** $\Delta H^{\circ}_{rxn} = -125$ kJ, $\Delta S_{rxn} = -253$ J/K, $T = 555$ K   **Find:** ΔG and spontaneity

       Conceptual Plan: J/K $\rightarrow$ kJ/K then $\Delta H^{\circ}_{rxn}, \Delta S_{rxn}, T \rightarrow \Delta G$

$$\frac{1 \text{ kJ}}{1000 \text{ J}} \qquad\qquad \Delta G = \Delta H_{rxn} - T\Delta S_{rxn}$$

Solution: $-253 \dfrac{J}{K} \times \dfrac{1 \text{ kJ}}{1000 \text{ J}} = -0.253 \text{ kJ/K}$ then

$$\Delta G = \Delta H_{rxn} - T\Delta S_{rxn} = -125 \text{ kJ} - (555 \text{ K})\left(-0.253 \dfrac{\text{kJ}}{\text{K}}\right) = +15 \text{ kJ} = +1.5 \times 10^4 \text{ J};$$

so the reaction is nonspontaneous.

Check: The units (J/K) are correct. The magnitude of the answer ($+15$ kJ) makes sense because the larger term is positive; so the reaction is nonspontaneous.

17.15   **Given:** $\Delta H^\circ_{rxn} = -2217 \text{ kJ}$, $\Delta S^\circ_{rxn} = +101.1 \text{ J/K}$, $T = 25 \,^\circ\text{C}$ **Find:** ΔG and spontaneity
Conceptual Plan: $^\circ\text{C} \rightarrow \text{K}$ then $\text{J/K} \rightarrow \text{kJ/K}$ then $\Delta H^\circ_{rxn}, \Delta S_{rxn}, T \rightarrow \Delta G$

$$K = 273.15 + {}^\circ C \qquad \dfrac{1 \text{ kJ}}{1000 \text{ J}} \qquad \Delta G = \Delta H_{rxn} - T\Delta S_{rxn}$$

Solution: $T = 273.15 + 25 \,^\circ\text{C} = 298 \text{ K}$ then $+101.1 \dfrac{J}{K} \times \dfrac{1 \text{ kJ}}{1000 \text{ J}} = +0.1011 \dfrac{\text{kJ}}{\text{K}}$ then

$$\Delta G = \Delta H_{rxn} - T\Delta S_{rxn} = -2217 \text{ kJ} - (298 \text{ K})\left(0.1011 \dfrac{\text{kJ}}{\text{K}}\right) = -2247 \text{ kJ} = -2.247 \times 10^6 \text{ J}; \text{ so the reaction is}$$

spontaneous.

Check: The units (kJ) are correct. The magnitude of the answer (-2250 kJ) makes sense because both terms are negative; so the reaction is spontaneous.

17.17

ΔH	ΔS	ΔG	Low Temp.	High Temp.
–	+	–	**Spontaneous**	Spontaneous
–	–	**Temp. dependent**	Spontaneous	Nonspontaneous
+	+	Temp. dependent	Nonspontaneous	**Spontaneous**
+	–	+	**Nonspontaneous**	**Nonspontaneous**

17.19   The molar entropy of a substance increases with increasing temperatures. The kinetic energy and the molecular motion increase. The substance will have access to an increased number of energy levels.

17.21   (a) $CO_2(g)$ because it has greater molar mass/complexity.
(b) $CH_3OH(g)$ because it is in the gas phase.
(c) $CO_2(g)$ because it has greater molar mass/complexity.
(d) $SiH_4(g)$ because it has greater molar mass.
(e) $CH_3CH_2CH_3(g)$ because it has greater molar mass/complexity.
(f) $NaBr(aq)$ because a solution has more entropy than a solid crystal.

17.23   (a) $He(g) < Ne(g) < SO_2(g) < NH_3(g) < CH_3CH_2OH(g)$. All are in the gas phase. From He to Ne, there is an increase in molar mass; beyond that, the molecules increase in complexity.
(b) $H_2O(s) < H_2O(l) < H_2O(g)$. Entropy increases as we go from a solid to a liquid to a gas.
(c) $CH_4(g) < CF_4(g) < CCl_4(g)$. Entropy increases as the molar mass increases.

17.25   (a)   **Given:** $C_2H_4(g) + H_2(g) \rightarrow C_2H_6(g)$ **Find:** ΔS°_{rxn}
Conceptual Plan: $\Delta S^\circ_{rxn} = \sum n_p S^\circ(\text{products}) - \sum n_r S^\circ(\text{reactants})$
Solution:

Reactant/Product	S°(J/mol · K from Appendix IIB)
$C_2H_4(g)$	219.3
$H_2(g)$	130.7
$C_2H_6(g)$	229.2

Be sure to pull data for the correct formula and phase.

$$\Delta S^\circ_{rxn} = \sum n_p S^\circ(\text{products}) - \sum n_r S^\circ(\text{reactants})$$
$$= [1(S^\circ(C_2H_6(g)))] - [1(S^\circ(C_2H_4(g))) + 1(S^\circ(H_2(g)))]$$
$$= [1(229.2 \text{ J/K})] - [1(219.3 \text{ J/K}) + 1(130.7 \text{ J/K})]$$
$$= [229.2 \text{ J/K}] - [350.0 \text{ J/K}]$$
$$= -120.8 \text{ J/K} \quad \text{The moles of gas are decreasing.}$$

Check: The units (J/K) are correct. The answer is negative, which is consistent with 2 moles of gas going to 1 mole of gas.

(b)   **Given:** $C(s) + H_2O(g) \rightarrow CO(g) + H_2(g)$ **Find:** ΔS°_{rxn}
Conceptual Plan: $\Delta S^\circ_{rxn} = \sum n_p S^\circ(\textbf{products}) - \sum n_r S^\circ(\textbf{reactants})$
Solution:

Reactant/Product	S°(J/mol · K from Appendix IIB)
$C(s)$	5.7
$H_2O(g)$	188.8
$CO(g)$	197.7
$H_2(g)$	130.7

Be sure to pull data for the correct formula and phase.

$$\Delta S^\circ_{rxn} = \sum n_p S^\circ(\text{products}) - \sum n_r S^\circ(\text{reactants})$$
$$= [1(S^\circ(CO(g))) + 1(S^\circ(H_2(g)))] - [1(S^\circ(C(s))) + 1(S^\circ(H_2O(g)))]$$
$$= [1(197.7 \text{ J/K}) + 1(130.7 \text{ J/K})] - [1(5.7 \text{ J/K}) + 1(188.8 \text{ J/K})]$$
$$= [328.4 \text{ J/K}] - [194.5 \text{ J/K}]$$
$$= +133.9 \text{ J/K} \quad \text{The moles of gas are increasing.}$$

Check: The units (J/K) are correct. The answer is positive, which is consistent with 1 mole of gas going to 2 moles of gas.

(c)   **Given:** $CO(g) + H_2O(g) \rightarrow H_2(g) + CO_2(g)$ **Find:** ΔS°_{rxn}
Conceptual Plan: $\Delta S^\circ_{rxn} = \sum n_p S^\circ(\textbf{products}) - \sum n_r S^\circ(\textbf{reactants})$
Solution:

Reactant/Product	S°(J/mol · K from Appendix IIB)
$CO(g)$	197.7
$H_2O(g)$	188.8
$H_2(g)$	130.7
$CO_2(g)$	213.8

Be sure to pull data for the correct formula and phase.

$$\Delta S^\circ_{rxn} = \sum n_p S^\circ(\text{products}) - \sum n_r S^\circ(\text{reactants})$$
$$= [1(S^\circ(H_2(g))) + 1(S^\circ(CO_2(g)))] - [1(S^\circ(CO(g))) + 1(S^\circ(H_2O(g)))]$$
$$= [1(130.7 \text{ J/K}) + 1(213.8 \text{ J/K})] - [1(197.7 \text{ J/K}) + 1(188.8 \text{ J/K})]$$
$$= [344.5 \text{ J/K}] - [386.5 \text{ J/K}]$$
$$= -42.0 \text{ J/K}$$

The change is small because the number of moles of gas is constant.

Check: The units (J/K) are correct. The answer is small and negative, which is consistent with a constant number of moles of gas. Water molecules are bent, and carbon dioxide molecules are linear; so the water has more complexity. Also, carbon monoxide is more complex than is hydrogen gas.

(d)   **Given:** $2 H_2S(g) + 3 O_2(g) \rightarrow 2 H_2O(l) + 2 SO_2(g)$ **Find:** ΔS°_{rxn}
Conceptual Plan: $\Delta S^\circ_{rxn} = \sum n_p S^\circ(\textbf{products}) - \sum n_r S^\circ(\textbf{reactants})$

Solution:

Reactant/Product	$S°$(J/mol · K from Appendix IIB)
$H_2S(g)$	205.8
$O_2(g)$	205.2
$H_2O(l)$	70.0
$SO_2(g)$	248.2

Be sure to pull data for the correct formula and phase.

$$\Delta S°_{rxn} = \sum n_p S°(\text{products}) - \sum n_r S°(\text{reactants})$$
$$= [2(S°(H_2O(l))) + 2(S°(SO_2(g)))] - [2(S°(H_2S(g))) + 3(S°(O_2(g)))]$$
$$= [2(70.0 \text{ J/K}) + 2(248.2 \text{ J/K})] - [2(205.8 \text{ J/K}) + 3(205.2 \text{ J/K})]$$
$$= [636.4 \text{ J/K}] - [1027.2 \text{ J/K}]$$
$$= -390.8 \text{ J/K}$$

The number of moles of gas is decreasing.

Check: The units (J/K) are correct. The answer is negative, which is consistent with a decrease in the number of moles of gas.

17.27 **Given:** $CH_2Cl_2(g)$ formed from elements in standard states **Find:** $\Delta S°$ and rationalize sign
Conceptual Plan: Write a balanced reaction, then $\Delta S°_{rxn} = \sum n_p S°(\text{products}) - \sum n_r S°(\text{reactants})$
Solution: $C(s) + H_2(g) + Cl_2(g) \rightarrow CH_2Cl_2(g)$

Reactant/Product	$S°$(J/mol · K from Appendix IIB)
$C(s)$	5.7
$H_2(g)$	130.7
$Cl_2(g)$	223.1
$CH_2Cl_2(g)$	270.2

Be sure to pull data for the correct formula and phase.

$$\Delta S°_{rxn} = \sum n_p S°(\text{products}) - \sum n_r S°(\text{reactants})$$
$$= [1(S°(CH_2Cl_2(g)))] - [1(S°(C(s))) + 1(S°(H_2(g))) + 1(S°(Cl_2(g)))]$$
$$= [1(270.2 \text{ J/K})] - [1(5.7 \text{ J/K}) + 1(130.7 \text{ J/K}) + 1(223.1 \text{ J/K})]$$
$$= [270.2 \text{ J/K}] - [359.5 \text{ J/K}]$$
$$= -89.3 \text{ J/K}$$

The moles of gas are decreasing.

Check: The units (J/K) are correct. The answer is negative, which is consistent with 2 moles of gas going to 1 mole of gas.

17.29 **Given:** methanol (CH_3OH) combustion at 25 °C **Find:** $\Delta H°_{rxn}$, $\Delta S°_{rxn}$, $\Delta G°_{rxn}$, and spontaneity
Conceptual Plan: Write a balanced reaction then $\Delta H°_{rxn} = \sum n_p H°_f (\text{products}) - \sum n_r H°_f (\text{reactants})$ **then**
$\Delta S°_{rxn} = \sum n_p S°(\text{products}) - \sum n_r S°(\text{reactants})$ **then °C → K then J/K → kJ/K then**

$$K = 273.15 + °C \qquad \frac{1 \text{ kJ}}{1000 \text{ J}}$$

$\Delta H°_{rxn}, \Delta S°_{rxn}, T \rightarrow \Delta G°.$

$$\Delta G = \Delta H_{rxn} - T\Delta S_{rxn}$$

Solution: Combustion is combined with oxygen to form carbon dioxide and water.
$2 CH_3OH(l) + 3 O_2(g) \rightarrow 2 CO_2(g) + 4 H_2O(g)$

Reactant/Product	$\Delta H°_f$ (kJ · mol from Appendix IIB)
$CH_3OH(l)$	−238.6
$O_2(g)$	0.0
$CO_2(g)$	−393.5
$H_2O(g)$	−241.8

Be sure to pull data for the correct formula and phase.

$$\Delta H^\circ_{rxn} = \sum n_p \Delta H^\circ_f \text{ (products)} - \sum n_r \Delta H^\circ_f \text{ (reactants)}$$
$$= [2(\Delta H^\circ_f (CO_2(g))) + 4(\Delta H^\circ_f (H_2O(g)))] - [2(\Delta H^\circ_f (CH_3OH(l))) + 3(\Delta H^\circ_f (O_2(g)))]$$
$$= [2(-393.5 \text{ kJ}) + 4(-241.8 \text{ kJ})] - [2(-238.6 \text{ kJ}) + 3(0.0 \text{ kJ})]$$
$$= [-1754.2 \text{ kJ}] - [-477.2 \text{ kJ}]$$
$$= -1277.0 \text{ kJ then}$$

Reactant/Product	S°(J/mol · K from Appendix IIB)
$CH_3OH(l)$	126.8
$O_2(g)$	205.2
$CO_2(g)$	213.8
$H_2O(g)$	188.8

Be sure to pull data for the correct formula and phase.

$$\Delta S^\circ_{rxn} = \sum n_p S^\circ \text{(products)} - \sum n_r S^\circ \text{(reactants)}$$
$$= [2(S^\circ(CO_2(g))) + 4(S^\circ(H_2O(g)))] - [2(S^\circ(CH_3OH(l))) + 3(S^\circ(O_2(g)))]$$
$$= [2(213.8 \text{ J/K}) + 4(188.8 \text{ J/K})] - [2(126.8 \text{ J/K}) + 3(205.2 \text{ J/K})]$$
$$= [1182.8 \text{ J/K}] - [869.2 \text{ J/K}]$$
$$= 313.6 \text{ J/K}$$

then $T = 273.15 + 25\,°C = 298 \text{ K}$ then $+313.6 \dfrac{J}{K} \times \dfrac{1 \text{ kJ}}{1000 \text{ J}} = +0.3136 \text{ kJ/K}$ then

$$\Delta G = \Delta H_{rxn} - T\Delta S_{rxn} = -1277.0 \text{ kJ} - (298 \text{ K})\left(+0.3136 \dfrac{kJ}{K}\right) = -1370.5 \text{ kJ} = -1.3705 \times 10^6 \text{ J; so the reac-}$$
tion is spontaneous.

Check: The units (kJ, J/K, and kJ) are correct. Combustion reactions are exothermic, and we see a large negative enthalpy. We expect a large positive entropy because we have an increase in the number of moles of gas. The free energy is the sum of two negative terms; so we expect a large negative free energy, and the reaction is spontaneous.

17.31   (a)   **Given:** $N_2O_4(g) \rightarrow 2\,NO_2(g)$ at 25 °C
Find: ΔH°_{rxn}, ΔS°_{rxn}, ΔG°_{rxn}, and spontaneity. Can temperature be changed to make it spontaneous?
Conceptual Plan: $\Delta H^\circ_{rxn} = \sum n_p H^\circ_f \text{ (products)} - \sum n_r H^\circ_f \text{ (reactants)}$ then
$\Delta S^\circ_{rxn} = \sum n_p S^\circ \text{(products)} - \sum n_r S^\circ \text{(reactants)}$ then °C → K then J/K → kJ/K then

$$K = 273.15 + °C \qquad \dfrac{1 \text{ kJ}}{1000 \text{ J}}$$

$\Delta H^\circ_{rxn}, \Delta S^\circ_{rxn}, T \rightarrow \Delta G^\circ$

$$\Delta G = \Delta H_{rxn} - T\Delta S_{rxn}$$

Solution:

Reactant/Product	ΔH°_f (kJ/mol from Appendix IIB)
$N_2O_4(g)$	9.16
$NO_2(g)$	33.2

Be sure to pull data for the correct formula and phase.

$$\Delta H^\circ_{rxn} = \sum n_p \Delta H^\circ_f \text{ (products)} - \sum n_r \Delta H^\circ_f \text{ (reactants)}$$
$$= [2(\Delta H^\circ_f (NO_2(g)))] - [1(\Delta H^\circ_f (N_2O_4(g)))]$$
$$= [2(33.2 \text{ kJ})] - [1(9.16 \text{ kJ})]$$
$$= [66.4 \text{ kJ}] - [9.16 \text{ kJ}]$$
$$= +57.2 \text{ kJ then}$$

Reactant/Product	S°(J/mol · K from Appendix IIB)
$N_2O_4(g)$	304.4
$NO_2(g)$	240.1

Be sure to pull data for the correct formula and phase.

$$\Delta S^\circ_{rxn} = \sum n_p S^\circ(\text{products}) - \sum n_r S^\circ(\text{reactants})$$
$$= [2(S^\circ(NO_2(g)))] - [1(S^\circ(N_2O_4(g)))]$$
$$= [2(240.1 \text{ J/K})] - [1(304.4 \text{ J/K})]$$
$$= [480.2 \text{ J/K}] - [304.4 \text{ J/K}]$$
$$= +175.8 \text{ J/K then } T = 273.15 + 25 \,^\circ\text{C} = 298 \text{ K then}$$

$$+175.8 \frac{J}{K} \times \frac{1 \text{ kJ}}{1000 \, J} = +0.1758 \text{ kJ then}$$

$$\Delta G^\circ = \Delta H^\circ_{rxn} - T\Delta S^\circ_{rxn} = +57.2 \text{ kJ} - (298 \, K)\left(+0.1758 \frac{\text{kJ}}{K}\right) = +4.8 \text{ kJ} = +4.8 \times 10^3 \text{ J; so the reaction}$$

is nonspontaneous. It can be made spontaneous by raising the temperature.

Check: The units (kJ, J/K, and kJ) are correct. The reaction requires the breaking of a bond, so we expect that this will be an endothermic reaction. We expect a positive entropy change because we are increasing the number of moles of gas. Because the positive enthalpy term dominates at room temperature, the reaction is nonspontaneous. The second term can dominate if we raise the temperature high enough.

(b)   **Given:** $NH_4Cl(s) \rightarrow HCl(g) + NH_3(g)$ at 25 °C
Find: $\Delta H^\circ_{rxn}, \Delta S^\circ_{rxn}, \Delta G^\circ_{rxn}$, and spontaneity. Can temperature be changed to make it spontaneous?
Conceptual Plan: $\Delta H^\circ_{rxn} = \sum n_p H^\circ_f(\text{products}) - \sum n_r H^\circ_f(\text{reactants})$ then

$\Delta S^\circ_{rxn} = \sum n_p S^\circ(\text{products}) - \sum n_r S^\circ(\text{reactants})$ then °C → K then J/K → kJ/K then

$$K = 273.15 + \,^\circ\text{C} \qquad \frac{1 \text{ kJ}}{1000 \text{ J}}$$

$\Delta H^\circ_{rxn}, \Delta S^\circ_{rxn}, T \rightarrow \Delta G^\circ$

$$\Delta G = \Delta H_{rxn} - T\Delta S_{rxn}$$

Solution:

Reactant/Product	ΔH°_f (kJ/mol from Appendix IIB)
$NH_4Cl(s)$	−314.4
$HCl(g)$	−92.3
$NH_3(g)$	−45.9

Be sure to pull data for the correct formula and phase.
$$\Delta H^\circ_{rxn} = \sum n_p \Delta H^\circ_f(\text{products}) - \sum n_r \Delta H^\circ_f(\text{reactants})$$
$$= [1(\Delta H^\circ_f(HCl(g))) + 1(\Delta H^\circ_f(NH_3(g)))] - [1(\Delta H^\circ_f(NH_4Cl(g)))]$$
$$= [1(-92.3 \text{ kJ}) + 1(-45.9 \text{ kJ})] - [1(-314.4 \text{ kJ})]$$
$$= [-138.2 \text{ kJ}] - [-314.4 \text{ kJ}]$$
$$= +176.2 \text{ kJ then}$$

Reactant/Product	S°(J/mol · K from Appendix IIB)
$NH_4Cl(s)$	94.6
$HCl(g)$	186.9
$NH_3(g)$	192.8

Be sure to pull data for the correct formula and phase.
$$\Delta S^\circ_{rxn} = \sum n_p S^\circ(\text{products}) - \sum n_r S^\circ(\text{reactants})$$
$$= [1(S^\circ(HCl(g))) + 1(S^\circ(NH_3(g)))] - [1(S^\circ(NH_4Cl(g)))]$$
$$= [1(186.9 \text{ J/K}) + 1(192.8 \text{ J/K})] - [1(94.6 \text{ J/K})]$$
$$= [379.7 \text{ J/K}] - [94.6 \text{ J/K}]$$
$$= +285.1 \text{ J/K}$$

then $T = 273.15 + 25 \,^\circ\text{C} = 298 \text{ K then } +285.1 \dfrac{J}{K} \times \dfrac{1 \text{ kJ}}{1000 \, J} = +0.2851 \text{ kJ/K then}$

$$\Delta G^\circ = \Delta H^\circ_{rxn} - T\Delta S^\circ_{rxn} = +176.2 \text{ kJ} - (298 \, K)\left(+0.2851 \frac{\text{kJ}}{K}\right) = +91.2 \text{ kJ} = +9.12 \times 10^4 \text{ J};$$

so the reaction is nonspontaneous. It can be made spontaneous by raising the temperature.

Check: The units (kJ, J/K, and kJ) are correct. The reaction requires the breaking of a bond, so we expect that this will be an endothermic reaction. We expect a positive entropy change because we are increasing the number of moles of gas. Because the positive enthalpy term dominates at room temperature, the reaction is non-spontaneous. The second term can dominate if we raise the temperature high enough.

(c) **Given:** $3 H_2(g) + Fe_2O_3(s) \rightarrow 2 Fe(s) + 3 H_2O(g)$ at 25 °C **Find:** ΔH°_{rxn}, ΔS°_{rxn}, ΔG°_{rxn}, and spontaneity. Can temperature be changed to make it spontaneous?

Conceptual Plan: $\Delta H^\circ_{rxn} = \sum n_p H^\circ_f \text{(products)} - \sum n_r H^\circ_f \text{(reactants)}$ then

$\Delta S^\circ_{rxn} = \sum n_p S^\circ \text{(products)} - \sum n_r S^\circ \text{(reactants)}$ then °C → K then J/K → kJ/K then

$$K = 273.15 + °C \qquad \frac{1\ kJ}{1000\ J}$$

ΔH°_{rxn}, ΔS°_{rxn}, $T \rightarrow \Delta G^\circ$

$$\Delta G = \Delta H_{rxn} - T\Delta S_{rxn}$$

Solution:

Reactant/Product	ΔH°_f (kJ/mol from Appendix IIB)
$H_2(g)$	0.0
$Fe_2O_3(s)$	−824.2
$Fe(s)$	0.0
$H_2O(g)$	−241.8

Be sure to pull data for the correct formula and phase.

$$\begin{aligned}
\Delta H^\circ_{rxn} &= \sum n_p \Delta H^\circ_f \text{(products)} - \sum n_r \Delta H^\circ_f \text{(reactants)} \\
&= [2(\Delta H^\circ_f (Fe(s))) + 3(\Delta H^\circ_f (H_2O(g)))] - [3(\Delta H^\circ_f (H_2(g))) + 1(\Delta H^\circ_f (Fe_2O_3(s)))] \\
&= [2(0.0\ kJ) + 3(-241.8\ kJ)] - [3(0.0\ kJ) + 1(-824.2\ kJ)] \\
&= [-725.4\ kJ] - [-824.2\ kJ] \\
&= +98.8\ kJ \text{ then}
\end{aligned}$$

Reactant/Product	S°(J/mol · K from Appendix IIB)
$H_2(g)$	130.7
$Fe_2O_3(s)$	87.4
$Fe(s)$	27.3
$H_2O(g)$	188.8

Be sure to pull data for the correct formula and phase.

$$\begin{aligned}
\Delta S^\circ_{rxn} &= \sum n_p S^\circ \text{(products)} - \sum n_r S^\circ \text{(reactants)} \\
&= [2(S^\circ(Fe(s))) + 3(S^\circ(H_2O(g)))] - [3(S^\circ(H_2(g))) + 1(S^\circ(Fe_2O_3(s)))] \\
&= [2(27.3\ J/K) + 3(188.8\ J/K)] - [3(130.7\ J/K) + 1(87.4\ J/K)] \\
&= [621.0\ J/K] - [479.5\ J/K] \\
&= +141.5\ J/K
\end{aligned}$$

then $T = 273.15 + 25\ °C = 298\ K$ then $+141.5\ \dfrac{J}{K} \times \dfrac{1\ kJ}{1000\ J} = +0.1415\ kJ/K$ then

$$\Delta G^\circ = \Delta H^\circ_{rxn} - T\Delta S^\circ_{rxn} = +98.8\ kJ - (298\ K)\left(+0.1415\ \frac{kJ}{K}\right) = +56.6\ kJ = +5.66 \times 10^4\ J;$$

so the reaction is nonspontaneous. It can be made spontaneous by raising the temperature.

Check: The units (kJ, J/K, and kJ) are correct. The reaction requires the breaking of a bond, so we expect that this will be an endothermic reaction. We expect a positive entropy change because there is no change in the number of moles of gas, but the product gas is more complex. Because the positive enthalpy term dominates at room temperature, the reaction is nonspontaneous. The second term can dominate if we raise the temperature high enough. This process is the opposite of rusting, so we are not surprised that it is nonspontaneous.

(d) **Given:** $N_2(g) + 3 H_2(g) \rightarrow 2 NH_3(g)$ at 25 °C
Find: ΔH°_{rxn}, ΔS°_{rxn}, ΔG°_{rxn}, and spontaneity. Can temperature be changed to make it spontaneous?

$$\Delta S^\circ_{rxn} = \sum n_p S^\circ(\text{products}) - \sum n_r S^\circ(\text{reactants})$$
$$= [2(S^\circ(NO_2(g)))] - [1(S^\circ(N_2O_4(g)))]$$
$$= [2(240.1 \text{ J/K})] - [1(304.4 \text{ J/K})]$$
$$= [480.2 \text{ J/K}] - [304.4 \text{ J/K}]$$
$$= +175.8 \text{ J/K then } T = 273.15 + 25 \text{ °C} = 298 \text{ K then}$$

$$+175.8 \frac{J}{K} \times \frac{1 \text{ kJ}}{1000 \text{ J}} = +0.1758 \text{ kJ then}$$

$$\Delta G^\circ = \Delta H^\circ_{rxn} - T\Delta S^\circ_{rxn} = +57.2 \text{ kJ} - (298 \text{ K})\left(+0.1758 \frac{\text{kJ}}{K}\right) = +4.8 \text{ kJ} = +4.8 \times 10^3 \text{ J; so the reaction}$$

is nonspontaneous. It can be made spontaneous by raising the temperature.

Check: The units (kJ, J/K, and kJ) are correct. The reaction requires the breaking of a bond, so we expect that this will be an endothermic reaction. We expect a positive entropy change because we are increasing the number of moles of gas. Because the positive enthalpy term dominates at room temperature, the reaction is non-spontaneous. The second term can dominate if we raise the temperature high enough.

(b) **Given:** $NH_4Cl(s) \rightarrow HCl(g) + NH_3(g)$ at 25 °C

Find: $\Delta H^\circ_{rxn}, \Delta S^\circ_{rxn}, \Delta G^\circ_{rxn}$, and spontaneity. Can temperature be changed to make it spontaneous?

Conceptual Plan: $\Delta H^\circ_{rxn} = \sum n_p H^\circ_f(\text{products}) - \sum n_r H^\circ_f$ (reactants) then

$\Delta S^\circ_{rxn} = \sum n_p S^\circ(\text{products}) - \sum n_r S^\circ(\text{reactants})$ then °C → K then J/K → kJ/K then

$$K = 273.15 + °C \qquad \frac{1 \text{ kJ}}{1000 \text{ J}}$$

$\Delta H^\circ_{rxn}, \Delta S^\circ_{rxn}, T \rightarrow \Delta G^\circ$

$$\Delta G = \Delta H_{rxn} - T\Delta S_{rxn}$$

Solution:

Reactant/Product	ΔH°_f (kJ/mol from Appendix IIB)
$NH_4Cl(s)$	−314.4
$HCl(g)$	−92.3
$NH_3(g)$	−45.9

Be sure to pull data for the correct formula and phase.

$$\Delta H^\circ_{rxn} = \sum n_p \Delta H^\circ_f (\text{products}) - \sum n_r \Delta H^\circ_f (\text{reactants})$$
$$= [1(\Delta H^\circ_f (HCl(g))) + 1(\Delta H^\circ_f (NH_3(g)))] - [1(\Delta H^\circ_f (NH_4Cl(g)))]$$
$$= [1(-92.3 \text{ kJ}) + 1(-45.9 \text{ kJ})] - [1(-314.4 \text{ kJ})]$$
$$= [-138.2 \text{ kJ}] - [-314.4 \text{ kJ}]$$
$$= +176.2 \text{ kJ then}$$

Reactant/Product	S° (J/mol · K from Appendix IIB)
$NH_4Cl(s)$	94.6
$HCl(g)$	186.9
$NH_3(g)$	192.8

Be sure to pull data for the correct formula and phase.

$$\Delta S^\circ_{rxn} = \sum n_p S^\circ(\text{products}) - \sum n_r S^\circ(\text{reactants})$$
$$= [1(S^\circ(HCl(g))) + 1(S^\circ(NH_3(g)))] - [1(S^\circ(NH_4Cl(g)))]$$
$$= [1(186.9 \text{ J/K}) + 1(192.8 \text{ J/K})] - [1(94.6 \text{ J/K})]$$
$$= [379.7 \text{ J/K}] - [94.6 \text{ J/K}]$$
$$= +285.1 \text{ J/K}$$

then $T = 273.15 + 25 °C = 298 \text{ K then} +285.1 \frac{J}{K} \times \frac{1 \text{ kJ}}{1000 \text{ J}} = +0.2851 \text{ kJ/K then}$

$$\Delta G^\circ = \Delta H^\circ_{rxn} - T\Delta S^\circ_{rxn} = +176.2 \text{ kJ} - (298 \text{ K})\left(+0.2851 \frac{\text{kJ}}{K}\right) = +91.2 \text{ kJ} = +9.12 \times 10^4 \text{ J;}$$

so the reaction is nonspontaneous. It can be made spontaneous by raising the temperature.

Check: The units (kJ, J/K, and kJ) are correct. The reaction requires the breaking of a bond, so we expect that this will be an endothermic reaction. We expect a positive entropy change because we are increasing the number of moles of gas. Because the positive enthalpy term dominates at room temperature, the reaction is non-spontaneous. The second term can dominate if we raise the temperature high enough.

(c)   **Given:** $3 H_2(g) + Fe_2O_3(s) \rightarrow 2 Fe(s) + 3 H_2O(g)$ at 25 °C   **Find:** $\Delta H°_{mx}$, $\Delta S°_{rxn}$, $\Delta G°_{rxn}$, and spontaneity. Can temperature be changed to make it spontaneous?

Conceptual Plan: $\Delta H°_{rxn} = \sum n_p H°_f \text{ (products)} - \sum n_r H°_f \text{ (reactants) then}$

$\Delta S°_{rxn} = \sum n_p S° \text{(products)} - \sum n_r S° \text{(reactants) then } °C \rightarrow K \text{ then } J/K \rightarrow kJ/K \text{ then}$

$$K = 273.15 + °C \qquad \frac{1 \text{ kJ}}{1000 \text{ J}}$$

$\Delta H°_{rxn}, \Delta S°_{rxn}, T \rightarrow \Delta G°$

$$\Delta G = \Delta H_{rxn} - T\Delta S_{rxn}$$

Solution:

Reactant/Product	$\Delta H°_f$ (kJ/mol from Appendix IIB)
$H_2(g)$	0.0
$Fe_2O_3(s)$	−824.2
$Fe(s)$	0.0
$H_2O(g)$	−241.8

Be sure to pull data for the correct formula and phase.

$\Delta H°_{rxn} = \sum n_p \Delta H°_f \text{ (products)} - \sum n_r \Delta H°_f \text{ (reactants)}$

$\quad = [2(\Delta H°_f (Fe(s))) + 3(\Delta H°_f (H_2O(g)))] - [3(\Delta H°_f (H_2(g))) + 1(\Delta H°_f (Fe_2O_3(s)))]$

$\quad = [2(0.0 \text{ kJ}) + 3(−241.8 \text{ kJ})] - [3(0.0 \text{ kJ}) + 1(−824.2 \text{ kJ})]$

$\quad = [−725.4 \text{ kJ}] - [−824.2 \text{ kJ}]$

$\quad = +98.8 \text{ kJ then}$

Reactant/Product	S°(J/mol · K from Appendix IIB)
$H_2(g)$	130.7
$Fe_2O_3(s)$	87.4
$Fe(s)$	27.3
$H_2O(g)$	188.8

Be sure to pull data for the correct formula and phase.

$\Delta S°_{rxn} = \sum n_p S° \text{(products)} - \sum n_r S° \text{(reactants)}$

$\quad = [2(S°(Fe(s))) + 3(S°(H_2O(g)))] - [3(S°(H_2(g))) + 1(S°(Fe_2O_3(s)))]$

$\quad = [2(27.3 \text{ J/K}) + 3(188.8 \text{ J/K})] - [3(130.7 \text{ J/K}) + 1(87.4 \text{ J/K})]$

$\quad = [621.0 \text{ J/K}] - [479.5 \text{ J/K}]$

$\quad = +141.5 \text{ J/K}$

then $T = 273.15 + 25 °C = 298 \text{ K}$ then $+141.5 \dfrac{J}{K} \times \dfrac{1 \text{ kJ}}{1000 \text{ J}} = +0.1415 \text{ kJ/K then}$

$\Delta G° = \Delta H°_{rxn} - T\Delta S°_{rxn} = +98.8 \text{ kJ} - (298 \text{ K})\left(+0.1415 \dfrac{\text{kJ}}{\text{K}}\right) = +56.6 \text{ kJ} = +5.66 \times 10^4 \text{ J};$

so the reaction is nonspontaneous. It can be made spontaneous by raising the temperature.

Check: The units (kJ, J/K, and kJ) are correct. The reaction requires the breaking of a bond, so we expect that this will be an endothermic reaction. We expect a positive entropy change because there is no change in the number of moles of gas, but the product gas is more complex. Because the positive enthalpy term dominates at room temperature, the reaction is nonspontaneous. The second term can dominate if we raise the temperature high enough. This process is the opposite of rusting, so we are not surprised that it is nonspontaneous.

(d)   **Given:** $N_2(g) + 3 H_2(g) \rightarrow 2 NH_3(g)$ at 25 °C
Find: $\Delta H°_{rxn}$, $\Delta S°_{rxn}$, $\Delta G°_{rxn}$, and spontaneity. Can temperature be changed to make it spontaneous?

Conceptual Plan: $\Delta H^\circ_{rxn} = \sum n_p H^\circ_f \text{(products)} - \sum n_r H^\circ_f \text{(reactants)}$ then

$\Delta S^\circ_{rxn} = \sum n_p S^\circ \text{(products)} - \sum n_r S^\circ \text{(reactants)}$ then °C → K then J/K → kJ/K then

$$K = 273.15 + °C \qquad \frac{1\ kJ}{1000\ J}$$

$\Delta H^\circ_{rxn}, \Delta S^\circ_{rxn}, T \rightarrow \Delta G^\circ$

$$\Delta G = \Delta H_{rxn} - T\Delta S_{rxn}$$

Solution:

Reactant/Product	ΔH°_f (kJ · mol from Appendix IIB)
$N_2(g)$	0.0
$H_2(g)$	0.0
$NH_3(g)$	−45.9

Be sure to pull data for the correct formula and phase.

$$\begin{aligned}
\Delta H^\circ_{rxn} &= \sum n_p \Delta H^\circ_f \text{(products)} - \sum n_r \Delta H^\circ_f \text{(reactants)} \\
&= [2(\Delta H^\circ_f(NH_3(g)))] - [1(\Delta H^\circ_f(N_2(g))) + 3(\Delta H^\circ_f(H_2(g)))] \\
&= [2(-45.9\ kJ)] - [1(0.0\ kJ) + 3(0.0\ kJ)] \\
&= [-91.8\ kJ] - [0.0\ kJ] \\
&= -91.8\ kJ \text{ then}
\end{aligned}$$

Reactant/Product	S°(J/mol · K from Appendix IIB)
$N_2(g)$	191.6
$H_2(g)$	130.7
$NH_3(g)$	192.8

Be sure to pull data for the correct formula and phase.

$$\begin{aligned}
\Delta S^\circ_{rxn} &= \sum n_p S^\circ \text{(products)} - \sum n_r S^\circ \text{(reactants)} \\
&= [2(S^\circ(NH_3(g)))] - [1(S^\circ(N_2(g))) + 3(S^\circ(H_2(g)))] \\
&= [2(192.8\ J/K)] - [1(191.6\ J/K) + 3(130.7\ J/K)] \\
&= [385.6\ J/K] - [583.7\ J/K] \\
&= -198.1\ J/K
\end{aligned}$$

then $T = 273.15 + 25\ °C = 298\ K$ then $-198.1\ \dfrac{J}{K} \times \dfrac{1\ kJ}{1000\ J} = -0.1981\ kJ/K$ then

$$\Delta G^\circ = \Delta H^\circ_{rxn} - T\Delta S^\circ_{rxn} = -91.8\ kJ - (298\ K)\left(-0.1981\dfrac{kJ}{K}\right) = -32.8\ kJ = -3.28 \times 10^4\ J;$$

so the reaction is spontaneous.

Check: The units (kJ, J/K, and kJ) are correct. The reaction forms more bonds than it breaks, so we expect that this will be an exothermic reaction. We expect a negative entropy change because we are decreasing the number of moles of gas. Because the negative enthalpy term dominates at room temperature, the reaction is spontaneous. The second term can dominate if we raise the temperature high enough.

17.33   (a)   **Given:** $N_2O_4(g) \rightarrow 2\ NO_2(g)$ at 25 °C   **Find:** ΔG_{rxn} and spontaneity and compare to Problem 17.31
Determine which method would show how free energy changes with temperature.
Conceptual Plan: $\Delta G^\circ_{rxn} = \sum n_p \Delta G^\circ_f \text{(products)} - \sum n_r \Delta G^\circ_f \text{(reactants)}$ **then compare to Problem 17.31**
Solution:

Reactant/Product	ΔG°_f (kJ/mol from Appendix IIB)
$N_2O_4(g)$	99.8
$NO_2(g)$	51.3

Be sure to pull data for the correct formula and phase.

$$\begin{aligned}
\Delta G^\circ_{rxn} &= \sum n_p \Delta G^\circ_f \text{(products)} - \sum n_r \Delta G^\circ_f \text{(reactants)} \\
&= [2(\Delta G^\circ_f(NO_2(g)))] - [1(\Delta G^\circ_f(N_2O_4(g)))] \\
&= [2(51.3\ kJ)] - [1(99.8\ kJ)] \\
&= [102.6\ kJ] - [99.8\ kJ] \\
&= +2.8\ kJ
\end{aligned}$$

So the reaction is nonspontaneous. The value is similar to Problem 17.31.

Check: The units (kJ) are correct. The free energy of the products is greater than that of the reactants; so the answer is positive, and the reaction is nonspontaneous. The answer is the same as in Problem 17.31 within the error of the calculation.

(b)   **Given:** $NH_4Cl(s) \rightarrow HCl(g) + NH_3(g)$ at 25 °C
       Find: ΔG°_{rxn} and spontaneity and compare to Problem 17.31
       Conceptual Plan: $\Delta G^{\circ}_{rxn} = \sum n_p \Delta G^{\circ}_f \text{(products)} - \sum n_r \Delta G^{\circ}_f \text{(reactants)}$ **then compare to Problem 17.31**
       Solution:

Reactant/Product	ΔG°_f (kJ/mol from Appendix IIB)
$NH_4Cl(s)$	−202.9
$HCl(g)$	−95.3
$NH_3(g)$	−16.4

Be sure to pull data for the correct formula and phase.

$$\Delta G^{\circ}_{rxn} = \sum n_p \Delta G^{\circ}_f \text{(products)} - \sum n_r \Delta G^{\circ}_f \text{(reactants)}$$
$$= [1(\Delta G^{\circ}_f (HCl(g))) + 1(\Delta G^{\circ}_f (NH_3(g)))] - [1(\Delta G^{\circ}_f (NH_4Cl(g)))]$$
$$= [1(-95.3 \text{ kJ}) + 1(-16.4 \text{ kJ})] - [1(-202.9 \text{ kJ})]$$
$$= [-111.7 \text{ kJ}] - [-202.9 \text{ kJ}]$$
$$= +91.2 \text{ kJ}$$

So the reaction is nonspontaneous. The result is the same as in Problem 17.31.

Check: The units (kJ) are correct. The answer matches the one in Problem 17.31.

(c)   **Given:** $3 H_2(g) + Fe_2O_3(s) \rightarrow 2 Fe(s) + 3 H_2O(g)$ at 25 °C
       Find: ΔG°_{rxn} and spontaneity and compare to Problem 17.31
       Conceptual Plan: $\Delta G^{\circ}_{rxn} = \sum n_p \Delta G^{\circ}_f \text{(products)} - \sum n_r \Delta G^{\circ}_f \text{(reactants)}$ **then compare to Problem 17.31**
       Solution:

Reactant/Product	ΔG°_f (kJ/mol from Appendix IIB)
$H_2(g)$	0.0
$Fe_2O_3(s)$	−742.2
$Fe(s)$	0.0
$H_2O(g)$	−228.6

Be sure to pull data for the correct formula and phase.

$$\Delta G^{\circ}_{rxn} = \sum n_p \Delta G^{\circ}_f \text{(products)} - \sum n_r \Delta G^{\circ}_f \text{(reactants)}$$
$$= [2(\Delta G^{\circ}_f (Fe(s))) + 3(\Delta G^{\circ}_f (H_2O(g)))] - [3(\Delta G^{\circ}_f (H_2(g))) + 1(\Delta G^{\circ}_f (Fe_2O_3(s)))]$$
$$= [2(0.0 \text{ kJ}) + 3(-228.6 \text{ kJ})] - [3(0.0 \text{ kJ}) + 1(-742.2 \text{ kJ})]$$
$$= [-685.8 \text{ kJ}] - [-742.2 \text{ kJ}]$$
$$= +56.4 \text{ kJ}$$

So the reaction is nonspontaneous. The value is similar to that in Problem 17.31.

Check: The units (kJ) are correct. The answer is the same as in Problem 17.31 within the error of the calculation.

(d)   **Given:** $N_2(g) + 3 H_2(g) \rightarrow 2 NH_3(g)$ at 25 °C
       Find: ΔG°_{rxn} and spontaneity and compare to Problem 17.31
       Conceptual Plan: $\Delta G^{\circ}_{rxn} = \sum n_p \Delta G^{\circ}_f \text{(products)} - \sum n_r \Delta G^{\circ}_f \text{(reactants)}$ **then compare to Problem 17.31**
       Solution:

Reactant/Product	ΔG°_f (kJ/mol from Appendix IIB)
$N_2(g)$	0.0
$H_2(g)$	0.0
$NH_3(g)$	−16.4

Be sure to pull data for the correct formula and phase.

$$\Delta G^{\circ}_{rxn} = \sum n_p \Delta G^{\circ}_f \text{(products)} - \sum n_r \Delta G^{\circ}_f \text{(reactants)}$$
$$= [2(\Delta G^{\circ}_f (NH_3(g)))] - [1(\Delta G^{\circ}_f (N_2(g))) + 3(\Delta G^{\circ}_f (H_2(g)))]$$

$$= [2(-16.4 \text{ kJ})] - [1(0.0 \text{ kJ}) + 3(0.0 \text{ kJ})]$$
$$= [-32.8 \text{ kJ}] - [0.0 \text{ kJ}]$$
$$= -32.8 \text{ kJ}$$

So the reaction is spontaneous. The result is the same as in Problem 17.31.

Check: The units (kJ) are correct. The answer matches the one in Problem 17.31.
Values calculated by the two methods are comparable. The method using $\Delta H°$ and $\Delta S°$ is longer, but it can be used to determine how $\Delta G°$ changes with temperature.

17.35   **Given:** $2 \text{ NO}(g) + \text{O}_2(g) \rightarrow 2 \text{ NO}_2(g)$ **Find:** $\Delta G°_{rxn}$ and spontaneity at (a) 298 K, (b) 715 K, and (c) 855 K
Conceptual Plan: $\Delta H°_{rxn} = \sum n_p H°_f \text{ (products)} - \sum n_r H°_f \text{ (reactants)}$ then
$\Delta S°_{rxn} = \sum n_p S° \text{(products)} - \sum n_r S° \text{(reactants)}$ then J/K $\rightarrow$ kJ/K then $\Delta H°_{rxn}, \Delta S°_{rxn}, T \rightarrow \Delta G°$

$$\frac{1 \text{ kJ}}{1000 \text{ J}} \qquad\qquad \Delta G = \Delta H_{rxn} - T\Delta S_{rxn}$$

Solution:

Reactant/Product	$\Delta G°_f$ (kJ/mol from Appendix IIB)
NO(g)	91.3
O$_2$(g)	0.0
NO$_2$(g)	33.2

Be sure to pull data for the correct formula and phase.

$\Delta H°_{rxn} = \sum n_p \Delta H°_f \text{ (products)} - \sum n_r \Delta H°_f \text{ (reactants)}$
$= [2(\Delta H°_f (\text{NO}_2(g)))] - [2(\Delta H°_f (\text{NO } (g))) + 1(\Delta H°_f (\text{O}_2(g)))]$
$= [2(33.2 \text{ kJ})] - [2(91.3 \text{ kJ}) + 1(0.0 \text{ kJ})]$
$= [66.4 \text{ kJ}] - [182.6 \text{ kJ}]$
$= -116.2 \text{ kJ}$ then

Reactant/Product	$S°$(J/mol · K from Appendix IIB)
NO(g)	210.8
O$_2$(g)	205.2
NO$_2$(g)	240.1

Be sure to pull data for the correct formula and phase.

$\Delta S°_{rxn} = \sum n_p S° \text{(products)} - \sum n_r S° \text{(reactants)}$
$= [2(S°(\text{NO}_2(g)))] - [2(S°(\text{NO } (g))) + 1(S°(\text{O}_2(g)))]$
$= [2(240.1 \text{ J/K})] - [2(210.8 \text{ J/K}) + 1(205.2 \text{ J/K})]$
$= [480.2 \text{ J/K}] - [626.8 \text{ J/K}]$

$= -146.6 \text{ J/K}$ then $-146.6 \dfrac{J}{K} \times \dfrac{1 \text{ kJ}}{1000 J} = -0.1466 \text{ kJ/K}$

(a) $\Delta G° = \Delta H°_{rxn} - T\Delta S°_{rxn} = -116.2 \text{ kJ} - (298 \text{ K})\left(-0.1466 \dfrac{\text{kJ}}{\text{K}}\right) = -72.5 \text{ kJ} = -7.25 \times 10^4 \text{ J}$; so the reaction is spontaneous.

(b) $\Delta G° = \Delta H°_{rxn} - T\Delta S°_{rxn} = -116.2 \text{ kJ} - (715 \text{ K})\left(-0.1466 \dfrac{\text{kJ}}{\text{K}}\right) = -11.4 \text{ kJ} = -1.14 \times 10^4 \text{ J}$; so the reaction is spontaneous.

(c) $\Delta G° = \Delta H°_{rxn} - T\Delta S°_{rxn} = -116.2 \text{ kJ} - (855 \text{ K})\left(-0.1466 \dfrac{\text{kJ}}{\text{K}}\right) = +9.1 \text{ kJ} = +9.1 \times 10^3 \text{ J}$; so the reaction is nonspontaneous.

Check: The units (kJ) are correct. The enthalpy term dominates at low temperatures, making the reaction spontaneous. As the temperature increases, the decrease in entropy starts to dominate and in the last case the reaction is nonspontaneous.

17.37   Because the first reaction has Fe$_2$O$_3$ as a product and the reaction of interest has it as a reactant, we need to reverse the first reaction. When the reaction direction is reversed, the sign of ΔG changes.

$$\text{Fe}_2\text{O}_3(s) \rightarrow 2 \text{ Fe}(s) + 3/2 \text{ O}_2(g) \qquad\qquad \Delta G° = +742.2 \text{ kJ}$$

Because the second reaction has 1 mole of CO as a reactant and the reaction of interest has 3 moles of CO as a reactant, we need to multiply the second reaction and the ΔG by 3.

$$3[CO(g) + 1/2\,O_2(g) \rightarrow CO_2(g)] \qquad\qquad \Delta G° = 3(-257.2\ \text{kJ}) = -771.6\ \text{kJ}$$

Hess's law states the ΔG of the net reaction is the sum of the ΔG of the steps. The rewritten reactions are:

$$
\begin{array}{ll}
Fe_2O_3(s) \rightarrow 2\,Fe(s) + 3/2\,\cancel{O_2(g)} & \Delta G° = +742.2\ \text{kJ} \\
3\,CO(g) + 3/2\,\cancel{O_2(g)} \rightarrow 3\,CO_2(g) & \Delta G° = -771.6\ \text{kJ} \\
\hline
Fe_2O_3(s) \rightarrow 3\,CO(g) \rightarrow 2\,Fe(s) + 3\,CO_2(g) & \Delta G°_{rxn} = -29.4\ \text{kJ}
\end{array}
$$

Free Energy Changes, Nonstandard Conditions, and the Equilibrium Constant

17.39 (a) **Given:** $I_2(s) \rightarrow I_2(g)$ at 25.0 °C   **Find:** $\Delta G°_{rxn}$
Conceptual Plan: $\Delta G°_{rxn} = \sum n_p \Delta G°_f\ (\text{products}) - \sum n_r \Delta G°_f\ (\text{reactants})$
Solution:

Reactant/Product	$\Delta G°_f$ (kJ/mol from Appendix IIB)
$I_2(s)$	0.0
$I_2(g)$	19.3

Be sure to pull data for the correct formula and phase.

$$
\begin{aligned}
\Delta G°_{rxn} &= \sum n_p \Delta G°_f\ (\text{products}) - \sum n_r \Delta G°_f\ (\text{products}) \\
&= [1(\Delta G°_f\ (I_2(g)))] - [1(\Delta G°_f\ (I_2(s)))] \\
&= [1(19.3\ \text{kJ})] - [1(0.0\ \text{kJ})] \\
&= +19.3\ \text{kJ; so the reaction is nonspontaneous.}
\end{aligned}
$$

Check: The units (kJ) are correct. The answer is positive because gases have higher free energy than do solids and the free energy change of the reaction is the same as free energy of formation of gaseous iodine.

(b) **Given:** $I_2(s) \rightarrow I_2(g)$ at 25.0 °C (i) $P_{I_2} = 1.00$ mmHg; (ii) $P_{I_2} = 0.100$ mmHg   **Find:** ΔG_{rxn}
Conceptual Plan: °C $\rightarrow$ K and mmHg $\rightarrow$ atm then $\Delta G°_{rxn}, P_{I_2}, T \rightarrow \Delta G_{rxn}$

$$K = 273.15 + °C \qquad \frac{1\ \text{atm}}{760\ \text{mmHg}} \qquad \Delta G_{rxn} = \Delta G°_{rxn} + RT\ln Q\ \text{where}\ Q = P_{I_2}$$

Solution: $T = 273.15 + 25.0\ °C = 298.2$ K and (i) $1.00\ \cancel{\text{mmHg}} \times \dfrac{1\ \text{atm}}{760\ \cancel{\text{mmHg}}} = 0.0013\underline{1}579$ atm

then $\Delta G_{rxn} = \Delta G°_{rxn} + RT\ln Q = \Delta G°_{rxn} + RT\ln P_{I_2} =$

$+19.3\ \text{kJ} + \left(8.314\ \dfrac{\cancel{J}}{\cancel{K} \cdot \text{mol}}\right)\!\left(\dfrac{1\ \text{kJ}}{1000\ \cancel{J}}\right)(298.2\ \cancel{K})\ \ln(0.0013\underline{1}579) = +2.9\ \text{kJ; so the reaction is}$
nonspontaneous.

Then (ii) $0.100\ \cancel{\text{mmHg}} \times \dfrac{1\ \text{atm}}{760\ \cancel{\text{mmHg}}} = 0.00013\underline{1}579$ atm then

$\Delta G_{rxn} = \Delta G°_{rxn} + RT\ln Q = \Delta G°_{rxn} + RT\ln P_{I_2} =$

$+19.3\ \text{kJ} + \left(8.314\ \dfrac{\cancel{J}}{\cancel{K} \cdot \text{mol}}\right)\!\left(\dfrac{1\ \text{kJ}}{1000\ \cancel{J}}\right)(298.2\ \cancel{K})\ \ln(0.00013\underline{1}579) = -2.9\ \text{kJ; so the reaction is}$
spontaneous.

Check: The units (kJ) are correct. The answer is positive at higher pressure because the pressure is higher than the vapor pressure of iodine. Once the desired pressure is below the vapor pressure (0.31 mmHg at 25.0 °C), the reaction becomes spontaneous.

(c) Iodine sublimes at room temperature because there is an equilibrium between the solid and the gas phases. The vapor pressure is low (0.31 mmHg at 25.0 °C), so a small amount of iodine can remain in the gas phase, which is consistent with the free energy values.

17.41 **Given:** $CH_3OH(g) \rightleftharpoons CO(g) + 2\,H_2(g)$ at 25.0 °C, $P_{CH_3OH} = 0.855$ atm, $P_{CO} = 0.125$ atm, $P_{H_2} = 0.183$ atm
Find: ΔG

Conceptual Plan:

$$\Delta G^{\circ}_{rxn} = \sum n_p \Delta G^{\circ}_f \text{ (products)} - \sum n_r \Delta G^{\circ}_f \text{ (reactants) then } ^{\circ}C \rightarrow K \text{ then } \Delta G^{\circ}_{rxn}, P_{CH_3OH}, P_{CO}, P_{H_2}, T \rightarrow \Delta G$$

$$K = 273.15 + ^{\circ}C \qquad \Delta G_{rxn} = \Delta G^{\circ}_{rxn} + RT \ln Q \qquad where \; Q = \frac{P_{CO}P^2_{H_2}}{P_{CH_3OH}}$$

Solution:

Reactant/Product	ΔG°_f (kJ/mol from Appendix IIB)
$CH_3OH(g)$	-162.3
$CO(g)$	-137.2
$H_2(g)$	0.0

Be sure to pull data for the correct formula and phase.

$$\begin{aligned}
\Delta G^{\circ}_{rxn} &= \sum n_p \Delta G^{\circ}_f \text{ (products)} - \sum n_r \Delta G^{\circ}_f \text{ (reactants)} \\
&= [1(\Delta G^{\circ}_f (CO(g))) + 2(\Delta G^{\circ}_f (H_2(g)))] - [1(\Delta G^{\circ}_f (CH_3OH(g)))] \\
&= [1(-137.2 \text{ kJ}) + 2(0.0 \text{ kJ})] - [1(-162.3 \text{ kJ})] \\
&= [-137.2 \text{ kJ}] - [-162.3 \text{ kJ}] \\
&= +25.1 \text{ kJ}
\end{aligned}$$

$$T = 273.15 + 25.0 \,^{\circ}C = 298.2 \text{ K then } Q = \frac{P_{CO}P^2_{H_2}}{P_{CH_3OH}} = \frac{(0.125)(0.183)^2}{0.855} = 0.00489\underline{6}05 \text{ then}$$

$$\Delta G_{rxn} = \Delta G^{\circ}_{rxn} + RT \ln Q = +25.1 \text{ kJ} + \left(8.314 \frac{J}{K \cdot mol}\right)\left(\frac{1 \text{ kJ}}{1000 \text{ J}}\right)(298.2 \text{ K}) \ln (0.00489\underline{6}05) = +11.9 \text{ kJ}$$

So the reaction is nonspontaneous.

Check: The units (kJ) are correct. The standard free energy for the reaction was positive and the fact that Q was less than 1 made the free energy smaller, but the reaction at these conditions is still not spontaneous.

17.43 (a) **Given:** $2 CO(g) + O_2(g) \rightleftharpoons 2 CO_2(g)$ at $25.0 \,^{\circ}C$ **Find:** K

Conceptual Plan:

$$\Delta G^{\circ}_{rxn} = \sum n_p \Delta G^{\circ}_f \text{ (products)} - \sum n_r \Delta G^{\circ}_f \text{ (reactants) then } ^{\circ}C \rightarrow K \text{ then } \Delta G^{\circ}_{rxn}, T \rightarrow K$$

$$K = 273.15 + ^{\circ}C \qquad \Delta G^{\circ}_{rxn} = -RT \ln K$$

Solution:

Reactant/Product	ΔG°_f (kJ/mol from Appendix IIB)
$CO(g)$	-137.2
$O_2(g)$	0.0
$CO_2(g)$	-394.4

Be sure to pull data for the correct formula and phase.

$$\begin{aligned}
\Delta G^{\circ}_{rxn} &= \sum n_p \Delta G^{\circ}_f \text{ (products)} - \sum n_r \Delta G^{\circ}_f \text{ (reactants)} \\
&= [2(\Delta G^{\circ}_f (CO_2(g)))] - [2(\Delta G^{\circ}_f (CO(g))) + 1(\Delta G^{\circ}_f (O_2(g)))] \\
&= [2(-394.4 \text{ kJ})] - [2(-137.2 \text{ kJ}) + 1(0.0 \text{ kJ})] \\
&= [-788.8 \text{ kJ}] - [-274.4 \text{ kJ}] \\
&= -514.4 \text{ kJ}
\end{aligned}$$

$$T = 273.15 + 25.0 \,^{\circ}C = 298.2 \text{ K then}$$

$\Delta G^{\circ}_{rxn} = -RT \ln K$ Rearrange to solve for K.

$$K = e^{\frac{-\Delta G^{\circ}_{rxn}}{RT}} = e^{\frac{-(-514.4 \text{ kJ}) \times \frac{1000 \text{ J}}{1 \text{ kJ}}}{\left(8.314 \frac{J}{K \cdot mol}\right)(298.2 \text{ K})}} = e^{207.483} = 1.28 \times 10^{90}$$

Check: The units (none) are correct. The standard free energy for the reaction was very negative, so we expect a very large K. The reaction is spontaneous, so mostly products are present at equilibrium.

(b) **Given:** $2 H_2S(g) \rightleftharpoons 2 H_2(g) + S_2(g)$ at $25.0 \,^{\circ}C$ **Find:** K

Conceptual Plan:

$$\Delta G^{\circ}_{rxn} = \sum n_p \Delta G^{\circ}_f \text{ (products)} - \sum n_r \Delta G^{\circ}_f \text{ (reactants) then } ^{\circ}C \rightarrow K \text{ then } \Delta G^{\circ}_{rxn}, T \rightarrow K$$

$$K = 273.15 + ^{\circ}C \qquad \Delta G^{\circ}_{rxn} = -RT \ln K$$

Solution:

Reactant/Product	ΔG_f° (kJ/mol from Appendix IIB)
$H_2S(g)$	-33.4
$H_2(g)$	0.0
$S_2(g)$	79.7

Be sure to pull data for the correct formula and phase.

$$\Delta G_{rxn}^\circ = \sum n_p \Delta G_f^\circ (\text{products}) - \sum n_r \Delta G_f^\circ (\text{reactants})$$
$$= [2(\Delta G_f^\circ (H_2(g))) + 1(\Delta G_f^\circ (S_2(g)))] - [2(\Delta G_f^\circ (H_2S(g)))]$$
$$= [2(0.0 \text{ kJ})] + 1(79.7 \text{ kJ})] - [2(-33.4 \text{ kJ})]$$
$$= [79.7 \text{ kJ}] - [-66.8 \text{ kJ}]$$
$$= +146.5 \text{ kJ} \qquad\qquad T = 273.15 + 25.0\,^\circ C = 298.2 \text{ K then}$$

$\Delta G_{rxn}^\circ = -RT \ln K$ Rearrange to solve for K.

$$K = e^{\frac{-\Delta G_{rxn}^\circ}{RT}} = e^{\dfrac{-146.5\,\cancel{kJ} \times \frac{1000\,J}{1\,\cancel{kJ}}}{\left(8.314 \frac{J}{K \cdot mol}\right)(298.2\,K)}} = e^{-59.0908} = 2.17 \times 10^{-26}$$

Check: The units (none) are correct. The standard free energy for the reaction was positive, so we expect a small K. The reaction is nonspontaneous, so mostly reactants are present at equilibrium.

17.45   **Given:** $CO(g) + 2\,H_2(g) \rightleftharpoons CH_3OH(g)$ $K_p = 2.26 \times 10^4$ at 25 °C
        Find: ΔG_{rxn}° at (a) standard conditions; (b) at equilibrium; and (c) $P_{CH_3OH} = 1.0$ atm, $P_{CO} = P_{H_2} = 0.010$ atm
        Conceptual Plan: °C → K then (a) K, T → ΔG_{rxn}° then (b) at equilibrium $\Delta G_{rxn} = 0$ then

$$K = 273.15 + \,^\circ C \qquad\qquad \Delta G_{rxn}^\circ = -RT \ln K$$

        (c) $\Delta G_{rxn}^\circ, P_{CH_3OH}, P_{CO}, P_{H_2}, T$ → ΔG

$$\Delta G_{rxn} = \Delta G_{rxn}^\circ + RT \ln Q \quad \text{where } Q = \frac{P_{CH_3OH}}{P_{CO} P_{H_2}^2}$$

Solution: $T = 273.15 + 25\,^\circ C = 298$ K then

(a) $\Delta G_{rxn}^\circ = -RT \ln K = -\left(8.314 \dfrac{J}{K \cdot mol}\right)\left(\dfrac{1 \text{ kJ}}{1000\,J}\right)(298\,K) \ln(2.26 \times 10^4) = -24.8$ kJ

(b)   at equilibrium, $\Delta G_{rxn} = 0$

(c) $Q = \dfrac{P_{CH_3OH}}{P_{CO} P_{H_2}^2} = \dfrac{1.0}{(0.010)(0.010)^2} = 1.0 \times 10^6$ then

$$\Delta G_{rxn} = \Delta G_{rxn}^\circ + RT \ln Q = -24.8 \text{ kJ} + \left(8.314 \dfrac{J}{K \cdot mol}\right)\left(\dfrac{1 \text{ kJ}}{1000\,J}\right)(298\,K) \ln(1.0 \times 10^6) = +9.4 \text{ kJ}$$

Check: The units (kJ) are correct. The K was greater than 1, so we expect a negative standard free energy for the reaction. At equilibrium, by definition, the free energy change is zero. Because the conditions give a $Q > K$, the reaction needs to proceed in the reverse direction, which means that the reaction is spontaneous in the reverse direction.

17.47   **(a)**   **Given:** $2\,CO(g) + O_2(g) \rightleftharpoons 2\,CO_2(g)$ at 25.0 °C   **Find:** K at 525 K
            Conceptual Plan: $\Delta H_{rxn}^\circ = \sum n_p H_f^\circ (\text{products}) - \sum n_r H_f^\circ (\text{reactants})$ then
            $\Delta S_{rxn}^\circ = \sum n_p S^\circ (\text{products}) - \sum n_r S^\circ (\text{reactants})$ then J/K → kJ/K then $\Delta H_{rxn}^\circ, \Delta S_{rxn}^\circ, T$ → ΔG

$$\frac{1 \text{ kJ}}{1000\,J} \qquad\qquad \Delta G = \Delta H_{rxn} - T\Delta S_{rxn}$$

            then $\Delta G_{rxn}^\circ, T$ → K

$$\Delta G_{rxn}^\circ = -RT \ln K$$

            Solution:

Reactant/Product	ΔH_f° (kJ/mol from Appendix IIB)
$CO(g)$	-110.5
$O_2(g)$	0.0
$CO_2(g)$	-393.5

Be sure to pull data for the correct formula and phase.

$\Delta H^{\circ}_{rxn} = \sum n_p \Delta H^{\circ}_f \text{ (products)} - \sum n_r \Delta H^{\circ}_f \text{ (reactants)}$

$= [2(\Delta H^{\circ}_f (CO_2(g)))] - [2(\Delta H^{\circ}_f (CO(g))) + 1(\Delta H^{\circ}_f (O_2(g)))]$

$= [2(-393.5 \text{ kJ})] - [2(-110.5 \text{ kJ}) + 1(0.0 \text{ kJ})]$ then

$= [-787.0 \text{ kJ}] - [-221.0 \text{ kJ}]$

$= -566.0 \text{ kJ}$

Reactant/Product	S°(J/mol · K from Appendix IIB)
CO(g)	197.7
O$_2$(g)	205.2
CO$_2$(g)	213.8

Be sure to pull data for the correct formula and phase.

$\Delta S^{\circ}_{rxn} = \sum n_p S^{\circ}\text{(products)} - \sum n_r S^{\circ}\text{(reactants)}$

$= [2(S^{\circ}(CO_2(g)))] - [2(S^{\circ}(CO(g))) + 1(S^{\circ}(O_2(g)))]$

$= [2(213.8 \text{ J/K})] - [2(197.7 \text{ J/K}) + 1(205.2 \text{ J/K})]$

$= [427.6 \text{ J/K}] - [600.6 \text{ J/K}]$ then

$= -173.0 \text{ J/K}$

$-173.0 \dfrac{J}{K} \times \dfrac{1 \text{ kJ}}{1000 \text{ J}} = -0.1730 \text{ kJ/K}$ then

$\Delta G^{\circ} = \Delta H^{\circ}_{rxn} - T\Delta S^{\circ}_{rxn} = -566.0 \text{ kJ} - (525 \text{ K})\left(-0.1730 \dfrac{kJ}{K}\right) = -475.2 \text{ kJ} = -4.752 \times 10^5 \text{ J}$ then

$\Delta G^{\circ}_{rxn} = -RT \ln K$ Rearrange to solve for K.

$K = e^{\frac{-\Delta G^{\circ}_{rxn}}{RT}} = e^{\frac{-(-4.752 \times 10^5 \text{ J})}{\left(8.314 \frac{J}{K \cdot mol}\right)(525 \text{ K})}} = e^{108.870} = 1.91 \times 10^{47}$

Check: The units (none) are correct. The free energy change was very negative, indicating a spontaneous reaction. This results in a very large K.

(b)   **Given:** $2 H_2S(g) \rightleftharpoons 2 H_2(g) + S_2(g)$ at 25.0 °C   **Find:** K at 525 K

Conceptual Plan: $\Delta H^{\circ}_{rxn} = \sum n_p H^{\circ}_f \text{ (products)} - \sum n_r H^{\circ}_f \text{ (reactants)}$ then

$\Delta S^{\circ}_{rxn} = \sum n_p S^{\circ}\text{(products)} - \sum n_r S^{\circ}\text{(reactants)}$ then J/K → kJ/K then $\Delta H^{\circ}_{rxn}, \Delta S_{rxn}, T \rightarrow \Delta G$

$\dfrac{1 \text{ kJ}}{1000 \text{ J}}$ $\Delta G = \Delta H_{rxn} - T\Delta S_{rxn}$

then $\Delta G^{\circ}_{rxn}, T \rightarrow K$

$\Delta G^{\circ}_{rxn} = -RT \ln K$

Solution:

Reactant/Product	ΔH°_f (kJ/mol from Appendix IIB)
H$_2$S(g)	−20.6
H$_2$(g)	0.0
S$_2$(g)	128.6

Be sure to pull data for the correct formula and phase.

$\Delta H^{\circ}_{rxn} = \sum n_p \Delta H^{\circ}_f \text{ (products)} - \sum n_r \Delta H^{\circ}_f \text{ (reactants)}$

$= [2(\Delta H^{\circ}_f (H_2(g))) + 1(\Delta H^{\circ}_f (S_2(g)))] - [2(\Delta H^{\circ}_f (H_2S(g)))]$

$= [2(0.0 \text{ kJ}) + 1(128.6 \text{ kJ})] - [2(-20.6 \text{ kJ})]$

$= [128.6 \text{ kJ}] - [-41.2 \text{ kJ}]$

$= +169.8 \text{ kJ}$

Reactant/Product	S°(J/mol · K from Appendix IIB)
H$_2$S(g)	205.8
H$_2$(g)	130.7
S$_2$(g)	228.2

Be sure to pull data for the correct formula and phase.

$$\Delta S^\circ_{rxn} = \sum n_p S^\circ(\text{products}) - \sum n_r S^\circ(\text{reactants})$$
$$= [2(S^\circ(H_2(g))) + 1(S^\circ(S_2(g)))] - [2(S^\circ(H_2S(g)))]$$
$$= [2(130.7 \text{ J/K}) + 1(228.2 \text{ J/K})] - [2(205.8 \text{ J/K})]$$
$$= [489.6 \text{ J/K}] - [411.6 \text{ J/K}]$$
$$= +78.0 \text{ J/K}$$

then $+78.0 \dfrac{J}{K} \times \dfrac{1 \text{ kJ}}{1000 \text{ } J} = +0.0780 \text{ kJ/K}$ then

$$\Delta G^\circ = \Delta H^\circ_{rxn} - T\Delta S^\circ_{rxn} = +169.8 \text{ kJ} - (525 \text{ K})\left(+0.0780 \dfrac{kJ}{K}\right) = +128.\underline{8}5 \text{ kJ} = +1.28\underline{8}5 \times 10^5 \text{ J}$$ then

$$\Delta G^\circ_{rxn} = -RT \ln K$$ Rearrange to solve for K.

$$K = e^{\frac{-\Delta G^\circ_{rxn}}{RT}} = e^{\frac{-1.28\underline{8}5 \times 10^5 \text{ } J}{\left(8.314 \frac{J}{K \cdot mol}\right)(525 \text{ K})}} = e^{-29.\underline{5}199} = 1.51 \times 10^{-13}$$

Check: The units (none) are correct. The free energy change is positive, indicating a nonspontaneous reaction. This results in a very small K.

Cumulative Problems

17.49   (a)   + because vapors have higher entropy than do liquids.

(b)   − because solids have less entropy than do liquids.

(c)   − because there is only one microstate for the final macrostate and there are six microstates for the initial macrostate.

17.51   (a)   **Given:** $N_2(g) + O_2(g) \rightarrow 2 \text{ NO}(g)$ **Find:** ΔG°_{rxn} and K_p at 298 K

Conceptual Plan: $\Delta H^\circ_{rxn} = \sum n_p H^\circ_f(\text{products}) - \sum n_r H^\circ_f(\text{reactants})$ then

$\Delta S^\circ_{rxn} = \sum n_p S^\circ(\text{products}) - \sum n_r S^\circ(\text{reactants})$ then $^\circ C \rightarrow K$ then J/K $\rightarrow$ kJ/K then

$$K = 273.15 + {}^\circ C \qquad \dfrac{1 \text{ kJ}}{1000 \text{ J}}$$

$\Delta H^\circ_{rxn}, \Delta S^\circ_{rxn}, T \rightarrow \Delta G$ then $\Delta G^\circ_{rxn}, T \rightarrow K$

$$\Delta G = \Delta H_{rxn} - T\Delta S_{rxn} \qquad \Delta G^\circ_{rxn} = -RT \ln K$$

Solution:

Reactant/Product	ΔH°_f (kJ/mol from Appendix IIB)
$N_2(g)$	0.0
$O_2(g)$	0.0
$NO(g)$	91.3

Be sure to pull data for the correct formula and phase.

$$\Delta H^\circ_{rxn} = \sum n_p \Delta H^\circ_f(\text{products}) - \sum n_r \Delta H^\circ_f(\text{reactants})$$
$$= [2(\Delta H^\circ_f(NO(g)))] - [1(\Delta H^\circ_f(N_2(g))) + 1(\Delta H^\circ_f(O_2(g)))]$$
$$= [2(91.3 \text{ kJ})] - [1(0.0 \text{ kJ}) + 1(0.0 \text{ kJ})]$$
$$= [182.6 \text{ kJ}] - [0.0 \text{ kJ}]$$
$$= +182.6 \text{ kJ}$$ then

Reactant/Product	S° (J/mol · K from Appendix IIB)
$N_2(g)$	191.6
$O_2(g)$	205.2
$NO(g)$	210.8

Be sure to pull data for the correct formula and phase.

$$\Delta S^\circ_{rxn} = \sum n_p S^\circ(\text{products}) - \sum n_r S^\circ(\text{reactants})$$
$$= [2(S^\circ(NO(g)))] - [1(S^\circ(N_2(g))) + 1(S^\circ(O_2(g)))]$$
$$= [2(210.8 \text{ J/K})] - [1(191.6 \text{ J/K}) + 1(205.2 \text{ J/K})]$$
$$= [421.6 \text{ J/K}] - [396.8 \text{ JK}]$$
$$= +24.8 \text{ J/K}$$

then $+24.8 \dfrac{J}{K} \times \dfrac{1 \text{ kJ}}{1000 \text{ J}} = +0.0248 \text{ kJ/K}$ then

$$\Delta G° = \Delta H°_{rxn} - T\Delta S°_{rxn} = +182.6 \text{ kJ} - (298 \text{ K})\left(0.0248 \dfrac{\text{kJ}}{\text{K}}\right) = +175.2 \text{ kJ} = +1.752 \times 10^5 \text{ J}$$

then $\Delta G°_{rxn} = -RT \ln K$ Rearrange to solve for K.

$$K = e^{\frac{-\Delta G°_{rxn}}{RT}} = e^{\left(\frac{-1.752 \times 10^5 \text{ J}}{8.314 \frac{\text{J}}{\text{K} \cdot \text{mol}}\right)(298 \text{ K})}} = e^{-70.7144} = 1.95 \times 10^{-31};$$ so the reaction is nonspontaneous, and at equilibrium, mostly reactants are present.

Check: The units (kJ and none) are correct. The enthalpy is twice the enthalpy of formation of NO. We expect a very small entropy change because the number of moles of gas is unchanged. Because the positive enthalpy term dominates at room temperature, the free energy change is very positive and the reaction in the forward direction is nonspontaneous. This results in a very small K.

(b)   **Given:** $N_2(g) + O_2(g) \rightarrow 2 \text{ NO}(g)$ **Find:** $\Delta G°_{rxn}$ at 2000 K
Conceptual Plan: Use results from part (a) $\Delta H°_{rxn}, \Delta S_{rxn}, T \rightarrow \Delta G$ then $\Delta G°_{rxn}, T \rightarrow K$
$$\Delta G = \Delta H_{rxn} - T\Delta S_{rxn} \qquad \Delta G°_{rxn} = -RT \ln K$$

Solution: $\Delta G = \Delta H_{rxn} - T\Delta S_{rxn} = +182.6 \text{ kJ} - (2000 \text{ K})\left(0.0248 \dfrac{\text{kJ}}{\text{K}}\right) = +133.0 \text{ kJ} = +1.330 \times 10^5 \text{ J}$

then $\Delta G°_{rxn} = -RT \ln K$ Rearrange to solve for K.

$$K = e^{\frac{-\Delta G°_{rxn}}{RT}} = e^{\left(\frac{-1.330 \times 10^5 \text{ J}}{8.314 \frac{\text{J}}{\text{K} \cdot \text{mol}}\right)(2000 \text{ K})}} = e^{-7.998557} = 3.36 \times 10^{-4};$$ so the forward reaction is becoming more spontaneous.

Check: The units (kJ and none) are correct. As the temperature rises, the entropy term becomes more significant. The free energy change is reduced, and the K increases. The reaction is still nonspontaneous.

17.53   **Given:** $C_2H_4(g) + X_2(g) \rightarrow C_2H_4X_2(g)$ where X = Cl, Br, and I
Find: $\Delta H°_{rxn}, \Delta S°_{rxn}, \Delta G°_{rxn}$ and K at 25 °C and spontaneity trends with X and temperature
Conceptual Plan: $\Delta H°_{rxn} = \sum n_p H°_f \text{(products)} - \sum n_r H°_f \text{(reactants)}$ then
$\Delta S°_{rxn} = \sum n_p S°\text{(products)} - \sum n_r S°\text{(reactants)}$ then °C → K then J/K → kJ/K then
$$K = 273.15 + °C \qquad \dfrac{1 \text{ kJ}}{1000 \text{ J}}$$

$\Delta H°_{rxn}, \Delta S°_{rxn}, T \rightarrow \Delta G$ then $\Delta G°_{rxn}, T \rightarrow K$
$$\Delta G = \Delta H_{rxn} - T\Delta S_{rxn} \qquad \Delta G°_{rxn} = -RT \ln K$$

Solution:

Reactant/Product	$\Delta H°_f$ (kJ/mol from Appendix IIB)
$C_2H_4(g)$	52.4
$Cl_2(g)$	0.0
$C_2H_4Cl_2(g)$	−129.7

Be sure to pull data for the correct formula and phase.

$$\begin{aligned}
\Delta H°_{rxn} &= \sum n_p \Delta H°_f \text{(products)} - \sum n_r \Delta H°_f \text{(reactants)} \\
&= [1\Delta H°_f (C_2H_4Cl_2)(g))] - [1(\Delta H°_f (C_2H_4(g))) + 1(\Delta H°_f (Cl_2(g)))] \\
&= [1(-129.7 \text{ kJ})] - [1(52.4 \text{ kJ}) + 1(0.0 \text{ kJ})] \\
&= [-129.7 \text{ kJ}] - [52.4 \text{ kJ}] \\
&= -182.1 \text{ kJ then}
\end{aligned}$$

Reactant/Product	$S°$ (J/mol · K from Appendix IIB)
$C_2H_4(g)$	219.3
$Cl_2(g)$	223.1
$C_2H_4Cl_2(g)$	308.0

Be sure to pull data for the correct formula and phase.

$$\Delta S^{\circ}_{\text{rxn}} = \sum n_p S^{\circ}(\text{products}) - \sum n_r S^{\circ}(\text{reactants})$$
$$= [1(S^{\circ}(C_2H_4Cl_2(g)))] - [1(S^{\circ}(C_2H_4(g))) + 1(S^{\circ}(Cl_2(g)))]$$
$$= [1(308.0 \text{ J/K})] - [1(219.3 \text{ J/K}) + 1(223.1 \text{ J/K})]$$
$$= [308.0 \text{ J/K}] - [442.4 \text{ J/K}]$$
$$= -134.4 \text{ J/K}$$

then $T = 273.15 + 25\,^{\circ}C = 298$ K then $-134.4\,\dfrac{J}{K} \times \dfrac{1 \text{ kJ}}{1000\,J} = -0.1344$ kJ/K then

$$\Delta G^{\circ} = \Delta H^{\circ}_{\text{rxn}} - T\Delta S^{\circ}_{\text{rxn}} = -182.1 \text{ kJ} - (298\text{ K})\left(-0.1344\,\frac{\text{kJ}}{\text{K}}\right) = -142.0 \text{ kJ} = -1.420 \times 10^5 \text{ J then}$$

$$\Delta G^{\circ}_{\text{rxn}} = -RT \ln K \text{ Rearrange to solve for } K.$$

$$K = e^{\frac{-\Delta G^{\circ}_{\text{rxn}}}{RT}} = e^{\frac{-(-1.420 \times 10^5\,J)}{\left(8.314\frac{J}{K\cdot \text{mol}}\right)(298\,K)}} = e^{57.\underline{3}14} = 7.78 \times 10^{24}; \text{ so the reaction is spontaneous.}$$

Reactant/Product	ΔH°_f (kJ/mol from Appendix IIB)
$C_2H_4(g)$	52.4
$Br_2(g)$	30.9
$C_2H_4Br_2(g)$	−38.3

Be sure to pull data for the correct formula and phase.

$$\Delta H^{\circ}_{\text{rxn}} = \sum n_p \Delta H^{\circ}_f(\text{products}) - \sum n_r \Delta H^{\circ}_f(\text{reactants})$$
$$= [1(\Delta H^{\circ}_f(C_2H_4Br_2(g)))] - [1\Delta H^{\circ}_f(C_2H_4(g))) + 1(\Delta H^{\circ}_f(Br_2(g)))]$$
$$= [1(-38.3 \text{ kJ})] - [1(52.4 \text{ kJ}) + 1(30.9 \text{ kJ})]$$
$$= [-38.3 \text{ kJ}] - [83.3 \text{ kJ}]$$
$$= -121.6 \text{ kJ then}$$

Reactant/Product	S°(kJ/mol · K from Appendix IIB)
$C_2H_4(g)$	219.3
$Br_2(g)$	245.5
$C_2H_4Br_2(g)$	330.6

Be sure to pull data for the correct formula and phase.

$$\Delta S^{\circ}_{\text{rxn}} = \sum n_p S^{\circ}(\text{produts}) - \sum n_r S^{\circ}(\text{reactants})$$
$$= [1(S^{\circ}(C_2H_4Br_2(g)))] - [1(S^{\circ}(C_2H_4(g))) + 1(S^{\circ}(Br_2(g)))]$$
$$= [1(330.6 \text{ J/K})] - [1(219.3 \text{ J/K})] + 1(245.5 \text{ J/K})]$$
$$= [330.6 \text{ J/K}] - [464.8 \text{ J/K}]$$
$$= -134.2 \text{ J/K}$$

then $-134.2\,\dfrac{J}{K} \times \dfrac{1 \text{ kJ}}{1000\,J} = -0.1342$ kJ/K

then $\Delta G^{\circ} = \Delta H^{\circ}_{\text{rxn}} - T\Delta S^{\circ}_{\text{rxn}} = -121.6 \text{ kJ} - (298\text{ K})\left(-0.1342\,\dfrac{\text{kJ}}{\text{K}}\right) = -81.608 \text{ kJ} = -8.1\underline{6}08 \times 10^4 \text{ J}$

then $\Delta G^{\circ}_{\text{rxn}} = -RT \ln K$

Rearrange to solve for K. $K = e^{\frac{-\Delta G^{\circ}_{\text{rxn}}}{RT}} = e^{\frac{-(-8.1608 \times 10^4\,J)}{\left(8.314\frac{J}{K\cdot \text{mol}}\right)(298\,K)}} = e^{32.9\underline{3}87} = 2.02 \times 10^{14}; \text{ so the reaction is spontaneous.}$

Reactant/Product	ΔH°_f (kJ/mol from Appendix IIB)
$C_2H_4(g)$	52.4
$I_2(g)$	62.42
$C_2H_4I_2(g)$	66.5

Be sure to pull data for the correct formula and phase.

$$\Delta H^\circ_{rxn} = \sum n_p \Delta H^\circ_f \text{ (products)} - \sum n_r \Delta H^\circ_f \text{ (reactants)}$$
$$= [1(\Delta H^\circ_f (C_2H_4I_2(g)))] - [1\Delta H^\circ_f (C_2H_4(g))) + 1(\Delta H^\circ_f (I_2(g)))]$$
$$= [1(66.5 \text{ kJ})] - [1(52.4 \text{ kJ}) + 1(62.42 \text{ kJ})]$$
$$= [66.5 \text{ kJ}] - [114.\underline{8}2 \text{ kJ}]$$
$$= -48.\underline{3}2 \text{ kJ then}$$

Reactant/Product	S°(kJ/mol · K from Appendix IIB)
$C_2H_4(g)$	219.3
$I_2(g)$	260.69
$C_2H_4I_2(g)$	347.8

Be sure to pull data for the correct formula and phase.

$$\Delta S^\circ_{rxn} = \sum n_p S^\circ \text{(products)} - \sum n_r S^\circ \text{(reactants)}$$
$$= [1(S^\circ(C_2H_4I_2(g)))] - [1(S^\circ(C_2H_4(g))) + 1(S^\circ(I_2(g)))]$$
$$= [1(347.8 \text{ J/K})] - [1(219.3 \text{ J/K}) + 1(260.69 \text{ J/K})]$$
$$= [347.8 \text{ J/K}] - [479.\underline{9}9 \text{ J/K}]$$
$$= -132.2 \text{ J/K}$$

$$\text{then} -132.2 \frac{J}{K} \times \frac{1 \text{ kJ}}{1000 \text{ } J} = -0.1322 \text{ kJ/K}$$

$$\text{then } \Delta G^\circ = \Delta H^\circ_{rxn} - T\Delta S^\circ_{rxn} = -48.\underline{3}2 \text{ kJ} - (298 \text{ K})\left(-0.1322 \frac{kJ}{K}\right) = -8.\underline{9}244 \text{ kJ} = -8.\underline{9}244 \times 10^3 \text{ J}$$

$$\text{then } \Delta G^\circ_{rxn} = -RT \ln K \text{ Rearrange to solve for } K.$$

$$K = e^{\frac{-\Delta G^\circ_{rxn}}{RT}} = e^{\frac{-(-8.9244 \times 10^3 \, J)}{\left(8.314 \frac{J}{K \cdot mol}\right)(298 \, K)}} = e^{3.\underline{6}021} = 37 \text{ and the reaction is spontaneous.}$$

Cl_2 is the most spontaneous in the forward direction; I_2 is the least. The entropy change in the reactions is very constant. The spontaneity is determined by the standard enthalpy of formation of the dihalogenated ethane. Higher temperatures make the forward reactions less spontaneous.

Check: The units (kJ and none) are correct. The enthalpy change becomes less negative as we move to larger halogens. The enthalpy term dominates at room temperature, and the free energy change is the same sign as the enthalpy change. The more negative the free energy change, the larger the K.

17.55 (a) **Given:** $N_2O(g) + NO_2(g) \rightleftharpoons 3 \text{ NO}(g)$ at 298 K **Find:** ΔG°_{rxn}
Conceptual Plan: $\Delta G^\circ_{rxn} = \sum n_p \Delta G^\circ_f \text{ (products)} - \sum n_r \Delta G^\circ_f \text{ (reactants)}$
Solution:

Reactant/Product	ΔG°_f(kJ/mol from Appendix IIB)
$N_2O(g)$	103.7
$NO_2(g)$	51.3
$NO(g)$	87.6

Be sure to pull data for the correct formula and phase.

$$\Delta G^\circ_{rxn} = \sum n_p \Delta G^\circ_f \text{ (produts)} - \sum n_r \Delta G^\circ_f \text{ (reactants)}$$
$$= [3(\Delta G^\circ_f (NO(g)))] - [1(\Delta G^\circ_f (N_2O(g))) + 1(\Delta G^\circ_f (NO_2(g)))]$$
$$= [3(87.6 \text{ kJ})] - [1(103.7 \text{ kJ}) + 1(51.3 \text{ kJ})]$$
$$= [262.8 \text{ kJ}] - [155.0 \text{ kJ}]$$
$$= +107.8 \text{ kJ}$$

The reaction is nonspontaneous.

Check: The units (kJ) are correct. The standard free energy for the reaction was positive, so the reaction is nonspontaneous.

(b) **Given:** $P_{N_2O} = P_{NO_2} = 1.0$ atm initially **Find:** P_{NO} when reaction ceases to be spontaneous
Conceptual Plan: Reaction will no longer be spontaneous when $Q = K$, **so** $\Delta G^\circ_{rxn}, T \rightarrow K.$

$$\Delta G^\circ_{rxn} = -RT \ln K$$

Then solve the equilibrium problem to get gas pressures. Because $K \ll 1$, the amount of NO generated will be very, very small compared to 1.0 atm; within experimental error, $P_{N_2O} = P_{NO_2} = 1.0$ atm. Simply solve for P_{NO}.

$$K = \frac{P_{NO}^3}{P_{N_2O}P_{NO_2}}$$

Solution: $\Delta G_{rxn}^\circ = -RT \ln K$ Rearrange to solve for K.

$$K = e^{\frac{-\Delta G_{rxn}^\circ}{RT}} = e^{\frac{-(+107.8 \text{ kJ}) \times \frac{1000 \text{ J}}{1 \text{ kJ}}}{\left(8.314 \frac{J}{K \cdot mol}\right)(298 \text{ K})}} = e^{-43.5103} = 1.27 \times 10^{-19} \text{ Because } K = \frac{P_{NO}^3}{P_{N_2O}P_{NO_2}}, \text{ rearrange to}$$

solve for P_{NO}. $P_{NO}^3 = \sqrt[3]{K\, P_{N_2O}P_{NO_2}} = \sqrt[3]{(1.27 \times 10^{-19})(1.0)(1.0)} = 5.0 \times 10^{-7}$ atm

Note that the assumption that P_{NO} was very, very small was valid.

Check: The units (atm) are correct. Because the free energy change was positive, the K was very small. This leads us to expect that very little NO will be formed.

(c) **Given:** $N_2O(g) + NO_2(g) \rightleftharpoons 3\,NO(g)$ **Find:** temperature for spontaneity

Conceptual Plan: $\Delta H_{rxn}^\circ = \sum n_p H_f^\circ \text{(products)} - \sum n_r H_f^\circ \text{(reactants)}$ then

$\Delta S_{rxn}^\circ = \sum n_p S^\circ \text{(products)} - \sum n_r S^\circ \text{(reactants)}$ then J/K $\rightarrow$ kJ/K then ΔH_{rxn}°, $\Delta S_{rxn} \rightarrow T$

$$\frac{1 \text{ kJ}}{1000 \text{ J}} \qquad \Delta G = \Delta H_{rxn} - T\Delta S_{rxn}$$

Solution:

Reactant/Product	ΔH_f° (kJ/mol from Appendix IIB)
$N_2O(g)$	81.6
$NO_2(g)$	33.2
$NO(g)$	91.3

Be sure to pull data for the correct formula and phase.

$$\begin{aligned}
\Delta H_{rxn}^\circ &= \sum n_p \Delta H_f^\circ \text{(products)} - \sum n_r \Delta H_f^\circ \text{(reactants)} \\
&= [3(\Delta H_f^\circ (NO(g)))] - [1(\Delta H_f^\circ (N_2O(g))) + 1(\Delta H_f^\circ (NO_2(g)))] \\
&= [3(91.3 \text{ kJ})] - [1(81.6 \text{ kJ}) + 1(33.2 \text{ kJ})] \\
&= [273.9 \text{ kJ}] - [114.8 \text{ kJ}] \\
&= +159.1 \text{ kJ then}
\end{aligned}$$

Reactant/Product	S° (J/mol · K from Appendix IIB)
$N_2O(g)$	220.0
$NO_2(g)$	240.1
$NO(g)$	210.8

Be sure to pull data for the correct formula and phase.

$$\begin{aligned}
\Delta S_{rxn}^\circ &= \sum n_p S^\circ \text{(products)} - \sum n_r S^\circ \text{(reactants)} \\
&= [3(S^\circ (NO(g)))] - [1(S^\circ (N_2O(g))) + 1(S^\circ (NO_2(g)))] \\
&= [3(210.8 \text{ J/K})] - [1(220.0 \text{ J/K}) + 1(240.1 \text{ J/K})] \\
&= [632.4 \text{ J/K}] - [460.1 \text{ J/K}] \\
&= +172.3 \text{ J/K}
\end{aligned}$$

then $+172.3 \dfrac{J}{K} \times \dfrac{1 \text{ kJ}}{1000 \text{ J}} = +0.1723$ kJ/K. Because $\Delta G = \Delta H_{rxn} - T\Delta S_{rxn}$, set $\Delta G = 0$ and rearrange to solve

for T. $T = \dfrac{\Delta H_{rxn}}{\Delta S_{rxn}} = \dfrac{+159.1 \text{ kJ}}{0.1723 \dfrac{kJ}{K}} = +923.4$ K

Check: The units (K) are correct. The reaction can be made more spontaneous by raising the temperature because the entropy change is positive (increase in the number of moles of gas).

17.57   (a)   **Given:** ATP(aq) + H$_2$O(l) → ADP(aq) + P$_i$(aq) ΔG°_{rxn} = −30.5 kJ at 298 K   **Find:** K

Conceptual Plan: $\Delta G^\circ_{rxn}, T \rightarrow K$

$$\Delta G^\circ_{rxn} = -RT \ln K$$

Solution: $\Delta G^\circ_{rxn} = -RT \ln K$ Rearrange to solve for K.

$$K = e^{\frac{-\Delta G^\circ_{rxn}}{RT}} = e^{\dfrac{-(-30.5\ \cancel{kJ}) \times \frac{1000\ J}{1\ \cancel{kJ}}}{\left(8.314\frac{J}{\cancel{K}\cdot mol}\right)(298\ \cancel{K})}} = e^{12.3104} = 2.22 \times 10^5$$

Check: The units (none) are correct. The free energy change is negative, and the reaction is spontaneous. This results in a large K.

(b)   **Given:** oxidation of glucose drives reforming of ATP   **Find:** ΔG°_{rxn} of oxidation of glucose and moles ATP formed per mole of glucose

Conceptual Plan: Write a balanced reaction for glucose oxidation then
$$\Delta G^\circ_{rxn} = \sum n_p \Delta G^\circ_f \text{ (products)} - \sum n_r \Delta G^\circ_f \text{ (reactants) then } \Delta G^\circ_{rxn}s \rightarrow \text{ moles ATP/mole glucose.}$$

$$\frac{\Delta G^\circ_{rxn} \text{ glucose oxidation}}{\Delta G^\circ_{rxn} \text{ ATP hydrolysis}}$$

Solution: C$_6$H$_{12}$O$_6$(s) + 6 O$_2$(g) → 6 CO$_2$(g) + 6 H$_2$O(l)

Reactant/Product	ΔG°_f (kJ/mol from Appendix IIB)
C$_6$H$_{12}$O$_6$(s)	−910.4
O$_2$(g)	0.0
CO$_2$(g)	−394.4
H$_2$O(l)	−237.1

Be sure to pull data for the correct formula and phase.

$$\begin{aligned}
\Delta G^\circ_{rxn} &= \sum n_p \Delta G^\circ_f \text{ (products)} - \sum n_r \Delta G^\circ_f \text{ (reactants)} \\
&= [6(\Delta G^\circ_f (CO_2(g))) + 6(\Delta G^\circ_f (H_2O(l)))] - [1(\Delta G^\circ_f (C_6H_{12}O_6(s))) + 6(\Delta G^\circ_f (O_2(g)))] \\
&= [6(-394.4\ kJ) + 6(-237.1\ kJ)] - [1(-910.4\ kJ) + 6(0.0\ kJ)] \\
&= [-3789.0\ kJ] - [-910.4\ kJ] \\
&= -2878.6\ kJ
\end{aligned}$$

So the reaction is very spontaneous. $\dfrac{2878.6\ \dfrac{kJ\ \text{generated}}{\text{mole glucose oxidized}}}{30.5\ \dfrac{kJ\ \text{needed}}{\text{mole ATP reformed}}} = 94.4\ \dfrac{\text{mole ATP reformed}}{\text{mole glucose oxidized}}$

Check: The units (mol) are correct. The free energy change for the glucose oxidation is large compared to the ATP hydrolysis, so we expect to reform many moles of ATP.

17.59   (a)   **Given:** 2 CO(g) + 2 NO(g) → N$_2$(g) + 2 CO$_2$(g)   **Find:** ΔG°_{rxn} and effect of increasing T on ΔG

Conceptual Plan: $\Delta G^\circ_{rxn} = \sum n_p \Delta G^\circ_f \text{ (products)} - \sum n_r \Delta G^\circ_f \text{ (reactants)}$

Solution:

Reactant/Product	ΔG°_f (kJ/mol from Appendix IIB)
CO(g)	−137.2
NO(g)	87.6
N$_2$(g)	0.0
CO$_2$(g)	−394.4

Be sure to pull data for the correct formula and phase.

$$\begin{aligned}
\Delta G^\circ_{rxn} &= \sum n_p \Delta G^\circ_f \text{ (products)} - \sum n_r \Delta G^\circ_f \text{ (reactants)} \\
&= [1(\Delta G^\circ_f (N_2(g))) + 2(\Delta G^\circ_f (CO_2(g)))] - [2(\Delta G^\circ_f (CO(g))) + 2(\Delta G^\circ_f (NO(g)))] \\
&= [1(0.0\ kJ) + 2(-394.4\ kJ)] - [2(-137.2\ kJ) + 2(87.6\ kJ)] \\
&= [-788.8\ kJ] - [-99.2\ kJ] \\
&= -689.6\ kJ
\end{aligned}$$

Because the number of moles of gas is decreasing, the entropy change is negative; ΔG will become less negative with increasing temperature.

Check: The units (kJ) are correct. The free energy change is negative because the carbon dioxide has such a low free energy of formation.

(b)   **Given:** $5 H_2(g) + 2 NO(g) \rightarrow 2 NH_3(g) + 2 H_2O(g)$ **Find:** ΔG°_{rxn} and effect of increasing T on ΔG
Conceptual Plan: $\Delta G^\circ_{rxn} = \sum n_p \Delta G^\circ_f \text{(products)} - \sum n_r \Delta G^\circ_f \text{(reactants)}$
Solution:

Reactant/Product	ΔG°_f (kJ/mol from Appendix IIB)
$H_2(g)$	0.0
$NO(g)$	87.6
$NH_3(g)$	−16.4
$H_2O(g)$	−228.6

Be sure to pull data for the correct formula and phase.
$$\Delta G^\circ_{rxn} = \sum n_p \Delta G^\circ_f \text{(products)} - \sum n_r \Delta G^\circ_f \text{(reactants)}$$
$$= [2(\Delta G^\circ_f (NH_3(g))) + 2(\Delta G^\circ_f (H_2O(g)))] - [5(\Delta G^\circ_f (H_2(g))) + 2(\Delta G^\circ_f (NO(g)))]$$
$$= [2(-16.4 \text{ kJ}) + 2(-228.6 \text{ kJ})] - [5(0.0 \text{ kJ}) + 2(87.6 \text{ kJ})]$$
$$= [-490.0 \text{ kJ}] - [175.2 \text{ kJ}]$$
$$= -665.2 \text{ kJ}$$

Because the number of moles of gas is decreasing, the entropy change is negative; so ΔG will become less negative with increasing temperature.

Check: The units (kJ) are correct. The free energy change is negative because ammonia and water have such a low free energy of formation.

(c)   **Given:** $2 H_2(g) + 2 NO(g) \rightarrow N_2(g) + 2 H_2O(g)$ **Find:** ΔG°_{rxn} and effect of increasing T on ΔG
Conceptual Plan: $\Delta G^\circ_{rxn} = \sum n_p \Delta G^\circ_f \text{(products)} - \sum n_r \Delta G^\circ_f \text{(reactants)}$
Solution:

Reactant/Product	ΔG°_f (kJ/mol from Appendix IIB)
$H_2(g)$	0.0
$NO(g)$	87.6
$N_2(g)$	0.0
$H_2O(g)$	−228.6

Be sure to pull data for the correct formula and phase.
$$\Delta G^\circ_{rxn} = \sum n_p \Delta G^\circ_f \text{(products)} - \sum n_r \Delta G^\circ_f \text{(reactants)}$$
$$= [1(\Delta G^\circ_f (N_2(g))) + 2(\Delta G^\circ_f (H_2O(g)))] - [2(\Delta G^\circ_f (H_2(g))) + 2(\Delta G^\circ_f (NO(g)))]$$
$$= [1(0.0 \text{ kJ}) + 2(-228.6 \text{ kJ})] - [2(0.0 \text{ kJ}) + 2(87.6 \text{ kJ})]$$
$$= [-457.2 \text{ kJ}] - [175.2 \text{ kJ}]$$
$$= -632.4 \text{ kJ}$$

Because the number of moles of gas is decreasing, the entropy change is negative; so ΔG will become less negative with increasing temperature.

Check: The units (kJ) are correct. The free energy change is negative because water has such a low free energy of formation.

(d)   **Given:** $2 NH_3(g) + 2 O_2(g) \rightarrow N_2O(g) + 3 H_2O(g)$ **Find:** ΔG°_{rxn} and effect of increasing T on ΔG
Conceptual Plan: $\Delta G^\circ_{rxn} = \sum n_p \Delta G^\circ_f \text{(products)} - \sum n_r \Delta G^\circ_f \text{(reactants)}$
Solution:

Reactant/Product	ΔG°_f (kJ/mol from Appendix IIB)
$NH_3(g)$	−16.4
$O_2(g)$	0.0
$N_2O(g)$	103.7
$H_2O(g)$	−228.6

Be sure to pull data for the correct formula and phase.
$$\Delta G^\circ_{rxn} = \sum n_p \Delta G^\circ_f \text{(products)} - \sum n_r \Delta G^\circ_f \text{(reactants)}$$

$$= [1(\Delta G_f^\circ (N_2O(g))) + 3(\Delta G_f^\circ (H_2O(g)))] - [2(\Delta G_f^\circ (NH_3(g))) + 2(\Delta G_f^\circ (O_2(g)))]$$
$$= [1(103.7 \text{ kJ}) + 3(-228.6 \text{ kJ})] - [2(-16.4 \text{ kJ}) + 2(0.0 \text{ kJ})]$$
$$= [-582.1 \text{ kJ}] - [-32.8 \text{ kJ}]$$
$$= -549.3 \text{ kJ}$$

Because the number of moles of gas is constant, the entropy change will be small and slightly negative; so the magnitude of ΔG will decrease with increasing temperature.

Check: The units (kJ) are correct. The free energy change is negative because water has such a low free energy of formation. The entropy change is negative once the S° values are reviewed ($\Delta S_{rxn} = -9.6$ J/K).

17.61 With one exception, the formation of any oxide of nitrogen at 298 K requires more moles of gas as reactants than are formed as products. For example, 1 mole of N_2O requires 0.5 mole of O_2 and 1 mole of N_2. 1 mole of N_2O_3 requires 1 mole of N_2 and 1.5 moles of O_2, and so on. The exception is NO, where 1 mole of NO requires 0.5 mole of O_2 and 0.5 mole of N_2: $\frac{1}{2} N_2(g) + \frac{1}{2} O_2(g) \rightarrow NO(g)$. This reaction has a positive ΔS because what is essentially mixing of the N and O has taken place in the product.

Challenge Problems

17.63 (a) **Given:** glutamate(aq) + $NH_3(aq)$ → glutamine(aq) + $H_2O(l)$ $\Delta G_{rxn}^\circ = 14.2$ kJ at 298 K $\quad$ **Find:** K
Conceptual Plan: $\Delta G_{rxn}^\circ, T \rightarrow K$
$$\Delta G_{rxn}^\circ = -RT \ln K$$
Solution: $\Delta G_{rxn}^\circ = -RT \ln K$ Rearrange to solve for K.

$$K = e^{\frac{-\Delta G_{rxn}^\circ}{RT}} = e^{\frac{-(+14.2 \text{ kJ}) \times \frac{1000 \text{ J}}{1 \text{ kJ}}}{\left(8.314 \frac{\text{J}}{\text{K} \cdot \text{mol}}\right)(298 \text{ K})}} = e^{-5.73142} = 3.24 \times 10^{-3}$$

Check: The units (none) are correct. The free energy change is positive, and the reaction is nonspontaneous. This results in a small K.

(b) **Given:** pair ATP hydrolysis with glutamate/NH_3 reaction $\quad$ **Find:** show coupled reactions, ΔG_{rxn}° and K
Conceptual Plan: Use the reaction mechanism shown, where A = NH_3 and B = glutamate ($C_5H_8O_4N^-$), then calculate ΔG_{rxn}° by adding free energies of reactions then $\Delta G_{rxn}^\circ, T \rightarrow K$.
$$\Delta G_{rxn}^\circ = -RT \ln K$$

Solution:

$NH_3(aq) + ATP(aq) + \cancel{H_2O(l)} \rightarrow NH_3\text{—}\cancel{P_i(aq)} + ADP(aq)$	$\Delta G_{rxn}^\circ = -30.5$ kJ
$\cancel{NH_3\text{—}P_i(aq)} + C_5H_8O_4N^-(aq) \rightarrow C_5H_9O_3N_2^-(aq) + \cancel{H_2O(l)} + P_i(aq)$	$\Delta G_{rxn}^\circ = +14.2$ kJ
$NH_3(aq) + C_5H_8O_4N^-(aq) + ATP(aq) \rightarrow C_5H_9O_3N_2^-(aq) + ADP(aq) + P_i(aq)$	$\Delta G_{rxn}^\circ = -16.3$ kJ

then $\Delta G_{rxn}^\circ = -RT \ln K$ Rearrange to solve for K.

$$K = e^{\frac{-\Delta G_{rxn}^\circ}{RT}} = e^{\frac{-(-16.3 \text{ kJ}) \times \frac{1000 \text{ J}}{1 \text{ kJ}}}{\left(8.314 \frac{\text{J}}{\text{K} \cdot \text{mol}}\right)(298 \text{ K})}} = e^{6.57902} = 7.20 \times 10^2$$

Check: The units (none) are correct. The free energy change is negative, and the reaction is spontaneous. This results in a large K.

17.65 (a) **Given:** $\frac{1}{2} H_2(g) + \frac{1}{2} Cl_2(g) \rightarrow HCl(g)$, define standard state as 2 atm $\quad$ **Find:** ΔG_f°
Conceptual Plan: $\Delta G_f^\circ, P_{H_2}, P_{Cl_2}, P_{HCl}, T \rightarrow$ new ΔG_f°
$$\Delta G_{rxn} = \Delta G_{rxn}^\circ + RT \ln Q \text{ where } Q = \frac{P_{HCl}}{P_{H_2}^{1/2} P_{Cl_2}^{1/2}}$$

Solution: $\Delta G_{rxn}^\circ = -95.3$ kJ/mol and $Q = \dfrac{P_{HCl}}{P_{H_2}^{1/2} P_{Cl_2}^{1/2}} = \dfrac{2}{2^{1/2} 2^{1/2}} = 1$ then

$$\Delta G_{rxn} = \Delta G_{rxn}^\circ + RT \ln Q = -95.3 \frac{\text{kJ}}{\text{mol}} + \left(8.314 \frac{\text{J}}{\text{K} \cdot \text{mol}}\right)\left(\frac{1 \text{ kJ}}{1000 \text{ J}}\right)(298 \text{ K}) \ln(1) =$$

$$-95.3 \text{ kJ/mol} = -95,300 \text{ J/mol}$$

Because the number of moles of reactants and products are the same, the decrease in volume affects the entropy of both equally; so there is no change in ΔG_f°.

Check: The units (kJ) are correct. The Q is 1, so ΔG_f° is unchanged under the new standard conditions.

(b)   **Given:** $N_2(g) + \frac{1}{2} O_2(g) \rightarrow N_2O(g)$, define standard state as 2 atm   **Find:** ΔG_f°
     Conceptual Plan: $\Delta G_f^\circ, P_{N_2}, P_{O_2}, P_{N_2O}, T \rightarrow$ **new** ΔG_f°

$$\Delta G_{rxn} = \Delta G_{rxn}^\circ + RT \ln Q \text{ where } Q = \frac{P_{N_2O}}{P_{N_2} P_{O_2}^{1/2}}$$

     Solution: $\Delta G_f^\circ = +103.7$ kJ/mol and $Q = \dfrac{P_{N_2O}}{P_{N_2} P_{O_2}^{1/2}} = \dfrac{2}{2 \, 2^{1/2}} = \dfrac{1}{\sqrt{2}}$ then

$$\Delta G_{rxn} = \Delta G_{rxn}^\circ + RT \ln Q = 103.7 \, \frac{\text{kJ}}{\text{mol}} + \left(8.314 \, \frac{\text{J}}{\text{K} \cdot \text{mol}}\right)\left(\frac{1 \text{ kJ}}{1000 \text{ J}}\right)(298 \text{ K}) \ln\left(\frac{1}{\sqrt{2}}\right) =$$

$+102.8$ kJ/mol $= +102,800$ J/mol

The entropy of the reactants (1.5 mol) is decreased more than the entropy of the product (1 mol). Because the product is relatively more favored at lower volume, ΔG_f° is less positive.

Check: The units (kJ) are correct. The Q is less than 1, so ΔG_f° is reduced under the new standard conditions.

(c)   **Given:** $1/2 \, H_2(g) \rightarrow H(g)$, define standard state as 2 atm   **Find:** ΔG_f°
     Conceptual Plan: $\Delta G_f^\circ, P_{H_2}, P_H, T \rightarrow$ **new** ΔG_f°

$$\Delta G_{rxn} = \Delta G_{rxn}^\circ + RT \ln Q \text{ where } Q = \frac{P_H}{P_{H_2}^{1/2}}$$

     Solution: $\Delta G_f^\circ = +203.3$ kJ/mol and $Q = \dfrac{P_H}{P_{H_2}^{1/2}} = \dfrac{2}{2^{1/2}} = \sqrt{2}$ then

$$\Delta G_{rxn} = \Delta G_{rxn}^\circ + RT \ln Q = +203.3 \, \frac{\text{kJ}}{\text{mol}} + \left(8.314 \, \frac{\text{J}}{\text{K} \cdot \text{mol}}\right)\left(\frac{1 \text{ kJ}}{1000 \text{ J}}\right)(298 \text{ K}) \ln(\sqrt{2}) =$$

$+204.2$ kJ/mol $= +204,200$ J/mol

The entropy of the product (1 mol) is decreased more than the entropy of the reactant (1/2 mol). Because the product is relatively less favored, ΔG_f° is more positive.

Check: The units (kJ) are correct. The Q is greater than 1, so ΔG_f° is increased under the new standard conditions.

17.67   (a)   **Given:** $NH_4NO_3(s) \rightarrow HNO_3(g) + NH_3(g)$ **Find:** ΔG_{rxn}°
       Conceptual Plan: $\Delta G_{rxn}^\circ = \sum n_p \Delta G_f^\circ (\text{products}) - \sum n_r \Delta G_f^\circ (\text{reactants})$
       Solution:

Reactant/Product	ΔG_f° (kJ/mol from Appendix IIB)
$NH_4NO_3(s)$	-183.9
$HNO_3(g)$	-73.5
$NH_3(g)$	-16.4

Be sure to pull data for the correct formula and phase.

$$\begin{aligned}
\Delta G_{rxn}^\circ &= \sum n_p \Delta G_f^\circ (\text{products}) - \sum n_r \Delta G_f^\circ (\text{reactants}) \\
&= [1(\Delta G_f^\circ (HNO_3(g))) + 1(\Delta G_f^\circ (NH_3(g)))] - [1(\Delta G_f^\circ (NH_4NO_3(s)))] \\
&= [1(-73.5 \text{ kJ}) + 1(-16.4 \text{ kJ})] - [1(-183.9 \text{ kJ})] \\
&= [-89.9 \text{ kJ}] - [-183.9 \text{ kJ}] \\
&= +94.0 \text{ kJ}
\end{aligned}$$

Check: The units (kJ) are correct. The free energy change is positive because ammonium nitrate has such a low free energy of formation.

(b)   **Given:** $NH_4NO_3(s) \rightarrow N_2O(g) + 2 \, H_2O(g)$ **Find:** ΔG_{rxn}°
       Conceptual Plan: $\Delta G_{rxn}^\circ = \sum n_p \Delta G_f^\circ (\text{products}) - \sum n_r \Delta G_f^\circ (\text{reactants})$

Solution:

Reactant/Product	ΔG_f° (kJ/mol from Appendix IIB)
$NH_4NO_3(s)$	-183.9
$N_2O(g)$	103.7
$H_2O(g)$	-228.6

Be sure to pull data for the correct formula and phase.

$$\Delta G_{rxn}^\circ = \sum n_p \Delta G_f^\circ \text{(products)} - \sum n_r \Delta G_f^\circ \text{(reactants)}$$
$$= [1(\Delta G_f^\circ (N_2O(g))) + 2(\Delta G_f^\circ (H_2O(g)))] - [1(\Delta G_f^\circ (NH_4NO_3(s)))]$$
$$= [1(103.7 \text{ kJ}) + 2(-228.6 \text{ kJ})] - [1(-183.9 \text{ kJ})]$$
$$= [-353.5 \text{ kJ}] - [-183.9 \text{ kJ}]$$
$$= -169.6 \text{ kJ}$$

Check: The units (kJ) are correct. The free energy change is negative because water has such a low free energy of formation.

(c) **Given:** $NH_4NO_3(s) \rightarrow N_2(g) + \frac{1}{2}O_2(g) + 2 H_2O(g)$ **Find:** ΔG_{rxn}°
Conceptual Plan: $\Delta G_{rxn}^\circ = \sum n_p \Delta G_f^\circ \text{(products)} - \sum n_r \Delta G_f^\circ \text{(reactants)}$
Solution:

Reactant/Product	ΔG_f° (kJ/mol from Appendix IIB)
$NH_4NO_3(s)$	-183.9
$N_2(g)$	0.0
$O_2(g)$	0.0
$H_2O(g)$	-228.6

Be sure to pull data for the correct formula and phase.

$$\Delta G_{rxn}^\circ = \sum n_p \Delta G_f^\circ \text{(products)} - \sum n_p \Delta G_f^\circ \text{(reactants)}$$
$$= [1(\Delta G_f^\circ (N_2(g))) + 1/2(\Delta G_f^\circ (O_2(g))) + 2(\Delta G_f^\circ (H_2O(g)))] - [1(\Delta G_f^\circ (NH_4NO_3(s)))]$$
$$= [1(0.0 \text{ kJ}) + 1/2(0.0 \text{ kJ}) + 2(-228.6 \text{ kJ})] - [1(-183.9 \text{ kJ})]$$
$$= [-457.2 \text{ kJ}] - [-183.9 \text{ kJ}]$$
$$= -273.3 \text{ kJ}$$

Check: The units (kJ) are correct. The free energy change is negative because water has such a low free energy of formation.

The second and third reactions are spontaneous, so we would expect decomposition products of N_2O, N_2, O_2, and H_2O in the gas phase. It is still possible for ammonium nitrate to remain as a solid because the thermodynamics of the reaction say nothing of the kinetics of the reaction (reaction can be extremely slow). Because all of the products are gases, the decomposition of ammonium nitrate will result in a large increase in volume (explosion). Some of the products aid in combustion, which could facilitate the combustion of materials near the ammonium nitrate. Also, N_2O is known as laughing gas, which has anesthetic and toxic effects on humans. The solid should not be kept in tightly sealed containers.

17.69 **Given:** ΔH_{vap}° table **Find:** ΔS_{vap}; then compare values
Conceptual Plan: °C $\rightarrow$ K then ΔH_{vap}°, $T \rightarrow \Delta S_{vap}$

$$K = 273.15 + °C \qquad \Delta S_{vap} = \frac{-\Delta H_{vap}}{T}$$

Solution:

Diethyl ether: $T = 273.15 + 34.6 = 307.8$ K then $\Delta S_{vap} = \dfrac{\Delta H_{vap}}{T} = \dfrac{26.5 \text{ kJ}}{307.8 \text{ K}} = 0.0861$ kJ/K $= 86.1$ J/K

Acetone: $T = 273.15 + 56.1 = 329.3$ K then $\Delta S_{vap} = \dfrac{\Delta H_{vap}}{T} = \dfrac{29.1 \text{ kJ}}{329.3 \text{ K}} = 0.0884$ kJ/K $= 88.4$ J/K

Benzene: $T = 273.15 + 79.8 = 353.0$ K then $\Delta S_{vap} = \dfrac{\Delta H_{vap}}{T} = \dfrac{30.8 \text{ kJ}}{353.0 \text{ K}} = 0.0873$ kJ/K $= 87.3$ J/K

Chloroform: $T = 273.15 + 60.8 = 334.0$ K then $\Delta S_{vap} = \dfrac{\Delta H_{vap}}{T} = \dfrac{29.4 \text{ kJ}}{334.0 \text{ K}} = 0.0880$ kJ/K $= 88.0$ J/K

Ethanol: $T = 273.15 + 77.8 = 351.0 \text{ K then } \Delta S_{vap} = \dfrac{\Delta H_{vap}}{T} = \dfrac{38.6 \text{ kJ}}{351.0 \text{ K}} = 0.110 \text{ kJ/K} = 110. \text{ J/K}$

Water: $T = 273.15 + 100 = 373.15 \text{ K then } \Delta S_{vap} = \dfrac{\Delta H_{vap}}{T} = \dfrac{40.7 \text{ kJ}}{373.15 \text{ K}} = 0.109 \text{ kJ/K} = 109 \text{ J/K}$

The first four values are very similar because they have similar intermolecular forces between molecules (dispersion forces and/or dipole–dipole interactions). The values for ethanol and water are higher because the intermolecular forces between molecules are stronger due to hydrogen bonding. Because of this, more energy is dispersed when these interactions are broken.

Conceptual Problems

17.71   (c) The spontaneity of a reaction says nothing about the speed of a reaction. It only states which direction the reaction will go as it approaches equilibrium.

17.73   (b) has the largest decrease in the number of microstates from the initial to the final state. In (a), there are initially

$\dfrac{9!}{4! \, 4! \, 1!} = 90$ microstates and $\dfrac{9!}{3! \, 3! \, 3!} = 1680$ microstates at the end; so $\Delta S > 0$. In (b), there are initially

$\dfrac{9!}{4! \, 2! \, 3!} = 1260$ microstates and $\dfrac{9!}{6! \, 3! \, 0!} = 84$ microstates at the end; so $\Delta S < 0$. In (c), there are initially

$\dfrac{9!}{3! \, 4! \, 2!} = 1260$ microstates and $\dfrac{9!}{3! \, 4! \, 2!} = 1260$ microstates at the end; so $\Delta S = 0$. Also, the final state in (b) has the least entropy.

17.75   (c) Because the vapor pressure of water at 298 K is 23.78 mmHg or 0.03129 atm. As long as the desired pressure (0.010 atm) is less than the equilibrium vapor pressure of water, the reaction will be spontaneous.

17.77   (c) The relationship between ΔG_{rxn}° and K is $\Delta G_{rxn}^{\circ} = -RT \ln K$. When $K > 1$, then the natural log of K is positive and $\Delta G_{rxn}^{\circ} < 0$. When $Q = 336$, the second term in $\Delta G_{rxn} = \Delta G_{rxn}^{\circ} + RT \ln Q$ is positive, and so at high temperature this term can dominate and make $\Delta G_{rxn} > 0$.

Questions for Group Work

17.79   The average of all of the dice will be 3.5 (one-sixth will be 1; one-sixth will be 2, one-sixth will be 3, …) or

$$\dfrac{\left(\frac{1}{6} \times 1 \times 10^6\right) + \left(\frac{1}{6} \times 2 \times 10^6\right) + \left(\frac{1}{6} \times 3 \times 10^6\right) + \left(\frac{1}{6} \times 4 \times 10^6\right) + \left(\frac{1}{6} \times 5 \times 10^6\right) + \left(\frac{1}{6} \times 6 \times 10^6\right)}{10^6} =$$

$\dfrac{1}{6}(1 + 2 + 3 + 4 + 5 + 6) = \dfrac{1}{6}(21) = 3.5$

It is very unlikely $\left(\left(\dfrac{1}{6}\right)^{10^6}\right)$ that the sum would be one million after the earthquake because they would all have to

be 1s. It is just as unlikely that the sum would be six million after the earthquake because they would all have to be 6s. The total would be close to 3.5 million (1 million times the average); this illustrates the second law because the numbers on the dice are maximizing their dispersal.

17.81 $3 \, O_2(g) + 6 \, H_2(g) + 6 \, C(s, \text{graphite}) \rightarrow C_6H_{12}O_6(s, \text{glucose})$

	ΔH_f°(kJ/mol)	S°(J/K · mol)
$O_2(g)$	0	205.2
$H_2(g)$	0	130.7
$C(s, \text{graphite})$	0	5.7
$C_6H_{12}O_6(s, \text{glucose})$	−1273.3	212.1

$$\Delta H^{\circ}_{rxn} = \sum n_P \Delta H^{\circ}_f (\text{products}) - \sum n_R \Delta H^{\circ}_f (\text{reactants})$$
$$= [1(\Delta H^{\circ}_f (C_6H_{12}O_6(s, \text{glucose})))] - [3(\Delta H^{\circ}_f (O_2(g)) + 6(\Delta H^{\circ}_f (H_2(g)) + 6(\Delta H^{\circ}_f (C(s, \text{graphite})))]$$
$$= [1(-1273.3 \text{ kJ})] - [3(0.0 \text{ kJ}) + 6(0.0 \text{ kJ}) + 6(0.0 \text{ kJ})]$$
$$= [-1273.3 \text{ kJ}] - [0.0 \text{ kJ}]$$
$$= -1273.3 \text{ kJ} = \Delta H^{\circ}_f(C_6H_{12}O_6 (s, \text{glucose})$$

$$\Delta S^{\circ}_{rxn} = \sum n_P S^{\circ}(\text{products}) - \sum n_R S^{\circ}(\text{reactants})$$
$$= [1(S^{\circ}(C_6H_{12}O_6(s, \text{glucose})))] - [3(S^{\circ}(O_2(g)) + 6(S^{\circ}(H_2(g)) + 6(S^{\circ}(C(s, \text{graphite})))]$$
$$= [1(212.1 \text{ J/K})] - [3(205.2 \text{ J/K}) + 6(130.7 \text{ J/K}) + 6(5.7 \text{ J/K})]$$
$$= [-212.1 \text{ J/K}] - [1434.0 \text{ J/K}]$$
$$= -1221.9 \text{ kJ}$$

ΔH°_f is zero for an element in its standard state at 25 °C. S° is zero only for a perfect crystal at 0 K.

18 Electrochemistry

Balancing Redox Reactions

18.1   **Conceptual Plan: Separate the overall reaction into two half-reactions: one for oxidation and one for reduction. → Balance each half-reaction with respect to mass in the following order: (1) Balance all elements other than H and O, (2) balance O by adding H_2O, and (3) balance H by adding H^+. → Balance each half-reaction with respect to charge by adding electrons. (The sum of the charges on both sides of the equation should be made equal by adding electrons as necessary.) → Make the number of electrons in both half-reactions equal by multiplying one or both half-reactions by a small whole number. → Add the two half-reactions together, canceling electrons and other species as necessary. → Verify that the reaction is balanced with respect to both mass and charge.**

Solution:

(a)   Separate: $K(s) \rightarrow K^+(aq)$ and $Cr^{3+}(aq) \rightarrow Cr(s)$

Balance elements: $K(s) \rightarrow K^+(aq)$ and $Cr^{3+}(aq) \rightarrow Cr(s)$

Add electrons: $K(s) \rightarrow K^+(aq) + e^-$ and $Cr^{3+}(aq) + 3\,e^- \rightarrow Cr(s)$

Equalize electrons: $3\,K(s) \rightarrow 3\,K^+(aq) + 3\,e^-$ and $Cr^{3+}(aq) + 3\,e^- \rightarrow Cr(s)$

Add half-reactions: $3\,K(s) + Cr^{3+}(aq) + \cancel{3\,e^-} \rightarrow 3\,K^+(aq) + \cancel{3\,e^-} + Cr(s)$

Cancel electrons: $3\,K(s) + Cr^{3+}(aq) \rightarrow 3\,K^+(aq) + Cr(s)$

Check:

Reactants	Products
3 K atoms	3 K atoms
1 Cr atom	1 Cr atom
+3 charge	+3 charge

(b)   Separate: $Al(s) \rightarrow Al^{3+}(aq)$ and $Fe^{2+}(aq) \rightarrow Fe(s)$

Balance elements: $Al(s) \rightarrow Al^{3+}(aq)$ and $Fe^{2+}(aq) \rightarrow Fe(s)$

Add electrons: $Al(s) \rightarrow Al^{3+}(aq) + 3\,e^-$ and $Fe^{2+}(aq) + 2\,e^- \rightarrow Fe(s)$

Equalize electrons: $2\,Al(s) \rightarrow 2\,Al^{3+}(aq) + 6\,e^-$ and $3\,Fe^{2+}(aq) + 6\,e^- \rightarrow 3\,Fe(s)$

Add half-reactions: $2\,Al(s) + 3\,Fe^{2+}(aq) + \cancel{6\,e^-} \rightarrow 2\,Al^{3+}(aq) + \cancel{6\,e^-} + 3\,Fe(s)$

Cancel electrons: $2\,Al(s) + 3\,Fe^{2+}(aq) \rightarrow 2\,Al^{3+}(aq) + 3\,Fe(s)$

Check:

Reactants	Products
2 Al atoms	2 Al atoms
3 Fe atom	3 Fe atom
+6 charge	+6 charge

(c)   Separate: $BrO_3^-(aq) \rightarrow Br^-(aq)$ and $N_2H_4(g) \rightarrow N_2(g)$

Balance non-H & O elements: $BrO_3^-(aq) \rightarrow Br^-(aq)$ and $N_2H_4(g) \rightarrow N_2(g)$

Balance O with H_2O: $BrO_3^-(aq) \rightarrow Br^-(aq) + 3\,H_2O(l)$ and $N_2H_4(g) \rightarrow N_2(g)$

Balance H with H^+: $BrO_3^-(aq) + 6\,H^+(aq) \rightarrow Br^-(aq) + 3\,H_2O(l)$ and

$$N_2H_4(g) \rightarrow N_2(g) + 4\,H^+(aq)$$

Add electrons:

$BrO_3^-(aq) + 6\,H^+(aq) + 6\,e^- \rightarrow Br^-(aq) + 3\,H_2O(l)$ and $N_2H_4(g) \rightarrow N_2(g) + 4\,H^+(aq) + 4\,e^-$

Equalize electrons:

$2\,BrO_3^-(aq) + 12\,H^+(aq) + 12\,e^- \rightarrow 2\,Br^-(aq) + 6\,H_2O(l)$ and $3\,N_2H_4(g) \rightarrow 3\,N_2(g) + 12\,H^+(aq) + 12\,e^-$

Add half-reactions: $2\,BrO_3^-(aq) + \cancel{12\,H^+(aq)} + 3\,N_2H_4(g) + \cancel{12\,e^-} \rightarrow 2\,Br^-(aq) + 6\,H_2O\,(l) + 3\,N_2(g)$
$+ \cancel{12\,H^+(aq)} + \cancel{12\,e^-}$

Cancel electrons & others: $2\,BrO_3^-(aq) + 3\,N_2H_4(g) \rightarrow 2\,Br^-(aq) + 6\,H_2O\,(l) + 3\,N_2(g)$

Check:

Reactants	Products
2 Br atoms	2 Br atoms
6 O atoms	6 O atoms
12 H atoms	12 H atoms
6 N atoms	6 N atoms
−2 charge	−2 charge

18.3   **Conceptual Plan: Separate the overall reaction into two half-reactions: one for oxidation and one for reduction. Balance each half-reaction with respect to mass in the following order: (1) Balance all elements other than H and O, (2) balance O by adding H_2O, and (3) balance H by adding H^+. → Balance each half-reaction with respect to charge by adding electrons. (The sum of the charges on both sides of the equation should be made equal by adding electrons as necessary.) → Make the number of electrons in both half-reactions equal by multiplying one or both half-reactions by a small whole number. → Add the two half-reactions together, canceling electrons and other species as necessary. → Verify that the reaction is balanced with respect to both mass and charge.**

Solution:

(a)   Separate: $PbO_2(s) \rightarrow Pb^{2+}(aq)$ and $I^-(aq) \rightarrow I_2(s)$

Balance non-H & O elements: $PbO_2(s) \rightarrow Pb^{2+}(aq)$ and $2\,I^-(aq) \rightarrow I_2(s)$

Balance O with H_2O: $PbO_2(s) \rightarrow Pb^{2+}(aq) + 2\,H_2O(l)$ and $2\,I^-(aq) \rightarrow I_2(s)$

Balance H with H^+: $PbO_2(s) + 4\,H^+(aq) \rightarrow Pb^{2+}(aq) + 2\,H_2O(l)$ and $2\,I^-(aq) \rightarrow I_2(s)$

Add electrons: $PbO_2(s) + 4\,H^+(aq) + 2\,e^- \rightarrow Pb^{2+}(aq) + 2\,H_2O(l)$ and $2\,I^-(aq) \rightarrow I_2(s) + 2\,e^-$

Equalize electrons: $PbO_2(s) + 4\,H^+(aq) + 2\,e^- \rightarrow Pb^{2+}(aq) + 2\,H_2O(l)$ and $2\,I^-(aq) \rightarrow I_2(s) + 2\,e^-$

Add half-reactions: $PbO_2(s) + 4\,H^+(aq) + \cancel{2\,e^-} + 2\,I^-(aq) \rightarrow Pb^{2+}(aq) + 2\,H_2O(l) + I_2(s) + \cancel{2\,e^-}$

Cancel electrons & others: $PbO_2(s) + 4\,H^+(aq) + 2\,I^-(aq) \rightarrow Pb^{2+}(aq) + 2\,H_2O(l) + I_2(s)$

Check:

Reactants	Products
1 Pb atom	1 Pb atom
2 O atoms	2 O atoms
4 H atoms	4 H atoms
2 I atoms	2 I atoms
+2 charge	+2 charge

(b)   Separate: $MnO_4^-(aq) \rightarrow Mn^{2+}(aq)$ and $SO_3^{2-}(aq) \rightarrow SO_4^{2-}(aq)$

Balance non-H & O elements: $MnO_4^-(aq) \rightarrow Mn^{2+}(aq)$ and $SO_3^{2-}(aq) \rightarrow SO_4^{2-}(aq)$

Balance O with H_2O: $MnO_4^-(aq) \rightarrow Mn^{2+}(aq) + 4\,H_2O(l)$ and $SO_3^{2-}(aq) + H_2O(l) \rightarrow SO_4^{2-}(aq)$

Balance H with H^+:

$MnO_4^-(aq) + 8\,H^+(aq) \rightarrow Mn^{2+}(aq) + 4\,H_2O(l)$ and $SO_3^{2-}(aq) + H_2O(l) \rightarrow SO_4^{2-}(aq) + 2\,H^+(aq)$

Add electrons: $MnO_4^-(aq) + 8\,H^+(aq) + 5\,e^- \rightarrow Mn^{2+}(aq) + 4\,H_2O(l)$ and
$SO_3^{2-}(aq) + H_2O\,(l) \rightarrow SO_4^{2-}(aq) + 2\,H^+(aq) + 2\,e^-$

Equalize electrons: $2\,MnO_4^-(aq) + 16\,H^+(aq) + 10\,e^- \rightarrow 2\,Mn^{2+}(aq) + 8\,H_2O(l)$ and
$5\,SO_3^{2-}(aq) + 5\,H_2O(l) \rightarrow 5\,SO_4^{2-}(aq) + 10\,H^+(aq) + 10\,e^-$

Add half-reactions: $2\,MnO_4^-(aq) + 6\,\cancel{16}\,H^+(aq) + \cancel{10\,e^-} + 5\,SO_3^{2-}(aq) + \cancel{5\,H_2O(l)} \rightarrow$
$2\,Mn^{2+}(aq) + 3\,\cancel{8}\,H_2O(l) + 5\,SO_4^{2-}(aq) + \cancel{10\,H^+(aq)} + \cancel{10\,e^-}$

Cancel electrons: $2\,MnO_4^-(aq) + 6\,H^+(aq) + 5\,SO_3^{2-}(aq) \rightarrow 2\,Mn^{2+}(aq) + 3\,H_2O\,(l) + 5\,SO_4^{2-}(aq)$

Check:

Reactants	Products
2 Mn atoms	2 Mn atoms
23 O atoms	23 O atoms
6 H atoms	6 H atoms
5 S atoms	5 S atoms
−6 charge	−6 charge

(c)   Separate: $S_2O_3^{2-}(aq) \rightarrow SO_4^{2-}(aq)$ and $Cl_2(g) \rightarrow Cl^-(aq)$

Balance non-H & O elements: $S_2O_3^{2-}(aq) \rightarrow 2\ SO_4^{2-}(aq)$ and $Cl_2(g) \rightarrow 2\ Cl^-(aq)$

Balance O with H_2O: $S_2O_3^{2-}(aq) + 5\ H_2O(l) \rightarrow 2\ SO_4^{2-}(aq)$ and $Cl_2(g) \rightarrow 2\ Cl^-(aq)$

Balance H with H^+: $S_2O_3^{2-}(aq) + 5\ H_2O(l) \rightarrow 2\ SO_4^{2-}(aq) + 10\ H^+(aq)$ and $Cl_2(g) \rightarrow 2\ Cl^-(aq)$

Add electrons:

     $S_2O_3^{2-}(aq) + 5\ H_2O(l) \rightarrow 2\ SO_4^{2-}(aq) + 10\ H^+(aq) + 8\ e^-$ and $Cl_2(g) + 2\ e^- \rightarrow 2\ Cl^-(aq)$

Equalize electrons:

     $S_2O_3^{2-}(aq) + 5\ H_2O(l) \rightarrow 2\ SO_4^{2-}(aq) + 10\ H^+(aq) + 8\ e^-$ and $4\ Cl_2(g) + 8\ e^- \rightarrow 8\ Cl^-(aq)$

Add half-reactions:

     $S_2O_3^{2-}(aq) + 5\ H_2O(l) + 4\ Cl_2(g) + \cancel{8\ e^-} \rightarrow 2\ SO_4^{2-}(aq) + 10\ H^+(aq) + \cancel{8\ e^-} + 8\ Cl^-(aq)$

Cancel electrons: $S_2O_3^{2-}(aq) + 5\ H_2O(l) + 4\ Cl_2(g) \rightarrow 2\ SO_4^{2-}(aq) + 10\ H^+(aq) + 8\ Cl^-(aq)$

Check:

Reactants	Products
2 S atoms	2 S atoms
8 O atoms	8 O atoms
10 H atoms	10 H atoms
8 Cl atoms	8 Cl atoms
−2 charge	−2 charge

18.5   **Conceptual Plan: Separate the overall reaction into two half-reactions: one for oxidation and one for reduction. → Balance each half-reaction with respect to mass in the following order: (1) Balance all elements other than H and O, (2) balance O by adding H_2O, (3) balance H by adding H^+, and (4) neutralize H^+ by adding enough OH^- to neutralize each H^+. Add the same number of OH^- ions to each side of the equation. → Balance each half-reaction with respect to charge by adding electrons. (The sum of the charges on both sides of the equation should be made equal by adding electrons as necessary.) → Make the number of electrons in both half-reactions equal by multiplying one or both half-reactions by a small whole number. → Add the two half-reactions together, canceling electrons and other species as necessary. → Verify that the reaction is balanced with respect to both mass and charge.**

Solution:

(a)   Separate: $ClO_2(aq) \rightarrow ClO_2^-(aq)$ and $H_2O_2(aq) \rightarrow O_2(g)$

Balance non-H & O elements: $ClO_2(aq) \rightarrow ClO_2^-(aq)$ and $H_2O_2(aq) \rightarrow O_2(g)$

Balance O with H_2O: $ClO_2(aq) \rightarrow ClO_2^-(aq)$ and $H_2O_2(aq) \rightarrow O_2(g)$

Balance H with H^+: $ClO_2(aq) \rightarrow ClO_2^-(aq)$ and $H_2O_2(aq) \rightarrow O_2(g) + 2\ H^+(aq)$

Neutralize H^+ with OH^-:

     $ClO_2(aq) \rightarrow ClO_2^-(aq)$ and $H_2O_2(aq) + 2\ OH^-(aq) \rightarrow O_2(g) + \underbrace{2\ H^+(aq) + 2\ OH^-(aq)}_{2\ H_2O(l)}$

Add electrons: $ClO_2(aq) + e^- \rightarrow ClO_2^-(aq)$ and $H_2O_2(aq) + 2\ OH^-(aq) \rightarrow O_2(g) + 2\ H_2O(l) + 2\ e^-$

Equalize electrons:

     $2\ ClO_2(aq) + 2\ e^- \rightarrow 2\ ClO_2^-(aq)$ and $H_2O_2(aq) + 2\ OH^-(aq) \rightarrow O_2(g) + 2\ H_2O(l) + 2\ e^-$

Add half-reactions:

     $2\ ClO_2(aq) + \cancel{2\ e^-} + H_2O_2(aq) + 2\ OH^-(aq) \rightarrow 2\ ClO_2^-(aq) + O_2(g) + 2\ H_2O(l) + \cancel{2\ e^-}$

Cancel electrons: $2\ ClO_2(aq) + H_2O_2(aq) + 2\ OH^-(aq) \rightarrow 2\ ClO_2^-(aq) + O_2(g) + 2\ H_2O(l)$

Check:

Reactants	Products
2 Cl atoms	2 Cl atoms
8 O atoms	8 O atoms
4 H atoms	4 H atoms
−2 charge	−2 charge

(b)   Separate: $MnO_4^-(aq) \rightarrow MnO_2(s)$ and $Al(s) \rightarrow Al(OH)_4^-(aq)$

Balance non-H & O elements: $MnO_4^-(aq) \rightarrow MnO_2(s)$ and $Al(s) \rightarrow Al(OH)_4^-(aq)$

Balance O with H_2O: $MnO_4^-(aq) \rightarrow MnO_2(s) + 2\ H_2O(l)$ and $Al(s) + 4\ H_2O(l) \rightarrow Al(OH)_4^-(aq)$

Balance H with H^+:

$MnO_4^-(aq) + 4\ H^+(aq) \rightarrow MnO_2(s) + 2\ H_2O(l)$ and $Al(s) + 4\ H_2O(l) \rightarrow Al(OH)_4^-(aq) + 4\ H^+(aq)$

Neutralize H^+ with OH^-: $MnO_4^- + \underbrace{4\ H^+(aq) + 4\ OH^-(aq)}_{2\ 4\ H_2O\ (l)} \rightarrow MnO_2(s) + 2\ \cancel{H_2O(l)} + 4\ OH^-(aq)$

and $Al(s) + \cancel{4\,H_2O(l)} + 4\,OH^-(aq) \rightarrow Al(OH)_4^-(aq) + \underbrace{4\,H^+(aq) + 4\,OH^-(aq)}_{\cancel{4\,H_2O(l)}}$

Add electrons: $MnO_4^-(aq) + 2\,H_2O(l) + 3\,e^- \rightarrow MnO_2(s) + 4\,OH^-(aq)$ and
$$Al(s) + 4\,OH^-(aq) \rightarrow Al(OH)_4^-(aq) + 3\,e^-$$

Equalize electrons: $MnO_4^-(aq) + 2\,H_2O(l) + 3\,e^- \rightarrow MnO_2(s) + 4\,OH^-(aq)$ and
$$Al(s) + 4\,OH^-(aq) \rightarrow Al(OH)_4^-(aq) + 3\,e^-$$

Add half-reactions:
$MnO_4^-(aq) + 2\,H_2O(l) + \cancel{3e^-} + Al(s) + \cancel{4\,OH^-(aq)} \rightarrow MnO_2(s) + \cancel{4\,OH^-(aq)} + Al(OH)_4^-(aq) + \cancel{3e^-}$
Cancel electrons: $MnO_4^-(aq) + 2\,H_2O(l) + Al(s) \rightarrow MnO_2(s) + Al(OH)_4^-(aq)$

Check:

Reactants	Products
1 Mn atom	1 Mn atom
6 O atoms	6 O atoms
4 H atoms	4 H atoms
1 Al atom	1 Al atom
−1 charge	−1 charge

(c)　Separate: 　　　　　　　　　$Cl_2(g) \rightarrow Cl^-(aq)$　and　$Cl_2(g) \rightarrow ClO^-(aq)$
Balance non-H & O elements: 　$Cl_2(g) \rightarrow 2\,Cl^-(aq)$　and　$Cl_2(g) \rightarrow 2ClO^-(aq)$
Balance O with H_2O: $Cl_2(g) \rightarrow 2\,Cl^-(aq)$　and　$Cl_2(g) + 2\,H_2O(l) \rightarrow 2\,ClO^-(aq)$
Balance H with H^+: $Cl_2(g) \rightarrow 2\,Cl^-(aq)$ and $Cl_2(g) + 2\,H_2O(l) \rightarrow 2\,ClO^-(aq) + 4\,H^+(aq)$
Neutralize H^+ with OH^-:
　　$Cl_2(g) \rightarrow 2\,Cl^-(aq)$ and $Cl_2(g) + \cancel{2\,H_2O(l)} + 4\,OH^-(aq) \rightarrow 2\,ClO^-(aq) + \underbrace{4\,H^+(aq) + 4\,OH^-(aq)}_{2\,\cancel{4}\,H_2O(l)}$

Add electrons: $Cl_2(g) + 2\,e^- \rightarrow 2\,Cl^-(aq)$ and $Cl_2(g) + 4\,OH^-(aq) \rightarrow 2\,ClO^-(aq) + 2\,H_2O(l) + 2\,e^-$
Equalize electrons: $Cl_2(g) + 2\,e^- \rightarrow 2\,Cl^-(aq)$ and $Cl_2(g) + 4\,OH^-(aq) \rightarrow 2\,ClO^-(aq) + 2\,H_2O(l) + 2\,e^-$
Add half-reactions: $Cl_2(g) + \cancel{2e^-} + Cl_2(g) + 4\,OH^-(aq) \rightarrow 2\,Cl^-(aq) + 2\,ClO^-(aq) + 2\,H_2O(l) + \cancel{2e^-}$
Cancel electrons: $2\,Cl_2(g) + 4\,OH^-(aq) \rightarrow 2\,Cl^-(aq) + 2\,ClO^-(aq) + 2\,H_2O(l)$
Simplify: $Cl_2(g) + 2\,OH^-(aq) \rightarrow Cl^-(aq) + ClO^-(aq) + H_2O(l)$

Check:

Reactants	Products
2 Cl atoms	2 Cl atoms
2 O atoms	2 O atoms
2 H atoms	2 H atoms
−2 charge	−2 charge

Voltaic Cells, Standard Cell Potentials, and Direction of Spontaneity

18.7　**Given:** voltaic cell overall redox reaction
Find: Sketch voltaic cell, labeling anode, cathode, all species, and direction of electron flow
Conceptual Plan: Separate the overall reaction into two half-cell reactions and add electrons as needed to balance reactions. Put the anode reaction on the left (oxidation = electrons as product) and the cathode reaction on the right (reduction = electrons as reactant). Electrons flow from anode to cathode.
Solution:

(a)　$2\,Ag^+(aq) + Pb(s) \rightarrow 2\,Ag(s) + Pb^{2+}(aq)$ separates to $2\,Ag^+(aq)$
$\rightarrow 2\,Ag(s)$ and $Pb(s) \rightarrow Pb^{2+}(aq)$ then add electrons to balance to get the cathode reaction—$2\,Ag^+(aq) + 2\,e^- \rightarrow 2\,Ag(s)$—and the anode reaction—$Pb(s) \rightarrow Pb^{2+}(aq) + 2\,e^-$.
Because we have $Pb(s)$ as the reactant for the oxidation, it will be our anode. Because we have $Ag(s)$ as the product for the reduction, it will be our cathode. Simplify the cathode reaction, dividing all terms by 2.

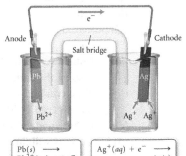

(b) $2 ClO_2(g) + 2 I^-(aq) \rightarrow 2 ClO_2^-(aq) + I_2(s)$ separates to $2 ClO_2(g)$
      $\rightarrow 2 ClO_2^-(aq)$ and $2 I^-(aq) \rightarrow I_2(s)$ then add electrons to balance to
      get the cathode reaction—$2 ClO_2(g) + 2 e^- \rightarrow 2 ClO_2^-(aq)$—and
      the anode reaction—$2 I^-(aq) \rightarrow I_2(s) + 2 e^-$.
      Because we have $I^-(aq)$ as the reactant for the oxidation, we will
      need to use Pt as our anode. Because we have $ClO_2^-(aq)$ as the prod-
      uct for the reduction, we will need to use Pt as our cathode. Because
      $ClO_2(g)$ is our reactant for the reduction, we need to use an electrode
      assembly like that used for a SHE. Simplify the cathode reaction,
      dividing all terms by 2.

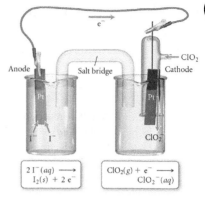

(c) $O_2(g) + 4 H^+(aq) + 2 Zn(s) \rightarrow 2 H_2O(l) + 2 Zn^{2+}(aq)$ sepa-
      rates to $O_2(g) + 4 H^+(aq) \rightarrow 2 H_2O(l)$ and $2 Zn(s) \rightarrow 2 Zn^{2+}(aq)$
      then add electrons to balance to get the cathode reaction—
      $O_2(g) + 4 H^+(aq) + 4 e^- \rightarrow 2 H_2O(l)$—and the anode reaction—
      $2 Zn(s) \rightarrow 2 Zn^{2+}(aq) + 4 e^-$.
      Because we have $Zn(s)$ as the reactant for the oxidation, it will be our
      anode. Because we have $H_2O(l)$ as the product for the reduction, we will
      need to use Pt as our cathode. Because $O_2(g)$ is our reactant for the re-
      duction, we need to use an electrode assembly like that used for a SHE.
      Simplify the anode reaction, dividing all terms by 2.

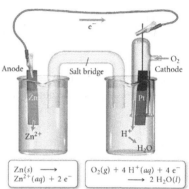

18.9   **Given:** overall reactions from Problem 7   **Find:** E°_{cell}
        **Conceptual Plan: Use Table 18.1 to look up half-reactions from the solution of Problem 7. Calculate the
        standard cell potential by subtracting the electrode potential of the anode from the electrode potential of the
        cathode:** $E^\circ_{cell} = E^\circ_{cathode} - E^\circ_{anode}$.
        Solution:
        (a) $Ag^+(aq) + e^- \rightarrow Ag(s)$ $E^\circ_{red} = 0.80 V = E^\circ_{cathode}$ and $Pb(s) \rightarrow Pb^{2+}(aq) + 2 e^- E^\circ_{red} = -0.13 V = E^\circ_{anode}$.
              Then $E^\circ_{cell} = E^\circ_{cathode} - E^\circ_{anode} = 0.80 V - (-0.13 V) = 0.93 V$.
        (b) $ClO_2(g) + e^- \rightarrow ClO_2^-(aq)$ $E^\circ_{red} = 0.95 V = E^\circ_{cathode}$ and $2 I^-(aq) \rightarrow I_2(s) + 2 e^- E^\circ_{red} = +0.54 V = E^\circ_{anode}$.
              Then $E^\circ_{cell} = E^\circ_{cathode} - E^\circ_{anode} = 0.95 V - 0.54 V = 0.41 V$.
        (c) $O_2(g) + 4 H^+(aq) + 4 e^- \rightarrow 2 H_2O(l)$ $E^\circ_{red} = 1.23 V$ and $Zn(s) \rightarrow Zn^{2+}(aq) + 2 e^- E^\circ_{red} = -0.76 V = $
              E°_{anode}. Then $E^\circ_{cell} = E^\circ_{cathode} - E^\circ_{anode} = 1.23 V - (-0.76 V) = 1.99 V$.

        Check: The units (V) are correct. All of the voltages are positive, which is consistent with a voltaic cell.

18.11   **Given:** voltaic cell drawing
        Find: (a) Determine electron flow direction, anode, and cathode; (b) write balanced overall reaction and calculate
        E°_{cell}; (c) label electrodes as $+$ and $-$; and (d) find directions of anions and cations from salt bridge.
        **Conceptual Plan: Look at each half-cell and write a reduction reaction by using electrode and solution compo-
        sition and adding electrons to balance. Look up half-reactions and standard reduction potentials in Table 18.1.
        Because this is a voltaic cell, the cell potentials must be assigned to give a positive E°_{cell}. Calculate the standard
        cell potential by subtracting the electrode potential of the anode from the electrode potential of the cathode,
        $E^\circ_{cell} = E^\circ_{cathode} - E^\circ_{anode}$, choosing the electrode assignments to give a positive E°_{cell}.**
        **(a)   Label the electrode where the oxidation occurs as the anode. Label the electrode where the reduction oc-
               curs as the cathode. Electrons flow from anode to cathode.**
        **(b)   Take two half-cell reactions and multiply the reactions as necessary to equalize the number of electrons
               transferred. Add the two half-cell reactions and cancel electrons and any other species.**
        (c)   Label anode as ($-$) and cathode as ($+$).
        **(d)   Cations will flow from the salt bridge toward the cathode, and the anions will flow from the salt bridge
               toward the anode.**

Solution:

left side: $Fe^{3+}(aq) \rightarrow Fe(s)$; right side: $Cr^{3+}(aq) \rightarrow Cr(s)$. Add electrons to balance $Fe^{3+}(aq) + 3e^- \rightarrow Fe(s)$ and right side—$Cr^{3+}(aq) + 3e^- \rightarrow Cr(s)$. Look up cell standard reduction potentials: $Fe^{3+}(aq) + 3e^- \rightarrow Fe(s)$ $E°_{red} = -0.036$ V and $Cr^{3+}(aq) + 3e^- \rightarrow Cr(s)$ $E°_{red} = -0.73$ V.

To get a positive cell potential, the second reaction is the oxidation reaction (anode). $E°_{cell} = E°_{cathode} - E°_{anode} = -0.036$ V $- (-0.73$ V$) = + 0.69$ V (a, c, and d).

(b) Add two half-reactions with the second reaction reversed.

$Fe^{3+}(aq) + \cancel{3e^-} + Cr(s) \rightarrow Fe(s) + Cr^{3+}(aq) + \cancel{3e^-}$

Cancel electrons to get $Fe^{3+}(aq) + Cr(s) \rightarrow Fe(s) + Cr^{3+}(aq)$.

Check: All atoms and charge are balanced. The units (V) are correct. The cell potential is positive, which is consistent with a voltaic cell.

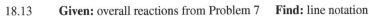

18.13 **Given:** overall reactions from Problem 7   **Find:** line notation

Conceptual Plan: Use the solution from Problem 7. Write the oxidation half-reaction components on the left and the reduction on the right. A double vertical line (‖), indicating the salt bridge, separates the two half-reactions. Substances in different phases are separated by a single vertical line (|), which represents the boundary between the phases. For some redox reactions, the reactants and products of one or both of the half-reactions may be in the same phase. In these cases, the reactants and products are separated from each other with a comma in the line diagram. Such cells use an inert electrode, such as platinum (Pt) or graphite, as the anode or cathode (or both).

Solution:

(a)   Reduction reaction: $Ag^+(aq) + e^- \rightarrow Ag(s)$; oxidation reaction: $Pb(s) \rightarrow Pb^{2+}(aq) + 2e^-$ so
      $Pb(s)|Pb^{2+}(aq)\|Ag^+(aq)|Ag(s)$

(b)   Reduction reaction: $ClO_2(g) + e^- \rightarrow ClO_2^-(aq)$; oxidation reaction: $2I^-(aq) \rightarrow I_2(s) + 2e^-$ so
      $Pt(s)|I^-(aq)|I_2(s)\|ClO_2(g)|ClO_2^-(aq)|Pt(s)$

(c)   Reduction reaction: $O_2(g) + 4H^+(aq) + 4e^- \rightarrow 2H_2O(l)$; oxidation reaction: $Zn(s) \rightarrow Zn^{2+}(aq) + 2e^-$
      so $Zn(s)|Zn^{2+}(aq)\|O_2(g)|H^+(aq), H_2O(l)|Pt(s)$

18.15 **Given:** $Sn(s)|Sn^{2+}(aq)\|NO_3^-(aq), H^+(aq)|NO(g)|Pt(s)$

Find: Sketch voltaic cell, labeling anode, cathode, all species, direction of electron flow, and $E°_{cell}$

Conceptual Plan: Separate overall reaction into two half-cell reactions, knowing that the oxidation half-reaction components are on the left and the reduction half-reaction components are on the right. Add electrons as needed to balance reactions. Multiply the half-reactions by the appropriate factors so that an equal number of electrons are transferred. Add the half-cell reactions and cancel electrons. Put anode reaction on the left (oxidation = electrons as product) and cathode reaction on the right (reduction = electrons as reactant). Electrons flow from anode to cathode. Look up half-reactions in Table 18.1. Calculate the standard cell potential by subtracting the electrode potential of the anode from the electrode potential of the cathode:

$E°_{cell} = E°_{cathode} - E°_{anode}.$

Solution: Oxidation reaction (anode): $Sn(s) \rightarrow Sn^{2+}(aq) + 2e^-$ $E°_{red} = -0.14$ V; reduction reaction (cathode): $NO_3^-(aq) + 4H^+(aq) + 3e^- \rightarrow NO(g) + 2H_2O(l)$ $E°_{red} = 0.96$ V. $E°_{cell} = E°_{cathode} - E°_{anode} = 0.96$ V $- (-0.14$ V$) = 1.10$ V. Multiply the first reaction by 3 and the second reaction by 2 so that 6 electrons are transferred. $3Sn(s) \rightarrow 3Sn^{2+}(aq) + 6e^-$ and $2NO_3^-(aq) + 8H^+(aq) + 6e^- \rightarrow 2NO(g) + 4H_2O(l)$. Add the two half-reactions and cancel electrons. $3Sn(s) + 2NO_3^-(aq) + 8H^+(aq) + \cancel{6e^-} \rightarrow 3Sn^{2+}(aq) + \cancel{6e^-} + 2NO(g) + 4H_2O(l)$. So balanced reaction is $3Sn(s) + 2NO_3^-(aq) + 8H^+(aq) \rightarrow 3Sn^{2+}(aq) + 2NO(g) + 4H_2O(l)$.

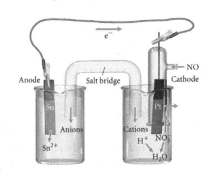

Check: All atoms and charge are balanced. The units (V) are correct. The cell potential is positive, which is consistent with a voltaic cell.

18.17 **Given:** overall reactions   **Find:** spontaneity in forward direction

Conceptual Plan: Separate the overall reaction into two half-cell reactions and add electrons as needed to balance reactions. Look up half-reactions in Table 18.1. Calculate the standard cell potential by subtracting

the electrode potential of the anode from the electrode potential of the cathode: $E°_{cell} = E°_{cathode} - E°_{anode}$. If $E°_{cell} = 0$, the reaction is spontaneous in the forward direction.

Solution:

(a) $Ni(s) + Zn^{2+}(aq) \rightarrow Ni^{2+}(aq) + Zn(s)$ separates to $Ni(s) \rightarrow Ni^{2+}(aq)$ and $Zn^{2+}(aq) \rightarrow Zn(s)$. Add electrons. $Ni(s) \rightarrow Ni^{2+}(aq) + 2\,e^-$ and $Zn^{2+}(aq) + 2\,e^- \rightarrow Zn(s)$. Look up cell potentials. Ni is oxidized, so $E°_{red} = -0.23$ V $= E°_{anode}$. Zn^{2+} is reduced, so $E°_{cathode} = -0.76$ V. Then $E°_{cell} = E°_{cathode} - E°_{anode} = -0.76$ V $- (-0.23$ V$) = -0.53$ V, so the reaction is nonspontaneous.

(b) $Ni(s) + Pb^{2+}(aq) \rightarrow Ni^{2+}(aq) + Pb(s)$ separates to $Ni(s) \rightarrow Ni^{2+}(aq)$ and $Pb^{2+}(aq) \rightarrow Pb(s)$. Add electrons. $Ni(s) \rightarrow Ni^{2+}(aq) + 2\,e^-$ and $Pb^{2+}(aq) + 2\,e^- \rightarrow Pb(s)$. Look up cell potentials. Ni is oxidized, so $E°_{red} = -0.23$ V $= E°_{anode}$. Pb^{2+} is reduced, so $E°_{red} = -0.13$ V $= E°_{cathode}$. Then $E°_{cell} = E°_{cathode} - E°_{anode} = -0.13$ V $- (-0.23$ V$) = +0.10$ V, so the reaction is spontaneous.

(c) $Al(s) + 3\,Ag^+(aq) \rightarrow Al^{3+}(aq) + 3\,Ag(s)$ separates to $Al(s) \rightarrow Al^{3+}(aq)$ and $3\,Ag^+(aq) \rightarrow 3\,Ag(s)$. Add electrons. $Al(s) \rightarrow Al^{3+}(aq) + 3\,e^-$ and $3\,Ag^+(aq) + 3\,e^- \rightarrow 3\,Ag(s)$. Simplify the Ag reaction to $Ag^+(aq) + e^- \rightarrow Ag(s)$. Look up cell potentials. Al is oxidized, so $E°_{red} = -1.66$ V $E°_{anode}$. Ag^+ is reduced, so $E°_{red} = 0.80$ V $= E°_{cathode}$. Then $E°_{cell} = E°_{cathode} - E°_{anode} = 0.80$ V $- (-1.66$ V$) = +2.46$ V, so the reaction is spontaneous.

(d) $Pb(s) + Mn^{2+}(aq) \rightarrow Pb^{2+}(aq) + Mn(s)$ separates to $Pb(s) \rightarrow Pb^{2+}(aq)$ and $Mn^{2+}(aq) \rightarrow Mn(s)$. Add electrons. $Pb(s) \rightarrow Pb^{2+}(aq) + 2\,e^-$ and $Mn^{2+}(aq) + 2\,e^- \rightarrow Mn(s)$. Look up cell potentials. Pb is oxidized, so $E°_{red} = -0.13$ V $= E°_{anode}$. Mn^{2+} is reduced, so $E°_{red} = -1.18$ V $= E°_{cathode}$. Then $E°_{cell} = E°_{cathode} - E°_{anode} = -1.18$ V $- (-0.13$ V$) = -1.05$ V, so the reaction is nonspontaneous.

Check: The units (V) are correct. If the voltage is positive, the reaction is spontaneous. If the voltage is negative, the reaction is nonspontaneous.

18.19   For a metal to be able to reduce an ion, it must be below it in Table 18.1 (need positive $E°_{cell} = E°_{cathode} - E°_{anode}$). So we need a metal that is below Mn^{2+} but above Mg^{2+}. Aluminum is the only one in the table that meets those criteria.

18.21   In general, metals whose reduction half-reactions lie below the reduction of H^+ to H_2 in Table 18.1 will dissolve in acids, while metals above it will not. (a) Al and (c) Pb meet that criterion. To write the balanced redox reactions, pair the oxidation of the metal with the reduction of H^+ to H_2 ($2\,H^+(aq) + 2\,e^- \rightarrow H_2(g)$). For Al, $Al(s) \rightarrow Al^{3+}(aq) + 3\,e^-$. To balance the number of electrons transferred, we need to multiply the Al reaction by 2 and the H^+ reaction by 3. So $2\,Al(s) \rightarrow 2\,Al^{3+}(aq) + 6\,e^-$ and $6\,H^+(aq) + 6\,e^- \rightarrow 3\,H_2(g)$. Adding the two reactions: $2\,Al(s) + 6\,H^+(aq) + 6\,e^- \rightarrow 2\,Al^{3+}(aq) + 6\,e^- + 3\,H_2(g)$. Simplify to $2\,Al(s) + 6\,H^+(aq) \rightarrow 2\,Al^{3+}(aq) + 3\,H_2(g)$. For Pb, $Pb(s) \rightarrow Pb^{2+}(aq) + 2\,e^-$. Because each reaction involves two electrons, we can add the two reactions. $Pb(s) + 2\,H^+(aq) + 2\,e^- \rightarrow Pb^{2+}(aq) + 2\,e^- + H_2(g)$. Simplify to $Pb(s) + 2\,H^+(aq) \rightarrow Pb^{2+}(aq) + H_2(g)$.

18.23   Nitric acid (HNO_3) oxidizes metals through the following reduction half-reaction: $NO_3^-(aq) + 4\,H^+(aq) + 3\,e^- \rightarrow NO(g) + 2\,H_2O(l)$ $E°_{red} = 0.96$ V. Because this half-reaction is above the reduction of H^+ in Table 18.1, HNO_3 can oxidize metals (copper, for example) that cannot be oxidized by HCl. (a) Cu, which is below nitric acid in the table, will be oxidized, but (b) Au, which is above nitric acid in the table (and has a reduction potential of 1.50 V), will not be oxidized. To write the balanced redox reactions, pair the oxidation of the metal with the reduction of nitric acid: $NO_3^-(aq) + 4\,H^+(aq) + 3\,e^- \rightarrow NO(g) + 2\,H_2O(l)$. For Cu, $Cu(s) \rightarrow Cu^{2+}(aq) + 2\,e^-$. To balance the number of electrons transferred, we need to multiply the Cu reaction by 3 and the nitric acid reaction by 2. So $3\,Cu(s) \rightarrow 3\,Cu^{2+}(aq) + 6\,e^-$ and $2\,NO_3^-(aq) + 8\,H^+(aq) + 6\,e^- \rightarrow 2\,NO(g) + 4\,H_2O(l)$. Adding the two reactions: $3\,Cu(s) + 2\,NO_3^-(aq) + 8\,H^+(aq) + 6\,e^- \rightarrow 3\,Cu^{2+}(aq) + 6\,e^- + 2\,NO(g) + 4\,H_2O(l)$. Simplify to $3\,Cu(s) + 2\,NO_3^-(aq) + 8\,H^+(aq) \rightarrow 3\,Cu^{2+}(aq) + 2\,NO(g) + 4\,H_2O(l)$.

18.25   **Given:** overall reactions   **Find:** $E°_{cell}$ and spontaneity in forward direction
Conceptual Plan: Separate the overall reaction into two half-cell reactions and add electrons as needed to balance reactions. Look up half-reactions in Table 18.1. Calculate the standard cell potential by subtracting the electrode potential of the anode from the electrode potential of the cathode: $E°_{cell} = E°_{cathode} - E°_{anode}$. If $E°_{cell} > 0$, the reaction is spontaneous in the forward direction.
Solution:

(a) $2\,Cu(s) + Mn^{2+}(aq) \rightarrow 2\,Cu^+(aq) + Mn(s)$ separates to $2\,Cu(s) \rightarrow 2\,Cu^+(aq)$ and $Mn^{2+}(aq) \rightarrow Mn(s)$. Add electrons. $2\,Cu(s) \rightarrow 2\,Cu^+(aq) + 2\,e^-$ and $Mn^{2+}(aq) + 2\,e^- \rightarrow Mn(s)$. Simplify the Cu reaction to $Cu(s) \rightarrow Cu^+(aq) + e^-$. Look up cell potentials. Cu is oxidized, so $E°_{red} = +0.52$ V $= E°_{anode}$. Mn^{2+} is reduced, so $E^\circ_{red} = -1.18$ V $= E^\circ_{cathode}$. Then $E^\circ_{cell} = E^\circ_{cathode} - E^\circ_{anode} = -1.18$ V $- 0.52$ V $= -1.70$ V, so the reaction is nonspontaneous.

(b) $MnO_2(s) + 4 H^+(aq) + Zn(s) \rightarrow Mn^{2+}(aq) + 2 H_2O(l) + Zn^{2+}(aq)$ separates to $MnO_2(s) + 4 H^+(aq)$ $\rightarrow Mn^{2+}(aq) + 2 H_2O(l)$ and $Zn(s) \rightarrow Zn^{2+}(aq)$. Add electrons. $MnO_2(s) + 4 H^+(aq) + 2 e^- \rightarrow Mn^{2+}$ $(aq) + 2 H_2O(l)$ and $Zn(s) \rightarrow Zn^{2+}(aq) + 2 e^-$. Look up cell potentials. Zn is oxidized, so $E^\circ_{red} = -0.76$ V $= E^\circ_{anode}$. Mn is reduced, so $E^\circ_{red} = 1.21$ V $= E^\circ_{cathode}$. Then $E^\circ_{cell} = E^\circ_{cathode} - E^\circ_{anode} = 1.21$ V $- (-0.76$ V$) = +1.97$ V, so the reaction is spontaneous.

(c) $Cl_2(g) + 2 F^-(aq) \rightarrow 2 Cl^-(aq) + F_2(g)$ separates to $Cl_2(g) \rightarrow 2 Cl^-(aq)$ and $2 F^-(aq) \rightarrow F_2(g)$. Add electrons. $Cl_2(g) + 2 e^- \rightarrow 2 Cl^-(aq)$ and $2 F^-(aq) \rightarrow F_2(g) + 2 e^-$. Look up cell potentials. F^- is oxidized, so $E^\circ_{red} = 2.87$ V $= E^\circ_{anode}$. Cl is reduced, so $E^\circ_{red} = 1.36$ V $= E^\circ_{cathode}$. Then $E^\circ_{cell} = E^\circ_{cathode} - E^\circ_{anode} = 1.36$ V $- 2.87$ V $= -1.51$ V, so the reaction is nonspontaneous.

Check: The units (V) are correct. If the voltage is positive, the reaction is spontaneous.

18.27   (a) Pb^{2+}. The strongest oxidizing agent is the one with the reduction reaction that is closest to the top of Table 18.1 (most positive, least negative reduction potential).

Cell Potential, Free Energy, and the Equilibrium Constant

18.29   **Given:** overall reactions   **Find:** ΔG°_{rxn} and spontaneity in forward direction
Conceptual Plan: Separate the overall reaction into two half-cell reactions and add electrons as needed to balance reactions. Look up half-reactions in Table 18.1. Calculate the standard cell potential by subtracting the electrode potential of the anode from the electrode potential of the cathode: $E^\circ_{cell} = E^\circ_{cathode} - E^\circ_{anode}$. Then calculate ΔG°_{rxn} using $\Delta G^\circ_{rxn} = -nFE^\circ_{cell}$.
Solution:

(a) $Pb^{2+}(aq) + Mg(s) \rightarrow Pb(s) + Mg^{2+}(aq)$ separates to $Pb^{2+}(aq) \rightarrow Pb(s)$ and $Mg(s) \rightarrow Mg^{2+}(aq)$. Add electrons. $Pb^{2+}(aq) + 2 e^- \rightarrow Pb(s)$ and $Mg(s) \rightarrow Mg^{2+}(aq) + 2 e^-$. Look up cell potentials. Mg is oxidized, so $E^\circ_{red} = -2.37$ V $= E^\circ_{anode}$. Pb^{2+} is reduced, so $E^\circ_{red} = -0.13$ V $= E^\circ_{cathode}$. Then E°_{cell} $= E^\circ_{cathode} - E^\circ_{anode} = -0.13$ V $- (-2.37$ V$) = +2.24$ V. $n = 2$, so $\Delta G^\circ_{rxn} = -nFE^\circ_{cell}$

$$= -2 \text{ mole } e^- \times \frac{96,485 \text{ C}}{\text{mole } e^-} \times 2.24 \text{ V} = -2 \times 96,485 \text{ C} \times 2.24 \frac{\text{J}}{\text{C}} = -4.32 \times 10^5 \text{ J} = -432 \text{ kJ}.$$

(b) $Br_2(l) + 2 Cl^-(aq) \rightarrow 2 Br^-(aq) + Cl_2(g)$ separates to $Br_2(g) \rightarrow 2 Br^-(aq)$ and $2 Cl^-(aq) \rightarrow Cl_2(g)$. Add electrons. $Br_2(g) + 2 e^- \rightarrow 2 Br^-(aq)$ and $2 Cl^-(aq) \rightarrow Cl_2(g) + 2 e^-$. Look up cell potentials. Cl is oxidized, so $E^\circ_{red} = 1.36$ V $= E^\circ_{anode}$. Br is reduced, so $E^\circ_{red} = 1.09$ V $= E^\circ_{cathode}$. Then $E^\circ_{cell} = E^\circ_{cathode}$ $-E^\circ_{anode} = 1.09$ V $- 1.36$ V $= -0.27$ V. $n = 2$, so $\Delta G^\circ_{rxn} = -nFE^\circ_{cell}$

$$= -2 \text{ mole } e^- \times \frac{96,485 \text{ C}}{\text{mole } e^-} \times -0.27 \text{ V} = -2 \times 96,485 \text{ C} \times -0.27 \frac{\text{J}}{\text{C}} = 5.2 \times 10^4 \text{ J} = 52 \text{ kJ}.$$

(c) $MnO_2(s) + 4 H^+(aq) + Cu(s) \rightarrow Mn^{2+}(aq) + 2 H_2O(l) + Cu^{2+}(aq)$ separates to $MnO_2(s) + 4 H^+(aq)$ $\rightarrow Mn^{2+}(aq) + 2 H_2O(l)$ and $Cu(s) \rightarrow Cu^{2+}(aq)$. Add electrons. $MnO_2(s) + 4 H^+(aq) + 2 e^- \rightarrow$ $Mn^{2+}(aq) + 2 H_2O(l)$ and $Cu(s) \rightarrow Cu^{2+}(aq) + 2 e^-$. Look up cell potentials. Cu is oxidized, so $E^\circ_{red} = 0.34$ V $= E^\circ_{anode}$. Mn is reduced, so $E^\circ_{red} = 1.21$ V $= E^\circ_{cathode}$. Then $E^\circ_{cell} = E^\circ_{cathode} - E^\circ_{anode} = 1.21$ V $- 0.34$ V $= +0.87$ V. $n = 2$, so $\Delta G^\circ_{rxn} = -nFE^\circ_{cell} = -2 \text{ mole } \times \frac{96,485 \text{ C}}{\text{mole}} \times 0.87 \text{ V} =$

$$-2 \times 96,485 \text{ C} \times 0.87 \frac{\text{J}}{\text{C}} = -1.7 \times 10^5 \text{ J} = -1.7 \times 10^2 \text{ kJ}.$$

Check: The units (kJ) are correct. If the voltage is positive, the reaction is spontaneous and the free energy change is negative.

18.31   **Given:** overall reactions from Problem 29   **Find:** K
Conceptual Plan: °C $\rightarrow$ K then ΔG°_{rxn}, $T = K$
$$K = 273.15 + °C \qquad \Delta G^\circ_{rxn} = -RT \ln K$$
Solution: $T = 273.15 + 25 °C = 298$ K then

(a) $\Delta G^\circ_{rxn} = -RT \ln K$. Rearrange to solve for K.

$$K = e^{\frac{-\Delta G^\circ_{rxn}}{RT}} = e^{\dfrac{-(-432\ \cancel{kJ}) \times \frac{1000\ J}{1\ \cancel{kJ}}}{\left(8.314\ \frac{J}{K\cdot mol}\right)(298\ K)}} = e^{\underline{1}74.364} = 5.31 \times 10^{75}$$

(b) $\Delta G^\circ_{rxn} = -RT \ln K$. Rearrange to solve for K.

$$K = e^{\frac{-\Delta G^\circ_{rxn}}{RT}} = e^{\dfrac{-(+52\ \cancel{kJ}) \times \frac{1000\ J}{1\ \cancel{kJ}}}{\left(8.314\ \frac{J}{K\cdot mol}\right)(298\ K)}} = e^{-2\underline{0}.998} = 7.67 \times 10^{-10}$$

(c) $\Delta G^\circ_{rxn} = -RT \ln K$. Rearrange to solve for K.

$$K = e^{\frac{-\Delta G^\circ_{rxn}}{RT}} = e^{\dfrac{-(-170\ \cancel{kJ}) \times \frac{1000\ J}{1\ \cancel{kJ}}}{\left(8.314\ \frac{J}{K\cdot mol}\right)(298\ K)}} = e^{6\underline{8}.616} = 6.3 \times 10^{29}$$

Check: The units (none) are correct. If the voltage is positive, the reaction is spontaneous, the free energy change is negative, and the equilibrium constant is large.

18.33   **Given:** $Ni^{2+}(aq) + Cd(s) \rightarrow$ **Find:** K

Conceptual Plan: Write two half-cell reactions and add electrons as needed to balance the reactions. Look up half-reactions in Table 18.1. Calculate the standard cell potential by subtracting the electrode potential of the anode from the electrode potential of the cathode: $E^\circ_{cell} = E^\circ_{cathode} - E^\circ_{anode}$**, then** $^\circ C \rightarrow K$ **then** $E^\circ_{cell}, n, T \rightarrow K$**.**

$K = 273.15 + {}^\circ C$ $\Delta G^\circ_{rxn} = -RT \ln K = -nFE^\circ_{cell}$

Solution: $Ni^{2+}(aq) + 2\ e^- \rightarrow Ni(s)$ and $Cd(s) \rightarrow Cd^{2+}(aq) + 2\ e^-$. Look up cell potentials. Cd is oxidized, so $E^\circ_{red} = -0.40\ V = E^\circ_{anode}$. Ni^{2+} is reduced, so $E^\circ_{red} = -0.23\ V = E^\circ_{cathode}$. Then $E^\circ_{cell} = E^\circ_{cathode} - E^\circ_{anode} = -0.23\ V -(-0.40\ V) = +0.17\ V$. The overall reaction is $Ni^{2+}(aq) + Cd(s) \rightarrow Ni(s) + Cd^{2+}(aq)$. $n = 2$ and $T = 273.15 + 25\ ^\circ C = 298\ K$ then $\Delta G^\circ_{rxn} = -RT \ln K = -nFE^\circ_{cell}$. Rearrange to solve for K.

$$K = e^{\frac{nFE^\circ_{cell}}{RT}} = e^{\dfrac{2\ \cancel{mol\ e^-} \times \frac{96{,}485\ \cancel{C}}{\cancel{mole\ e^-}} \times 0.17\ \frac{J}{\cancel{C}}}{\left(8.314\ \frac{J}{K\cdot mol}\right)(298\ K)}} = e^{1\underline{3}.241} = 5.6 \times 10^5$$

Check: The units (none) are correct. If the voltage is positive, the reaction is spontaneous and the equilibrium constant is large.

18.35   **Given:** $n = 2$ and $K = 25$ **Find:** ΔG°_{rxn} and E°_{cell}

Conceptual Plan: $K, T \rightarrow \Delta G^\circ_{rxn}$ **and** $\Delta G^\circ_{rxn}, n \rightarrow E^\circ_{cell}$

$\Delta G^\circ_{rxn} = -RT \ln K$ $\Delta G^\circ_{rxn} = -nFE^\circ_{cell}$

Solution: $\Delta G^\circ_{rxn} = -RT \ln K = -\left(8.314\ \dfrac{J}{K \cdot mol}\right)(298\ K)\ \ln 25 = -7.9\underline{7}500 \times 10^3\ J = -8.0\ kJ$ and

$\Delta G^\circ_{rxn} = -nFE^\circ_{cell}$. Rearrange to solve for E°_{cell}.

$$E^\circ_{cell} = \frac{\Delta G^\circ_{rxn}}{-nF} = \frac{-7.9\underline{7}500 \times 10^3\ J}{-2\ \cancel{mole^-} \times \dfrac{96{,}485\ C}{\cancel{mole^-}}} = 0.041\frac{V \cdot \cancel{C}}{\cancel{C}} = 0.041\ V$$

Check: The units (kJ and V) are correct. If $K > 1$, the voltage is positive and the free energy change is negative.

Nonstandard Conditions and the Nernst Equation

18.37   **Given:** $Sn^{2+}(aq) + Mn(s) \rightarrow Sn(s) + Mn^{2+}(aq)$

Find: (a) E°_{cell}; (b) E_{cell} when $[Sn^{2+}] = 0.0100\ M$; $[Mn^{2+}] = 2.00\ M$; and (c) E_{cell} when $[Sn^{2+}] = 2.00\ M$; $[Mn^{2+}] = 0.0100\ M$

Conceptual Plan: (a) Separate the overall reaction into two half-cell reactions and add electrons as needed to balance the reactions. Look up half-reactions in Table 18.1. Calculate the standard cell potential by subtracting the electrode potential of the anode from the electrode potential of the cathode: $E°_{cell} = E°_{cathode} - E°_{anode}$. **(b) and (c)** $E°_{cell}$, $[Sn^{2+}]$, $[Mn^{2+}]$, $n \rightarrow E_{cell}$

$$E_{cell} = E°_{cell} - \frac{0.0592\ V}{n} \log Q \quad \text{where} \quad Q = \frac{[Mn^{2+}]}{[Sn^{2+}]}$$

Solution:

(a) Separate the overall reaction to $Sn^{2+}(aq) \rightarrow Sn(s)$ and $Mn(s) \rightarrow Mn^{2+}(aq)$. Add electrons. $Sn^{2+}(aq) + 2\ e^- \rightarrow Sn(s)$ and $Mn(s) \rightarrow Mn^{2+}(aq) + 2\ e^-$. Look up cell potentials. Mn is oxidized, so $E°_{red} = -1.18\ V = E°_{anode}$. Sn^{2+} is reduced, so $E°_{red} = -0.14\ V = E°_{cathode}$. Then $E°_{cell} = E°_{cathode} - E°_{anode} = -0.14\ V - (-1.18\ V) = +1.04\ V$.

(b) $Q = \dfrac{[Mn^{2+}]}{[Sn^{2+}]} = \dfrac{2.00\ M}{0.0100\ M} = 200.$ and $n = 2$ then

$$E_{cell} = E°_{cell} - \frac{0.0592\ V}{n} \log Q = 1.04\ V - \frac{0.0592\ V}{2} \log 200. = +0.97\ V$$

(c) $Q = \dfrac{[Mn^{2+}]}{[Sn^{2+}]} = \dfrac{0.0100\ M}{2.00\ M} = 0.00500$ and $n = 2$ then

$$E_{cell} = E°_{cell} - \frac{0.0592\ V}{n} \log Q = 1.04\ V - \frac{0.0592\ V}{2} \log 0.00500 = +1.11\ V$$

Check: The units (V, V, and V) are correct. The Sn^{2+} reduction reaction is above the Mn^{2+} reduction reaction, so the standard cell potential will be positive. Having more products than reactants reduces the cell potential. Having more reactants than products raises the cell potential.

18.39 **Given:** $Pb(s) \rightarrow Pb^{2+}(aq, 0.10\ M) + 2\ e^-$ and $MnO_4^-(aq, 1.50\ M) + 4\ H^+(aq, 2.0\ M) + 3\ e^- \rightarrow MnO_2(s) + 2\ H_2O(l)$ **Find:** E_{cell}
Conceptual Plan: Look up half-reactions in Table 18.1. Calculate the standard cell potential by subtracting the electrode potential of the anode from the electrode potential of the cathode: $E°_{cell} = E°_{cathode} - E°_{anode}$. **Equalize the number of electrons transferred by multiplying the first reaction by 3 and the second reaction by 2. Add the two half-cell reactions and cancel the electrons.**
Then $E°_{cell}$, $[Pb^{2+}]$, $[MnO_4^-]$, $[H^+]$, $n \rightarrow E_{cell}$.

$$E_{cell} = E°_{cell} - \frac{0.0592\ V}{n} \log Q \quad \text{where} \quad Q = \frac{[Pb^{2+}]^3}{[MnO_4^-]^2[H^+]^8}$$

Solution: Pb is oxidized, so $E°_{red} = -0.13\ V = E°_{anode}$. Mn is reduced, so $E°_{red} = 1.68\ V = E°_{cathode}$. Then $E°_{cell} = E°_{cathode} - E°_{anode} = 1.68\ V - (-0.13\ V) = +1.81\ V$. Equalizing the electrons: $3\ Pb(s) \rightarrow 3\ Pb^{2+}(aq) + 6\ e^-$ and $2\ MnO_4^-(aq) + 8\ H^+(aq) + 6\ e^- \rightarrow 2\ MnO_2(s) + 4\ H_2O(l)$. Adding the two reactions: $3\ Pb(s) + 2\ MnO_4^-(aq) + 8\ H^+(aq) + 6\ e^- \rightarrow 3\ Pb^{2+}(aq) + 6\ e^- + 2\ MnO_2(s) + 4\ H_2O(l)$. Cancel the electrons: $3\ Pb(s) + 2\ MnO_4^-(aq) + 8\ H^+(aq) \rightarrow 3\ Pb^{2+}(aq) + 2\ MnO_2(s) + 4\ H_2O(l)$. So $n = 6$ and $Q = \dfrac{[Pb^{2+}]^3}{[MnO_4^-]^2[H^+]^8} = \dfrac{(0.10)^3}{(1.50)^2(2.0)^8}$

$= 1.\underline{7}361 \times 10^{-6}$. Then $E_{cell} = E°_{cell} - \dfrac{0.0592\ V}{n} \log Q = 1.81\ V - \dfrac{0.0592\ V}{6} \log 1.\underline{7}361 \times 10^{-6} = +1.87\ V$.

Check: The units (V) are correct. The MnO_4^- reduction reaction is above the Pb^{2+} reduction reaction, so the standard cell potential will be positive. Having more reactants than products raises the cell potential.

18.41 **Given:** Zn/Zn^{2+} and Ni/Ni^{2+} half-cells in voltaic cell; initially, $[Ni^{2+}] = 1.50\ M$ and $[Zn^{2+}] = 0.100\ M$
Find: (a) initial E_{cell}, (b) E_{cell} when $[Ni^{2+}] = 0.500\ M$, and (c) $[Ni^{2+}]$ and $[Zn^{2+}]$ when $E_{cell} = 0.45\ V$
Conceptual Plan:

(a) **Write two half-cell reactions and add electrons as needed to balance reactions. Look up half-reactions in Table 18.1. Calculate the standard cell potential by subtracting the electrode potential of the anode from the electrode potential of the cathode:** $E°_{cell} = E°_{cathode} - E°_{anode}$. **Choose the direction of the half-cell reactions so that** $E°_{cell} > 0$. **Add two half-cell reactions and cancel electrons to generate overall reaction. Define Q based on overall reaction. Then** $E°_{cell}$, $[Ni^{2+}]$, $[Zn^{2+}]$, $n \rightarrow E_{cell}$.

$$E_{cell} = E°_{cell} - \frac{0.0592\ V}{n} \log Q$$

(b)   When $[Ni^{2+}] = 0.500$ M, then $[Zn^{2+}] = 1.100$ M. **(Because the stoichiometric coefficients for** $Ni^{2+} : Zn^{2+}$ **are 1:1 and the** $[Ni^{2+}]$ **drops by 1.00 M, the other concentration must rise by 1.00 M.) Then** $E^{\circ}_{cell}, [Ni^{2+}], [Zn^{2+}], n \rightarrow E_{cell}$

$$E_{cell} = E^{\circ}_{cell} - \frac{0.0592 \text{ V}}{n} \log Q$$

(c) $E^{\circ}_{cell}, E_{cell}, n \rightarrow [Zn^{2+}]/[Ni^{2+}] \rightarrow [Ni^{2+}], [Zn^{2+}]$

$$E_{cell} = E^{\circ}_{cell} - \frac{0.0592 \text{ V}}{n} \log Q \qquad [Ni^{2+}] + [Zn^{2+}] = 1.50 \text{ M} + 0.100 \text{ M} = 1.60 \text{ M}$$

Solution:

(a) $Zn^{2+}(aq) + 2 e^- \rightarrow Zn(s)$ and $Ni^{2+}(aq) + 2 e^- \rightarrow Ni(s)$. Look up cell potentials. For Zn, $E^{\circ}_{red} = -0.76$ V. For Ni, $E^{\circ}_{red} = -0.23$ V. To get a positive E°_{cell}, Zn is oxidized; so $E^{\circ}_{red} = -0.76$ V $= E^{\circ}_{anode}$. Ni^{2+} is reduced, so $E^{\circ}_{red} = -0.23$ V $= E^{\circ}_{cathode}$. Then $E^{\circ}_{cell} = E^{\circ}_{cathode} - E^{\circ}_{anode} = -0.23$ V $- (-0.76$ V$) = +0.53$ V. Adding the two half-cell reactions: $Zn(s) + Ni^{2+}(aq) + 2\,\cancel{e^-} \rightarrow Zn^{2+}(aq) + 2\,\cancel{e^-} + Ni(s)$. The overall reaction

is $Zn(s) + Ni^{2+}(aq) \rightarrow Zn^{2+}(aq) + Ni(s)$. Then $Q = \dfrac{[Zn^{2+}]}{[Ni^{2+}]} = \dfrac{0.100}{1.50} = 0.0666667$ and $n = 2$. Then

$$E_{cell} = E^{\circ}_{cell} - \frac{0.0592 \text{ V}}{n} \log Q = 0.53 \text{ V} - \frac{0.0592 \text{ V}}{2} \log 0.0666667 = +0.56 \text{ V}.$$

(b) $Q = \dfrac{[Zn^{2+}]}{[Ni^{2+}]} = \dfrac{1.100}{0.500} = 2.20$ then

$$E_{cell} = E^{\circ}_{cell} - \frac{0.0592 \text{ V}}{n} \log Q = 0.53 \text{ V} - \frac{0.0592 \text{ V}}{2} \log 2.20 = +0.52 \text{ V}$$

(c) $E_{cell} = E^{\circ}_{cell} - \dfrac{0.0592 \text{ V}}{n} \log Q$ so 0.45 V $= 0.53$ V $- \dfrac{0.0592 \text{ V}}{2} \log Q \rightarrow 0.08 \cancel{V} = \dfrac{0.0592 \cancel{V}}{2} \log Q \rightarrow$

$\log Q = 2.70270 \rightarrow Q = 10^{2.70270} = 504.31$. Then $Q = 504.31 = \dfrac{[Zn^{2+}]}{1.60 \text{ M} - [Zn^{2+}]}$. Solving for $[Zn^{2+}]$:

$(504.31)(1.60 \text{ M} - [Zn^{2+}]) = [Zn^{2+}] \rightarrow [Zn^{2+}] = \dfrac{806.896 \text{ M}}{505.31} = 1.59683 \text{ M} = 1.60 \text{ M}$ then

$[Ni^{2+}] = 1.60 \text{ M} - 1.59683 \text{ M} = 0.003 \text{ M}.$

Check: The units (V, V, and M) are correct. The standard cell potential is positive, and because there are more reactants than products, this raises the cell potential. As the reaction proceeds, reactants are converted to products; so the cell potential drops for parts (b) and (c).

18.43   **Given:** Zn/Zn^{2+} concentration cell, with $[Zn^{2+}] = 2.0$ M in one half-cell and $[Zn^{2+}] = 1.0 \times 10^{-3}$ M in other half-cell

Find: Sketch a voltaic cell, labeling the anode, the cathode, the reactions at electrodes, all species, and the direction of electron flow.

Conceptual Plan: In a concentration cell, the half-cell with the higher concentration is always the half-cell where the reduction takes place (contains the cathode). The two half-cell reactions are the same, but reversed. Put anode reaction on the left (oxidation = electrons as product) and cathode reaction on the right (reduction = electrons as reactant). Electrons flow from anode to cathode.

Solution:

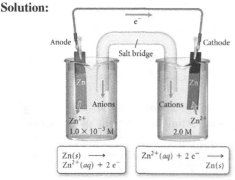

Check: The figure looks similar to the right side of Figure 18.10.

18.45   **Given:** Sn/Sn^{2+} concentration cell with $E_{cell} = 0.10$ V   **Find:** ratio of $[Sn^{2+}]$ in two half-cells

       Conceptual Plan: Determine n, then $E°_{cell}$, $E°_{cell}$, $n \rightarrow Q$ = ratio of $[Sn^{2+}]$ in two half-cells.

$$E_{cell} = E°_{cell} - \frac{0.0592 \text{ V}}{n} \log Q$$

       Solution: Because $Sn^{2+}(aq) + 2 e^- \rightarrow Sn(s)$, $n = 2$. In a concentration cell, $E°_{cell} = 0$ V. So

$$E_{cell} = E°_{cell} - \frac{0.0592 \text{ V}}{n} \log Q, \text{ so } 0.10 \text{ V} = 0.00 \text{ V} - \frac{0.0592 \text{ V}}{2} \log Q \rightarrow 0.10 \text{ V} = -\frac{0.0592 \text{ V}}{2} \log Q \rightarrow$$

$$\log Q = -3.\underline{3}784 \rightarrow Q = 10^{-3.3784} = 4.2 \times 10^{-4} = \frac{[Sn^{2+}](ox)}{[Sn^{2+}](red)}.$$

       Check: The units (none) are correct. Because the concentration in the reduction reaction half-cell is always greater than the concentration in the oxidation half-cell in a voltaic concentration cell, the Q or ratio of two cells is less than 1.

Batteries, Fuel Cells, and Corrosion

18.47   **Given:** alkaline battery   **Find:** optimum mass ratio of Zn to MnO_2

       Conceptual Plan: Look up alkaline battery reactions. Use stoichiometry to get mole ratio. Then

$$Zn(s) + 2 OH^-(aq) \rightarrow Zn(OH)_2(s) + 2e^- \qquad \frac{1 \text{ mol Zn}}{2 \text{ mol } MnO_2}$$

$$2 MnO_2(s) + 2 H_2O(l) + 2 e^- \rightarrow 2 MnO(OH)(s) + 2 OH^-(aq)$$

       mol Zn → g Zn Zn then mol MnO_2 → g MnO_2.

$$\frac{65.38 \text{ g Zn}}{1 \text{ mol Zn}} \qquad \frac{1 \text{ mol } MnO_2}{86.94 \text{ g } MnO_2}$$

       Solution: $\dfrac{1 \text{ mol Zn}}{2 \text{ mol } MnO_2} \times \dfrac{65.38 \text{ g Zn}}{1 \text{ mol Zn}} \times \dfrac{1 \text{ mol } MnO_2}{86.94 \text{ g } MnO_2} = 0.3760 \dfrac{\text{g Zn}}{\text{g } MnO_2}$

       Check: The units (mass ratio) are correct. Because more moles of MnO_2 are needed and the molar mass is larger, the ratio is less than 1.

18.49   **Given:** $CH_4(g) + 2 O_2(g) \rightarrow CO_2(g) + 2 H_2O(g)$ **Find:** $E°_{cell}$

       Conceptual Plan: $\Delta G°_{rxn} = \sum n_p \Delta G°_f$ (products) $- \sum n_r \Delta G°_f$ (reactants) and determine n then

       $\Delta G°_{rxn}$, $n \rightarrow E°_{cell}$

$$\Delta G°_{rxn} = -nFE°_{cell}$$

       Solution:

Reactant/Product	$\Delta G°_f$ (kJ/mol from Appendix IIB)
$CH_4(g)$	-50.5
$O_2(g)$	0.0
$CO_2(g)$	-394.4
$H_2O(g)$	-228.6

       Be sure to pull data for the correct formula and phase.

$$\Delta G°_{rxn} = \sum n_p \Delta G°_f \text{ (products)} - \sum n_r \Delta G°_f \text{ (reactants)}$$
$$= [1(\Delta G°_f (CO_2(g))) + 2(\Delta G°_f (H_2O(g)))] - [1(\Delta G°_f (CH_4(g))) + 2(\Delta G°_f (O_2(g)))]$$
$$= [1(-394.4 \text{ kJ}) + 2(-228.6 \text{ kJ})] - [1(-50.5 \text{ kJ}) + 2(0.0 \text{ kJ})]$$
$$= [-851.6 \text{ kJ}] - [-50.5 \text{ kJ}]$$
$$= -801.1 \text{ kJ} = -8.011 \times 10^5 \text{ J}$$

       Also, because one C atom goes from an oxidation state of -4 to $+4$ and four O atoms are going from 0 to -2, $n = 8$ and $\Delta G°_{rxn} = -nFE°_{cell}$. Rearrange to solve for $E°_{cell}$.

$$E°_{cell} = \frac{\Delta G°_{rxn}}{-nF} = \frac{-8.011 \times 10^5 \text{ J}}{-8 \text{ mol } e^- \times \dfrac{96,485 \text{ C}}{\text{mol } e^-}} = 1.038 \frac{V \cdot C}{C} = 1.038 \text{ V}$$

       Check: The units (V) are correct. The cell voltage is positive, which is consistent with a spontaneous reaction.

18.51   When iron corrodes or rusts, it oxidizes to Fe^{2+}. For a metal to be able to protect iron, it must be more easily oxidized than iron or be below it in Table 18.1. (a) Zn and (c) Mn meet that criterion.

Electrolytic Cells and Electrolysis

18.53   **Given:** electrolytic cell sketch
         Find: (a) Label the anode and cathode and indicate half-reactions, (b) indicate direction of electron flow, and (c) label battery terminals and calculate minimum voltage to drive reaction.
         Conceptual Plan: (a) Write two half-cell reactions and add electrons as needed to balance reactions. Look up half-reactions in Table 18.1. Calculate the standard cell potential by subtracting the electrode potential of the anode from the electrode potential of the cathode: $E°_{cell} = E°_{cathode} - E°_{anode}$**. Choose the direction of the half-cell reactions so that** $E°_{cell} < 0$**. (b) Electrons flow from anode to cathode. (c) Each half-cell reaction moves forward, so direction of the concentration changes can be determined.**
         Solution:

(a) $Ni^{2+}(aq) + 2e^- \rightarrow Ni(s)$ and $Cd^{2+}(aq) + 2e^- \rightarrow Cd(s)$.
       Look up cell potentials. For Ni, $E°_{red} = -0.23$ V. For Cd,
       $E°_{red} = -0.40$ V. To get a negative cell potential, Ni is oxidized; so
       $E°_{red} = -0.23$ V $= E°_{anode}$. Cd^{2+} is reduced, so $E°_{red} = -0.40$ V $=$
       $E°_{cathode}$. Then $E°_{cell} = E°_{cathode} - E°_{anode} = -0.40$ V $- (-0.23$ V$) =$
       -0.17 V. Because oxidation occurs at the anode, Ni is the anode
       and the reaction is $Ni(s) \rightarrow Ni^{2+}(aq) + 2e^-$. Because reduction
       takes place at the cathode, Cd is the cathode and the reaction is
       $Cd^{2+}(aq) + 2e^- \rightarrow Cd(s)$.

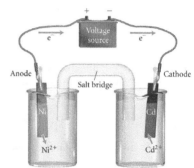

(c)   Because reduction is occurring at the cathode, the battery terminal closest to the cathode is the negative terminal. Because the cell potential from part (a) is $= -0.17$ V, a minimum of 0.17 V must be applied by the battery.

       Check: The reaction is nonspontaneous because the reduction of Ni^{2+} is above Cd^{2+}. Electrons still flow from the anode to the cathode. The reaction can be made spontaneous with the application of electrical energy.

18.55   **Given:** electrolysis cell to electroplate Cu onto a metal surface
         Find: Draw a cell and label the anode and cathode and write half-reactions.
         Conceptual Plan: Write two half-cell reactions and add electrons as needed to balance reactions. The cathode reaction will be the reduction of Cu^{2+} **to the metal. The anode will be the reverse reaction.**
         Solution:

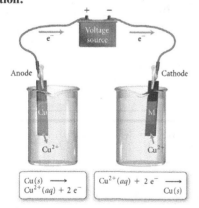

       Check: The metal to be plated is the cathode because metal ions are converted to Cu(s) on the surface of the metal.

18.57   **Given:** Cu electroplating of 225 mg Cu at a current of 7.8 A (7.8 C/s); $Cu^{2+}(aq) + 2e^- \rightarrow Cu(s)$ **Find:** time
         Conceptual Plan: mg Cu $\rightarrow$ g Cu $\rightarrow$ mol Cu $\rightarrow$ mol e$^-$ $\rightarrow$ C $\rightarrow$ s

$$\frac{1\,g}{1000\,mg} \quad \frac{1\,mol\,Cu}{63.55\,g\,Cu} \quad \frac{2\,mol\,e^-}{1\,mol\,Cu} \quad \frac{96,485\,C}{1\,mol\,e^-} \quad \frac{1\,s}{7.8\,C}$$

Solution: $225\ \cancel{mg\ Cu} \times \dfrac{1\ g\ \cancel{Cu}}{1000\ \cancel{mg\ Cu}} \times \dfrac{1\ \cancel{mol\ Cu}}{63.55\ g\ \cancel{Cu}} \times \dfrac{2\ \cancel{mol\ e^-}}{1\ \cancel{mol\ Cu}} \times \dfrac{96,485\ \cancel{C}}{1\ \cancel{mol\ e^-}} \times \dfrac{1\ s}{7.8\ \cancel{C}} = 88\ s$

       Check: The units (s) are correct. Because far less than a mole of Cu is electroplated, the time is short.

18.59   **Given:** Na electrolysis, 1.0 kg in one hour   **Find:** current

Conceptual Plan: Na$^+$(*l*) + e$^-$ → Na(*l*) $\dfrac{kg\ Na}{h}$ → $\dfrac{g\ Na}{h}$ → $\dfrac{mol\ Na}{h}$ → $\dfrac{mol\ e^-}{h}$ → $\dfrac{C}{h}$ → $\dfrac{C}{min}$ → $\dfrac{C}{s}$

$\dfrac{1000\ g}{1\ kg}$ $\dfrac{1\ mol\ Na}{22.99\ g\ Na}$ $\dfrac{1\ mol\ e^-}{1\ mol\ Na}$ $\dfrac{96{,}485\ C}{1\ mol\ e^-}$ $\dfrac{1\ h}{60\ min}$ $\dfrac{1\ min}{60\ s}$

Solution:

$\dfrac{1.0\ \cancel{kg\ Na}}{1\ \cancel{h}} \times \dfrac{1000\ \cancel{g\ Na}}{1\ \cancel{kg\ Na}} \times \dfrac{1\ \cancel{mol\ Na}}{22.99\ \cancel{g\ Na}} \times \dfrac{1\ \cancel{mol\ e^-}}{1\ \cancel{mol\ Na}} \times \dfrac{96{,}485\ C}{1\ \cancel{mol\ e^-}} \times \dfrac{1\ \cancel{h}}{60\ \cancel{min}} \times \dfrac{1\ \cancel{min}}{60\ s} = 1.2 \times 10^3\ \dfrac{C}{s} = 1.2 \times 10^3\ A$

Check: The units (A) are correct. Because the amount per hour is so large, we expect a very large current.

Cumulative Problems

18.61   **Given:** $MnO_4^-(aq) + Zn(s) \rightarrow Mn^{2+}(aq) + Zn^{2+}(aq)$, 0.500 M KMnO$_4$, and 2.85 g Zn
Find: balance equation and volume KMnO$_4$ solution
Conceptual Plan: Separate the overall reaction into two half-reactions: one for oxidation and one for reduction. → Balance each half-reaction with respect to mass in the following order: (1) Balance all elements other than H and O, (2) balance O by adding H$_2$O, and (3) balance H by adding H$^+$. → Balance each half-reaction with respect to charge by adding electrons. (The sum of the charges on both sides of the equation should be made equal by adding electrons as necessary.) → Make the number of electrons in both half-reactions equal by multiplying one or both half-reactions by a small whole number. → Add the two half-reactions together, canceling electrons and other species as necessary. → Verify that the reaction is balanced with respect to both mass and charge.
Then g Zn → mol Zn → mol MnO$_4^-$ → L MnO$_4^-$ → mL MnO$_4^-$.

$\dfrac{1\ mol\ Zn}{65.38\ g\ Zn}$ $\dfrac{2\ mol\ MnO_4^-}{5\ mol\ Zn}$ $\dfrac{1\ L\ MnO_4^-}{0.500\ mol\ MnO_4^-}$ $\dfrac{1000\ mL\ MnO_4^-}{1\ L\ MnO_4^-}$

Solution:

Separate: $MnO_4^-(aq) \rightarrow Mn^{2+}(aq)$ and $Zn(s) \rightarrow Zn^{2+}(aq)$
Balance non-H & O elements: $MnO_4^-(aq) \rightarrow Mn^{2+}(aq)$ and $Zn(s) \rightarrow Zn^{2+}(aq)$
Balance O with H$_2$O: $MnO_4^-(aq) \rightarrow Mn^{2+}(aq) + 4\ H_2O(l)$ and $Zn(s) \rightarrow Zn^{2+}(aq)$
Balance H with H$^+$: $MnO_4^-(aq) + 8\ H^+(aq) \rightarrow Mn^{2+}(aq) + 4\ H_2O(l)$ and $Zn(s) \rightarrow Zn^{2+}(aq)$
Add electrons: $MnO_4^-(aq) + 8\ H^+(aq) + 5\ e^- \rightarrow Mn^{2+}(aq) + 4\ H_2O(l)$ and $Zn(s) \rightarrow Zn^{2+}(aq) + 2\ e^-$
Equalize electrons:
$2\ MnO_4^-(aq) + 16\ H^+(aq) + 10\ e^- \rightarrow 2\ Mn^{2+}(aq) + 8\ H_2O(l)$ and $5\ Zn(s) \rightarrow 5\ Zn^{2+}(aq) + 10\ e^-$
Add half-reactions:
$2\ MnO_4^-(aq) + 16\ H^+(aq) + \cancel{10\ e^-} + 5\ Zn(s) \rightarrow 2\ Mn^{2+}(aq) + 8\ H_2O(l) + 5\ Zn^{2+}(aq) + \cancel{10\ e^-}$
Cancel electrons: $2\ MnO_4^-(aq) + 16\ H^+(aq) + 5\ Zn(s) \rightarrow 2\ Mn^{2+}(aq) + 8\ H_2O(l) + 5\ Zn^{2+}(aq)$

$2.85\ \cancel{g\ Zn} \times \dfrac{1\ \cancel{mol\ Zn}}{65.38\ \cancel{g\ Zn}} \times \dfrac{2\ \cancel{mol\ MnO_4^-}}{5\ \cancel{mol\ Zn}} \times \dfrac{1\ \cancel{L\ MnO_4^-}}{0.500\ \cancel{mol\ MnO_4^-}} \times \dfrac{1000\ mL\ MnO_4^-}{1\ \cancel{L\ MnO_4^-}} = 34.9\ mL\ MnO_4^- =$

$= 34.9\ mL\ KMnO_4$

	Reactants	Products
Check:	2 Mn atoms	2 Mn atoms
	8 O atoms	8 O atoms
	16 H atoms	16 H atoms
	5 Zn atoms	5 Zn atoms
	+14 charge	+14 charge

The units (mL) are correct. Because far less than a mole of zinc is used, less than a mole of permanganate is consumed; so the volume is less than a liter.

18.63   **Given:** beaker with Al strip and Cu^{2+} ions   **Find:** Draw sketch after Al is submerged for a few minutes.
Conceptual Plan: Write two half-cell reactions and add electrons as needed to balance reactions. Look up half-reactions in Table 18.1. Calculate the standard cell potential by subtracting the electrode potential of the anode from the electrode potential of the cathode: $E°_{cell} = E°_{cathode} - E°_{anode}$. If $E°_{cell} > 0$, the reaction is spontaneous in the forward direction and Al will dissolve and Cu will deposit.

Solution: $Al(s) \rightarrow Al^{3+}(aq)$ and $Cu^{2+}(aq) \rightarrow Cu(s)$. Add electrons. $Al(s) \rightarrow Al^{3+}(aq) + 3\ e^-$ and $Cu^{2+}(aq) + 2\ e^- \rightarrow Cu(s)$. Look up cell potentials. Al is oxidized, so $E°_{anode} = E°_{red} = -1.66\ V$. Cu^{2+} is reduced, so $E°_{cathode} = E°_{red} = 0.34\ V$. Then $E°_{cell} = E°_{cathode} - E°_{anode} = 0.34\ V - (-1.66\ V) = 2.00\ V$, so the reaction is spontaneous. Al will dissolve to generate $Al^{3+}(aq)$, and $Cu(s)$ will deposit.

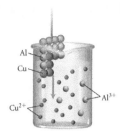

Check: The units (V) are correct. If the voltage is positive, the reaction is spontaneous; so Al will dissolve and Cu will deposit.

18.65   **Given:** (a) 2.15 g Al, (b) 4.85 g Cu, and (c) 2.42 g Ag in 3.5 M HI
        Find: If metal dissolves, write a balanced reaction and the minimum amount of HI needed to dissolve the metal.
        Conceptual Plan: In general, metals whose reduction half-reactions lie below the reduction of H^+ to H_2 in Table 18.1 will dissolve in acids, while metals above it will not. Stop here if metal does not dissolve. To write the balanced redox reactions, pair the oxidation of the metal with the reduction of H^+ to H_2 ($2H^+(aq) + 2e^- \rightarrow H_2(g)$). Balance the number of electrons transferred. Add the two reactions. Cancel electrons. Then g metal $\rightarrow$ mol metal $\rightarrow$ mol H^+ $\rightarrow$ L HI $\rightarrow$ mL HI.

$$\mathcal{M} \quad\quad \frac{x\ mol\ H^+}{y\ mol\ metal} \quad \frac{1\ L\ HI}{3.5\ mol\ HI} \quad \frac{1000\ mL\ HI}{1\ L\ HI}$$

        Solution:
    (a)   Al meets this criterion. For Al, $Al(s) \rightarrow Al^{3+}(aq) + 3\ e^-$. We need to multiply the Al reaction by 2 and the H^+ reaction by 3. So $2\ Al(s) \rightarrow 2\ Al^{3+}(aq) + 6\ e^-$ and $6\ H^+(aq) + 6\ e^- \rightarrow 3\ H_2(g)$. Adding the half-reactions: $2\ Al(s) + 6\ H^+(aq) + 6\ e^- \rightarrow 2\ Al^{3+}(aq) + 6\ e^- + 3\ H_2(g)$. Simplify to $2\ Al(s) + 6\ H^+(aq) \rightarrow 2\ Al^{3+}(aq) + 3\ H_2(g)$. Then

$$2.15\ g\ Al \times \frac{1\ mol\ Al}{26.98\ g\ Al} \times \frac{6\ mol\ H^+}{2\ mol\ Al} \times \frac{1\ L\ HI}{3.5\ mol\ HI} \times \frac{1000\ mL\ HI}{1\ L\ HI} = 68.3\ mL\ HI$$

    (b)   Cu does not meet this criterion, so it will not dissolve in HI.
    (c)   Ag does not meet this criterion, so it will not dissolve in HI.

        Check: Only metals with negative reduction potentials will dissolve. The volume of acid needed is fairly small because the amount of metal is much less than 1 mole and the concentration of acid is high.

18.67   **Given:** $Pt(s)\,|\,H_2(g, 1\ atm)\,|\,H^+(aq, ?\ M)\,||\,Cu^{2+}(aq, 1.0\ M)\,|\,Cu(s)$, $E_{cell} = 355\ mV$ **Find:** pH
        Conceptual Plan: Write half-reactions from line notation. Look up half-reactions in Table 18.1. Calculate the standard cell potential by subtracting the electrode potential of the anode from the electrode potential of the cathode: $E°_{cell} = E°_{cathode} - E°_{anode}$. Add the two half-cell reactions and cancel the electrons. Then mV $\rightarrow$ V then $E°_{cell}, E_{cell}, P_{H_2}, [Cu^{2+}], n \rightarrow [H^+] \rightarrow$ pH.

$$\frac{1\ V}{1000\ mV} \quad\quad\quad E_{cell} = E°_{cell} - \frac{0.0592\ V}{n}\log Q \quad pH = -\log[H^+]$$

        Solution: The half-reactions are $H_2(g) \rightarrow 2\ H^+(aq) + 2\ e^-$ and $Cu^{2+}(aq) + 2\ e^- \rightarrow Cu(s)$. H is oxidized, so $E°_{red} = 0.00\ V = E°_{anode}$. Cu is reduced, so $E°_{red} = 0.34\ V = E°_{cathode}$. Then $E°_{cell} = E°_{cathode} - E°_{anode} = 0.34\ V - 0.00\ V = +0.34\ V$. Adding the two reactions: $H_2(g) + Cu^{2+}(aq) + 2\ e^- \rightarrow 2\ H^+(aq) + 2\ e^- + Cu(s)$. Cancel the electrons: $H_2(g) + Cu^{2+}(aq) \rightarrow 2\ H^+(aq) + Cu(s)$. Then $355\ mV \times \frac{1\ V}{1000\ mV} = 0.355\ V$. So

$n = 2$ and $Q = \dfrac{[H^+]^2}{P_{H_2}[Cu^{2+}]} = \dfrac{(x)^2}{(1)(1.0)} = x^2$. Then $E_{cell} = E°_{cell} - \dfrac{0.0592\ V}{n}\log Q$. Substitute values and

solve for x. $0.355\ V = 0.34\ V - \dfrac{0.0592\ V}{2}\log x^2 \rightarrow 0.015\ V = -\dfrac{0.0592\ V}{2}\log x^2 \rightarrow -0.50676 = \log x^2 \rightarrow$

$x^2 = 10^{-0.50676} = 0.31134 \rightarrow x = 0.55798$ then $pH = -\log[H^+] = -\log[0.55798] = 0.25338 = 0.3$

        Check: The units (none) are correct. The pH is acidic, which is consistent with dissolving a metal in acid.

18.69   **Given:** Mg oxidation and Cu^{2+} reduction; initially, $[Mg^{2+}] = 1.0 \times 10^{-4}\ M$ and $[Cu^{2+}] = 1.5\ M$ in 1.0 L half-cells   **Find:** (a) initial E_{cell}, (b) E_{cell} after 5.0 A for 8.0 h, and (c) how long battery can deliver 5.0 A
        Conceptual Plan:
    (a)   **Write the two half-cell reactions and add electrons as needed to balance reactions. Look up half-reactions in Table 18.1. Calculate the standard cell potential by subtracting the electrode potential of the**

anode from the electrode potential of the cathode: $E°_{cell} = E°_{cathode} - E°_{anode}$. Add the two half-cell reactions, cancel electrons, and determine n. Then $E°_{cell}$, $[Mg^{2+}]$, $[Cu^{2+}]$, $n \rightarrow E_{cell}$.

$$E_{cell} = E°_{cell} - \frac{0.0592\ V}{n} \log Q$$

(b) $h \rightarrow min \rightarrow s \rightarrow C \rightarrow mol\ e^- \rightarrow mol\ Cu\ reduced \rightarrow [Cu^{2+}]$ and

$$\frac{60\ min}{1\ h} \quad \frac{60\ s}{1\ min} \quad \frac{5.0\ C}{1\ s} \quad \frac{1\ mol\ e^-}{96,485\ C} \quad \frac{1\ mol\ Cu^{2+}}{2\ mol\ e^-}\ since\ V = 1.0\ L \quad [Cu^{2+}] = [Cu^{2+}] - \frac{mol\ Cu^{2+}\ reduced}{1.0\ L}$$

mol Cu reduced $\rightarrow$ **mol Mg oxidized** $\rightarrow$ **$[Mg^{2+}]$**

$$\frac{1\ mol\ Mg\ oxidized}{1\ mol\ Cu^{2+}\ reduced}\ because\ V = 1.0\ L \qquad [Mg^{2+}] = [Mg^{2+}] + \frac{mol\ Mg\ oxidized}{1.0\ L}$$

(c) $[Cu^{2+}] \rightarrow mol\ e^- \rightarrow C \rightarrow s \rightarrow min \rightarrow h$

$$\frac{1\ mol\ e^-}{2\ mol\ Cu^{2+}} \quad \frac{96,485\ C}{1\ mol\ e^-} \quad \frac{1\ s}{5.0\ C} \quad \frac{1\ min}{60\ s} \quad \frac{1\ h}{60\ min}$$

Solution:

(a)   Write half-reactions and add electrons. $Cu^{2+}(aq) + 2\ e^- \rightarrow Cu(s)$ and $Mg(s) \rightarrow Mg^{2+}(aq) + 2\ e^-$. Look up cell potentials. Mg is oxidized, so $E°_{red} = -2.37\ V = E°_{anode}$. Cu^{2+} is reduced, so $E°_{red} = 0.34\ V = E°_{cathode}$. Then $E°_{cell} = E°_{cathode} - E°_{anode} = 0.34\ V - (-2.37\ V) = +2.71\ V$. Add the two half-cell reactions: $Cu^{2+}(aq) + 2e^- + Mg(s) \rightarrow Cu(s) + Mg^{2+}(aq) + 2e^-$. Simplify to

$Cu^{2+}(aq) + Mg(s) \rightarrow Cu(s) + Mg^{2+}(aq)$. So $Q = \dfrac{[Mg^{2+}]}{[Cu^{2+}]} = \dfrac{1.0 \times 10^{-4}}{1.5} = 6.6667 \times 10^{-5}$ and $n = 2$.

Then $E_{cell} = E°_{cell} - \dfrac{0.0592\ V}{n} \log Q = 2.71\ V - \dfrac{0.0592\ V}{2} \log 6.6667 \times 10^{-5} = +2.83361\ V = +2.83\ V$.

(b) $8.0\ h \times \dfrac{60\ min}{1\ h} \times \dfrac{60\ s}{1\ min} \times \dfrac{5.0\ C}{1\ s} \times \dfrac{1\ mol\ e^-}{96,485\ C} \times \dfrac{1\ mol\ Cu^{2+}}{2\ mol\ e^-} = 0.74623\ mol\ Cu^{2+}$ and

$[Cu^{2+}] = [Cu^{2+}] - \dfrac{mol\ Cu^{2+}\ reduced}{1.0\ L} = 1.5\ M - \dfrac{0.74623\ mol\ Cu^{2+}}{1.0\ L} = 0.75377\ M\ Cu^{2+}$

and $0.74623\ mol\ Cu^{2+} \times \dfrac{1\ mol\ Mg\ oxidized}{1\ mol\ Cu^{2+}\ reduced} = 0.74623\ mol\ Mg\ oxidized$ and

$[Mg^{2+}] = [Mg^{2+}] + \dfrac{mol\ Mg\ oxidized}{1.0\ L} = 1.0 \times 10^{-4}\ M + \dfrac{0.74623\ mol\ Mg\ oxidized}{1.0\ L}$

$= 0.74633\ M\ Mg^{2+}$

$Q = \dfrac{[Mg^{2+}]}{[Cu^{2+}]} = \dfrac{0.74633}{0.75377} = 0.99013$ and $n = 2$ then

$E_{cell} = E°_{cell} - \dfrac{0.0592\ V}{n} \log Q = 2.71\ V - \dfrac{0.0592\ V}{2} \log 0.99013 = +2.71013\ V = +2.71\ V$

(c)   In 1.0 L, there are initially 1.5 moles of Cu^{2+}. So

$1.5\ mol\ Cu^{2+} \times \dfrac{2\ mol\ e^-}{1\ mol\ Cu^{2+}} \times \dfrac{96,485\ C}{1\ mol\ e^-} \times \dfrac{1\ s}{5.0\ C} \times \dfrac{1\ min}{60\ s} \times \dfrac{1\ h}{60\ min} = 16\ h$.

Check: The units (V, V, and h) are correct. The Cu^{2+} reduction reaction is above the Mg^{2+} reduction reaction, so the standard cell potential will be positive. Having more reactants than products increases the cell potential. As the reaction proceeds, the potential drops. The concentrations drop by $\frac{1}{2}$ in 8 hours (part (b)), so all of it is consumed in 16 hours.

18.71   **Given:** $Cu(s) \mid CuI(s) \mid I^-(aq, 1.0\ M) \parallel Cu^+(aq, 1.0\ M) \mid Cu(s)$, $K_{sp}(CuI) = 1.1 \times 10^{-12}$ **Find:** E_{cell}
Conceptual Plan: Write half-reactions from line notation. Because this is a concentration cell, $E°_{cell} = 0.00\ V$.
Then K_{sp}, $[I^-] \rightarrow [Cu^+](ox)$ then $E°_{cell}$, $[Cu^+](ox)$, $[Cu^+](red)$, $n \rightarrow E_{cell}$.

$$K_{sp} = [Cu^+][I^-] \qquad\qquad E_{cell} = E°_{cell} - \frac{0.0592\ V}{n} \log Q$$

Solution: The half-reactions are $Cu(s) \rightarrow Cu^+(aq) + e^-$ and $Cu^+(aq) + e^- \rightarrow Cu(s)$. Because this is a concentration cell, $E°_{cell} = 0.00\ V$ and $n = 1$. Because $K_{sp} = [Cu^+][I^-]$, rearrange to solve for $[Cu^+](ox)$.

$$[Cu^+](ox) = \frac{K_{sp}}{[I^-]} = \frac{1.1 \times 10^{-12}}{1.0} = 1.1 \times 10^{-12} \text{ M then}$$

$$Q = \frac{[Cu^+](ox)}{[Cu^+](red)} = \frac{1.1 \times 10^{-12}}{1.0} = 1.1 \times 10^{-12} \text{ then}$$

$$E_{cell} = E°_{cell} - \frac{0.0592 \text{ V}}{n} \log Q = 0.00 \text{ V} - \frac{0.0592 \text{ V}}{1} \log (1.1 \times 10^{-12}) = 0.71 \text{ V}$$

Check: The units (V) are correct. Because $[Cu^+](ox)$ is so low and $[Cu^+](red)$ is high, the Q is very small; so the voltage increase compared to the standard value is significant.

18.73   **Given:** (a) disproportionation of $Mn^{2+}(aq)$ to $Mn(s)$ and $MnO_2(s)$ and (b) disproportionation of $MnO_2(s)$ to $Mn^{2+}(aq)$ and $MnO_4^-(s)$ in acidic solution   **Find:** $\Delta G°_{rxn}$ and K
Conceptual Plan: Separate the overall reaction into two half-reactions: one for oxidation and one for reduction. → Balance each half-reaction with respect to mass in the following order: (1) Balance all elements other than H and O, (2) balance O by adding H_2O, and (3) balance H by adding H^+. → Balance each half-reaction with respect to charge by adding electrons. (The sum of the charges on both sides of the equation should be made equal by adding electrons as necessary.) → Make the number of electrons in both half-reactions equal by multiplying one or both half-reactions by a small whole number. → Add the two half-reactions together, canceling electrons and other species as necessary. → Verify that the reaction is balanced with respect to both mass and charge. Look up half-reactions in Table 18.1. Calculate the standard cell potential by subtracting the electrode potential of the anode from the electrode potential of the cathode: $E°_{cell} = E°_{cathode} - E°_{anode}$. Then calculate $\Delta G°_{rxn}$ using $\Delta G°_{rxn} = -nFE°_{cell}$. Finally, °C → K then $\Delta G°_{rxn}, T → K$.

$$K = 273.15 + °C \qquad \Delta G°_{rxn} = -RT \ln K$$

Solution:

(a)   Separate: $Mn^{2+}(aq) \rightarrow MnO_2(s)$ and $Mn^{2+}(aq) \rightarrow Mn(s)$
Balance non-H & O elements: $Mn^{2+}(aq) \rightarrow MnO_2(s)$ and $Mn^{2+}(aq) \rightarrow Mn(s)$
Balance O with H_2O: $Mn^{2+}(aq) + 2 H_2O(l) \rightarrow MnO_2(s)$ and $Mn^{2+}(aq) \rightarrow Mn(s)$
Balance H with H^+: $Mn^{2+}(aq) + 2 H_2O(l) \rightarrow MnO_2(s) + 4 H^+(aq)$ and $Mn^{2+}(aq) \rightarrow Mn(s)$
Add electrons: $Mn^{2+}(aq) + 2 H_2O(l) \rightarrow MnO_2(s) + 4 H^+(aq) + 2 e^-$ and $Mn^{2+}(aq) + 2 e^- \rightarrow Mn(s)$
Equalize electrons: $Mn^{2+}(aq) + 2 H_2O(l) \rightarrow MnO_2(s) + 4 H^+(aq) + 2 e^-$ and $Mn^{2+}(aq) + 2 e^- \rightarrow Mn(s)$
Add half-reactions: $Mn^{2+}(aq) + 2 H_2O(l) + Mn^{2+}(aq) + 2\cancel{e^-} \rightarrow MnO_2(s) + 4 H^+(aq) + 2\cancel{e^-} + Mn(s)$
Cancel electrons: $2 Mn^{2+}(aq) + 2 H_2O(l) \rightarrow MnO_2(s) + 4 H^+(aq) + Mn(s)$
Look up cell potentials. Mn is oxidized in the first half-cell reaction, so $E°_{anode} = E°_{red} = +1.21$ V. Mn is reduced in the second half-cell reaction, so $E°_{cathode} = E°_{red} = -1.18$ V. Then
$E°_{cell} = E°_{cathode} - E°_{anode} = -1.18$ V $- 1.21$ V $= -2.39$ V. $n = 2$, so

$$\Delta G°_{rxn} = -nFE°_{cell} = -2 \text{ } \cancel{\text{mole}^-} \times \frac{96{,}485 \text{ C}}{\cancel{\text{mole}^-}} \times -2.39 \text{ V} = -2 \times 96{,}485 \text{ } \cancel{C} \times -2.39 \frac{J}{\cancel{C}} =$$

4.61198×10^5 J $= 461$ kJ and $T = 273.15 + 25 \text{ °C} = 298$ K then
$\Delta G°_{rxn} = -RT \ln K$. Rearrange to solve for K.

$$K = e^{\frac{-\Delta G°_{rxn}}{RT}} = e^{\frac{-4.61198 \times 10^5 \cancel{J}}{\left(8.314 \frac{\cancel{J}}{K \cdot mol}\right)(298 \cancel{K})}} = e^{-186.149} = 1.43 \times 10^{-81}$$

Check: Reactants   Products
                2 Mn atoms   2 Mn atoms
                2 O atoms   2 O atoms
                4 H atoms   4 H atoms
                +4 charge   +4 charge
The units (kJ and none) are correct. If the voltage is negative, the reaction is nonspontaneous, the free energy change is very positive, and the equilibrium constant is extremely small.

(b)   Separate: $MnO_2(s) \rightarrow Mn^{2+}(aq)$ and $MnO_2(s) \rightarrow MnO_4^-(aq)$
Balance non-H & O elements: $MnO_2(s) \rightarrow Mn^{2+}(aq)$ and $MnO_2(s) \rightarrow MnO_4^-(aq)$
Balance O with H_2O: $MnO_2(s) \rightarrow Mn^{2+}(aq) + 2 H_2O(l)$ and $MnO_2(s) + 2 H_2O(l) \rightarrow MnO_4^-(aq)$

Balance H with H^+:

$MnO_2(s) + 4 H^+(aq) \rightarrow Mn^{2+}(aq) + 2 H_2O(l)$ and $MnO_2(s) + 2 H_2O(l) \rightarrow MnO_4^-(aq) + 4 H^+(aq)$

Add electrons: $MnO_2(s) + 4 H^+(aq) + 2 e^- \rightarrow Mn^{2+}(aq) + 2 H_2O(l)$ and $MnO_2(s) + 2 H_2O(l) \rightarrow$
$$MnO_4^-(aq) + 4 H^+(aq) + 3 e^-$$

Equalize electrons: $3 MnO_2(s) + 12 H^+(aq) + 6 e^- \rightarrow 3 Mn^{2+}(aq) + 6 H_2O(l)$ and
$$2 MnO_2(s) + 4 H_2O(l) \rightarrow 2 MnO_4^-(aq) + 8 H^+(aq) + 6 e^-$$

Add half-reactions: $3 MnO_2(s) + 4 \overset{12}{\cancel{12}} \overset{}{H^+(aq)} + \cancel{6 e^-} + 2 MnO_2(s) + \overset{2}{\cancel{4 H_2O(l)}} \rightarrow$
$$3 Mn^{2+}(aq) + \overset{2}{\cancel{6}} H_2O(l) + 2 MnO_4^-(aq) + \overset{}{\cancel{8 H^+(aq)}} + \cancel{6 e^-}$$

Cancel electrons & species: $5 MnO_2(s) + 4 H^+(aq) \rightarrow 3 Mn^{2+}(aq) + 2 H_2O(l) + 2 MnO_4^-(aq)$

Look up cell potentials. Mn is reduced in the first half-cell reaction, so $E^\circ_{cathode} = E^\circ_{red} = 1.21$ V. Mn is oxidized in the second half-cell reaction, so $E^\circ_{anode} = E^\circ_{red} = +1.68$ V. Then $E^\circ_{cell} = E^\circ_{cathode} - E^\circ_{anode}$
$= 1.21$ V $- 1.68$ V $= -0.47$ V. $n = 6$, so

$$\Delta G^\circ_{rxn} = -nFE^\circ_{cell} = -6 \text{ mol } e^- \times \frac{96{,}485 \text{ C}}{\text{mol } e^-} \times -0.47 \text{ V} = -6 \times 96{,}485 \text{ C} \times -0.47 \frac{\text{J}}{\text{C}}$$

$= 2.\underline{7}209 \times 10^5$ J $= 270$ kJ $= 2.7 \times 10^2$ kJ. $T = 273.15 + 25 \,°C = 298$ K then $\Delta G^\circ_{rxn} = -RT \ln K$.

Rearrange to solve for K. $K = e^{\frac{-\Delta G^\circ_{rxn}}{RT}} = e^{\frac{-2.\underline{7}209 \times 10^5 \text{ J}}{\left(8.314 \frac{\text{J}}{\text{K} \cdot \text{mol}}\right)(298 \text{ K})}} = e^{-109.82} = 2.0 \times 10^{-48}$

Check:

Reactants	Products
5 Mn atoms	5 Mn atoms
10 O atoms	10 O atoms
4 H atoms	4 H atoms
+4 charge	+4 charge

The units (kJ and none) are correct. If the voltage is negative, the reaction is nonspontaneous, the free energy change is very positive, and the equilibrium constant is extremely small. The voltage is less than in part (a), so the free energy change is not as large and the equilibrium constant is not as small.

18.75   **Given:** metal, M, 50.9 g/mol, 1.20 g of metal reduced in 23.6 minutes at 6.42 A from molten chloride
Find: empirical formula of chloride
Conceptual Plan: $\text{min} \rightarrow \text{s} \rightarrow \text{C} \rightarrow \text{mol } e^-$ and $\text{g M} \rightarrow \text{mol M}$ then $\text{mol } e^-, \text{mol M} \rightarrow \text{charge} \rightarrow MCl_x$

$$\frac{60 \text{ s}}{1 \text{ min}} \quad \frac{6.42 \text{ C}}{1 \text{ s}} \quad \frac{1 \text{ mol } e^-}{96{,}485 \text{ C}} \qquad \frac{1 \text{ mol M}}{50.9 \text{ g M}} \qquad \frac{1 \text{ mol } e^-}{1 \text{ mol M}}$$

Solution: $23.6 \text{ min} \times \frac{60 \text{ s}}{1 \text{ min}} \times \frac{6.42 \text{ C}}{1 \text{ s}} \times \frac{1 \text{ mol } e^-}{96{,}485 \text{ C}} = 0.0942190 \text{ mol } e^-$ and

$1.20 \text{ g M} \times \frac{1 \text{ mol M}}{50.9 \text{ g M}} = 0.0235756 \text{ mol M}$ then $\frac{0.0942190 \text{ mol } e^-}{0.0235756 \text{ mol M}} = 3.99646 \frac{e^-}{M}$

So the empirical formula is MCl_4.

Check: The units (none) are correct. The result was an integer within the error of the measurements. The formula is typical for a metal salt. It could be vanadium, which has a +4 oxidation state.

18.77   **Given:** 0.535 g impure Sn; dissolve to form Sn^{2+} and titrate with 0.0344 L of 0.0448 M NO_3^- to generate
NO   **Find:** percent by mass Sn
Conceptual Plan: Use balanced reaction from Problem 18.4(c) then
$L \rightarrow \text{mol } NO_3^- \rightarrow \text{mol Sn} \rightarrow \text{g Sn} \rightarrow$ percent by mass Sn.

$$M = \frac{\text{mol}}{L} \qquad \frac{3 \text{ mol Sn}}{2 \text{ mol } NO_3^-} \qquad \frac{118.71 \text{ g Sn}}{1 \text{ mol Sn}} \quad \text{percent by mass Sn} = \frac{\text{g Sn}}{\text{g sample}} \times 100\%$$

Solution: $2 NO_3^-(aq) + 8 H^+(aq) + 3 Sn^{2+}(aq) \rightarrow 2 NO(g) + 4 H_2O(l) + 3 Sn^{4+}(aq)$

$0.0344 \text{ L} \times \frac{0.0448 \text{ mol } NO_3^-}{1 \text{ L}} \times \frac{3 \text{ mol Sn}}{2 \text{ mol } NO_3^-} \times \frac{118.71 \text{ g Sn}}{1 \text{ mol Sn}} = 0.2744195 \text{ g Sn}$ then

$\text{percent by mass Sn} = \frac{\text{g Sn}}{\text{g sample}} \times 100\% = \frac{0.2744195 \text{ g Sn}}{0.535 \text{ g sample}} \times 100\% = 51.3\%$ by mass Sn

Check: The units (% by mass) are correct. The result was a number less than 100%.

18.79 **Given:** $[A^{2+}]$ and $[B^{2+}]$ in table and $\Delta G^{\circ}_{rxn} = -14.0$ kJ **Find:** E°_{cell}, K, Q, E_{cell}, and ΔG_{rxn}

Conceptual Plan: Determine n; ΔG°_{rxn}, **then** $n \rightarrow E^{\circ}_{cell}$ **and** ΔG°_{rxn}, $T \rightarrow K$ **and**

$$A(s) + B^{2+}(aq) \rightarrow A^{2+}(aq) + B(s) \quad \Delta G^{\circ}_{rxn} = -nFE^{\circ}_{cell} \qquad \Delta G^{\circ}_{rxn} = -RT \ln K$$

For each set of conditions: $[A^{2+}]$, $[B^{2+}] \rightarrow Q$ **then** E°_{cell}, $[A^{2+}]$, $[B^{2+}]$, $n \rightarrow E_{cell}$ **and** ΔG°_{rxn}, Q, $T \rightarrow \Delta G_{rxn}$

$$Q = \frac{[A^{2+}]}{[B^{2+}]} \qquad E_{cell} = E^{\circ}_{cell} - \frac{0.0592 \text{ V}}{n} \log Q \qquad \Delta G_{rxn} = \Delta G^{\circ}_{rxn} + RT \ln Q$$

Solution: Since the charge of both A and B change by 2 in the reaction, $n = 2$. $\Delta G^{\circ}_{rxn} = -nFE^{\circ}_{cell}$ Rearrange to solve

for E°_{cell}. $E^{\circ}_{cell} = \dfrac{\Delta G^{\circ}_{rxn}}{-nF} = \dfrac{-1.40 \times 10^4 \text{ J}}{-2 \text{ mole} \times \dfrac{96,485 \text{ C}}{\text{mole}}} = 0.07\underline{2}5501 \dfrac{\text{V} \cdot \cancel{C}}{\cancel{C}} = 0.0726 \text{ V}.$

$\Delta G^{\circ}_{rxn} = -RT \ln K$. Rearrange to solve for K. $K = e^{\frac{-\Delta G^{\circ}_{rxn}}{RT}} = e^{\dfrac{-(-1.40 \times 10^4 \cancel{J})}{\left(8.314\dfrac{\cancel{J}}{\text{K} \cdot \text{mol}}\right)(298 \text{ K})}} = e^{+5.6\underline{5}0694} = 28\underline{4}.4888 = 284.$

1: $Q = \dfrac{[A^{2+}]}{[B^{2+}]} = \dfrac{1.00 \text{ M}}{1.00 \text{ M}} = 1.00$

$E_{cell} = E^{\circ}_{cell} - \dfrac{0.0592 \text{ V}}{n} \log Q = 0.07\underline{2}5501 \text{ V} - \dfrac{0.0592 \text{ V}}{2} \log(1) = +0.0726 \text{ V}$ and

$\Delta G_{rxn} = \Delta G^{\circ}_{rxn} + RT \ln Q = -14.0 \text{ kJ} + \left(8.314 \dfrac{\cancel{J}}{\text{K} \cdot \text{mol}}\right)\left(\dfrac{1 \text{ kJ}}{1000 \cancel{J}}\right)(298 \text{ K}) \ln(1) = -14.0 \text{ kJ}$

These are standard state conditions, so $E^{\circ}_{cell} = E_{cell}$ and $\Delta G^{\circ}_{rxn} = \Delta G_{rxn}$.

2: $Q = \dfrac{1.00 \times 10^{-4} \text{ M}}{1.00 \text{ M}} = 1.00 \times 10^{-4}$

$E_{cell} = 0.07\underline{2}5501 \text{ V} - \dfrac{0.0592 \text{ V}}{2} \log(1.00 \times 10^{-4}) = +0.19\underline{0}9501 \text{ V} = +0.1910 \text{ V}$ and

$\Delta G_{rxn} = -14.0 \text{ kJ} + \left(8.314 \dfrac{\cancel{J}}{\text{K} \cdot \text{mol}}\right)\left(\dfrac{1 \text{ kJ}}{1000 \cancel{J}}\right)(298 \text{ K}) \ln(1.00 \times 10^{-4}) = -36.8 \text{ kJ}$

3: $Q = \dfrac{1.00 \text{ M}}{1.00 \times 10^{-4} \text{ M}} = 1.00 \times 10^4$

$E_{cell} = 0.07\underline{2}5501 \text{ V} - \dfrac{0.0592 \text{ V}}{2} \log(1.00 \times 10^4) = -0.04\underline{5}8499 \text{ V} = -0.0458 \text{ V}$ and

$\Delta G_{rxn} = -14.0 \text{ kJ} + \left(8.314 \dfrac{\cancel{J}}{\text{K} \cdot \text{mol}}\right)\left(\dfrac{1 \text{ kJ}}{1000 \cancel{J}}\right)(298 \text{ K}) \ln(1.00 \times 10^4) = +8.8 \text{ kJ}$

4: $Q = \dfrac{1.00 \text{ M}}{3.52 \times 10^{-3} \text{ M}} = 28\underline{4}.0909 = 284$

$E_{cell} = 0.07\underline{2}5501 \text{ V} - \dfrac{0.0592 \text{ V}}{2} \log(28\underline{4}.0909) = -0.0000\underline{7}224 \text{ V} = -0.0001 \text{ V}$ and

$\Delta G_{rxn} = -14.0 \text{ kJ} + \left(8.314 \dfrac{\cancel{J}}{\text{K} \cdot \text{mol}}\right)\left(\dfrac{1 \text{ kJ}}{1000 \cancel{J}}\right)(298 \text{ K}) \ln(28\underline{4}.0909) = -0.0\underline{0}347 \text{ kJ} = +0.0 \text{ kJ}$

These are equilibrium conditions, so $E_{cell} = 0$ and $\Delta G_{rxn} = 0$.

Experiment	$[B^{2+}]$	$[A^{2+}]$	Q	E_{cell}	ΔG_{rxn}
1	1.00 M	1.00 M	**1.00**	**+ 0.0726 V**	**− 14.0 kJ**
2	1.00 M	1.00×10^{-4} M	**1.00×10^{-4}**	**+ 0.1910 V**	**− 36.8 kJ**
3	1.00×10^{-4} M	1.00 M	**1.00×10^4**	**− 0.0458 V**	**+ 8.8 kJ**
4	3.52×10^{-3} M	1.00 M	**284**	**− 0.0001 V**	**+ 0.0 kJ**

Check: The units (V, none, 4 sets of none, V, and kJ) are correct. ΔG°_{rxn} was negative, so $K > 1$ and $E^{\circ}_{cell} > 0$. At standard state conditions, $E^{\circ}_{cell} = E_{cell}$ and $\Delta G^{\circ}_{rxn} = \Delta G_{rxn}$. These are equilibrium conditions, so $E_{cell} = 0$ and $\Delta G_{rxn} = 0$.

Challenge Problems

18.81 **Given:** hydrogen–oxygen fuel cell; 1.2×10^3 kWh of electricity/month $\quad$ **Find:** V of $H_2(g)$ at STP/month

Conceptual Plan: Write half-reactions. Look up half-reactions at pH 7. The reaction on the left is the oxidation. Calculate the standard cell potential by subtracting the electrode potential of the anode from the electrode potential of the cathode: $E^\circ_{cell} = E^\circ_{cathode} - E^\circ_{anode}$. **Add the two half-cell reactions and cancel the electrons. Then**

$$kWh \rightarrow J \rightarrow C \rightarrow mol\ e^- \rightarrow mol\ H_2 \rightarrow V.$$

$$\frac{3.60 \times 10^6\ J}{1\ kWh} \quad \frac{1\ C}{1.23\ J} \quad \frac{1\ mol\ e^-}{96,485\ C} \quad \frac{2\ mol\ H_2}{4\ mol\ e^-} \quad at\ STP\ \frac{22.414\ L}{1\ mol\ H_2}$$

Solution: $2\ H_2(g) + 4\ OH^-(aq) \rightarrow 4\ H_2O(l) + 4\ e^-$ where $E^\circ_{red} = -0.83\ V = E^\circ_{anode}$ and $O_2(g) + 2\ H_2O(l) + 4\ e^- \rightarrow 4\ OH^-(aq)$ where $E^\circ_{red} = 0.40\ V = E^\circ_{cathode}$. $E^\circ_{cell} = E^\circ_{cathode} - E^\circ_{anode} = 0.40\ V - (-0.83\ V) = 1.23\ V$ $= 1.23\ J/C$ and $n = 4$. Net reaction is $2\ H_2(g) + O_2(g) \rightarrow 2\ H_2O(l)$. Then

$$1.2 \times 10^3\ \cancel{kWh} \times \frac{3.60 \times 10^6\ \cancel{J}}{1\ \cancel{kWh}} \times \frac{1\ \cancel{C}}{1.23\ \cancel{J}} \times \frac{1\ \cancel{mol\ e^-}}{96,485\ \cancel{C}} \times \frac{2\ \cancel{mol\ H_2}}{4\ \cancel{mol\ e^-}} \times \frac{22.414\ L}{1\ \cancel{mol\ H_2}} = 4.1 \times 10^5\ L$$

Check: The units (L) are correct. A large volume is expected because we are trying to generate a large amount of electricity.

18.83 **Given:** Au^{3+}/Au electroplating; surface area $= 49.8\ cm^2$, Au thickness $= 1.00 \times 10^{-3}$ cm, density $= 19.3\ g/cm^3$; at 3.25 A $\quad$ **Find:** time

Conceptual Plan: Write the half-cell reaction and add electrons as needed to balance reactions. Then surface area, thickness $\rightarrow V \rightarrow g\ Au \rightarrow mol\ Au \rightarrow mol\ e^- \rightarrow C \rightarrow s.$

$$V = surface\ area \times thickness \quad \frac{19.3\ g\ Au}{1\ cm^3\ Au} \quad \frac{1\ mol\ Au}{196.97\ g\ Au} \quad \frac{3\ mol\ e^-}{1\ mol\ Au} \quad \frac{96,485\ C}{1\ mol\ e^-} \quad \frac{1\ s}{3.25\ C}$$

Solution: Write the half-reaction and add electrons. $Au^{3+}(aq) + 3\ e^- \rightarrow Au(s)$.

$V = surface\ area \times thickness = (49.8\ cm^2)(1.00 \times 10^{-3}cm) = 0.0498\ cm^3$ then

$$0.0498\ \cancel{cm^3\ Au} \times \frac{19.3\ \cancel{g\ Au}}{1\ \cancel{cm^3\ Au}} \times \frac{1\ \cancel{mol\ Au}}{196.97\ \cancel{g\ Au}} \times \frac{3\ \cancel{mol\ e^-}}{1\ \cancel{mol\ Au}} \times \frac{96,485\ \cancel{C}}{1\ \cancel{mol\ e^-}} \times \frac{1\ s}{3.25\ \cancel{C}} = 435\ s$$

Check: The units (s) are correct. Because the layer is so thin, there is far less than a mole of gold; so the time is not very long. To be an economical process, it must be fairly quick.

18.85 **Given:** $C_2O_4^{2-} \rightarrow CO_2$ and $MnO_4^-(aq) \rightarrow Mn^{2+}(aq)$, 50.1 mL of MnO_4^- to titrate 0.339 g $Na_2C_2O_4$, 4.62 g U sample titrated by 32.5 mL MnO_4^-; and $UO^{2+} \rightarrow UO_2^{2+}$ $\quad$ **Find:** percent U in sample

Conceptual Plan: Separate the overall reaction into two half-reactions: one for oxidation and one for reduction. $\rightarrow$ **Balance each half-reaction with respect to mass in the following order: (1) Balance all elements other than H and O, (2) balance O by adding** H_2O, **and (3) balance H by adding** H^+. $\rightarrow$ **Balance each half-reaction with respect to charge by adding electrons. (The sum of the charges on both sides of the equation should be made equal by adding electrons as necessary.)** $\rightarrow$ **Make the number of electrons in both half-reactions equal by multiplying one or both half-reactions by a small whole number.** $\rightarrow$ **Add the two half-reactions together, canceling electrons and other species as necessary.** $\rightarrow$ **Verify that the reaction is balanced with respect to both mass and charge. Then**

$$mL\ MnO_4^- \rightarrow L\ MnO_4^- \text{ and } g\ Na_2C_2O_4 \rightarrow mol\ Na_2C_2O_4 \rightarrow mol\ MnO_4^- \text{ then}$$

$$\frac{1\ L\ MnO_4^-}{1000\ mL\ MnO_4^-} \quad \frac{1\ mol\ Na_2C_2O_4}{134.00\ g\ Na_2C_2O_4} \quad \frac{2\ mol\ MnO_4^-}{5\ mol\ Na_2C_2O_4}$$

$$L\ MnO_4^-, mol\ MnO_4^- \rightarrow M\ MnO_4^- \text{ then write U half-reactions and balance as above.} \rightarrow$$

$$M = \frac{mol\ MnO_4^-}{L}$$

Make the number of electrons in both half-reactions equal by multiplying one or both half-reactions by a small whole number. $\rightarrow$ **Add the two half-reactions together, canceling electrons and other species as necessary.** $\rightarrow$ **Verify that the reaction is balanced with respect to both mass and charge.**

Then $mL\ MnO_4^-, M\ MnO_4^- \rightarrow mol\ MnO_4^- \rightarrow mol\ U \rightarrow g\ U$ **then** $g\ U, g\ sample \rightarrow \%\ U.$

$$M = \frac{mol\ MnO_4^-}{L} \quad \frac{5\ mol\ U}{2\ mol\ MnO_4^-} \quad \frac{238.03\ g\ U}{1\ mol\ U} \qquad percent\ U = \frac{g\ U}{g\ sample} \times 100\%$$

Solution:

Separate: $\qquad\qquad\qquad\qquad\quad MnO_4^-(aq) \rightarrow Mn^{2+}(aq) \qquad$ and $\quad C_2O_4^{2-}(aq) \rightarrow CO_2(g)$

Balance non-H & O elements: $\ MnO_4^-(aq) \rightarrow Mn^{2+}(aq) \qquad$ and $\quad C_2O_4^{2-}(aq) \rightarrow 2\ CO_2(g)$

Balance O with H_2O: $MnO_4^-(aq) \rightarrow Mn^{2+}(aq) + 4 H_2O(l)$ and $C_2O_4^{2-}(aq) \rightarrow 2 CO_2(g)$
Balance H with H^+: $MnO_4^-(aq) + 8 H^+(aq) \rightarrow Mn^{2+}(aq) + 4 H_2O(l)$ and $C_2O_4^{2-}(aq) \rightarrow 2 CO_2(g)$
Add electrons: $MnO_4^-(aq) + 8 H^+(aq) + 5 e^- \rightarrow Mn^{2+}(aq) + 4 H_2O(l)$ and $C_2O_4^{2-}(aq) \rightarrow 2 CO_2(g) + 2 e^-$
Equalize electrons:
$2 MnO_4^-(aq) + 16 H^+(aq) + 10 e^- \rightarrow 2 Mn^{2+}(aq) + 8 H_2O(l)$ and $5 C_2O_4^{2-}(aq) \rightarrow 10 CO_2(g) + 10 e^-$
Add half-reactions:
$2 MnO_4^-(aq) + 16 H^+(aq) + \cancel{10 e^-} + 5 C_2O_4^{2-}(aq) \rightarrow 2 Mn^{2+}(aq) + 8 H_2O(l) + 10 CO_2(g) + \cancel{10 e^-}$
Cancel electrons: $2 MnO_4^-(aq) + 16 H^+(aq) + 5 C_2O_4^{2-}(aq) \rightarrow 2 Mn^{2+}(aq) + 8 H_2O(l) + 10 CO_2(g)$

then $50.1 \text{ mL } \cancel{MnO_4^-} \times \dfrac{1 \text{ L } MnO_4^-}{1000 \text{ mL } \cancel{MnO_4^-}} = 0.0501 \text{ L } MnO_4^-$

$0.399 \text{ g } \cancel{Na_2C_2O_4} \times \dfrac{1 \text{ mol } \cancel{Na_2C_2O_4}}{134.00 \text{ g } \cancel{Na_2C_2O_4}} \times \dfrac{2 \text{ mol } MnO_4^-}{5 \text{ mol } \cancel{Na_2C_2O_4}} = 0.0011\underline{9}10448 \text{ mol } MnO_4^-$

$M = \dfrac{0.0011\underline{9}10448 \text{ mol } MnO_4^-}{0.0501 \text{ L}} = 0.023773345 \text{ M } MnO_4^-$

Separate: $MnO_4^-(aq) \rightarrow Mn^{2+}(aq)$ and $UO^{2+}(aq) \rightarrow UO_2^{2+}(aq)$
Balance non-H & O elements: $MnO_4^-(aq) \rightarrow Mn^{2+}(aq)$ and $UO^{2+}(aq) \rightarrow UO_2^{2+}(aq)$
Balance O with H_2O: $MnO_4^-(aq) \rightarrow Mn^{2+}(aq) + 4 H_2O(l)$ and $UO^{2+}(aq) + H_2O(l) \rightarrow UO_2^{2+}(aq)$
Balance H with H^+:
$MnO_4^-(aq) + 8 H^+(aq) \rightarrow Mn^{2+}(aq) + 4 H_2O(l)$ and $UO^{2+}(aq) + H_2O(l) \rightarrow UO_2^{2+}(aq) + 2 H^+(aq)$
Add electrons: $MnO_4^-(aq) + 8 H^+(aq) + 5 e^- \rightarrow Mn^{2+}(aq) + 4 H_2O(l)$ and
$\qquad\qquad UO^{2+}(aq) + H_2O(l) \rightarrow UO_2^{2+}(aq) + 2 H^+(aq) + 2 e^-$
Equalize electrons: $2 MnO_4^-(aq) + 16 H^+(aq) + 10 e^- \rightarrow 2 Mn^{2+}(aq) + 8 H_2O(l)$ and
$\qquad\qquad 5 UO^{2+}(aq) + 5 H_2O(l) \rightarrow 5 UO_2^{2+}(aq) + 10 H^+(aq) + 10 e^-$
Add half-reactions: $2 MnO_4^-(aq) + 6 \cancel{16}H^+(aq) + \cancel{10 e^-} + 5 UO^{2+}(aq) + 5\cancel{H_2O(l)} \rightarrow$
$\qquad\qquad 2 Mn^{2+}(aq) + 3 \cancel{8} H_2O(l) + 5 UO_2^{2+}(aq) + \cancel{10 H^+(aq)} + \cancel{10 e^-}$
Cancel electrons & species:
$\qquad\qquad 2 MnO_4^-(aq) + 6 H^+(aq) + 5 UO^{2+}(aq) \rightarrow 2 Mn^{2+}(aq) + 3 H_2O(l) + 5 UO_2^{2+}(aq)$

$32.5 \text{ mL } \cancel{MnO_4^-} \times \dfrac{0.023773345 \text{ mol } \cancel{MnO_4^-}}{1000 \text{ mL } \cancel{MnO_4^-}} \times \dfrac{5 \text{ mol } \cancel{U}}{2 \text{ mol } \cancel{MnO_4^-}} \times \dfrac{238.03 \text{ g U}}{1 \text{ mol } \cancel{U}} = 0.459\underline{7}750 \text{ g U}$ then

$\text{percent U} = \dfrac{\text{g U}}{\text{g sample}} \times 100\% = \dfrac{0.459\underline{7}750 \text{ g U}}{4.62 \text{ g sample}} \times 100\% = 9.95\%$

Check: first reaction

	Reactants	Products
	2 Mn atoms	2 Mn atoms
	28 O atoms	28 O atoms
	16 H atoms	16 H atoms
	10 C atoms	10 C atoms
	+4 charge	+4 charge
second reaction	Reactants	Products
	2 Mn atoms	2 Mn atoms
	13 O atoms	13 O atoms
	6 H atoms	6 H atoms
	5 U atoms	5 U atoms
	+14 charge	+14 charge

The reactions are balanced. The units (%) are correct. The percentage is between 0 and 100%.

18.87   **Given:** 215 mL of a 0.500 M NaCl solution, initially at pH = 7.00; after 15 minutes, a 10.0 mL aliquot is titrated
with 22.8 mL 0.100 M HCl   **Find:** current (A)
Conceptual Plan: Titration is neutralizing base generated in the hydrolysis, so
mL HCl, M HCl, mL aliquot → mol OH^- in aliquot → mol OH^- in solution then min → s then

$\qquad M_{Acid}V_{Acid} = M_{Base}V_{Base} \qquad\qquad M_1V_1 = M_2V_2 \qquad\qquad \dfrac{1 \text{ min}}{60 \text{ s}}$

mol OH^- in solution, s $\rightarrow$ mol e^-/s $\rightarrow$ C/s.

$$\frac{2 \text{ mol } e^-}{2 \text{ mol } OH^-} \qquad \frac{96{,}485 \text{ C}}{1 \text{ mol } e^-}$$

Solution: $2 \text{ NaCl}(aq) + 2 \text{ H}_2\text{O}(l) \rightarrow \text{H}_2(g) + \text{Cl}_2(g) + 2 \text{ Na}^+(aq) + 2 \text{ OH}^-(aq)$

$M_{Acid}V_{Acid} = M_{Base}V_{Base}$ so $22.8 \text{ mL HCl} \times \dfrac{0.100 \text{ mol HCl}}{1000 \text{ mL HCl}} \times \dfrac{1 \text{ mol } OH^-}{1 \text{ mol HCl}} = 0.00228 \text{ mol } OH^-$

$0.00228 \text{ mol } OH^- \text{ in aliquot} \times \dfrac{215 \text{ mL}}{10.0 \text{ mL}} = 0.04902 \text{ mol } OH^- \text{ in solution}$

$\dfrac{0.04902 \text{ mol } OH^- \text{ in solution}}{15 \text{ min}} \times \dfrac{1 \text{ min}}{60 \text{ s}} \times \dfrac{2 \text{ mol } e^-}{2 \text{ mol } OH^-} \times \dfrac{96{,}485 \text{ C}}{1 \text{ mol } e^-} = 5.2552 \dfrac{\text{C}}{\text{s}} = 5.3 \text{ A}$

Check: The units (A) are correct. The current is reasonable for an electrolysis process.

18.89   **Given:** SHE   **Find:** pH to get half-cell potential $= -0.122$ V
Conceptual Plan: Write the half-cell reaction. The standard half-cell potential is 0.00 V. Define Q based on half-cell reaction. Then $E^\circ_{\text{half-cell}}, n$ $\rightarrow$ $[H^+]$ $\rightarrow$ pH.

$$E_{\text{half-cell}} = E^\circ_{\text{half-cell}} - \frac{0.0592 \text{ V}}{n} \log Q \qquad \text{pH} = -\log [H^+]$$

Solution: $2 \text{ H}^+(aq) + 2 \text{ e}^- \rightarrow \text{H}_2(g)$ $E^\circ_{\text{half-cell}} = 0.00$ V, $n = 2$, and $Q = \dfrac{1}{[H^+]^2}$.

$E_{\text{half-cell}} = E^\circ_{\text{half-cell}} - \dfrac{0.0592 \text{ V}}{n} \log Q$, so $-0.122 \text{ V} = 0.00 \text{ V} - \dfrac{0.0592 \text{ V}}{2} \log [H^+]^{-2} \rightarrow$

$4.12162 = \log [H^+]^{-2} \rightarrow [H^+]^{-2} = 10^{4.12162} = 1.32318 \times 10^4 \rightarrow [H^+] = 0.00869342$ M

$\text{pH} = -\log [H^+] = -\log(0.00869342) = 2.06081 = 2.06$

Check: The units (none) are correct. There is an inverse second-order dependence in $[H^+]$, so we expect an acidic pH.

Conceptual Problems

18.91   (a)   Looking for anion reductions that are between the reduction potentials of Cl_2 and Br_2. The only one that meets that criterion is the dichromate ion.

18.93   Since $K < 1$, the reaction must be nonspontaneous under standard conditions. Therefore, E°_{cell} is negative and $\Delta G^\circ_{\text{rxn}}$ is positive.

Questions for Group Work

18.95   Choose any two half-reaction from Table 18.1 and follow the conceptual plan in Problem 18.17 to get a positive cell potential.

18.97   Specific answer will vary. In general, a device could have a known cell as one half-reaction, and the unknown copper sample as the other half cell. $E_{\text{cell}} = E^\circ_{\text{cell}} + RT \ln Q$ can be solved for the unknown Cu^{2+}. 1 mV uncertainty in voltage may correspond to approximately 1×10^{-6} M uncertainty in concentration.

19 Radioactivity and Nuclear Chemistry

Radioactive Decay and Nuclide Stability

19.1   **Conceptual Plan: Begin with the symbol for a parent nuclide on the left side of the equation and the symbol for a particle on the right side (except for electron capture).** → **Equalize the sum of the mass numbers and the sum of the atomic numbers on both sides of the equation by writing the appropriate mass number and atomic number for the unknown daughter nuclide.** → **Using the periodic table, deduce the identity of the unknown daughter nuclide from the atomic number and write its symbol.**

Solution:

(a)   U-234 (alpha decay) $^{234}_{92}\text{U} \rightarrow ^{?}_{?}? + ^{4}_{2}\text{He}$ then $^{234}_{92}\text{U} \rightarrow ^{230}_{90}? + ^{4}_{2}\text{He}$ then $^{234}_{92}\text{U} \rightarrow ^{230}_{90}\text{Th} + ^{4}_{2}\text{He}$

(b)   Th-230 (alpha decay) $^{230}_{90}\text{Th} \rightarrow ^{?}_{?}? + ^{4}_{2}\text{He}$ then $^{230}_{90}\text{Th} \rightarrow ^{226}_{88}? + ^{4}_{2}\text{He}$ then $^{230}_{90}\text{Th} \rightarrow ^{226}_{88}\text{Ra} + ^{4}_{2}\text{He}$

(c)   Pb-214 (beta decay) $^{214}_{82}\text{Pb} \rightarrow ^{?}_{?}? + ^{0}_{-1}\text{e}$ then $^{214}_{82}\text{Pb} \rightarrow ^{214}_{83}? + ^{0}_{-1}\text{e}$ then $^{214}_{82}\text{Pb} \rightarrow ^{214}_{83}\text{Bi} + ^{0}_{-1}\text{e}$

(d)   N-13 (positron emission) $^{13}_{7}\text{N} \rightarrow ^{?}_{?}? + ^{0}_{+1}\text{e}$ then $^{13}_{7}\text{N} \rightarrow ^{13}_{6}? + ^{0}_{+1}\text{e}$ then $^{13}_{7}\text{N} \rightarrow ^{13}_{6}\text{C} + ^{0}_{+1}\text{e}$

(e)   Cr-51 (electron capture) $^{51}_{24}\text{C} + ^{0}_{-1}\text{e} \rightarrow ^{?}_{?}?$ then $^{51}_{24}\text{Cr} + ^{0}_{-1}\text{e} \rightarrow ^{51}_{23}?$ then $^{51}_{24}\text{Cr} + ^{0}_{-1}\text{e} \rightarrow ^{51}_{23}\text{V}$

Check: (a) $234 = 230 + 4$, $92 = 90 + 2$, and thorium is atomic number 90. (b) $230 = 226 + 4$, $90 = 88 + 2$, and radium is atomic number 88. (c) $214 = 214 + 0$, $82 = 83 - 1$, and bismuth is atomic number 83. (d) $13 = 13 + 0$, $7 = 6 + 1$, and carbon is atomic number 6. (e) $51 + 0 = 51$, $24 - 1 = 23$, and vanadium is atomic number 23.

19.3   **Given:** Th-232 decay series: $\alpha, \beta, \beta, \alpha$ **Find:** balanced decay reactions

Conceptual Plan: Begin with the symbol for a parent nuclide on the left side of the equation and the symbol for a particle on the right side. → **Equalize the sum of the mass numbers and the sum of the atomic numbers on both sides of the equation by writing the appropriate mass number and atomic number for the unknown daughter nuclide.** → **Using the periodic table, deduce the identity of the unknown daughter nuclide from the atomic number and write its symbol.** → **Use the product of this reaction to write the next reaction.**

Solution:

Th-232 (alpha decay) $^{232}_{90}\text{Th} \rightarrow ^{?}_{?}? + ^{4}_{2}\text{He}$ then $^{232}_{90}\text{Th} \rightarrow ^{228}_{88}? + ^{4}_{2}\text{He}$ then $^{232}_{90}\text{Th} \rightarrow ^{228}_{88}\text{Ra} + ^{4}_{2}\text{He}$

Ra-228 (beta decay) $^{228}_{88}\text{Ra} \rightarrow ^{?}_{?}? + ^{0}_{-1}\text{e}$ then $^{228}_{88}\text{Ra} \rightarrow ^{228}_{89}? + ^{0}_{-1}\text{e}$ then $^{228}_{88}\text{Ra} \rightarrow ^{228}_{89}\text{Ac} + ^{0}_{-1}\text{e}$

Ac-228 (beta decay) $^{228}_{89}\text{Ac} \rightarrow ^{?}_{?}? + ^{0}_{-1}\text{e}$ then $^{228}_{89}\text{Ac} \rightarrow ^{228}_{90}? + ^{0}_{-1}\text{e}$ then $^{228}_{89}\text{Ac} \rightarrow ^{228}_{90}\text{Th} + ^{0}_{-1}\text{e}$

Th-228 (alpha decay) $^{228}_{90}\text{Th} \rightarrow ^{?}_{?}? + ^{4}_{2}\text{He}$ then $^{228}_{90}\text{Th} \rightarrow ^{224}_{88}? + ^{4}_{2}\text{He}$ then $^{228}_{90}\text{Th} \rightarrow ^{224}_{88}\text{Ra} + ^{4}_{2}\text{He}$

Thus, the decay series is $^{232}_{90}\text{Th} \rightarrow ^{228}_{88}\text{Ra} + ^{4}_{2}\text{He}$, $^{228}_{88}\text{Ra} \rightarrow ^{228}_{89}\text{Ac} + ^{0}_{-1}\text{e}$, $^{228}_{89}\text{Ac} \rightarrow ^{228}_{90}\text{Th} + ^{0}_{-1}\text{e}$, $^{228}_{90}\text{Th} \rightarrow ^{224}_{88}\text{Ra} + ^{4}_{2}\text{He}$.

Check: $232 = 228 + 4$, $90 = 88 + 2$, and radium is atomic number 88. $228 = 228 + 0$, $88 = 89 - 1$, and actinium is atomic number 89. $228 = 228 + 0$, $89 = 90 - 1$, and thorium is atomic number 90. $228 = 224 + 4$, $90 = 88 + 2$, and radium is atomic number 88.

19.5   **Conceptual Plan: Equalize the sum of the mass numbers and the sum of the atomic numbers on both sides of the equation by writing the appropriate mass number and atomic number for the unknown species.** → **Using the periodic table and the list of particles, deduce the identity of the unknown species from the atomic number and write its symbol.**

Solution:

(a) $^{?}_{?}? \rightarrow \, ^{217}_{85}At \, + \, ^{4}_{2}He$ becomes $^{221}_{87}? \rightarrow \, ^{217}_{85}At \, + \, ^{4}_{2}He$ then $^{221}_{87}Fr \rightarrow \, ^{217}_{85}At \, + \, ^{4}_{2}He$

(b) $^{241}_{94}Pu \rightarrow \, ^{241}_{95}Am \, + \, ^{?}_{?}?$ becomes $^{241}_{94}Pu \rightarrow \, ^{241}_{95}Am \, + \, ^{0}_{-1}?$ then $^{241}_{94}Pu \rightarrow \, ^{241}_{95}Am \, + \, ^{0}_{-1}e$

(c) $^{19}_{11}Na \rightarrow \, ^{19}_{10}Ne \, + \, ^{?}_{?}?$ becomes $^{19}_{11}Na \rightarrow \, ^{19}_{10}Ne \, + \, ^{0}_{1}?$ then $^{19}_{11}Na \rightarrow \, ^{19}_{10}Ne \, + \, ^{0}_{+1}e$

(d) $^{75}_{34}Se \, + \, ^{?}_{?}? \rightarrow \, ^{75}_{33}As$ becomes $^{75}_{34}Se \, + \, ^{0}_{-1}? \rightarrow \, ^{75}_{33}As$ then $^{75}_{34}Se \, + \, ^{0}_{-1}e \rightarrow \, ^{75}_{33}As$

Check: (a) $221 = 217 + 4, 87 = 85 + 2$, and francium is atomic number 87. (b) $241 = 241 + 0, 94 = 95 - 1$, and the particle is a beta particle. (c) $19 = 19 + 0, 11 = 10 + 1$, and the particle is a positron. (d) $75 = 75 + 0, 34 - 1 = 33$, and the particle is an electron.

19.7 (a) Mg-26: stable, N/Z ratio is close to 1, acceptable for low Z atoms
(b) Ne-25: not stable, N/Z ratio is much too high for low Z atom
(c) Co-51: not stable, N/Z ratio is less than 1, much too low
(d) Te-124: stable, N/Z ratio is acceptable for this Z

19.9 Sc, V, and Mn each have an odd number of protons. Atoms with an odd number of protons typically have fewer stable isotopes than those with an even number of protons.

19.11 (a) Mo-109, $N = 67, Z = 42, N/Z = 1.6$, beta decay, because N/Z is too high
(b) Ru-90, $N = 46, Z = 44, N/Z = 1.0$, positron emission, because N/Z is too low
(c) P-27, $N = 12, Z = 15, N/Z = 0.8$, positron emission, because N/Z is too low
(d) Rn-196, $N = 110, Z = 86, N/Z = 1.3$, positron emission, because N/Z is too low

19.13 (a) Cs-125, $N/Z = 70/55 = 1.3$; Cs-113, $N/Z = 58/55 = 1.1$; Cs-125 will have the longer half-life because it is closer to the proper N/Z
(b) Fe-62, $N/Z = 36/26 = 1.4$; Fe-70, $N/Z = 44/26 = 1.7$; Fe-62 will have the longer half-life because it is closer to the proper N/Z

The Kinetics of Radioactive Decay and Radiometric Dating

19.15 **Given:** U-235, $t_{1/2}$ for radioactive decay $= 703$ million years **Find:** t to $\dfrac{1}{8}$ of initial amount

Conceptual Plan: radioactive decay implies first-order kinetics, $t_{1/2} \rightarrow k$ then

$$t_{1/2} = \frac{0.693}{k}$$

$m_{\text{U-235 0}}, m_{\text{U-235 } t}, k \rightarrow t$

$$\ln N_t = -kt + \ln N_0$$

Solution: $t_{1/2} = \dfrac{0.693}{k}$; rearrange to solve for k. $k = \dfrac{0.693}{t_{1/2}} = \dfrac{0.693}{703 \times 10^6 \text{ yr}} = 9.8\underline{5}7752 \times 10^{-10} \text{ yr}^{-1}$. Because

$\ln m_{\text{U-235 } t} = -kt + \ln m_{\text{U-235 0}}$, rearrange to solve for t.

$$t = -\frac{1}{k} \ln \frac{m_{\text{U-235 } t}}{m_{\text{U-235 0}}} = -\frac{1}{9.857752 \times 10^{-10} \text{ yr}^{-1}} \ln \frac{1}{8} = 2.11 \times 10^9 \text{ yr}$$

Check: The units (yr) are correct. Because 1/2 will be left after one half-life, 1/4 will be left after two half-lives, and 1/8 will be left after three half-lives $= 3 \times 7.03 \times 10^8 = 2.11 \times 10^9$.

19.17 **Given:** $t_{1/2}$ for isotope decay $= 3.8$ days; 1.55 g isotope initially **Find:** mass of isotope after 5.5 days
Conceptual Plan: radioactive decay implies first-order kinetics, $t_{1/2} \rightarrow k$ then

$$t_{1/2} = \frac{0.693}{k}$$

$m_{\text{isotope 0}}, t, k \rightarrow m_{\text{isotope } t}$

$$\ln N_t = -kt + \ln N_0$$

Solution: $t_{1/2} = \dfrac{0.693}{k}$; rearrange to solve for k. $k = \dfrac{0.693}{t_{1/2}} = \dfrac{0.693}{3.8 \text{ days}} = 0.18\underline{2}37 \text{ day}^{-1}$. Because

$\ln N_t = -kt + \ln N_0 = -(0.1\underline{8}237 \text{ day}^{-1})(5.5 \text{ day}) + \ln (1.55 \text{ g}) = -0.5\underline{6}478 \rightarrow N_t = e^{-0.56478} = 0.57 \text{ g}$.

Check: The units (g) are correct. The amount is consistent with a time between one and two half-lives.

19.19   **Given:** F-18 initial decay rate $= 1.5 \times 10^5/\text{s}$, $t_{1/2}$ for F-18 $= 1.83$ h   **Find:** t to decay rate of $1.0 \times 10^2/\text{s}$
       Conceptual Plan: radioactive decay implies first-order kinetics, $t_{1/2} \rightarrow k$ **then** Rate_0, Rate_t, $k \rightarrow t$

$$t_{1/2} = \frac{0.693}{k} \qquad\qquad \ln \frac{\text{Rate}_t}{\text{Rate}_0} = -k\,t$$

       Solution: $t_{1/2} = \dfrac{0.693}{k}$; rearrange to solve for k. $k = \dfrac{0.693}{t_{1/2}} = \dfrac{0.693}{1.83 \text{ h}} = 0.378\underline{6}89 \text{ h}^{-1}$. Because

$\ln \dfrac{\text{Rate}_t}{\text{Rate}_0} = -k\,t$, rearrange to solve for t.

$$t = -\frac{1}{k} \ln \frac{\text{Rate}_t}{\text{Rate}_0} = -\frac{1}{0.378\underline{6}89 \text{ h}^{-1}} \ln \frac{1.0 \times 10^2/\cancel{s}}{1.5 \times 10^5/\cancel{s}} = 19.3 \text{ h}$$

       Check: The units (h) are correct. The time is between 10 and 11 half-lives, and the rate is just under $1/2^{10}$ of the original amount.

19.21   **Given:** boat analysis, C-14/C-12 $= 72.5\%$ of living organism   **Find:** t
       Other: $t_{1/2}$ for decay of C-14 $= 5730$ years
       Conceptual Plan: radioactive decay implies first-order kinetics, $t_{1/2} \rightarrow k$ **then 72.5% of** $m_{\text{C-14 }0}$, $k \rightarrow t$

$$t_{1/2} = \frac{0.693}{k} \qquad\qquad \ln N_t = -k\,t + \ln N_0$$

       Solution: $t_{1/2} = \dfrac{0.693}{k}$; rearrange to solve for k. $k = \dfrac{0.693}{t_{1/2}} = \dfrac{0.693}{5730 \text{ yr}} = 1.2\underline{0}942 \times 10^{-4} \text{ yr}^{-1}$ then

$[\text{C-14}]_t = 0.725[\text{C-14}]_0$. Because $\ln m_{\text{C}-14\,t} = -k\,t + \ln m_{\text{C}-14\,0}$, rearrange to solve for t.

$$t = -\frac{1}{k} \ln \frac{m_{\text{C-14}\,t}}{m_{\text{C-14}\,0}} = -\frac{1}{1.2\underline{0}942 \times 10^{-4} \text{ yr}^{-1}} \ln \frac{0.725 \, \cancel{m_{\text{C-14}\,0}}}{\cancel{m_{\text{C-14}\,0}}} = 2.66 \times 10^3 \text{ yr}$$

       Check: The units (yr) are correct. The time to 72.5% decay is consistent with a time less than one half-life.

19.23   **Given:** skull analysis, C-14 decay rate $= 15.3$ dis/min $\cdot$ g C in living organisms and 0.85 dis/min $\cdot$ g C in skull
       Find: t **Other:** $t_{1/2}$ for decay of C-14 $= 5730$ years
       Conceptual Plan: radioactive decay implies first-order kinetics, $t_{1/2} \rightarrow k$ **then** Rate_0, Rate_t, $k \rightarrow t$

$$t_{1/2} = \frac{0.693}{k} \qquad\qquad \ln \frac{\text{Rate}_t}{\text{Rate}_0} = -k\,t$$

       Solution: $t_{1/2} = \dfrac{0.693}{k}$; rearrange to solve for k. $k = \dfrac{0.693}{t_{1/2}} = \dfrac{0.693}{5730 \text{ yr}} = 1.2\underline{0}942 \times 10^{-4} \text{ yr}^{-1}$

Because $\ln \dfrac{\text{Rate}_t}{\text{Rate}_0} = -k\,t$, rearrange to solve for t.

$$t = -\frac{1}{k} \ln \frac{\text{Rate}_t}{\text{Rate}_0} = -\frac{1}{1.2\underline{0}942 \times 10^{-4} \text{ yr}^{-1}} \ln \frac{0.85 \text{ } \cancel{\text{dis/min}} \cdot \text{g C}}{15.3 \text{ } \cancel{\text{dis/min}} \cdot \text{g C}} = 2.39 \times 10^4 \text{ yr}$$

       Check: The units (yr) are correct. The rate is 6% of initial value, and the time is consistent with a time just more than four half-lives.

19.25   **Given:** rock analysis, 0.438 g Pb-206 to every 1.00 g U-238, no Pb-206 initially   **Find:** age of rock
       Other: $t_{1/2}$ for decay of U-238 to Pb-206 $= 4.5 \times 10^9$ years
       Conceptual Plan: radioactive decay implies first-order kinetics, $t_{1/2} \rightarrow k$ **then**

$$t_{1/2} = \frac{0.693}{k}$$

g Pb-206 $\rightarrow$ **mol Pb-206** $\rightarrow$ **mol U-238** $\rightarrow$ **g U-238 then** $m_{\text{U-238}\,t}$, $k \rightarrow t$

$$\frac{1 \text{ mol Pb-206}}{206 \text{ g Pb-206}} \qquad \frac{1 \text{ mol U-238}}{1 \text{ mol Pb-206}} \qquad \frac{238 \text{ g U-238}}{1 \text{ mol U-238}} \qquad\qquad \ln N_t = -k\,t + \ln N_0$$

       Solution: $t_{1/2} = \dfrac{0.693}{k}$; rearrange to solve for k. $k = \dfrac{0.693}{t_{1/2}} = \dfrac{0.693}{4.5 \times 10^9 \text{ yr}} = 1.5\underline{4} \times 10^{-10} \text{ yr}^{-1}$ then

$$0.438 \text{ } \cancel{\text{g Pb-206}} \times \frac{1 \text{ } \cancel{\text{mol Pb-206}}}{206 \text{ } \cancel{\text{g Pb-206}}} \times \frac{1 \text{ } \cancel{\text{mol U-238}}}{1 \text{ } \cancel{\text{mol Pb-206}}} \times \frac{238 \text{ g U-238}}{1 \text{ } \cancel{\text{mol U-238}}} = 0.50\underline{6}039 \text{ g U-238. Because}$$

$\ln \dfrac{m_{\text{U-238}\,t}}{m_{\text{U-238}\,0}} = -k\,t$, rearrange to solve for t.

$$t = -\frac{1}{k} \ln \frac{m_{\text{U-238 } t}}{m_{\text{U-238 } 0}} = -\frac{1}{1.54 \times 10^{-10} \text{ yr}^{-1}} \ln \frac{1.00 \text{ g U-238}}{(1.00 + 0.506039) \text{ g U-238}} = 2.7 \times 10^9 \text{ yr}$$

Check: The units (yr) are correct. The amount of Pb-206 is less than half the initial U-238 amount, and time is less than one half-life.

Fission and Fusion

19.27   **Given:** U-235 fission induced by neutrons to Xe-144 and Sr-90   **Find:** number of neutrons produced
         Conceptual Plan: Write the species given on the appropriate side of the equation. → **Equalize the sum of the mass numbers and the sum of the atomic numbers on both sides of the equation by writing the stoichiometric coefficient in front of the desired species.**
         Solution: $^{235}_{92}\text{U} + ^{1}_{0}\text{n} \rightarrow ^{144}_{54}\text{Xe} + ^{90}_{38}\text{Sr} + ?^{1}_{0}\text{n}$ becomes $^{235}_{92}\text{U} + ^{1}_{0}\text{n} \rightarrow ^{144}_{54}\text{Xe} + ^{90}_{38}\text{Sr} + 2 ^{1}_{0}\text{n}$, so two neutrons are produced.
         Check: $235 + 1 = 144 + 90 + 2, 92 + 0 = 54 + 38 + 0$, and no other particle is necessary to balance the equation.

19.29   **Given:** fusion of two H-2 atoms to form He-3 and one neutron   **Find:** balanced equation
         Conceptual Plan: Write the species given on the appropriate side of the equation. → **Equalize the sum of the mass numbers and the sum of the atomic numbers on both sides of the equation by writing the stoichiometric coefficient in front of the desired species.**
         Solution: $2 ^{2}_{1}\text{H} \rightarrow ^{3}_{2}\text{He} + ^{1}_{0}\text{n}$
         Check: $2(2) = 3 + 1, 2(1) = 2 + 0$, and no other particle is necessary to balance the equation.

19.31   **Given:** U-238 bombarded by neutrons to form U-239, which undergoes two beta decays to form Pu-239
         Find: balanced equations
         Conceptual Plan: Write the species given on the appropriate side of the equation. → **Equalize the sum of the mass numbers and the sum of the atomic numbers on both sides of the equation by writing the stoichiometric coefficient in front of the desired species.** → **Use the product of this reaction to write the next reaction until the process is complete.**
         Solution: $^{238}_{92}\text{U} + ? ^{1}_{0}\text{n} \rightarrow ^{239}_{92}\text{U}$ becomes $^{238}_{92}\text{U} + ^{1}_{0}\text{n} \rightarrow ^{239}_{92}\text{U}$ then
         beta decay $^{239}_{92}\text{U} \rightarrow ^{?}_{?}? + ^{0}_{-1}\text{e}$ becomes $^{239}_{92}\text{U} \rightarrow ^{239}_{93}? + ^{0}_{-1}\text{e}$ then $^{239}_{92}\text{U} \rightarrow ^{239}_{93}\text{Np} + ^{0}_{-1}\text{e}$ then
         beta decay $^{239}_{93}\text{Np} \rightarrow ^{?}_{?}? + ^{0}_{-1}\text{e}$ becomes $^{239}_{93}\text{Np} \rightarrow ^{239}_{94}? + ^{0}_{-1}\text{e}$ then $^{239}_{93}\text{Np} \rightarrow ^{239}_{94}\text{Pu} + ^{0}_{-1}\text{e}$
         The entire process is $^{238}_{92}\text{U} + ^{1}_{0}\text{n} \rightarrow ^{239}_{92}\text{U}, ^{239}_{92}\text{U} \rightarrow ^{239}_{93}\text{Np} + ^{0}_{-1}\text{e}, ^{239}_{93}\text{Np} \rightarrow ^{239}_{94}\text{Pu} + ^{0}_{-1}\text{e}$.
         Check: $238 + 1 = 239, 92 + 0 = 92$, and no other particle is necessary to balance the equation. $239 = 239 + 0$, $92 = 93 - 1$, and neptunium is atomic number 93. $239 = 239 + 0, 93 = 94 - 1$, and plutonium is atomic number 94.

Energetics of Nuclear Reactions, Mass Defect, and Nuclear Binding Energy

19.33   **Given:** 1.0 g of matter converted to energy   **Find:** energy
         Conceptual Plan: g → **kg** → **E**
         $\frac{1 \text{ kg}}{1000 \text{ g}}$ $E = mc^2$
         Solution: $1.0 \text{ g} \times \frac{1 \text{ kg}}{1000 \text{ g}} = 0.0010 \text{ kg}$ then $E = mc^2 = (0.0010 \text{ kg})\left(2.9979 \times 10^8 \frac{\text{m}}{\text{s}}\right)^2 = 9.0 \times 10^{13} \text{ J}$
         Check: The units (J) are correct. The magnitude of the answer makes physical sense because we are converting a large quantity of amus to energy.

19.35   **Given:** (a) O-16 = 15.9949145 amu, (b) Ni-58 = 57.935346 amu, and (c) Xe-129 = 128.904780 amu
         Find: mass defect and nuclear binding energy per nucleon
         Conceptual Plan: $^{A}_{Z}X$, isotope mass → **mass defect** → **nuclear binding energy per nucleon**
         mass defect $= Z(\text{mass } ^{1}_{1}\text{H}) + (A\text{-}Z)(\text{mass } ^{1}_{0}\text{n}) - \text{mass of isotope}$ $\frac{931.5 \text{ MeV}}{(1 \text{ amu})(A \text{ nucleons})}$
         Solution: mass defect $= Z(\text{mass } ^{1}_{1}\text{H}) + (A\text{-}Z)(\text{mass } ^{1}_{0}\text{n}) - \text{mass of isotope}$

(a) O-16 mass defect $= 8(1.00783 \text{ amu}) + (16 - 8)(1.00866 \text{ amu}) - 15.9949145 \text{ amu} =$

$0.1370055 \text{ amu} = 0.13701 \text{ amu}$ and $0.1370055 \text{ amu} \times \dfrac{931.5 \text{ MeV}}{(1 \text{ amu})(16 \text{ nucleons})} = 7.976 \dfrac{\text{MeV}}{\text{nucleon}}$

(b) Ni-58 mass defect $= 28(1.00783 \text{ amu}) + (58 - 28)(1.00866 \text{ amu}) - 57.935346 \text{ amu} =$

$0.543694 \text{ amu} = 0.54369 \text{ amu}$ and $0.543694 \text{ amu} \times \dfrac{931.5 \text{ MeV}}{(1 \text{ amu})(58 \text{ nucleons})} = 8.732 \dfrac{\text{MeV}}{\text{nucleon}}$

(c) Xe-129 mass defect $= 54(1.00783 \text{ amu}) + (129 - 54)(1.00866 \text{ amu}) - 128.904780 \text{ amu} = 1.16754 \text{ amu}$

and $1.16754 \text{ amu} \times \dfrac{931.5 \text{ MeV}}{(1 \text{ amu})(129 \text{ nucleons})} = 8.431 \dfrac{\text{MeV}}{\text{nucleon}}$

Check: The units (amu and MeV/nucleon) are correct. The mass defect increases with an increasing number of nucleons, but the MeV/nucleon does not change by as much (on a relative basis).

19.37 **Given:** $^{235}_{92}\text{U} + ^{1}_{0}\text{n} \rightarrow ^{144}_{54}\text{Xe} + ^{90}_{38}\text{Sr} + 2\, ^{1}_{0}\text{n}$, U-235 $= 235.043922$ amu, Xe-144 $= 143.9385$ amu, and Sr-90 $= 89.907738$ amu **Find:** energy per g of U-235
Conceptual Plan: mass of products and reactants $\rightarrow$ mass defect $\rightarrow$ mass defect/g of U-235 then

$$\text{mass defect} = \textstyle\sum \text{mass of reactants} - \sum \text{mass of products} \qquad \dfrac{\text{mass defect}}{235.043922 \text{ g U-235}}$$

g $\rightarrow$ kg $\rightarrow$ E

$$\dfrac{1 \text{ kg}}{1000 \text{ g}} \qquad E = mc^2$$

Solution: mass defect $= \sum \text{mass of reactants} - \sum \text{mass of products};$ notice that we can cancel a neutron from each side to get $^{235}_{92}\text{U} \rightarrow ^{144}_{54}\text{Xe} + ^{90}_{38}\text{Sr} + ^{1}_{0}\text{n}$ and
mass defect $= 235.043922 \text{ g} - (143.9385 \text{ g} + 89.907738 \text{ g} + 1.00866 \text{ g}) = 0.189024 \text{ g}$

then $\dfrac{0.189024 \text{ g}}{235.043922 \text{ g U-235}} \times \dfrac{1 \text{ kg}}{1000 \text{ g}} = 8.04207 \times 10^{-7} \dfrac{\text{kg}}{\text{g U-235}}$ then

$E = mc^2 = \left(8.04207 \times 10^{-7} \dfrac{\text{kg}}{\text{g U-235}}\right)\left(2.9979 \times 10^{8}\dfrac{\text{m}}{\text{s}}\right)^2 = 7.228 \times 10^{10} \dfrac{\text{J}}{\text{g U-235}}$

Check: The units (J) are correct. A large amount of energy is expected per gram of fuel in a nuclear reactor.

19.39 **Given:** $2\, ^{2}_{1}\text{H} \rightarrow ^{3}_{2}\text{He} + ^{1}_{0}\text{n}$, H-2 $= 2.014102$ amu, and He-3 $= 3.016029$ amu **Find:** energy per g reactant
Conceptual Plan: mass of products and reactants $\rightarrow$ mass defect $\rightarrow$ mass defect/g of H-2 then

$$\text{mass defect} = \textstyle\sum \text{mass of reactants} - \sum \text{mass of products} \qquad \dfrac{\text{mass defect}}{2(2.014102 \text{ g H-2})}$$

g $\rightarrow$ kg $\rightarrow$ E

$$\dfrac{1 \text{ kg}}{1000 \text{ g}} \qquad E = mc^2$$

Solution: mass defect $= \sum \text{mass of reactants} - \sum \text{mass of products}$ and mass defect $= 2(2.014102 \text{ g}) - (3.016029 \text{ g} + 1.00866 \text{ g}) = 0.003515 \text{ g}$

then $\dfrac{0.003515 \text{ g}}{2(2.014102 \text{ g H-2})} \times \dfrac{1 \text{ kg}}{1000 \text{ g}} = 8.72597 \times 10^{-7} \dfrac{\text{kg}}{\text{g H-2}}$ then

$E = mc^2 = \left(8.72597 \times 10^{-7} \dfrac{\text{kg}}{\text{g H-2}}\right)\left(2.9979 \times 10^{8}\dfrac{\text{m}}{\text{s}}\right)^2 = 7.84 \times 10^{10} \dfrac{\text{J}}{\text{g H-2}}$

Check: The units (J) are correct. A large amount of energy is expected per gram of fuel in a fusion reaction.

Effects and Applications of Radioactivity

19.41 **Given:** 75 kg human exposed to 32.8 rad and falling from chair **Find:** energy absorbed in each case
Conceptual Plan: rad, kg $\rightarrow$ J and assume $d = 0.50$ m chair height then mass, $d \rightarrow$ J

$$1 \text{ rad} = \dfrac{0.01 \text{ J}}{1 \text{ kg body tissue}} \qquad\qquad E = F \cdot d = m\,g\,d$$

Solution: $32.8 \text{ rad} = 32.8 \dfrac{0.01 \text{ J}}{1 \text{ kg body tissue}} \times 75 \text{ kg} = 25 \text{ J}$ and

$$E = F \cdot d = m\,g\,d = 75 \text{ kg} \times 9.8\,\frac{\text{m}}{\text{s}^2} \times 0.50 \text{ m} = 370 \text{ kg}\frac{\text{m}^2}{\text{s}^2} = 370 \text{ J}$$

Check: The units (J and J) are correct. Allowable radiation exposures are low because the radiation is very ionizing and thus damaging to tissue. Falling may have more energy, but it is not ionizing.

19.43 **Given:** $t_{1/2}$ for F-18 = 1.83 h, 65% of F-18 makes it to the hospital traveling at 60.0 miles/hour **Find:** distance between hospital and cyclotron

Conceptual Plan: $t_{1/2} \rightarrow k$ then $m_{\text{F-18 }0}, m_{\text{F-18 }t}, k \rightarrow t$ then h $\rightarrow$ mi

$$t_{1/2} = \frac{0.693}{k} \qquad \ln\frac{m_{\text{F-18 }t}}{m_{\text{F-18 }0}} = -k\,t \qquad \frac{60.0 \text{ mi}}{1 \text{ h}}$$

Solution: $t_{1/2} = \dfrac{0.693}{k}$; rearrange to solve for k. $k = \dfrac{0.693}{t_{1/2}} = \dfrac{0.693}{1.83 \text{ h}} = 0.378689 \text{ h}^{-1}$. Because

$\ln\dfrac{m_{\text{F-18 }t}}{m_{\text{F-18 }0}} = -k\,t$, rearrange to solve for t.

$$t = -\frac{1}{k}\ln\frac{m_{\text{F-18 }t}}{m_{\text{F-18 }0}} = -\frac{1}{0.378689 \text{ h}^{-1}}\ln\frac{0.65\,m_{\text{F-18 }0}}{m_{\text{F-18 }0}} = 1.1376 \text{ h then}$$

$$1.1376 \text{ h} \times \frac{60.0 \text{ mi}}{1 \text{ h}} = 68 \text{ mi}$$

Check: The units (mi) are correct. The time is less than one half-life, so the distance is less than 1.83 times the speed of travel.

Cumulative Problems

19.45 **Given:** (a) Ru-114, (b) Ra-216, (c) Zn-58, and (d) Ne-31 **Find:** Write a nuclear equation for the most likely decay.
Conceptual Plan: Referring to the Valley of Stability graph in Figure 19.4, decide on the most likely decay mode depending on N/Z (too large = beta decay, too low = positron emission). $\rightarrow$ Write the symbol for the parent nuclide on the left side of the equation and the symbol for a particle on the right side. $\rightarrow$ Equalize the sum of the mass numbers and the sum of the atomic numbers on both sides of the equation by writing the appropriate mass number and atomic number for the unknown daughter nuclide. $\rightarrow$ Using the periodic table, deduce the identity of the unknown daughter nuclide from the atomic number and write its symbol.
Solution:
(a) Ru-114 ($N/Z = 1.6$) will undergo beta decay $^{114}_{44}\text{Ru} \rightarrow {}^{?}_{?}? + {}^{0}_{-1}\text{e}$ then $^{114}_{44}\text{Ru} \rightarrow {}^{114}_{45}? + {}^{0}_{-1}\text{e}$ then $^{114}_{44}\text{Ru} \rightarrow {}^{114}_{45}\text{Rh} + {}^{0}_{-1}\text{e}$

(b) Ra-216 ($N/Z = 1.4$) will undergo positron emission $^{216}_{88}\text{Ra} \rightarrow {}^{?}_{?}? + {}^{0}_{+1}\text{e}$ then $^{216}_{88}\text{Ra} \rightarrow {}^{216}_{87}? + {}^{0}_{+1}\text{e}$ then $^{216}_{88}\text{Ra} \rightarrow {}^{216}_{87}\text{Fr} + {}^{0}_{+1}\text{e}$

(c) Zn-58 ($N/Z = 0.9$) will undergo positron emission $^{58}_{30}\text{Zn} \rightarrow {}^{?}_{?}? + {}^{0}_{+1}\text{e}$ then $^{58}_{30}\text{Zn} \rightarrow {}^{58}_{29}? + {}^{0}_{+1}\text{e}$ then $^{58}_{30}\text{Zn} \rightarrow {}^{58}_{29}\text{Cu} + {}^{0}_{+1}\text{e}$

(d) Ne-31 ($N/Z = 2$) will undergo beta decay $^{31}_{10}\text{Ne} \rightarrow {}^{?}_{?}? + {}^{0}_{-1}\text{e}$ then $^{31}_{10}\text{Ne} \rightarrow {}^{31}_{11}? + {}^{0}_{-1}\text{e}$ then $^{31}_{10}\text{Ne} \rightarrow {}^{31}_{11}\text{Na} + {}^{0}_{-1}\text{e}$

Check: (a) $114 = 114 + 0$, $44 = 45 - 1$, and rhodium is atomic number 45. (b) $216 = 216 + 0$, $88 = 87 + 1$, and francium is atomic number 87. (c) $58 = 58 + 0$, $30 = 29 + 1$, and copper is atomic number 29. (d) $31 = 31 + 0$, $10 = 11 - 1$, and sodium is atomic number 11.

19.47 **Given:** Bi-210, $t_{1/2} = 5.0$ days, 1.2 g Bi-210, 209.984105 amu, 5.5% absorbed
Find: beta emissions in 13.5 days and dose (in Ci)
Conceptual Plan: $t_{1/2} \rightarrow k$ then $m_{\text{Bi-210 }0}, t, k \rightarrow m_{\text{Bi-210 }t}$ then

$$t_{1/2} = \frac{0.693}{k} \qquad \ln N_t = -k\,t + \ln N_0$$

$g_0, g_t \rightarrow$ g decayed $\rightarrow$ mol decayed $\rightarrow$ beta decays then day $\rightarrow$ h $\rightarrow$ min $\rightarrow$ s then

$$g_0 - g_t = \text{g decayed} \qquad \frac{1 \text{ mol Bi-210}}{209.984105 \text{ g Bi-210}} \qquad \frac{6.022 \times 10^{23} \text{ beta decays}}{1 \text{ mol Bi-210}} \qquad \frac{24 \text{ h}}{1 \text{ day}} \quad \frac{60 \text{ min}}{1 \text{ h}} \quad \frac{60 \text{ s}}{1 \text{ min}}$$

beta decays, s $\rightarrow$ beta decays/s $\rightarrow$ Ci available $\rightarrow$ Ci absorbed

$$\text{take ratio} \qquad \frac{1 \text{ Ci}}{\dfrac{3.7 \times 10^{10} \text{ decays}}{\text{s}}} \qquad \frac{5.5 \text{ Ci absorbed}}{100 \text{ Ci emitted}}$$

Solution: $t_{1/2} = \dfrac{0.693}{k}$; rearrange to solve for k. $k = \dfrac{0.693}{t_{1/2}} = \dfrac{0.693}{5.0 \text{ days}} = 0.1386 \text{ day}^{-1}$. Because

$\ln m_{\text{Bi-210 } t} = -kt + \ln m_{\text{Bi-210 } 0} = -(0.1386 \text{ day}^{-1})(13.5 \text{ day}) + \ln (1.2 \text{ g}) = -1.6888 \rightarrow$

$m_{\text{Bi-210 } t} = e^{-1.6888} = 0.18474 \text{ g}$ then $g_0 - g_t = \text{g decayed} = 1.2 \text{ g} - 0.18474 \text{ g} = 1.0153 \text{ g Bi-210}$

then $1.0153 \text{ g Bi-210} \times \dfrac{1 \text{ mol Bi-210}}{209.984105 \text{ g Bi-210}} \times \dfrac{6.022 \times 10^{23} \text{ beta decays}}{1 \text{ mol Bi-210}} = 2.9117 \times 10^{21} \text{ beta decays}$

$= 2.9 \times 10^{21} \text{ beta decays then } 13.5 \text{ day} \times \dfrac{24 \text{ h}}{1 \text{ day}} \times \dfrac{60 \text{ min}}{1 \text{ h}} \times \dfrac{60 \text{ s}}{1 \text{ min}} = 1.1664 \times 10^6 \text{ s then}$

$\dfrac{2.9117 \times 10^{21} \text{ beta decays}}{1.1664 \times 10^6 \text{ s}} \times \dfrac{1 \text{ Ci}}{\dfrac{3.7 \times 10^{10} \text{ decays}}{\text{s}}} = 6.7468 \times 10^4 \text{ Ci emitted} \times \dfrac{5.5 \text{ Ci absorbed}}{100 \text{ Ci emitted}} = 3700 \text{ Ci}$

Check: The units (decays and Ci) are correct. The amount that decays is large because the time is over three half-lives and we have a relatively large amount of the isotope. Because the decay is large, the dosage is large.

19.49   **Given:** Ra-226 (226.025402 amu) decays to Rn-224, $t_{1/2} = 1.6 \times 10^3 \text{yr}$, 25.0 g Ra-226, $T = 25.0 \,^{\circ}\text{C}$, $P = 1.0$ atm
Find: V of Rn-224 gas produced in 5.0 day
Conceptual Plan: day $\rightarrow$ yr then $t_{1/2} \rightarrow k$ then $m_{\text{Ra-226 } 0}\, t, k \rightarrow m_{\text{Ra-226 } t}$

$\dfrac{1 \text{ yr}}{365.24 \text{ day}} \qquad t_{1/2} = \dfrac{0.693}{k} \qquad \ln N_t = -k\,t + \ln N_0$

then $g_0, g_t \rightarrow$ g decayed $\rightarrow$ mol decayed $\rightarrow$ mol Rn-224 formed then $^{\circ}\text{C} \rightarrow$ K then $P, n, T \rightarrow V$

$g_0 - g_t = \text{g decayed} \quad \dfrac{1 \text{ mol Ra-226}}{226.025402 \text{ g Ra-226}} \quad \dfrac{1 \text{ mol Rn-224}}{1 \text{ mol Ra-226}} \qquad \text{K} = {^{\circ}\text{C}} + 273.15 \qquad PV = nRT$

Solution: $5.0 \text{ day} \times \dfrac{1 \text{ yr}}{365.24 \text{ day}} = 0.013690 \text{ yr}$ then $t_{1/2} = \dfrac{0.693}{k}$; rearrange to solve for k.

$k = \dfrac{0.693}{t_{1/2}} = \dfrac{0.693}{1.6 \times 10^3 \text{ yr}} = 4.33125 \times 10^{-4} \text{ yr}^{-1}$. Because

$\ln m_{\text{Ra-226 } t} = -kt + \ln m_{\text{Ra-226 } 0} = -(4.33125 \times 10^{-4} \text{ yr}^{-1})(0.013690 \text{ yr}) + \ln (25.0 \text{ g}) = 3.21887 \rightarrow$

$m_{\text{Ra-226 } t} = e^{3.21887} = 24.999854 \text{ g}$ then
$g_0 - g_t = \text{g decayed} = 25.0 \text{ g} - 24.999854 \text{ g} = 0.000146 \text{ g Ra-226 then}$

$0.000146 \text{ g Ra-226} \times \dfrac{1 \text{ mol Ra-226}}{226.025402 \text{ g Ra-226}} \times \dfrac{1 \text{ mol Rn-224}}{1 \text{ mol Ra-226}} = 6.5584 \times 10^{-7} \text{ mol Rn-224 then}$

$T = 25.0 \,^{\circ}\text{C} + 273.15 = 298.2 \text{ K}$ then $PV = nRT$. Rearrange to solve for V.

$V = \dfrac{nRT}{P} = \dfrac{6.5584 \times 10^{-7} \text{ mol} \times 0.08206 \dfrac{\text{L} \cdot \text{atm}}{\text{mol} \cdot \text{K}} \times 298.2 \text{ K}}{1.0 \text{ atm}} = 1.6049 \times 10^{-5} \text{ L} = 1.6 \times 10^{-5} \text{ L}$. Two

significant figures are reported as requested in the problem.

Check: The units (L) are correct. The amount of gas is small because the time is so small compared to the half-life.

19.51   **Given:** $^0_{+1}\text{e} + ^{\ 0}_{-1}\text{e} \rightarrow 2\,^0_0\gamma$ **Find:** energy (in kJ/mol)
Conceptual Plan:
mass of products and reactants $\rightarrow$ mass defect (g) $\rightarrow$ kg $\rightarrow$ kg/mol $\rightarrow E$ (J/mol) $\rightarrow E$ (kJ/mol)

$\text{mass defect} = \sum \text{mass of reactants} - \sum \text{mass of products} \quad \dfrac{1 \text{ kg}}{1000 \text{ g}} \quad 2 \text{ mol} \quad E = mc^2 \quad \dfrac{1 \text{ kJ}}{1000 \text{ J}}$

Solution: mass defect $= \sum \text{mass of reactants} - \sum \text{mass of products} = (0.00055 \text{ g} + 0.00055 \text{ g}) - 0 \text{ g} =$

0.00110 g then $\dfrac{0.00110 \text{ g}}{2 \text{ mol}} \times \dfrac{1 \text{ kg}}{1000 \text{ g}} = 5.50 \times 10^{-7} \dfrac{\text{kg}}{\text{mol}}$ then

$E = mc^2 = \left(5.50 \times 10^{-7} \dfrac{\text{kg}}{\text{mol}}\right)\left(2.9979 \times 10^8 \dfrac{\text{m}}{\text{s}}\right)^2 = 4.94307 \times 10^{10} \dfrac{\text{J}}{\text{mol}} \times \dfrac{1 \text{ kJ}}{1000 \text{ J}} = 4.94 \times 10^7 \dfrac{\text{kJ}}{\text{mol}}$

Check: The units (kJ/mol) are correct. A large amount of energy is expected per mole of mass lost. The photon is in the gamma ray region of the electromagnetic spectrum.

19.53 **Given:** $^3\text{He} = 3.016030$ amu   **Find:** nuclear binding energy per atom
Conceptual Plan: $^A_Z X$, **isotope mass** $\rightarrow$ **mass defect** $\rightarrow$ **nuclear binding energy per nucleon**

$$\text{mass defect} = Z(\text{mass } ^1_1\text{H}) + (A\text{-}Z)(\text{mass } ^1_0\text{n}) - \text{mass of isotope} \qquad \frac{931.5 \text{ MeV}}{1 \text{ amu}}$$

Solution: mass defect $= Z(\text{mass } ^1_1\text{H}) + (A\text{-}Z)(\text{mass } ^1_0\text{n}) - \text{mass of isotope}$
He-3 mass defect $= 2(1.00783 \text{ amu}) + (3 - 2)(1.00866 \text{ amu}) - 3.016030 \text{ amu} = 0.00829 \text{ amu}$

and $0.00829 \text{ amu} \times \dfrac{931.5 \text{ MeV}}{1 \text{ amu}} = 7.72 \text{ MeV}$

Check: The units (MeV) are correct. The number of nucleons is small, so the MeV is not that large.

19.55 **Given:** $t_{1/2}$ for decay of $^{238}\text{U} = 4.5 \times 10^9$ years, 1.6 g rock, 29 dis/s all radioactivity from U-238
Find: percent by mass ^{238}U in rock
Conceptual Plan: $t_{1/2} \rightarrow k$ **and** $\text{s} \rightarrow \text{min} \rightarrow \text{h} \rightarrow \text{day} \rightarrow \text{yr}$ **then Rate,** $k \rightarrow N \rightarrow \text{mol } ^{238}\text{U} \rightarrow \text{g } ^{238}\text{U}$

$$t_{1/2} = \frac{0.693}{k} \qquad \frac{1 \text{ min}}{60 \text{ s}} \quad \frac{1 \text{ h}}{60 \text{ min}} \quad \frac{1 \text{ day}}{24 \text{ h}} \quad \frac{1 \text{ yr}}{365.24 \text{ day}} \qquad \text{Rate} = k\,N \quad \frac{1 \text{ mol dis}}{6.022 \times 10^{23} \text{ dis}} \quad \frac{238 \text{ g } ^{238}\text{U}}{1 \text{ mol } ^{238}\text{U}}$$

then g ^{238}U, g rock $\rightarrow$ **percent by mass ^{238}U**

$$\text{percent by mass } ^{238}\text{U} = \frac{\text{g } ^{238}\text{U}}{\text{g rock}} \times 100\%$$

Solution: $t_{1/2} = \dfrac{0.693}{k}$; rearrange to solve for k. $k = \dfrac{0.693}{t_{1/2}} = \dfrac{0.693}{4.5 \times 10^9 \text{ yr}} = 1.54 \times 10^{-10} \text{ yr}^{-1}$ and

$1 \text{ s} \times \dfrac{1 \text{ min}}{60 \text{ s}} \times \dfrac{1 \text{ h}}{60 \text{ min}} \times \dfrac{1 \text{ day}}{24 \text{ h}} \times \dfrac{1 \text{ yr}}{365.24 \text{ day}} = 3.16889554 \times 10^{-8} \text{ yr}$. Rate $= kN$. Rearrange to
solve for N.

$$N = \frac{\text{Rate}}{k} = \frac{\dfrac{29 \text{ dis}}{3.16889554 \times 10^{-8} \text{ yr}}}{1.54 \times 10^{-10} \text{ yr}^{-1}} = 5.9425 \times 10^{18} \text{ dis then}$$

$5.9425 \times 10^{18} \text{ dis} \times \dfrac{1 \text{ mol dis}}{6.022 \times 10^{23} \text{ dis}} \times \dfrac{238 \text{ g } ^{238}\text{U}}{1 \text{ mol } ^{238}\text{U}} = 2.3486 \times 10^{-3} \text{g } ^{238}\text{U then}$

$\text{percent by mass } ^{238}\text{U} = \dfrac{\text{g } ^{238}\text{U}}{\text{g rock}} \times 100\% = \dfrac{2.3486 \times 10^{-3} \text{ g } ^{238}\text{U}}{1.6 \text{ g rock}} \times 100\% = 0.15\%$

Check: The units (%) are correct. The mass percent is low because the dis/s is low.

19.57 **Given:** $V = 1.50$ L, $P = 745$ mmHg, $T = 25.0 \,^\circ\text{C}$, 3.55% Rn-220 by volume, $t_{1/2} = 55.6$ s
Find: number of alpha particles emitted in 5.00 min
Conceptual Plan: **mmg** $\rightarrow$ **atm and $^\circ$C** $\rightarrow$ **K then** $P, V, T \rightarrow n_{\text{Total}} \rightarrow n_{\text{Rn-220}}$ **and min** $\rightarrow$ **s**

$$\frac{1 \text{ atm}}{760 \text{ mmHg}} \qquad K = \,^\circ\text{C} + 273.15 \qquad PV = nRT \quad \frac{3.55 \text{ mol Rn-220 particles}}{100 \text{ mol gas particles}} \quad \frac{60 \text{ s}}{1 \text{ min}}$$

then $t_{1/2} \rightarrow k$ **then** $n_{\text{Rn-220 }0}, t, k \rightarrow n_{\text{Rn-220 }t} \rightarrow$ **number of particles remaining** $\rightarrow$ **particles emitted**

$$t_{1/2} = \frac{0.693}{k} \qquad \ln N_t = -k\,t + \ln N_0 \qquad \frac{6.022 \times 10^{23} \text{ particles}}{1 \text{ mol}}$$

Solution: $745 \text{ mmHg} \times \dfrac{1 \text{ atm}}{760 \text{ mmHg}} = 0.9802632 \text{ atm and } T = 25.0 \,^\circ\text{C} + 273.15 = 298.2 \text{ K then}$

$PV = nRT$. Rearrange to solve for n.

$$n = \frac{PV}{RT} = \frac{0.9802632 \text{ atm} \times 1.50 \text{ L}}{0.08206 \dfrac{\text{L} \cdot \text{atm}}{\text{mol} \cdot \text{K}} \times 298.2 \text{ K}} = 0.06008898 \text{ mol gas particles}$$

then $0.06008898 \text{ mol gas particles} \times \dfrac{3.55 \text{ mol Rn-220 particles}}{100 \text{ mol gas particles}} = 0.002133159 \text{ mol Rn-220 particles}$

$5.00 \text{ min} \times \dfrac{60 \text{ s}}{1 \text{ min}} = 300. \text{ s then } t_{1/2} = \dfrac{0.693}{k}$ and rearrange to solve for k.

$k = \dfrac{0.693}{t_{1/2}} = \dfrac{0.693}{55.6 \text{ s}} = 0.01246403 \text{ s}^{-1}$. Because

$\ln m_{\text{Rn-220 }t} = -k\,t + \ln m_{\text{Rn-220 }0} = -(0.01246403 \text{ s}^{-1})(300. \text{ s}) + \ln (0.002133159 \text{ mol}) = -9.889360 \rightarrow$

$m_{\text{Rn-220 }t} = e^{-9.889360} = 5.071139 \times 10^{-5}$ mol alpha particles remaining

The number of alpha particles emitted would be the difference between this and the initial number of moles.

$0.002133158 \text{ mol} - 0.00005071139 \text{ mol} = 0.002082447 \text{ mol}$

$0.002082447 \text{ mol} \times \dfrac{6.022 \times 10^{23} \text{ particles}}{1 \text{ mol}} = 1.254050 \times 10^{21} \text{ particles} = 1.25 \times 10^{21} \text{ particles}$

Check: The units (particles) are correct. The number of particles is far less than a mole, because we have far less than a mole of gas.

19.59   **Given:** $^{0}_{+1}e + {}^{0}_{-1}e \rightarrow 2\,{}^{0}_{0}\gamma$ **Find:** wavelength of gamma ray photons
Conceptual Plan:

mass of products and reactants $\rightarrow$ mass defect (g) $\rightarrow$ kg $\rightarrow$ kg/mol $\rightarrow$ E (J/mol) $\rightarrow$ E (kJ/mol)

$\text{mass defect} = \sum \text{mass of reactants} - \sum \text{mass of products} \qquad \dfrac{1 \text{ kg}}{1000 \text{ g}} \quad 2 \text{ mol} \qquad E = mc^2 \qquad \dfrac{1 \text{ kJ}}{1000 \text{ J}}$

This energy is for 2 moles of γ, so E(J/2 mol γ) $\rightarrow$ E(J/γ photon) $\rightarrow$ λ.

$\dfrac{1 \text{ mol } \gamma}{6.022 \times 10^{23} \, \gamma \text{ photons}} \qquad E = \dfrac{h\,c}{\lambda}$

Solution: mass defect $= \sum \text{mass of reactants} - \sum \text{mass of products} = (0.00055 \text{ g} + 0.00055 \text{ g}) - 0 \text{ g} =$

0.00110 g then $\dfrac{0.00110 \text{ g}}{2 \text{ mol}} \times \dfrac{1 \text{ kg}}{1000 \text{ g}} = 5.50 \times 10^{-7} \dfrac{\text{kg}}{\text{mol}}$ then

$E = mc^2 = \left(5.50 \times 10^{-7} \dfrac{\text{kg}}{\text{mol}}\right)\left(2.9979 \times 10^{8} \dfrac{\text{m}}{\text{s}}\right)^2 = 4.94307 \times 10^{10} \dfrac{\text{J}}{\text{mol}} \times \dfrac{1 \text{ kJ}}{1000 \text{ J}} = 4.94 \times 10^{7} \dfrac{\text{kJ}}{\text{mol}}$

$E = 4.94307 \times 10^{10} \dfrac{\text{J}}{\text{mol } \gamma} \times \dfrac{1 \text{ mol } \gamma}{6.022 \times 10^{23} \gamma \text{ photons}} = 8.20835 \times 10^{-14} \dfrac{\text{J}}{\gamma \text{ photons}}.$ Then $E = \dfrac{h\,c}{\lambda}.$ Rearrange

to solve for λ. $\lambda = \dfrac{h\,c}{E} = \dfrac{(6.626 \times 10^{-34} \text{ J} \cdot \text{s})\left(2.9979 \times 10^{8} \dfrac{\text{m}}{\text{s}}\right)}{8.20835 \times 10^{-14} \dfrac{\text{J}}{\gamma \text{ photons}}} = 2.42 \times 10^{-12} \text{ m} = 2.42 \text{ pm}$

Check: The units (m or pm) are correct. A large amount of energy is expected per mole of mass lost. The photon is in the gamma ray region of the electromagnetic spectrum.

19.61   **Given:** $^{2}_{1}\text{H} + {}^{2}_{1}\text{H} \rightarrow {}^{3}_{2}\text{He} + {}^{1}_{0}\text{n}$ releases 3.3 MeV; $^{2}_{1}\text{H} + {}^{2}_{1}\text{H} \rightarrow {}^{3}_{1}\text{H} + {}^{1}_{1}\text{p}$ releases 4.0 MeV
Find: The energy change for $^{3}_{2}\text{He} + {}^{1}_{0}\text{n} \rightarrow {}^{3}_{1}\text{H} + {}^{1}_{1}\text{p}$ and explain why this can happen at a much lower temperature.
Conceptual Plan: Use Hess's law to calculate the energy change and give the two reactions.
Solution:

$^{3}_{2}\text{He} + {}^{1}_{0}\text{n} \rightarrow {}^{2}_{1}\text{H} + {}^{2}_{1}\text{H} \qquad \Delta E = 3.3 \text{ MeV}$

$^{2}_{1}\text{H} + {}^{2}_{1}\text{H} \rightarrow {}^{3}_{1}\text{H} + {}^{1}_{1}\text{p} \qquad \Delta E = -4.0 \text{ MeV}$

$\overline{^{3}_{2}\text{He} + {}^{1}_{0}\text{n} \rightarrow {}^{3}_{1}\text{H} + {}^{1}_{1}\text{p} \qquad \Delta E = -0.7 \text{ MeV}}$

The energy change is much less, and there is no coulombic barrier for collision with a neutron; so the process can occur at lower temperatures.

Check: The units (MeV) are correct. Because one reaction releases energy and one requires energy, the resulting energy change is much smaller in magnitude.

Challenge Problems

19.63   **(a)**   **Given:** 72,500 kg Al(s) and 10 Al(s) + 6 NH$_4$ClO$_4$(s) $\rightarrow$ 4 Al$_2$O$_3$(s) + 2 AlCl$_3$(s) + 12 H$_2$O(g) + 3 N$_2$(g)
and 608,000 kg O$_2$(g) that reacts with hydrogen to form gaseous water
Find: energy generated ($\Delta H^{\circ}_{\text{rxn}}$)
Conceptual Plan: Write a balanced reaction for O$_2$(g) then

$\Delta H^{\circ}_{\text{rxn}} = \sum n_{\text{P}} \Delta H^{\circ}_{\text{f}} (\text{products}) - \sum n_{\text{r}} \Delta H^{\circ}_{\text{f}} (\text{reactants})$ then

kg → g → mol → energy then add the results from the two reactions.

$$\frac{1000 \text{ g}}{1 \text{ kg}} \qquad \mathcal{M} \qquad \Delta H^{\circ}_{\text{rxn}}$$

Solution:

Reactant/Product	ΔH°_{f} (kJ/mol from Appendix IIB)
Al(s)	0.0
$NH_4ClO_4(s)$	−295
$Al_2O_3(s)$	−1675.7
$AlCl_3(s)$	−704.2
H_2O (g)	−241.8
$N_2(g)$	0.0

Be sure to pull data for the correct formula and phase.

$\Delta H^{\circ}_{\text{rxn}} = \sum n_p \Delta H^{\circ}_f \text{ (products)} - \sum n_r \Delta H^{\circ}_f \text{ (reactants)}$

$= [4(\Delta H^{\circ}_f (Al_2O_3(s))) + 2(\Delta H^{\circ}_f (AlCl_3(s))) + 12(\Delta H^{\circ}_f (H_2O(g))) + 3(\Delta H^{\circ}_f (N_2(g)))] +$
$\quad -[10(\Delta H^{\circ}_f (Al(s))) + 6(\Delta H^{\circ}_f (NH_4ClO_4(s)))]$

$= [4(-1675.7 \text{ kJ}) + 2(-704.2 \text{ kJ}) + 12(-241.8 \text{ kJ}) + 3(0.0 \text{ kJ})] - [10(0.0 \text{ kJ}) + 6(-295 \text{ kJ})]$

$= [-11012.8 \text{ kJ}] - [-1770. \text{ kJ}]$

$= -9242.8 \text{ kJ}$

then $72{,}500 \text{ kg Al} \times \dfrac{1000 \text{ g Al}}{1 \text{ kg Al}} \times \dfrac{1 \text{ mol Al}}{26.98 \text{ g Al}} \times \dfrac{9242.8 \text{ kJ}}{10 \text{ mol Al}} = 2.483703 \times 10^9 \text{ kJ}$

balanced reaction: $H_2(g) + \frac{1}{2} O_2(g) \rightarrow H_2O(g)$ $\Delta H^{\circ}_{\text{rxn}} = \Delta H^{\circ}_f (H_2O(g)) = -241.8$ KJ/mol then

$608{,}000 \text{ kg } O_2 \times \dfrac{1000 \text{ g } O_2}{1 \text{ kg } O_2} \times \dfrac{1 \text{ mol } O_2}{32.00 \text{ g } O_2} \times \dfrac{241.8 \text{ kJ}}{0.5 \text{ mol } O_2} = 9.1884 \times 10^9$ kJ. So the total is

2.483703×10^9 kJ $+ 9.1884 \times 10^9$ kJ $= 1.1672103 \times 10^{10}$ kJ $= 1.167 \times 10^{10}$ kJ.

Check: The units (kJ) are correct. The answer is very large because the reactions are very exothermic and the weight of reactants is so large.

(b) **Given:** $^1_1H + ^{-1}_{-1}p + ^{0}_{+1}e \rightarrow ^0_0\gamma$

Find: mass of antimatter to give same energy as part (a)

Conceptual Plan: Because the reaction is an annihilation reaction, no matter will be left; so the mass of antimatter is the same as the mass of the hydrogen. So kJ → J → kg → g

$$\frac{1000 \text{ J}}{1 \text{ kJ}} \qquad E = mc^2 \qquad \frac{1000 \text{ g}}{1 \text{ kg}}$$

Solution: 1.1672103×10^{10} kJ $\times \dfrac{1000 \text{ J}}{1 \text{ kJ}} = 1.1672103 \times 10^{13}$ J. Because $E = mc^2$, rearrange to solve for m.

$$m = \frac{E}{c^2} = \frac{1.1672103 \times 10^{13} \text{ kg} \frac{m^2}{s^2}}{\left(2.9979 \times 10^8 \frac{m}{s}\right)^2} = 1.299 \times 10^{-4} \text{ kg} \times \frac{1000 \text{ g}}{1 \text{ kg}} = 0.1299 \text{ g total matter, } 0.0649 \text{ g}$$

each of matter and antimatter.

Check: The units (g) are correct. A small mass is expected because nuclear reactions generate a large amount of energy.

19.65 **Given:** $^{235}_{92}U \rightarrow ^{206}_{82}Pb$ and $^{232}_{90}Th \rightarrow ^{206}_{82}Pb$ **Find:** decay series

Conceptual Plan: Write the species given on the appropriate side of the equation. → Equalize the sum of the mass numbers and the sum of the atomic numbers on both sides of the equation by writing the stoichiometric coefficient in front of the desired species.

Solution: $^{235}_{92}U \rightarrow ^{?}_{82}Pb + ? \, ^4_2He + ? \, ^0_{-1}e$ becomes $^{235}_{92}U \rightarrow ^{207}_{82}Pb + 7 \, ^4_2He + 4 \, ^0_{-1}e$.

$^{232}_{90}Th \rightarrow ^{?}_{82}Pb + ? \, ^4_2He + ? \, ^0_{-1}e$ becomes $^{232}_{90}Th \rightarrow ^{208}_{82}Pb + 6 \, ^4_2He + 4 \, ^0_{-1}e$.

U-235 forms Pb-207 in 7 α-decays and 4 β-decays, and Th-232 forms Pb-208 in 6 α-decays and 4 β-decays.

Check: $235 = 207 + 7(4) + 4(0)$, and $92 = 82 + 7(2) + 4(-1)$. $232 = 208 + 6(4) + 4(0)$, and $90 = 82 + 6(2) + 4(-1)$. The mass of the Pb can be determined because alpha particles are large and need to be included as integer values. To make the masses balance requires more alpha particles than can be supported by the number of protons in the total equation. To account for this, an appropriate number of beta decays is added.

Conceptual Problems

19.67   7. Because $1/2^6 = 1.6\%$ and $1/2^7 = 0.8\%$.

19.69   The gamma emitter is a greater threat while you sleep because it can penetrate more tissue. The alpha particles will not penetrate the wall to enter your bedroom. The alpha emitter is a greater threat if you ingest it because it is more ionizing.

Questions for Group Work

19.71   See Table 19.1; All processes conserve total mass number and total charge, but they differ in the specific particles consumed and produced.

19.73 $^{238}_{92}U \rightarrow \, ^{234}_{90}Th + \, ^4_2He$; $^{234}_{90}Th \rightarrow \, ^{234}_{91}Pa + \, ^0_{-1}e$; $^{234}_{91}Pa \rightarrow \, ^{234}_{92}U + \, ^0_{-1}e$.